GOLF CLUB DESIGN, FITTING, ALTERATION AND REPAIR

the principles and procedures

by Ralph Maltby

This is the Revised 4th Edition Published in January, 1995
3rd Edition Published in September, 1990
2nd Edition Published in May, 1982
1st Edition Published in September, 1974

Brief quotations may be used in critical articles and reviews. For any other reproduction of the book, however, including electronic, mechanical, photocopying, recording or other means, written permission must be obtained from the author.

ISBN 0-927956-05-5

©Copyright 1995 by Ralph D. Maltby
Published by: Ralph Maltby Enterprises, Inc.
Book Manufactured in the United States of America
BOOK TRADE DISTRIBUTION BY:
Ralph Maltby Enterprises, Inc.
4820 Jacksontown Road
PO Box 3008
Newark, OH 43058-3008

To my wife Donna and
our daughters, Tracy,
Kelly and Cathy.

Only myself and especially
my family can fully comprehend
the magnitude of this project
and for their understanding,
patience and support, I am
grateful.

TABLE OF CONTENTS

APPENDICES

INTRODUCTION

The golf business has enjoyed dynamic growth and is continuing to expand and change daily. There are more golfers, more golf courses, more rounds of golf played and more interest than ever before in this fast growing sport for both youngsters and adults of all ages. Because of this dynamic growth and the opportunities which exist, the golf club manufacturers have substantially increased expenditures in research to advance their knowledge in equipment technology, improve their manufacturing methods and develop better merchandising techniques.

Advances in golf club technology have fostered a variety of advertising claims and products that have succeeded in confusing both the golf professional and the golfer. To fully understand and interpret the manufacturer's claims, the pro and the golfer must have a succinct body of knowledge for reference. This book was written with that purpose in mind. It will, I hope, eliminate the confusion by providing a solid background in all aspects of golf club design from a technical but practical standpoint.

The repair section includes information on all wood and iron club repairs and alterations. It is written to provide step by step "how to" instructions for the golf professional, or small or large repair shop. It can even be utilized by the average home handyman to do their own repairs. Alterations such as changing the facing on woods, changing lofts and lies on iron clubs and changing swingweight are included in the repair section because these procedures require repair shop facilities.

The golf club design section applies to both woods and irons and includes discussions on specifications, definitions of terms, important head shape and style features, design information on components and also an explanation of balancing and matching methods. To insure a more concise understanding of golf club mechanics, much of the design information is included in the repair and alteration chapters, but only where it would directly relate and help the reader to more fully understand what is happening. Because of this interrelation of information, it is best to read all 66 chapters and the appendices, in total, to obtain a more complete understanding of golf clubs.

Much of the golf professional's business is selling golf equipment, and this includes recommending and fitting golf clubs to customers. This book provides the professional with the basic knowledge of golf club mechanics and then shows how to apply this knowledge to the proper fitting of golf clubs. The fitting section first references the appropriate parts of the book that apply to each fitting variable such as loft, lie, grip size and swingweight. It then provides detailed explanations of fitting, coupled with handy reference tables which apply to each fitting variable.

There are many other tables in this book to provide valuable information, most of which has been developed solely for this book and is not available elsewhere. The book also has an extensive appendix which includes names and addresses of golf club manufacturers and the manufacturer's standard loft, lie and length specifications.

The golf professional, club repairman and clubmaker today who maintains a firm grasp on all phases of this business has the best chance of being successful. Increased knowledge about golf clubs can help their business significantly and will promote the lasting satisfaction in thoroughly knowing all aspects of the profession by providing the best service, best products and best quality for their customers.

Ralph Maltby
January, 1995

ACKNOWLEDGEMENTS

A special thanks must go to a number of GolfWorks® employees who contributed valuable information to this revised edition. We have generated considerable data at the GolfWorks Testing, Research and Fitting Facility in our daily work with new club designs, new components, our fitting programs and schools. Much of this new information was included in this book and would not have been possible without the additional help of Mark Wilson and Greg Johnson; for their expert help I am grateful.

Also, I want to especially thank my daughter, Tracy, who took two years off from her busy life to head up and coordinate this entire project. Utilizing the latest in computer technology Tracy transferred this entire revised 4th edition over to a 100% electronic format. She also gathered much of the updated material in the book from suppliers, manufacturers and other sources. Most importantly she kept me and the project moving along so that it would be finished on time.

Finally, I want to thank my daughter, Cathy, for helping us input extensive information into the computer and my wife, Donna, for her expert and tireless proofing of this revised manuscript.

Following is a list of companies who have been especially helpful in providing information for this revised edition.

Aldila
Club-Kit, Inc.
Coastcast Corporation
Dynamic Precision Casting Mfg., Co., Ltd.
Eaton Corporation (Golf Pride Grip Division)
Grafalloy
True Temper Sports Inc.
United States Golf Association (USGA)

A Few Important Club Assembly Do's and Don'ts

Do's

- When epoxying or gluing any two surfaces together, always apply epoxy or glue to both surfaces.

- Always install a shaft locking screw to pin the steel shaft to a persimmon or laminated wood head.

- Always wear eye protection. Lead, epoxy, plastic, rubber and wood sometimes snap, crackle, pop and spit when heat is applied. Solvents such as acetone, gasoline, trichlorethylene, stain and polyurethane can also splash in your eyes.

- Wear a dust respirator when sanding wood heads or during any buffing or grinding operation.

- Use a proper paint respirator when spraying finish materials.

Don'ts

- Don't smoke when working on golf clubs. When you light your propane torch you know it is lit, but when you smoke a cigarette you're not always aware it is lit.

- Don't store any flammable solvent next to heat, sparks or open flames.

- Don't remove loose screws with your fingers because golf screws have razor sharp edges!

To Keep in Mind

- Build or fit every club with the same care and patience that you would devote to building or fitting your own.

- Do it once, do it right and strive to do the best possible job.

- The golf club assembly sections in this book are intended to be used as a professional manual of shop instruction. It is beyond the scope of this book to teach common sense and the skills needed to operate ordinary hand and power tools safely and correctly. Always practice safety, good housekeeping and common sense at all times around the shop.

SECTION

ONE

GOLF WOOD CLUB REPAIRS AND ALTERATIONS

CHAPTER 1

REFINISHING WOODS
WOOD, GRAPHITE, METAL

Refinishing is considered one of the more difficult and therefore "advanced skill" types of repair. It can, however, be mastered quite easily; but, like the golf swing, it requires some practice to develop a sound technique. Refinishing can be done using many different methods, for example, the methods for sanding a clubhead range from time-consuming hand sanding to the use of motorized machinery for maximum speed. Regardless of the method, if done correctly, the end result can be the same.

Refinishing "woods" has become a bit more complex with the introduction of inorganic materials (stainless steel, aluminum, exotic alloys, graphite and plastic) into the traditional persimmon and laminated maple club lines. Fortunately, in most cases, the refinishing steps are similar. The steps required for refinishing materials other than wood are covered in the latter part of the chapter.

Almost all finishes consist of a water- or alcohol-based dye stain, a wood filler (which is either oil, water or urethane base) applied over or under the stain, a colorcote (usually only with black finishes) and three to five coats of a clear polyurethane applied by either dipping or spraying.

A word about polyurethane coatings. There are two basic types of polyurethane available — moisture cure and oil modified. There are many variations, however, of these two types which are commercially available through hardware and paint stores. Unless the polyurethane has been developed expressly for golf club heads, you would be wise to avoid the store-bought types. This type of polyurethane may look good for a short while, but may soon crack, chip or peel upon impact with the topped ball or "fat" shot. If you are pioneering a new brand, test it thoroughly; otherwise, stick with a reputable maker or supplier of specially formulated polyurethanes for golf woods.

■ IMPORTANT NOTE: Product compatibility is always a question. Use the table at the end of this chapter if you use either The GolfWorks® products or Club-Kit products. Also, different products require different drying times. Again, the table at the end of this chapter should be used as a guide in determining correct drying times for both room temperature and force dry conditions.

Many times a golf club is received with simple instructions for a straight refinish. Never assume the club requires a simple refinish! You should thoroughly inspect the club to determine if it requires other head repairs. Failure to perform this clubhead inspection may lead to future problems with the customer. For instance, if a new finish is applied to a clubhead with a loose insert or soleplate, the finish will eventually peel or chip around these components. The customer will not understand this, however, and will come back to you demanding an explanation. Your reputation will be hurt simply because you neglected to inspect the clubhead before refinishing and inform the customer of the possible consequences should the additional necessary repairs not be completed. Decisions such as these should always be made by the customer so there are no hidden costs or surprises when the club is picked up.

In addition to the head inspection, there are other features on a golf club that should be noted prior to a refinish. These features, plus the general head inspection, are covered extensively in this chapter. Remember this: your goal as a refinisher is to apply a finish to the clubhead that is as good, if not better, than the original factory finish.

1-1 Check and record the swingweight. Refinishing will reduce the swingweight 1-2 points. This loss of weight must be compensated by preferably adding additional weight under the soleplate or as a last resort down the shaft. See Chapter 14 for weighting procedures.

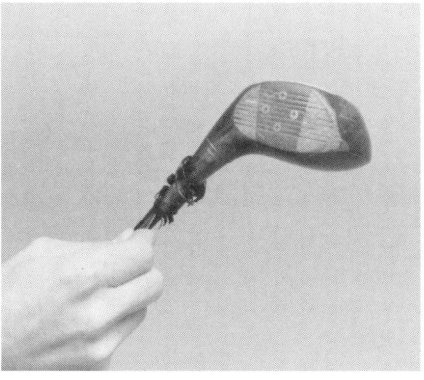

1-2 Carefully cut through the whipping and remove. Do not make deep cuts in the hosel. If the club has a plastic whipping cover, do not remove it unless you desire to convert to whipping.

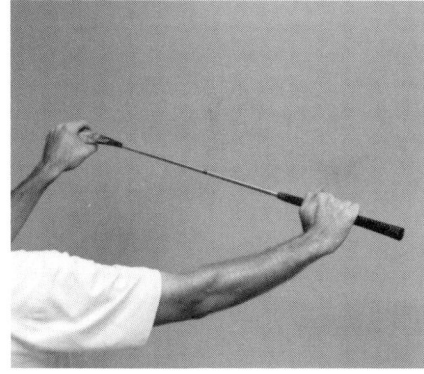

1-3 Inspect the head to see if it is loose on the shaft. Grasp the head in one hand and the grip in the other, then twist in opposite directions. Sometimes you may only hear a squeak, which indicates the head is loose. See Chapter 8 to repair a loose wood head.

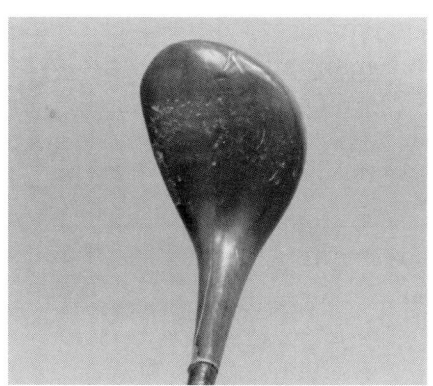

1-4 Inspect the hosel for cracks. Minor hairline cracks are okay as long as the shaft is bonded securely to the head. Major cracks will require removal and reinstallation of the shaft to properly repair the crack. Refer to Chapter 9 for repairing cracks in the hosel.

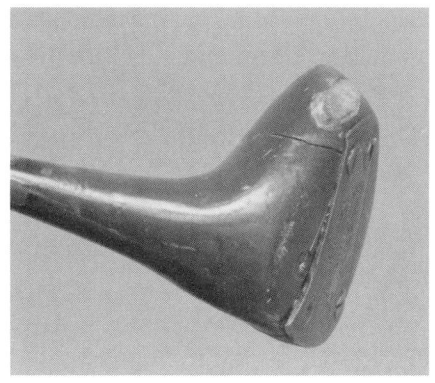

1-5 Examine the head for any cracks or breaks. The head shown above will eventually break into two pieces. See Chapter 9 for repairing cracked or broken heads.

1-6 Look carefully at this photo. This condition is known as **"dry rot"** or **"weathering."** Chapter 4 will show you how to repair this rotted area.

1-7 If the club has a brass or lead back-weight, check to make sure it is set properly. A loose brass weight will need to be reset, while the lead weight will most likely need to be replaced. Chapter 15 outlines both repair procedures.

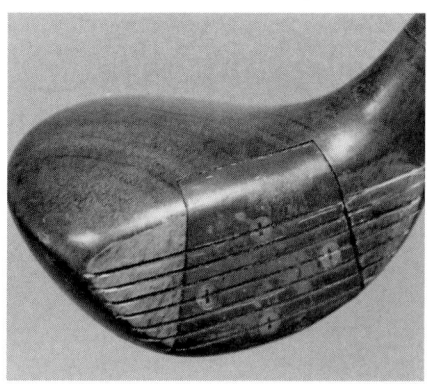

1-8 Inspect for a loose insert and reset if necessary. Follow the instructions shown in Chapter 3.

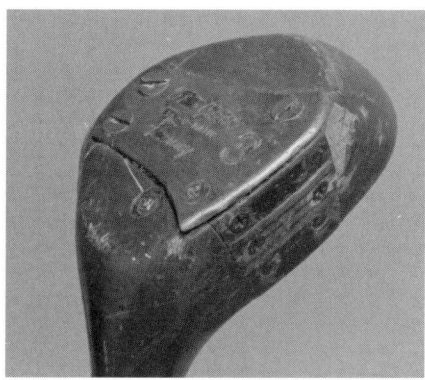

1-9 Inspect for a loose or open soleplate. If necessary, reset as outlined in Chapter 2. **Note: A very loose soleplate or insert can be an indication that a crack in the head is beginning to form.**

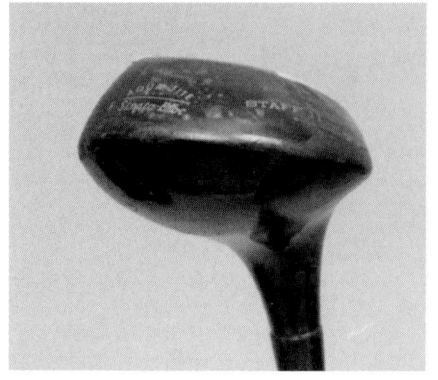

1-10 Before the finish is removed, the **color should be recorded** (if the head is to be refinished in the same color). **Make note of the decal(s) and the decal position.** Recording this information will make it much easier to remember it at a later stage.

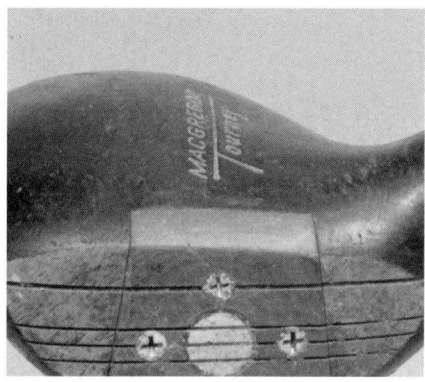

1-11 If the clubhead has a stamping in the crown or wood area of the sole, make a note of the paint color used to fill the stamping.

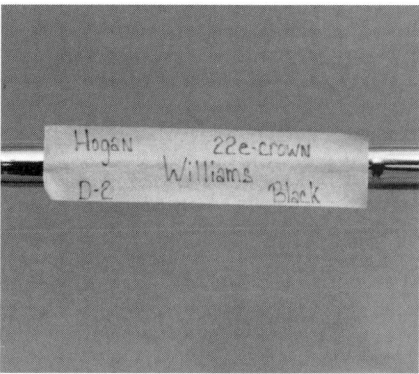

1-12 Attach a piece of tape (masking tape works well) to the shaft and record the club's swingweight, color, decal, type, decal color (if applicable), decal placement and the customer's name. This is an efficient practice regardless of the size of your shop.

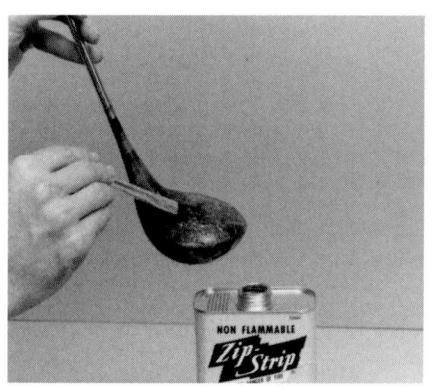

1-13 Old polyurethane, varnish, shellac or lacquer finish is best removed by brushing a paste stripper onto the head.

1-14 Be careful to keep stripper off plastic inserts, whipping covers and ferrules. Prolonged contact will allow the stripping agent to ruin the plastic parts. Stripper has no effect on inserts such as fiber, melamine, gamma fire and phenolic.

1-15 Stripper is now available in an aerosol can. The same precautions must still be taken concerning plastic components. Because you are unable to control the application as easily as with a brush, be sure to cover the insert and plastic whipping cover. Ferrules should also be covered. Masking tape works well for this.

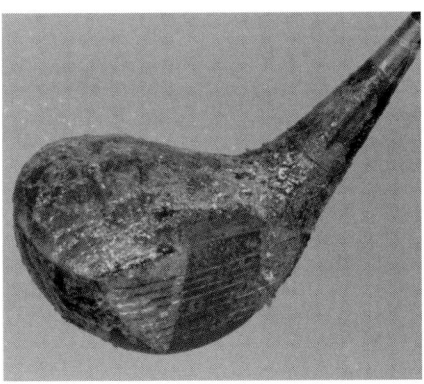

1-16 After the stripper has been on the finish for a few minutes, minor surface rippling to major bubbling will occur. Stripper and loosened finish should then be removed with...

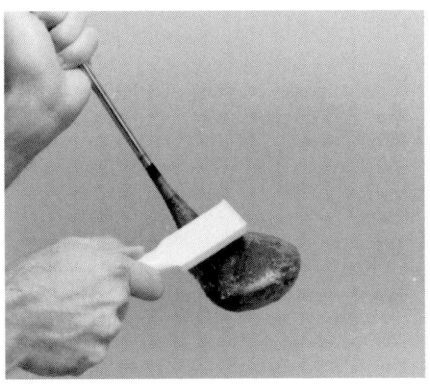

1-17 ... a stiff bristle Stripping Brush or ...

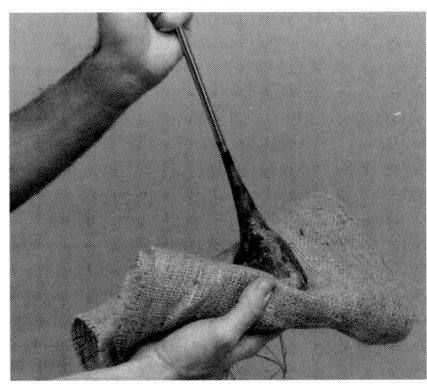

1-18 ... vigorous wiping with burlap or ...

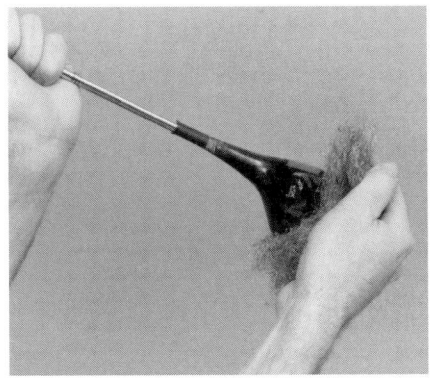

1-19 ... coarse steel wool. **Note: The stripper can cause skin irritation. Immediately wash off any stripper. Disposable plastic gloves work very well for stripping operations.**

1-20 Another method which is very quick is to remove the finish with **Scotch-Brite™ Wheels.** These wheels will remove the finish without removing the wood. They are most effective when used in conjunction with the paste stripper. Instructions for their use are found at the end of this chapter.

1-21 Observe properly stripped clubheads. Small patches of finish left on the head are acceptable, as our goal here is to remove the majority of the finish. Sandpaper usage will be lessened as a result of removing most of the finish with a stripper.

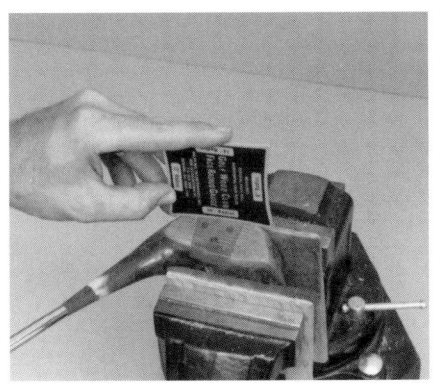

1-22 To check and record the horizontal face bulge, place a Face Radius Gauge horizontally across the bottom of the face and slide the gauge upward towards the top of the face.

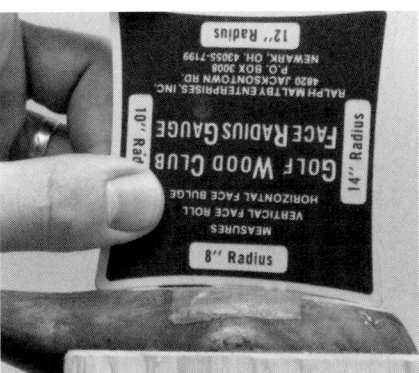

1-23 In this photo, the face does not adequately conform to the 8" radius side; therefore, the face is flatter or has less radius than 8".

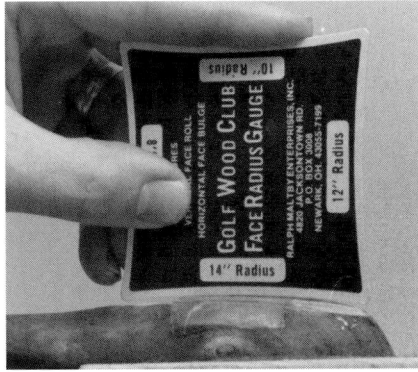

1-24 Shown here, the face has more curvature or radius than the 14" side. Somewhere in between these two readings is the measurement that will allow the clubface to properly match up to one side of the gauge.

13

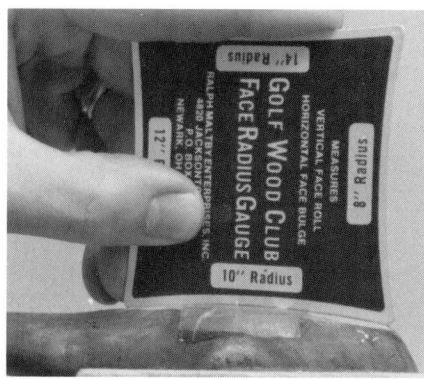

1-25 With the 10" radius side of the gauge resting on the face, the two radius match. This is referred to as a 10" radius horizontal face bulge or 10" bulge.

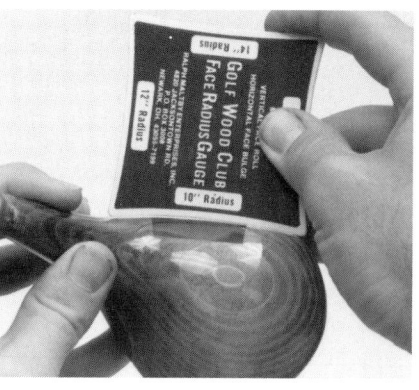

1-26 Most manufacturers intentionally leave the top, heel portion of the face higher or flatter in radius. This is done for cosmetic purposes, and the bulge reading should not be taken along the top line of the face. Also, do not file this slightly higher area more than is necessary. This area affects the look of the face in the playing position.

1-27 Another reading to take is the vertical face roll. Again, we look for the side that allows the face to fit flush against the gauge. In this case, the 12" radius side properly fits.

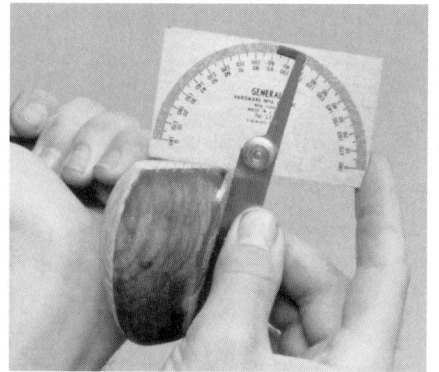

1-28 Loft should also be checked. Loft is always specified in degrees. Hold the arm of the protractor tight against the soleplate and adjust the protractor head so that it touches the face at ½ its vertical height. This photo shows the protractor head resting below the halfway point so the loft it is indicating would be less or stronger than the heads actual loft.

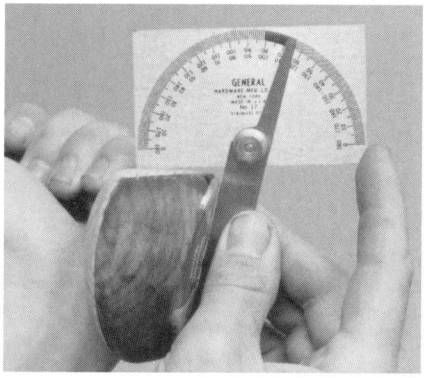

1-29 This photo shows the protractor head resting above the halfway point so the loft reading of the protractor is greater or weaker than the actual loft.

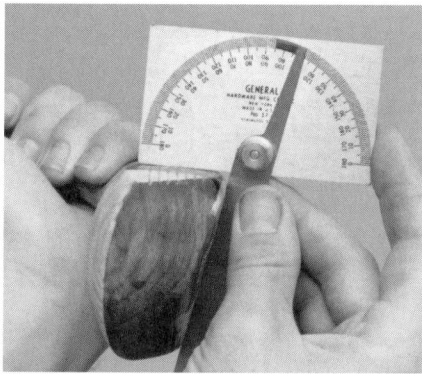

1-30 The correct positioning of the protractor head is shown here. The degree of loft is read directly off the gauge. **Note: The gauge arm is flat on the sole and the gauge head is touching the clubface at ½ its vertical height.**

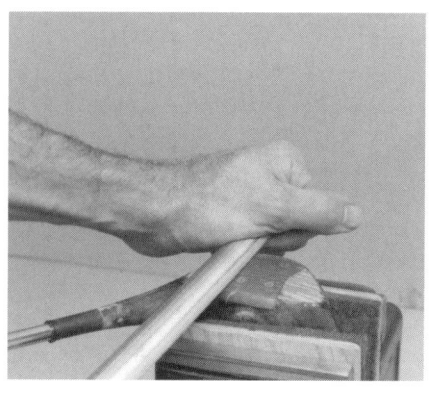

1-31 Once the bulge, roll and loft angle have been determined, your goal will be to remove the finish without changing these readings, unless desired. Select a medium or fine cut file and file across the face from the heel …

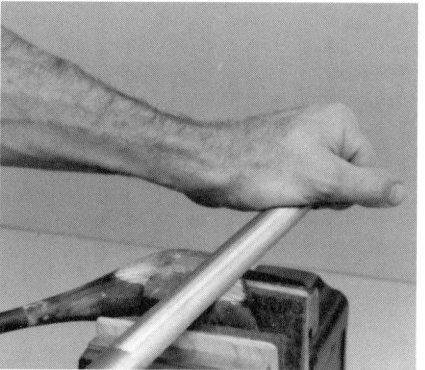

1-32 … towards the toe. It is best to move the file away from the hosel to prevent accidental marring of the hosel. Work the file in a radiusing motion for best results.

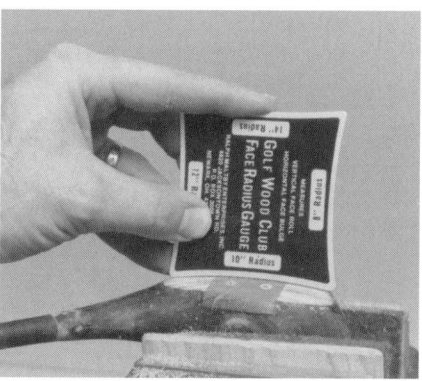

1-33 As you file, periodically check the face bulge and roll to make sure these specifications are as desired.

14

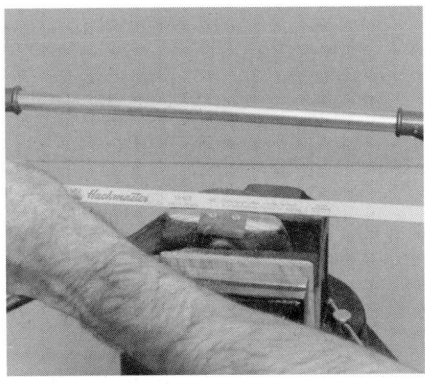

1-34 Use a rigid hacksaw and specially made, narrow width blade to clean out or slightly deepen existing face lines. The best approach is to begin at a heel side scoring line and use short cutting strokes as the blade is drawn through the line. **KEEP THE HACKSAW BLADE INSIDE THE LINES.**

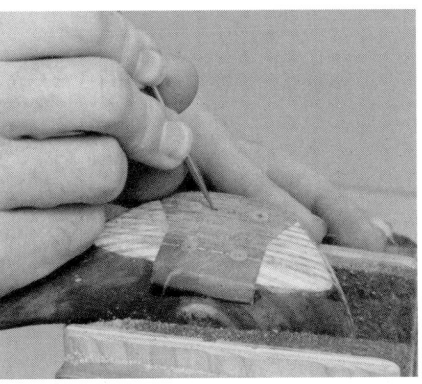

1-35 A **scriber** works well for cleaning the scoring lines in between and around the insert screws, however, it should not be used to deepen the lines.

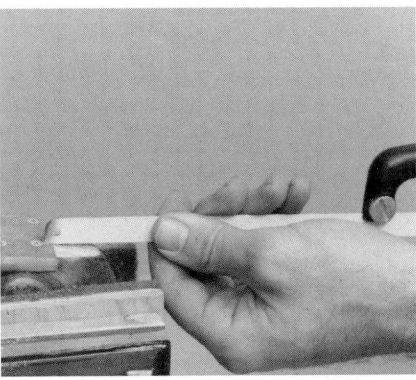

1-36 A **Mini Hacksaw** is available that will hold a blade that has been ground to a point. This enables you to deepen scoring lines around the screws.

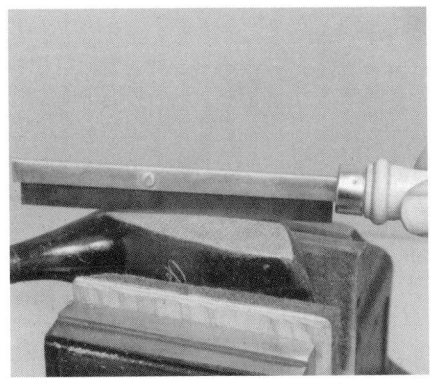

1-37 Cutting special narrow face lines on a number of older (1920's, 30's and some 1940's) woods requires the use of a **Razor Saw** to cut them to a proper, original width as the face scoring is very narrow.

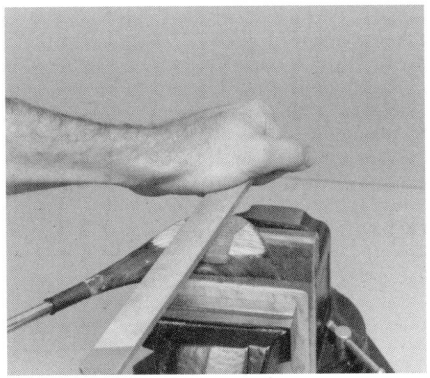

1-38 Next, lightly file the face with a flat mill or fine cut file. This will remove deeper marks left from the use of the coarse cut file. No further smoothing of the face is necessary at this time.

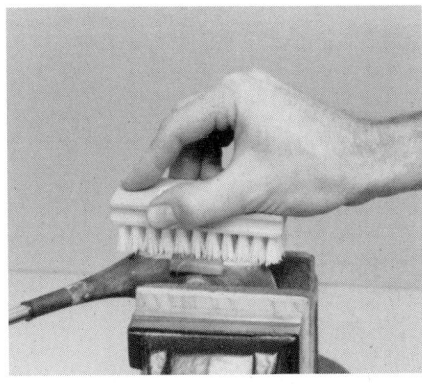

1-39 Brush the face to remove debris from the face lines and screw head recesses.

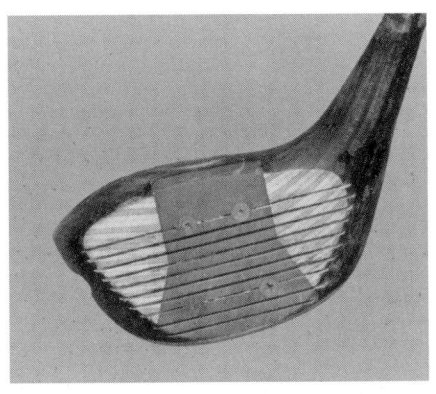

1-40 A properly prepared face will look like this. Note the clean, well-defined scoring lines.

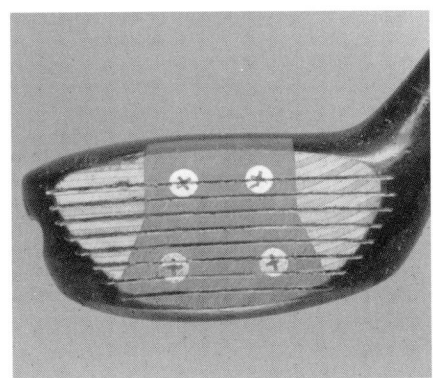

1-41 This photo shows a sure sign of a novice at work. Cutting face lines through the insert screws is an **unacceptable practice.**

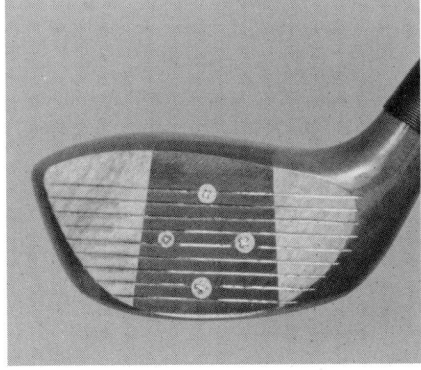

1-42 Sometimes original insert screws are damaged or the heads have become too small as a result of excessive filing. Most screws are easily turned out using a small **Reed and Prince screwdriver.** If difficulties are encountered refer to Chapter 3 for further instructions on removing face screws.

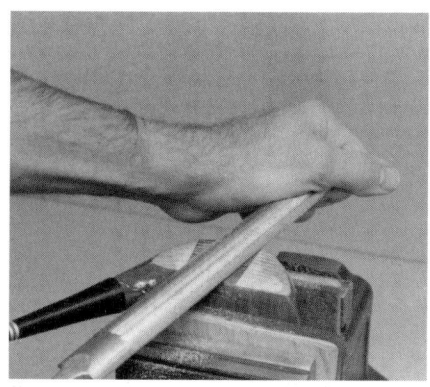

1-43 Once the screws are removed, the face is filed as previously shown.

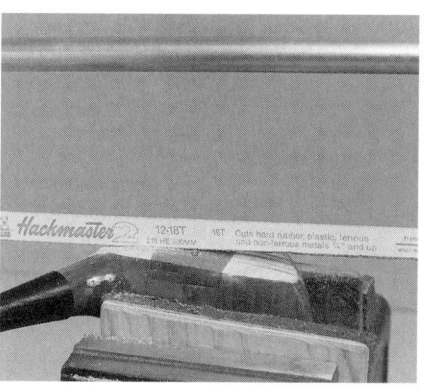

1-44 Also, cut in scoring lines as shown in photo 1-34.

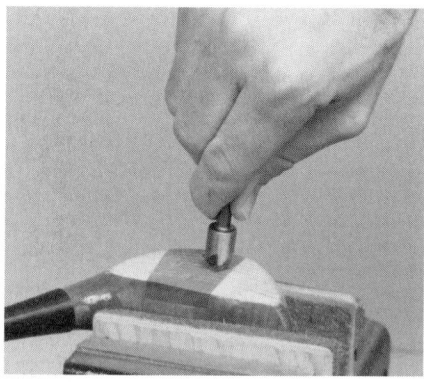

1-45 Next, insert a countersink into the screw hole. Hold the shank in your fingers as shown and twirl the countersink quickly. This is all that is necessary to enlarge the holes to accept the small face screw heads. **BE CAREFUL NOT TO MAKE HOLES WIDER THAN SCREW HEADS.** The countersink may be held in a drill chuck for faster work.

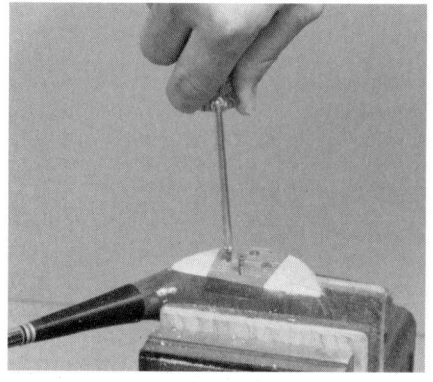

1-46 Install new insert screws. A very small dab of epoxy on the screw tip will permanently lock it in place, if desired. See Table 3-1 in Chapter 3 for recommended screw size. If the insert screw pilot hole is too shallow, use a ³⁄₃₂" drill bit to deepen the hole.

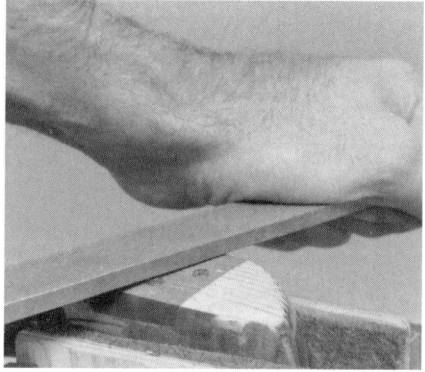

1-47 File the screw heads flush with the face. A properly countersunk hole will allow the head of the screw to be seated slightly above the face. This will give a professional look once the heads are filed flush with the face.

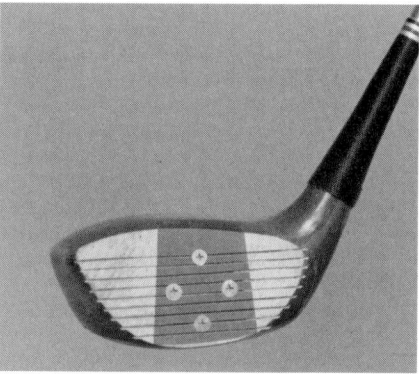

1-48 The face is shown here with new insert screws. The additional effort required to replace the screws was well worth it. Note the screw slots have been positioned parallel and perpendicular to the scoring lines. This is a nice, professional touch.

1-49 Next, the soleplate needs to be resurfaced. Clean the soleplate stampings first. Remove dirt, paint and old finish from the stamping using a scriber or sharpened awl. **Keep the tool inside the stamping.**

1-50 Position the clubhead in a vise as shown. Draw a fine cut file across the soleplate from the heel towards the toe. Remove as many scratches, dings and dents as possible without removing stampings. Usually, all but the very deepest dings can be removed.

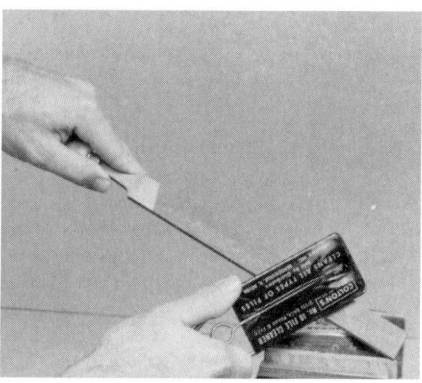

1-51 Lengthy filing will cause "loading." This occurs when metal collects between the teeth of the file. Failure to remove these metal clots will result in deep gouges inflicted on the soleplate as the file is drawn across the plate. **A good file cleaner should be kept close by and used frequently.**

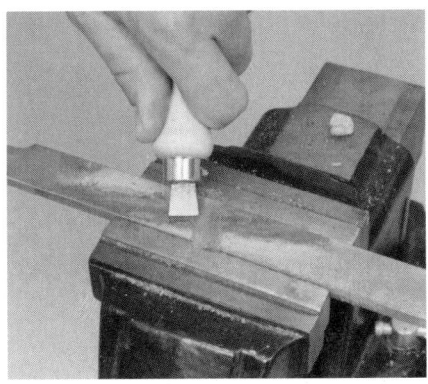

1-52 Stubborn metal or old epoxy can be removed using a piece of soft brass. Tighten the file in the vise and push the brass across the file face. This will push the residue from the file. A piece from an old brass soleplate works well for this.

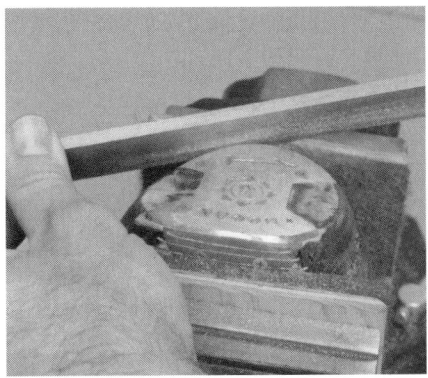

1-53 Not only must the bottom of the soleplate be refurbished, but the sides of the soleplate as well. This photo shows the trailing edge and …

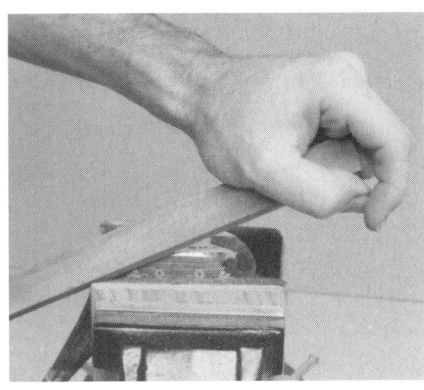

1-54 … the leading edge being filed. Use a radiusing motion with the file for best results. Maintain a defined edge around the soleplate.

1-55 A properly resurfaced soleplate will look like this. Note the file marks are running in the same direction on the bottom of the plate (toe to heel).

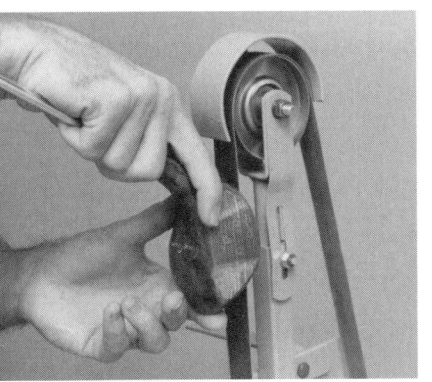

1-56 An alternative to filing is to use a belt sander. Using this machine will substantially speed up this step. For safest and fastest results, hold the club as shown. **Always wear eye protection when working around motorized machinery.**

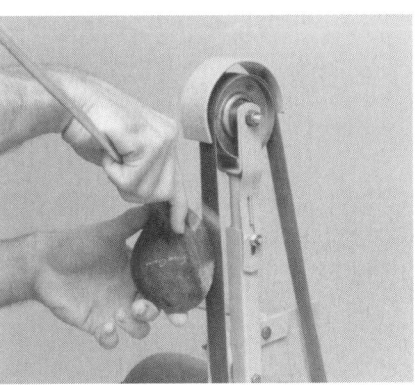

1-57 As before, lightly sand the leading edge …

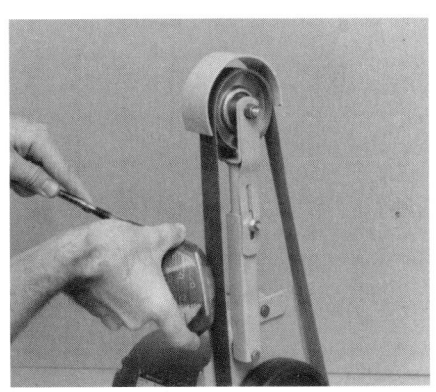

1-58 … and the trailing edge. **As with any motorized operation, a little practice first on junk golf clubs is highly recommended.**

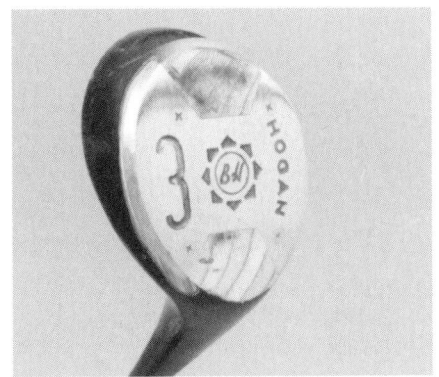

1-59 This is a good example of how the bottom and edges of a soleplate should look after grinding. A smooth and uniform filing or grinding will save excess sanding and sandpaper wear later.

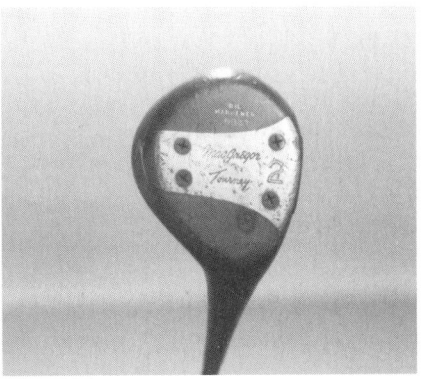

1-60 Here is the typical valuable classic club. Most of these soleplate dings can be removed. The deep ding by the number stamp should not be removed as most of the number would be removed in the process. The value of the club would then drop.

1-61 To preserve a wood stamping, apply paste stripper once again to the stamping after the finish is removed. Refinishing a classic club is an acceptable practice as long as proper care is taken to preserve the head stampings and maintain originality.

1-62 Wait five minutes then wipe the stripper from the head. Be careful to keep the stripper off plastic inserts.

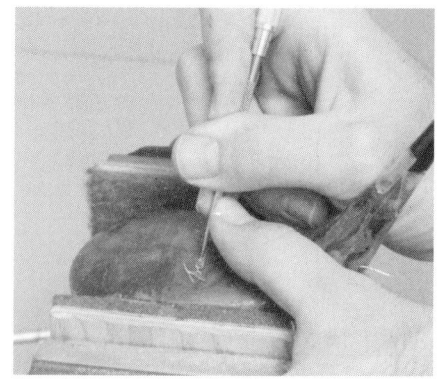

1-63 Re-etching the stamping involves a two-step process. First, simply etch the old paint from the stamp. The second step requires the stamp to be deepened. Carefully push the scriber through the stamp. **DO NOT ALLOW THE SCRIBER TO SLIDE OUT OF THE STAMP WHILE ETCHING.**

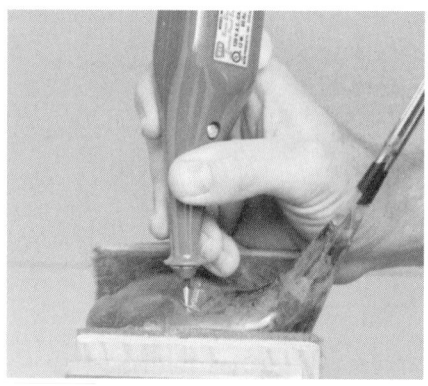

1-64 An inexpensive **Electric Vibrator Engraver** will also work, as long as the engraver has a fine point. Some engravers have a point that is too blunt and serious damage will result to the stamping. With the proper point, set engraver knob on "FINE" setting and proceed slowly and carefully.

1-65 A properly etched stamping will look like this. The paint has been removed and the stamping deepened. It is necessary to deepen the stamping as some depth will be lost through the sanding step. The discoloration around the stamp is normal and will sand out. The clubhead is now ready for sanding.

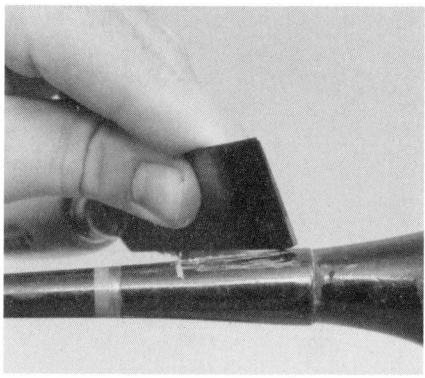

1-66 A club with a plastic whipping cover requires additional steps before sanding. Most covers have several coats of polyurethane. Scrape the cover lightly with a knife. If the scrapings are black, there is no polyurethane coating. If the scrapings are clear or yellow, there is a polyurethane coating.

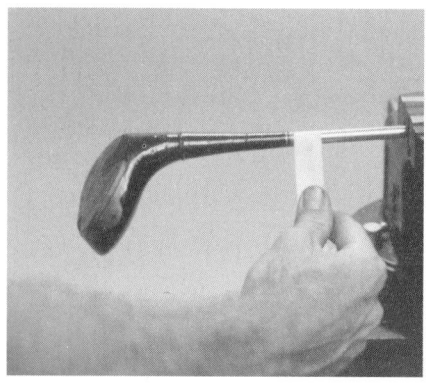

1-67 If there is no polyurethane coating, proceed to photo 1-73. If your cover has a coating it must be removed before the clubhead is sanded. First, wrap a layer of masking tape around the shaft above the plastic ferrule.

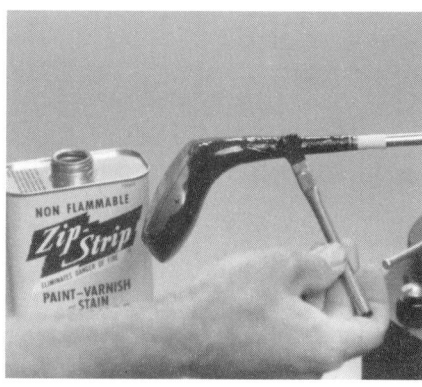

1-68 Brush on a light coat of stripper. Cover both the ferrule and the whipping cover.

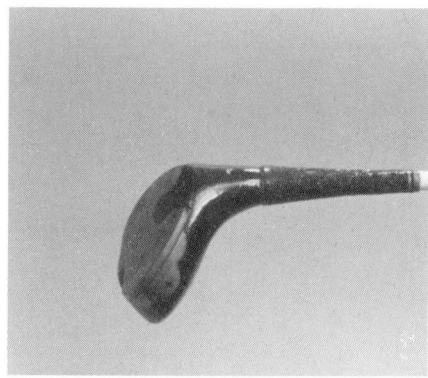

1-69 Leave the stripper on the cover and ferrule until minor surface rippling is noticed. This will usually occur within the first 25 seconds after application. The purpose of the stripper is to soften the polyurethane without damaging the plastic.

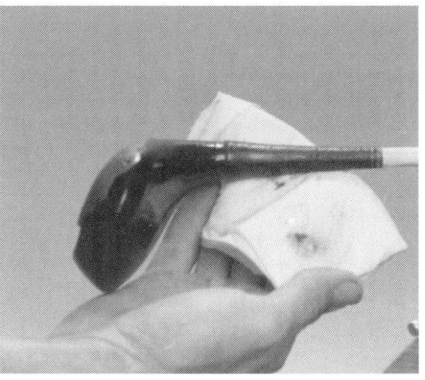

1-70 Once you notice the minor rippling, wipe the stripper off the plastic cover and ferrule. If you wait too long, the stripper will eat into the plastic. Never leave the stripper on the cover longer than 40 seconds.

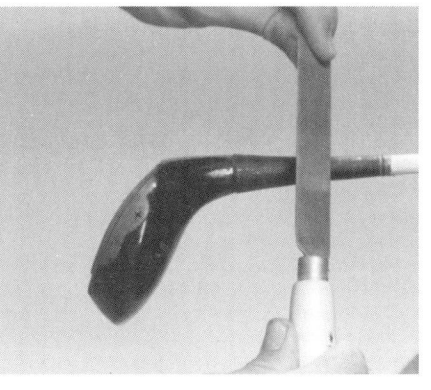

1-71 The softened polyurethane may now be removed through filing or light scraping with a **Detail Knife.** Be careful not to dig into the plastic.

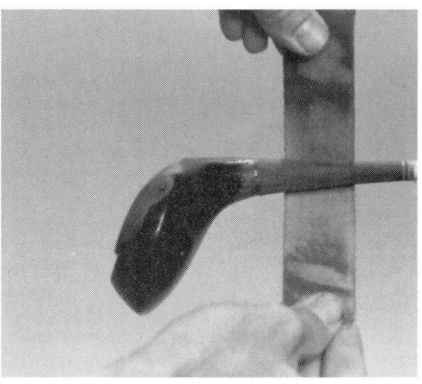

1-72 Lightly sand the cover with 150 grit sandpaper. Sanding will remove the scratches and flat spots left from filing or scraping.

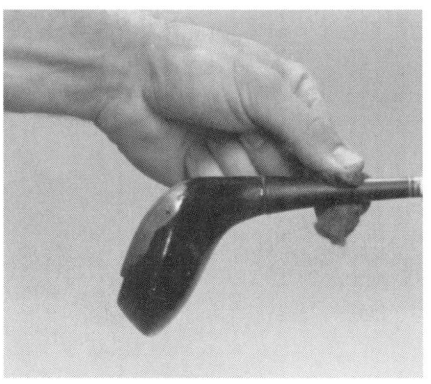

1-73 Rub the cover and ferrule with fine 000 steel wool. Steel wool will eliminate the scratches left from the use of the sandpaper. The ferrule should be very smooth but somewhat dull in appearance after this step.

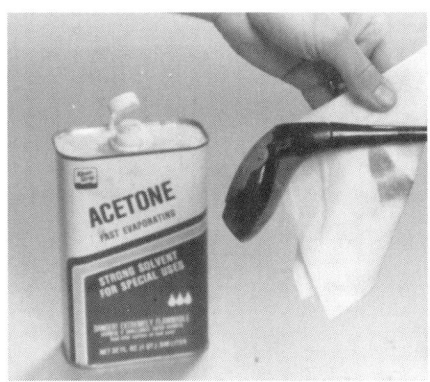

1-74 Dampen a paper towel with acetone and quickly wipe the cover and ferrule. This will bring out the attractive deep plastic gloss.

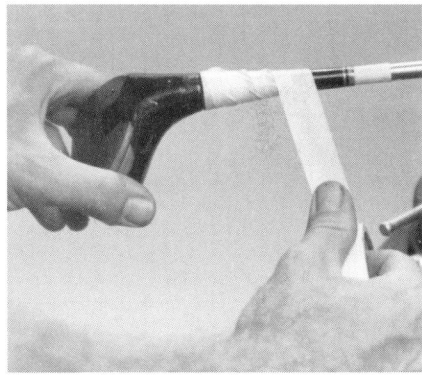

1-75 Wrap the cover and ferrule with masking tape. During the ensuing sanding steps, take great care to avoid the cover. Later, after sanding, refer to photos 1-104 and 1-105 which show how to finish the area where the wood head and plastic hosel cover meet.

1-76 The Golf Club Refinishing Machine utilizes double sponge-backed sanding drums. These sanding procedures apply to all sanding sleeve type sanders, both sponge rubber and pneumatic. It also applies to sanding cones and sanding belts as shown in photos 1-101 and 1-102.

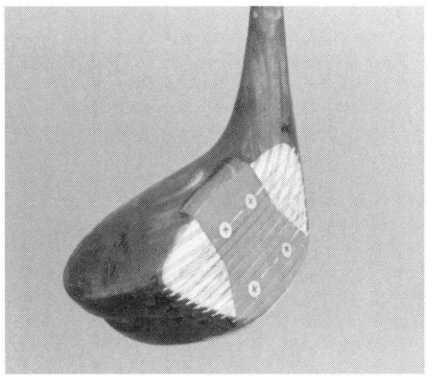

1-77 The goal here is to preserve the original shape of the clubhead. Use 80 to 100 grit sandpaper for rough sanding. Use 120-150 paper for fine sanding and 180 to 220 for very fine sanding.

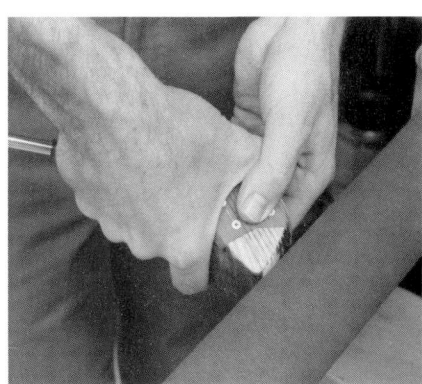

1-78 Grasp the clubhead as shown. Rotate the toe into the sanding sleeve from the edge of the face ...

19

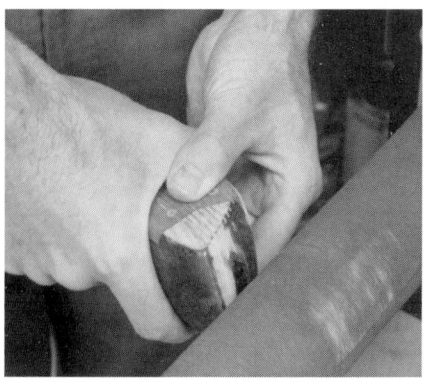

1-79 … outward to the middle of the toe. Sand from the top line around the toe down to the bottom line around the sole. **DO NOT SAND ON THE FACE.**

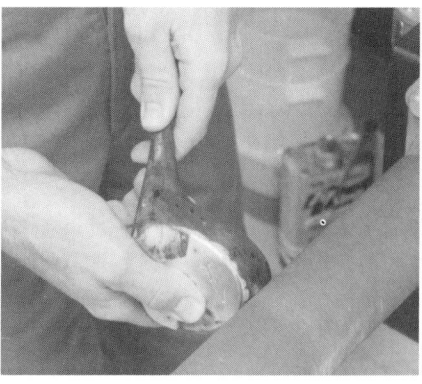

1-80 Position the club as shown. Sand from the middle of the toe to the back side of the club and …

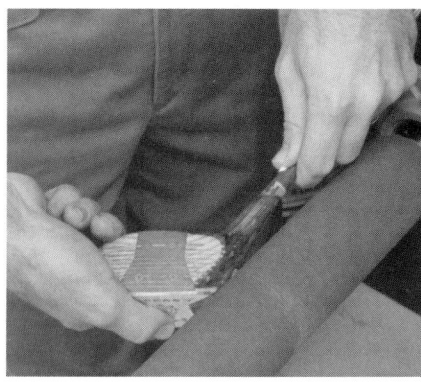

1-81 … around to the back of the hosel. Now sand up to the heel side of the face.

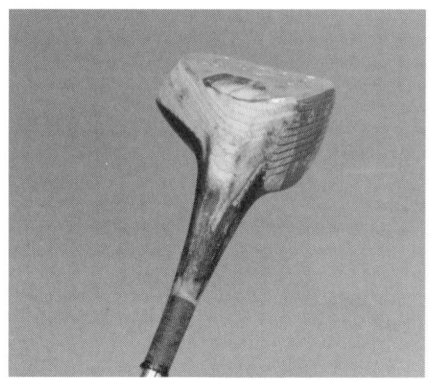

1-82 The side portion of the club should look like this. It is not necessary to remove all of the color at this point. Simply remove the majority of the leftover finish and most of the color while preserving the shape of the clubhead.

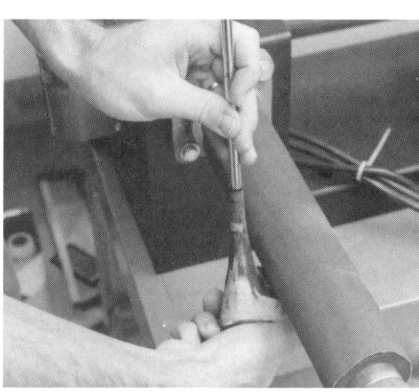

1-83 Hold the clubhead as shown. Place the back top portion of the clubhead against the sanding sleeve and …

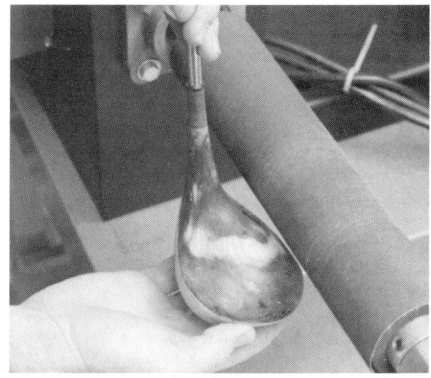

1-84 … rotate the clubhead away from the sleeve. This will create a sanded area from the back of the club to the front. Sanding from back to front will ensure that the sanding marks are running parallel with the grain on persimmon heads.

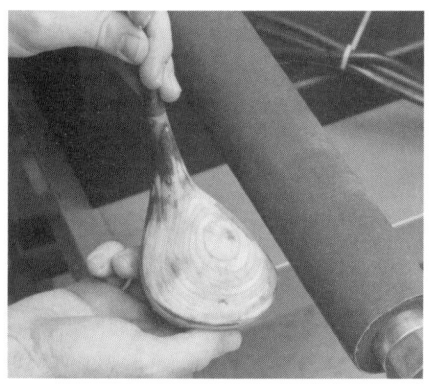

1-85 Repeat the back to front movement across the top of the clubhead until the entire top is sanded.

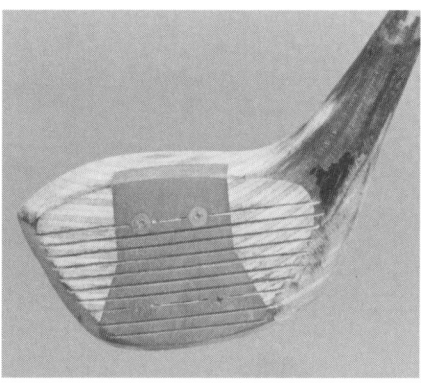

1-86 When sanding the top of the clubhead, great care must be taken along the line separating the face from the top of the clubhead.

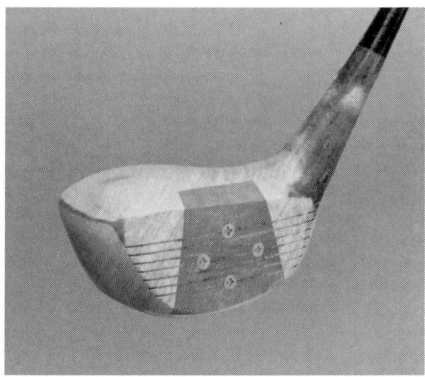

1-87 This line should not be straight or concave as shown here. Rather, the line should have a smooth symmetrical look as shown in the previous photo. Every effort should be made to avoid pulling this top line down. **The rule of thumb for sanding is again applied: preserve the original clubhead shape.**

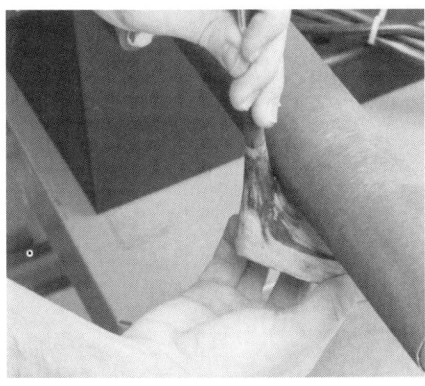

1-88 The hosel should now be sanded (except clubs with whipping covers). Place the hosel lightly against the sanding sleeve, supporting the head with one hand while holding the shaft with the other hand.

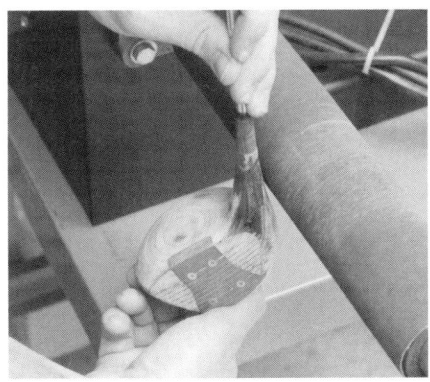

1-89 Smoothly rotate the hosel while light to medium pressure is maintained against the sleeve.

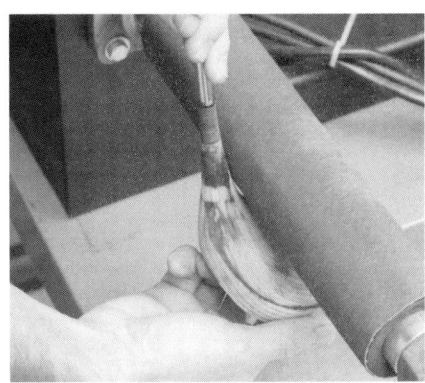

1-90 Continue to rotate the head while sanding the hosel. Keep the club constantly turning to eliminate the chance of flat spots in the hosel. The entire hosel, from the top down to the hosel/head radius is sanded.

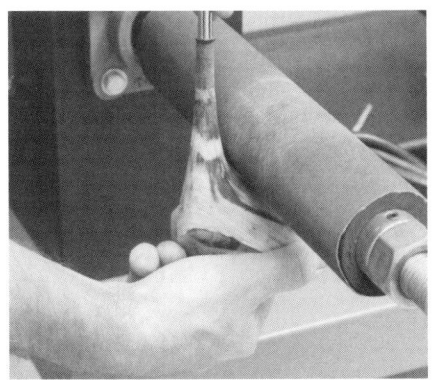

1-91 When sanding the base of the hosel (hosel radius), move the sleeve over the top of the head to ensure a smooth transition from the hosel into the head area. This eliminates ridges.

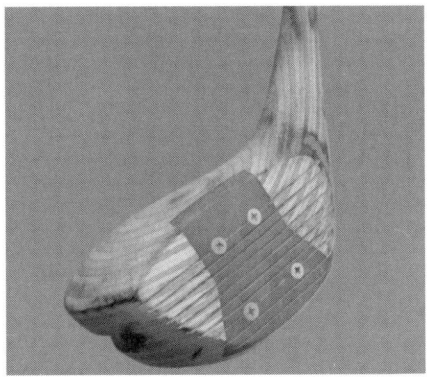

1-92 The sanded hosel should look like this. Note the presence of a stained area in the hosel. This indicates that the outside curvature of the sanding sleeve did not fit perfectly into the hosel radius. Never force the sleeve into the hosel radius. Light hand sanding will remove this excess finish.

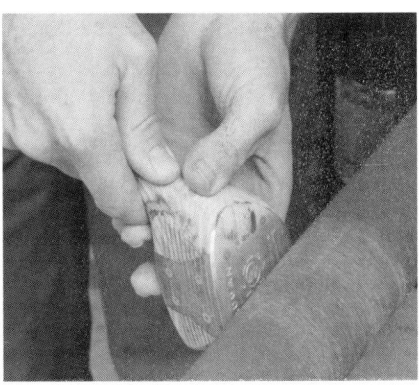

1-93 Even though the sole has been filed, we must still machine sand the sole to make sure the sanding and filing marks are running in one direction — from heel to toe. Sanding will also blend in the filing marks.

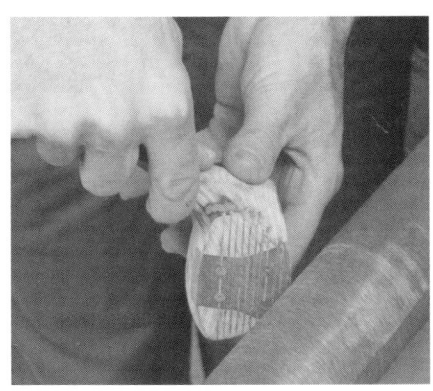

1-94 The leading edge and trailing edge are also lightly sanded. This again will blend in the filing marks.

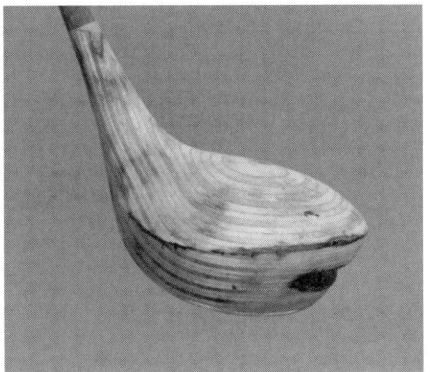

1-95 The rough-sanded club should look like this. Notice there is finish around the edges of the clubhead. This is acceptable at this stage, as this indicates the shape has not been altered. The previous sanding steps would now be repeated using the medium 120 or 150 grit paper, followed by the 180 or 220 paper.

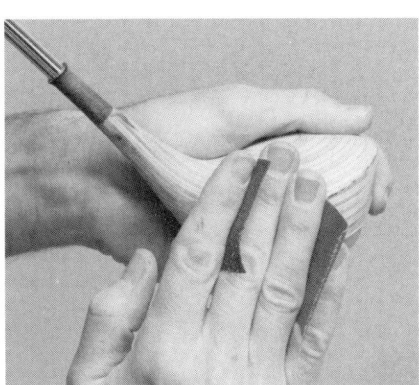

1-96 After the final sanding, the edges will be sharp. Lightly radius the edges with a strip of 180 or 220 grit paper as shown. Radiusing the edges is often referred to as "blocking."

1-97 Some refinishers prefer to use a **Sand-O-Flex** for the blocking step. The sharp edge is turned into the rotating "loose" sandpaper, thus removing the sharp edge. Be sure to use a very fine grit loading.

1-98 Machine sanding the hosel will some-times create ridges in the hosel. These are easily removed by holding the clubhead as shown. Rotate the club while sanding the hosel up and down. **"Blocking" the edges and this step are the final sanding detailing steps which assure that everything is completely blended together.**

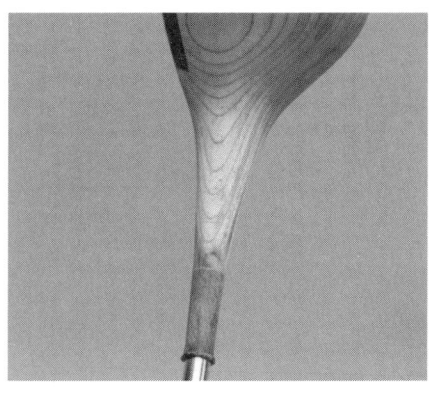

1-99 A properly sanded hosel will be smooth and possess a nice even taper from top to bottom. There should be no bulges or irregularities. This club is now ready for face masking as detailed in photos 1-115 through 1-123.

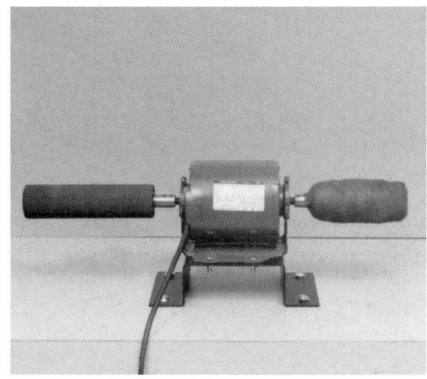

1-100 An alternative to the Golf Club Refinishing Machine is the **Economy Sanding Machine.** This unit is ideal for shops with limited space. It can easily be mounted to a sturdy bench and is then ready for use.

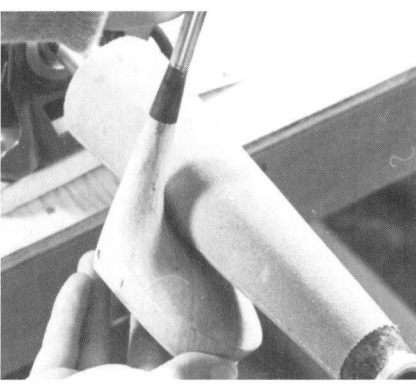

1-101 The old finish can also be removed on a sanding cone using 80 or 100 grit paper. Use 120 or 150 grit for medium sanding and 180 or 220 for final sanding. Although excel-lent results can be obtained with a cone, it has two drawbacks. First, the replacement sanding sleeves are expensive and second, the felt backing does not conform to the head shape as easily as the sponge rubber type backing.

1-102 A 3" wide by 132" long sanding belt is used to remove old finish. The same grits are used as in the previous sanding steps. A belt idler unit is located on the floor. The sander is powered by a ⅓ H.P. motor. Belts are commercially available.

1-103 A **Sand-O-Flex wheel** can also be used to strip off old finish and final sand the head. For best results, use model 550A Sand-O-Flex powered by a ½ H.P. motor at 1725 RPM. Model 350 Sand-O-Flex can be used with a ⅓ H.P. motor, but is slower in removing the finish than the 550A model.

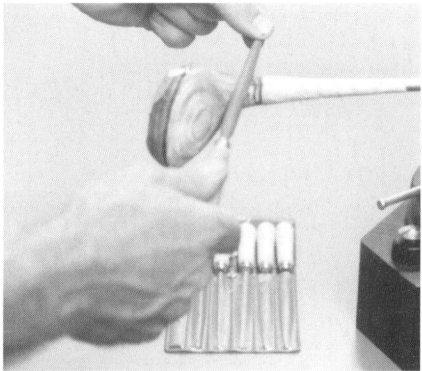

1-104 After sanding a club with a plastic whipping cover, there will be some finish around the base of the cover. This cannot be removed on a sanding machine. Place the club in a vise as shown and lightly file the excess finish from the hosel. A small flat file works best.

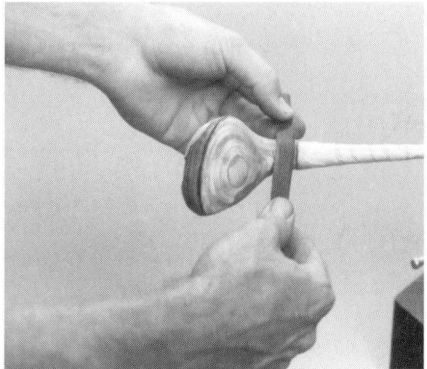

1-105 After the finish is removed, lightly sand the hosel with 180 grit or finer paper. This will blend in any file marks and/or flat spots.

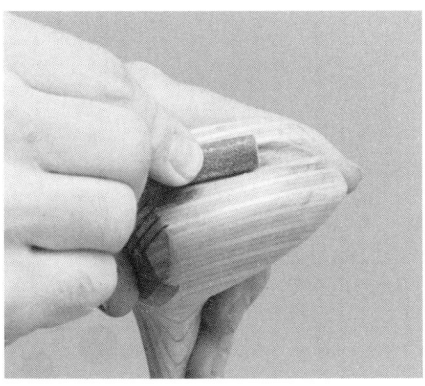

1-106 Occasionally, you will find a slot running through the toe or back portion of a club. A slot is best cleaned by first running a ½" or smaller round file through the slot. Then, lightly sand the slot with fine sandpaper wrapped around the file.

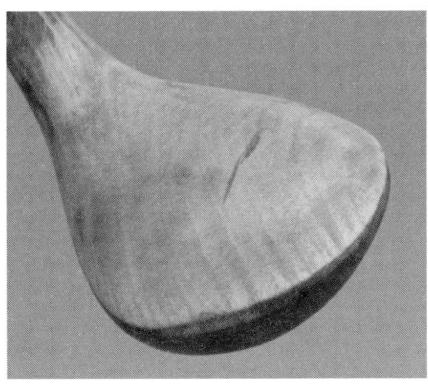

1-107 You may not be able to sand out some deep indentations in the wood head. The dent can sometimes be repaired by using the following technique which works best on persimmon heads.

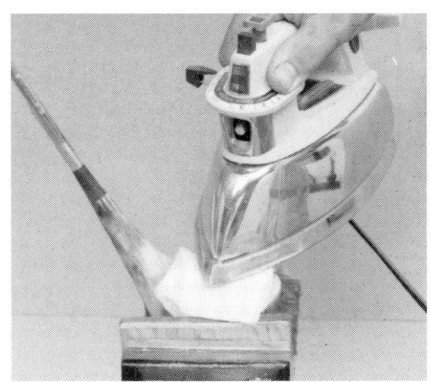

1-108 Lay a wet cloth over the damaged area. Iron the cloth directly over the dent. The dent will be infused with moisture and the steam created will raise the wood grain. This step is best performed after the rough sanding step. Once the wood grain has raised, proceed to the next sanding step.

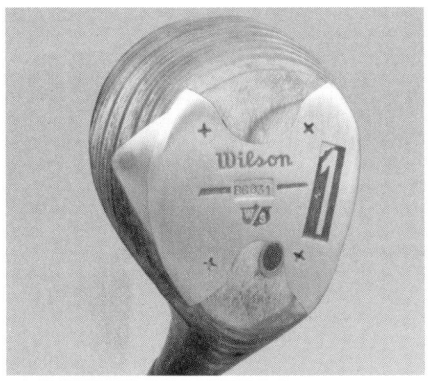

1-109 Some refinishers prefer a satin look to the soleplate. This is best accomplished by…

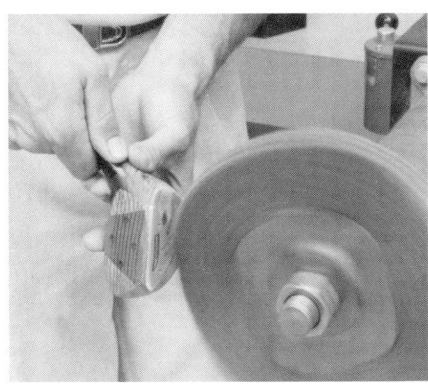

1-110 … lightly pressing the soleplate against the face of a **Scotch-Brite™ Wheel.** This step is performed just prior to the stain application.

1-111 In rare cases, a customer may wish to have the soleplate polished. Proceed as follows to buff the soleplate: apply buffing compound to the **Stitched Buffing Wheel.** (See Table 1-2 at the end of this chapter for selection of proper buffing compound.)

1-112 Buff the soleplate to the desired lustre. After polishing, remove the buffing compound from the soleplate by wiping with alcohol. Be careful not to get compound on the wood portion of the sole unless the wood will be covered with an opaque paint. If compound residue remains on the wood, wipe the wood with alcohol or acetone.

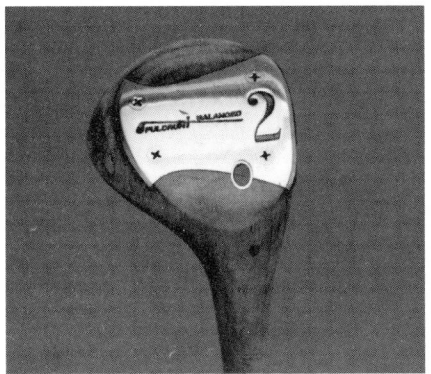

1-113 The results of a polished soleplate can be outstanding, however, the ensuing coats of finish adhere best to a somewhat rougher surface. Adhesion problems may occur as a result of polishing the metal.

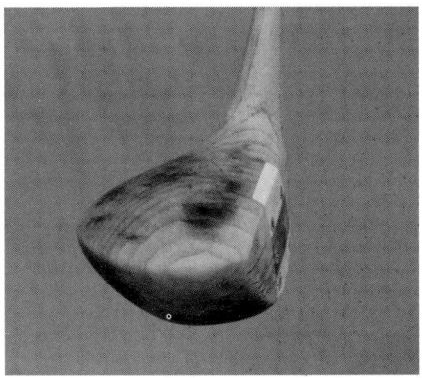

1-114 This is a professionally sanded clubhead. Note some of the original stain is still present in the wood. There are three possible reasons for this …

1. The refinisher will stain the club using an identical color. Therefore, it is not necessary to remove all of the original stain.

2. A colorcote will be applied to the head. This means a coating of opaque paint will cover the old stain.

3. The original factory staining did not evenly penetrate the wood. This can be caused by imperfect sanding, wood imperfection or various absorption differences in the grain hardness, or inconsistency in the stain itself.

Many beginning refinishers will look at the club pictured in photo 1-114 and immediately assume more sanding is necessary. This is not the case. Further sanding will only reduce the size of the clubhead and, in the end, some of the stain would probably still be present.

Pursuing this course could also ruin the club. Some refinishers have been known to press the stained area against the face of a sander until the area is clean. This creates a clean head but the clubhead shape is less than desirable.

Be reasonable in your expectations of what will and will not sand out. Also, adopt a policy of advising your customer of the possible consequences should the decision be made to change the color of the club from a dark stain to a lighter stain.

Some commercial bleaching agents can help remove excess stain. Experiment carefully with a bleach before attempting to use it on a customer's club.

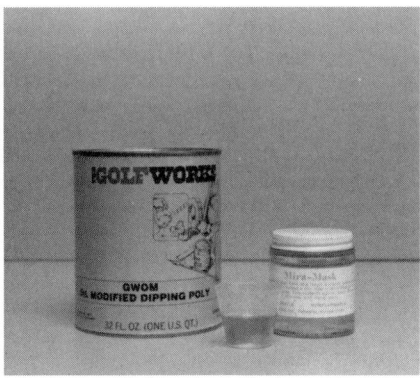

1-115 Before the clubhead can be stained, a protective coating must be applied to the face and insert. The material used for coating can be polyurethane, primer sealer or Mira-Mask, a product made expressly for this. Old, thickened polyurethane works best. The poly seeps into the wood pores and prevents stain penetration into the face.

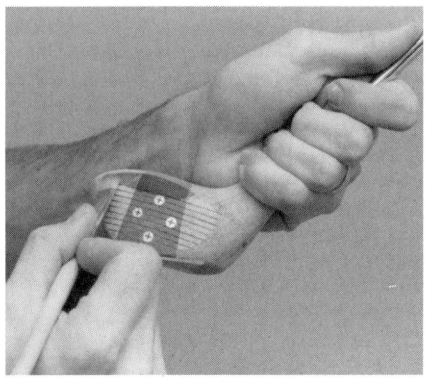

1-116 The material is spread onto the face using either a stiff bristled artist's brush or your finger. Here we are using the brush. Apply a small portion of the masking material to the upper portion of the face. Spread this evenly along the top of the face out to the toe. Keep the masking material in the face outline only.

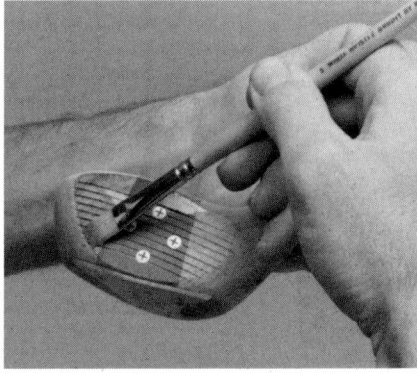

1-117 Brush the mask from the top of the toe to the bottom of the face. This is the easiest portion of the face to mask, as there should be a well-defined line between the face and toe portion of the clubhead. Note the brush is always inside the face. This helps prevent accidental spreading outside the face.

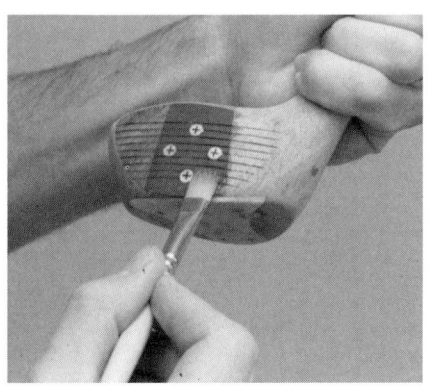

1-118 We're halfway finished. Notice the insert is also covered. Stain can penetrate deeply into fibrous type inserts. It will not penetrate into plastic, aluminum or epoxy inserts. Until you are able to identify the different insert types, all inserts should be masked.

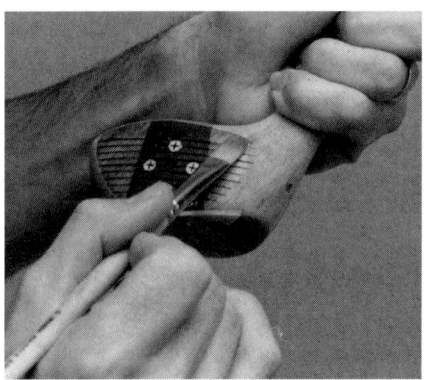

1-119 Brush the mask from the insert back toward the heel. This area is more difficult to mask, as the line between the face and hosel area is not always defined. Some refinishers choose to pencil in the shape of the face prior to masking.

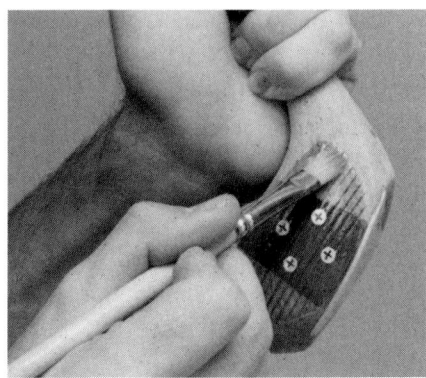

1-120 Spread the mask from the bottom of the face to the top of the face, working the mask slowly back into the heel area until the desired shape is achieved. Practice will help develop an "eye" for a properly shaped face.

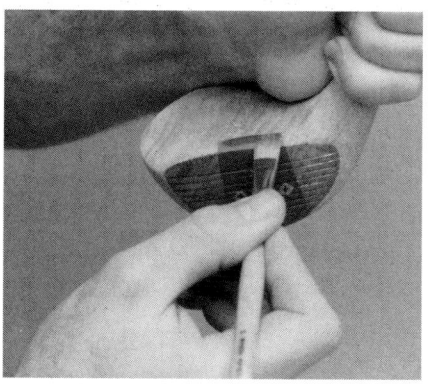

1-121 Carefully apply the mask to the top of the insert. Remember, any area coming in contact with the mask will not take stain. Keep the mask on the insert.

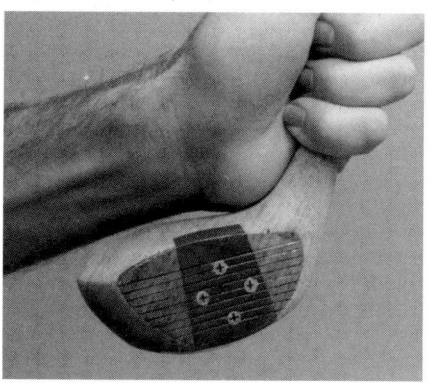

1-122 This is a properly masked face. The toe and heel of the face are well defined, with good shape.

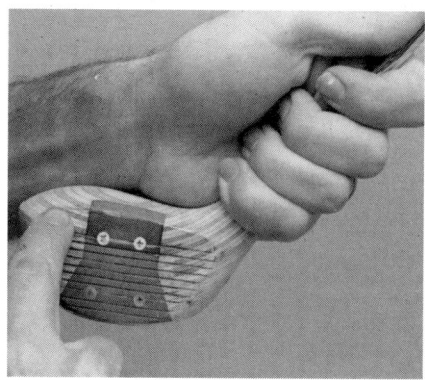

1-123 Some refinishers prefer to apply the mask with a finger. Although somewhat messier, they feel more in control using a finger instead of a brush. Experiment and see which method you like best. Results can be comparable. **Now the clubhead is ready for staining.**

1-124 Water or alcohol base stains work best. Table 1-4 at the end of this chapter offers complete information on various refinishing products regarding compatibility, application type and average drying times. At The GolfWorks®, we feel it is easier to work with water base stains.

1-125 For even stain coverage, completely submerge the clubhead into a container of stain for five seconds. Repeated dippings will produce a darker color. For best results, wait a few minutes between coats. The plastic container shown is most convenient for holding stains and fillers for both storage and dipping.

1-126 Remove the clubhead from the stain and allow the excess stain to drip back into the can. Note the stain does not penetrate the masked face.

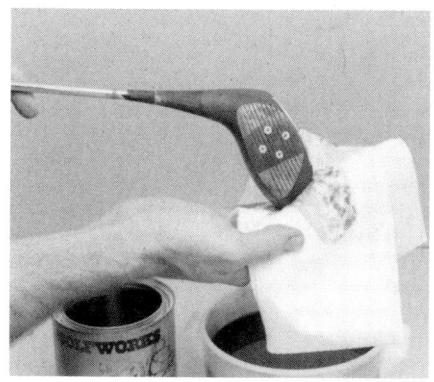

1-127 Wait 30 seconds then use a paper towel to blot the excess stain from the head. **DO NOT WIPE THE STAIN, BLOT IT.** Excess stain will also collect in the scoring lines. Place the paper towel at the end of the face and force the collected stain onto the towel by blowing along the scoring lines.

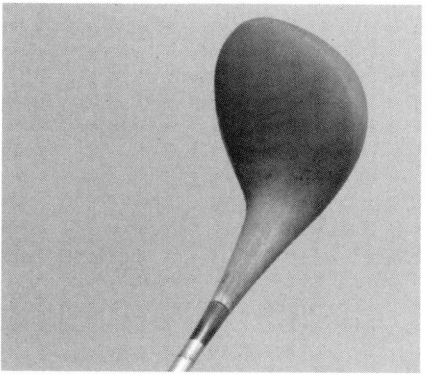

1-128 Stain dries quickly. Immediately after the clubhead is removed from the stain, it has a bright shine. As the stain dries, the clubhead will take on a duller, drier look as shown. This is to be expected. The clubhead may be advanced to the next step after drying. Drying times will vary from 4 to 12 hours depending on the stain type and drying temperature. See Table 1-4.

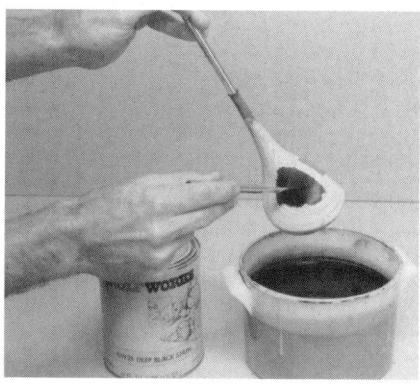

1-129 Stain may also be applied by brushing. It is difficult, however, to achieve a uniform even color through brushing. Brushing stain is best if you wish to highlight or gradually tone an area with concentrated stain.

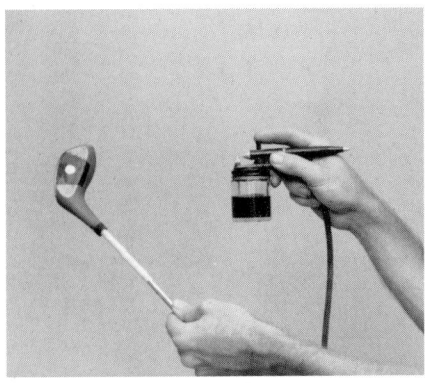

1-130 Stain can also be applied by spraying, using an airbrush and a small compressor. The disposable spraying unit with screw-on jars also works quite well and will spray up to 16 ounces of stain in one aerosol pack.

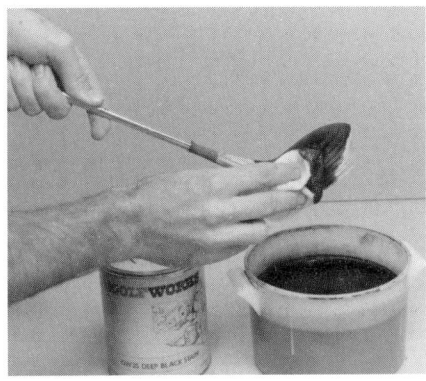

1-131 Stain can be applied by blotting or wiping. Cotton cloth or cheesecloth works very well.

1-132 Filling the clubhead is the next finishing step. Fillers are available in an oil, polyurethane or water base. See Table 1-4. The most common and easiest to work with are the oil base fillers.

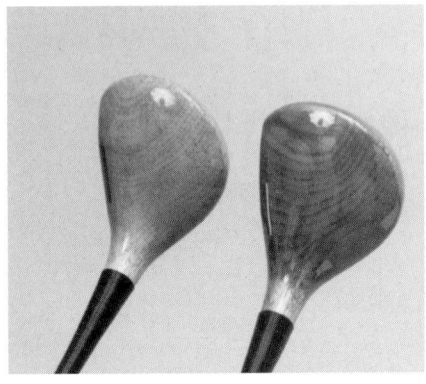

1-133 The filler serves to fill in the open pores in the wood head and provides a relatively smooth surface for the upcoming finish coats. Natural and less intense black filler are used the most. Natural retains the existing stain color while less intense black darkens the existing stain color by a few shades.

1-134 Dip the toe of the clubhead into the filler. It is not necessary to submerge the entire clubhead. Note the use of plastic gloves. Using these gloves will prevent the filler from coming in contact with your hands. Filler can stain skin and clothes.

1-135 Remove the toe of the clubhead from the container. Wipe the filler over the entire head. Be sure to cover all wood areas with the filler.

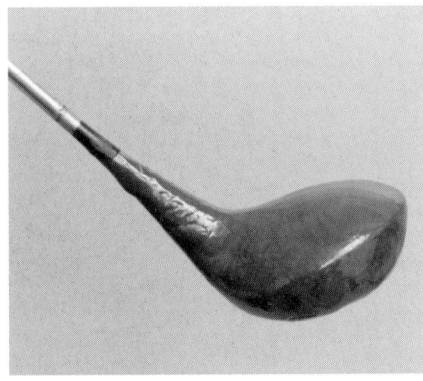

1-136 The covered clubhead will look like this. Do not remove the excess filler until the filler has "flashed off" for at least 10 minutes but not longer than 15 minutes. "Flash off" refers to the solvent evaporation the filler undergoes when exposed to the air. As solvents evaporate, the filler becomes a more solid coating.

1-137 If Mira-Filler is used, which is a polyurethane base filler, it may be first tinted with Mira-Stain. Note a portion of the filler has been removed from the can prior to changing the color. You won't want to color the entire can.

1-138 After the 10 minute "flash off" period, the filler will look quite different. It will have a dull cast to it.

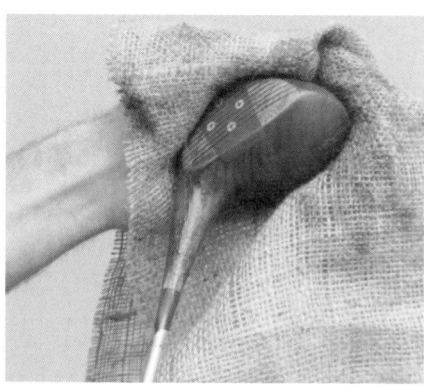

1-139 The excess filler is now wiped from the head with burlap, cheesecloth or other coarse cloth. Rub the head briskly. Failure to remove excess filler is the number one cause of finish adhesion problems.

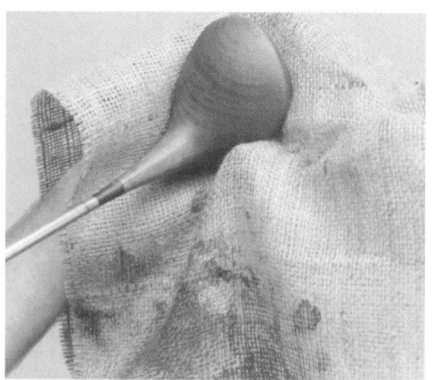

1-140 Wipe only with clean burlap. The clubhead surface should feel smooth and polished after wiping.

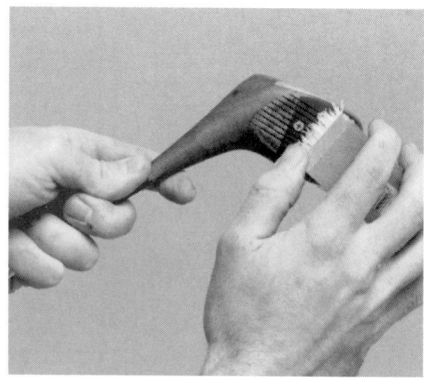

1-141 Filler will collect in the scoring lines. Brush scoring lines briskly with a **stiff bristled brush** to remove excess. The clubhead is advanced to the next step after drying. Oil type fillers require 6-12 hours and polyurethane fillers require 2-5 hours. See Table 1-4.

1-142 The clubhead will look dull at this stage. Every step hereafter will improve the cosmetics dramatically.

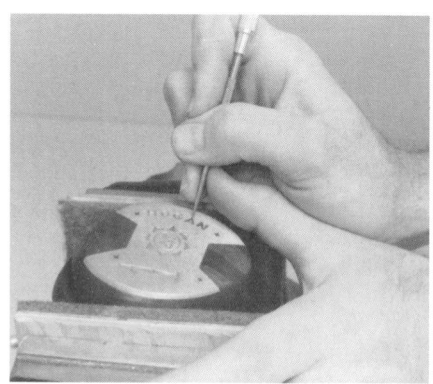

1-143 Filler will also collect in the wood and metal stampings. **Carefully pick the excess filler from the soleplate stampings using a scriber or sharpened awl.** Keep the instrument inside the stamping. Sometimes, brisk brushing with a stiff fingernail brush will remove all filler from the soleplate engravings.

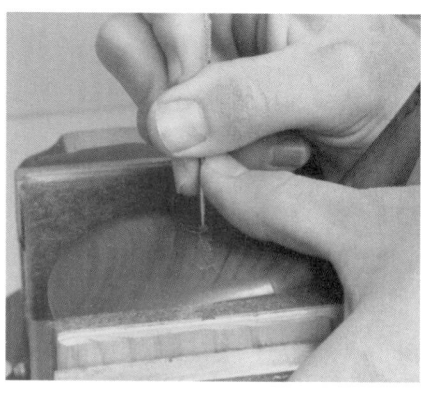

1-144 Wood stampings must also be cleaned. Use the same procedure as shown in photos 1-63 through 1-65. Again, take great care with this step. Do not wait longer than 4 hours before cleaning stampings, as the filler will become hard and more difficult to remove.

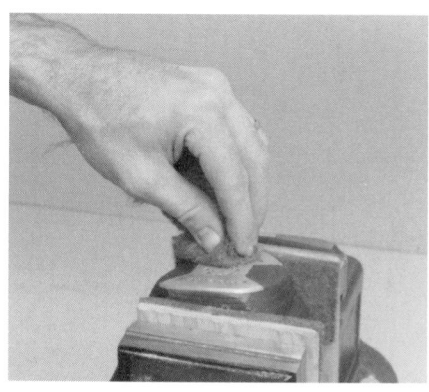

1-145 After the filler has dried, the residue left on the soleplate (and backweight) must be removed. This residue can be removed by rubbing with fine 000 steel wool. When steel wooling the soleplate, rub from heel to toe and back again. You should never rub from side to side.

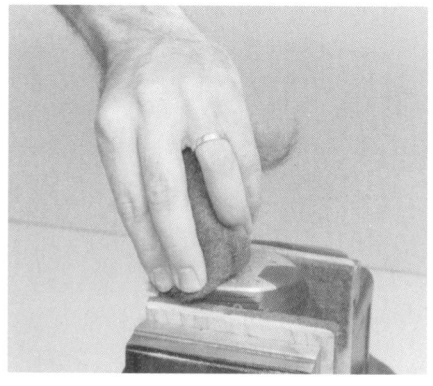

1-146 The leading edge and trailing edge of the soleplate must also be cleaned. Keep the steel wool on the metal surface — rubbing the wood portion of the club may remove some of the color.

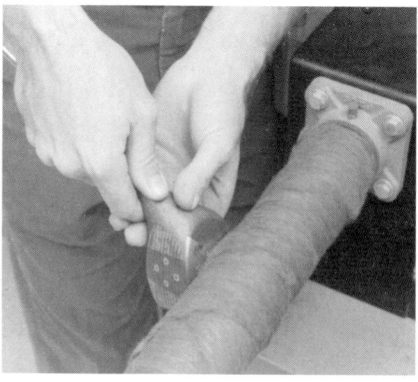

1-147 The Golf Club Refinishing Machine is easily converted for steel wooling. Slide the steel wool sleeve on and tighten the nut. Press the soleplate and backweight lightly against the turning steel wool. Filler residue is quickly removed.

27

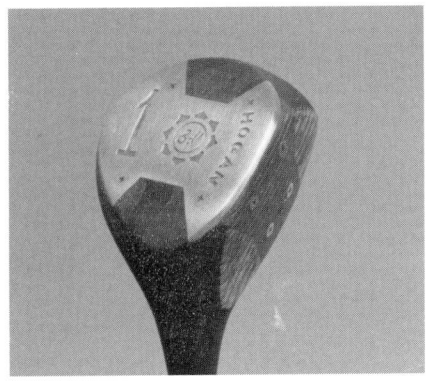

1-148 The soleplate and backweight will now look much better. There is a small amount of oil packed into the steel wool which prevents the steel wool from oxidizing. Traces of this oil have now been thinly deposited over the soleplate, backweight and anywhere the steel wool has touched the head.

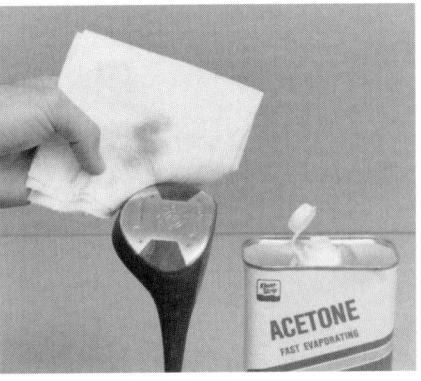

1-149 To remove the oily residue, dampen a paper towel with acetone. Wipe the towel over the soleplate and backweight only. Also, using some naphtha, lightly wipe the wood surrounding the soleplate and backweight. Do not use acetone for this.

The refinishing steps discussed thus far are identical for clubs of all colors. At this point, however, the refinishing steps will vary depending upon whether or not the club is to receive a colorcote. The purpose of a colorcote is to cover or hide the wood grain, or any surface imperfections with an opaque coating. Black or blue finished clubs normally receive this paint color coating, while clubs of other colors usually do not.

If the club will be colorcoted, continue on to step 1-150.

If the club will not be colorcoted, continue on to step 1-196.

1-150 On a colorcoted club, the soleplate, backweight and top of the insert must be covered prior to paint application. Either a clear cellophane tape or masking tape can be used. **Cellophane tape** is preferred because it is easier to see through, but will sometimes leave a sticky residue on the metal. Masking tape will not leave a residue, however, it is more difficult to see through.

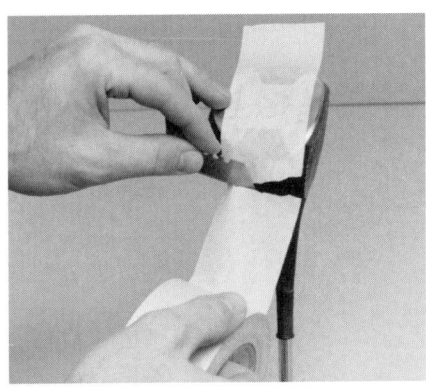

1-151 Lay a piece of tape across the sole-plate. The tape should be at least 2" wide and extend over the heel and toe portion of the sole.

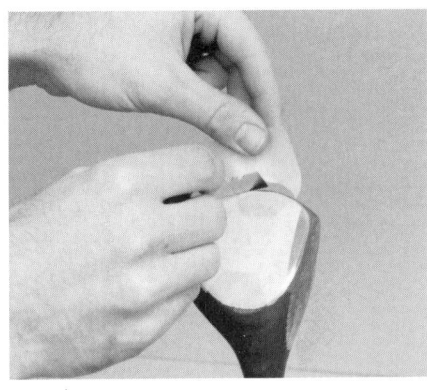

1-152 With a razor blade, carefully cut around the edge of the sole through the tape.

1-153 The bottom of the club should look like this. The masking tape being used here is 2" wide.

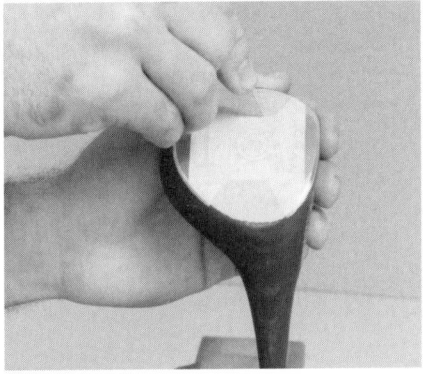

1-154 Now, carefully trace around the edge of the toe portion of the soleplate and...

1-155 ...around the heel portion of the sole-plate. Do not allow the razor blade to slip onto the metal, as a permanent scratch will result. **Note: Best results are obtained by using a very sharp blade.**

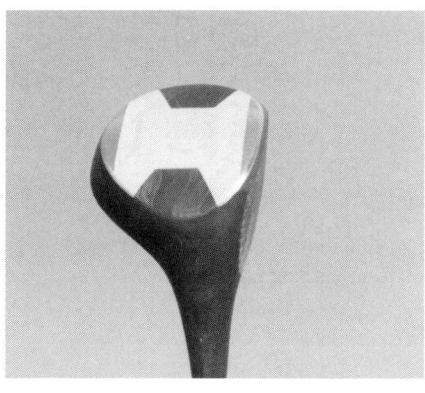

1-156 A properly outlined soleplate will look like this. Note the precise cuts that have been made around the heel and toe. A jagged edge will give an unprofessional appearance.

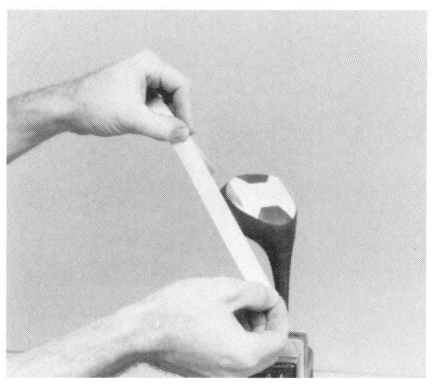

1-157 The trailing and leading edges must also be covered. Tear off a 5" piece of ½" or ¾" masking tape.

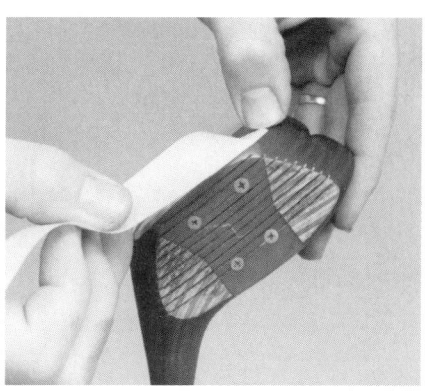

1-158 Place one end of the tape against a soleplate corner. Lay the edge of the tape against the edge of the soleplate. Wrap the tape around the leading edge, keeping the tape edge butted against the soleplate edge.

1-159 Once the tape has been positioned around the front edge, place your thumbnail against the tape and inside the soleplate corner, then...

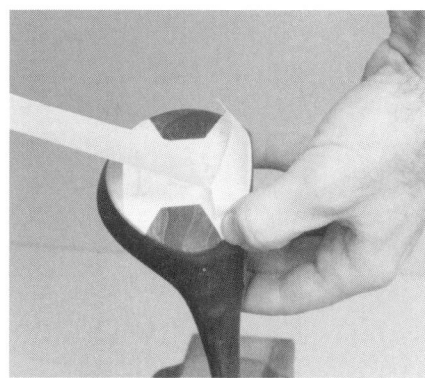

1-160 ...quickly tear the excess tape. A razor blade also works well for this.

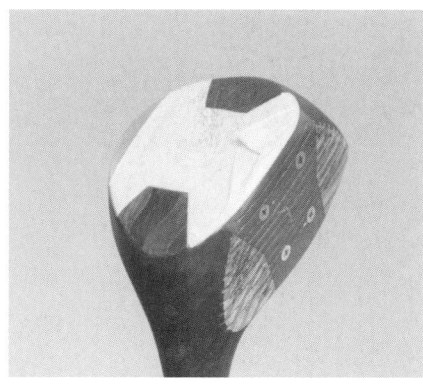

1-161 Fold the remaining portion of tape onto the soleplate. This will cover any exposed area of the soleplate on this side. Repeat steps shown in photo 1-157 through 1-161 for trailing edge.

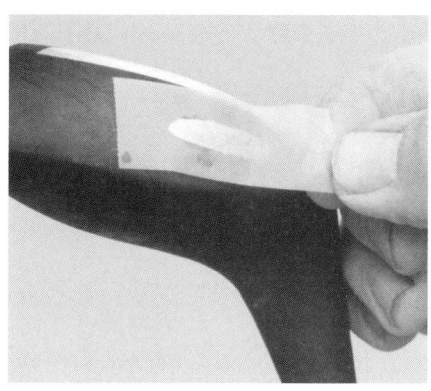

1-162 Any backweights must also be covered. Again, clear cellophane or masking tape will work. Shown here is cellophane tape.

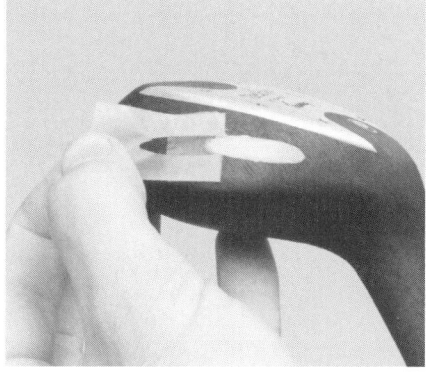

1-163 Tear off a strip of tape that will completely cover the weight. Carefully trace around the edge of the weight and remove the excess tape.

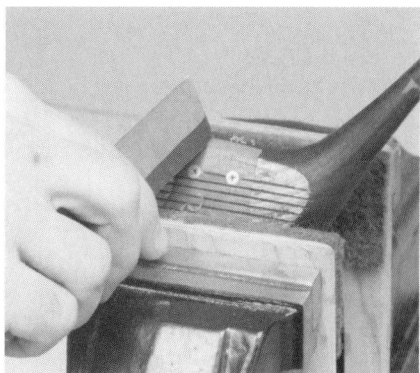

1-164 Scrape the top of the insert lightly with a **Detail Knife** to remove the polyurethane mask.

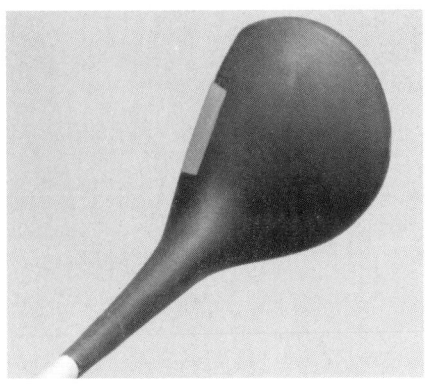

1-165 If the insert you are working with is made of ABS plastic, do the following. After scraping the top of the insert...

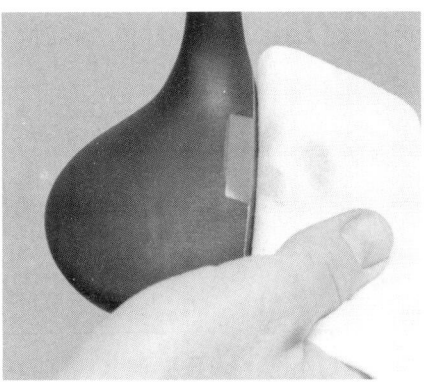

1-166 ...dampen a paper towel or cloth with acetone and wipe the top of the insert. This will substantially brighten the plastic.

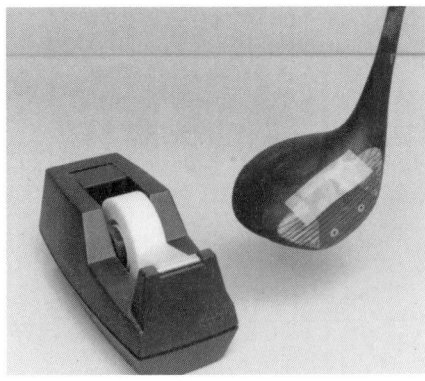

1-167 Next, lay a strip of tape across the top of the insert. One edge of the tape should butt up to the back edge of the insert. Cellophane tape should be used for this.

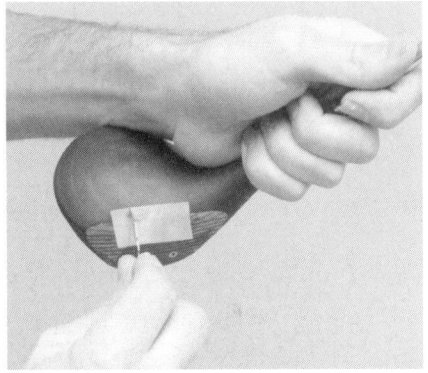

1-168 With a razor blade, cut and remove the excess tape around the sides of the insert. The extra tape overhanging the face may be folded down onto the face.

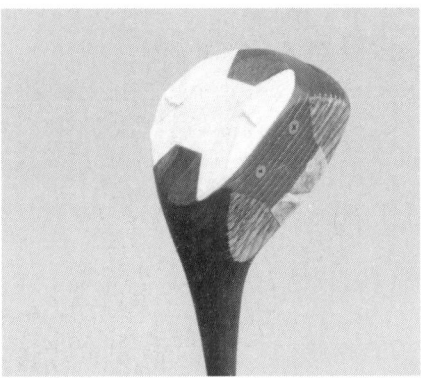

1-169 The club is now ready to be colorcoted. The face does not need a tape masking because a polyurethane coating is already masking it.

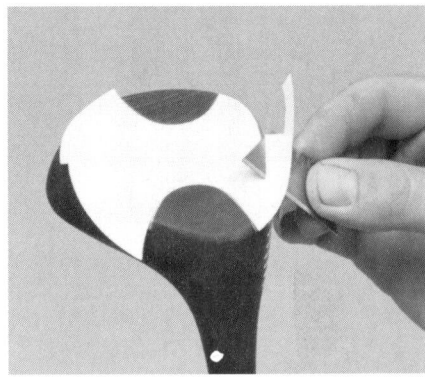

1-170 Some woodhead manufacturers sell die-cut soleplate masks to fit their own brands. This is the easiest way to mask a soleplate. Once the mask is applied to the soleplate, the edges must still be masked as already shown, using ½" or ¾" masking tape or cellophane tape.

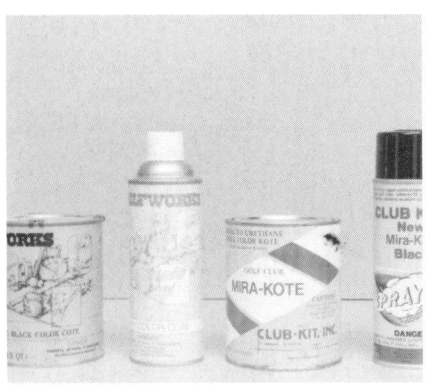

1-171 Colorcote may be applied by brushing, dipping or spraying. There are different types of colorcotes available. Check Table 1-4 at the end of this chapter for product compatibility.

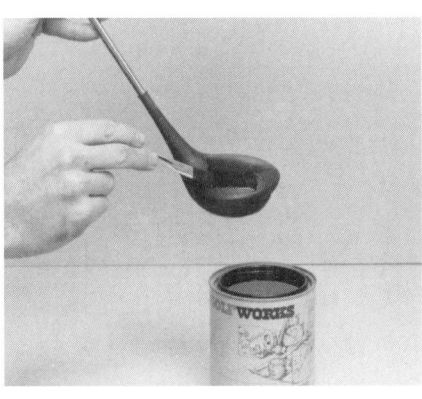

1-172 A few refinishers choose to brush the colorcote onto the head. It is difficult to achieve an even coat without streaks using this method. It works, but it is not recommended.

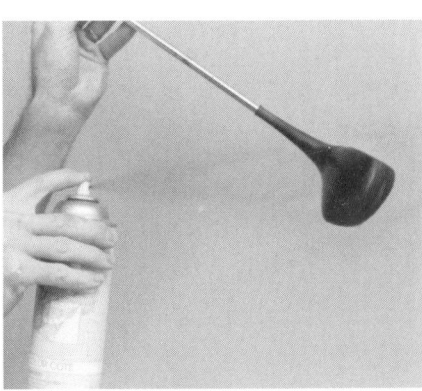

1-173 Spraying the colorcote allows the refinisher to control the depth of the coat and achieve an even coat. When spraying the colorcote from an aerosol can, keep the can approximately 15" from the clubhead surface.

30

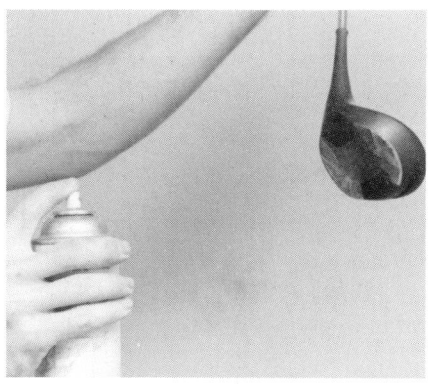

1-174 For best results, adopt a spraying technique that utilizes broad sweeping motions with the can. Turn the clubhead to expose unsprayed areas of the head.

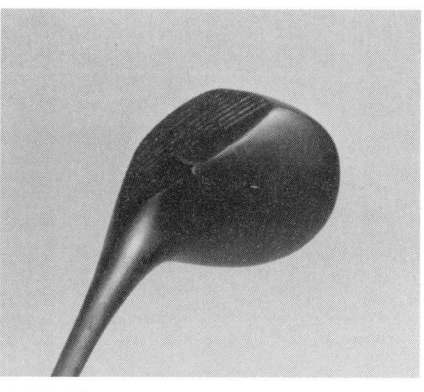

1-175 The main concern is to avoid a heavy build-up. A properly sprayed surface will not have a glossy look. Instead, the sprayed surface will have a rough, dull appearance. This is normal and no steps should be taken to smooth it out.

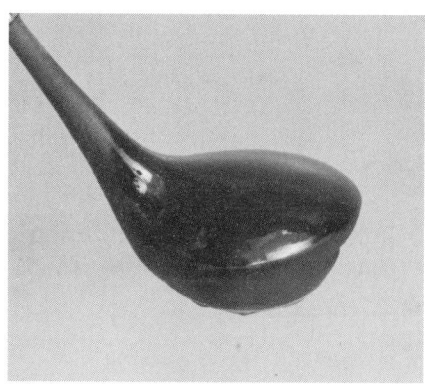

1-176 This is an example of a clubhead that has received a coating that is too heavy. If left as is, problems will develop once the next finish coat is applied. The entire head should be wiped with an acetone dampened towel to remove all the colorcote, and then reapply.

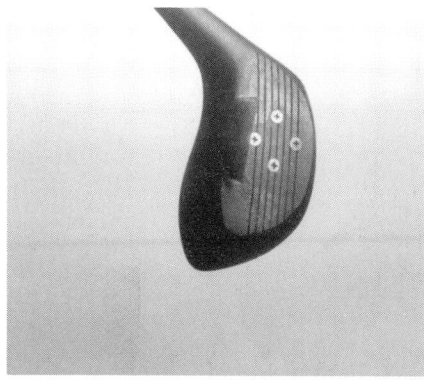

1-177 There is a fine line between too light and just right. Generally, if you are still able to see through to the face, the coating is too light. Although the above club has a coat that is too light, this can be remedied by spraying an additional light coat. **Several light coats are far better than one heavy coat.**

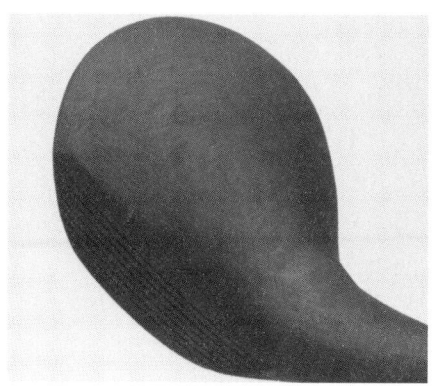

1-178 Do not be fooled if you can see the laminations on laminated maple heads. Applying more coats is a common mistake. These rings will disappear as the polyurethane coats are applied later. The lamination glue lines and the wood are not the same roughness, causing the colorcote to look smoother on each glue line vertically enhancing the lamination layers.

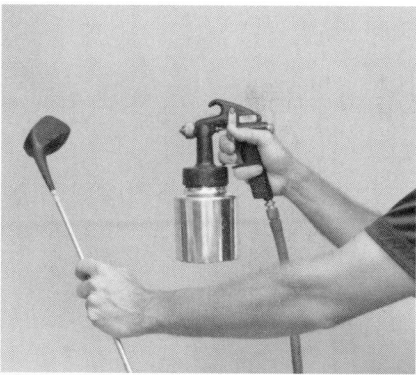

1-179 Colorcote may also be applied with an airbrush or commercial spray gun. The aerosol can method is more economical and the results are basically the same. See Table 1-4 at the end of this chapter for drying times.

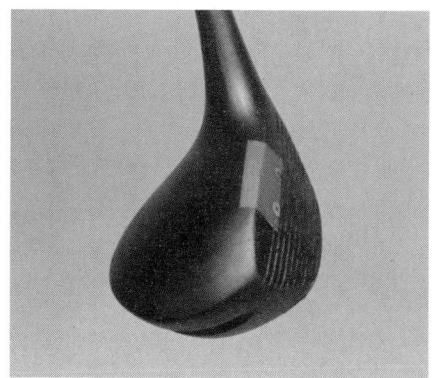

1-180 After the colorcote has dried, remove the tape that covers the top of the insert. There should now be a sharp, well defined line between the insert and the colorcoted wood.

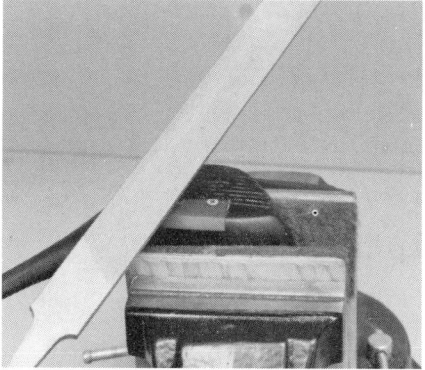

1-181 Fasten the shaft or the head securely in a vise. Select a fine cut file. Note the use of clean felt vise pads to protect the finish. The purpose of this step is to create a reasonably clean face by removing the colorcote, if used, and the polyurethane face mask.

1-182 File carefully toward the toe. Gentle strokes are sufficient to clean the face. Remember, you are only cleaning off the face with the file and removing very little material from the face itself.

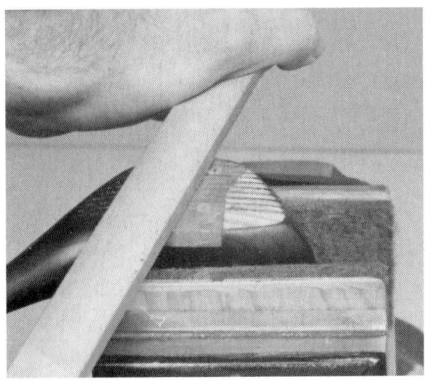

1-183 File back in the direction of the heel until the insert is clean.

1-184 Carefully work the file into the heel area. Cleaning the heel side of the face is far more difficult than the toe side. If you file into the hosel, you will have to touchup the affected area with stain and/or colorcote.

1-185 The tool shown here is called a **Detail Knife.** The Detail Knife is used to create a sharp, well-defined face.

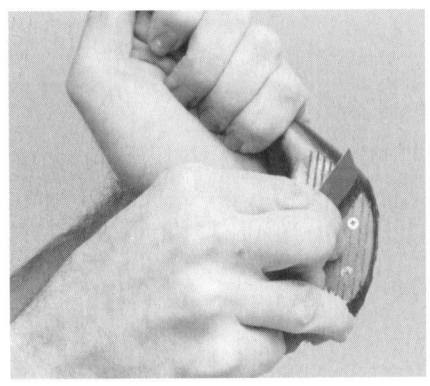

1-186 The club may be fastened in a vise, or held as shown. Scrape with the back side of the blade, not the cutting edge. Begin at the bottom of the heel side of the face and work...

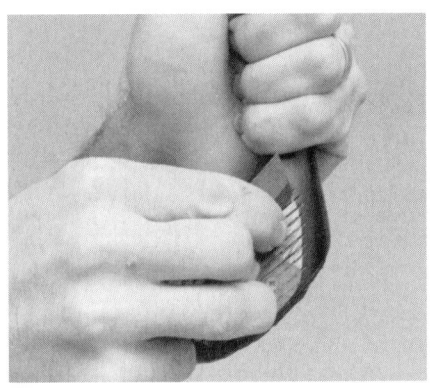

1-187 ...up toward the top of the face. Short scraping strokes work best.

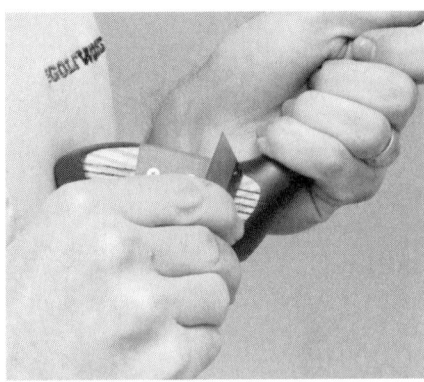

1-188 Turn the corner at the top of the face and...

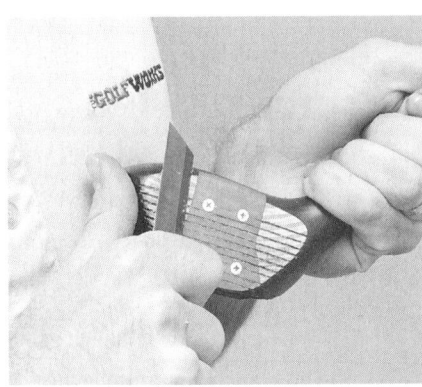

1-189 ...continue across the top of the face toward the toe.

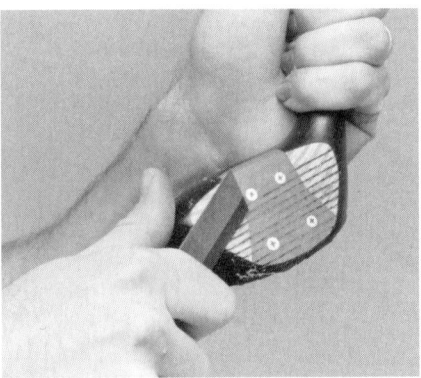

1-190 After reaching the toe, place the blade at the bottom of the face and scrape toward the top.

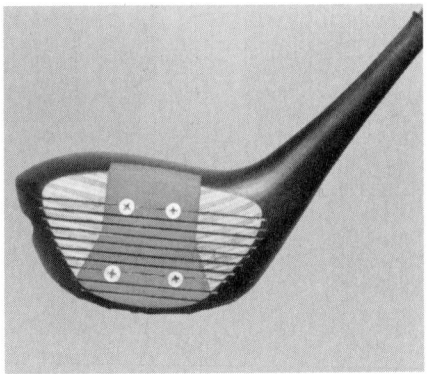

1-191 This is how a properly detailed face, which was colorcoted should look. Note the symmetrical look of the face. Drawing the knife repeatedly across the face will remove all of the file marks and create a smooth face. No face sanding will be necessary.

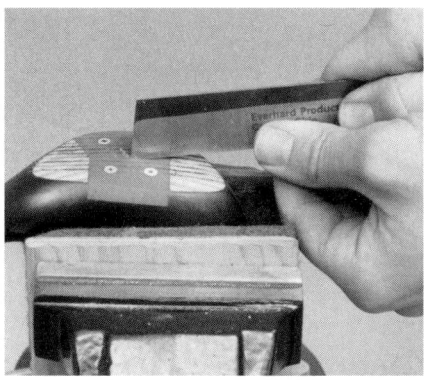

1-192 The sharp edge of the Detail Knife may be used for removing build-up in the scoring lines. **The Detail Knife is one of the refinisher's best friends and is one of the secrets to professional refinishes.**

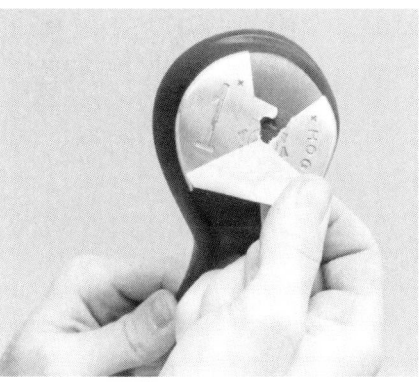

1-193 Now that the face is detailed, remove the tape from the soleplate and backweight.

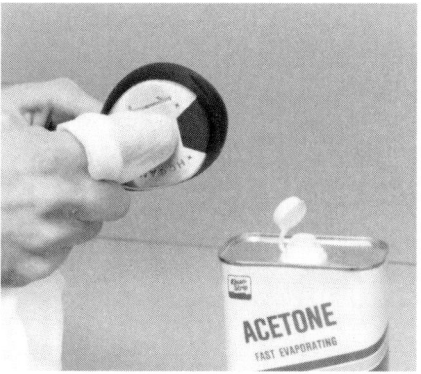

1-194 Occasionally, the colorcote will bleed onto the soleplate. This is easily removed with a piece of cheesecloth and acetone. Wrap the cloth tightly around your index finger, dampen with acetone and wipe off the excess. Keep the dampened cloth on the soleplate only. If it comes in contact with the wood, the colorcote, if any, will be removed.

1-195 As with the face, our goal is to have a well defined outline between the colorcoted wood and the soleplate. Avoid a fuzzy definition. This club is now ready for the next finishing step. Proceed to photo 1-201.

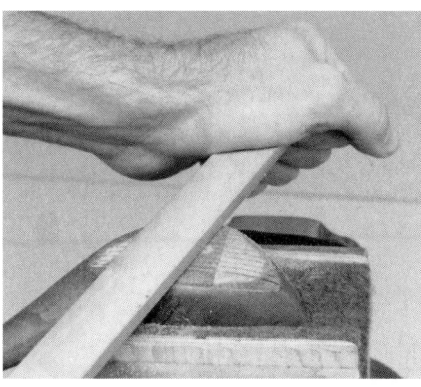

1-196 A club that was not colorcoted must also have the face cleaned. This is easier to do than with colorcoted clubs because the outline of the face is clearly seen.

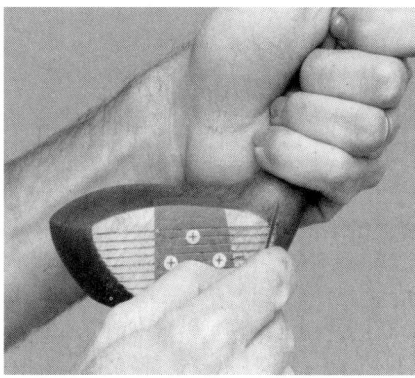

1-197 Proceed detailing the face in basically the same manner as for colorcoted clubs. **Review photos 1-185 through 1-191 for use of the Detail Knife which works best for outlining faces professionally.**

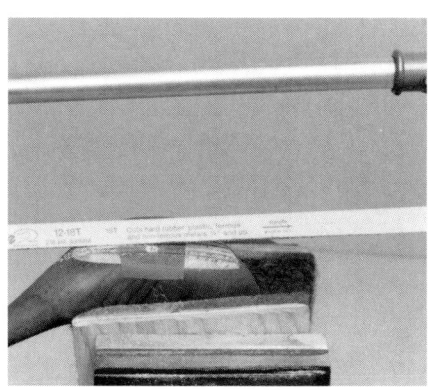

1-198 Scoring lines can be cleaned with a hacksaw blade. Keep the blade in the scoring lines. Note: An old broken piece of a scoring line blade held in the fingers will also work well.

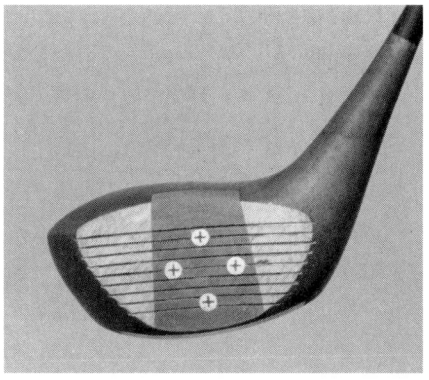

1-199 This is what a properly detailed face looks like on a non-colorcoted club.

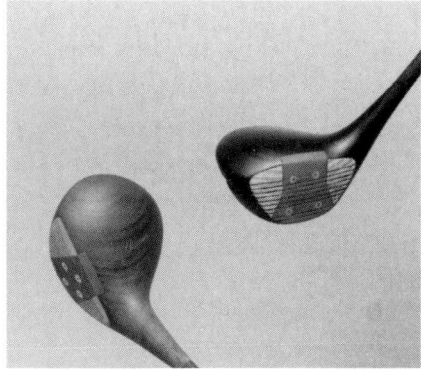

1-200 Colorcoted clubs and non-colorcoted clubs follow identical steps from this point forward.

1-201 The two most widely used types of polyurethane are Moisture Cure (MC) and Oil Modified (OM). The OM poly will be used here because it best serves the average refinisher and is easier to work with when learning refinishing techniques. Read "Additional Information" at the end of this chapter for descriptions of the various polyurethane types.

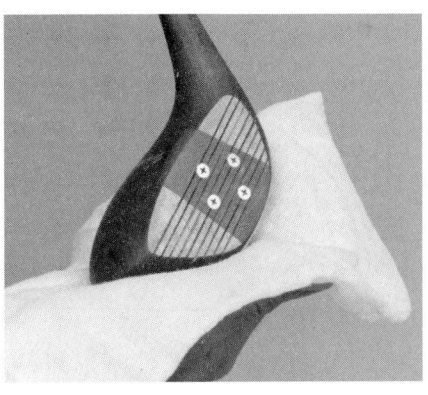

1-202 First, lightly wipe the head with a tack rag to remove any dust particles, lint, etc. An alternative to the tack rag is the use of naphtha. Wipe the head lightly with a towel dampened with this solvent. This will remove a wide range of contaminants.

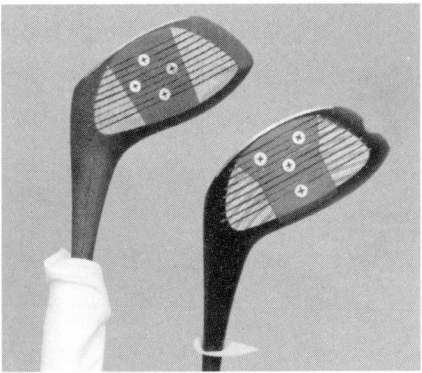

1-203 Fold a paper towel and attach it to the shaft with tape, positioning it at the top of the hosel. This towel will collect the poly runoff. Another method used to catch the polyurethane as it runs off the head is to use small rubber "dippers" available from club repair suppliers. They stretch over the grip and are slid down the shaft into position.

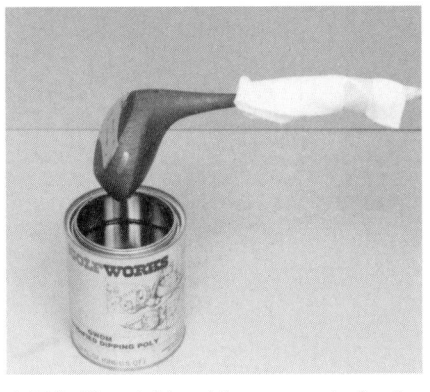

1-204 The clubhead is now ready for the first dipping. Note the level of the poly in the can is approximately 1½" below the rim. This will allow the clubhead to fully submerge without poly overflow. The can will arrive full. Pour enough out to reach the level shown. Excess poly can be used for masking faces.

1-205 Submerge the entire clubhead into the can and then...

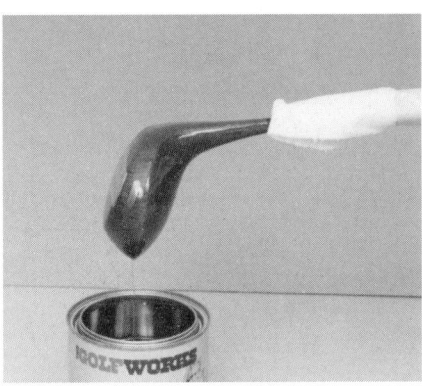

1-206 ...remove the club as **quickly** as possible. Speed in dipping is essential. Allow excess poly to run off the head and back into the can until the poly stops running and begins to drip. Immediately after the poly begins to drip...

1-207 ...turn the head up with the face cocked slightly open. This will facilitate proper poly runoff and flow from the head. It is important that the first poly coat be as thin as possible. After the toe has been turned up...

1-208 ...using your finger, wipe the poly down the uncovered hosel and blow briskly across the clubhead surface toward the hosel. This will decrease the thickness of the poly coating. A poly coat that is too thick will invite solvent entrapment problems which are explained in detail at the end of this chapter in the "Additional Information For Refinishing Woods" section.

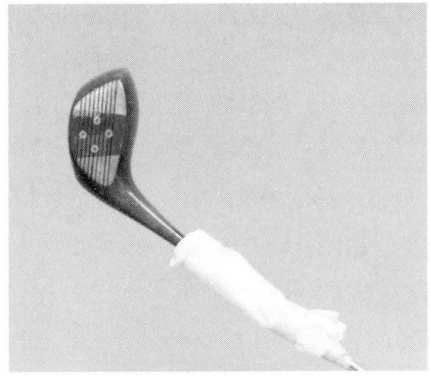

1-209 Hold the clubhead in this position until the runoff stops (usually 60 to 90 seconds). It is important to hold the clubhead as shown in this photo.

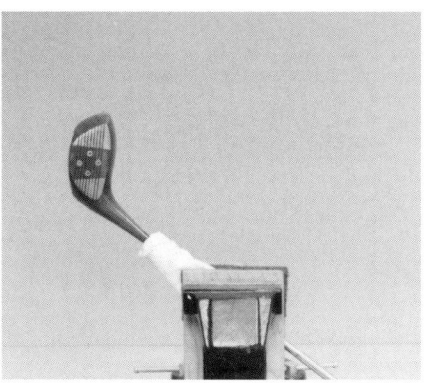

1-210 Now the clubhead may be placed in a drying rack or held in a vise for 30 minutes. Most of the solvents in the poly will evaporate during this drying period.

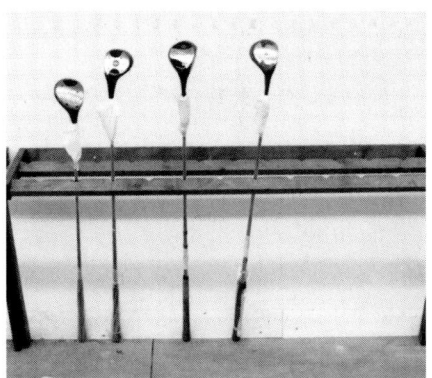

1-211 The club may then be placed under force dry conditions to accelerate the curing process or left at room temperature to dry. Table 1-4 at the end of this chapter provides average drying time information.

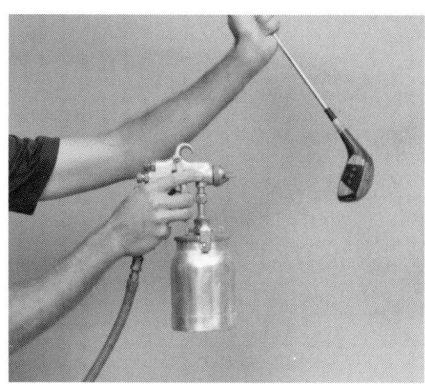

1-212 As an alternative to dipping, polyurethane is often applied by using adequate spray equipment consisting of a compressor, spray gun and spray booth.

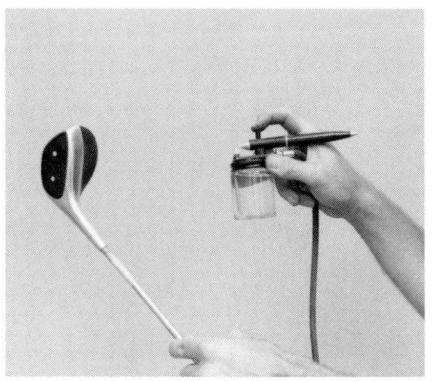

1-213 An inexpensive **Airbrush** can also be used effectively. A fine nozzle works best for proper spray dispersion.

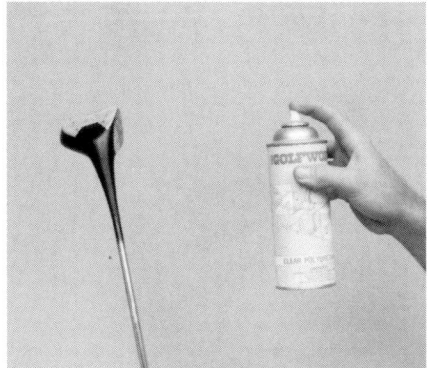

1-214 Polyurethane is also available in an aerosol can. Serious refinishers doing any sort of volume work should avoid this as an alternative to dipping. The aerosol poly can, however, can be used effectively for touchup purposes and should be kept on hand even in larger shops.

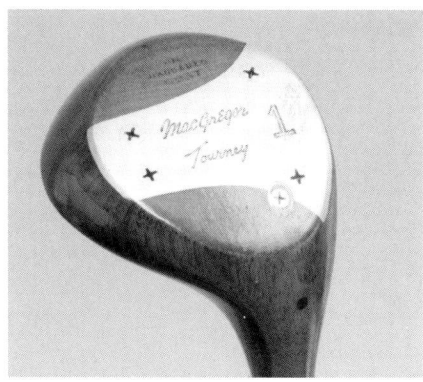

1-215 After the first poly coat has dried, wood and metal stampings should be paint-filled. Additional coats of poly will fill in the stamping and make paint-filling later on impossible.

1-216 Scoring line paint and lacquer sticks are commonly used for filling stampings. Lacquer sticks are preferred because they are easier to work with and are not as messy as paint. Also, lacquer sticks dry quickly.

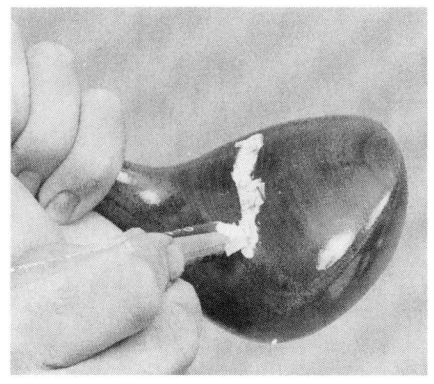

1-217 Lightly rub the **lacquer stick** into the stamping until the stamping is completely filled.

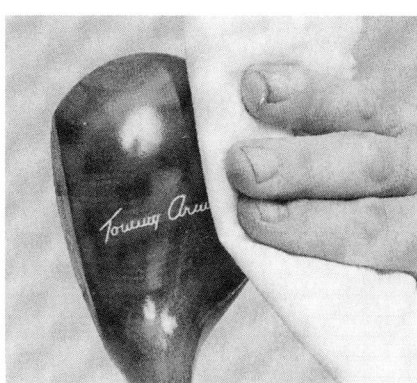

1-218 Immediately after filling the stamping, wipe the excess from the head with a paper towel. Do not smear the paint all over the head.

1-219 Any residue left around the stamping is easily removed by…

1-220 …rubbing lightly with 000 steel wool.

1-221 This is a sample of a properly filled wood stamping. **Allow the lacquer stick to dry a minimum of 2 hours before applying the second coat of poly.** There are solvents that must evaporate before the next poly coat is applied.

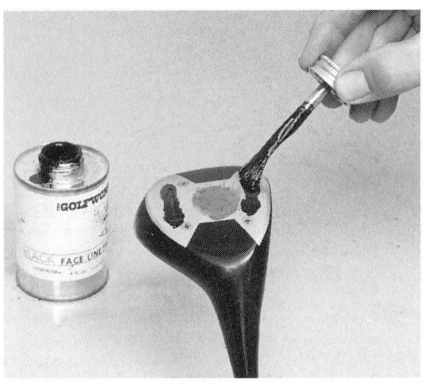

1-222 The soleplate stampings are also filled in the same manner. Scoring line paint and a brush are used to fill the stampings this time. Simply fill the stampings and wipe away the excess with a paper towel.

1-223 The photo shows properly paint-filled soleplate stampings. When paint-filling stampings, try to use original colors.

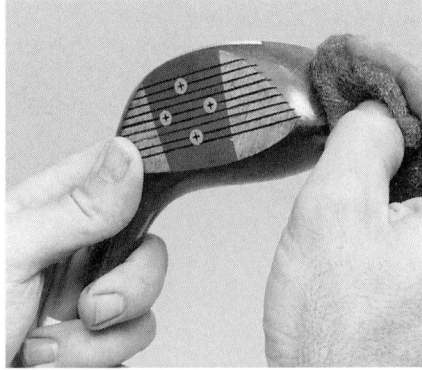

1-224 **After the polyurethane coating has dried and after any stampings are paint-filled, lightly steel wool the surface with 000 steel wool.** Abrading the surface allows the next polycoat a better "hold." This light abrading will turn the high gloss finish to a dull satin look. Do not steel wool the clubhead edges to prevent going through this first thin coat of poly.

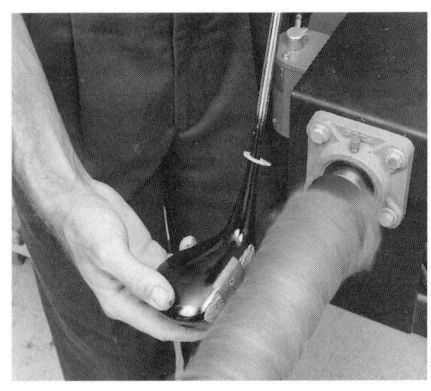

1-225 Machine steel wooling with 000 steel wool is faster. A light touch is required when working with a machine. Take the same care with the clubhead edges.

1-226 **If a decal(s) is needed, proceed as follows:** Fold a paper towel in half and place it on a flat surface. Saturate the paper towel with water, but do not allow the water to puddle.

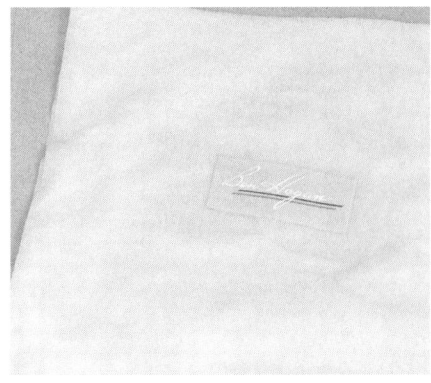

1-227 Place the decal with the image up and the back of the decal in complete contact with the wet towel. Allow the decal to absorb moisture and soften for a minute or two. When the decal slides freely on the paper backing, it may then be applied to the head. Dampen the area of the head where the decal will be applied.

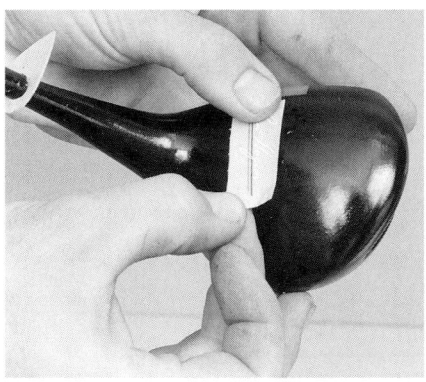

1-228 Slide the decal off the backing and onto the desired location. See "Additional Information" at the end of this chapter for more information on positioning decals. Note the positioning of the hands. A thumb is placed on one end of the decal while...

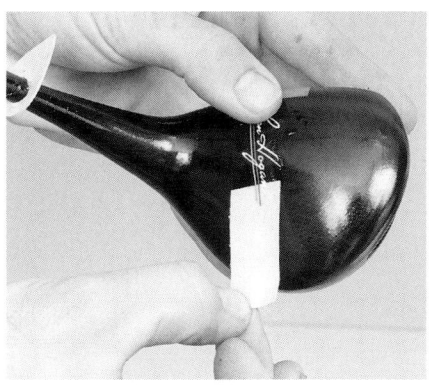

1-229 ...the backing is pulled out from underneath the decal. If the decal is a reverse image type, substitute decal solvent for water. It is not possible to slide reverse image decals in place. Reverse image decals are placed in their exact position and the backing paper is lifted off the decal.

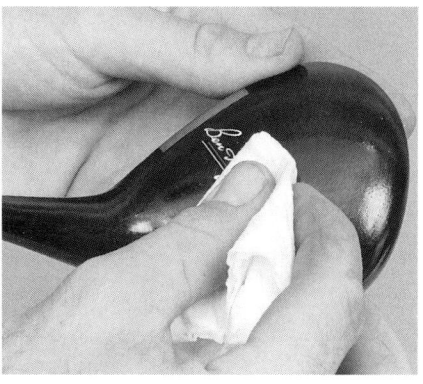

1-230 Water slide-off type decals may be moved around on the clubhead surface up to 45 seconds before permanently setting. Once the decal is set, pat the decal firmly with a damp paper towel or cloth. This will force out any air bubbles from beneath the decal.

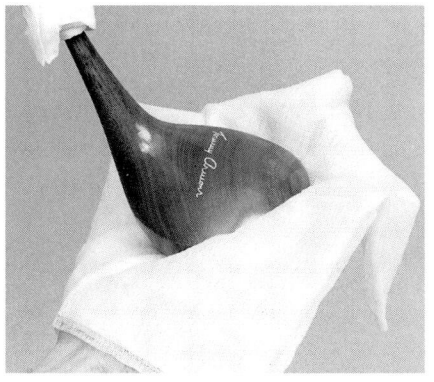

1-231 The clubhead is wiped with a **tack rag** or **naphtha** once again before the second poly coating.

1-232 Dip the second coat of polyurethane. Turn the club up once the poly runoff begins to drip. It is not necessary to blow on the finish after the first poly coat.

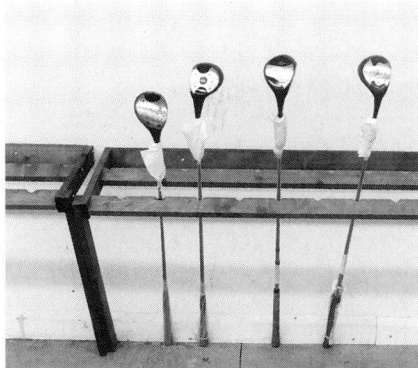

1-233 Allow the club to dry in this position at room temperature for one hour. A **Golf Club Drying Rack** as shown works best.

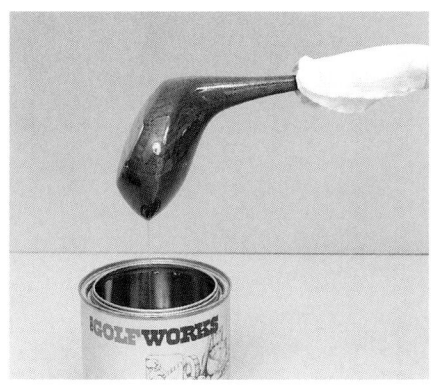

1-234 After the one-hour drying period, dip the third coat of polyurethane. Do not abrade the surface before dipping this coat. The second coat is tacky enough to give the third coat a good bonding surface.

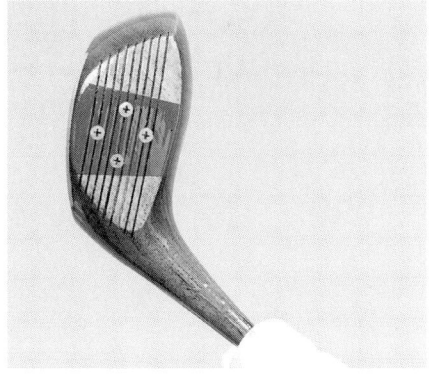

1-235 After the initial 30 minute "flash-off" period, again place the club under room temperature dry or force dry conditions.

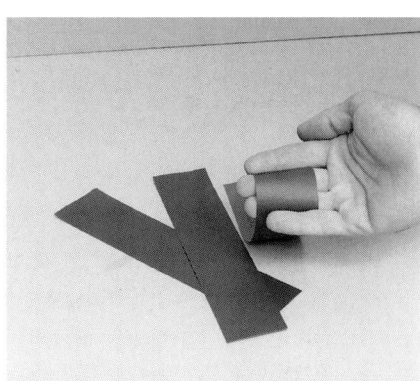

1-236 After the third coat is completely dry, the poly will have a sufficient build-up to allow some leveling of the surface. **A 400 grit silicone-backed wet or dry paper works best.** Cut strips of sandpaper approximately 1½" wide and wrap around the two middle fingers as shown.

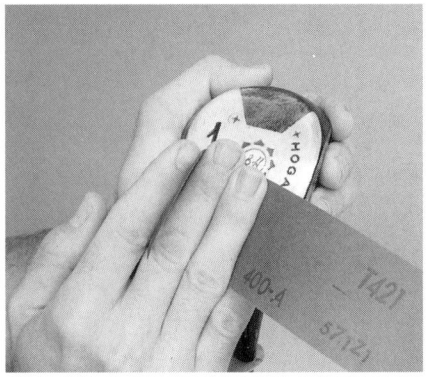

1-237 Use a circular sanding motion for best results. Sand the entire clubhead until the finish begins to look like dust or chalk. If the finish "balls," this is an indication that the poly has not dried long enough. Hand sanding between coats is the secret to a super smooth finish and the deepest gloss.

1-238 If you find a run or sag on the surface, concentrate sanding directly on top of this polyurethane build-up. Be careful not to sand the surrounding area, as the finish is much thinner there.

1-239 Sand lightly over decals and do not sand the clubhead edges.

1-240 This is an example of a properly sanded head. The small high gloss areas must be left as is. These spots indicate low points in the finish. If these small areas are sanded at this stage, you will sand through the poly into the wood.

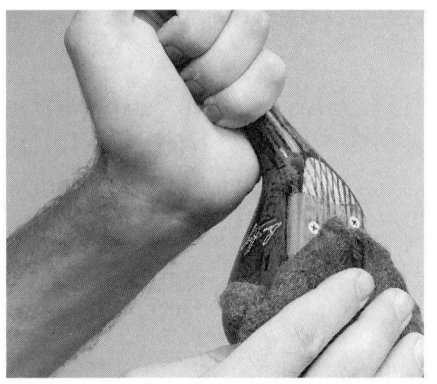

1-241 Next, either hand or machine steel wool the entire head with fine 000 grade to smooth out the hand-sanding marks. Note that steel wooling does not take the place of hand sanding. Both are necessary for an excellent finish.

1-242 This is the same head after steel wooling. Note the even, dull appearance.

1-243 Tack rag the head or wipe with Naphtha.

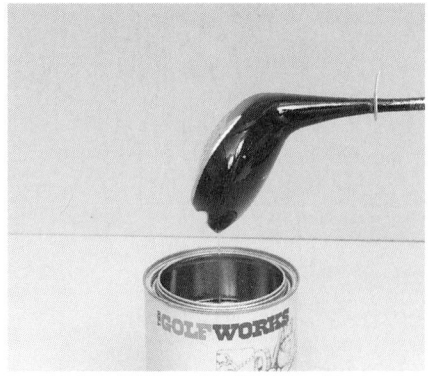

1-244 Dip the fourth polyurethane coat using the same techniques as used for the previous coats. After the 30 minute "flash-off" period, allow the club to thoroughly dry under room temperature or force dry conditions as before.

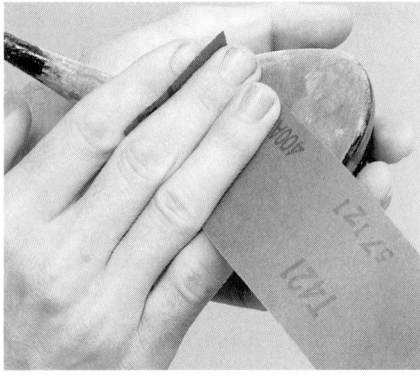

1-245 After the poly has dried, hand sand the clubhead with 400 or 600 grit sandpaper.

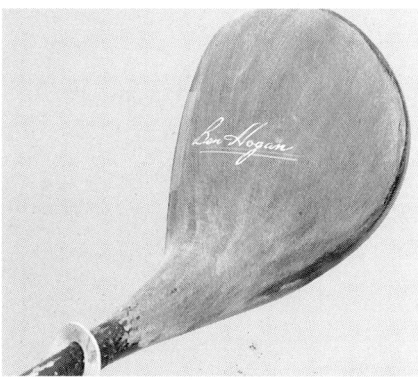

1-246 This is a properly sanded club. Note the even, gray appearance. This indicates there are no low spots and the polyurethane coatings have been leveled properly. Steel wool the clubhead and then lightly wipe the head with the tack rag or naphtha.

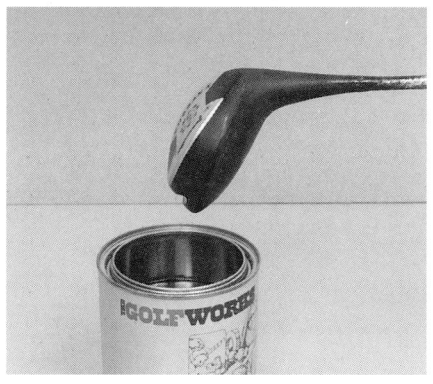

1-247 Dip the fifth and final coat. After the 30 minute "flash-off" period, allow the club to dry overnight under room temperature or force dry conditions.

1-248 If there is a small run or surface imperfection on the final poly coat, it is not necessary to sand, steel wool and apply another coat. To rid the surface of this problem, wait three days for the poly to fully cure and then…

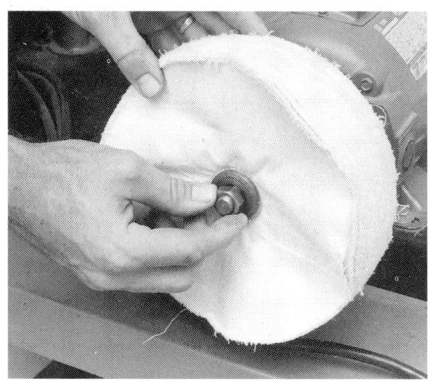

1-249 …put 2 or 3 **unstitched buffing wheels** together and attach them to a motor shaft and an arbor. The buffing wheel should spin no faster than 1725 R.P.M. A slower speed, between 600–900 R.P.M., is preferred. Friction created when operating at higher speeds increases the likelihood of buffing through the finish.

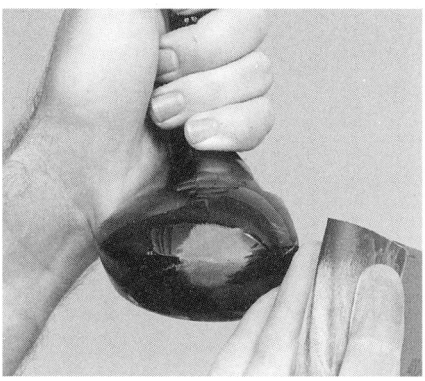

1-250 First, remove the run or imperfection from the surface through controlled sanding. Note the 400 or 600 grit sandpaper is wrapped around one finger instead of two.

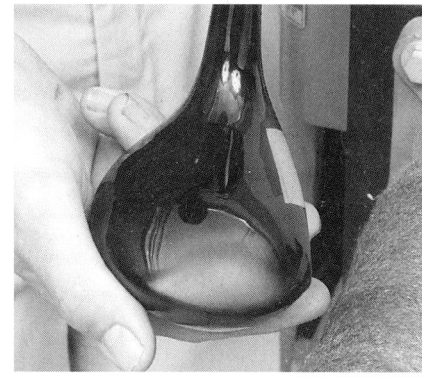

1-251 Lightly steel wool this area to blend in the sanding marks.

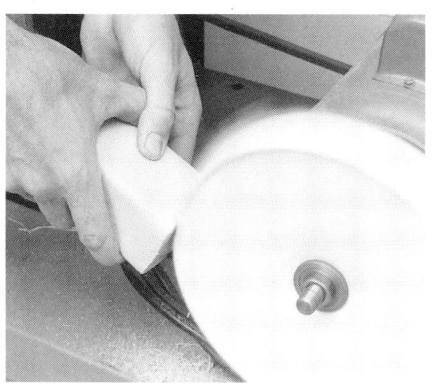

1-252 Apply **Glanz Wach** to the **unstitched buffing wheels** as they are turning. Apply just enough Glanz Wach to coat the wheels.

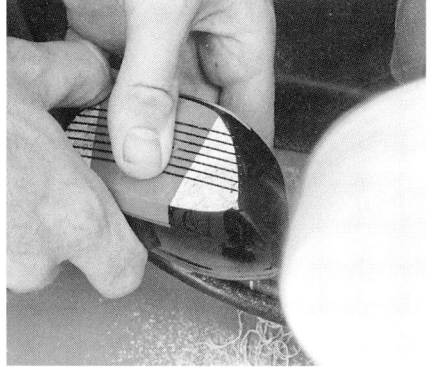

1-253 Lightly press the flawed area of the clubhead against the buffing wheel. Keep the clubhead moving at all times. After buffing the area in one direction…

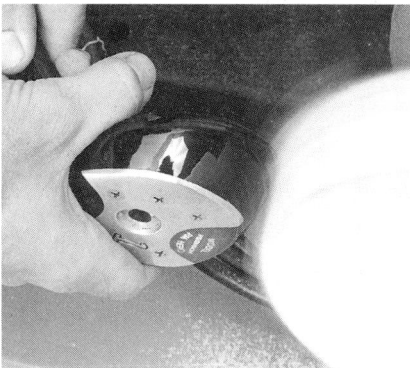

1-254 …lightly buff in the other direction. Repeat this until the scratches from the sandpaper and steel wool are completely gone and the repaired area has a high gloss.

1-255   The repaired area will look as if another coating of polyurethane was applied. This procedure works because enough surface friction (heat) is created to rearrange the surface molecules and polish to a bright gloss. Because so much heat is generated, the clubhead must be constantly moving to avoid burning through the finish.

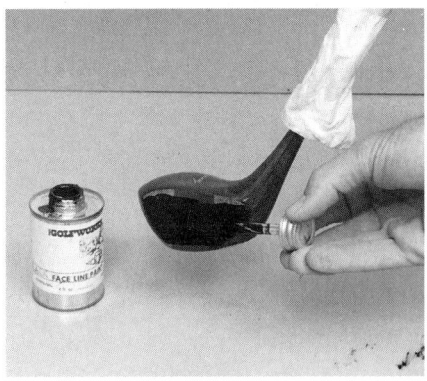

1-256 Face lines are paint-filled by wiping or brushing quick drying enamel into the grooves. Scoring line paint is available from golf component suppliers.

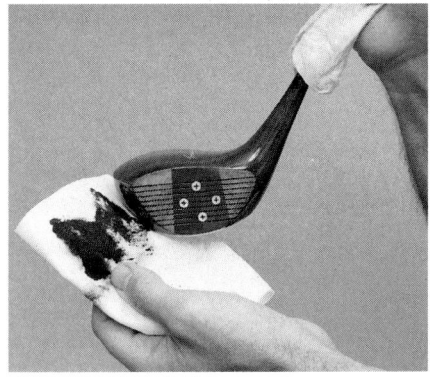

1-257 Wipe off the excess paint with a paper towel which is alternately folded back and forth to expose a clean surface. Allow the face paint to dry 12 hours. If all the paint is not removed, wipe again with a paper towel lightly dampened with naphtha.

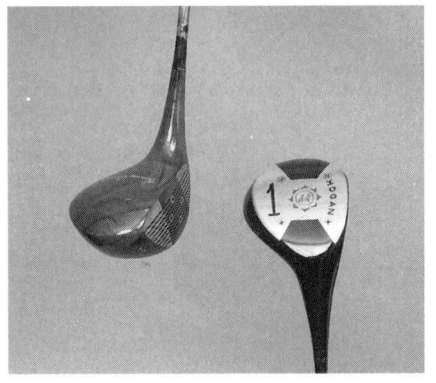

1-258   This is the finished product. With practice you can achieve a finished clubhead that is far better than most factory finishes. The club is now ready to be whipped. See Chapter 6 for the correct whipping procedure.

1-259 If the club has a plastic whipping cover, first cut through the polyurethane underneath the cover.

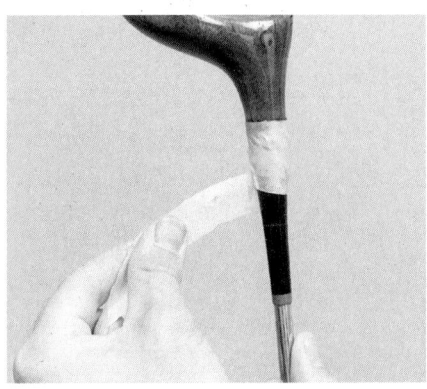

1-260 Next, unwind the masking tape covering that was wrapped prior to sanding the head.

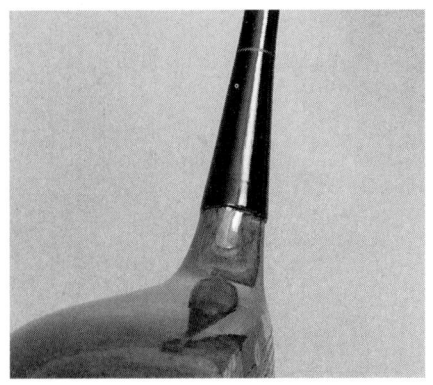

1-261 This is the best a refinisher can expect from a club with a plastic whipping cover. Removing tape prior to dipping the poly would result in heavy runs on the cover. If the plastic needs to be touched up with acetone, do not allow it to come in contact with the polyurethane.

1-262   Refinishing Graphite, Lexan and Plastic Heads. In recent years, woods have been manufactured from materials other than the traditional persimmon or laminated maple. One of these new materials is graphite. Do not be intimidated by a graphite or similar head, as most of the steps for refinishing them are identical to those for conventional woods.

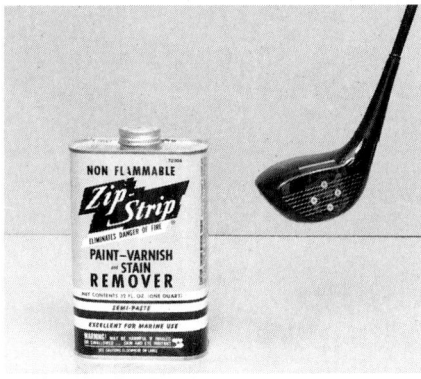

1-263 Never apply a stripping agent to a graphite head. Many graphite heads have a plastic content. The stripper will attack the plastic and permanently damage the head. Therefore, sand the old finish off the head. These steps also apply to plastic molded heads.

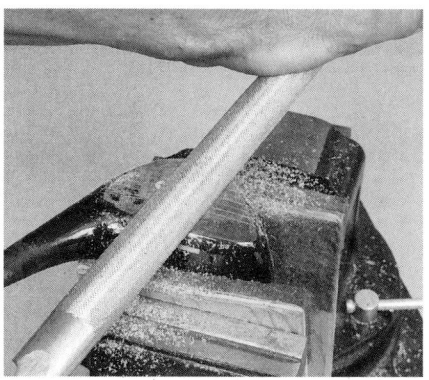

1-264 Remove the whipping, file the face (see photos 1-22 through 1-33), recut the scoring lines (photo 1-34) and file the soleplate (photos 1-50 through 1-59) to remove nicks.

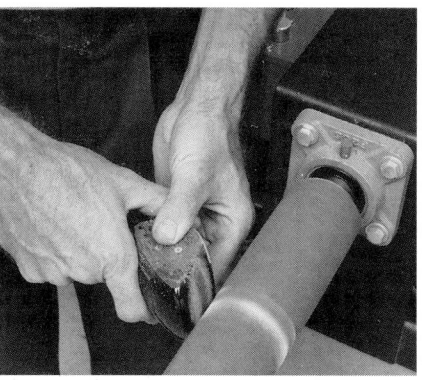

1-265 The procedure for sanding a graphite head is identical to those steps shown in photos 1-78 through 1-99. The key in sanding graphite is to keep the sandpaper sharp. Use 100, 150 and 220 grit sandpaper.

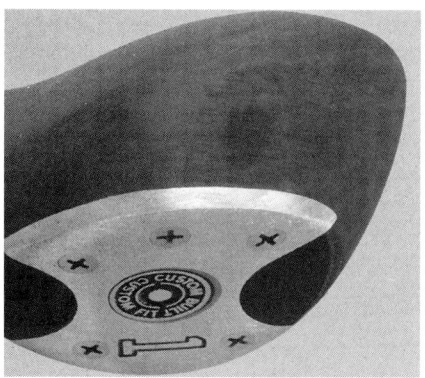

1-266 If the clubhead is sanded with dull, worn paper, a sag in the graphite may result. To remove this sag, sand the area with sharp paper until the sag disappears.

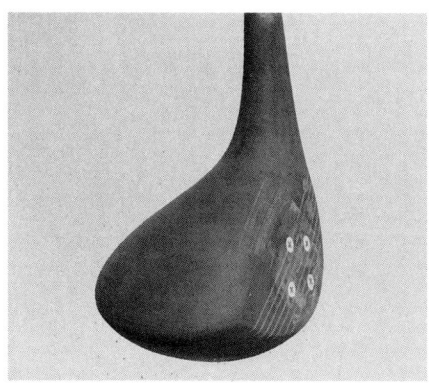

1-267 This is a properly sanded head. Even though we have used very fine sandpaper during the last sanding step, there are still scratches that need to be removed.

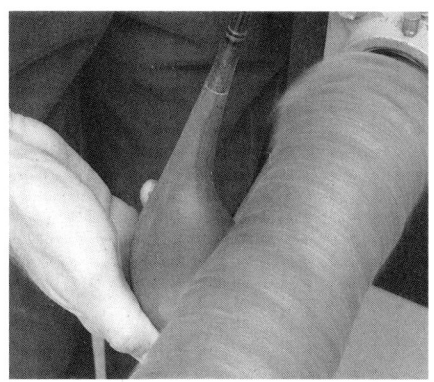

1-268 Vigorously steel wool the entire head to reduce the scratches left from sanding. Keep the steel wool moving over the head to avoid sags created by too much heat. The steel wool that works best is 000 grade.

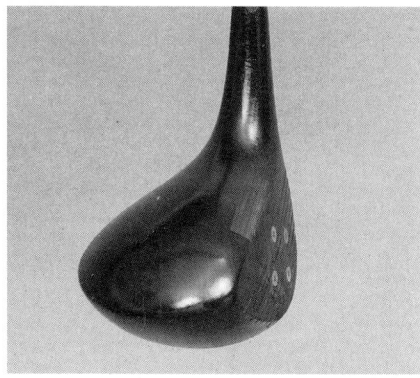

1-269 The graphite head should look like this after steel wooling. Graphite heads are not stained or filled. If the clubhead had a colorcote…

1-270 …follow the tape masking steps as shown in photos 1-150 through 1-163. A polyurethane mask on the face is not needed.

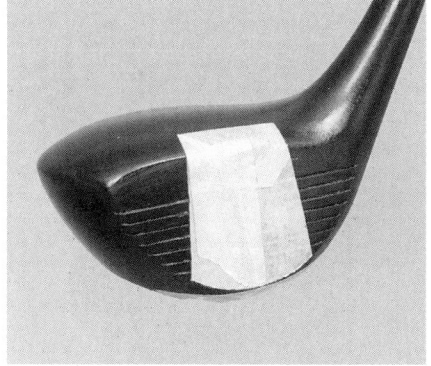

1-271 Some manufacturers tape the entire insert prior to applying the colorcote. The reason behind this step is to colorcote the toe and heel portion of the face and to leave the natural graphite fiber pattern visible in the insert only.

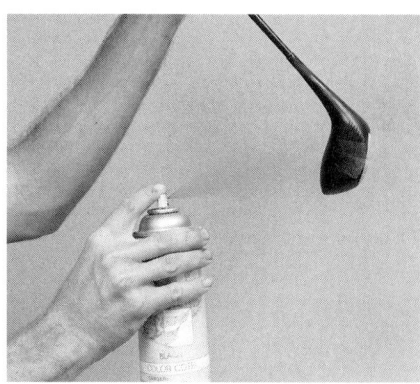

1-272 Apply the colorcote following the steps outlined in photos 1-171 through 1-179.

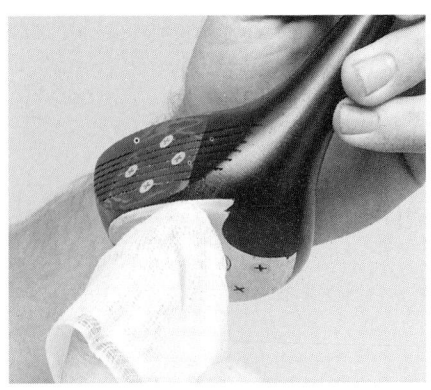

1-273 After the colorcote is applied and dried, the tape is removed. If the colorcote has bled on the soleplate, follow the steps outlined in photos 1-194 and 1-195.

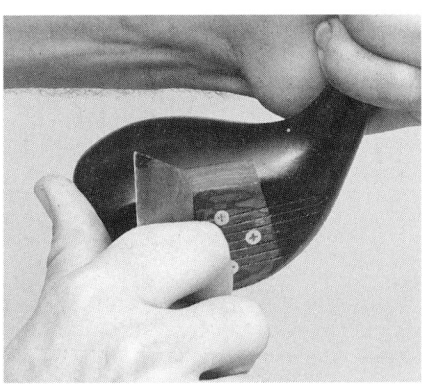

1-274 If the colorcote bleeds onto the insert, lightly scrape the insert with the Detail Knife. If you do not want the toe and heel portion of the face to be covered, follow the facing steps as shown in photos 1-181 through 1-192.

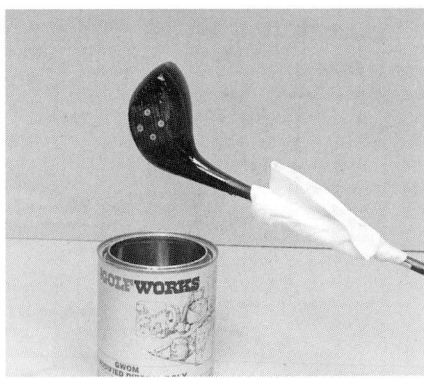

1-275 The remaining finishing steps are identical to those shown in photos 1-201 through 1-257.

1-276 The finished graphite clubhead should look like this. Apply whipping as shown in Chapter 6.

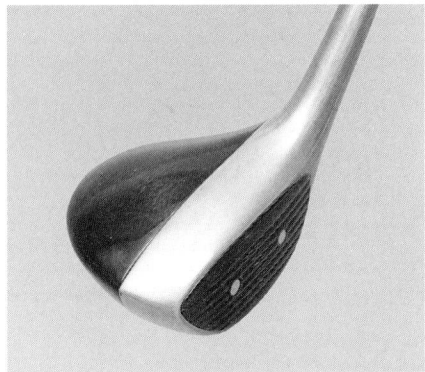

1-277 Refinishing Metal and Wood Combination Woods. This is an aluminum shell with wood inlay type of "wood." The refinishing steps are similar to conventional wood heads. Apply a stripping agent to the entire head. (Stripper should not be applied to the face of those models with plastic inserts.)

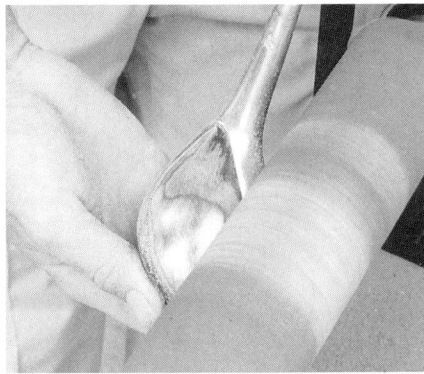

1-278 Carefully sand the entire head with 150 or 220 grit sandpaper. Sanding steps are the same as those shown in photos 1-78 through 1-99. The face is also sanded on models with an aluminum face. Models with a plastic face must be filed first and then lightly sanded by hand.

1-279 This is the final sanded head. Notice the sanding marks are clearly visible. No matter how careful you are, there is no way to develop a consistent sanding pattern that will blend in with the head material. Because of this...

1-280 ...work the entire head with **Scotch-Brite™ wheels.** This will develop an attractive satin finish on the head. Instructions for using Scotch-Brite™ wheels are found at the end of this chapter.

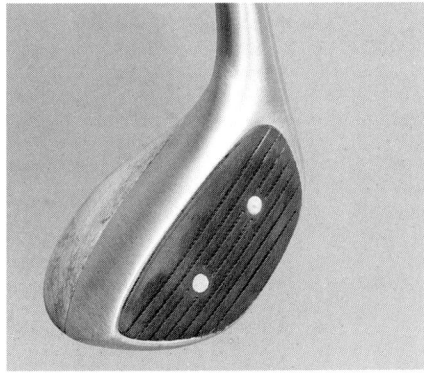

1-281 This is an example of the aluminum head with a **"Scotch-Brite™" satin finish.** The wood inlay is now stained and filled in the desired color. Follow the steps shown in photos 1-124 through 1-143. It is not necessary to submerge the head into the stain. Blotting the stain is the preferred method.

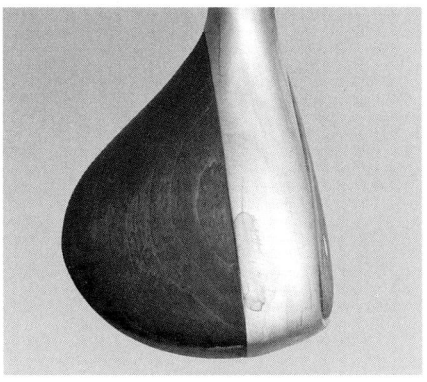

1-282 Any stain or filler residue left on the aluminum shell is easily removed by…

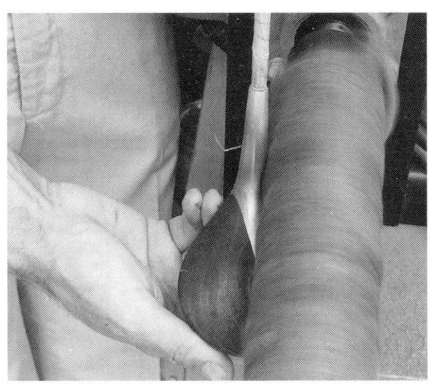

1-283 …steel wooling the aluminum shell and then…

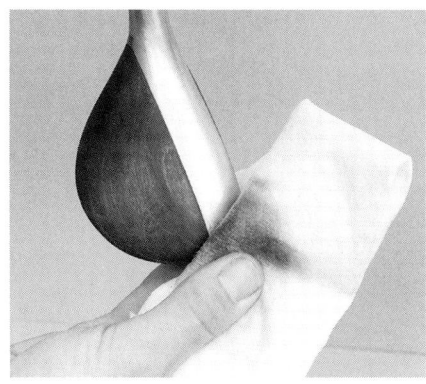

1-284 …wiping the head with a paper towel or cloth that has been dampened with acetone or naphtha. If the club has a plastic insert, avoid wiping the insert. Instead, lightly hand sand the insert with 400 grit sandpaper.

1-285 The clubhead is now ready for the application of polyurethane. Refer to photo 1-202 for steps to apply polyurethane to the clubhead.

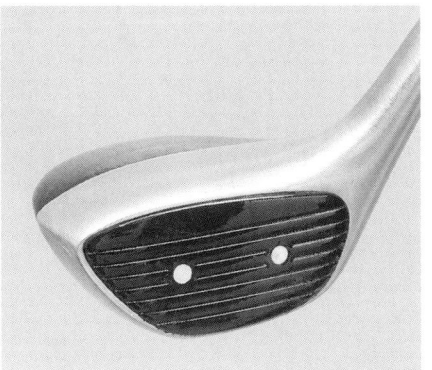

1-286 This is the finished club. These models do not normally require whipping.

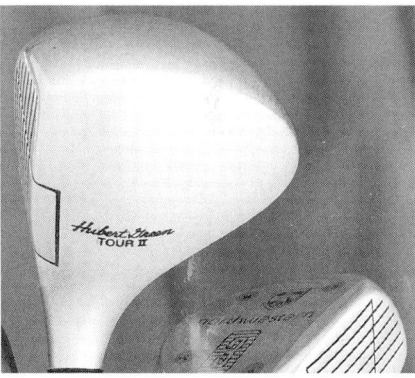

1-287 Some Northwestern woods are made of a "Byzanium C-4 Alloy." The steps for refinishing this club are identical to those just shown for aluminum shells with wood inlays except that no wood inlay is present.

1-288 Refinishing Metal Woods. The finish found on most stainless steel metal woods is identical to the finish found on stoves and refrigerators. This type of finish requires a two component polyurethane that will not easily peel from the polished steel surface. This method of applying finish is suggested for metal woods having an opaque coating of paint, such as blue or black.

1-289 Another method used to refinish metal woods requires the finish to be stripped to the bare metal. This method is suggested for use on clear coated, sandblast gray metal woods. Both methods require the use of polishing and sandblasting equipment.

1-290 This method is suggested for use on clear coated, sandblast gray metal woods. Apply stripper to the entire clubhead. Remove "bubbled" clear finish with a stiff bristled brush, coarse steel wool, Scotch-Brite™ wheel or burlap.

1-291 Examine the clubhead surface. Deeper scratches and nicks can be removed. **Note: Some metal wood refinishers remove the head from the shaft for better control during sanding and buffing operations. See Chapter 7 for head removal.**

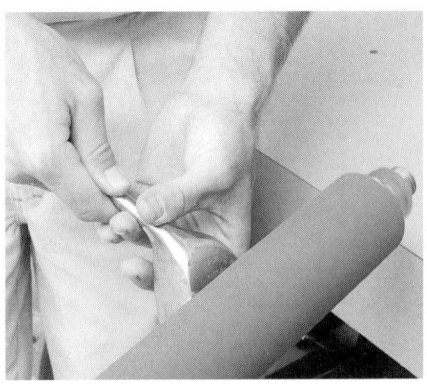

1-292 Machine sand area with small nicks and scratches using 240 grit sandpaper. Sand just enough to remove imperfections.

1-293 The sanded surface should now look like this.

1-294 Polishing the Metal Wood. These instructional steps are offered in conjunction with The Buffing Shop, a 20 piece buffing kit offered by The GolfWorks®. These steps are also applicable for any set-up using the proper buffing materials and buffer.

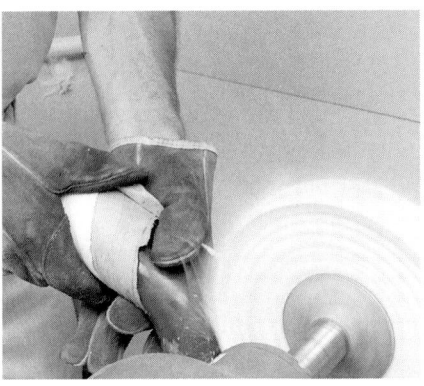

1-295 Place 4 spiral-sewn buffing wheels over a motor shaft to create a 1" wide wheel. Apply a coating of #173 glue compound to the stitched wheels. Hold the compound against the face of the wheel and turn the wheel on for 10–15 seconds while applying. Let the glue dry for one minute before proceeding. Note the use of leather gloves for this and all other buffing steps.

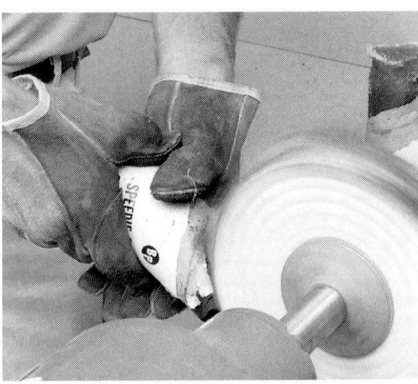

1-296 Apply the #200 lea compound, turning on the wheel for 10 seconds at a time or until you get an even coating on the buffing sections. Wait 5 minutes before buffing.

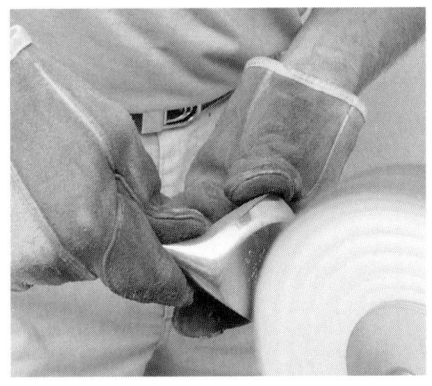

1-297 Begin buffing, using a forward rolling motion while maintaining firm control of the head. Move the head across the face of the wheel in a different direction from the previous sanding step. Buff those areas of the clubhead that will not be sandblasted. Normally this is the soleplate…

1-298 …face and sometimes the toe and heel.

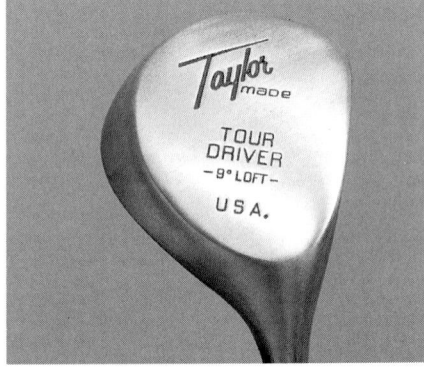

1-299 This photo shows the same head after the buffing step.

1-300 Assemble 2 sisal buff sections to the other side of the buffer. Apply the black sisal compound against the face of the turning wheel. Apply a smooth coating of compound.

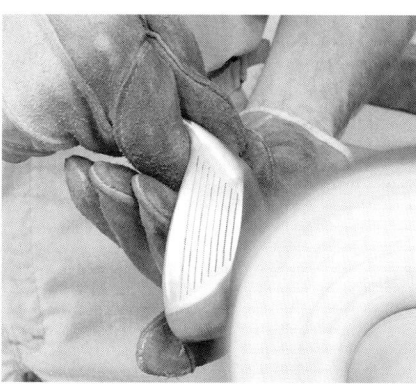

1-301 Buff the head again. Note the angle of the head against the wheel to change the direction of the scratches from the previous buffing step. This is the key to a professional job. Use very firm pressure.

1-302 This photograph shows the head after buffing with the black compound. Scratches are becoming much finer and the surface is getting shinier.

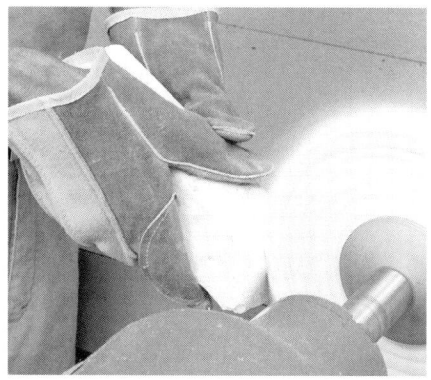

1-303 Next, place a clean set of four spiral-sewn buffing sections on the machine. Apply white polishing compound to the turning wheel for 5 seconds.

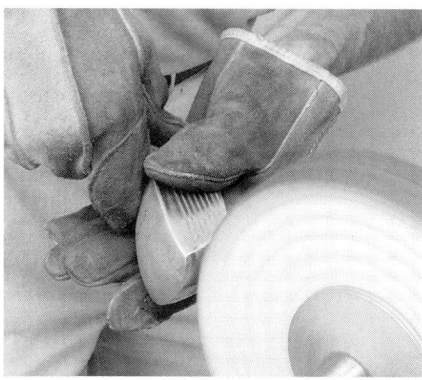

1-304 Using very firm pressure, move the polished areas over the face of the wheel. Again, use a downward rolling motion.

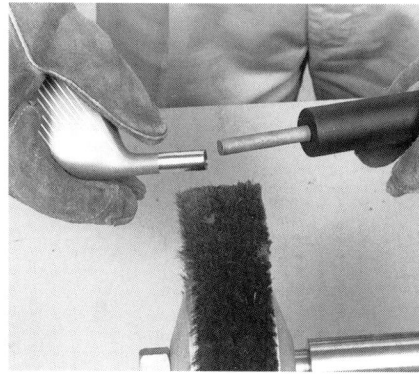

1-305 Some metal woods have a polished hosel as well. Spin the hosel against the wheel to polish, if required. Inserting a **Hosel Turner** into the hosel will allow extra control while polishing.

1-306 This photo shows a properly polished clubhead. All scratches have been removed to provide a mirror-like, factory new appearance.

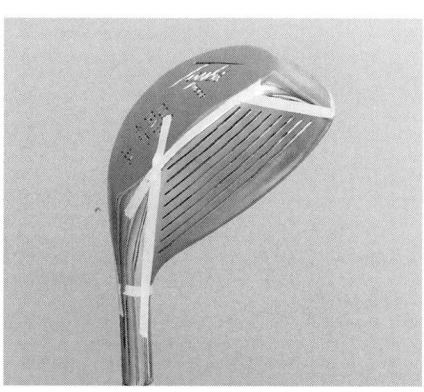

1-307 Carefully apply tape over the polished areas. Use ⅛" masking tape to accurately outline these areas.

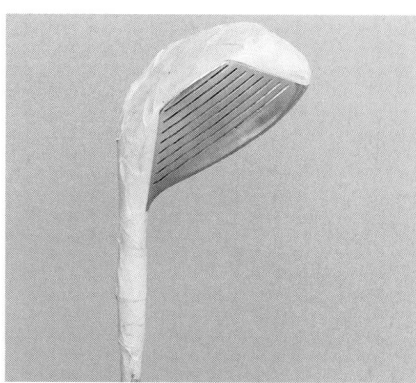

1-308 Apply ¾" masking tape to fill in the remaining exposed polished metal surface. Make sure the tape is tight. Club is now ready for sandblasting.

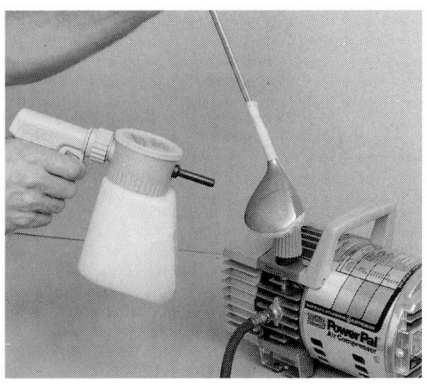

1-309 Sandblast the exposed surface by using 150 grade aluminum oxide sand at 40 to 60 P.S.I. A sandblast cabinet is best suited for this procedure, but a sandblast gun with tank-type compressor or the pictured **Power Pal compressor and accessory sandblast gun** will do the job.

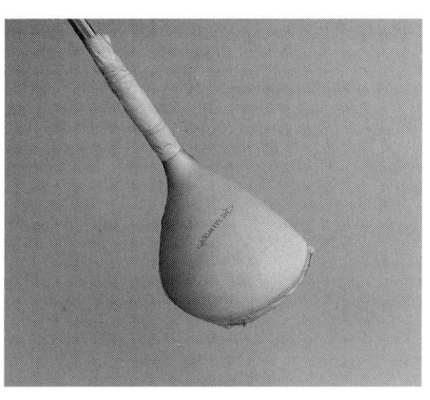

1-310 This photo shows the sandblasted head. Note the even appearance of the surface of the head. Try not to touch the head at this point.

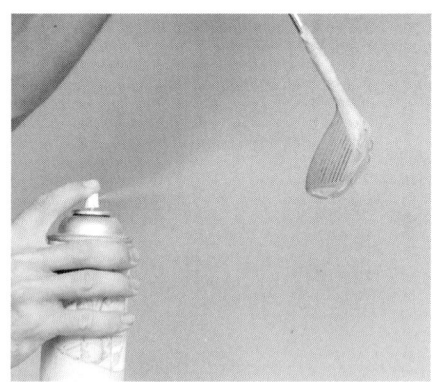

1-311 Without removing the tape, apply 2 or 3 light coats of **Primer Sealer.** Allow 30 minutes drying time at room temperature between coats or bake the finish at 300 degrees. Baking will improve adhesion between finish and metal. The Primer Sealer is not applied to any polished metal surfaces as it will quickly wear off.

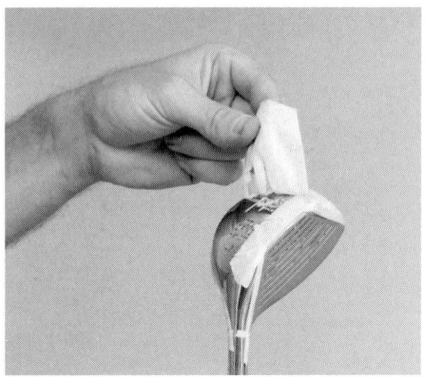

1-312 Carefully pull the tape from the head. There should be a defined line between the polished and sandblasted areas.

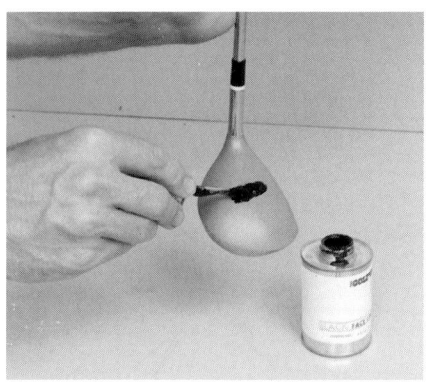

1-313 Paint-fill all stampings with the appropriate color paint. The coating of Primer Sealer prevents the paint from accumulating on the head itself. After applying, quickly wipe the excess paint from the head. A paper towel dampened with Grip Solvent or naphtha works well.

1-314 This photo shows the finished clubhead. A professional job can be expected.

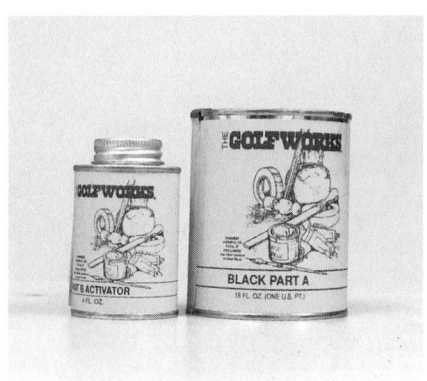

1-315 This next method for refinishing metal woods utilizes The GolfWorks® two component polyurethane, which is identical to the materials used by major manufacturers. This method is suggested for metal woods having an opaque coating, such as blue or black. First, polish, tape and sandblast the metal wood following steps 1-294 through 1-310.

1-316 Some heads will have pit marks, as shown, that must be filled prior to applying the opaque coating. Common automobile putty is a good product for filling these imperfections. Simply apply the putty into the pit, allow it to dry the prescribed time and then scrape away the excess using a razor blade. Then, lightly sand the area with 100 grit sandpaper.

1-317 Mix the appropriate amount of the two-component polyurethane, following the instructions on the outside of each can. Note that the working life of the mixed product is very short. Mix only the amount that you intend to use within 1 hour. Pour the mixture into a commercial spray gun cannister and prepare the gun for spraying. Note: For smaller jobs the **Sprā Tool** aerosol unit works well and is available from The GolfWorks®.

46

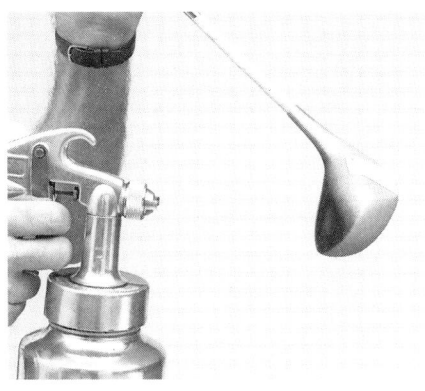

1-318 Coat the head with the opaque coating of your choice. Two coats are required with a 15 minute drying time between each coat. No surface preparation is required between coats. **Minimum temperature required for application and drying is 70°F. Allow the head to dry overnight.** See Table 1-4 for Force Dry conditions.

1-319 Next, lightly steel wool the entire head with 000 steel wool. Then, spray two coats of clear finish, waiting 15 minutes between coats. **Allow the head to dry at room temperature overnight.** After drying, carefully peel the tape from the head. Note, you may carefully trace around the edge of the tape with a razor blade before peeling the tape.

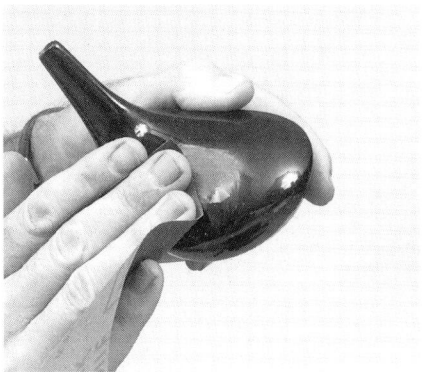

1-320 After the tape has been removed, lightly sand the finish coated portion of the head using 800 grit sandpaper. Be careful not to sand the high-polished surface(s). Sanding will remove any imperfections in the finish and is usually required to create a smooth, uniform surface.

1-321 Now, buff the head to remove the scratches left from sanding. See photos 1-252 through 1-255 for buffing procedure. Proper buffing will create a high-gloss, mirror-like finish. Also, buff the edges of the finish around the polished metal surface(s). This will "feather" the edges to remove any obvious step. The clear finish is very durable and you should not buff through it unless you press too hard.

1-322 The properly buffed head will look like this. Proper buffing will create a high-gloss, mirror-like finish. The edges of the polyurethane have been blended with the metal and any runs or sags in the polyurethane are gone. It is absolutely flawless in appearance yet provides a durable finish.

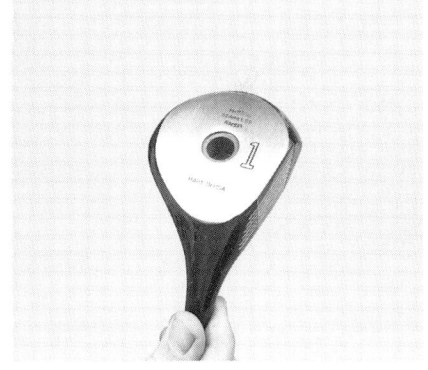

1-323 Important Point: If the metal wood you are finishing has a satin finish on the non-sandblasted areas, remove the tape before applying the 2 clear polyurethane coats. The polyurethane will adhere to that "scratched," satin surface. After the polyurethane dries, lightly sand the entire head and buff as previously described.

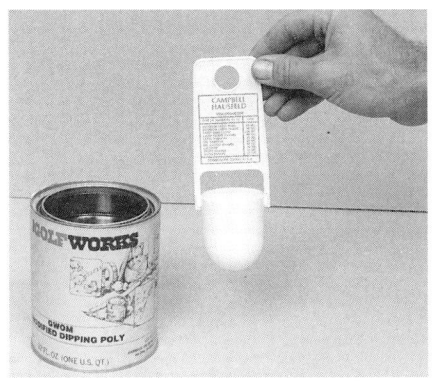

1-324 How to use a Viscosimeter. The viscosimeter will enable the refinisher to determine when the viscosity of the polyurethane is too thick for use as a clubhead coating.

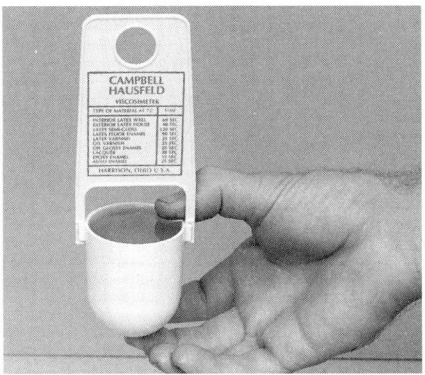

1-325 Cover the opening in the bottom of the cup with your finger or a piece of tape. Pour finish material into the cup until level with the rim.

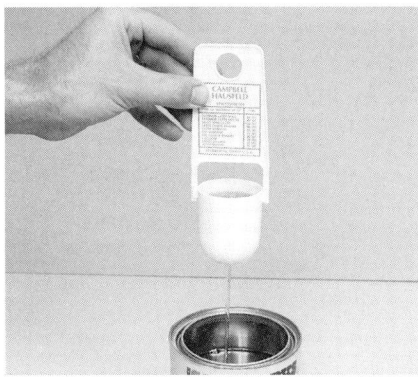

1-326 With an eye on the clock or a watch, remove your finger or tape from the opening. Count how many seconds it takes for the contents to empty. When polyurethane registers in the low 30 second range, open a new can and use this old thickened poly for masking faces. **A good rule of thumb to use is: Anything from 16-29 seconds is usable.**

47

ADDITIONAL INFORMATION FOR
REFINISHING WOODS

TABLE 1-1
Selecting the Proper Steel Wool Grade

Grade	Texture	Usage
0000	Superfine	This grade is used for most all steel wooling operations such as leveling between coats, cleaning soleplates, etc. Ribbon is the most common type used.
000	Extra Fine ◄———	
00	Very Fine	
0	Fine	
1	Medium	
2	Medium Coarse	
3	Coarse ◄———	Used for removing old, softened finish after the stripper has been brushed on the head. Pads are most commonly used.

TABLE 1-2
Selecting the Proper Buffing Compound

Grit	Compound	When to Use
Coarse	Black Emery Cake	■ If an extra heavy cutting action is necessary, such as removing rust, heavy nicks, deep scratches.
Medium	Tripoli Brown	■ For buffing items of aluminum, pewter, brass, copper, wood, bone, plastic and painted surfaces. Medium cutting action.
Fine	White Rouge	■ For buffing stainless steel, cast brass, aluminum, chromium, nickel and all steel articles to a bright luster. Fine cutting action.
Very Fine	Red Rouge	■ For buffing silverplate, gold, sterling silver and all sorts of precious metals to a bright luster. Works well on dull chrome golf shafts.

TABLE 1-3
Selecting the Proper Sandpaper Grit

Grit	Texture	Usage
40	Coarse	Sandpaper in this category is too abrasive for wood head refinishing. Coarse sandpaper is used to grind raw forgings or castings to weight by manufacturers.
50		
60	Medium	
80*	Medium	*Represents one possible sanding system. Would be useful for those repairmen who do not use a stripping agent to remove the finish from the clubhead prior to sanding.
100†		
120*		
150†	Fine	†Represents another sanding system. This system would be ideal for the repairman who does use a stripping agent and does not need the coarser 80 grit paper for finish removal.
180*		
220†	Very Fine	
240	Very Fine	Is generally too fine for head sanding prior to stain application. This grade of paper tends to close wood pores if dull and prevent stain absorption.
280		
400	Extra Fine	Used between coats of polyurethane for leveling.
500	Extra Fine	Sometimes used prior to the final polyurethane coat or when sanding runs or sags before steel wooling and buffing.
600		

Procedure for Installing Sandpaper, Steel Wool and Scotch-Brite™ Wheels on Sanding Machines, Sanding Arbors and Steel Wool Arbors

This procedure has been added to eliminate much of the confusion and frustration in properly installing sanding cloth, steel wool and Scotch-Brite™ wheels on refinishing and conditioning machines. The procedure is fast and really quite simple, however, like many things, it is best to actually see how it is done to avoid all the trial and error in learning.

The world of sandpaper and sanding cloth types, grits and sizes can also be confusing. For sanding wood, either cloth-backed garnet or aluminum oxide cloth works best. Paper-backed sandpaper will not work satisfactorily; you must use a cloth backing. The grits that are most common in golf club refinishing are 80, 100, 120, 150 and 180. See Table 1-3.

The best all around steel wool for golf clubs is 000 grade, which is quite fine. It is best obtained in spools or packages of "ribbon" and not in "pads." Scotch-Brite™ wheels or discs of a medium grade are ideally suited for the removal of finish from a golf club head. The advantage of a Scotch-Brite™ wheel or disc is they remove the majority of the finish without damaging any identifying stampings. Also, when used in conjunction with a paste stripper, the life of the wheel or disc is greatly expanded.

■ **Remember, always wear eye protection when working around any abrasive materials.**

1-327 Installing Sanding Cloth. First, wrap a strip of 2" double-coated tape around the sponge rubber drum.

1-328 The 2" strip of tape is approximately 7" long and should be overlapped as shown.

1-329 Place another strip of 2" double-coated tape on the opposite end.

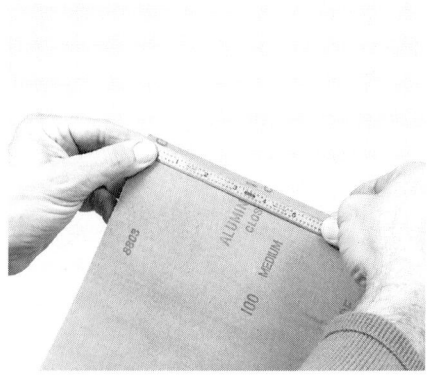

1-330 Use a ruler to measure the width of the strip to be torn off. Measurement may be a little different on each make of sander.

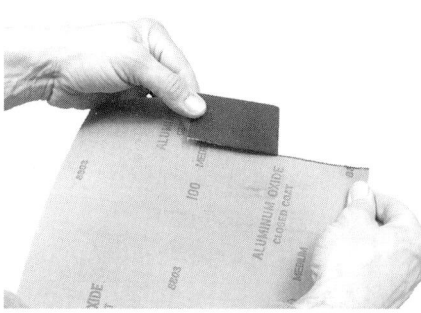

1-331 You can first determine how much should be cut off by wrapping the sanding cloth around the sanding drum. It should overlap approximately ¾" to 1". Save the strips you tear off for general bench work.

1-332 Using a good quality "contact" cement, brush the back side of the sanding cloth with a liberal amount. **Be sure to brush the cement up to the edge of the sanding cloth.**

1-333 Turn the sanding cloth over and coat the sanding surface with a liberal amount of cement. **Be sure to brush the cement up to the edge of the sanding cloth. Allow the contact cement to dry.**

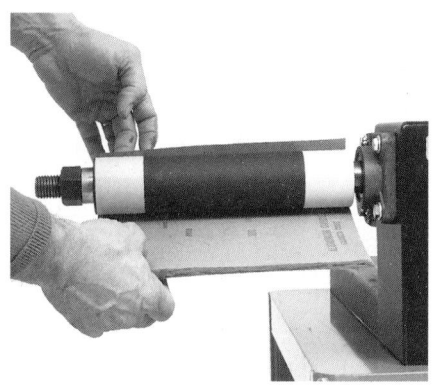

1-334 Place the sanding cloth in position.

1-335 Work the sanding cloth around the sanding drum, keeping it tight against the drum.

1-336 Squeeze in on the sanding drum and pull the sanding cloth up and over itself in the center only and press in place.

1-337 Repeat instructions in 1-336 on right side of cloth.

1-338 Repeat squeezing on the left side of the cloth. Note: Squeezing down on the sponge rubber drum as the sanding cloth is pressed into place helps to make it install tighter.

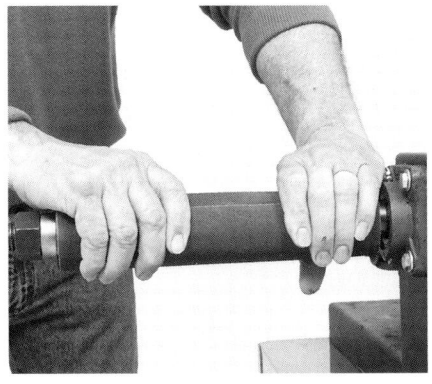

1-339 Squeeze down tightly on the cemented seam to obtain a good bond.

1-340 Assembled sanding cloth should look like this. Notice how the cloth overlaps which is proper because the sanding drum rotates downward in front and up in the back (counterclockwise when facing the nut).

1-341 Installing Steel Wool. Wrap steel wool around the drum.

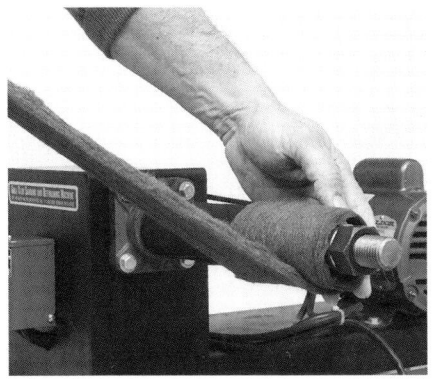

1-342 As the steel wool overlaps itself, be sure it is tight.

1-343 Rotate the drum by hand and "wind on" the remaining portion of the steel wool ribbon, keeping it as tight as possible.

1-344 Spread apart the end of the steel wool using your fingers.

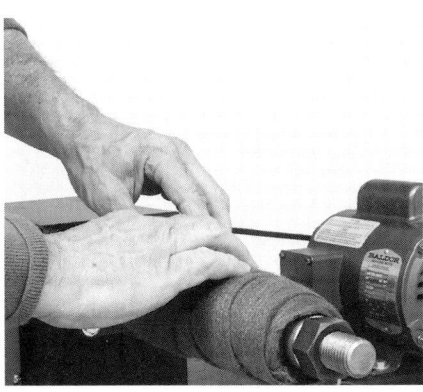

1-345 Press the spread apart ends down, as well as you can.

1-346 Place either one or two hands around the steel wool and turn the motor on. Your hand will shape the steel wool and lock it in place so it will not spin off. Note: If you do not want to use your hands, a rounded dowel will also work.

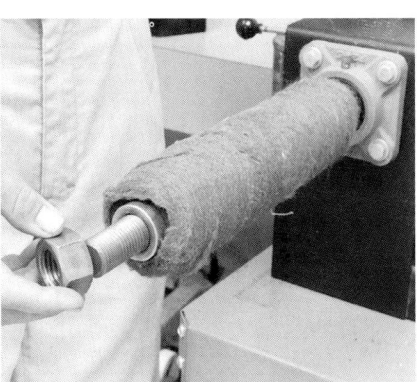

1-347 Installing Scotch-Brite™ Wheels. Remove the end nut from the motor shaft or arbor. The GolfWorks® Sanding Machine has a 1" diameter shaft.

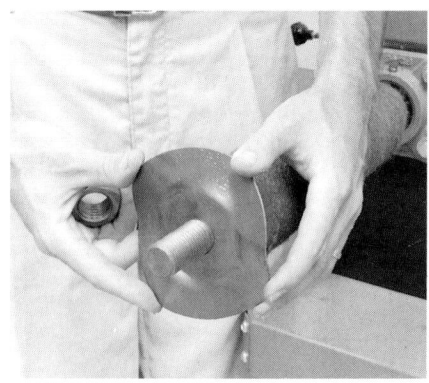

1-348 Slide 1 wavy washer over the shaft. Note: Special adapters are available so washers and wheels will also fit a ⅝" or ½" motor shaft.

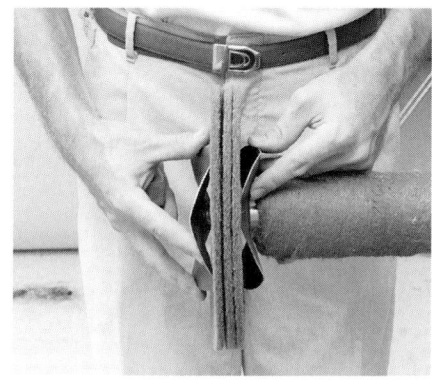

1-349 Slide 2 or 3 Scotch-Brite™ wheels over the shaft. Then, slide the second wavy washer over the shaft. Note the positioning of the second washer in relation to the first.

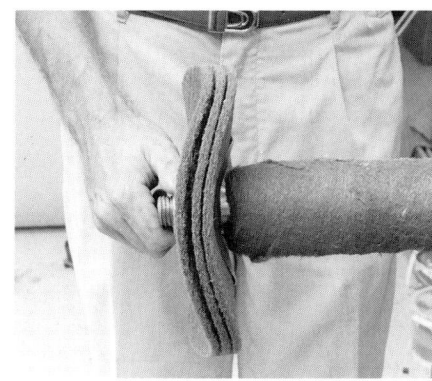

1-350 Reinstall the end nut and tighten. If the wavy washers have been positioned properly, the effective working area on the wheels has been greatly expanded when the motor is switched on. The wheels are ready for use.

Preserving Wood Head Stampings

It is important to understand how wood head stampings were put in originally at the factory and the best way of preserving them. From time to time, confusion exists regarding stamping in both the crown and the sole of wood heads such as "Tommy Armour, oil hardened, 693T," etc. The value of these clubs largely depends on the readability and recognizability of the stamps in today's classic club market. (See photo 1-351)

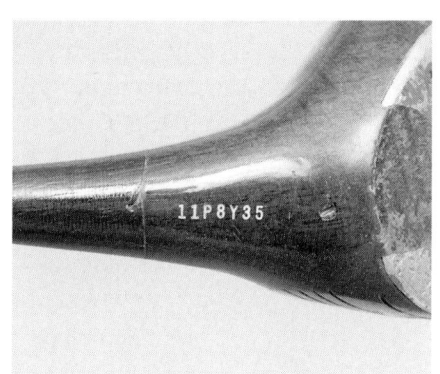

1-351

First of all, when the stamps were put on at the factory, they were stamped after the first and sometimes second clear coat of varnish (often lacquer). Remember that the club had already been stained, filed and colorcoted if the finish was to be black. When the old finish is removed during refinishing, a portion of the original stamp is removed with it because the stamp is partially in the finish as well as in the wood. Next, when the club is sanded to remove scratches and nicks, a little more of the stamp is removed. If a club has been previously refinished and is now going to be refinished again, still more of the stamp will be removed. Because of this, the stamping must be deepened before the sanding step as shown in photos 1-61 through 1-65.

The person at the factory who originally stamped the clubs would sometimes stamp them very deep and other times quite shallow. This would depend on two factors: first, how hard the stamp was hit and second, how hard the persimmon in that particular head was. Also, a number of times human error would enter in and the stamp would be cocked slightly to one side or the other, thus resulting in a deep stamp on one side and shallow on the other.

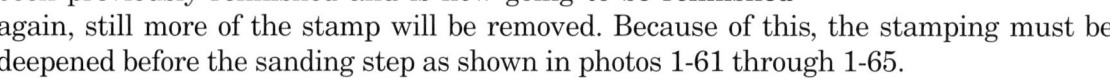

1-352

Your intention should be to restore these stampings as best you can during refinishing. Obviously, you cannot restore these stamps to factory newness unless you had all the hundreds of stamps used in the past (for instance, there were 8 different Tommy Armour stamps used for stamping the MacGregor heads). If you become proficient, however, with a scriber or electric engraver, you can closely match the quality of a newly stamped head.

It is very difficult if not impossible to professionally restore a hosel stamping. (See photo 1-352) Hosel stampings are usually very shallow because the operator at the factory did not dare exert much force when stamping this relatively fragile area.

Often the stamping will disappear completely once the finish is removed because the stamp was only as deep as the finish itself. Classic club collectors generally agree, if the condition of the finish warrants a refinish, the value of the club will not drop simply because the hosel stamping is lost. It is an accepted fact that the depth of the hosel stamping does not allow it to be saved.

When a club that has a wood head stamping comes in for refinishing, be sure to look it over closely to evaluate the condition of the stampings so that if necessary, you can immediately bring them to the customer's attention. Many people feel that these stampings are restamped during refinishing. Personnel in The GolfWorks® Repair Department use this policy: If you can see it, we can save it. With practice, you should adopt this policy also.

Oil Hardening

Oil hardening is a name given to a process whose sole purpose is to seal the pores of a persimmon or laminated wood turning, and help prevent the shrinking or swelling of that head due to moisture absorption or loss. The material used for this process can be boiled linseed oil, Nelsonite, resin or slight variations of these three materials. These materials are applied to a head by immersion or impregnation using both vacuum and pressure.

Virtually every head you encounter has been "oil hardened" and there is not a need for the head to again undergo this process. Some repairmen mistakenly believe dipping the sanded head in oil or Nelsonite will magically "harden" the wood, but this is just not so. Remember, the oil hardening process seals the wood from moisture loss or absorption, but does nothing to actually harden the wood. The finish will have difficulty adhering to a clubhead surface that has been re-oiled.

Moisture Cure Polyurethane vs. Oil Modified Polyurethane

Moisture cure and oil modified polyurethane represent the two most common types of poly used on golf clubs today. Each offers an excellent coating system, yet each is different in shelf life, color, odor and curing time.

Moisture cure poly is used by approximately 95% of all golf club manufacturers and about 70% of golf club refinishers. What makes moisture cure poly very attractive is that the color is water clear. What makes moisture cure poly less attractive to some users is the tight environmental control that must be maintained during its use to ensure the product will work properly. As evidenced by the name, moisture cure poly requires the moisture in the air to aid in the curing of the poly.

The moisture acts as a drying mechanism as the poly resin pulls the moisture molecules from the air. These molecules, in fact, become part of the poly coating. The tendency of the moisture cure poly coating to dry from the top to the bottom can cause a problem. If the top of the poly coat dried too quickly or if too heavy a coating has been applied, then as many as 8 different solvents can be trapped underneath this dried film of poly. The purpose of these solvents is to aid in the blending, curing, adhesion and drying of the poly. The refinisher, however, does not realize there are any trapped solvents until the second coat of poly is applied on top of the first coat. If the solvents in the first coat have not evaporated, the solvents in the second coat will eat through the top layer of the first coat. This causes a reaction between these solvents that manifests itself in the form of common wrinkling of the poly coat.

The drying characteristics of the oil modified poly are different from the moisture cure poly. Oil modified poly is made by inter-reacting the poly with a vegetable oil. The type of vegetable oil used determines the color, clarity and the flexibility of the finish. The addition of oil leads to a very slight amber color that is most noticeable on aluminum soleplates. This is the only drawback to oil modified poly. The drying characteristics of oil modified poly are from the bottom of the coat to the top. Primarily for this reason, you should not experience the trapped solvent problem with the oil modified poly. The other factor for this is that the poly resins are grabbing oxygen molecules from the air to aid in the curing of the poly. Oxygen will allow the solvents to evaporate much more freely than moisture will.

■ Which Polyurethane to Choose

The decision you make as to which type of polyurethane to choose should be based upon three points:
1. Color—Moisture cure poly is water clear while oil modified poly has a very slight amber color, usually only slightly noticeable on aluminum soleplates and white inserts.
2. Working Difficulty—Oil modified poly is the easiest to work with because of the nature of the curing process. Unless the proper drying conditions are created in the use of the moisture cure poly, the refinisher may experience problems.
3. Shelf Life—After the can is first opened, oil modified poly has at least a 4 to 6 month shelf life with reasonable care and proper storage. Moisture cure poly, with the use of a preservative should last 4 to 8 weeks.

For the shop that works with a small number of clubs or for the part-time refinisher, the oil modified poly would suit their needs better than the moisture cure poly. For a full-time shop that has a large volume of work, the moisture cure poly would be the correct choice. The large volume shop will be refinishing enough clubs that the shop would run out of the moisture cure poly before it cures to a level that makes it too thick for use. Whichever poly you choose, both will give the refinisher an excellent finishing system with professional results.

■ How to Obtain Shelf Life

One problem which re-occurs concerns short shelf life of polyurethanes. This is especially true if the refinsher dips the heads because of the constant removing and reinstalling of the lid. Also, a number of smaller users may not use the polyurethane soon enough before it sets up. It should be noted that we have not found golf club polyurethanes to be defective other than accidental dirt contamination during the can filling operation. It has usually been mishandling on the user's part which allows for rapid thickening. There are a number of things you can do.
1. Always store polyurethanes in a cool location and never near direct sunlight. If material will not be used sooner than a week or two, put it in the refrigerator. This will greatly retard thickening. Remember that you must allow the material sufficient time to normalize at room temperature before using it (usually 12 hours minimum). Never use polyurethane below 65°F. An aquarium thermometer or darkroom thermometer is handy for checking the temperature prior to use.
2. Only keep the lid off the can for the absolute minimum time. Air is the number one enemy of polyurethane and wet, humid air is even worse if you are using a moisture cure polyurethane.
3. When you receive a new can of polyurethane, pour enough in a small container so that the level in the quart can is approximately 1" below the top. This will keep the polyurethane from running over the top. As you use it, pour the remainder back into the can to maintain this 1" level. As the level goes below 1", drop marbles into the can to maintain the 1" level. This will always assure you of the minimum amount of air space in the can. Never transfer polyurethane into glass jars or plastic containers because glass lets in light which affects uncured polyurethane, and plastic containers let in air which promotes thickening.

Also, once you have used a little over ½ or up to ⅔ of a can and you do not have sufficient material to dip a head in, throw the remainder out or use it for masking faces. Never add new material to old material. The old material will accelerate thickening and also, after so many dippings it becomes contaminated. You should be able to dip 20-50 clubs with 3-4 coats with one quart of polyurethane.

4. If you use spraying polyurethane or spray-dipping polyurethane, it is best to squeeze and deform the can (with the cap or lid off) as you use it up to maintain its level right up to the top. This will eliminate all air from the can which is best.

Compatibility of Various Finishing Products & Drying Times

TABLE 1-4
Compatibility of Various Finishing Products & Drying Times

Product	Application	Drying Times Room Temp.	Force Dry*	Compatibility Comments and General Notes
GOLFWORKS® SYSTEMS				
GolfWorks® Water Base Stains	dip, brush, wipe, or spray	4-6 hrs.	1 hr.	Can be used with anything. Dipping provides uniform coating.
GolfWorks® Oil Base Fillers	dip or brush and rub	12 hrs.	6 hrs.	Can be used with any polyurethane. Burnish well with burlap or coarse cloth when wiping. Do not steel wool.
GolfWorks® Rapid Dry Aerosol Color Cote	aerosol	4-6 hrs.	2 hrs.	Must be used only with GolfWorks® Oil Modified or Moisture Cure Polyurethane. Do not apply heavy coat. Several light coats are superior to one heavy coat. Do not sand or steel wool.
GolfWorks® Opaque Color Cote	spray or brush	24 hrs.	12 hrs.	Must be used only with GolfWorks® Oil Modified or Moisture Cure Polyurethane. Do not apply a heavy coat. If brushing, apply quickly to avoid streaks.
GolfWorks® Primer Sealer, Aerosol	aerosol	4 hrs.	1 hr.	Can be used with any polyurethane but specially formulated for Moisture Cure type polyurethane. Do not sand or steel wool.
GolfWorks® Primer Sealer, Spraying	spray	4 hrs.	1 hr.	Can be used with any polyurethane but specially formulated for Moisture Cure type polyurethane. Also commonly used over sandblasted surface of metal wood. Do not sand or steel wool.
GolfWorks® Oil Modified Dipping Polyurethane	dip or spray	8 hrs.	4 hrs.	Do not apply on top of Moisture Cure Polyurethane. Usually requires 5-6 coats for a quality finish.
GolfWorks® Moisture Cure Dipping Polyurethane	dip or spray	12-24 hrs.	8 hrs.	Do not apply on top of Mira-Dip or Mira Filler. Can be applied over other polyurethanes or fillers.
GolfWorks® Moisture Cure Spraying Polyurethane	spray	12-24 hrs.	8 hrs.	Do not apply on top of Mira-Dip or Mira Filler. Can be applied over other polyurethanes or fillers.
GolfWorks® Moisture Cure Aerosol Polyurethane	aerosol	12-24 hrs.	8 hrs.	Do not apply on top of Mira-Dip or Mira Filler. Can be applied over other polyurethanes or fillers.
GolfWorks® Two-Component Polyurethane	spray	12-24 hrs	12 hrs.	Used for metal wood refinishing. Very durable. Professional refinishers can spray all coats with room drying time of 15 minutes between each coat up to a total of 4 coats.

*Force dry conditions: 30% to 50% relative humidity, 90% to 100% temperature.

TABLE 1-4 cont.
Compatibility of Various Finishing Products & Drying Times

Product	Application	Drying Times Room Temp.	Force Dry*	Compatibility Comments and General Notes
		CLUB-KIT SYSTEM		
Mira-Stains (alcohol base)	dip, brush, wipe, or spray	3-6 hrs.	1 hr.	Can be used with anything. Dipping provides uniform coating.
Mira-Filler (polyurethane base)	dip or brush and rub	5 hrs.	2 hrs.	Use only with Mira-Dip.
Mira-Kote (polyurethane base)	spray or brush	12 hrs.	8 hrs.	Use only with Mira-Dip. Do not apply heavy coat. Several light coats superior to one heavy coat.
Mira-Kote Aerosol (polyurethane base)	aerosol	12 hrs.	8 hrs.	Same as above.
Dem-Kote Enamel	aerosol	4 hrs.	2 hrs.	Same as above.
Mira-Dip Oil Modified Polyurethane	dip or spray	8 hrs.	4 hr.	Do not apply on top of Moisture Cure polyurethanes. Usually requires 5-6 coats for quality finish.
Mira-Spray Aerosol Oil Modified Polyurethane	aerosol	8 hrs.	4 hrs.	Do not apply on top of Moisture Cure Polyurethanes.

*Force dry conditions: 30% to 50% relative humidity, 90% to 100% temperature.

How Moisture Cure Polyurethane Dries and Cures

The drying and curing information presented in the beginning of this section pertains mostly to moisture cure (MC) polyurethane. This is because a coating of moisture cure polyurethane dries from the top to the bottom. This drying action differs from a coating of oil modified polyurethane because oil modified dried from the bottom of the coat to the top. The information presented, however, concerning the inter-reaction between solvents is applicable to all types of polyurethane. Also, the 6 tips given at the end of this section can be used to assist in trouble free refinishing, regardless of which type of polyurethane you use.

Understanding how polyurethane cures is a vital step in becoming a knowledgeable and competent golf club refinisher. With this knowledge, you will be able to troubleshoot finish problems should they occur. The following diagrams are for explanation purposes only. They depict the flow and movement of the polyurethane on the clubhead.

Diagram #1 shows a wood head just after the application of the polyurethane. The dashed lines represent the solids as they flow over the head and the arrows represent the solvents that are naturally present in the polyurethane. The key to proper drying is the evaporation of all of the solvents that are in the coating. In the diagram, the solvents are beginning to evaporate or "flash off" the surface through the solids and out into the air. As of yet the solids have not begun to flow together and join to form the film coating, so there are plenty of avenues of escape for the solvents.

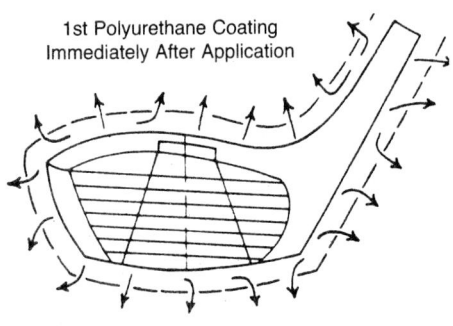

1st Polyurethane Coating
Immediately After Application

DIAGRAM 1

56

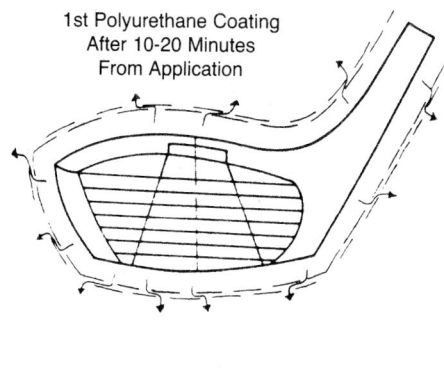

1st Polyurethane Coating
After 10-20 Minutes
From Application

DIAGRAM 2

In **Diagram #2** the solids of the polyurethane are beginning to join together to form what is called the film coat. This is represented by the overlapping of the dashed lines seen in the diagram. This joining together begins to cut off the access to evaporation of the solvents, since at this point they have to work their way around and through the solids to get to the surface. During this time (10 to 20 minutes after application) there is a chance that many tiny bubbles may appear on the surface of the polyurethane. These bubbles are caused by a very rapid film coat set-up that "squeezes" down the solvents and naturally present gases. Not having the adequate time to come to the surface normally, these solvents and gases "collide" with the solids and burst to become bubbles on the surface. Too rapid of a film coat set-up is usually caused by humidity being too high. This can be alleviated by reducing the humidity or by the addition of a retarder solvent which slows the film coat set-up.

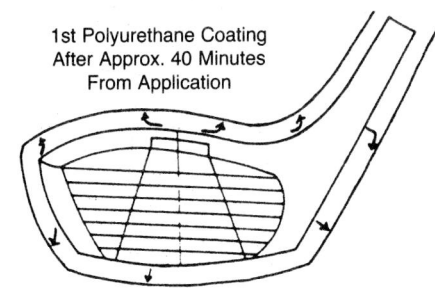

1st Polyurethane Coating
After Approx. 40 Minutes
From Application

DIAGRAM 3

Approximately 40 minutes after application of the polyurethane, the film or solid coating has joined together and shut off further evaporation of the solvents. In **Diagram #3**, if there are solvents remaining (arrows) they are considered to be trapped and no longer have the opportunity to evaporate into the air. This condition is called "solvent entrapment" and is the cause of over 90% of the finish application problems.

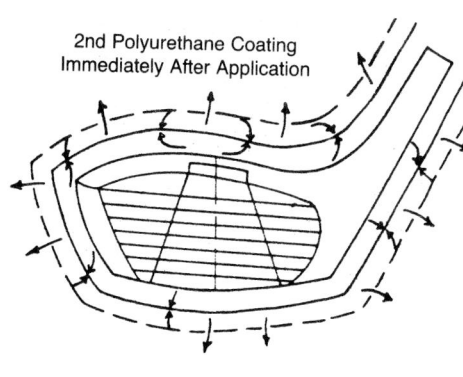

2nd Polyurethane Coating
Immediately After Application

DIAGRAM 4

Once the second coat of the polyurethane is applied, its solvents immediately begin to evaporate. At the same time its solvents are designed to penetrate or "eat" into the preceding coat. See **Diagram #4**. This is the real key to the adhesion properties of polyurethane. When the succeeding coat "eats" into the first coat and meets any unevaporated or trapped solvents, a chemical reaction occurs in the solid layer which results in a breaking down of that solid coating. This reaction may be small or quite extensive and take the form of "wrinkles" or cracking on the surface of the head. In other words, this condition can occur anywhere unevaporated solvents are trapped. In several cases, the head will have to be started over as a result of this problem.

The preceding diagrams and explanation have covered the reasons for many of the problems seen during the application of finish coats. Now it is important to go over some of the preventative measures that may be followed to eliminate the possibility of solvent entrapment. We know the key element in the curing of the polyurethane is getting rid of the solvents present in the polyurethane. This may be accomplished by either speeding up their evaporation or by cutting down on the amount of solvents that flow over the head. The chart below covers the options available to you to control these 2 points.

To Speed Evaporation	To Cut Down the Volume of Solvents
• Elevation of temperature in drying area (max. 100°F)	• Keep polyurethane fresh for better flow
• Add Retarders to hold film coat open longer (in high humidity only)	• Do not use thickened or colder polyurethane
• Apply finish to warmer head (min. 70°F, max. 110°F)	• Do not apply polyurethane to cold head
	• Do not add thinner to improve flow

Thinners are solvents and our goal is to rid the head of solvents.

If you study the methods of drying and understand the control you may exercise over those methods, trouble free finishing will not be difficult to achieve.

In an effort to smooth out the problems that can be caused by refinishing in a workshop environment that is colder than the suggested 70°F temperature, we recommend that you follow these tips:

■ Try to keep your clubs in a warmer area of the shop during the application of the finish coats. Primer/Sealer and polyurethane coatings require higher temperatures to dry properly. The use of a drying box heated with small light bulbs will work well to increase the temperature around your clubs. A shallow pan of water in the box will add humidity, if necessary, for moisture cure type polyurethane. Oil modified polys do not require levels of high humidity.

■ Before applying the polyurethane, make sure the polyurethane is over 70°F. Polyurethane that is cold will not flow on the head adequately and thus a heavier coating will result. This, in turn, may cause solvent entrapment.

■ Try to keep the temperature of the heads themselves at least at 70°F. Dipping or spraying a cold head can create unwanted problems in refinishing.

■ If you cannot dry the polyurethane coats at higher temperatures use this tip to aid in the cure of each finish coat. Twelve to 15 hours after dipping the polyurethane, sand the entire head with 400 grit wet/dry sandpaper and set the club aside for another 12 hours to cure. This 400 sanding will break through the partially cured solid layer and help to further expose potentially trapped solvents to the air for evaporation. After the additional 12 hour drying period, GENTLY 400 sand again, taking care not to break through the finish. Then steel wool and apply the next coat of polyurethane.

■ Thinning your polyurethane in colder air temperatures can create more problem than if it is done in the summer. We recommend restricting the addition of thinner in the winter unless you are able to keep the shop warm.

■ Increasing polyurethane flow may be accomplished by raising the temperature of the poly. This can be done by filling a sink with 3-4 inches of hot water. Set the can down in the sink of warm water and leave it for 20 minutes prior to using. Raising the temperature of the polyurethane will thus make the polyurethane thinner and a better flow will result.

Tips for Applying Decals

There is more to applying decals than simply sliding them in place. The position of the decal is extremely important because if improperly positioned, the decal can make the club appear hooked or excessively open. Also, if the decal is not positioned at the middle of the insert, it gives the club an unbalanced look when addressed with a golf ball and may even cause problems in ball alignment and consequently solid contact at impact.

When a decal is properly positioned, it should line up with the middle of the insert and tail away to an "open" position with the clubface. See Figure 1-353.

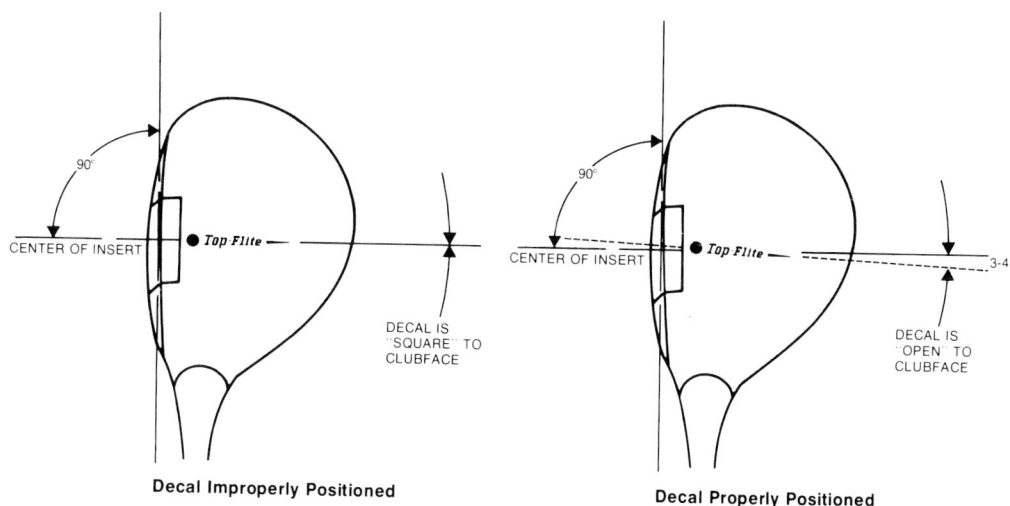

Decal Improperly Positioned   Decal Properly Positioned

FIG. 1-353
Proper decal positioning

The longer a decal happens to be, the more important it is to "tail away." Of course on the short decals such as arrows, dots, small initials or in general those less than ½" long, the importance of tilting the decal open is minimal. Always position the decal, however, at the end of the insert.

A problem that occurs from time to time when installing decals is the appearance of "trapped air" underneath or a blotched grayness look to the decal. This is usually caused by soaking and/or sliding the decal around too much, thereby removing the water soluble glue which bonds the decal to the head. Also, some decals have less glue than others. The best remedy to eliminate grayness is to put down 4 or 5 paper towels, one on top of the other, and soak them with water. See photo 1-226. Do not oversoak or to the point where water is puddling on top of the paper towels. Now, lay the decals face up on the toweling so that the water from the toweling is absorbed into the decal backing paper. This will release the decal's glue from the backing without removing the backing, so that the decal can be slid off onto the head.

NOTES

_____

_____

_____

_____

_____

_____

_____

_____

_____

CHAPTER 2

SOLEPLATE REMOVAL AND RESETTING LOOSE OR OPEN SOLEPLATES

Rarely will someone bring in a club to have the soleplate reset unless it is about to fall off, or has already taken flight down the fairway. This is unfortunate because a loose soleplate makes the club susceptible to moisture damage. You will usually detect an open or loose soleplate when a club is brought in for some other repair, usually a refinishing job or a rattle.

Developing skills in removing a soleplate is important because many wood head repairs start with this operation as the first step. For instance, if a swing-weight change is necessary, the soleplate is usually removed to gain access to the soleplate cavity, where weight is either added or removed. Other reasons for removing a soleplate are:

a.   On a loose or open soleplate, the soleplate must be removed and then reset with epoxy to ensure good adhesion between the soleplate and the head. Also, this prevents moisture from swelling or shrinking the clubhead.

b.   To repair a deep nick or gouge on a soleplate, it is best accomplished by removing the soleplate and hammering the defect from the underneath side of the soleplate.

c.   An insert that is loose or needs replaced can usually only by removed by first removing the soleplate. This allows the Insert Remover Tool or chisel to be driven underneath the insert from the bottom of the insert cavity, which is normally hidden by the soleplate.

d.   A rattle in the head is likely caused by a loose weight under the soleplate. Obviously, the soleplate must be removed before the loose object can be fixed.

The time and effort required to remove a soleplate can range from fast and simple to time consuming and quite difficult. Difficulties occur because various types of high strength epoxies are now in use. Also, golf club manufacturers have become very clever in attaching soleplates to their clubheads using various mechanical means.

To further complicate matters, some customers request that the soleplate be reset without benefit of a refinish. This means you must remove and reset the soleplate while doing as little damage as possible to the finish. If damage is done, you must then repair the damaged finish so the club is presentable to the owner. The touchup steps without a complete refinish can be found in Chapter 16.

Soleplate removal and installation requires very little in the way of materials and equipment. You will need a size assortment of brass flathead screws, epoxy, wooden toothpicks, Phillips #1 and #2 screwdrivers, and both large and small Reed and Prince (Frearson) screwdrivers. A Reed and Prince (Frearson) screwdriver looks similar to Phillips #1 and #2 screwdrivers, however, the former has different angle points and sharper inside radiuses where the cross is formed. "Frearson" is the correct technical name used to refer to a Reed and Prince style screw or screwdriver. Most all golf clubhead manufacturers use the Reed and Prince (Frearson) type cross head screws exclusively, and most golf club repairmen use the Phillips type screwdriver to remove them. This accounts for many ruined screw heads and much frustration. Reed and Prince (Frearson) screwdrivers are usually not available in local hardware stores and must be obtained from a golf repair supply company.

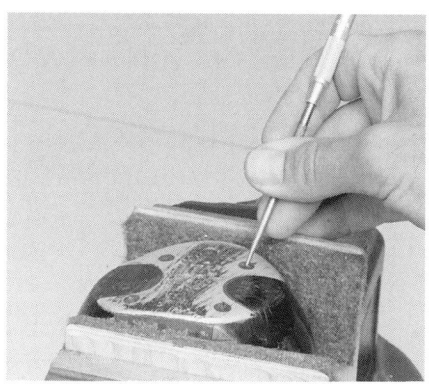

2-1 Using a sharp scriber, dental pick, awl or other pointed tool, thoroughly clean all dirt, old finish and paint from the screw head's recess. This allows the screwdriver to get a better "bite" and reduces the chance of "stripping" out the screw head recess.

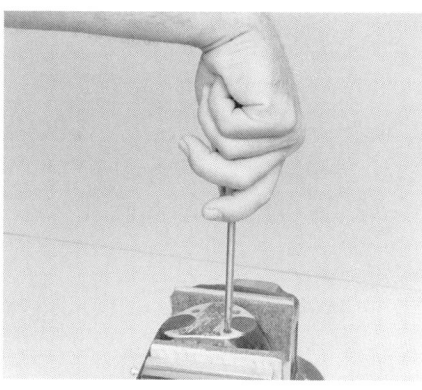

2-2 Hold the screwdriver perfectly square, press down firmly and turn the screw out (counterclockwise). It is a good idea to tap the top of the screwdriver with a hammer to be certain it seats solidly. Note: Most all soleplate screws are Reed and Prince (Frearson) and not Phillips types. Also note that recent Ping woods use special screws that are easily removed using a Torx Bit, available from The GolfWorks®.

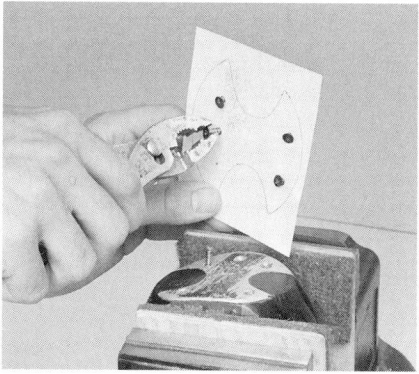

2-3 If the clubhead will not be refinished, place screws so they can be put back in their original holes. A piece of cardboard or pegboard works well for this. If the clubhead is to be refinished discard the screws and use new ones. If the screws will not come out, refer to photos 2-25 through 2-34. Note: Pliers protect fingers from sharp screw edges when placing the screws in the cardboard.

2-4 If the clubhead's finish is still covering the sole, carefully cut around the outline of the soleplate with a razor blade. This will allow the soleplate to be removed without pulling up the surrounding finish.

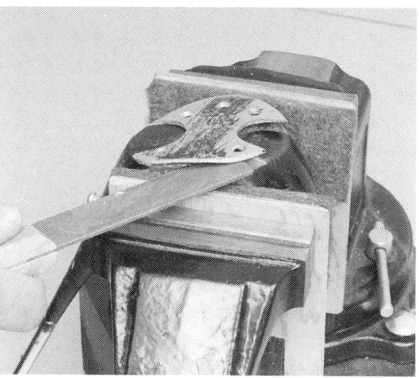

2-5 Pry up the soleplate, carefully using a strong, sharp knife. Tap the knife lightly if necessary. If the soleplate will not come off ...

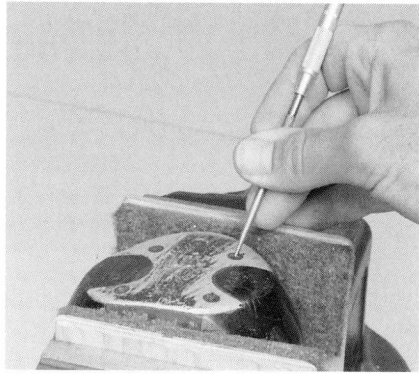

2-6 ... tap a small wood chisel, with the bevel up, under the leading edge of the soleplate. If the soleplate still will not come off, heat will need to be applied to soften the epoxy bond.

2-7 Using an **Electric Heat Gun,** direct the heat against the soleplate keeping the nozzle elevated 1" to 2" from the plate. After a minute or two, the soleplate should lift off.

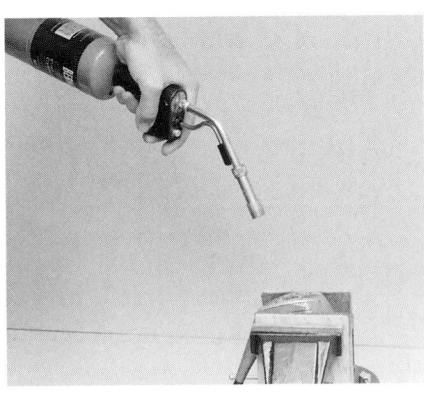

2-8 An alternate method is to use a **Propane Torch,** directing the tip of the flame against the middle of the soleplate. Heat will spread throughout the soleplate, softening the epoxy and allowing for easy removal. This method usually requires the club to be refinished unless great care is taken.

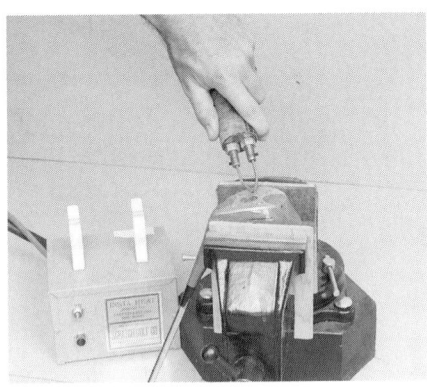

2-9 Still another method is to use an **Electric Screw Extractor.** Touch the electrode tips against the soleplate. If you wish to preserve the finish, place the electrode tips against the soleplate but inside the countersunk area of the screw pilot hole.

2-10 **With the soleplate now removed, gently remove dirt and epoxy** using a medium grade file. Be careful not to damage the sides of the soleplate cavity when filing. File deep enough into the cavity to remove most of the old epoxy.

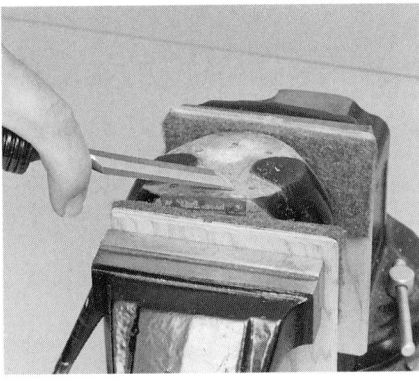

2-11 A sharp chisel also works well in removing dirt, glue or epoxy.

2-12 **Remove dirt, old glue or epoxy from the soleplate by using a file or chisel.** Before installing the soleplate with epoxy, test fit the soleplate to the head. If the soleplate does not seat properly, further filing is needed. Refer to photo 2-40 if the soleplate is bent.

2-13 **Mix the epoxy and apply to both the soleplate cavity and the back of the soleplate.** In most cases, there will be a slight gap between the soleplate and the wood. A color paste dispersion can be mixed in with the epoxy to match the color of the stained wood. This will help camouflage the epoxy line if it shows slightly.

2-14 **Place the soleplate back into the soleplate cavity.** If necessary, lightly tap the soleplate with a hammer. When the soleplate screws are installed they will draw the soleplate down against the head thus eliminating small gaps.

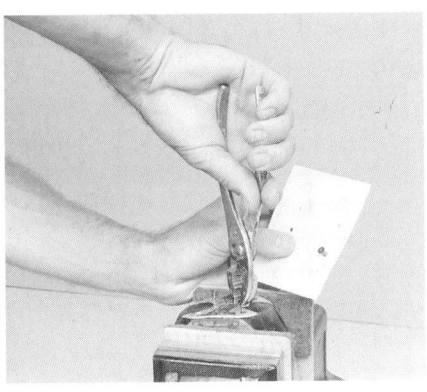

2-15 If the original screws are reused, make sure they are returned to the exact holes in which they were removed. Note: Pliers protect fingers from sharp screw edges when placing the screws back in the proper holes.

2-16 Turn the screws down until they have been turned back to their original positions. A snug fit should be achieved. If the screws are stripped, refer to photos 2-35 through 2-39.

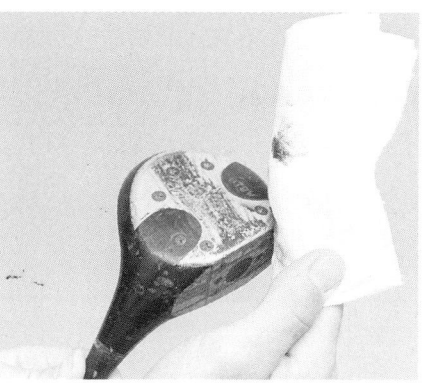

2-17 If the clubhead is not to be refinished, carefully wipe the excess epoxy from the head. If the club is to be refinished, the epoxy may either be wiped off or left to cure and filed from the head later.

2-18 If new screws are used, turn them into the holes until a snug fit is achieved. If the screws are stripped, refer to photos 2-35 through 2-39.

2-19 Note the original screws have been turned down to their original positions. The heads are perfectly flush with the soleplate surface. Before returning this club to the customer, the clubhead should receive at least one coating of polyurethane. Refer to Chapter 16 for touchup steps.

2-20 If new screws have been used, file the heads flush with the soleplate using a fine mill file. The filing motion should be from heel to toe to maintain proper "graining."

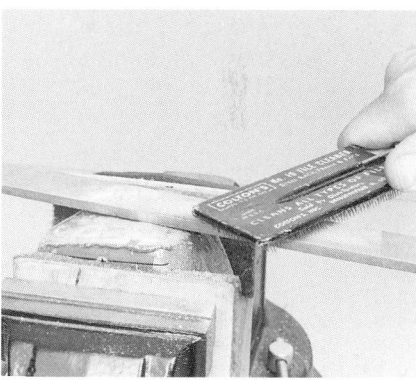

2-21 Use a file cleaner to clean off any metal shaving buildup. Metal particles stuck between the teeth of the file will gouge the soleplate.

2-22 Pushing a piece of soft brass through the teeth of the file works amazingly well in removing stubborn metal particles or dried epoxy.

2-23 Blend in the leading and trailing edges of the soleplate as needed to obtain a flush fit.

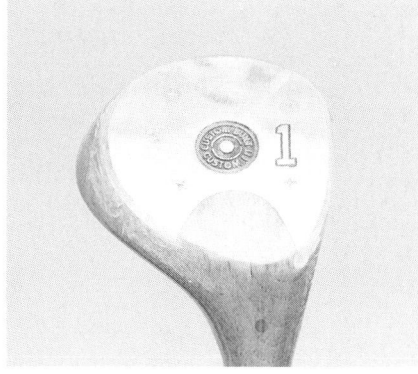

2-24 The soleplate is reset and the sole area is filed smooth. This club is now ready for refinishing. Refer to Chapter 1 for wood head refinishing procedures.

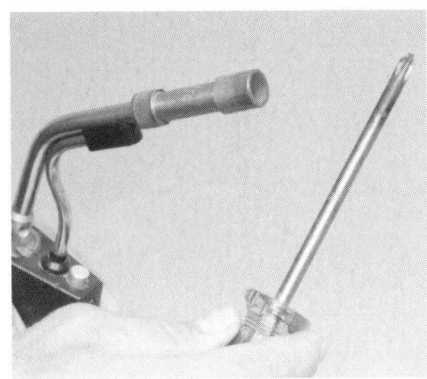

2-25 Instructions for removing difficult screws. If a soleplate screw will not turn, it is usually a result of the epoxy bond. Heat must be applied to the screw to soften the epoxy. One method is to heat the tip of an old Reed & Prince or Phillips screwdriver with a propane torch. After the tip of the screwdriver turns red …

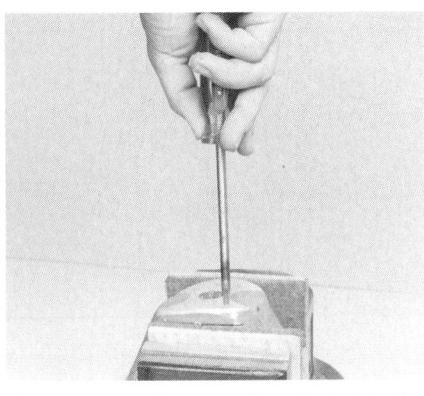

2-26 … place the screwdriver tip inside the screw head recess. Allow the tip to rest inside the recess for 45 seconds, then try to turn the screw. Repeated application of the heated screwdriver tip may be necessary before the screw will turn.

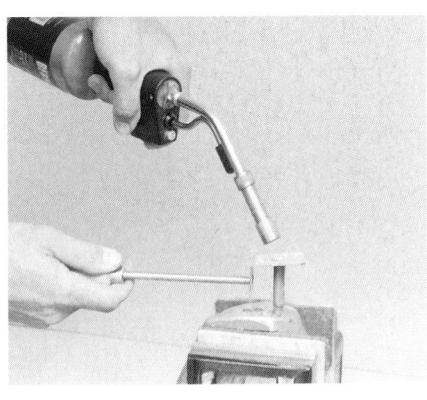

2-27 To use a Screw Heater, place the copper tube over the head of the screw. Direct the flame down the copper tube for 10-15 seconds or until the epoxy softens enough to allow the screw to be removed.

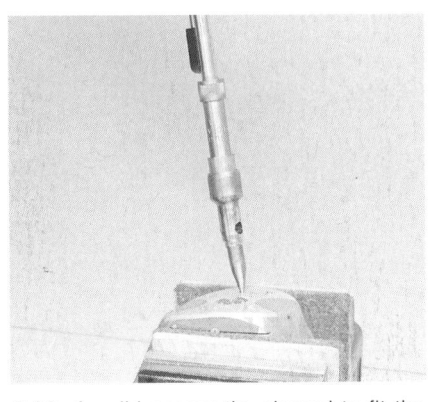

2-28 A solid copper tip, shaped to fit the screwdriver head recess, can be mounted to the top of a propane torch. The flame from the torch heats the copper tip so the screw becomes hot without burning the finish.

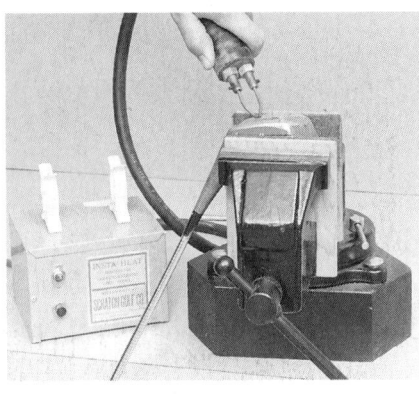

2-29 Information on the use of the Electric Screw Extractor. This is absolutely the best and fastest method to heat epoxied screws. Place both electrode tips against the head of the screw. An arc is created that instantly heats the screw. Now, simply turn out the screw.

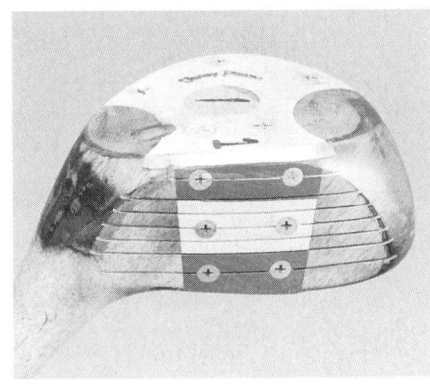

2-30 Although rare, if the soleplate screw will not turn but appears to be loose, check to see if the insert screw has been installed through the soleplate screw thus mechanically locking it in place.

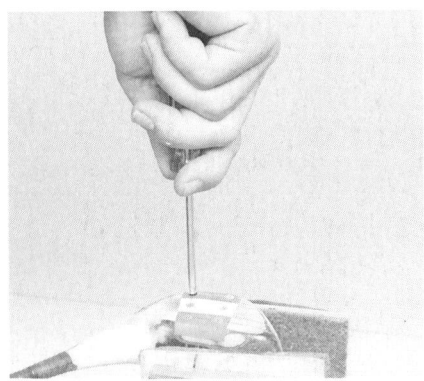

2-31 If it appears the insert screw is locking the soleplate screw, remove the insert screw and then remove the soleplate screw.

2-32 To remove a screw with a ruined head, first drill a ⁵⁄₆₄" diameter pilot hole into the center of the screw head. Drill the hole ⅛" to ¼" deep. Heat the screw using one of the methods shown in photos 2-25 through 2-29.

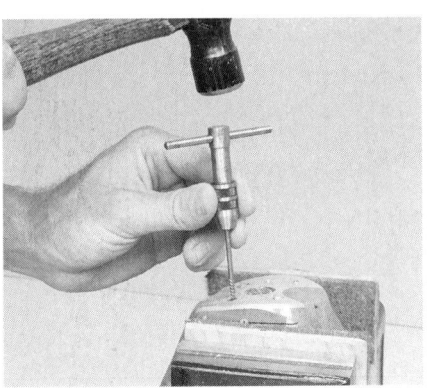

2-33 Next, place a #1 size screw extractor in a "T" handle wrench. Tap the extractor into the drilled hole to obtain a good "bite." If the extractor will not bite, drill the hole deeper.

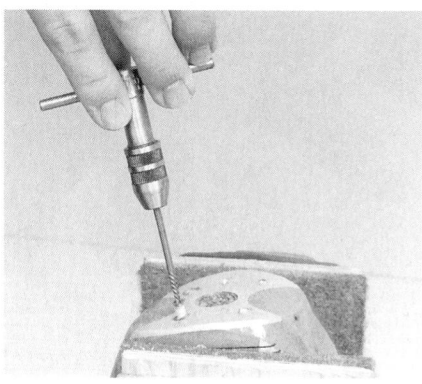

2-34 Gently and with even pressure, turn the handle counterclockwise to back the screw out. This method will also work if the head snaps off. Simply drill into the middle of the body of the screw.

2-35 If the screw threads are stripped in a wood head, push one or more toothpicks into the screw hole. Break each toothpick flush with the surface.

2-36 Dip the tip of the screw in epoxy.

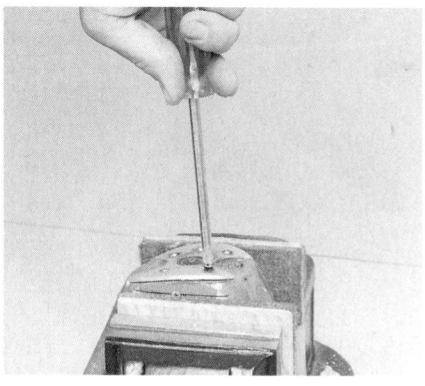

2-37 Install the screw in the normal manner. If the threads strip again, repeat the procedure.

2-38 More toothpicks take up more space in the screw hole. Fine strands of steel wool can also be used. Pack the steel wool into the hole using an awl or scriber.

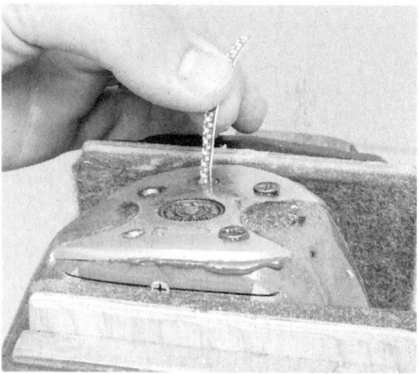

2-39 A Stripped Screw Repair Kit is also available. Cut one or two thin strips of perforated metal and fit them into the stripped hole. Next, insert the soleplate screw in the normal manner.

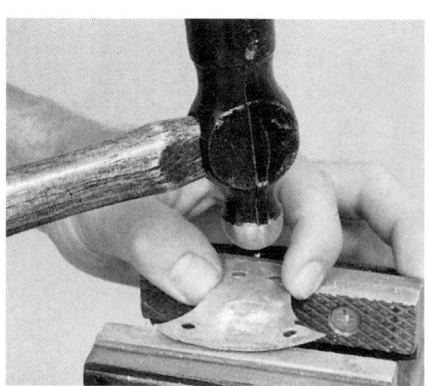

2-40 To rebend or to form a soleplate to make it fit properly, lay it across vise jaws and tap gently with a hammer. Repeatedly test fit the soleplate into the cavity until the proper shape is achieved.

2-41 How to remove a soleplate from a Toney Penna golf club. This photo shows the threaded steel or aluminum sleeve with brass or aluminum "Master Screw." The sleeve is epoxied into the wood head and then the Master Screw is screwed in place with epoxy.

2-42 To remove the soleplate, heat must first be applied to the Master Screw to soften the epoxy bond. Use either a Screw Heater or ...

2-43 ... a propane torch ...

2-44 ... or better yet, the **Electric Screw Extractor**.

2-45 Once the Master Screw is very hot, attempt to turn it out using a chisel that has been ground to fit the curved slot in the Master Screw or ...

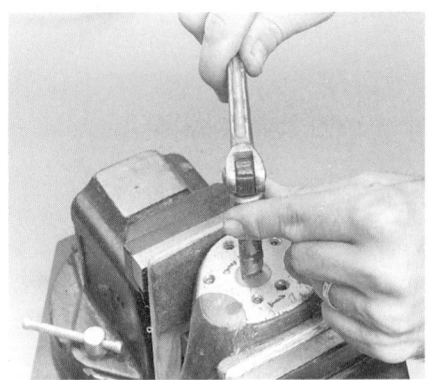

2-46 ... use a Breaker Bar or Ratchet with a slotted socket. This creates tremendous leverage and the Master Screw will usually turn out.

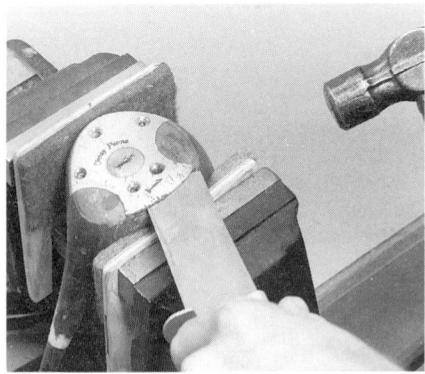

2-47 If the Master Screw will not turn, insert a strong knife or chisel under the leading edge of the soleplate and slowly pry the soleplate up. The soleplate screws are removed first. If the soleplate will not come up, apply more heat until ...

2-48 ... the soleplate, metal sleeve and Master Screw come out as one unit. Sometimes this requires repeated heatings at higher temperatures.

2-49 The **Double Screw Extractor** works great when a screw will not come out with the **#1 size screw extractor**. Position the extractor over the broken screw.

2-50 Drill down to the depth of the screw hole, usually ⅝". The resulting plug should come out when the extractor is removed from the hole. If it does not, however, remove the plug with a narrow screwdriver or similar object. The hole will be ¼" in diameter.

2-51 Tap a ¼" dowel rod coated with epoxy into the hole or fill the hole with only epoxy. After the epoxy dries, drill the pilot hole using the appropriate sized bit as found in Table 2-2. Now proceed with normal installation steps.

66

ADDITIONAL INFORMATION FOR SOLEPLATE REMOVAL AND RESETTING LOOSE SOLEPLATES

TABLE 2-1
Screw Head Styles

 Slotted

 Reed & Prince (Frearson)

Phillips

Phillips and Reed & Prince (Frearson) screwdrivers come in a number of sizes. Club repairmen should have 2 or 3 slotted screwdriver sizes and the #1 and #2 sizes in both Phillips and Reed & Prince types.

TABLE 2-2
Standard Wood Screw Diameters

Screw Number Size	Shank Diameter	General Golf Club Use	Drill Size to Use so Screw Threads Properly
4	.112	Standard size face insert screw	3/32"
5	.125	Oversize face insert screw	7/64"
6	.138	Very large face insert screw	#32
7	.151	Standard size soleplate screw	1/8"
8	.164	Oversize soleplate screw	9/64"
9	.177	Backweight screw (older clubs)	#25
10	.190	Backweight screw (old H&B)	#19

Club manufacturers use both the #7 and #8 soleplate screws. It is always best to have both sizes handy.

TABLE 2-3
Drill Selection Chart

• Back screw pilot drill	1/8"
• Screw extractor pilot drill	5/64"
• Drill to cut shaft backscrew	7/32"
• Pilot drill for #7 soleplate screws	1/8"
• Pilot drill for #8 soleplate screws	9/64"
• Pilot drill for #4 face insert screws	3/32"
• Pilot drill for #5 face insert screws	7/64"
• Hosel pin drill for irons - most modern	1/8"
• Hosel pin drill for irons - older models	3/32"

CHAPTER 3

INSERT REMOVAL AND RESETTING LOOSE INSERTS

Most golfers are not aware that their inserts are loose. A loose insert is usually discovered by the repairman when the club is brought in for a refinish or other clubhead work. If the club is to be refinished, a loose insert must first be repaired to eliminate insert movement. The slightest movement can cause a hairline crack to develop in the finish around the insert, usually after impact with a ball. Also, a loose insert will allow moisture to enter the head during periods of high humidity and allow moisture to leave the head during periods of low humidity. This change in moisture content causes the head to alternately swell and shrink slightly, which in turn causes cracking, delamination and general deterioration of the bonding between the head and its components.

Insert materials will usually be one of the following: original fiber, cycolac (ABS), acrylic, epoxy, phenolic laminate, graphite, aluminum, Gamma-fire, melamine or Ferro-Ligno.

The following removal techniques will work on all of the above-mentioned insert materials, with the exception of a pour-in-place epoxy insert. Steps required for the removal of epoxy inserts are found in Chapter 4.

A number of clubs have face insert screws, although many newer models do not. If a screw is used, it is most likely a #4 or #5 brass screw. It is a good idea to keep a supply of both on hand. We stock both the #4 x ⅝" and #5 x ¾" sizes, and find that the larger #5 size is quite handy for replacing stripped out #4 screws.

3-1 This photo shows a clubhead with a loose insert. A loose insert is identified by a gap between the insert and the insert cavity. The gap can be at the sides of the insert or along the top line of the insert or both.

3-2 First, remove the soleplate as outlined in Chapter 2.

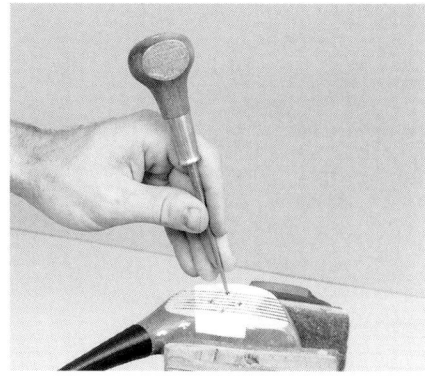

3-3 Carefully clean out all dirt, paint and old finish from the screw head recesses with a scriber, dental pick, awl or other pointed tool.

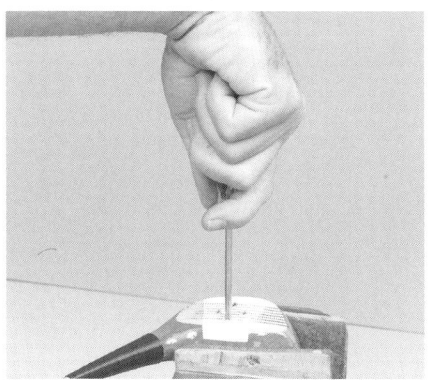

3-4 Hold the screwdriver perfectly square, press down firmly and turn the screw out (counterclockwise). Insert screws are usually not installed with epoxy and will therefore, turn out easily. If difficulty is experienced, refer to photos 3-5 through 3-15 for methods of removing stubborn face insert screws.

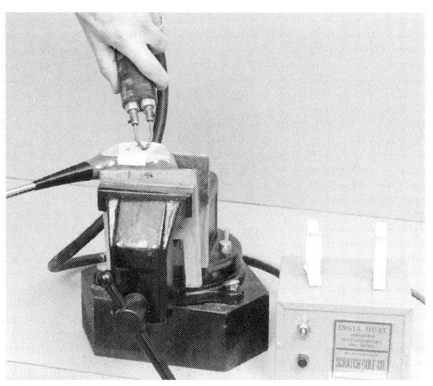

3-5 Use of the Electric Screw Extractor is the fastest and easiest way to remove stubborn screws. When the two electrode tips make contact with the head of the screw, heat is immediately applied. After a few seconds of contact, simply turn the screw out with a screwdriver. The longer the tips make contact with the screw, the hotter the screw becomes.

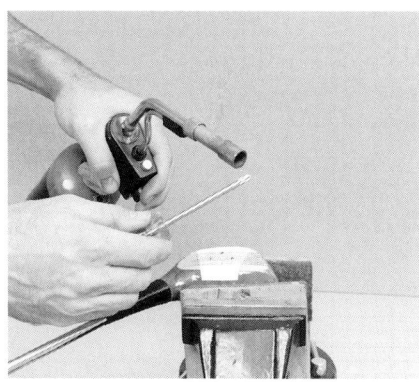

3-6 Another method is to heat the tip of an old screwdriver with a propane torch. After the tip is quite hot, place it in the screw head for 30 seconds and then try to twist the screw out. This method works surprisingly well for insert screw removal.

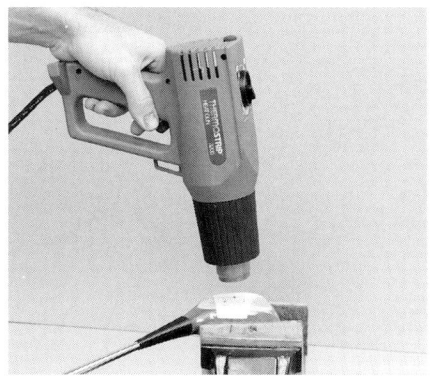

3-7 An **Electric Heat Gun** will also heat the screw enough to break the epoxy bond. Of course, this method heats the entire face so use care in not applying too much heat.

3-8 Method for removing a "stripped" screw head. A stripped screw head is generally caused by failure to properly clean the screw head recess before attempting to turn the screw or by using the incorrect type or size of screwdriver.

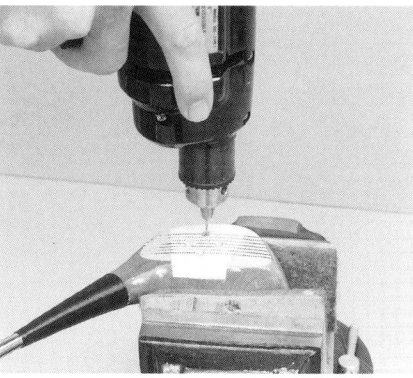

3-9 First, using a ⁵⁄₆₄" drill bit, drill a hole at least ³⁄₁₆" deep into the middle of the screw head. If necessary, heat the head of the screw using one of the methods already shown.

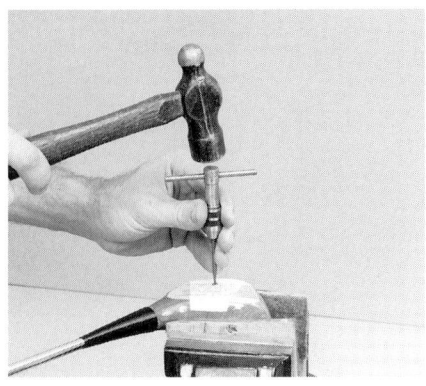

3-10 Next, place a **#1 size screw extractor** into the drilled hole and tap lightly until it gets a good "bite." The extractor works best when held in a **"T" handle Tap Wrench** as shown.

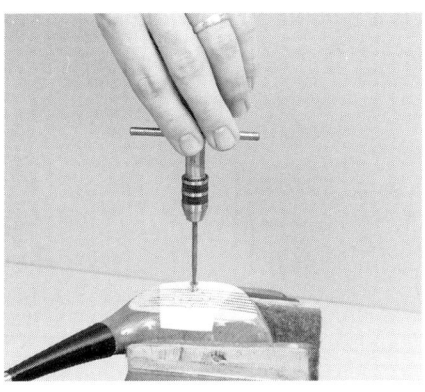

3-11 Turn the extractor counterclockwise to remove the screw. Do not use force. If the screw will not turn, use more heat and try again.

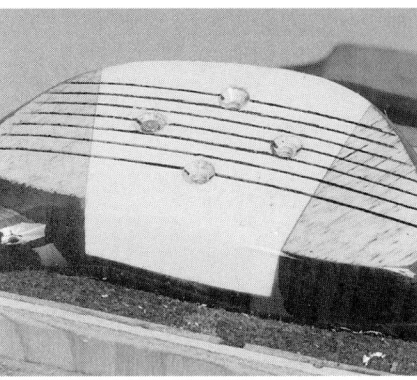

3-12 If the head of an insert screw breaks while attempting removal, the drill and extractor method will usually not work. The best method for dealing with this difficult situation is …

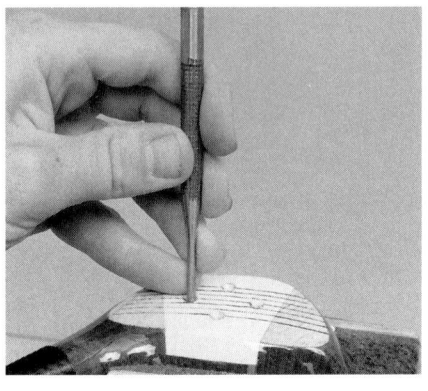

3-13 … place a ⅛" or ³⁄₃₂" **pin punch** on top of the broken screw and …

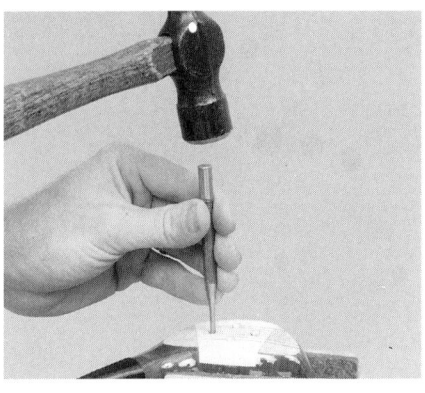

3-14 … drive the broken screw at least ½" below the surface of the face.

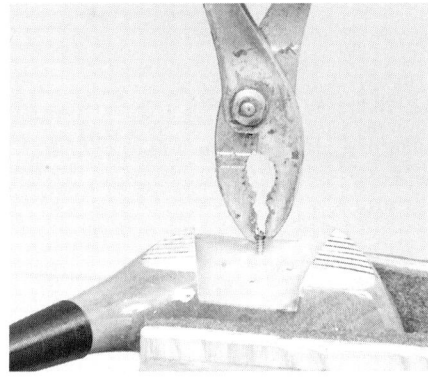

3-15 An alternative method: Once the other insert screws are removed, pry the insert over the broken screw shank. After the insert is removed, grasp the broken screw with a pair of pliers and turn it out.

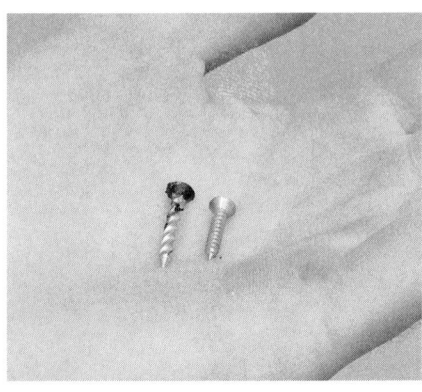

3-16 A few manufacturers use a different type of insert screw known as a drive screw. Note the difference in the threading of the two screws. The drive screw must be turned and pulled from the head simultaneously.

3-17 Unfortunately, this type of screw is not easily recognized. Experience will indicate which manufacturers use this screw. If you suspect a club has a drive screw …

3-18 … drill into the screw head as shown in photo 3-9. Next, heat the screw head as shown in photos 3-5 through 3-7. Quickly, while the screw is still hot, tap the #1 size screw extractor into the hole. Once the extractor is seated in the hole, turn the extractor counterclockwise while pulling up slightly on the screw.

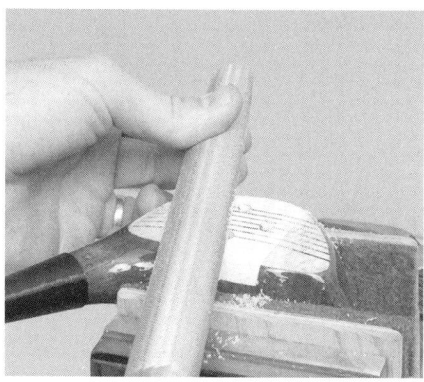

3-19 After the insert screws are removed, lightly file through the polyurethane coating on the face. Concentrate the filing on the face where the insert edge meets the wood. Any fine or medium grade file works best.

3-20 Polyurethane adheres very well to the face. If it is not removed from around the insert, some of the wood may be pulled from the head when the insert is removed.

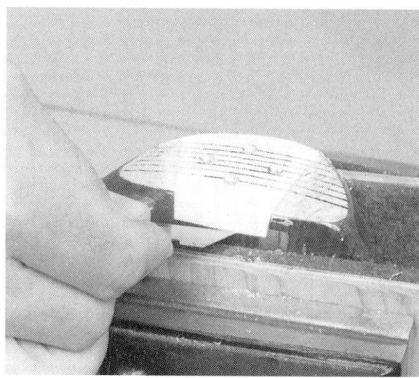

3-21 Carefully cut around the top of the insert. This step will help prevent wood from being pulled from the head and it will not allow polyurethane to be torn from the head. Only cut deep enough to penetrate the clear finish.

3-22 If you suspect there is a tight fit between the insert and the insert cavity, carefully tap a razor blade between the insert and insert cavity. This will create a very thin gap and help with insert removal. Do not tap the razor blade deeper than ⅛". Use the razor blade on both sides.

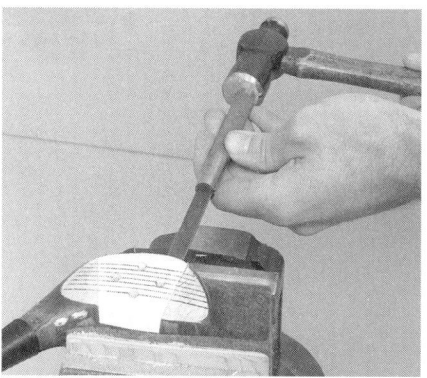

3-23 Place an **Insert Remover Tool** at the bottom of the insert cavity. Start at the side of the insert. Gently tap the top of the tool. As the insert lifts from the head, watch the sides of the face to see if any wood is coming up with the insert. If the wood begins to lift, repeat the step shown in photo 3-22.

3-24 Once approximately two-thirds of the side of the insert is free…

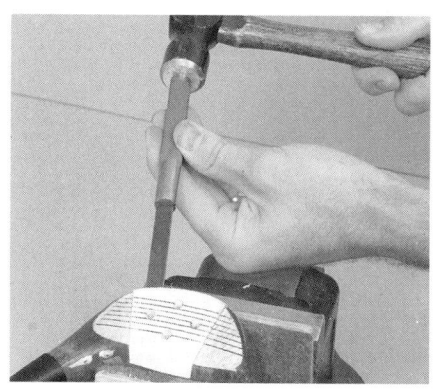

3-25 … remove the tool and reinsert it under the other side, Again, lightly tap until two-thirds of the insert is free.

3-26 At this point, there is a lot of pressure created at the top of the insert cavity between the insert and the wood. To alleviate this pressure, tap the top of the insert lightly with a hammer. The insert should pop out. If it does not, repeat the previous steps. Do not attempt to pry the insert out. Serious damage to the wood around the top of the insert may result.

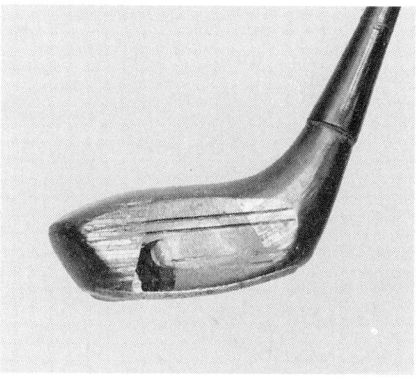

3-27 The method shown in the previous photos will work on every insert material with the exception of a pour-in-place epoxy insert. This type of insert is installed into the insert cavity in the form of a liquid which hardens and becomes solid. Most epoxy inserts cannot be removed without destroying the insert. Refer to Chapter 4 for correct removal and replacement steps.

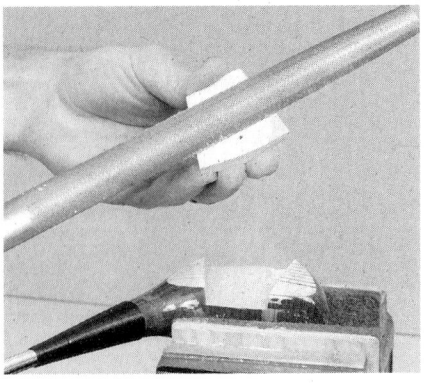

3-28 Once the insert is removed, file the back and sides of the insert to remove excess epoxy or any foreign material.

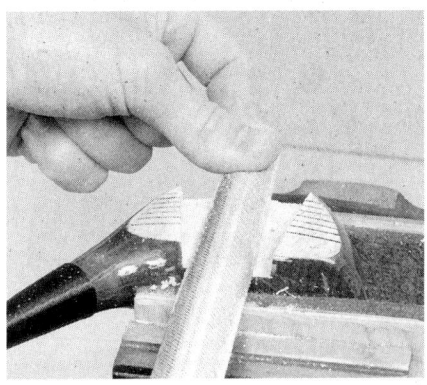

3-29 Excess epoxy in the insert cavity should also be removed. A file may be used to remove this excess, but be very careful when filing along the top edge of the insert cavity. Maintain a straight edge and do not file too deeply.

3-30 Epoxy may also be removed using a chisel. Heating the tip of the chisel before scraping will help soften the epoxy and make it much easier to remove. A propane torch is good for heating the chisel tip.

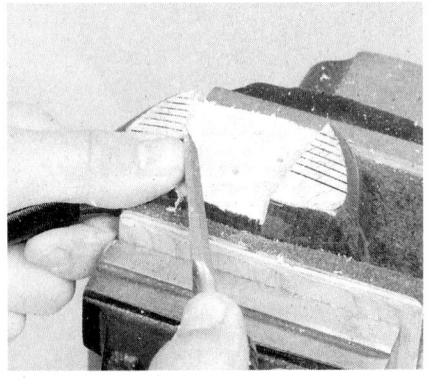

3-31 The sides of the insert cavity are also carefully cleaned. A chisel works best for this area.

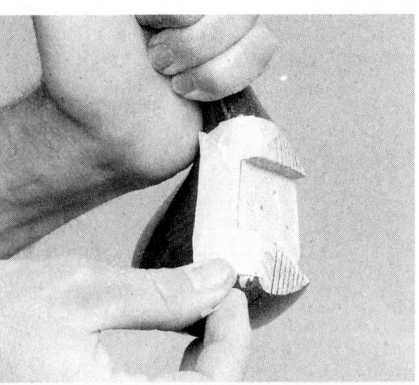

3-32 If the clubhead is not to be refinished after resetting the insert, carefully lay two layers of ¾" masking tape around the top of the insert cavity. The tape will protect the finish from the epoxy adhesive.

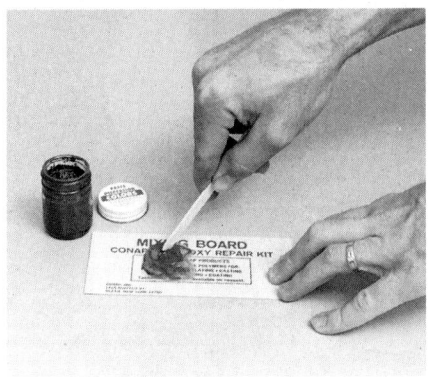

3-33 Mix an appropriate amount of epoxy. It is a good idea to mix a colored paste dispersion with the epoxy so that the color will match the stained wood. This will camouflage an epoxy line behind the top of the insert cavity. A high shear strength epoxy is used for this step. **GolfWorks®** or **Conap®** epoxy works very well.

3-34 Apply epoxy to the back and sides of both the insert and the insert cavity.

3-35 Place the insert in the bottom half of the cavity and ...

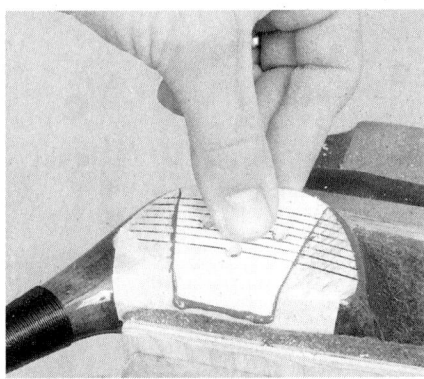

3-36 ... push the insert up into the proper location. This will force epoxy around the sides of the insert and guarantee a good seal. Make sure the scoring lines in the insert and face are properly aligned. Note that some people will temporarily install an insert screw into the bottom hole to properly align the scoring lines.

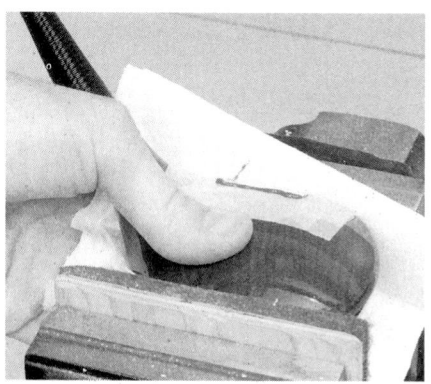

3-37 Place a paper towel across the face and position the clubhead in the vise as shown. Tighten the vise jaws until snug but not tight. Allow the epoxy to harden before removing. Note the use of a **Felt Vise Pad** to protect the back of the clubhead.

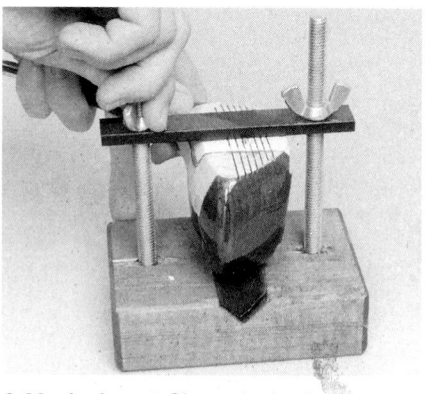

3-38 An **Insert Clamp** is the best way to tighten a newly epoxied insert into the insert cavity. Use of the Insert Clamp will keep the vise free for other activities and also allow better visibility of the clamping process. It is a good idea to have enough Insert Clamps on hand to reset an entire day's work.

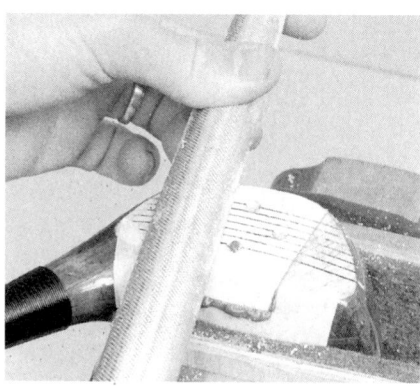

3-39 **After the epoxy hardens,** remove the head from the vise or Insert Clamp. Carefully file the excess epoxy from the face, using a medium cut file. Do not file into the wood yet.

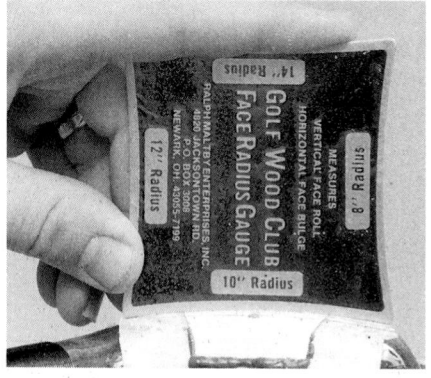

3-40 **Check the bulge and roll** and make any necessary corrections with the medium or fine cut file. Refer to Chapter 1, photos 1-22 through 1-30 for correct face measuring techniques and filing steps.

3-41 After filing, recut the scoring lines using the same technique as shown in photo 1-34 in Chapter 1.

3-42 Next, clean out the insert screw pilot holes with a ³⁄₃₂" drill bit. The depth to drill depends upon the length of the screw to be used. See Table 3-1 for other pilot drill sizes.

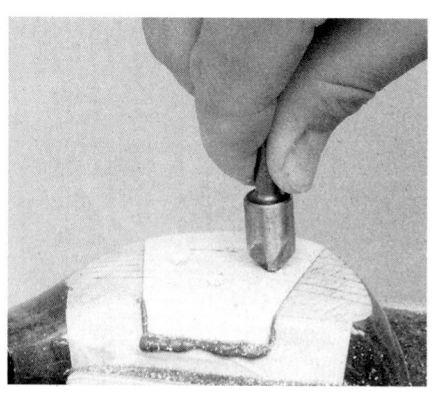

3-43 After drilling, recountersink the holes if necessary. Hold the shank as shown, and twirl quickly. **DO NOT MAKE HOLES WIDER THAN THE SCREW HEADS.**

3-44 The **Automatic Countersink** is very fast and efficient for both insert and soleplate screws. It is used mainly for high volume repair or production work.

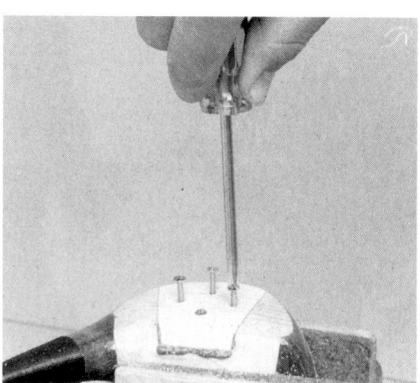

3-45 Next, install new insert screws.

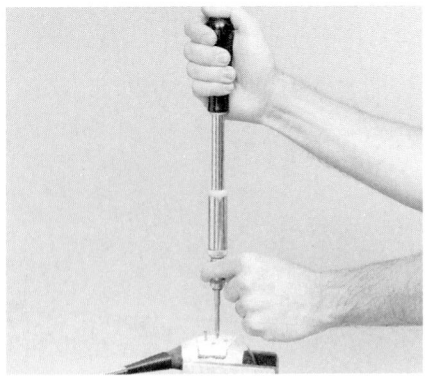

3-46 A **Ratchet Screwdriver** saves time by allowing the operator to turn the screws into the head at a very fast rate.

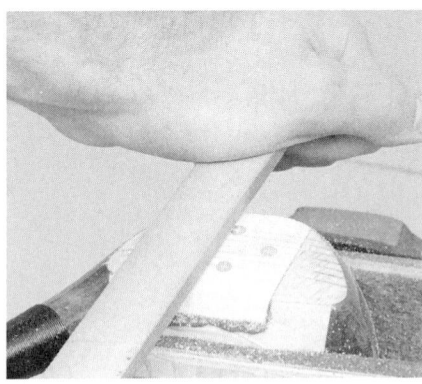

3-47 **File the screw heads flush with the face.** A properly countersunk hole will allow the head of the screw to be seated slightly above the face. This will give a professional look once the heads are filed down flush. Use a fine cut file when filing insert screws.

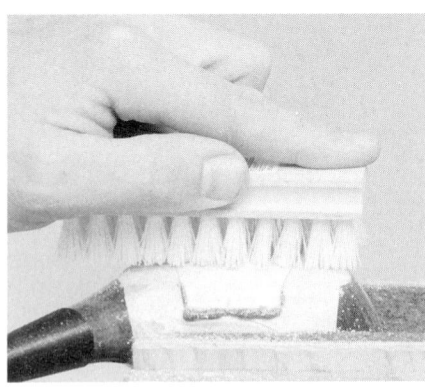

3-48 **Brush the face clean** with a stiff bristled brush after filing.

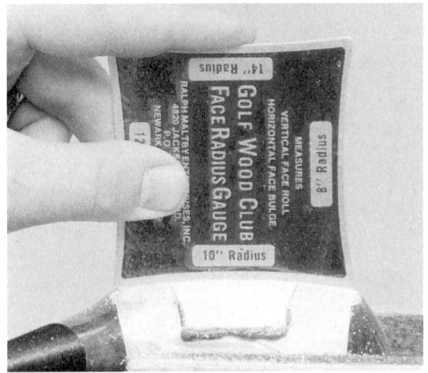

3-49 **Final check the bulge and the roll.**

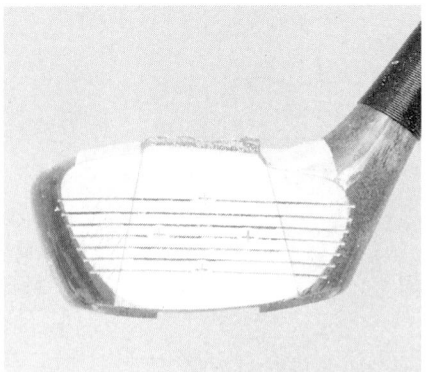

3-50 This is how the face should look after filing. Note the screw slots are positioned perpendicular and parallel to the scoring lines. If the clubhead is to be refinished, reinstall the soleplate as outlined in Chapter 2 and proceed with the refinishing steps as shown in Chapter 1.

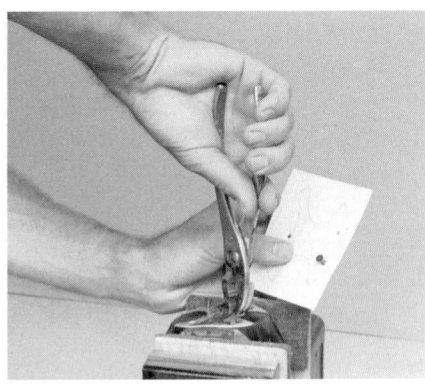

3-51 If the club must be returned to the customer without the benefit of a refinish, reinstall the soleplate as outlined in Chapter 2, photos 2-10 through 2-17. Touchup steps are shown in Chapter 16.

3-52 **INFORMATION ON SPECIAL INSERTS.** Some H&B Power Bilt models have three headless brass screws running through the insert and into the wood. The quickest method for removal is to first drill into the center of the screw with a 5/64" drill.

3-53 Next, heat the screw with an **Electric Screw Extractor** and then quickly tap a #1 size extractor into the hole. Note: Alternate methods to heat the screw are to use an Electric Heat Gun or a 3/16" diameter flat end heating rod and a propane torch.

3-54 Turn the extractor and "T" handle Tap Wrench counterclockwise while pulling up. As you can see, this screw is very much like the drive screw pictured in photo 3-16.

74

3-55 INFORMATION ON SPECIAL INSERTS. To remove old MacGregor inserts with the screw-in aluminum firing pin, first remove the 4 screws and cut only the center face line deeper, but not wider, with a scoring line hacksaw blade.

3-56 Heat the aluminum pin with the **Screw Heater, Electric Screw Extractor or Electric Heat Gun.**

3-57 Place a chisel or conventional large screwdriver in the middle scoring line. Turn the aluminum pin counterclockwise and screw it out.

3-58 The aluminum pin is then removed. Note the use of a pair of pliers as the screw will be very hot. The insert can now be removed as previously shown.

3-59 INFORMATION ON SPECIAL INSERTS. To remove a two-piece insert from an old Ben Hogan head, use normal procedures and remove both the red fiber insert and the white fiber insert backing piece from the insert cavity. To reinstall, epoxy both pieces back in at the same time.

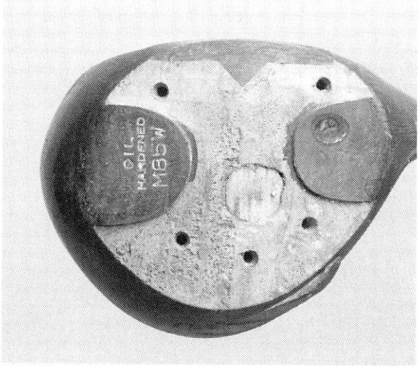

3-60 INFORMATION ON SPECIAL INSERTS. To remove all MacGregor Eye-O-Matic inserts with "V" back, proceed as follows. The insert is usually loose at its edges but the "V" is still secure to the head. Note: Some repairmen choose to simply fill any gaps around the insert with epoxy if the "V" is secure to the head. This is due to removal difficulty.

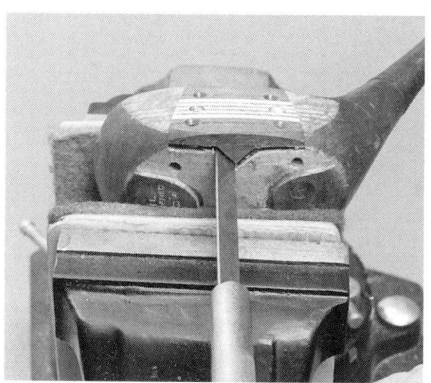

3-61 First, place an Insert Remover Tool beneath the flat back side of the insert. Tap the head of the tool several times, remove the tool and now place it under the "V" portion of the insert as shown above. Again tap the insert tool several times and continue to repeat these steps until …

3-62 … the insert comes out. Patience is the key in removing this type of insert.

3-63 INFORMATION ON SPECIAL INSERTS. This concerns old MacGregor Eye-O-Matic type inserts with three fiber dowel pins running through the insert into the wood. The best removal method is to slide the special Insert Remover Tool underneath the insert and cut through the dowels. Now follow the normal insert removal procedure.

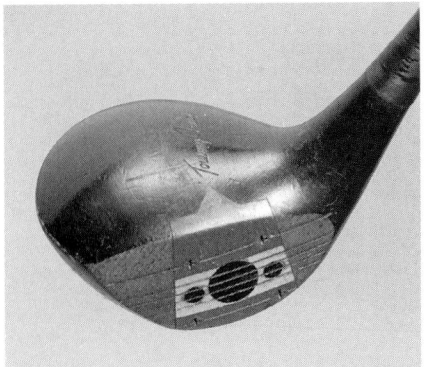

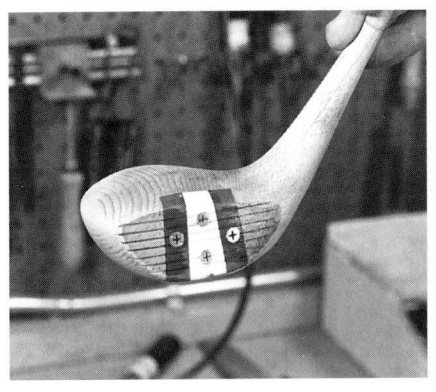

3-64 The three dowels are also found in the "V" back insert type. Follow the instructions as shown in photos 3-60 through 3-62. Simply cut through the dowels while removing the insert as shown in photo 3-63.

3-65   INFORMATION ON SPECIAL INSERTS. An old Spalding 3-piece insert will come out easily, however, it will come out in 3 pieces. During reassembly, epoxy the three pieces back together. Some repairmen will install each piece with an insert screw to ensure the pieces do not slide out of place.

ADDITIONAL INFORMATION FOR INSERT REMOVAL AND RESETTING LOOSE INSERTS

TABLE 3-1
Standard Wood Screw Diameters

Screw Number Size	Shank Diameter	General Golf Club Use	Drill Size to Use so Screw Threads Properly
→ 4	.112	Standard size face insert screw	3/32"
→ 5	.125	Oversize face insert screw	7/64"
→ 6	.138	Very large face insert screw	#32
7	.151	Standard size soleplate screw	1/8"
8	.164	Oversize soleplate screw	9/64"
9	.177	Backweight screw (older clubs)	#25
10	.190	Backweight screw (old H&B)	#19

Golf clubs manufactured from 1940 and on use mostly #4 and #5 face insert screws. Most are brass, however, some were made of aluminum. The #6 screw was used in a few 1920's and 1930's models and is quite rare to find.

TABLE 3-2
Drill Selection Chart

• Back screw pilot drill	1/8"
→ • Screw extractor pilot drill	5/64"
• Drill to cut shaft backscrew	7/32"
• Pilot drill for #7 soleplate screws	1/8"
• Pilot drill for #8 soleplate screws	9/64"
→ • Pilot drill for #4 face insert screws	3/32"
→ • Pilot drill for #5 face insert screws	7/64"
• Hosel pin drill for irons - most modern	1/8"
• Hosel pin drill for irons - older models	3/32"

CHAPTER 4

REPLACING OLD INSERTS WITH EPOXY POUR-IN-PLACE INSERTS AND REPAIRING DAMAGED FACES

Many times you will be faced with an unrepairable face insert which must be replaced. Epoxy, pour-in-place inserts are one alternative for replacement. This insert material was developed because it is impossible to stock the hundreds of different shapes and colors of inserts used by golf club manufacturers. The versatility of pour-in-place epoxy inserts is probably the most important characteristic of this material. Inserts can be poured in any shape or size with a myriad of color combinations available.

This high-impact strength, pour-in-place epoxy can also be used to repair damaged faces on woods. Often, due to moisture absorption and excessive toe or heel shots, a wood face will dry rot or weather. Eventually, a defect in the face develops where the rotten wood is worn from the face causing some concavity. When a ball is struck from this irregular surface, an errant shot can result. If properly repaired, the clear epoxy will reflect the wood surface beneath the epoxy, and the repair is hardly noticeable. Many valuable and cherished wood clubs have been saved using this procedure.

Epoxy inserts also allow for customizing. Photos in this chapter show how to take advantage of the versatility of this material by placing a medallion, logo, coin, photo, etc. inside the epoxy insert. Customizing inserts adds a unique touch to a club and can give the club a truly one-of-a-kind look.

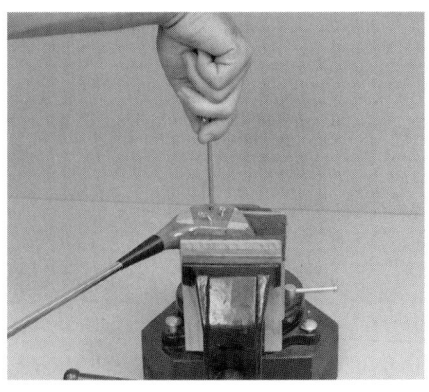

4-1 Remove the old insert and insert screws, if any, as outlined in Chapter 3. Also, remove the soleplate as outlined in Chapter 2.

4-2 For difficult to remove inserts, make two vertical cuts approximately ⅛" in from each side of the insert cavity. Note the use of a conventional hacksaw blade. The conventional raked teeth blade will move more freely through the insert material without binding.

4-3 This photo shows the insert after cutting. **Do not cut through the top line of the insert cavity into the wood.**

4-4 Place a chisel or **Insert Remover Tool** underneath the middle of the insert. Tap the head of the tool sharply with a hammer.

4-5 The middle portion of the insert will "pop out" leaving only the sides still attached to the insert cavity.

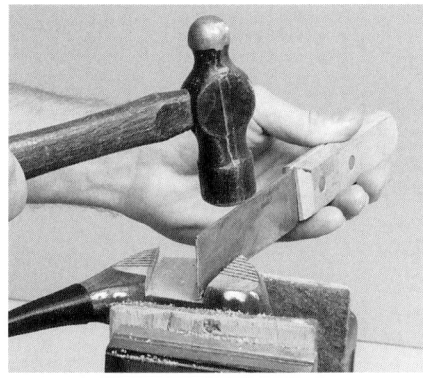

4-6 Place a sharp knife on the line between the cavity and the insert. Tap lightly on the edge of the knife with a hammer until the sliver of insert falls into the cavity. Note: The stiff bladed **"Super Knife"** sold for cutting off old grips works very well for this.

4-7 An alternative to a knife is a stiff razor blade. Employ the same technique as shown in the previous photo.

4-8 All portions of the insert are now removed. Remove any old epoxy from the cavity using a file or wood chisel.

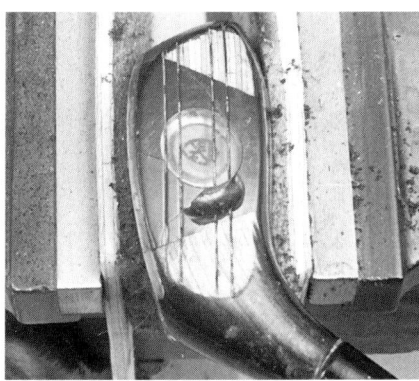

4-9 Take note of the decorative piece inside this insert. If proper care is taken this can be saved and reused in the new insert. The existing epoxy insert can be removed using the following method.

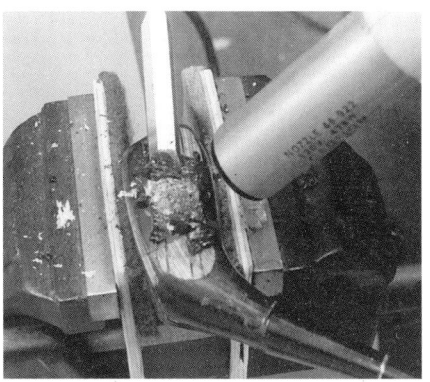

4-10 An **Electric Heat Gun** produces anywhere from 125° to 1000°F. Directing this heat against the epoxy insert will quickly soften the epoxy. The softened epoxy can then be easily dug from the cavity using a chisel.

4-11 Continue to dig at the epoxy until …

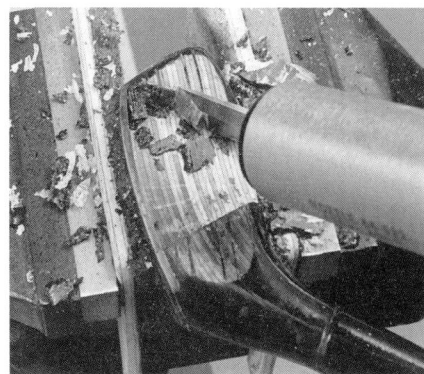

4-12 … all the epoxy is removed. Note the medallion has been salvaged for reuse. Use care not to burn the wood with the Heat Gun.

4-13 After the insert is removed from the club (and if the soleplate was also removed), temporarily reinstall the soleplate without epoxy. The reinstalled soleplate will provide a perfect shaped radius for the poured insert.

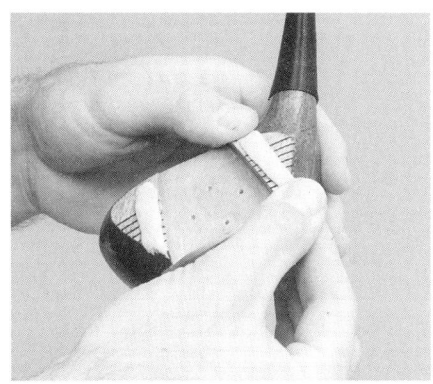

4-14 Press a tiny amount of Mortite putty in the face lines on either side of the cavity. This is necessary to keep the liquid epoxy from flowing out of the cavity through the lines.

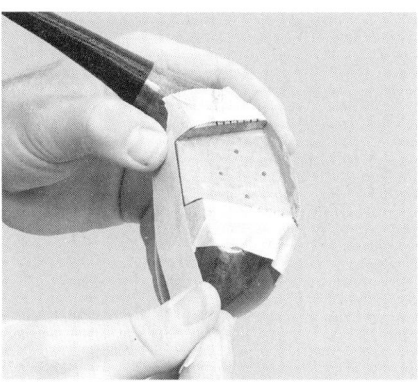

4-15 If the clubhead will not be refinished (it is strongly recommended that it be refinished), outline the entire insert cavity with ¾" masking tape. The tape will protect the finish from the epoxy and also provide a depth gauge later on when filing the insert. Be careful not to allow the tape to lay over the cavity.

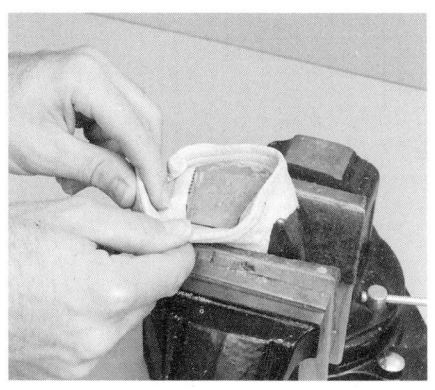

4-16 Form the Mortite putty dam. Press Mortite down tightly around the edges to prevent leaks.

4-17 The finished dam should look like this. Crude in appearance, but very effective. Be sure the putty does not occupy any space that the insert should occupy.

4-18 The club can now be placed in a vise or…

79

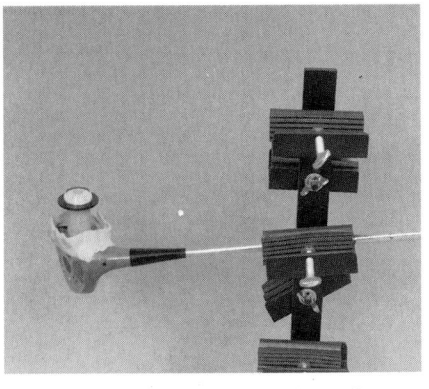

4-19 … a handy **Insert Tree**. Note the use of a **Bubble Level** to ensure the cavity will be filled evenly. Remove the Bubble Level before pouring the insert.

4-20 High-impact strength epoxy is available in different colors and quantities, depending upon need. High-impact strength epoxy is used instead of high shear strength epoxy because the face must withstand the shock of the ball at impact.

4-21 Epoxy resin (base) and activator are mixed together to create the insert mixture. Resins are available in different colors. For smaller users, buy only the clear resin and mix different colored paste dispersions into it to produce the required color. When working with a precolored base, always mix the base thoroughly until …

4-22 … the coloring agent in the bottom of the can is blended in with the upper contents of the can. Note the difference in the color of the base that is on the stick compared to the previous photo. The pigment obviously settles out in the can during storage.

4-23 Pour the appropriate amount of base into a container. Note the use of metric cups to ensure an accurate measurement. **Read the Additional Information on Pouring Inserts at the end of this chapter for specific amounts to use. (See Pages 91-93.)**

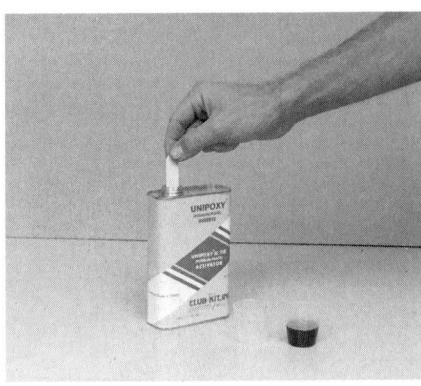

4-24 Slowly stir the activator in the can. **Do not shake the can as it will cause bubbles to form.**

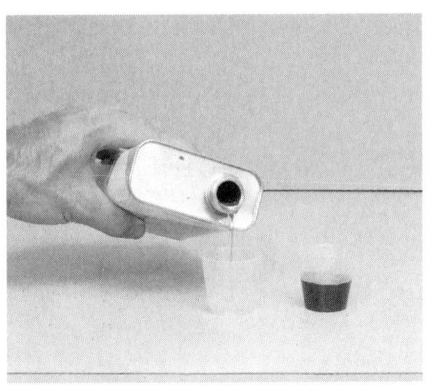

4-25 Pour the appropriate amount of activator into a separate metric cup.

4-26 Once the exact amounts have been poured, pour the activator into the cup holding the base.

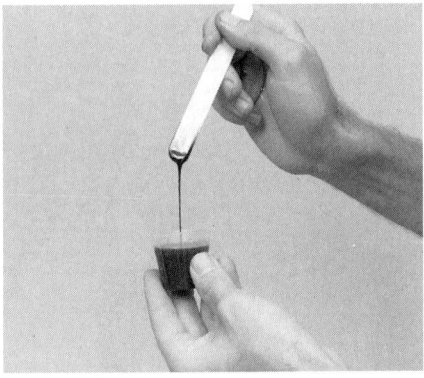

4-27 Fold the epoxy thoroughly, according to the instructions. A folding motion introduces fewer air bubbles than a stirring motion. It will also do a better job of combining the base and the activator.

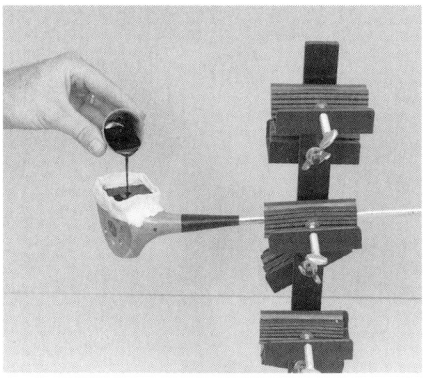

4-28 Pour the epoxy material into the cavity approximately 1½ times the thickness of the original insert. 15 cc's of material will pour one small insert, 22½ cc's a medium insert and 30 cc's a large insert (Wilson). Some full face inserts will require an even greater amount of material.

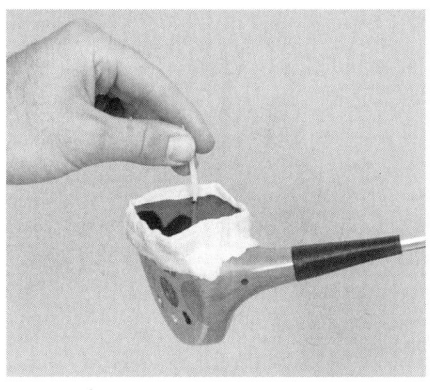

4-29 Using a toothpick or mix stick, swirl around the edges of the insert cavity to release any trapped air bubbles. Do not use a match or pass an open flame across the insert to release the bubbles. Allow the insert to cure in this position, usually overnight.

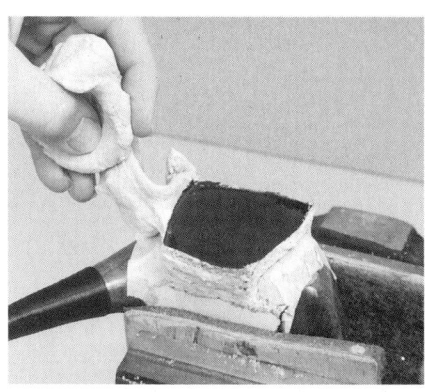

4-30 After the insert has cured, Mortite putty is removed and saved, as it can be used over and over again. Do not remove the masking tape. **If the insert is quite soft it means the mixture quantities of base and activator were not in a proper proportion, it was not mixed well enough or the temperature was below 65°F.**

4-31 Use a medium or coarse wood rasp (preferably 10" length) to rough shape the insert. Leave the middle of the insert "high" while filing the edges of the insert flush with the wood. Reaching the masking tape when filing provides a good indication that you should slow down and use caution so as not to file too deep and remove too much wood from the face. Always use a file handle to prevent possible injury to your hands.

4-32 Use of a **Belt Sander** with a coarse belt is a quick alternative to filing. Be very careful, however, as mistakes can occur faster.

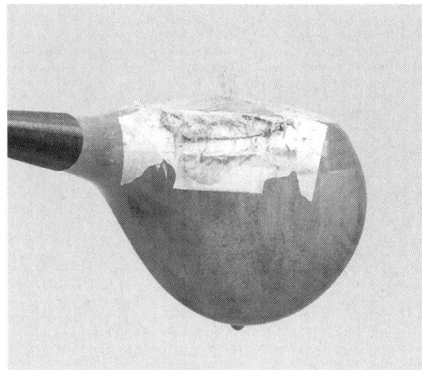

4-33 After rough shaping, the profile of the face should look like this. If there is a low spot in the middle of the insert, excessive filing of the toe and heel will be necessary to achieve the proper bulge and roll. This, in turn, will reduce the face progression and potentially ruin the look of the club.

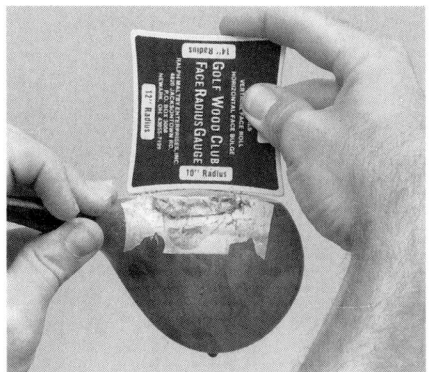

4-34 Check the horizontal face bulge with the Face Radius Gauge. Check at different points from the top to the bottom of the face. Chapter 1 shows how to use this gauge properly (photos 1-22 through 1-27).

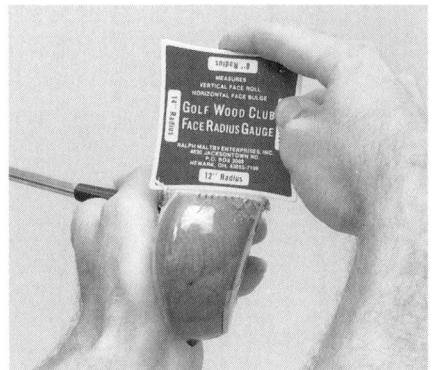

4-35 Check the vertical face roll with the Face Radius Gauge. Check at different points from the toe to the heel.

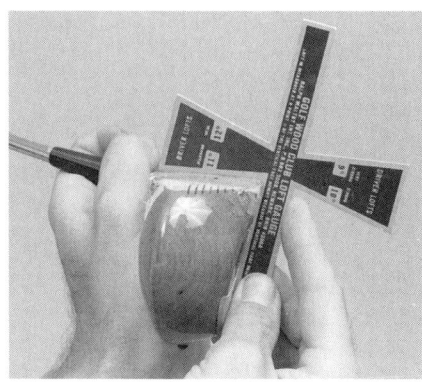

4-36 Check the loft using a protractor or a Loft Gauge. See Chapter 10 for a thorough explanation of measuring loft.

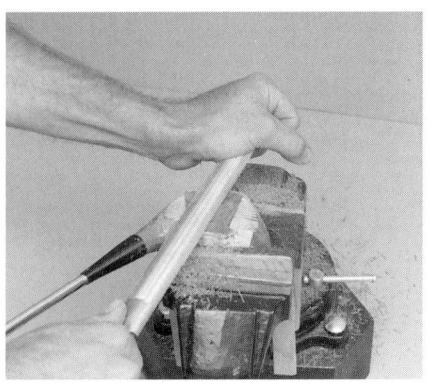

4-37 The purpose in facing the club is to bring the high spots down to the low spots without removing very much wood, if any. With that in mind, file the face with a 10" medium cut wood file (not a rasp). Concentrate the file on the high points in the face using a radiusing motion until…

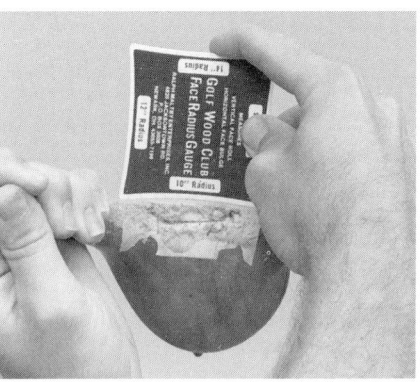

4-38 …the desired bulge radius is achieved and …

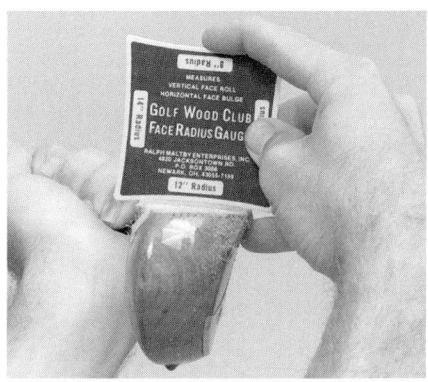

4-39 … the desired roll radius is achieved. Check the loft also. If the original bulge and roll are maintained, very little of the wood in the heel and toe will be filed away and as a result, the loft should be unaffected.

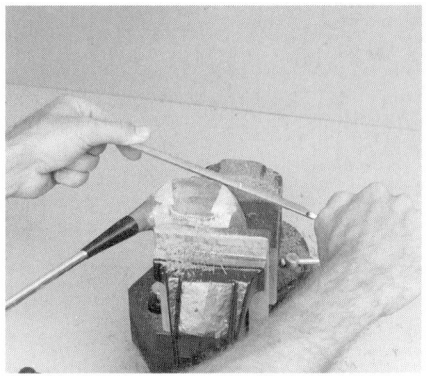

4-40 Next, radius the leading edge of the insert with the file.

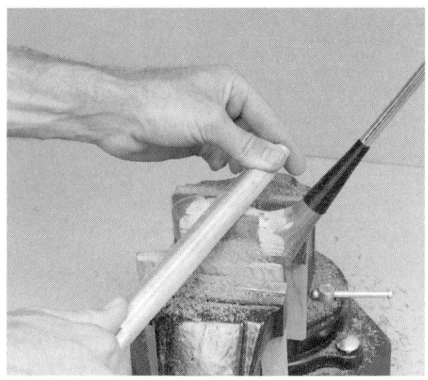

4-41 Change the position of the club in the vise pads and rough file the top of the insert with a medium cut wood file until the file cuts into the masking tape. The wood rasp can also be used here, but be sure to change files upon reaching or nearing the masking tape.

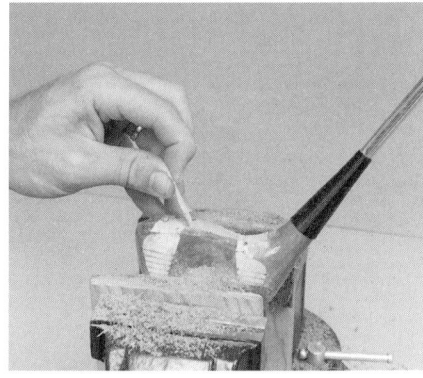

4-42 If the club will not be refinished, care must be taken not to file through the finish. Carefully peel off the tape from around the top of the insert cavity and…
Note: A new piece of ¾" masking tape can be applied at this time, approximately ¼" back from the insert top edge to prevent inadvertent file nicks in the crown of the wood.

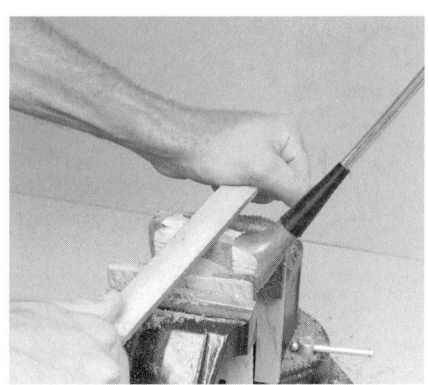

4-43 … lightly file the excess epoxy with a fine mill file. Continue to file the epoxy insert until…

4-44 … the top of the insert is flush with the surrounding finish. Minor surface abrasions are easily repaired. Refer to Chapter 16 for touchup steps if the club is not to be refinished. Note: Some repairmen find it easier to shape the top of the insert with a **Detail Knife** once the level of the insert is close to the wood surface.

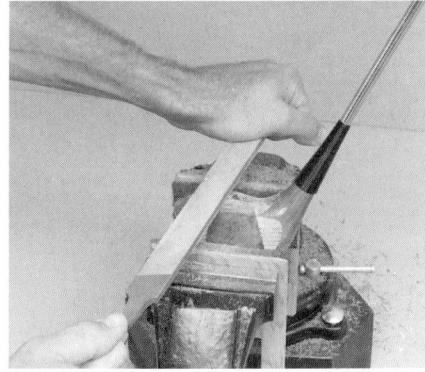

4-45 If the golf club is to be refinished, smooth file the top of the insert flush with the clubhead using a fine cut flat or mill file.

4-46 Note the shape of the top line. Care should be taken to preserve this symmetrical look of the wood head.

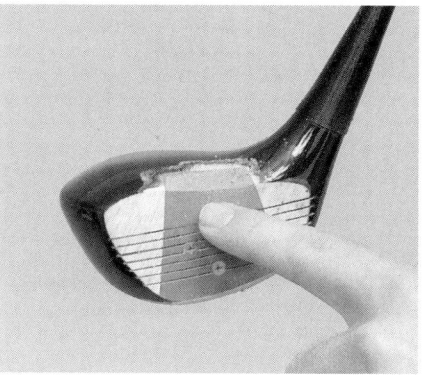

4-47 Avoid this top line shape. Too much material was removed from the middle of the insert caused by an improper filing angle.

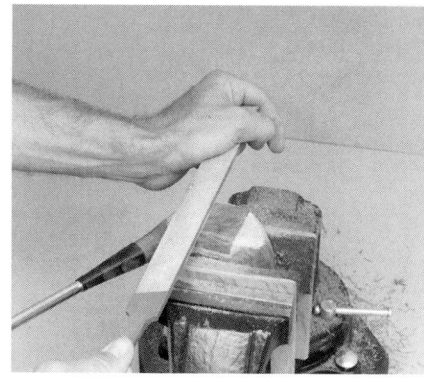

4-48 Smooth file the face with a fine cut flat or mill file. Remove all previous filing marks from the insert and the face. If a medallion or other cosmetic article is to be installed, refer to photo 4-64 to begin the proper steps.

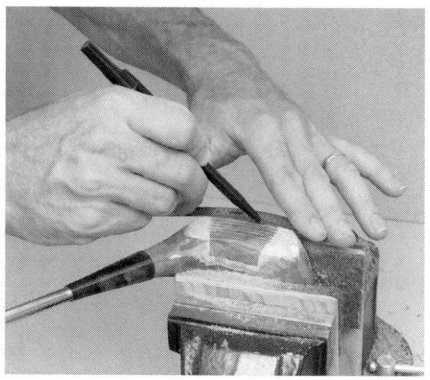

4-49 Next, draw all the face lines on the insert using a 6" flexible metal scale and a sharp pencil. Use care in connecting the old face lines in the toe and heel of the clubface.

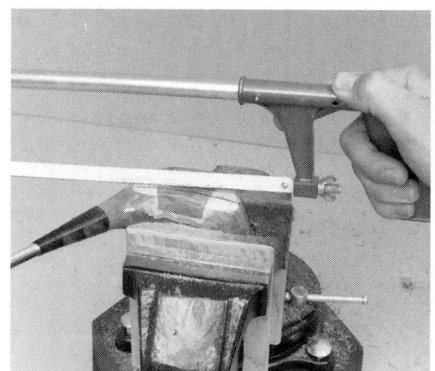

4-50 Place the hacksaw blade in the heel side scoring line. Using short cutting strokes, **cut across the face following the drawn line.** Note the use of a special made hacksaw blade with no rake or offset so proper scoring line width is maintained.

4-51 The newly cut scoring lines should look like this.

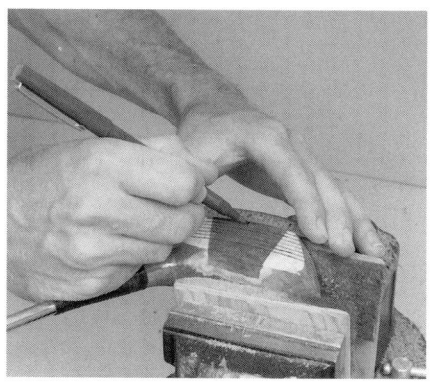

4-52 Installing Insert Screws. Determine the screw pattern. Most clubs use a diamond screw pattern. Place a 6" scale on the bottom scoring line and find the midpoint between the sides of the insert. Make a mark with a pen, pencil or sharp awl. Repeat this step to the top scoring line.

4-53 Place the scale along the middle scoring line. Make a mark ¼" from each side of the insert.

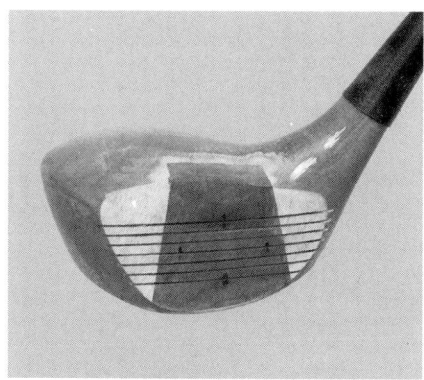

4-54 This photo shows a properly marked insert. **Note:** The screw pattern is altered if the face has more than 7 lines. In the case of a 9 line face, the top and bottom lines are left blank. The screws are installed in the second and eighth line instead of as shown above.

4-55 Using the marks as a guide, drill into the insert with a ³⁄₃₂" bit. The depth of the hole is determined by the length of the insert screw. The #4 x ⅝" brass cross slot screw is the industry standard for insert screws.

4-56 After drilling, open the holes with a countersink. Countersinking the pilot hole will allow the head of the screw to seat flush with the insert. If properly countersunk, the top of the screw head should be slightly higher than the surface of the insert before filing the screw heads.

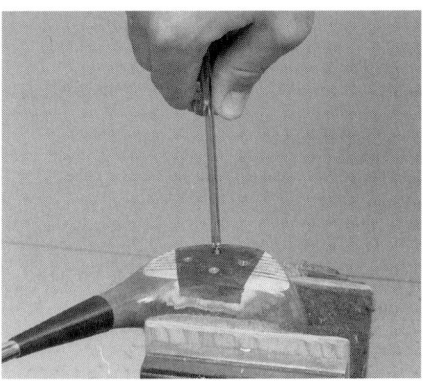

4-57 Carefully turn in the new insert screws. Note: If desired, a small dab of epoxy can be placed on each screw tip for added security.

4-58 File the screw heads flush with the insert using a fine cut mill file. After filing, rub a finger across the face. The screw heads should not be felt.

4-59 All filing marks are removed by lightly **scraping the face with the back edge of the Detailing Knife.**

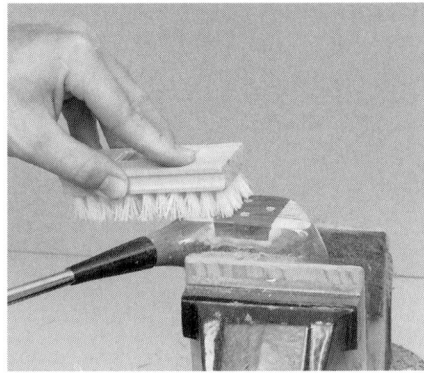

4-60 Brush the dust and other particles from the scoring lines with a stiff bristled brush.

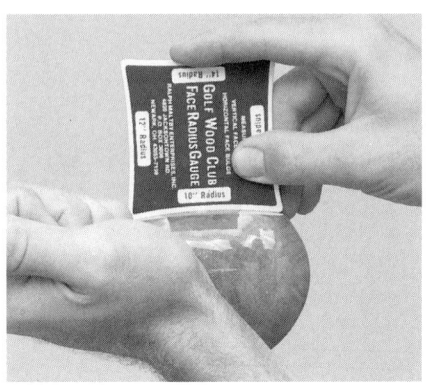

4-61 Final check for proper bulge …

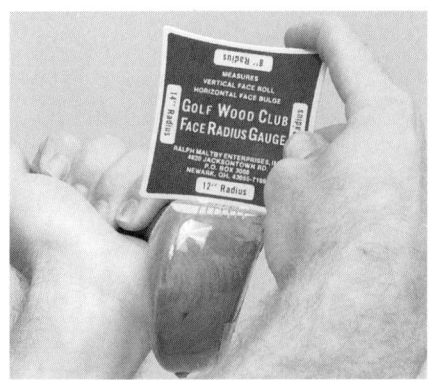

4-62 … check for proper roll and …

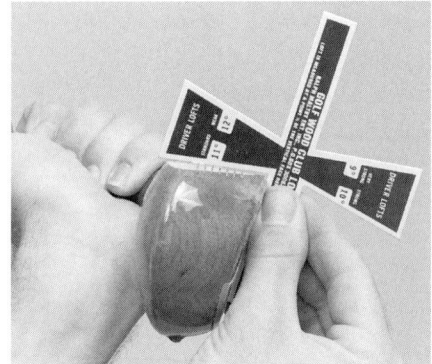

4-63 … check for proper loft. The club is now ready for swingweighting and soleplate installation. See Chapters 14 and 2 respectively for these procedures. If the club is not going to be refinished, see Chapter 16 for touchup steps. See Chapter 1 if it will be refinished.

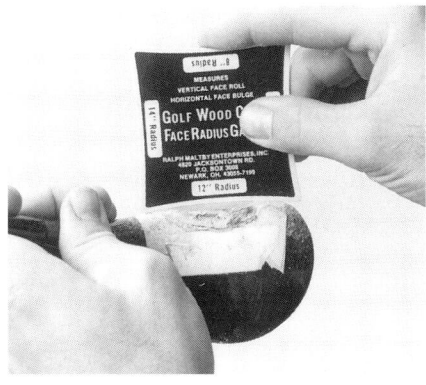

4-64 Customizing an insert. These steps are performed after the bulge, roll and loft are set but before the scoring lines are cut.

4-65 Locate the middle of the insert. Measure along a horizontal line and find the midpoint in the insert. Mark this point with a pencil or pen.

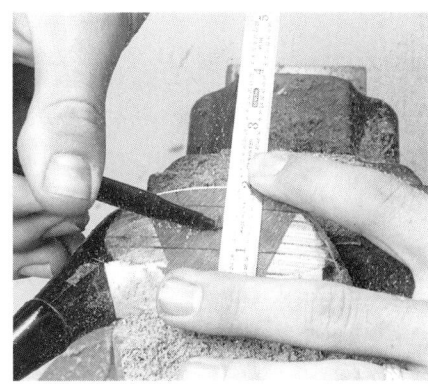

4-66 Measure on a vertical line from the top to the bottom of the insert and find the mid-point. Mark this point. If necessary, extend the points until a cross hair is formed. The cross hair determines the entry point of the drill bit.

4-67 Using the cross hair as a guide, drill into the insert using a ⅛" bit. Drill approximately ¾" into the insert.

4-68 Depending upon the diameter of the medallion or decorative piece, select the proper size bit. In this case a ⅝" wood bit is used. Drill to a depth that will allow at least ⅛" clearance between the top of the medallion and the insert surface. Do not drill through the insert into the wood unless absolutely necessary.

4-69 Place the medallion, logo, coin, emblem, photo, etc., in the recess.

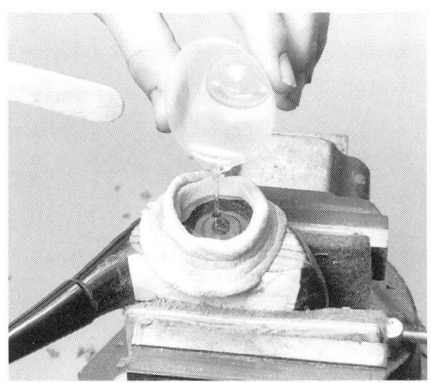

4-70 Form a Mortite putty dam around the hole, mix the clear insert epoxy and pour it into the recess.

4-71 Stir a toothpick around in the epoxy to release any trapped air bubbles. Allow the epoxy to cure, usually overnight is best.

4-72 After curing, remove the Mortite putty dam.

4-73 Excess epoxy may be carefully cut from the face using a hacksaw. **DO NOT CUT INTO THE FACE.**

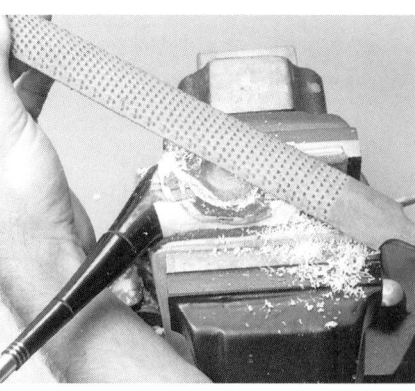

4-74 Using a medium to coarse cut wood rasp, file the remaining epoxy until the rasp begins to just scratch the face. Check the bulge and roll and …

4-75 … continue to file the face. Use a medium cut wood file until all of the excess is removed.

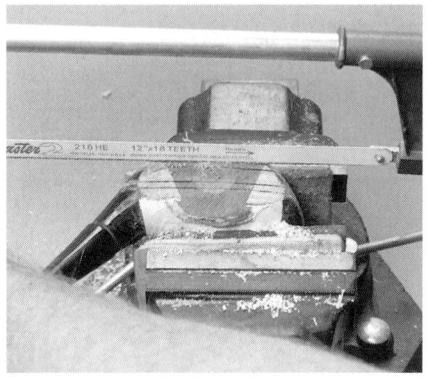

4-76 Draw and cut scoring lines as outlined in photos 4-49 through 4-51.

4-77 The finished insert will look as good if not better than new after finishing.

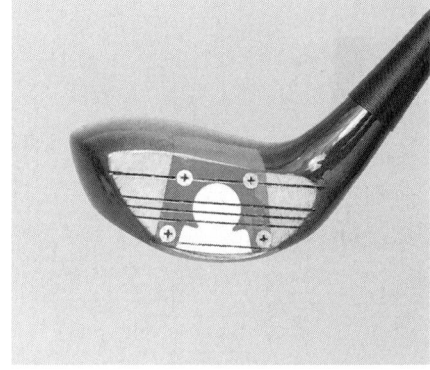

4-78 MacGregor "Keysite" Inserts can also be reproduced using a ⅝" wood bit and a **Dremel tool**. Carefully draw the insert outline on the face before drilling and cutting.

4-79 Repairing a dry rotted face. This photo shows a fairly typical dry rotted face. The following steps illustrate the clear epoxy face repair method.

4-80 Select a sharp chisel and lightly pry and scrape the rotten wood from the face. Do not damage the insert. The unrotted or good wood will be lighter in color and hence more difficult to remove. Use this as your guide in how much and what wood should be removed.

4-81 To remove the chisel marks and create a uniform surface, file the cavity with a fine file and then lightly sand the cavity with 150 or 180 grit sandpaper.

86

4-82 This photo shows a properly prepared area. It is not necessary to remove the entire side of the face. Only the rotted area must be removed. Also, there is no depth limitation. The area can be very shallow or quite deep.

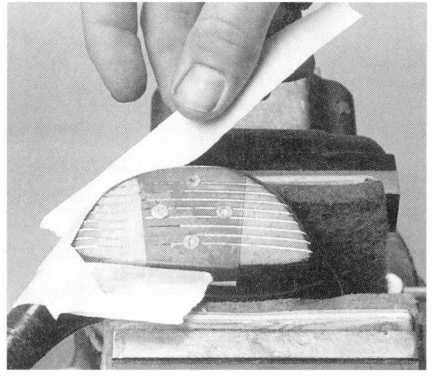

4-83 If the club is not to be refinished, outline the edge of the face with ¾" masking tape to protect the finish. This step is unnecessary if the club is to be refinished.

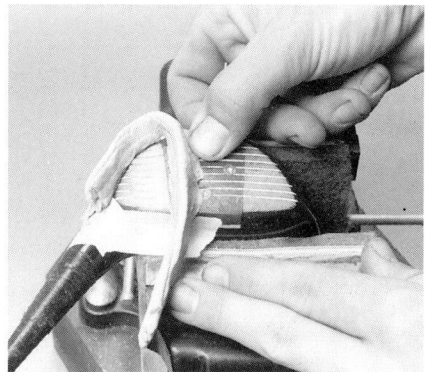

4-84 Form a Mortite putty dam around the cavity. Make sure the putty is pressed firmly around the cavity, especially into the scoring lines to prevent leaks.

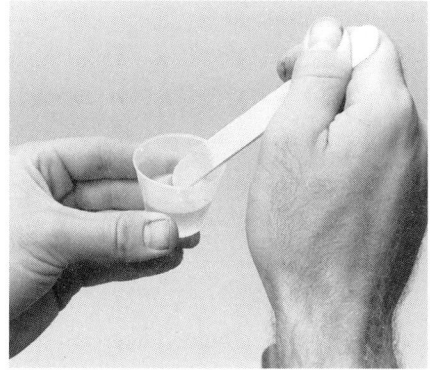

4-85 Prepare and fold the clear epoxy. Some repairmen choose to add persimmon or maple dust to the mixture. If the wood is properly repaired, however, the epoxy will reflect the wood surface underneath and the repair will hardly be noticed.

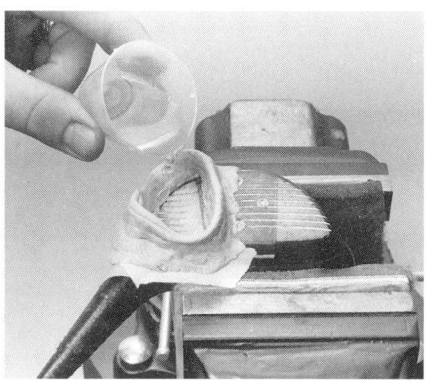

4-86 Pour the epoxy into the cavity approximately 1½ times the depth of the cavity. Allow the epoxy to cure overnight. Do not forget to stir the epoxy with a toothpick, after pouring, to free any entrapped air bubbles.

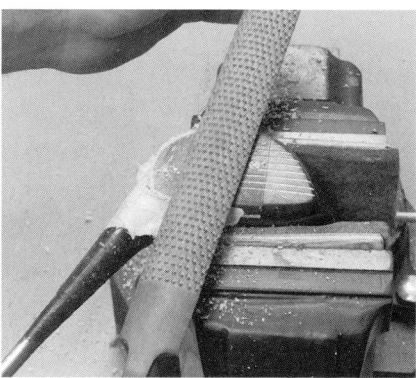

4-87 After the epoxy has cured, remove the Mortite putty. File the excess epoxy with a wood rasp.

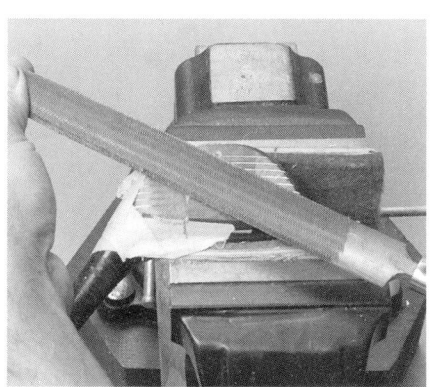

4-88 Once the rasp begins to scratch into the face, begin filing with a wood file.

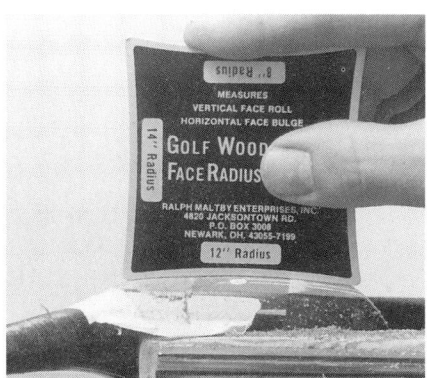

4-89 Check the bulge and the roll.

4-90 Continue to file, bringing down the high spots until …

4-91 ... the correct face bulge and roll are achieved.

4-92 Recut the scoring lines through the epoxy face repair. Follow the steps shown in photos 4-49 through 4-51.

4-93 This **Mini Hacksaw** is a handy tool when cutting scoring lines around the insert screws. Remember, never cut through the insert screw. This would be a sure sign of unprofessional work.

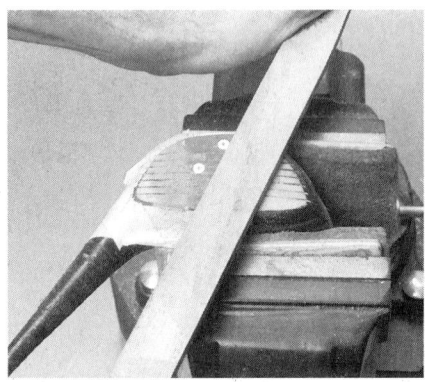

4-94 File the entire face, lightly blending in all the scratches and creating a uniform surface, using a fine file.

4-95 If the face would look better by replacing the insert screws, follow these instructions.

4-96 Remove the screws as outlined in Chapter 3. If any additional filing is needed, do so now.

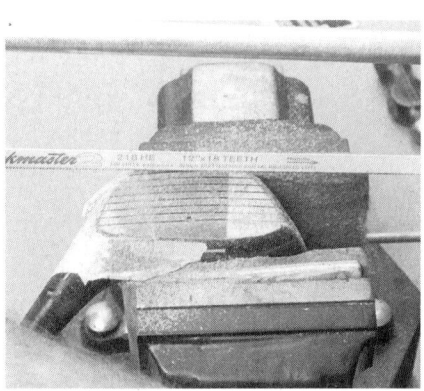

4-97 If necessary, recut the scoring lines.

4-98 Using a ³/₃₂" drill bit, clean out each screw hole.

4-99 Re-countersink the hole. Note the use of the **Automatic Countersink**. This tool is very fast and gives precise results. You can also use a hand-held countersink as previously shown.

4-100 After installing new screws and filing the heads flush with the insert surface, remove any tape from the head and the club is now ready for finishing steps. Refer to Chapter 16 for touchup steps if the club is not to be refinished. Chapter 1 shows complete refinishing steps.

4-101 Repairing a chip broken from the toe or heel.

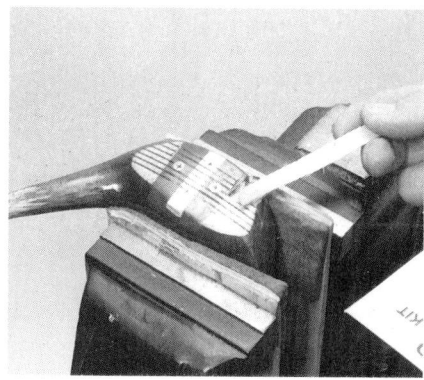

4-102 Mix and apply appropriate high shear strength epoxy to the cavity. **GolfWorks®** or **Conap®** epoxy works very well.

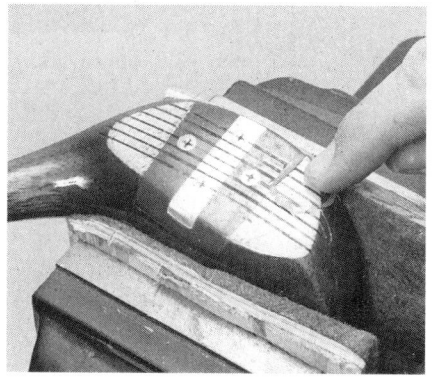

4-103 After applying epoxy to the chip as well, press the chip into its original location.

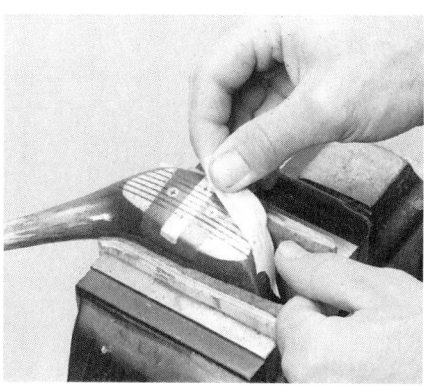

4-104 To ensure the piece does not move, lay a piece of masking tape across the repaired area.

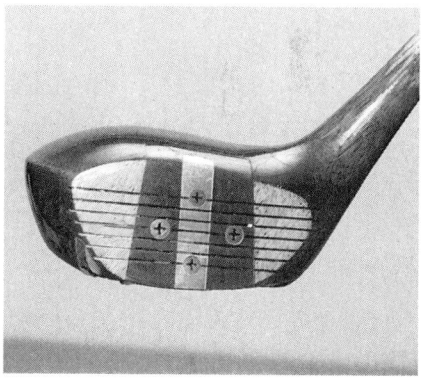

4-105 After the epoxy has cured, file the excess epoxy from the face and recut any affected scoring lines. The club is now ready for complete refinishing or touchup steps.

4-106 This photo shows a deep gouge in the face. This is often caused by hitting a rock and is commonly found in fairway woods. This may be repaired by filling with a clear, pour-in-place epoxy as shown in photos 4-79 through 4-92. An alternative is to use ...

4-107 ... the **Plug Cutter** method. Using ½" Plug Cutter, make some laminated maple or persimmon plugs. Use old heads or turnings.

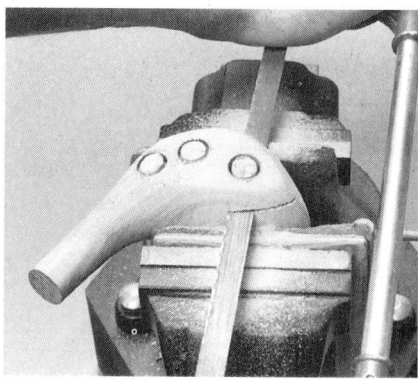

4-108 Cut through the head using a hacksaw to free the plugs.

4-109 Next, use a ½" twist drill or speedbore flat type bit and drill out the defective area. Drill ⅜" to ½" deep.

4-110 This photo shows the clubface after drilling.

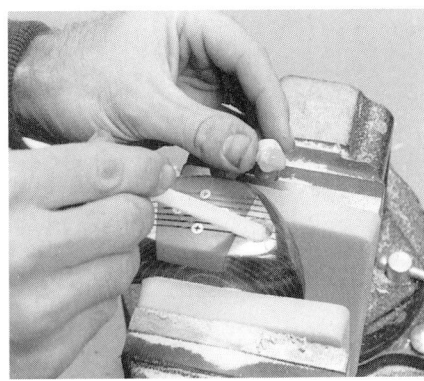

4-111 Apply high shear strength epoxy to the plug and the hole. Use as clear an epoxy as possible to hide the glue line.

4-112 Insert the wooden plug into the hole. Make sure laminations are aligned properly in the case of laminated maple heads. Allow the epoxy to cure.

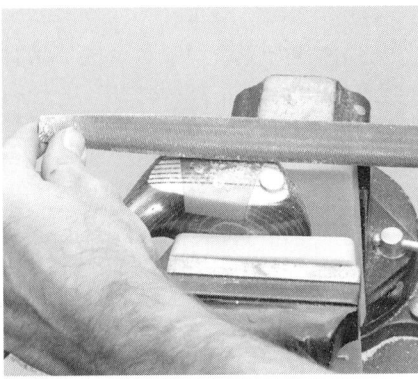

4-113 After the epoxy has cured, file the plug flush with the face. Use a coarse rasp or medium cut wood file. Finish up with a fine file and file the entire face to blend in everything.

4-114 The face should look like this after filing.

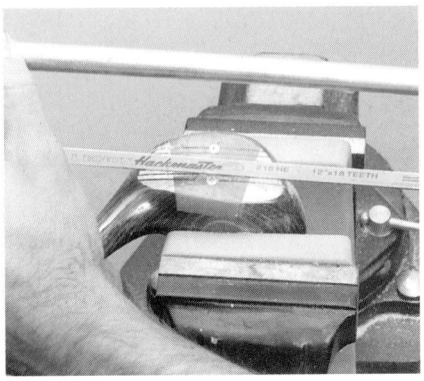

4-115 Finally, recut the scoring lines as necessary.

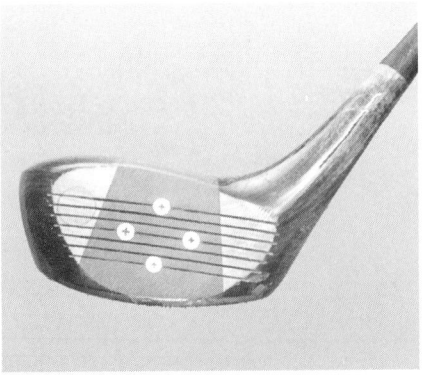

4-116 This photo shows the finished club, ready for refinish or touchup.

NOTES

_____
_____
_____
_____
_____
_____
_____
_____
_____
_____

ADDITIONAL INFORMATION FOR REPLACING OLD INSERTS WITH EPOXY POUR-IN-PLACE INSERTS AND REPAIRING DAMAGED FACES

Detailed Mixing Instructions for Club-Kits IC-110® (Volume Method)

Step #1: Stir each component well (activator and base) in its original container before taking out smaller quantities to use. The coloring pigments in the base tend to settle out over a period of time making this stirring step quite important if you intend to get the same color and opacity every time you use it. The base is heavier and if not stirred properly will have a poor mix.

Step #2: Measure out the desired amount of base per Table 4-1. Use a metric cup as the exact or near exact measurement is important. Next, pour in the correct amount of activator over the base.

Step #3: Immediately begin to fold the material together similar to mixing a cake batter. This procedure is very important as the lighter activator tends to float on the heavier base and normal stirring is not adequate. After one minute of folding, begin stirring. Stir to approximately 75 revolutions. Do not stir briskly or whip the insert material as an excess of air bubbles will cause air entrapment during curing and the finished insert will look like a sponge. Some bubbles are normal and will float out during the cure.

Step #4: IC-110® insert material is now ready to pour.

TABLE 4-1 Volume Method Mixing Chart by Insert Size for Club-Kit IC-110®			
Insert Size	**Amount of Base 2:1**	**Amount of Activator 1:2**	**Total Amount**
Small (Most MacGregor and most fiber inserts)	10 cc's	5 cc's	15 cc's
Medium (Most Spalding 1962 and later and early Wilson inserts)	15 cc's	7½ cc's	22½ cc's
Large (Wilson and First Flight)	20 cc's	10 cc's	30 cc's

CC stands for cubic centimeters. Metric cups are available through golf club repair supply houses and are graduated in cc's, ounces, drams, etc.

NOTES

_____

_____

_____

_____

_____

Additional Mixing Instructions Using the Weight Method

Some repair shops doing a large volume of work prefer to weigh the base and activator on a gram scale and mix accordingly. If you prefer to use this method the following mathematics will help. See Table 4-2.

By Weight: 68 grams of base to 27 grams of activator. (Note: This is the correct ratio by weight, hence any combination in this ratio by weight would be correct.)

The ratio by weight stated above of 68 grams base to 27 grams activator would make an insert of 95 grams or 3.35 ounces. (95 grams divided by 28.35 grams per ounce = 3.35 ounces)

The mathematics ratio is stated as the activator being 28.4% of the base or it can be stated that the base portion is 71.6% of the activator.

$$\begin{array}{r} 28.4\% \text{ Activator} \\ \textbf{By Weight:} \quad \underline{71.6\% \text{ Base}} \quad\quad\quad \\ 100\% \text{ IC-110}^® \text{ mixed} \end{array}$$

So, for a 28.35 gram insert (1 ounce) which is equivalent to a Wilson size insert you would multiply 28.35 x 28.4% = 8.05 grams activator. Now subtract 8.05 grams from 28.35 grams and you get 20.3 grams of base.

$$\begin{array}{r} 8.05 \text{ grams activator } (28.4\%) \\ \textbf{By Weight:} \quad \underline{20.30 \text{ grams base } (71.6\%)} \quad\quad \\ 28.35 \text{ grams IC-110}^® (1 \text{ ounce}) (100\%) \end{array}$$

TABLE 4-2
Weight Method
Mixing Chart by Insert Size for Club-Kit IC-110®

Insert Size	Amount of Base (71.6%)	Amount of Activator (28.4%)	Total Amount (100%)
Small (Most MacGregor and most fiber inserts)	10.15 gr.	4.02 gr.	14.17 gr. (½ ounce)
Medium (Most Spalding 1962 and later and early Wilson inserts)	15.22 gr.	6.03 gr.	21.25 gr. (¾ ounce)
Large (Wilson and First Flight)	20.3 gr.	8.05 gr.	28.35 gr. (1 ounce)

1. To convert grams to ounces divide by 28.35.
2. To convert ounces to grams multiply by 28.35.
3. 28.35 grams = 1 ounce.

Mixing Instructions for Adding Color Paste to Clear IC-110®

Many repair shops use clear non-pigmented IC-110® along with the various color paste dispersions and mix their own colors. To properly mix in the color paste dispersions, follow step 1 under mixing instructions and then proceed as follows. Add not more than 5% by weight of the desired color to the base only. For a 30 cc insert which is comprised of 20 cc's base and 10 cc's activator you only need to add color paste in the approximate amount that it would take to coat one of your fingernails ¹⁄₁₆" thick, this is approximately 1 cc of color paste.

Mix the color paste and base throughly for at least one minute, scavenging the sides of the mixing container while mixing. IMPORTANT NOTE: For compatibility use only Club-Kit color paste dispersions with Club-Kit IC-110® epoxy. Now proceed with steps 2 through 4 under mixing instructions.

Points to Remember when Pouring Inserts

■ Never pour an insert when surrounding temperature is less than 65°F.

■ Never use a match or open flame to draw air bubbles to the surface as epoxy is flammable. Swirling with a toothpick or other object after pouring will work best to release entrapped air bubbles.

■ Never add additional activator in the hope of speeding up the cure. This will only cause the insert to remain rubbery. Follow mixing instructions exactly.

■ Never try to speed up the cure by placing the club in direct sunlight, under sunlamps, in an oven or on a radiator. This could cause the insert to break into flame or boil thus causing deep craters after curing.

■ If the insert seems cured, but during filing it softens, DO NOT be concerned. Let the insert cure for one more day then continue. The heat buildup from filing will always soften the insert to some degree.

NOTES

_____

_____

_____

_____

_____

_____

_____

_____

_____

_____

_____

_____

_____

_____

CHAPTER 5

REPLACING OLD INSERTS WITH PREFABRICATED INSERTS

A prefabricated insert differs from an epoxy pour-in-place insert in that the prefabricated insert is solid in composition when installed into an insert cavity. Some pre-shaping of the insert is usually necessary to ensure a proper fit. Because of this, installing a prefabricated insert requires different techniques and skills for proper installation versus the liquid epoxy pour-in-place type inserts.

Replacing an old insert with a new prefabricated insert is desirable if the old insert is not original or is worn or damaged beyond repair. For example, the older "classic" clubs were manufactured with "original" type fiber inserts. Replacing this type of insert with something other than original fiber will ordinarily lower the value of this classic club.

Prefabricated inserts are available in many different materials. Cycolac, original fiber, phenolic laminate, melamine, graphite, Gamma Fire (green glass) and aluminum are the most common. These insert materials are usually available in sheets, bars, squares and ready to install precut shapes.

It should be noted that even though the hardness of inserts vary, hardness makes no significant difference in the distance a ball carries. For further information on this see Chapter 47, Golf Wood Club Design: Insert Materials.

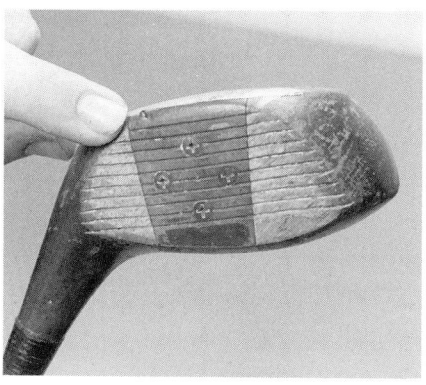

5-1 Old inserts often need to be replaced because of delaminations in the insert, a large ding or a poor fit in the insert cavity caused by the wood head swelling due to moisture absorption.

5-2 First, remove the soleplate as outlined in Chapter 2.

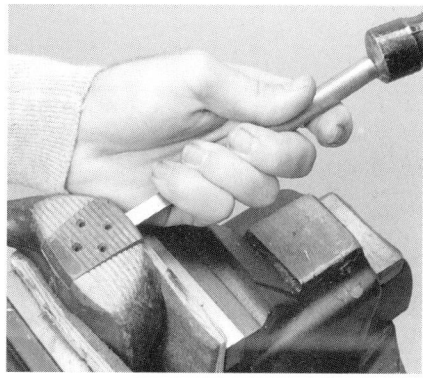

5-3 Next, remove the insert as outlined in Chapter 3.

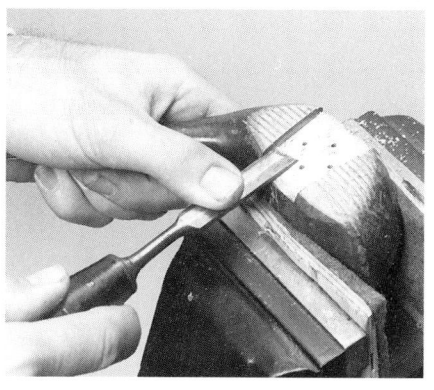

5-4 Remove all epoxy buildup and other debris from the insert cavity. Maintain a sharp top line.

5-5 Replacement insert materials are available in various forms.

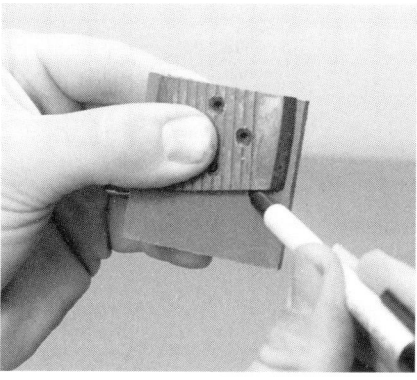

5-6 The old insert may be used as a pattern to cut out the new insert. Place the insert against the new material. Note one side of the insert is butted up against one side of the new material. This eliminates unnecessary work in cutting two angles since only one cut will now be made. Next, draw a line down one side of the insert tracing it onto the material.

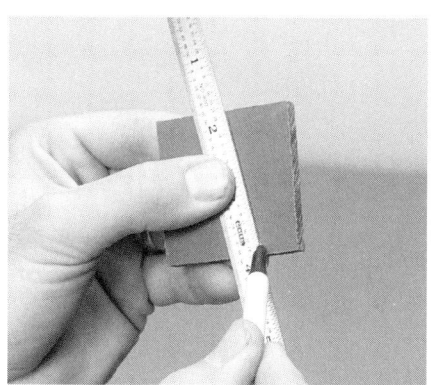

5-7 After drawing the line, a good idea is to use a straight edge to check the straightness of the line.

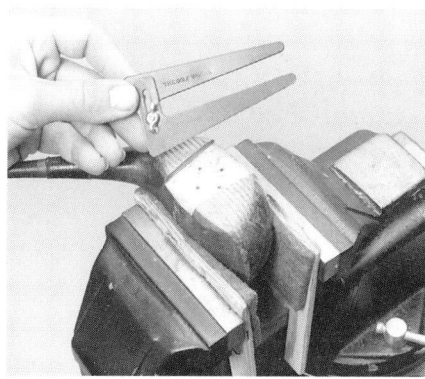

5-8 Sometimes the old insert is damaged or lost. In this case the **Insert Pattern Copier** simplifies insert angle copying and ensures a perfect fit into the insert cavity.

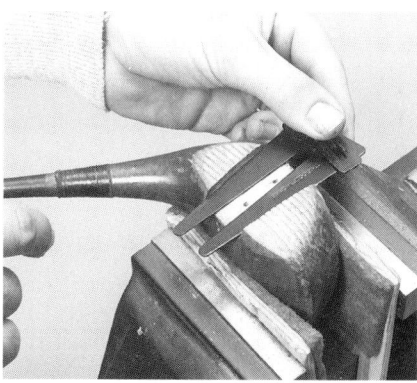

5-9 To use this tool, loosen the wing nut and place the arms inside the insert cavity. Spread the arms apart so each arm is flush against the side of the cavity. Tighten the wing nut.

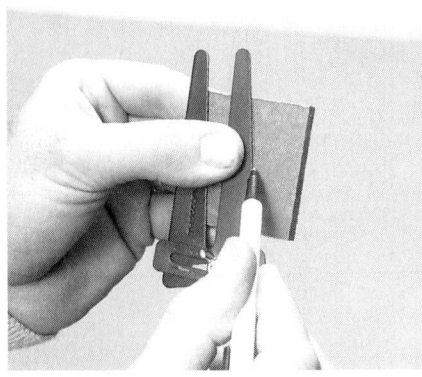

5-10 Place the Insert Copier against the new insert material and draw a line. Note one of the arms is flush against the side of the material eliminating one unnecessary cut.

5-11 Fasten the insert material securely in a vise so the drawn line is vertical. Using a hacksaw, cut to the outside of the line. This will ensure the new insert will be slightly larger than the cavity, allowing some modification if the insert shape is not perfect.

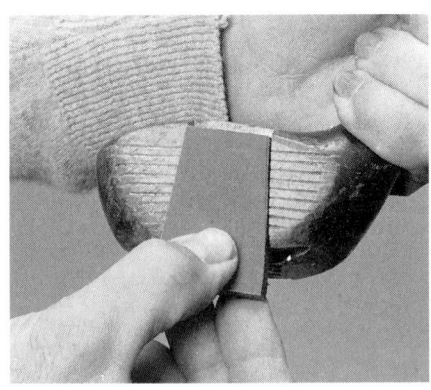

5-12 Test fit the insert in the cavity to be sure it fits.

5-13 This photo shows a perfect fit along one side of the cavity but…

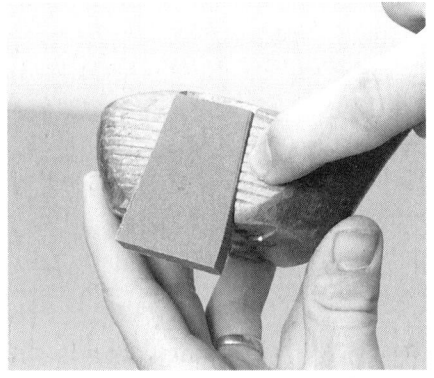

5-14 …a gap exists along the opposite side. Use a file to lower the high point of the insert side. This will provide a perfect fit to both sides of the insert. To do this…

5-15 …place the insert between the vise jaws with the poor fitting side up.

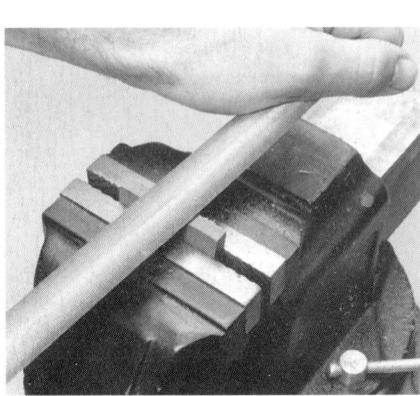

5-16 File along the side of the insert working the high spot down. Periodically test fit the insert while filing until…

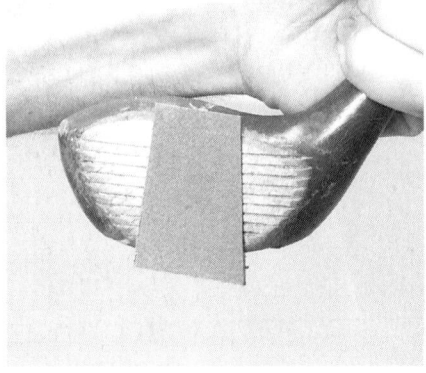

5-17 …the insert fits properly. A properly fit insert will have no noticeable gaps between the insert and the insert cavity walls.

5-18 Remove the insert from the cavity and abrade the back of the insert with a wood file or sandpaper. This provides a better bonding surface for the epoxy.

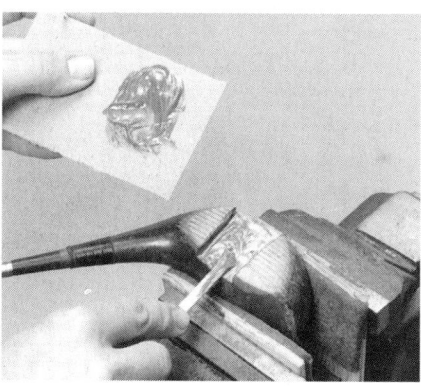

5-19 Mix and apply a shear strength epoxy to the insert cavity and the back of the insert. Note that a brown paste dispersion has been added to the epoxy to camouflage any glue line.

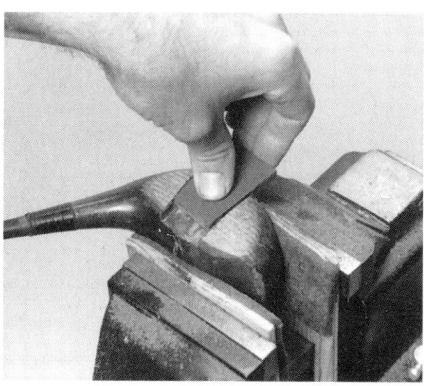

5-20 Place the insert in the bottom half of the cavity and...

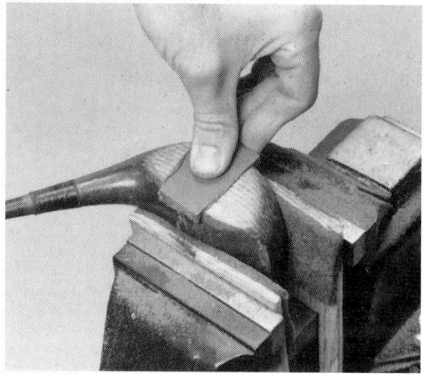

5-21 ...push the insert up into the cavity until a tight fit is achieved. This method of installation ensures the epoxy is forced around all sides of the insert and the cavity.

5-22 Place the club in an **Insert Clamp** or vise until the epoxy cures. After the epoxy cures, follow the steps shown in photos 5-35 through 5-53 for finishing steps.

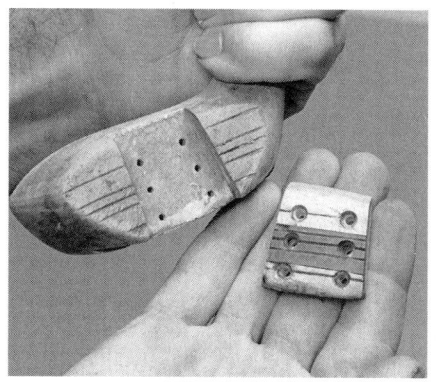

5-23 Installing two color horizontal bar inserts. This photo shows another classic club, but this time there is a horizontal bar running through the insert. This type of insert is a bit more difficult to duplicate.

5-24 After the soleplate and insert are removed, carefully clean the insert cavity, removing all epoxy buildup.

5-25 The horizontal bar will usually be either ½" or ⅝" wide. The smaller ½" bars are commonly found in the fairway woods while the wider ⅝" bars are found in the drivers.

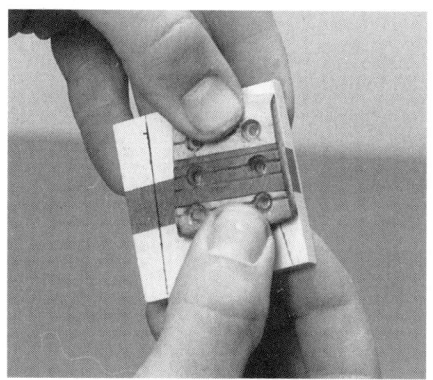

5-26 The original insert is best used as a pattern. Position the old insert on the new material so the bars are running parallel. Draw a line down both sides of the old insert onto the new material. This photo shows why one side of the old insert cannot be laid against the side of the new material. The bars would not run parallel with each other.

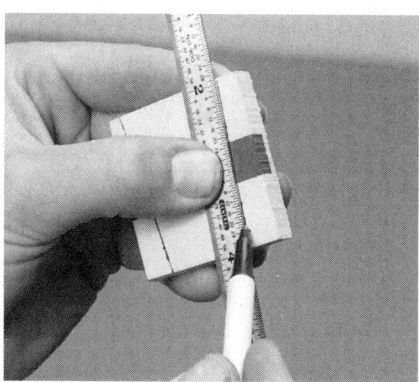

5-27 A straight edge can be used to guarantee that the lines are straight.

5-28 Place the new material between the vise jaws and tighten securely. The drawn lines should be vertical while held in the vise to make accurate cutting easier. Use a hacksaw and cut outside the drawn lines. This will ensure the insert will be larger than intended to allow for final fitting in the insert cavity itself.

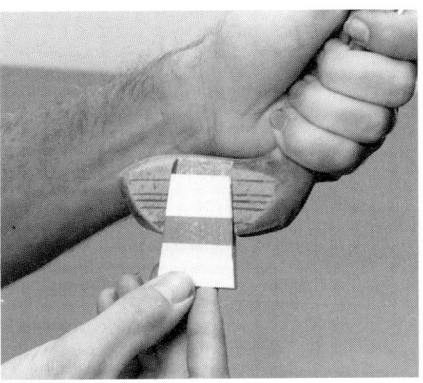

5-29 Place the insert into the cavity to check for initial fit.

5-30 File where necessary to create a tight fit without gaps between the insert and the insert cavity.

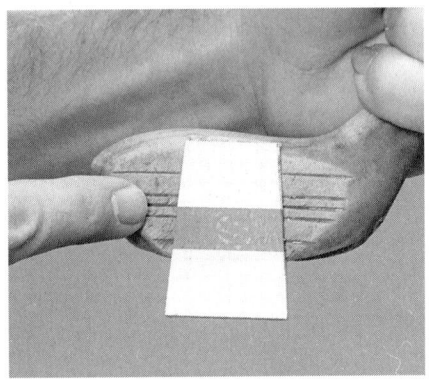

5-31 Periodically check the position of the insert within the cavity while filing. This photo shows the horizontal bar running parallel with the scoring lines. All that is needed now is to file an equal amount from each side of the insert so the insert will move up the cavity, positioning the horizontal bar in its original location.

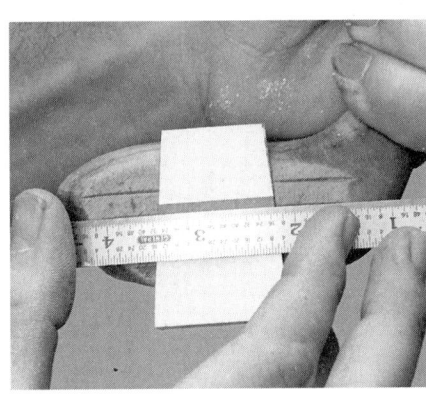

5-32 After final filing, the insert is positioned perfectly in the cavity. Note, the bar is parallel with the scoring lines. This is important for a professional look and fit.

5-33 Roughen the back of the insert with a wood file or sandpaper.

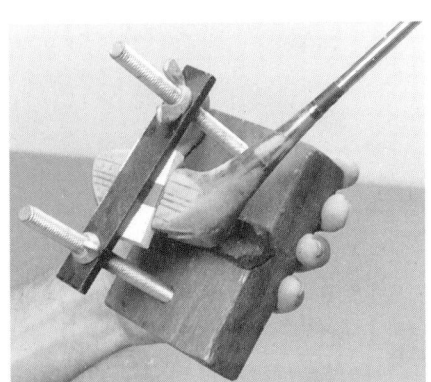

5-34 Mix and apply epoxy to both the insert and the cavity. Install the insert as previously shown.

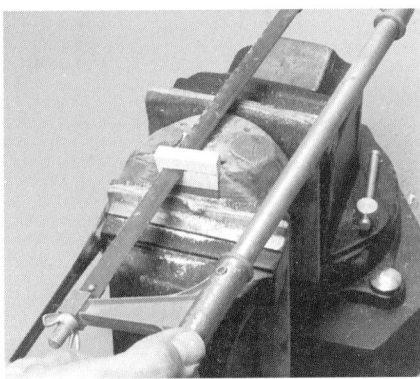

5-35 After the epoxy has cured, the excess insert material is easily removed with a hacksaw.

5-36 Use a wood file to file the remaining portion of the insert. Use a radiusing motion to follow the contour of the sole.

5-37 The bottom of the insert should look like this after filing.

5-38 Reposition the club in the vise and cut or file the top of the insert. Be careful not to mar the hosel.

5-39 Using a wood file, carefully file the remaining portion of the insert flush with the top of the head.

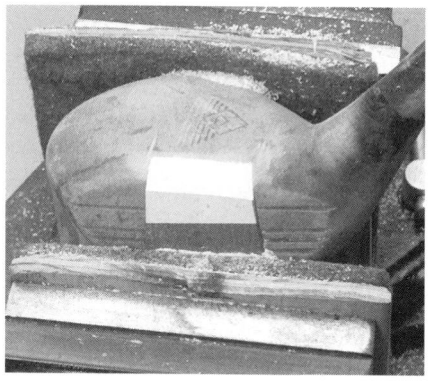

5-40 The top of the insert should look like this. The insert top line should blend in perfectly with the entire face top line from toe to heel.

5-41 Next, place the club in the vise as shown. Using a wood file, remove any excess insert material and epoxy. Concentrate filing on the sides of the insert while intentionally leaving the middle of the insert slightly higher than the rest of the face. The tendency for a novice is usually to file too much from the middle of the insert.

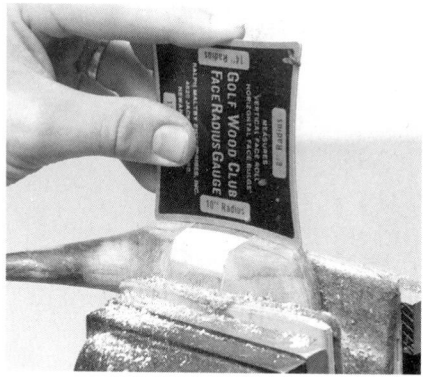

5-42 Check horizontal face bulge and...

5-43 ...vertical face roll while filing. Also, check the loft with a protractor or loft gauge. Refer to the tables at the end of Chapter 10 for proper bulge, roll and loft specifications.

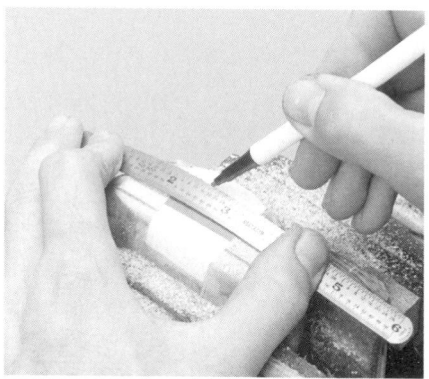

5-44 A 6" scale is used to draw lines across the face. Make sure the drawn lines match up to the proper heel and toe scoring lines.

5-45 Carefully cut through the insert using the drawn lines as a guide. Note the use of the special hacksaw blade without sides on the teeth (no rake).

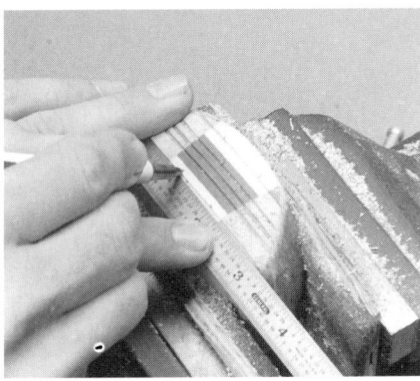

5-46 Measure and mark locations for insert screw pilot holes. A six screw configuration is here. Marks are made ¼" from the sides of the insert on the top, middle and bottom scoring lines. Chapter 4 shows photos for installing a four screw diamond pattern.

5-47 Drill into the insert using a ³⁄₃₂" **bit.** The depth of the pilot hole is determined by the insert screw. The #4 x ⅝" brass screw is commonly used and is shown here.

5-48 After drilling, the pilot hole is **counter-sunk.** The diameter of the countersunk hole should be slightly smaller than the diameter of the insert screw head. This will allow the top of the installed screw head to be seated slightly above the face before filling.

5-49 This photo shows an **Automatic Countersink** in use. The Automatic Countersink can be set to various diameters (depths) for quick work when opening up insert or soleplate pilot holes.

5-50 To prevent a screw head from possibly snapping off, it is a good idea to drill through the insert only with a ⅛" bit. This will alleviate excess pressure between the insert and the screw by providing clearance for the screw shank.

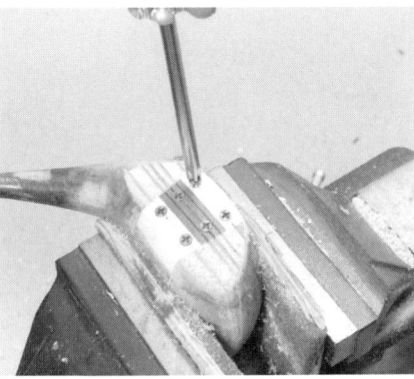

5-51 Next, install the screws. Align the slots of the screw heads parallel and perpendicular with the scoring lines. The top of the screw head should be slightly above the level of the insert.

5-52 File the screw heads flush with the insert using a fine file. Rub a finger across the face. If the screw heads are filled properly, the heads will barely be felt.

5-53 Brush the face with a stiff bristled brush to remove all loose particles from the screw heads and facelines.

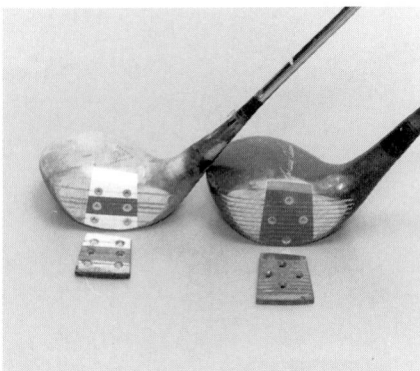

5-54 This photo shows the completed horizontal bar insert, as well as the solid color insert replaced in photos 5-5 through 5-22. After the soleplates are reinstalled following the procedures shown in Chapter 2, the clubs are ready for refinishing or touchup. See Chapter 16 for touchup steps or Chapter 1 for complete refinishing.

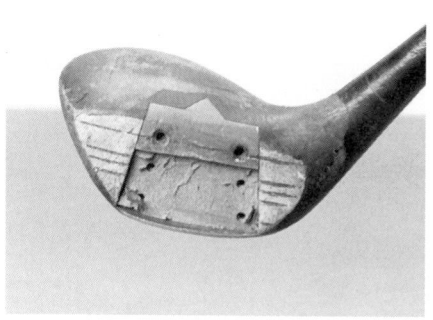

5-55 Replacing "V" back inserts. This photo shows a bar type insert with a notch in the back. This insert is commonly referred to as a three piece "V" back insert.

5-56 First, remove the soleplate. See Chapter 2 for procedures.

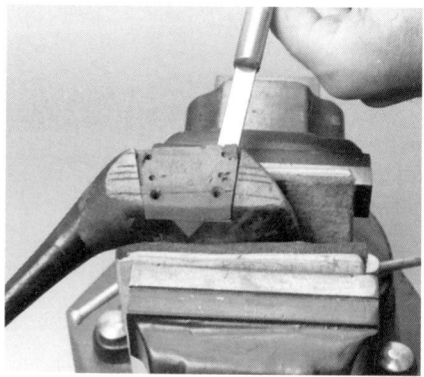

5-57 Next, remove the insert following the steps outlined in Chapter 3.

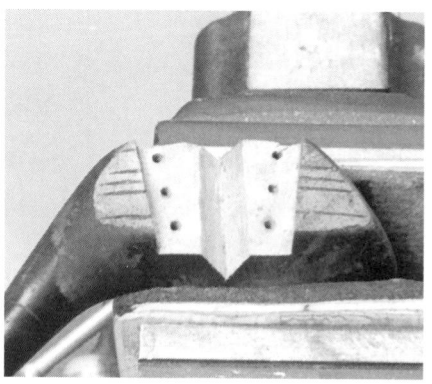

5-58 Clean the exposed insert cavity of old epoxy using a chisel and file.

5-59 Cut a ½" narrow bar of insert material. The piece should be long enough to fit the entire length of the "V" notch.

5-60 Mix and apply shear strength epoxy to the notch and ½" bar. Note the use of a colored paste dispersion to match the insert or stain color.

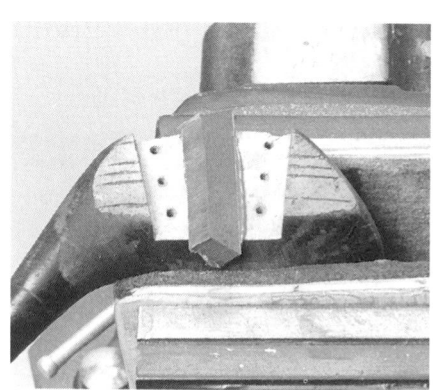

5-61 Place the ½" bar in the "V" notch, sliding it back and forth to seat it properly.

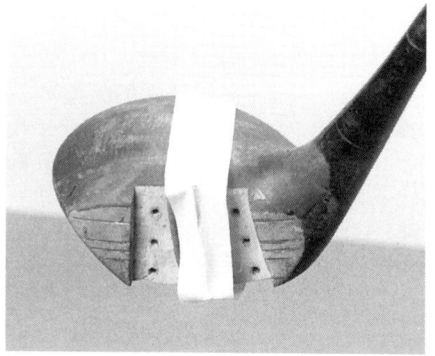

5-62 Masking tape or a wide rubber band should be used to maintain pressure against the new "V" bar. Allow the epoxy to cure.

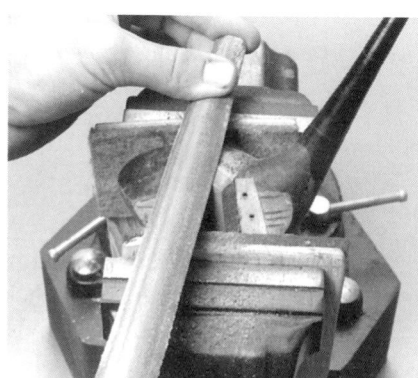

5-63 After the epoxy has cured, file the excess insert material flush with the top line of the club using a wood file.

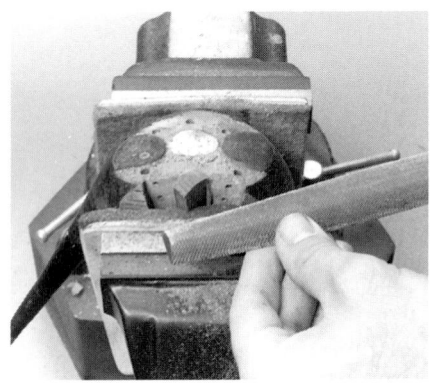

5-64 File the bottom of the insert flush with the soleplate cavity. Use a radiusing motion with the wood file.

5-65 This photo shows a properly filed insert at the sole.

5-66 A wood file is used to file the "V" bar flush with the insert cavity. Excess may be cut with a hacksaw before filing. Be careful.

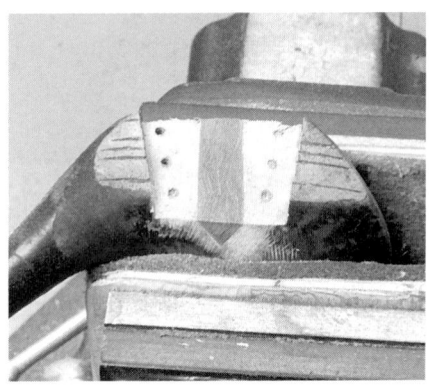

5-67 This photo shows the insert piece properly filed flush with the insert cavity. Make sure to maintain a straight top line.

5-68 Finally, determine the bar width and follow the finishing steps shown in photos 5-23 through 5-54.

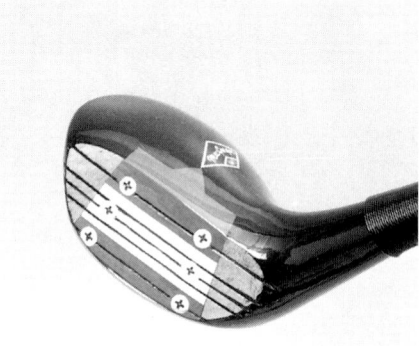

5-69 This is the finished installation. The owner will be amazed at the results.

ADDITIONAL INFORMATION FOR REPLACING OLD INSERTS WITH PREFABRICATED INSERTS

There are a number of different materials used for inserts in golf clubs. The more common and widely used materials are listed below. The order in which they appear reflects the ease the repairman would encounter when working with each material. Characteristics taken into consideration when making the list were: bonding properties, how easy the insert cuts with a hacksaw, how easily the insert can be filed and how much wear your tools will experience after working with the material.

1. ABS plastic (injection molded) like cycolac
2. Epoxy (prepoured in molds or poured in the head itself)
3. Fiber-original type (compressed vulcanized paper)
4. Phenolic fiber (compressed linen or cotton fibers bonded with phenolic resins)
5. Aluminum (either sheet, bar, extrusion or casting)
6. Green or red glass types (fiberglass and resin) like Gamma Fire

There are other insert materials but they are only used in small quantities or by one manufacturer. Some of these are stainless steel (investment cast), brass, nylon, graphite and Ligno Ferro® laminated wood inserts. New materials emerge on the market daily, so rest assured that this listing is not a complete one.

ABS Plastic Insert Materials - Cycolac

This is the most popular insert type used today. The most common type of ABS material used is called cycolac. ABS plastics are popular for insert usage because they are very stable and relatively tough. They are also compatible with the various adhesives used to cement them into the head and also with polyurethane finishes used on today's golf wood heads.

ABS inserts are manufactured by a method known as injection molding. The ABS material is purchased in a pellet form, dumped into a hopper and injected into a multi-cavity steel mold under tremendous heat and pressure. The insert cools, solidifies and is removed from the mold. Because of the preciseness of tooling for injection molded parts, many combinations of colors and different designs are possible.

Face screws are not required to hold ABS inserts in golf heads, however, some manufacturers put them in for added assurance and decorative purposes.

Epoxy Insert Material

Epoxy inserts are three to four times more expensive than ABS plastic inserts because of both the raw material cost and the manufacturing method. They are also a harder material and possess a slightly harder feel and different sound to the accomplished golfer. Epoxy first became popular as a repair shop item. Since epoxy is a liquid, it could be mixed with an activator, poured into the face cavity, allowed to cure and then it could be filed down into a new insert. This proved valuable in replacing lost or broken inserts that were otherwise not available. The most popular epoxy insert material used today by repair shops is Club-Kit's IC-110®. Later on, manufacturers used epoxy as an insert material mostly in their premium lines to add additional product differentiation from the less expensive models. Some manufacturers are now using epoxy inserts with medallions, logos or emblems cast into them and covered over with clear epoxy to enhance the cosmetics of the club. It should be noted here that ABS plastic inserts can also be made with recessed medallions with clear epoxy poured over the top for the same three dimensional effect.

Epoxy inserts are cast from a two component liquid, one component being the base and the other component being the activator. These two components are mixed in the exact proportions necessary and poured into silicon molds. After the epoxy cures, they are easily removed from a mold which can be used over and over again. Epoxy inserts can also be directly poured into the insert cavity. These epoxy pour-in-place inserts do not require screws, however, they can be used for decorative purposes.

Fiber Inserts — Original Type

Original type fiber inserts are made of a compressed, vulcanized paper. They are being used less and less each year in newly manufactured golf woods. There are a number of reasons. First, fiber is a porous material affected by moisture and temperature. These conditions can cause fiber to warp, shrink, expand and sometimes delaminate. This is why during manufacture original type fiber inserts should be kept in a humidity and temperature controlled environment until they are ready to be assembled. Even after the polyurethane finish has cured on the entire head, fiber inserts can be affected to the degree of actually being able to feel and see a hairline crack all around the edge of the insert, especially on the top of the insert. Second, fiber inserts require the use of face screws because without them the insert has a tendency to warp and ultimately break the epoxy or resin bond used to glue it in place. Third, because of the fiber's inherent instability causing swelling and shrinking, many owners simply send the clubs back for repair or replacement, assuming that the club is defective. Fourth, fiber inserts produce a club which is unquestionably inferior regarding durability with no apparent offsetting performance benefits. The main consumption of fiber inserts today is in restoration and replacement on older, classic clubs.

Phenolic Fiber Inserts

Phenolic inserts are made from compressed linen or cotton fibers which are bound together with a phenolic resin. These inserts are relatively new in the golf industry and are often confused with original type fiber inserts. The phenolic inserts are easily recognized by their distinctive swirl pattern which is created during the four-way roll facing process in manufacture. When putting on four-way roll, the file cuts through varying layers of impregnated cloth leaving a swirl. Almost every company today producing so-called copies of the classic woods are using this insert. It is most popular in red with a white horizontal bar through the center.

This is a very durable, attractive insert and makes a good replacement for original type fiber inserts.

Aluminum Inserts

Aluminum has been used for some time as an insert material and is quite acceptable. Most of the aluminum materials used today are the softer type so they work easier in production. Look at a few finished woods with aluminum inserts, however, and you will usually spot one where the face bulge is not a constant radius. This is caused by the hand filing operation during manufacture which is required to set the correct bulge, roll and properly outline the face. During this operation, the file removes wood more quickly than it does aluminum, thus a small drop-off or dip occurs on each side of the insert. Aluminum inserts usually require the use of screws because it is very difficult to get superior adhesion between aluminum and wood unless adequate preparation and roughening is done immediately before assembly. A good tip for aluminum insert installation is to sandblast the back and sides of the insert prior to installation.

Gamma Fire Inserts (Green Glass)

Green and red glass inserts, marketed as Gamma Fire, were introduced in the 1970's and remained fairly popular into the mid 80's. This insert is durable and bonds exceptionally well to wood with epoxy adhesives. It is easy to cut to size and it files well during facing. It has a tendency, however, to dull saw blades and files very rapidly. This is caused mainly by the abrasion of the glass fibers.

Glass inserts are much heavier than ABS plastic inserts. A glass insert of the same installed size as an ABS insert is approximately 9 swingweight points heavier or slightly over ½ ounce additional in weight.

NOTES

_____

_____

_____

_____

_____

_____

_____

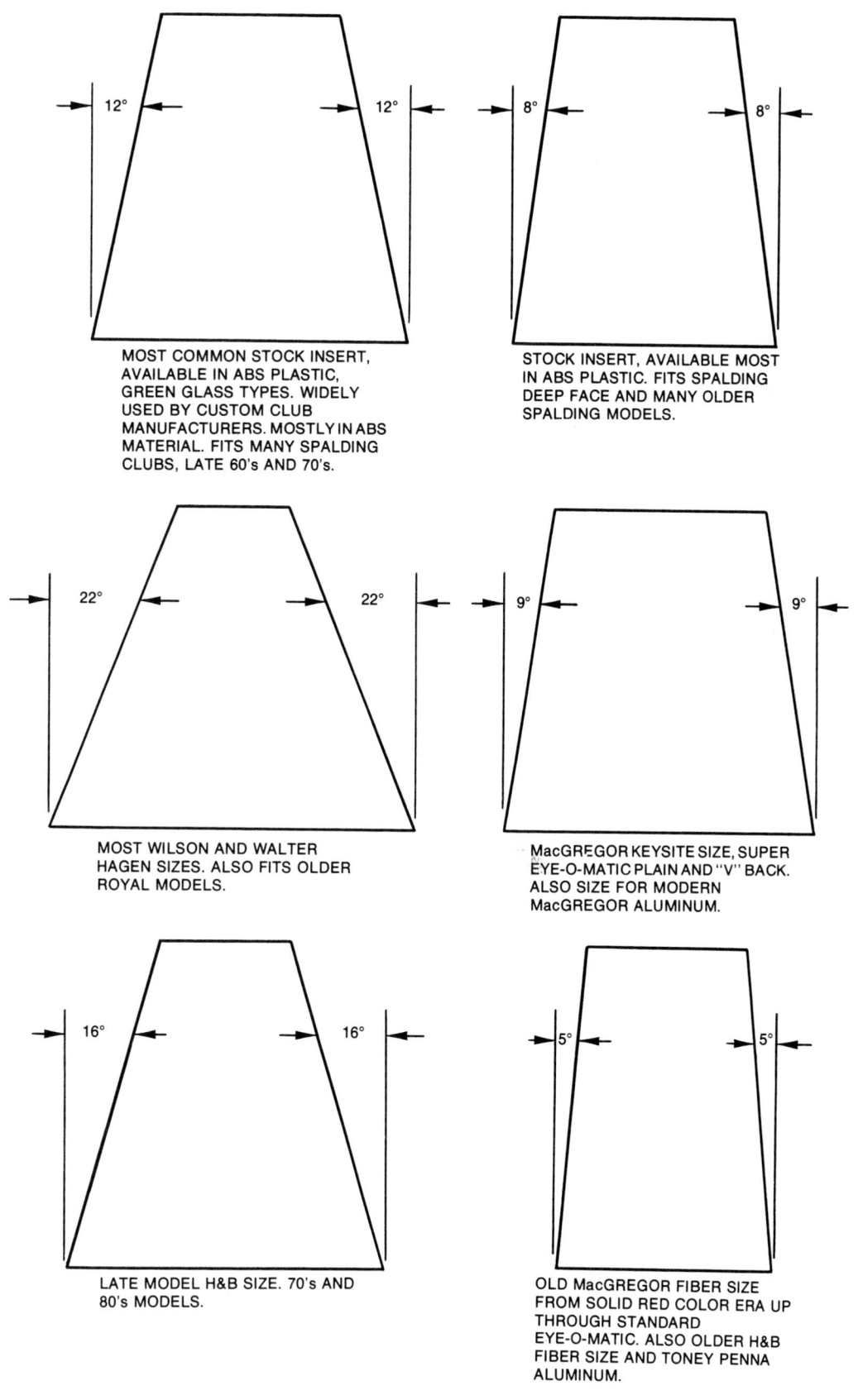

12°   12°
MOST COMMON STOCK INSERT, AVAILABLE IN ABS PLASTIC, GREEN GLASS TYPES. WIDELY USED BY CUSTOM CLUB MANUFACTURERS. MOSTLY IN ABS MATERIAL. FITS MANY SPALDING CLUBS, LATE 60's AND 70's.

8°   8°
STOCK INSERT, AVAILABLE MOST IN ABS PLASTIC. FITS SPALDING DEEP FACE AND MANY OLDER SPALDING MODELS.

22°   22°
MOST WILSON AND WALTER HAGEN SIZES. ALSO FITS OLDER ROYAL MODELS.

9°   9°
MacGREGOR KEYSITE SIZE, SUPER EYE-O-MATIC PLAIN AND "V" BACK. ALSO SIZE FOR MODERN MacGREGOR ALUMINUM.

16°   16°
LATE MODEL H&B SIZE. 70's AND 80's MODELS.

5°   5°
OLD MacGREGOR FIBER SIZE FROM SOLID RED COLOR ERA UP THROUGH STANDARD EYE-O-MATIC. ALSO OLDER H&B FIBER SIZE AND TONEY PENNA ALUMINUM.

FIG. 5-70
Insert size and shape variations

CHAPTER 6

APPLYING WHIPPING TO WOODS

Applying new whipping to the neck of a golf wood is a common operation in any repair shop. Whipping will be replaced on almost every golf club that is refinished, reshafted, reheaded or needs a split neck repaired. Since the whipping is exposed on most wood and graphite hosels (and some metal wood hosels), it is susceptible to accidental breakage. Whipping is necessary on wood and graphite hosels to help prevent the hosel from splitting due to the stress on the hosel area during the golf swing. Whipping is also found on some metal wood hosels, but the whipping serves only as a cosmetic feature. The addition of whipping to a metal wood tends to make the club more appealing to some traditionalist golfers.

There are many different types and sizes of whipping available. The .023 diameter nylon whipping, available in many colors, is suggested instead of waxed or pitched linen types, mono-filament types, or the smaller .020, .019 or .016 diameter whippings. The larger .023 diameter braided nylon whipping is stronger and more durable than other whipping types, as a strand of .023 nylon whipping is composed of three smaller strands braided together and then covered with a sheathing. Also, it looks much better when installed over a hosel with minor imperfections such as small dents, dings or any unevenness that may occur with age. Also, nylon type whippings seem to be more compatible with today's modern polyurethane wood club finishes than some of the other types, namely waxed and pitched types which tend to inhibit proper curing of modern finishing materials.

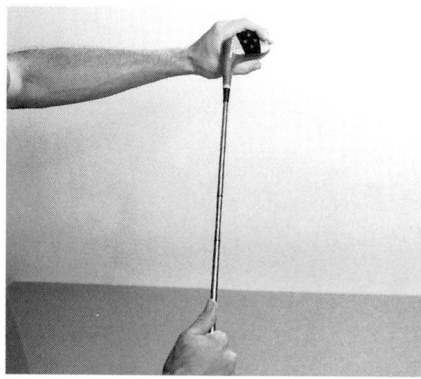

6-1 When a golf club comes in with loose or no whipping, always check to see if the shaft is loose in the hosel. Many times this is the cause for the whipping to fail. Refer to Chapter 7 for shaft tightening procedures if the shaft is loose.

6-2 When removing old whipping, use a sharp knife or razor blade. When cutting through the whipping, always cut away from the clubhead. This eliminates the chance of ruining the finish should you slip.

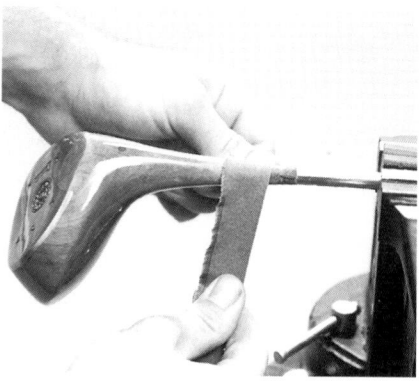

6-3 Large irregularities or bulges on the hosel surface may be removed using a flat mill file. Follow up the filing by sanding with a fine grade of sandpaper. When shaping the hosel, the goal should be to obtain a smooth tapered look from the top of the ferrule to the bottom of the hosel where it blends into the head. **Be careful not to sand below the point where the whipping will end.**

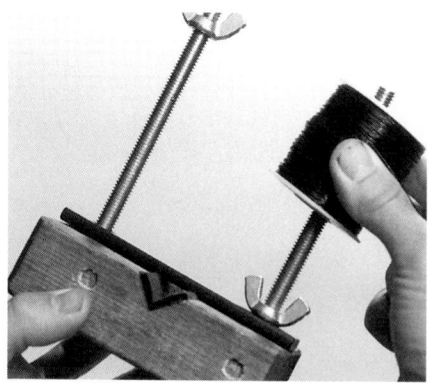

6-4 Whipping a hosel is easier if the whipping spool is stationary. The **Insert Clamp** does double duty as a stable base from which to unravel the whipping without twisting it.

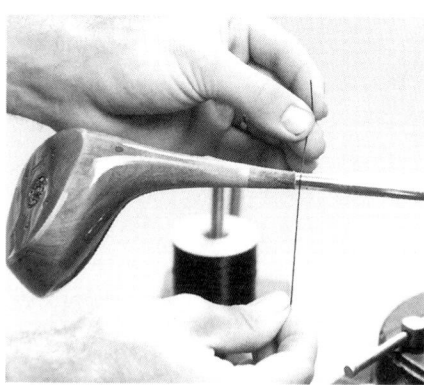

6-5 To whip a club, first lay the strand of whipping across the shaft approximately ⅛" above the ferrule and …

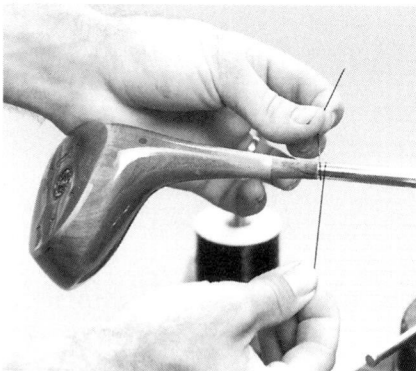

6-6 … completely encircle the shaft with the whipping.

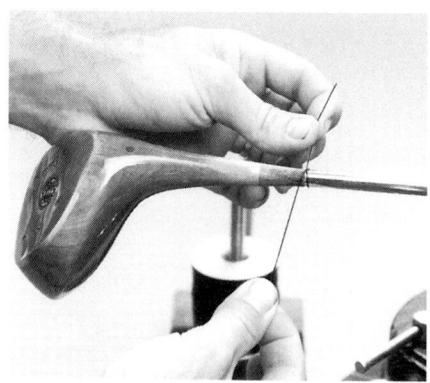

6-7 Holding the whipping as shown, take the strand held in your right hand and cross over the top of the whipping that encircles the shaft (the cut end of the whipping). This overlapping will secure the initial whipping loop to the shaft.

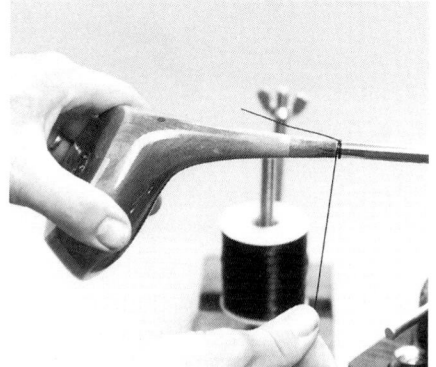

6-8 While applying light pressure with your right hand, grasp the clubhead with the left hand and turn the head, while feeding the whipping over the top of the short strand to lay straight down the very back of the hosel and …

6-9 … continue to turn the clubhead another two revolutions, Now, cut off flush the visible portion of whipping that is laying along the back of the hosel. Doing this eliminates a possible gap in the whipping because the next turn will butt perfectly against the preceding one.

107

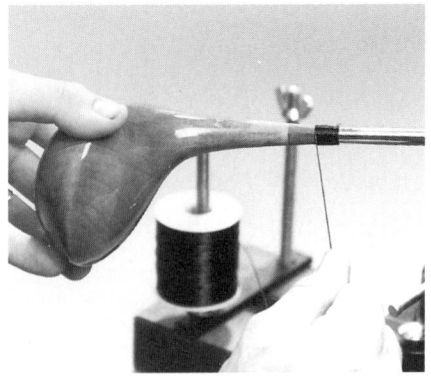

6-10 Continue to rotate the clubhead while feeding the whipping on the hosel. Note the position of the right hand in relation to the whipping already on the shaft. Feeding the whipping onto the hosel at this angle will help eliminate gaps. Use a medium tension.

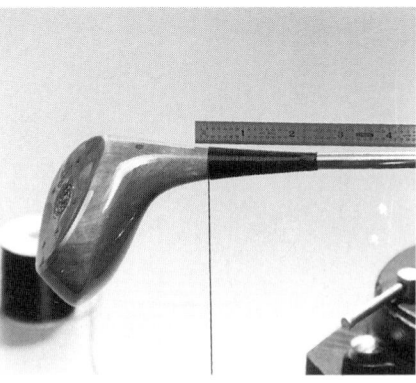

6-11 Use a ruler (6" scale works well) to measure the finished whipping length desired. The average whipping length is 2½", however, with the various length hosels, it is better to end the whipping…

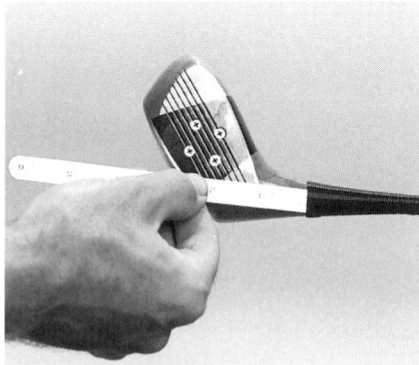

6-12 … at a point one inch from the top of the face measured at the heel.

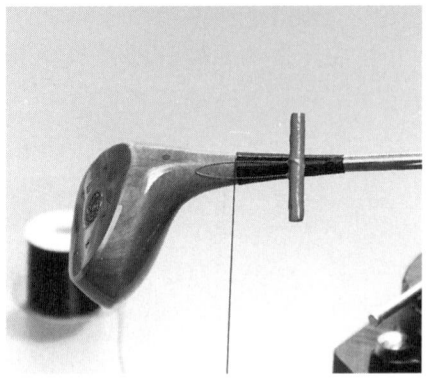

6-13 When the whipping is wound to a point approximately ¼" from the desired end, insert a **Loop Puller** (or a doubled-over piece of whipping) underneath the next turn of whipping as shown. Position the puller so that it lies alongside the centerline of the back of the hosel, not directly on it.

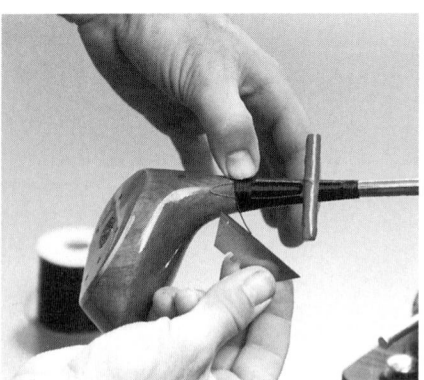

6-14 Wind the whipping six turns over the puller then cut the strand free from the spool while holding the whipping in place with your finger.

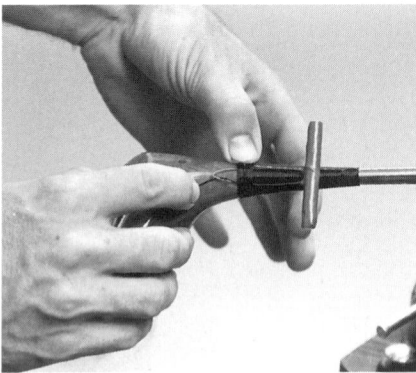

6-15 Next, feed the cut end of the whipping through the loop puller end. Continue to hold the whipping in place with your finger.

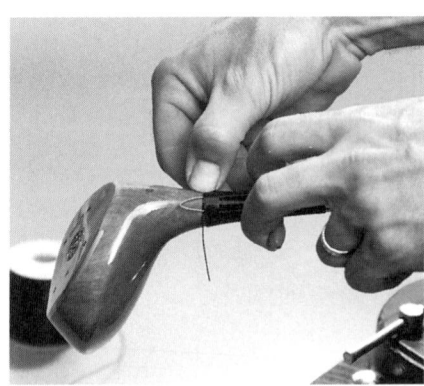

6-16 Place a thumb on the back of the hosel directly over the last strand of whipping. While holding the whipping in place, drop the end of the strand and grasp the puller with the other hand. Duplicate the hand positions as shown in the photo and …

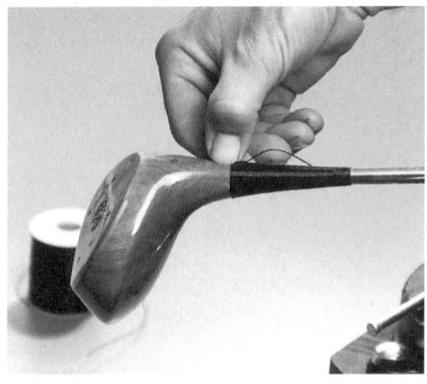

6-17 … quickly pull the loop through. Firmly planting the thumb on the back of the hosel will prevent the pulled-through strand from sliding to the side of the hosel.

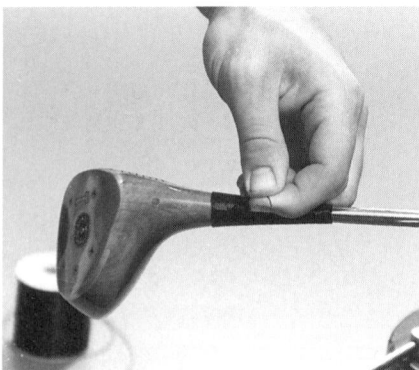

6-18 If the strand is not positioned along the back center of the hosel, pull the strand around until properly positioned.

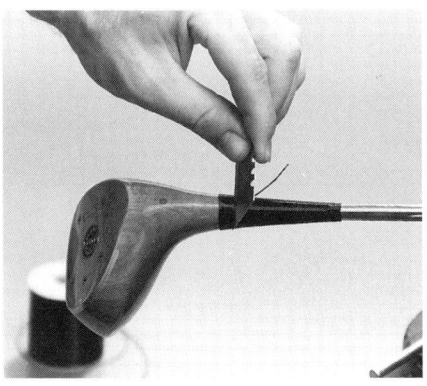

6-19 Carefully cut the excess whipping from the hosel. A sharp knife or razor blade will provide a flush cut.

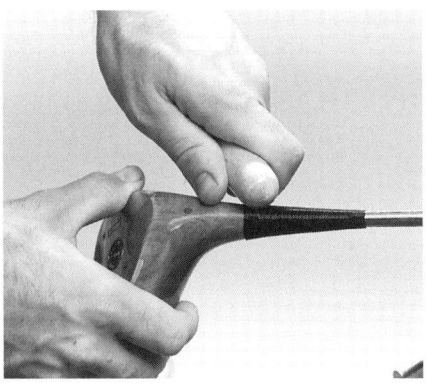

6-20 If the whipping has "raised up" as a result of pulling the strand through, rub the raised part back in place with a smooth firm object such as a wooden knife handle or plastic screwdriver handle, etc.

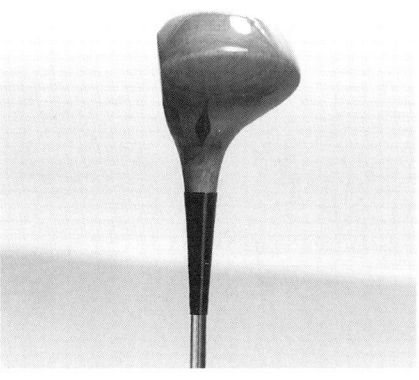

6-21 This is how the whipping should look. Note the smoothly tapered hosel. Whipping will either enhance the look of a properly tapered hosel or magnify any irregularities.

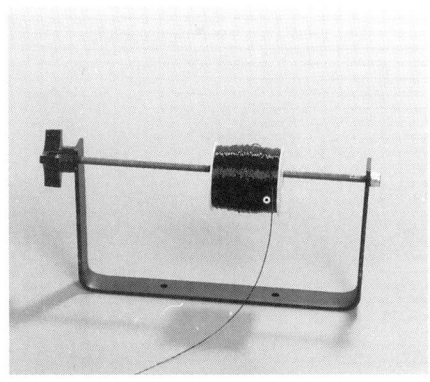

6-22 As an alternative to the **Insert Clamp**, this **Whipping Spool Holder** will allow the whipping to be fed from the spool at a high speed. The holder can be permanently mounted so the whipping will always be ready to use.

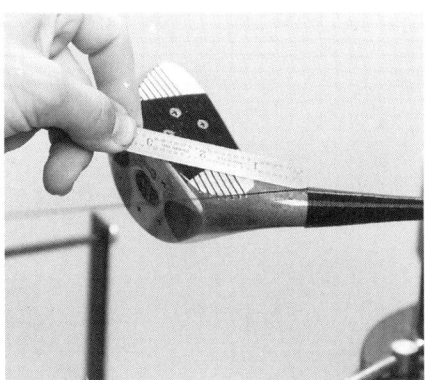

6-23 Another way of tying off the whipping is to use the loop-over method. Once the whipping has been wound to the desired length, cut the whipping approximately 12" longer from this point and …

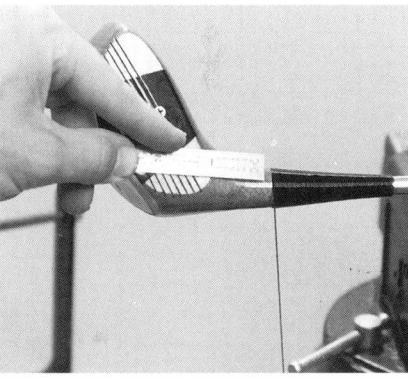

6-24 … unwind 9 turns of the whipping from the hosel. You should now have approximately 18" - 20" of excess whipping.

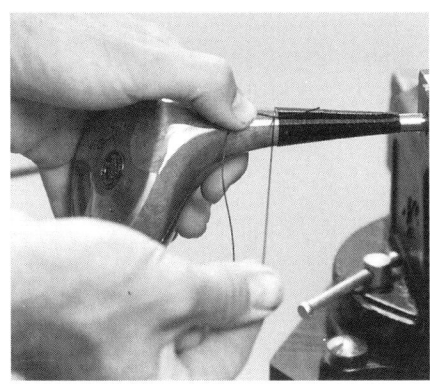

6-25 Take the very end of the whipping and lay it along the back of the neck, slightly off center and …

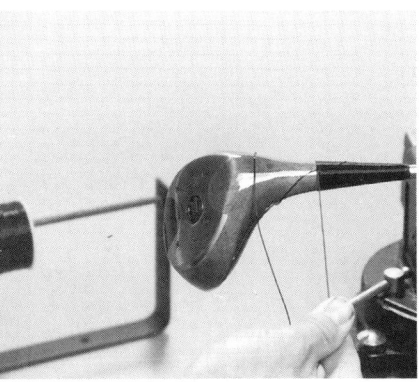

6-26 … wrap the whipping around the hosel over the top of the strand, thus locking the strand in place.

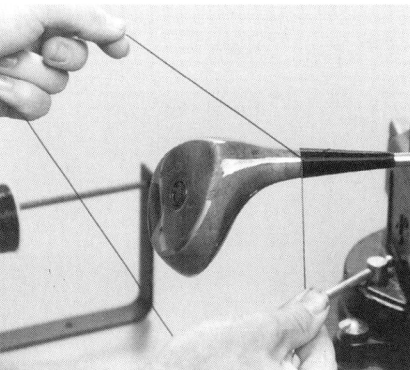

6-27 Continue to wind the whipping over the strand while, each time, passing the loop over the clubhead…

109

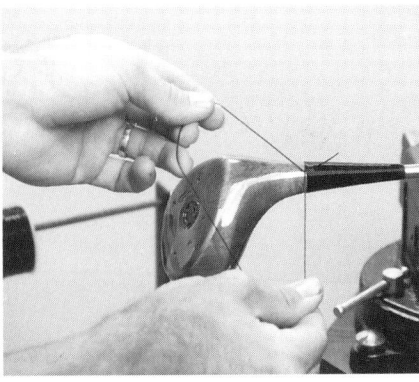

6-28 ... until the loop of whipping will no longer pass over the head. This will leave the 9 turns of whipping over the strand. Remember, we previously unwound 9 turns of whipping.

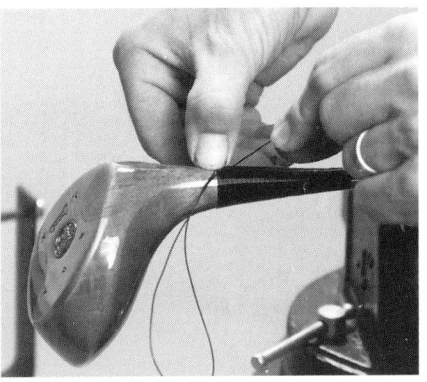

6-29 Place your thumb directly on the back of the hosel over the whipping. Grasp the end of the whipping in your hand and ...

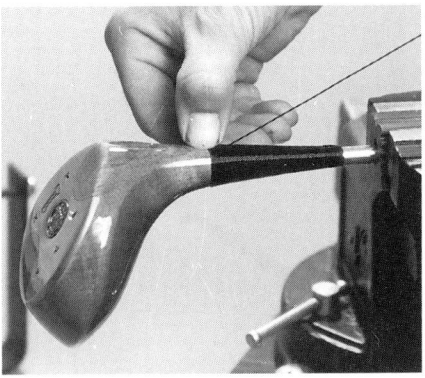

6-30 ... pull the whipping tight underneath and through the last 9 windings. Position the strand so that it runs straight up the back of the hosel. Positioning the strand on the back of the hosel will keep this slight lump in the whipping out of sight when the golfer is addressing the ball.

6-31 Cut the strand flush with the whipping. Note: The only drawback to this method is the waste of the 12" strand.

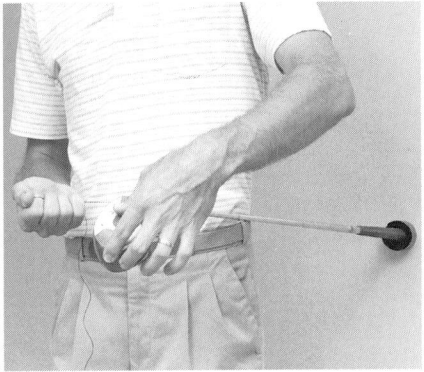

6-32 A quicker way of winding whipping is to fasten a spray can cap to a wall. Insert the butt of the club into the cap and support the shaft with your side as shown. Rotate the head with one hand while winding on whipping with the other. The tension created while pulling on the whipping will keep the shaft tight against your side.

6-33 If hammering a nail into your wall is not possible, attach the cap to the base of the vise or workbench.

6-34 For higher volume work, the **Motorized Whipping Machine** with a variable speed drive, controlled by a foot pedal, works very well. Use of this machine will allow the operator to whip approximately 60 clubs per hour.

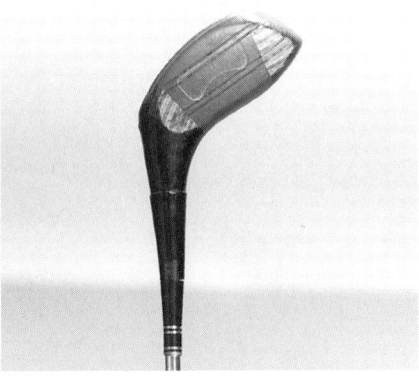

6-35 The condition of this whipping cover is typical of clubs that use a plastic molded cover over a string whipping. The plastic eventually breaks down from repeated contact with iron heads or the side of the golf bag. Replacement of a whipping cover requires removal of the shaft, so many repairmen...

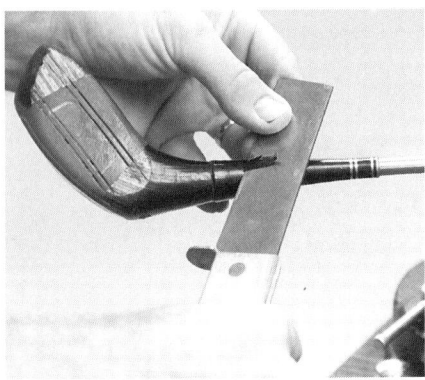

6-36 ... choose to cut through the cover, being careful not to cut into the wood hosel or mar the finish. If only one club in a set is bad, the cover should be replaced to match the set. Of course, all this depends on the customer's desires.

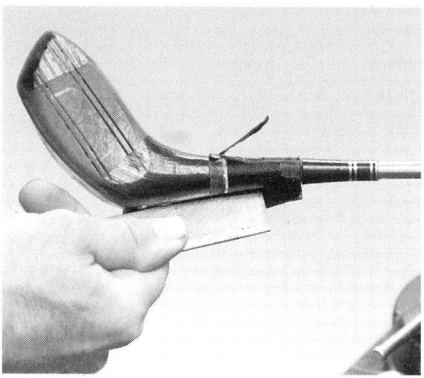

6-37 Peel the cover from the hosel, thus exposing the whipping below.

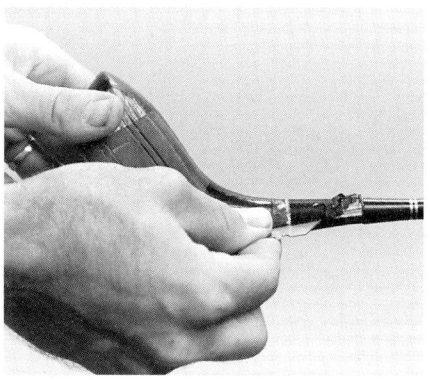

6-38 Cut through the whipping and remove it also. The whipping found below the plastic whipping cover is much thinner than the type of whipping found on most other clubs. This whipping is equivalent to 8 pound test fishing line and is usually a mono-filament type.

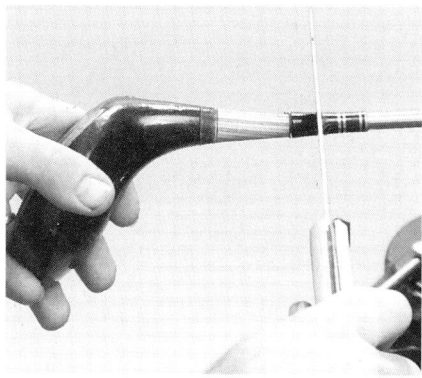

6-39 Place the knife on top of the ferrule perpendicular to the shaft. The knife should be placed ½" to ¾" from the top of the hosel. Cut through the plastic and remove the top half.

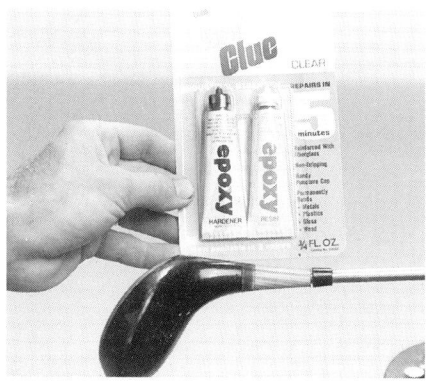

6-40 If a gap exists between the ferrule and the hosel, a quick-setting epoxy will work well to fill the gap.

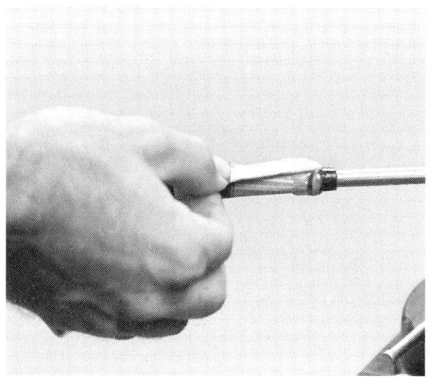

6-41 After the epoxy has been mixed, force the epoxy down into the gap and allow the epoxy to cure.

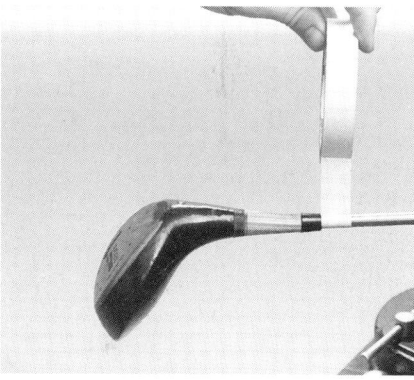

6-42 Wrap a piece of ¾" masking tape around the shaft just above the ferrule. This will protect the chrome-plated shaft during the ensuing filing steps.

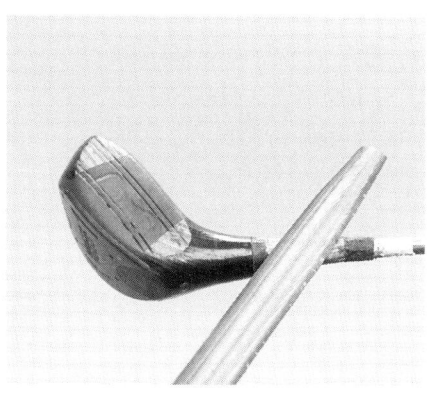

6-43 The oversized ferrule must now be filed down in diameter to provide a smooth taper from the shaft to the hosel for the whipping. Rough shape the ferrule with a coarse file. Do not cut into the hosel or through the tape.

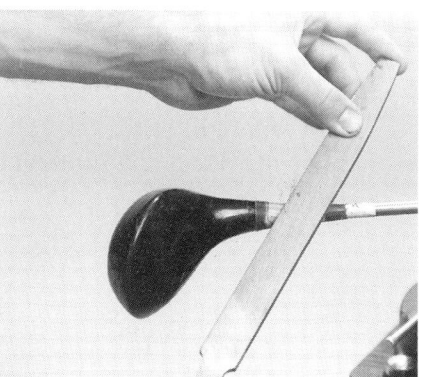

6-44 With most of the excess plastic removed, change to a fine file for final shaping. Blend the top of the ferrule into the shaft so there is no noticeable "step" between the shaft and the ferrule. The bottom of the ferrule should be even or flush with the hosel.

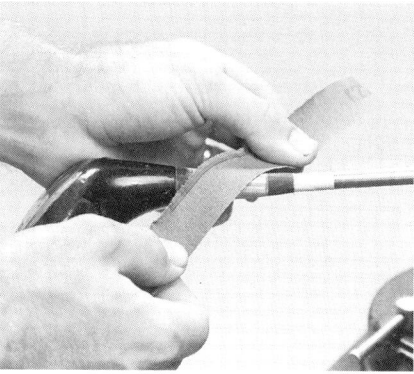

6-45 Next, use a fine grade of sandpaper to blend in the file marks and to remove any flat spots left from filing. If there is a buildup of finish at the base of the plastic cover, this too must be smoothed out. The fine file and sandpaper work well to do this.

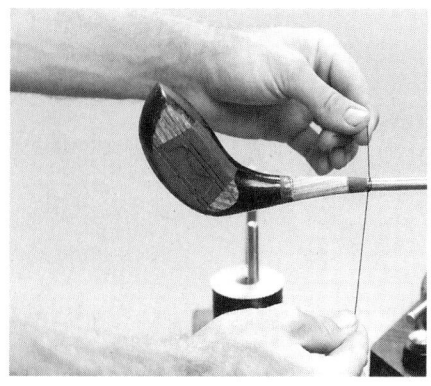

6-46 The hosel is now prepared for the application of the whipping. Now follow the same steps as performed in photos 6-5 through 6-21.

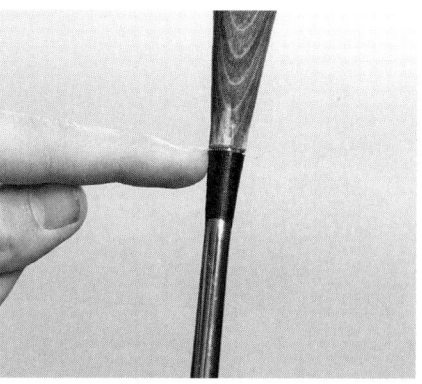

6-47 Oftentimes, whipping will loosen because the ferrule separates from the hosel. The resulting gap allows a strand of whipping to fall into it, which lessens the whipping tension, causing it to loosen and/or ultimately unravel.

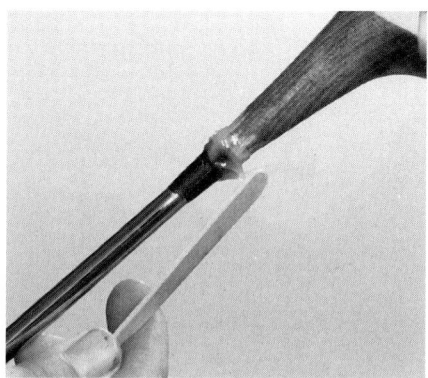

6-48 If you find a gap between the ferrule and hosel, always fill it with epoxy before whipping the hosel.

6-49 Older golf clubs require different types of whipping for proper restoration of the era. The two most common types are waxed linen and pitched linen.

6-50 Application of a modern, plastic-covered whipping to an old club would be aesthetically incorrect. To preserve the original appearance, pitched linen whipping should be used. The steps for application are the same as detailed in photos 6-5 through 6-21.

6-51 When regripping an antique club with leather, the bottom of the leather grip should be finished off with the pitched linen whipping. Again, the same procedure is used to apply the whipping to the shaft and leather grip as is used for the hosel.

ADDITIONAL INFORMATION FOR APPLYING WHIPPING TO WOOD CLUBS

Whipping is sold by the spool. The smallest amount available is 50 yards which is usually adequate to whip about 9 clubs. Table 6-1 has been developed as an aid in purchasing the correct amount of whipping by anticipated usage. The table was calculated using .023" diameter whipping. It takes an average of 16 feet of whipping for each wood club.

TABLE 6-1			
Average Number of Clubs Per Spool of Whipping			
Spool Yardage Size	[1]Approximate Number of Clubs From Each Spool	[2]Approximate Cost Per Spool	Average Cost Per Club
50 yards	9 Clubs	$ 2.55	28¢ Per Club
200 yards	37 Clubs	$ 7.65	20½¢ Per Club
500 yards	93 Clubs	—	—
1000 yards	187 Clubs	—	—
2000 yards	375 Clubs	$51.00	13½¢ Per Club
4000 yards	750 Clubs	$82.50	11¢ Per Club

[1]Based on .023" diameter whipping @ 16 feet per club.
[2]Based on .023" diameter braided or twisted nylon or orlon whipping @ 1994 prices in The GolfWorks® catalog.

CHAPTER 7

RESHAFTING WOOD CLUBS AND CHANGING HOSEL BORE SIZES

The time and technique required to reshaft woods (wood, metal or graphite) varies as much as the golf swing itself. With the rising popularity of metal wood heads, graphite heads and composite shafts, the techniques for reshafting have become more involved. One prerequisite necessary, however, for any successful reshafting job is patience! Never rush or force any reshaft as this can only result in disaster or additional repair work to correct the mistake. There will be times when a wood club reshaft will take as little as fifteen minutes or as much as one hour, or in rare cases, over an hour. At first, you may become frustrated at the amount of time required for a supposedly simple reshaft job. But, have patience. The more times you do this, the more confidence you will acquire and subsequently, even the hardest reshafts will become much easier and faster.

It is important to have a good understanding of golf shaft specifications to enable you to accurately identify the shaft in a club and also the replacement shaft. Refer to the Golf Shaft Specifications and Reference Tables in Chapters 56, 57 and 59. For more information on the design characteristics of various types of shafts see Chapters 55 and 58.

When replacing a shaft, the four most important features of the shaft to be matched are listed here in order of importance. (Note that the fourth feature, torque, is only applicable if you are replacing a composite shaft.)

1) Shaft Flex
2) Shaft Pattern
3) Shaft Weight
4) Shaft Torque

The definition of shaft flex is "a comparative measurement of a shaft's resistance to bending under a given load." This measurement is commonly taken from a shaft deflection board and divided into five different flexes: L (ladies'), A (flexible), R or T (medium), S (stiff) and X (extra stiff), with "X" being the most stiff and "L" being the most flexible. A less commonly used machine for measuring flex is the Frequency Analyzer. Information on this very accurate flex tool is found in Chapter 63. Matching the shaft flex is important so an entire set will be consistent. If one or more shafts are not matched properly in flex, the clubface will be delivered into the ball at an angle different from the rest of the clubs.

The shaft pattern identifies the shaft type (Dynamic™, TT Lite™ Jet Step™, etc.) through an arrangement of step downs. Shaft type indicates the bend point (flex point) on a golf shaft. The bend point is the point on a shaft that experiences the greatest bending or deflection when placed on a deflection board, or where the shaft will bend most during a swing. A golf shaft will either have a low, mid or high bend point. A high bend point means most of the bending during the swing occurs above the middle of the shaft with the tip section of the shaft remaining relatively firm. A mid bend point means most of the bending occurs near the middle of the shaft and a low bend point indicates most of the bending occurs below the middle of the shaft with the butt section of the shaft remaining relatively firm. This is important because the bend point does much to determine the trajectory of a golf shot among other things.

Shaft weight simply means the overall weight of a golf shaft. The weight of a golf shaft will fall into these categories: standard weight, lightweight and very lightweight.

Shaft torque is an indication of the degree to which a shaft will twist along its longitudinal axis. The higher the torque reading, the more easily the shaft will twist. Refer to Chapters 58 and 60 for more information on torque. It should be noted that without a fairly sophisticated machine you will not be able to measure the torque of a golf shaft. If you know the flex, however, and name of the shaft (i.e. Aldila HM-40, GolfWorks® Distance Master, Grafalloy Nitro Flex, etc.), then you can refer to the charts in Chapter 59 to find the corresponding torque. If the shaft is a private label shaft like Daiwa's TRX-80 or Taylor Made's Twist Flex, your best bet to determine the torque is to call the company. When attempting to match torque, it is not necessary that the torque readings be identical. No player, through feel or performance, can tell the difference between two shafts having nominal differences in torque. For example, if you were to replace a 2.8° torque shaft with one having 3.5° torque, assuming everything else to be the same, there would be no measurable difference in performance.

In addition to covering the reshafting steps, this chapter also shows how to change hosel bores to accept different shaft tip sizes. An inexpensive and effective way to change bore sizes, or just to clean them out, is by a method called step drilling. Step drilling utilizes a set of three different drill sizes for taper bores or only one drill size for unitized (parallel) bores. Also available are a series of different size tapered reamers to match the various sized taper tip shafts.

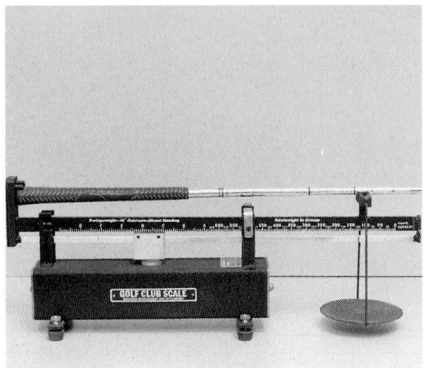

7-1 If possible, **check and record the swingweight.** Your goal is to return the club to its original condition unless otherwise requested.

7-2 Measure the club length. If only part of the club is available, measure another club from the same set to determine this club's length or set the length at the industry standard. Industry standard specifications on length are found in Table 7-1 at the end of this chapter.

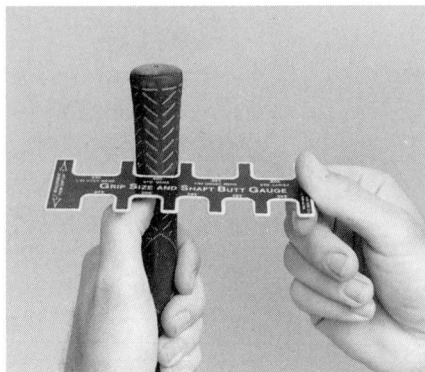

7-3 The grip size is also measured and the grip type should be noted if the same type of grip is to be used.

114

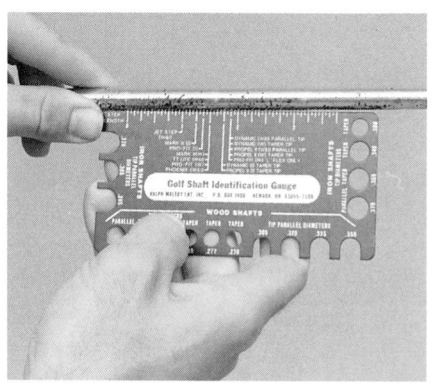

7-4 If possible, determine the shaft flex, pattern and weight. (See the introduction to this chapter and see Chapters 56, 57 and 59 for more information.) Note the use of the **Golf Shaft Identification Gauge.** Try to match the original shaft unless otherwise requested.

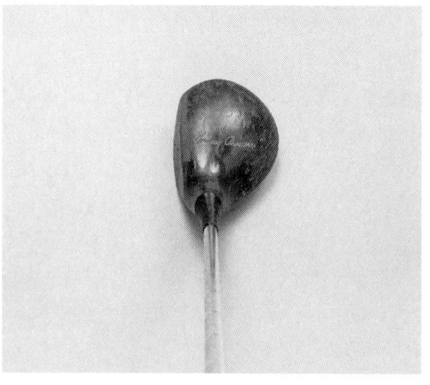

7-5 Observe the face angle. Alterations to the face angle are often made at the factory, or by an individual, by bending the shaft at the hosel. Installing the new straight shaft into the hosel will return the face to its original hosel bore angle. See Chapter 12 for a more complete understanding of face angle and how to rebend a shaft, if desired.

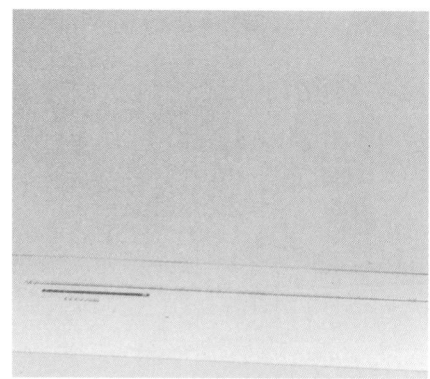

7-6 Reshafting woods having steel, aluminum or titanium shafts. Reshafting requires the use of three different length $7/32$" drill bits. A "jobbers" length, 12" length and 47" length drill bits are widely used in wood reshafting. Note: Always use the shortest possible drill bit.

7-7 The two types of shaft assemblies for a wood are a "through-bore" (club on the right), and a "blind-bore" (club on the left). On a through-bore, the shaft penetrates through the sole. The shaft stops at a distance of $1/2$" from the sole on a blindbore.

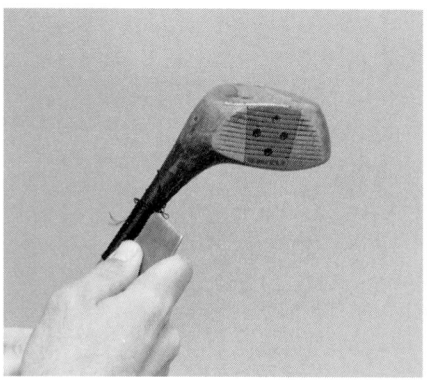

7-8 Remove the old hosel whipping with a sharp knife. On clubs with plastic whipping covers, do not remove them unless you intend to replace them with whipping.

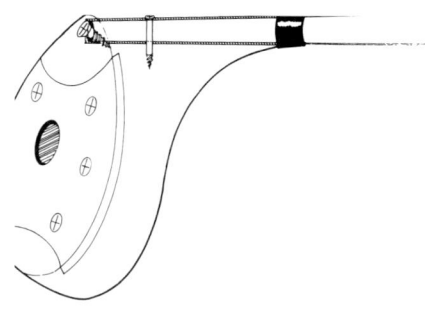

7-9 Depending upon the type of assembly, there can be as many as three locking mechanisms holding the shaft in place. They are: 1) a tip screw, 2) a back screw and 3) epoxy or glue.

7-10 Procedure for removing a tip screw. The tip screw, if installed, is a #4 size screw. Clean the screw head recess with a scriber or an awl.

7-11 Attempt to turn the screw out using a small **Reed & Prince (Frearson) screwdriver.** Tip screws are seldom glued or epoxied in place, however, if one fails to turn …

7-12 … drill into the center of the screw head, $3/16$" deep using a $5/64$" **diameter bit.**

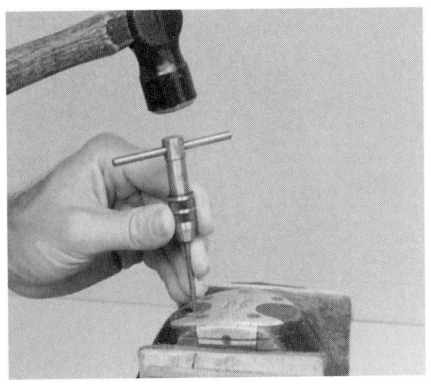

7-13 Tap a **#1 size extractor** into the hole and …

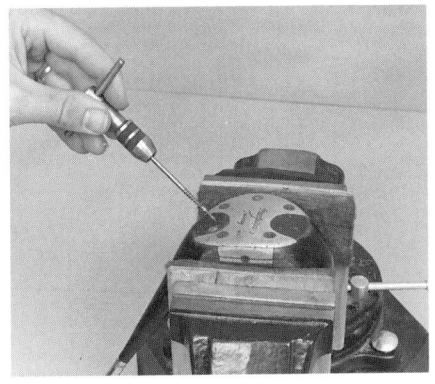

7-14 … turn the extractor counterclockwise to remove the screw. (Note the use of a "**T**" **handle Tap Wrench.**) If the head of the screw twists off, drive the remainder of the screw into the head with a ⅛" **pin punch.**

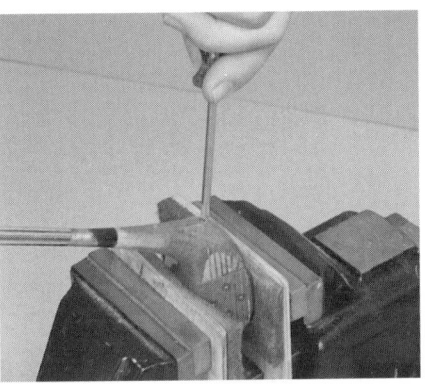

7-15 Procedure for removing a backscrew: Some backscrew heads are visible versus recessed and covered, therefore, the entire screw is easily removed using a small Reed and Prince screwdriver as shown.

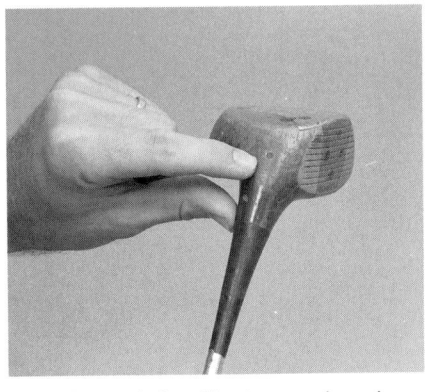

7-16 The majority of backscrews have been punched below the surface of the hosel and then covered with a wood filler or epoxy. A few clubs do not have a backscrew (usually graphite shafts). Always look for the telltale epoxy or filler patch on the back of the hosel.

7-17 Using a ⅛" bit, drill through the filler until contact is made with the head of the backscrew.

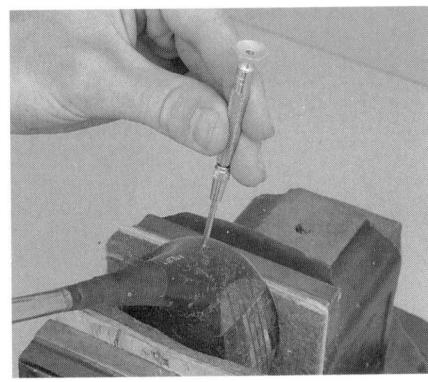

7-18 The head of the backscrew will usually have a straight slot or a cross slot configuration. Most manufacturers, however, drive the backscrew into the head as if it were a nail. Attempts to turn the backscrew out will usually fail. A **jeweler's screwdriver** is your best bet for trying to remove the backscrew by turning it counterclockwise.

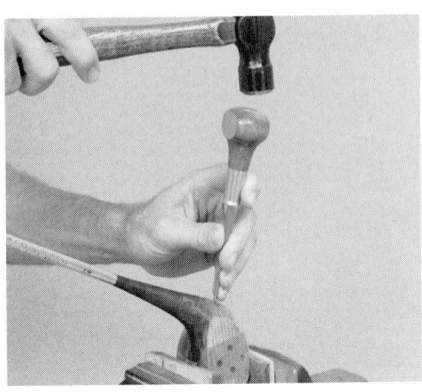

7-19 If this method fails, place the tip of an awl or scriber on the middle of the backscrew head and make a slight indentation. This shallow depression will allow the drill bit to start drilling in the middle of the screw head and help prevent "walking."

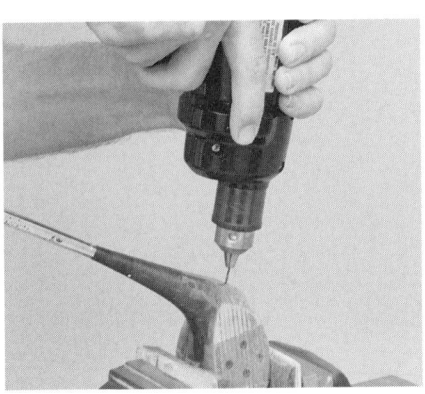

7-20 Using a ⁵⁄₆₄" **bit,** drill ³⁄₁₆" into the center of the backscrew.

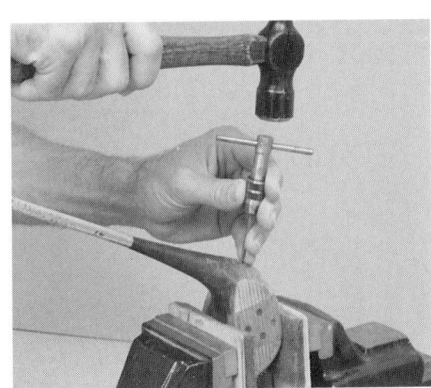

7-21 Gently tap a **#1 size extractor** into the hole. Note the use of a "**T**" **handle tap wrench.**

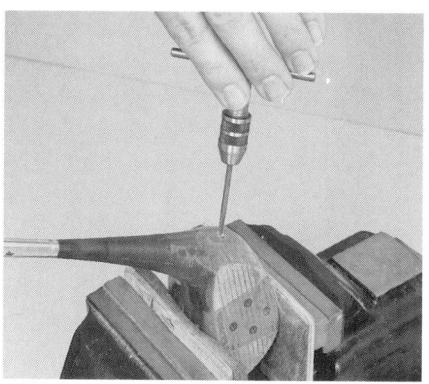

7-22 Once the extractor tip "bottoms out" in the drilled hole, slowly turn the extractor counterclockwise while simultaneously pulling upwards on the handle.

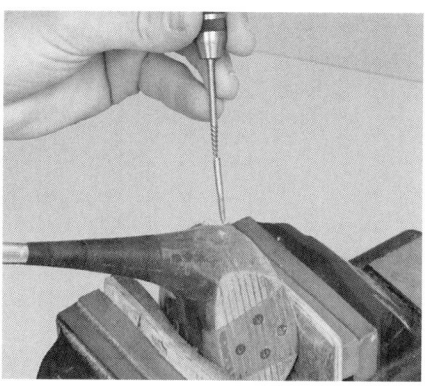

7-23 If the hole was drilled properly, the backscrew should come out as shown. If the extractor turns but the backscrew does not, drill deeper and try again. The advantage here is that the backscrew comes out intact. The next method to be shown will leave half of the backscrew in the head.

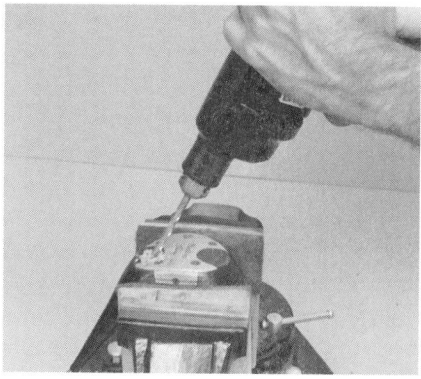

7-24 The drill through method: On a through-bore type shaft assembly, drill through the wood plug in the tip of the shaft using a 7/32" bit. Note: Do not allow the drill bit to walk off the tip of the shaft as this can damage the finish around the shaft tip.

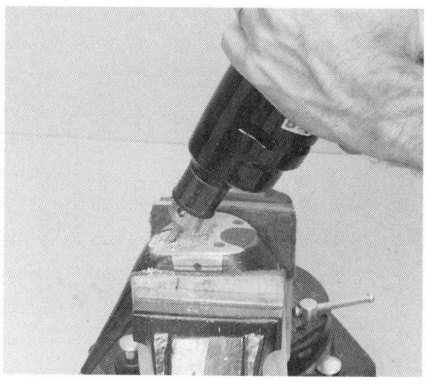

7-25 Drill down to the backscrew and then continue drilling completely through the backscrew, cutting it in half. When drilling through the backscrew, do not allow the drill chuck to come in contact with or damage the sole area.

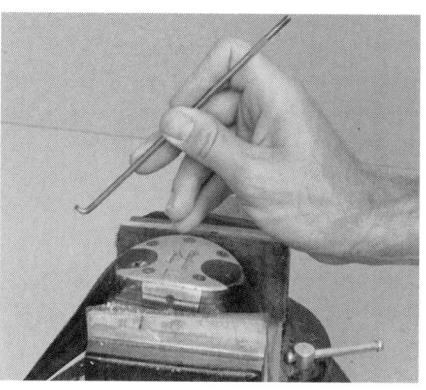

7-26 After you have drilled through the backscrew, the head portion of the screw will sometimes pop up and can be removed easily. If the head portion of the backscrew does not pop up, a **backscrew hook** can be used to help.

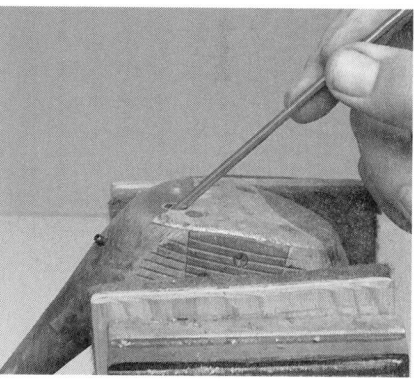

7-27 Insert the hook end of the backscrew hook into the shaft tip and "fish around" in the shaft until the hook catches the top half of the backscrew and forces it partially out. Now, the backscrew can be easily removed.

7-28 If the top half of the backscrew is stubborn and still will not come out, place the club in the vise as shown. Place the tip of a 1/8" pin punch on top of the backscrew head and ...

7-29 ... drive the top half of the backscrew down into the shaft. The top half should then tumble out the tip of the shaft. If it does not, redrill with a 7/32" bit and then punch the remaining portion of the backscrew into the shaft tip.

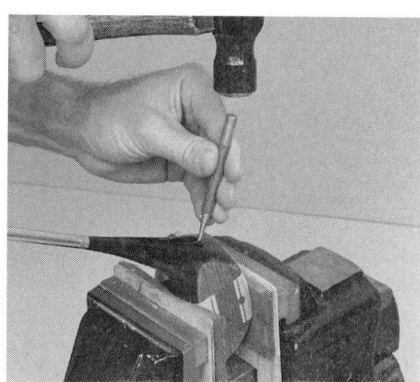

7-30 With the top half of the backscrew removed, reinsert the 1/8" pin punch and punch the bottom half of the backscrew through the shaft and into the wood. This will then clear the shaft of the lower half of the backscrew. Proceed to photo 7-44 for the next steps.

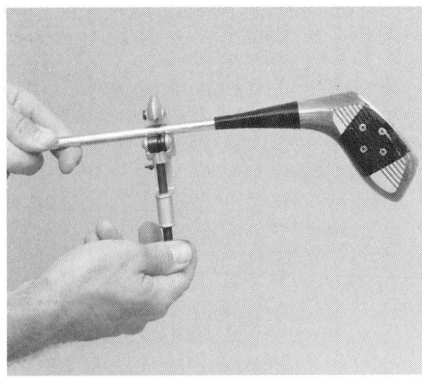

7-31 To remove the backscrew from a blind-bore club, proceed as follows. If the shaft will not be saved, cut the shaft approximately 4" above the top of the hosel using a tubing cutter or a **friction cutoff wheel.** See Chapter 21, photos 21-172 through 21-176 for information on using the friction wheel.

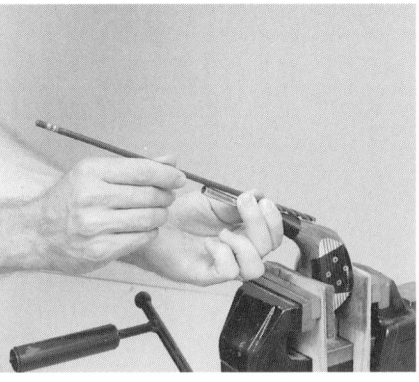

7-32 Next, place the clubhead in a vise as shown. Place the **12" long,** 7/32" drill bit against the outside of the hosel. The tip of the drill bit should be even with the backscrew hole.

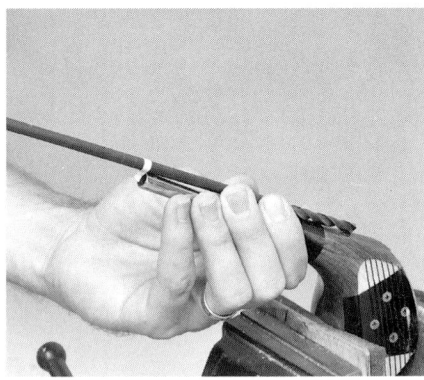

7-33 Place a piece of masking tape around the drill bit at a point even with the top of the shaft.

7-34 Install the drill bit into the drill chuck, and then place the bit inside the shaft.

7-35 Drill inside the shaft until the wrapping of tape around the bit disappears inside the shaft. This indicates the backscrew has been drilled in half. If the tape disappears more than ½" inside the shaft, the tip of the drill bit may come through the bottom of the club. If this happens, you have just turned the club into a through-bore model.

7-36 Once the backscrew has been drilled in half, place the clubhead in a vise as shown. Punch the top half of the backscrew into the shaft tip using a ⅛" **pin punch.**

7-37 Turn the club upside down and the top half of the backscrew should tumble out of the shaft. If it does not, place the head back in the vise, redrill and repunch until the backscrew is removed.

7-38 After the top half of the backscrew is removed, punch the bottom half of the backscrew into the wood head using the ⅛" pin punch. Proceed to photo 7-44.

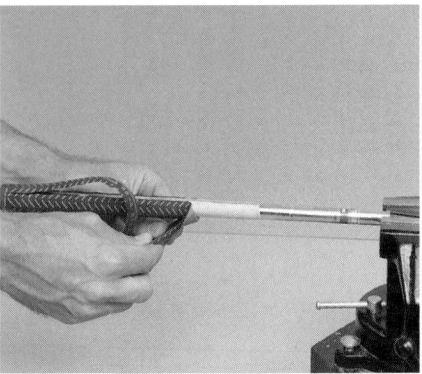

7-39 If you wish to save the shaft, as when repairing a loose head, first remove the grip. Use either a knife or, if the grip is to be saved, use a **Pressurized Grip Remover.** See Chapter 23, photos 23-31 through 23-37 for use of the Grip Remover.

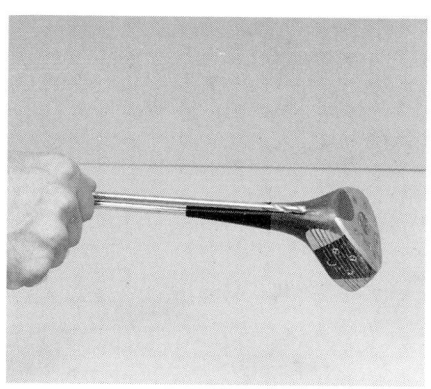

7-40 Place a 47" long ⁷⁄₃₂" bit against the back of the club so that the tip of the drill is even with the backscrew.

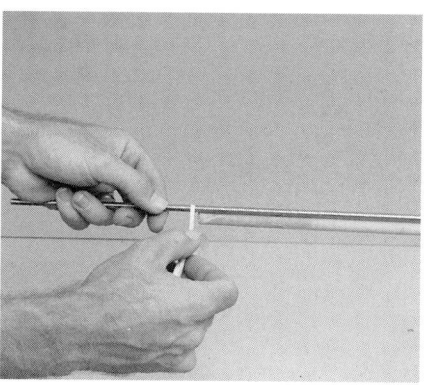

7-41 Place a wrapping of masking tape around the drill bit even with the top of the shaft.

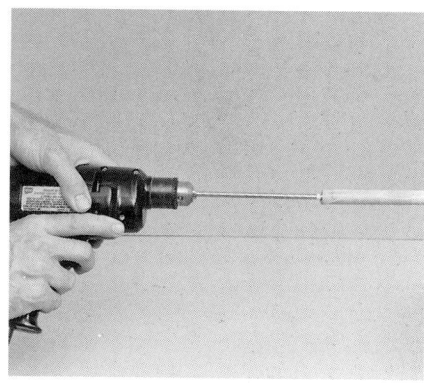

7-42 Place the long drill bit inside the shaft and drill until the wrapping of tape disappears below the top of the shaft. This indicates the backscrew has been cut in half.

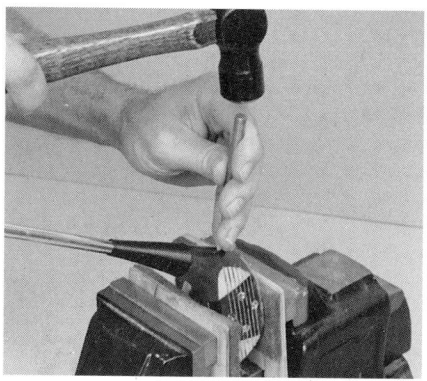

7-43 Follow the punching and, if necessary, redrilling steps until the backscrew is removed as previously shown in photos 7-36 through 7-38.

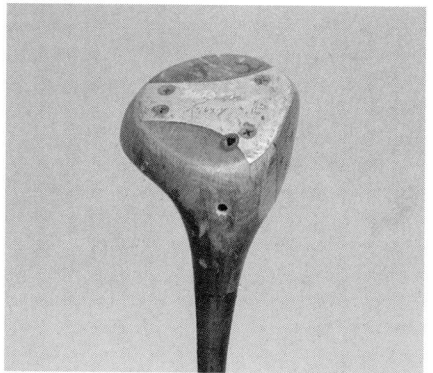

7-44 Once the backscrew is removed, the final locking mechanism must be dealt with before the shaft can be removed. On older golf clubs, white glue, fish glue or pitch tar were used allowing easy shaft removal. If epoxy was used, heat will be needed to soften the epoxy.

7-45 An **Aluminum Lock Tight Shaft Holder** is used to securely hold the shaft in the vise. Next, if necessary, use a ⁷⁄₃₂" drill inside the shaft tip to remove any foreign material such as glue, rubber or lead, etc.

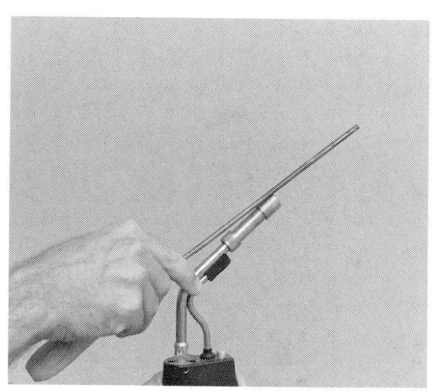

7-46 Heat the end of a **Heating Rod** using a propane torch. Note how the end of the rod is positioned in relation to the flame. This will heat a much broader portion of the rod than when the rod is placed perpendicular to the flame.

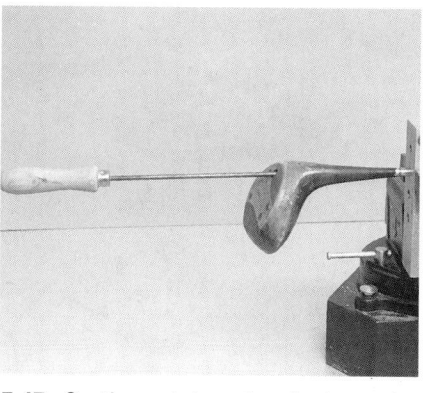

7-47 On through-bore heads, insert the rod inside the shaft from the sole. **On a blind-bore head** with a short shaft, insert the rod from the top of the shaft to the bottom of the hosel bore.

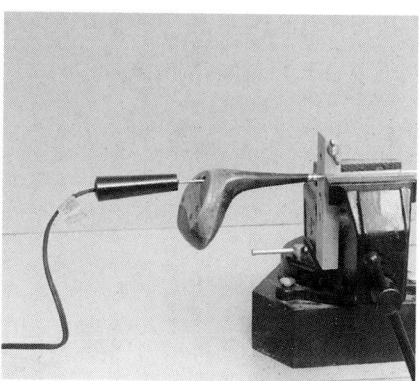

7-48 A fast alternative to the propane torch and Heating Rod method is the **Electric Heating Rod.** Plug it into an electrical outlet, wait 30 seconds and insert it into the shaft. After another few seconds, the head is ready for removal.

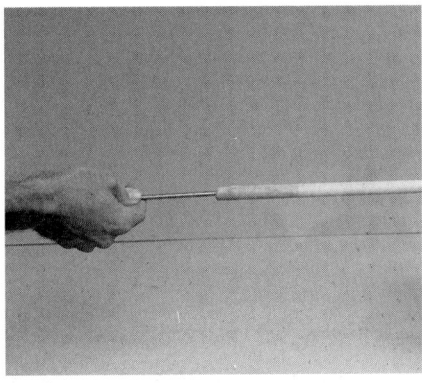

7-49 On blind-bore models with the entire shaft, heat the smooth end of a 47" drill bit and insert it into the shaft until it bottoms out. A 47" rod can also be used.

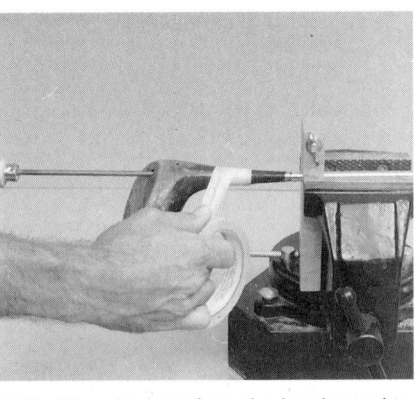

7-50 Allow the heat from the heating rod to penetrate the epoxy surrounding the shaft for one to two minutes. In the meantime, apply 5 or 6 turns of masking tape to the hosel to prevent it from splitting during wood head removal.

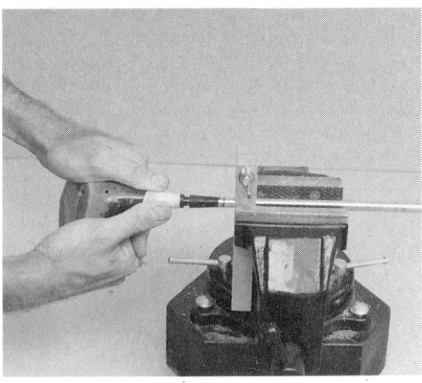

7-51 Grasp the head with both hands and attempt to gently twist the wood head. Turn the head one complete revolution around the shaft. Now remove the head by gently, but firmly, twisting and pulling simultaneously. **Proceed to photo 7-59 if the shaft comes out. Continue on to the next photo if the shaft is broken off inside the hosel.**

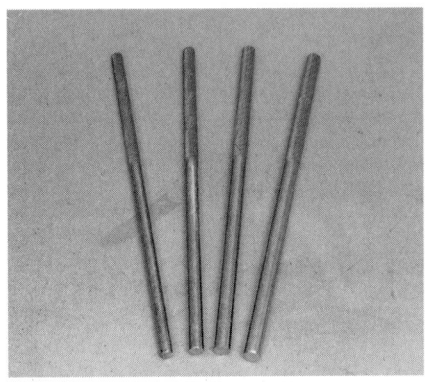

7-52 Shaft extractors are available to fit all shaft tip diameters. Extractors represent the best way of removing shafts broken off inside the wood head hosel.

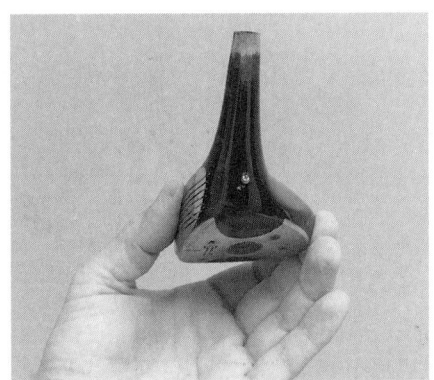

7-53 To use a shaft extractor. Be certain that the backscrew is removed from the head before using the shaft extractors. The number one cause for extractor failure is a backscrew left within the walls of the shaft. Refer to photo 7-15 through 7-30 for backscrew removal steps.

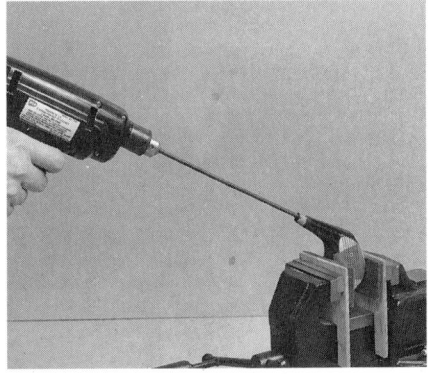

7-54 After the backscrew is removed, completely clean all epoxy or other foreign materials from inside the tip of the shaft. A 7/32" drill bit works best. DO NOT DRILL THROUGH THE BOTTOM OF THE CLUB ON A BLIND-BORE TYPE WOOD.

7-55 Place the smooth end of the extractor between the vise jaws and tighten securely.

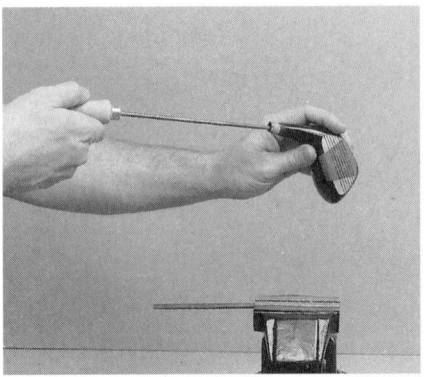

7-56 Heat the end of a **heating rod** and insert the rod inside the shaft to soften the epoxy. Make sure the tip of the rod is pushed to the bottom of the hosel. Repeated heating of the rod may be necessary to break the epoxy bond.

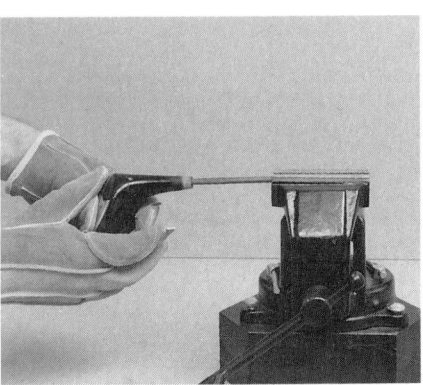

7-57 After heating and while the shaft is still hot, push the shaft over the extractor. Push and turn the head clockwise until you feel the shaft "lock" onto the extractor. It may require a firm push to lock the extractor into the shaft.

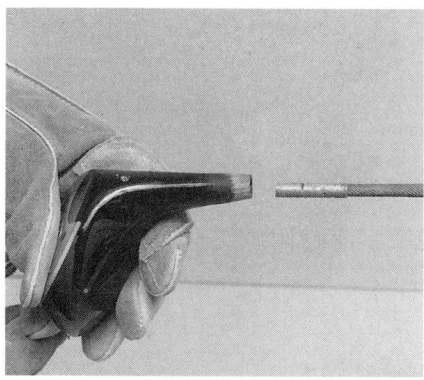

7-58 After locking in the extractor, turn the head while simultaneously pulling on the head. The head should pull free from the shaft while the shaft remains attached to the extractor as shown above. Remove the shaft from the extractor by pulling the shaft out with a pair of pliers.

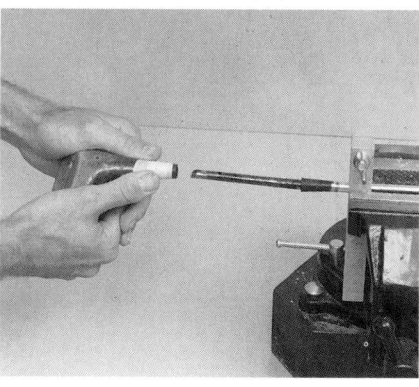

7-59 The wood head is now removed. Be sure your grasp is firm and you pull the head straight back so as not to split the hosel.

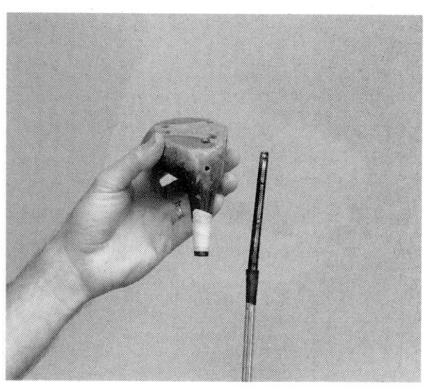

7-60 As stated before, check to see if the shaft has a bend in the tip end. This indicates a face angle change has been made either intentionally or unintentionally. Instructions for altering the face angle once the new shaft is installed are found in Chapter 12. **TIP: A bent shaft tip can be easily detected by rolling the shaft on a flat surface.**

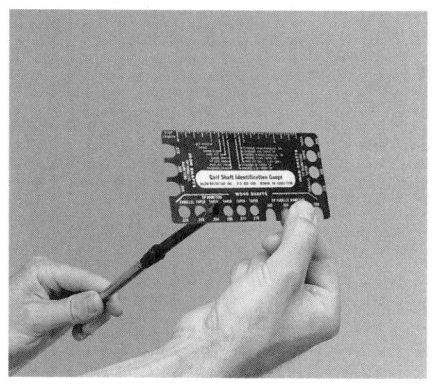

7-61 Use the **Golf Shaft Identification Gauge, micrometer or vernier caliper** to determine the size of the removed shaft tip and replacement shaft tip.

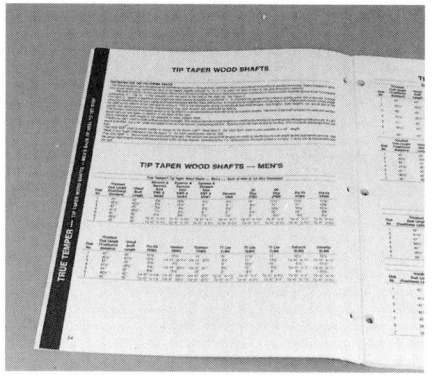

7-62 The tables in Chapter 57 give **back of heel to first step dimensions** for commercially available shafts. This measurement is vital if you want the new shaft to perform as it was designed. When this measurement is altered, the shaft will either play more flexible or more stiff.

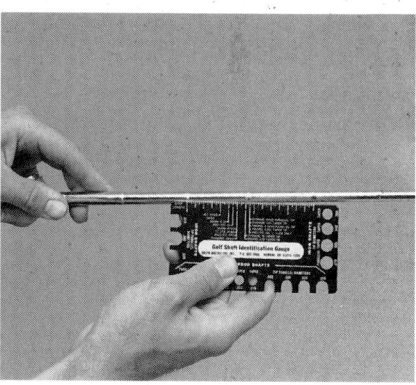

7-63 First, determine the type of shaft (Dynamic™, Pro-Fit™, TT Lite™, etc.) required. This is known either from customer input, shaft band data, use of the Golf Shaft Identification Gauge or measuring the shaft's step length, tip size, butt size, tip section length and tip parallel measurement, and matching these specifications up with those shown in Chapter 56.

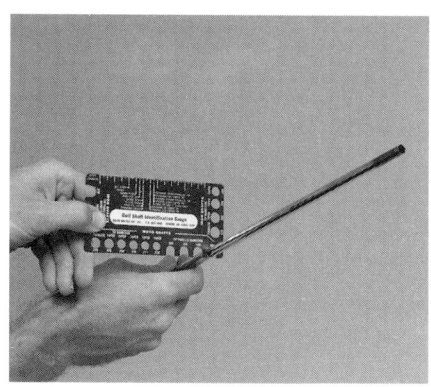

7-64 Next, you need to know if you are working with a tapered tip shaft or a parallel tip shaft. A **tapered tip shaft** is a shaft with a tip section that changes in diameter. First, take a measurement just below the first step. Measurement reads .350 dia. as shown in the photo.

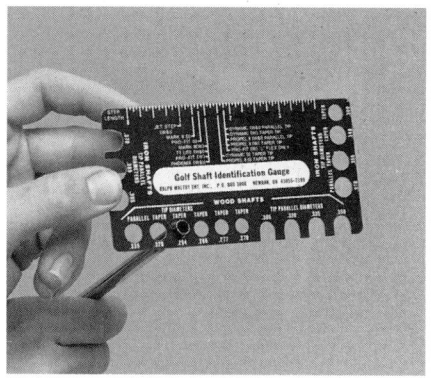

7-65 Another measurement is taken at the shaft's tip end. This measurement reads .294 dia. Therefore, this is a taper tip shaft.

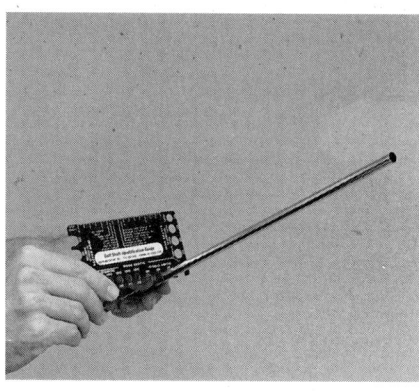

7-66 A parallel tip (unitized) shaft has a constant tip diameter from the tip to the first step. Again, a measurement is taken just below the first step. Measurement reads .335 dia. as shown in the photo.

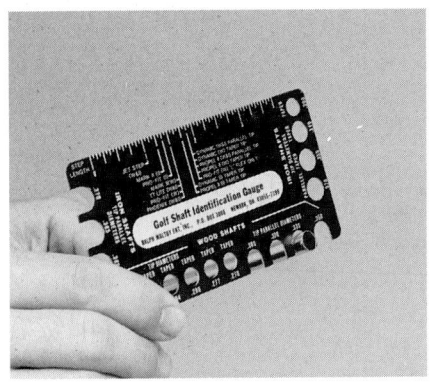

7-67 Another measurement is taken at the shaft tip. This measurement reads .335 dia. also. The tip section has a constant diameter from below the first step to its tip end, so it is a parallel tip (Unitized) shaft.

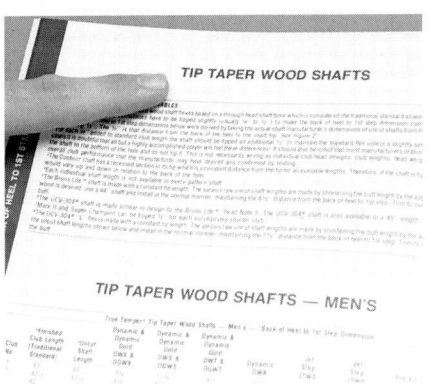

7-68 With the shaft type and tip type known, refer to the tables in Chapter 57. **The tables are divided into a tapered tip group and a parallel tip group.** Look for the grouping of tables that fits your shaft tip construction.

7-69 Then, look for the individual table that includes your type of shaft **(Dynamic™, TT Lite™, Pro Pel™, Microtaper™, etc.)**

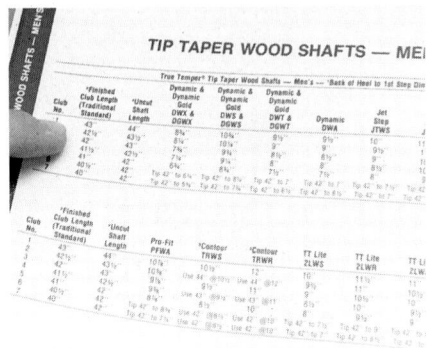

7-70 Next, look at the first column labeled **Club Number.** Look down the column until you come across the club number with which you are working (driver, 3 wood, etc.)

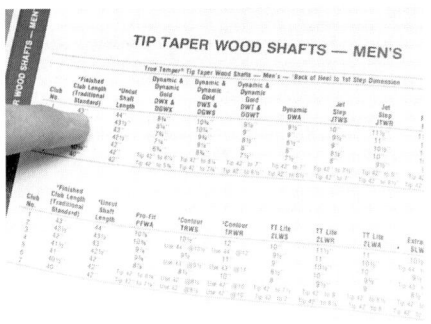

7-71 Next, look straight across the page to the next column labeled **Finished Club Length.** This reading gives you the industry standard length for your club.

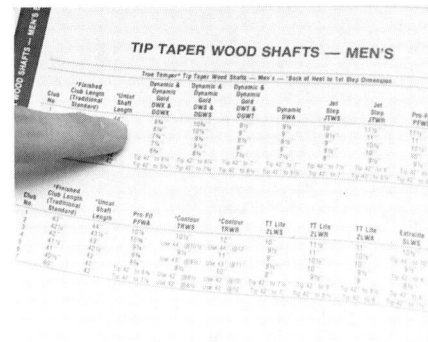

7-72 The next column labeled **Uncut Shaft Length** gives the recommended raw length shaft you need to select from your stock of shafts for this length club.

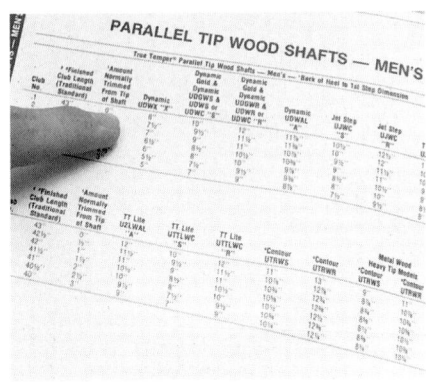

7-73 If you are working with a parallel tip shaft, you will find a column labeled **Amount Normally Trimmed From Tip Of Shaft.** Because virtually all parallel tip shafts are available in only one length, there is no reason to indicate which length shaft to choose.

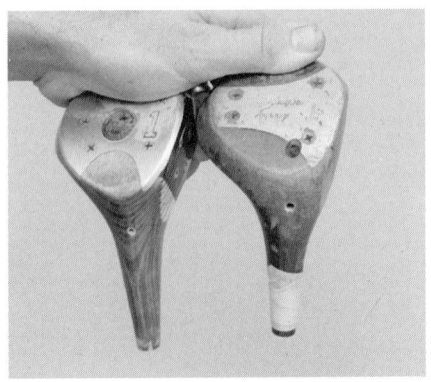

7-74 Some repairmen stop at this stage, grab the recommended shaft and install it into the head. The reason this should not be done is obvious after looking at the photo. One of the clubs is a **through-bore** and one is a **blind-bore.** If the same length shaft is installed in both clubs, without tip trimming, they will play differently.

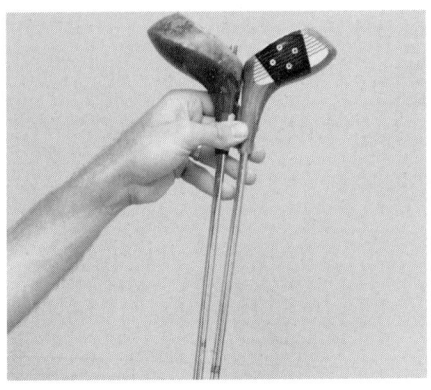

7-75 This photo shows why. The distance from the back of the heel to the first step varies enough to make the club on the left play ¼ flex stiffer than the club on the right. Therefore, the **back of heel to first step dimension** must be followed closely to ensure proper shaft performance unless you specifically wish a club to perform differently.

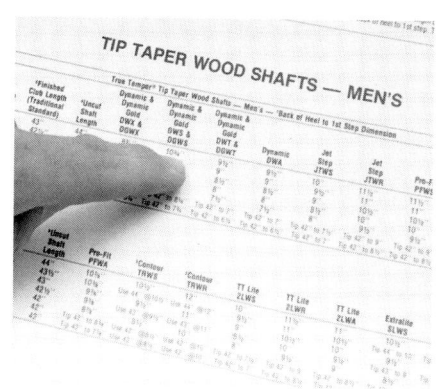

7-76 Again, look straight across the page until you reach the column heading that describes the type and flex of shaft with which you are working. This figure is the distance you need with this shaft for the **back of the heel to the first step.**

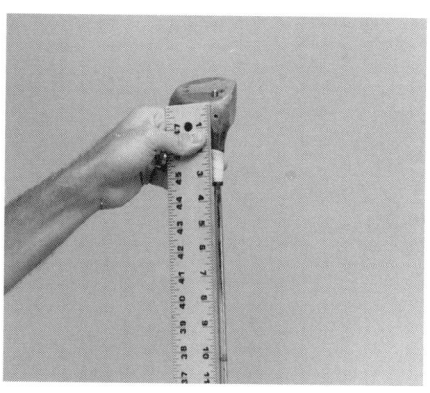

7-77 Take the recommended shaft and temporarily install it into the head and measure the **back of heel to first step distance.** (If the tip of the shaft will not penetrate to the bottom of the hosel bore, refer to photos 7-80 through 7-88 for step drilling procedure.)

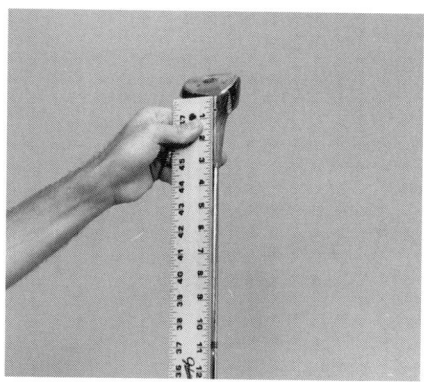

7-78 If the **back of the heel to first step distance** is longer than the recommended distance, either select a shorter shaft or cut the difference from the tip of the shaft. Note: Cutting material from a tapered tip shaft may require the hosel bore to be enlarged.

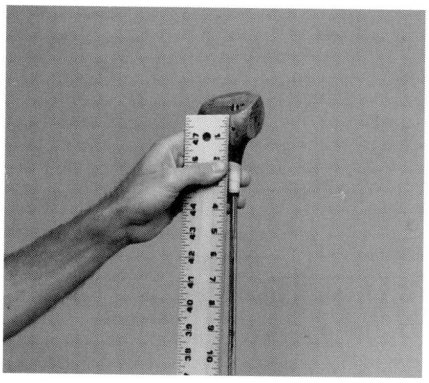

7-79 If the **back of heel to first step distance** is shorter than the recommended distance, a longer shaft is needed. This is correct because the difference in length between most shafts of the same pattern and flex is made up solely in the tip section. Hence, a longer shaft has a longer tip section.

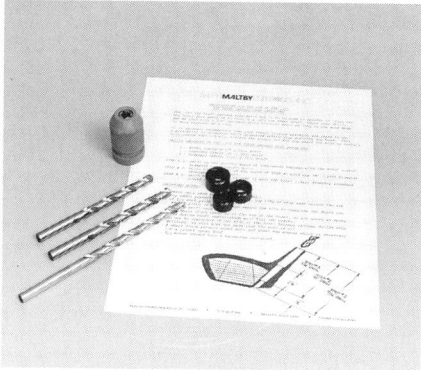

7-80 Step drilling procedure. This photo shows a set of 3 step drills used for cleaning out or enlarging a bore to accept a **taper tip shaft.** Drill bits are available to accommodate any taper tip or parallel tip shaft. Also shown are two types of drill stops which can be used instead of masking tape to control the depth more positively.

7-81 First, place the head in the vise between a set of **felt or urethane vise pads.** Wrap 6 or 7 layers of ¾" masking tape tightly around the hosel to prevent possible splitting.

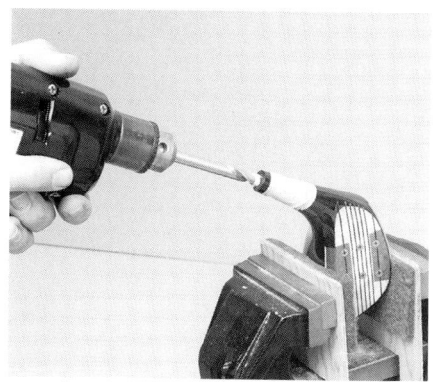

7-82 Using the smallest drill in the set, drill to the bottom of the bore or completely through as necessary. Note wrapping of the tape around the drill bit. Premeasuring the depth of the hosel bore and then placing a wrapping of tape around the bit at the same length is a good idea. Stop drilling when the tape is even with the top of the hosel.

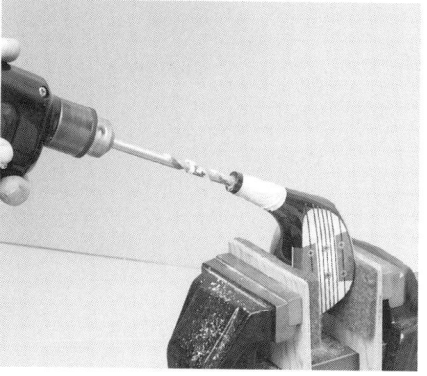

7-83 Using the next largest size drill, drill to within a specified distance from the bottom of the first drill. Follow the instructions that came with the drill set.

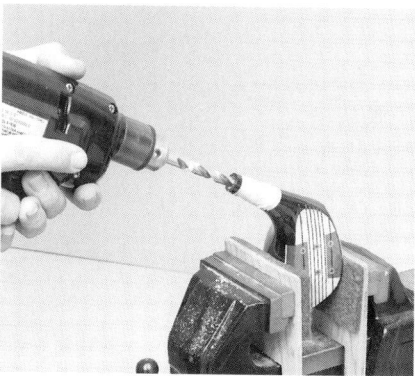

7-84 Finally, using the largest size drill, drill to within a specified distance from the depth of the 2nd drill.

123

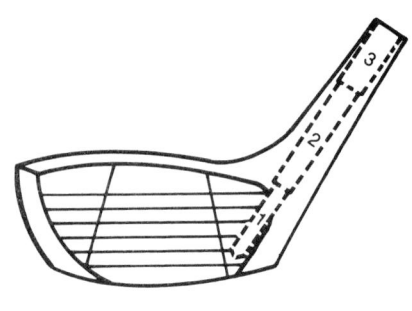

7-85 The inside of the drilled hosel will look like this, hence the term **"step drilling."** A blind-bore head is shown, but the step drills also work as well on through-bore types.

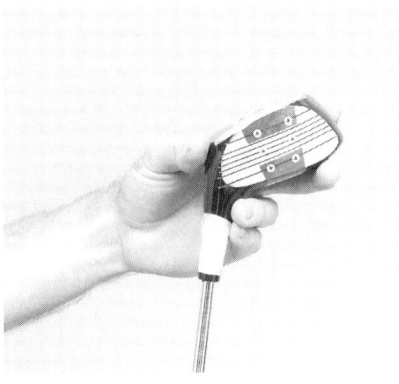

7-86 Test the shaft for proper fit. A properly fit shaft is one that is not tight or binding but snug enough so that it has no sideways movement or slope.

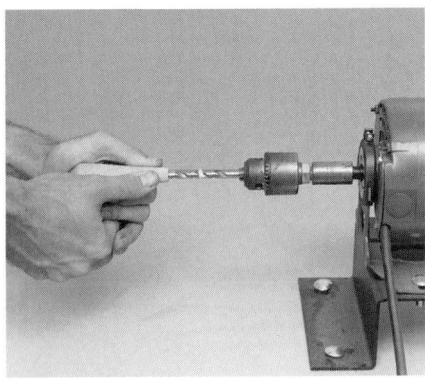

7-87 This is how we clean out bores using step drills and reamers in our repair department. The bench motor shown with the drill chuck attached by means of a "Motor Arbor."

7-88 A **tapered reamer drill** is also available to enlarge the existing hosel bore sizes. Reamers are very expensive and are commonly used for boring blank wood heads when making custom woods.

7-89 Shaft installation. Once the proper shaft is chosen and any needed modifications have been made, abrade the tip of the shaft with the use of a belt sander, grinding stone, emery cloth or file. Abrading the shaft tip gives the epoxy a better bonding surface.

7-90 Choose an appropriate ferrule. Ferrules are labeled according to the shaft tip size they match. Both a standard ferrule and a "shanked" ferrule are available. It is not necessary to file the top of the shanked ferrule, thus saving some time in finishing the job later on.

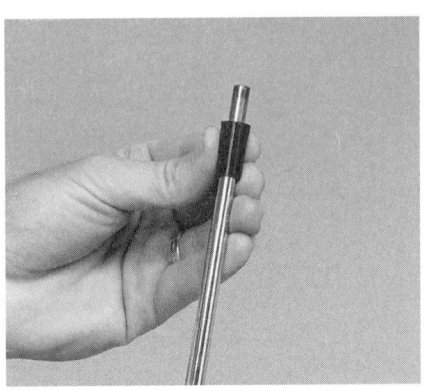

7-91 If the ferrule will not slide far enough up the shaft tip, refer to Chapter 21, photos 21-117 through 21-127 for ways to do this.

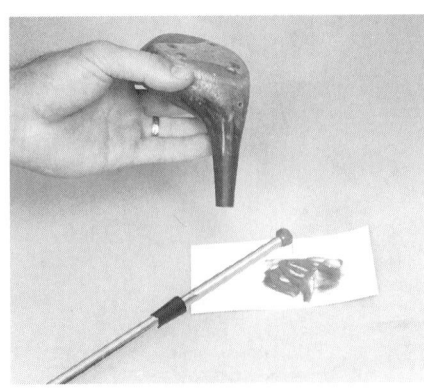

7-92 After mixing a shear strength epoxy, dip the tip of the shaft into the epoxy and then insert the shaft into the hosel. Note the use of a colored paste dispersion mixed in with the epoxy. This will help camouflage any epoxy line.

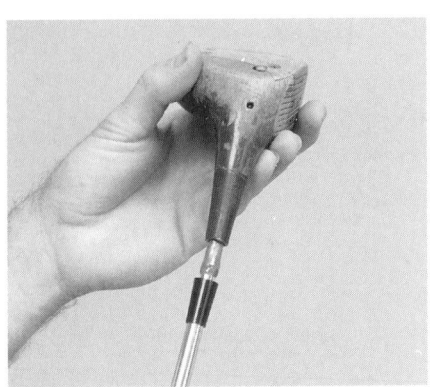

7-93 For best results, simultaneously turn and push the shaft into the hosel. This method will coat both the outside of the shaft and the inside of the hosel walls.

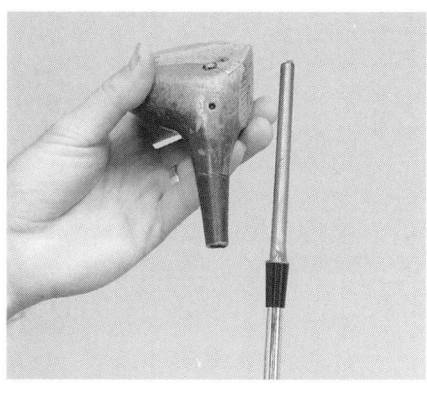

7-94 Withdraw the shaft from the hosel to ensure the tip is adequately covered with epoxy and then reinstall the shaft.

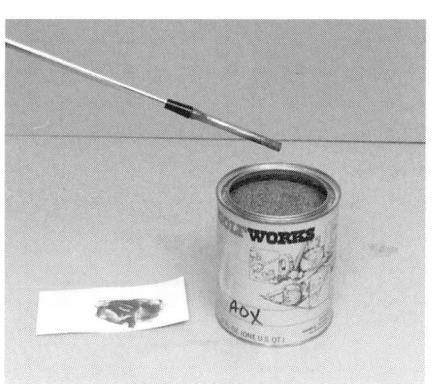

7-95 If the shaft is very loose, remove the shaft from the hosel and dip the tip of the shaft into **Aluminum Oxide Sand.**

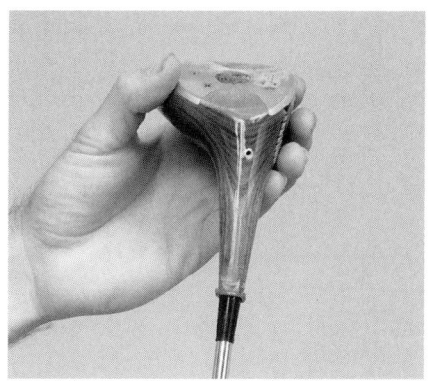

7-96 Reinstall the shaft into the hosel. The sand will take up the excess space and provide an excellent bonding surface for the epoxy.

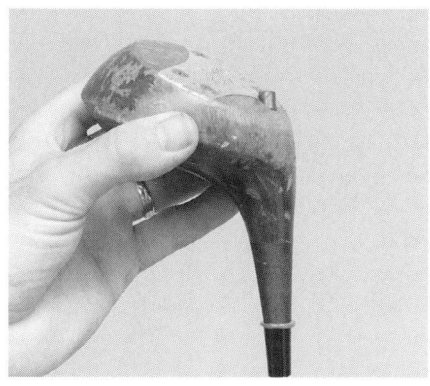

7-97 In the case of a through-bore wood, push the shaft through the sole of the wood until the entire tip of the shaft is just protruding from the sole.

7-98 Place a tapered wood plug in the shaft opening and …

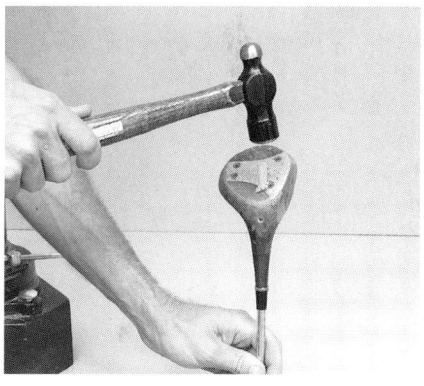

7-99 … drive the plug down into the shaft until the plug "mushrooms" against the sole. This indicates the plug has been driven far enough into the shaft tip.

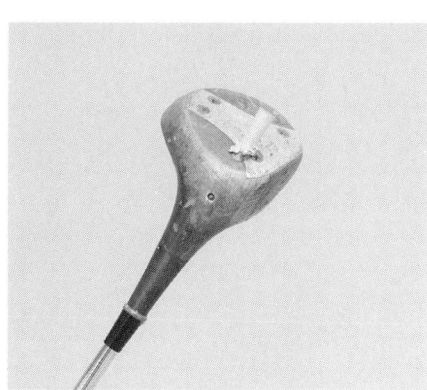

7-100 Allow the epoxy to cure before proceeding to the next step.

7-101 To remove the excess wood plug, tap lightly until the plug breaks from the shaft tip or cut the excess with a hacksaw.

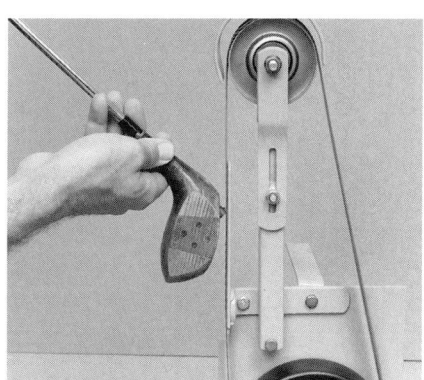

7-102 The remaining portion of the shaft tip protruding from the sole must now be removed. One way is by carefully pressing the tip against the face of a coarse or medium grit belt on a **belt sander.**

7-103 Carefully filing with a medium grade file is another way to remove the protruding shaft tip.

7-104 After the majority of the shaft tip is removed, switch to a fine cut mill file to take the shaft tip down perfectly flush with the sole.

7-105 This photo shows a properly filed shaft. Note the tapered wood plug has completely filled the inside of the shaft.

7-106 Determine the color of the head and select a color matching stain. Blot the surface of the bare wood with a towel that has been dampened with the stain.

7-107 The stained wood plug should now match the surrounding wood color.

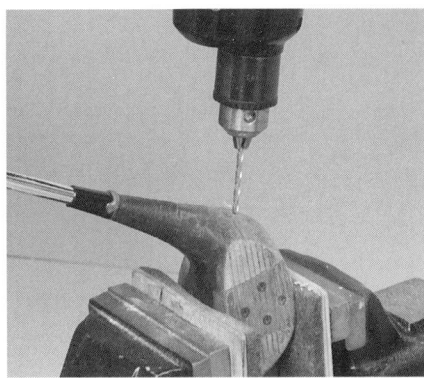

7-108 Installing a backscrew. Using a ⅛" drill bit, (cobalt bits work best), drill into the backscrew hole cleaning out the excess epoxy. Do not attempt to drill through the shaft. Instead …

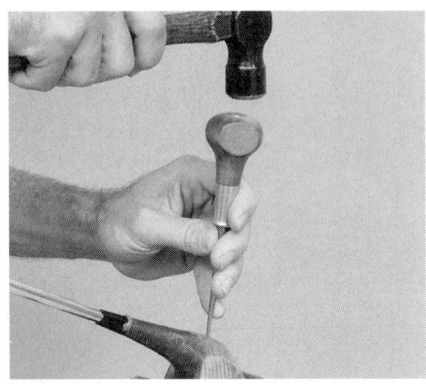

7-109 … insert a sharpened awl into the hole and drive the tip of the awl through the top of the shaft. Remove the awl and …

7-110 … reinstall the ⅛" bit and drill a clear passage through the top of the shaft. Do not attempt to drill through the bottom of the shaft. Instead …

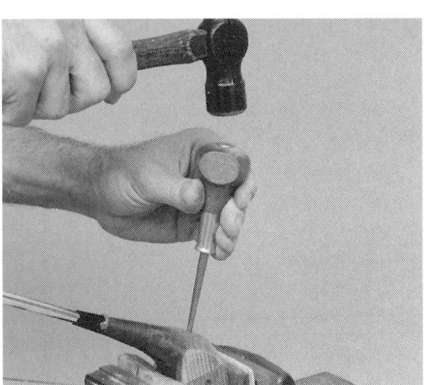

7-111 … insert the awl and drive it through the bottom of the shaft.

126

7-112 Insert the ⅛" bit into the hole and drill a clear passage through the shaft into the wood below the shaft. The proper depth of the hole is dependent upon the length of the backscrew (drill the hole ⅛" deeper if you want the backscrew to be seated below the surface of the hosel after backscrew installation).

7-113 If the bit encounters an old backscrew under the shaft – have patience! The bit will seek the softer material around the backscrew and eventually will veer off to the side of the old backscrew creating a clear hole for the new backscrew.

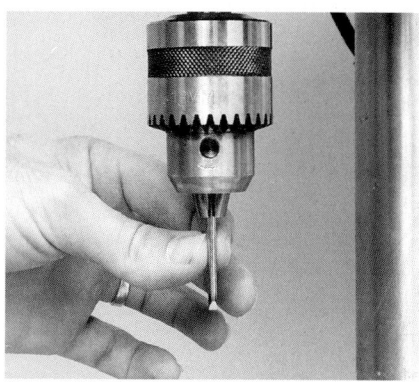

7-114 A last alternative to the punch and drill method is the use of a drill blank and a drill press. Install a ⅛" **drill blank** into the chuck. Note: The drill blank tip is ground the same as a flat screwdriver tip.

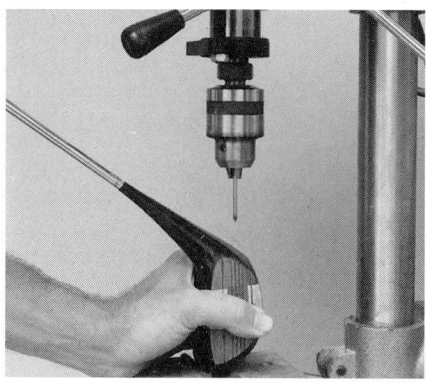

7-115 Place the toe of the club underneath the blank. Note the use of a padded block of wood to protect the finish on the toe.

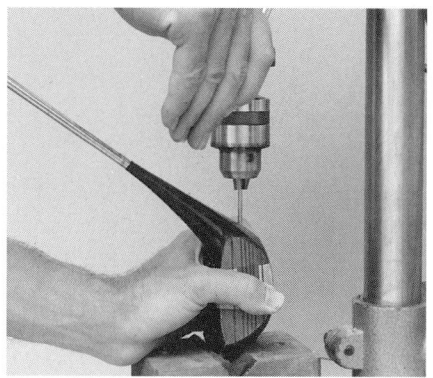

7-116 Move the drill blank into the backscrew hole and through the shaft. You will be amazed at how fast and easy this is.

7-117 Next, select either a standard backscrew with a standard size head or, a headless backscrew. Should you ever have to remove this backscrew, the headless are much easier to remove (yes, headless) and are therefore the preferred choice.

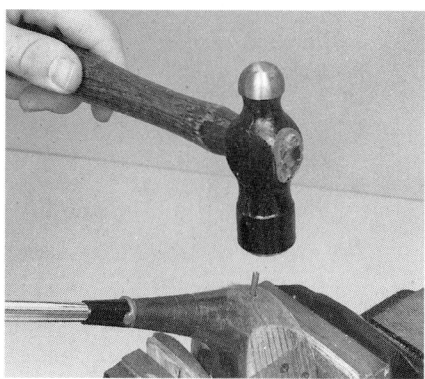

7-118 Place the backscrew into the hole and lightly tap the head of the backscrew until it is flush with the surface of the hosel.

7-119 Some repairmen like to leave the head exposed on the back of the hosel.

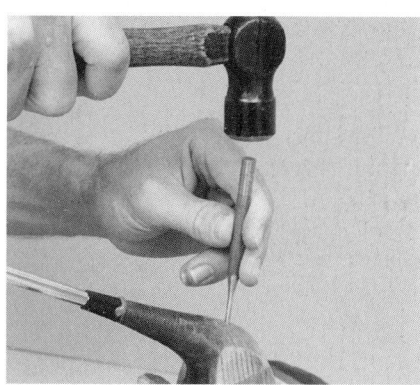

7-120 If you want the backscrew below the surface of the hosel, as is usually the case, drive it ⅛" below the surface using a ⅛" pin punch and a hammer.

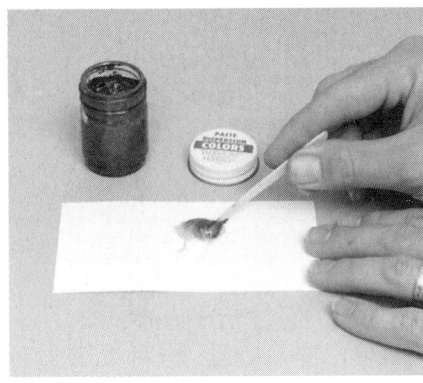

7-121 Mix a quick setting epoxy and as an added touch, mix in a paste dispersion that will color the epoxy to match the color of the wood.

7-122 Fill the backscrew hole with the epoxy. A toothpick or tongue depressor works well for this.

7-123 After the epoxy hardens, remove the excess using either a file or …

7-124 … a sharp razor blade.

7-125 The filled backscrew hole should now look like this.

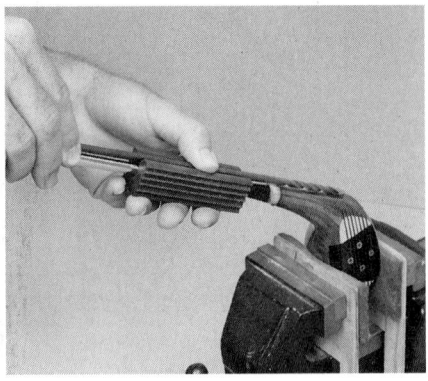

7-126 To install a backscrew in a wood head that did not have one before, use one of the following two methods. **First method:** Place a **Rubber Shaft Clamp** around the shaft above the ferrule and place a 12" x 7/32" drill bit in the Clamp so it is parallel with the shaft.

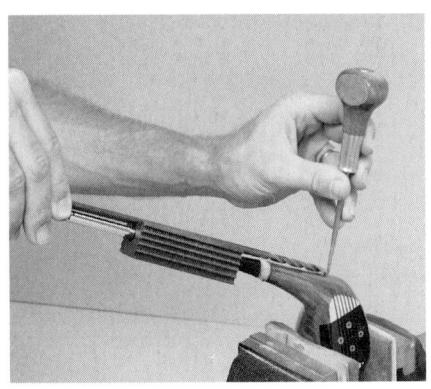

7-127 If the bit is running parallel with the shaft, it will show you exactly where the center of the shaft is in relation to the bottom of the hosel bore. Make a slight indentation into the finish with a sharpened awl or scriber 3/4" above the back of the heel.

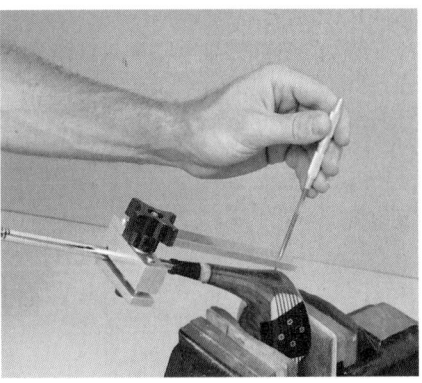

7-128 Second method: The Backscrew Locator Tool works under the same principle as the previous method but is easier and faster to use.

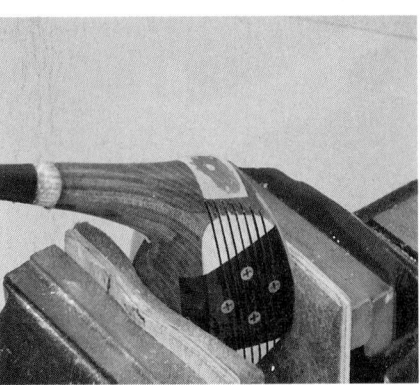

7-129 Next, after making the indentation in the finish, place a layer of cellophane tape across the mark.

7-130 Using a ⅛" drill bit, drill through the tape into the wood. The drill bit should be angled slightly toward the sole of the club to ensure the bit does not drill through the top of the head. The tape will prevent the finish from tearing as the bit passes through.

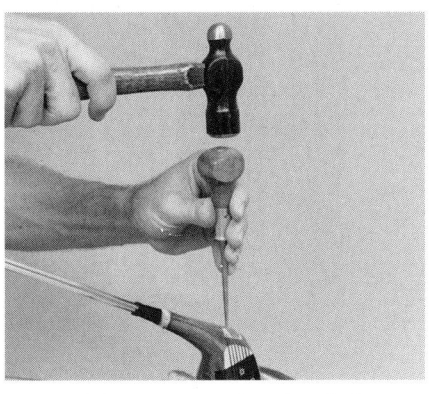

7-131 After encountering the shaft, stop drilling and use the alternating punch and drill method as shown in photos 7-108 through 7-116 for drilling the hole for the backscrew.

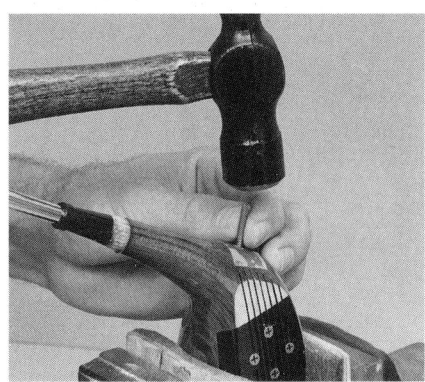

7-132 Refer to photos 7-117 through 7-125 for installation of the backscrew and camouflaging the backscrew hole.

7-133 Tapering the hosel and the ferrule. Place the shaft between a rubber shaft clamp and fasten it in a vise as shown. Wrap tape around the shaft above the ferrule.

7-134 Remove the excess plastic epoxy using a medium grade file. Be careful not to file through the tape and scratch the chromed shaft.

7-135 After rough shaping with the medium file, final shape the hosel area with a fine file. Create a taper from the top of the ferrule into the hosel.

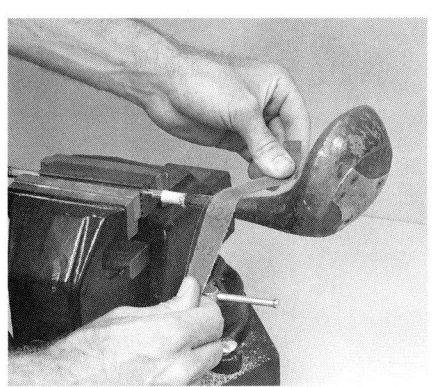

7-136 After filing, lightly sand the hosel to remove any ridges or flat spots in the hosel. Note: Do not sand below a point where the whipping will not cover.

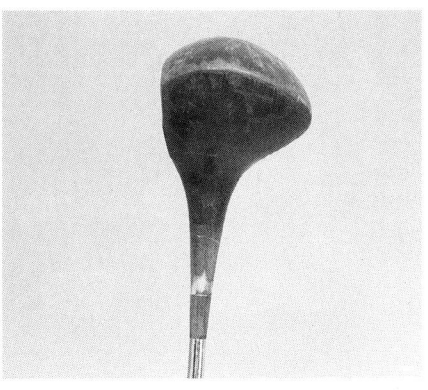

7-137 Look carefully at the hosel to see if a proper taper exists from the top of the ferrule into the base of the hosel. If there are any irregularities, file or sand as necessary to create a proper blended taper.

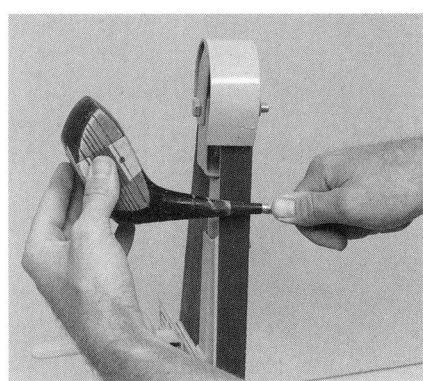

7-138 A fast alternative to the filing and sanding method is to use a belt sander. Using a medium grade belt, slowly rotate the club while pressing the hosel against the face of the sandpaper. Continue to sand until the proper taper is achieved.

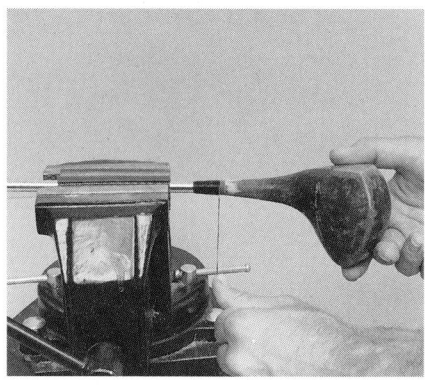

7-139 Apply new whipping as shown in Chapter 6.

7-140 To measure for correct length, sole the club on the ground as shown. Slide a **48" ruler** behind the shaft and ...

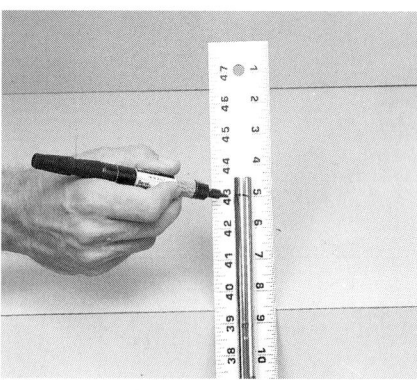

7-141 ... make a mark on the shaft ⅛" below the desired final length. Note: The grip cap will make up the ⅛" difference.

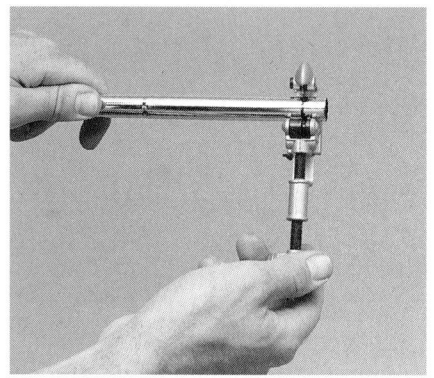

7-142 Cut the shaft using a Tubing Cutter or ...

7-143 ... **a friction wheel.** See Chapter 21, photos 21-172 through 21-176 for correct cutting procedure.

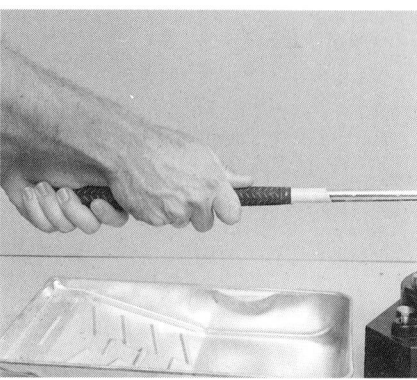

7-144 Install the proper grip following the steps outlined in Chapter 23.

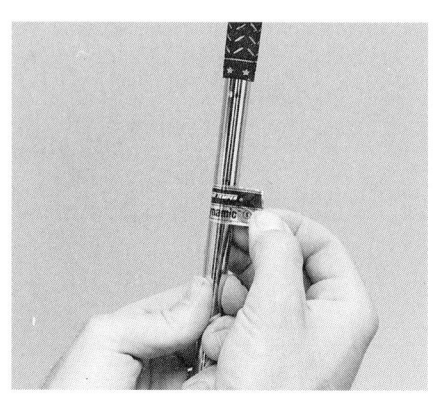

7-145 Apply the shaft band.

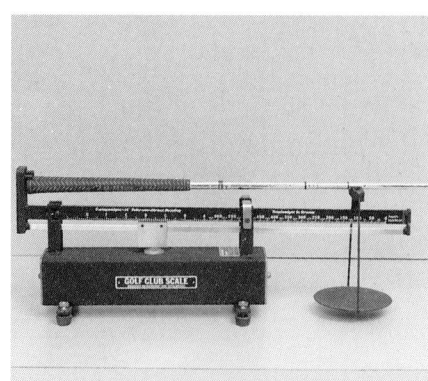

7-146 Check the swingweight. If it needs to be changed, refer to Chapter 14 for procedures.

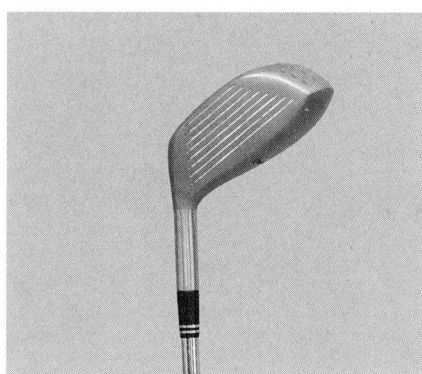

7-147 Reshafting metal wood heads having steel, aluminum or titanium shafts. First, determine if a rivet has been installed through the hosel and the shaft (very rare). If there is a rivet, drive it through the hosel using the same procedures as shown in Chapter 21, photos 21-6 through 21-9.

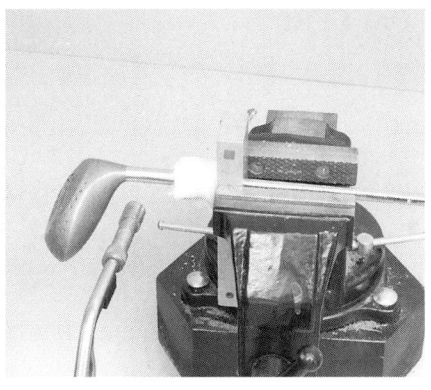

7-148 Check to see if a coating of paint and/or polyurethane is covering the hosel. If no coating is covering the hosel, heat the hosel area using a propane torch. Note the use of a wet paper towel wrapped around the ferrule. This will protect the ferrule from melting should you wish to save it. Note: An **Electric Heat Gun** can also be used.

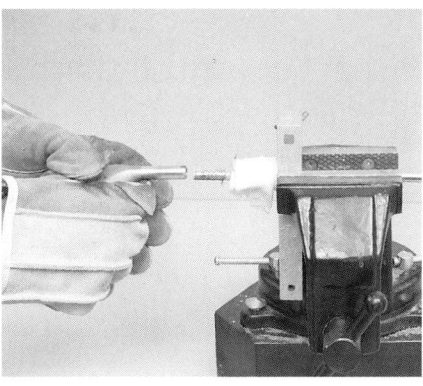

7-149 After 10-15 seconds of heating, grasp the head with your gloved hands and attempt to turn the head from the shaft. Apply more heat if the head will not turn.

7-150 If the hosel is covered with paint and/or polyurethane, use the **Heating Rod** and propane torch as shown in photos 7-46 through 7-51. After heating, remove the head.

7-151 Once the head is removed, select the appropriate shaft. Refer to photos 7-61 through 7-79 for determining the proper back of heel to first step dimensions before permanently installing a steel shaft. Any parallel tip steel shaft is suitable since golf shaft manufacturers have designed thicker walls in the tip section specifically for metal woods. If given the option, choose special tip reinforced shafts for metal woods.

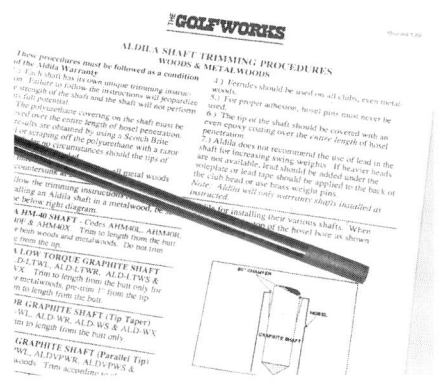

7-152 The diameters of most titanium and composite shafts are not reduced along the shaft using step downs, therefore, there are no back of heel to first step dimensions to ensure proper shaft flexibility. Instead, most of these shafts have their own specific trimming instructions which should always be included with your shaft order. If the instructions recommend trimming from the tip, proceed with this step now.

7-153 All metal woods that will be shafted with a composite shaft should have the inside hosel edge modified by countersinking with an 18° or 20° countersink. The gap between the modified hosel edge and the shaft will be filled with epoxy which will help reduce the stress placed upon the shaft.

7-154 This is an 18° carbide coated steel countersink installed in a normal drill. It is very durable which makes it a good choice for the high volume user. An 18° carbon steel countersink, which is less expensive, would be good for a low volume shop.

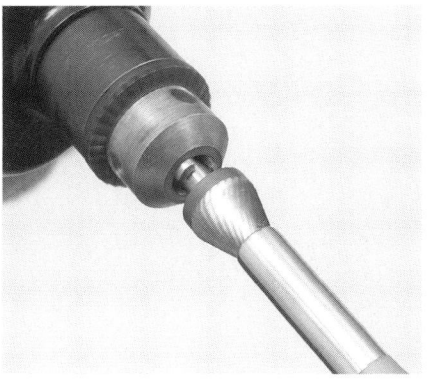

7-155 To use, simply insert the countersink into the hosel and activate the drill until a bevel is created.

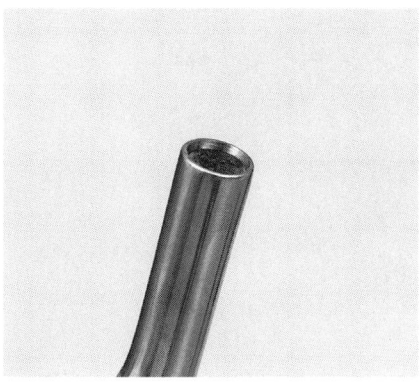

7-156 This photo shows the inside hosel edge after countersinking. The entire job takes only a couple of seconds.

7-157 Whichever shaft you use, temporarily install it into the hosel to check the fit. When temporarily installing the shaft, also check to make sure the shaft penetrates to the bottom of the hosel bore. On metal woods this is usually 1¼". This is very important.

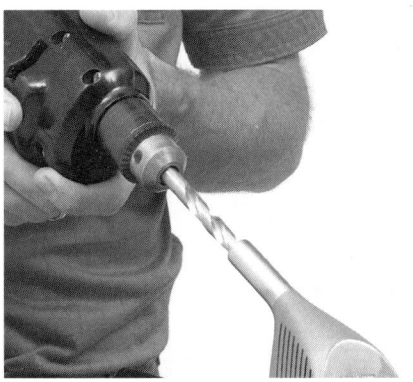

7-158 The most effective method for cleaning a hosel bore is to tighten the metal wood in a vise using a pair of vise pads. Select a letter "R" drill bit and drill into the hosel bore using an electric drill. Note: Most metal woods will have a thin metal "shoulder" in the hosel approximately 1½" from the top of the hosel. Do not drill through this shoulder. For hosel-less metal woods, the shaft will go to the sole, or all the way through.

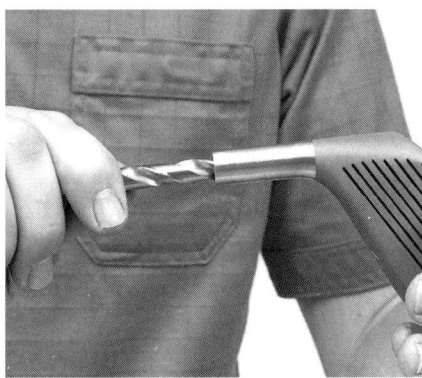

7-159 An alternative to the electric drill method is to hand turn the "R" drill into the hosel. This is slower, but you will be better able to feel the drill turning against the metal shoulder. This shoulder ensures that the tip of the shaft is set a consistent distance from the top of the hosel on every club. Do not drill through this shoulder.

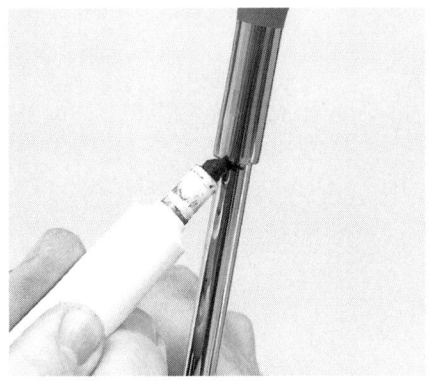

7-160 Abrading the Shaft Tip. Once any corrections have been made to the shaft tip, it must be abraded to provide the epoxy with a good bonding surface. To determine how much of the shaft tip should be abraded, insert it into the hosel, then mark the shaft with a felt tip pen even with the top of the hosel.

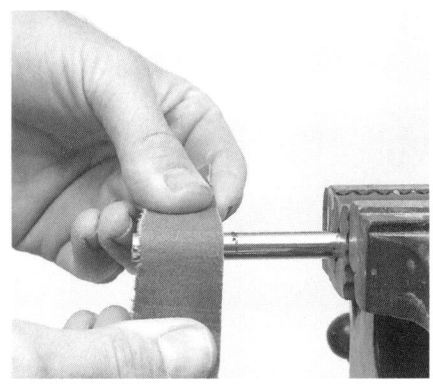

7-161 Remove the shaft from the hosel and abrade the steel or titanium shaft to within ⅛" of the mark. If the metal wood you are using requires a ferrule, abrade the shaft another ½" above the mark. Place the shaft in a **Rubber Shaft Clamp** and tighten it in your vise. Lightly sand the shaft using coarse sandpaper or emery cloth. Refer to photo 7-165 for instructions on treating a composite shaft tip.

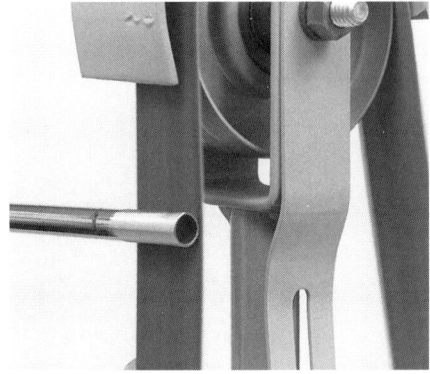

7-162 A fast alternative to hand sanding the shaft is to use a **1" x 42" or 2" x 48" Belt Sander.** Lightly place the tip of the shaft against the turning belt and rotate the shaft rapidly.

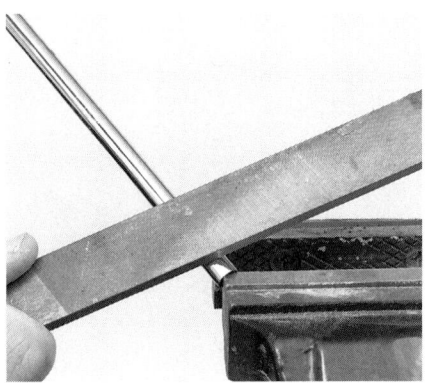

7-163 A fine file or grinding stone can also be used to abrade the titanium or steel shaft tip.

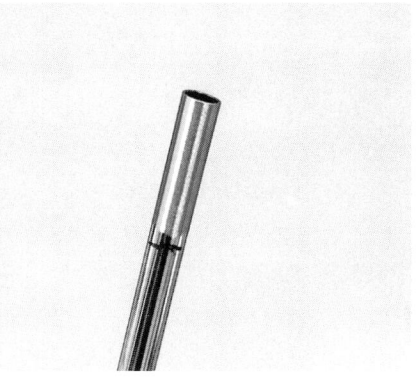

7-164 The tip of the shaft should look like this. The tip of composite shafts should not be abraded with a belt sander, file, etc. The polyurethane covering that portion of the shaft tip that will be installed into the hosel should be removed for good adhesion, however, the removal of more than the polyurethane coating will damage the shaft fibers.

7-165   A Scotch-Brite™ Wheel does an effective job of removing the polyurethane without damaging the fibers. (See Chapter 58 for information on manufacturing graphite shafts.)

7-166 Rotate the shaft against the turning wheel until the polyurethane coating is removed. Do not pause while rotating the shaft because of the risk of cutting the fibers. Do not press too firmly. Light pressure works best. Machine set-up shows a ⅓ HP motor that turns at 1725 RPM.

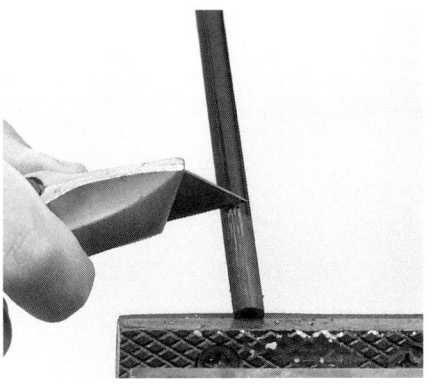

7-167 A razor blade also works well, but is slower. Hold the razor blade perpendicular to the shaft and scrape back and forth while rotating the shaft.

7-168 If you are working with a metal wood that had a ferrule, select the appropriate style ferrule.

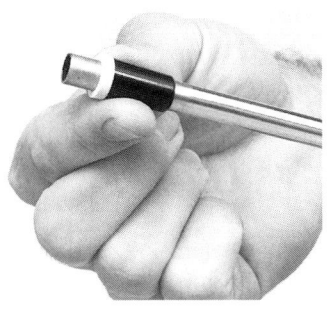

7-169 Slide the ferrule onto the shaft. The ferrule should be set far enough up the shaft tip to allow the shaft to penetrate to the bottom of the hosel bore. If the ferrule will not slide far enough up the shaft tip, refer to Chapter 21, photos 21-117 through 21-127 for ways to do this.

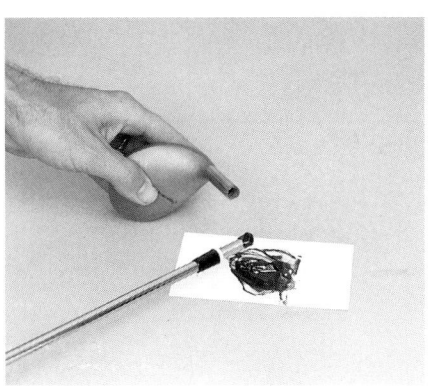

7-170 Mix the shear strength epoxy and dip the tip of the shaft into the epoxy.

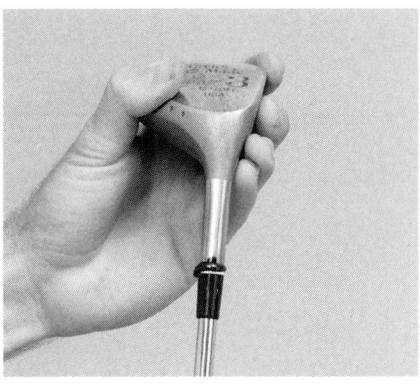

7-171 Insert the tip of the shaft into the metal wood hosel. Push the shaft to the bottom of the hosel bore while simultaneously rotating the shaft. This will help coat both the hosel bore and the shaft tip. Make sure the shaft tip penetrated to the bottom of the hosel bore. If not, shaft breakage can occur.

7-172 Remove the shaft from the hosel and check to make sure the shaft is well covered. If not, apply more epoxy. This photo shows adequate epoxy coverage. Note: If the shaft already has a shaft band, make sure the shaft is turned so that the band's identifying markings are facing toward the front before permanently setting the shaft.

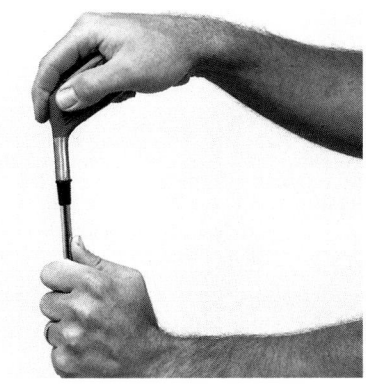

7-173 Reinstall the shaft into the hosel. Place one hand on the head and the other on the shaft and hit the shaft butt against a concrete floor or steel plate. This will: (1) position the tip of the shaft to the bottom of the hosel bore, and (2) drive the ferrule (if installed) to the proper position on the shaft.

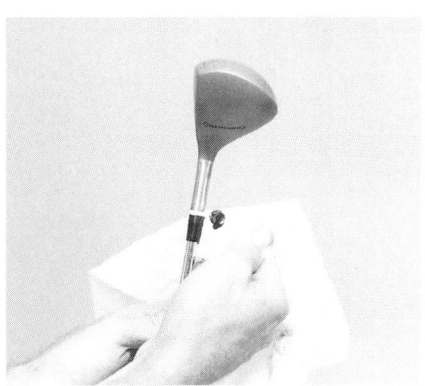

7-174 Wipe the excess epoxy from the hosel and ferrule, if one was installed. Allow the epoxy to cure before proceeding.

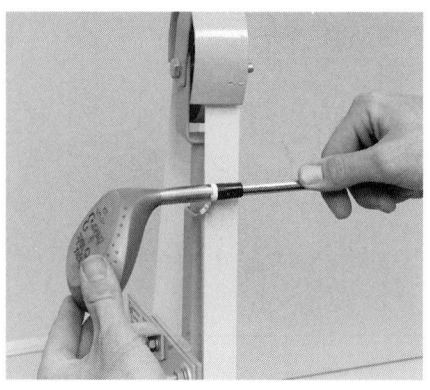

7-175 After the epoxy hardens, follow the steps shown in Chapter 21, photos 21-134 through 21-149 for reducing the size of the ferrule. If a rivet must be installed, refer to Chapter 21, photos 21-150 through 21-167.

7-176 If whipping is to be applied to the hosel, refer to photos 7-133 through 7-138 for proper tapering of the ferrule prior to application of the whipping. Note: It will not be necessary to file the metal hosel, only the ferrule is filed and sanded.

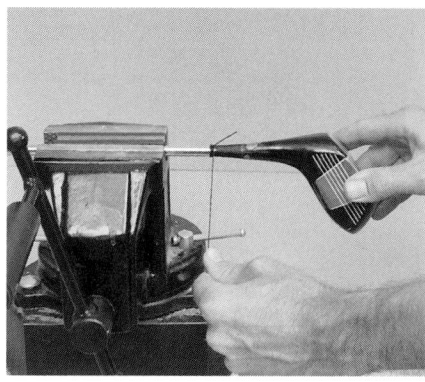

7-177 Apply whipping as shown in Chapter 6.

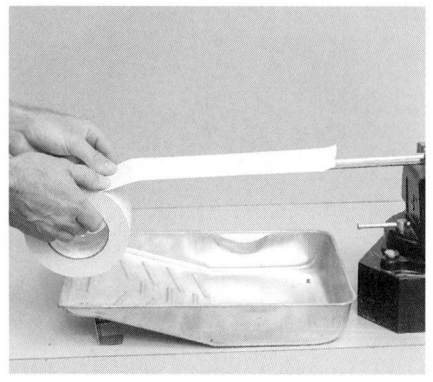

7-178 Cut the shaft butt end to proper length following the procedures shown in photos 7-140 through 7-143. **Install the grip as shown in Chapter 23.**

7-179 Removing a graphite shaft from a metal, laminated maple or persimmon wood head. The easiest and most consistent method to remove graphite shafts is with the use of **The GolfWorks® Graphite Shaft Extractor** as shown above. The Graphite Shaft Extractor should be placed in a vise for use. Note that the Extractor works great on short hosel, through-bore metal woods like the Callaway Big Bertha.

7-180 When using the Graphite Shaft Extractor, first, remove the whipping by using a sharp knife or razor blade. When cutting through whipping, always cut away from the clubhead. This eliminates the chance of ruining the finish should you slip. In the case of a metal wood, remove the ferrule as outlined in the next photo.

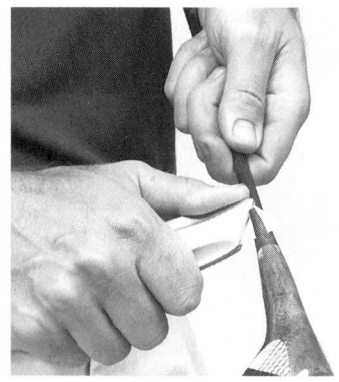

7-181 Remove the ferrule by carefully cutting with a detail knife or use a chisel. Note: Be very careful as the graphite shaft can damage easily.

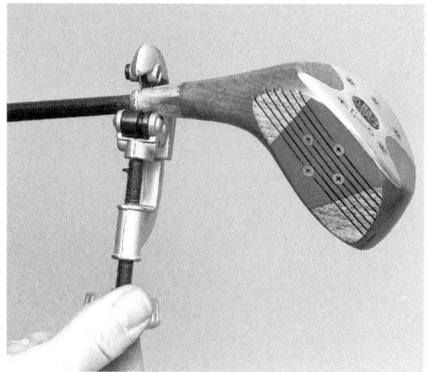

7-182 When working with **wood heads** the first ½" of the hosel must be cut off. The cut edge will serve as a "shoulder" for the extractor to push against in order to force the head off the shaft. A **Tubing Cutter** works well to create a straight shoulder. Note this step is not necessary for a metal wood head.

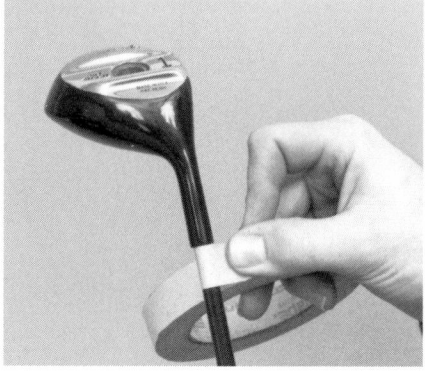

7-183 Wrap ¾" masking tape once around the shaft just above the hosel.

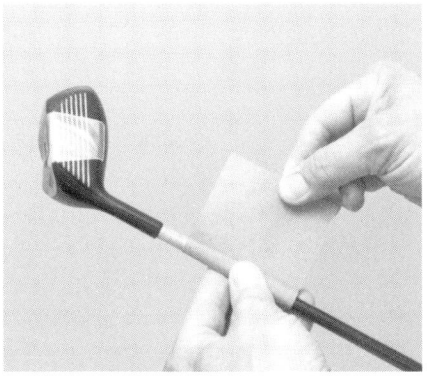

7-184 Next, wrap the 3" x 4" brown piece of paper around the shaft above the tape wrapping.

7-185 Place an adjustable hose clamp around the top of the hosel on a wood head and tighten until snug. The hose clamp will prevent the wood from "mushrooming" when the shaft is removed. Note: The hose clamp is not necessary on a metal wood head.

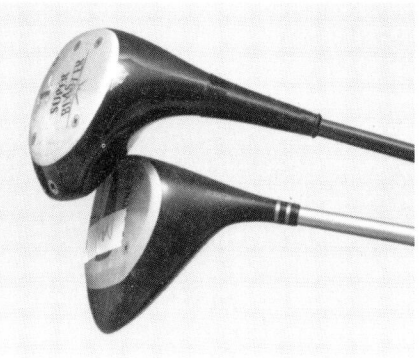

7-186 A graphite shaft can be removed from a graphite head using the same procedure as shown here if the graphite hosel is fairly large or wide like the GolfWorks® SuperBlaster. If working with a graphite head having a narrower hosel, typical of a Yonex A.D.X., then the shaft should be drilled from the head as shown in photos 7-199 and 7-201.

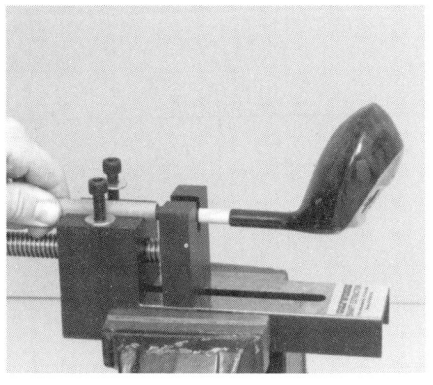

7-187 Place the shaft in the **Graphite Shaft Extractor** with the head up as shown above. Allow ½" of the shaft to extend in front of the unit.

7-188 Place the top clamp piece under the two allen screws. Tighten the screws evenly with the provided Hex Key until snug. Do not overtighten, as damage to the shaft can occur.

7-189 Place the Steel Collar, included with the **Graphite Shaft Extractor**, over the shaft.

7-190 Tighten the large hex head bolt with the provided ratchet wrench. Tighten until snug.

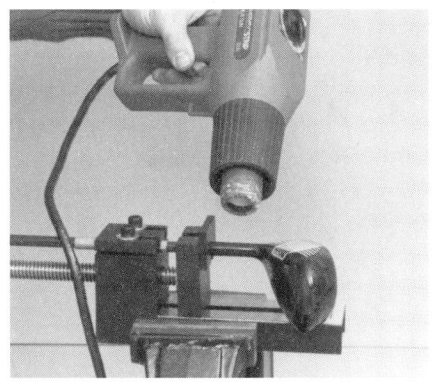

7-191 Heat the hosel area using an **Electric Heat Gun** or some other commercially available heating gun (if using The GolfWork's® Heat Gun, the correct temperature setting is between the 230 and 450 settings with the fan set on high). **Keep the Heat Gun moving at all times so as not to damage the finish.** Move the Heat Gun back and …

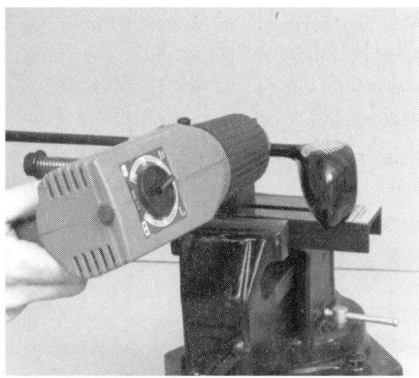

7-192 … forth as well as around the entire hosel. When heating wood hosels, concentrate more of the heat at the bottom of the hosel. Five to eight minutes is the correct heating time for wood heads and three minutes for a metal wood head. Maintain the constantly moving Heat Gun at least 4" to 5" away from the head at all times.

7-193 After heating the recommended period, turn the ratchet wrench a half turn. If you feel the head release from the shaft continue to turn until the head is removed. If the head does not release, reheat the hosel for a short period and try again. Continue this until the head is removed. Do not twist the head to remove as this will cause damage to the graphite fibers in the shaft.

7-194 Removing a graphite shaft from a metal, laminated maple or persimmon wood head when a Graphite Shaft Extractor is not available. Note: The success rate using this method is about 70% and in most cases the club will need to be refinished after this procedure. First, place the graphite shaft in a rubber shaft clamp and fasten the clamp in a vise.

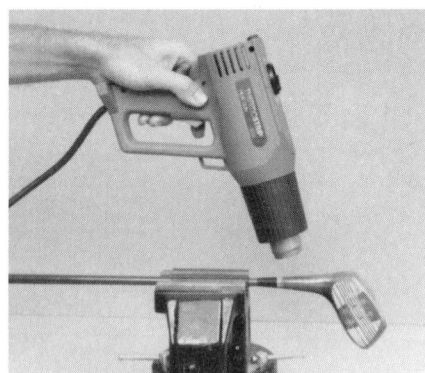

7-195 Using an **Electric Heat Gun**, apply heat to the back of the hosel working from the top to the ...

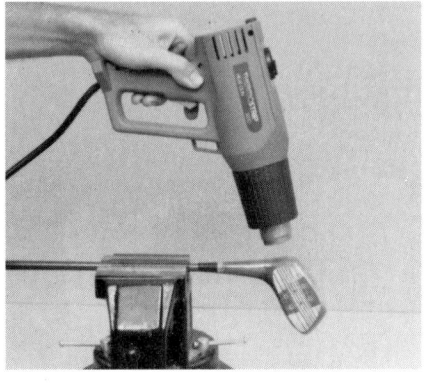

7-196 ... bottom of the hosel (heel portion of the head). Keep the Heat Gun moving. More time should be spent with the gun directed at the bottom of the hosel. The wood is much thicker in this section of the hosel and it will take more heat to penetrate the wood to soften the epoxy.

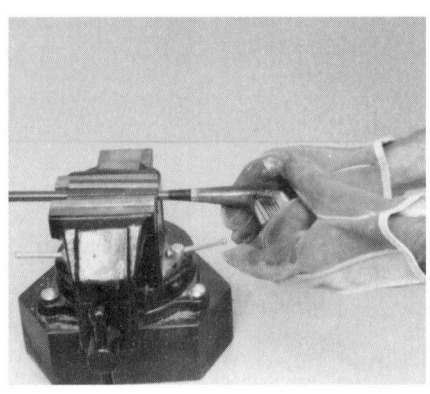

7-197 After moving the gun back and forth for two minutes, grasp the head with a gloved hand and carefully try to turn the head. Continue this action, with the gun pointed at the hosel, until the head ...

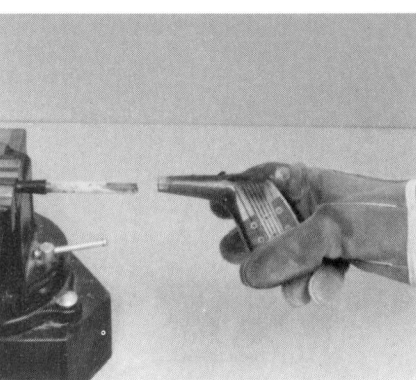

7-198 ... turns around the shaft and can be pulled off. The real challenge with this type of reshaft is to soften the epoxy holding the shaft in place before the epoxy holding the graphite fibers together is destroyed.

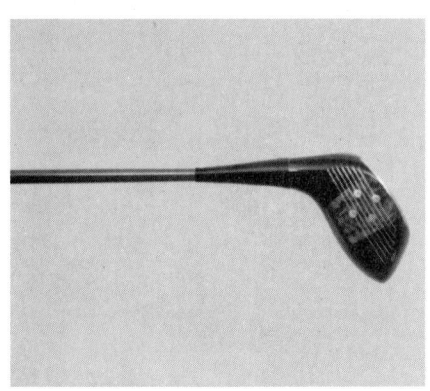

7-199 Removing a graphite shaft from a graphite head when a GolfWorks® Graphite Shaft Extractor is not available or if working with a narrow hoseled graphite head. Decide which of the components, head or shaft, you wish to save since the heat required to soften the epoxy holding the shaft in the head will also destroy either the head or the shaft.

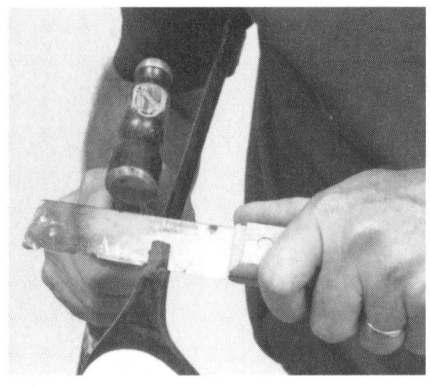

7-200 If the shaft is to be saved, carefully cut or saw the head from the shaft.

7-201 If the head is to be saved, cut the shaft even with the top of the hosel and then drill the remaining portion of the shaft from the hosel. Begin with a small drill bit and then increase the size until the hosel bore is large enough to accept the new shaft. The head is then ready for shafting using normal steps.

136

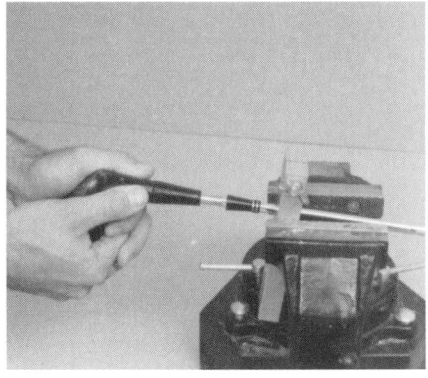

7-202 For a head with a plastic whipping cover, steps for the removal of the head are the same as demonstrated in photos 7-15 through 7-51. The plastic whipping cover will remain on the head when the head is pulled from the shaft.

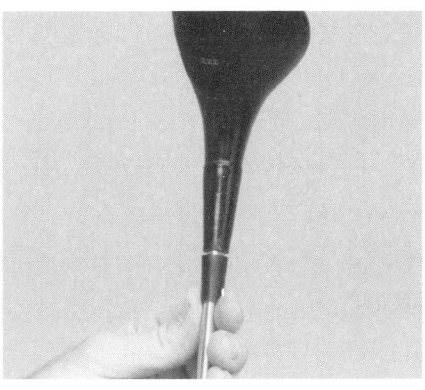

7-203 When installing the head onto the shaft, select the ferrule that is larger than the top of the whipping cover. Wipe the excess epoxy from the cover and the ferrule. Allow the epoxy to harden.

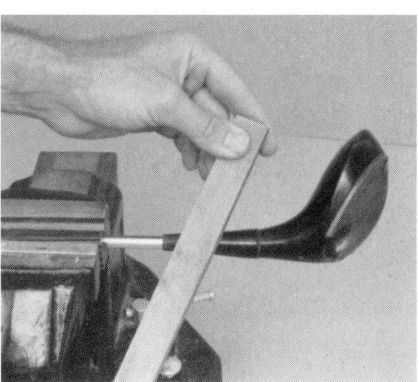

7-204 After the epoxy hardens, file the excess plastic until the ferrule is flush with the top of the whipping cover. Use a fine file. Do not "taper" the ferrule. There should be a noticeable step from the shaft up to the top of the ferrule.

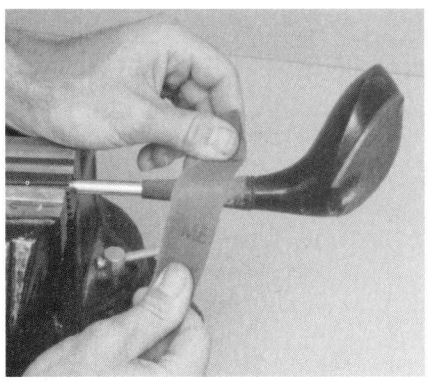

7-205 After filing, lightly sand the ferrule and whipping cover until both pieces are blended together. Remove any polyurethane from the whipping cover to ensure a uniform finish.

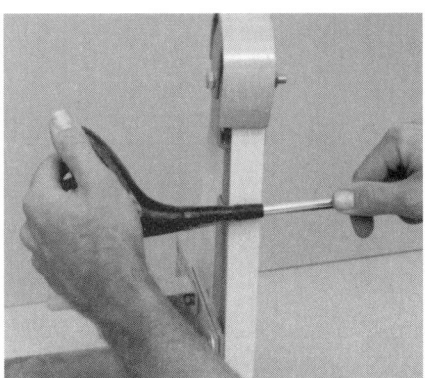

7-206 An alternative to the filing and sanding method is to use a **Cloth Linen Belt** on the **Belt Sander.** Refer to Chapter 21, photos 21-142 through 21-146 for procedure.

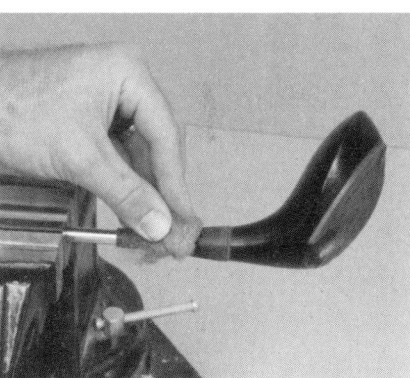

7-207 Next, lightly steel wool the ferrule and cover with 000 steel wool.

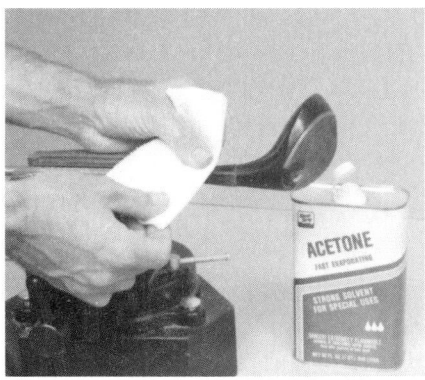

7-208 Wipe the cover and ferrule with a paper towel dampened with acetone.

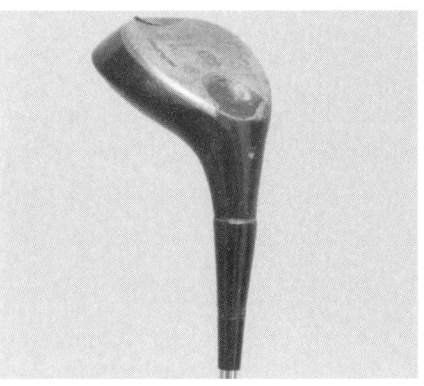

7-209 The finished ferrule and whipping cover should look like this.

NOTES

_____

_____

_____

_____

_____

_____

_____

_____

_____

_____

_____

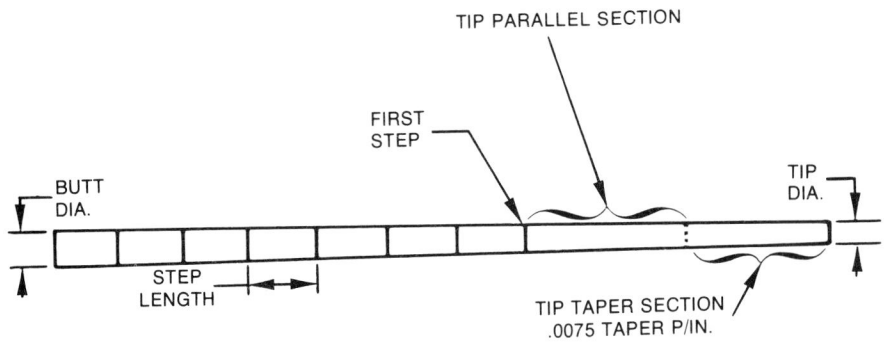

FIG. 7-210
Golf shaft terminology

ADDITIONAL INFORMATION FOR WOOD RESHAFTING

TABLE 7-1
Wood Club Lengths – Men's and Ladies'

Woods	Men's Standard	Ladies' Standard	Ladies' Petite
1	43"	42"	41½"
2	42½"	41½"	41"
3	42"	41"	40½"
4	41½"	40½"	40"
5	41"	40"	39½"
6	40½"	39½"	39"
7	40"	39"	38½"
8	39½"	38½"	38"
9	39"	38"	37½"

The most popular length variations for men are ½" shorter or longer than standard and 1" longer than standard. The most popular length variations for ladies are ½" shorter or longer than standard.

TABLE 7-2
Drill Selection Chart

• Back screw pilot drill	⅛"
• Screw extractor pilot drill	5/64"
• Drill to cut shaft back screw	7/32"
• Pilot drill for #7 soleplate screws	⅛"
• Pilot drill for #8 soleplate screws	9/64"
• Pilot drill for #4 face screws	3/32"
• Pilot drill for #5 face screws	7/64"

TABLE 7-3
Determining Shaft Flex by Color on Butt End of Shaft

Designation	Flex	Color
X	Extra Stiff	Green
S	Stiff	Red
R or T	Medium	Black
A	Flexible	Yellow
L	Ladies (very flexible)	Blue

Combination flex shafts such as UDWC, UDWAL, UJWC & U2LWAL do not have a color code on the butt end.

TABLE 7-4
Standard Wood Screw Diameters

Screw Number Size	Shank Diameter	General Golf Club Use	Drill Size to Use so Screw Threads Properly
4	.112	Standard size face insert screw	3/32"
5	.125	Oversize face insert screw	7/64"
6	.138	Very large face insert screw	#32
7	.151	Standard size soleplate screw	1/8"
8	.164	Oversize soleplate screw	9/64"
9	.177	Backweight screw (older clubs)	#25
10	.190	Backweight screw (old H&B)	#19

The majority of manufacturers use a #5 backscrew, however, some companies use a 3/32" or 1/8" headless nail.

Step Drilling Instructions and Drill Sizes by Tip Sizes

When boring hosels for new shafts or reshafting, many repair shops find it difficult or very expensive to obtain the proper size drills and reamers to match every wood shaft tip size available. Also, they run into special problems such as enlarging hosel holes to accept "tipped" shafts or hosels which need to be bored to accept another shaft size, or in most cases, hosels which just need to be cleaned out so that the replacement shaft will fit properly. Step drilling will solve this problem. See photos 7-80 through 7-88 for the procedure. Listed below are the drill sizes needed for the various shaft tip sizes.

Step Drilling Instructions and Sizes for .270" Taper Tip Shafts

Step #1: Drill to desired length or completely through with "J" (.277") diameter extra length drill.

Step #2: Drill to within ½" of depth as stated in Step #1 with "L" (.290") diameter standard length drill.

Step #3: Drill top within 2½" of depth as stated in Step #1 with "N" (.302") diameter standard length drill.

Step Drilling Instructions and Sizes for .277" Taper Tip Shafts

Step #1: Drill to desired length or completely through with 9/32 (.281") diameter extra length drill.

Step #2: Drill to within ½" of depth as stated in Step #1 with "M" (.295") diameter standard length drill.

Step #3: Drill to within 2¼" of depth as stated in Step #1 with 5/16 (.312") diameter standard length drill.

Step Drilling Instructions and Sizes for .294" Taper Tip Shafts

Step #1: Drill to desired length or completely through with 19/64" (.296") diameter extra length drill.

Step #2: Drill to within 3/8" of depth as stated in Step #1 with 5/16" (.312") diameter standard length drill.

Step #3: Drill to within 2" of depth as stated in Step #1 with 21/64" (.328") diameter standard length drill.

Step Drilling Instructions and Sizes for .320" Taper Tip Shafts

Step #1: Drill to desired length or completely through with "P" (.323") diameter extra length drill.

Step #2: Drill to within ½" of depth as stated in Step 1 with "R" (.339") diameter standard length drill.

Step #3: Drill to within 2½" of depth as stated in Step #1 with "T" (.358") diameter standard length drill.

Step Drilling Instructions and Size for .335" Unitized Parallel Tip Shafts

Step #1: Drill to desired length or completely through with "R" (.339") diameter extra length drill.

NOTES

_____

_____

_____

_____

_____

_____

_____

_____

_____

_____

_____

_____

_____

_____

_____

_____

CHAPTER 8

TIGHTENING LOOSE WOOD HEADS

Finding a loose wood head is fairly common, especially with persimmon woods. This is because persimmon is characterized as an open-grain wood, and therefore, is more susceptible to moisture absorption. As a wood head takes on moisture, it swells or expands. The loss of moisture in a head causes the head to shrink or contract. This movement, however slight, is sometimes enough to cause the epoxy holding the shaft in the hosel to fail. Once the epoxy bond fails, only the existence of a backscrew will keep the shaft in place. Even with the backscrew in place, however, some movement of the shaft is inevitable once the epoxy fails. Aside from the possibility of someone getting hurt from a flying wood head, a loose head can affect a golfer's game.

Finding a loose metal or composite head is also fairly common. Often this is caused by faulty shaft tip preparation. Another reason for looseness is either an inadequate bonding strength epoxy was used or the proportion of base to activator was incorrect. Some club assemblers attempt to accelerate the curing of the epoxy by mixing in additional activator (hardener) to the epoxy base. While this does quicken the pace of epoxy curing, it also causes the epoxy to be too brittle.

To determine if a wood head is loose, grasp the head in one hand and the grip in your other hand. Twist the grip and head in opposite directions and note if the head is loose. You may not always be able to feel or visually detect a loose head because, in many cases, the head and shaft are still firmly bonded at the bottom, but loose through the upper portion of the neck. This can usually be detected by a squeaky sound when the head and grip are twisted in opposite directions. Always check for a loose head on every club brought to you for any type of repair.

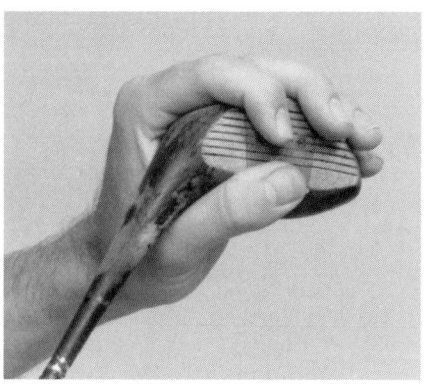

8-1 To determine if a wood head is loose, **grasp the head in one hand and the grip in your other hand** and attempt to twist each in opposite directions.

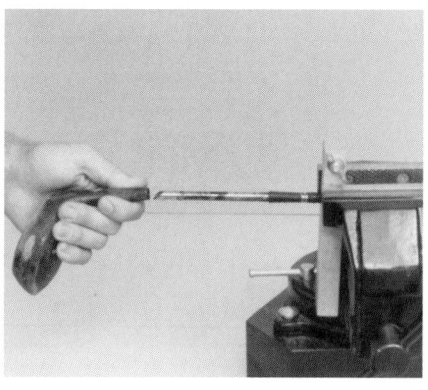

8-2 As outlined in Chapter 7 remove the head from the shaft. Note that these steps are also applicable for metal or composite heads.

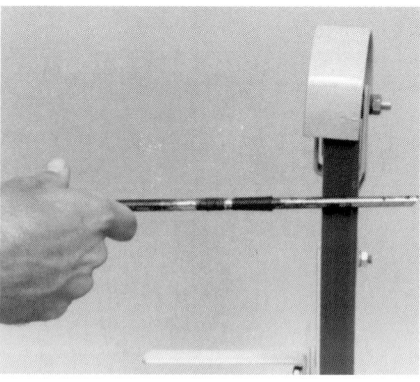

8-3 Remove the old epoxy and rough up the tip of the shaft using a belt sander, grinding wheel, file or emery cloth.

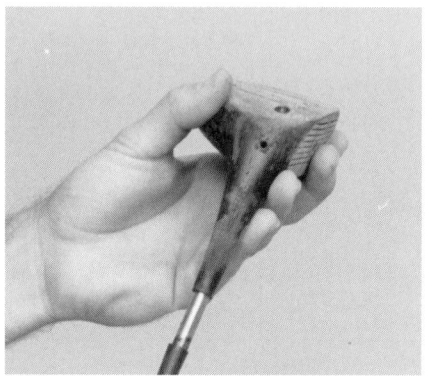

8-4 Temporarily reinstall the shaft to check the fit. If the head is very loose on the shaft, a shim must be used to take up the excess space.

8-5 The three most commonly used shimming materials are brass shims, paper shims and aluminum oxide sand.

8-6 If a brass or paper shim is chosen, cut a tapered shim approximately 3" long, as shown.

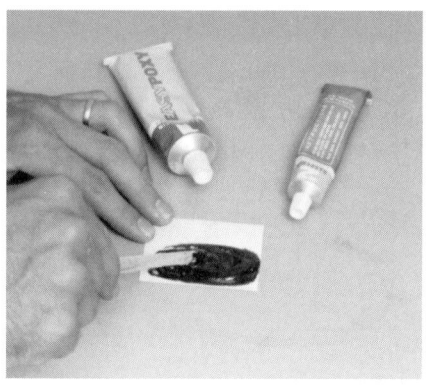

8-7 Mix a shear strength epoxy. **Conap®** or **GolfWorks® Shafting Epoxy** is extremely strong.

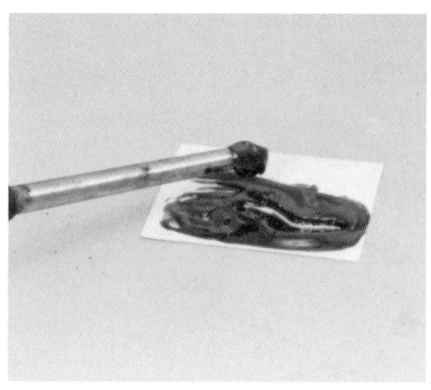

8-8 Dip the tip of the shaft into the epoxy and...

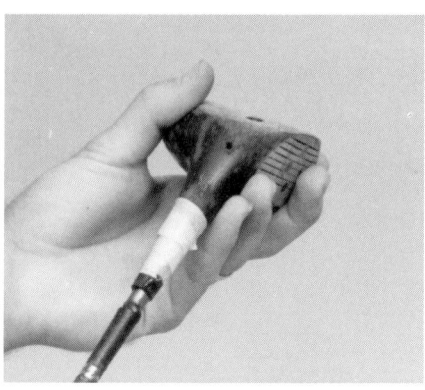

8-9 ...insert the tip of the shaft into the hosel. Simultaneously push and turn the shaft to completely coat the shaft and hosel walls. **Note: It is always a good idea to wrap the hosel with masking tape to prevent splitting.**

142

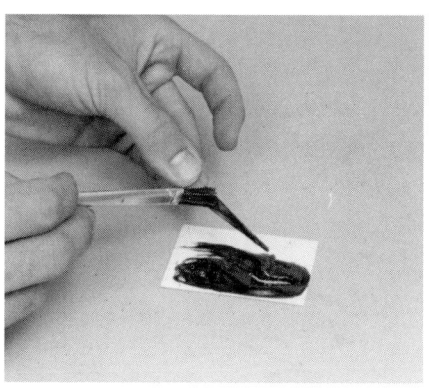

8-10 If a tapered shim is used, apply epoxy to both sides of the shim.

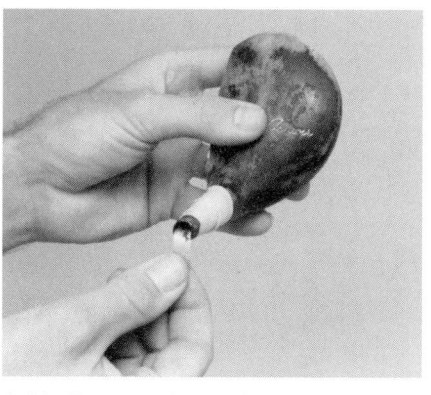

8-11 Remove the shaft from the hosel. Press the shim into the hosel hole — small end first. Leave the large end protruding about ¼" above the end of the hosel.

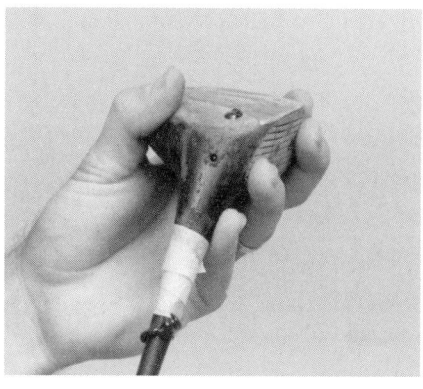

8-12 Reinstall the shaft while slowly twisting, until it bottoms out. The protruding portion of the shim should go down with the shaft.

8-13 If **Aluminum Oxide Sand** is used, coat the shaft and hosel with epoxy as detailed in photos 8-7 through 8-9 and then dip the tip of the shaft into the sand.

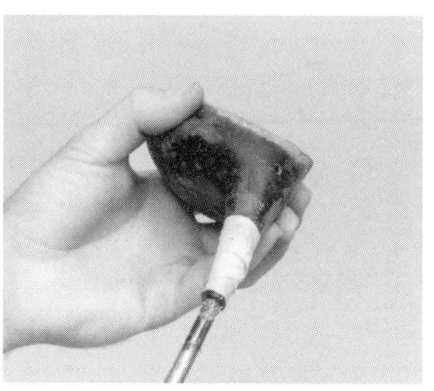

8-14 Finally, install the shaft into the hosel. The sand will effectively take up excess space while providing a good bonding surface for the epoxy.

8-15 After the epoxy has hardened, drill and install the backscrew if the club had one before. Refer to Chapter 7 photos 7-108 through 7-125 for the procedure. **Note: Many repairmen choose to install a new backscrew regardless of whether or not a club had one before, unless a graphite shaft is being used. Graphite shafts do not need a backscrew.**

NOTES

_____

_____

_____

_____

_____

_____

_____

_____

CHAPTER 9

REPAIRING CRACKED, CHIPPED OR BROKEN WOOD HEADS

There was a time when a cracked or broken wood head was either replaced or the entire club was discarded. This is not the case today with the availability of high strength epoxies. The proper epoxy must be a high shear strength type that cures with some flexibility. In addition, the epoxy should also accept a coloring agent such as colored paste dispersions. This will allow the repairman to alter the color of the epoxy to match the color of the stained wood. This is very effective for camouflaging an epoxy line.

Basically, there are three types of breaks which you will encounter, and all three require a different method of repair.

The first kind of break or crack, and probably the most common, is the hairline crack or cracks extending from under the whipping or ferrule down the hosel. Usually, this crack works its way down the hosel to its weakest part, namely the shaft locking screw hole. It is usually caused by a loose whipping, loose shaft-to-head bond, constant wood swelling from moisture and wood shrinking from drying out, or whoever assembled the club was not careful during the shaft installation step and cracked the hosel.

The second kind of break (usually found in persimmon heads), is one which starts on one side of the face insert, extends under the soleplate, to a backweight if one exists and then eventually around the entire head. The crack takes this route because it is always cracking in the direction of the weakest part of the head. Routing the head for the various components during manufacture weakens the wood head. This type of break will commonly break into two to five different pieces. Do not be intimidated by the prospect of refitting these back together though. If the proper epoxy is used, the club will rarely rebreak along the same cracks.

The third kind of break can really be referred to as a chip, and usually represents a piece of wood chipped out of the toe, the face or around the soleplate. Sometimes, in the case of laminated heads, it is a delamination of the wood in the sole area caused by moisture being absorbed into the wood because the finish has been chipped or worn off.

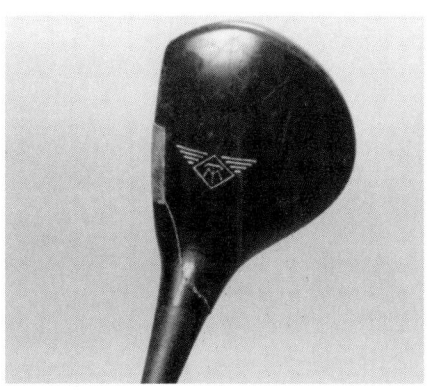

9-1 A typical crack running from behind the insert, across the head, up the side of the hosel …

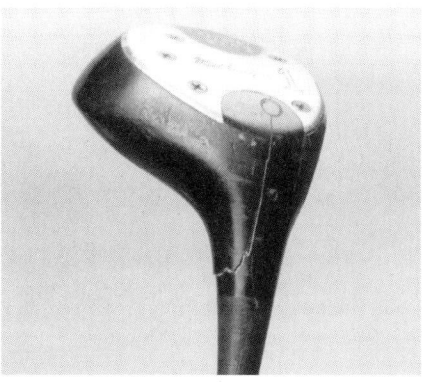

9-2 … back down the hosel and under the soleplate. Cracks have a tendency to seek out the weakest parts of the head. During manufacture, the removal of wood from the head for the placement of the insert, soleplate and lead weight will generally be where the breaks occur.

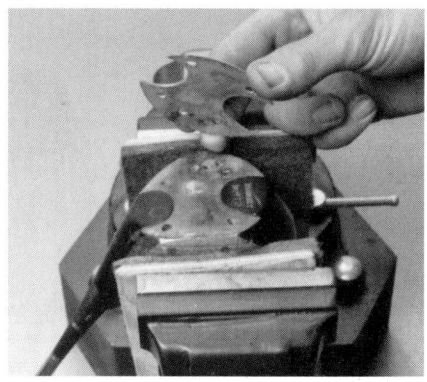

9-3 To fix a cracked wood head. First, remove the soleplate as outlined in Chapter 2.

9-4 Next, remove the face insert as outlined in Chapter 3. Some cracks run parallel to the face and the removal of the insert is not necessary unless the insert is loose.

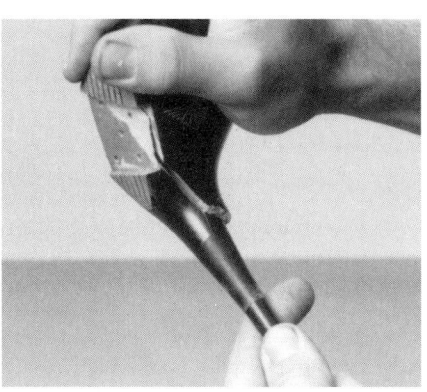

9-5 Grasp the head in both hands or in a vise and …

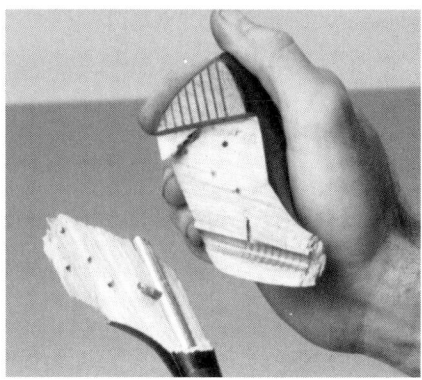

9-6 … break it into two or more pieces. Note: The club must be completely broken apart at any crack to properly fix it.

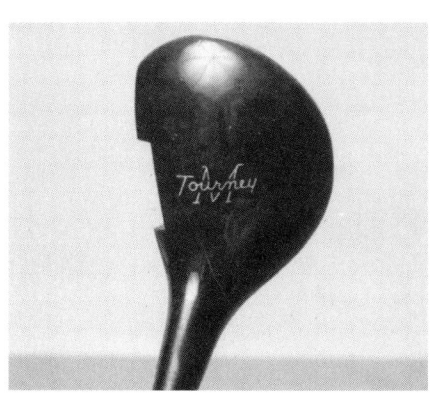

9-7 Occasionally a break must be persuaded to come apart. To do this …

9-8 … place a chisel in the crack and hammer lightly until the head comes apart. This is especially useful when a crack has not extended completely around the head. The break you create will usually follow the same line the crack would eventually develop into.

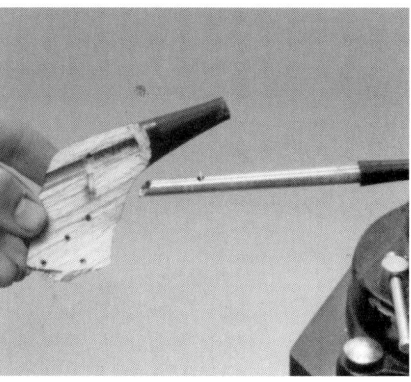

9-9 Temporarily piece the halves back together to see if the shaft interferes with a proper fit. If the shaft does interfere, remove the shaft as outlined in Chapter 7.

9-10 In one half of the broken head, drill a series of holes approximately ⅛" deep using a ⅛" diameter drill bit.

9-11 Do the same in the other half of the head. If more than two pieces exist, drill a series of holes in each piece.

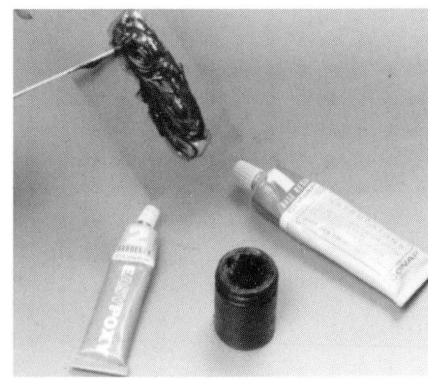

9-12 Mix up a shear strength epoxy, such as Conap® epoxy. Note the addition of a colored paste dispersion to match the stain color of the head. This will help camouflage the epoxy line when refinishing the club. If the club will be refinished in black, there is no need for concern.

9-13 Miracle-Man® epoxy manufactured by Club-Kit® is also an excellent bonding epoxy for broken heads. It does not change color very well, however, when mixing in a colored paste dispersion.

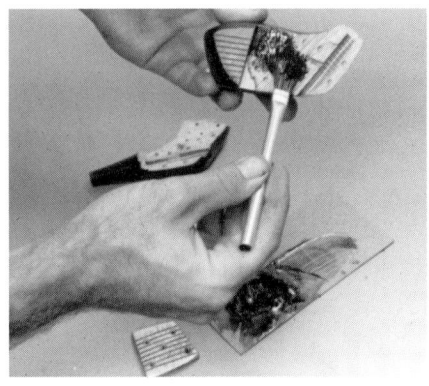

9-14 Coat one half of the broken head thoroughly with epoxy. Be sure to get the epoxy in all the ⅛" drilled holes.

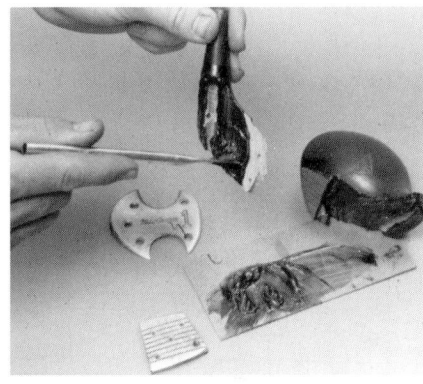

9-15 Also coat the other half and any other pieces.

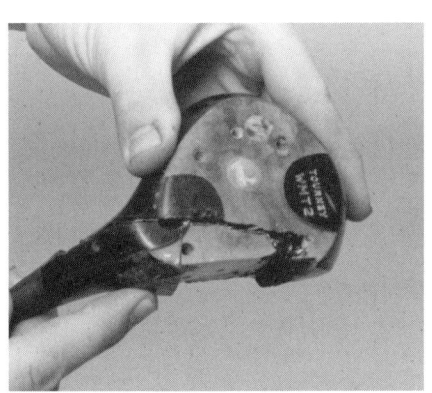

9-16 Line up both halves and press together. Do not squeeze out all the epoxy because the epoxy develops its maximum strength if it has a thin glue line.

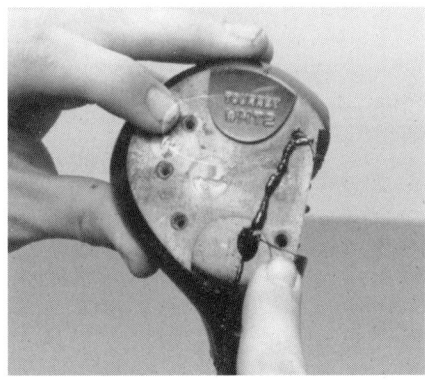

9-17 Where practical, the insert and/or soleplate can be temporarily installed to help draw the pieces in proper alignment. This photo shows the type of break that would benefit from the temporary placement of the insert and/or soleplate.

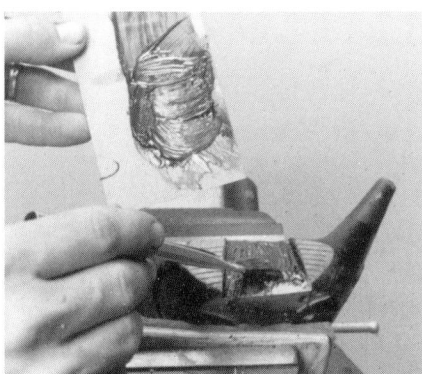

9-18 If a proper fit is achieved with the insert, it may be permanently installed with epoxy. The clubhead will require swing-weighting so do not permanently install the soleplate.

9-19 Pay particular attention to the scoring lines. Installing the insert can be a great help in ensuring the lines are properly aligned.

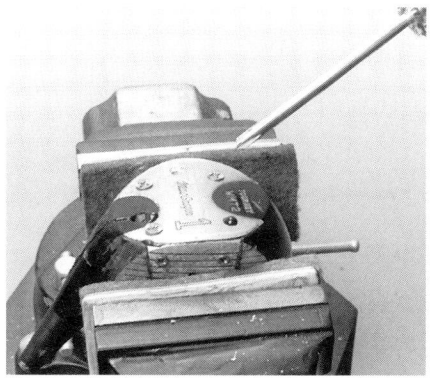

9-20 Temporarily install the soleplate if it will help draw the pieces together.

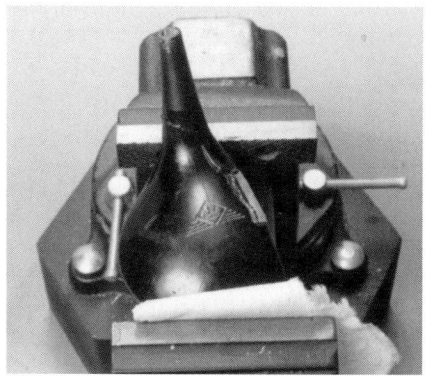

9-21 Strategically place the epoxied clubhead between the vise jaws and carefully tighten the vise until the epoxy begins to ooze out. Note: A paper towel is used to protect the head from the rough surface of the vise jaws yet allowing the jaws to firmly grasp the head without slippage.

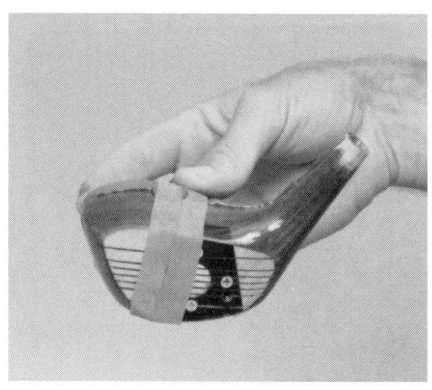

9-22 An alternative to the vise is placing a rubber band around the clubhead to hold it together and in the proper position.

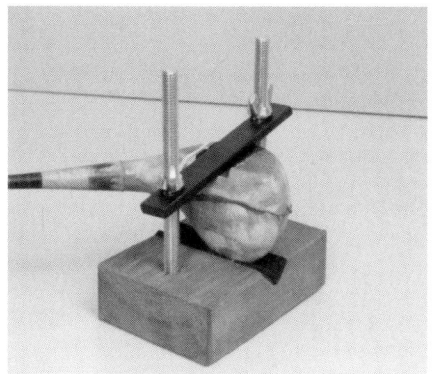

9-23 A **Face Insert Clamp** works very well to hold everything together.

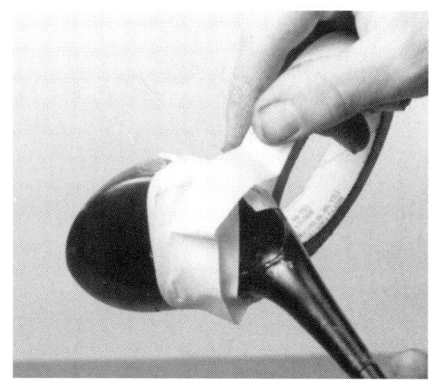

9-24 Masking tape can also be used.

9-25 After the epoxy has hardened, if the shaft was removed, clean out the hosel using the proper size drill bits and reinstall the shaft. See Chapter 7 for shaft installation procedures.

9-26 Next, remove the soleplate screws and then ...

9-27 ... remove the soleplate.

147

9-28 File the excess epoxy from the face, using a medium cut or fine cut file. If the insert was not previously reset, it should now be epoxied back in place.

9-29 Periodically check the bulge, roll and loft until it is correct. See Chapter 1 photos 1-22 through 1-30 for facing procedure.

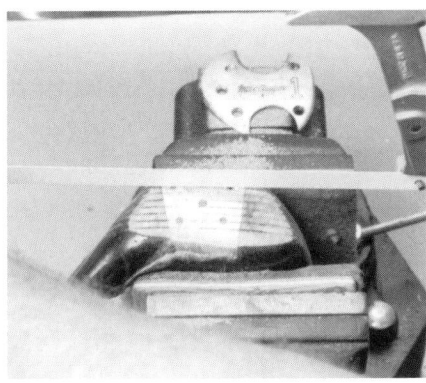

9-30 Recut the scoring lines using a proper blade with no rake on the teeth.

9-31 Redrill the screw holes using a 3/32" drill bit.

9-32 Recountersink the screw holes and install the new insert screws as outlined in Chapter 3, photos 3-42 through 3-46.

9-33 File the screw heads flush with the insert using a fine cut file. Recheck the bulge, roll and loft to insure these specifications have not been changed.

9-34 The club is now ready for swingweighting and soleplate installation.

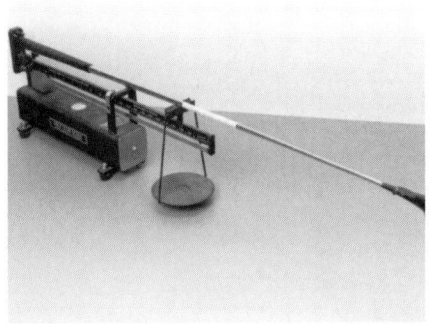

9-35 Place the soleplate in the soleplate cavity and check the swingweight. The soleplate screws can temporarily be installed or simply compensate for the lack of screws. Example: 5 #8 soleplate screws are equivalent to 3 swingweight points.

9-36 Make any necessary adjustments in swingweight following the instructions from Chapter 14.

9-37 Clean the soleplate cavity of excess epoxy using a medium cut file.

9-38 Temporarily reinstall the soleplate and redrill the screw holes for the soleplate screws using a ⅛" drill bit.

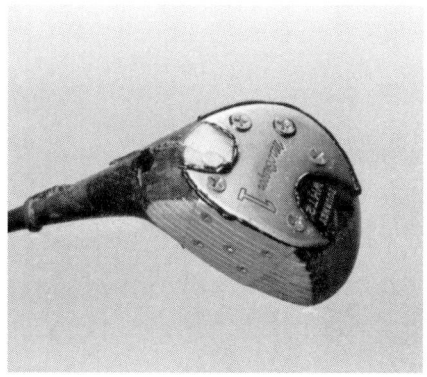

9-39 Mix the epoxy, apply it to the cavity and the soleplate and install the soleplate. The club is now ready for refinishing. If the epoxy was mixed properly, the club will not break along the original crack again. If the wood is very brittle, however, the clubhead may crack along a different line in the future.

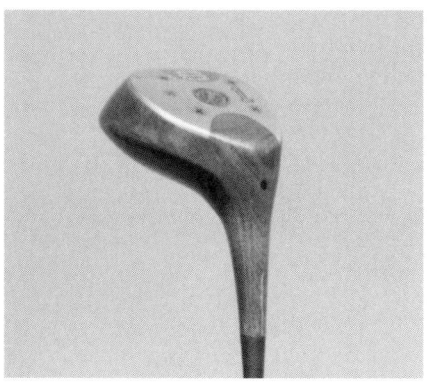

9-40 Another type of crack in a wood club is a split neck.

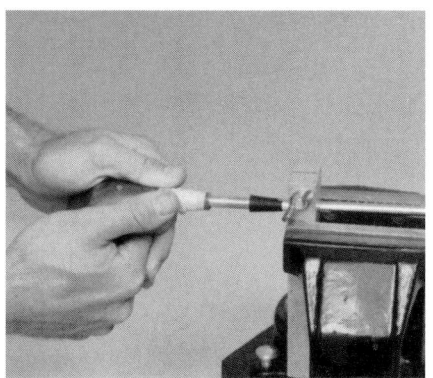

9-41 To properly repair a split neck the head must be removed from the shaft as outlined in Chapter 7.

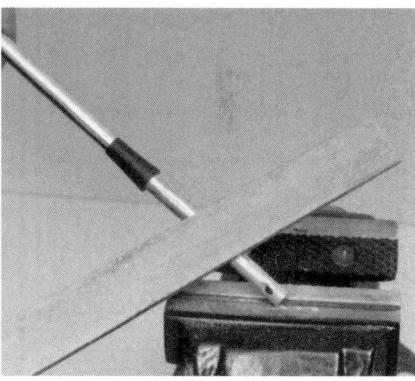

9-42 Abrade the tip of the shaft using a belt sander, grinding wheel, file or a piece of emery cloth.

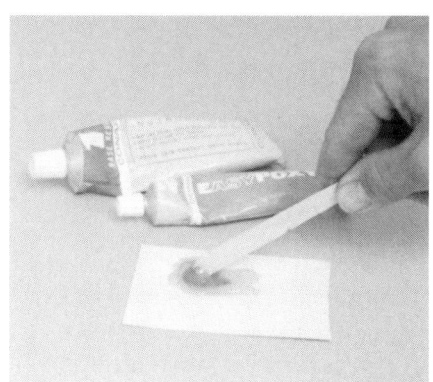

9-43 Mix the appropriate shear strength epoxy such as Conap® or GolfWorks® shafting epoxy.

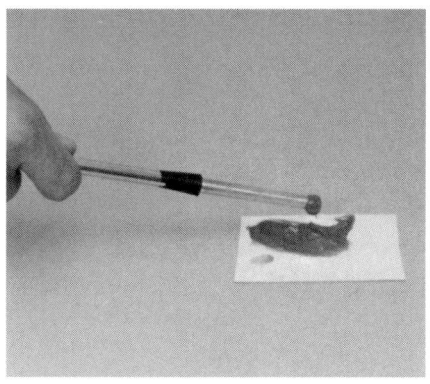

9-44 Dip the tip of the shaft into the epoxy and...

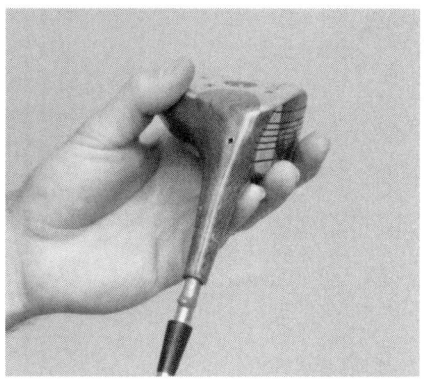

9-45 ... install the shaft into the hosel. For best results, simultaneously push and turn the shaft to effectively coat the shaft tip and the hosel wall.

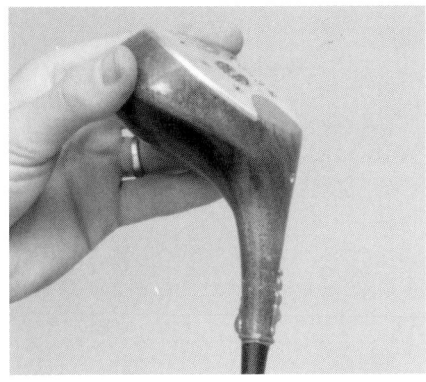

9-46 The result of turning the shaft during installation is that the epoxy is forced through and out the cracks. This effectively seals the cracks.

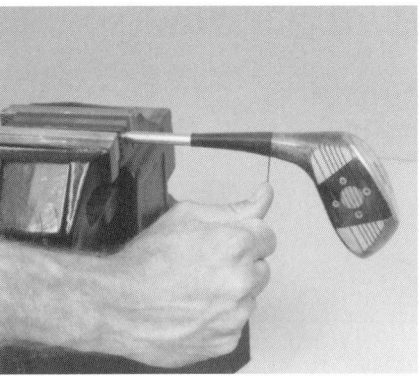

9-47 After the epoxy has hardened, smooth the neck, install the shaft locking screw and apply the whipping.

9-48 A delamination in the sole area is quite common and usually caused by moisture absorption due to the loss of the polyurethane coating.

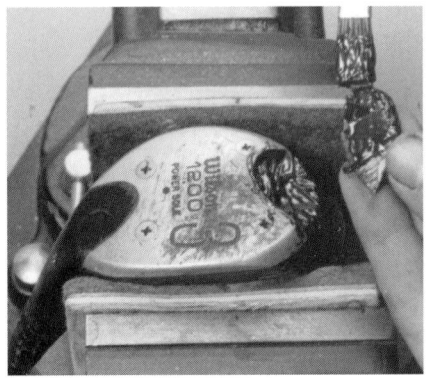

9-49 If the chip is removed, apply epoxy to the chip and the damaged area.

9-50 Place the chip back in place. To secure, place a piece of tape across the chip or clamp the bottom of the club between vise jaws.

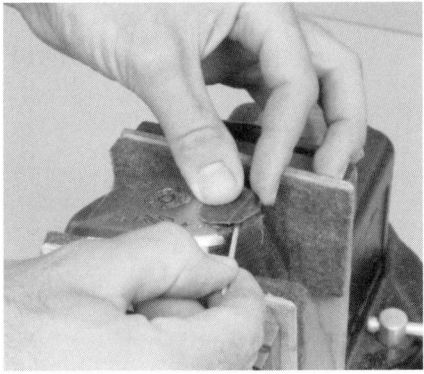

9-51 If enough epoxy can be forced under the delaminated piece, it is not necessary to completely remove the piece and then reinstall. Force the epoxy under the piece with a toothpick as shown. A layer of tape should then be applied until the epoxy hardens.

9-52 If the chip from the sole is lost, make a dam around the damaged area using masking tape or ...

9-53 ... Mortite putty.

9-54 It is not necessary to use an impact strength epoxy for this job. Any shear strength epoxy will work. Conap® or GolfWorks® brand epoxy works well. Mix and apply enough epoxy to fill in the cavity.

150

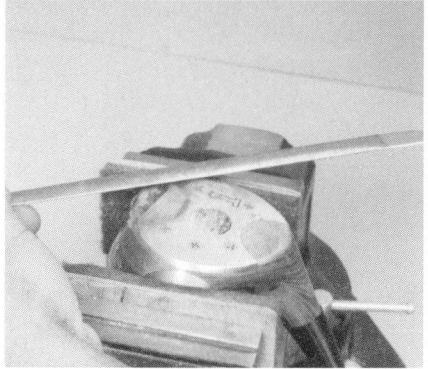

9-55 After the epoxy hardens, file the excess and shape it to match the contour of the head using a fine cut file.

9-56 The club is now ready for touchup or refinishing. Note that a colored paste dispersion was used to camouflage the repaired area.

ADDITIONAL INFORMATION FOR REPAIRING CRACKED, CHIPPED OR BROKEN WOOD HEADS

Epoxy

To a golf club repairman, it is critical that any components epoxied together remain together. The thought of a customer swinging a club with a head that has just flown off the shaft is enough to make any repairman feel very uneasy. This potentially embarrassing situation need never be faced if the repairman uses the correct type of epoxy and follows a few simple rules when assembling components.

Impact strength and shear strength represent the two types of epoxies used in golf club repair. Shear strength epoxy is used whenever a component will likely experience twisting or pulling effects (i.e. shaft in or over a hosel), soleplate or insert placement, etc. The twisting properties may be obvious, as in the case of the tremendous torque experienced between the shaft and the hosel during impact, or not so obvious as in the case of the insert resisting movement during impact.

Impact strength epoxy is used solely when casting a new insert (See Chapter 4). The insert must be unyielding and able to withstand the impact of the ball against the insert, hence the term impact strength. Some repairmen erroneously believe they should also use an impact strength epoxy when resetting an insert. This is not true because the insert itself is impact resistant, the epoxy holding the insert in place must have shear strength properties in order to resist the oblique impact of the ball. This indirect impact produces shifting stress on the entire insert that must be avoided hence the need for shear strength epoxy.

In order to ensure the components remain epoxied together, the repairman must follow a few simple rules:

1. Make certain the quantities of base and activator are measured precisely before mixing them together.
2. Make sure the surfaces of all components are prepared properly.
3. Do not use epoxy if the contents of the epoxy container or the surrounding area are below 65°F.
4. Slowly mix the contents of each container before using whenever applicable. Depending upon the container this may not be possible in some case.

Always follow the instructions that accompany your favorite brand of epoxy. Mixing instructions will inform you not only of the mixing ratio but also, in most cases, recommend measuring by weight or volume. Cheating on the mixing instructions (adding more activator in an attempt to speed curing) will always result in the epoxy either being too brittle or never achieving proper hardness.

When epoxying golf club components, make sure all surfaces are properly abraded following the directions found in each of the appropriate chapters of this book. Also, make sure the surfaces are free of oil, dirt, fingerprints or other surface contaminates. This is best achieved by wiping with a degreasing solvent such as Trichlorethylene or Naphtha. Allow a few minutes drying time to allow the solvents to evaporate before applying epoxy.

The table below gives curing times for the epoxies offered by the GolfWorks® under both room temperature and heat lamp conditions. To use the heat lamp, be sure it is positioned 15" from the repair, using a 300 or 400 watt light bulb. The strength of a heat-cured bond will not be as great as that achieved through the use of a moderate curing temperature.

TABLE 9-1
Various Shear Strength Epoxy Curing Times

Type and Time to Harden and/or Cure		K20	Conap K22	K26	GolfWorks® General Purpose High Strength Epoxy	Truset APOX & BPOX	Club-Kit Miracle-Man
Rm. Temp.	Hrs. to Harden (72°F)	2	2	2	8-10	1	3
Rm. Temp.	Hrs. to Cure (72°F)	24	24	24	24	6	8
Heat Lamp	Cure (minutes)	20-30	20-30	20-30	45	60	Not Recommended

NOTES

_____

_____

_____

_____

_____

_____

_____

_____

_____

CHAPTER 10

CHANGING THE LOFT, BULGE AND ROLL

Occasionally you will be required to change the loft, bulge or roll of a golf wood clubface. The amount of change which can be done to a wood face depends entirely on the particular make or model of golf club. Also, more alteration can be done on a driver face versus a #5 wood face. This should not pose a problem, however, since most face alterations will be requested for the driver.

Before getting into the actual procedure of altering the face, it is necessary to review the exact definitions of loft, bulge and roll.

Loft: The angle of the face and a line perpendicular to the sole line measured in degrees to a point ½ the distance of the face height and located on the centerline of the face.

Horizontal Face Bulge: The radius bulge of the face is measured from the heel to the toe in a horizontal plane along the face. It is usually the same at any point vertically up or down the face.

Vertical Face Roll: The radius roll of the face is measured from the top to the bottom of the face in a vertical plane. It is usually the same at any point along the face from the heel to the toe.

No matter which specification you intend to alter (loft, bulge or roll) the other two will probably be affected. Because of this it is necessary that you obtain some gauges to accurately measure loft, bulge and roll. The recommended gauges would be those specifically made to measure golf clubfaces as they save considerable time and eliminate interpolation required with other types of gauges. The photos in this chapter show the proper gauges to use.

The steps shown for measuring loft, bulge and roll are also applicable for metal and composite heads. These specifications, however, cannot be altered except in rare cases.

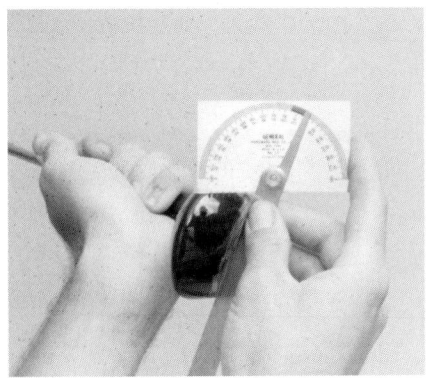

10-1 Using a machinist's protractor, hold the arm of the protractor tight against the soleplate and adjust the protractor head so it touches the face at ½ its vertical height. Loft is always specified in degrees.

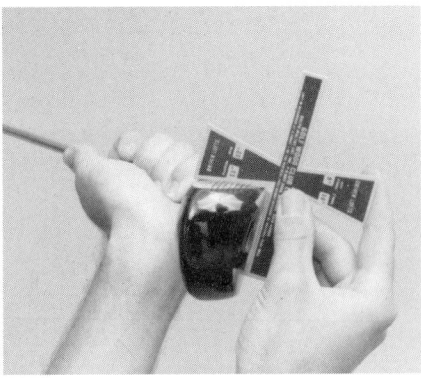

10-2 Using a fixed loft gauge, find the loft where one arm of the gauge is resting flush against the soleplate and the other is resting against the face at ½ its vertical face height.

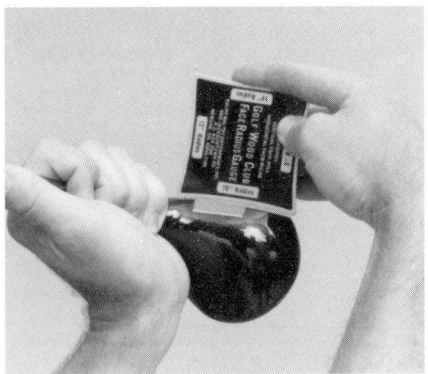

10-3 Bulge is measured with a **Face Radius Gauge**. See Chapter 1, photos 1-22 through 1-27 for a thorough explanation of measuring bulge. Bulge is always specified in inches of radius.

10-4 Roll is also measured with a **Face Radius Gauge**. See Chapter 1, photos 1-22 through 1-27 for a thorough explanation of measuring roll. Roll is always specified in inches of radius.

10-5 Record the loft, bulge and roll before beginning work.

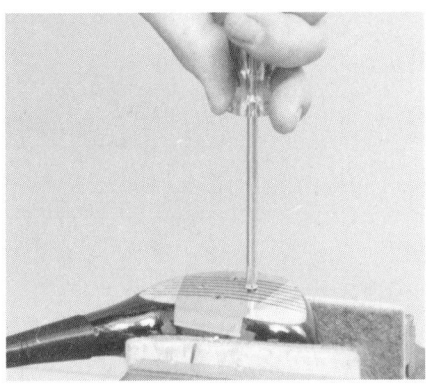

10-6 First, remove the insert screws. See Chapter 3, photos 3-3 through 3-19 for insert screw removal procedure.

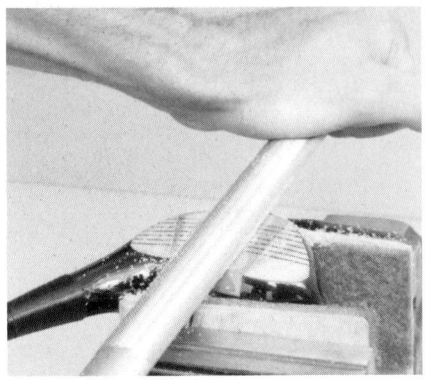

10-7 If the bulge is to be reduced (this means the amount of curvature from the heel to the toe is decreased or made flatter), concentrate your filing in the middle area of the face. A medium or coarse cut file works best depending on how much material is to be removed.

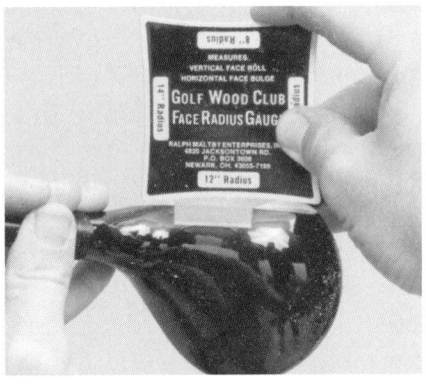

10-8 After carefully filing, the reduced horizontal face bulge is measured.

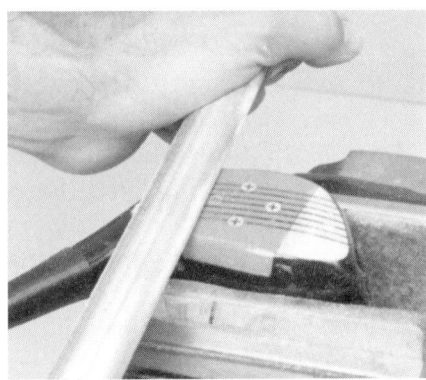

10-9 If the bulge is to be increased (this means the amount of curvature from the heel to the toe is increased or made more round), concentrate your filing on the heel and toe portion of the face.

154

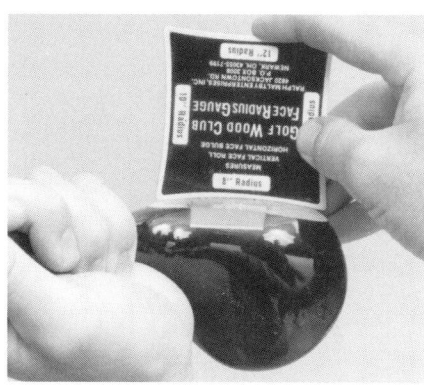

10-10 After carefully filing, the increased horizontal face bulge is measured. Slide the gauge up and down the face checking it from the top to the bottom. On some wood head models, it is necessary for the horizontal bulge to flatten out slightly in the upper heel portion of the face. This gives a better look in the playing position and avoids filing the face into the hosel. This will not affect playability.

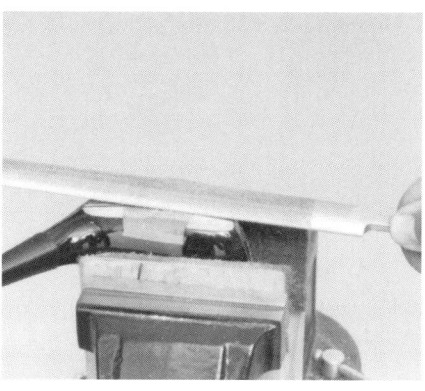

10-11 To reduce vertical face roll, concentrate your filing from the heel to the toe, along the middle of the face.

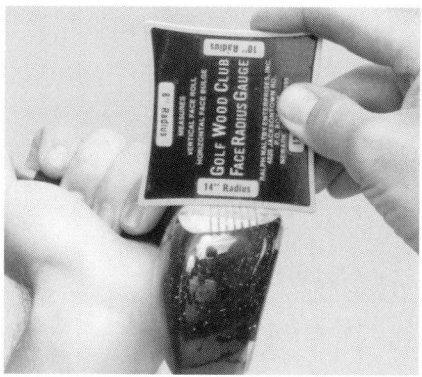

10-12 After carefully filing, the decreased vertical face roll is measured.

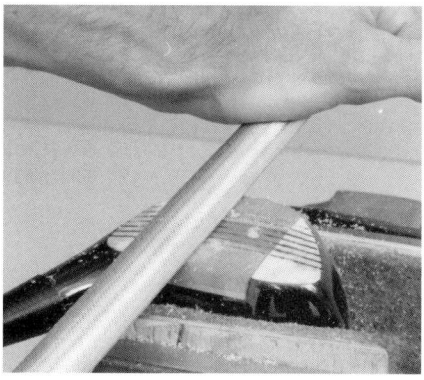

10-13 To increase vertical face roll, concentrate your filing from the heel to the toe, above and below the middle of the face.

10-14 After carefully filing, the increased vertical roll is measured.

10-15 To increase loft (this adds more loft to increase ball trajectory), file as shown working along the middle of the face to the top of the face. Keep checking the bulge, roll and loft as you file.

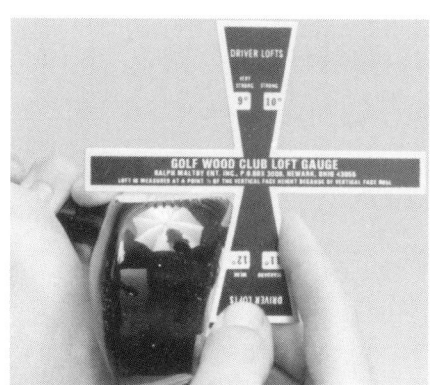

10-16 After carefully filing, the increase in loft is measured.

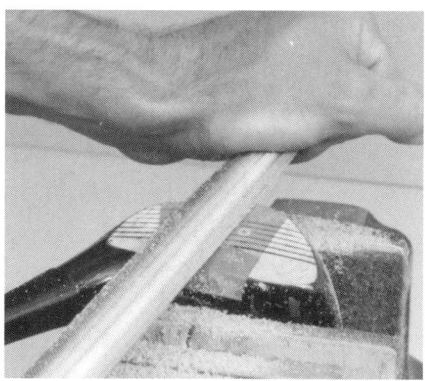

10-17 To decrease the loft (this reduces loft to lower ball trajectory), concentrate your filing from the middle of the face to the bottom of the face working horizontally across the face. Keep checking the bulge, roll and loft as you file.

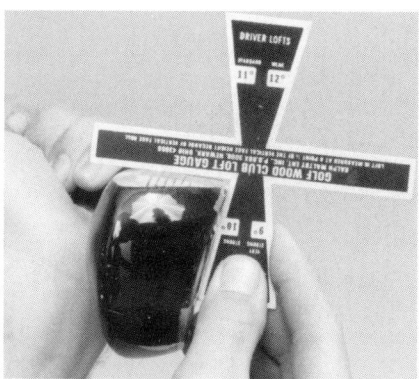

10-18 After carefully filing, the decrease in loft is measured.

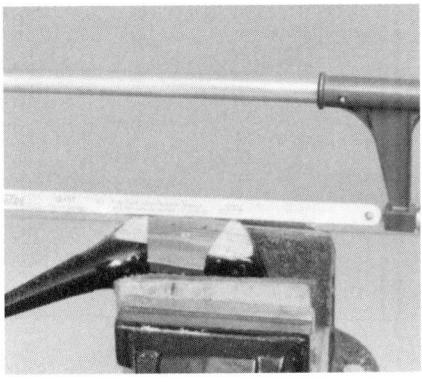

10-19 Recut new scoring lines if necessary.

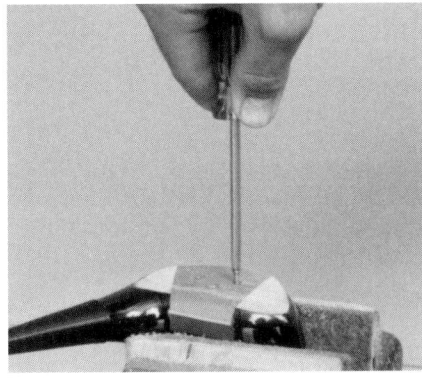

10-20 Reinstall new insert screws if necessary.

10-21 Lightly sand the face with fine sandpaper and lightly scrape with a **Detailing Knife.**

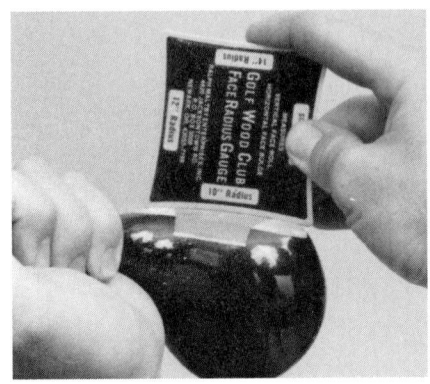

10-22 Final check the bulge, roll and loft to ensure the specifications have not changed because of the final detail steps. See Chapter 16 for finish touchup around the sole and around the insert.

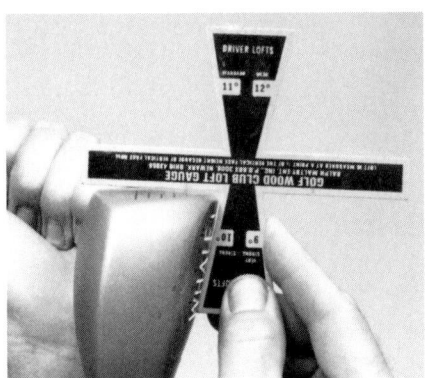

10-23 Some woods are now manufactured that have very radiused soles, which makes it difficult to measure loft using a fixed loft gauge or protractor.

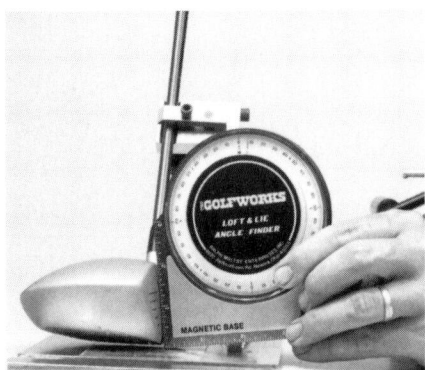

10-24 For such a wood, place the golf club in the **Golf Club Gauge** or measuring unit of the **Metal Wood Bending Machine.** Set the club so it measures 0° face angle then lean the **Magnetic Protractor** against the face at its vertical and horizontal centerline and record the loft.

ADDITIONAL INFORMATION FOR CHANGING LOFT, BULGE AND ROLL
How to Read a Machinist's Protractor When Measuring Wood Head Lofts

Photo 10-1 shows how to correctly hold a protractor for measuring the loft of a wood. It is important to develop a good technique that will allow you to get exact repeatability no matter how many times you recheck the same club. The method easiest to use when taking a loft reading is to hold the protractor arm on the sole of the club and hold the club up directly in front of a good light source such as a window or light fixture. While in this position, adjust the head of the protractor to touch the face at ½ its vertical height.

There are a number of different types and styles of protractors available. Some have square heads, some have round heads and a number of them have differing graduation callout markings although every one is marked in one degree increments. Look at Fig. 10-25 which shows a head with 3 sets of callout graduations.

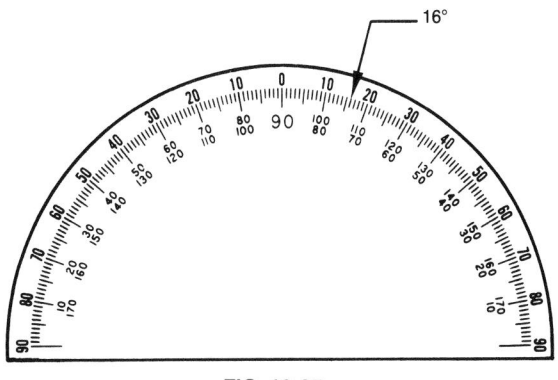

FIG. 10-25
Protractor head readings

This is not very common as most protractor heads will not have the top row with 0° in the middle and increasing to 90° in each direction. Most protractors have the bottom two rows of callout graduations thus when taking a wood loft reading with this type, you would have to do a little additional calculating.

Look again at Fig. 10-25. Most of the readings taken for loft will be on the right side of the protractor head or right of the 0° or 90° mark. When reading toward the right or left, notice you will be increasing from 90° or decreasing from 90°. If you happen to have a 0° mark you can read loft directly off this scale. As stated earlier, however, most protractors only have the bottom two callout designations. Notice the 16° callout in Fig. 10-25. It is 16 one degree increments to the right of 90°. Hence the wood head would have 16° loft. The bottom scale callouts would have you reading 16° as either 106° or 74°. Of course, subtracting 74° from 90° would be 16° and subtracting 90° from 106° would be 16°. See Fig. 10-26. It is easiest just to count the graduations in units of 10's, 5's and 1's when reading the protractor to obtain loft radius.

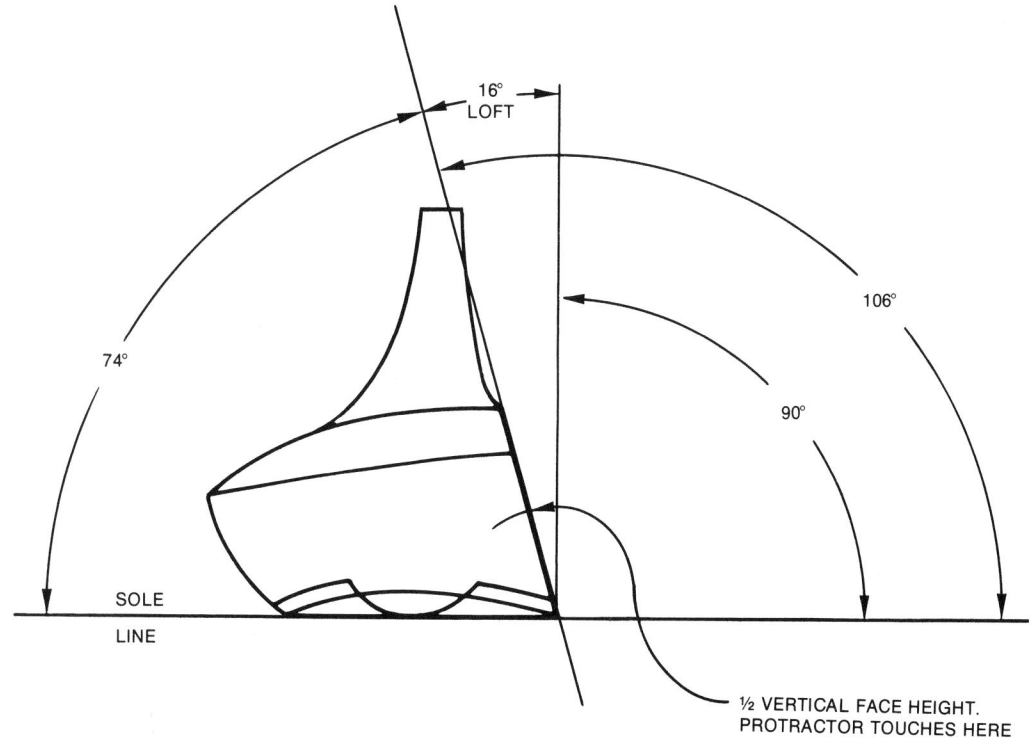

FIG. 10-26
Defining protractor readings when measuring loft

TABLE 10-1
Chart For Determining Strong, Standard and Weak Loft Specifications
Men's and Ladies' – Wood Club Lofts

Woods	Men's			Ladies'		
	Strong Lofts	Standard Lofts	Weak Lofts	Strong Lofts	Standard Lofts	Weak Lofts
1	10°	11°	12°	11°	12°	13°
2	12°	13°	14°	13°	14°	15°
3	15°	16°	17°	16°	17°	18°
4	18°	19°	20°	19°	20°	21°
5	21°	22°	23°	22°	23°	24°
6	24°	25°	26°	25°	26°	27°
7	27°	28°	29°	28°	29°	30°
8	30°	31°	32°	31°	32°	33°
9	33°	34°	35°	34°	35°	36°

TABLE 10-2
Chart For Determining Bulge and Roll Specifications
Wood Clubs

Club No.	Vertical Face Roll	Horizontal Face Roll
1	12" Radius	10" Radius
2	14" Radius	12" Radius
3	14" Radius	12" Radius
4	14" Radius	12" Radius
5	16" Radius	14" Radius
6	16" Radius	14" Radius
7	18" Radius	16" Radius

NOTES

CHAPTER 11

CHANGING THE LIE OF WOOD CLUBS

This chapter will show you how to alter the lie of a golf wood using a rather simple procedure of bending the shaft slightly. As golfers are learning the importance of having the clubhead in the correct lie position at impact, the demand for this service is increasing. Naturally, the ideal solution for the golfer with an incorrect wood lie is to order custom woods with the correct lie specifications. The shaft bending method described in this chapter, however, will work satisfactorily if the detailed procedure is followed carefully. Note that bending the shaft does not negatively impact the performance of the shaft.

The amount of bend that can be made in a shaft depends upon the shaft material. Standard weight shafts made of carbon steel, such as True Temper's® Dynamic Gold™, ProFit™, Jet Step™, Comet™ or Apollo's AP44 can be safely bent as much as 4°. Lightweight steel shafts such as True Temper's® Dynamic Lite™, Unitized Dynamic Gold™, Dynalite™, TT Lite™, Flex-Flow™ or Apollo's Spectre, Match Flex, Shadow or Brunswick's Precision FM can be bent a maximum of 2°. Lightweight steel shafts tend to have thinner walls and larger diameters and therefore are more easily broken or kinked than a standard weight steel shaft. Attempting a bend of more than 2° on a lightweight steel shaft should not be attempted. Shafts that fall into the super lightweight category (i.e. True Temper's® Extralite™, Gold Plus™, Brunswick Golf's® UCV-304™ or Apollo's Acculite) cannot be bent without breaking or kinking the shaft and as such altering these shafts should not be attempted. Shafts made of composite materials such as graphite, fiberglass or aramid-fiber, cannot be permanently bent and this also should not be attempted. Titanium shafts can be bent up to 2°.

11-1 A bending block is the most effective way of changing a wood club's lie. This block is made from strong hardwood and has a 1" wide x 1" deep notch which is padded with 2 pieces of leather from an old grip. Use in a vise or bolt securely to a workbench as shown. Plans for making your own bending block are found in Figure 11-10 at the end of this chapter.

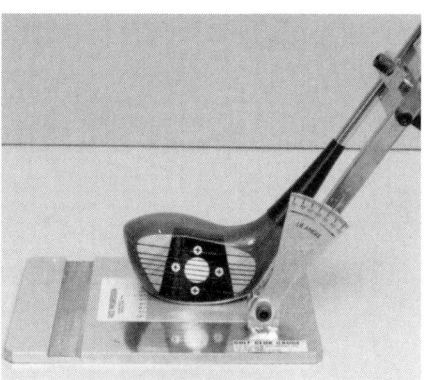

11-2 The lie can be changed by eye, however, the use of an accurate measuring gauge, such as this Golf Club Gauge, will eliminate guesswork.

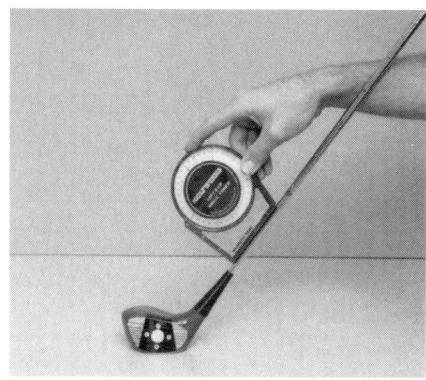

11-3 Another method for measuring lie is to rest the middle of the sole of the clubhead on a flat surface. Next, place a Magnetic Protractor on the tip section of the shaft. Read the lie directly off the protractor. This method is reasonably accurate.

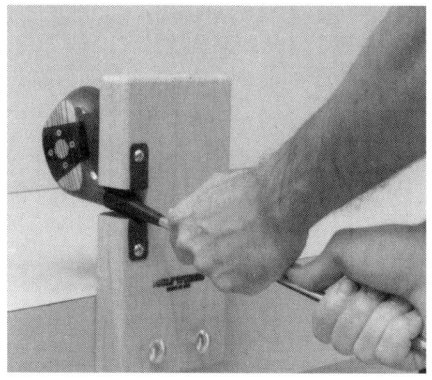

11-4 To flatten the lie, place the club in the block as shown. Note the location where the shaft is being bent. The bend in the shaft should be made at a point where the top of the hosel meets the ferrule. Hold hands close to the block and apply short bursts of downward pressure to the shaft. Practice on old clubs first. Whipping should be left on the hosel to prevent the hosel from splitting.

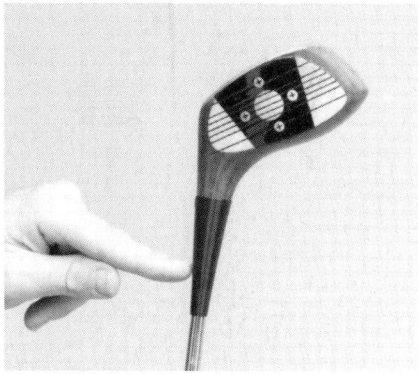

11-5 This photo shows where the bend in the shaft is made. This point is approximately 1" from the top of the whipping.

11-6 To make the lie more upright, place the club in the block as shown. With the toe of the club pointing downward, hold hands close to the block and apply short bursts of downward pressure to the shaft.

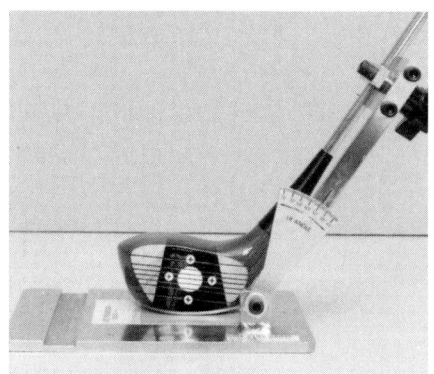

11-7 The altered club should again be measured to ensure the proper lie change has been made.

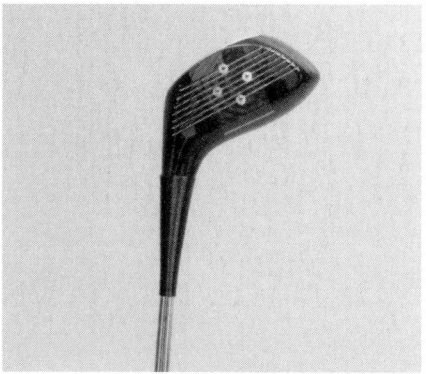

11-8 Because the shaft is being bent and not the hosel, steel shafted graphite heads may also be bent. The same steps as outlined previously apply.

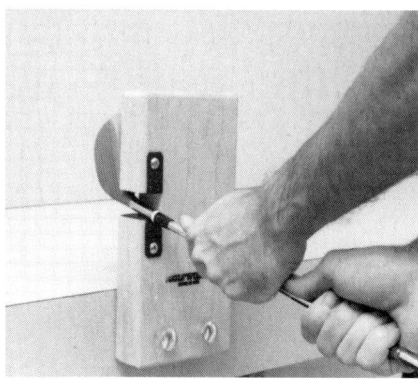

11-9 Steel shafted metal woods can also be bent. Because of the lack of whipping to camouflage the bend, however, the angle created on the shaft is more obvious.

TABLE 11-1
Wood Club Lies – Men's and Ladies'

Woods	Men's			Ladies'		
	[1]Flat Lies	[1]Standard Lies	[1]Upright Lies	[2]Flat Lies	[2]Standard Lies	[2]Upright Lies
1	53°	55°	57°	51°	53°	55°
2	53½°	55½°	57½°	51½°	53½°	55½°
3	54°	56°	58°	52°	54°	56°
4	54½°	56½°	58½°	52½°	54½°	56½°
5	55°	57°	59°	53°	55°	57°
6	55½°	57½°	59½°	53½°	55½°	57½°
7	56°	58°	60°	54°	56°	58°
8	56½°	58½°	60½°	54½°	56½°	58½°
9	57°	59°	61°	55°	57°	59°

[1] Lies shown are for standard length woods (i.e., 43" driver). For each ½" added to standard length, subtract 1° in lie (flatter) and for each ½" subtracted from standard length, add 1° in lie (upright).
[2] Same as Note 1 above but based on a standard length set with a 42" driver.

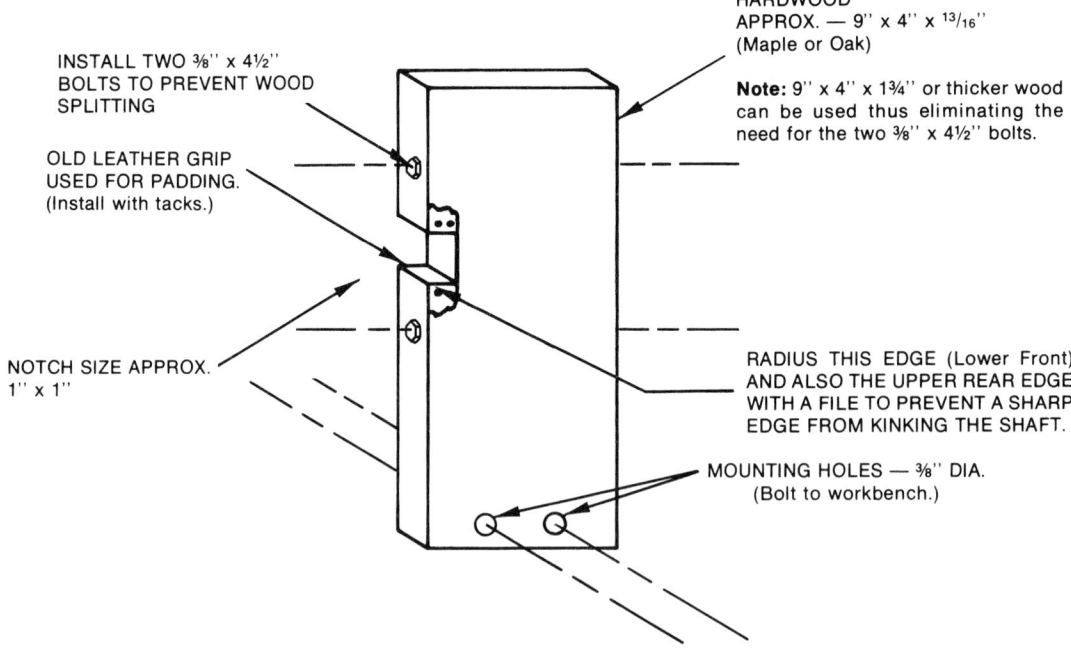

FIG. 11-10
A device you can make to alter lie of wood clubs

162

CHAPTER 12

CHANGING THE FACE ANGLE ON WOODS (SQUARE, OPEN, CLOSED)

Adjusting the face angle on woods is accomplished by either bending the shaft or precisely removing material from certain areas of the face. This change in face angle is usually made to provide a positive change in the direction and/or shape of a golf shot. It should be understood, however, that when the facing is altered, one or more other specifications may be affected significantly enough to cause an undesirable side effect in performance. To change the face angle of a metal wood, see Chapter 13.

The amount of bend that can be made in a shaft depends upon the shaft material. Standard weight shafts made of carbon steel such as True Temper's® Dynamic Gold™, ProFit™, Jet Step™, Comet™ or Apollo's AP44 can be safely bent as much as 4°. Lightweight steel shafts such as True Temper's® TT Lite™, Unitized Dynamic Gold™, Dynalite™, Dynamic Lite™, Flex-Flow™ or Apollo's Spectre, Match Flex, Shadow or Brunswick's Precision FM can be bent a maximum of 2°. Lightweight steel shafts tend to have thinner walls and larger diameters and therefore are more easily broken or kinked than a standard weight steel shaft. Do not attempt to bend a lightweight steel shaft more than 2°. Shafts that fall into the very lightweight category – i.e., True Temper's® Gold Plus™, Extralite™, Brunswick Golf's® UCV-304™ or Apollo's Acculite – cannot be bent without breaking or kinking the shaft and as such altering these shafts should not be attempted. Shafts made of composite materials such as graphite, fiberglass or aramid-fiber, simply cannot be permanently bent and this also should not be attempted. Titanium shafts can be bent a maximum of 2°.

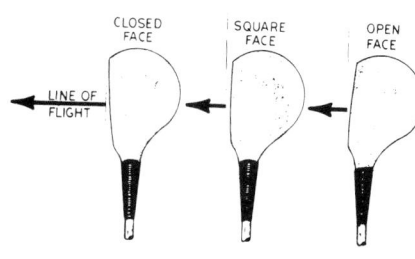

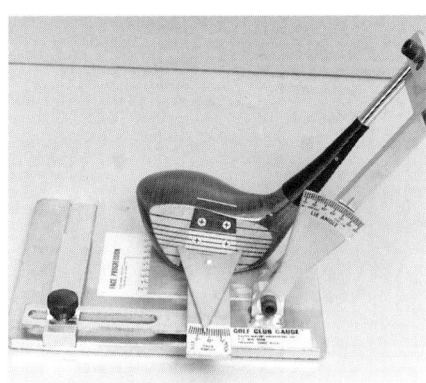

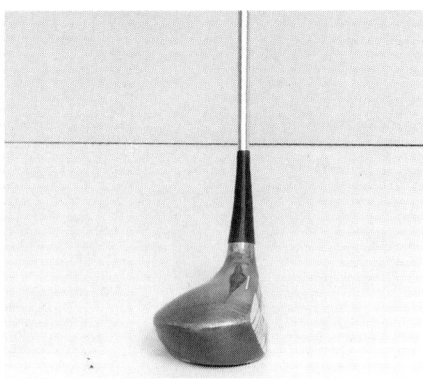

12-1 The above drawing defines a closed, square and open clubface. "Open" is sometimes referred to as "Slice" and "Closed" is referred to as "Hook." It should be noted that when the club is in the playing position, what the face angle appears to the golfer and what the face angle actually measures are two different observations. A club will normally appear to have a more closed face angle – usually a difference of 2°.

12-2 An accurate gauge, such as the **Golf Club Gauge**, must be used to determine the actual face angle. Note the indicator shows the face to be open by 2°. An actual 2° open reading will give the club the appearance of being straight-faced or "square" in the playing position.

12-3 Here is another method for determining the actual face angle. Lean the club against a wall so that the shaft is vertical but the club is in a normal lie playing position. Observe the face from the position shown in this photo (in front of the club). By looking at the clubface from this direction, you are bypassing the factors that give the club the appearance of being 2° more hooked than it really is.

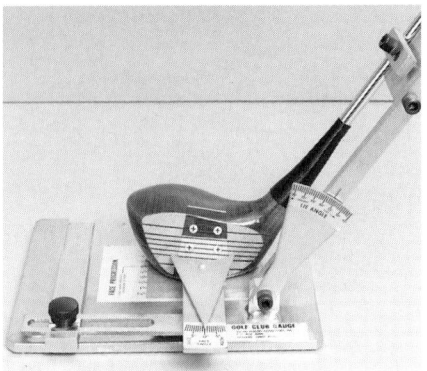

12-4 Closing the face angle. To close a 2° open face, the clubface is pointed downward in the shaft bending block and the shaft is bent downward as shown. See Chapter 11 for the bending procedures and information on the **Shaft Bending Block.**

12-5 After bending the shaft, the gauge now shows the face to be 0° or square. When the club is placed in the playing position, however, it will appear to be closed to the golfer.

12-6 Opening the face angle. Point the face up and bend downward on the shaft. If the owner does not like the change, the face angle can be easily returned to its original angle.

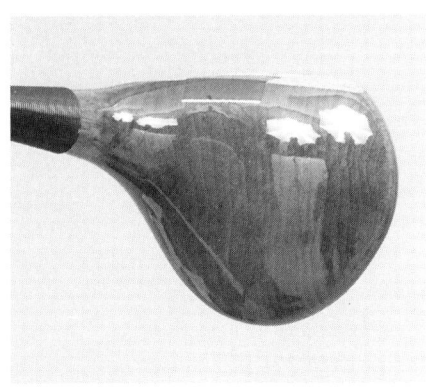

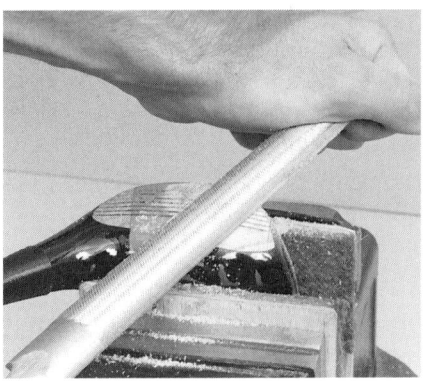

12-7 Another way to change the face angle can be achieved by filing the face. Usually 1° or 2° is the maximum and depends on each particular clubhead shape and top line progression.

12-8 To open the face angle, file from the middle of the insert out to the toe. Periodically check the bulge, roll and loft to ensure these face specifications remain the same. Virtually every clubface can be opened through filing. A 1° change requires approximately ⅛" of material removed from the edge of the face. This amount decreases proportionately as you near the center of the face.

12-9 This photo shows the filed clubface. Note it is sometimes necessary to remove the insert screw(s) before filing. See Chapter 3, photos 3-3 through 3-18 for insert screw removal. See Chapter 16 for touchup steps after filing.

12-10 To close the face angle, file from the middle of the insert back toward the heel. Maintain the correct bulge, roll and loft. Closing the face through filing requires some material to be removed from the top line along the hosel. Many clubfaces cannot be closed due to a lack of top line progression.

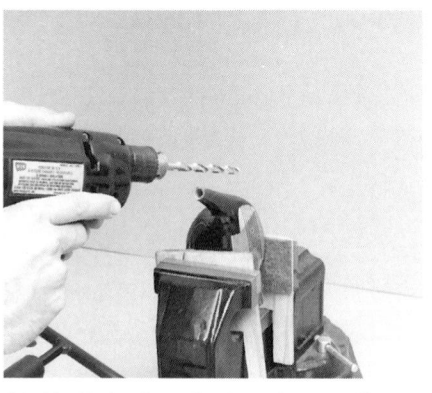

12-11 Reboring the hosel can affect a plus or minus 1° change in the face angle. This is a difficult procedure and should only be tried by the experienced club repairman. The repairman is making use of the existing hosel bore and does not plug the bore before redrilling.

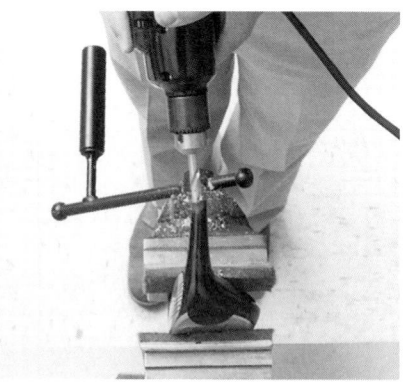

12-12 To close the face angle, drill into the hosel with the appropriate size drill bit. Favor the back side of the hosel with the end of the bit while drilling. **Note: Either apply whipping or masking tape around the hosel to prevent splitting during drilling.**

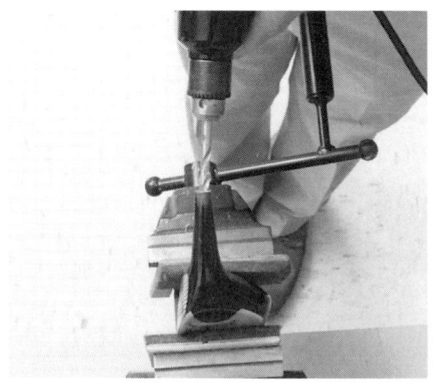

12-13 To open the face angle, drill into the hosel with the appropriate size drill bit. Favor the face side of the hosel with the end of the bit while drilling.

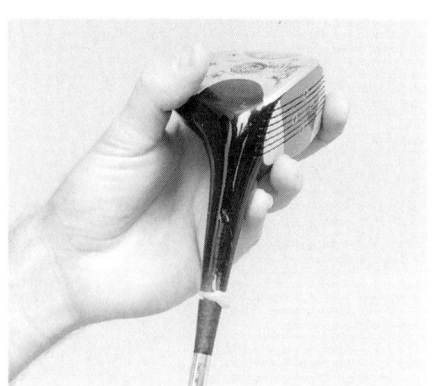

12-14 When reinstalling the shaft, make sure the shaft is shifted to the proper angle. It may be necessary to use a shim to take up the excess space in the hosel. See Chapter 8 for installing a loose shaft.

NOTES

_____

_____

_____

_____

_____

_____

_____

_____

CHAPTER 13

CHANGING THE LIE AND FACE ANGLE ON METAL WOODS

Chapters 11 and 12 explained changing lie and face angle on wood clubs. To alter these same specifications on a metal wood, the hosel is bent slightly using the GolfWorks® Metal Wood Bending Machine. Bending a metal wood should be done slowly and accurately following the instructions given in this chapter. You will find that some clubs bend easier than others due to differences in casting and heat treating. As a precautionary note, the Metal Wood Bending Machine can only alter metal woods in which the shaft does not penetrate below the top of the crown (See Figure 13-19). Attempting to bend a hosel in which the shaft penetrates further than the top of the crown will result in a bend in the hosel bore that will not allow extraction or installation of the shaft.

■IMPORTANT NOTE: Since the walls of metal woods are very thin, when tightening the metal wood in the bending unit, proceed slowly and tighten firmly, but do not overtighten, as damage to the walls may occur. Correct tightening of the head in the bending unit is a matter of "feel" which will be developed only with practice. Slight movement of the head during bending will not cause a problem. It is wise to use a discarded head to practice on until you become comfortable with this procedure.

See Chapter 39 for a more thorough understanding of the effects of changing the face angle on a wood club. Chapter 36 will provide more information on lie and its effect on golf ball direction.

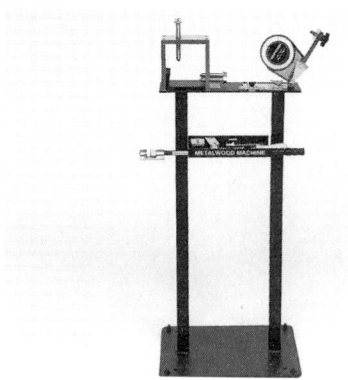

13-1 The **GolfWorks® Metal Wood Bending Machine** is the most effective way of changing a metal wood's lie and face angle.

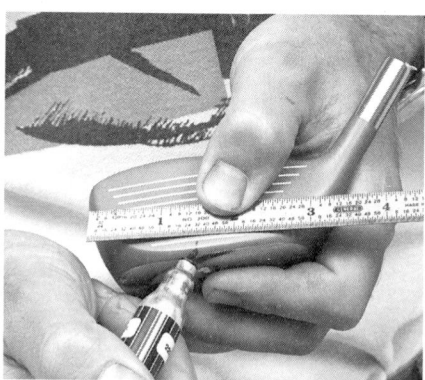

13-2 To measure the lie angle. Using a 6" ruler, locate the center of the club face and mark it lightly with a pencil or other instrument that is easily removed. A thin strip of tape also works well.

13-3 Place the club in the machine. If the head is not assembled with a shaft, place the **Hosel Support Rod** into the hosel and attach it to the shaft holder on the arm assembly. The two pieces of paper shown in the photo are slid in from both ends to determine if the club is soled exactly at the center of its face. This is the absolute lie measurement position.

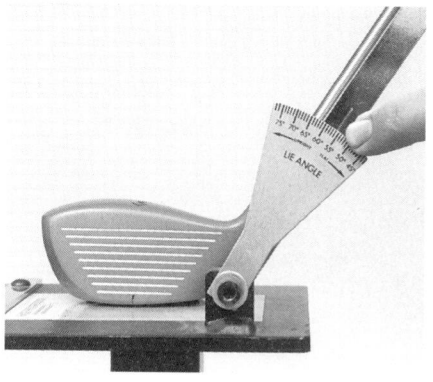

13-4 The lie angle can now be read directly from the lie indicator and recorded.

13-5 Measuring the face angle. Double-check that the sole of the metal wood is touching and sitting flat on the base.

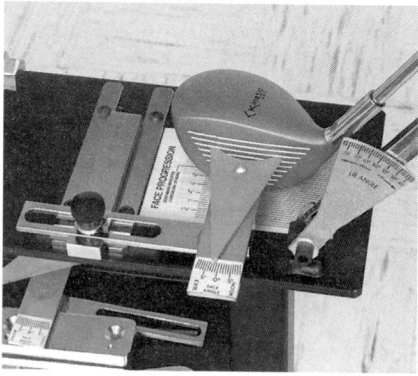

13-6 Place the "face angle" assembly on the gauge. To properly position the "face angle" assembly, loosen the thumbscrew and adjust the cross slide right or left until the two indicator points are equidistant from either side of the face centerline. Tighten the thumbscrew.

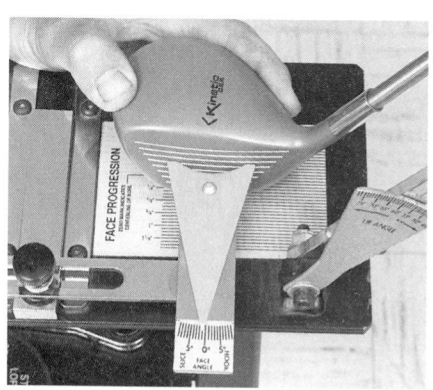

13-7 Slide the indicator in until both points touch the club face. Note the face angle reading and record it. Be sure one or both of the indicator points do not drop into a face line as this will cause an incorrect reading. (A "hook" reading refers to a "closed face," a 0° reading is a "square face," and a "slice" reading is an "open face.")

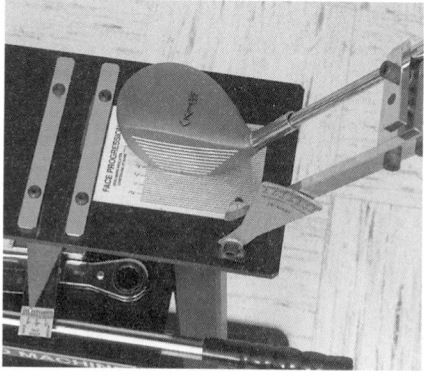

13-8 Measuring the face progression. The face progression is read with the club face in the square position (0° angle reading). The face progression measurement is noted at the farthest forward portion of the bottom leading edge of the club face.

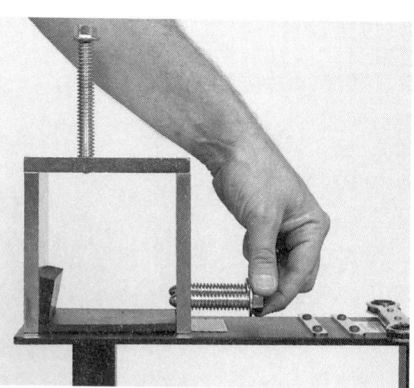

13-9 Bending the metal wood. Unscrew the three Acme Threaded Bolts far enough to allow positioning of the metal wood head.

167

13-10 Place the metal wood head into the bending unit, toe first, with the face against the angled rubber bumper. Position the head so the heel aligns with the rear edge of the Black Polyethylene Sole Rest on which the head sits.

13-11 Place the Back Clamping Plate with Rubber Pad against the back of the club and tighten the two Acme Threaded Bolts, being sure that the tips of the bolts fit into the dimples on the back of the Clamping Plate.

13-12 Place the Top Clamping Plate with Rubber Pads on the crown of the head so that the three dimples are parallel to the face. Thread the bolt through the front one of the three holes in the top of the unit and hand tighten so the tip of the rod fits into the center dimple of the Top Clamping Plate. (The other holes in the top of the unit allow for positioning fairway heads or heads with different shapes.)

13-13 Tighten all Acme Threaded Bolts with the ¾" Ratchet Wrench.

13-14 If bending an unshafted club, be sure to install the **Hosel Support Rod** before proceeding. Never attempt to bend a head without using some type of hosel support as the hosel will be squeezed out of round and ruined.

13-15 Turn the handle to open the jaws on the Metal Wood Bending Bar. Position the bending bar low around the hosel and then tighten. When bending the hosel, the head will move slightly because of the give that the rubber pads allow.

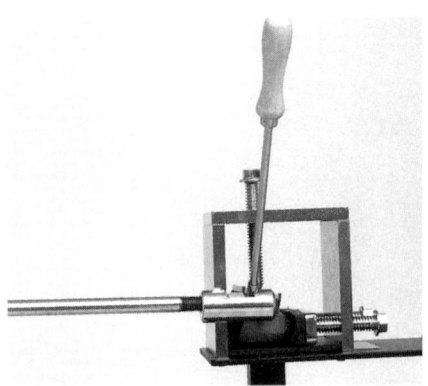

13-16 To alter the face angle, place the bending bar in position as shown, with the bar parallel to the front of the machine (at right angles to the face of the club). To hook (close) the face, push down on the bending bar. To open (slice) the face, pull up on the bending bar.

13-17 To alter the lie angle, place the bending bar in position as shown, with the bar at right angles to the front of the machine (parallel with the face of the club). To flatten the lie, push down on the bending bar. To make the lie more upright, pull up on the bending bar.

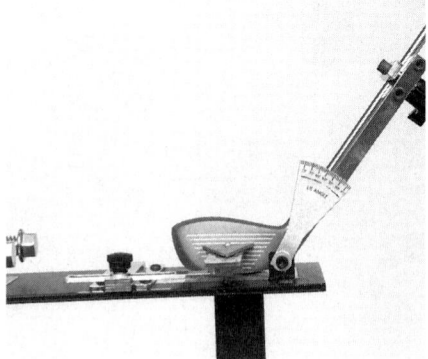

13-18 Remove the head from the bending unit and measure the angles again to be sure your work is accurate.

168

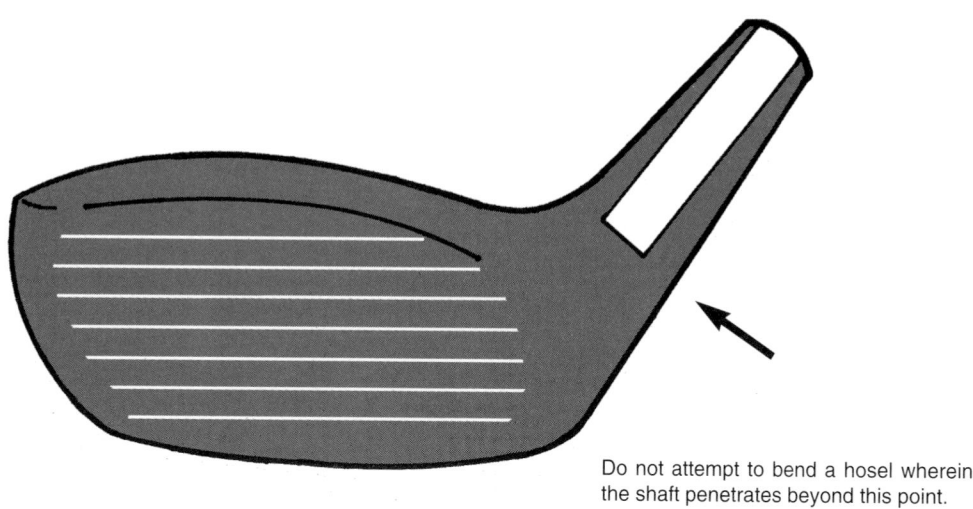

Do not attempt to bend a hosel wherein the shaft penetrates beyond this point.

FIG. 13-19
Only alter metal woods where the shaft does not penetrate below the top of the crown

NOTES

169

CHAPTER 14

CHANGING THE SWINGWEIGHT OF WOODS (WOOD, METAL, GRAPHITE)

Changing the swingweight of wood clubs requires the use of a swingweight scale. Various types and models of swingweight scales are shown in photos 14-38 through 14-47. Other tools required are standard shop tools such as screwdrivers, a drill, drill bits and a propane torch. Weighting materials, such as various forms of lead, are needed to add weight to the head if an increase in swingweight is desired.

The most common material used by club manufacturers for weighting wood heads is lead. Lead is available at most hardware stores, plumbing supply houses or golf repair supplies dealers.

The need to increase or decrease the swingweight will fall under two categories:

1) The owner of the club wishes to increase or decrease the total weight of the club by increasing or decreasing the swingweight or wishes to change the relative stiffness (flex feel) of the golf shaft by increasing or decreasing the swingweight. When the swingweight is increased (weight added to the head), the shaft feels more flexible. When the swingweight is decreased (weight removed from the head), the shaft feels stiffer. Consequently, increasing or decreasing swingweight (headweight) to raise or lower the total weight will also change the relative stiffness of the shaft.

2) Virtually every repair will affect the club's swingweight. For instance, refinishing a club will usually lower the swingweight 1-2 swingweight points. Regripping can change the swingweight if the new grip is not the same weight as the old grip. Reshafting a club will change the swingweight if the same shaft length and weight are not maintained. Acquiring the knowledge and skill that will allow you to change swingweight is very important.

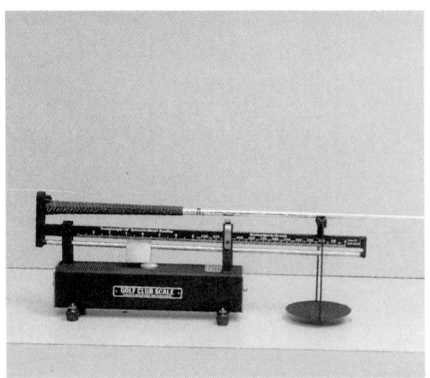

14-1 Before any change in swingweight takes place, the existing swingweight must be determined, using a swingweight scale. See photos 14-38 through 14-47 for various types and models of swingweight scales.

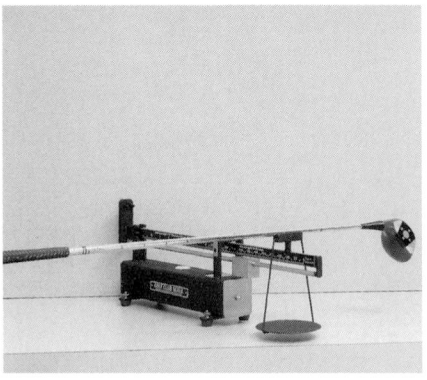

14-2 It is also a good idea to check and record the golf club's total weight. Again, photos 14-38 through 14-47 will tell you which swingweight scales also measure total weight.

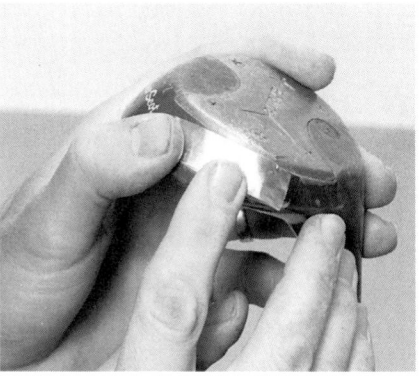

14-3 **The simplest method to increase swingweight is by adding lead tape to the back of the head.** This can also be used on a trial basis if the customer wishes to see what the added weight feels like before making a permanent weight increase under the soleplate. **A strip of ½" lead tape 4½" long will increase swingweight 1 point.**

14-4 **Rub the tape to burnish it and make it conform and stick to the curved surface of the head.** A wooden or plastic tool handle works well. This is also the best way to increase swingweight in a metal wood.

14-5 **Swingweight can also be increased or decreased by adding or removing weight from under the soleplate.** First, the soleplate must be removed as outlined in Chapter 2.

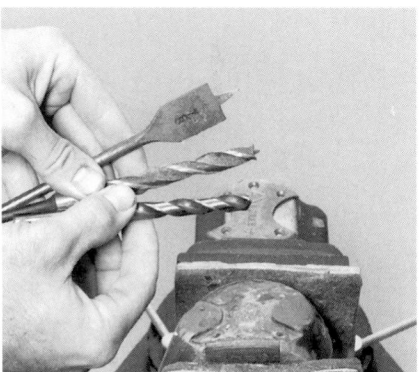

14-6 Twist drills with ¼" shanks or flat type wood bits work well for drilling wood heads. Sizes recommended are ¼", ⅜", 7/16" and ½" diameter twist drills or ¼", ⅜", 7/16", ½", ¾" and 1" diameter flat bore bits.

14-7 To remove weight and decrease swingweight, drill the weight out from under the soleplate. A hole ⅜" in diameter and ¼" deep drilled in the old lead weight, will reduce the swingweight by approximately 2 or 3 points.

14-8 **In some cases, a lead backweight can be used for a slight reduction.** Simply drill into the center of the weight with an appropriate size bit until the proper weight has been removed. Periodically check the swingweight while drilling. Of course this may not be cosmetically appealing.

14-9 To add weight and increase swing-weight, various forms of lead can be used. Included are lead powder, shot, rod or wire, sheet, discs and lead ingots. In some cases a lead ladle is needed to hold molten lead.

171

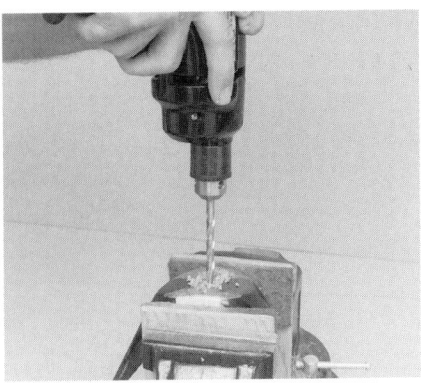

14-10 The ¼" lead rod works well under the soleplate. A ¼" length of ¼" diameter rod will increase the swingweight 1 point. Drill into the head with a ¹⁷⁄₆₄" bit. Insert the appropriate length of lead rod into the hole and …

14-11 … place the tip of a cross point screwdriver onto the top of the lead rod. Gently hammer the tip into the lead. This will peen the lead and secure it in position. If desired, epoxy can also be used to hold the lead plug in place.

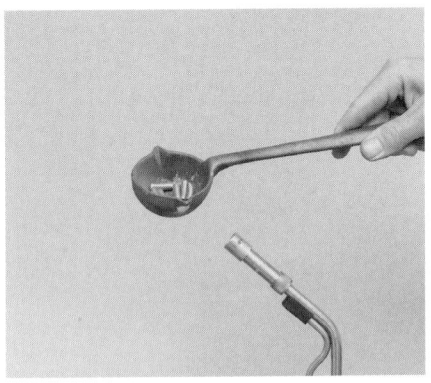

14-12 If large increases in weight are needed, drill a ¾" or 1" hole into the center of the head. Drop several pieces of lead or lead rod into a ladle and heat with a propane torch. Wear eye protection as lead can spit and pop if moisture is present.

14-13 Pour the molten lead into the cavity.

14-14 Use a wood chisel to remove any excess lead, making it flush with the soleplate cavity.

14-15 Lead should always be peened to prevent rattling. Use a machinist's ball peen hammer. Also, a cross point screwdriver tip can be gently hammered into the lead to peen and secure it.

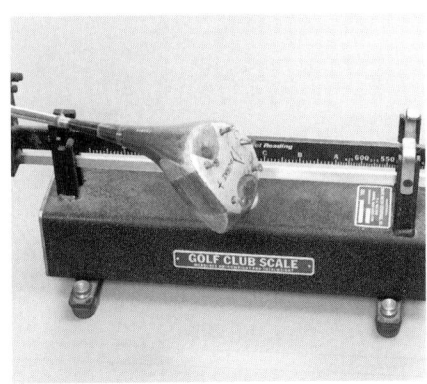

14-16 If weight was either added or removed, install the soleplate loosely as shown to check the swingweight. Note the use of all the screws in the soleplate.

14-17 If the swingweight is incorrect, reweight. If it is okay, reinstall the soleplate as outlined in Chapter 2. See Chapter 16 for touchup steps or refer to Chapter 1 for complete refinishing steps.

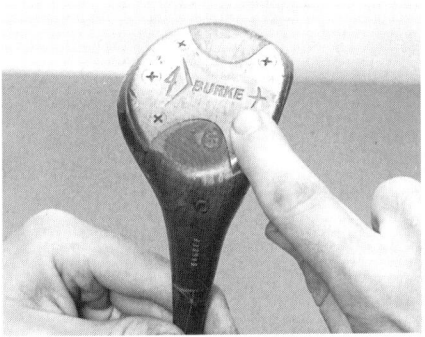

14-18 TIP: If the original soleplate screws are to be reused, take a swingweight reading before and after the soleplate and screws are removed. The swingweight change can be calculated and now simply make the weight change, check the swingweight and reinstall the soleplate and screws. It should not be necessary to check the swingweight with the soleplate on as the plate and screws are a constant.

172

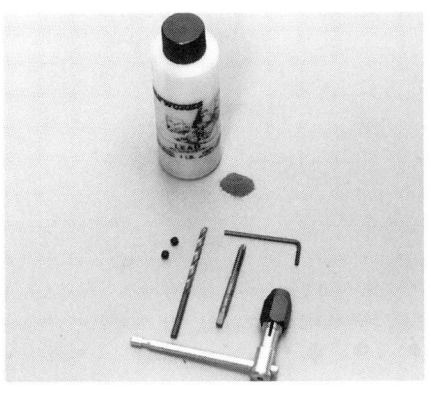

14-19 Installing a weight port in the soleplate of a wood or metal wood. A **Weight Port Installation Kit** and **Lead Powder** are required to accomplish this alteration.

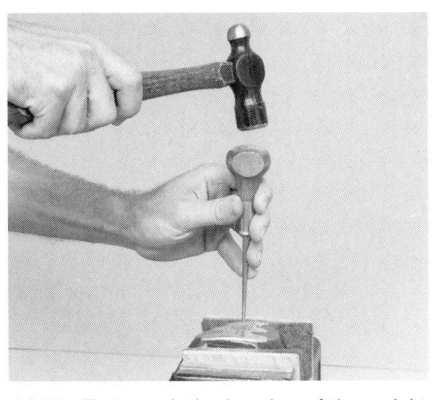

14-20 First, mark the location of the weight port with a center punch or awl and hammer.

14-21 Next, drill the proper size hole per the table at the end of this chapter. Shown above is a #3 drill which is the tap drill size for ¼-28 threads. Be careful not to drill too deeply.

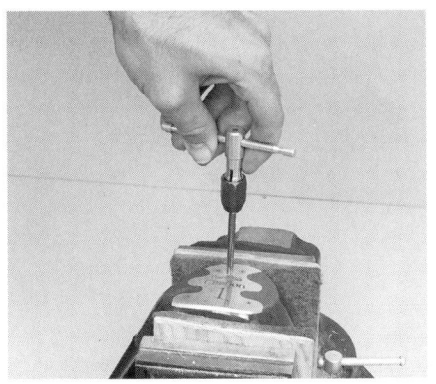

14-22 Place the tap in the tap wrench and screw it into the hole. It will cut the threads as it goes in (¼-28 tap shown).

14-23 Using a ⅛" hex key wrench, install a ¼-28 x ³⁄₁₆" long socket set screw flush with the soleplate. Check the swingweight after installation.

14-24 If more weight is needed, and it usually is, remove the soleplate as outlined in Chapter 2. Drill under the set screw location with a ¼" or ½" bit. **DO NOT DRILL TOO DEEP.** Reinstall the soleplate and pour lead powder through the hole and replace the set screw.

14-25 An alternative to the weight port is to use a trick some manufacturers use. First, locate a number or letter stamping that is large enough to allow a ⅛" bit to pass through. It is also helpful if the drilled hole is located in the center of the soleplate and in line with the cavity under the soleplate.

14-26 Drill through the soleplate with a ⅛" bit.

14-27 Lead powder can be poured through the hole into the cavity.

14-28 The hole is now filled with an aluminum colored or black epoxy. Carefully cut or file the excess epoxy to complete what can be a very slick method for weight increases in selected cases.

14-29 Once finished, the camouflaged hole is hardly noticed. Installing a set screw or drilling through a soleplate is an acceptable practice for some clubs and may be requested by customers wishing to make their own future changes. Avoid the two previously described methods, however, when working with antique or classic clubs.

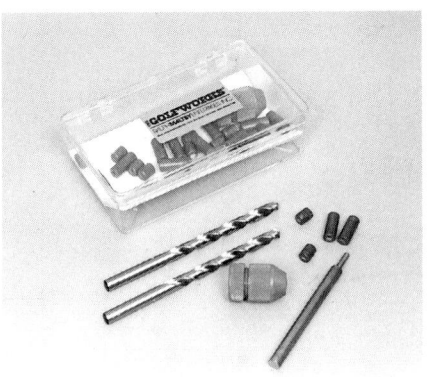

14-30 The **Changeable Swingweight Kit** for woods allows swingweight increases without the installation of a set screw.

14-31 First, remove a soleplate screw, drill a ¼" diameter hole to accommodate either a ⁵⁄₁₆" or ⅝" long lead cylinder. ⁵⁄₁₆" cylinder = 1 swingweight point. ⅝" cylinder = 2 swingweight points.

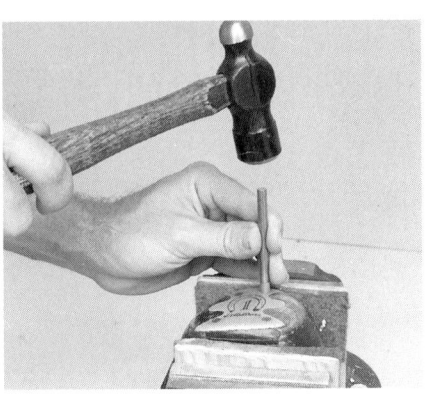

14-32 After drilling, install the lead cylinder with a special punch which is included with the kit. It is not necessary to install the lead cylinder with epoxy since the screw will expand the lead cylinder to fit securely.

14-33 Because the lead cylinders are pre-drilled, simply reinstall the original screw with a dab of epoxy on the tip end of the screw. The reinstalled screw should fit flush with the soleplate.

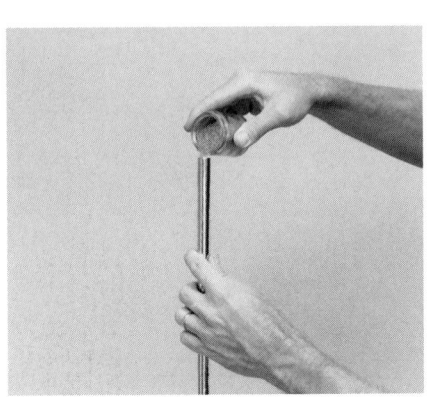

14-34 See Chapter 18, photos 18-7 through 18-12 for steps to increase swingweight by adding lead powder or lead rod down the shaft.

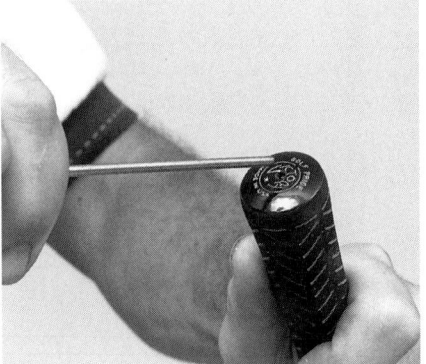

14-35 Note: A **Weight Checker Rod** can be used to determine the amount of weight down the shaft of a club without pulling the head or grip off. Simply push the rod through the grip cap hole until it bottoms out.

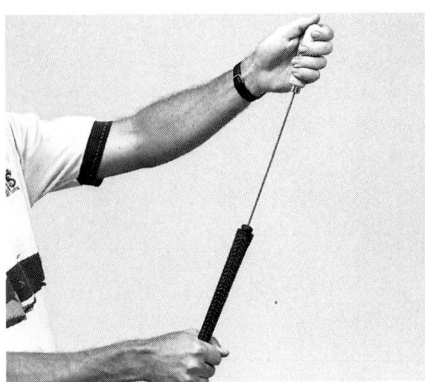

14-36 Push the rubber stopper against the grip cap, pull out the rod and use the "tip to stopper length" to determine how far up the shaft any lead or epoxy may be located.

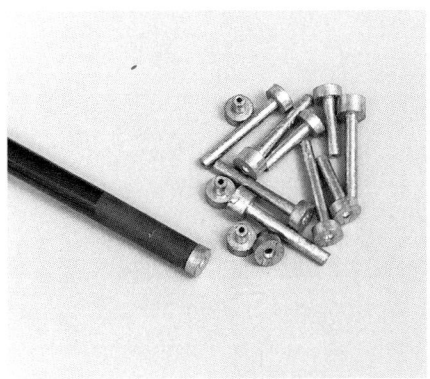

14-37 These lead **Plug-Wates** are used to add weight to the tip of steel and composite shafts. They come in 2, 4, 6, 8 and 10 gram weights. They are especially useful for weighting metal woods.

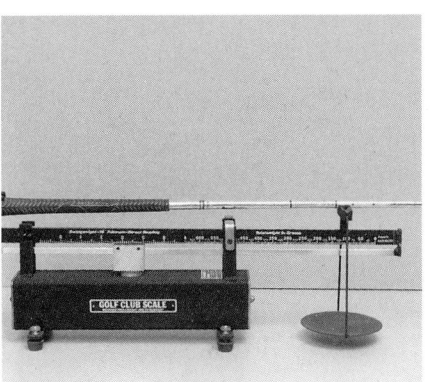

14-38 The GolfWorks® Swingweight Scale measures swingweight in Lorythmic units (D0, D1, D2, etc.) and total weight in ounces and grams. 14" fulcrum. The scale also has a tray for weighing individual components during club assembly.

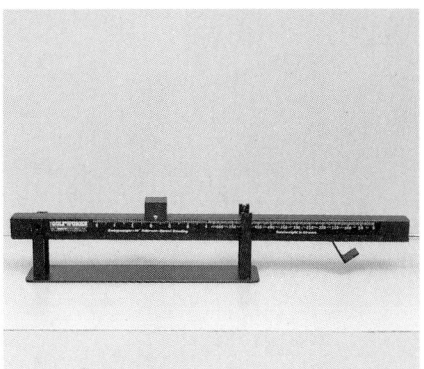

14-39 The GolfWorks® Low Cost Swingweight Scale measures swingweight in Lorythmic units (D0, D1, D2, etc.) and total weight in ounces and grams. 14" fulcrum.

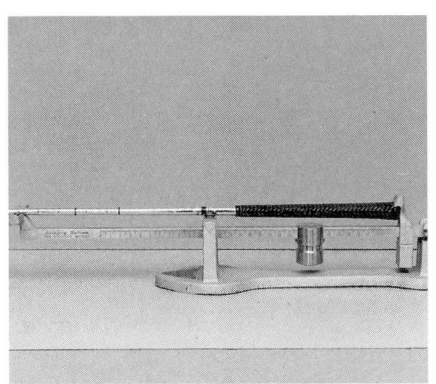

14-40 The Official Swingweight Scale measures in ounces (20.3, 20.4, 20.5, etc.) and total weight in ounces and grams. A conversion chart is used with this scale to convert the readings to Lorythmic units. 12" fulcrum. The name is a misnomer as virtually every manufacturer uses the Lorythmic reading type scales with 14" fulcrums.

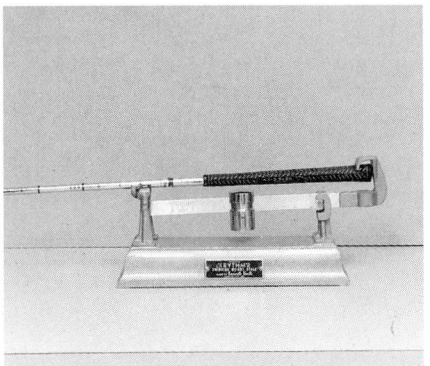

14-41 The Lorythmic Swingweight Scale measures swingweight only in Lorythmic units (D0, D1, D2, etc.). This is the original swingweight scale developed in the late 1920's. 14" fulcrum.

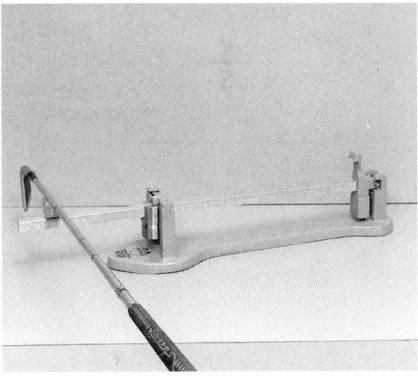

14-42 The Prorythmic Swingweight Scale measures swingweight in Lorythmic units (D0, D1, D2, etc.) and total weight in ounces and grams. 14" fulcrum. This photo shows the total weight being measured.

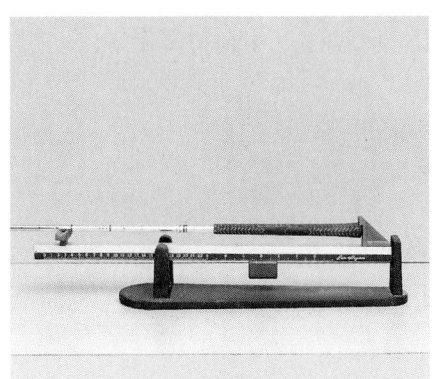

14-43 The Ben Hogan Co. Swingweight Scale measures swingweight in Lorythmic units (D0, D1, D2, etc.) and total weight in ounces and grams. 14" fulcrum.

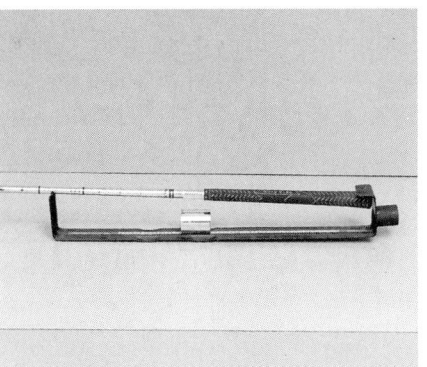

14-44 The Ping Swingweight Scale measures swingweight in Lorythmic units (D0, D1, D2, etc.) and total weight in ounces. 14" fulcrum.

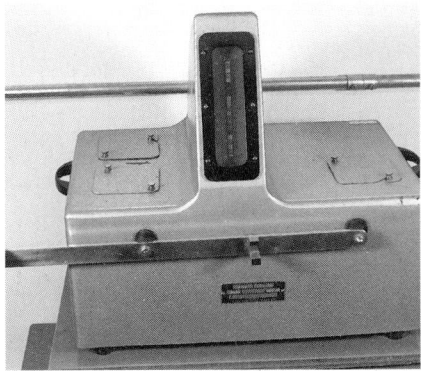

14-45 The Shadowgraph Swingweight Scale. This is an electronic scale which measures swingweight only. It is Lorythmic (D0, D1, D2, etc.) and is designed for production use because of its rapid dampening characteristic. 14" fulcrum.

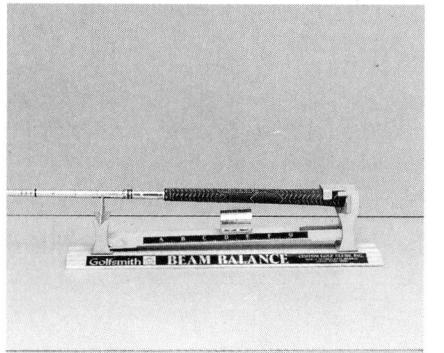

14-46 The Golfsmith Swingweight Scale measures swingweight only. Measures in Lorythmic units (D0, D1, D2, etc.). 14" fulcrum.

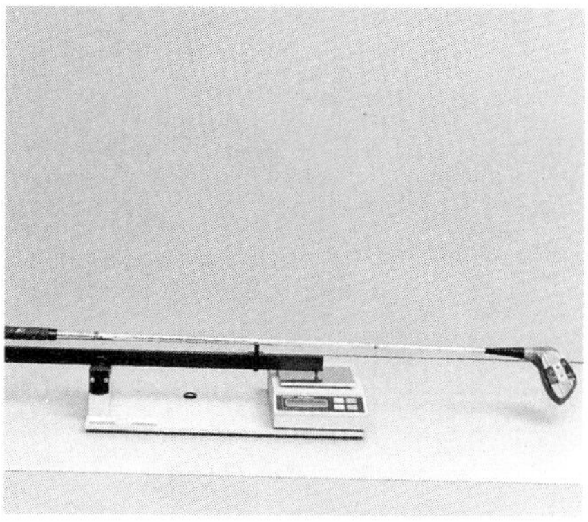

14-47 The O'Haus Electronic Swingweight Scale. This scale measures swingweight in Lorythmic units (D0, D1, D2, etc.) and total weight in ounces or grams. 14" fulcrum.

ADDITIONAL INFORMATION FOR CHANGING SWINGWEIGHT OF WOOD CLUBS

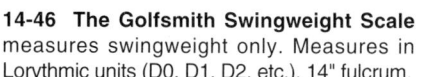

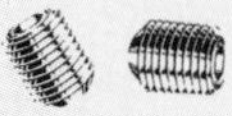

TABLE 14-1
Weight Port Screw – Installation Data

¹Weight Port Screw Size	Tap Drill Size	²Tap Size	Hex Key Wrench Size	Coarse or Fine Thread
#8-32 x ³⁄₁₆" lg.	#29	#8-32	⁵⁄₆₄"	Coarse
#10-24 x ³⁄₁₆" lg.	#25	#10-24	³⁄₃₂"	Coarse
#10-32 x ³⁄₁₆" lg.	#21	#10-32	³⁄₃₂"	Fine
¼-20 x ³⁄₁₆" lg.	#7	¼-20	⅛"	Coarse
¼-28 x ³⁄₁₆" lg.	#3	¼-28	⅛"	Fine
⁵⁄₁₆-18 x ¼" lg.	F	⁵⁄₁₆-18	⁵⁄₃₂"	Coarse
⁵⁄₁₆-24 x ¼" lg.	I	⁵⁄₁₆-24	⁵⁄₃₂"	Fine

¹ Weight port screws are actually "Socket Head Set Screws."
² The first number is the "Outside Thread Diameter" and the second number denotes the "Threads Per Inch."

Some Helpful Hints Pertaining to Swingweight

• For every ½" increase in a club's length, the swingweight will increase by 3 points.

• For every ½" decrease in a club's length, the swingweight will decrease by 3 points.

• If you would like to check a club's swingweight before installing the grip and any tape, allow 9 points (10 points for leather, cord or oversize rubber) for these components. Example: Ungripped club swingweights at E-0 and will probably be D-1 after gripping with an average weight 1¾ ounce rubber grip.

• Finishing a clubhead usually increases the swingweight from 1½ to 2 points (stain, filler, colorcote, clear finish and whipping).

• Every 4 swingweights are equivalent to approximately ¼ ounce (7.09 grams). A swingweight point in a wood head is approximately .065 ounces (2 grams). See Fig. 14-48.

• A swingweight point in the grip end of a wood is approximately .13 ounces (4 grams) or twice as much as is required in the head end. If .13 ounces is added to the grip end, the swingweight will decrease by 1 point. This is called "counterbalancing." Also, .13 ounces taken out of the grip end will increase the swingweight by 1 point. See Fig. 14-48.

176

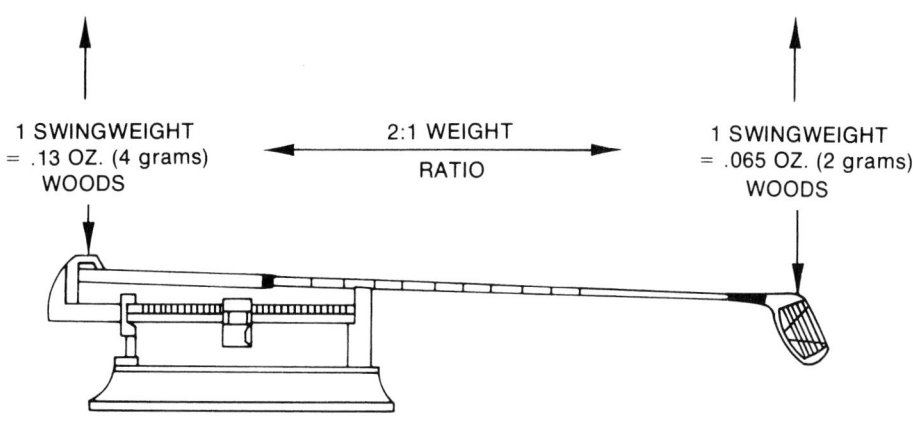

FIG. 14-48
Approximate swingweight equivalents for grip and head ends of club

• The lighter the shaft, the heavier the head weight must be to obtain the same swingweight that you would get with a heavier shaft. Even though the head weight is heavier with the lighter shaft, the total weight of the club will still be less. For a general rule of thumb, use the following: For each 1 ounce reduction in shaft weight, a wood club will lose approximately 5 swingweight points. This, of course, assumes that the grip weight and shaft length are exactly the same. Example: A set of D-2 woods with Dynamic™ taper tip shafts (4⅜ ounces) are reshafted with Extralite™ taper tip shafts (3⅜ ounces). Without reweighting the heads, the swingweight would now be C-7. Approximately 5/16 ounce of weight would have to be added to the heads to achieve a D-2 swingweight. The Extralite™ shaft is 1 ounce lighter, leaving a net reduction in total club weight of 11/16 ounce. For a comparative look at what happened, refer to the driver example in Table 14-2. The design chapters in this book will explain technically why head weights must be increased when changing to or using lighter shafts.

	Driver Before Change: Dynamic™ Taper Tip Shaft	**Driver After Change: Extralite™ Taper Tip Shaft**	**Difference From Change**	**Club Specs: Reweighted to D-2**	**Net Change In Club**
TABLE 14-2 **Effect of Different Weight Shafts on Driver Head Weight,** **Total Weight and Swingweight**					
Shaft Weight (ounces)	4.37	3.37	– 1	3.37	– 1
Head Weight (ounces)	7	7	Same	7.31	+.31
Grip Weight (ounces)	1.75	1.75	Same	1.75	None
Total Weight (ounces)	13.12	12.12	– 1	12.43	– .69
Swingweight	D-2	C-7	– 5	D-2	+ 5

Note: A 1 ounce reduction in shaft weight for an iron club would decrease swingweight by 3 points because of the shorter shaft length. Refer to Chapter 18 for more information.

• Installing face screws or replacing them with a larger size will affect swingweight. Table 14-3 has been developed for you to use as a guideline for face insert screw weights and swingweight equivalents.

TABLE 14-3
Effect of Face Insert Screw Weights on Swingweight

Description:	Brass Screw Size	Weight Per Screw	Weight of 4 Screws	Swingweight Equivalent[2]	Weight of 5 Screws	Swingweight Equivalent	Weight of 6 Screws	Swingweight Equivalent
Standard Face Insert Screw	#4 x ⅝ Lg.	.6 grams	2.4 grams	+ 1¼	3 grams	+ 1½	3.6 grams	+ 1¾
Oversize Face Insert Screw	#5 x ¾ Lg.	.95 grams	3.8 grams	+1⅞	4.8 grams	+ 2⅜	5.7 grams	+ 2⅞
Standard Soleplate Screw[1]	#7 x ¾ Lg.	1.43 grams	5.7 grams	+ 2⅞	7.1 grams	+ 3½	8.6 grams	+ 4⅜

[1] In some older clubs standard soleplate screws were also used in the face.
[2] Swingweight equivalent means the number of swingweight points a club will change.

• The #5 x 1⅛" steel shaft locking screw weighs 1.45 grams and is equivalent to ¾ of a swingweight point.

• The tapered hardwood plug on through bore shafts weighs 1.52 grams and is equivalent to ¾ of a swingweight point.

• A dollar bill weighs 1 gram and is equivalent to ½ of a swingweight point. A dime weighs 2 grams and is equivalent to 1 point. A quarter weighs 6 grams and is equivalent to 3 points.

•A cycolac (ABS plastic) or fiber insert weighs approximately 14 grams in a driver or an equivalent of 7 swingweights. A Gamma Fire™ insert (green glass) of the same size weighs approximately 32 grams in a driver or an equivalent of 16 swingweights. If you change a standard plastic insert to a Gamma Fire™ insert, you can plan on increasing swingweight by almost 9 points. Therefore, to maintain the original swingweight, you must remove a little over 9⁄16 ounce (17 grams) from the head.

• If you use ½" wide lead tape, it takes approximately a 4½" long piece to weigh 2 grams or be equivalent to 1 swingweight point.

• An average length whipping of .022" braided or twisted nylon will weigh approximately 1.5 grams or an equivalent of ¾ swingweight point.

• To convert grams to ounces, divide by 28.35.

• To convert ounces to grams, multiply by 28.35. 1 ounce = 28.35 grams.

TABLE 14-4
Swingweight Conversion Chart
Official Swingweight Scale vs. Lorythmic Swingweight Scale

Official Swingweight Scale Reading	Lorythmic Scale Swingweight		Official Swingweight Scale Reading	Lorythmic Scale Swingweight	
	Woods	Irons		Woods	Irons
18.33	C0	B8	20.00	D0	C8
18.4	0.4	8.4	20.05	0.3	8.3
18.45	0.7	8.7	20.1	0.6	8.6
			20.15	0.9	8.9
18.5	C1	B9	20.17	D1	C9
18.55	1.3	9.3			
18.6	1.6	9.6	20.2	1.2	9.2
			20.25	1.5	9.5
18.65	C2	C0	20.3	1.8	9.8
18.7	2.2	0.2	20.33	D2	D0
18.75	2.5	0.5			
18.8	2.8	0.8	20.35	2.1	0.1
			20.4	2.4	0.4
18.83	C3	C1	20.45	2.7	0.7
18.85	3.1	1.1	20.5	D3	D1
18.9	3.4	1.4			
18.95	3.7	1.7	20.55	3.3	1.3
			20.6	3.6	1.6
19.00	C4	C2	20.65	D4	D2
19.05	4.3	2.3			
19.1	4.6	2.6	20.7	4.2	2.2
19.15	4.9	2.9	20.75	4.5	2.5
			20.8	4.8	2.8
19.17	C5	C3	20.83	D5	D3
19.2	5.2	3.2			
19.25	5.5	3.5	20.85	5.1	3.1
19.3	5.8	3.8	20.9	5.4	3.4
			20.95	5.7	3.7
19.33	C6	C4	21.00	D6	D4
19.35	6.1	4.1			
19.4	6.4	4.4	21.05	6.3	4.3
19.45	6.7	4.7	21.1	6.6	4.6
			21.15	6.9	4.9
19.5	C7	C5	21.17	D7	D5
19.55	7.3	5.3			
19.6	7.6	5.6	21.2	7.2	5.2
19.65	7.9	5.9	21.25	7.5	5.5
			21.3	7.8	5.8
19.66	C8	C6	21.33	D8	D6
19.7	8.2	6.2			
19.75	8.5	6.5	21.35	8.1	6.1
19.8	8.8	6.8	21.4	8.4	6.4
			21.45	8.7	6.7
19.83	C9	C7	21.5	D9	D7
19.85	9.1	7.1			
19.9	9.4	7.4	21.55	9.3	7.3
19.95	9.7	7.7	21.6	9.6	7.6
			21.65	9.9	7.9
			21.66	E0	D8

CHAPTER 15

BRASS AND LEAD BACKWEIGHT REMOVAL, INSTALLATION AND REFITTING

Many of the woods manufactured in the past and even some today have some sort of backweight. Backweights can range from a hunk of brass screwed on the back of the club to a poured lead inset routed into the back. The latter is most indicative of early and classic type MacGregor® clubs. Backweights do become loose as in the case of brass backweights and they also shift, slide and mushroom as in the case of poured lead backweights. During the course of normal repairs, you run across these situations and it is necessary to offer a concise explanation of how to repair them.

Also, with the popularizing of custom club making and component assembly, it is also necessary to cover the installation of new lead and brass backweights in both new and used clubs.

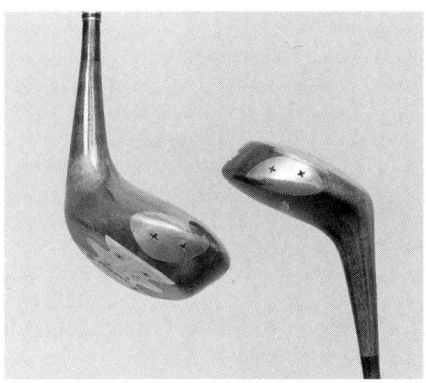

15-1 A loose brass backweight is usually identified by a rattling sound or the existence of a gap between the wood and the backweight.

15-2 To tighten a loose brass backweight, first clean out the screw head recesses using a scriber or sharpened awl.

15-3 If the screws will not turn out, heat them with a propane torch and a screw heater or …

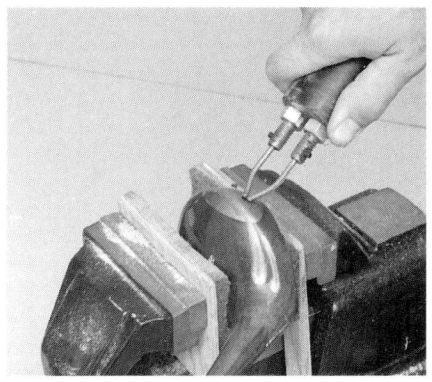

15-4 … use the **Electric Screw Extractor.**

15-5 Next, remove the screws. Screw heads may be either a straight slot, Phillips style or Frearson type.

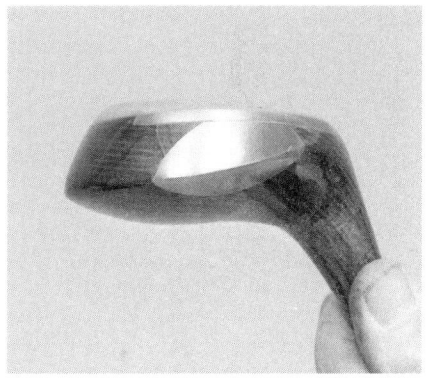

15-6 Some manufacturers are very clever in disguising the screws. This photo shows a backweight held on with a headless brass backweight screw. Virtually every backweight will have a screw of one type or another. Examine a backweight closely if it does not have an obvious slotted type screw.

15-7 Procedure for removing headless screws. Drill ⅛" deep into the center of the screw head with a 5⁄64" drill bit. Note: Making a slight indentation into the center of the head with an awl or a center punch will keep the bit from walking around and help start it correctly.

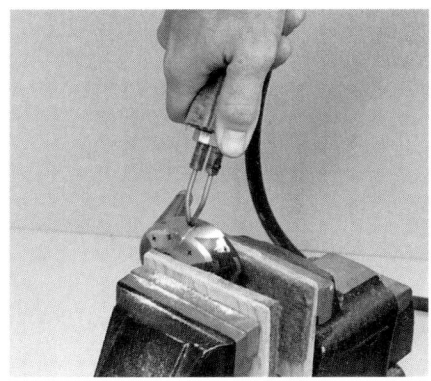

15-8 Heat the screw as previously shown.

15-9 Tap a #1 size extractor into the hole until it bites and turn the extractor counterclockwise. Note the use of the "T" handle Tap Wrench.

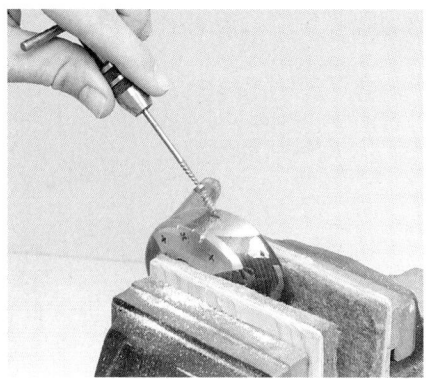

15-10 The screw is now removed.

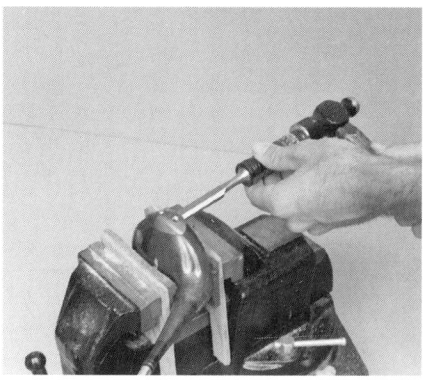

15-11 Next, insert a ½" wide or smaller wood chisel as shown and gently tap with a hammer. Heat the backweight if it will not come off easily. Avoid damaging the wood around the backweight. A heat gun works well for this.

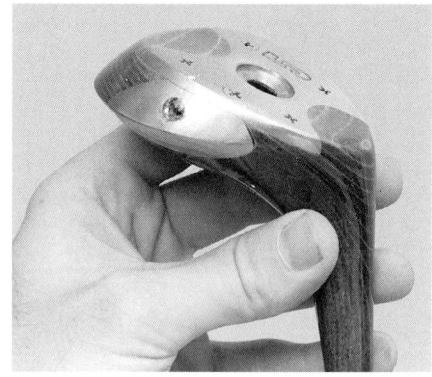

15-12 If the backweight rests against the soleplate, remove the soleplate as outlined in Chapter 2. The only reason to remove the soleplate is to gain access to the bottom of the backweight so it can be removed with the chisel if it will not come loose otherwise.

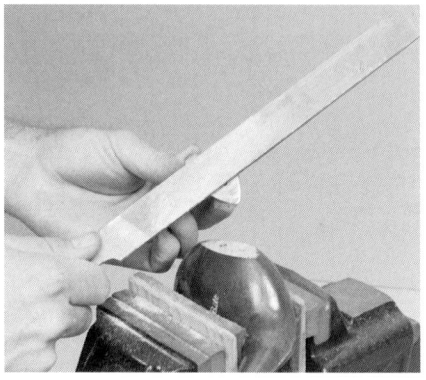

15-13 Remove the brass backweight. Use a smooth cut file to clean off all the old epoxy from the flat side of the backweight.

15-14 Carefully remove any glue from the flat portion of the wood. Maintain a perfectly flat surface.

15-15 Mix up some shear strength epoxy, apply it to the wood and …

15-16 … also apply epoxy to the back-weight.

15-17 Place the backweight in place and install the original screws or use new screws. If the backweight turns out of place as a result of turning the screws in …

15-18 … set the backweight in the desired position and lay a couple layers of masking tape across the backweight to ensure it does not move. This usually only occurs when a backweight has a single screw. Most back-weights utilize two screws for safety.

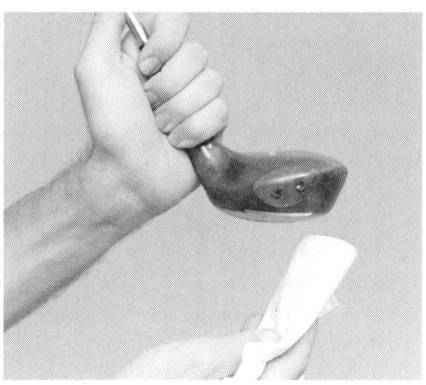

15-19 Wipe off all excess epoxy and reinstall the soleplate (if previously removed) as outlined in Chapter 2. The club is now ready for refinishing.

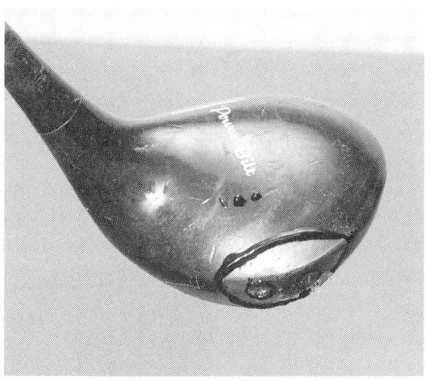

15-20 This photo shows another club with the backweight reinstalled. Note the epoxy that has been hydraulically squeezed up through the top of the club. Do not be alarmed if this happens. Persimmon is an open grain wood and the above reaction is quite common.

15-21 Installing a new brass backweight. First remove the soleplate. After the soleplate is removed, check to see if any weight can be removed from the head. The addition of a brass backweight will add ½ to 1½ ounces of weight to the head. This increase needs to be offset by the removal of the same amount of weight from the head.

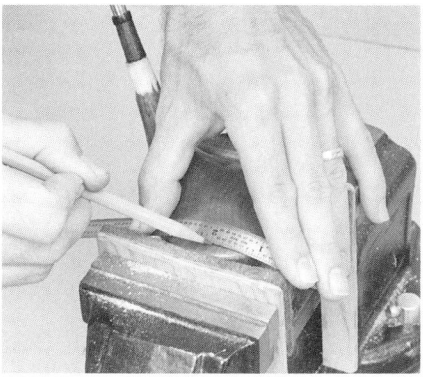

15-22 Next, mark the portion of wood to be sawed using a straight edge and pencil.

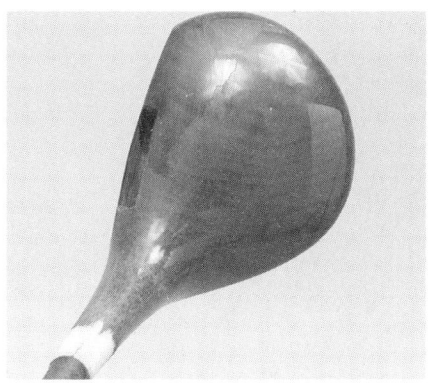

15-23 The line indicating where the cut is to be made should "appear" to be parallel to the face. In actuality, the line will be drawn slightly open to the face if it is to look parallel. If the line is drawn exactly parallel, it will appear to be closed relative to the face. See notes on this at the end of the chapter.

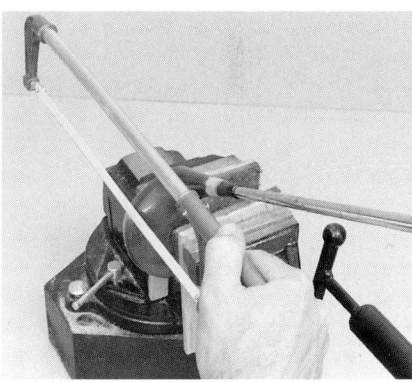

15-24 With a hacksaw or on a bandsaw, carefully follow the line and cut off the back portion of the wood.

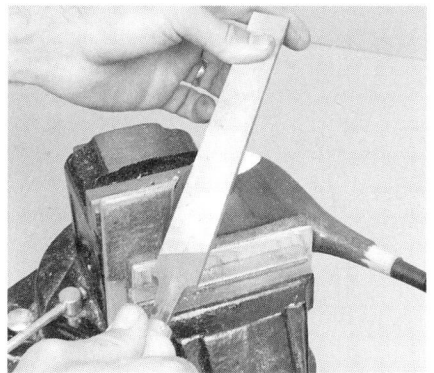

15-25 Use a file or a belt sander to make sure the sawed portion of the wood is absolutely flat.

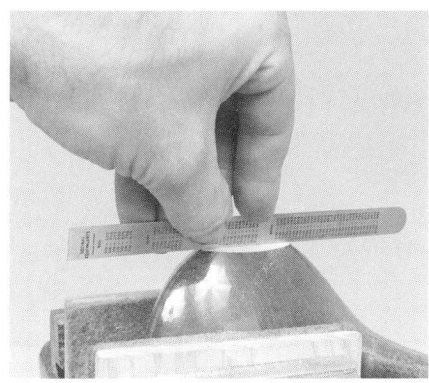

15-26 Check for absolute flatness first in one direction and ...

15-27 ... also in the other direction. A 6" steel scale works well for this.

15-28 Check the backweight for the proper fit and location. Minor changes can be made through filing if the backweight does not appear to be in the correct location.

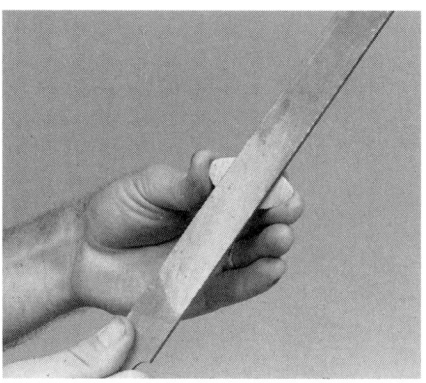

15-29 Lightly abrade the flat side of the backweight for better epoxy adhesion.

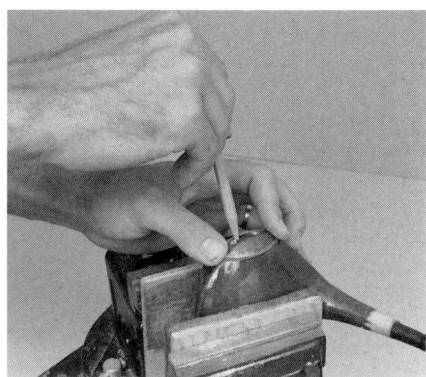

15-30 If a predrilled backweight is being used, place the backweight in position and mark the location of the screw holes using the holes in the backweight as a guide.

15-31 Drill the screw holes in the wood head. The drill bit size is determined by the size of the screw used. A ⅛" bit is normally used.

15-32 After applying the epoxy to both the backweight and the wood, lay the backweight in place.

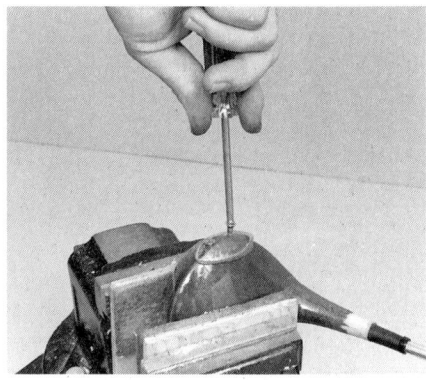

15-33 Apply a dab of epoxy to each screw and screw the backweight down tightly. A #7 brass screw is being used here.

15-34 Wipe off the excess epoxy. Allow the epoxy to cure. After the epoxy has cured, proceed to photo 15-42 for completion steps.

15-35 If an undrilled backweight is used, lay the backweight in place after applying epoxy to both the backweight and the wood.

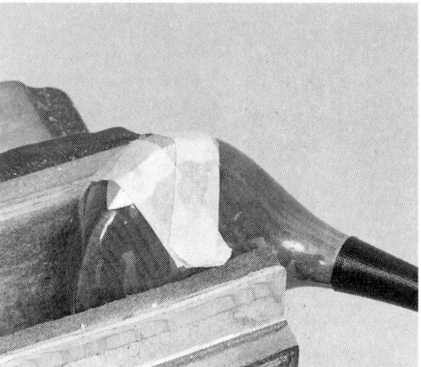

15-36 Lay a couple of layers of tape across the backweight and wood to ensure the backweight does not move. Allow the epoxy to cure.

184

15-37 After the epoxy has hardened, determine whether you wish to install one or two screws.

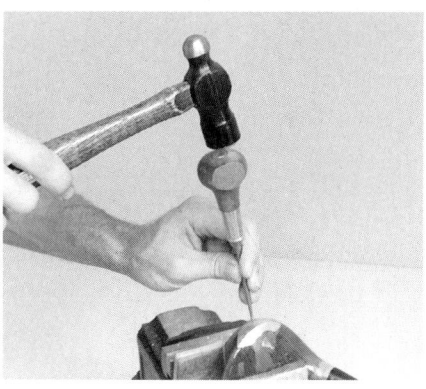

15-38 If one screw is installed, make a slight indentation into the center of the backweight but on the bottom half. Two screws require two indentations at points that are approximately equidistant from the center.

15-39 Drill through the backweight and into the head with a 9/64" drill bit. (This is the pilot drill for a #8 screw.)

15-40 Next, countersink the pilot holes to a depth that allows most of the screw head to seat below the surface of the backweight.

15-41 Install the appropriate screw. A #8 screw is being used here. A dab of epoxy is usually applied to the screw before installation.

15-42 After the epoxy has cured, file the backweight to shape using a medium cut file and then a fine cut file.

15-43 Sand the backweight smooth by hand or on a sanding machine using 150 grit to remove all scratches.

15-44 The finished backweight should look like this. Check the swingweight and make any necessary adjustments as shown in Chapter 14. Reinstall the soleplate as shown in Chapter 2 and then refer to Chapter 1 for refinishing steps.

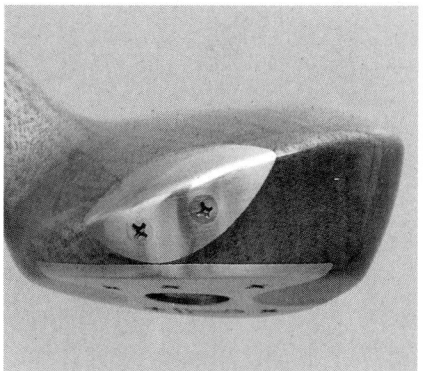

15-45 Aluminum backweights are also used. Aluminum is lighter than brass and is sometimes more desirable for larger model drivers that will not allow the addition of a heavy brass backweight.

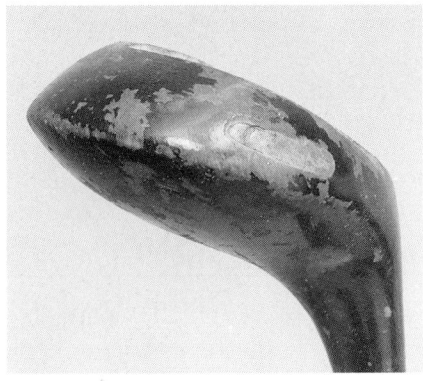

15-46 Procedure for repouring a lead backweight. Lead backweights sometimes fall out, become loose or mushroom and overflow like this one.

15-47 To remove this type of a backweight, drill a 7/32" hole at the point shown in the photo. Drill at the angle shown. Drill another hole on the opposite side. Occasionally a center hole should be drilled if the backweight has a center plug extending into the wood head.

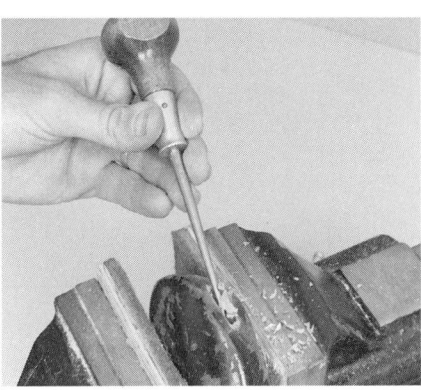

15-48 Using an awl or very narrow ¼" width wood chisel, gently tap and pry all of the ...

15-49 ... old lead from the cavity. The three previously drilled holes should be empty of all lead and debris as they will act as a mechanical lock when the new lead backweight is repoured.

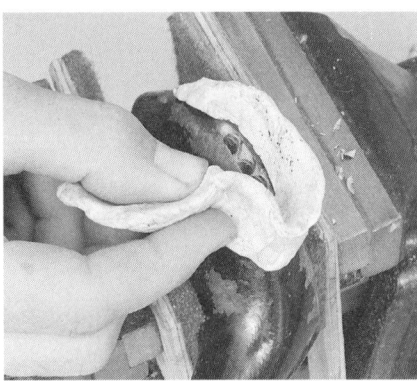

15-50 First, use Mortite putty to form a dam around the cavity.

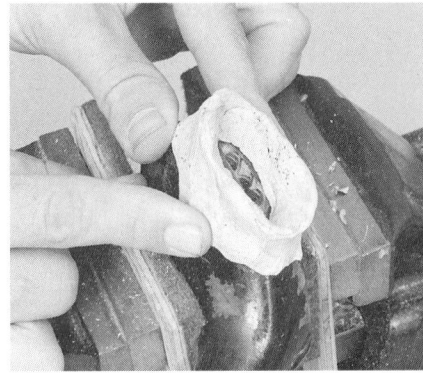

15-51 Press the putty down tight on the head and shape it like the old backweight. Do not allow any of the Mortite to rest inside the cavity.

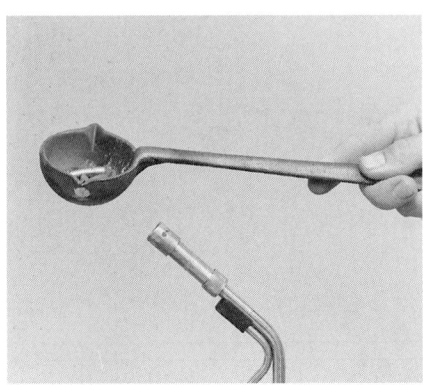

15-52 Place several pieces of lead material in a ladle and melt it using a propane torch.

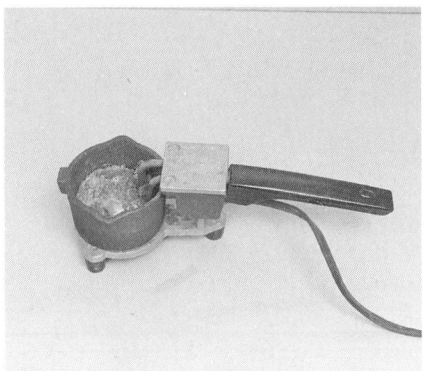

15-53 An alternative to melting the lead is to use the **Electric Hot Pot with stand.** This is very handy for keeping lead molten in a repair shop.

15-54 Carefully pour molten lead into the cavity. Lead can burn the head more than is necessary if it gets too hot. Before pouring, the lead should be just above the temperature at which it solidifies.

186

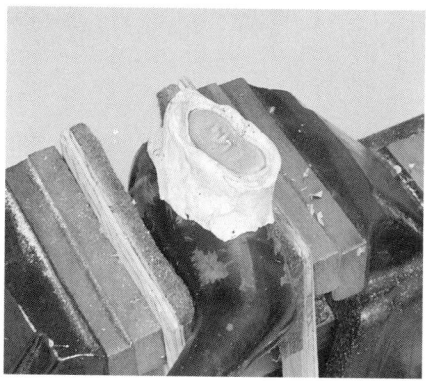

15-55 Allow the lead to cool for 5 to 10 minutes.

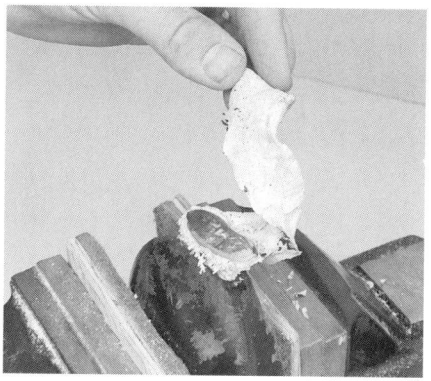

15-56 Remove the putty from the head.

15-57 Using a ball peen hammer, mushroom the lead in the middle and around the edges so that it becomes very tight in the cavity.

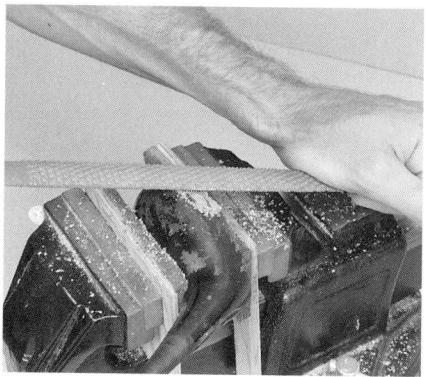

15-58 Use a "Rasp" or coarse cut file and rough shape the lead.

15-59 Next, switch to a fine file and smooth the lead so it blends perfectly with the wood.

15-60 Finally, sand the lead smooth.

15-61 Installing a new lead backweight. Use a pencil and straight edge to determine the outline and location. The shape and size is left up to the individual.

15-62 Using a ⁷⁄₃₂" drill bit, drill ⁵⁄₈" deep at the angle shown.

15-63 Drill another ⁷⁄₃₂" diameter hole in the opposite side at the angle shown.

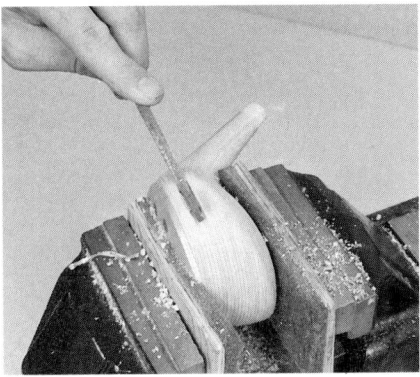

15-64 With a small round wood rasp, file back and forth to get the desired shape.

15-65 The cavity should look like this.

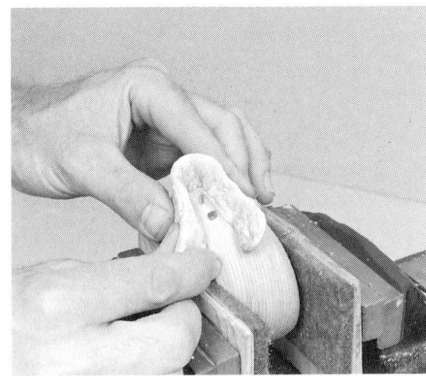

15-66 Next, form a dam with Mortite putty. Press the putty down tightly.

15-67 Be sure the dam is high enough and formed properly. Check to make sure no Mortite putty is in the cavity.

15-68 Pour in the molten lead.

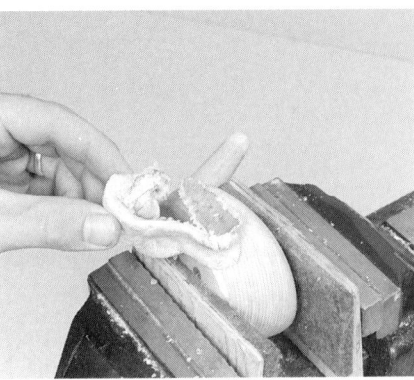

15-69 Remove the putty dam after allowing the lead to cool for 5 to 10 minutes.

15-70 Next, peen the lead in its middle and all around the edges to lock it tightly in the cavity.

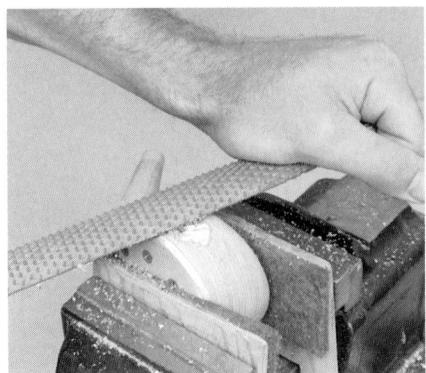

15-71 Rough shape the backweight with a rasp or coarse cut file. Then file the backweight with a fine cut file until smooth and flush with the wood.

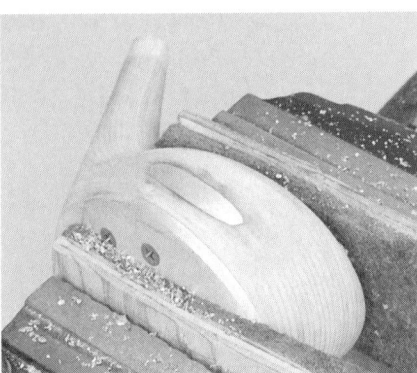

15-72 The finished lead backweight should look like this after it has been hand or machine sanded smooth. Refer to Chapter 1 for refinishing steps.

ADDITIONAL INFORMATION FOR BRASS AND LEAD BACKWEIGHT REMOVAL, INSTALLATION AND REFITTING

Installing a backweight on a head which previously did not have one requires that the backweight be properly lined up with the face. The most common mistake is to install the backweight parallel with the face. This of course seems to be the logical approach, but the result will be a backweight which will appear quite hooked in relation to the face. In actual fact, a backweight should be installed 4°-6° open to the face so that it appears parallel or square with the face. See Fig. 15-73.

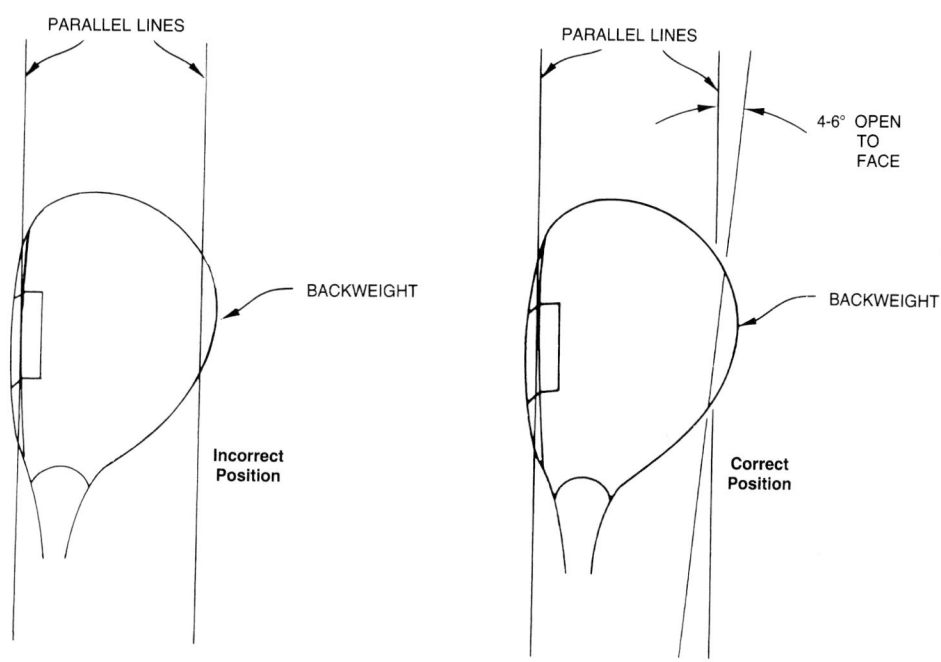

FIG. 15-73
Proper positioning for a backweight

The backweight location in the toe to heel direction should be as close to the center of the face as possible, however, this is dictated more by clubhead shape and back radius than by personal choice. The backweight will vary some from the face center position, but remember, the weight of all the head's components determines the center of gravity (center of mass) location in the heel to toe direction. Therefore, the center of gravity in the head can still be located on the face center in the heel and toe direction even though the backweight is slightly forward or back.

NOTES

_____

_____

_____

_____

_____

CHAPTER 16

FINISH REFURBISHING AND TOUCHUP TECHNIQUES

When you are working with a club that benefits from a refinish, the end result should be a club that appears as if it had just been finished at the factory. The challenge when working with a clubhead that does not benefit from a refinish is to present the repaired head in a condition that is as good if not better than when it was first given to you.

The difficulty with this challenge will range from fairly simple as in touching up a reshafted club; to very difficult as when refurbishing a clubhead that has had the insert reset or replaced and the soleplate reset. As more clubhead components are removed, and consequently more of the original finish is disturbed, the more difficult the touchup job becomes.

Touching up the finish on a repaired clubhead is absolutely necessary not only for the obvious cosmetic reasons, but also to ensure that the clubhead will not absorb moisture that results in a rotting of the wood in the exposed area. The following pages will aid you when refurbishing or touching up the finish after your clubhead repairs are complete.

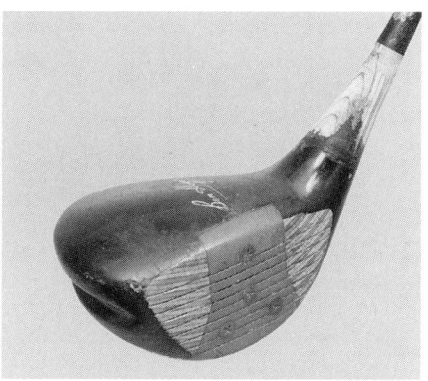

16-1 Finish refurbish and whip hosel. The purpose is to take an existing club with a dull, worn or marred finish and substantially improve it, while at the same time sealing the club from moisture absorption. The procedure benefits woods that are reshafted or rewhipped or simply a wood requiring a general clean-up or winterizing service.

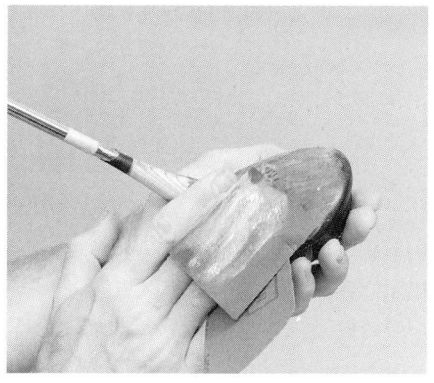

16-2 First, carefully hand sand the entire clubhead with 400 grade sandpaper. This will level an uneven surface. Be careful not to sand through the old finish.

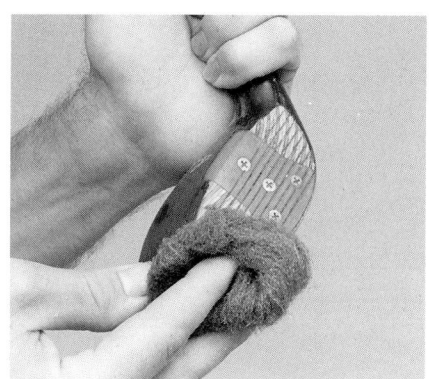

16-3 Hand or machine steel wool the head using 000 steel wool. Steel wooling will blend in the scratches left behind by the fine sandpaper. If necessary, touchup any bare spots with a matching stain color.

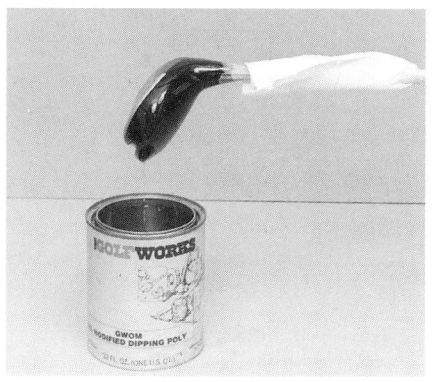

16-4 Next, wrap a paper towel around the shaft above the hosel. Dip the clubhead into the polyurethane. After the poly stops flowing from the head and begins to drip …

16-5 … turn the toe upright with the face slightly open as shown. Note: **Whitty Dippers**, a small stretchable disc, can be used instead of paper towels to prevent the polyurethane from running down the shaft.

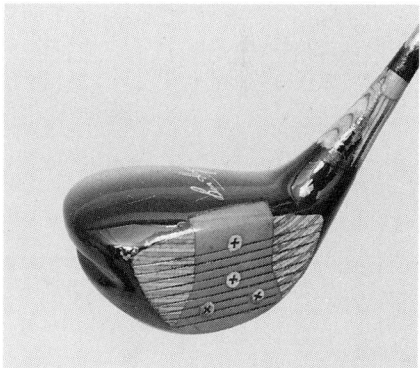

16-6 Allow the poly coating to cure overnight. Whipping can then be applied as shown in Chapter 6. This refurbish and new whipping can make a wood look like new.

16-7 How to touchup the face. This touchup technique applies to a wood whose face has been filed clean of the finish. Repairs that could cause this would be insert resetting or replacement, loft, bulge, roll or face angle alterations. First, remove the whipping if it is not already off the club.

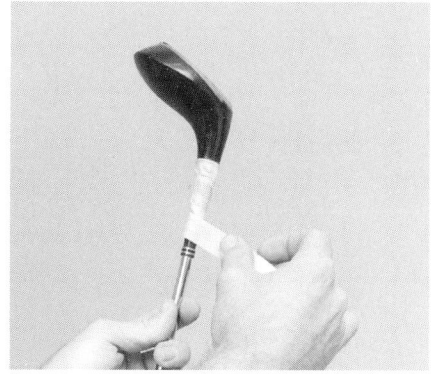

16-8 A club with a plastic whipping cover should be covered with masking tape.

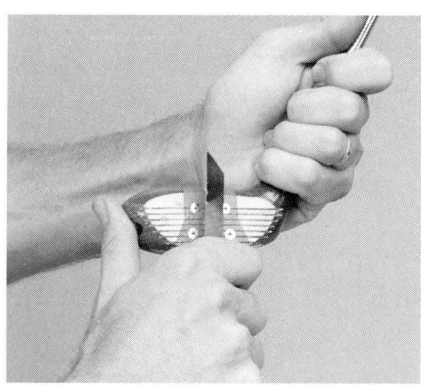

16-9 Scrape the entire face with the **Detail Knife.** This effectively removes all file or sandpaper marks and creates a smooth surface.

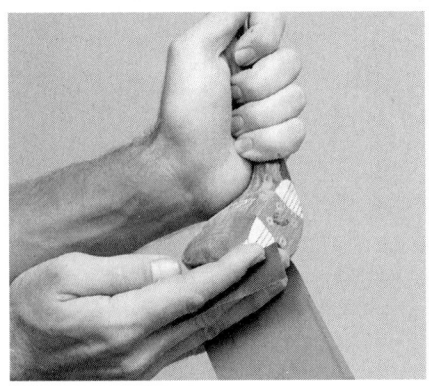

16-10 Hand sand the entire club with 400 grade sandpaper. Hand or machine steel wool the sanded surface using 000 steel wool.

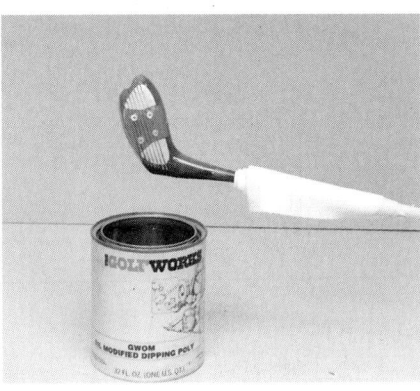

16-11 Dip a coat of polyurethane. Allow the coating to cure overnight.

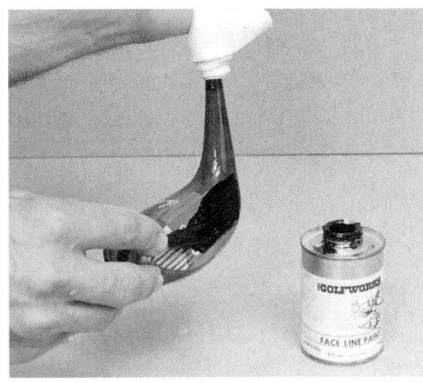

16-12 The face lines are paint filled by wiping or brushing a quick dry enamel into the grooves. Scoring line paint is available from most golf supply houses.

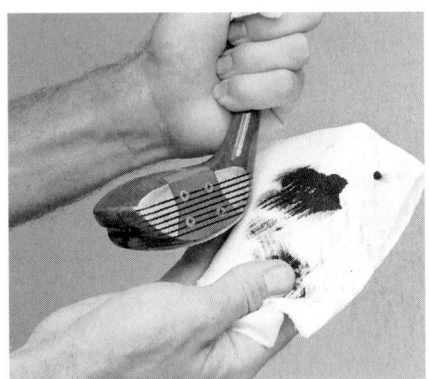

16-13 Wipe off the excess scoring line paint with a paper towel which is alternately folded back and forth to expose a clean surface. Dampening the towel with Naphtha or Grip Solvent and wiping across the face will remove stubborn paint. Allow the face paint to dry 12 hours.

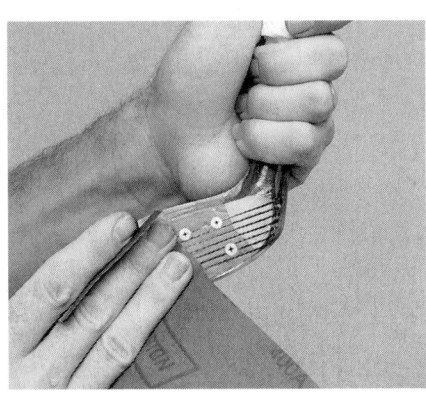

16-14 After the scoring line paint has dried, lightly hand sand the face and head with 400 grit sandpaper and then hand or machine steel wool the head with 000 steel wool.

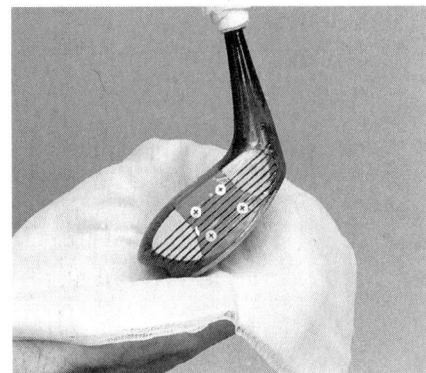

16-15 Prior to every polyurethane coating, lightly wipe the head with a tack rag to ensure all dust or steel wool particles are removed.

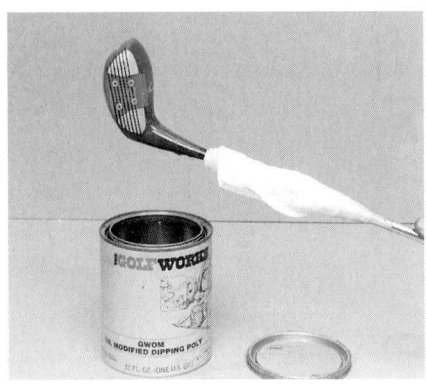

16-16 Dip a final coat of polyurethane. This two-coat dipping process is very effective in sealing the face from moisture. Some repairmen may wish to dip an additional coat for a more even clubface surface after once again sanding and steel wooling the head.

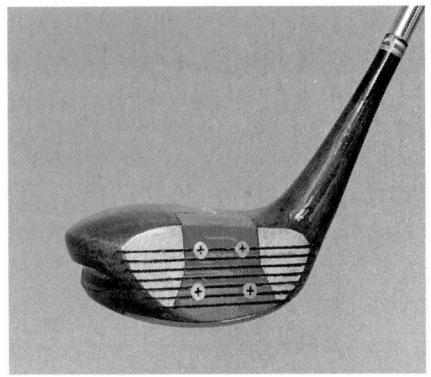

16-17 After the polyurethane has dried, the club is ready for whipping following the steps shown in Chapter 6.

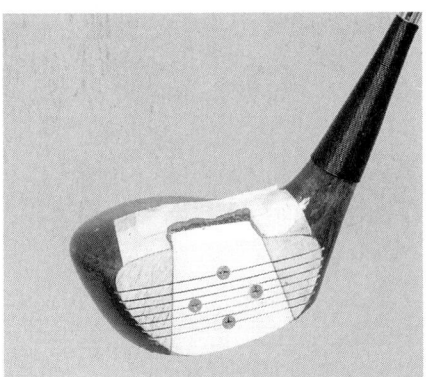

16-18 How to touchup around the top of the insert. This skill is needed when replacing or resetting an insert. Note the use of masking tape around the top of the insert. This protects the finish from epoxy.

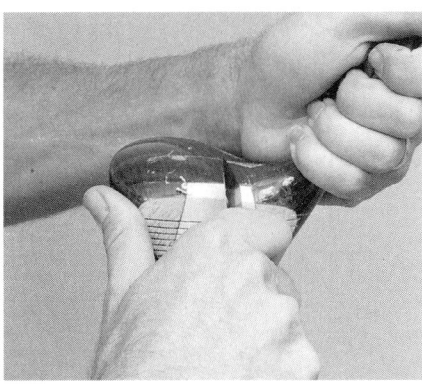

16-19 The top of the insert must be flush with the finish. Once the excess epoxy and any masking tape has been removed (see Chapter 4, photos 4-41 through 4-44 for removal of excess epoxy and tape), lightly scrape the top of the insert with a **Detail Knife** to bring the top of the insert down flush to the top of the finish.

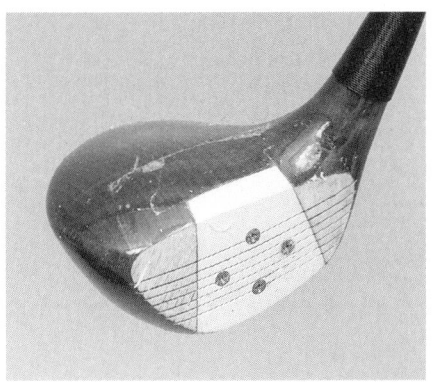

16-20 Once the level of the finish and the insert are even, minor scratches in the finish are easily removed by …

16-21 … hand sanding the area with 400 sandpaper. Remove the whipping before sanding. If sanded properly, this will remove the scratches left from filing or scraping. DO NOT SAND THROUGH THE FINISH.

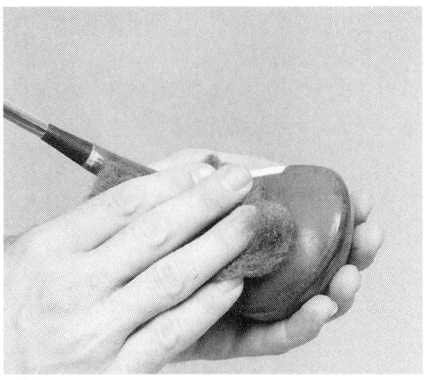

16-22 Next, lightly steel wool the sanded area with 000 steel wool.

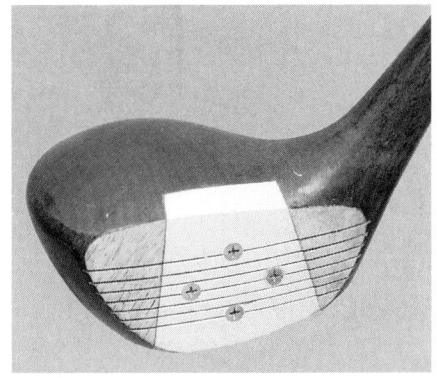

16-23 The club is now ready for touchup steps applicable to the face as shown in photos 16-7 through 16-17.

16-24 How to touchup a break in the finish. This photo shows an area of the club where too much filing or sanding has resulted in breaking through the finish into the bare wood. This procedure also applies when the stain or wood filler is inadvertently scraped from the head when detailing the face.

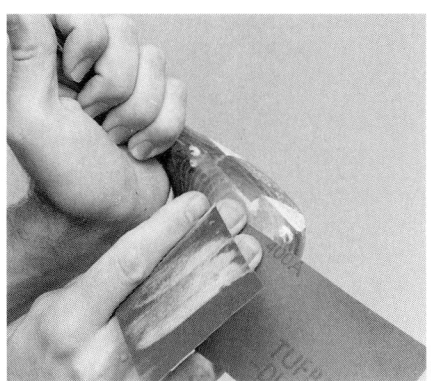

16-25 First, fine sand the damaged area with 400 grade paper to "feather in" the sharp edges of the poly. This step may enlarge the damaged area, however, it is necessary to create a smooth surface.

16-26 Next, select a stain that matches the color of the wood. Dip a paper towel or cloth into the stain and …

16-27 … blot the stained towel onto the damaged area. Open grain wood will accept stain and hopefully the newly stained area will match the rest of the club.

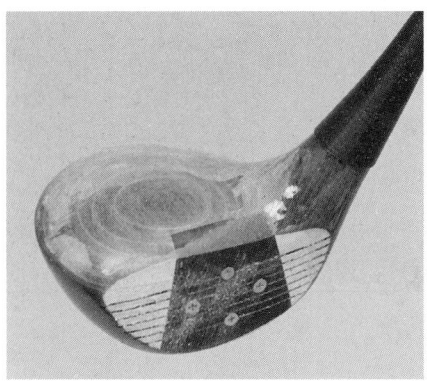

16-28 Often though, the newly stained area will be too light. Repeated staining will darken the color somewhat. Applying less intense black filler will help to darken the stain color slightly.

16-29 The best way to darken a light spot is as follows: Water base stains are available in dye powder form. Storing extra packets of the more popular colors in powder form will prove invaluable to you.

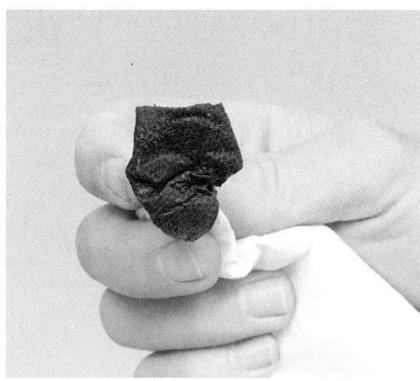

16-30 Dip the damp paper towel or cloth into the dye powder. Only a few grains are needed.

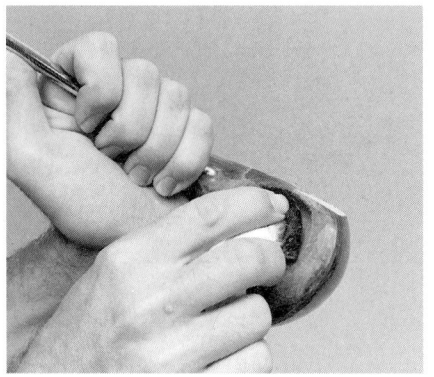

16-31 Rub the grains into the light area of the head.

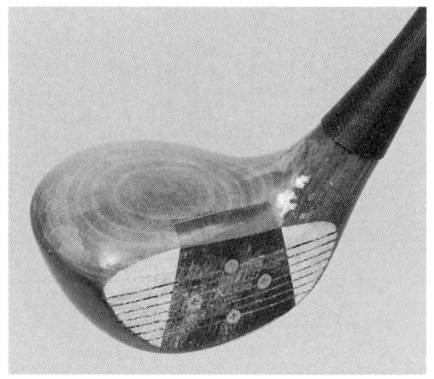

16-32 The difference in color will be dramatic. If the area is now too dark, simply rub the area with another paper towel dampened with plain water. This will dilute the intensity of the stain in the area. You will be amazed at the effectiveness of this step. This technique can be used anywhere on the clubhead.

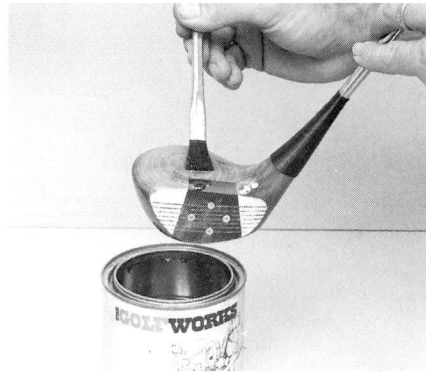

16-33 Brush two coats of poly over any bare areas allowing an overnight dry between each coat.

16-34 Next, remove the whipping if you have not already done so. Hand sand the entire head with 400 grit sandpaper, steel wool with 000 steel wool and dip two coats of clear polyurethane finish.

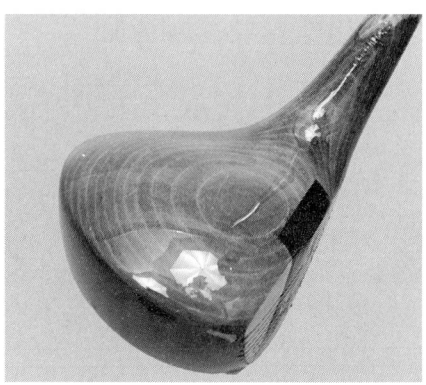

16-35 The repaired area should match in color with the rest of the head.

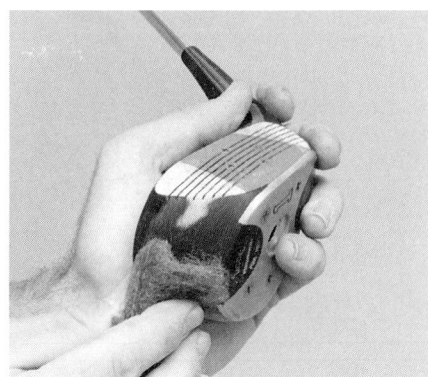

16-36 How to touchup bare spots on colorcoted heads. Colorcoted clubs are easier to fix than stained clubs. First, sand the affected area to "feather in" the finish around it. Next, 000 steel wool the area and ...

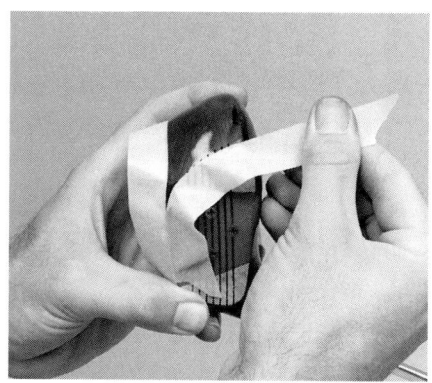

16-37 … apply masking tape over the clubface and sole area to prevent colorcote overspray from getting on them.

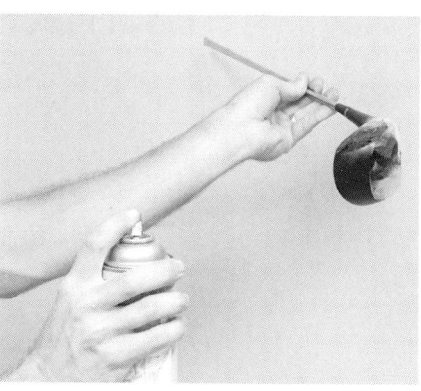

16-38 Spray a couple of light coats of colorcote on the bare area. Wait 15 minutes between each coat.

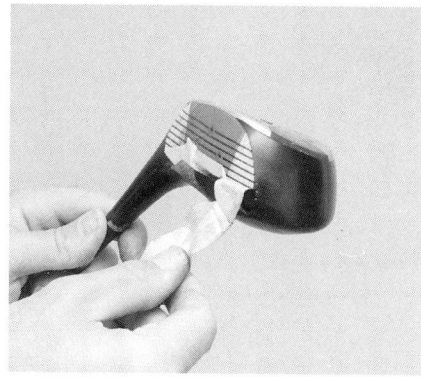

16-39 After 15 minutes of drying, remove the tape. Allow the colorcote to dry completely (see the drying times at the end of the chapter for various colorcotes). The club is then ready for polyurethane coats. See photos 16-33 and 16-34 for final finishing steps.

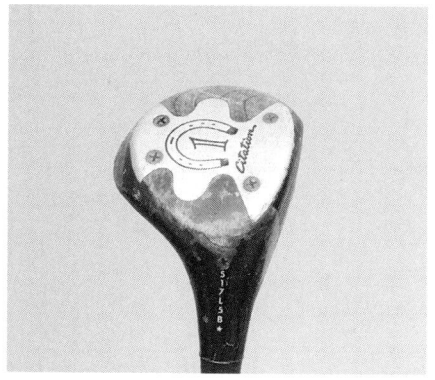

16-40 How to touchup the sole area. A skill that is required often because of the need to reset soleplates without completely refinishing the club. Also, after a through bore reshaft, the sole needs a touchup.

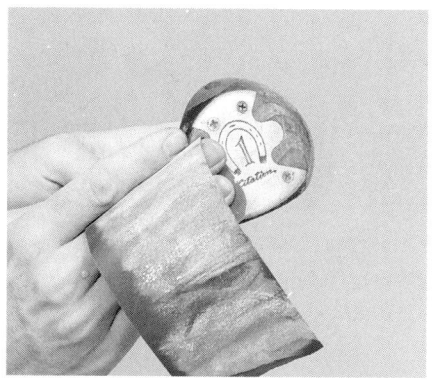

16-41 One alternative is to simply hand sand the sole area and entire head with 400 sandpaper.

16-42 Next, hand or machine steel wool the entire head using 000 steel wool.

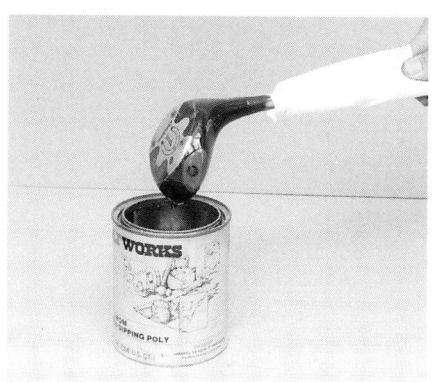

16-43 Dip a coat of polyurethane. This will properly reseal the head.

16-44 When the finish on the sole area is torn or sanded through, one must use another technique. First, using a mill or flat file, dress the soleplate to blend the entire sole area smooth and flush as required.

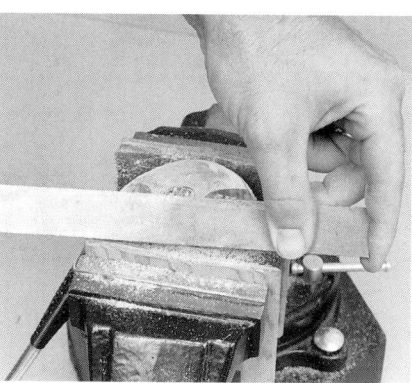

16-45 Next, blend in the leading and trailing edges of the soleplate as needed to obtain a flush fit.

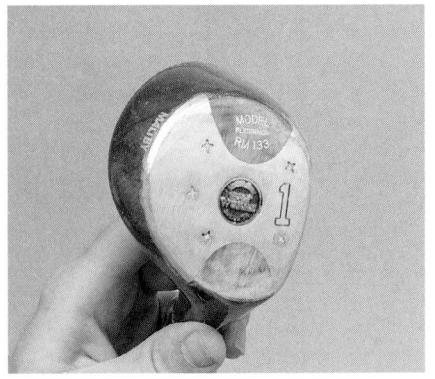

16-46 This photo shows the sole area filed smooth and properly blended parts flush with each other.

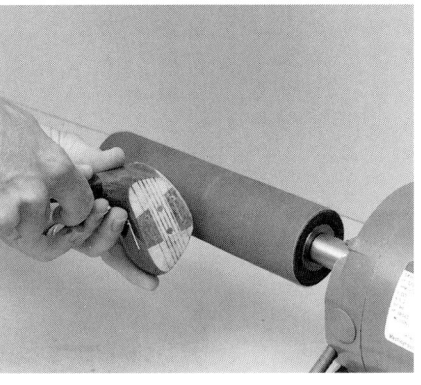

16-47 Sand the sole area by hand or machine using fine 150 grit sandpaper.

16-48 Lightly sand the edge of the polyurethane finish with 400 sandpaper. This will "feather in" the edge of the polyurethane so a smooth blending between the old and new coats will occur.

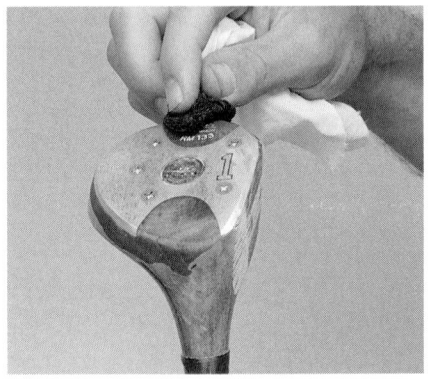

16-49 Select the color matching stain and blot the bare wood areas. Refer to photos 16-29 through 16-32 if the stain color is too light. Allow a 4-6 hour drying time.

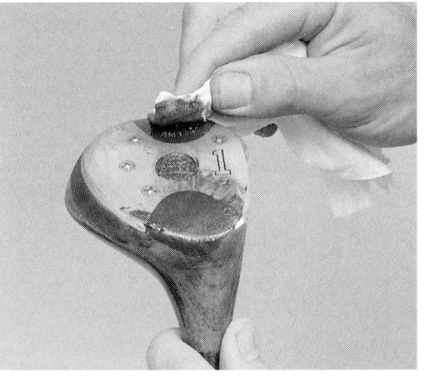

16-50 Next, apply either less intense black or natural filler to the exposed wood, depending upon whether you desire a slightly darker color or the present color. After filler has dried on the clubhead for 10 to 15 minutes, wipe the excess with burlap or terry cloth. Allow to dry overnight.

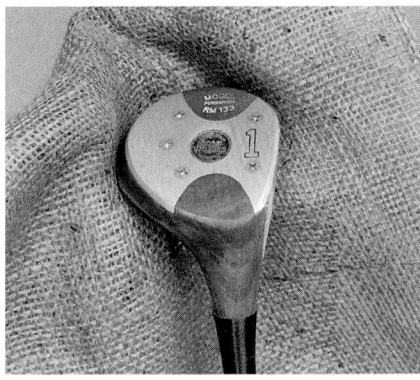

16-51 After the filler has dried, refer to Chapter 1, photos 1-145 through 1-149 for soleplate clean up steps. Hand sand and steel wool all areas of the head except the soleplate area. Apply 2 coats of polyurethane allowing an overnight dry between each coat and 000 steel wool before the second coat.

16-52 This photo shows the finished sole area. Note how it blends in with the rest of the club after two coats of poly. The contents of this chapter should allow you to confidently repair the finish on any area of the club.

NOTES

_____

_____

_____

_____

_____

_____

ADDITIONAL INFORMATION FOR
FINISH REFURBISHING AND
TOUCHUP TECHNIQUES – WOODS

TABLE 16-1
Compatibility of Various Finishing Products & Drying Times

Product	Application	Drying Times Room Temp.	Force Dry*	Compatibility Comments and General Notes
GOLFWORKS® SYSTEMS				
GolfWorks® Water Base Stains	dip, brush, wipe, or spray	4-6 hrs.	1 hr.	Can be used with anything. Dipping provides uniform coating.
GolfWorks® Oil Base Fillers	dip or brush and rub	12 hrs.	6 hrs.	Can be used with any polyurethane. Burnish well with burlap or coarse cloth when wiping. Do not steel wool.
GolfWorks® Rapid Dry Aerosol Color Cote	aerosol	4-6 hrs.	2 hrs.	Must be used only with GolfWorks® Oil Modified or Moisture Cure Polyurethane. Do not apply heavy coat. Several light coats are superior to one heavy coat. Do not sand or steel wool.
GolfWorks® Opaque Color Cote	spray or brush	24 hrs.	12 hrs.	Must be used only with GolfWorks® Oil Modified or Moisture Cure Polyurethane. Do not apply a heavy coat. If brushing, apply quickly to avoid streaks.
GolfWorks® Primer Sealer, Aerosol	aerosol	4 hrs.	1 hr.	Can be used with any polyurethane but specially formulated for Moisture Cure type polyurethane. Do not sand or steel wool.
GolfWorks® Primer Sealer, Spraying	spray	4 hrs.	1 hr.	Can be used with any polyurethane but specially formulated for Moisture Cure type polyurethane. Also commonly used over sandblasted surface of metal wood. Do not sand or steel wool.
GolfWorks® Oil Modified Dipping Polyurethane	dip or spray	8 hrs.	4 hrs.	Do not apply on top of Moisture Cure Polyurethane. Usually requires 5-6 coats for a quality finish.
GolfWorks® Moisture Cure Dipping Polyurethane	dip or spray	12-24 hrs.	8 hrs.	Do not apply on top of Mira-Dip or Mira Filler. Can be applied over other polyurethanes or fillers.
GolfWorks® Moisture Cure Spraying Polyurethane	spray	12-24 hrs.	8 hrs.	Do not apply on top of Mira-Dip or Mira Filler. Can be applied over other polyurethanes or fillers.
GolfWorks® Moisture Cure Aerosol Polyurethane	aerosol	12-24 hrs.	8 hrs.	Do not apply on top of Mira-Dip or Mira Filler. Can be applied over other polyurethanes or fillers.
GolfWorks® Two-Component Polyurethane	spray	12-24 hrs	12 hrs.	Used for metal wood refinishing. Very durable. Professional refinishers can spray all coats with room drying time of 15 minutes between each coat up to a total of 4 coats.

*Force dry conditions: 30% to 50% relative humidity, 90% to 100% temperature.

NOTE: Table 16-1 is continued on the next page.

Product	Application	Drying Times Room Temp.	Force Dry*	Compatibility Comments and General Notes
		CLUB-KIT SYSTEM		
Mira-Stains (alcohol base)	dip, brush, wipe, or spray	3-6 hrs.	1 hr.	Can be used with anything. Dipping provides uniform coating.
Mira-Filler (polyurethane base)	dip or brush and rub	5 hrs.	2 hrs.	Use only with Mira-Dip.
Mira-Kote (polyurethane base)	spray or brush	12 hrs.	8 hrs.	Use only with Mira-Dip. Do not apply heavy coat. Several light coats superior to one heavy coat.
Mira-Kote Aerosol (polyurethane base)	aerosol	12 hrs.	8 hrs.	Same as above.
Dem-Kote Enamel	aerosol	4 hrs.	2 hrs.	Same as above.
Mira-Dip Oil Modified Polyurethane	dip or spray	8 hrs.	4 hr.	Do not apply on top of Moisture Cure Cure polyurethanes. Usually requires 5-6 coats for quality finish.
Mira-Spray Aerosol Oil Modified Polyurethane	aerosol	8 hrs.	4 hrs.	Do not apply on top of Moisture Cure Polyurethanes.

*Force dry conditions: 30% to 50% relative humidity, 90% to 100% temperature.

NOTES

_____

_____

_____

_____

_____

_____

_____

_____

_____

_____

_____

_____

_____

SECTION TWO

GOLF IRON CLUB REPAIRS

CHAPTER 17

REFINISHING AND RESCORING IRONS

Refinishing iron heads can be broken down into two types of procedures, namely rechroming and refurbishing.

■ Rechroming

It is very unlikely that any golf club repair shop will have a facility for rechroming an iron head. This is due to EPA regulations and the enormous capital investment required to start up such an operation. The two basic alternatives are:

1) Send the club to someone who specializes in rechroming irons, or
2) Send the club back to the original manufacturer for rechroming.

In many cases though, the manufacturer will send the club to a reputable shop that specializes in rechroming irons.

To rechrome an iron head, the head is removed from the shaft and the old chrome and nickel are stripped off the head in strip tanks. The head is then ground and buffed on special machinery to remove nicks and scratches. After buffing, the face is outline masked and sandblasted. Next, the head is nickel plated and the face sandblasted once more and the head is now chrome plated. Lastly, the engravings in the head are paint-filled and the head is reinstalled on the shaft.

■ Refurbishing

Refurbishing an iron head can run the gauntlet from complete repolishing of a non-chrome plated head to simple paint-filling of the head stampings in any iron head. Regardless of which steps are chosen, each can substantially improve the appearance of an iron head.

Repolishing a non-chrome plated head requires the following materials:

- Eight 8" spiral-sewn buffing wheels – used for heavy and fine buffing work.
- Two 8" sisal buffing wheels – used for the intermediate buffing step.
- #200 lea compound – used when heavy cutting is required for the removal of nicks and scratches from the iron head.
- #173 glue compound – applied to the buffing wheels for the sole purpose of keeping the lea compound on the wheels.
- Black sisal compound – an intermediate abrasive that evens out deep scratches left from coarser grit buffing and/or removes minor scratches if the lea step was bypassed.
- White polishing compound – a fine abrasive that is used to polish the clubhead to a mirror finish, the last step in the repolishing process.

- A double shafted ⅓ or ½ H.P. motor with a minimum RPM of 1750 (3450 RPM recommended).
- Buffing wheel rake; used to remove old compound from the wheels.
- Heavy duty leather gloves; for protection because metal becomes very hot during the repolishing steps.
- Safety glasses or goggles; always wear eye protection.

■ Rescoring and Sandblasting Irons

The scoring lines on older clubs tend to wear, especially the lower ones on sand clubs. When an iron is being refurbished or rechromed, it is sometimes desirable to put the missing or worn lines back to like new condition. Also, it is possible to re-sandblast the face if you have the proper equipment.

This chapter shows you the methods of rescoring the traditional V-groove lines and sandblasting faces. Converting the V-groove scoring lines to the "box" groove scoring lines requires special milling equipment. The GolfWorks® offers this service.

17-1 Repolishing stainless steel heads. The following instructional steps are offered in conjunction with The Buffing Shop, a 20-piece buffing kit offered by The GolfWorks®. These steps are also applicable for any setup using the proper materials.

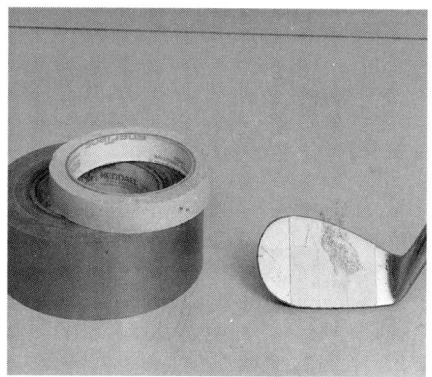

17-2 First, mask the sandblasted area of the face with duct tape or ¾" masking tape.

17-3 Assemble four ¼" stitched buff sections to one side of the buffer to make a 1" wide wheel.

17-4 Apply a coating of #173 glue compound to the stitched wheels. Hold the compound against the face of the wheel and turn the wheel on for 10-15 seconds while applying. Let the glue dry for one minute before proceeding. **Note the use of leather gloves for this and all the following steps.**

17-5 Next, apply the #200 lea compound, turning on the wheel for 10 seconds or until you get an even coating on the buffing sections. Wait 5 minutes before buffing. The longer the #200 compound is allowed to dry, the more abrasive it becomes. (This can be used to your advantage if deep nicks must be removed.)

17-6 This photo shows a typical stainless steel iron head before buffing. Note the nicks on the sole.

17-7 Begin buffing the head, pressing it firmly on the wheel using a forward rolling motion. **Note: Hold the head firmly as the heads can sometimes be pulled from your hands.**

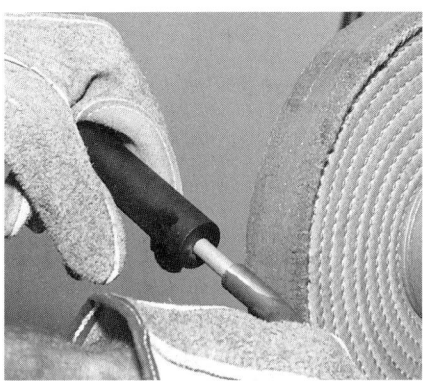

17-8 The hosel may also need buffing. Place a **Hosel Turner** in the hosel and spin the hosel against the wheel to buff. Spin evenly to maintain proper shape of the hosel.

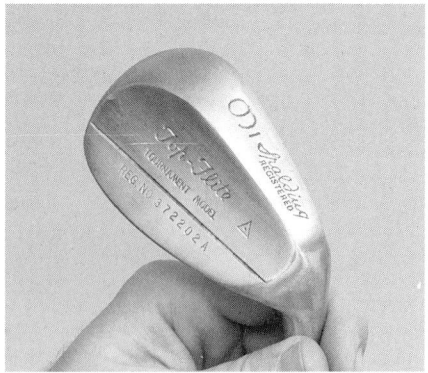

17-9 This photo shows the same head after the buffing step. Note the nicks are removed. Take care when buffing around head stampings. The value of a classic club will drop considerably if a head stamping is removed. Note: This finish is referred to as a satin finish and may be desired. If this is the case, proceed to photo 17-20 for final steps. If a high polish finish is desired, continue on to 17-10.

17-10 Next, assemble 2 sisal buff sections to the other side of the buffer.

17-11 Apply the black sisal compound against the face of the turning wheel. Apply a smooth coating of compound.

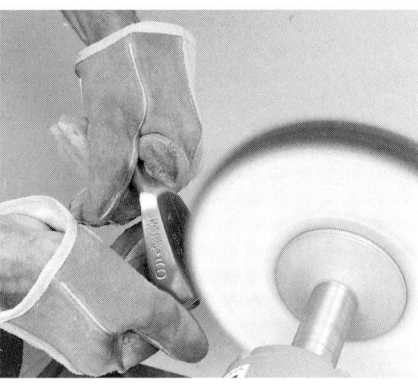

17-12 Begin to buff the iron, blending in the buffing scratches from the #200 compound. Move the head across the face of the wheel in a different direction from the previous buffing step. This will effectively remove previous scratches. It is possible to begin the repolishing steps at this point if the head is free of deep scratches or nicks.

17-13 This photo shows a head after the buffing step, using the black compound and sisal wheels.

17-14 Remove the wheels from either end and assemble a clean set of four stitched buff sections.

17-15 With the wheel turning, apply a smooth coating of the white polishing compound.

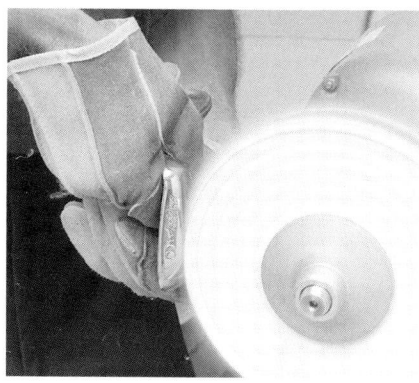

17-16 Buff the head to a mirror-like finish. The buffing direction should again be different from the previous buffing step. This is the final step in this procedure.

17-17 This photo shows a properly polished head. Remove the tape from the face of each club when the entire set is finished.

17-18 Stainless steel irons can also be refinished using an 8" diameter stitched buffing wheel 1" thick spinning at 1725 RPM. A 1/3 H.P. minimum motor is required. A set of 4 bar buffing compounds works well.

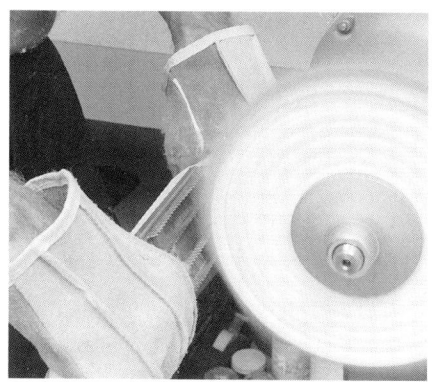

17-19 Each day as you begin a new buffing job, rake the wheels clean so most of the old abrasive compound is removed from the wheels. Simply hold the rake against the face of the wheel while the wheel is turning. **Hold the rake firmly.**

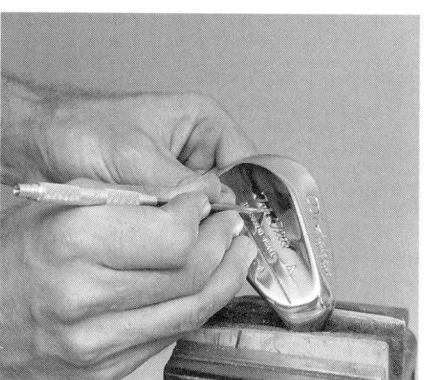

17-20 Paint-filling irons. Etch head stampings to remove old paint using a scriber or sharpened awl, if necessary. **Be careful not to slip.**

17-21 First, using either lacquer sticks, lacquer paint, or fast dry enamel, brush or wipe paint into the engravings.

17-22 With a folded cloth or paper towel, wipe off the excess paint. Let the paint dry. If lacquer is used, apply lacquer thinner to the towel before wiping off the excess paint.

17-23 Lacquer sticks work best. They are not messy and come in all colors.

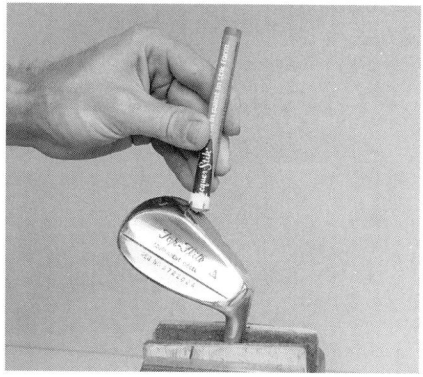

17-24 Rub the lacquer stick across the engraving or stamp and ...

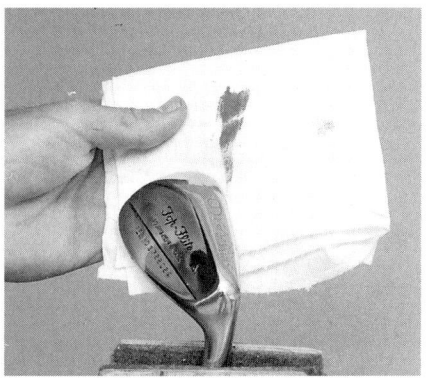

17-25 ...immediately wipe off the excess with a paper towel or clean cloth.

17-26 Scoring lines may also be paint-filled using the same procedure as described in photos 17-20 through 17-25. If the faces are to be sandblasted, paint-filling is performed after the sandblasting step. See photo 17-31 through 17-34 for sandblasting steps.

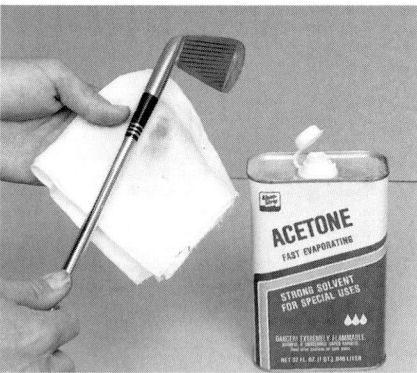

17-27 Plastic ferrules can be made to look brand new by wiping with an acetone dampened towel.

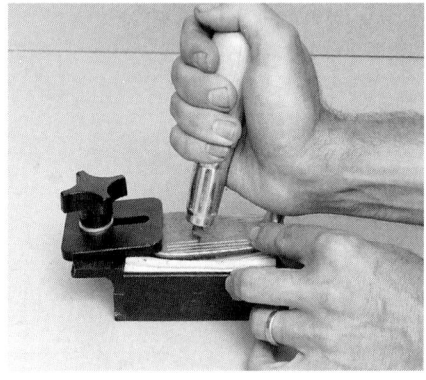

17-28 Rescoring irons. A carbide tipped rescoring tool is carefully dragged repeatedly through each groove until the proper depth is obtained. Note the use of a **Rescoring Nest** to firmly hold the head.

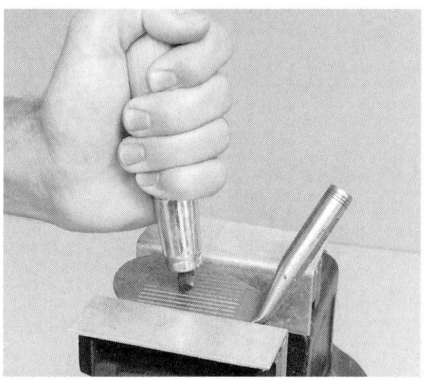

17-29 Iron heads can also be held in aluminum or brass vise pads.

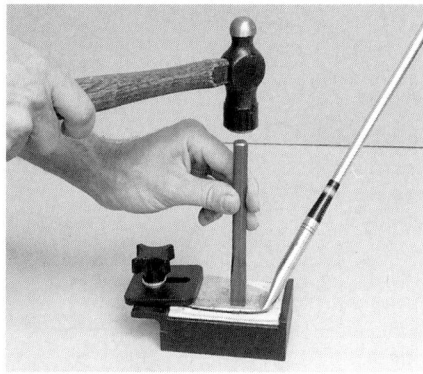

17-30 A ½" cold chisel will also work but the club must be secured in something like the **Rescoring Nest**. See Appendix 4 for USGA rules regarding iron face markings.

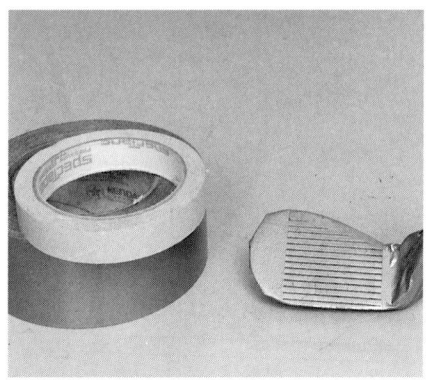

17-31 Re-sandblasting iron faces. First, use a heavy tape such as duct tape or several layers of masking tape to outline the face. This will protect the toe and heel portion of the face.

17-32 A small sandblasting cabinet works best. **The GolfWorks® Sandblaster** shown above is economically priced for the smaller golf club repair operation. It requires a 2 H.P., 13 gallon tank air compressor and a 5 gallon Shop-Vac to operate.

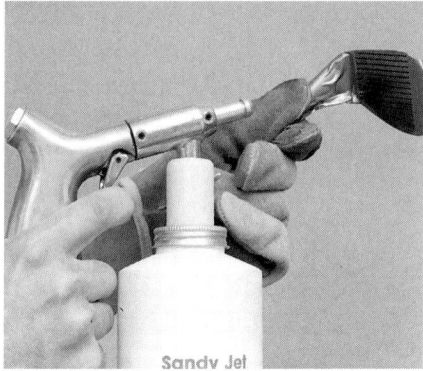

17-33 A **Sandblasting Gun** also works well and can be used with a ½ H.P. tank type air compressor.

17-34 The **Power Pal air compressor** is a smaller unit that works well for sandblasting and spraying purposes. A special optional sandblast gun is available.

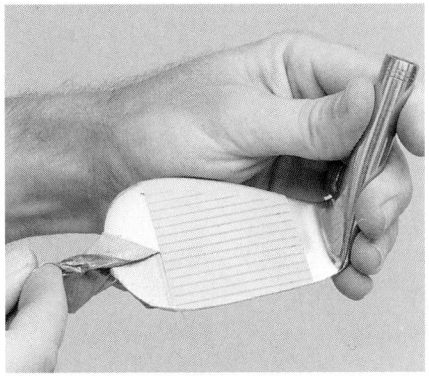

17-35 After the face has been sandblasted using a fine **aluminum oxide sand**, peel the protective duct or masking tape from the face.

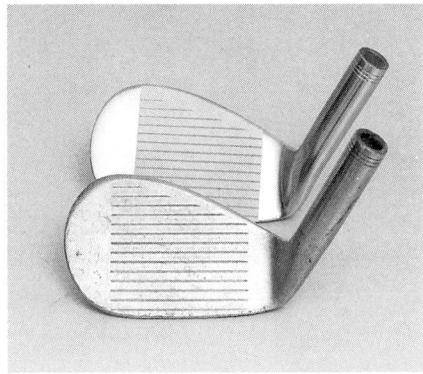

17-36 This photo shows the before and after of two irons from the same set. If the head was removed from the shaft before buffing, reinstall the head following the instructions in Chapter 21. In most cases, the shaft does not need to be removed.

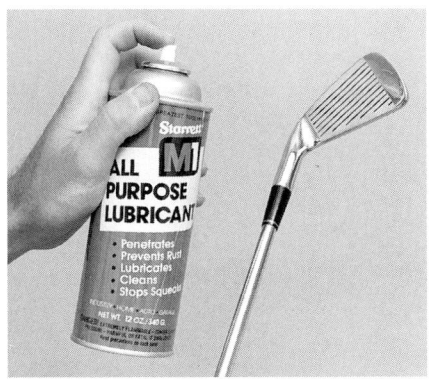

17-37 If the clubface that was sandblasted was carbon steel and not stainless steel, then the face will have to be protected from rust. Starrett M-1 is excellent. WD-40 and C.R.C. also work well.

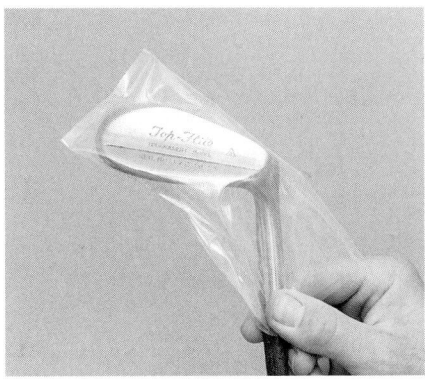

17-38 After buffing, winterizing, rechroming or refurbishing, it is a nice professional touch to bag the heads with a special plastic iron head bag.

17-39 **This is a M.I.G. Electric Welder** which wire feed welds in a pocket of Argon and CO_2 Gas for porosity-free welds. The GolfWorks® uses this for welding on broken hosels, fixing cracks and most general welding on damaged clubs sent in for repair.

17-40 **This is a T.I.G. Electric Welder (Tungsten Inert Gas).** This welder uses filler rods of any material (aluminum, brass, stainless steel, carbon steel, etc.) and welds in a pocket of pure Argon Gas. It also is a specialty welder we use to give us capabilities beyond M.I.G. welding.

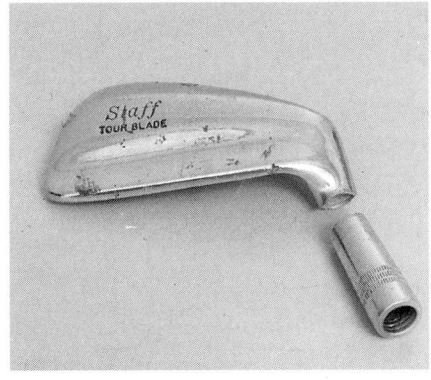

17-41 So, do not be intimidated by a club looking like this. A hosel that is broken—partially or completely—or has been drilled through can be repaired by us. Most major golf club manufacturers' repair departments send this type of work to The GolfWorks®.

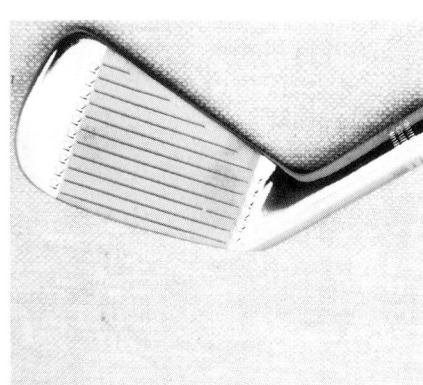

17-42 The same club as shown in the previous photo has been welded, ground and rechromed to play and look like new.

205

17-43 The GolfWorks® **Mini Vibratory** works very well for refinishing metal woods or irons having a vibratory finish like that found on Ping irons. Place the **Mini Vibratory** on a firm, smooth, level surface, place a cork in the hosel of each iron or metal wood and let it go to work. While the unit is refinishing your wood or iron, you can be working on something else. Tumbling time is normally 6 to 8 hours.

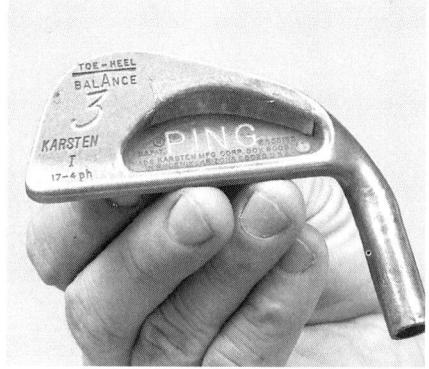

17-44 The above photo shows an iron before tumbling in the **Mini Vibratory**. Note the small scratches and general wear.

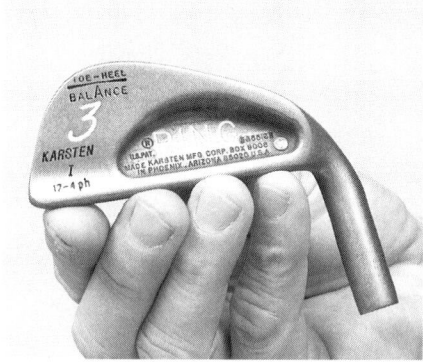

17-45 This photo shows the iron after tumbling in the **Mini Vibratory**.

RECHROMING AND REFINISHING:
A WAY TO INCREASE SALES AND PROFITS

In doing golf club repair, both the golf professional and the professional club repair shop provide much needed services for the golfer. With the hustle and bustle of running the everyday operations, seldom is there time for thought on expanding and capitalizing on new areas of club repair with the sole intention of increasing sales and profits.

Rechroming irons is an area which is virtually untapped and one which could provide a substantial increase in income. A number of people do not use the services available to them in rechroming irons because they do not understand the procedure, they are afraid of having the set ruined or they feel it just could not be profitable and worthwhile.

The profitability and economics of rechroming is probably the most important. People are keeping and playing their older sets of irons. Many are collecting these classics and hoarding them. Also, at times it is quite difficult to sell new irons and for that matter new clubs. Let's look at the figures and see how rechroming a set of irons compares against purchasing a new set. Current 1994 prices and cost comparisons are used. Costs should increase approximately 6% per year.

First of all, the wholesale cost of rechroming an iron head off the shaft is $12.50 each. If the head is sent in on the shaft, a $5.50 per club additional charge applies. The retail charge to your customer is $22.75 per club or 45% profit margin for a head off the shaft and a 21% margin for a head on the shaft. If you remove and install the head on the shaft, you can figure approximately one hour's labor. Some sets may take a little longer and some will take less time.

Take a look at Table 17-1, read it carefully and study it. Notice in line III and IV the retail shown for rechroming, reshafting and regripping a set is an average suggested retail. The average retail throughout the United States, taken from many repair lists is $57.75 per club with the range running from $40.00 to $65.00. It is easy to see that line IV (rechroming and reshafting) compares very favorably to line V and VI (selling a new set). It also points up that you should spend the 1 to 2 hours required to do the shafting and gripping to obtain the best profit. Having a set of heads rechromed and then reshafted and regripped will give your customer a brand new set of irons for very close to the wholesale cost of a new set of irons. But the best part is that in many cases, you make as much and usually more profit dollars than selling the new set of irons.

206

Another advantage of rechroming, reshafting and regripping an old set of irons is proper custom fitting. For example, an individual has a set of older well-liked irons, but through one or two changes – such as a longer or shorter length, a shaft flex or pattern change, larger or smaller grips or adjusting loft and lie – the individual would be even better fitted to the clubs. This can now be done quite easily and for very little or no additional cost. So, in essence, you have provided your customer with a brand new, properly fit, custom set of irons. See Ralph Maltby's *The Complete Golf Club Fitting Plan* for additional information on golf club fitting.

A number of golf professionals and repair shops have been able to promote rechroming successfully. This part of The GolfWorks'® business has grown dramatically to the point where we are now the largest iron refinishers and rechromers in the world. At times, during the heavy volume months, we will do more than 400 sets a week. We also do some warranty rechroming work for a few of the larger golf club manufacturers as well as many PGA Professionals. Major manufacturers also routinely send us irons that belong to PGA Tour Players for special work to be completed. Rechroming can take anywhere from 2 to 6 weeks depending on seasonality and the complexity of the work required.

TABLE 17-1
Rechroming Profitability and Cost Comparison Table

Line	Description	Cost Per Club	Retail Cost Per club	Cost Per Set of 9 Clubs	Retail Cost For 9 Clubs	% Gross Margin of Profit	$ Amount of Profit (9 Clubs)
I	Rechroming a head off the shaft	$12.50	$22.75	$112.50	$204.75	45%	$92.25
II	Rechroming a head on the shaft	$18.00	$22.75	$162.00	$204.75	21%	$42.75
III	**If We Do Everything** Rechroming & Reshafting ¹(Includes new grip and swingweighting)	$18.00 (rechrome) $18.95 (reshaft) $ 5.50 (regrip) $42.45	$22.75 $28.00 $ 7.00 $57.75	$382.05	$519.75	26.5%	$137.70
IV	**If We Rechrome and You Reshaft and Regrip** Rechroming & Reshafting ¹(Includes new grip and swingweighting)	$12.50 (rechrome) $ 3.95 (reshaft) $ 1.25 (regrip) $17.70 plus 2½ hrs. labor to reshaft, grip & swingweight	$22.75 $28.00 $ 7.00 $57.75	$159.30 plus 2½ hrs. labor	$519.75	69.3%	$360.45
V	²If you sell avg. priced set of irons for avg. discounted retail	$50.00	$65.00	$450.00	$585.00	23%	$135.00
VI	³If you sell a so called avg. priced set of irons for full retail	$50.00	$85.00	$450.00	$765.00	41.2%	$315.00

¹ Average retail prices nationwide for rechroming, reshafting and gripping are $57.75 per club. The range is from $40.00 to $65.00.
² Average discounted retail for irons in 1994 is est. @ $65.00 each. Average % gross margin based on wholesale of $50.00 to average discounted retail $65.00 is 23%.
³ Average catalog stated retail for irons in 1994 is $85.00 each. Average wholesale for irons in 1994 is $50.00 each. This would give a 41% margin of profit.

CHAPTER 18

CHANGING SWINGWEIGHTS OF IRON CLUBS

Seldom will a golfer bring in an iron(s) specifically for a swingweight change. Usually the swingweight will need adjustment because a change in shaft weight or length, or a change in grip size or weight, has lowered or raised the swingweight.

A recent positive trend in golf club repair is the redistribution of weight within a golf club. Repairmen and golfers are discovering that lead in the tip of the shaft will adversely affect the performance of the club. Lead is often placed in the tip section by the manufacturer to increase the swingweight. While this is a cosmetically acceptable practice, functionally it is not. The presence of lead in the tip of the shaft indicates the clubhead's center of gravity is no longer in the center of the head. Instead, the C of G is towards the hosel. Because of this, some clubs are virtually unplayable. A solid shot is only achieved when the ball's center of gravity is struck in line with the clubhead's center of gravity. If the club's C of G is moved too far toward the hosel, which is entirely possible, a golfer would have to almost shank the ball in order to align the C of G of both the ball and clubhead at impact. Because of this, removing lead from the hosel and redistributing it on the back of the head in the proper position is an improvement to any golf club.

There are very few irons on the market that are designed so swingweight can be changed in the head itself, such as with a weight port. Listed below are the five methods by which the swingweight of an iron club can be changed.

Method 1: Drill a small hole(s) in the head to reduce swingweight.

Method 2: Remove the shaft and drill out the metal from the bottom of the hosel to reduce swingweight.

Method 3: Add lead underneath the grip to achieve a lighter swingweight reading on the swingweight scale (counterbalancing).

Method 4: Add lead tape to the back of the head to increase swingweight.

Method 5: Put weight (usually steel or lead) in the tip of the shaft to increase swingweight.

Methods 1 and 4 alter the cosmetic appearance of the iron head, but are the most effective. Because weight is either being added or subtracted directly from the head, the center of gravity is maintained. Methods 2 and 5 will alter the center of gravity in the head. Method 2 will move the center of gravity down and slightly toward the toe. Method 5 will move the center of gravity up and toward the hosel. Method 3 is by far the worst choice, as it does nothing but increase the overall weight of the club while only fooling the swingweight scale into thinking the clubhead has been lightened. This is called counterbalancing.

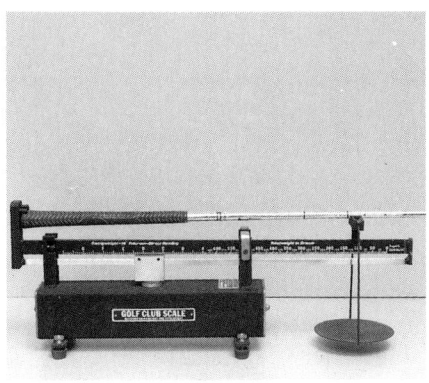

18-1 Before changing the swingweight, the existing swingweight must be determined, using a swingweight scale. It is also a good idea to check the total weight. See Chapter 14, photos 14-38 through 14-47 for the various types and models of swingweight scales and which scales also measure total weight.

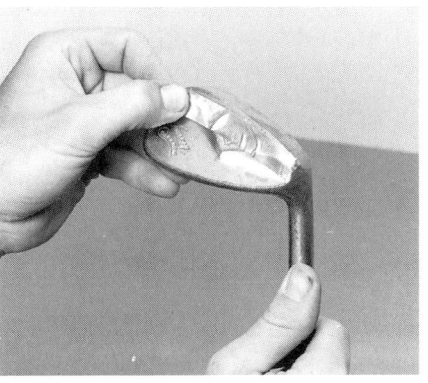

18-2 To increase swingweight, lead tape can be applied to the back of the clubhead. Be sure the tape is applied symmetrically and as low as possible behind the clubface. A 4½" strip of ½" wide lead tape will increase the swingweight by one point.

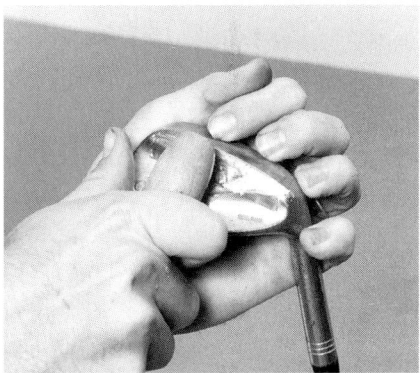

18-3 A wood or plastic tool handle is used to burnish the lead tape to the back of the iron. This helps the tape stick better and conform to any irregular surface.

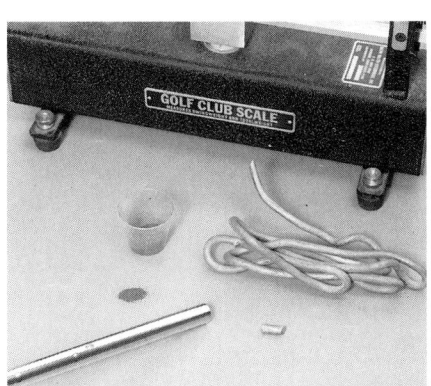

18-4 Lead rod or powder can also be used to increase swingweight. Use ¼" diameter lead rod for irons, ³⁄₁₆" diameter lead rod for woods.

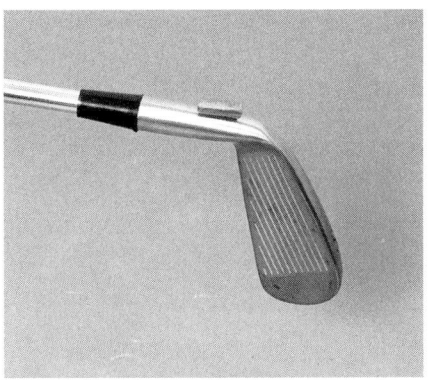

18-5 Lead rod can be first taped to the hosel while the club is on a swingweight scale to help determine the proper amount to use. A ¼" diameter rod cut to a ¼" length will increase the swingweight by 1 point.

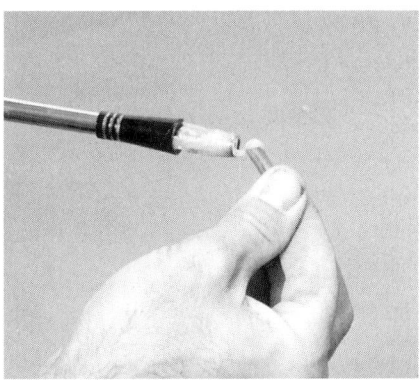

18-6 If you are making custom irons, or if the head is removed from the shaft, lead rod can be inserted directly into the tip of the shaft. Coat the lead rod generously with epoxy to prevent possible future rattles.

18-7 Lead rod can also be inserted from the butt end of the shaft if the head is not removed. Apply epoxy to lead rod and drop it down the shaft.

18-8 Next, drop a cork into the shaft (available from most golf repair supply dealers).

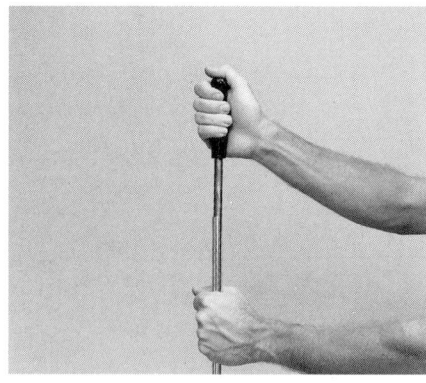

18-9 Ram the cork and lead rod as far into the tip of the shaft as possible using a **Ramrod**. The opposite end of a **47" drill bit** will also work.

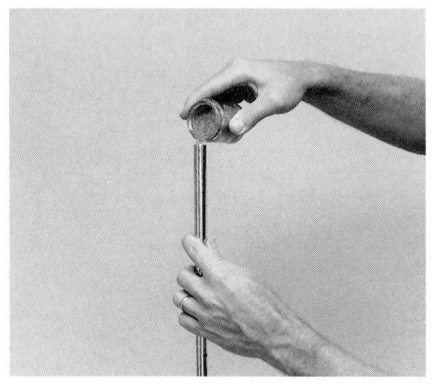

18-10 Lead shot or powder can be used instead of lead rod. First, pour the required amount through the butt end of the shaft.

18-11 Place a cork with a glob of epoxy on its bottom end inside the shaft and …

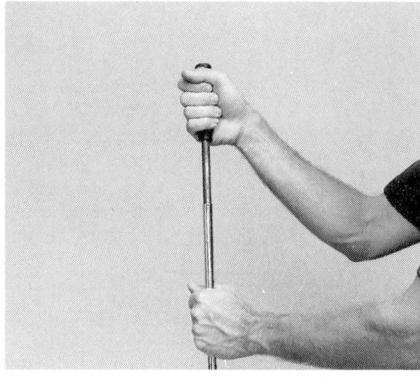

18-12 … ram the cork and lead powder or shot in place with the long **Ramrod** or the opposite end of a **47" drill bit.** Note: For every four swingweights (.28 ounces or 8 grams) added to the shaft tip or hosel, the clubhead's center of gravity will move ⅛" closer to the hosel and slightly higher up the face.

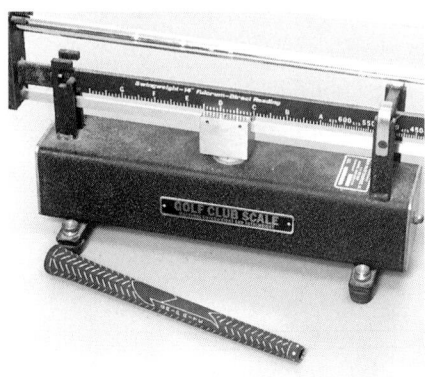

18-13 Check the final swingweight. If the grip was removed from the club to add weight down the shaft, it is a good idea to check for desired swingweight before reinstalling the grip. The grip can be taped to the top of the shaft to do this.

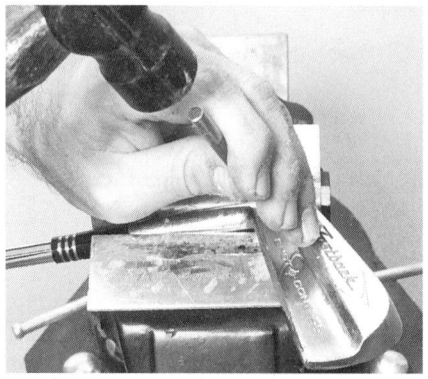

18-14 Swingweight can be reduced in irons by drilling holes in the head. First, center punch the head in the desired location.

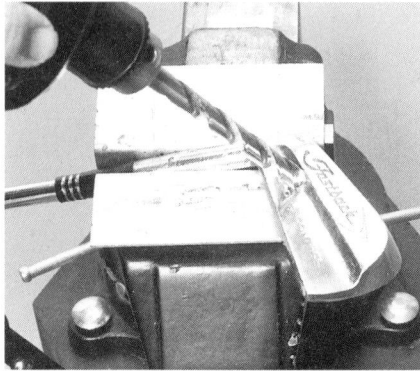

18-15 Next, drill the appropriate number of holes equal distances from the face centerline. A ³⁄₁₆" diameter hole x ¼" deep will reduce the swingweight by approximately 1 point.

210

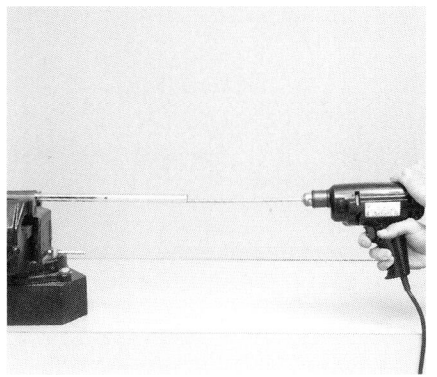

18-16 To remove the weight from the hosel of an assembled club. Using a 47" x 7/32" bit, drill into the bottom of the hosel bore. Drilling 3/16" deep is equivalent to a 1 swingweight point reduction. **Be careful not to drill too deep on some irons with short hosels and deep bores or you may drill through.**

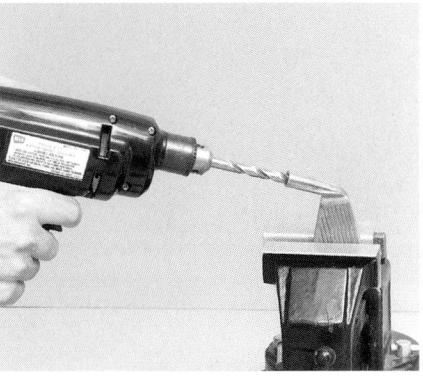

18-17 If the head is removed from the shaft, drill into the bottom of the hosel bore with a letter "T" bit. Drilling 1/8" deep is equivalent to a 1 swingweight point reduction.

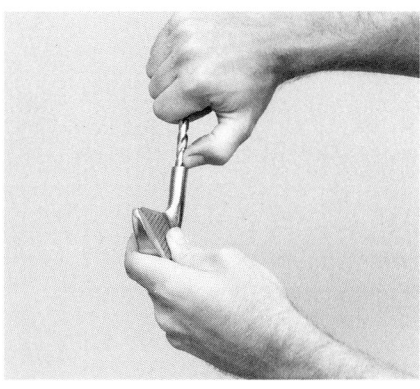

18-18 This photo shows a typical iron hosel. Before drilling, always premeasure the depth of the hosel bore.

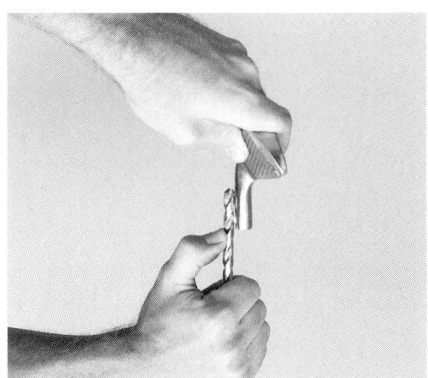

18-19 After measuring, place the desired drill bit outside the hosel to proper depth to determine if drilling is possible. Many repairmen have accidentally drilled through the side of the hosel. **Note: Drilling through the hosel wall can be repaired by welding.**

NOTES

_____

_____

_____

_____

_____

_____

_____

ADDITIONAL INFORMATION FOR CHANGING SWINGWEIGHTS OF IRON CLUBS

• For every ½" increase in a club's length, the swingweight will increase by 3 points.

• For every ½" decrease in a club's length, the swingweight will decrease by 3 points.

• If you would like to check a club's swingweight before installing the grip and any tape, allow 9 points (10 points for leather, cord or oversize rubber). Example: Ungripped club swingweights at E-0; it will probably be D-1 after gripping with an average-weight 1¾ ounce rubber grip.

• Every 4 swingweights are equivalent to slightly more than ¼ ounce (8 grams). A swingweight point in an iron head is approximately .07 ounce (2 grams). See Fig. 18-20.

• A swingweight point in the grip end of an iron is approximately .14 ounces (4 grams) or twice as much as is required in the head end. Adding .14 ounces to the grip end will decrease the swingweight by 1 point (this is called "counterbalancing") and .14 ounces taken out of the grip end will increase the swingweight by 1 point. See Fig. 18-20.

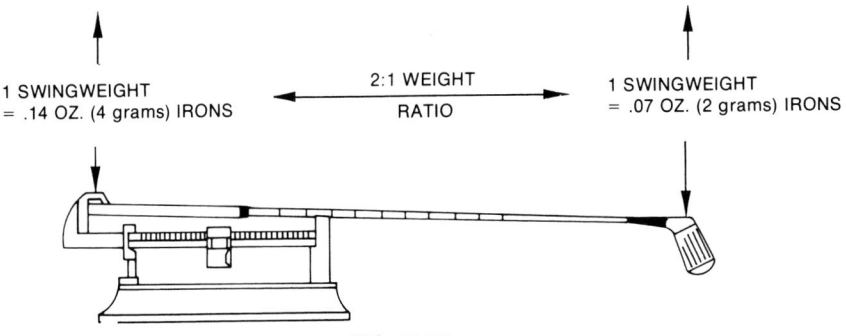

FIG. 18-20
Approximate swingweight equivalents for grip and head ends of club

• The lighter the shaft, the heavier the head weight must be to obtain the same swingweight that you would get with a heavier shaft. Even though the head weight is heavier with the lighter shaft, the total weight of the club will still be less. For a general rule of thumb use the following: For each 1 ounce reduction in shaft weight, an iron club will lose approximately 3 swingweight points. This, of course, assumes that the grip weight and shaft length are exactly the same. Example: A set of D-2 irons with Dynamic™ Taper Tip Shafts (4⅜ ounces) are reshafted with Extralite™ Taper Tip Shafts (3⅜ ounces). Without reweighting the heads, the swingweight would not be C-9. Approximately ¼ ounce of weight would have to be added to the heads to achieve a D-2 swingweight. The Extralite™ shaft is 1 ounce lighter than the Dynamic™ Taper Tip shaft but only ¼ ounce is added to the head leaving a net reduction in total club weight of ¾ ounce. For a comparative look at what just happened, refer to the #5 iron example in Table 18-1.

• A dollar bill weighs 1 gram and is equivalent to ½ of a swingweight point. A dime weighs 2 grams and is equivalent to 1 point. A quarter weighs 6 grams and is equivalent to 3 points.

	#5 Iron Before Change: Dynamic™ Taper Tip Shaft	#5 Iron After Change: Extralite™ Taper Tip Shaft	Difference From Change	Club Specs: Reweighted to D-2	Net Change In Club
TABLE 18-1 Effect of Different Weight Shafts on Driver Head Weight, Total Weight and Swingweight					
Shaft Weight (ounces)	4.37	3.37	− 1	3.37	− 1
Head Weight (ounces)	9.5	9.5	Same	9.75	+.25
Grip Weight (ounces)	1.75	1.75	Same	1.75	None
Total Weight (ounces)	15.62	14.62	− 1	14.87	− .75
Swingweight	D-2	C-9	− 3	D-2	+ 3

Note: A 1 ounce reduction in shaft weight for an wood club would decrease swingweight by 5 points because of the additional shaft length. Refer to Chapter 14 for more information.

• If you use ½" wide lead tape, it takes approximately a 4½" long piece to weigh 2 grams or be equivalent to 1 swingweight point.

• To convert grams to ounces, divide by 28.35.

• To convert ounces to grams, multiply by 28.35.

• 1 ounce = 28.35 grams.

212

TABLE 18-2
Swingweight Conversion Chart
Official Swingweight Scale vs. Lorythmic Swingweight Scale

Official Swingweight Scale Reading	Lorythmic Scale Swingweight		Official Swingweight Scale Reading	Lorythmic Scale Swingweight	
	Woods	Irons		Woods	Irons
18.33	C0	B8	20.00	D0	C8
18.4	0.4	8.4	20.05	0.3	8.3
18.45	0.7	8.7	20.1	0.6	8.6
			20.15	0.9	8.9
18.5	C1	B9	20.17	D1	C9
18.55	1.3	9.3			
18.6	1.6	9.6	20.2	1.2	9.2
			20.25	1.5	9.5
18.65	C2	C0	20.3	1.8	9.8
18.7	2.2	0.2	20.33	D2	D0
18.75	2.5	0.5			
18.8	2.8	0.8	20.35	2.1	0.1
			20.4	2.4	0.4
18.83	C3	C1	20.45	2.7	0.7
18.85	3.1	1.1	20.5	D3	D1
18.9	3.4	1.4			
18.95	3.7	1.7	20.55	3.3	1.3
			20.6	3.6	1.6
19.00	C4	C2	20.65	D4	D2
19.05	4.3	2.3			
19.1	4.6	2.6	20.7	4.2	2.2
19.15	4.9	2.9	20.75	4.5	2.5
			20.8	4.8	2.8
19.17	C5	C3	20.83	D5	D3
19.2	5.2	3.2			
19.25	5.5	3.5	20.85	5.1	3.1
19.3	5.8	3.8	20.9	5.4	3.4
			20.95	5.7	3.7
19.33	C6	C4	21.00	D6	D4
19.35	6.1	4.1			
19.4	6.4	4.4	21.05	6.3	4.3
19.45	6.7	4.7	21.1	6.6	4.6
			21.15	6.9	4.9
19.5	C7	C5	21.17	D7	D5
19.55	7.3	5.3			
19.6	7.6	5.6	21.2	7.2	5.2
19.65	7.9	5.9	21.25	7.5	5.5
			21.3	7.8	5.8
19.66	C8	C6	21.33	D8	D6
19.7	8.2	6.2			
19.75	8.5	6.5	21.35	8.1	6.1
19.8	8.8	6.8	21.4	8.4	6.4
			21.45	8.7	6.7
19.83	C9	C7	21.5	D9	D7
19.85	9.1	7.1			
19.9	9.4	7.4	21.55	9.3	7.3
19.95	9.7	7.7	21.6	9.6	7.6
			21.65	9.9	7.9
			21.66	E0	D8

CHAPTER 19

CHANGING LOFTS AND LIES OF IRON CLUBS

Altering lofts and lies of iron clubs is a relatively simple operation, but it does require special equipment. This special equipment is designed to do three things. First, to measure actual loft and lie angles; second, to provide a means of holding the head securely in position; and third, to provide a tool which attaches to the hosel and exerts enough leverage to bend the hosel, thus altering loft, lie, or both.

The lie of an iron can be altered without affecting any other specifications of that iron. When the loft of an iron is altered, however, three effects on other specifications occur.

The first two of the effects, hosel offset and face progression, are relatively minor changes and are usually not given consideration when making a loft change.

The third effect is to the sole inversion. Sole inversion is defined as the angle of the sole to the ground when the shaft is perpendicular to the ground and the face is square to the target. Sole inversion, or sole angle as it is sometimes called, is defined under three possible conditions: 1) scoop or dig sole, 2) square sole, and 3) bounce (or inverted) sole. Of these three, the scoop or dig sole is to be avoided if at all possible (photos 19-1 through 19-3 show the three conditions).

Unfortunately, most golfers who wish to have a loft adjustment will request that the loft be decreased so they can hit the ball farther. Therefore, always inspect the sole angle of the irons and determine if the decreased loft alteration will potentially ruin the clubs by creating a dig sole angle. If a loft alteration is made and you then deem it to be unfavorable, you can always bend the hosel back to its original loft position.

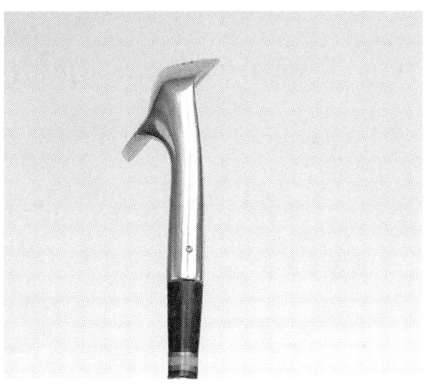

19-1 A scoop or dig sole. The trailing edge is lower than the leading edge. Try to avoid this as it results in fat type shots.

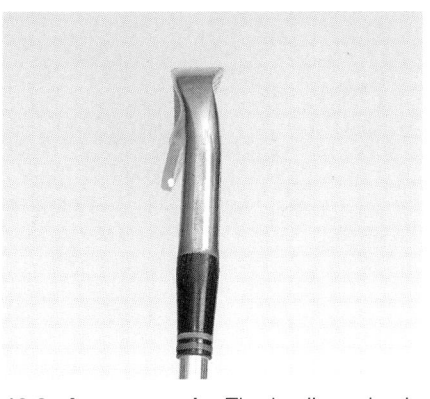

19-2 A square sole. The leading edge is even in height with the trailing edge.

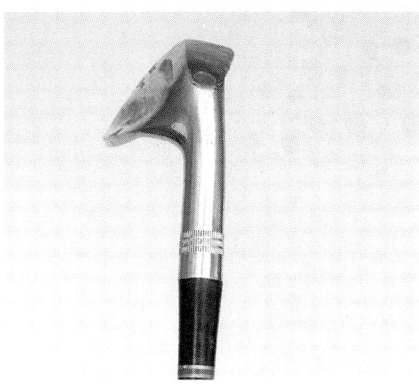

19-3 A bounce or inverted sole. The trailing edge is higher than the leading edge.

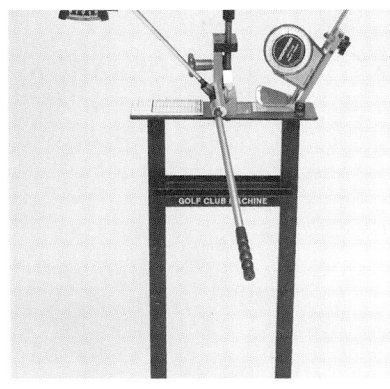

19-4 There are a number of different loft and lie machines available to fit various budgets. Shop and compare features carefully. This chapter will demonstrate the use of a loft and lie machine available from The GolfWorks®.

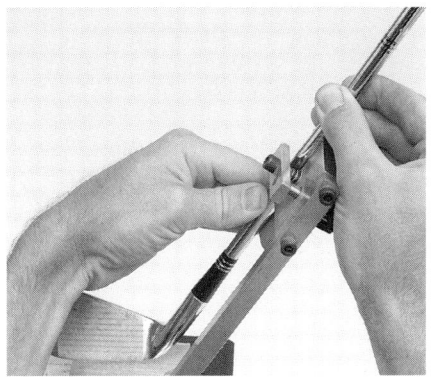

19-5 How to measure loft and lie. The clubhead must be in the correct lie position before measuring. Place the shaft in the V-Block and lower the head to the base. Pressure should be placed against the shaft while lowering the head to keep the shaft flush in the "V" groove. (The knob may be lightly tightened to accomplish this.)

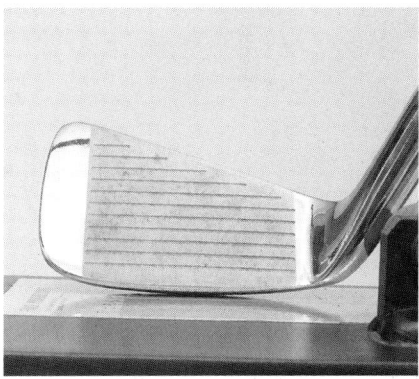

19-6 The correct lie position is achieved when the sole of the clubhead is touching the base at the center of the face. This can be determined either visually or...

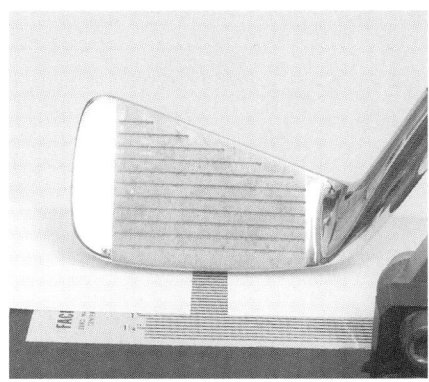

19-7 ...by slipping two pieces of paper underneath the sole, one from the toe side and one from the heel side, until snug. The papers should either meet at the face center-line or an equal distance away from the face centerline. This photo shows the clubhead in a correct lie position. The face centerline can be determined by eye or by measuring and finding the face mid-point.

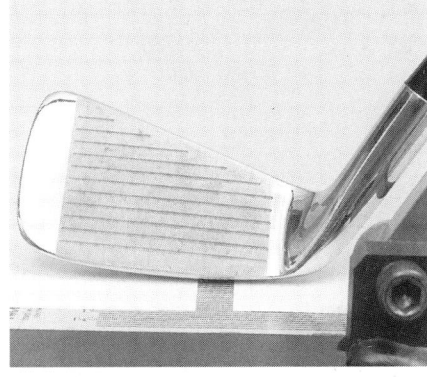

19-8 If the papers are forward or rearward of the face centerline, readjust the club until correct, using the two slips of paper as your guide.

19-9 After proper positioning of the clubhead, align the leading edge of the clubhead parallel to a line on the face progression sticker. This will ensure a correct loft reading. Now, tighten the knob holding the shaft in place.

19-10 Place the magnetic side of the Protractor against the Measuring Arm and read the actual lie angle in degrees. Record this specification on the Fitting Sheet.

19-11 Remove the Protractor from the arm. Place the Protractor's non-magnetic side on the clubface. Be sure the Protractor is flat against the face. Read and record the actual loft angle in degrees. Note: Be sure the leading edge of the face is still parallel with a line on the face progression sticker.

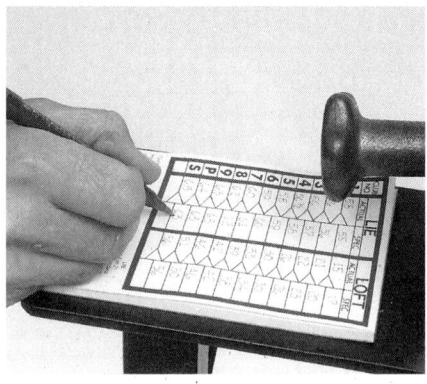

19-12 Continue to measure and record all loft and lie readings. Also, in the space provided on the pad, record the desired or manufacturer's specifications for comparison. Industry standard loft and lie readings are found in Tables 19-1 and 19-2 at the end of this chapter.

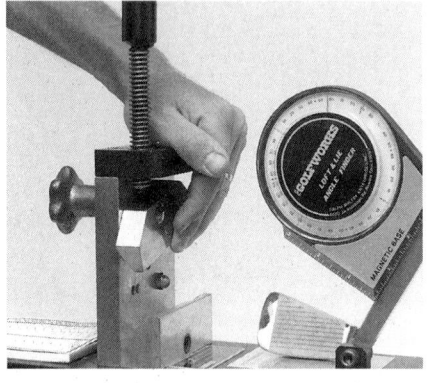

19-13 How to bend loft and/or lie. Loosen the steel mushroom knob (1) and unscrew the large double-handled clamping screw (2) until the Top Line Holddown (3) is raised up as far as it will go.

19-14 With the Top Line Holddown in this position, place the iron head into the Bending Unit, toe first, with the face flat against the major vertical piece (1). Be sure the toe of the club is against the Brass Acorn Head Stop Screw (2).

19-15 Lower the Top Line Holddown on to the top line of the iron head, keeping the Top Line Holddown flat against the major vertical steel piece. Be sure the Brass Plugs found on the underside of the Top Line Holddown are in contact with the top line of the head.

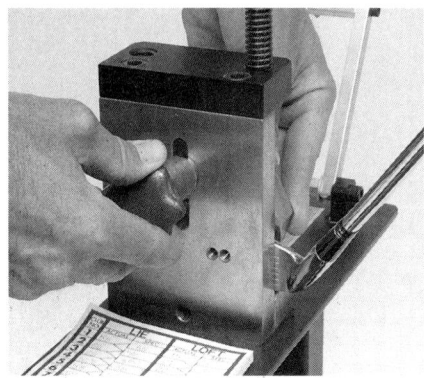

19-16 Secure the Top Line Holddown by tightening the steel mushroom knob until finger tight. Do not over tighten.

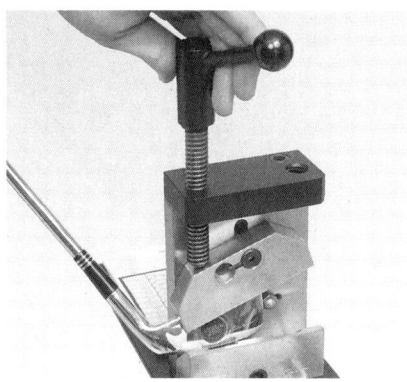

19-17 Screw the large double-handled clamping screw down to contact the Top Line Holddown and securely lock the iron head in the bending unit. Usually ½ turn of the clamping screw past snug is sufficient. The head is now secure and ready for bending.

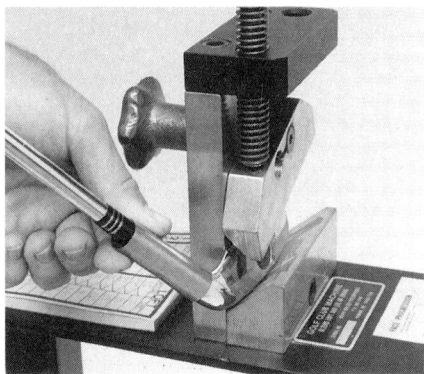

19-18 To prevent any possibility of a small hosel nick in newer clubs, attach a brass hosel protector clip to the hosel. This is usually not necessary with older irons.

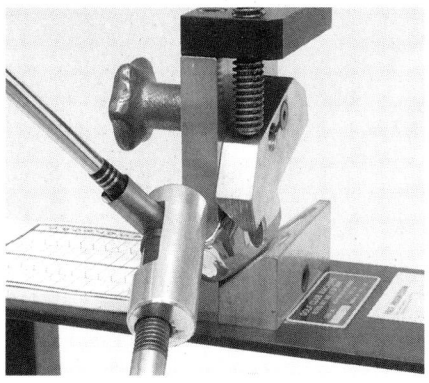

19-19 Place the bending bar around the hosel protector as low on the hosel as possible. Tighten the bending bar handle until snug around the hosel.

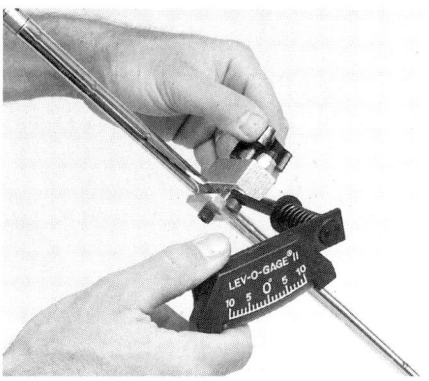

19-20 A protractor with a special clamping assembly can be placed around the shaft. This unit will allow you to see the amount of change you are making during the bending operation. This will eliminate the need to repeatedly move the club back and forth between the bending and measuring units.

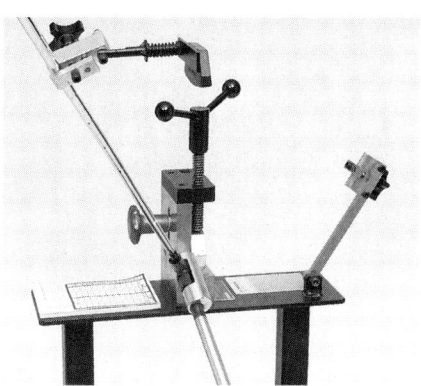

19-21 Altering lie. Position the protractor so it is perpendicular to the machine as shown and rotate until the protractor reads zero degrees.

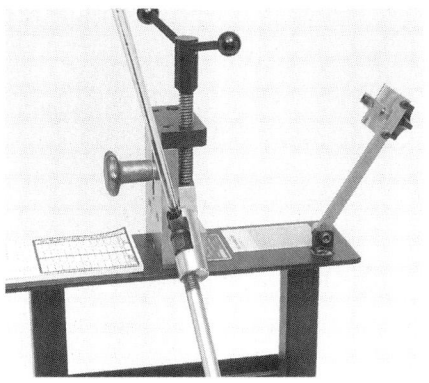

19-22 Swing the bending bar so that the bar is in line with the back of the iron's hosel. As you place each of the different lofted irons into your machine…

19-23 …the position of the bar will always stay in line with the back of the hosel. There will be a slight change with regard to its position relative to the side of the machine. The previous photo (19-22) showed the proper positioning of the bar on a less lofted club. The photo above shows the bar's placement on a higher lofted club and in line with the hosel.

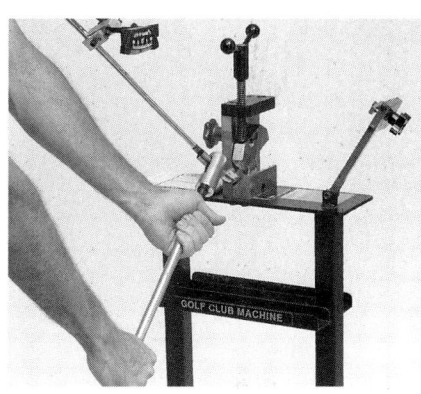

19-24 To make the lie more upright. Grasp the bar handle with both hands, as shown, and lift up towards, and in line with, the shaft of the club and the back of the hosel. Follow the lie change progress on the protractor.

19-25 To flatten the lie. Grasp the bar handle with both hands and push directly away from the shaft and the back of the hosel. The bend is not made vertically, but is made in line with the back of the hosel.

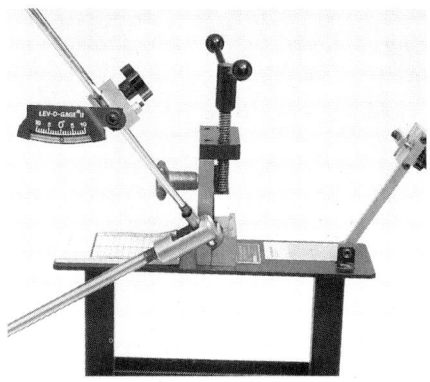

19-26 Changing the loft. Swing the measuring unit protractor around so it is parallel to the machine as shown and the protractor rotated so it reads zero degrees. Swing the bending bar around so it is even with the base of the machine or perpendicular to the face.

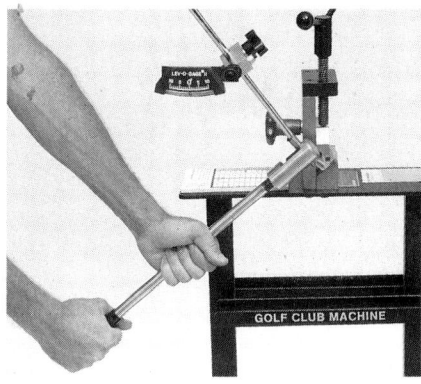

19-27 To increase the loft. Grasp the bar handle as shown and bend straight down. Follow the progress on the protractor.

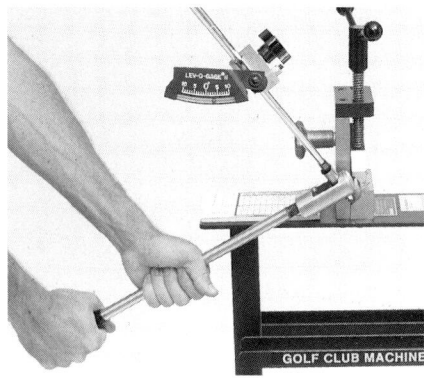

19-28 To decrease the loft. Grasp the bar handle as shown and bend straight up.

19-29 After bending, the club should be checked in the Measuring Unit for correct lie angle and...

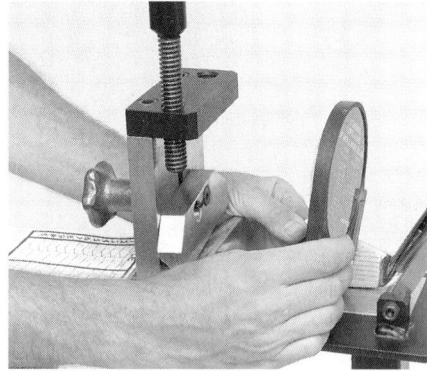

19-30 ...checked for the correct loft angle. It takes approximately 35 minutes to check, bend and recheck an entire set or irons. Note: After you gain confidence and find that the indicator assembly attached to the shaft is always correct, you can eliminate the recheck of lofts and lies. Then it will only take 20-25 minutes per set.

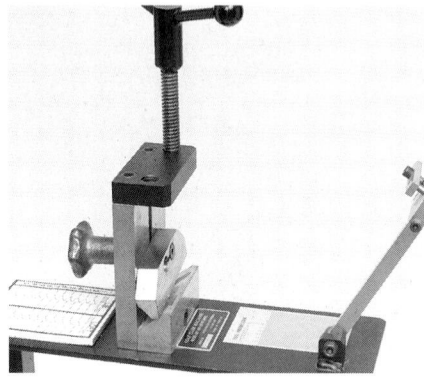

19-31 This machine can also be converted to bend left-handed irons. First, the double handled clamp is placed in the opposite hole.

19-32 Next, the Top Line Holddown is removed, and the pivot bolt is placed in the opposite hole. Next, the Top Line Holddown is reinstalled.

19-33 The brass acorn nut, which acts as a toe stop, is removed and placed in the opposite hole. This conversion takes less than 30 seconds to complete and makes this machine the most versatile on the market.

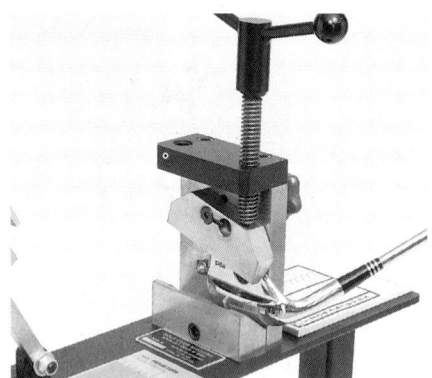

19-34 This photo shows a left-handed club being clamped in the Bending Unit. Left-handed clubs are measured and bent in the same manner as right-handed clubs.

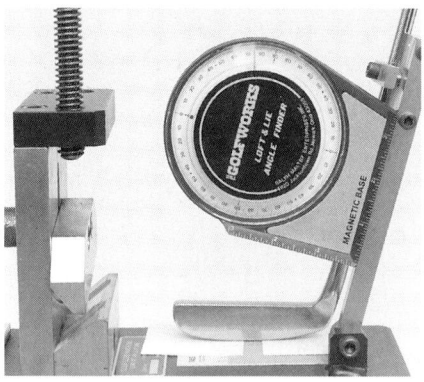

19-35 Putters can also be measured and altered in this machine. This photo shows the lie angle being checked.

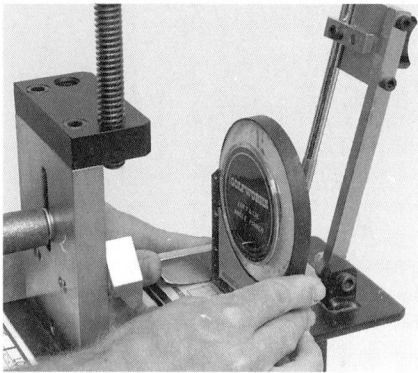

19-36 The loft angle is checked. Record these specifications on the Fitting Sheet.

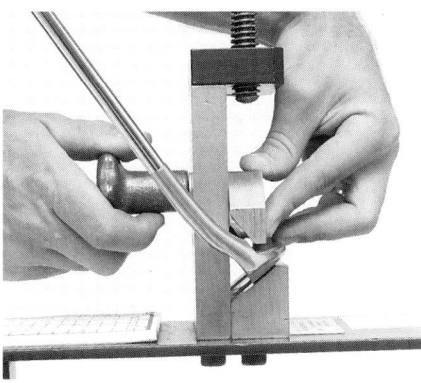

19-37 Place the head of the putter into the Bending Unit toe first with the sole of the putter flat against the Angled Wedge Plate (1). This means the face of the putter will not be flat against the Major Vertical Piece (2), as is the case with all iron clubs.

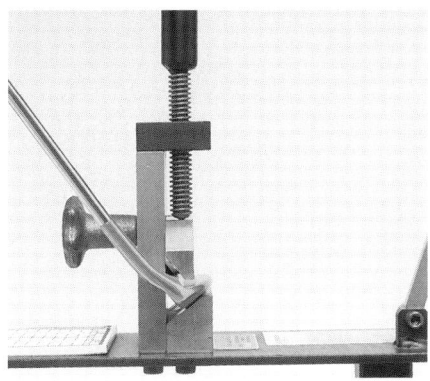

19-38 Lower the Top Line Holddown on top of the top line of the putter and tighten the steel mushroom knob. Tighten the double-handled clamping screw.

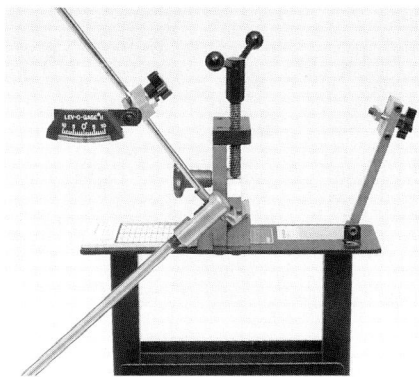

19-39 Install the brass hosel protector on the hosel as shown in photo 19-18. Attach the special protractor to the shaft as shown above.

19-40 Use the bending bar as previously shown to make lie and loft alterations.

19-41 Woods can also be measured on this machine. You can easily and accurately measure both the lie angle and the loft angle of wood clubs. Use the same procedure as was shown for irons. **Note: Take the loft measurement from a wood at half the vertical face height.**

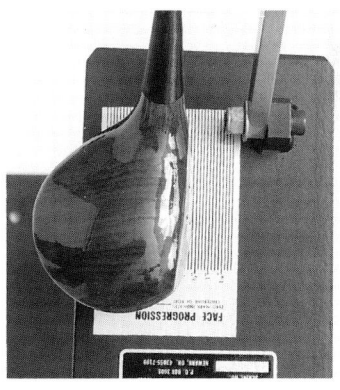

19-42 Face progression is easily determined for a wood and face angle can be visually determined using the straight face progression lines as a visual reference.

19-43 Measuring bounce on an iron head. Place the iron head properly in the Measuring Unit. Measure and record the loft angle as shown above. Be sure the leading edge of the face lines are square (parallel) to the lines on the face progression sticker.

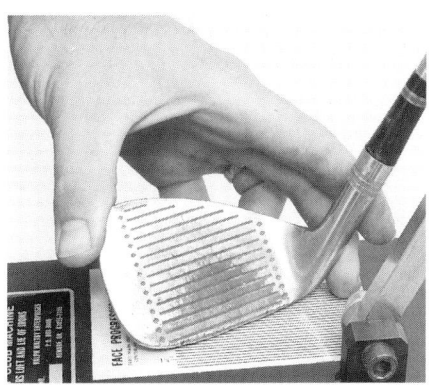

19-44 Next, rotate the iron head until the face leading edge is no longer elevated off the base but is touching the base. Another way of saying this is to simply rotate the clubhead until the sole of the club is sitting squarely (flat) on the machine base, thus eliminating all bounce.

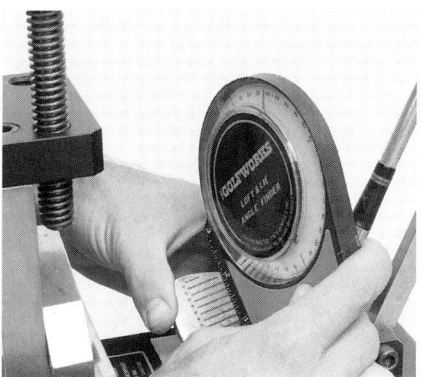

19-45 Now measure and record the new loft reading as shown. Subtract this reading from the previous reading to find the degree of bounce on an iron. Example: The first loft reading is 56°. The second loft reading is 48°. Then 56° - 48° = 8° bounce. Obviously we are measuring a sand club here.

19-46 The GolfWorks® is also offering an **Economy Loft and Lie Machine**. This unit will do everything the deluxe model will do. It is offered for the less frequent user.

ADDITIONAL INFORMATION FOR
CHANGING LOFT AND LIES OF IRON CLUBS

TABLE 19-1
Iron Club Lofts – Men's and Ladies'

Irons	Men's Strong Lofts	Men's Modern Standard Lofts	Men's Weak Lofts	Men's Traditional Standard	Ladies' Strong Lofts	Ladies' Modern Standard Lofts	Ladies' Weak Lofts	Ladies' Traditional Standard
1	15°	15°	17°	17°	–	–	–	–
2	18°	18°	20°	20°	19°	20°	22°	21°
3	21°	21°	24°	23°	22°	23°	25°	24°
4	23°	24°	28°	26°	25°	26°	28°	27°
5	27°	28°	32°	30°	29°	30°	32°	31°
6	31°	32°	36°	34°	33°	34°	36°	35°
7	35°	36°	40°	38°	37°	38°	40°	39°
8	39°	40°	44°	42°	41°	42°	44°	43°
9	43°	44°	48°	46°	45°	46°	48°	47°
PW	47°	48°	52°	50°	49°	50°	52°	51°
SW	54°	55°	56°	56°	55°	56°	58°	56°

TABLE 19-2
Iron Club Lies – Men's and Ladies'

Woods	Men's [1]Flat Lies	Men's [1]Standard Lies	Men's [1]Upright Lies	Ladies' [2]Flat Lies	Ladies' [2]Standard Lies	Ladies' [2]Upright Lies
1	53°	55°	57°	51°	53°	55°
2	54°	56°	58°	52°	54°	56°
3	55°	57°	59°	53°	55°	57°
4	56°	58°	60°	54°	56°	58°
5	57°	59°	61°	55°	57°	59°
6	58°	60°	62°	56°	58°	60°
7	59°	61°	63°	57°	59°	61°
8	60°	62°	64°	58°	60°	62°
9	61°	63°	65°	59°	61°	63°
PW	61°	63°	65°	59°	61°	63°
SW	61°	63°	65°	59°	61°	63°

[1] Lies shown are for standard men's length irons (i.e., 39" #2 iron). For each ½" added to standard length, subtract 1° in lie (flatter) and for each ½" subtracted from standard length, add 1° in lie (upright).
[2] Same as Note 1 above but based on a standard length set with a 38" #2 iron.

What Happens to an Iron
When Loft and Lie are Altered.

The lie of an iron club can be altered without usually affecting any other specification of that iron. However, adjusting the lie 3 to 4 degrees flatter will increase the swingweight by 1 point and adjusting the lie 3 to 4 degrees more upright will decrease the swingweight by 1 point simply because the clubhead is extended further from or closer to the fulcrum point on the swingweight scale. This slight change should not be considered when altering the lie because if a person truly needs the lie angle changed this much, the improvement in ball striking solidness and directional control will overwhelm an insignificant 1 point swingweight change. See Figure 19-47.

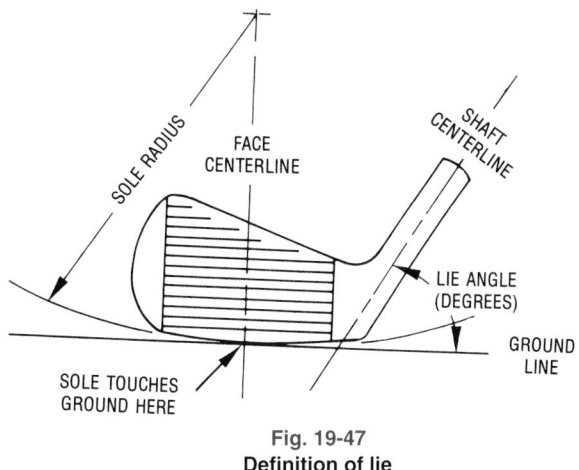

Fig. 19-47
Definition of lie

When the loft of an iron club is altered, three effects on other specifications occur with which you should be thoroughly familiar. First, the hosel offset will be progressed if the loft is decreased, and conversely, the hosel offset will be regressed if the loft is increased. As a result, the face progression has also been affected. Offset is measured differently than face progression and is illustrated in Figure 19-48. The change in hosel offset and subsequently face progression will make the iron appear a little differently to the golfer. These two changes, however, are rather minor.

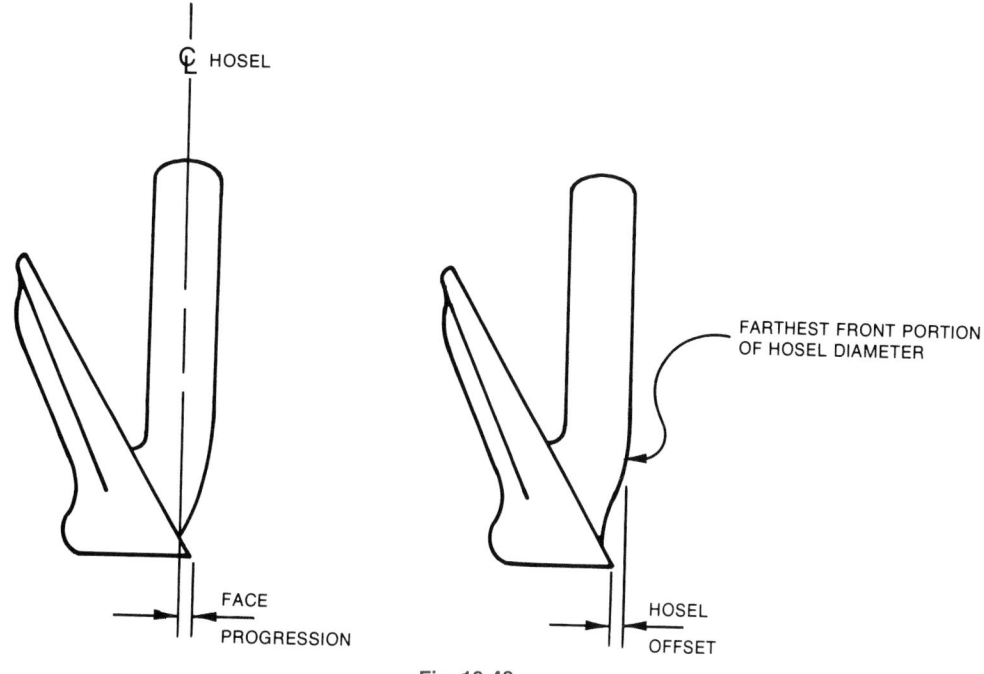

Fig. 19-48
Progression and offset comparison

221

The third, and more important, specification that is affected during a loft change is to the sole inversion. Sole inversion is defined as the angle of the sole to the ground when the shaft is perpendicular to the ground and the face is square to the target. See Figure 19-49. When most iron clubs are designed, the hosel-to-face angle and the face-to-sole angle are all directly related to one another. For instance, the angle of the face to the centerline of the hosel equals the loft. Also the angle of the face to the sole minus 90° would equal the loft only if a 0° sole inversion were part of the original design. See Figure 19-49. It should be apparent that when you bend a golf iron hosel in a bending machine, some part of this relationship of the original design specifications must be destroyed.

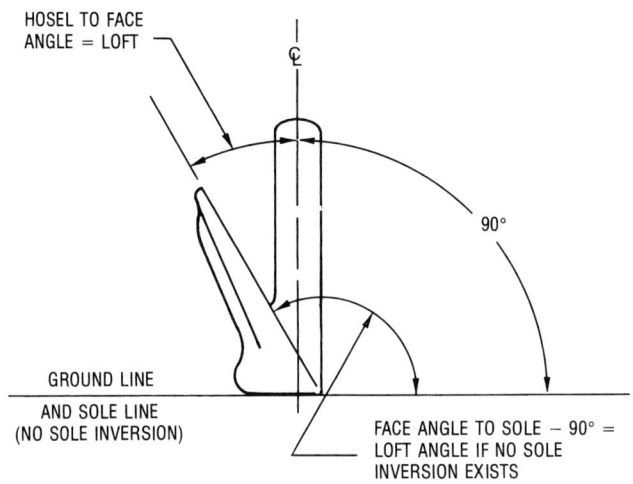

Fig. 19-49
Loft and sole inversion relationship

To more fully understand this, refer next to Figure 19-50 which shows a before and after comparison of the same iron shown in Figure 19-49 whose loft has been increased 3°, returned to normal, and then decreased 3°. Assume for discussion's sake, we have a 35° lofted #5 iron with no offset and a square sole angle or 0° sole angle. (See the top drawing in Figure 19-50.) Now look at the middle drawing in Figure 19-50, by bending in more loft, the leading edge of the clubface has protruded slightly forward and in this example is actually ahead of the farthest front portion of the hosel, providing what is called "Regressed Offset," or in layman's golfing terms a "front porch" look. Notice also what has happened to the sole angle. We now have 3° of bounce sole angle which happens to be exactly the same as the loft angle increase. Since the sole angle and loft angle are part of the same head, you cannot change either one without changing the other by the same amount.

Now look at the bottom drawing in Figure 19-50 where it shows the hosel bent to decrease the loft. The sole angle now has 3° scoop which is not a good situation since the club will now have a greater tendency to dig into the ground. Also, the hosel offset has changed to a "Progressed Offset" where the clubhead's leading edge is behind the leading edge of the hosel. Figure 19-50 is excellent for pointing out the importance of maintaining the proper interrelationships between specifications.

Let's go back to Figure 19-50 and once again note that if an iron was originally designed with 0° sole inversion (the sole line is perpendicular to the shaft) and its loft is increased, sole inversion in the form of "bounce" is created. See photo 19-3. Conversely, if the loft is decreased, sole inversion in the form of "scoop" or "dig" is created. See photo 19-1.

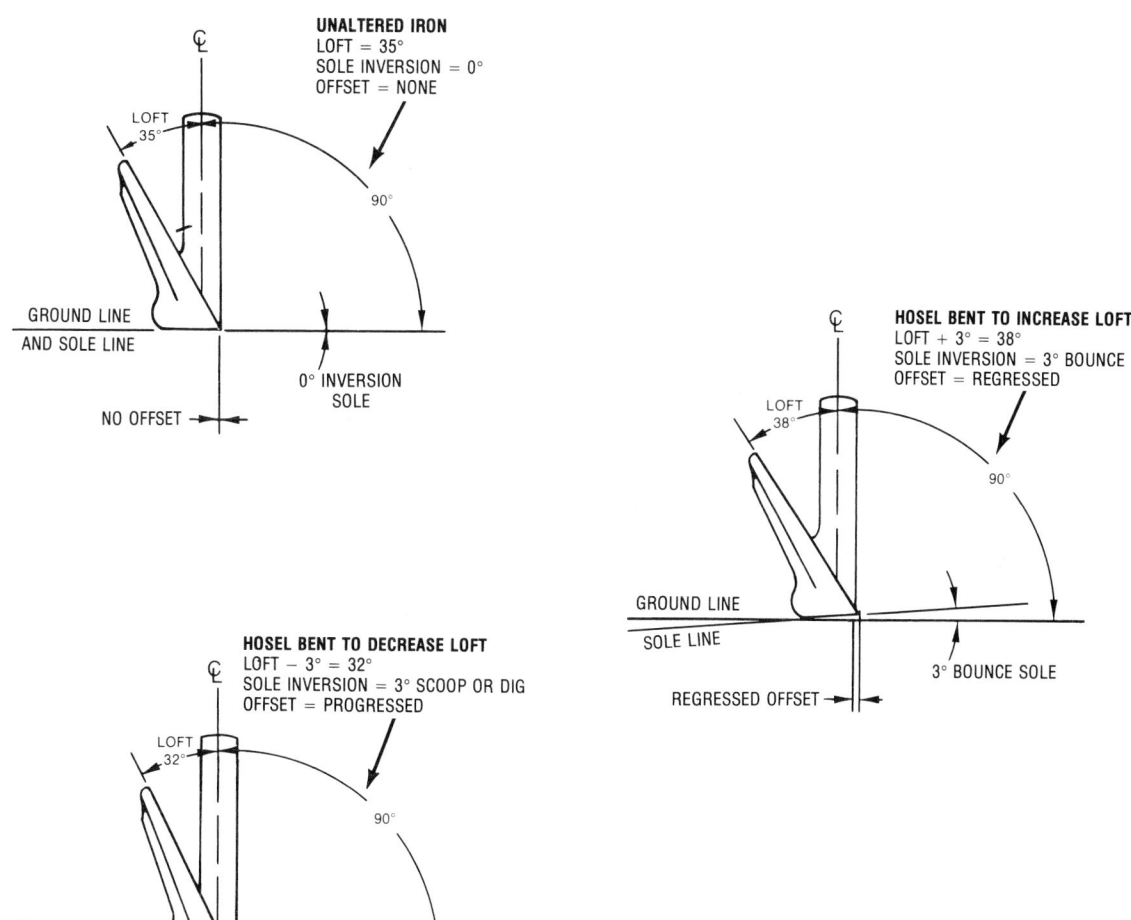

Fig. 19-50
Effect of altering iron lofts

Of these two sole angles, the scoop or dig condition is by far the worse and should be avoided. Unfortunately, most players ask to decrease loft so they can hit the ball farther, which can potentially create this undesirable scoop sole. Therefore, before you decide to decrease the loft on a set of irons, be sure to inspect the existing sole angle to see if the bend will unfavorably change the sole angle. To check the sole angle of any iron, hold the club in front of you as shown in Figure 19-51 with the shaft vertical and the leading edge of the sole pointed directly away from your sight line. Note the relationship of the leading and trailing edges of the sole to the shaft. If the leading edge is even with or above the trailing edge, you will be creating a scoop sole, a condition caused by strengthening the club's loft. This is not a good situation. This can cause the player to hit heavy or fat shots.

A good rule of thumb to use here is if you have various sole angles within the same set of irons (in other words a few have bounce soles, a few scoop soles and maybe a couple square soles), this would be a good indication that the lofts are out of specification. If you simply bend them back to the original loft specification, the sole angles should once again be consistent with one another throughout the set.

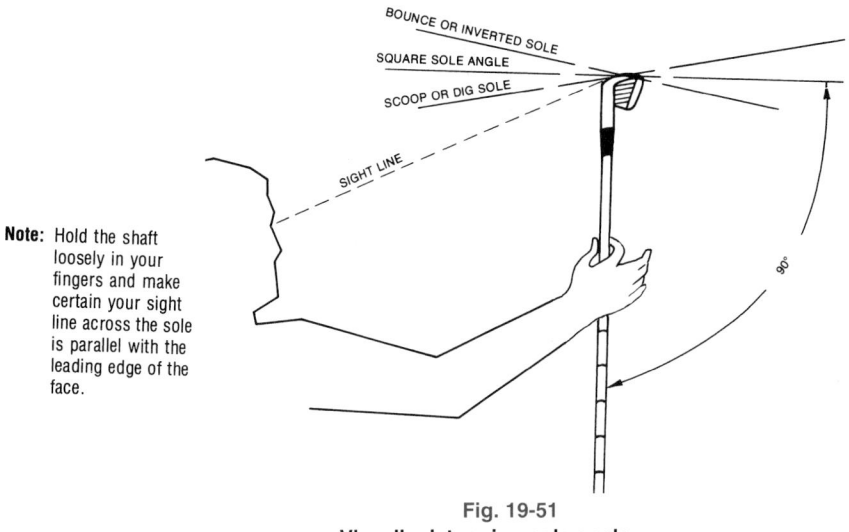

Note: Hold the shaft loosely in your fingers and make certain your sight line across the sole is parallel with the leading edge of the face.

Fig. 19-51
Visually determining sole angle

An advantage of altering the loft of irons is if any adverse effect on playability occurs, the iron can be restored to its original specifications quite easily. Keep in mind after reading this section that each individual manufacturer designs and builds irons in different ways. For instance, some manufacturers build an inversion or bounce sole into their iron clubs and others build their irons with a very pronounced sole camber (radius from front to back of sole and radius from heel to toe of sole). These particular sole designs would indicate slightly different results than the drawing shown here. However, the effect of each loft change can be easily calculated if you first measure an iron's original loft, offset and sole inversion, and then compare it to the altered readings. The point is, it is easy to make a club more unplayable by altering lofts without proper knowledge of the interrelationships of certain specifications. Figure 19-52 is included here to provide additional information on the playability of various sole designs.

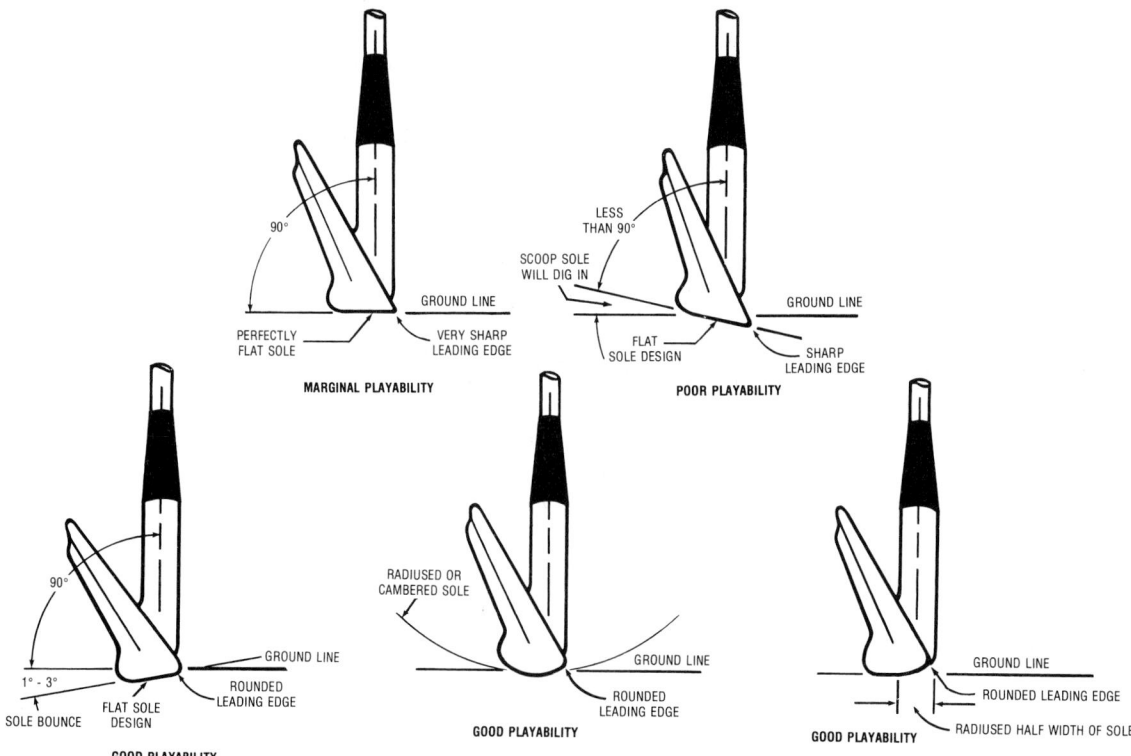

Fig. 19-52
Playability comparisons of various types of sole angles and designs

224

Tips and Suggestions When Altering Loft and Lie of Irons

1. Only allow authorized individuals and yourself to operate a loft and lie machine. It will generate more attention and consequently additional income if it is place in a sales traffic area so that your customers may see and ask about it. It can, however, only lead to problems if you allow just anyone to use the machine.

2. Most loft and lie machines utilize a manually operated Bending Bar while a few are motorized. With the manually operated Bending Bar, as you become more and more proficient you will obtain a feel for exactly how much pressure to exert on the Bending Bar to get the desired loft and lie.

3. Eighty to ninety percent of all investment cast clubs can also be bent to alter loft and lie. Most cast clubs can be bent as much as 4° in any direction; however, it is recommended that you stay within 2° in any direction to maintain a safety margin.

When you make the initial effort to bend the first cast club in a set that is questionable, remember that all bendable clubs will have a little springiness in the hosel as initial pressure is exerted on the Bending Bar. If this initial bend attempt produces a rigid rock hard feel with no springiness, then the set is suspect and you may break the hosel.

Some people seem to feel that heating or warming the hosel will allow it to bend more easily. The amount of heat required to actually help would surely discolor the hosel as it would need to be almost red hot. Also, if a cast club is made of a brittle material that will not bend, it will most likely break even though it was heated.

4. The use of a standard loft and lie chart for recording before and after readings is very helpful. The one shown in Figure 19-53 works quite well because it has a triangular area between readings which allows the recorder to mark down differences in each successive reading. This will tell you at a glance how evenly progressed the actual readings of loft and lie are through the set and will make it much easier during bending.

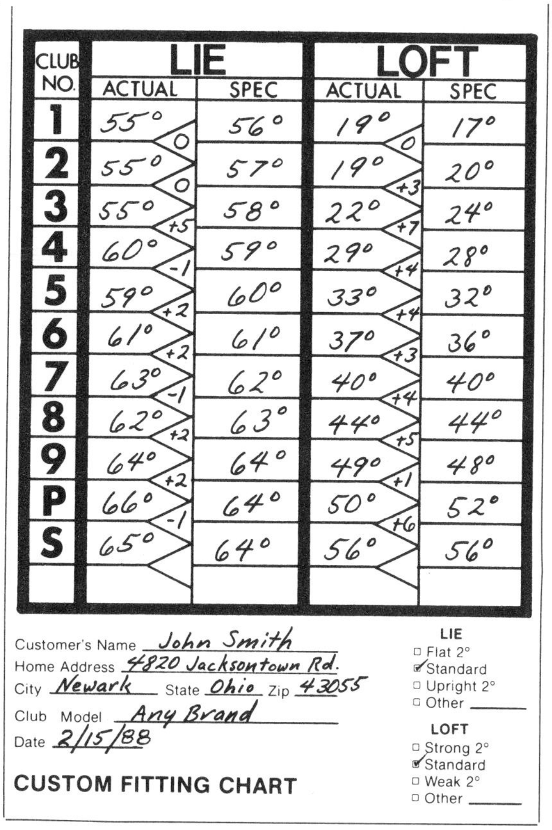

CLUB NO.	LIE ACTUAL	LIE SPEC	LOFT ACTUAL	LOFT SPEC
1	55°	56°	19°	17°
2	55°	57°	19°	20°
3	55°	58°	22°	24°
4	60°	59°	29°	28°
5	59°	60°	33°	32°
6	61°	61°	37°	36°
7	63°	62°	40°	40°
8	62°	63°	44°	44°
9	64°	64°	49°	48°
P	66°	64°	50°	52°
S	65°	64°	56°	56°

Customer's Name John Smith
Home Address 4820 Jacksontown Rd.
City Newark State Ohio Zip 43055
Club Model Any Brand
Date 2/15/88

CUSTOM FITTING CHART

LIE
☐ Flat 2°
☑ Standard
☐ Upright 2°
☐ Other _____

LOFT
☐ Strong 2°
☑ Standard
☐ Weak 2°
☐ Other _____

Fig. 19-53
Lie/Loft chart for recording specifications

5.   Generally the charge for altering the loft and/or lie of each club is between $2.50 and $4.50. The national average is $3.75. Some shops charge a flat fee of $23.00 to $36.00 per set.

When selling a new set of irons, the customer can be custom fit to a so-called stock set and of course, this service is usually on a "no charge" basis. This feature will increase your golf club sales.

6.   When bending an iron club hosel, the Bending Bar exerts a tremendous pressure on it. As such, a small mark is sometimes slightly noticeable. If you are bending a brand new set, never used, you should use a Brass Hosel Protector Clip available from The GolfWorks® or you can make your own from .10" thick brass or aluminum shim stock. Using a pair of scissors cut a piece of shim stock 1½" square and roll it into a cylinder as the one pictured in photo 19-18.

The Difference in Bending Machines

Numerous bending machines are available and careful shopping is necessary before purchasing one. Bending machines fall into two categories. One type measures and bends the iron hosel in the same fixture. It is very rare to find one of these machines that bends and measures accurately. The other type measures the loft and lie specifications and then bends the hosel in a separate fixture. The GolfWorks® Loft and Lie machines are in this latter category. Machines that bend and measure in separate fixtures give the correct loft and lie more accurately for all types of irons.

Let me explain why this is a very important point. When working the type of machine that measures and bends in the same fixture, the clubhead is locked in a holding vise. The position of the shaft in relation to one, or sometimes, two fixed measuring arms determines the loft and lie of the iron. This type of machine, however, can be inaccurate. The measuring arm gives the operator a loft or lie reading that can be off by as much as 2°. Remember that as the hosel offset increases, the reading from this type of machine will show the loft to be weaker than what it really is. Also, as the blade length increases or decreases, or as the scoring line length increases or decreases from a standard distance built into the machine, the lie reading will be read flatter or more upright than it actually is. Look closely at photos 19-54 and 19-55 for a clear understanding of these important points.

19-54 Both #9 irons with the same degree of lie. But the lie readings are different because the length of the scoring lines vary.

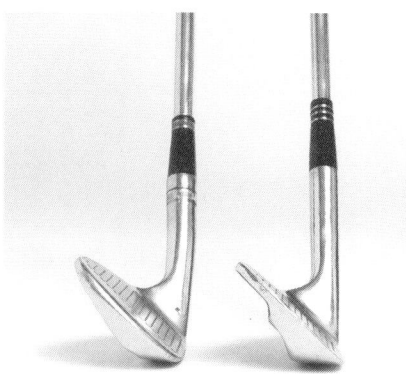

19-55 Both #9 irons with the same loft. But the club on the left has a weaker loft reading because it has a greater hosel offset. (The distance from the farthest front portion of the hosel to the farthest front portion of the leading edge of the face center.)

The point is, if every iron had the same amount of hosel offset and the exact same blade length and scoring line length, then a machine that measures and bends in the same fixture would be acceptable. However, different manufactured irons vary widely with these two features and the potential for inaccurate readings is enormous.

Only The GolfWorks® Golf Club Machines will provide the means to determine a truly accurate loft and lie reading, and then adjust these specifications accordingly.

The GolfWorks® Golf Club Machines allow the operator to sole the clubhead properly on the base of the machine. Remember, the definition of lie is the angle of the centerline of the shaft with the ground line, tangent to the sole at the centerline of the face. To achieve the correct lie reading, the sole of the clubhead must be resting at the point just below the center of the face. Once the club is soled properly, and only then, can the correct loft be read. The GolfWorks® Golf Club Machines enable the operator to achieve the correct soled position.

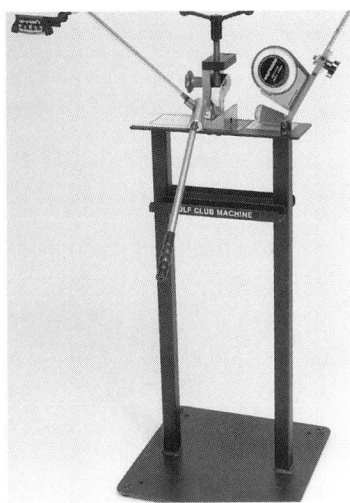

Fig. 19-56
The GolfWorks® Loft & Lie Machine

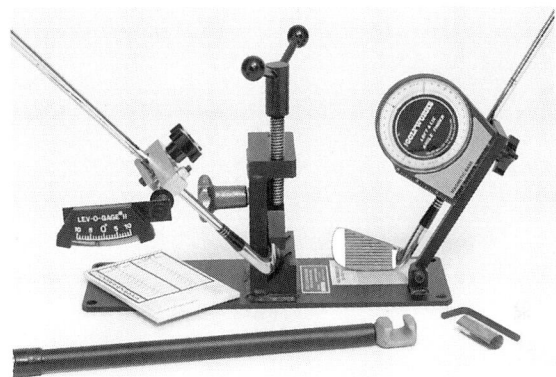

Fig. 19-57
The GolfWorks® Economy Model Loft & Lie Machine

NOTES

_____

_____

_____

_____

_____

_____

_____

_____

_____

CHAPTER 20

TIGHTENING LOOSE IRON HEADS

With today's modern bonding materials and assembly methods, loose iron heads on modern clubs have become more rare than in the past. This is fortunate because when a loose iron head is detected it is usually too late since the head has probably flown completely off the end of the shaft. Most of the loose irons heads you will find will be on the older clubs that have a pinned hosel. The pin, of course, will keep the head from flying completely off and it can also make it hard for you to detect if the head is loose. The best thing to do is to check the entire set by holding the clubhead in a vise equipped with aluminum or brass vise pads. With the clubhead firmly held, grasp the grip end with both hands and try to twist the shaft in both directions. If you cannot feel it move, listen carefully for a squeaking sound which indicates that the shaft is loose.

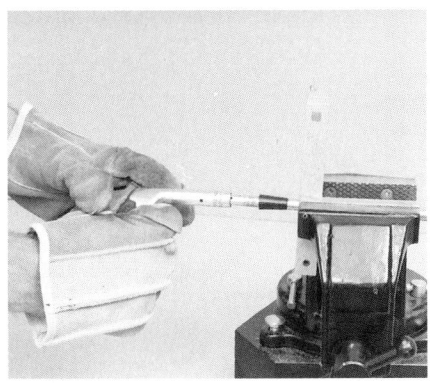

20-1 First, remove the head from the shaft. Refer to Chapter 21 for this procedure.

20-2 The choices for materials to fill the excess space in a hosel are brass or aluminum shims, or **Aluminum Oxide Sand.**

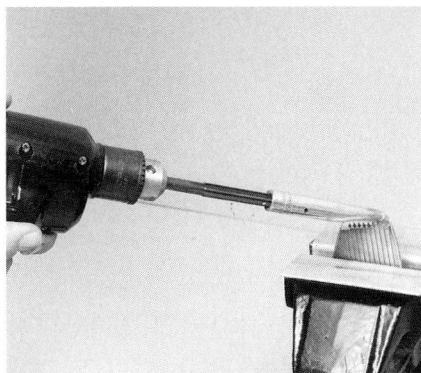

20-3 Before reinstalling the shaft, clean out all loose glue, dirt and scale from the hosel bore. A proper size hosel reamer, or step drills, work well for tapered hosel bores. A ⅜" drill bit is used for a hosel bored to fit a .370 parallel tip shaft.

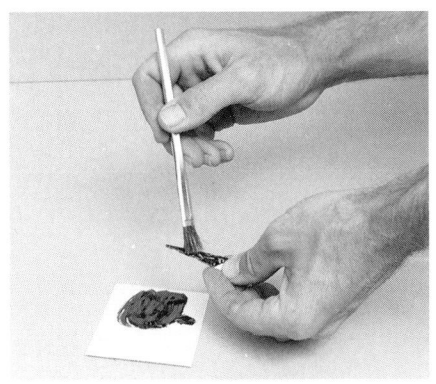

20-4 If a shim is used, apply a liberal amount of epoxy to both sides of the shim and also down the hosel bore.

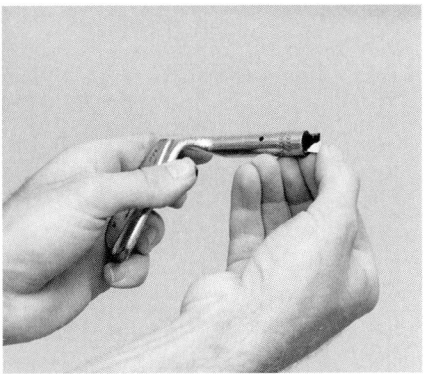

20-5 Push the shim into the hosel bore. A shim is not always necessary and sometimes epoxy alone will suffice. If the head turns freely about the shaft when the shaft is pushed to the bottom of the hosel bore, this is a good indication a shim is necessary.

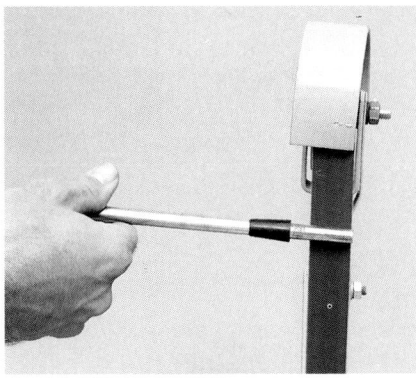

20-6 Roughen the shaft tip using a belt sander, grinding stone, file or emery cloth. Removing all the old epoxy will ensure good adhesion between the epoxy and the shaft.

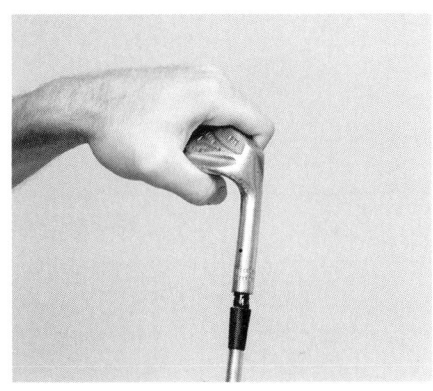

20-7 Put epoxy on the tip of the shaft and also inside the hosel. Push the shaft into the hosel hole. Make sure the shaft is turned properly so the grip is correctly aligned with the clubface. If the shaft doesn't penetrate to the bottom of the hosel bore, proceed to photo 20-8.

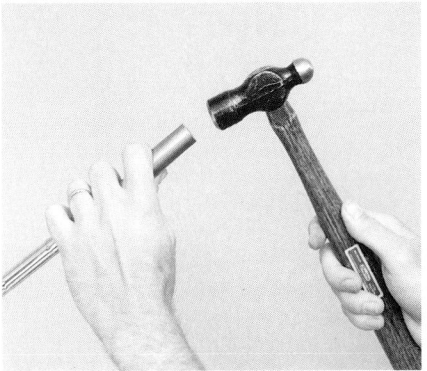

20-8 Using a **Shaft Driving Plug,** drive the shaft into the hosel as far as it will go. It is necessary to remove the grip and use the above method on "Taper Tip" shafts which are force fit. "Unitized" (parallel tip) shafts will usually bottom out in the hosel by pushing the shaft into the head or tapping the grip end against the floor.

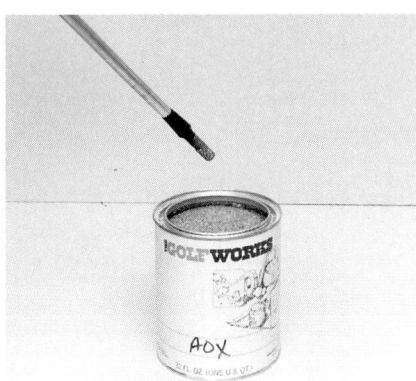

20-9 To use Aluminum Oxide Sand, coat the inside of the hosel and the outside of the shaft with epoxy, dip only the tip of the shaft into the sand and …

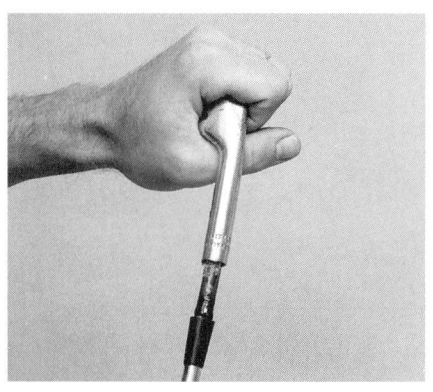

20-10 ...push the shaft into the hosel. Aluminum Oxide Sand is an excellent material because the sand acts as a good bonding surface for the epoxy. Therefore, this is the material we recommend for tightening loose shafts.

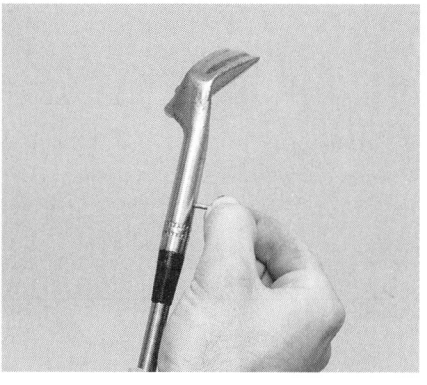

20-11 Another trick for ensuring the shaft is aligned properly in the hosel is to make sure the rivet hole, if present, is lined up from the outside of the hosel through the shaft. The procedure for installing a rivet is shown in Chapter 21.

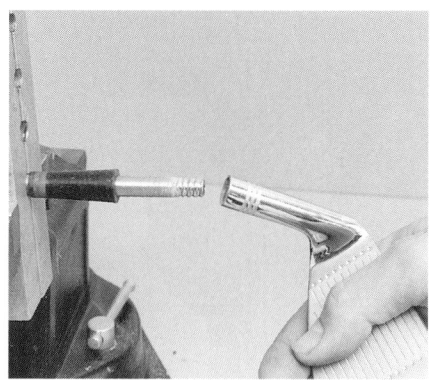

20-12 To tighten a screw-in type shaft. It is necessary to first remove it by turning the head clockwise.

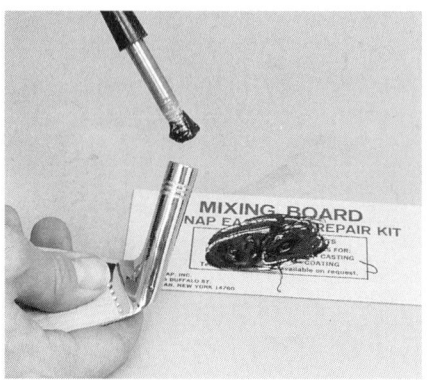

20-13 Next, apply epoxy to the shaft tip and inside the hosel.

20-14 Once epoxy is applied, simply screw the head back onto the shaft. If the head is forced past its original position, it will be necessary to reposition the grip on the shaft for proper alignment.

NOTES

_____

_____

_____

_____

_____

_____

_____

_____

CHAPTER 21

RESHAFTING IRON CLUBS AND CHANGING HOSEL BORE SIZES

Basically, reshafting irons is much easier than reshafting woods, especially if the correct equipment is used. Without correct equipment, however, reshafting irons can sometimes turn into a frustrating wrestling match. Fortunately, the appropriate tools and equipment are available to make even the potentially difficult reshafting job much easier. Along with covering reshafting iron clubs with a steel or graphite shaft and changing hosel bore sizes, putter reshafting is also explained in this chapter.

Ninety-nine percent of all iron head assemblies fall into an assembly category referred to as a "force fit" or "slip in" assembly. This describes a shaft that is placed in the hosel and secured with epoxy, a swaged fit, and/or a rivet. The other 1% represents assemblies where the shaft screws into a threaded hosel.

When replacing a steel shaft, the three most important features of the shaft to be matched are listed here in order of importance.

1) Shaft Flex
2) Shaft Pattern or Flex Point
3) Shaft Weight

The definition of a shaft flex is "a comparative measurement of a shaft's resistance to bending under a given load." This measurement is commonly taken from a shaft deflection board and divided into five different flexes: L (ladies'), A (flexible), R or T (medium), S (stiff) and X (extra stiff) with "X" being the stiffest and "L" being the most flexible. A less commonly used machine for measuring flex is the Frequency Analyzer. Information on this very accurate flex tool is found in Chapter 63. Matching shaft flex is important so the entire set will be consistent. If one or more shafts are not matched properly in flex, the clubface may be delivered into the ball at an angle that is different from the rest of the clubs.

Shaft pattern identifies the shaft type (Dynamic™, TT Lite™, Jet Step™, etc.) through an arrangement of step downs. Shaft type indicates the bend point (flex point) on a golf shaft. The bend point is the point on a shaft that experiences the greatest amount of bending or deflection when placed on a deflection board or where the shaft bends the most during a swing. A golf shaft will either have a low, mid or high bend point. A high bend point means most of the bending during the swing occurs above the middle of the shaft. A mid-bend point means most of the bending occurs near the middle of the shaft and a low bend point indicates most of the bending occurs below the middle of the shaft. This is important because the bend point or flex point does much to determine both the trajectory and directional control of a golf shot.

Shaft weight simply means the total weight of the golf shaft. The weight of a golf shaft will fall into these categories: standard weight, lightweight and very lightweight.

When replacing a graphite shaft, refer to the specifications on the shaft. Since graphite shafts do not have step downs to identify them and if no information is on the shaft, the customer must specify the flex point, flex, torque and weight of the graphite shaft desired. The characteristics of graphite shafts are explained in Chapter 58.

The methods, techniques and use of tools required to remove a shaft, regardless of the assembly procedure, are covered in this chapter. In addition to covering the reshafting steps, this chapter also shows how to change hosel bores to accept different shaft tip sizes. An inexpensive and effective way to change bore sizes, or just clean them out, is by a method called step drilling. Step drilling utilizes a set of three different drill sizes for taper bores or only one drill size for unitized (parallel bores).

Note: Removing an iron head can be a potentially dangerous repair if certain precautions are not followed. Always wear eye protection and never stand in front of an iron head when applying heat to the hosel. Trapped air between the tip of the shaft and the bottom of the hosel can turn into an explosive force when heated. Occasionally a head will fly off the shaft or a rubber plug will be forced from the top of the shaft through this rapid expansion of air.

21-1 If possible, check and record the swingweight before removing the shaft. Your goal is to return the club to the owner in as close to original condition as possible unless requested otherwise. **If the shaft is broken, check another club from the set.**

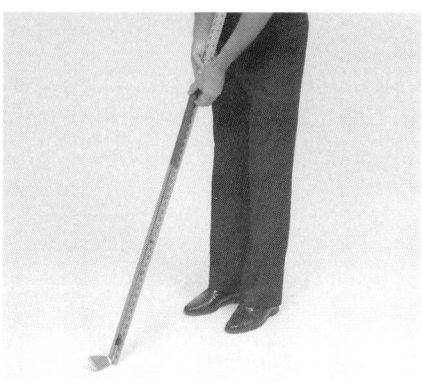

21-2 The length should also be recorded. Once again, if the shaft is broken, measure the club nearest to the broken one to determine its correct set length. **(Example: #6 iron is broken. Measure the length of both the #5 and #7 irons.)**

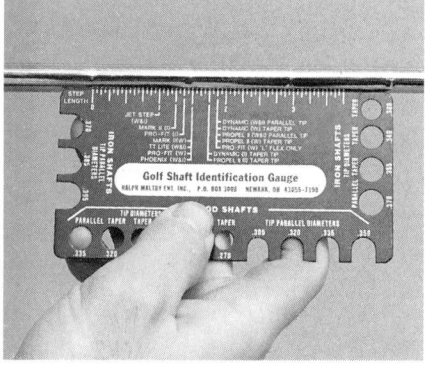

21-3 If you are to install the same type of shaft, the original shaft type must be identified. As is often the case, the shaft band may be missing. Shafts can be easily identified, however, by using the **Golf Shaft Identification Gauge.** If a non-commercial, proprietary shaft is present, refer to the end of Chapter 56, Proprietary Shaft Pattern Identification, to determine the characteristics and match for the shaft.

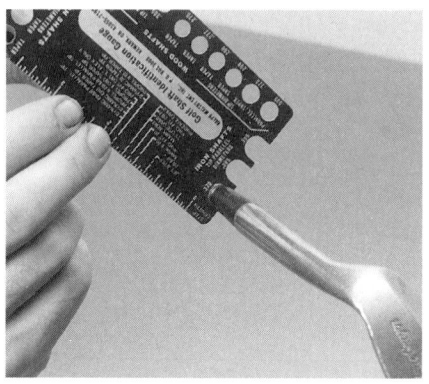

21-4 The **Golf Shaft Identification Gauge** can also be used to determine the shaft tip construction. That is, whether it is a taper tip or a parallel tip (unitized) shaft. The exact use of this gauge is explained later in this chapter.

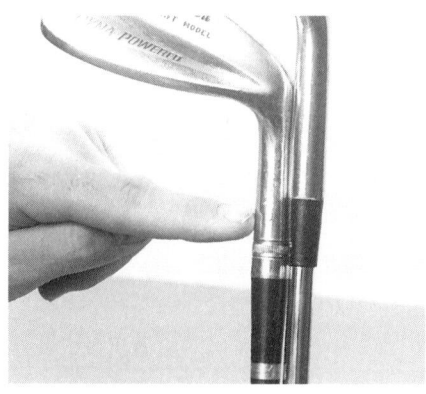

21-5 Determine if the shaft and hosel are pinned together. Sometimes a pin (rivet) will only penetrate one half of the hosel. The club on the right has no pin, while the club on the left does have a pin.

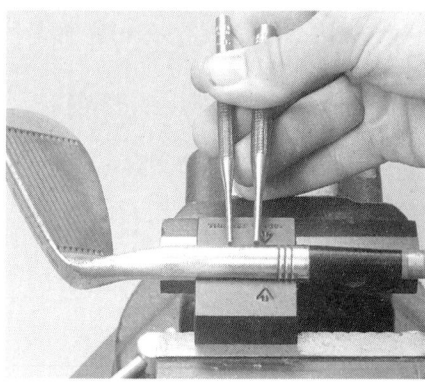

21-6 Depending upon the diameter of the pin, select either a ³⁄₃₂" or ⅛" pin punch. Note the use of a **Riveting Block.** This special tool allows the hosel to rest on a curved surface and provides a sturdy base. The pin is punched through an opening in the Block.

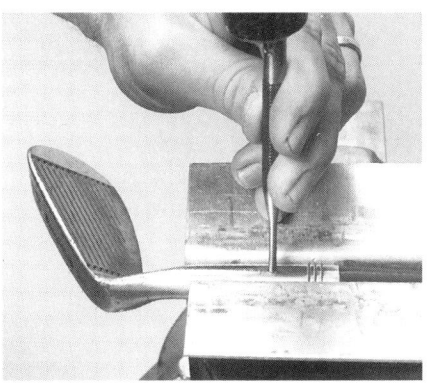

21-7 Place the tip of the **pin punch** squarely on top of the pin. If a **Riveting Block** is not available, make sure the hosel is placed securely between a pair of **aluminum or brass vise pads** before fastening in a vise.

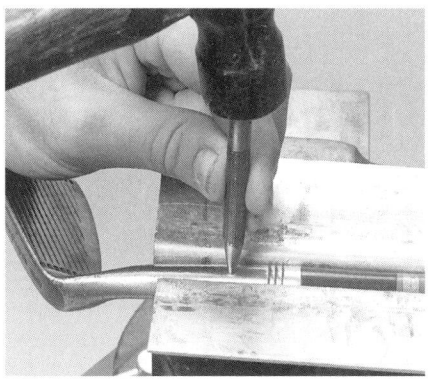

21-8 Drive the pin through the hosel.

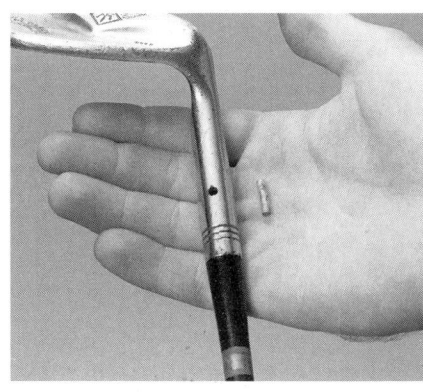

21-9 This photo shows an iron head with the pin removed. If the pin does not penetrate both sides of the hosel, then the pin must first be drilled through with a 7/32" drill bit from inside the shaft and the remainder of the pin punched inside the hosel.

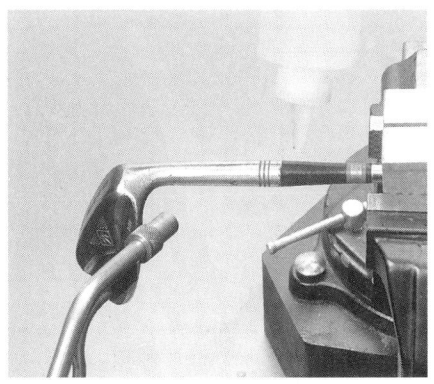

21-10 A Lock Tight Shaft Holder or Rubber Shaft Clamp should be used to hold the shaft securely. Heat the hosel at a point approximately 1" from the top of the hosel. If you wish to save the ferrule, simultaneously squirt water onto the plastic ferrule. The squirt bottle is very handy for this purpose. A bucket can be set on the floor to catch the water.

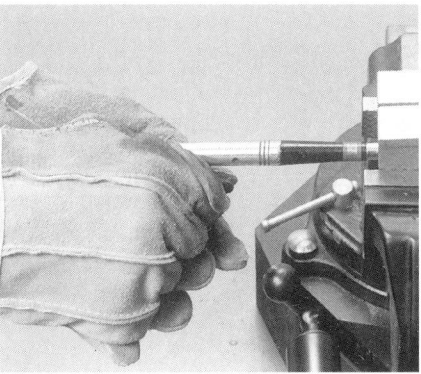

21-11 Next, grasp the iron head in your hands and attempt to turn and pull the head from the shaft. A pair of **leather gloves**, a pot holder glove or rags should be used to protect your hands.

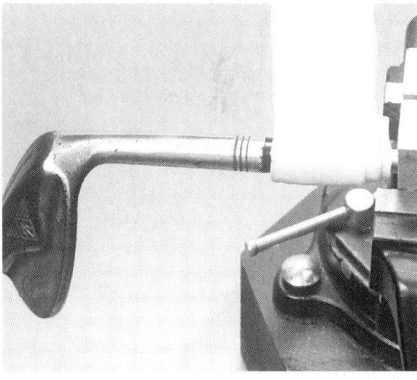

21-12 If the head fails to come off the shaft, the hosel must be reheated. An alternative to the squirt bottle is to soak a paper towel with water and then wrap the towel around the ferrule.

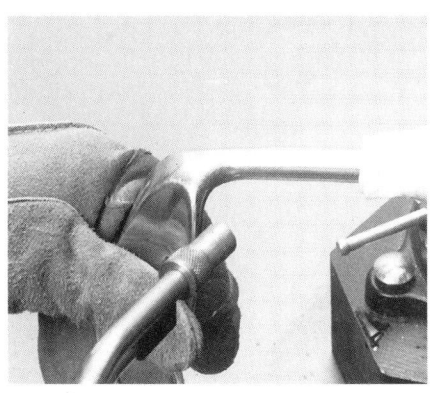

21-13 Direct more heat against the hosel. Do not worry if the hosel discolors. This is easily removed and will be shown later in this chapter.

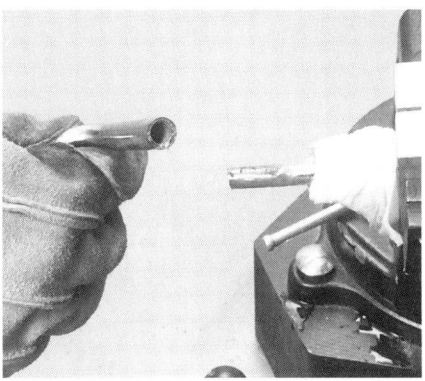

21-14 The head should now come loose from the shaft. If it does not, jump ahead to photo 21-23 and continue through the photos which apply to your particular situation.

21-15 If you wish to save the old ferrule, it will usually slip right off the shaft.

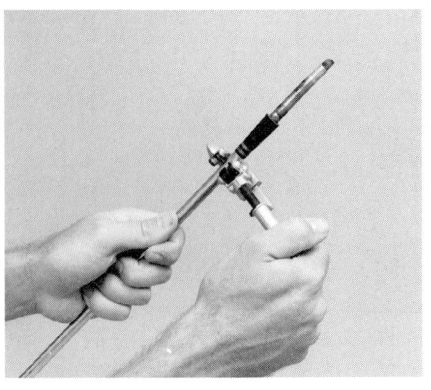

21-16 If the ferrule will not come off, then proceed as follows: First, cut the shaft off 1" or 2" above the ferrule using a tubing cutter or friction wheel.

21-17 Select a hole in the **Lock Tight Shaft Holder** that will allow the shaft to slide freely through it. Gently tap the shaft through the ferrule. Note the ferrule is removed up the shaft and not from the tip end.

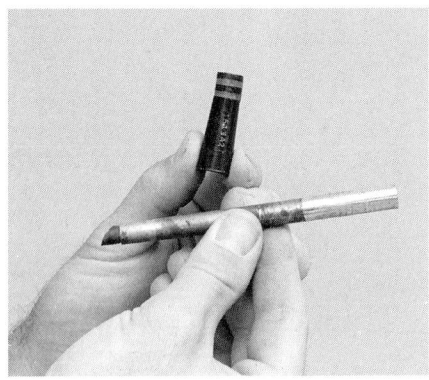

21-18 Ferrule is removed in perfect condition.

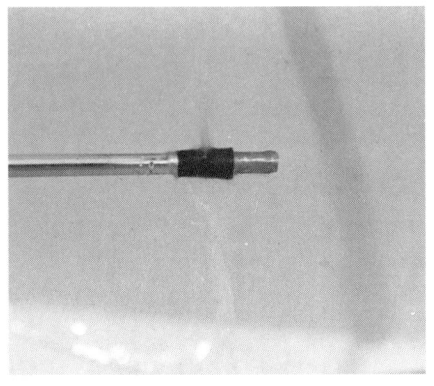

21-19 An alternative method is to soak the ferrule in hot water and attempt to remove it or wrap the ferrule with masking tape and attempt to pull it off with a pair of pliers. The hot water will soften the plastic but not burn it.

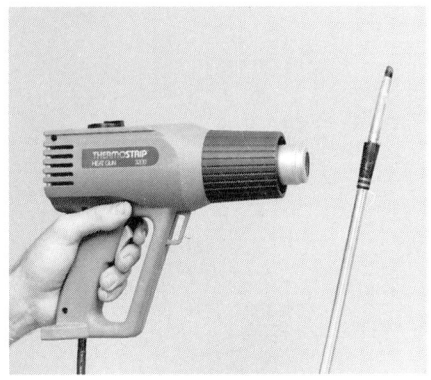

21-20 A **Heat Gun** will supply enough heat to soften the ferrule also and allow you to slide it off the shaft.

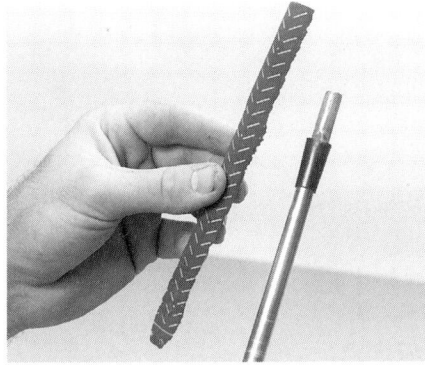

21-21 Another method for removing a ferrule is to cut a strip of rubber from an old rubber grip. The strip should be 7" long and ¾" wide.

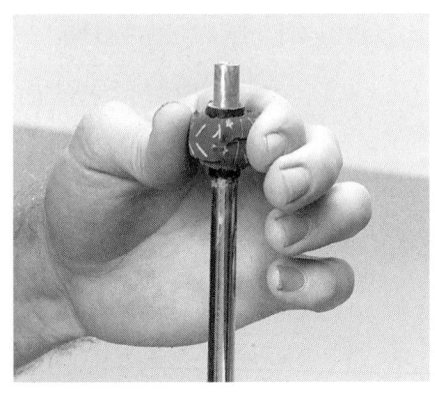

21-22 Wrap the rubber strip around the ferrule and then continue to turn the strip in the same direction after tightening. This will create tremendous pressure on the ferrule and it should turn from the shaft.

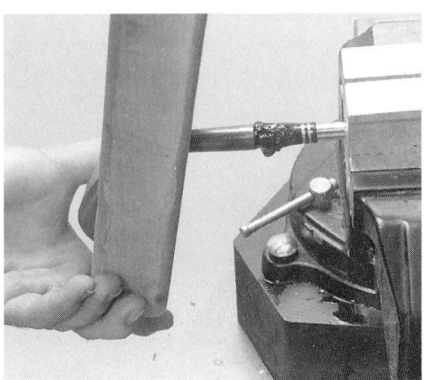

21-23 If a head fails to come off, apply more heat to the hosel. Next, place a **Hardwood Leverage Block** around the head and …

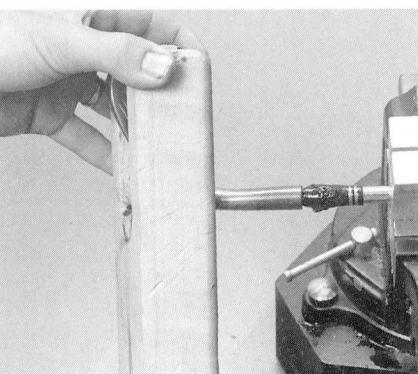

21-24 … attempt to turn the head. Once the head is turned, it will usually pull off the shaft. Note the melted condition of the plastic ferrule if not treated properly.

234

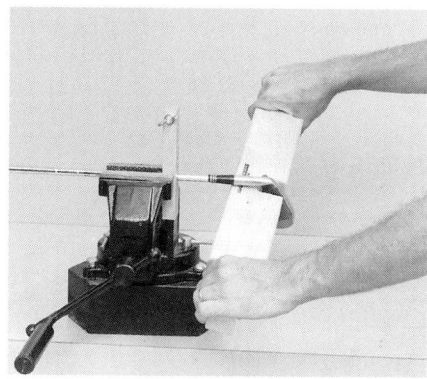

21-25 This **Leverage Block** allows the user to simultaneously turn and pull on the head. This is the recommended leverage block to use.

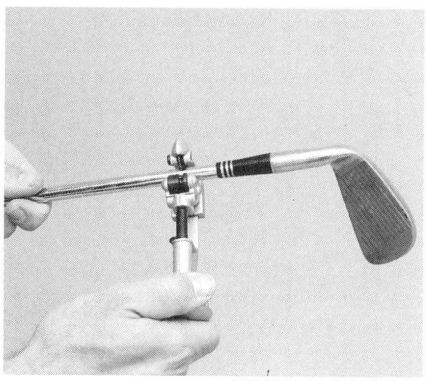

21-26 If the head would not come off as previously shown, cut the shaft off 1" to 1½" above the top of the hosel using a **tubing cutter.**

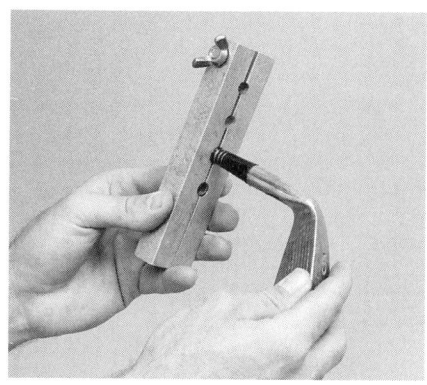

21-27 Place the protruding portion of the shaft secured in the **Lock Tight Shaft Holder.**

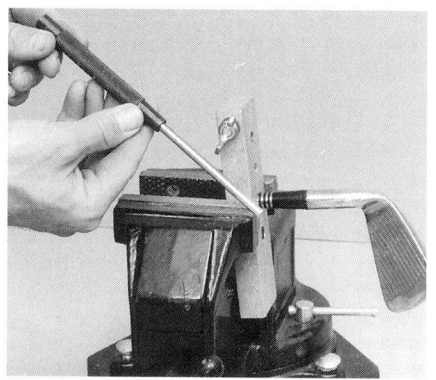

21-28 Use an **8" Long Pin Punch** and …

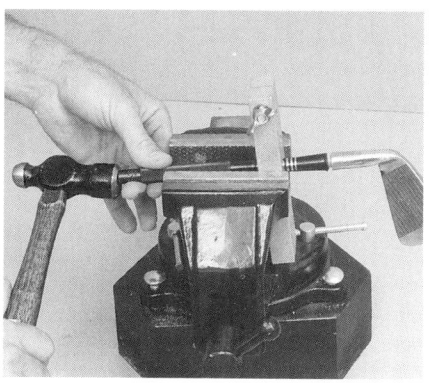

21-29 … insert the punch in the shaft and drive the head off. Sometimes it is first necessary to remove any lead and other foreign matter from inside the shaft by drilling it out with a $7/32$" or $1/4$" drill bit.

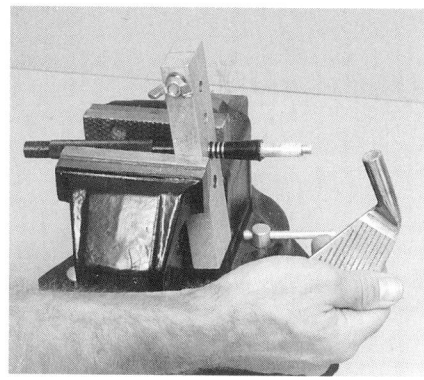

21-30 The head is now driven off the shaft.

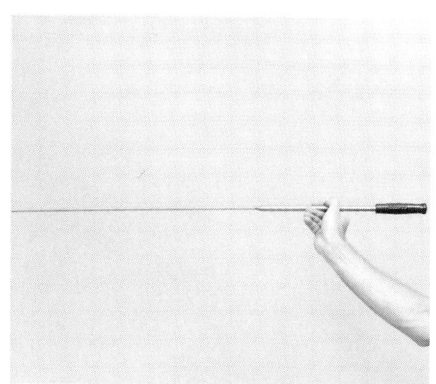

21-31 A **47" Ramrod** is an alternative to cutting the shaft short and using the 8" pin punch. Here's how it works.

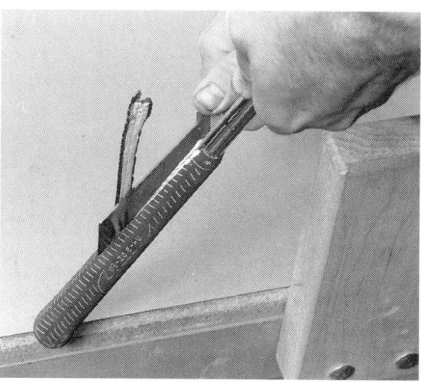

21-32 First, either cut the old grip off the shaft or …

21-33 … save the grip for future use by using the **Pressurized Grip Remover**, as shown, or with a syringe and a large hypodermic needle. Chapter 23, photos 23-31 through 23-37 shows the procedure for using the Grip Remover.

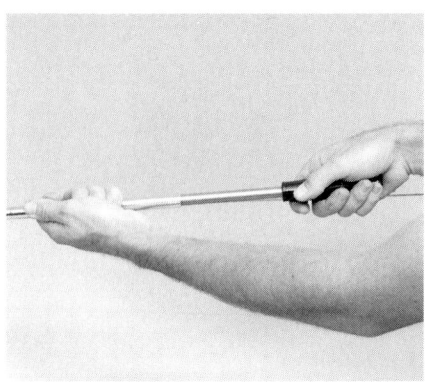

21-34 Insert the **47" Ramrod** down the shaft. Hold the shaft and knock the head off. Remember to first remove any foreign matter from inside the shaft tip with a **47" drill bit.**

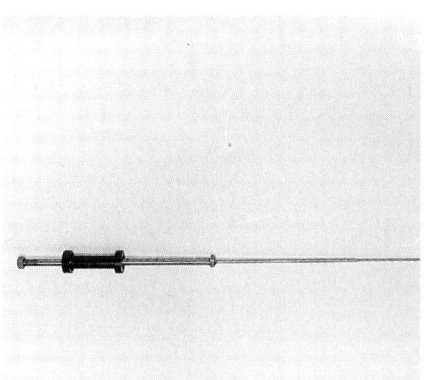

21-35 A **Sliding Weight Ramrod** works the same way as the regular ramrod except it has a heavy 6 lb. sliding weight. This produces a tremendous amount of ramming force against the bottom of the hosel.

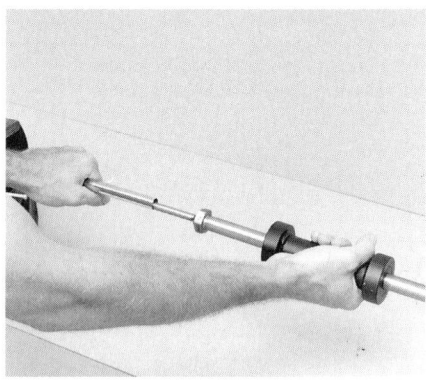

21-36 Place the **Sliding Weight Ramrod** inside the shaft, support the shaft with one hand and slide the weight forward against the stop for hammering action.

21-37 The **Iron Head Remover Tool** will remove the most stubborn iron head from a steel shaft. Often an older shaft will rust to the hosel, making it difficult to remove.

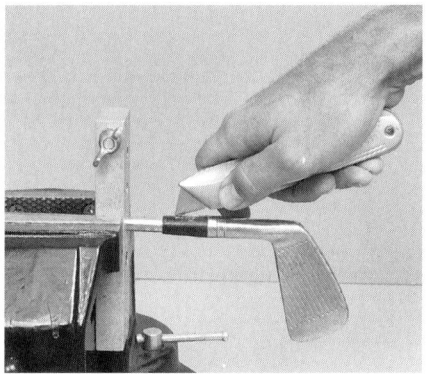

21-38 First the ferrule must be removed from the shaft. If you wish to reuse the ferrule, split the ferrule top and bottom into two halves with a sharp knife or razor blade.

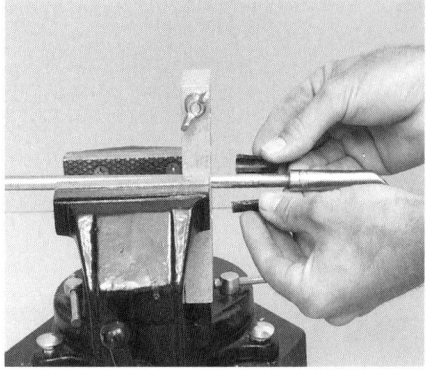

21-39 Remove the ferrule. Later, in photos 21-121 through 21-127 you will learn how to put the split ferrule together again. If you do not wish to save the ferrule …

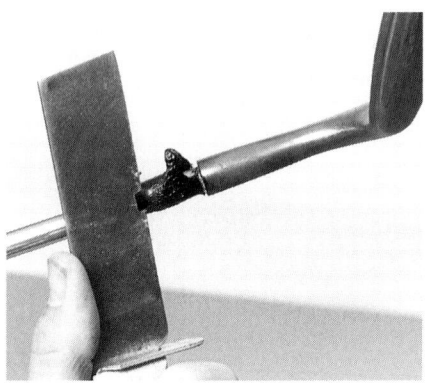

21-40 … simply cut it from the shaft.

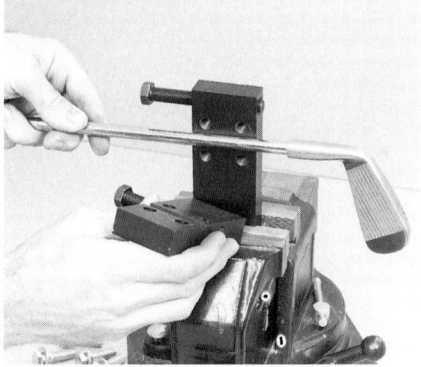

21-41 Secure the longer half of the **Iron Head Remover Tool** in a vise. Place the shaft in the specially grooved section and place the other half of the unit around the shaft.

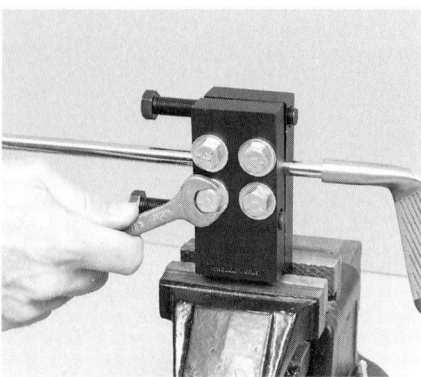

21-42 Tighten the four bolts evenly to secure the shaft. Allow at least a ¾" gap between the top of the hosel and the unit.

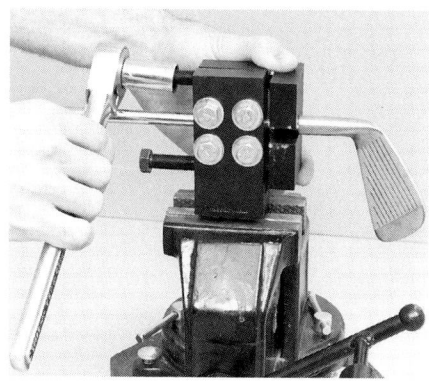

21-43 Place the **forcing plate** over the shaft and tighten the drive bolts until the forcing plate is snug against the top of the hosel. Note the use of a ratchet socket wrench.

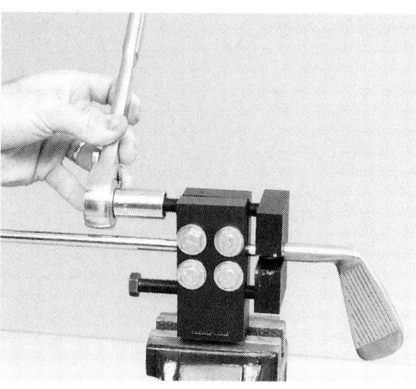

21-44 Alternately tighten the two drive bolts until the head is ...

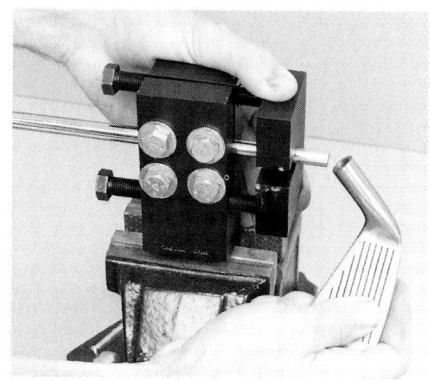

21-45 ... pushed off the shaft. **NOTE: Graphite shafts are easily removed using The GolfWorks® Graphite Shaft Extractor.** See Chapter 7, photos 7-179 through 7-193 for instructions. Also, graphite shafts can often be removed by heating the iron hosel briefly with a propane torch and then carefully twisting the head from the shaft.

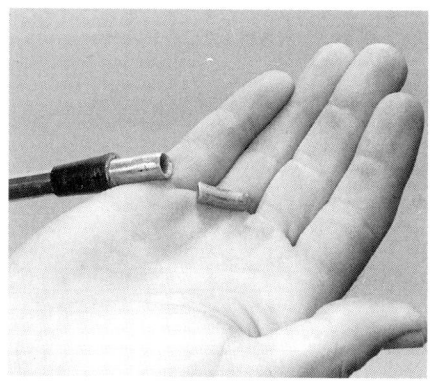

21-46 Occasionally you will find a lead slug or other weighted material inside the tip of the shaft. This indicates the manufacturer or another repairman found the swingweight too light and added weight down the shaft. If you find weight down the shaft, after reshafting, you will have to add weight to bring the swingweight back to original. See Chapter 18 for swingweighting procedures.

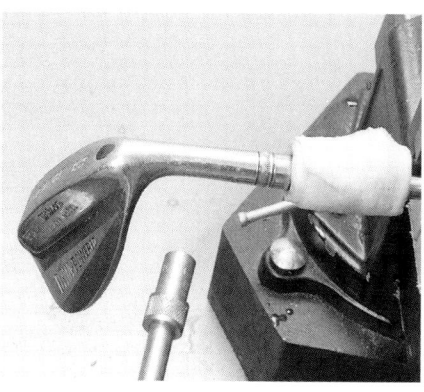

21-47 Some iron head models have a rubber or plastic plug extending down the hosel and through the sole. Heat the hosel as described previously. If the hosel contains a pin, refer to photos 21-6 through 21-9.

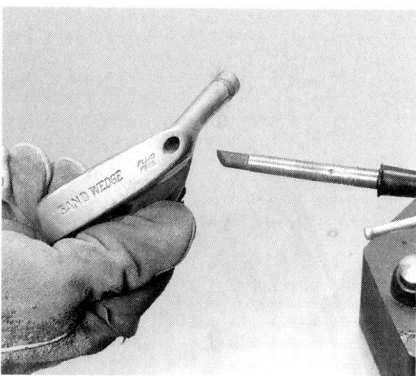

21-48 The head will pull off the shaft leaving the plug inside the shaft. If you wish to save the plug, tug at the plug with a pair of pliers. If the plug does not come out ...

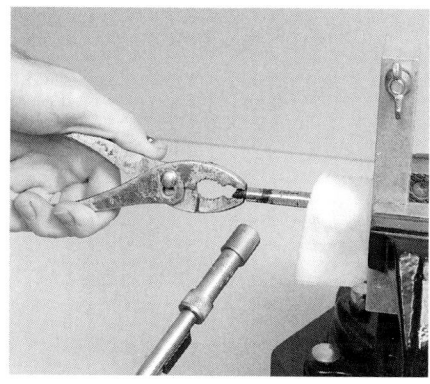

21-49 ... apply heat to the tip of the shaft while simultaneously pulling on the plug.

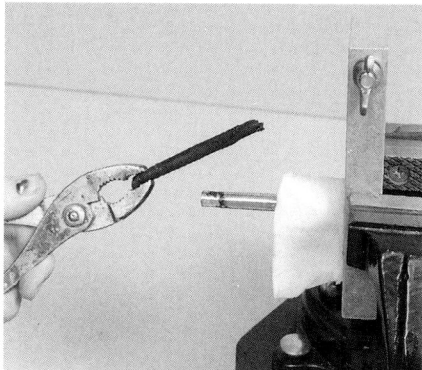

21-50 The plug is removed. As you can see, these plugs were often used in swingweighting lighter heads. Some plugs are quite short, others very long and some even had lead powder added to the rubber during molding.

21-51 Replacement plugs are available if you do not wish to save the original. See photos 21-188 through 21-193 for installation steps. These plugs are available in both red or black colors.

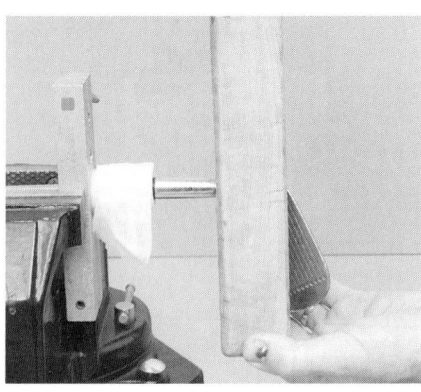

21-52 Occasionally you will encounter a model with the shaft screwed into a threaded hosel. You will note the head loosens while turning the head clockwise yet tightens when turned counterclockwise.

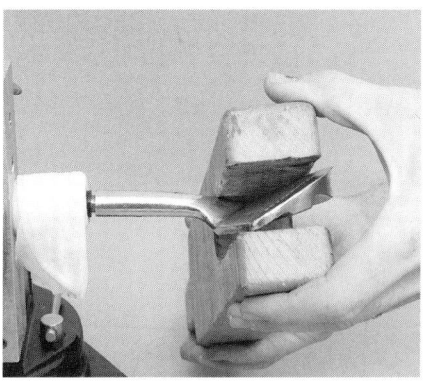

21-53 Simply continue to turn the head clockwise and ...

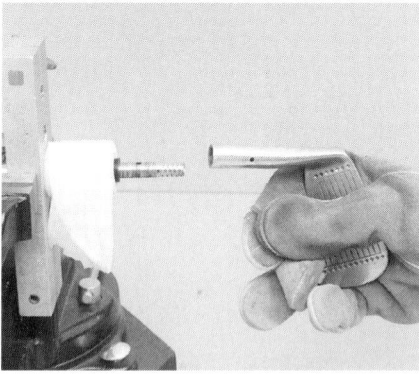

21-54 ... the head will turn off the shaft. If you are replacing this type of shaft, be aware that the hosel must be rebored to accept a larger tip diameter shaft. See photos 21-98 through 21-105 for hosel bore enlarging steps using the step drills.

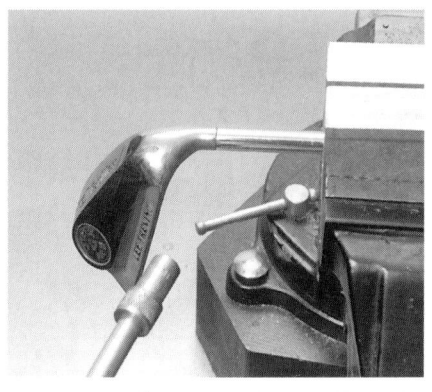

21-55 A shaft over hosel assembly is the easiest type to remove. You should rarely encounter a pin. Place a **Lock Tight Shaft Holder** around the shaft 3" above the tip of the shaft. Apply heat to the shaft.

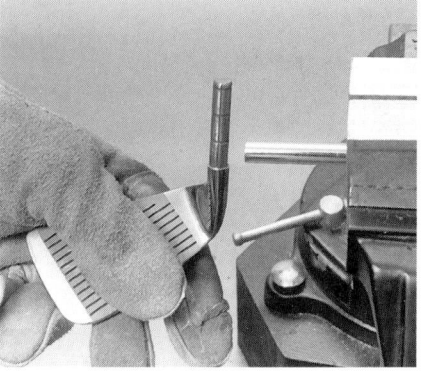

21-56 Twist the head loose with a **Hardwood Leverage Block** or gloved hands. Note the post extending from the iron head. A special shaft with an enlarged over hosel tip section is needed to properly reshaft this club.

21-57 Do not be intimidated if asked to **replace a hickory shaft.** Simply punch the pin through the hosel if one is present.

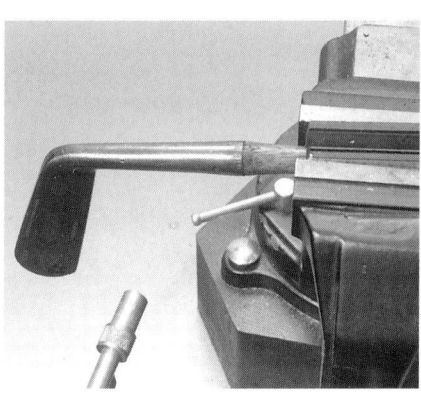

21-58 Heat the hosel briefly using a propane torch and ...

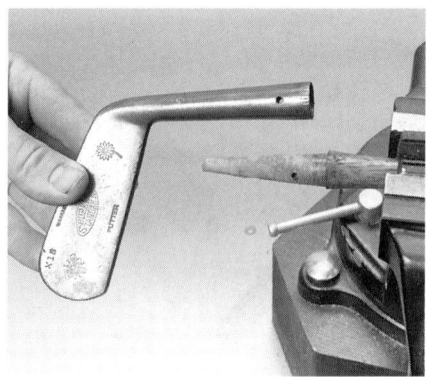

21-59 ... turn and pull the head from the shaft.

21-60 The procedure for removing a shaft broken off inside the hosel is to first heat the hosel with a **propane torch.**

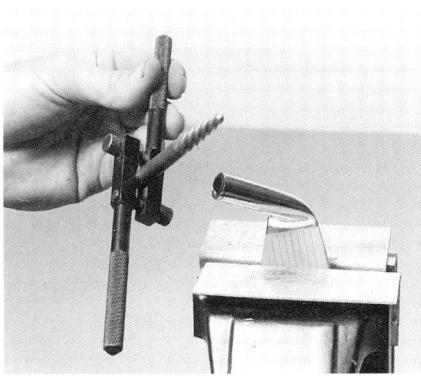

21-61 Select a screw type **extractor** of the proper size. Note the use of the special **extractor wrench.**

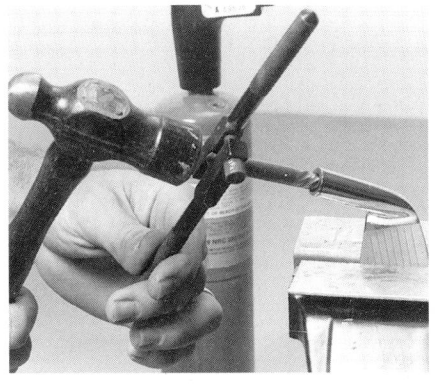

21-62 Tap the extractor inside the shaft until a snug fit is achieved.

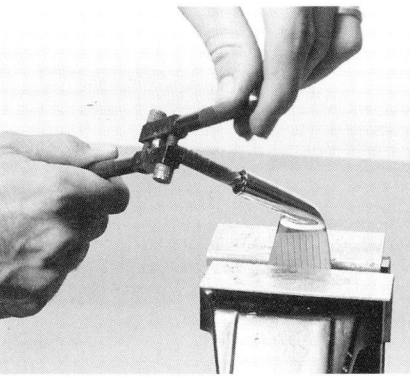

21-63 Turn the extractor wrench counter-clockwise while pulling and ...

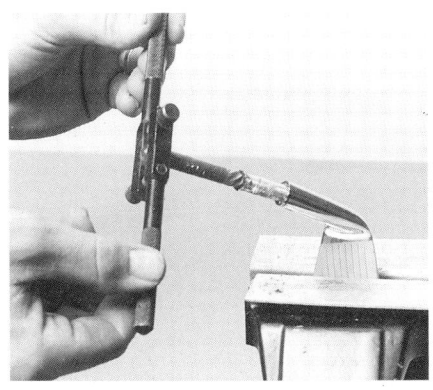

21-64 ... the shaft should come out of the hosel. The ridges along the side of the extractor "bite" into the walls of the shaft allowing the shaft to be pulled from the head along with the extractor. If the shaft does not pull from the head, reheat the hosel and try again.

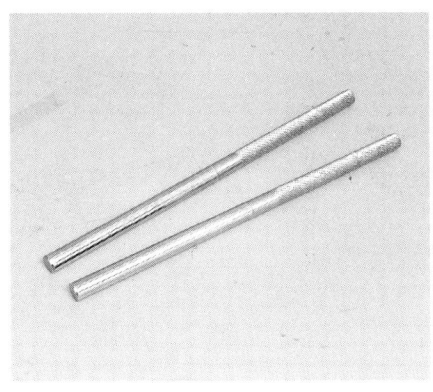

21-65 The GolfWorks® offers a set of Iron Shaft Extractors that work amazingly well. The extractors taper at the same rate as the inside of the shaft. They are available for .355 taper tip and .370 parallel tip iron shafts.

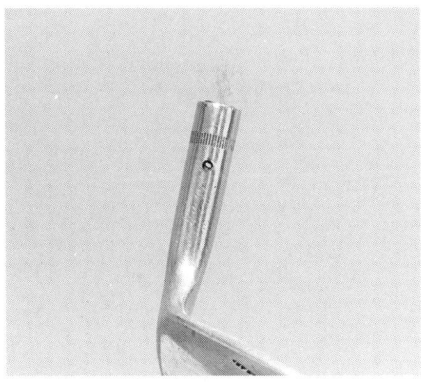

21-66 Be certain the pin (rivet) is removed from the hosel before using the **Iron Extractor.**

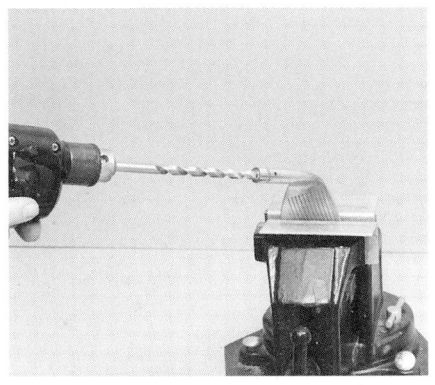

21-67 After the pin is removed, completely clean all the epoxy or other foreign material from inside the tip of the shaft. A ¼" drill bit works best.

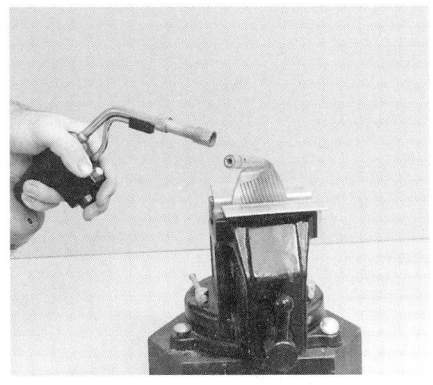

21-68 Heat the hosel using a propane torch. This will soften the epoxy and allow for easy shaft removal.

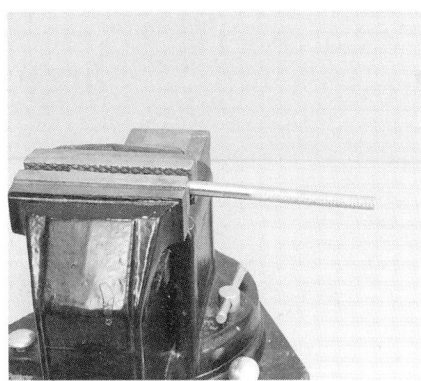

21-69 Place the smooth end of the extractor between the vise jaws and tighten securely.

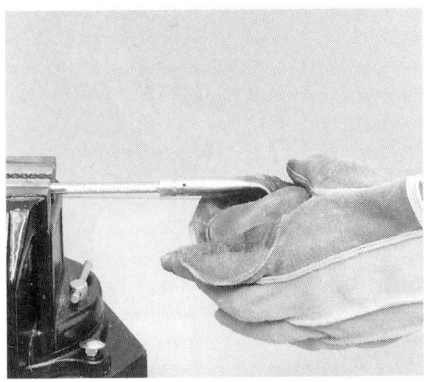

21-70 Push the shaft over the extractor. Push and turn the head clockwise until you feel the shaft "lock" onto the extractor. It may require a firm push to lock the extractor in the shaft. Note the use of leather gloves for protection from the heated hosel.

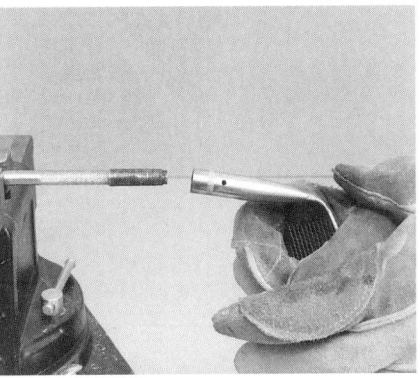

21-71 After locking in the extractor, turn the head counterclockwise while simultaneously pulling on the head. The head should pull free from the shaft while the shaft remains attached to the extractor. Remove the shaft from the extractor by pulling the shaft off with a pair of pliers.

21-72 If the extractor methods fail, the shaft must be drilled from the head. Use of an Iron Head Boring and Reaming Vise along with a drill press will make this job much safer, faster, easier and more accurate.

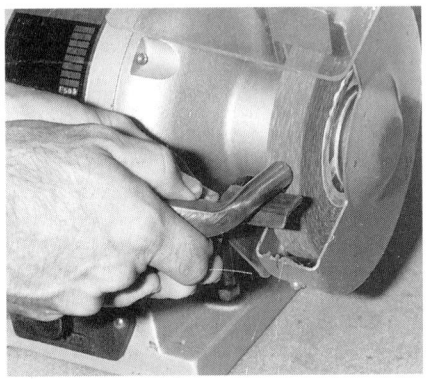

21-73 If any portion of the shaft extends out of the hosel, this must be ground flush with the top of the hosel. Do not grind into the hosel.

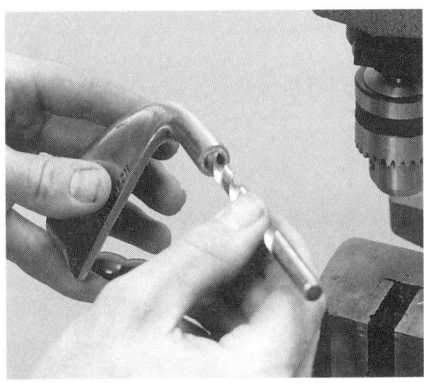

21-74 Select a drill bit that will fit snugly inside the shaft. Drill bits made from a **hard cobalt material** work best.

21-75 Place the hosel in the **Boring Vise.** Newer iron heads should have a brass hosel protector placed around the hosel for protection. Begin drilling and liberally apply **cutting oil** (not machine or lubricating oil) to both the drill bit and the hosel hole.

21-76 Drill to the bottom of the hosel bore. Note: Special Wilson and Hagen models with the black or red plugs are not a true "through bore" design. The shaft is not installed completely through the hosel.

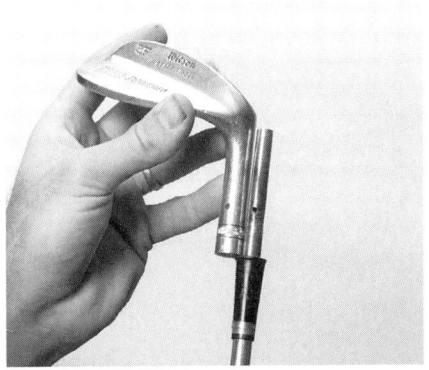

21-77 The original shaft used in this type of club is referred to as a "reduced tip" shaft. Instead of the common .355 tip diameter, this shaft is a .340. When replacing this shaft, do not rebore the hosel to the same depth as before. Instead, bore into the hosel to a depth of 1½" maximum. Drilling farther risks the chance of the drill bit coming through the side of the hosel.

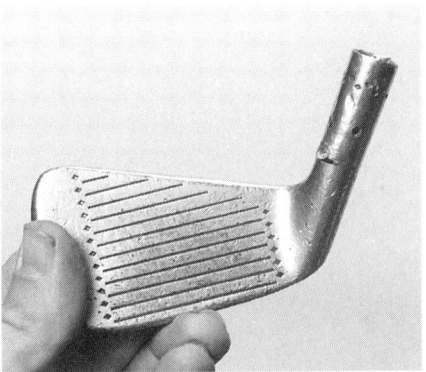

21-78 This photo shows the previously described iron head after an attempt to bore to the bottom of the hosel. Fortunately, this can be repaired by welding and rechroming. The GolfWorks® offers this service.

21-79 Next, select a drill bit that is slightly larger than the first and drill to the bottom of the hosel bore. Continue this procedure until ...

21-80 ... either the shaft tip comes out with the drill or the shaft is completely drilled from the hosel. Often the shaft tip will come out because of the heat created in the hosel by the spinning drill bit. Step drilling is also used to enlarge an existing bore size. See photos 21-98 through 21-105 for procedure.

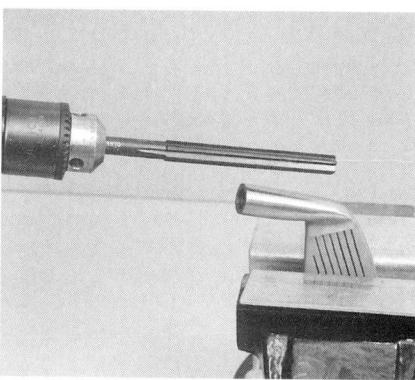

21-81 A .355 tapered reamer is great for cleaning out and resetting proper internal tapers in hosels. Never use the reamer, however, for removing broken shaft tips. If a drilling oil was used, clean all the oil from the hosel after drilling.

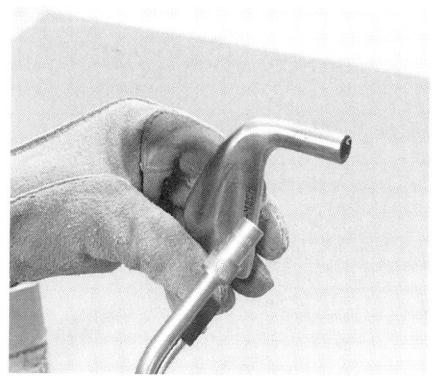

21-82 Iron hosels can also be super heated red hot in an attempt to remove the temper from the broken shaft tip. This is referred to as "annealing" the metal or reducing its hardness.

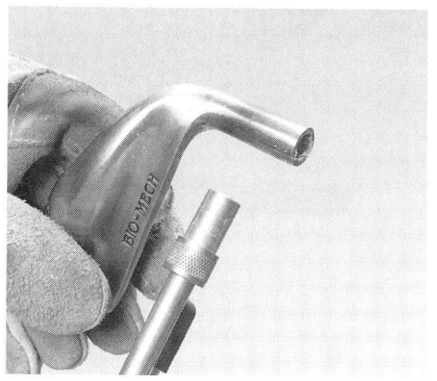

21-83 Apply heat to the hosel using a propane torch until the hosel turns red. Allow the hosel to return to room temperature and then drill the shaft from the hosel. This makes the shaft easier to drill. Heating the hosel does not functionally damage the hosel. Refer to photos 21-185 and 21-187 for removing hosel discoloration.

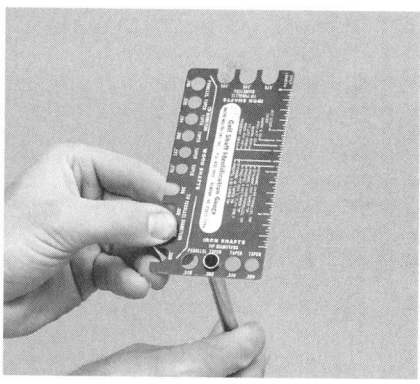

21-84 With the head off the shaft, use a **Golf Shaft Identification Gauge,** a micrometer or vernier caliper to determine the tip size of the removed shaft and replacement shaft.

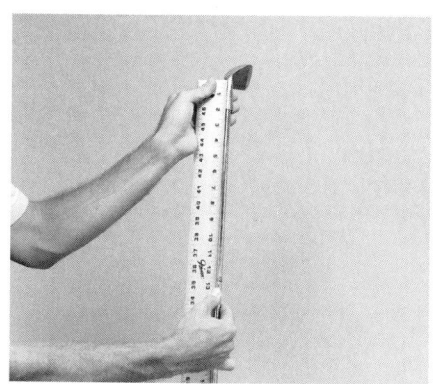

21-85 The tables in Chapter 57 give **back of heel to first step dimensions** for commercially available shafts. This measurement is important if you want the new shaft to perform as it was designed. When these measurements are altered, the shaft will either be more flexible or stiffer than original.

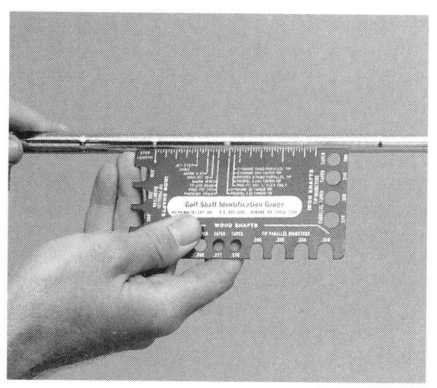

21-86 First determine what pattern (Dynamic™, Pro-Fit™, TT Lite™, etc.) shaft you will be working with. This information will come either from customer input, your determination of the original shaft pattern or by simply choosing a new shaft.

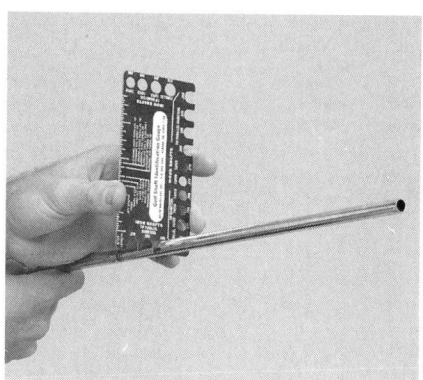

21-87 Next, you need to know if you are working with a tapered or a parallel (unitized) tip shaft. A tapered tip shaft is just that–tapered. The tip section increases in diameter from the tip to a point up from the tip. A parallel (unitized) tip shaft has a constant tip diameter from the tip to the first step. The **Shaft Identification Gauge** or a micrometer is used to determine the steps.

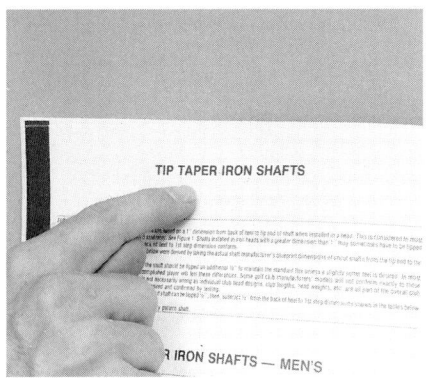

21-88 With the shaft pattern and tip construction known, refer to Chapter 57. The tables are divided into a **tapered tip group** and a **parallel tip group.** Look for grouping of tables that fits your shaft tip construction.

21-89 Next, look for the individual table that includes your **shaft pattern** – Dynamic™, TT Lite™, Pro Pel™, Microtaper™, etc. The tables are further subdivided into wood and iron shafts, as well as men's and ladies' shafts. Choose the table that is appropriate for your reshafting job.

21-90 Look at the first column labeled **Club Number.** Look down the column until you come across the club number with which you are working.

21-91 Next, look straight across the page to the next column labeled **Finished Club Length.** This reading gives you the industry standard length for your club (many modern clubs have a length that is ½" longer called **Modern Standard Length**). This is easily adjusted though by following the instructions at the bottom of the tables.

21-92 The next column labeled **Uncut Shaft Length** gives the recommended raw length shaft you need to select from your stock of shafts for this length club. If you are working with a parallel tip shaft, the column will read "Amount Normally Trimmed From Tip of Shaft." Parallel tip shafts come in only 1 length for each flex, so uncut shaft length is not applicable.

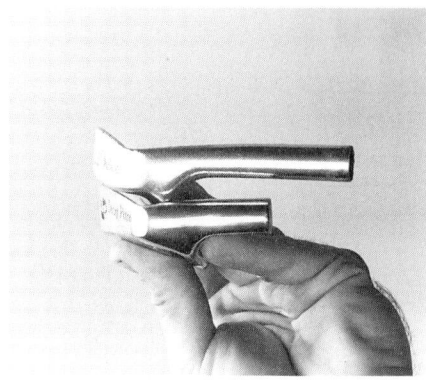

21-93 Some repairmen stop at this stage, grab the recommended shaft and install it into the head. The reason this should not be done should be obvious after looking at this photograph. Two clubs have very different hosel lengths and bore depths. If the same length shafts are installed in both clubs, without tip trimming, they will play very different.

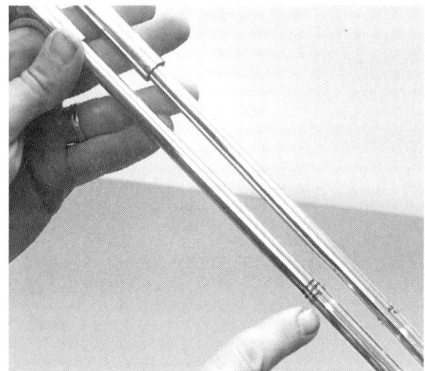

21-94 This photo shows why. The distance from the **back of the heel to the first step** varies enough to make the club on the bottom play much stiffer than the club on the top. Therefore, the **back of heel to first step dimension** must be followed closely to ensure proper shaft performance unless you specifically wish a club to perform differently.

21-95 Again, look straight across the page until you reach the column heading that describes the **pattern and flex shaft** with which you are working. This measurement gives the distance you need with this shaft from **back of the heel to the first step.**

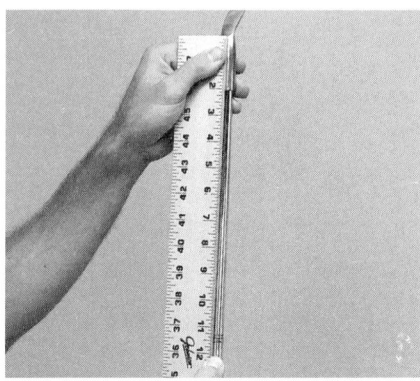

21-96 Next, take the recommended shaft, temporarily install it into the head and measure this distance. If the measurement you come up with is longer than this recommended **back of heel to first step dimension,** either select a shorter shaft or cut the difference from the tip of the shaft.

242

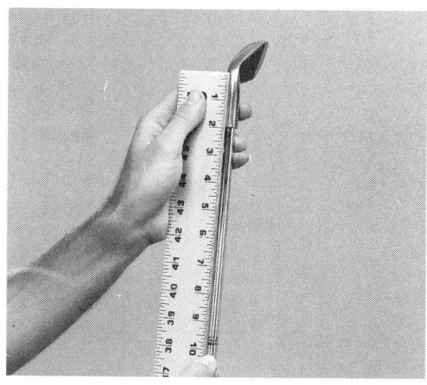

21-97 If the measurement is shorter than the recommended distance, a longer shaft is needed. This is correct because the difference in length between identical shafts is made up solely in the tip section. A longer shaft has a longer tip section.

21-98 Step drilling procedure for enlarging hosel bores. Step drilling is best performed when using a **Drill Press** in conjunction with the **Iron Head Boring and Reaming Vise.** Step drills used in this sequence are a special hard cobalt material which works best.

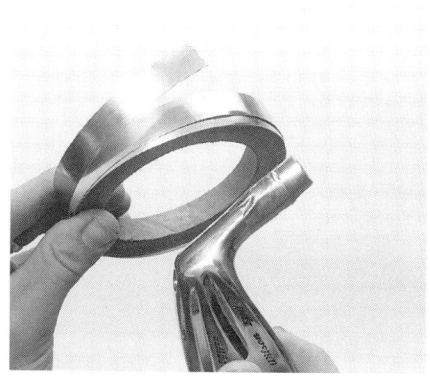

21-99 Place a **Brass Hosel Protector** or **Lead Tape** around the hosel to prevent possible scratches.

21-100 Fasten the hosel securely in the vise's vertical "V" groove. Drill to the bottom of the hosel hole using the smallest drill bit first. If working with a "through-bore" model, place a wrapping of tape or a **Drill Stop** around the bit no farther than 1½" up. This will ensure that you do not drill too far.

21-101 Drill to the bottom of the bore or until the tape is even with the top of the hosel. Always use **cutting oil** (not machine or lubricating oil) when drilling.

21-102 Next, drill to within a specified distance of the first bit using the next largest size bit.

21-103 Using the largest drill bit next, measure and ...

21-104 ... drill to within a specified distance of the second bit. Clean the hosel of any leftover cutting oil before installing the new shaft. Acetone works well for this.

21-105 The hosel has been bored to the desired depth and diameter and will now accept the larger shaft.

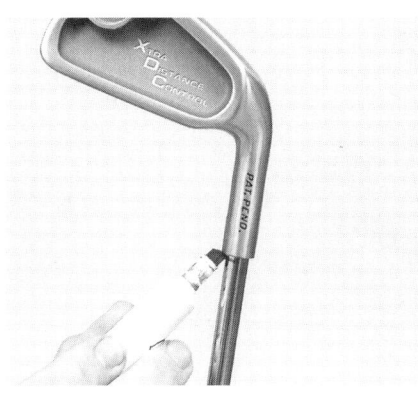

21-106 Abrading the Shaft Tip. After any necessary corrections have been made to the shaft tip, it must be abraded in order to provide the epoxy with a good bonding surface. To determine how much of the shaft tip should be abraded, first install it in the hosel and mark the shaft with a felt tip pen even with the top of the hosel.

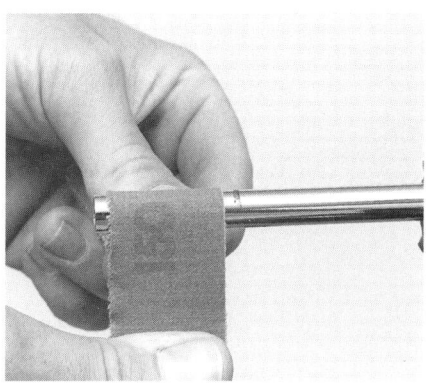

21-107 Remove the shaft and abrade to within ⅛" of the mark with a piece of 150 grit sandpaper. If the iron you are assembling requires a ferrule, abrade more of the shaft depending upon the length of the ferrule.

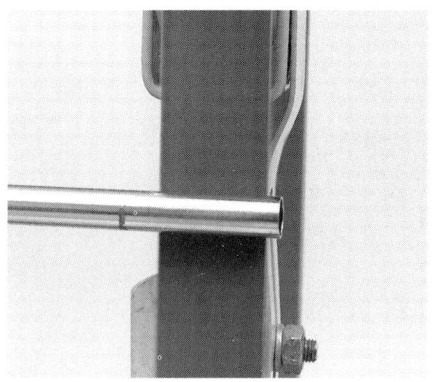

21-108 A **Belt Sander** is a fast alternative to hand sanding the tip of a steel or titanium shaft. Lightly place the tip of the shaft against the turning belt and rotate the shaft rapidly. A fine file, grinding stone or emery cloth can also be used.

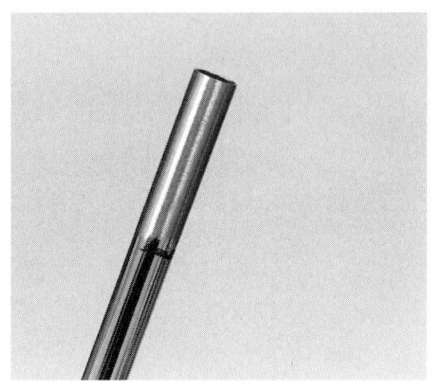

21-109 The tip of the shaft should look like this.

21-110 Graphite and other fibrous shafts are coated with polyurethane that should be removed from the portion of the shaft tip that will be installed into the hosel to provide good adhesion. A Scotch-Brite™ Wheel mounted to a motor shaft will do an effective job without damaging the graphite fibers. Caution: Do not use a file, belt sander, sandpaper, etc. These will damage the fibers and weaken the shaft.

21-111 Rotate the shaft against the turning wheel until the polyurethane coating is removed. Do not pause while rotating the shaft because of the risk of cutting the fibers. Light pressure works best. Machine set-up shows a ⅓ HP motor that turns at 1725 R.P.M.

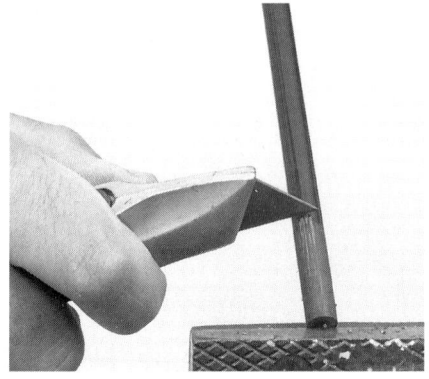

21-112 A razor blade will also work well. Hold the razor blade perpendicular to the shaft and scrape back and forth while rotating the shaft.

21-113 Regardless of which method is used, clean the shaft tip with a solvent to remove any oil that may be present. Oil reduces the bonding effectiveness of the epoxy.

21-114 If a composite shaft is being installed, the inside hosel edge should be countersunk using an 18° or 20° countersink, as shown. The subsequent gap will be filled with epoxy which will help reduce the stress placed upon the shaft.

244

21-115 Install the countersink into a normal drill. Next, insert the countersink into the hosel and activate the drill until a bevel is created. This photo shows the inside hosel edge after countersinking. The entire job takes only a couple of seconds.

21-116 The appropriate size and style of ferrule is chosen. Ferrules have various bore sizes according to the shaft tip size they match. Slide the ferrule on the shaft. If a ferrule is not to be installed, proceed to photo 21-128.

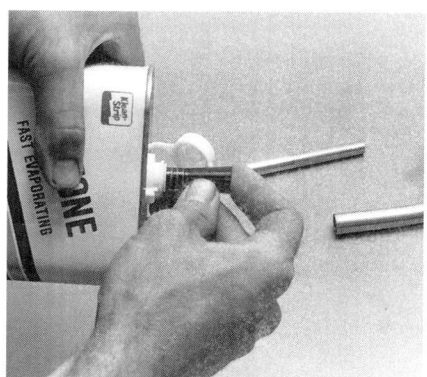

21-117 Sometimes the new ferrule will not slide on the shaft easily. Use this method: Place the ferrule against the mouth of a can of acetone and turn the can upside down so the acetone runs into the ferrule. Keep the other end of the ferrule closed off with your finger.

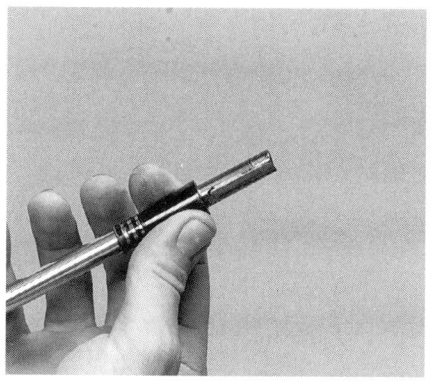

21-118 After 10 seconds, quickly remove the ferrule from the can and slide the ferrule down the shaft. If the acetone is not available in the small mouth can, dip the ferrule in an open container of acetone for a few seconds and then install it.

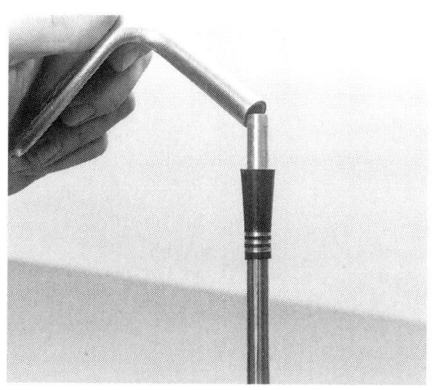

21-119 An alternative to the acetone method is to simply place the hosel over the shaft and force the ferrule down the shaft.

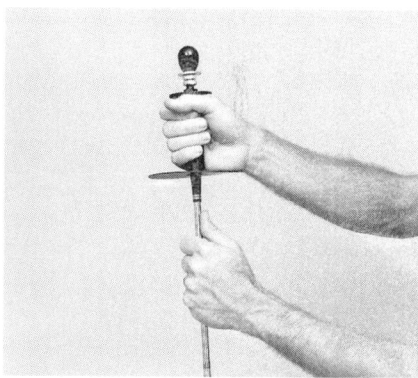

21-120 The **Ferrule Installer Tool** will accurately set an iron or wood ferrule to the proper depth. It is especially helpful when assembling more than one club and a series of ferrules must be set.

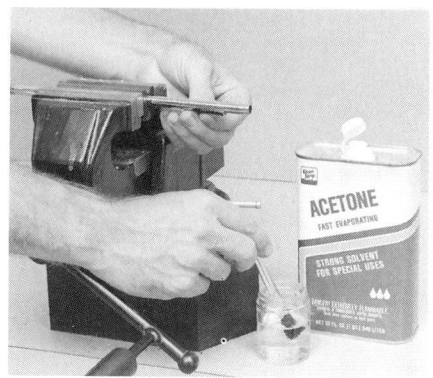

21-121 If the old ferrule was split with a razor knife to remove it, melt it back together with acetone. First, hold one half of the split ferrule under the shaft and …

21-122 … apply a liberal amount of acetone to the ferrule. Note that the ferrule is being assembled up close to the shaft tip. This is important with taper tip shafts.

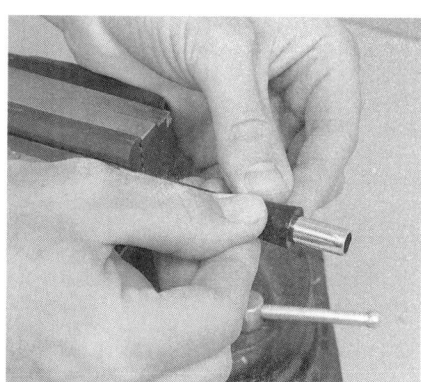

21-123 Dip the other half of the ferrule in the acetone and quickly stick the two halves together.

21-124 Rub the seams with acetone. This will further seal the 2 halves together.

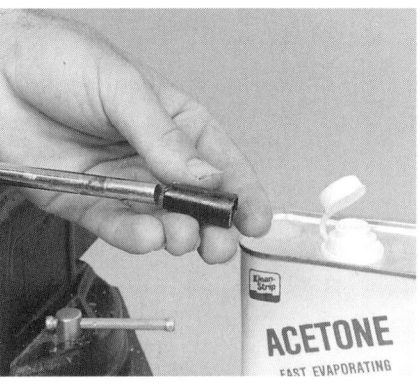

21-125 In approximately one minute, slip the ferrule off the shaft.

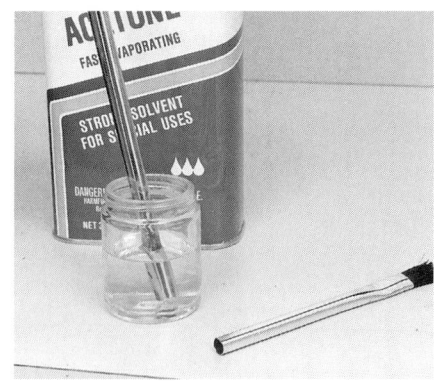

21-126 Dip the shaft tip in acetone and …

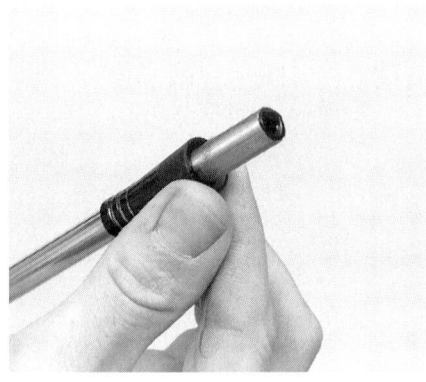

21-127 … slide the ferrule up into position.

21-128 **To install the shaft into the hosel.** First mix your epoxy. Dip the tip of the shaft into the epoxy and then insert the shaft into the hosel. A good high shear strength shafting epoxy is best for reshafting. GolfWorks® or Conap shafting epoxy works well.

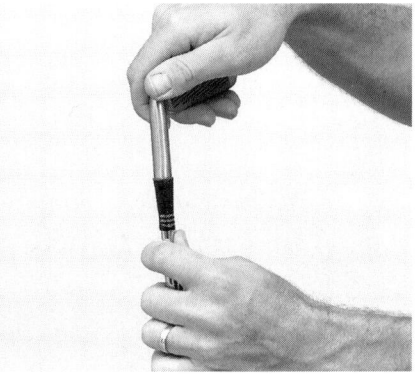

21-129 To set the shaft in place, grasp the head with one hand while supporting the shaft with the other and …

21-130 … hammer the butt of the shaft onto a steel plate or concrete floor.

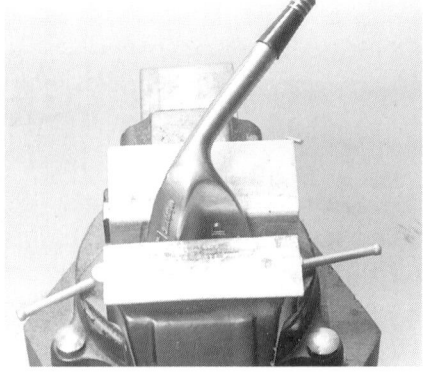

21-131 A practical alternative to hammering the shaft against the floor is to tighten the head securely in a vise. Place a pair of **aluminum or brass vise pads** over the vise jaws before tightening.

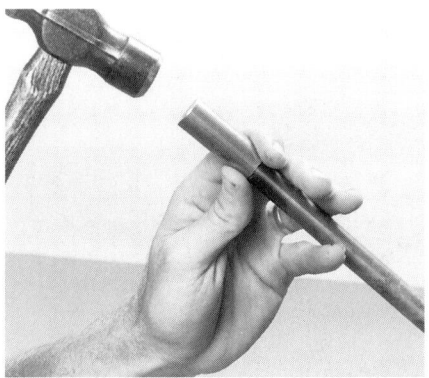

21-132 Insert a **Shaft Driving Plug** in the butt end of the shaft and drive the shaft in place.

246

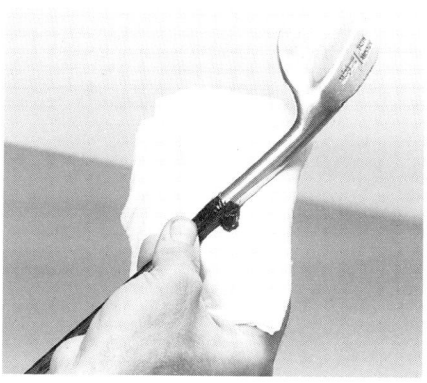

21-133 Wipe off any excess epoxy. Be sure the ferrule is seated flush against the hosel. If it is not, place the **Lock Tight Shaft Holder** above it and force the ferrule down into place. Allow the epoxy to cure for the recommended time.

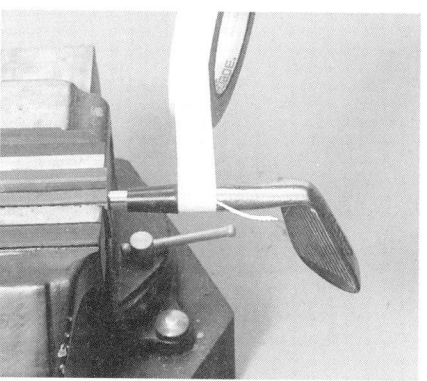

21-134 Reducing the Ferrule Diameter. The next step, after the epoxy has hardened, is to reduce the diameter of the ferrule so it matches the hosel. Place the shaft in a **Rubber Shaft Clamp** and tighten in a vise. Wrap a piece of ¾" masking tape around the hosel just below the ferrule.

21-135 Use a flat mill or fine file and lightly file the excess plastic down flush with the tape. The tape will protect the hosel from possible scratches.

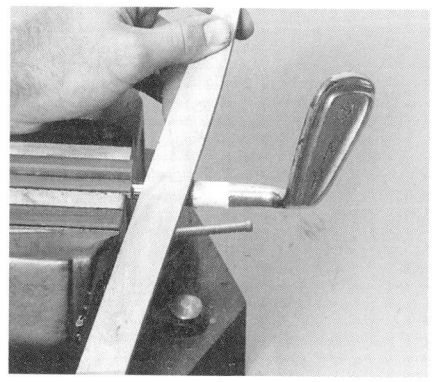

21-136 Continue to file while rotating the club. Care should be taken to ensure a proper taper in the ferrule. Do not file the top edge of the ferrule as a definite lip should remain.

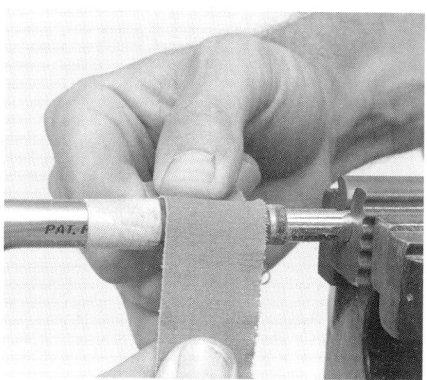

21-137 Filing will leave flat spots and ridges in the plastic. Lightly sand the ferrule with a 180 or 220 grit fine sandpaper.

21-138 At this point the ferrule will look rough and dull in appearance. This is normal at this stage.

21-139 Rub the ferrule with 000 steel wool. This will remove some of the scratches left from the sandpaper and make the ferrule smoother.

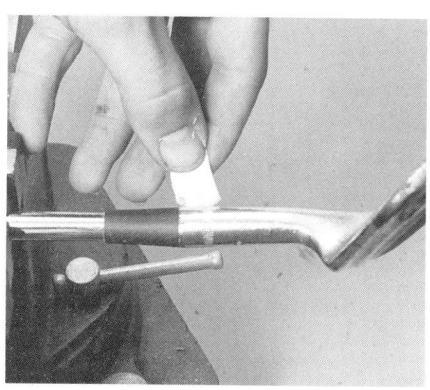

21-140 Remove the masking tape from the hosel.

21-141 Dampen a paper towel with **Acetone** and wipe the ferrule with the paper towel. This will restore the plastic ferrule to a shiny, like-new appearance.

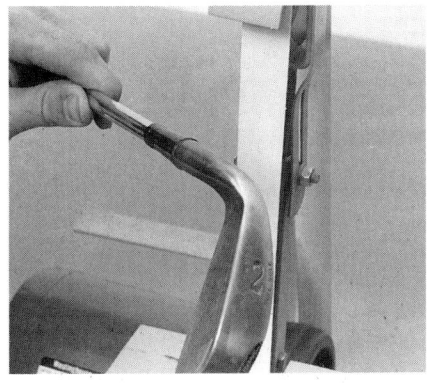

21-142 A much quicker way to reduce the diameter of the ferrule is with a **Belt Sander.** The belt used is a **Cloth Linen Belt.** This is a non-abrasive surface which removes the excess plastic through friction.

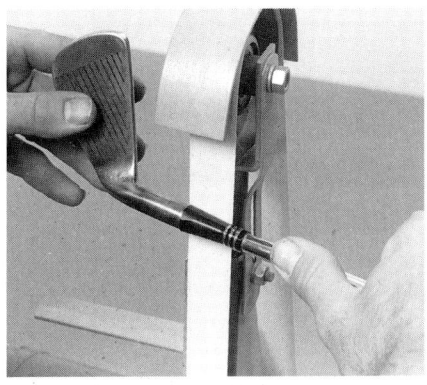

21-143 Hold the clubhead as shown and rotate the ferrule against the linen belt in …

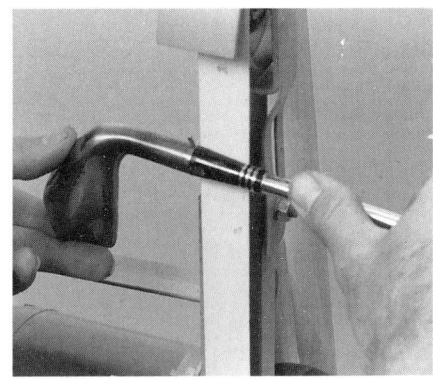

21-144 … the clockwise direction …

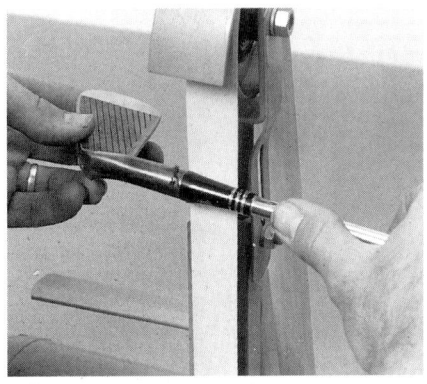

21-145 … as shown. This is very important. Turning the clubhead in the opposite direction will only burn and ruin the ferrule.

21-146 This photo shows a properly tapered ferrule using the **Cloth Linen Belt.**

21-147 Lightly steel wool the ferrule by hand or on the **Steel Wool Arbor.**

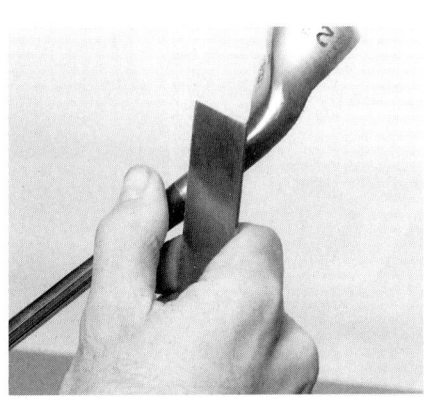

21-148 If there is any plastic or epoxy residue around the top of the hosel, carefully scrape or cut it from the hosel.

21-149 Wipe the ferrule with an **Acetone** dampened paper towel. This makes the ferrule look like new again.

21-150 Installing a new hosel pin. Depending upon what size was previously used, select either a ⅛" or ³⁄₃₂" drill bit. Note the hosel is tightened securely between aluminum vise pads. Brass pads will work well also. **Note: Graphite shafts are never pinned.**

248

21-151 Drill into the existing hole to clean out the excess epoxy. Do not attempt to drill through the shaft at this point.

21-152 Instead, place a sharpened **Awl** or **Prick Punch** into the hole and …

21-153 … drive the **Awl** through the top half of the shaft. Usually one sharp blow will do this.

21-154 After piercing the shaft, drill through the top half of the shaft. Do not attempt to drill through the bottom half. Instead …

21-155 … turn the club around and repeat the drilling, punching and …

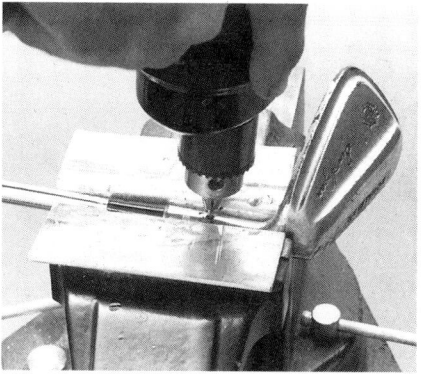

21-156 … drilling procedure. Once you have drilled through this half of the shaft, allow the drill bit to exit out the other side of the hosel. This will ensure there is a clear passage from one side of the hosel to the other.

21-157 Select the appropriate size hosel pin. Sharpening or beveling one end of the hosel pin will help the pin push through the hosel.

21-158 Place the pin in the hole and lightly tap the pin completely through the hosel.

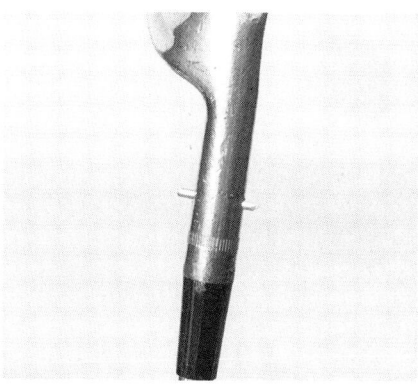

21-159 The photo shows the pin extending out both sides of the hosel.

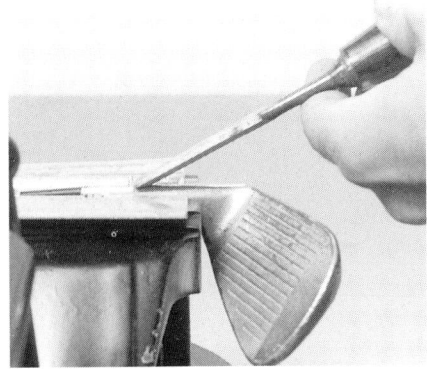

21-160 Remove the pin excess, yet leave a small portion sticking above the surface of the hosel on both sides. Tapping a **Chisel** quickly through the pin is one way to remove this excess.

21-161 Wire snips work well also for cutting the pin.

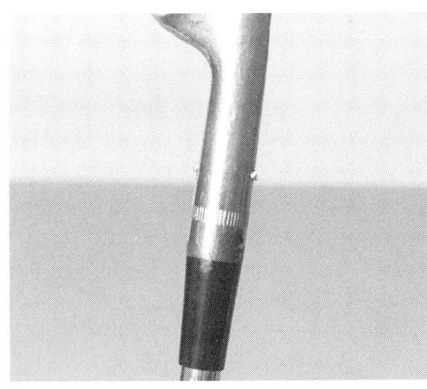

21-162 This photo shows some of the pin still extending above the surface.

21-163 Place the hosel on a hard surface such as the top of the vise jaws or vise anvil and repeatedly tap the pin lightly so it mushrooms outward against the hosel. The purpose of this tap is to fill in any gap between the pin and the pin hole wall and make the pin fit tightly.

21-164 Next, gently peen the other side.

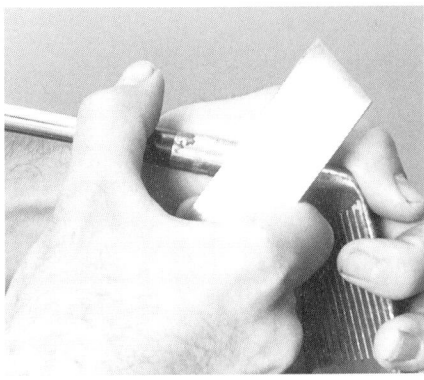

21-165 After peening, carefully cut through the flattened pin head with a sharp knife. Because the pin is made of aluminum, the pin will trim easily.

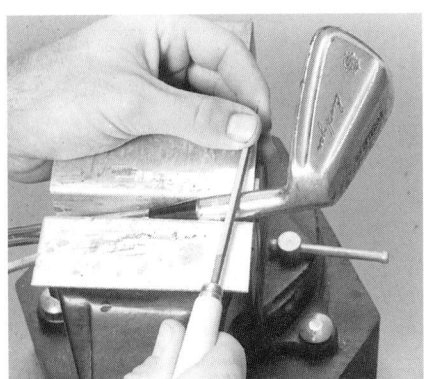

21-166 A small file also works well to remove the excess pin. Do not scratch the hosel.

21-167 This photo shows a properly installed pin. The ends of the pin should camouflage well with the side of the hosel. If desired, a light buff using a white polishing compound on a set of stitched buffing wheels will hide the pin entirely.

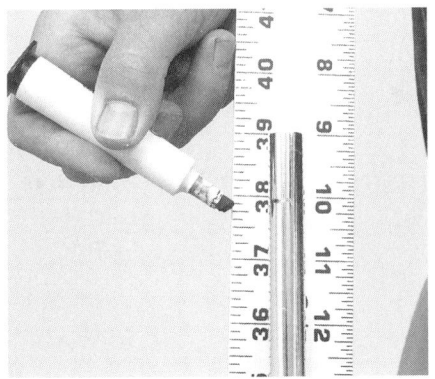

21-168 The club must now be cut to length. Lay a **48" long ruler** behind the club with the club in a correct address position. Mark the shaft at a point ⅛" below the desired final length (i.e., at 35⅜" if a 35½" length club is desired). The grip cap will account for the ⅛" difference after the grip is installed.

250

21-169 This photo shows a clubhead in the correct address position for measuring with a ruler positioned directly behind the head.

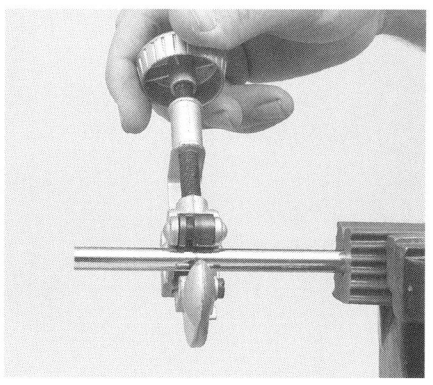

21-170 Cut the shaft with either a **Tubing Cutter** or …

21-171 … a **Friction Cutoff Wheel.** Always wear safety glasses when working around machines.

21-172 Procedure for cutting a shaft with the Friction Cutoff Wheel. Make a mark on the shaft against the spinning wheel. Next, push the shaft firmly into the wheel.

21-173 Keep pushing the shaft against the cutoff wheel until the edge of the wheel is through the shaft wall and then slowly rotate the shaft counterclockwise.

21-174 Keep turning the shaft counterclockwise into the wheel until the shaft section comes off. **Note: A cutoff wheel also works for graphite and titanium shafts.**

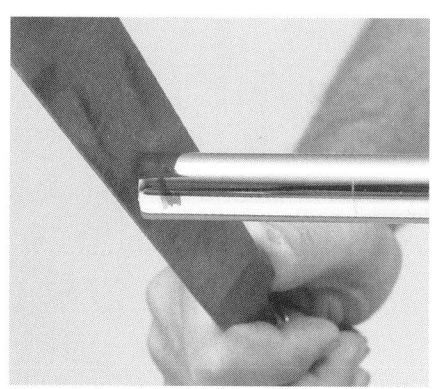

21-175 Cutting a steel or titanium shaft will usually result in a rough edge. Remove this rough edge by either lightly filing or …

21-176 … spinnning the shaft against the wheel of a bench grinder or belt sander. Note the shaft is positioned at a 45° angle to the grinding stone.

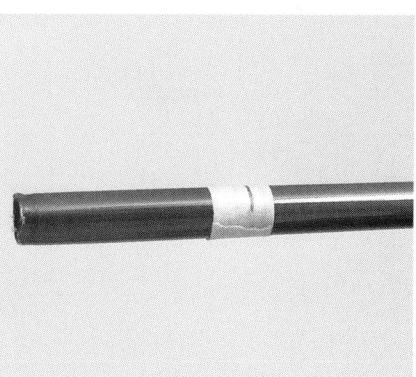

21-177 An alternative to the cutoff wheel for graphite is to cut the shaft with a common hacksaw. Place a wrapping of masking tape around the graphite shaft where you intend to make the cut. Clearly mark the tape where the cut will be made.

251

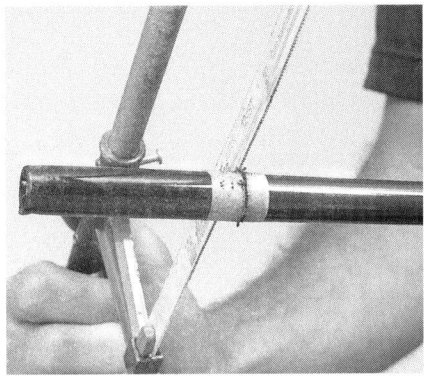

21-178 An important step is to first circumscribe the exterior of the shaft with the hacksaw. This step will prevent the shaft from splitting while cutting.

21-179 Once the shaft has been circumscribed, carefully cut into the shaft with the hacksaw.

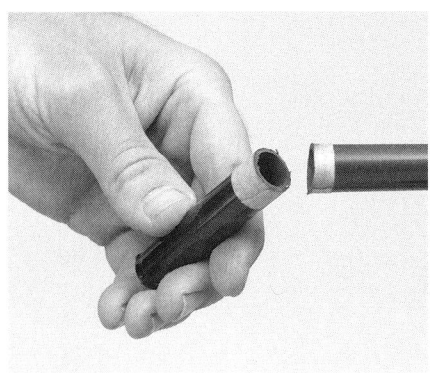

21-180 After cutting through the shaft there should not be any graphite splinters or torn pieces.

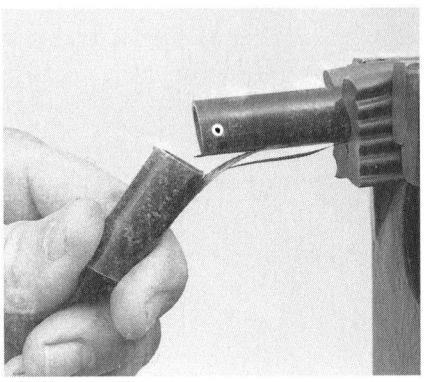

21-181 This is how a graphite shaft will usually look if the taping and circumscribing step is not followed when cutting with a hacksaw.

21-182 In addition to using the steel friction cutoff wheel, The GolfWorks® also uses this **Automatic Cutoff Saw** with a wheel. We use this on all shaft materials and it works especially well when cutting more than one shaft, as shown. An upgrade for volume repair shops is The GolfWorks® **Multi Shaft Cutoff Machine** which will cut an entire set.

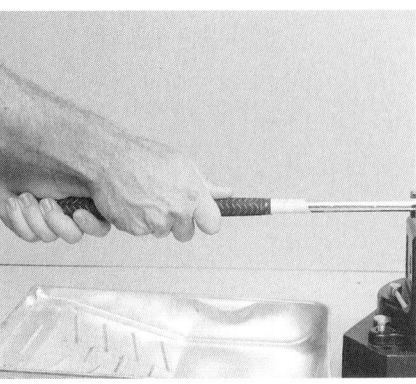

21-183 Install the grip as outlined in Chapter 23 and apply the appropriate shaft band.

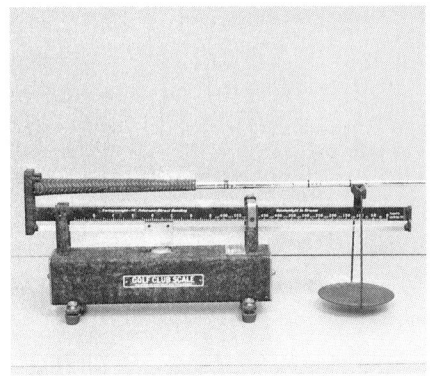

21-184 Finally, check the swingweight. If swingweight correction is needed, refer to Chapter 18 for procedure.

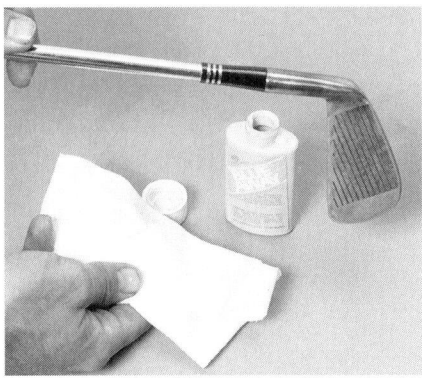

21-185 If the hosel was blued from excess heating during shaft removal, it can be made to look like new again. **Simichrome polish** or **Blue Away** is very effective. Simply rub fluid onto the hosel with a towel.

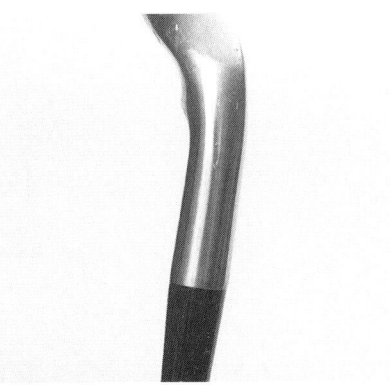

21-186 This photo shows the hosel after the product **Blue Away** has been used. For irons having a vibratory finish, like that found on Ping irons, the head can be placed in The GolfWorks® **Mini Vibratory** prior to shaft installation. Instructions for its use are found in Chapter 17, photos 17-43 through 17-45.

21-187 Applying the hosel against the face of a **stitched** or **unstitched buffing wheel** will also remove the discoloration. The **white compound** is best used for this buffing procedure. Note: This step should not be used on vibratory finished heads as the finish will be altered.

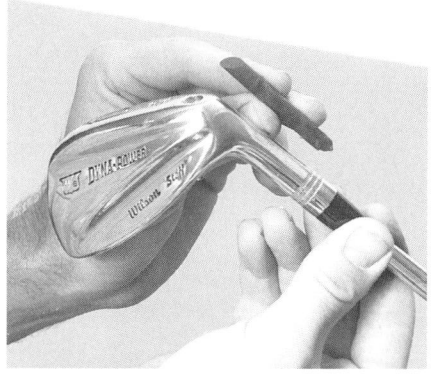

21-188 Procedure for installing rubber plugs. The original plug may be reinstalled or the easier step is to install an available replacement.

21-189 Dip the end of the plug into epoxy and then ...

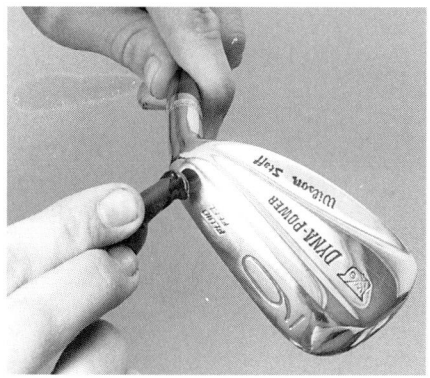

21-190 ... push the plug into the hole in the sole of the club. Push until a snug fit is achieved. A **Colored Paste Dispersion** has been mixed in with the epoxy to match the color of the plug.

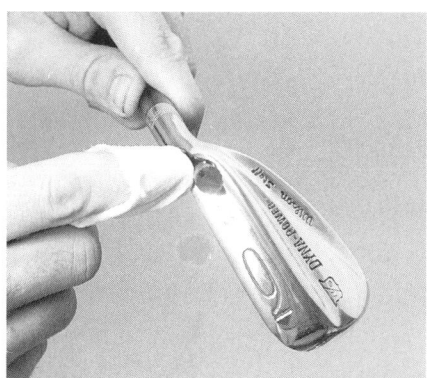

21-191 Wipe up the excess epoxy and allow the epoxy to cure.

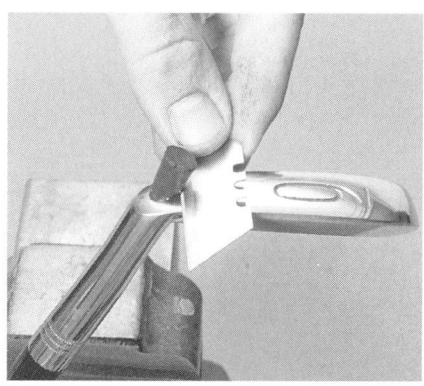

21-192 After the epoxy has hardened, slice through the protruding plug with a sharp knife or razor blade. Trim the plug as close to the sole as you can.

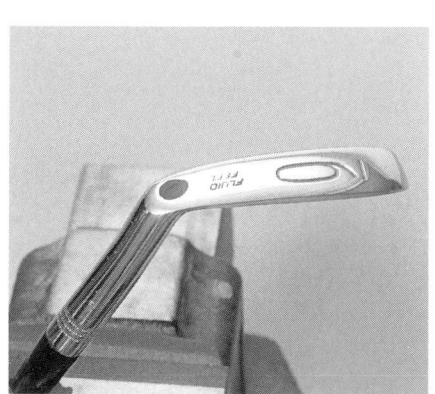

21-193 This photo shows the plug correctly trimmed.

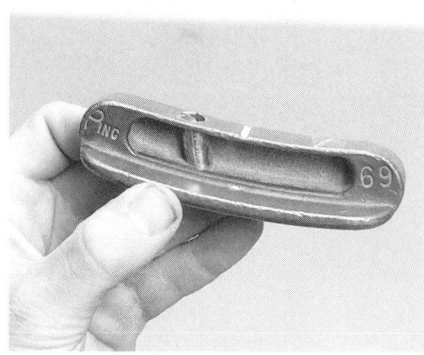

21-194 Some Ping® model putter heads are attached to the shaft in a unique manner. In addition to epoxy, a steel ball bearing was forced into the shaft tip. This expands the tip and makes the shaft very difficult to remove. If, after heating, the shaft will not pull free ...

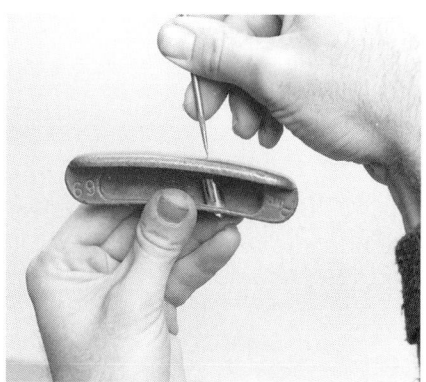

21-195 ... determine by eye where the tip of the shaft would extend through the sole of the putter (in some models the shaft will not extend through the sole but through an offset hosel).

21-196 Make a small indentation at this point with a sharp center punch or awl. Drill through the sole of the putter with a ⅛" drill bit. Drill until the bit meets the steel ball bearing. Note the head is held in a vise using polyurethane vise pads. **Aluminum or brass vise pads** will also work well.

21-197 Punch the ball bearing out through the shaft. The shaft will now come out easily. The hole in the sole should be filled in with a brass colored epoxy.

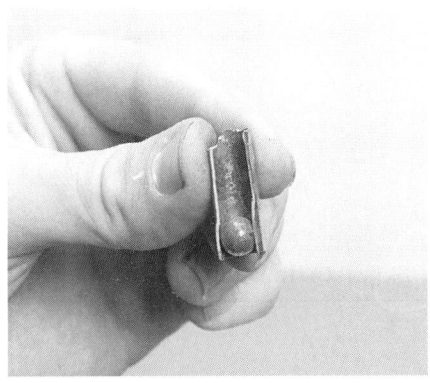

21-198 This photo shows the shaft tip with the hardened ball bearing. This can be a repairman's nightmare, however, it is a very clever way to ensure a shaft will not come loose. Note: When installing the new shaft a ball bearing is not needed.

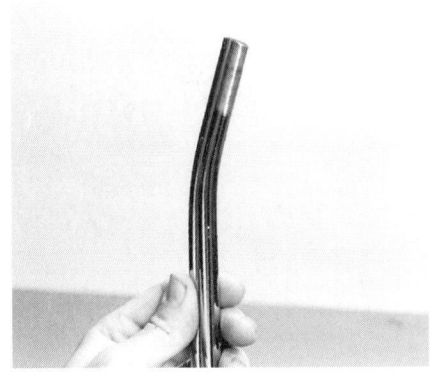

21-199 When reshafting putters, you will sometimes need to make a bend in the tip section of the new shaft to match the bend in the original.

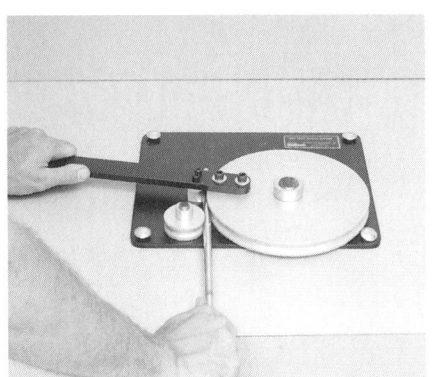

21-200 The Golf Shaft Bending Machine will make any degree bend at any point on the shaft. If you do not do enough work to justify the expense of this machine, you can have shafts custom bent for you by The GolfWorks®.

21-201 Installing a new hickory shaft in an antique iron. This photo shows a typical antique putter head with the tip of the new and old shaft.

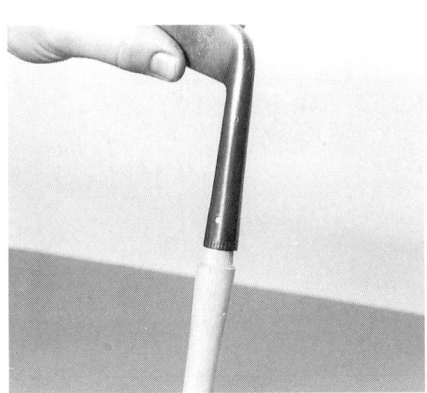

21-202 The tip of the new shaft must be shaped to fit the hosel. Test fit the shaft into the hosel and …

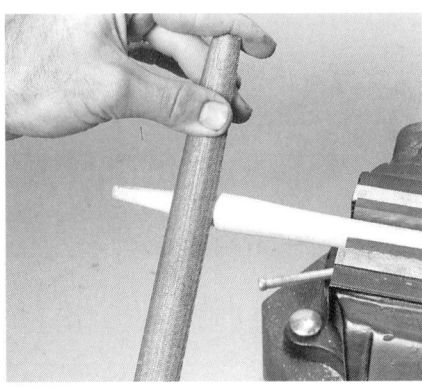

21-203 … file it until it fits or …

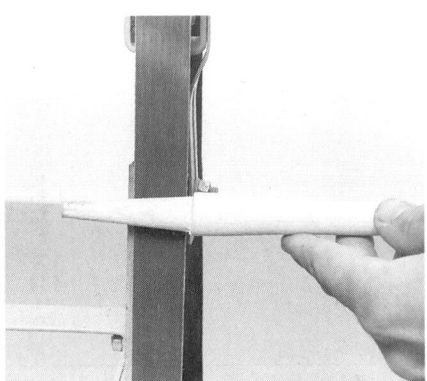

21-204 … sand until …

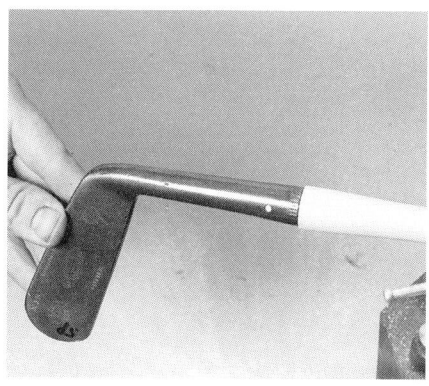

21-205 ... the tip fits snugly inside the hosel. Have patience as this can sometimes be a time consuming project. The results, however, are well worth the effort.

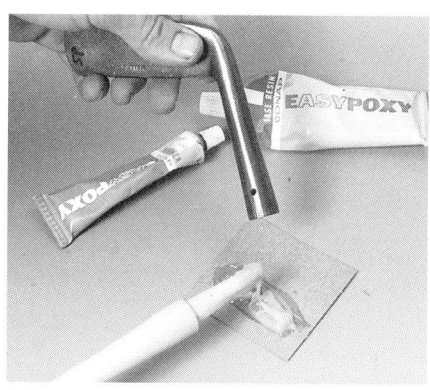

21-206 Mix up a shear strength shafting epoxy and coat the shaft tip as well as ...

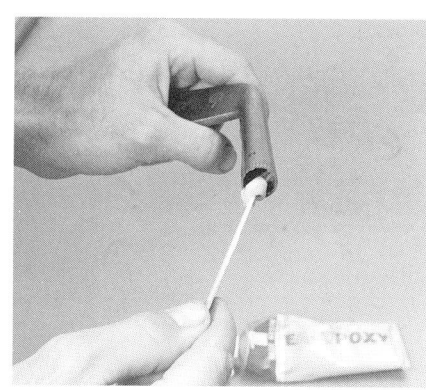

21-207 ... the hosel.

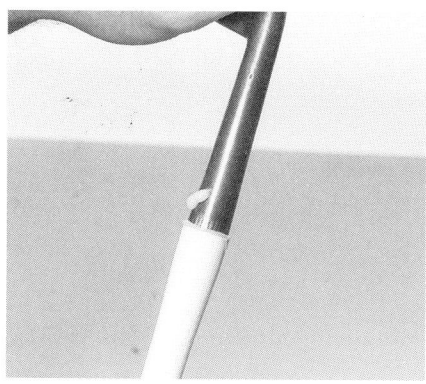

21-208 Install the shaft into the hosel and wipe off any excess epoxy. Allow the epoxy to cure.

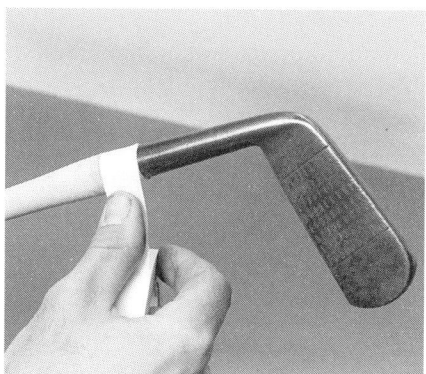

21-209 Next, wrap a layer of masking tape around the top of the hosel.

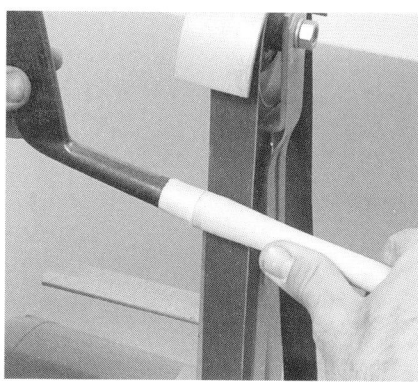

21-210 Using a **file** or preferably a **belt sander** with a **medium grade belt,** remove the excess wood so the shaft is flush with the hosel.

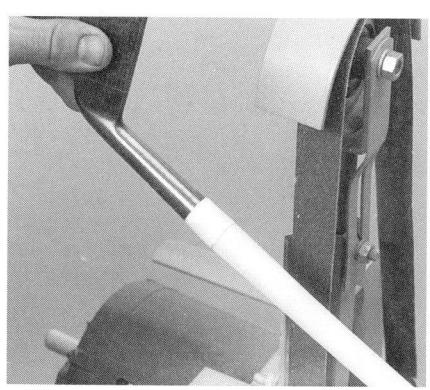

21-211 Continue to sand while maintaining a proper taper.

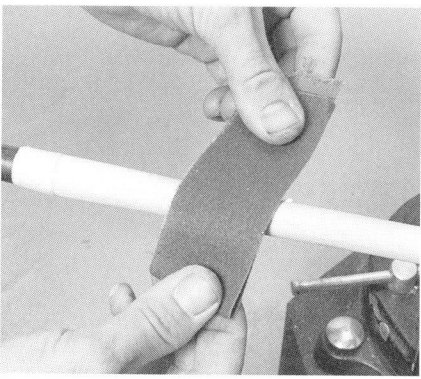

21-212 After shaping, lightly sand the hosel with a fine grade sandpaper. This will remove any irregularities in the wood surface.

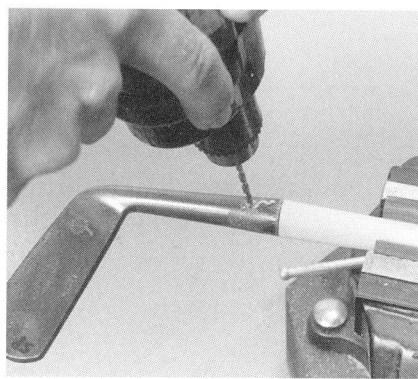

21-213 Drill through the pin hole into the shaft tip using the proper size drill bit. An ⅛" bit is usually required. After drilling through one side of the shaft ...

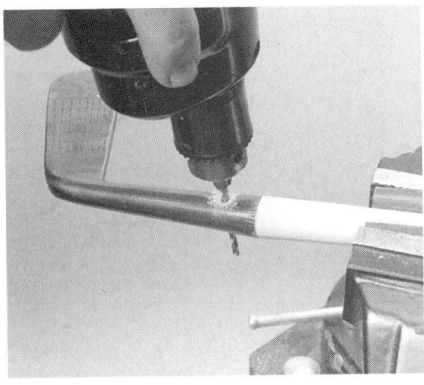

21-214 ... turn the club in the vise and drill into the other side of the shaft tip. Allow the drill bit to pass through the opposite side to create a clear passage for the pin.

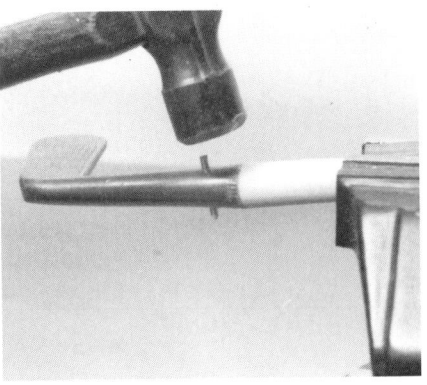

21-215 Tap an aluminum pin through the hosel and shaft.

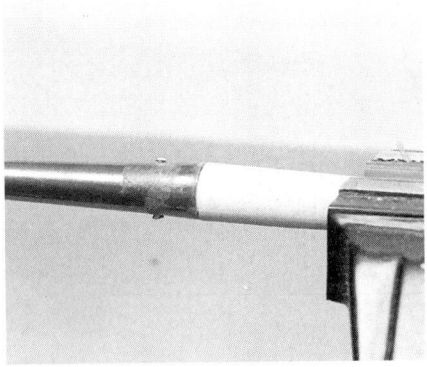

21-216 Trim the excess pin as shown in photos 21-159 through 21-161.

21-217 Peen the end of the pin flush with the hosel so any gap around the pin is eliminated. Repeat this operation to the other side.

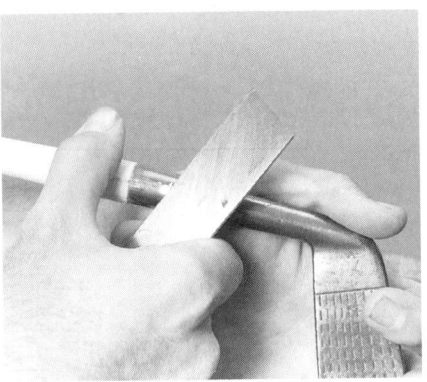

21-218 Next, cut through the excess using a sharp knife. Be careful!

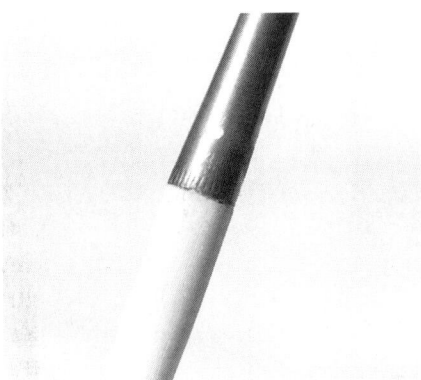

21-219 This photo shows the hosel and pin area after trimming.

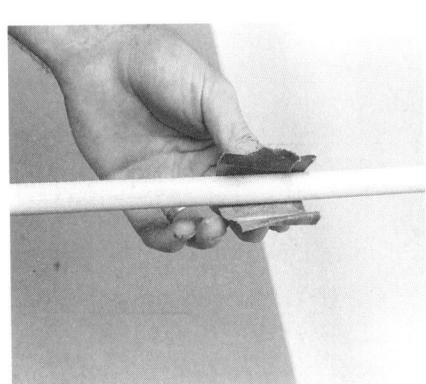

21-220 Lightly sand the entire shaft with a fine grade of sandpaper. 150 or 220 grit is preferred.

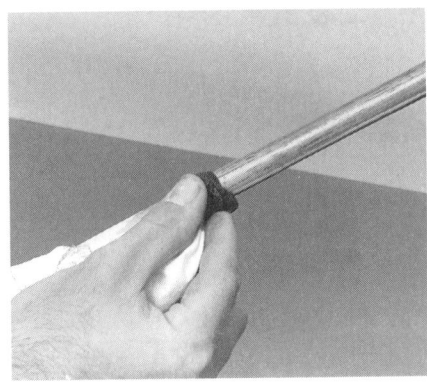

21-221 Apply a light brown stain such as walnut to the entire shaft. Allow the shaft to dry overnight.

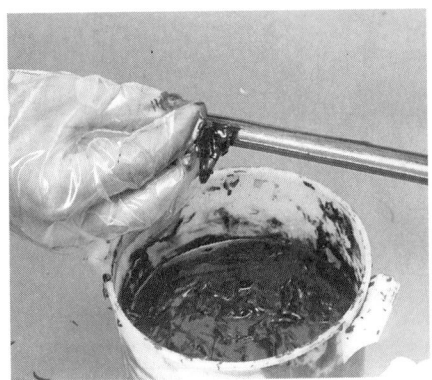

21-222 After the stain has dried, apply a filler to the shaft. The filler will plug up the pores of the wood and prevent moisture absorption. Leave the filler on the shaft for 7 minutes. This will allow the solvents to evaporate and the filler to harden.

21-223 Vigorously wipe the excess filler from the shaft using a piece of **Burlap** or **terry cloth.** Allow the shaft to dry overnight. Filler used can either be a **natural** or **less intense black filler** depending upon the shade you wish to achieve. See Chapter 1 if more information on filler is needed.

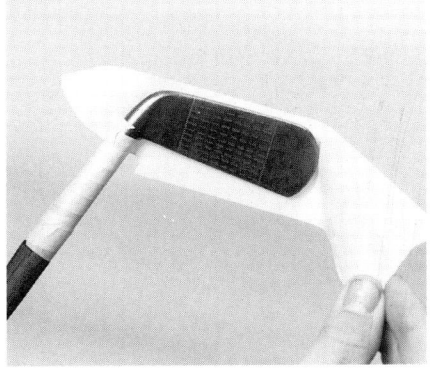

21-224 After an overnight dry, cover the head with a loose wrapping of masking tape or newspaper.

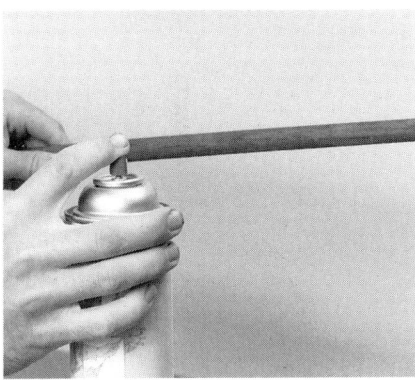

21-225 Apply a couple of light spray coats of **Primer Sealer** to the shaft. This will properly seal the shaft and give it a satin look. Allow the **Primer Sealer** to dry 30 minutes between each light coat.

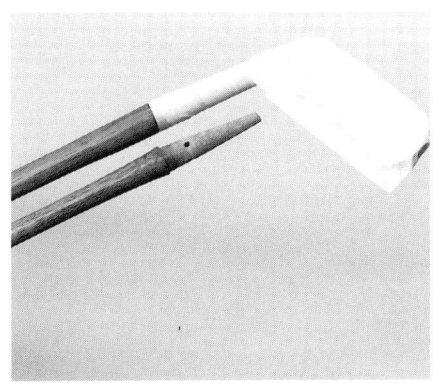

21-226 This photo shows the old and new shaft. If proper care is taken, the new shaft will look similar to the old one. Note the difference in shaft thickness. This is perfectly acceptable but if you wish a more flexible feel, reduce the diameter of the shaft. The club is now ready to be cut to length using a hacksaw. Install the grip as shown in Chapter 23.

NOTES

ADDITIONAL INFORMATION FOR RESHAFTING IRON CLUBS

	TABLE 21-1			
	Iron Club Lengths – Men's and Ladies'			
Irons	Men's Modern Standard	Men's Traditional Standard	Ladies' Standard	[1] Ladies' Petite
1	39½"	39"	38"	37½"
2	39"	38½"	37½"	37"
3	38½"	38"	37"	36½"
4	38"	37½"	36½"	36"
5	37½"	37"	36"	35½"
6	37"	36½"	35½"	35"
7	36½"	36"	35"	34½"
8	36"	35½"	34½"	34"
9	35½"	35"	34"	33½"
PW	35½"	35"	34"	33½"
SW	35½"	35"	34"	33½"

[1] Ladies' petite is usually ½" shorter than the traditional ladies' standard length. Some companies make ladies' petite 1" shorter than ladies' standard length.

TABLE 21-2	
Drill Selection Chart	
• Hosel pin drill for irons – most modern	1/8"
• Hosel pin drill for irons – older models	3/32"

TABLE 21-3		
Determining Shaft Flex by Color on Butt End of Shaft		
Designation	**Flex**	**Color**
X	Extra Stiff	Green
S	Stiff	Red
R or T	Medium	Black
A	Flexible	Yellow
L	Ladies (very flexible)	Blue

Combination flex shafts such as UDWC, UDWAL, UJWC & U2LWAL do not have a color code on the butt end.

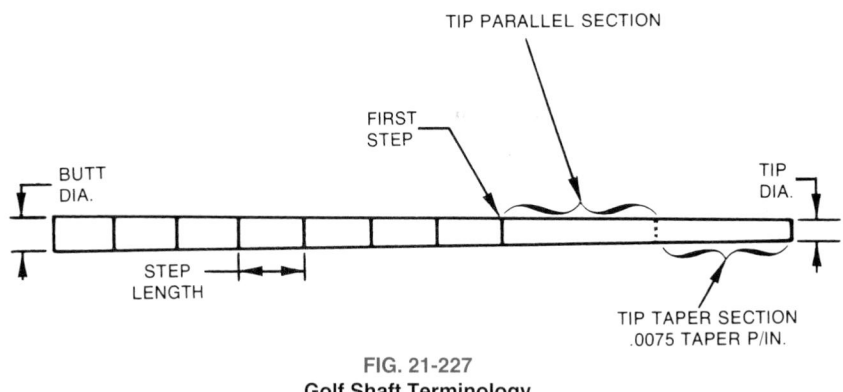

FIG. 21-227
Golf Shaft Terminology

Step Drilling Instructions and Drill Sizes by Tip Sizes

When boring hosels for new shafts or reshafting, many repair shops find it difficult or very expensive to obtain the proper size drills and reamers to match every iron shaft tip size available. Also, they run into special problems such as enlarging hosels holes to accept "tipped" shafts or hosels which need to be bored to accept another shaft size, or in most cases, hosels which just need to be cleaned out so that the replacement shaft will fit properly.

To solve this problem, step drilling is recommended. See figure 21-228. Step drilling can be described simply as a method utilizing a matched set of special drills, each a different size. The smallest drill is used first by drilling to the bottom of the hosel hole (or completely through as the case may be). The next larger size drill is then used and drilled part way down and finally the largest size is used and drilled to a lesser depth than the previous two. This system for creating the proper taper by utilizing steps has the advantage of providing areas for epoxy to collect thus eliminating the common occurrence of squeezing it all out, resulting in premature bond failure of head to shaft. Also, step drills can be easily resharpened, unlike reamers, and step drills are not damaged when they hit any remaining portion of the hardened shaft tip.

Step #1: Drill to bottom of hosel with smallest diameter cobalt drill bit.
Step #2: Drill to within a specified depth of the 1st drill using the next largest size 2nd cobalt drill bit.
Step #3: Drill to within a specified depth of the 2nd drill using the larger size 3rd cobalt drill bit.

FIG. 21-228
Step Drilling Procedure

Step Drilling Instructions and Sizes for .355" Taper Tip Shafts

Step #1: Drill to bottom of hosel bore with a "T" (.358") diameter special hard cobalt drill.

Step #2: Drill to within 3/8" of bottom of hosel bore with a "U" (.368") diameter special hard cobalt drill.

Step #3: Drill to within 1¼" of bottom of hosel bore with a 3/8" (.375") diameter special hard cobalt drill.

Step Drilling Instructions and Sizes for .300" Taper Tip Shafts

Step #1: Drill to bottom of hosel bore with a "N" (.302") diameter special hard cobalt drill.

Step #2: Drill to within 3/8" of bottom of hosel bore with a 5/16" (.312") diameter special hard cobalt drill.

Step #3: Drill to within 1¼" of bottom of hosel bore with a "O" (.316") diameter special hard cobalt drill.

Step Drilling Instructions and Sizes for .370" Unitized Parallel Tip Shafts

Step #1: Drill to bottom of hosel bore with the 3/8" (.375") diameter special hard cobalt drill.

Equipment Required in Step Drilling Irons

A 3/8" electric variable speed hand drill can be used to enlarge or open up hosel bores and also to clean out foreign particles before installing a new shaft. To drill out broken shafts, however, it is recommended that a drill press be used in conjunction with The GolfWorks® Iron Head Boring and Reaming Vise to securely hold the hosel in a vertical position. Also, during drilling apply a liberal amount of good quality cutting oil. DO NOT USE MOTOR OIL OR LIGHT MACHINE OIL. See photos 21-98 through 21-104.

Types of Drills Used in Step Drilling Irons

The best type of drills to use when step drilling irons is cobalt. The cobalt material is much tougher than high speed steel drill bits and is especially useful when drilling out broken shafts and stainless steel investment cast hosels. For irons, a standard length drill bit referred to as "jobbers length" is used. Cobalt drill bits are all but impossible to find in retail stores and with the worldwide shortage of this material, they are becoming increasingly difficult to obtain even from the drill manufacturers. The GolfWorks® sells complete sets of step drills packaged in a clear plastic box with instructions. See Figure 21-229.

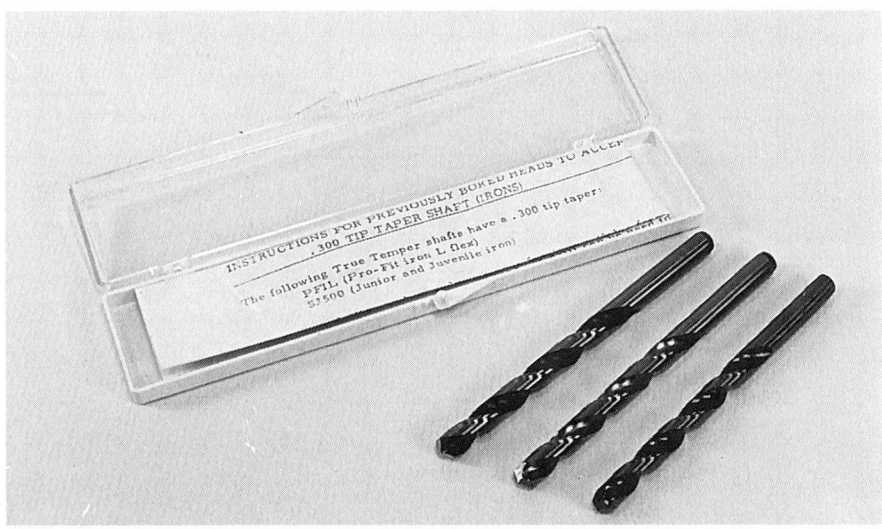

FIG. 21-229
Sets of step drills are available from "The GolfWorks®" for both woods and irons

Controlling Depth When Step Drilling Irons

A piece of masking tape wrapped around the drill bit will work quite well to indicate the proper depth for drilling. Another method is to use adjustable drill stops which come in two sizes, one size to fit ¹⁄₁₆" to ¼" drill bits and the other size to fit ¼" to ½" drill bits. See Figure 21-230. Also shown here are drill stop collars which come in various sizes and are usually sold in sets. These various drill stops are available from The GolfWorks® and many hardware stores.

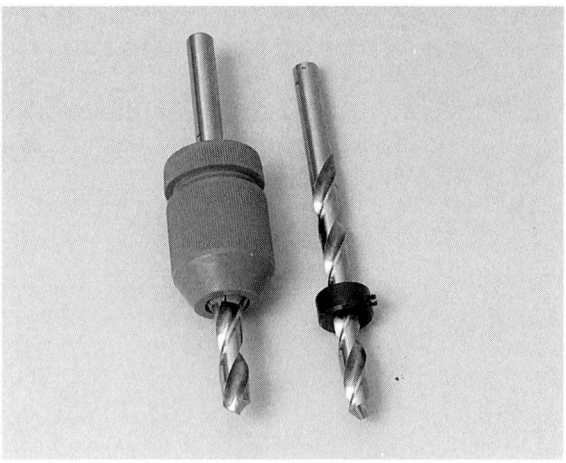

FIG. 21-230
Adjustable Drill Stops provide exact depth control when step drilling – 2 types are shown

Shaft Tip Sizes

The shaft tip sizes by type of shaft and by manufacturer are shown in Chapter 57.

Iron Head Reamer for Cleaning and Re-Sizing Hosel Bores

Reamers do have a few drawbacks when compared to step drilling. The first problem is that reamers are expensive, and they will sometimes break or chip if they hit an old piece of shaft or part of a stainless steel hosel rivet. They are also more difficult and costly to resharpen than step drills. Also if a shaft is "tipped," the reamer will not open the hosel hole up to the correct size unless you had a spare reamer that had the tip ground back the correct amount.

On the other hand, reamers are faster and more accurate for high speed production or even custom head manufacture. The GolfWorks® stocks the most popular .355" taper tip reamer. See photo 21-81. If you desire to have your own made up, the drawings and measurements are included here in Figure 21-231. Remember that most custom orders of this type require a minimum of 5 and many times 10 pieces of each size.

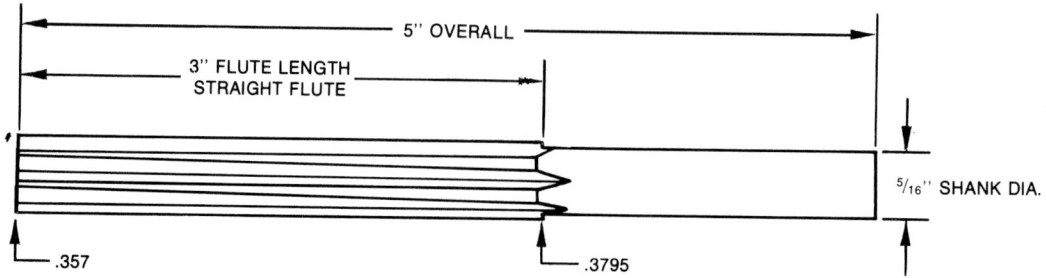

1. Material high speed steel

2. Taper per inch is .0075"

3. Tolerance: fractions ± .015", decimals ± .002

FIG. 21-231
Iron Head Reamer for .355" Taper Tip Shafts

SECTION

THREE

COMBINED GOLF WOOD AND
IRON CLUB REPAIRS

CHAPTER 22

ELIMINATING RATTLES AND SQUEAKS

It is usually rare when a customer brings in a golf club to have an annoying noise removed from it because golfers will put up with the distraction as long as the club holds together. When a customer brings in a club for such a repair, however, you can bet that the customer has come to the decision that the noise is costing valuable strokes out on the course. In some cases it is true that the noise can be traced to something which is affecting the shot. However, nine out of ten times, the noise has no mechanical bearing on the golf club's playability.

Most common causes for rattles:

Problem #1: An adhesive particle has come loose from the shaft tip end and is sliding up and down the shaft.

Problem #2: A piece of dirt or a small stone has entered the shaft through the hole in the rubber grip's end cap.

Problem #3: Some manufacturers use plastic grip end caps with either a plastic plug or a metal screw inside. These end caps occasionally come loose or the plug falls through and slides up and down the shaft.

Problem #4: Many manufacturers add a small lead slug to the tip end of the shaft during assembly to achieve the desired swingweight. Sometimes they break loose and rattle or slide up and down inside the shaft.

Problem #5: A loose soleplate on woods can sometimes rattle.

Problem #6: A loose lead weight under the soleplate on woods is one of the most common causes of a rattle.

Problem #7: A set screw sometimes falls into the hollow cavity of a metal wood, or a piece of foam breaks loose.

Most common causes for squeaks:

Problem #8: A loose, or partially loose, shaft in a wood club or iron club will squeak.

Problem #9: A grip that is loose on the shaft. Generally this looseness will be found in the top of the grip.

22-1 To test for a rattle in the head of the club, hold the shaft loosely and tap the head gently on a hard surface.

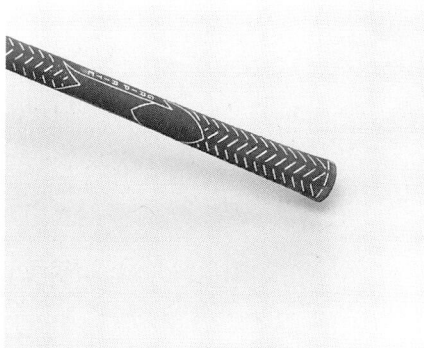

22-2 To test for a rattle in the grip end of the club, hold the head end loosely and bounce the grip on a hard surface.

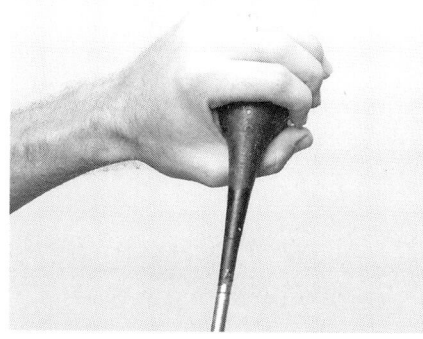

22-3 Sometimes a squeak can be caused by a loose head. Grasp the head in one hand and the shaft in the other. If you detect movement between the shaft and the head, the shaft will need to be removed and reinstalled properly.

22-4 To tighten a rattle under the soleplate, remove the soleplate as outlined in Chapter 2. If a lead weight is loose, it can be peened and tightened by tapping a cross point screwdriver into the lead plug.

22-5 Lead can also be peened by tapping with the round end of a ball peen hammer.

22-6 Refer to Chapter 2, photos 2-10 through 2-24, for soleplate reinstallation procedure.

22-7 Here is an example of a club that allows access to the weight cavity without removing the soleplate.

22-8 Remove the center screw. If necessary apply heat using the methods shown in Chapter 3, photos 3-5 through 3-7.

22-9 Lift the medallion from the soleplate. Some models do not have the center screw and heat must be applied to the medallion to soften the epoxy holding it in place.

22-10 Either stuff steel wool or cotton inside the cavity to deaden the sound or …

22-11 … remove the loose lead and/or epoxy from the cavity and …

22-12 … pour lead powder or molten lead back into the cavity. Although loose, lead powder offers no sound when free inside the cavity.

22-13 Apply epoxy to the medallion and the recess that holds the medallion. If necessary remove any old epoxy from the recess before new epoxy is applied.

22-14 Place the medallion back in the recess and install the original screw if the club had one.

22-15 Wipe off the excess epoxy. If no screw holds the medallion in place, lay a piece of masking tape across the medallion until the epoxy cures.

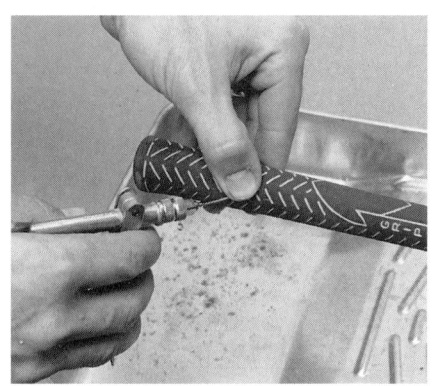

22-16 To remove a rattle inside the shaft, either cut off the grip or remove it with the **Pressurized Grip Remover.** See Chapter 23, photos 23-31 through 23-37. Always wear eye protection.

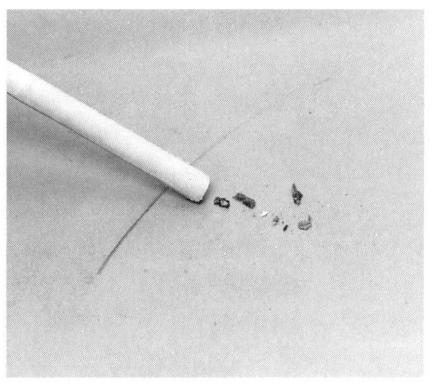

22-17 If particles are loose inside the shaft, pour them out.

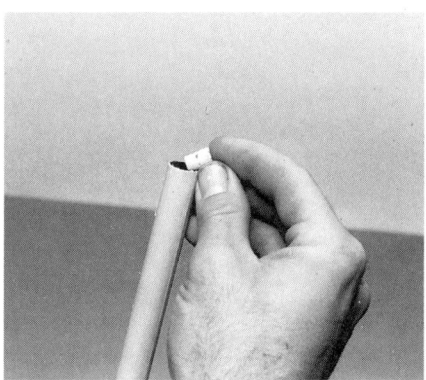

22-18 If loose particles of lead or another heavy substance is poured out of the shaft, this weight must be replaced. Ideally, the weight should be added under the soleplate and not down the shaft. When this is not possible, drop a cork with a glob of epoxy on it down the shaft to secure the weight.

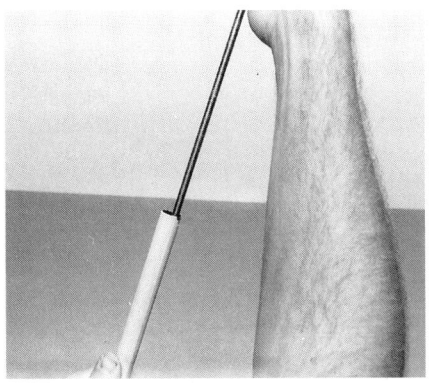

22-19 Ram the cork in place with a long drill rod or **Ramrod**. The opposite end of a **47" Drill Bit** will also work.

22-20 **To remove a rattle caused by a loose end cap,** first, remove it and apply epoxy to the stem. See Chapter 23 for additional information on removing end cap assemblies.

22-21 Insert the end cap into the shaft. Be careful not to use too much epoxy as the excess may later break off and cause another rattle. It may be necessary to completely replace the end cap. See Chapter 23 for correct replacement procedure.

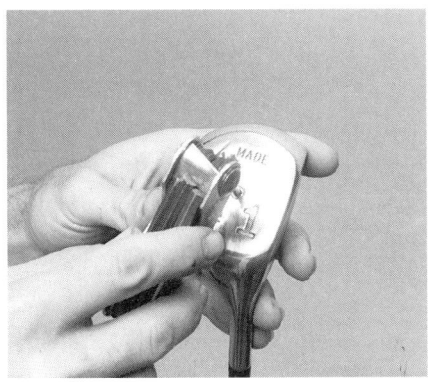

22-22 **To remove a set screw from inside a metal head,** it must be speared with a **Hex Key Wrench** and turned up through the threaded hole in the soleplate. This requires a degree of patience and luck.

22-23 If the set screw fails to come out, the cavity can be stuffed with cotton. This should deaden the offending sound. Steel wool can be used but be aware that the swingweight will increase.

22-24 **Loose foam in a metal head** can be dumped out through the set screw hole if the head has one. Loss of weight can be compensated for by adding steel wool or lead powder inside the head.

NOTES

_____

_____

_____

_____

_____

_____

_____

CHAPTER 23

INSTALLING GRIPS AND CHANGING GRIP SIZE

Grip replacement will probably be the most common golf club repair in your shop. Fortunately, it is also one of the most profitable and easy to perform, especially with slip-on rubber grips. With the various materials and components available, even leather regripping has become much easier and faster than it was just a few years ago.

There will be many instances when you will be asked to regrip a golf club with another type, style or size of grip. For instance, you may be requested to replace leather grips with rubber grips, or an 11" rubber grip with a 10" rubber grip, or a standard size grip with an oversize grip. When you change the grip size or change to another type or style of grip, you may unknowingly change the balance of the club by altering both the swingweight and the total weight. The weight of a golf grip can vary significantly because of style, length, material, size and manufacturer. This weight variance is often significant enough to affect both swingweight and total weight.

At this point read through the tables at the end of this chapter and study the information, keeping in mind the relationships that exist between the different tables. This information is valuable as handy reference material and will also provide a better understanding of the design relationship between the grip and the entire golf club.

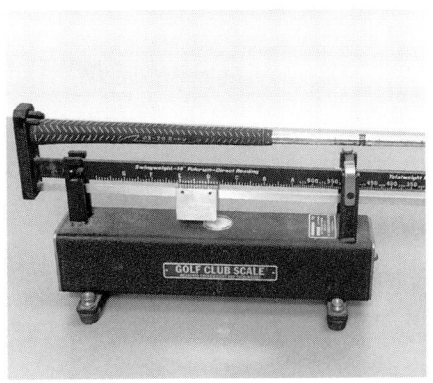

23-1 Before regripping any club, always check the swingweight. It is also a good idea to check the total weight.

23-2 If the grip size is not to be changed, the existing grip size must be accurately determined because it must be properly duplicated when installing the new grip. The **Grip Size and Shaft Butt Gauge** shown works very well and is the quickest method. Slip a gauge opening over the bottom of the grip. Slide the gauge up the grip until it becomes snug against the grip. Mark the spot with your thumb and …

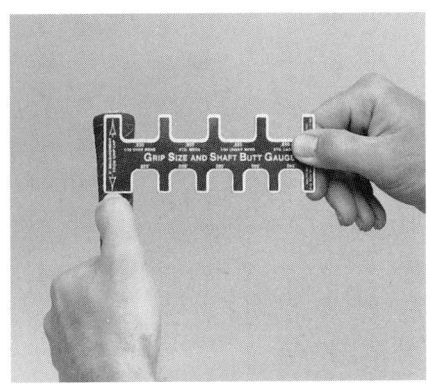

23-3 … slip the gauge off the grip and use the end of the gauge for the 2" measurement. This gauge measures the grip size at 2" from the end of the grip. One of the various grip gauge openings will allow it to slide up the grip, but will stop 2" from the top as shown in this photo. The actual size of the grip can be read at that opening.

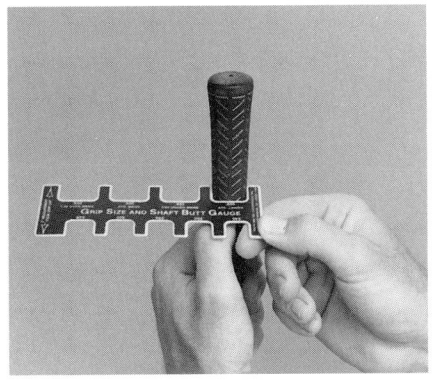

23-4 If the gauge opening stops below the 2" measurement, the grip is larger than the designated opening.

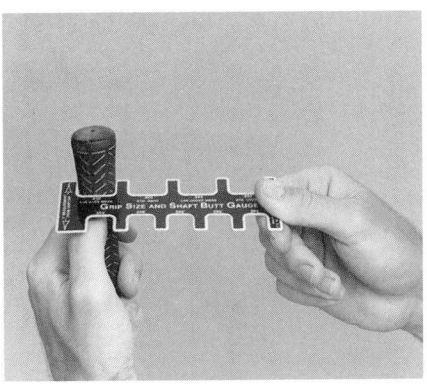

23-5 If the gauge stops above the 2" measurement, the grip is smaller than the designated opening.

23-6 A gauge for measuring the grip size underneath the right hand is also available. The **Grip Size Under Right Hand Gauge** is used by sliding the different size openings up the grip until one becomes snug at a point 5" from the top of the grip. The size would then be read directly from the gauge.

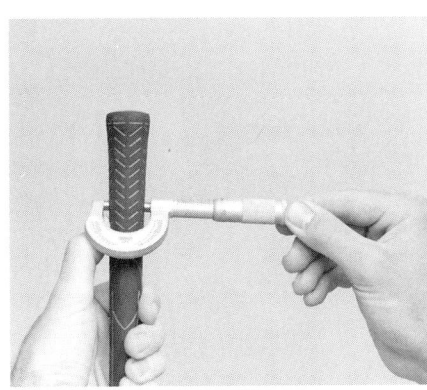

23-7 An alternative to a grip gauge is a micrometer. The only drawback to this method is once a reading has been taken you must refer to Table 23-2 (at the end of this chapter) to determine the equivalent grip size. Example: .930 = 1/32" over men's standard grip size.

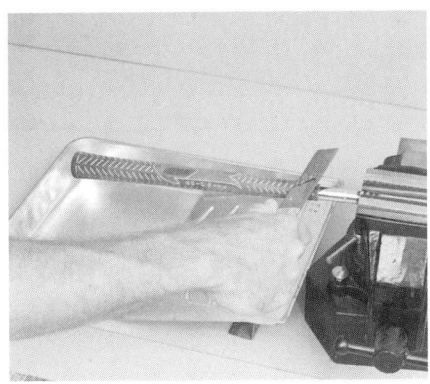

23-8 Removal of an old grip. Rubber grips can be cut off using a sharp knife. Cut underneath the lip of the grip and …

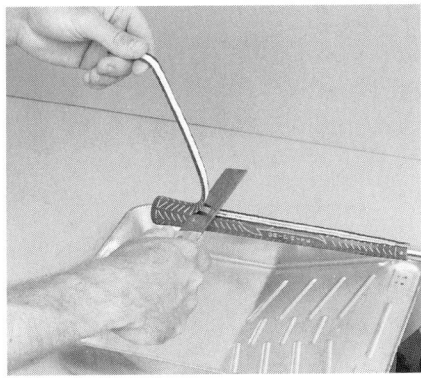

23-9 … pull back on the cut rubber piece while, simultaneously, slicing through the grip all the way to the grip cap. **Be very careful when using sharp knives.**

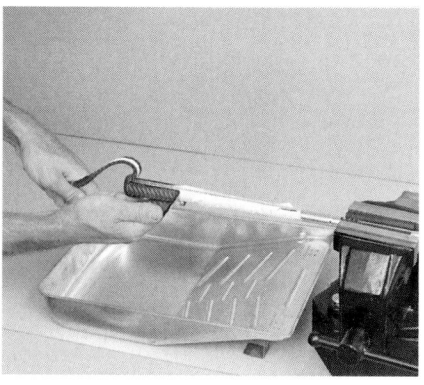

23-10 After cutting through the length of the grip, pull the remaining portion of the grip from the shaft.

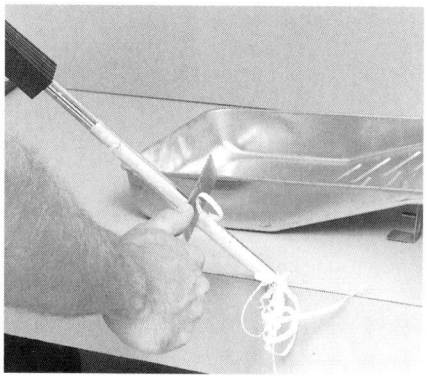

23-11 A quick way to remove any remaining tape is to place the butt of the shaft against the edge of the workbench or vise and push the knife through the tape while rotating the shaft.

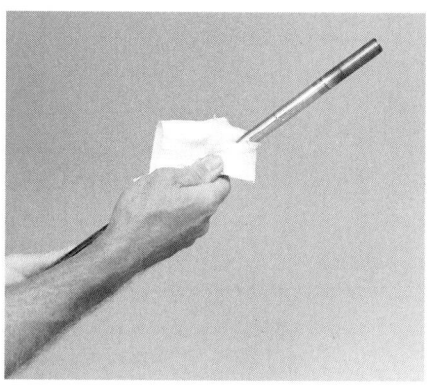

23-12 The final remaining tape residue is easily removed by wiping the butt of the shaft with a paper towel dampened in grip solvent or Naphtha.

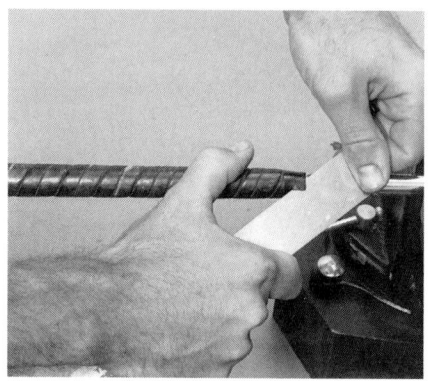

23-13 To remove leather wrap on grips, first cut through the plastic grip collar. Note: If you are going to regrip with leather, you can try to save the existing grip collar by grasping, twisting and pulling down simultaneously.

23-14 Next, unwrap the old leather grip and remove it.

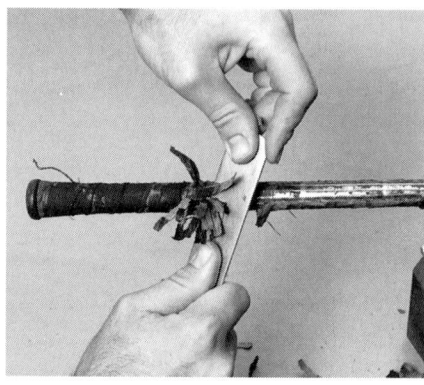

23-15 Cut off the old underlisting and remove all the old glue or tape from the shaft. Although current underlistings are made of rubber, you will find crepe paper or cardboard underlistings on many of the older clubs.

23-16 Many older clubs have plastic end caps. Sometimes, the entire end cap assembly will pull or screw out in one piece. Grasp the end cap lightly in vise jaws, or with pliers and gently twist and pull at the same time to remove it. If it will not come out all the way, warm the outside of the shaft with a propane torch on a low setting. Be careful.

23-17 This photo shows a removed end cap assembly. See Fig. 23-146 at the end of this chapter for a drawing of the anatomy of an end cap.

23-18 If the end cap will not pull out in one piece, attempt to pry out the plastic disc with a sharp knife.

23-19 In some cases, a screw will be found underneath the disc.

23-20 After turning the screw out, the end cap is easily removed. A tapered wooden plug, however, extends from the shaft.

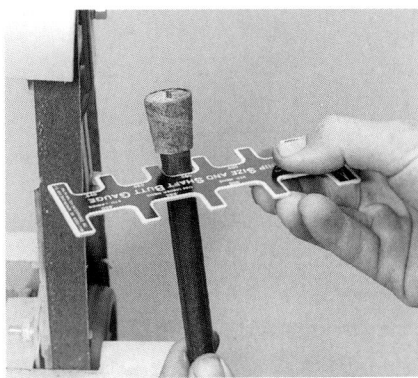

23-21 One alternative for the wooden plug is to grind it to the same diameter as the shaft butt. The **Belt Sander** shown works well. Measure the shaft with the **Grip Size and Shaft Butt Gauge** or a micrometer.

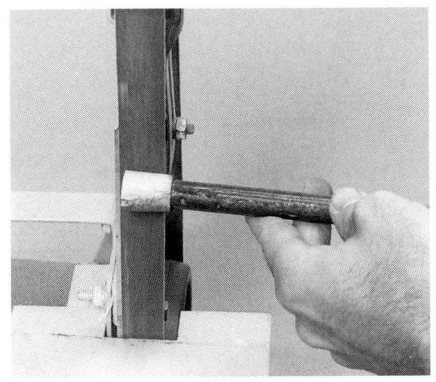

23-22 Next, grind the excess wood to the same diameter as the shaft butt.

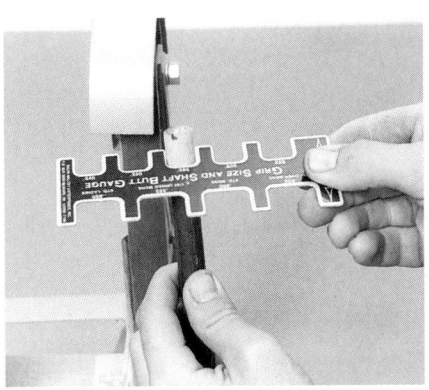

23-23 Periodically check the size until …

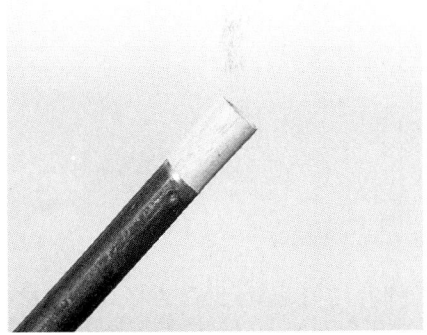

23-24 … the wooden plug is the same size as the shaft. The club is now ready for gripping.

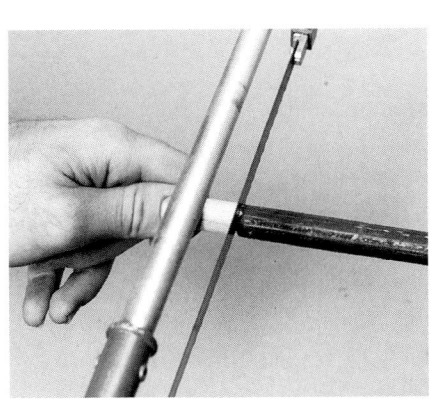

23-25 If you wish to remove the wooden plug, cut it even with the shaft using a hacksaw.

23-26 Drill through the plug with a ⅜" drill bit.

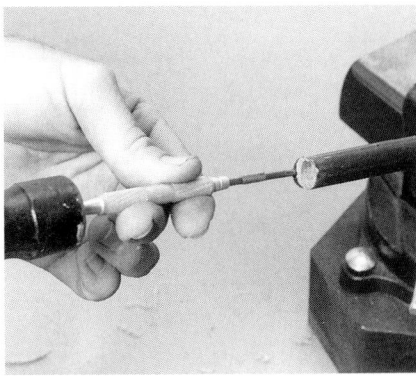

23-27 The sides of the plug are now easily collapsed inward with a scriber or awl. Dump the debris out of the shaft.

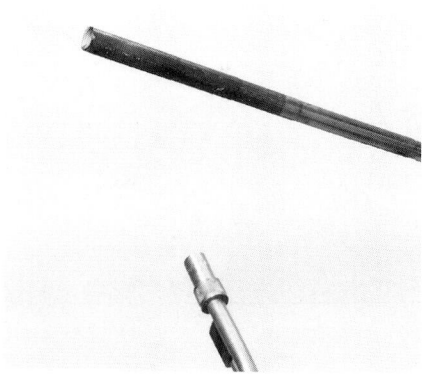

23-28 If the plug does not come out, heat the shaft butt briefly with a propane torch on a low setting.

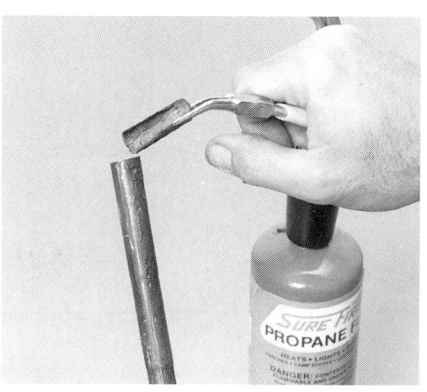

23-29 Remains of the wood plug can then be removed with a pair of **Needle Nose Pliers.**

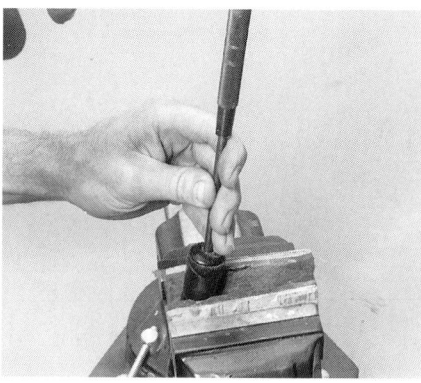

23-30 Sometimes, after removing the plastic disc in the end cap, you will find a plastic pin, brass pin or a hex socket set screw. Set screws will usually turn out with the proper size **Hex Key Wrench.** Pins must be driven through the end cap assembly with a long punch as shown. The remaining end cap can then be pulled or drilled from the shaft.

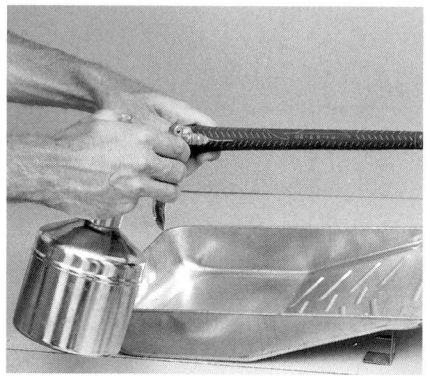

23-31 If, for some reason, it is requested that the old grip be saved, it can be removed using the **Pressurized Grip Remover** as shown, or with a syringe and a large hypodermic needle. **Always wear eye protection.** Push the needle slowly into the grip at a 45° angle until it touches the shaft. The needle should enter the grip approximately 2" from the grip cap. **Keep your fingers away from the end of the needle.**

23-32 Place your thumb over the entry point in the grip and inject solvent underneath the grip. Placing your thumb over the hole will prevent the solvent from squirting out.

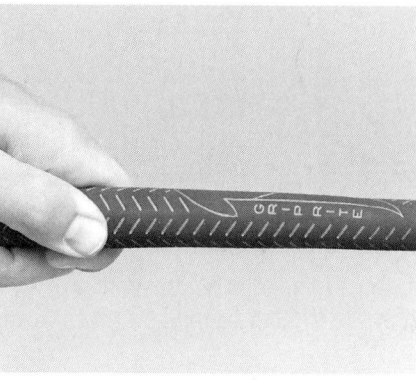

23-33 Once a portion of the grip is enlarged as a result of pumping in the solvent, remove the needle. Keep your thumb over the hole.

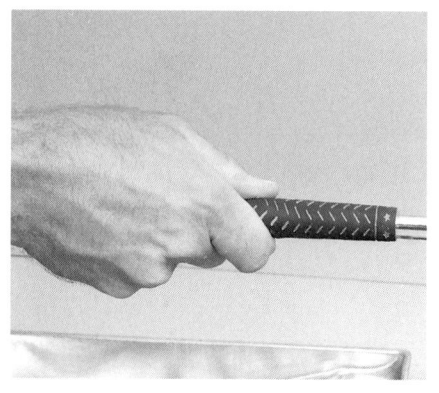

23-34 Work the solvent bubble down the length of the grip by pushing, prodding and twisting the grip at a point just below the bubble. This will allow the solvent to move down the entire length of the grip.

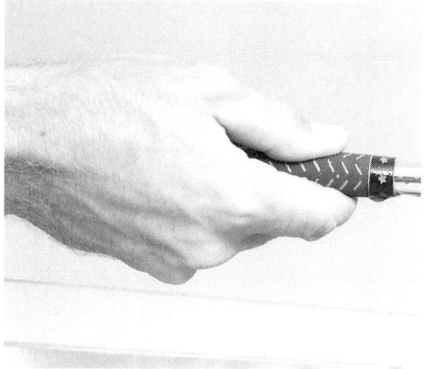

23-35 Continue to push and twist until the solvent squirts from the bottom of the grip.

23-36 Pull the grip from the shaft.

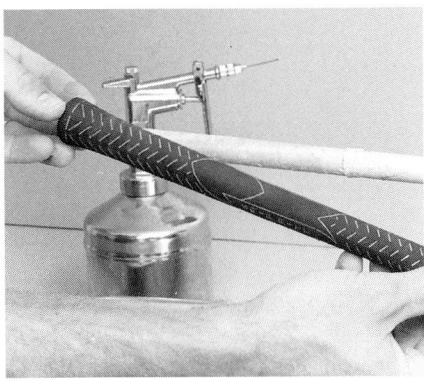

23-37 The grip is removed in perfect condition and can be reused. **A final caution: Be very careful using hypodermic needles and always wear eye protection.**

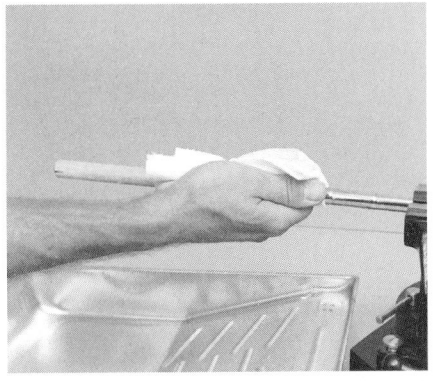

23-38 A fast way to remove slimy tape is by wrapping a paper towel around it while squeezing and pulling it towards the butt end of the shaft. You must remove all the tape and residue from the shaft.

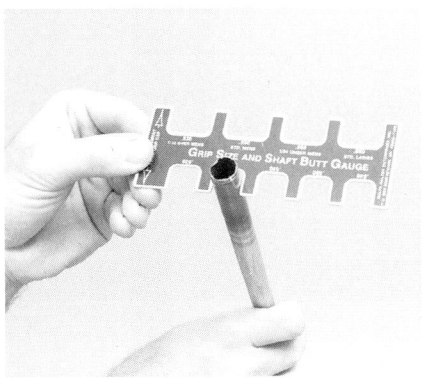

23-39 To install grips, first check the shaft butt size using the **Shaft Butt and Grip Size Gauge,** or ...

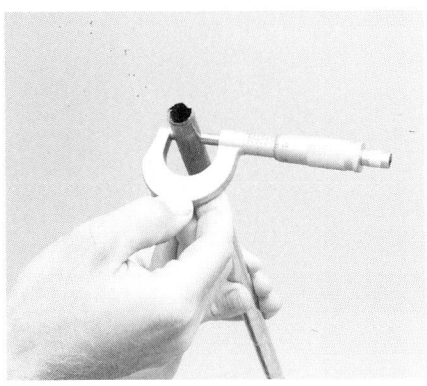

23-40 ... use a micrometer or vernier caliper.

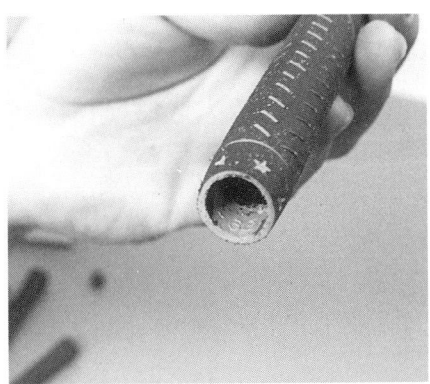

23-41 Next, determine the grip core size by looking inside the mouth of the grip. Look for a size designation such as M58, L56, 58, 60, M62R, etc. See Tables 23-3 through 23-6 and Fig. 23-144 at the end of this chapter for an understanding of these codes.

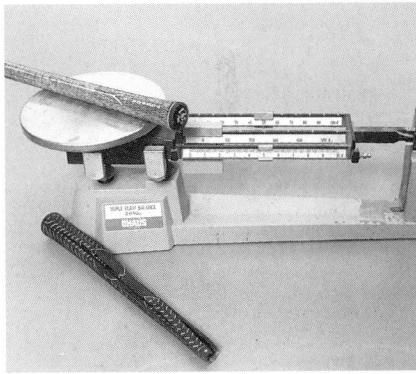

23-42 The old grip and the new grip can be weighed on an accurate scale to determine if the new grip is lighter or heavier. This weight can affect the club's swingweight. Table 23-10 at the end of this chapter gives various grip weights.

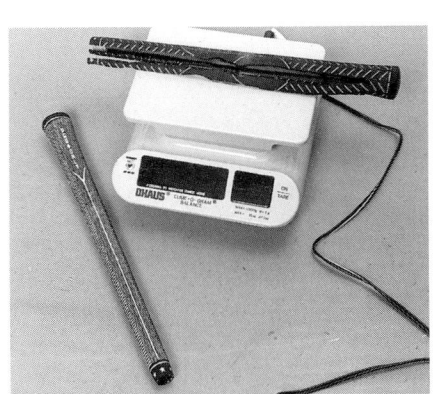

23-43 This photo shows an **O'Haus Electronic Gram-Ounce Scale** that is fast and convenient for weighing any component.

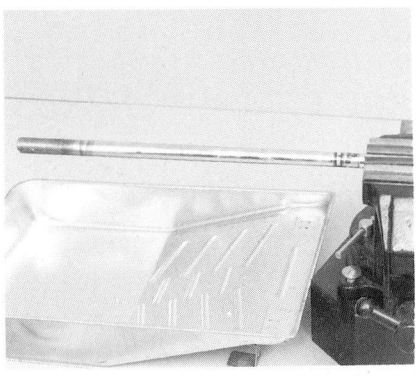

23-44 To install a slip on rubber grip, first place a shaft clamp around the shaft and tighten in a vise. The face of the club should point up vertically and in a square position. Note the use of a common paint roller pan to catch the excess solvent. Solvent can be reused.

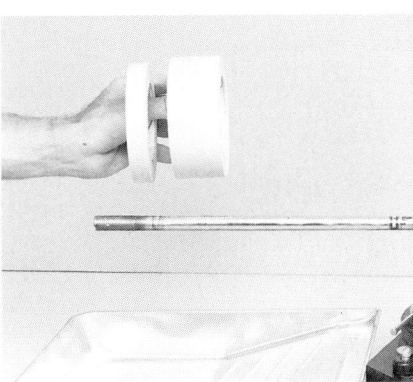

23-45 With the shaft butt size and grip core size known, additional layers of tape may be needed to achieve the desired grip size. If additional tape layers are necessary for build-up, use the regular ¾" or 2" wide masking tape. See the tables at the end of this chapter for information on how tape thickness and multiple tape layers affect grip size.

271

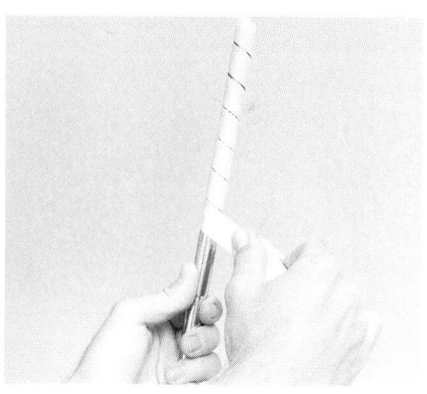

23-46 A single layer wrap of ¾" masking tape (not overwrapped), as shown, will increase grip size .01" which is slightly less than ¹⁄₆₄" (¹⁄₆₄" = .015).

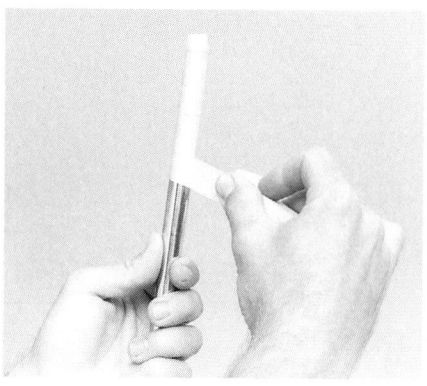

23-47 When ¾" masking tape is overlapped half-again on itself (this is referred to as an overlay wrap), the grip size will increase by .02" or slightly larger than ¹⁄₆₄". Both tape wraps used together (a single layer wrap and an overlapping wrap on top of it) are exactly .03" or ¹⁄₃₂" oversize.

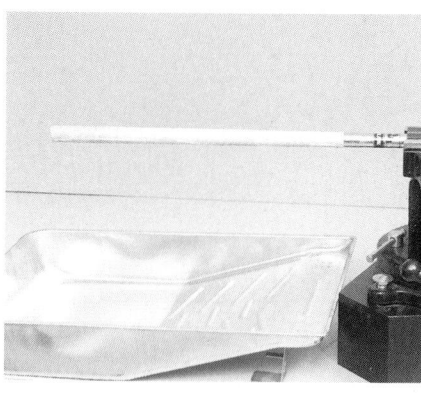

23-48 You can also use 2" wide masking tape for build-up. One layer will increase the grip size .01" which is slightly less than ¹⁄₆₄" (¹⁄₆₄" = .015).

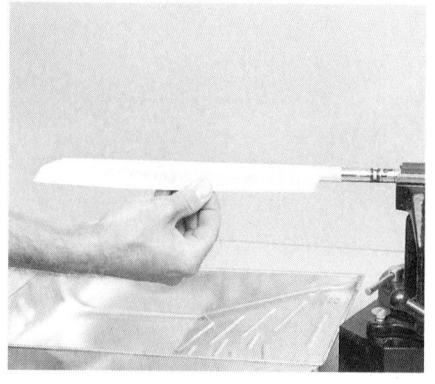

23-49 For more build-up, overlap layers of 2" wide masking tape. Two layers will increase grip size by .02" or slightly larger than ¹⁄₆₄". Three layers will increase grip size by .03 or ¹⁄₃₂" oversize.

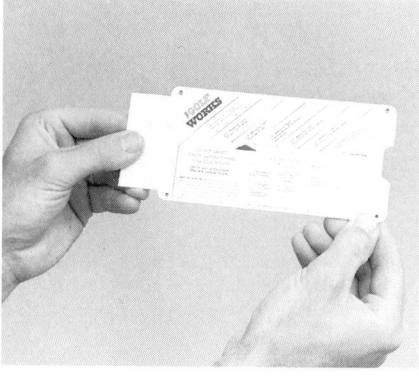

23-50 This photo shows a **Grip Slide Rule.** The Rule is used to calculate how to install oversize grips using build-up tape and core sizes and determine the amount of swing-weight change due to the grip change. In many cases it details several ways to wrap the build-up tape and swap core sizes to achieve the desired grip size.

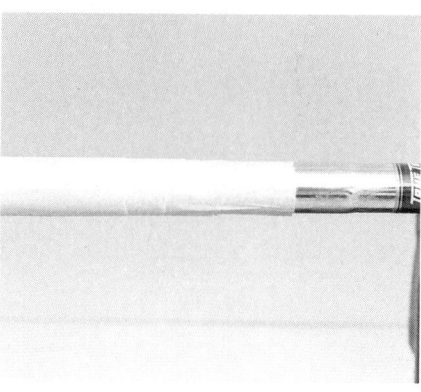

23-51 When placing multiple layers of tape on the shaft, stagger the length and placement of each piece of tape. This will eliminate any unsightly drop at the bottom of the grip and, also, avoid the formation of an additional rib where all pieces overlap in the same spot.

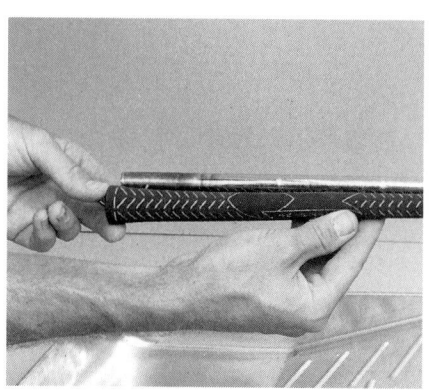

23-52 Once the build-up tape is applied, or if no build-up tape is required, hold the new grip up to the shaft to determine the approximate length of double-coated tape needed.

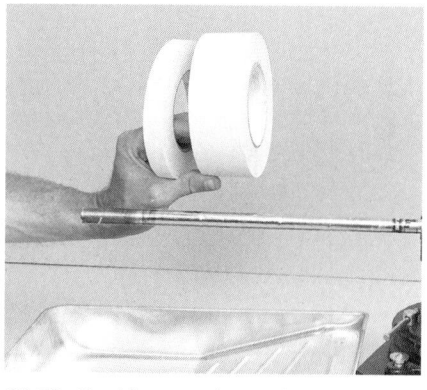

23-53 Double-coated tape is available in both ¾" or 2" wide tape.

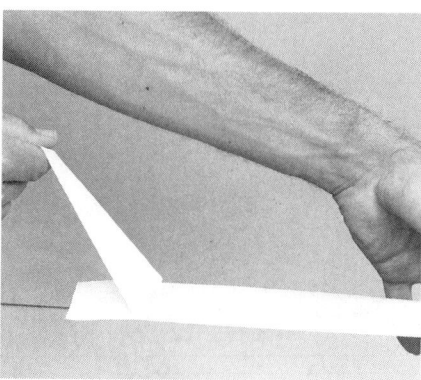

23-54 The use of 2" wide double-coated tape is shown. This is faster and more economical than using ¾" wide double-coated tape. Apply the tape lengthwise to the shaft. The tape should be slightly shorter than the grip length, yet still have approximately 1" extending over the butt end of the shaft.

272

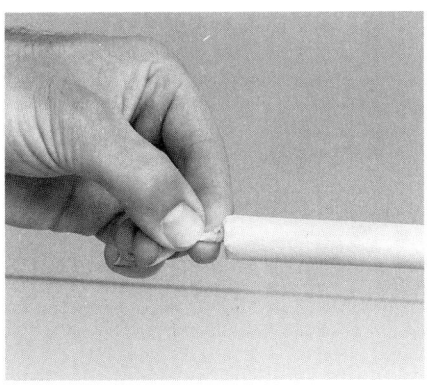

23-55 Carefully wrap the tape around the shaft. Twist or squeeze the end of the tape together as shown and push inside the butt end of the shaft. This prevents the solvent from entering the shaft during grip installation.

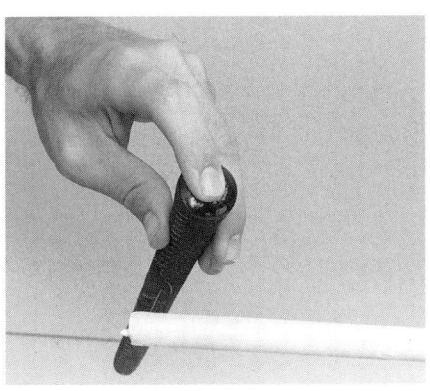

23-56 Block the vent hole in the butt end of the grip with your finger, golf tee or other pointed object.

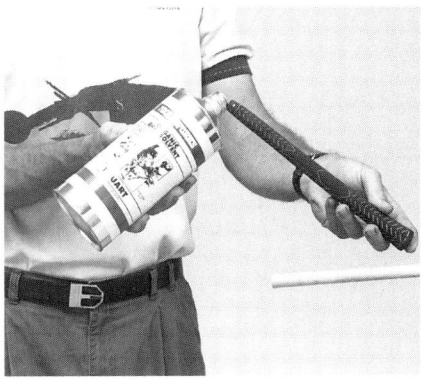

23-57 Squirt or pour a generous amount of grip solvent inside the grip. Pinch the open end of the grip with your fingers and shake to thoroughly wet the inside of the grip. The **GolfWorks® non-flammable 100% Organic Grip Solvent** is shown. Many shops still use naphtha, gasoline or lighter fluid. These are highly flammable and dangerous solvents and are not recommended.

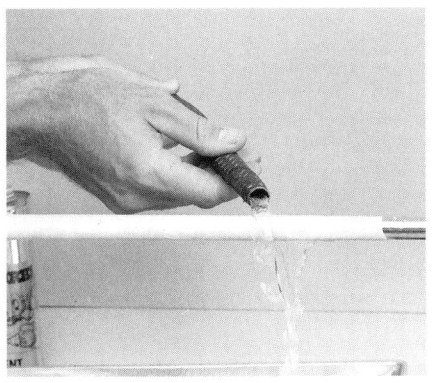

23-58 Grip solvent is then poured out of the grip over the entire length of the double-coated tape to wet it thoroughly. If necessary, squirt additional solvent onto the tape.

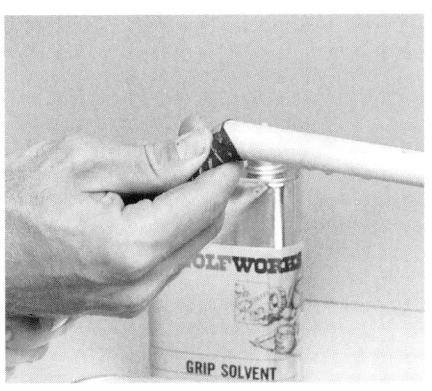

23-59 It is vitally important that the butt end of the shaft is wet, as this will make installation easier. Working quickly, position the open end of the grip just beneath the shaft butt and ...

23-60 ... start the grip up and over the shaft. Holding the grip as shown, slide it on until the end of the shaft stops at the top of the grip. Work quickly.

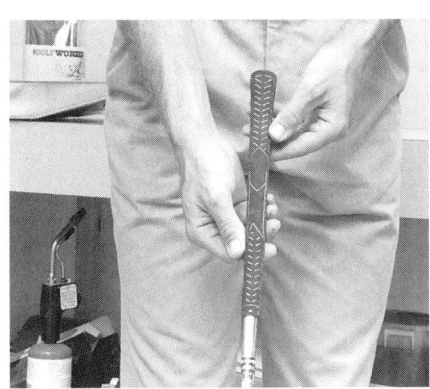

23-61 To properly align the grip, place the club in the playing position and sight down the grip and the center of the shaft. The grip should be aligned with the leading edge on woods and irons. The grip can be changed in alignment for 2 to 3 minutes after installation before the solvent evaporates.

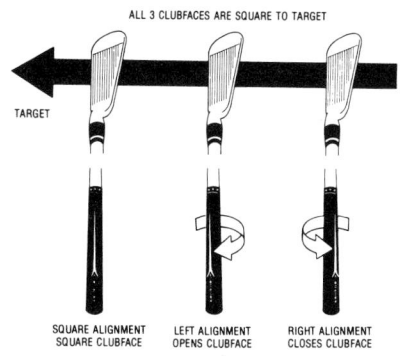

23-62 Be aware that some golfers like their grips turned slightly right or left. If possible, allow the golfer to check the first club and make any suggestions as to changes in alignment. The most common installation is perfectly square.

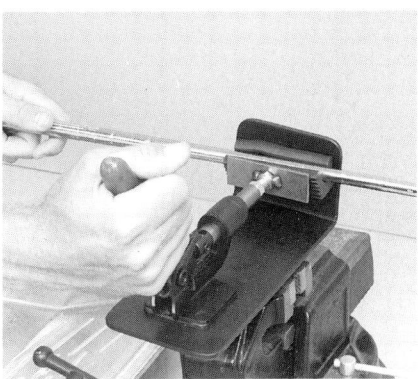

23-63 The photo shows a **Lever Action Shaft Holder.** Regripping can be performed much faster with this tool. The shaft is tightened and then released by simply lowering and raising the lever.

273

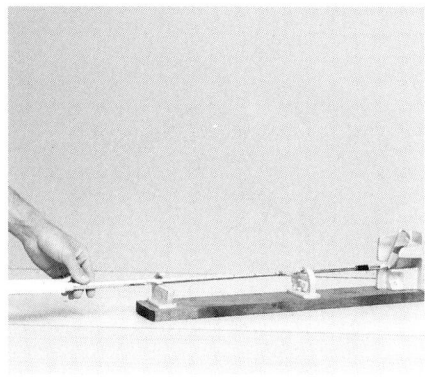

23-64 The **Automatic Gripper for Irons** will hold an iron head and most putters securely as the grip is installed. Because the face is automatically aligned properly, the grip will be in perfect alignment.

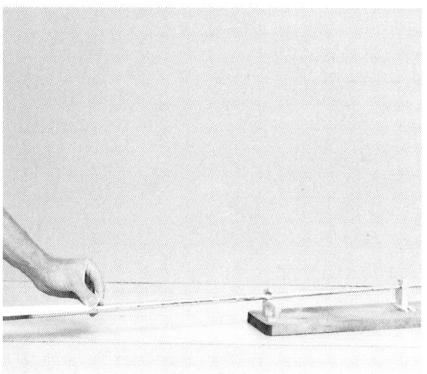

23-65 The **Automatic Gripper for Woods** works under the same principle, so the grip is aligned properly.

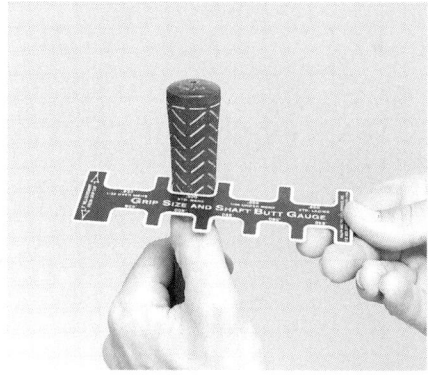

23-66 The grip size should be final checked** before returning the club to the customer using the **Grip Size and Shaft Butt Gauge.**

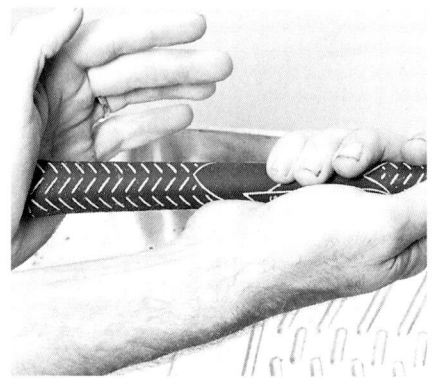

23-67 **To make a standard size grip smaller,** first slide the grip on in the normal manner. **Refer to Tables 23-4 through 23-6 at the end of this chapter on producing oversize and undersize grips by interchanging grip core sizes.**

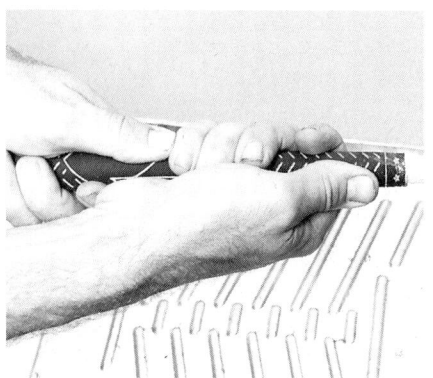

23-68 When sliding the grip on, stretch it past its normal stopping point, as shown. Use both hands to stretch the grip evenly over its entire length.

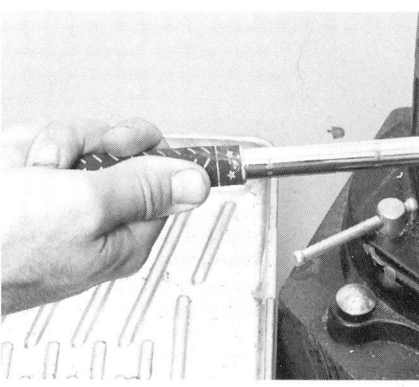

23-69 Hold it in this stretched position for approximately 1 minute or until the tape begins to set.

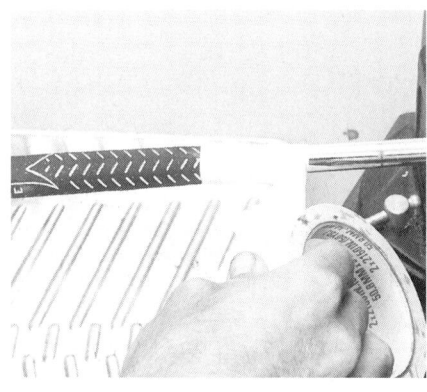

23-70 While still holding the grip, wrap a piece of masking tape around the bottom to hold the grip in place. A grip stretched ¾" will decrease in size by 1⁄64". Leave the tape on for a minimum of 2 hours. **Be sure to check the grip size with the gauge or micrometer before the solvent evaporates and the grip becomes firmly attached.**

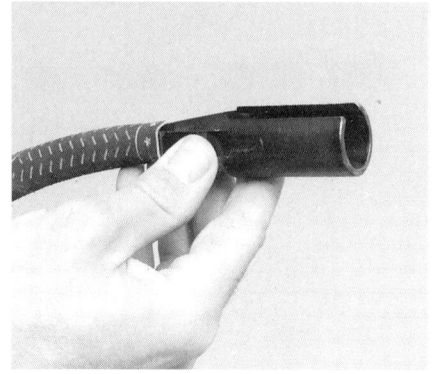

23-71 The **Grip Installer Tool** is very helpful when installing grips. First, slip fingers inside the mouth of the grip.

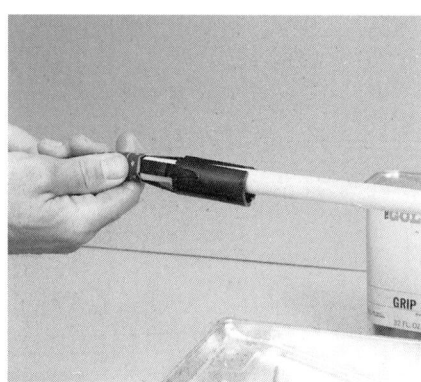

23-72 Pour solvent out of the grip and onto the tape. Slide the Grip Installer onto the shaft butt.

274

23-73 Continue sliding the grip on in a normal manner. The Grip Installer will slide right down with it. Also, the Grip Installer will enlarge the mouth of the grip for easier installation.

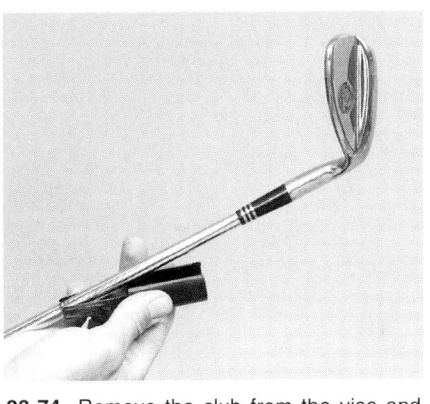

23-74 Remove the club from the vise and continue to slide the Grip Installer down the shaft until you can remove it through the notch in the side. This tool avoids any frustration in stretching smaller grips on larger shafts.

23-75 To install leather wrap-on grips, first install a grip collar. Grip collars are available in two types – rigid and stretchable plastic. The rigid grip collars are available in 4 sizes to match the common butt diameters. The stretchable collar comes in one size but can be stretched over all shaft butt sizes.

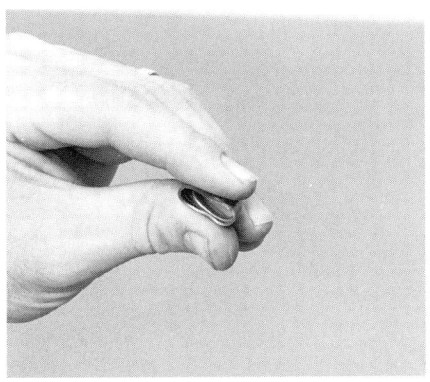

23-76 To install a stretchable grip collar, first roll the grip collar between your fingers to make it soft and pliable (or drop it in a glass of warm water for 2 minutes).

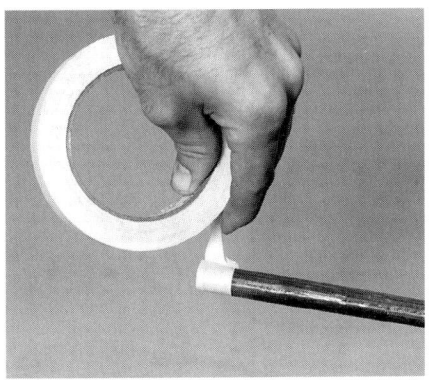

23-77 After wrapping a piece of tape around the shaft butt, push the grip collar on as far as it will go.

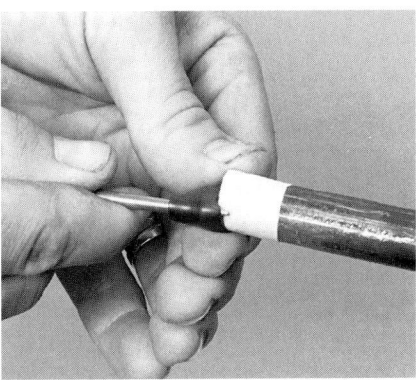

23-78 Using an awl or small screwdriver, lift and stretch the remaining portion over the end of the shaft.

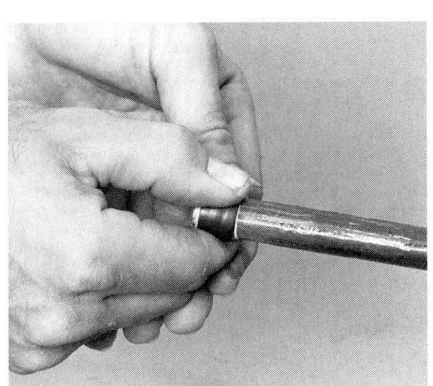

23-79 Slide the grip collar down the shaft.

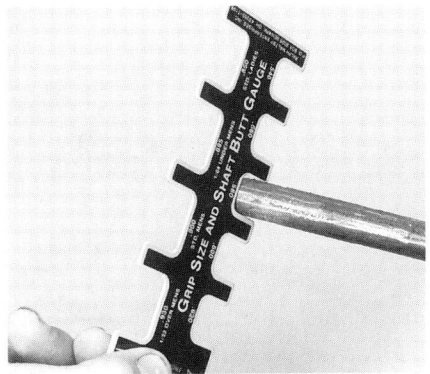

23-80 To install rigid grip collars, first measure the shaft butt and select the appropriate grip collar size. Note the use of the **Grip Size and Shaft Butt Gauge.**

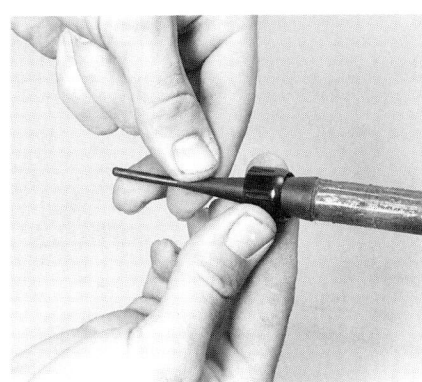

23-81 Place a **Grip Collar Starter** inside the mouth of the shaft. Slide the grip collar over it and ...

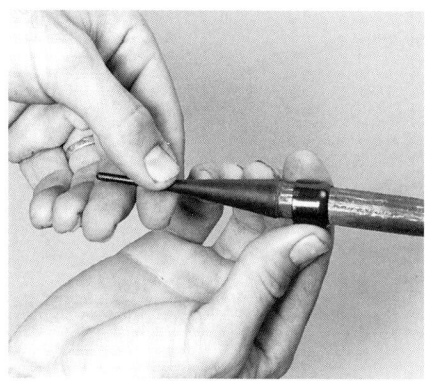

23-82 ... onto the shaft. Fast, simple and no cut fingers or cut grip collars. Note: The Grip Collar Starter also works well with stretchable grip collars.

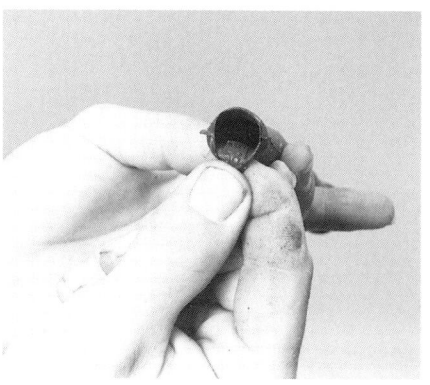

23-83 As with the rubber slip-on grip, check inside the mouth of the underlisting to determine its core size. Eaton® rubber underlistings will usually be designated with a RM58, RM60 or RM62. This indicates a Men's Reminder Rib. An SM in front of the numbers indicates a round grip (with no rib). See Fig. 23-144 for more information on number and letter designations found inside the grip.

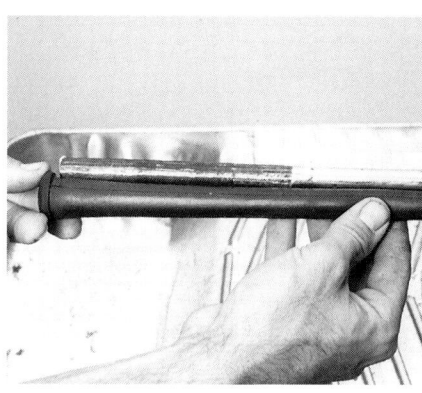

23-84 Next, hold the underlisting up to the shaft to determine the approximate tape length needed.

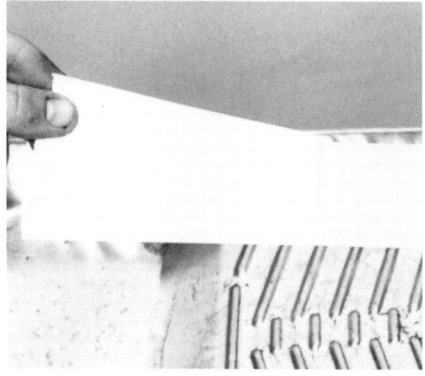

23-85 Use 2" double-coated tape as shown or use ¾" double-coated tape spiral wrapped around the shaft. Note: To build-up the size of the underlisting, the same procedure applies as shown in photos 23-45 through 23-51 for conventional rubber grips.

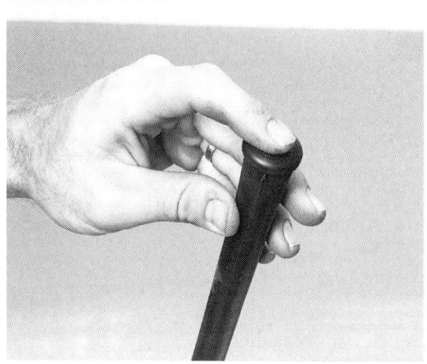

23-86 Plug the vent hole in the butt of the underlisting with your finger, golf tee or other pointed object.

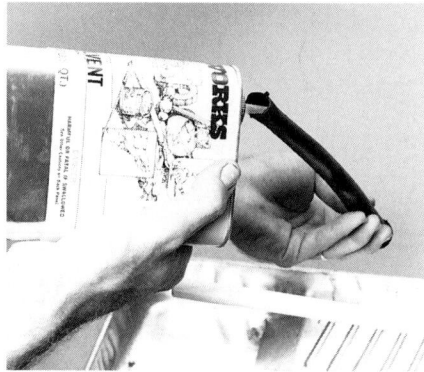

23-87 Apply grip solvent liberally inside the underlisting. Pinch off the open end of the underlisting and agitate it to thoroughly wet the interior of the underlisting.

23-88 Pour the excess solvent over the double-coated tape to actuate it. Additional solvent may be necessary to completely wet the tape.

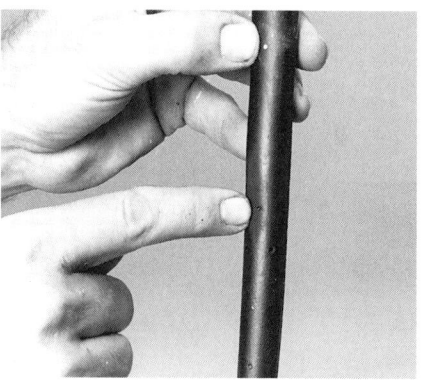

23-89 Quickly locate the rib on the underlisting and make sure it is positioned down the back of the shaft. The rib is easily identified by a series of mold markings running down the length of the back side. Note: You may wish to locate the back of the underlisting before applying solvent until you are familiar with this procedure.

23-90 Next, slide on the underlisting. The installation procedure is the same as shown in photos 23-59 and 23-60.

23-91 After the underlisting is installed, check to make sure the rib is straight down the back of the shaft. First, adjust the grip cap so the identifying markings are vertical when the club is in the address position. Next, ...

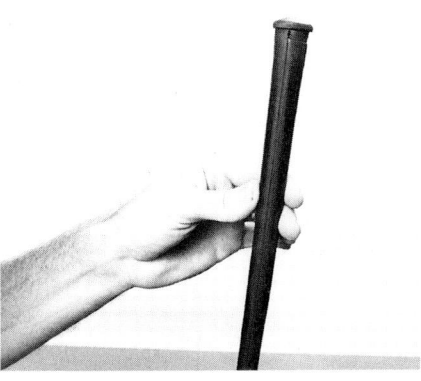

23-92 ...twist the rest of the underlisting so the seams running down the sides of the underlisting are placed straight down the shaft. This will ensure the rib is also properly aligned. Remember, the rib should run down the back of the shaft in line with the heel of the club. The seams will be aligned down the sides of the shaft. This ensures proper rib alignment.

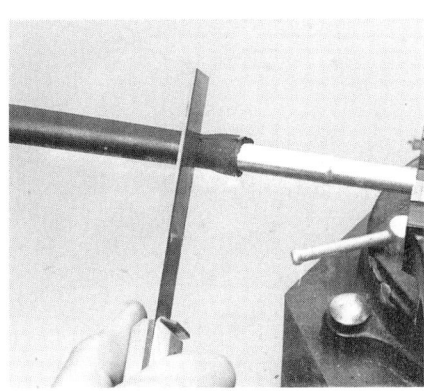

23-93 Once all of the solvent has evaporated and the grip cannot be turned, carefully cut the bell bottom off the underlisting using a sharp knife. Make a square cut.

23-94 This photo shows the bell bottom before installation. Its purpose it to aid the repairman when slipping the mouth of the grip over the shaft. Once the grip is on, it serves no other purpose and is cut off.

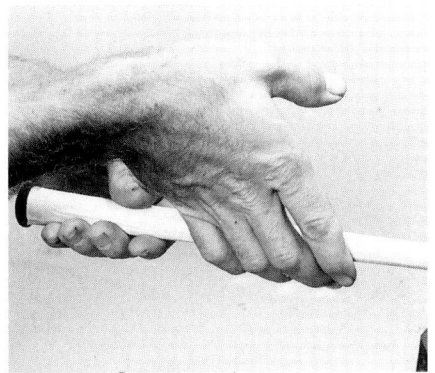

23-95 Now apply one strip of 2" double-coated tape to the underlisting. Tape should extend ¼" past the bottom of the underlisting. ¾" double-coated tape can also be used by spiral wrapping it around the underlisting.

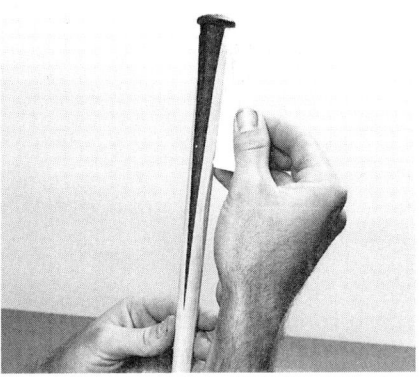

23-96 In most cases the 2" wide double-coated tape will not wrap around the entire underlisting. Although it is not necessary, a narrow piece of double-coated tape may be applied to cover the exposed rubber.

23-97 The leather strip has a squared end and a tapered end. It is with the tapered end that the wrapping begins.

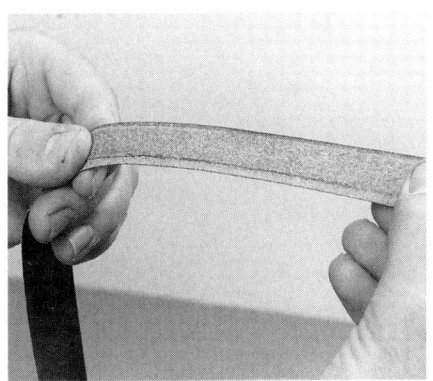

23-98 Also note the differences in the thickness of the strip. The thinner edges are referred to as the "skiving." The skiving is the part of the leather strip that is overlapped when wrapping the leather around the shaft.

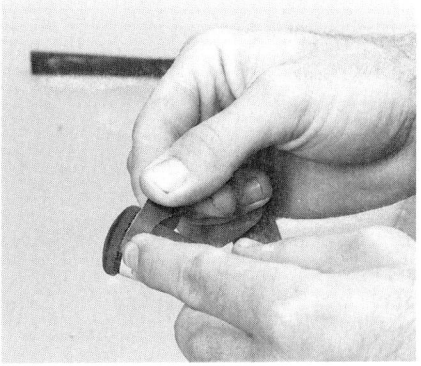

23-99 Start the tapered end of the leather strip in the rubber underlisting recess located just beneath the underlisting cap. Be sure the leather is tightly seated against the grip cap to eliminate any gaps.

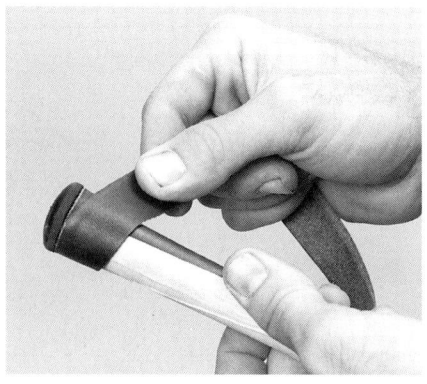

23-100 The club may be held loosely in a vise for turning or it can be held in your hands. After the strip has encircled the underlisting and slightly overlapped the tapered end, start the leather in a downward direction so the top edge of the leather overlaps the bottom edge, skiving over skiving.

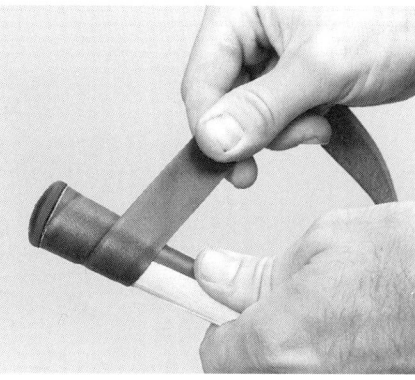

23-101 The correct wrapping procedure is to pull the leather strip with your right hand while turning the club with …

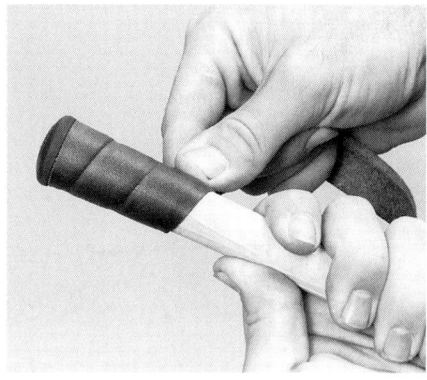

23-102 … your left. Wrap the grip using firm tension.

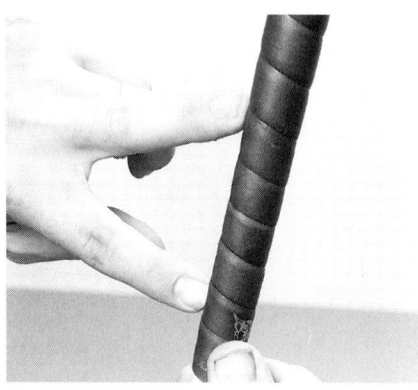

23-103 There are two different methods for wrapping a leather grip. One is called a groove or ribbed wrap, the other is called a smooth wrap. The top portion of the grip shown has been wrapped in a ribbed wrap where only a small portion of the skiving is overlapped. The bottom of the grip shown here is a smooth wrap where the entire skiving is overlapped. **Ribbed wrap is the preferred choice.**

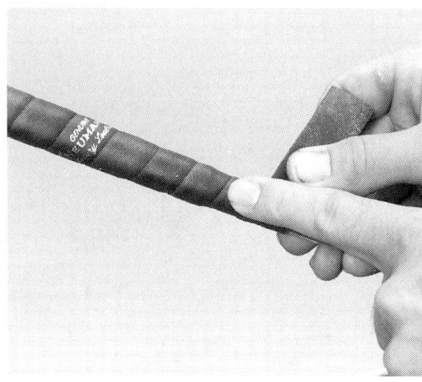

23-104 Wrap the leather 1" past the bottom of the underlisting.

23-105 Place a piece of ⅛" masking tape around the grip at a point approximately ⅜" below the bottom of the underlisting.

23-106 Using a sharp knife, cut the leather below the tape. This provides a built-in recess for positioning the grip collar.

23-107 Apply a light coating of contact cement to the bottom ⅜" of the leather.

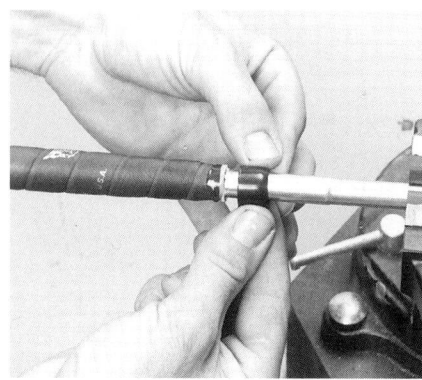

23-108 Position the grip collar below the grip.

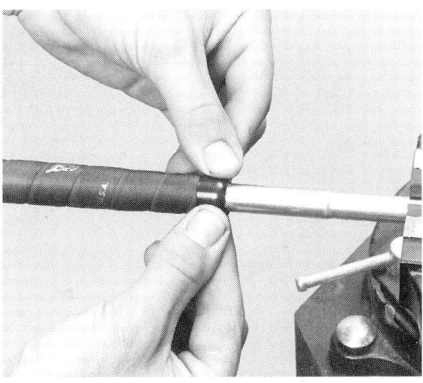

23-109 Push the grip collar to the desired position against the bottom of the underlisting over the narrow ⅜" of the leather.

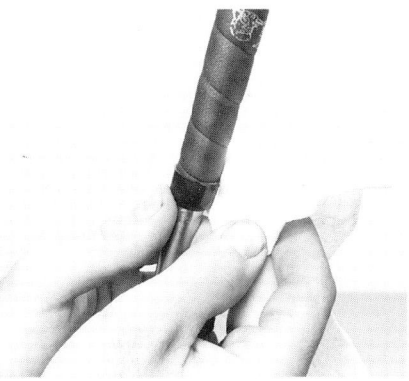

23-110 Wipe the excess cement from the collar. The rigid plastic collar gives a professional look.

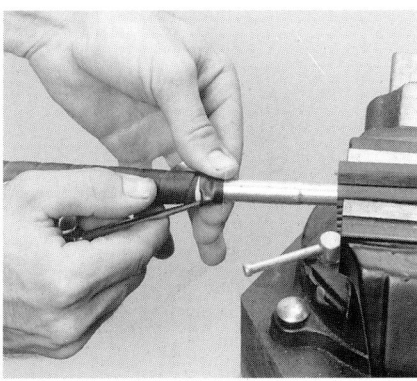

23-111 If installing a stretchable grip collar, stretch the collar over the grip, flush with the bottom of the underlisting. An awl or scriber can be used to position the collar properly.

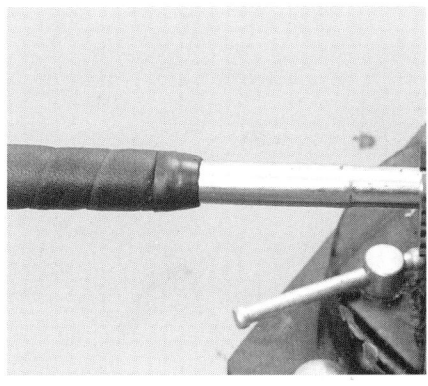

23-112 The stretch collar gives a similarly professional look.

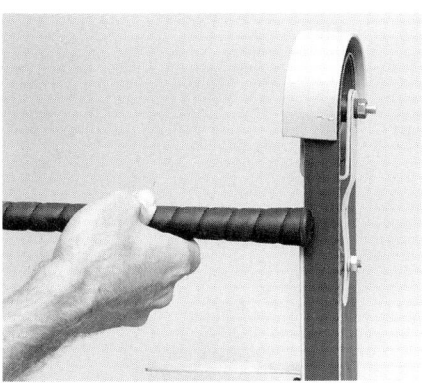

23-113 Rarely will the rubber end cap be flush with the grip diameter. It can carefully be turned down on a 1" belt sander or filed with a medium cut wood file. If the grip is accidentally nicked with the sander or file, use the appropriate color shoe polish for a touchup.

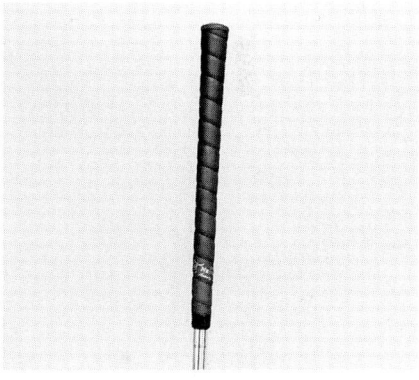

23-114 The finished grip should look like this. A groove or ribbed wrap is shown, and as previously stated, is the preferred method of wrapping a leather grip.

23-115 Final check the swingweight and make any necessary corrections as shown in Chapter 14.

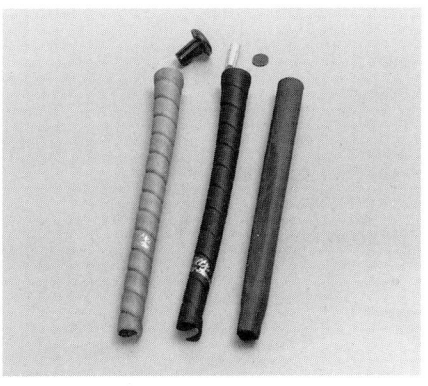

23-116 Directions for installing leather slip-on grips. The attraction of a leather slip-on grip is that it appears to lessen the work because the leather is already wrapped around an underlisting.

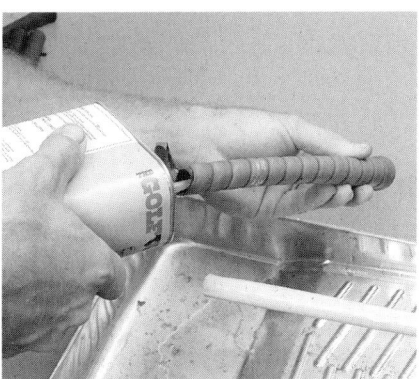

23-117 First, install the grip collar and apply tape as shown in photos 23-76 thorough 23-85. Plug the hole in the butt of the grip with your finger while squirting grip solvent inside the grip.

23-118 Pour the excess solvent over the double-coated tape. Additional solvent may be necessary to completely wet the tape.

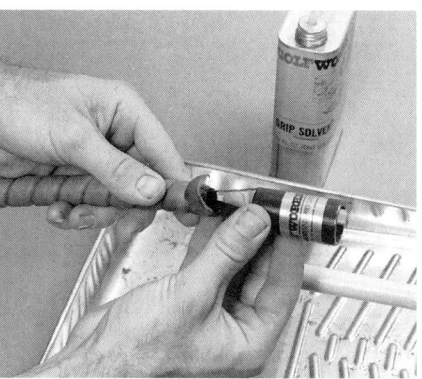

23-119 The slip-on leather grips do not have a ribbed back, so positioning is not a concern. slip the **Grip Installer Tool** inside the mouth of the grip before installation.

23-120 Push the **Grip Installer Tool** and the mouth of the grip over the shaft. Difficulties occur when the shaft butt is larger than the grip core size. Because the leather is wrapped around the underlisting, the underlisting resists expansion. **The Grip Installer Tool is a great help with this situation and should be considered a necessity.**

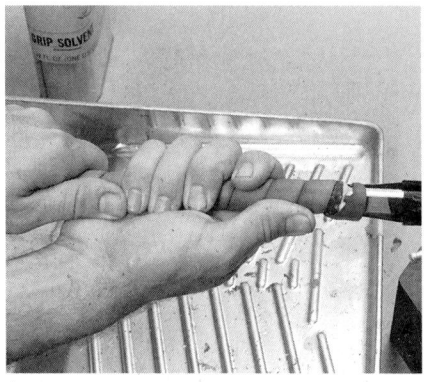

23-121 Once the grip is started on the shaft, turn the grip …

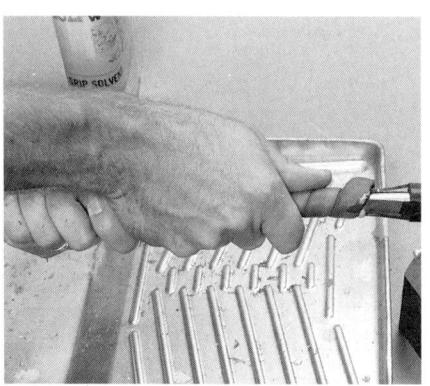

23-122 … clockwise while pushing. This helps as the wrapped underlisting will expand slightly and slide much easier down the shaft.

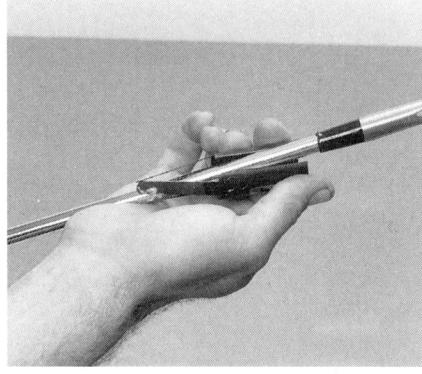

23-123 Once the top of the grip is flush with the shaft butt, slide the Installer Tool down the shaft and remove it.

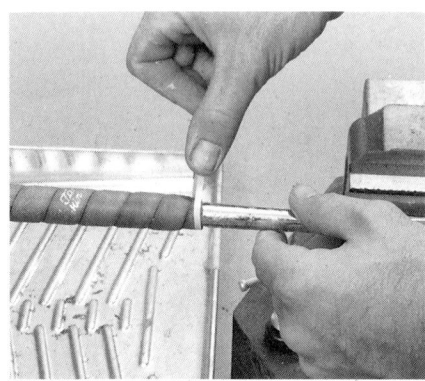

23-124 Once the solvent has evaporated and the grip can no longer turn, wrap the remaining portion of the leather around the shaft. Apply a strip of 1/8" masking tape around the bottom of the grip and finish off the bottom as shown in photos 23-105 through 23-112.

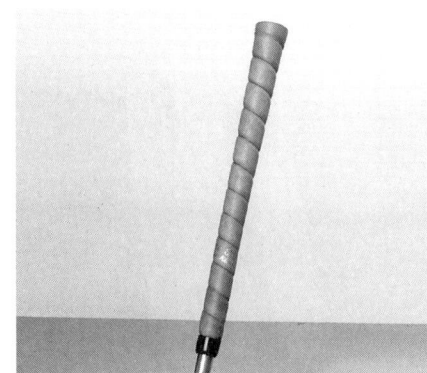

23-125 After installing the grip collar, the grip should look like this, ready for the end cap assembly.

23-126 End caps are available in four sizes: .560, .580, .600 and .620 to match the four common butt diameters. The lock pin and disc are usually included with the end cap.

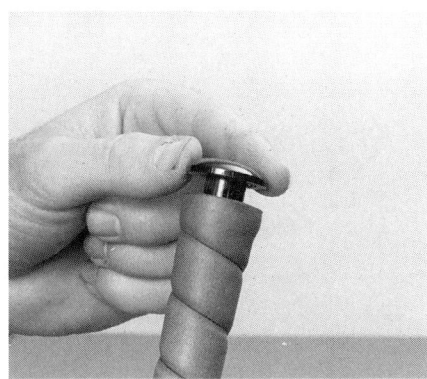

23-127 Select the appropriate end cap and push the plastic plug inside the shaft until the bottom of the cap fits flush with the top of the grip.

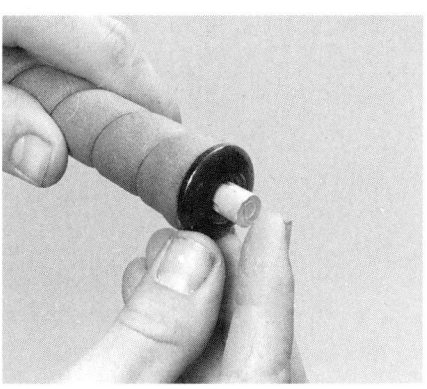

23-128 Place the lock pin inside the plug and tap in gently to the bottom of the plug. The end cap tightens as the pin is pushed farther down the plug, expanding it.

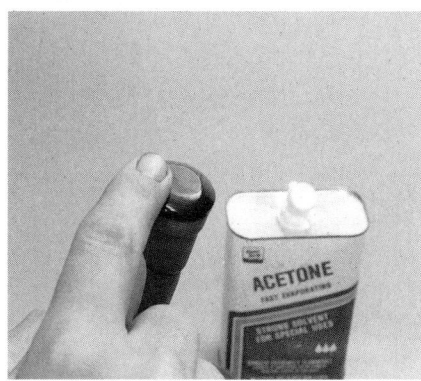

23-129 Secure the disc inside the end cap with a spot of epoxy or dampen the disc with acetone and quickly place it inside the cap. The acetone will temporarily soften the plastic and bond the plastic disc to the plastic end cap.

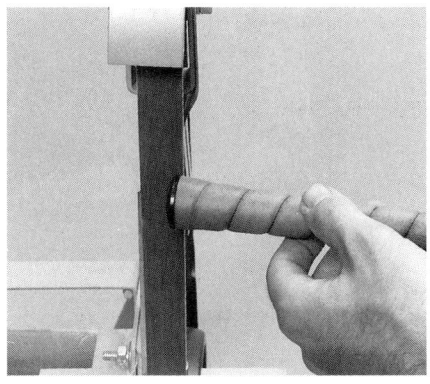

23-130 Rarely will the plastic end cap be flush with the outside of the grip. It can be turned down on a 1" or 2" Belt Sander as shown, or a medium cut file may be used. Use care in either procedure. If the grip is nicked with the sander or file, use the appropriate color shoe polish for touchup.

23-131 Use of clear plastic poly bags gives a professional touch to custom or regripped clubs. They also protect against dust, dirt, etc.

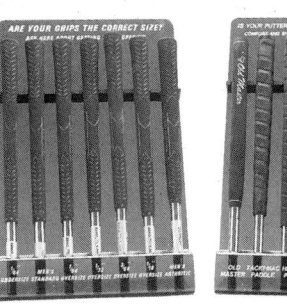

23-132 Special grip racks are available to display various grip sizes and putter grips to promote gripping services.

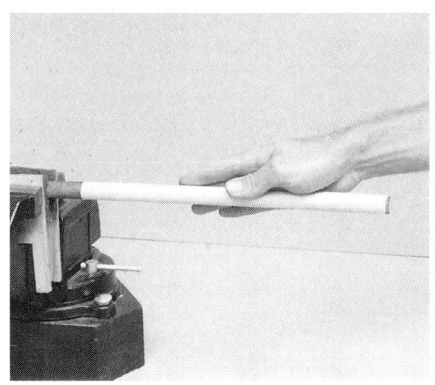

23-133 Applying leather to hickory shafts. Because of the large diameter of hickory shafts, a rubber underlisting is not necessary. Instead, apply a strip of 2" double-coated tape to the butt. If desired, ¾" double-coated tape can be spiral wrapped around the shaft.

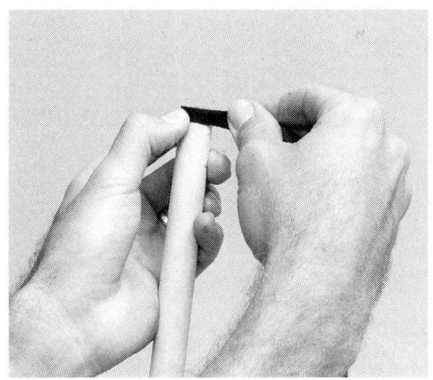

23-134 Place the tapered end of the leather wrap against the top of the shaft. In most cases you will be required to use a strip of leather that is longer than the standard leather strip. Extra long leather strips are available from most golf supply dealers.

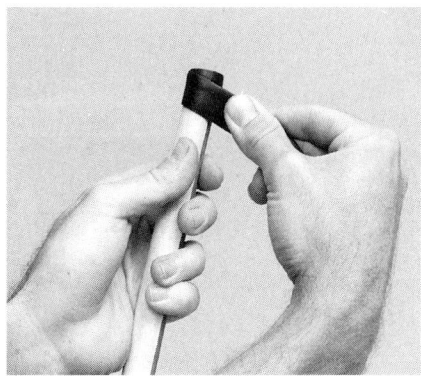

23-135 Encircle the top of the shaft with the leather. Once the beginning of the strip has been overlapped by the leather, start a downward wrapping of the leather. Follow the procedures as shown in photos 23-100 through 23-103.

23-136 Continue to wrap the leather down the shaft to the desired stopping point.

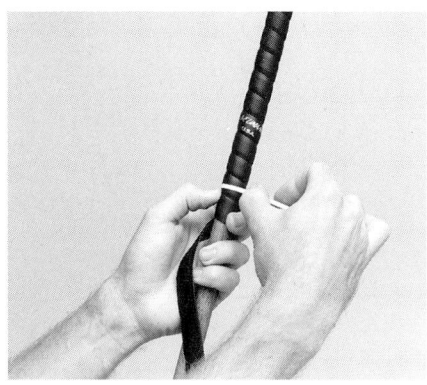

23-137 Once the desired stopping point has been reached, wrap a piece of ⅛" tape around the leather.

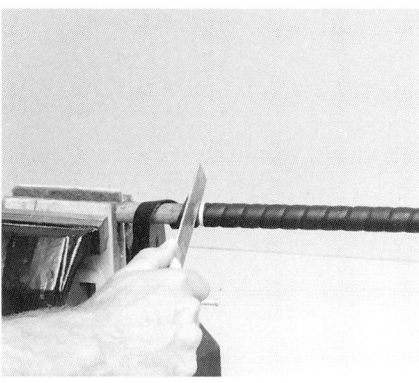

23-138 Using a sharp knife, cut through the leather and discard the excess piece.

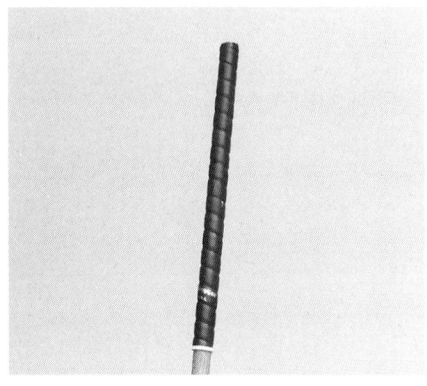

23-139 The leather grip should now look like this. Note the sharp drop from the leather to the shaft.

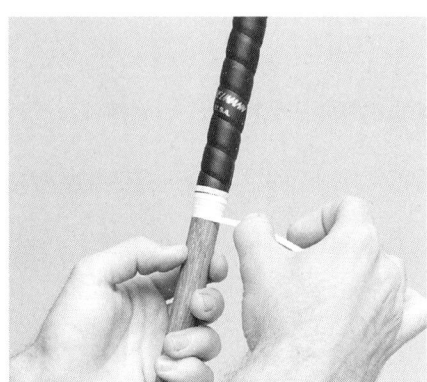

23-140 Using ⅛" masking tape, wrap the tape around the shaft to create a tapered section from the shaft to the grip.

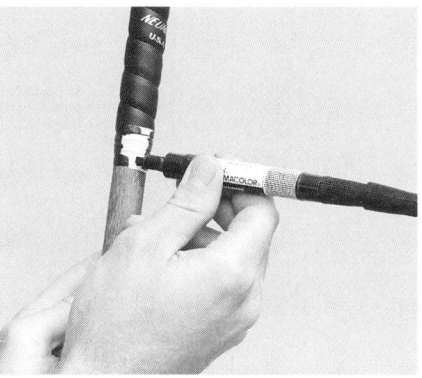

23-141 Camouflage the tape by coloring it with a black felt tip marker.

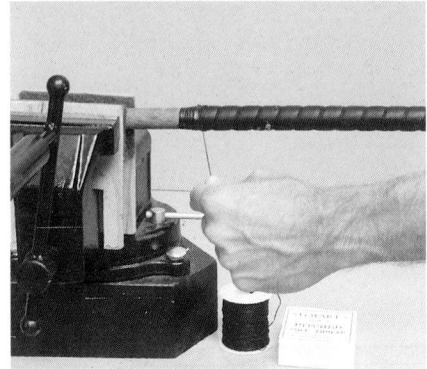

23-142 Finally, apply whipping over the tape from the bottom of the leather to the shaft. Use the same technique as shown in Chapter 6. The correct whipping to use is a pitched linen whipping.

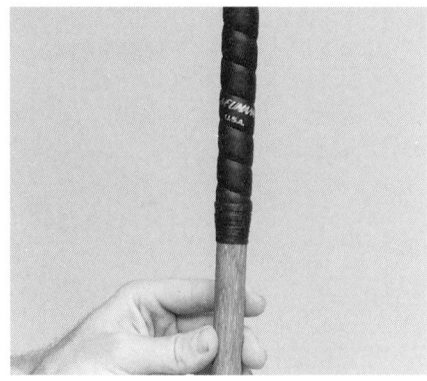

23-143 The bottom of the grip should look like this. Applying pitched whipping ensures a somewhat authentic look to the club.

The steps you have reviewed for installing a grip involved a tape that is activated by a special solvent. Currently, a new tape is being introduced by a number of different companies that requires water for tape activation. This water soluble tape holds great potential for future use. Most of the tapes introduced, however, fail when subjected to temperatures that are common in the summer months. The GolfWorks® is extensively testing all brands of water soluble tape, one of which has finally satisfied our demanding criteria for quality and performance. This new water soluble tape will be available through GolfWorks® publications beginning in 1995.

ADDITIONAL INFORMATION FOR INSTALLING GRIPS AND CHANGING GRIP SIZE
Increasing and Decreasing Grip Sizes by Interchanging Grip Core Sizes

Anyone can learn to put a grip on a golf club in a few minutes time. However, putting the grip on to the correct size and being able to explain a possible increase or decrease in swingweight and total weight to the customer can be quite a bit more involved. When I used to start off a repair class at The GolfWorks® with regripping, a great majority of students initially feel it is a waste of their time since they have been regripping clubs for years. As the lesson continues, however, their opinions rapidly change as they find a whole new understanding in regripping. The main thrust in the repair schools concerning regripping is to be able to determine exactly what size a certain grip will install to before the club is gripped. Many times I have seen someone cut off an old grip, install a new one, and if the size feels a little small they quickly slide it off and wrap on another layer of tape. This is totally unnecessary if you understand the code numbers used on grips and how they match up to the various size shaft butts.

The grip core size, sometimes referred to as the mandrel size, is located just inside the mouth of the grip. See photo 23-41 and Fig. 23-144. Each grip manufacturer identifies its grips differently. Eaton® Molded Products Co. is the largest grip manufacturer and consequently, this is the most popular "after market" replacement grip used today. Eaton's® code numbers inside the mouth of their grips are easy to interpret. Usually you will find a single letter designation followed by 2 numerals. The letter designation will be either (M) men's, (L) ladies' or (J) juniors'. The 2 numerals indicate the grip core size or mandrel size such as 58, 60 or 62. The grip core size is made to match a corresponding shaft butt size such as .580, .600 or .620. The proper interpretation of all these letters and numbers is this: an M58 grip installed on a .580 diameter butt shaft will measure to a men's standard diameter when using 1 layer of double-coated tape. Men's standard diameter is defined in Table 23-1.

If an M58 grip is installed on a .600 diameter butt shaft, the grip will measure slightly over $\frac{1}{64}$" larger than the men's standard size. If an M58 grip is installed on a .620 diameter butt shaft, the grip will measure slightly over $\frac{1}{32}$" larger than men's standard size. In each case stated above, the smaller grip core size is being stretched over the larger shaft butt sizes and consequently it is being stretched to a larger than standard size according to the designation inside the mouth of the grip.

A grip can be stretched quite a bit. As long as the grip core size is smaller than the shaft butt diameter, it can be used satisfactorily assuming it is understood that it will install oversize.

A grip core size can also be selected that is actually larger than the shaft butt diameter. This will cause the grip to be installed undersize. The grip core size should never be more than one size larger than the shaft butt size when making a grip undersize. For example: An M60 grip installed on a .580 diameter shaft butt will measure slightly less than $\frac{1}{64}$" smaller than men's standard size. There are also other methods of installing grips undersize. One method is shown in photos 23-67 through 23-70 whereby the grip is stretched farther down the shaft when installing it, causing it to decrease in size by approximately $\frac{1}{64}$" when stretched $\frac{3}{4}$ to 1" longer. The grip, however, must be stretched evenly over its entire length and not just stretched down at the bottom end.

Another method for reducing men's grip sizes is to use ladies' grips. The difference in standard men's grips and standard ladies' grips is slightly more than $\frac{3}{64}$". So, as an example, if an L58 grip is installed on a .580 diameter butt shaft, the grip will measure standard ladies' size and also $\frac{3}{64}$" undersize men's. If an L56 grip is installed on a .580 diameter butt shaft, the grip will measure slightly over $1/64$" larger than standard ladies' size and $1/32$" undersize men's.

Now refer to Tables 23-1, 23-2, 23-3, 23-4, 23-5 and 23-6 which put this information in quick-to-use form.

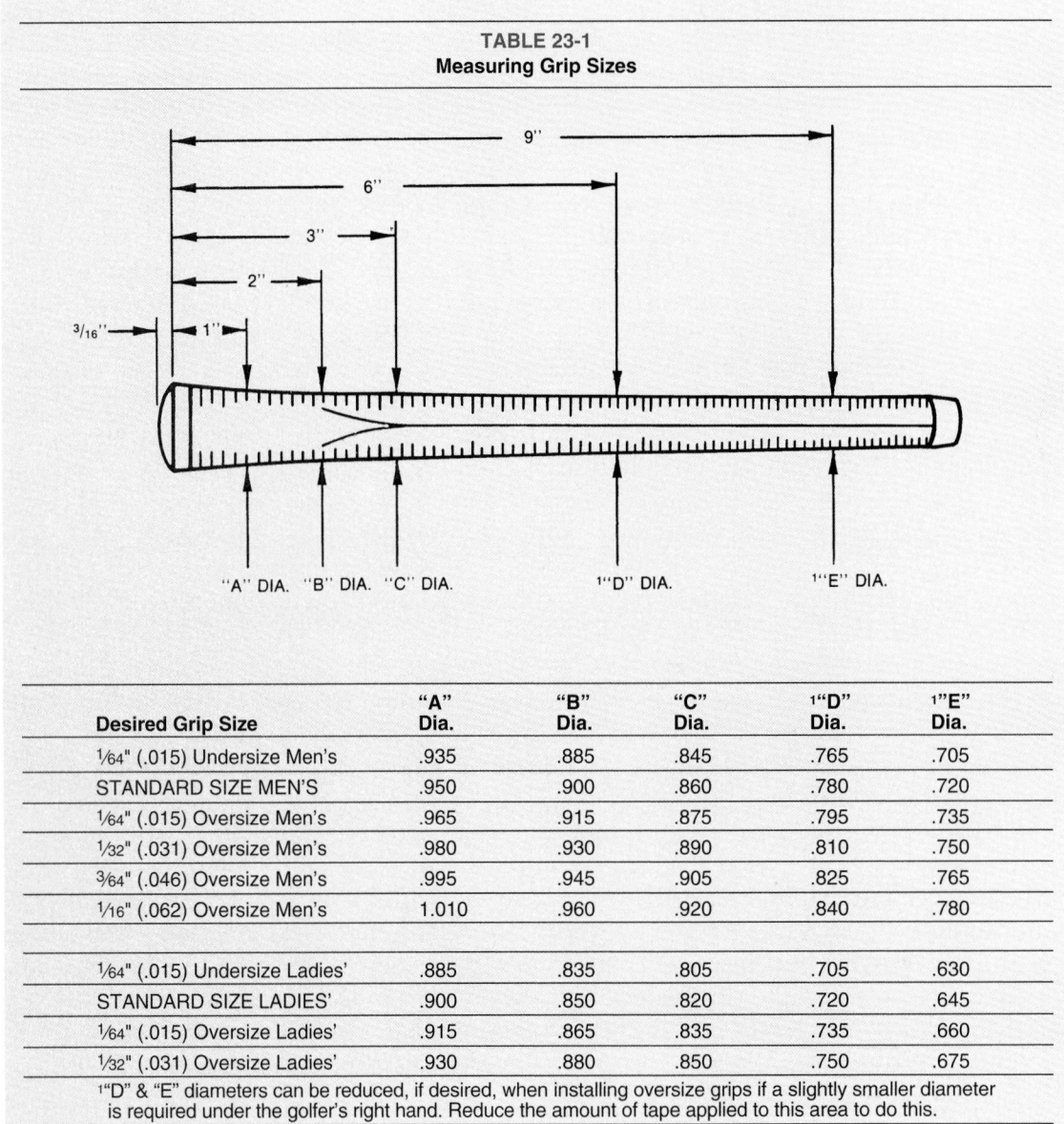

TABLE 23-1
Measuring Grip Sizes

Desired Grip Size	"A" Dia.	"B" Dia.	"C" Dia.	1"D" Dia.	1"E" Dia.
$1/64$" (.015) Undersize Men's	.935	.885	.845	.765	.705
STANDARD SIZE MEN'S	.950	.900	.860	.780	.720
$1/64$" (.015) Oversize Men's	.965	.915	.875	.795	.735
$1/32$" (.031) Oversize Men's	.980	.930	.890	.810	.750
$3/64$" (.046) Oversize Men's	.995	.945	.905	.825	.765
$1/16$" (.062) Oversize Men's	1.010	.960	.920	.840	.780
$1/64$" (.015) Undersize Ladies'	.885	.835	.805	.705	.630
STANDARD SIZE LADIES'	.900	.850	.820	.720	.645
$1/64$" (.015) Oversize Ladies'	.915	.865	.835	.735	.660
$1/32$" (.031) Oversize Ladies'	.930	.880	.850	.750	.675

1"D" & "E" diameters can be reduced, if desired, when installing oversize grips if a slightly smaller diameter is required under the golfer's right hand. Reduce the amount of tape applied to this area to do this.

TABLE 23-2
Grip Size Table @ 2" Down From Top of Grip

Designation	Relative Size	Measurement @ 2" Down From Top of Grip "B" Diameter	
		Men's Diameter	Ladies' Diameter
Extra Large	$1/16$" oversize	.960"	.910"
Very Large	$3/64$" oversize	.945"	.895"
Large	$1/32$" oversize	.930"	.880"
Slightly Larger	$1/64$" oversize	.915"	.865"
Average	Standard Size	.900"	.850"
Slightly Smaller	$1/64$" undersize	.885"	.835"
Very Small	$1/32$" undersize	.870"	.820"

TABLE 23-3
Matching Grip Size to Shaft Butt Diameter – Eaton® Grips

[2]When You Use an Eaton® Grip With Identification on Mouth of Grip as Follows:	[1]Shaft Butt Diameter to Produce Standard Grip Size
"M56"	.560
"M58"	.580
"M60"	.600
"M62"	.620
"L54"	.540
"L56"	.560
"L58"	.580
"L60"	.600
#12	.375
#16 or J50	.500
#17	.560
#18	.580
#19	.600
#20	.620

[1]To determine shaft butt diameter use either a vernier caliper, micrometer or the "Grip Size and Shaft Butt Gauge" available from The GolfWorks®.
[2]M (Men's), L (Ladies'), J (Junior)

TABLE 23-4
Producing Standard and Oversize Grips By Interchanging Grip Sizes – Eaton® Grips

Men's or Ladies' Sizes	Shaft Butt Diameter	To Produce Standard Size Grip Use the Following	[1]To Produce Oversize Grip (approx. 1/64" over) Use the Following	[1]To Produce Oversize Grip (approx. 1/32" over) Use the Following
Men's	.580	M58	Use additional tape	Use additional tape
	.600	M60	M58	[2]M56
	.620	M62	M60	M58
Ladies'	.560	L56	L54	M58
	.580	L58	L56	L54 or M60
	.600	L60	L58	L58 or M62

[1]If you do not happen to have these grip sizes to produce oversize grips, refer to Table 23-7 "Tape Wrapping Information to Produce Oversize Grips."
[2]M56 grips are only available in "Men's Crown" model from Eaton®.

TABLE 23-5
Producing Standard and Undersize Grips By Interchanging Grip Sizes – Eaton® Grips

Men's or Ladies' Sizes	Shaft Butt Diameter	To Produce Standard Size Grip Use the Following	To Produce Undersize Grip (approx. 1/64" under) Use the Following	To Produce Undersize Grip (approx. 1/32" under) Use the Following
Men's	.580	M58	M60 or M58 stretched down 3/4"	L56 or M60 stretched down 3/4"
	.600	M60	M62 or M60 stretched down 3/4"	L58 or M26 stretched down 3/4"
	.620	M62	L58 or M62 stretched down 3/4"	L60 or L58 stretched down 3/4"
Ladies'	.560	L56	L58 or L56 stretched down 3/4"	L58 stretched down 3/4"
	.580	L58	L60 or L58 stretched down 3/4"	L60 stretched down 3/4"
	.600	L60	L60 stretched down 3/4"	Not Advised

For procedure on stretching grips down to reduce their size, see photos 23-67 through 23-70.

TABLE 23-6
Producing Standard, Oversize and Undersize Grips
by Interchanging Grip Sizes – Tacki-Mac® Grips

Men's & Ladies' Sizes	Tacki-Mac® Model Number	Grip Core Size	[1]Shaft Butt Diameter					GolfWorks® Catalog Code Number	Pattern on Grip	Round or Rib
			.560	.580	.600	.620	.700			
Men's Standard	Model 11	58	No	Std.	+1/64	+1/32	No	MSB58	Knurled Wrap	Round
Men's Standard	Model 11	60	No	No	Std.	+1/64	No	MSB60	Knurled Wrap	Round
Men's Standard	Model 11	62	No	No	No	Std.	No	MSB62	Knurled Wrap	Round
Men's Oversize	Model 13	58	No	+1/32	+3/64	+1/16	No	MOB58	Golfer Wrap	Round
Men's Oversize	Model 13	60	No	No	+1/32	+3/64	No	MOB60	Golfer Wrap	Round
Men's Oversize	Model 13	62	No	No	No	+1/32	No	MOB62	Golfer Wrap	Round
Ladies' Standard	Model 33	56	Std.	+1/64	+1/32	+1/16	No	LSU56	Starburst Wrap	Round

[1]Above sizes are based upon installation without the use of double-coated tape. Sizes different from those above, however, can be made by using buildup tape and double-coated tape. See Table 23-7.

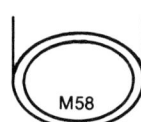

[1] **Check the letters and numbers in the mouth of the grip to determine the size.**
Each grip has a letter and an identifying number.

[2] **Grip Designations**
M58   Indicates that grip has a reminder rib (no "R" after number) and will install to standard men's grip size on a .580 diameter butt shaft.
M58R Indicates that grip is round ("R" after number) and will install to standard men's grip size on a .580 diameter butt shaft.

[3] **Underlisting Designations**
RM58 Indicates that underlisting has a reminder rib ("R") and will install to standard men's size (after leather is installed over it) on a .580 diameter butt shaft.
SM58 Indicates that underlisting is round ("S") and will install to standard men's size (after leather is installed over it) on a .580 diameter butt shaft.

Notes:

[1] Not every grip model is available in every size.

[2] The first letter in the mouth of the grip indicates the general use of the grip: M-Men's, L-Ladies', J-Juniors'. Refer to these and the code markings noted above. All other numbers and letters in the grips are for grip manufacturer's reference only.

[3] Underlistings can be built up and reduced in size using the same procedures and methods described for grips. Using buildup tape, interchanging grip core sizes and stretching down the underlisting are all acceptable methods. Remember, you should never buildup a leather grip by applying multiple layers of tape on top of the underlisting.

FIG. 23-144
Information for identifying Eaton® Grips and Underlistings

Increasing Grip Sizes by Applying Additional Buildup Tape

Buildup tape is nothing more than crepe masking tape. It is available in many widths but the most popular ones used in regripping are the ¾" and 2" widths. Each roll is 60 yards long, fairly inexpensive and easy to find in your local hardware department. A number of people use the expensive double-coated tape applied in multiple layers for building grips up. Not only is this three times more costly, but it is much more difficult to work with than ordinary masking tape.

Grip buildup procedures using masking tape are shown in photos 23-45 through 23-51. An important point to keep in mind when building grips up using tape is that the tape has a certain amount of weight and will, depending on how much is used, counterbalance the club (reduce swingweight by increasing grip end weight) and at the same time increase total weight, again depending on the amount of tape used. Table 23-7 has been developed to provide information on how much each layer of tape increases the grip size and its equivalent reduction in swingweight and increase in total weight.

TABLE 23-7
Tape Wrapping Information to Produce Oversize Grips

Description	[1]Increase in Diameter	Weight of Tape	[2]Swingweight Equivalent
¾" masking tape (overlap wrap)	.02" slightly more than 1/64"	.1 ounce	$-¾$
¾" masking tape (single layer wrap)	.01" slightly more than 1/64"	.05 ounce	$-⅓$
¾" masking tape (overlap wrap plus single layer wrap)	.03" exactly 1/32"	.15 ounce	-1
2" masking tape (each layer lengthwise)	.01" slightly less than 1/64"	.05 ounce	$-⅓$
¾" or 2" width double-coated tape (single layer wrap)	.01" slightly less than 1/64"	.05 ounce	$-⅓$

[1]For converting decimals to fractions, use the following:
    .015" = 1/64"   .031" = 1/32"   .046" = 3/64"   .062" = 1/16"
[2]Swingweight Equivalent. Example: Assume a D-2 driver with no changes other than one additional overlap wrapping of ¾" masking tape to increase the grip diameter. The resulting increased weight because of the additional tape will decrease the swingweight by approximately ¾. See Fig. 23-145. Swingweight equivalent is approximately the same for both woods and irons.

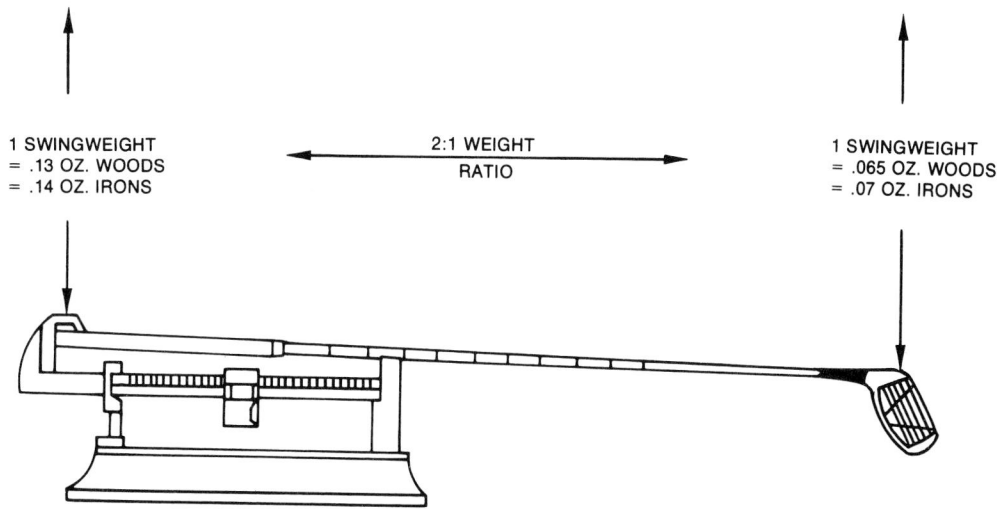

1 SWINGWEIGHT
= .13 OZ. WOODS
= .14 OZ. IRONS

2:1 WEIGHT
RATIO

1 SWINGWEIGHT
= .065 OZ. WOODS
= .07 OZ. IRONS

FIG. 23-145
Equivalent head weight and grip end weight to equal 1 swingweight

Most people that regrip use the ¾" width masking tape and ¾" width double-coated tape vs. the 2" width tape. The reason for this is more tradition than anything else. Most people have learned regripping procedures using the ¾" tape and have continued to use it. There is absolutely nothing wrong with using ¾" width tapes other than they are slightly costlier in material and require substantially more labor.

287

Study Tables 23-8 and 23-9, which provide cost comparison figures and the number of clubs you can expect to regrip from each roll of tape. One argument against using 2" tape is that some of the fine professional players feel where the tape overlaps that it increases the amount of rib under the grip. This is true, however, after making up a number of test grip sizes using both ¾" and 2" tapes, it takes at least a 1⁄32" additional buildup (3 lengths of 2" buildup plus 1 length of 2" double-coated) to be detected by feel in the reminder rib increase. For most of those detecting the increase, it was a more desirable feel. It should also be noted that during this test the individual had the opportunity to constantly switch back and forth from grip to grip thus making it easier to compare differences in feel. I seriously doubt if anyone can just pick up a regripped club and tell you that it feels as if 2" width tape was used instead of ¾". Also, you can apply the buildup tape by varying the position of the overlap so that it does not accumulatively buildup in only the rib area of the grip. I prefer to overlap the 2" tape at the rib since, as previously stated, it gives most players a better feeling to have a little larger rib.

TABLE 23-8
¾" and 2" Buildup Crepe Masking Tape: Usage and Cost Comparison

Tape Width	Tape Length	Amount of Tape Used Per Club	[2] Approx. Amount of Time To Apply Tape	No. of Clubs Per Roll of Tape	[1] Cost Per Roll of Tape	Cost of Tape Per Club
¾"	60 yards	25"	30 sec.	86.4	$1.10	1.27¢
2"	60 yards	9"	10 sec.	240	$2.70	1.12¢

[1] Cost based on average 1994 prices.
[2] Time varies with individual and technique.

Summary:
Cost wise, 2" tape is 13% less than ¾" when computed on a cost per club basis. If you use 2", you save approximately 36¢ per roll on a cost vs. number of clubs comparison with ¾".
Labor wise, 2" tape is approximately 3 times faster to install or a 66% saving in labor vs ¾" tape.

TABLE 23-9
¾" and 2" Double-Coated Tape: Usage and Cost Comparison

Tape Width	Tape Length	Amount of Tape Used Per Club	[2] Approx. Amount of Time To Apply Tape	No. of Clubs Per Roll of Tape	[1] Cost Per Roll of Tape	Cost of Tape Per Club
¾"	36 yards	25"	30 sec.	51.8	$3.50	6.75¢
2"	36 yards	9"	10 sec.	144	$7.25	5.03¢

[1] Cost based on average 1994 prices.
[2] Time varies with individual and technique.

Summary:
Cost wise, 2" tape is 25% less than ¾" when computed on a cost per club basis. If you use 2" double-coated tape, you save approximately $1.55 per roll on a cost vs. number of clubs comparison with ¾".
Labor wise, 2" tape is approximately 3 times faster to install or a 66% saving in labor vs ¾" tape.

A Specific Example to Help Understand How Regripping Affects Other Club Specifications

Now that an abundant amount of information has been compiled, it is time to explain how to apply this information using a specific example.

A customer requests that their present "Eagle" standard size rubber grip be changed to an "All Cord" grip 1⁄32" oversize on a D-3 driver. At this point, you should be able to calculate approximately what is going to happen to swingweight and total weight from this change.

1. The swingweight will decrease by approximately 3.5 swingweights.

2. The total weight or static weight will increase by approximately .45 ounces.

3. If desired, weight can be added to the head to readjust the club to its original D-3 swingweight by adding .23 ounces to the head weight. Of course, the total weight will again be increased by an additional .23 ounces for a total overall weight increase of .68 ounces.

The information listed above was determined at follows:

To Determine the Swingweight Change:

First, you assume that the present "Eagle" grip weighs approximately 1.65 ounces compared to an "All Cord" grip which weighs approximately 1.95 ounces (refer to Table 23-10). Next, from Table 23-7 you determine that it will take approximately .15 ounces of additional tape to achieve a $\frac{1}{32}$" (.031") oversize grip. (One overlap wrap weighing .1 ounces and increasing the diameter by .02" plus one single layer wrap weighing .05 ounces and increasing the diameter by .01", giving a total weight increase of .15 ounces for the tape and a total size increase of $\frac{1}{32}$" (.031).)

Next, calculate the increase in total weight:

$\frac{1}{32}$" oversize "All Cord" total grip weight (includes tape also)	2.10 oz.
Less the original "Eagle" total grip weight	1.65 oz.
TOTAL WEIGHT INCREASE FROM GRIP CHANGE	.45 oz.

Next, refer to Fig. 23-145 and note that a change of .13 ounces in the grip end weight or .065 ounce in head weight is equivalent to 1 swingweight (divide .45 ounces by .13 to obtain an answer of approximately a 3½ point swingweight decrease).

To Determine the Total Weight Change:

The total or static weight change has already been determined to be .45 ounces or the difference in weight between the original "Eagle" grip and the new "All Cord" grip plus the additional weight of the tape used to make it $\frac{1}{32}$" oversize.

Assume that it is desirable to restore the driver to its original swingweight. Again refer to Fig. 23-145 and you will see that for each swingweight decrease caused by the additional grip and weight that .065 ounce will have to be added to the head weight. So multiply the 3½ point swingweight decrease by .065 ounce to obtain an answer of .23 ounces of weight that must be added to the head to restore the original swingweight of D-3 in the example driver.

To make this more clear, a summary of the original specifications and the new specifications of the example driver are shown below to compare the net effect of the grip and size change on both swingweight and total weight.

Summary for the Example Used			
Description	Swingweight	Total Weight	Total Weight Increase From Original
Original Driver with "Eagle" grip (standard size)	D-3	13.25 oz.	0
Install $\frac{1}{32}$" oversize "All Cord" grip (No swingweight adjustment)	C-9½	13.70 oz.	+.45 oz.
Install $\frac{1}{32}$" oversize "All Cord" grip (swingweight adjusted by adding head weight)	D-3	13.93 oz.	+.68 oz.

TABLE 23-10
General Information on Grips

Grip Style, Model or Pattern	Grip Material	Manufacturer	Length of Grip	[1]Grip Weight[4] (Approx.)	Men's or Ladies'
Victory M58	Rubber and cork	Eaton®	10⅝"	1.83 oz.	Men's
Victory 2000 M58	Rubber and cork	Eaton®	10²³⁄₃₂"	1.83 oz.	Men's
Crown M58	Rubber and cork	Eaton®	11"	1.89 oz.	Men's
Arrow M58	Rubber and cork	Eaton®	10¾"	1.74 oz.	Men's
Classic Cushion M60	Rubber and cork	Eaton®	10⅜"	1.72 oz.	Men's
Tour Wrap M58	Rubber and cork	Eaton®	10²³⁄₃₂"	1.90 oz.	Men's
Dimple M58	Rubber and cork	Eaton®	10¹⁷⁄₃₂"	1.78 oz.	Men's
Victory 2000 Cord M58	Rubber and cord	Eaton®	10²⁷⁄₃₂"	1.86 oz.	Men's
Victory Velvet Cord M58	Rubber and cord	Eaton®	10⅞"	1.80 oz.	Men's
Crown Cord M58	Rubber and cord	Eaton®	10¹¹⁄₁₆"	1.95 oz	Men's
Classic Cord M58	Rubber and cord	Eaton®	10¹¹⁄₁₆"	1.95 oz.	Men's
Dimple Cord M58	Rubber and cord	Eaton®	10¹¹⁄₁₆"	1.80 oz.	Men's
Crown L56	Rubber and cork	Eaton®	10¹⁵⁄₃₂"	1.58 oz.	Ladies'
Dimple L56	Rubber and cork	Eaton®	10½"	1.50 oz.	Ladies'
Arrow L56	Rubber and cork	Eaton®	10¾"	1.55 oz.	Ladies'
Victory L56	Rubber and cork	Eaton®	10⅝"	1.74 oz.	Ladies'
Victory 2000 L56	Rubber and cork	Eaton®	10¹¹⁄₁₆"	1.83 oz.	Ladies'
Victory Cord L58	Rubber and cord	Eaton®	10¹³⁄₁₆"	1.66 oz.	Ladies'
Spiral Wrap Grip (slip-on type)	Leather	Lamkin®	10⅜"	1.75 oz.	Men's
Conquest 58	Rubber and cork	Lamkin®	10½"	1.75 oz.	Men's
Silhouette 590	Rubber and cork	Lamkin®	10½"	2.00 oz.	Men's
Silhouette 580	Rubber and cork	Lamkin®	10½"	2.00 oz.	Ladies'
Black Panel (slip-on type)	Leather	Lamkin®	10½"	1.75 oz.	Men's
Ultra Tac Tour	Rubber and cork	Lamkin®	10½"	1.75 oz.	Men's
Ultra Classic	Rubber and cork	Lamkin®	10½"	1.75 oz.	Men's
Seamless	Rubber	Lamkin®	10½"	1.65 oz.	Men's
[2]Chamois CM	Rubber	Avon®	10½"	1.87 oz.	Men's
Chamois CL	Rubber	Avon®	10½"	1.41 oz.	Ladies'
Charger 58	Rubber	Avon®	10½"	1.90 oz.	Men's
Nexus 58	Rubber	Avon®	10½"	1.90 oz.	Men's
Spiral Wrapped Grip (Hand wound type)	Cowhide or calf	Neumann®	10½"	[3]1.95 oz.	Men's
Underlisting	Rubber	Eaton®	10½"	1.20 oz.	Men's
Knurl Pattern 58	Krayton and rubber	Tacki-Mac®	10⅜"	1.80 oz.	Men's
³⁄₆₄" Oversize Herringbone 58	Krayton and rubber	Tacki-Mac®	10"	2.00 oz.	Men's
Tour Pro Perforated 58	Krayton and rubber	Tacki-Mac®	10¾"	1.70 oz.	Men's
³⁄₃₂" Oversize 58	Krayton and rubber	Tacki-Mac®	10"	2.70 oz.	Men's
Ladies' 58 (standard)	Krayton and rubber	Tacki-Mac®	9¾"	1.35 oz.	Ladies'

[1]Weights can vary due to the grip manufacturer's tolerances and also because of the different grip core sizes in each style that are available. As a very general rule, an M60 core size grip will weigh ¹⁄₂₀ ounce (1½ grams) lighter than an M58. An M62 core size grip will weigh ¹⁄₁₀ ounce (3 grams) lighter than an M60. Use the weights above as a comparative measure when changing from one grip type and/or size to another.

[2]"CM" inside the mouth of a chamois grip designates "Chamois Men's Size." Likewise a "CL" indicates "Chamois Ladies' Size."

[3]1.95 ounces includes the Neumann leather strip, one layer of double-coated tape and an Eaton® rubber underlisting.

[4]To convert grip weights to fractions, use the following:
   1.75 = 1¾, 1.5 = 1½, 1.65 = 1²¹⁄₃₂, 1.95 = 1⁶¹⁄₆₄, 1.45 = 1²⁹⁄₆₄, 1.6 = 1¹⁹⁄₃₂.
To convert grip weights to grams, multiply the weight shown above in ounces by 28.35.
Example: A 1.83 ounce Victory grip is 51.8 grams.

A Final Word on Regripping

The process of simply regripping a golf club takes place thousands of times every single day. It is very easy to learn how to regrip golf clubs by cutting off the old grip and slipping on a new one. Part of the purpose of this chapter, however, is to provide a sound working knowledge of why regripping can alter other club specifications. The information at the end of this chapter should answer the "why" aspect and give you the personal satisfaction of being able to explain to your customer what will happen to the golf club when it is brought in for regripping.

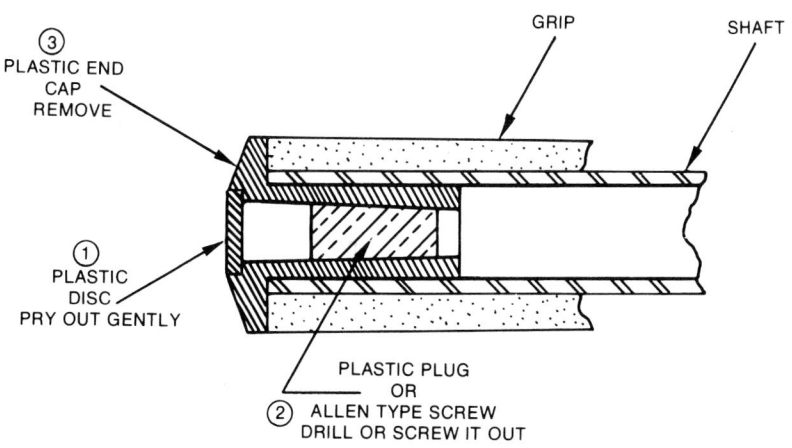

FIG. 23-146
Plastic end cap removal

NOTES

CHAPTER 24

CHANGING LENGTHS OF GOLF CLUBS

Changing the length of a golf club is a relatively simple procedure by itself. When a golf club's length is changed, however, various other specifications of the golf club are directly affected. More specifically, total weight, swingweight, shaft flex and lie are affected enough that when a length change is made, each one of these specifications should be considered and possibly adjusted. For a basic comparison, consider the following example of an average driver changed only by increasing it ½" in length from 43" to 43½".

Total weight: Increased by 3⁄16 to ¼ ounce.

Swingweight: Increases 3 swingweights (shorter clubs are less affected).

Shaft Flex: Will feel slightly more flexible.

Lie: Although the actual absolute lie angle remains the same, the ½" increase in club length will make the club appear 1° more upright and the toe will be slightly higher off the ground.

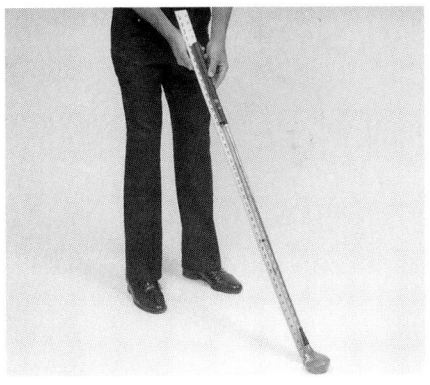

24-1 First, accurately measure the club length. This photo shows the club in a normal lie position with a **48" rule**r placed close behind it. The length is read from the top of the grip cap.

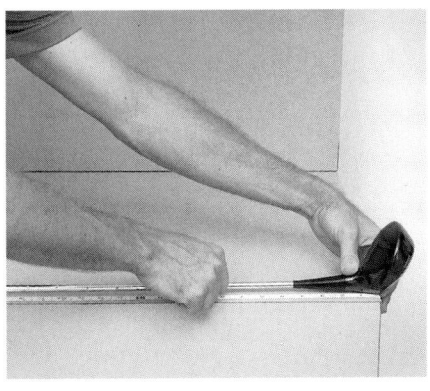

24-2 Another way to measure club length is to install a self-adhesive measuring tape to the top of the workbench. The drawback here is that this fails to pick up the distance between the bottom of the sole radius and the back of the heel. This method, however, is good for comparative length check (i.e. differences in lengths from one club to another).

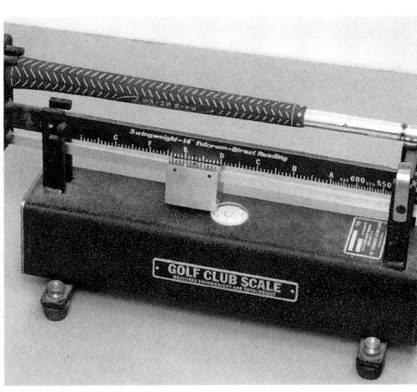

24-3 Check the swingweight before changing the club length.

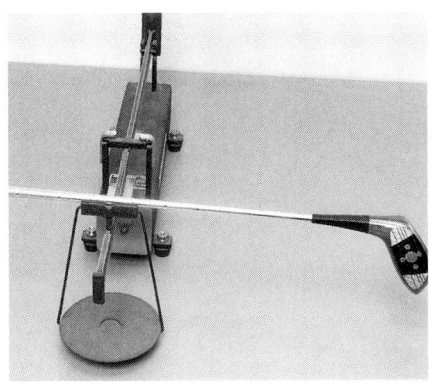

24-4 Check the total weight before changing the club length.

24-5 Check the grip size if either the old grip or a new one is to be installed.

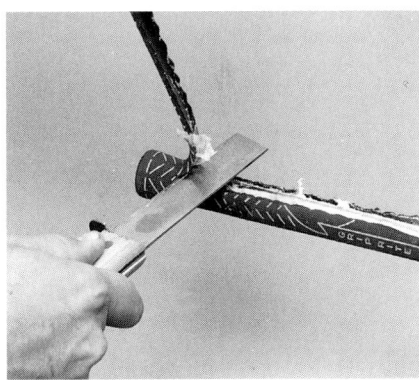

24-6 Remove the grip by cutting it off, or …

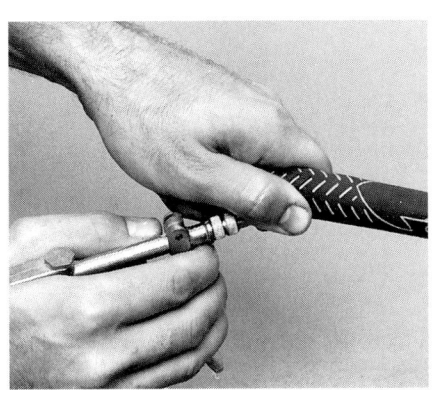

24-7 … remove the grip using a **Pressurized Grip Remover** which injects solvent under the grip through a hypodermic needle. Wear eye protection. For procedure, see Chapter 23, photos 23-31 through 23-37.

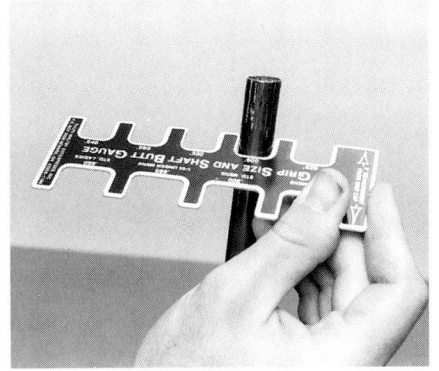

24-8 Determine the shaft butt size. Shown is the **Grip Size and Shaft Butt Gauge**. A vernier caliper or micrometer will also work.

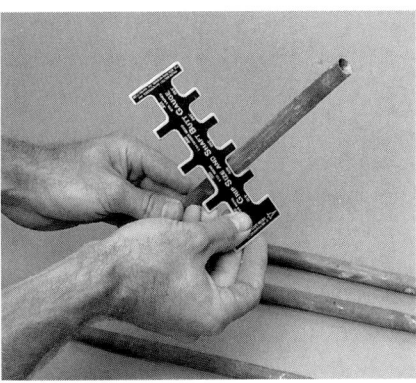

24-9 To lengthen a steel shaft, first check the size of the steel shaft butt extension to be sure it matches the butt size. Steel butt extensions are available to fit .560, .580, .600 and .620 shaft butts.

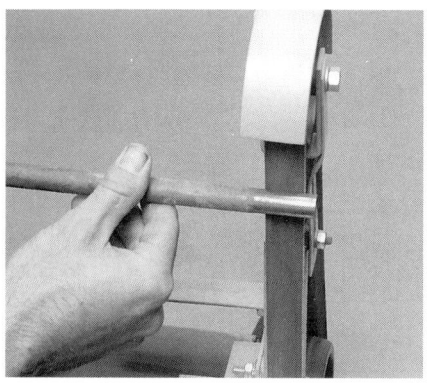

24-10 Light abrading of the reduced section of the shaft extension will ensure good adhesion between the epoxy and extension.

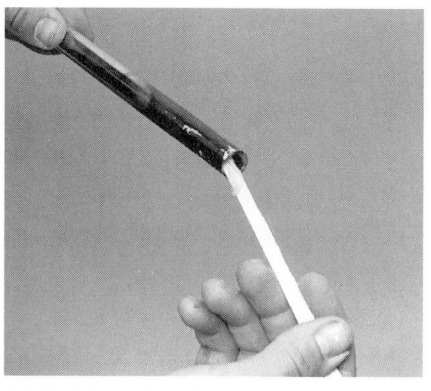

24-11 Mix and apply epoxy inside the shaft butt. Any high shear strength shafting type epoxy is sufficient.

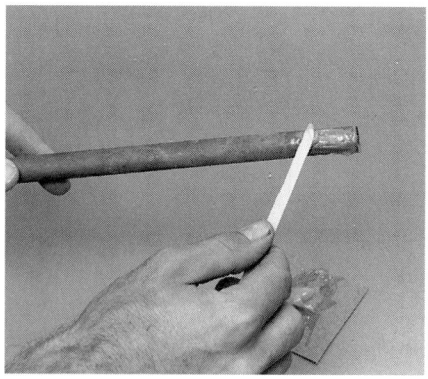

24-12 Apply epoxy to the outside of the reduced section of the shaft extension.

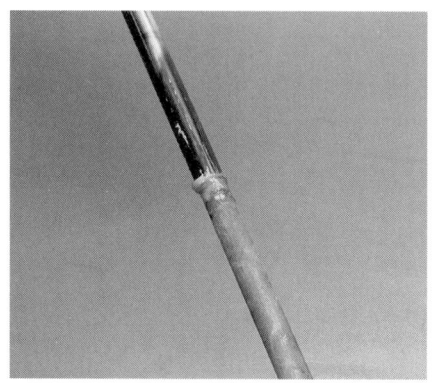

24-13 Install the reduced section of the extension inside the shaft butt. Push the extension down into the shaft until the enlarged portion of the extension rests against the shaft butt. Wipe off any excess epoxy.

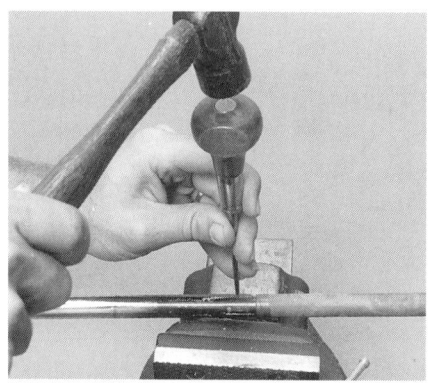

24-14 Make 2 or 3 indentations around the top of the shaft with an awl to ensure the extension will not come loose. Make marks 1" down from the top of the shaft.

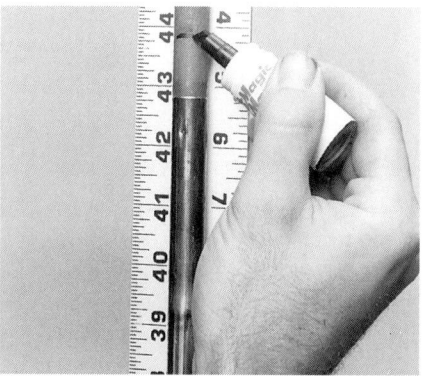

24-15 After the epoxy has cured, measure and make a mark on the extension where you wish to make your cut. Remember to make the mark ⅛" below the desired length as the grip cap will account for an additional ⅛".

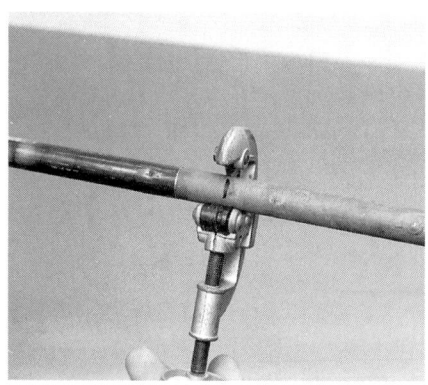

24-16 Cut the shaft extension using a **Tubing Cutter**, the edge of a grinding wheel or a steel friction wheel.

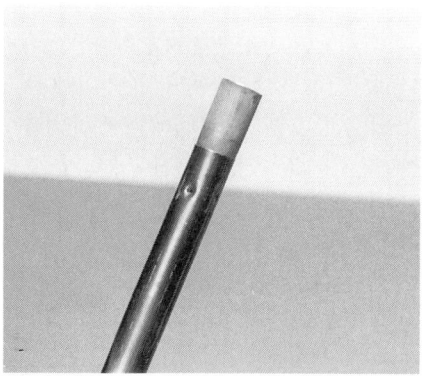

24-17 This photo shows the installed extension cut to length.

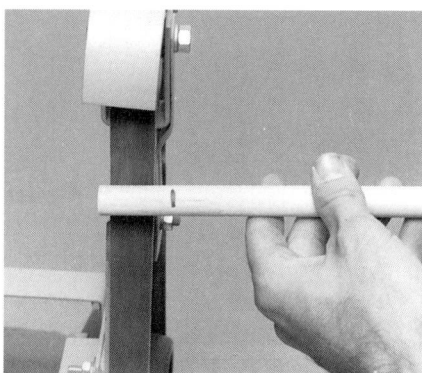

24-18 ⅝" diameter hardwood dowels can also be used as a substitute for steel shaft butt extensions. This photo shows the end of a dowel being turned down on a **1" x 42" Belt Sander** to fit inside the shaft butt.

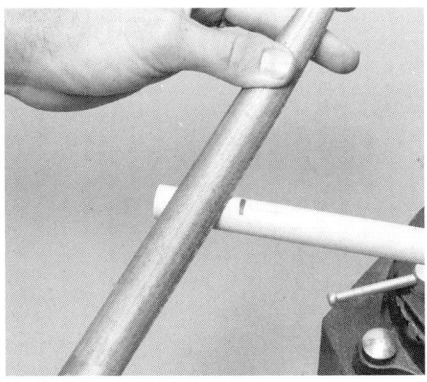

24-19 A wood rasp or coarse cut file can also be used to turn down the end of a wood dowel. Note the mark on the extension. Make sure the reduced section which fits inside the shaft butt is a minimum of 1½" long and preferably 2" long.

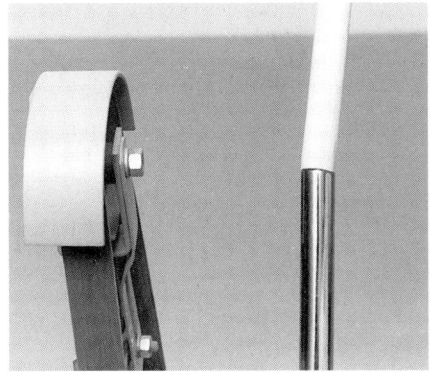

24-20 Periodically test fit the dowel in the shaft butt. When the extension fits snugly inside the shaft …

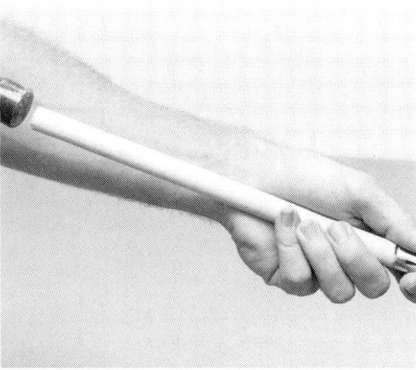

24-21 … mix and apply epoxy to both the inside of the shaft and to the reduced section of the dowel. Drive the reduced section of the dowel into the shaft butt.

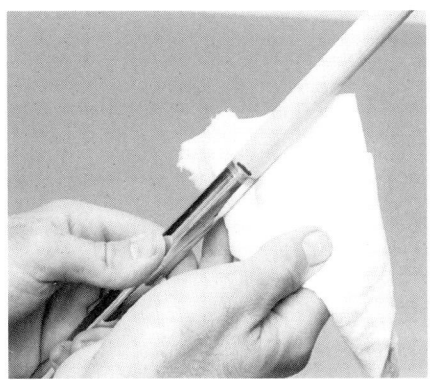

24-22 Wipe the excess epoxy from the shaft and extension. Allow the epoxy to cure.

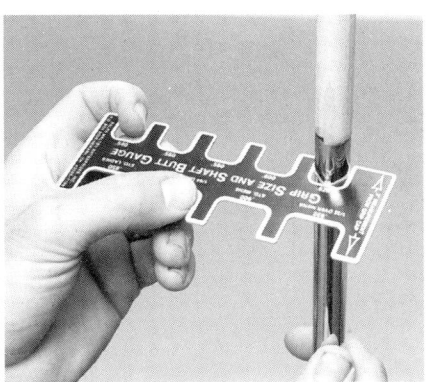

24-23 After the epoxy has cured, measure the shaft butt diameter.

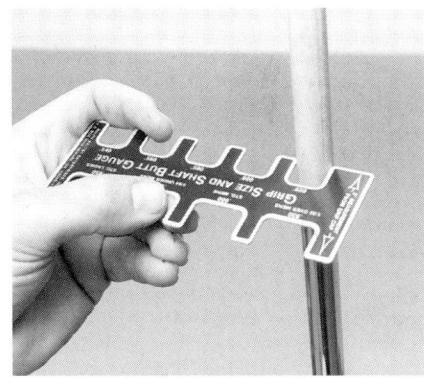

24-24 Measure the extension diameter also.

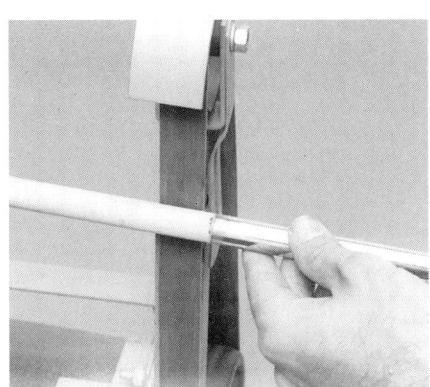

24-25 Using a file or belt sander, blend the wood to conform to the outside diameter of the shaft. Make as uniform as possible.

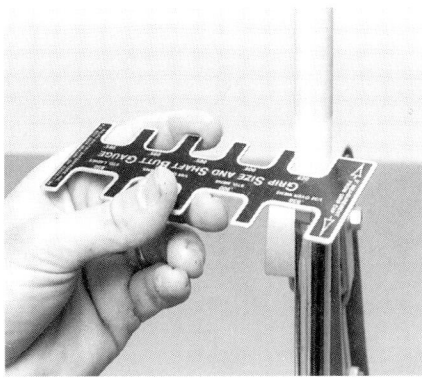

24-26 The extension has been reduced to the proper diameter.

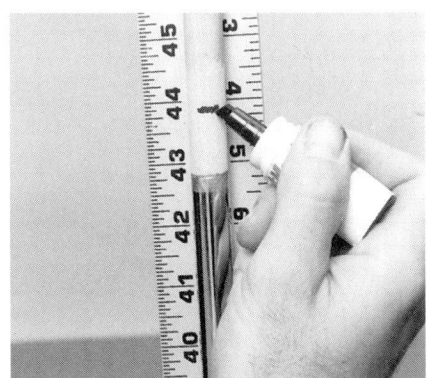

24-27 Next, mark the wood dowel at the desired length and …

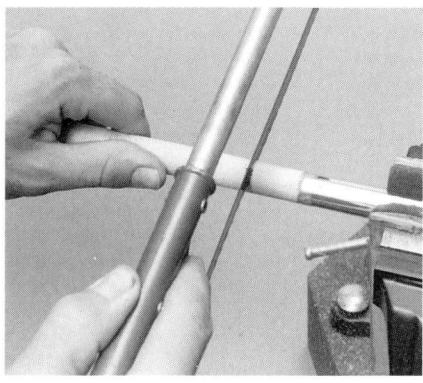

24-28 ...cut, using a saw. Note: Lengthening clubs more than 2" using wood dowels is not recommended.

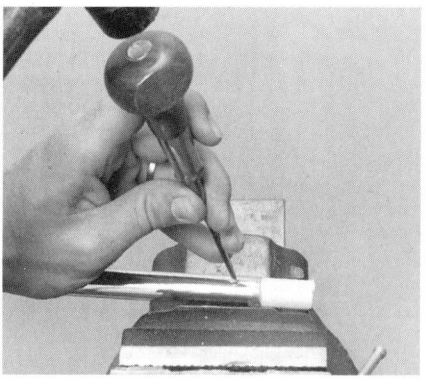

24-29 Pierce the shaft at 3 places around the shaft using a sharp **Awl** or **Prick Punch**. These punch marks are made 1" down from the top of the steel shaft.

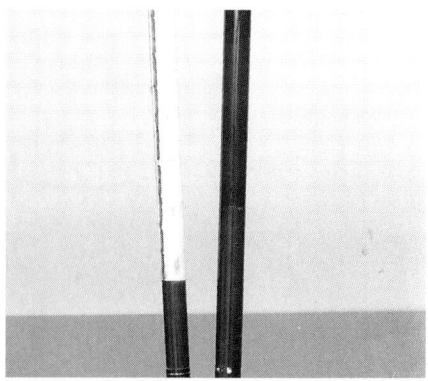

24-30 Composite shafts, such as graphite, can also be extended. Steel extensions are not available because of the smaller inside diameter of a graphite shaft. Instead, save old or broken graphite shafts and use these as extensions or The GolfWorks® offers a lightweight butt extension made of maple specifically for graphite shafts.

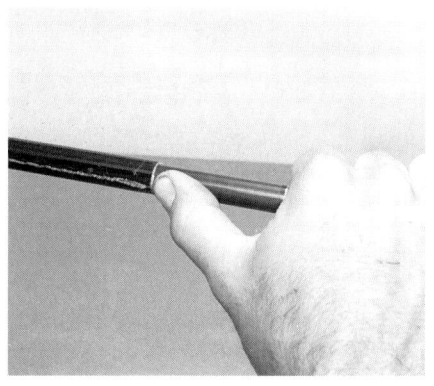

24-31 When using an old graphite shaft, push the old graphite shaft into the butt of the shaft to be extended until a snug fit is achieved. Make the old shaft even with the top of the original shaft.

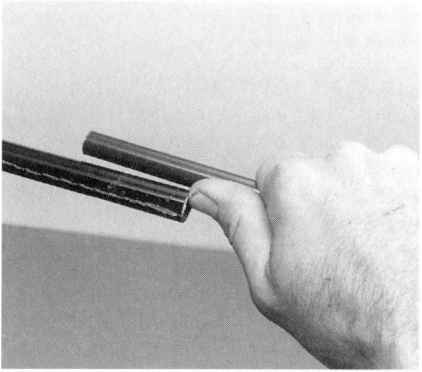

24-32 Pull the old shaft out and make another mark 3" down from the first mark. Lightly abrade that portion of the shaft extension that will fit inside the shaft that is to be extended. Cut the excess portion of the shaft below the 3" mark.

24-33 Apply epoxy to the abraded section and fit inside the graphite shaft. Push the graphite extension inside the shaft until a snug fit is achieved. This should be very close to the original mark on the extension.

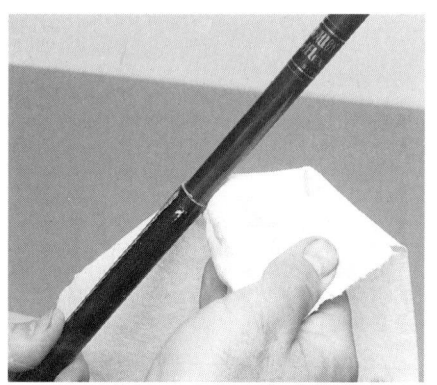

24-34 Remove any excess epoxy and allow the epoxy to cure.

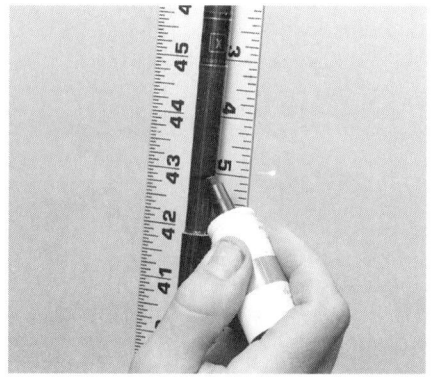

24-35 Mark the graphite extension at the point where you wish to make your cut. Remember to make the mark ⅛" below the desired overall length as the grip cap will account for an additional ⅛".

24-36 Cut the extension using a hacksaw.

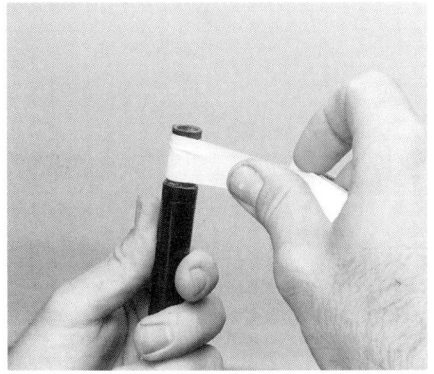

24-37 The extension can now be built up to match the outside diameter of the shaft, using several layers of masking tape.

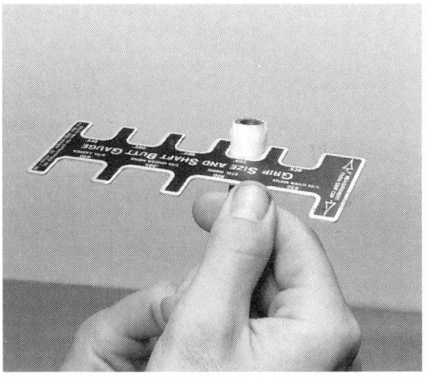

24-38 Measure the extension diameter to ensure it is the same diameter as the shaft. No piercing is required on composite shafts as this would tend to weaken them.

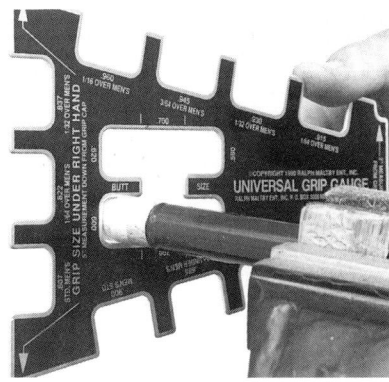

24-39 When using The GolfWorks® maple butt extensions for graphite shafts, they only come in a .600 diameter. To fit a smaller diameter, it is necessary to turn down the section that fits into the shaft using a belt sander or file ...

24-40 ... and sandpaper will work sufficiently to reduce the size.

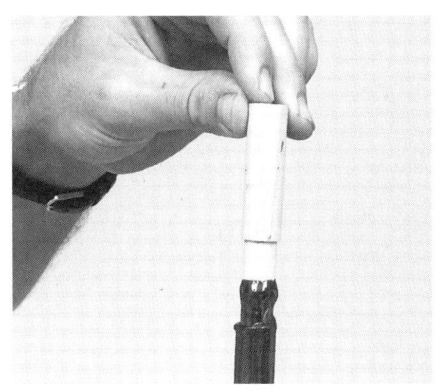

24-41 When the desired diameter is reached, apply epoxy to the butt extension and inside the shaft and then push while rotating the extension inside the shaft until a snug fit is achieved. Pull the extension from the shaft and check to see that a fairly uniform coating of epoxy exists. Now, reinstall the shaft.

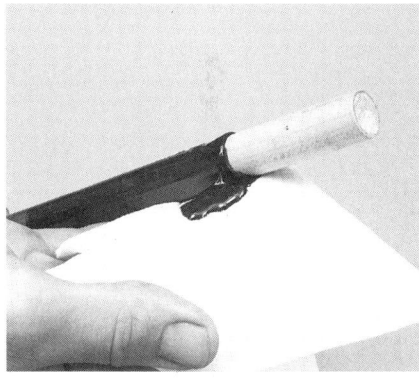

24-42 Remove any excess epoxy and allow the epoxy to cure.

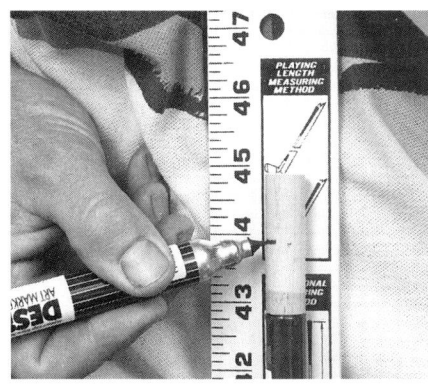

24-43 To cut the extension to length, mark the maple shaft extension at the point where you wish to make your cut. Remember to make the mark ⅛" below the desired overall length as the grip cap will account for an additional ⅛". **Note: The club length can only be extended a maximum of 2" using the maple butt extensions.**

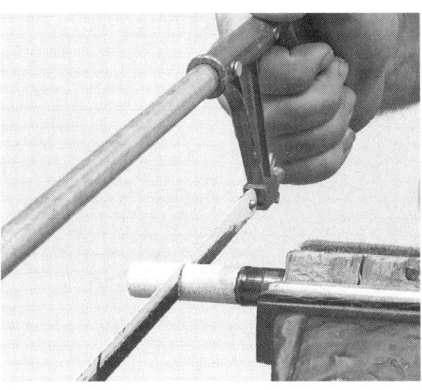

24-44 Cut the extension using a hacksaw.

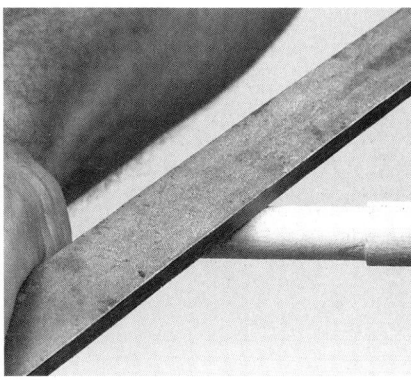

24-45 Once completed, measure the extension diameter to ensure it is the same diameter as the shaft. Use a file and sandpaper if more reducing is necessary. No piercing is required on composite shafts as this would tend to weaken the shaft.

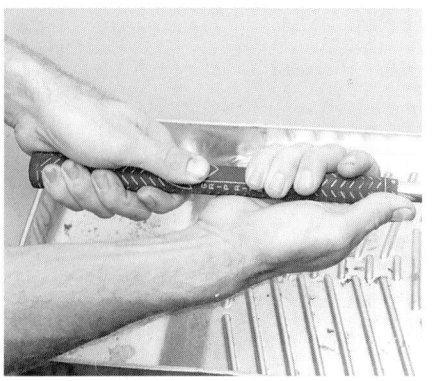

24-46 Install the grip and check the grip size as outlined in Chapter 23.

24-47 Final check the new length using a 48" ruler.

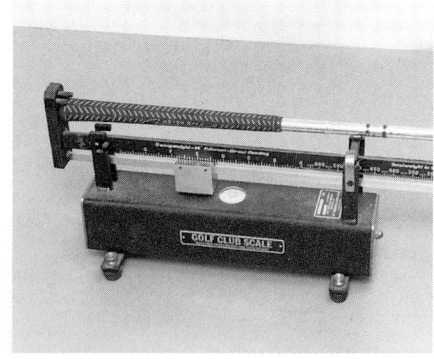

24-48 Final check the swingweight. If weight is to be removed, refer to Chapter 14 for woods and Chapter 18 for irons. Remember that an increase in length will cause the swingweight to go up. Actual head weight, however, remains the same. Use your own judgment as to whether a change in swingweight is necessary.

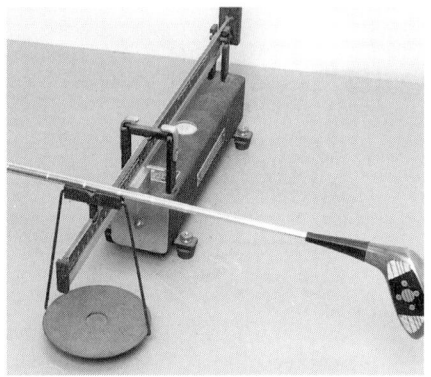

24-49 Final check the total weight. Note that any change does not require an adjustment to be made.

NOTES

_____

_____

_____

_____

_____

_____

ADDITIONAL INFORMATION FOR CHANGING LENGTHS OF GOLF CLUBS

When it comes to golf clubs and their components, it sometimes seems that all of the different references to the use of the word "length" can be very confusing. To help you understand "length," this glossary of terms should be studied.

Playing Length – The length of the finished golf club when measured from the ground line to the edge of the grip cap while the club is held in the playing position. This length is determined by placing a 48" ruler in back of the club as shown in Fig. 24-50.

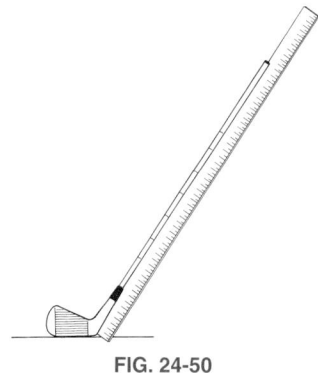

FIG. 24-50

298

Raw shaft Length – The length of the raw, uncut golf shaft, from the tip to the butt end.

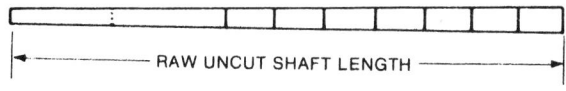

RAW UNCUT SHAFT LENGTH

FIG. 24-51

Tip Length – Also called tip section length, the distance from the raw shaft tip to the first step down.

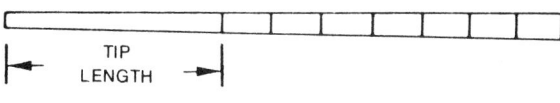

TIP LENGTH

FIG. 24-52

Traditional Length Method – The distance from the back of the heel of the golf club to the top of the grip cap. Note the difference in measuring methods as shown in Fig. 24-50 and 24-53. The playing length method compensates for sole radius and the traditional length method does not.

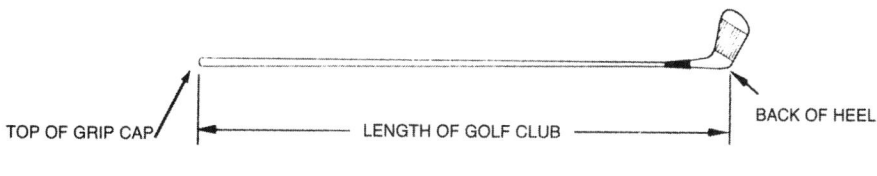

TOP OF GRIP CAP / LENGTH OF GOLF CLUB / BACK OF HEEL

FIG. 24-53

Standard Length – The golf industry's accepted playing lengths of golf clubs. See Table 24-1 for wood clubs and Table 24-2 for iron clubs.

TABLE 24-1 Wood Club Lengths – Men's and Ladies'			
Woods	Men's Standard	Ladies' Standard	Ladies' Petite
1	43"	42"	41½"
2	42½"	41½"	41"
3	42"	41"	40½"
4	41½"	40½"	40"
5	41"	40"	39½"
6	40½"	39½"	39"
7	40"	39"	38½"
8	39½"	38½"	38"
9	39"	38"	37½"

The most popular length variations for men are ½" shorter or longer than standard and 1" longer than standard. The most popular length variations for ladies are ½" shorter or longer than standard.

Irons	Men's Modern Standard	Men's Traditional Standard	Ladies' Standard	[1] Ladies' Petite
1	39½"	39"	38"	37½"
2	39"	38½"	37½"	37"
3	38½"	38"	37"	36½"
4	38"	37½"	36½"	36"
5	37½"	37"	36"	35½"
6	37"	36½"	35½"	35"
7	36½"	36"	35"	34½"
8	36"	35½"	34½"	34"
9	35½"	35"	34"	33½"
PW	35½"	35"	34"	33½"
SW	35½"	35"	34"	33½"

TABLE 24-2
Iron Club Lengths – Men's and Ladies'

[1]Ladies' petite is usually ½" shorter than the traditional ladies' standard length. Some companies make ladies' petite 1" shorter than ladies' standard length.

NOTES

CHAPTER 25

STRAIGHTENING BENT SHAFTS

There are many types of bent shafts which can be straightened to like-new condition with no adverse effect in performance whatsoever. Basically, the only type of bent shafts which cannot be straightened are those with dings, dents, kinks, creases or more specifically are no longer circular in cross section. A handy device for straightening many types of bent shafts is the Shaft Bending Block, which is offered by The GolfWorks® or you can make your own as shown at the end of Chapter 11.

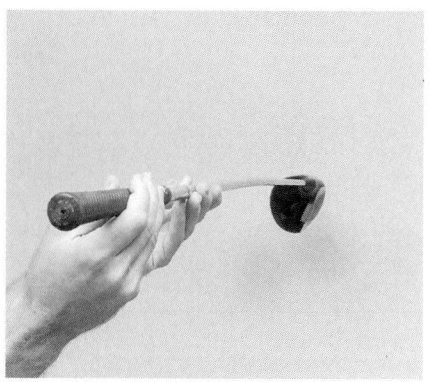

25-1 Sight down the shaft to determine the bend location.

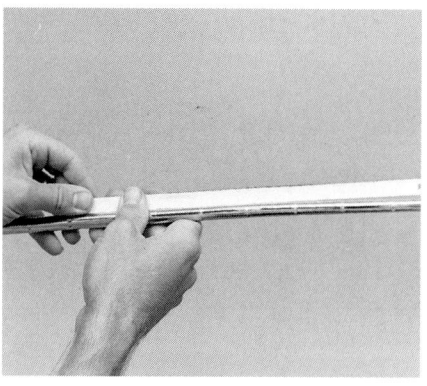

25-2 Placing a straight edge against the shaft can help you determine exactly where the bend is located.

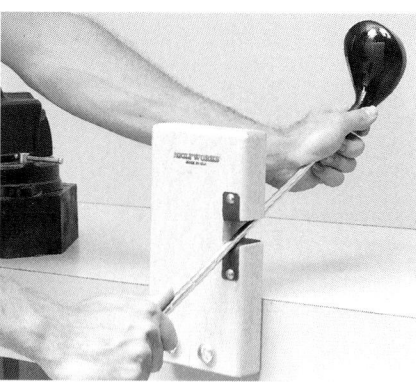

25-3 Using the **Shaft Bending Block,** apply downward pressure with hands apart as shown. Change the shaft position in the Block as you slowly work along the bend.

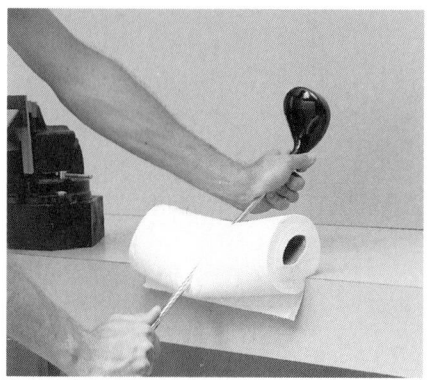

25-4 Another method may be used. Place a thick roll of paper towels against the edge of a bench. Work the bend back and forth over the towels until the bend disappears. check for straightness constantly while alternating bending so as not to over-bend the shaft.

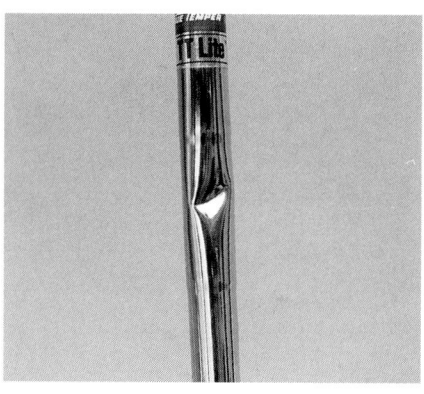

25-5 A crease or kink in the shaft indicates the shaft must be replaced due to structural damage.

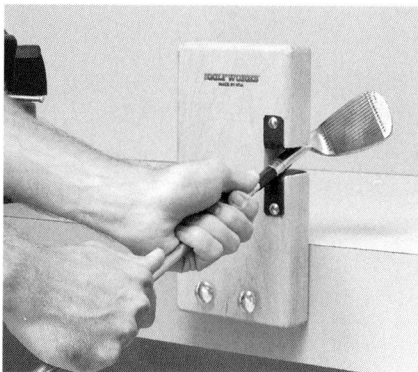

25-6 Sometimes an iron shaft will be bent at the neck. The assumption is to replace the shaft, however, the shaft can often be straightened easily as shown. Be sure the hosel just hangs over the edge of the Bending Block. Slight downward pressure will return the shaft to a straight condition. This repair would also apply to metal woods.

NOTES

302

CHAPTER 26

GOLF CLUB CARE AND MAINTENANCE

This chapter is written for two purposes. First, it is intended to give the proper recommendations for the care and maintenance of each golf club component; and secondly, to provide this information for golf professionals and repair shops in the hopes that it will be taught and passed along to the general golfing populace. Very little has been written on this subject and of that which has, some is wrong and the rest incomplete. Like many things in golf, much of the information we use today has been passed along from times past with the origin unknown, the information sometimes unproven and certainly not representative of modern materials used in golf today.

The proper care and maintenance of golf clubs can definitely make a difference in their playability. For instance, wood heads which are not properly sealed or dried after play can swingweight heavier by picking up moisture in the wet, humid months or climates and swingweight lighter in the dry, arid months or climates. Worn, slick grips which in many cases can be rejuvenated, will be hard to hold onto during the swing and can cause directional control problems and unsolid hits. This also applies to dirty grips which can become slick and cause the same problems.

■ Grips – Rubber and Leather

There are two basic material types used in making golf grips; rubber and leather. The rubber varieties actually are either made of all rubber, rubber and cork, rubber and Kraton or rubber and cord. Leather used in making golf grips is made from either calfskin or cowhide – the difference being in the suppleness of the grip (calfskin is more supple) and the age of the cow. Predominately, the rubber grips are manufactured by Lamkin® and Avon®, the rubber and cork and the rubber and cord by Eaton® and Lamkin® and the rubber and Kraton by Tacki-Mac®.

■ Cleaning Rubber Type Grips

The general procedure for every type rubber grip is to periodically clean with liquid detergent soap and water, rinse thoroughly and towel dry. This will remove any dust, dirt, sweat or hand oils which accumulate on the grips from normal play. The frequency of this cleaning varies with the geographical location, the climate and season, amount of play or practice, and of course, with each individual. It is good practice, however, to clean rubber type grips every five rounds or less.

If the grips are quite dirty, have not been cleaned for some time and are beginning to show signs of becoming slick, detergent soap will not work. To clean grips in this condition use a good scouring cleanser and scrub the grip vertically (up and down) using a nail brush. See Fig. 26-1. Rinse the grip under running lukewarm water and towel dry.

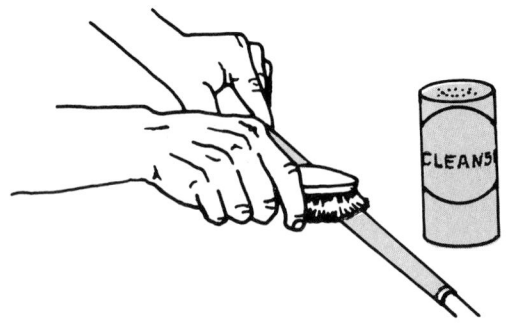

FIG. 26-1
Cleaning the grip with a nail brush and cleanser

■ Rejuvenating Worn Rubber Grips

Many times instead of replacing a grip, it can be successfully rejuvenated to a like new feel. First, it must be closely inspected for any cracking or checking and of course, indentations caused by wear (usually from the thumbs). If any of these conditions are present, then it would be best to replace the grip. However, if the main problem is the grip feels hard and is quite slippery, denoted by a semi-gloss surface appearance, it can be rejuvenated by using a coarse grade sandpaper or emery cloth. Sand the grip vertically from the top to the bottom until the semi-gloss glaze disappears on the grip and the original appearance returns.

Next, scrub the grip thoroughly with a nail brush and cleanser as previously described. Thoroughly rinse in lukewarm water, towel dry and check to see if the grip has a new or original feel. If it is still slippery feeling you probably did not sand it long enough. If this is the case, repeat the sanding and scrubbing steps and dry the grip again. If it still feels slippery then it needs to be replaced.

■ Special Recommendations for Specific Rubber Grip Types

Rubber and Kraton grips (Tacki-Mac®) will never need sanding because they do not buildup a slick glaze like other rubber grips. This type grip when new, however, has a small amount of mold release agent on it which can make it less tacky. To bring out the full tackiness on this grip, scrub after installing with a good cleanser, rinse thoroughly in lukewarm water and towel dry. The grips will now have a much tackier feel and will only periodically require cleaning in a mild detergent soap to maintain this tackiness.

Rubber and cord grips when new may tend to feel hard. This is more true of some models than others. Regardless, if they feel hard to you here is what to do. Take a coarse piece of sandpaper or emery cloth and sand vertically up and down the grip.

The amount of sanding depends on how soft a feel you want. You are not actually softening the grip, but giving it a velvety feel and as soon as it is rinsed off thoroughly under running water and toweled dry you will have the feeling of a softer, velvety, stickier grip. Hard to describe, but it works. Tour player Roger Maltbie uses the all cord velvet grip and after installation he meticulously sands each grip for over 5 minutes to achieve the feel he wants.

■ Cleaning Leather Grips

I have experimented cleaning dirty leather grips with virtually all available materials, lotions and potions; many of which work quite well. However, I still feel the best method is to obtain a small nail or hand brush and a bottle of liquid dish-washing detergent. Wet the grip with lukewarm water, squirt some liquid detergent on the nail brush and thoroughly scrub the leather grip. Rinse the grip well under warm running water until all signs of soap bubbles disappear. Using a lint-free towel (an old one) dry the grip by patting it. Do not rub dry. Let the grip air dry for a least five more minutes and grip it. If cleaned properly the grip should almost stick to your hand or glove. The Neumann calf grip responds to this type of cleaning better than any other leather grip, but you will get noticeable results with any leather grip.

■ Rejuvenating Leather Grips

Leather tends to become hard and slick over a period of time and particularly so if they have not been periodically cleaned, kept from extremes of heat and cold or left wet in the golf bag to dry.

The first step in rejuvenating leather grips is to clean them as explained above. If the grip is especially dirty and the dirt is deeply ground in then it may be necessary to scrub it once or even twice with a steel wool soap pad and rinse thoroughly.

Next, apply a good leather conditioner and/or preservative. Rub in well using your hand or a soft cloth which is saturated with leather conditioner. Wipe off all excess conditioner and allow the grip to dry overnight.

The grips should now feel quite tacky with most or all of the original suppleness restored.

■ Golf Shafts – Chrome Plated Steel

Normal care and maintenance of golf shafts only requires an occasional wiping with a damp rag followed by a brisk up and down rub with a dry towel. For extra protection a coat of metal polish or wax works well.

On many older clubs or clubs which have not been cared for, the shafts tend to accumulate surface rust and in more severe cases are heavily rusted and pitted. The first step in cleaning these shafts is to steel wool them using 000 grade which is quite fine. Do not use anything coarser such as 00 or 0 grade (which is probably what you would find around the house) as it will scratch the chrome. 000 steel wool the shaft until all traces of rust color have been removed. In most cases of neglect, the shaft is only surface rusted and the steel wool will remove it all. If the shaft is pitted or the chrome is flaking off after steel wooling the shaft should be replaced.

All shafts having rust removed should be waxed or have metal polish applied.

■ Golf Shafts – Graphite

Care must be taken with graphite shafts because they have a tendency to scratch and wear when they rub against the top ring of a golf bag. Recent advances in the durability of the polyurethane coating on a graphite shaft, however, are beginning to make this less of a problem. If you are concerned about possible scratching, a good idea is to place a piece of foam rubber or a fur liner inside the top portion of the golf bag. Longer neck head covers are also recommended to protect graphite shafts.

If a graphite shaft is beginning to dull and show signs of scratching, gently rub the entire shaft, first with grade 00 steel wool and then with grade 000 or 0000 steel wool until most scratches disappear. Apply one or two coats of a good furniture or carnuba paste wax, let dry for a few minutes and rub off. Repeat this procedure as often as needed.

Of course, if the shaft is in good condition, just wipe it off with a damp cloth, dry it and apply a coat of wax. Never use abrasives to clean a graphite shaft.

Another option to clean up a graphite shaft would be to completely refinish the shaft. The GolfWorks® offers a **Graphite Shaft Refinishing Kit** which contains a two component polyurethane (your choice of color), 3 sheets of 150 grit sanding cloth, 1 roll of steel wool and the **Sprā Tool** with an aerosol attachment. See the simple step-by-step instructions below.

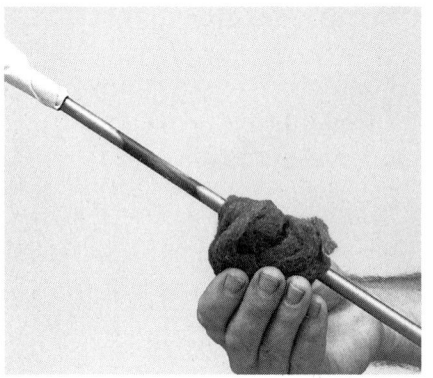

26-2 Refinishing a Graphite Shaft. First, prepare the shaft by sanding with 150 grit sandpaper until smooth and then rub with the steel wool. **NOTE: If refinishing the graphite shaft on an assembled club, cover the head and the grip with tape.**

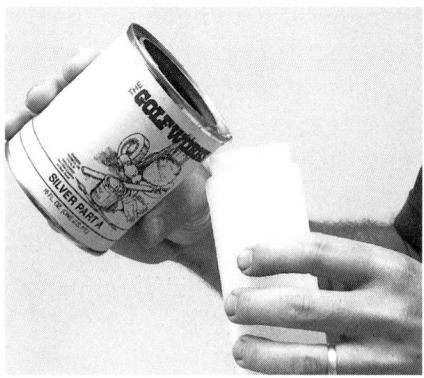

26-3 Using the two component polyurethane, mix three parts "A" to one part "B", by volume. After mixing, "sweat in" for 30 - 45 minutes, then remix. ("Sweat in" is the incubation period required to compatibalize the two parts before application.) After "sweat in," pour into the **Sprā Tool** aerosol unit or a regular spray gun.

26-4 After "sweat-in," spray a thin, wet coat of the colored epoxy paint to the prepared areas. Two or three coats are recommended. Allow to dry at least 15, but no longer than 30 minutes between each coat. Cure the finished shafts for 24 hours at 90°F - 100°F or for one week at room temperature. Note: Normally thinning is not required, however, acetone may be used if necessary.

■ Iron Heads

Scoring lines and engravings on irons are most easily cleaned with a hand or nail brush. Let water run over the head or soak it for a few seconds to loosen the dried soil and then scrub the entire head with a nail brush.

If the irons were put away wet or have been generally uncared for which usually results in slight surface rust, then it is recommended to use a piece of 000 steel wool and lightly rub over the entire head. 000 steel wool will not scratch chrome or stainless steel if moderate pressure is used during rubbing.

If desired, a good chrome polish or wax can be applied.

■ Wood Heads

A wood head is more easily susceptible to damage than any other golf club component. Moisture is its No. 1 enemy and because a wood head is glued and screwed together moisture has many areas where it can easily enter the club.

Once again, using the soft bristled hand or fingernail brush and water scrub all dirt from the face lines and soleplate engravings. Immediately towel dry and apply one or two coats of a good furniture paste wax to the entire head.

If a wood club has noticeable gaps around the insert and/or soleplate it would be a good idea to have these reset and the head refinished.

■ Materials Required for Golf Club Care
 1. Soft bristled hand or nail brush
 2. Paste Wax (good furniture grade)
 3. Chrome or metal polish
 4. Leather preservative (for leather grips only)
 5. 000 grade steel wool ribbon or pads
 6. One or two pieces coarse sandpaper or emery cloth (rubber grips only)
 7. Liquid dishwashing detergent
 8. Steel wool soap pads (leather grips only)
 9. Scouring cleanser (rubber grips only)
10. Soft cloth or cheesecloth

NOTES

NOTES ON REPAIR

SECTION

FOUR

GETTING STARTED IN GOLF CLUB REPAIR AND CUSTOM CLUBMAKING

CHAPTER 27

SETTING UP AND EQUIPPING THE REPAIR SHOP

Providing a good work flow is a fundamental goal when setting up a repair shop. Regardless of the shop's size or the volume of work, it should be organized to allow the work to commence at a certain point and then easily move through the shop in progressive stages until finished. With this in mind, careful positioning of the various tools and machines will contribute to a smooth operation that maximizes the use of your space and time. Examine the floor drawing on the next page for an idea of how an ideal work flow can be established.

Professionally operated repair shops typically have a desk, counter or small bench located next to the shop entrance. This serves as the nerve center for the entire shop. Here, customers are received, incoming clubs examined, records of accounts stored, outgoing clubs inspected and finally, clubs are packaged for shipment or customer pickup. Obviously, this area is a vital part of an organized shop. Once the incoming clubs have been inspected, appropriately tagged for identification and noted in a work log, they are moved to the workbench. Even if the size or location of your shop precludes a convenient customer reception space, a desk is still an important place for transacting certain business procedures in a well run shop.

Most club repair is performed at or near a vise fastened to the middle portion of the workbench. A sheet of pegboard should be attached to the back of the bench or hung on the wall behind it. Tools and gauges used most often (i.e. files, screwdrivers, face radius gauges, etc.) should be hung on pegboard hooks within easy reach of the vise. A Swingweight Scale should be conveniently located on the bench near the vise during repair operations. *(See A)* Less frequently used tools and gauges can be hung on the outer edges of the pegboard. Larger tools can be stored along the back of the bench top. The front of the bench top should not be used for tool storage as clubhead components will be placed there during club disassembly and reassembly steps.

A small open shelving unit should be arranged either to the immediate right or left of the workbench. *(See B)* This is used for storing screws, rivets, corks and other sundries the repairman must have within easy reach. Adequate stock of these supplies must be continuously maintained to avoid inefficient work stoppages.

A sturdy 4' x 4' bench should be located next to the shelving unit and built sturdy enough to hold a 1" x 42" Belt Sander, Bench-type Drill Press, Club Holder, and a spare Electric Motor. *(See C)* The use of this machinery will substantially speed up many repair tasks. The Belt Sander is used to shape ferrules, sand wood hosels, abrade shaft tips, remove excess epoxy around inserts, grind indentations from soleplates and many more chores. The Drill Press is used with the Iron Head Boring and Reaming Vise for removing broken shaft tips and enlarging hosel bores in irons. Installing a drill blank into the chuck provides the repairman with a quick means of drilling backscrew holes into wood head hosels. The Club Holder will secure a club in a fixed position while the vise is used for other purposes. Specifically, clubs with freshly poured inserts must be held in the correct position until the epoxy has cured. The Electric Motor has many uses. A Drill Chuck may be attached to an arbor, which in turn, is fastened to the motor shaft. The chuck is used to hold drill bits when a wood hosel bore requires enlargement. Also, a Shaft Cutoff Wheel or Unstitched Buffing Wheel can be attached to the motor if needed. The bench is also a good place to put the Mini Vibratory, a small vibratory that restores the vibratory finish on Ping type heads.

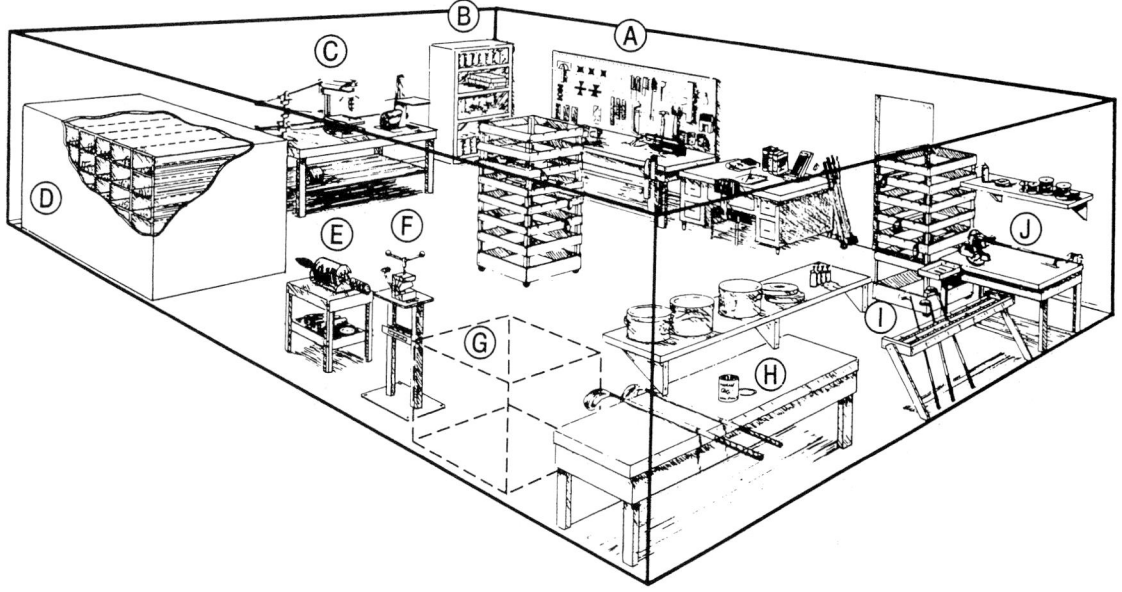

A logical storage location for shaft and grip inventory is next to the small bench. *(See D)* A large plywood rack can be built to hold both shafts and grips with enough built-in bins to sort them by type. The shaft and grip rack can be extended far enough out into the room to serve as a separating wall between the repair and finishing areas of the shop.

If space is available, a Golf Club Rack should be placed in the middle of the room to hold clubs during various drying stages in the repair-refinishing process. The rack can be set up in such a way as to allow clubs to be placed on the rack from any side of the room. For instance, clubs can be placed on the rack on the side of the room facing the workbench after components have been reset. Clubs with a fresh coating of stain or filler may be placed on the rack until dry. It is not necessary to have clubs scattered around the shop; instead, make full use of the Golf Club Rack.

After all repairs have been performed and the wood clubs are ready for refinishing, the next step requires sanding the wood heads. The Sanding Machine is positioned next to the shaft rack. *(See E)* Some repair shops place a curtain around the Sanding Machine to isolate the dust from other areas of the shop. The use of a vacuum system hooked to the sander will substantially reduce this problem. Other shops choose to place a large buffer with a pedestal for metal wood and iron refinishing here, instead of the Sanding Machine. Sanding wood heads is then performed on the Economy Sanding Machine which is mounted on the bench mentioned previously. Now, it becomes obvious that the work flow is moving in a circular pattern through the shop.

The next step in the refinishing process is the application of stain, filler and subsequent finish coats. Because clubhead sanding can create a large amount of dust, the sanding machine area should be placed as far away as possible from the finish application area. Yet, the shop must maintain an easy work flow. To accomplish this, the flow is only slightly interrupted by placing the Loft and Lie Machine next to the sanding area. *(See F)* Ample space is required when using the Loft and Lie Machine and this placement provides a good break between the sanding and finishing application stages. The lie and face angle of metal woods are adjusted by using the Economy Metal Wood Bending Machine in your vise.

To separate the two areas even more, some shops will build a drying box and place it in line next to the Loft and Lie Machine. The drying box provides an enclosed space that is dust free for clubheads with freshly coated finishes. The box can also have heat and humidity level controls for the curing process. *(See G)* This space can also be used to place a sandblast cabinet for blasting metal woods and iron faces.

Next in the line of flow is a small 8' bench with a shelf mounted on top. *(See H)* The bench should be placed far enough away from the wall to allow clubs to lie lengthwise across the bench top. An 8' shelf will neatly hold all the finish containers the repairman will use. A drying rack may be conveniently placed next to the finishing bench. *(See I)* This rack will hold the clubs during the important room temperature flash-off period that is required before they are placed under warmer conditions.

Another 4' bench is used to hold a Whipping Machine. Also, it can be used to set up a gripping station. *(See J and note the paint pan overhanging the edge of the bench to catch excess gripping solvent for reuse.)* This is a good spot to place a frequency analyzer for determining the flex of golf shafts. At this point, the repair-refinishing cycle is complete. After a thorough inspection, the club can be whipped and prepared for customer delivery or pickup. The rack conveniently located next to the door serves as a holding area until delivery.

While we have used an advanced repair shop as our model, those repairmen wishing to get started on a smaller scale should utilize as many of these ideas as is practical to achieve a smooth work flow.

■ How Much Space is Needed?

Now we will discuss things which I like to refer to as "Specific Generalities." This means that it is virtually impossible to cover each and every situation in exact quantitative terms on how to get properly set up repairing golf clubs.

In many instances the question, "How much space is needed?" should have been asked, "How much space is available?"

In a very general way, the following minimum square footage's for each situation should be used as a guideline only.

(A) Regripping, rewhipping, fixing loose inserts and soleplates, minor touchup and dipping one coat of finish to seal clubhead.
Minimum: 60 square feet
Examples of adequate room sizes would be: 10' x 6', 8½' x 7', etc.
Comments: Room would contain bench, vise, wall pegboard, tools and supplies to do above operations.

(B) Everything listed in (A) plus reshafting.
Minimum: 84 square feet
Examples of adequate room sizes would be: 10' x 8½', 12' x 7', etc.
Comments: Additional space is needed for shaft storage and additional tools and supplies needed for reshafting.

(C) Everything listed in both (A) and (B) plus refinishing.
Minimum: 144 square feet
Examples of adequate room sizes would be: 12' x 12', 10' x 14½', 8' x 18', etc.
Comments: Addition of refinishing supplies, shelves, sanding or polishing equipment. Drying between coats must be in another location. If drying is included in the same room, 200 square feet would be minimum.

(D) A full service repair shop doing virtually all repairs including reshafting, refinishing, adjusting lofts and lies of irons and lie and face angle of metal woods.

1. Small volume full service shop with mostly hand tools, some motorized equipment and minimum supplies.
Minimum: 324 square feet
Examples of adequate room sizes would be: 18' x 18', 12' x 27', etc.

2. Medium volume full service shop with additional motorized equipment and good stock of supplies.
Minimum: 400 square feet
Examples of adequate room sizes would be: 20' x 20', 13' x 30', 16' x 25', etc.

3. Large volume full service shop complete with most specialized equipment available. Excellent stock of supplies.
Minimum: 600 square feet
Examples of adequate room sizes would be: 20' x 30', 25' x 24', 18' x 34', etc.

■ What Machines, Tools, Components and Supplies are Needed?

On the following pages is a listing of the machines, tools, components and supplies that are needed in a repair shop. This listing consists of three groups – Machines and Tools, Supplies and Components. Each group is then subdivided into three categories – Beginning, Intermediate and Advanced. This will help determine your specific needs when equipping a repair shop. Each category is specifically geared toward the needs of a beginning, intermediate or advanced repair shop.

Do not feel you must confine yourself to only one category throughout the groups. For instance, if you wish to concentrate on the most profitable repairs – reshafting and regripping – you may want to outfit yourself with those machines, tools, supplies and components from the advanced categories for reshafting and regripping. Selections for other repairs can be made from the beginning or intermediate categories. Realistically consider the services you will be offering and make your choices from the appropriate category.

Beginning Category: regripping, reshafting, changing club lengths and club assembly. Bulge, role, loft and face angle alterations also.

Intermediate Category: regripping, reshafting, refinishing woods and metal woods, club assembly and all club alterations. Machines are introduced to speed club repair services, and a larger inventory of components and supplies are listed to provide greater variety for a larger clientele.

Advanced Category: regripping, reshafting, refinishing woods, metal woods and stainless steel irons, club assembly and all club alterations. A wide array of machinery is used to provide a very efficient operation. Also, a large variety of components and supplies to cover virtually any request.

MACHINES AND TOOLS
Beginning

1 Clubmaker's Vise
1 Propane Torch Kit
1 Lock Tight Shaft Holder
1 Screw Heater
1 Whipping Loop Puller
1 Swingweight Scale
1 Electric Drill
1 pr. Wooden Vise Pads
1 pr. Aluminum Vise Pads
1 Shaft Vise Clamp
1 Shaft Bending Block
1 Grip Size and Shaft Butt Gauge
1 Leverage Block
1 Face Radius Gauge
1 Grip Slide Rule
1 Aluminum Ruler
1 Wood File
1 Flat File

1 File Cleaner
1 Screwdriver
1 Mini Hacksaw with Blade
1 Mill Knife
1 $\frac{1}{8}$" Pin Punch
1 $\frac{3}{32}$" Pin Punch
1 Scratch Awl
1 8" Long Punch
1 pr. Leather Buffing Gloves
1 Driving Plug
1 $\frac{19}{64}$" Taper Length Drill
1 $\frac{5}{16}$" Standard Length Drill
1 $\frac{21}{64}$" Standard Length Drill
1 "R" Taper Length Drill
1 "T" Standard Length Drill
1 "T" Cobalt Standard Length Drill
1 "U" Cobalt Standard Length Drill

1 $\frac{3}{8}$" Cobalt Standard Length Drill
1 $\frac{1}{16}$" Drill
1 $\frac{1}{8}$" Drill
1 $\frac{3}{32}$" Drill
1 $\frac{7}{32}$" Drill
1 12" x $\frac{7}{32}$" Extension Drill
1 #1 Extractor & Wrench Set
1 Heating Rod
1 Golf Shaft Cutter
1 Ball Peen Hammer
1 Grip Collar Starter
1 Hacksaw Blade
1 Drill Stand
1 Protractor
1 Shaft Tipping Gauge
1 Grip Size Under Right Hand Gauge

Intermediate

1 Clubmaker's Vise
1 Propane Torch Kit
1 Lock Tight Shaft Holder
1 Screw Heater
1 Propane Torch Tip
1 Whipping Loop Puller
1 Economy Loft & Lie Machine
1 Swingweight Scale
1 Economy Sanding Machine
1 1" x 42" Belt Sander
2 Ferrule Turning Belt
1 Buffing Wheel Rake
2 Unstitched Buffing Wheels
1 Electric Drill
1 pr. Wooden Vise Pads
1 pr. Aluminum Vise Pads
1 Rubber Shaft Vise Clamp
1 Shaft Bending Block
1 Grip Size Shaft Butt Gauge
1 Leverage Block
1 Square Head Protractor
1 Mini Vibratory
1 Graphite Shaft Extractor
1 Tape Stripper
1 Electric Heat Gun
1 Economy Metal Wood

  Bending Machine
1 Golf Club Gauge
1 Face Radius Gauge
1 Loft Gauge
1 Shaft I.D. Gauge
1 Grip Slide Rule
1 48" Aluminum Ruler
1 Insert Pattern Copier
1 Insert Remover Tool
1 Wood File
1 Flat File
1 File Cleaner
1 #1 Phillips Screwdriver
1 #2 Phillips Screwdriver
1 Hacksaw with Blade
1 Mini Hacksaw with Blade
1 Mill Knife
2 $\frac{1}{8}$" Pin Punch
2 $\frac{3}{32}$" Pin Punch
1 Scratch Awl
1 8" Long Punch
1 Backscrew Hook & Scriber
1 pr. Leather Buffing Gloves
1 Driving Plug
1 $\frac{19}{64}$" Taper Length Drill
1 $\frac{5}{16}$" Standard Length Drill
1 $\frac{21}{64}$" Standard Length Drill

1 "T" Cobalt Standard Length Drill
1 "U" Cobalt Standard Length Drill
1 $\frac{3}{8}$" Cobalt Standard Length Drill
1 "T" Standard Length Drill
1 "R" Taper Length Drill
1 12" x $\frac{7}{32}$" Extension Drill
1 47" x $\frac{7}{32}$" Drill
1 Ram Rod
1 Tap Wrench
1 Screw Extractor Set
1 Countersink
1 Drill Stand
1 $\frac{1}{2}$" wood Chisel
1 Heating Rod
1 6" Scale With Clip
1 Weight Checker Rod
1 Ball Peen Hammer
1 Grip Collar Starter
1 Rasp
1 Round File
1 Fractional Drill Set
1 Shaft Tipping Gauge
1 Grip Size Under Right Hand Gauge

Advanced

1	Clubmaker's Vise	1	Protractor	1	Binocular Magnifier
1	Sure Fire Propane Torch	1	Golf Club Gauge	1	Pressurized Grip Remover
1	Super Lock Tight Shaft Holder	1	Face Radius Gauge	1	Driving Plug
1	Electric Extractor	1	Driver Loft Gauge	1	.294 Set Step Drills
1	Whipping Loop Puller	1	Fairway Loft Gauge	1	.320 Set Step Drills
1	Golf Club Machine	1	Shaft I.D. Gauge	1	.335 Set Step Drills
1	Golf Club Scale	1	Grip Slide Rule	1	.355 Set Step Drills
1	Accurate Shop Scale	1	48" Aluminum Ruler	1	Iron Head Reamer
1	Economy Sanding Machine	1	Golf Club Drying Rack	1	⅛" Drill Blank
1	Sanding Sleeve for Economy Sanding	1	Electric Heat Gun	1	12" x 7/32" Extension Drill
4	Face Insert Clamps	1	Bench Grinder	1	47" x 7/32" Drill
1	1" x 42" Belt Sanding Machine	1	Drill Press	1	47" Ram Rod
1	⅓ H.P. Motor	1	Insert Pattern Copier	1	Cutting & Drilling Oil
1	Buffing Wheel Rake	1	Insert Remover Tool	1	Extractor Wrench
2	Unstitched Loose Buffing Wheels	1	Ferrule Installer Tool	1	Screw & Shaft Extractor Set
1	Scotch-Brite™ Wheel	1	Wood Rasp	1	Countersink
1	Electric Drill	1	Round Wood File	1	Drill Stand
1	Motor Switch	1	Flat File	1	Drill Chuck & Key
1	8' Motor Cord	4	File Handles	1	Motor Shaft ARbor
1	4-Outlet Plug Box	1	File Cleaner	1	½" Wood Chisel
1	Club Holder	1	Wood File	1	Heating Rod
1	pr. Bent Nose pliers	1	Spiral Ratchet Screwdriver	1	6" Steel Scale
1	Eaton Metal Shaft Clamp	1	#1 Phillips Screwdriver	1	Iron Head Boring and Reaming Vise
1	Lever Action Shaft Holder	1	#2 Phillips Screwdriver	1	Dremel Moto Tool
1	Shaft Bending Block	1	Small Reed and Prince Screwdriver	1	Ball Peen Hammer
1	SandBlast Cabinet	1	Large Reed and Prince	1	Grip Collar Knife
1	Graphite Shaft Extractor	1	Hacksaw with Blade	1	Fractional Drill Set
1	Economy Metal Wood Bending Machine	1	Mini Hacksaw with Blade	1	Electric Heating Rod
1	Grip Size and Butt Gauge	1	Mill Knife	1	Shaft Extractor Set
1	Leverage Block	2	⅛" Pin Punch	1	Compressor and Accessories
		2	3/32" Pin Punch	1	Buffing Shop with ¾ H.P. Buffer
		1	Scratch Awl	1	Weight Checker Rod
		1	8" Long Punch		
		1	Backscrew Hook & Scriber		

SUPPLIES
Beginning

Wood and Iron Ferrules to fit:
   .277, .294, .335, .355 and
   .370 shaft tip diameters
   (1 dozen of each)
1 qt. - Acetone
End Cap Assemblies to fit:
   .580, .600 and .620
   shaft butt diameters
   (1dozen of each)
Plastic Bell Grip Collars to fit:
   .580, .600 and .620
   shaft butt diameters
   (1 dozen of each)
50 yards - Whipping

4 - Molded Whipping Covers
50 - #8 x ⅝" Brass Screws
50 - #4 x ⅝" Brass Screws
50 - #5 x 1¼" Steel Backscrews
25 - Wood Corks
25 - Iron Corks
1 roll - Lead Tape
1 lb. - Powdered Lead
12 - Tapered Wood Plugs
25 - ⅛" Hosel Rivets
1 can - Oil Modified or
   Moisture Cure Polyurethane
1 - Black Faceline Scoring Paint
10 sheets - 400 grit Sandpaper

000 Steel Wool
5 - Epoxy Application Brushes
1 - Tack Rag
1 - Shear Strength Epoxy
1 roll - Single-Coated 2" Wide Tape
1 roll - Double-Coated 2" Wide Tape
1 qt. - Grip Solvent
100 - Repair Tags
10 - Graphite Extensions
10 - Steel Extensions

Intermediate

12 - Cycolac Inserts
4 squares - Fiber Inserts
Wood and Iron Ferrules to fit:
.277, .294, .335, .355 and
.370 shaft tip diameters
(3 dozen of each)
End Cap Assemblies to fit:
.580, .600 and .620
shaft butt diameters
(1 dozen of each)
Plastic Bell Grip Collars to fit:
.580, .600 and .620
shaft butt diameters
(1 dozen .560, 2 dozen
.580, .600 and .620)
Trim Rings (assortment of
colors to match all shaft
sizes)
200 yards - Whipping
4 - Whipping Covers
50 - #7 x ¾" Steel Screws
50 - #5 x ¾" Aluminum Screws
50 - #7 x ¾" Brass Screws
100 - #8 x ⅝" Brass Screws
50 - #5 x ¾" Brass Screws
100 - #4 x ⅝" Brass Screws
100 - #5 x 1¼" Steel
Backscrews
25 - Wood Corks
25 - Iron Corks
1 roll - Lead Tape
Lead Rod - 1 lb. ¼" diameter
1 lb. - Powdered Lead
100 - Tapered Wood Plugs

100 - ⅛" Hosel Rivets
100 - 3⁄32" Hosel Rivets
12 - Black Rubber Hosel Plugs
12 - Red Rubber Hosel Plugs
4 - Brass Backweights
3 - 1" x 42" Linen Ferrule
Turning Belts
1 can - Contact Adhesive
10 sheets - 100 grit Sandpaper
10 sheets - 150 grit Sandpaper
10 sheets - 240 grit Sandpaper
20 sheets - 400 grit Sandpaper
1 lb. roll - 000 Steel Wool
1 pr. - Leather Gloves
Stains: cherry, black, walnut,
armour mahogany and
burgundy
Filler: natural and less intense
black
Colorcotes: black and blue -
aerosol
1 can - Polyurethane
1 can - Polyurethane
Preservative
Faceline Scoring Paint - black
and white
1 qt. - Acetone
1 qt. - Paste Stripper
1 tube - Chrome Polish
1 bar - Glanz Wach
3 - 1" x 42" Coarse Sanding
Belts
3 - 1" x 42" Linen Ferrule
Turning Belts

100 - Epoxy Mix Sticks
7 - Dipping Containers (for
stains and filler)
20 pairs - Plastic Gloves
25 - Metric Cups
5 - Stiff Bristled Brushes
3 - Face Masking Brushes
10 - Epoxy Application Brushes
3 - Tack Rags
30 yards - Burlap
Cheesecloth
Pour-in-Place Epoxy - red,
black and clear
Mortite Putty
Shear Strength Epoxy
1 gallon - Grip Solvent
1 roll - Single-Coated 2" Wide
Tape
1 roll - Single-Coated ¾" Wide
Tape
2 rolls - Double-Coated 2"
Wide Tape
Color Paste Dispersions -
black and brown
Lacquer Rub-in Sticks -
white, red, black and gold
1 qt. - Aluminum Oxide Sand
100 - Poly Grip Protector Bags
50 - Poly Wood Head Bags
50 - Repair Brochures
100 - Repair Tags
25 - Graphite Extensions
25 - Steel Extensions

Advanced

12 - Cycolac Inserts
4 squares - Fiber Inserts
4 squares - Phenolic Inserts
4 squares - Fiber Two-color
Inserts
1 - Graphite Insert
1 - Aluminum Insert
Wood and Iron Ferrules to fit:
.277, .294, .335, .355 and
.370 shaft tip diameters
(100 of each)
End Cap Assemblies to fit: .560,
.580, .600 and .620 shaft butt
diameters (1 dozen of each)
Plastic Bell Grip Collars to fit:
.560, .580, .600 and .620
shaft butt diameters
(1 doz. .560, 2 doz. .580,
.600 and .620)

Trim Rings - assortment of
colors to match all shaft sizes
200 yards - Whipping
4 - Whipping Covers
50 - #7 x ¾" Steel Screws
50 - #5 x ¾" Aluminum Screws
50 - #7 x ¾" Brass Screws
100 - #8 x ⅝" Brass Screws
50 - #5 x ¾" Brass Screws
100 - #4 x ⅝" Brass Screws
100 - #5 x 1¼" Steel
Backscrews
25 - Wood Corks
25 - Iron Corks
1 roll - Lead Tape
Lead Rod - 1 lb. ¼" diameter
1 lb. - Powdered Lead
100 - Tapered Wood Plugs
100 - ⅛" Hosel Rivets

100 - 3⁄32" Hosel Rivets
12 - Black Rubber Hosel Plugs
12 - Red Rubber Hosel Plugs
4 - Brass Backweights
5 - 1" x 42" Linen Ferrule
Turning Belts
1 can - Contact Adhesive
10 sheets - 100 grit Sandpaper
10 sheets - 150 grit Sandpaper
10 sheets - 240 grit Sandpaper
40 sheets - 400 grit Sandpaper
1 lb. roll - 000 Steel Wool
1 pr. - Leather Gloves
Stains: cherry, black, walnut,
armour mahogany,
burgundy, buckskin, dark
blue and rosewood
Filler: natural and less intense
black

Color Cotes: black and blue
  aerosol
1 can - Polyurethane
1 can - Polyurethane
  Preservative
Faceline Scoring Paint - black,
  red and white
1 qt. - Acetone
1 qt. - Paste Stripper
1 tube - Chrome Polish
1 bar - Glanz Wach
10 - 1" x 42" Coarse Sanding
  Belts (for Belt Sander)
10 - 1" x 42" Linen Ferrule
  Turning Belts
100 - Epoxy Mix Sticks
10 - Dipping Containers (for
  stains and filler)
20 pairs - Plastic Gloves

25 - Metric Cups
5 - Stiff Bristled Brushes
3 - Face Masking Brushes
10 - Epoxy Application Brushes
5 - Tack Rags
30 yards - Burlap
Cheesecloth
Pour-in-Place Epoxy - red,
  black and clear
Mortite Putty
1 gallon - Grip Solvent
1 roll - Single-Coated 2" Wide
  Tape
1 roll - Single-Coated ¾"
  Wide Tape
2 rolls - Double-Coated 2"
  Wide Tape
Color Paste Dispersions -
  black and brown

Lacquer Rub-in Sticks - white,
  red, black and gold
1 qt. - Aluminum Oxide Sand
100 - Poly Grip Protector Bags
50 - Poly Wood Head Bags
50 - Repair Brochures
200 - Repair Tags
1 - Dust Respirator
1 pr. - Soft Flex Goggles
8 - 8" Spiral-sewn Buffing
  Wheels
2 - 8" Sisal Buffing Wheels
1 bar - White Polishing
  Compound
1 bar - Sisal Compound
1 bar - Lea Compound
1 bar - Glue Compound
25 - Graphite Extensions
25 - Steel Extensions

COMPONENTS
(Shafts & Grips)
Beginning Grips

24 - V260
24 - VG60
14 - VVC60
14 - PWMR60
4 - JBV

14 - MSB60
14 - DIM60
14 - CHMS
14 - GOHE60
4 - POP58

1 - ELPG
4 - GRP58
4 - TWP58
12 - LVGG58
12 - LVGP58

Intermediate Grips

48 - VG60
12 - VG62
24 - VGR60
48 - PWMR60
12 - DIM60
24 - VVC60
24 - V260
14 - VHC60
12 - GOHE60
4 - JBV

5 - POP58
5 - GRP58
5 - PAB58
12 - LVGG58
12 - LVGP58
1 - RTG
12 - NPPL
12 - RU60
12 - SM60
2 - ELPG

14 - TENX60
14 - TWC60
14 - MSB60
12 - MWMR60
4 - FMAC
14 - CPCU
14 - CHMS
14 - PWLR56
5 - OMPG

Advanced Grips

48 - DIM60
1 case - VG60
24 - VG62
24 - VGR60
24 - VHC60
14 - TWC60
48 - VVC60
48 - PWMR60
48 - MWMR60
24 - GOHE60
14 - V2560
14 - JBV

24 - V260
24 - SWMR60
9 - JRV50
14 - TENX60
14 - MSB60
14 - FMAC
14 - CPCU
24 - CHMS
14 - V2C60
10 - OMPG
5 - CHPS
10 - POP58

10 - GPP58
5 - ELPG
5 - TSPG
5 - PSP58
5 - CLP58
24 - LVGG58
12 - LVGP58
12 - PWLR60
14 - NPPL
2 - L60
12 - RU60
14 - TWG58

Beginning Shafts

Taper Tip Woods
1 - 44" DWS
1 - 44" DWT
Taper Tip Irons
2-35", 1-35½", 1-36", 1-36½",
   1-37", 1-37½", 1-38" 1-38½",
   1-39" - DIS
1-35" - DIT
1-YSTG

Parallel Tip Woods
2 - UDWCH
4 - UTTLWCH
1 - U2LWAL
1 - UPMWC
Parallel Tip Irons
1 - UDIC
9 - UTTLIC
1 - UDICO

1 - U2LIAL
1 - UPMIC
1 - YST370
1 - UDIXM

Total Shafts = 37

Intermediate Shafts

Taper Tip Woods
1 - 44" DGWS300
1 - DWX
1 - 44", 1-43", 1-42" DWS
1 - 44" DWT
Taper Tip Irons
1 - 35", 1-36", 1-37", 1-38",
   1-39" DIS
1 - 35", 1-36", 1-37", 1-38",
   1-39" DIT
1 - YSTG

Parallel Tip Woods
3 - UDGWS300
3 - UDWCH
3 - U2LWAL
3 - UTTLWC
3 - UPMWC
Parallel Tip Irons
2 - UDIC
1 - U2LIAL
1 - UDICO
9 - UTTLIC

9 - UPMIC
2 - YST370
1 - UDIXM

Total Shafts = 57

Advanced Shafts

Taper Tip Woods
1-44" DGWS100
1-44" DGWS300
1-44" DGWS500
1-44" DGWX100
1-44", 1-43", 1-42½", 1-42" DWS
1-44", 1-43", 1-42" DWT
Taper Tip Irons
1-35" through 39" increments
   (9) DIS
2-35", 1-36", 1-37", 1-38",
   1-39" DIT
2 - YSTG

Parallel Tip Woods
3 - UDGWS300
4 - UDWCH
4 - UTTLWC
3 - U2LWAL
3 - UPMWC
1 - ALTWRS
1 - ALTWL
1 - UEI7WS
Parallel Tip Irons
1 - UDGIS100
1 - UDGIS300
1 - UDGIS500

1 - UDIX
10 - UDIC
1 - UDIAL
1 - UDICO
10 - UTTLIC
10 - UPMIC
2 - YST370
1 - ALTIRS
2 - UDIXM

Total Shafts = 89

NOTES

_____

_____

_____

_____

_____

_____

CHAPTER 28

GOLF CLUB REPAIR TOOLS AND AIDS YOU CAN MAKE

There are a number of tools, fixtures and aids you can make. Some of the items shown in this chapter are available commercially while others must be made. There is usually a greater amount of satisfaction and enjoyment derived from building some or all of these items yourself, not to mention the money saved.

Each item shown in this chapter is self-explanatory and enough detail is given so the item can be built. Full detailed working drawings were impractical so basic dimensional sketches and material lists only are shown along with photographs where necessary. A few of the items have complex or hard to find parts which may require welding or special machining. In these instances a part number is listed indicating the component is available from The GolfWorks® if you cannot make it yourself.

Shaft Bending Block

The shaft bending block is used to straighten bowed and slightly bent shafts, to alter face angles and lies on wood clubs or to straighten shafts bent at the top of an iron hosel. Its use is best shown in Chapters 11, 12 and 26.

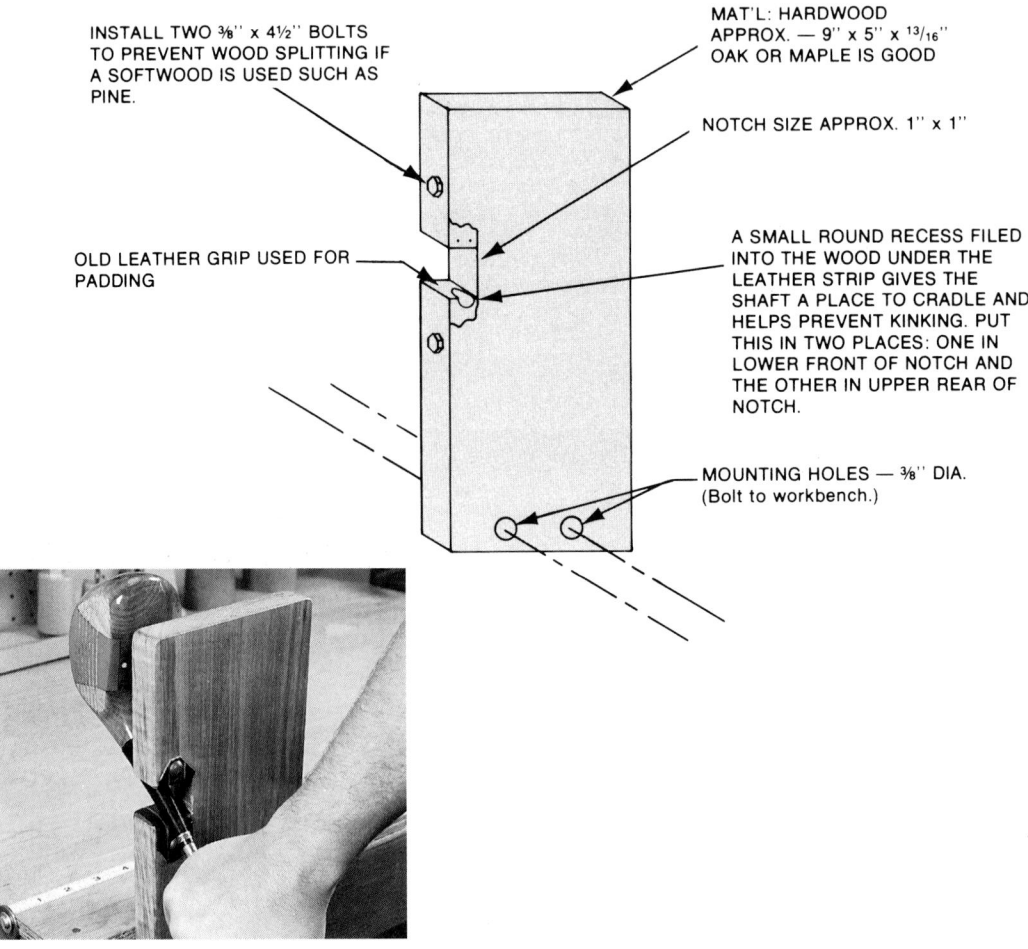

INSTALL TWO ⅜'' x 4½'' BOLTS TO PREVENT WOOD SPLITTING IF A SOFTWOOD IS USED SUCH AS PINE.

MAT'L: HARDWOOD APPROX. — 9'' x 5'' x ¹³/₁₆'' OAK OR MAPLE IS GOOD

NOTCH SIZE APPROX. 1'' x 1''

OLD LEATHER GRIP USED FOR PADDING

A SMALL ROUND RECESS FILED INTO THE WOOD UNDER THE LEATHER STRIP GIVES THE SHAFT A PLACE TO CRADLE AND HELPS PREVENT KINKING. PUT THIS IN TWO PLACES: ONE IN LOWER FRONT OF NOTCH AND THE OTHER IN UPPER REAR OF NOTCH.

MOUNTING HOLES — ⅜'' DIA. (Bolt to workbench.)

Shaft Driving Plug

The shaft driving plug fits into the butt end of the shaft and allows the shaft to be driven into the iron head without damaging the butt end of the shaft. See Chapters 20 and 21 for proper use.

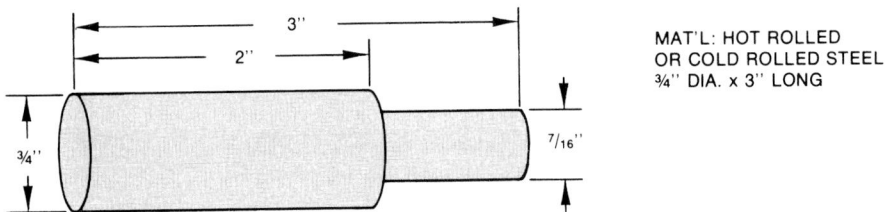

3''

2''

¾''

⁷/₁₆''

MAT'L: HOT ROLLED OR COLD ROLLED STEEL ¾'' DIA. x 3'' LONG

NOTE: If you do not have access to a lathe to turn the end down try this: Cut a piece of ¾'' dia. round 2'' long. Next cut a ⁷/₁₆'' dia. round 1½'' long. Drill ⁷/₁₆'' dia. x ½'' deep in the end of the ¾'' dia. piece and epoxy the two together.

Heating Rod

The heating rod is a very simple tool used to heat wood club shafts inside the hosel for easier removal. The heat from the rod heats the shaft tip which in turn softens the epoxy or glue holding it in place. The heating rod tip is pre-heated with a propane torch. If necessary the heating rod tip can be heated red hot for more difficult shaft removal.

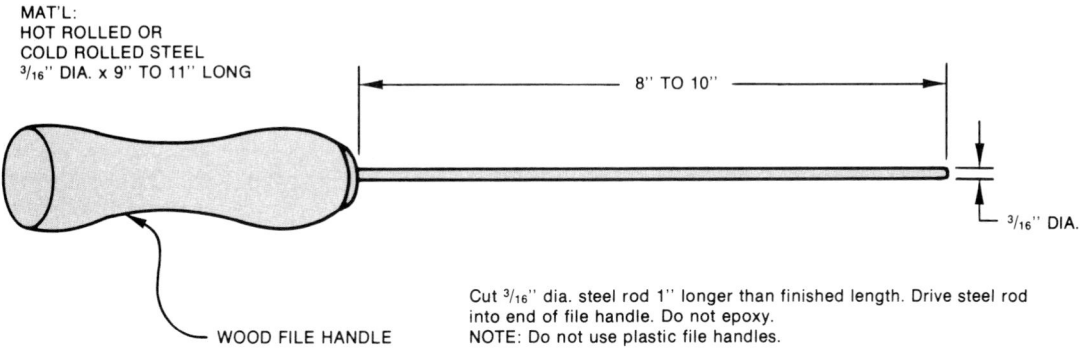

MAT'L:
HOT ROLLED OR
COLD ROLLED STEEL
3/16" DIA. x 9" TO 11" LONG

8" TO 10"

3/16" DIA.

WOOD FILE HANDLE

Cut 3/16" dia. steel rod 1" longer than finished length. Drive steel rod into end of file handle. Do not epoxy.
NOTE: Do not use plastic file handles.

Hardwood Leverage Block

This tool is used to break iron heads loose from the head during reshafting. It is a very valuable tool. Its use is fully explained in Chapter 21.

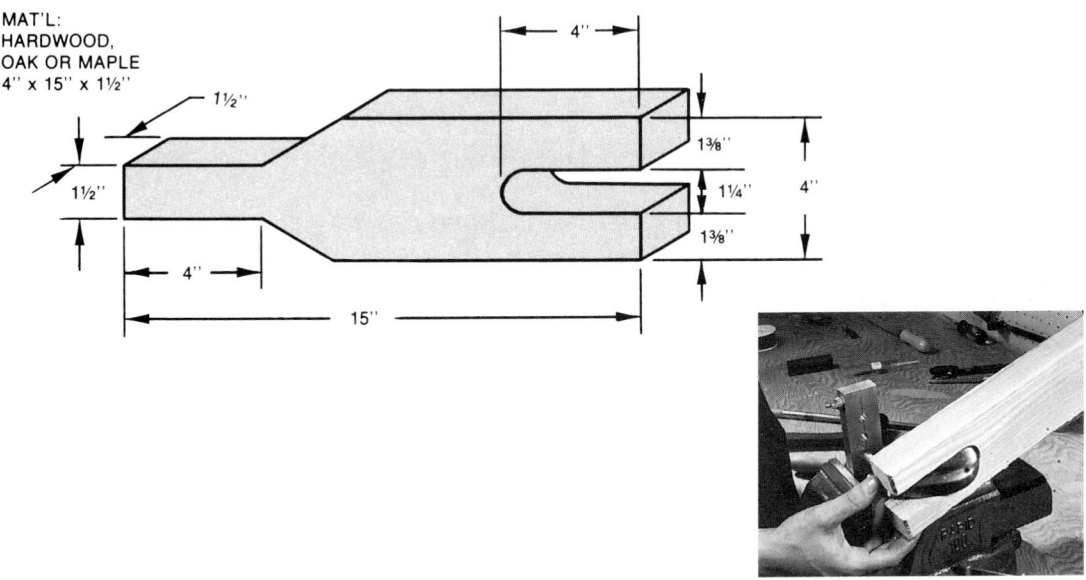

MAT'L:
HARDWOOD,
OAK OR MAPLE
4" x 15" x 1½"

1½"

1½"

4"

4"

1⅜"

1¼"

1⅜"

4"

15"

Wood and Felt Vise Pads

This is an absolute necessity in any repair shop. These vise pads fit in the jaws of the vise to protect the woodhead. The proper method of holding a woodhead in the vise pads when performing various functions is adequately shown in Chapters 1 through 15.

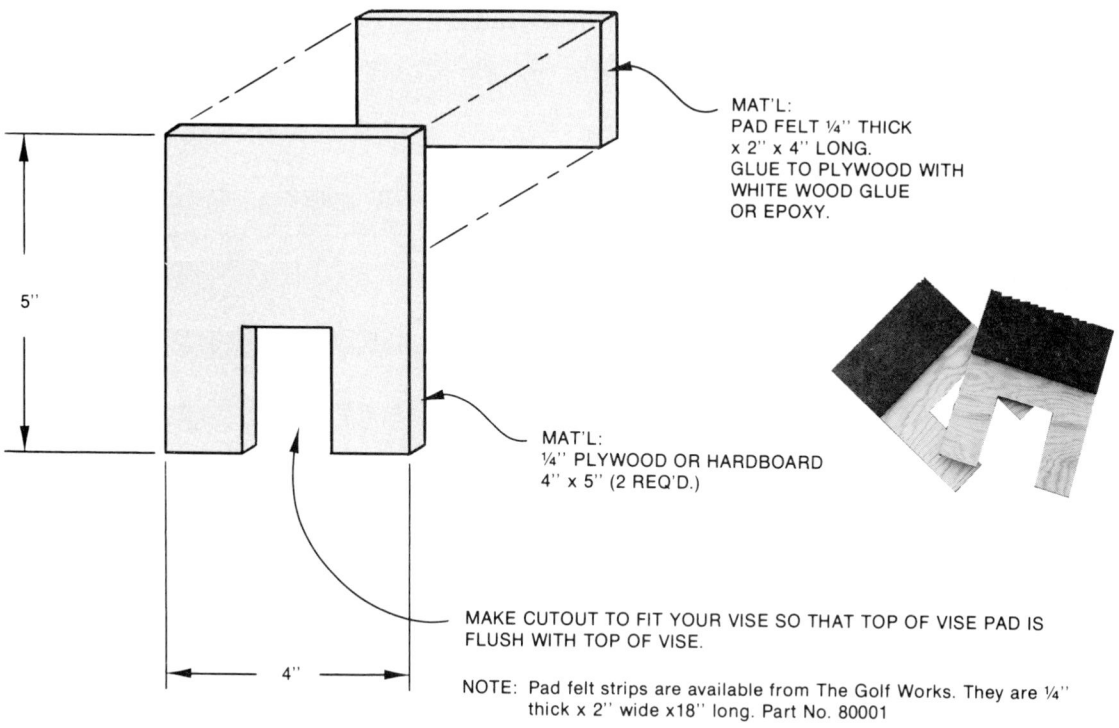

MAT'L:
PAD FELT ¼'' THICK
x 2'' x 4'' LONG.
GLUE TO PLYWOOD WITH
WHITE WOOD GLUE
OR EPOXY.

5''

MAT'L:
¼'' PLYWOOD OR HARDBOARD
4'' x 5'' (2 REQ'D.)

4''

MAKE CUTOUT TO FIT YOUR VISE SO THAT TOP OF VISE PAD IS
FLUSH WITH TOP OF VISE.

NOTE: Pad felt strips are available from The Golf Works. They are ¼''
thick x 2'' wide x18'' long. Part No. 80001

Whipping Loop Puller

This nifty little gadget makes it faster and easier to tie off whippings on wood clubs. Its use is shown in Chapter 6, Photos 6-28 through 6-33.

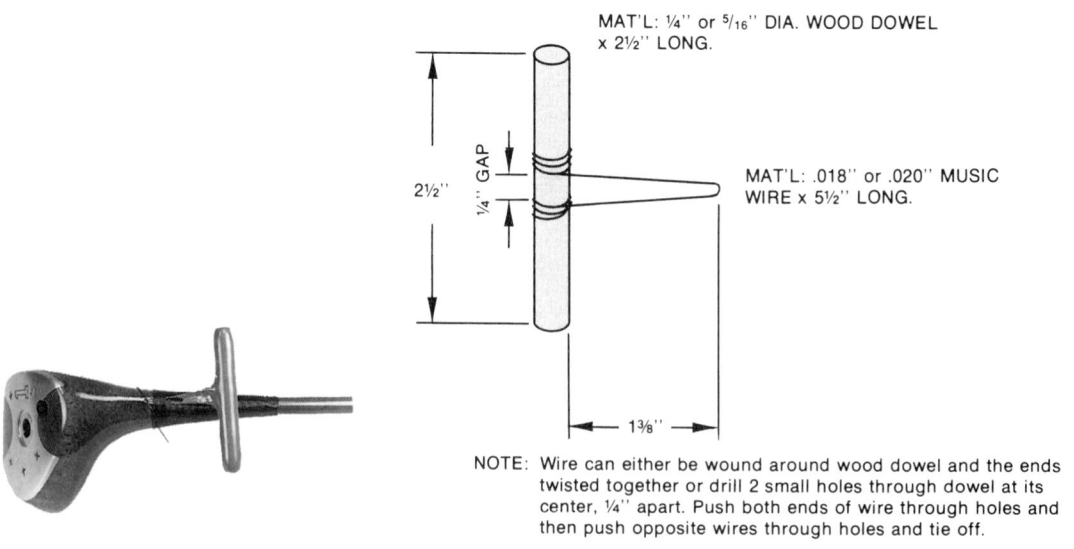

MAT'L: ¼'' or ⁵/₁₆'' DIA. WOOD DOWEL
x 2½'' LONG.

2½''

¼'' GAP

MAT'L: .018'' or .020'' MUSIC
WIRE x 5½'' LONG.

1⅜''

NOTE: Wire can either be wound around wood dowel and the ends
twisted together or drill 2 small holes through dowel at its
center, ¼'' apart. Push both ends of wire through holes and
then push opposite wires through holes and tie off.

Face Insert Clamp

This clamp is used for gluing in inserts in new woods and resetting loose inserts in older clubs. This versatile clamp holds the insert tightly in place with just enough pressure to eliminate too wide a glue line or correct a warped insert. It works with any size head, large or small. It also works great for gluing split heads together and gluing on brass, aluminum or plastic backweights.

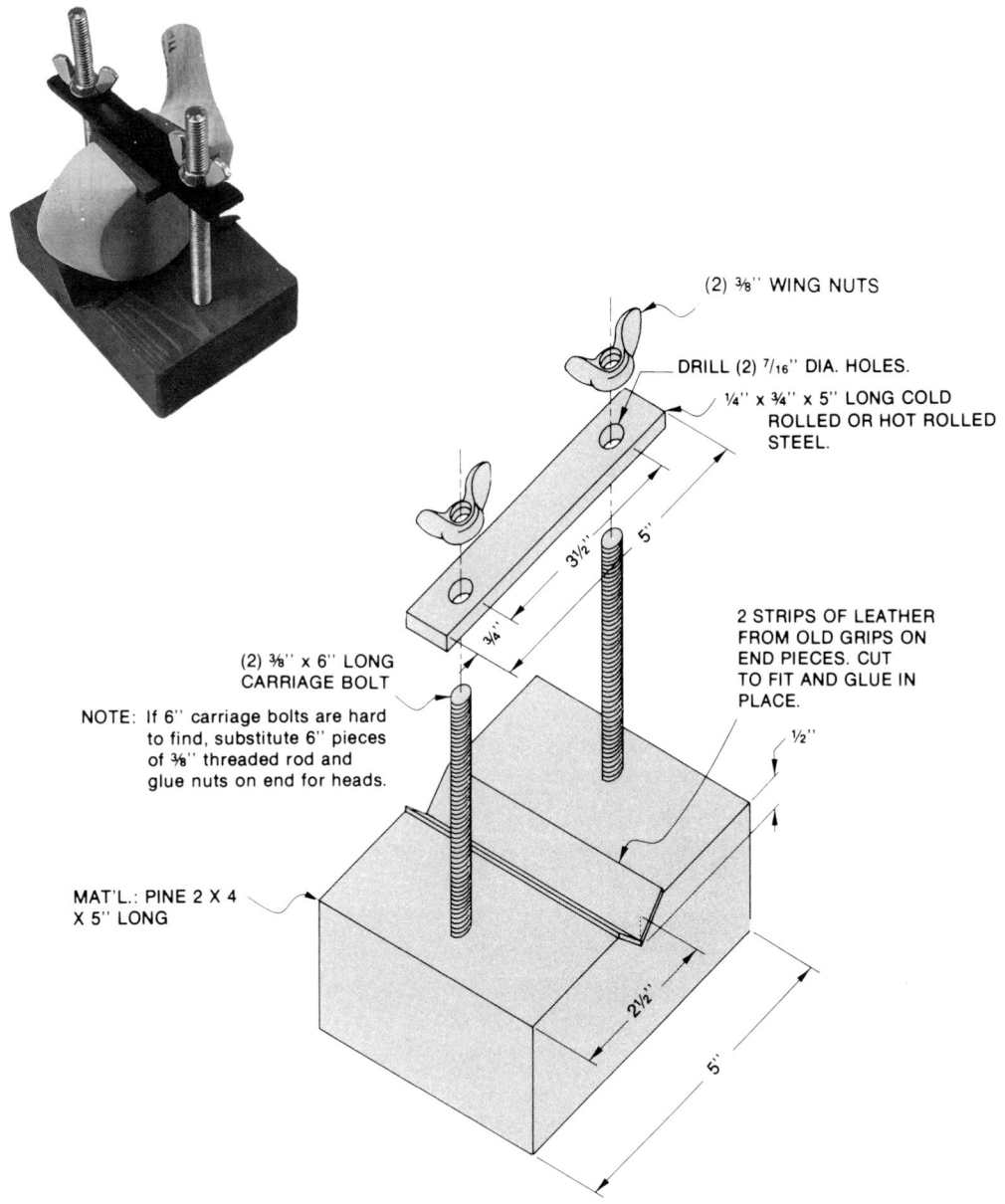

(2) ⅜'' WING NUTS

DRILL (2) ⁷/₁₆'' DIA. HOLES.

¼'' x ¾'' x 5'' LONG COLD ROLLED OR HOT ROLLED STEEL.

3½''

5''

¾''

(2) ⅜'' x 6'' LONG CARRIAGE BOLT

NOTE: If 6'' carriage bolts are hard to find, substitute 6'' pieces of ⅜'' threaded rod and glue nuts on end for heads.

2 STRIPS OF LEATHER FROM OLD GRIPS ON END PIECES. CUT TO FIT AND GLUE IN PLACE.

½''

MAT'L.: PINE 2 X 4 X 5'' LONG

2½''

5''

Workbench

This is the main part of any workshop. Without it, any repair operation would be an exercise in frustration. Workbenches can be quite elaborate and expensive or very basic and inexpensive as the one shown here. This workbench makes a good starter bench and later on if you want to replace it with something bigger or fancier it will double as a table for laying out clubs, mounting bench motors or other accessories. This is the same bench I built when starting out in the repair business and I still have it in use today.

BILL OF MATERIALS:

- 1-   2' x 8' Sheet of plywood or particleboard
- 8-   2 x 4's x 8' long
- 16-   ⅜" x 3½" lg. Carriage bolts w/nuts & washers
- ¼ lb.   3d common nails for top and shelf
- 1 lb.   10d common nails for 2 x 4's

CONSTRUCTION NOTES:

1. Build end frame leg assemblies first.
2. Next, nail on 8' long 2 x 4's.
3. Put in remaining 4 braces (21" long 2 x 4).
4. Paint frame color desired. Grey or brown are good colors.
5. Last, nail on top and shelf and apply 1 clear coat of varnish or poly.

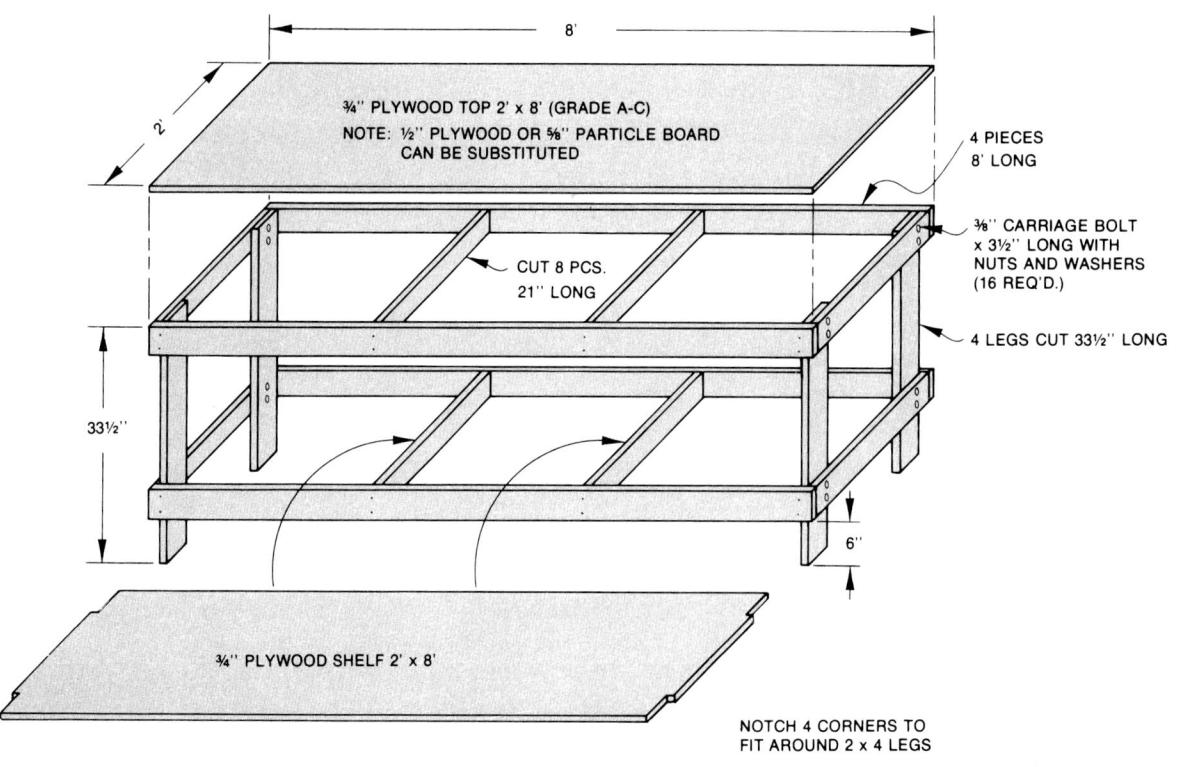

8'

2'

¾" PLYWOOD TOP 2' x 8' (GRADE A-C)
NOTE: ½" PLYWOOD OR ⅝" PARTICLE BOARD CAN BE SUBSTITUTED

4 PIECES 8' LONG

⅜" CARRIAGE BOLT x 3½" LONG WITH NUTS AND WASHERS (16 REQ'D.)

CUT 8 PCS. 21" LONG

4 LEGS CUT 33½" LONG

33½"

6"

¾" PLYWOOD SHELF 2' x 8'

NOTCH 4 CORNERS TO FIT AROUND 2 x 4 LEGS

Shaft Storage Rack

Keeping golf shafts organized and easy to find can be a real problem. We solved it in our repair department by building the rack below. It has 77 openings, each with a capacity of 80 shafts which gives a total shaft storage capacity of 6,160 shafts.

The rack is constructed of 1" x 2" pine firring strips for the grid and ½" plywood for the outside covering. There are two grids in the rack, one for the front and the other 30" back from the front. The depth of the rack is 34" so the rear grid is positioned 4" forward of the plywood back. The height and width of the rack can be made to suit your needs. Also, the size of each opening in the rack shown is 5" x 5" and holds 80 shafts. If the opening size is reduced to 3½" x 3½", each opening will hold 40 shafts. This also can be tailored to suit your needs.

Construction is quite simple:

First, the grids are built on the floor to the desired height, width and opening size.

Next, a 2 x 4 frame is built around the bottom of the front and rear grids and also around the top. This now gives you a free standing form.

Last, the ½" plywood is cut and nailed on both sides, the back and top of the rack.

The rack can now be painted if desired. Identification stickers such as DIS 39", DWT 44", etc. can be placed under each opening for easy shaft selection.

Ramrods

There are two types of ramrods used in club repair; the first type has no moving parts and is used to knock heads off irons, drive powdered lead and corks in place and tighten loose weights in the shafts of both woods and irons.

The second type has a movable weight which acts as a sliding ram. This type of ramrod generates a tremendous impact force and is mainly used for knocking off stubborn iron heads. Chapter 21 demonstrates the use of both ramrods.

MAT'L: ½'' DIA. & ¼'' DIA. COLD ROLLED STEEL

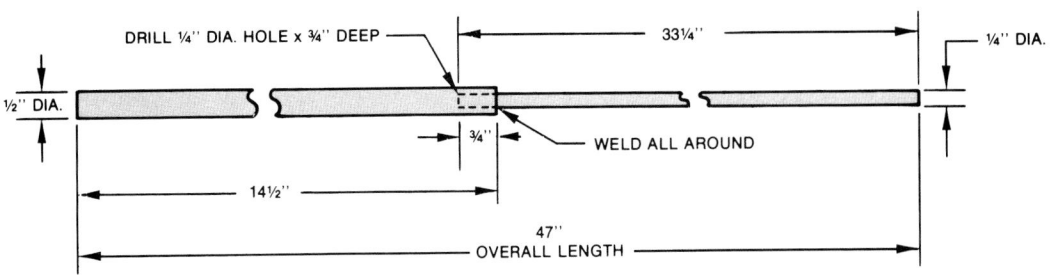

DRILL ¼'' DIA. HOLE x ¾'' DEEP

33¼''

¼'' DIA.

½'' DIA.

¾''

WELD ALL AROUND

14½''

47''
OVERALL LENGTH

IF DESIRED, A ½'' I.D. BICYCLE HANDLEBAR GRIP CAN BE INSTALLED

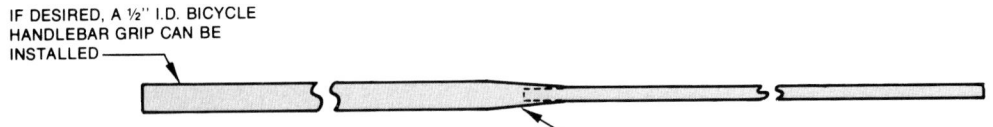

After welding, file or grind to blend both pieces of steel together. This prevents any possible lip from catching on the butt end of the shaft during use.

2½'' O.D. HOT ROLLED STEEL x 1½'' LONG. DRILL A ⅞'' HOLE IN ITS CENTER (2 PIECES)

¾'' PIPE x 4¼'' LONG

¾'' DIA. x 18'' LONG HEX HD CONSTRUCTION BOLT
DRILL ⁷/₁₆'' DIA. HOLE x ½'' DEEP IN BOLT HEAD, INSERT ⁷/₁₆'' DIA. ROD, WELD ALL AROUND.

¾'' NUT

⁷/₁₆'' DIA.

26''

¼'' DIA.

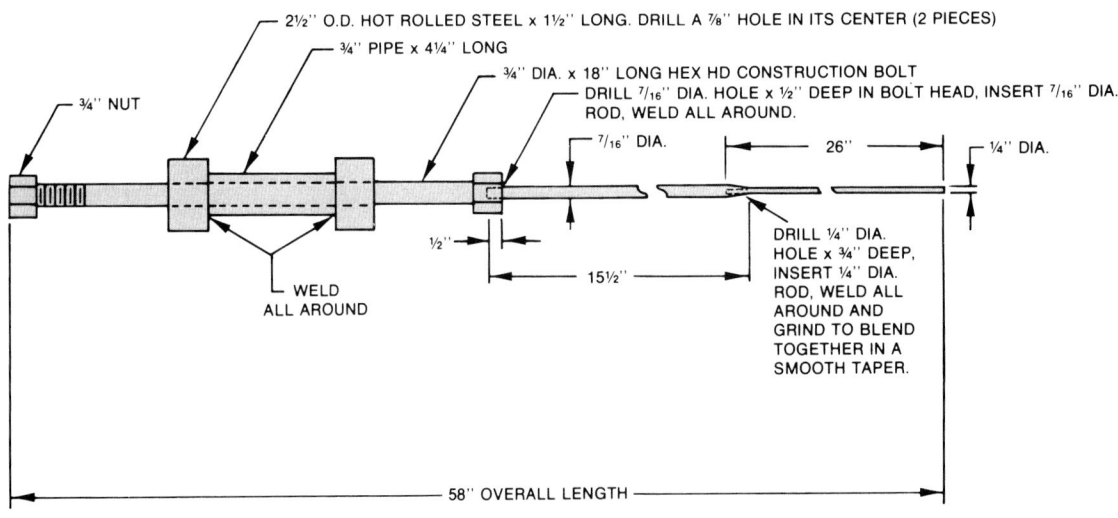

½''

15½''

WELD ALL AROUND

DRILL ¼'' DIA. HOLE x ¾'' DEEP, INSERT ¼'' DIA. ROD, WELD ALL AROUND AND GRIND TO BLEND TOGETHER IN A SMOOTH TAPER.

58'' OVERALL LENGTH

NOTE: The ¾'' dia. x 18'' long construction bolt and nut are available from The Golf Works. Part No. 80020

Whipping Spool Holder

Whether you whip a club by hand or use a machine, the whipping spool holder keeps the whipping tangle free and always where you want it. This holder will accommodate up to 4,000 yard spools or hold as little as a 50 yard spool.

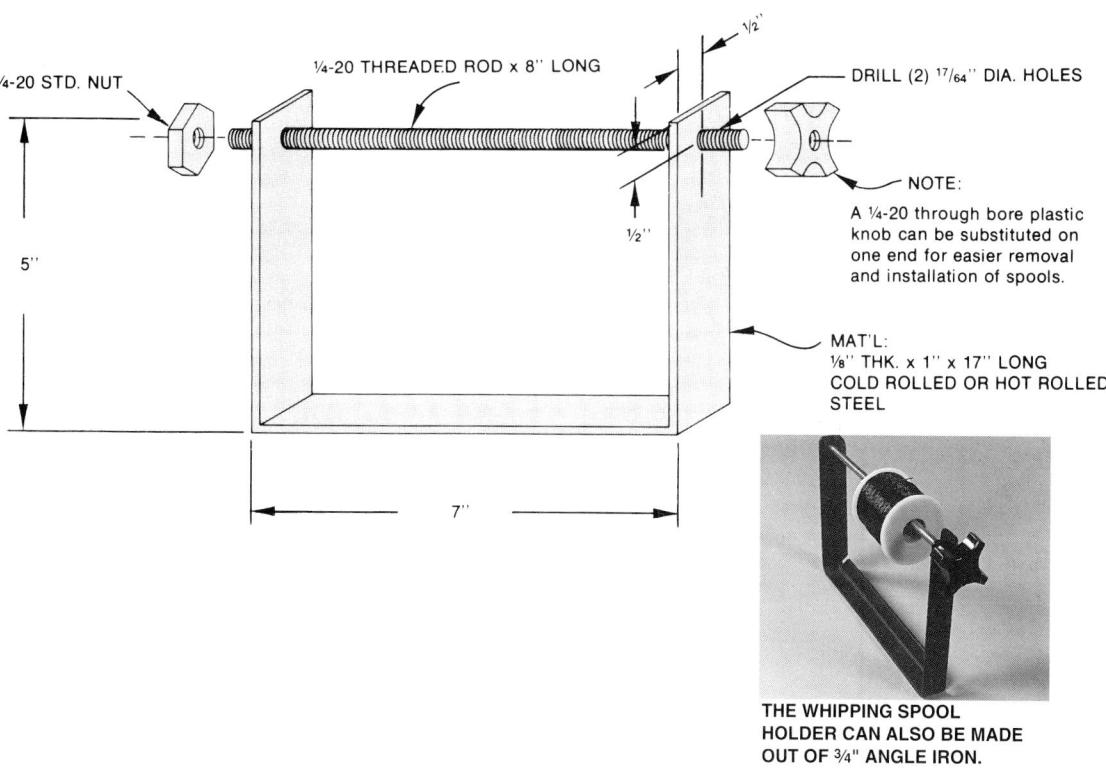

1/4-20 STD. NUT

1/4-20 THREADED ROD x 8" LONG

1/2"

DRILL (2) $^{17}/_{64}$" DIA. HOLES

NOTE:
A 1/4-20 through bore plastic knob can be substituted on one end for easier removal and installation of spools.

5"

1/2"

MAT'L:
1/8" THK. x 1" x 17" LONG COLD ROLLED OR HOT ROLLED STEEL

7"

THE WHIPPING SPOOL HOLDER CAN ALSO BE MADE OUT OF 3/4" ANGLE IRON.

Club Racks

The photo below shows 2 types of club racks which are great for organizing and keeping track of repair and custom clubs. They also work well as drying racks in the finishing department.

They can be built from 1" x 2" pine to your own requirements. Casters add mobility and are available at most hardware stores.

CHAPTER 29

HOW TO EXPAND AND GET ADDITIONAL BUSINESS

There are many different ways to expand the existing repair shop business and also a number of logical related areas of expansion such as custom club making and fitting. During my years in the golf business I have heard a number of good ideas and tips for expanding and growing and this chapter is designed to pass these ideas along to you. These ideas will be beneficial to you whether you are a golf professional or a hobbyist who has entered the business of club repair.

INDIVIDUAL SPECIALS AND PROMOTIONS

■ Regripping Specials
1. Offer a discount when regripping a full set of clubs.
2. Regrip the putter for free if the entire set is regripped.
3. Offer a special regripping service on one type of grip. Most grips can be purchased at a reduced cost when ordering in case quantities. These savings can be passed on to the customer in the form of a "special," when clubs are regripped with this particular grip.
4. Fit the customer to the proper grip size for free, before regripping a set of clubs. This service can improve the golf game not only through the use of new grips, but also by using grips that are the correct size.

■ Grip Promotion
1. Display racks are available that promote different grip types on shaft butts. This allows the golfer to choose from not only different styles but also materials. Keep this display fresh by changing the grips twice a year. This will encourage frequent grip changes as the customer is exposed to the latest grip. Mens, ladies and putter grips make a good display.
2. Another display rack can be filled with all conceivable grip sizes. Golfers are naturally curious about different grip sizes and are attracted to this display. Golfers are fitted for correct grip size using the grips from this display.

■ Reshafting Specials

1. Offer a discount when reshafting a full set.
2. Offer a reshafting service for one shaft type. As with grips, shafts may be purchased in larger quantities at a reduced cost. Pass these savings to the customer in the form of a "special."
3. Offer to reshaft the 5 iron at cost to encourage full set reshafting after the 5 iron has been tried.

■ Shaft Promotion

1. Build 4 or 5 drivers with identical shaft patterns but each with a different flex. Strike a deal with the local pro shop to display these clubs. Allow golfers to take the clubs to the range or course for a trial. This is a great way to increase reshafting services. A profitable arrangement can be worked out so both you and the golf professional can benefit.
2. Same concept as above, but build 4 or 5 drivers with different shaft patterns and materials. Best way to increase reshafting services is to not use all conventional shafts. Try the latest composite or very lightweight steel shafts.
3. Also same concept, but build three graphite shafted drivers with different torque readings like 2°, 4.5° and 7°. Players can see for themselves which torque benefits them the most.

■ Loft and Lie Specials

1. Offer to check the loft and lie for free. Most sets will require adjusting. When the customer sees the recorded specifications, they will usually want to take advantage of your bending service.
2. Offer a free lie fitting service in return for loft and lie adjustment.

■ Loft and Lie Promotion

1. Demonstrate the importance of correctly fitted lofts and lies with a professional presentation at the golf course, range or organizational meetings. The most effective demonstration is using an iron with a hole drilled through the face and a shaft pushed into the hole. See GolfWorks® literature for more information.
2. Build a very upright and very flat 7 iron. Allow golfers to hit shots with both to see the effect on ball flight. (Greater loft produces more significant results, easier to hit.)

GENERAL PROMOTIONS AND INFORMATION

■ Golf Teacher's During a Lesson: Check Golf Club Condition and Proper Fit

When giving a lesson, a golf teacher has an ideal opportunity to inspect the pupil's golf clubs. The teacher may notice that the woods are in need of refinishing or a shaft is loose or bent. Clubs that need refinishing could be affected by moisture absorption or drying out which can alter the swingweight, delaminate, swell or shrink the wood itself. The golf professional can check the fit of the pupil's equipment and recommend any alterations that will improve its performance. New grips might be suggested, longer or shorter lengths, a change in loft or lies. With all the variations in hand size, playing abilities, swing planes and each manufacturer's own individual specifications, it can be estimated that over 90% of the golfers today would benefit from a proper fitting session that would determine the correct alterations to make on their golf clubs. Additionally, a lesson is a great way to promote club assembly, which is a very profitable area.

■ Checking Club Storage and "Winterizing"

Contact golf courses or clubs with bag storage facilities and arrange a time when you may look through each bag and inspect all the clubs. If all clubs are in need of repair leave a tag behind detailing the necessary work. Many times the owner will be appreciative of the attention given to their equipment and will contact you for the work.

Also through contacting golf courses or clubs you can arrange to offer winterizing to all of the bags in storage over the winter. For example, the club can bill the members a small additional charge on top of their bag storage fee. You can split an agreed percentage with the club or professional. Winterizing usually consists of a general sprucing and cleaning up of the entire set of woods and irons. Here's what is included: steel wool, touchup bare spots and dip or spray 1 coat of polyurethane on wood heads, replace frayed whipping if necessary, scrub grips, steel wool shafts, buff iron heads, wipe acetone on plastic ferrules, sandblast metal woods and perhaps repaint graphite shafts. Finally, wipe the golf bag clean, apply saddle soap or a special lubricant to the zippers, and put the clubs back in the bag.

Note: A good idea is to cover the bag and clubs to protect them from dust and dirt during the storage period. The large paper or clear plastic bags that dry cleaners use work perfectly for this and are only a few pennies apiece.

So, if you're ready to reach out for a little extra business and provide more assistance to your golfers or customers then you're ready for the extra repair business. It's another way to pursue increased self-satisfaction and more profit. Most all golfers appreciate this winterizing service simply because they are usually too busy to think of it on their own during the off season.

■ Do Club Repair for Other Golf Courses and Shops

If you want to grow quickly in the repair business, go out and talk with golf professionals or possibly the local sporting goods store, discount store or department store who sells golf equipment and make a pitch for their business emphasizing service, usually 5 working days on normal repairs and 10 working days on wood head refinishing. Show a sample of your wood and metal wood refinishing work and leave a few business cards and a price list with both wholesale and retail prices.

■ Authorized Repair Service Centers

Some manufacturers have established authorized repair service centers throughout the United States. If a repair facility is needed in your area and you write the golf manufacturers, you may be contacted by a company representative who will usually stop in and check your facility to see if you can handle the work load and if the quality of your work is adequate. The company representative will probably explain how many specific repair items that you would have to maintain in inventory.

■ Rejuvenating "Trade-ins"

A golf professional or discount store usually accepts trade-ins from customers when they purchase new golf clubs. The traded-in clubs can be made much more valuable if the woods are refinished and the irons refurbished. Of course, the condition of the clubs and their potential value must be considered very closely before more money is invested in them. Do not rule out some half-way measures such as buffing the shafts to remove rust and dirt, replacing broken or frayed whippings, sand blasting metal woods, dipping or spraying a coat of finish over a lightly steel wooled wood head and cleaning the face grooves in both woods and irons and paint filling them. Trade-ins are not very desirable commodities at many country clubs because of the type of clientele. In many cases the professional at this type of club will be willing to sell his used clubs in the peak of condition. Usually, the key to success in building this particular part of the business is local newspaper advertising in the classified section. This will help build a clientele fairly quickly and from then on sales will result by word of mouth to the new golfer and also the golfer on a budget who wants to buy good used pro-line golf clubs.

■ Advertising

Local newspaper advertising, if practical for your situation, can give a substantial boost to your business. Preferably, this would not be a classified ad but would be a regular ad inserted into the sports section of the newspaper. The Monday edition would be ideal since Monday sports pages carry all of the final results of the weekend's events, including the final round coverage of professional golf tournaments. The ad will be seen by a great number of golfers. The size of the ad depends on how much money you have to spend. However, stay small at first and advertise a few specials for the more common repairs such as refinishing or a special price on regripping only if the entire set is done. If you build custom woods, advertise it. It is also a good idea to state your capabilities in the ad such as complete golf club repair facilities, custom fitting, custom clubs, used clubs, and if you accept trade-ins.

Another way to increase repair and alteration business is to arrange to have a sign put up in a pro shop or discount store. Tell the customers that you do this type of work and better yet list the services that you have available. Rarely will you see a sign in a pro shop telling golfers that they can have their clubs repaired or altered. Have the sign put up, it's the least expensive form of advertising you can do and one which will reward you with increased customer awareness of your services. Many golf professionals are happy to do this for a percentage of income.

■ Assemble Your Own Custom Woods and Irons

The mere fact that golfers will spend approximately 600 million dollars on new golf clubs each year gives a strong indication why so many new golf club companies are displaying their wares at the January PGA Merchandise Show in Florida each year. Custom golf club manufacturing is on the upswing and there is still plenty of room for new entries into this field, especially on the local level. The whole secret here is to offer the members of your club and other local golfers a top quality custom fitted set of golf clubs that perform and are durable and they can get them serviced.

Building custom clubs is not difficult if you purchase metal wood heads and iron heads because, except for raw materials, you will not have to purchase any other equipment than that used to repair golf clubs.

If you develop a sound approach to the proper fitting of golf clubs, fully understand the mechanics and design of golf clubs and you can put that extra something into your own individual custom clubs with the highest quality of workmanship, you will surely have an excellent chance at successfully building a very profitable custom club portion of the business.

The following information was developed to show the profitability and feasibility of getting into custom golf club assembly. It could help you re-evaluate your approach to merchandising golf clubs.

The wholesale costs of golf clubs have skyrocketed. The retail market for golf clubs has become so competitively priced that a reasonable operating profit is very difficult to obtain unless you purchase in large quantities at deal prices and sell at very low profit margins. The main problem with this is you are trading dollars and assume a high risk on a larger inventory that may not sell.

It is a good idea to carry nationally advertised golf club brands and have them available for customers who ask for them; however, if volume and a decent profit are to return, coupled with a reduced inventory and reduced cash outlay, you must look at assembling or as we call it "custom building and custom fitting" golf clubs. It is fun, easy, profitable and rewarding. With just a few sets of heads, a few different shafts and grip types you have in your inventory hundreds of possible set variations that can be custom fit to your customer and custom assembled for delivery in two days or less. Think of it! A very small inventory cost with hundreds of sets available almost immediately.

Let's look at some cost comparisons:

A study of 1994 wholesale costs from published manufacturers' price lists shows an average iron cost of $44.00, metal wood cost of $80.00 and persimmon wood cost of $85.00.

A study of discounted prices nationally, given by the larger volume buyers, shows that irons retail for about $82.00 each, metal woods about $141.00 each and persimmon woods about $155.00 each.

It is quite easy to see the dilemma the small to medium shop encounters in purchasing just a few sets from each manufacturer at normal wholesale costs. They simply cannot compete unless the customer's loyalty is greater than the desire to purchase the same product at a lower cost elsewhere.

Here are the figures, based on 1994 prices, if you purchase finished persimmon wood, metal wood, iron heads and components from the GolfWorks® and assemble the clubs yourself:

Persimmon Woods – Finished Head

(15 finished, 6 insert colors and 4 models to choose from.)	$ 30.00
Grip	$ .95
Tape and Solvent	$ .09
Shaft	$ 4.45
Ferrule	$ .14
Whipping	$ .27
Epoxy	$ .15
Lead Powder	$ .12
Total Component Cost	**$ 36.17**

Metal Woods – Finished Head

(11 models from which to choose. Includes "Custom Built, Custom Fit" medallion and weights.)	$ 22.00
Grip	$ .95
Tape and Solvent	$ .09
Shaft	$ 4.75
Ferrule (not always needed)	$ .14
Epoxy	$ .15
Total Component Cost	**$ 28.08**

Iron Head

(Includes "Custom Built, Custom Fit" medallion and weights.)	$ 9.90
Grip	$ .95
Tape and Solvent	$ .09
Shaft	$ 3.95
Ferrule (not always needed)	$ .14
Epoxy	$ .15
Total Component Cost	**$ 15.18**

As you can see the clubs that you build yourself reduce your costs substantially. No matter how you figure your labor, the amount of time to assemble clubs from finished components is minimal and your actual profits will still be spectacular. Couple this with the fact that the clubs are actually built and fit to your customer's specifications;

there is no lead or anything added down the shaft or counterbalanced in the grip end and from some suppliers the finished club can bear your own name, company name, country club or logo in a high quality medallion, decal or stamp. You should keep at least one set of partially finished custom clubs in your shop. For example, the heads would be finished and assembled on shafts but no other work performed. The customer who is attracted to the set can be fit for length, grip type and size, swingweight, face angle on woods (through slight bending of the shaft) and lie of both the woods and irons (again through bending)

Now let's look at what you can assemble a set for:

4 Persimmon Woods	$ 144.68
4 Metal Woods	$ 112.32
8 Irons	$ 121.44
9 Irons	$ 136.62
or	
4 Persimmon Woods and 9 Irons	$ 281.30
4 Metal Woods and 9 Irons	$ 248.94

Compare this price with the manufacturers' wholesale price of $736.00 to purchase 4 Persimmon woods and 9 Irons. As you can see, this is less than ½ the cost of 4 & 9 sets from major golf club manufacturers at their average 1994 published wholesale costs!

Also, it is less than ½ the cost of 4 & 9 average discounted retail cost nationally.

You can determine your own selling costs depending on your particular market, but I think you will agree that the smart, aggressive merchandiser can bring the words "profit," "fitting" and "clubmaking" back into selling golf clubs. And to top it all off, you can now service what you sell and your customers will look to you as a knowledgeable clubmaker whose expertise should surely gain greater admiration and respect.

One Final Word

The repair business and the other related aspects discussed in this chapter can provide the reader with a wonderful opportunity for increasing personal or company income. Pro only merchandise policies have broken down with the majority of sales being now made by the off-course discounter. Consumers can now have their repair needs satisfied at locations as diverse as the most elite private course to the basement workshop of a good friend. It is expected that this trend will continue for many years.

CHAPTER 30

REPAIR SHOPS AND REPAIR PRICE LISTS FROM AROUND THE COUNTRY

Repair Shops

I have always felt fortunate to have the opportunity to visit many repair shops throughout the United States and also other parts of the world. Whether a large shop or a small one it seems that I always go away with some new idea that can be shared with other club repairmen. This chapter includes photographs from a number of such shops that were kind enough to allow us to "look in" on their operations. The old adage "a picture is worth a thousand words" certainly applies here.

30-1
R. C. Russell of Bridge City, Texas makes efficient use of every available square inch of space in his full service repair shop. Note the four electric drills in homemade holders. R. C.'s volume is so great that he finds it worthwhile to keep each of these drills ready with commonly used attachments so he doesn't have to change attachments so frequently.

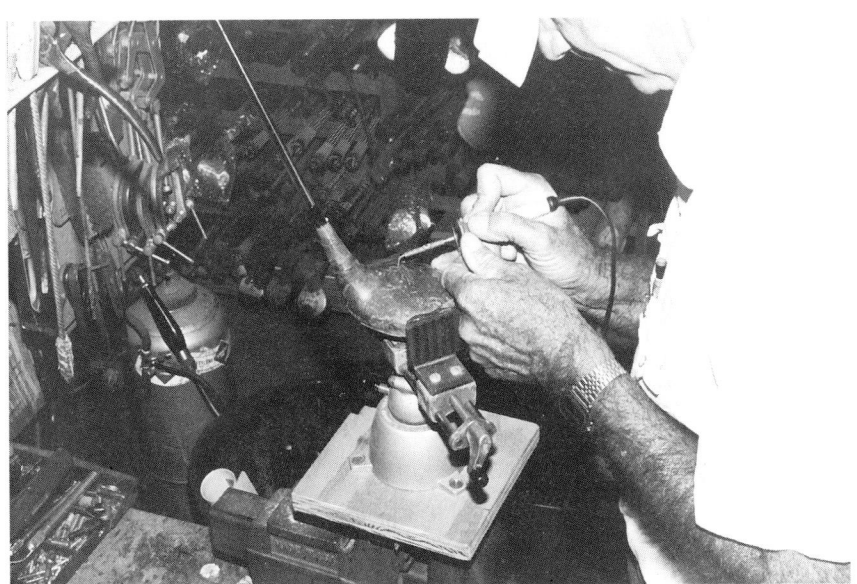

30-2
R. C. Russell carefully etches wood stampings by clamping the head in a Panavise. The Panavise allows R. C. to adjust the position of the head to better access parts of the stamping.

30-3
Many types of shafts are kept in separate cubicles in this shaft holder that R. C.
built using plans found in this book.

30-4
Old cardboard boxes make good grip storage containers. Golf ball dozen boxes are
also handy for small parts or saving old components and parts. Put old Spalding parts
in a Spalding golf ball box, old MacGregor parts in a MacGregor golf ball box, etc.

30-5
This is a portion of the author's original repair shop. Note the 4 foot tall wood vise for working on wood clubs. The pegboard caps and jars organized the many small parts such as ferrules, rings, screws, etc. A repair shop should be kept fairly neat and be well planned to facilitate a good work flow.

30-6
This photo shows part of the Model Repair Shop originally set up at The GolfWorks®. This model repair shop was quite extensive and was used to give customers a first hand look at an efficient set up.

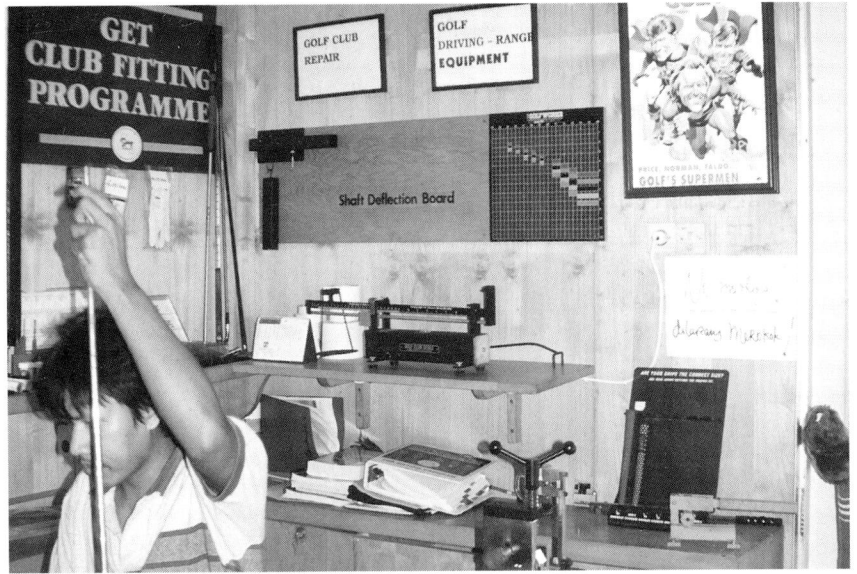

30-7

This is a photo of a repair shop in Singapore. Note the beautiful wood paneling, shelves and workbench. The owner of this shop must keep a neat appearance because he allows his customers to enter the shop to drop off and pick up their clubs. Note The GolfWorks® Loft and Lie Machine in the middle of the floor. Such an open location encourages customers to have their iron specifications checked and adjusted.

30-8

Russ Swanson of Cape Cod, Massachusetts keeps a neat shop. Note the rack on the right that holds clubs in process or for customer pick-up. The finishing supplies are efficiently placed on shelves in the back, ready for use.

30-9
Like many repair shops, Russ also fits and assembles custom clubs. Note the many professional features of this part of his shop where the customers are custom fitted, like the swing analyzer, camcorder, checkered back drop, posters and assembled GolfWork's® clubs ready for sale.

30-10
In Montreal, Quebec, Claude DeSautels separates his repair area from a custom fitting/retail area with large glass windows. This allows customers to view the repair operations without interfering with work. Allowing the customer to see the extent of the repair operations increases new club sales also. The customer naturally assumes the worker has great golf club knowledge and is qualified to recommend new clubs.

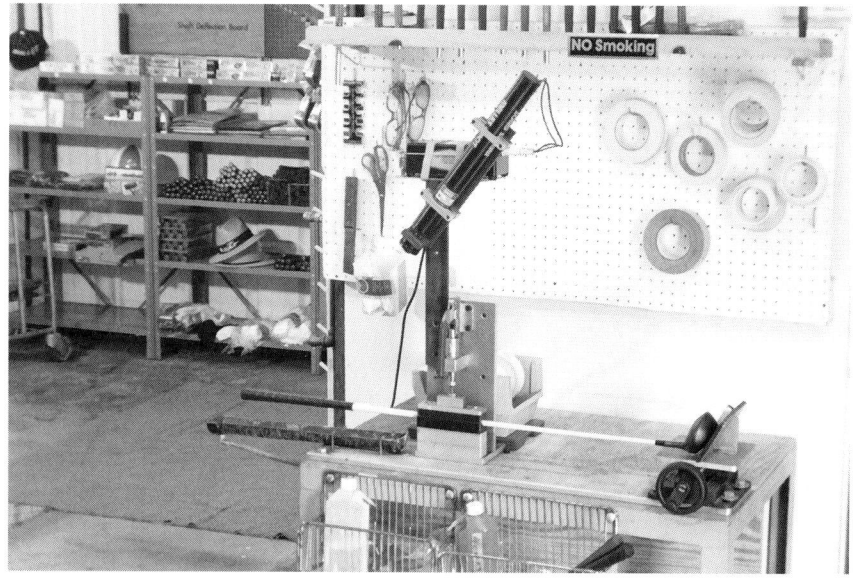

30-11
Jim Brown's shop in Youngstown, Ohio contains a piece of sophisticated machinery that is seldom seen in most shops, a grip laser alignment machine. When the club is placed in the clamping device, a laser beam shows the exact center of the shaft to serve as an alignment aid. The beam shows if the grip is twisted.

30-12
Jim also uses a frequency analyzer to better match the flex of shafts he is reshafting or installing in new clubs. The analyzer is placed on its own table on the right side of the photo. Note also The GolfWorks® swingweight scale and shaft deflection board.

30-13
Jim has a wide range of clubheads from which to choose for customers of all playing abilities. Note also the overhead shaft storage, which frees up more space on the floor.

30-14
Larry Wolfe of Columbus, Ohio keeps a good quality Binks spray booth in his shop. Here he applies the finish coats to woods and metal woods. Note that Larry properly wears a respirator to filter out solvents and fumes from the air he breathes.

30-15
This photo is of a large volume repair shop in Jakarta, Indonesia. Along the edge of the table the owner has attached a row of "V" shaped recesses so that shafts and clubs will not slide and fall down – a common problem for repair shops.

30-16
The clubhouse at Muirfield Village in Dublin, Ohio was recently expanded and a new club repair room was added. This is where The GolfWorks® performs club repair during each Memorial Golf Tournament.

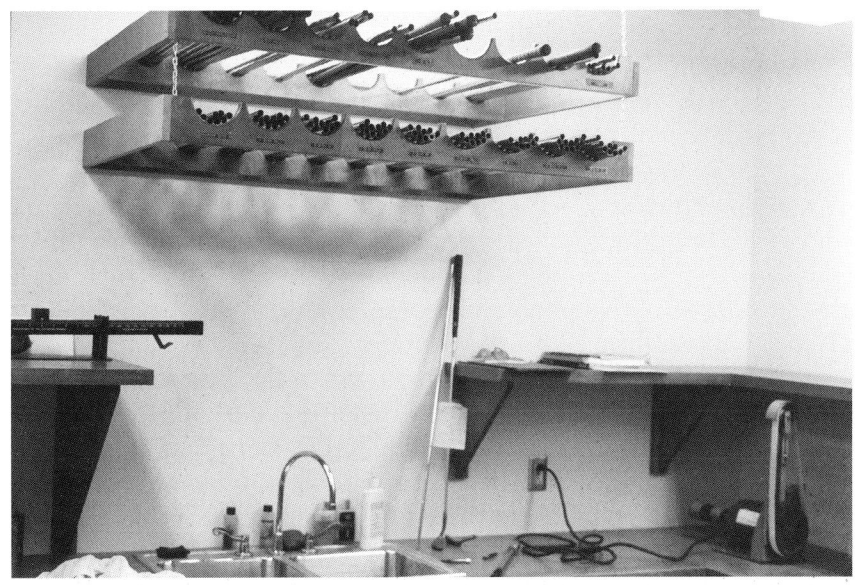

30-17
Note the overhead shaft storage cylinders at the repair room at Muirfield Village. A convenient feature of this room is the sink so hot iron heads can be quickly cooled under running water.

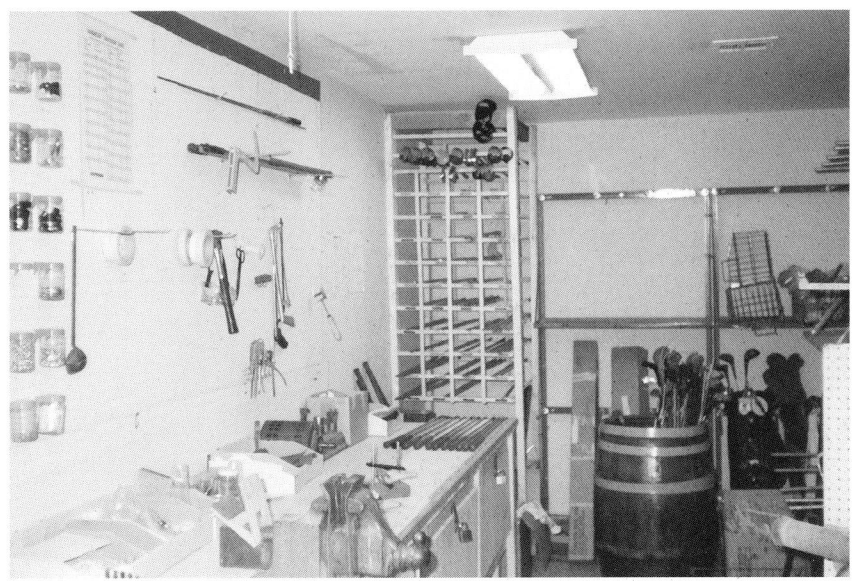

30-18
David Kohlman's shop in Evansville, Indiana. This photo shows a small portion of the shop. Note the club storage and shaft rack built into one corner.

Repair Price Lists

When someone decides to start a repair business, probably the single most important element is the price list. All of the repair volume one could handle will not make up for undercharging which can mean no profits or even a loss. On the other hand, high prices and no repair volume can also spell disaster.

Repair prices vary quite a bit from area to area. Location, reputation, economic conditions and the amount of golfers are a few of the influences that determine pricing. This is something that you will need to research in your own area.

This chapter's purpose is to show you some of the repair price lists and various ways to describe repairs from around the country. Of course, it must be understood as you read the prices that they are current as of June, 1994. Increases in raw materials, labor and overhead may have a significant influence on prices in the near future.

An important consideration in setting up a repair price list is whether or not to have a wholesale and a retail price. If you are doing other golf professionals repair work, they will request your wholesale price so they can in turn put a markup on the repair to their customer. If you are doing repair strictly for the consumer or players at one golf course, then you only need a retail price list.

The repair price lists that follow vary from simple single page descriptions to the very complete listing of The GolfWorks®. These examples will give you a guide for listing and describing the repairs that you will do.

The price list below is a simple one. This is from an East Coast golf shop.

REPAIR PRICE LIST

	Suggested Retail Price
Refinishing	$30.00
Reshafting (includes rubber grip)	
Steel:	
Irons	$20.00
Woods	$25.00
Graphite:	
Irons	$60.00 - 80.00
Woods	$65.00 - 100.00
Remove broken shaft (inside hosel)	$10.00
Reset Lies and Lofts - Irons	$ 4.00 per club
Lies and Face Angle	$ 6.00 per club
New Inserts (poured, cycolac or phenolic)	$22.00
(does not include refinishing)	
Reset Soleplate	$10.00
Reset Shaft	$15.00
Lengthen Club (does not include grip)	$ 4.00
Graphite	$10.00
Shorten Club	$ 1.00
Grips:	
Rubber	$ 5.00 - 6.00
Cord	$ 8.00

This repair price list is from a shop located in the Midwest.

REPAIR PRICE LIST

REFINISHING

Any stained or painted color	$20.00
Reset soleplate and insert	$ 6.00
Reset soleplate only	$ 3.00
Stainless metal woods - sandblast	$13.00
or with one coat of poly	$16.00
Metal wood	$20.00
Repair split or broken head w/ refinish only	$45.00

REPLACE INSERT

Fiber, Cycolac, Pour-in-Place Epoxy	$28.00
with reseal	$22.00
Insert only	$17.00
Repair insert & reseal	$22.00
Custom Insert (keysite, 2 color, firing pin)	$32.00
Repair custom insert & reseal	$26.00
Aluminum insert	$35.00
Graphite insert	$40.00

GENERAL REPAIRS

Weight port in metal wood	$ 8.00
Foam metal head for rattle	$15.00
with refinish	$20.00
Change swingweight	$ 5.00
when soleplate has to be removed	$16.50
Replace whipping	$ 3.00
Tighten Loose Head	$ 9.00
Repair split neck	$12.00
Change hosel bore (larger only)	$ 3.50
Remove shaft inside hosel	$ 8.00
Repair damaged face	$ 9.50
Reset soleplate and reseal	$16.00
Reset sole and insert and reseal	$18.00
Reset backweight and reseal	$17.00
Change face angle, roll, or bulge and reseal	$17.00
Touch-up and reseal	$14.00
Scribe top of club	$ 6.00
Change lie or angle on metal wood	$ 3.00
Change length - includes grip (Chamois add $1.00, cord add $1.50 and leather add $12.50)	
longer	$ 9.00
shorter	$ 5.00
Steel extension with no grip	$ 5.00
Extend graphite with no grip	$ 9.00

This is a repair price list from a shop located in the Southwest.

REPAIR PRICE LIST

REFINISH	(Includes soleplate removal & swingweight adjustment)	$ 25.00
	Metal Woods - Sandblast Finish	$ 15.00
	Repair face; extra	$ 6.00
	Reset insert; extra	$ 5.00
	Replace insert; extra	$ 7.50
	Replace custom insert; extra	$ 9.00
	Repair split head; extra	$ 11.00
	Change loft &/or face angle	$ 3.00
RESHAFT	Dynamic, TT Lite, Jet Step, Pro Fit	$ 15.00
	Dynamic Gold	$ 18.00
	Aldila Low Torque	$ 34.00
	Aldila HM-40 - Titanium - Alloy 2000, Harrison	$ 72.00
	HM-30	$ 44.00
	Hogan Apex	$ 18.00
	Gold Plus	$ 20.00
	Shaft furnished by customer	$ 7.50
	Offset Putter	$ 16.50
REGRIP	Golf Pride - Rubber	$ 3.50
	Avon Chamois, Tour Wrap	$ 4.00
	All Cord & Half Cord	$ 4.50
	Neumann Leather	$ 16.00
REPAIRS	Change Swingweight Woods	$ 6.00
	Change Swingweight Irons	$ 4.00
	Reset insert	$ 7.00
	Replace insert & reseal	$ 12.00
	Reset soleplate	$ 6.00
	Replace whipping thread	$ 2.50
	Change length - Includes swingweight adjustment woods	$ 8.00
	Change length - Irons	$ 6.00
	Change length with new grip add	$ 1.50
	Tighten loose head - woods	$ 7.50
	Tighten loose head - irons	$ 4.00
	Set loft/lie single	$ 4.00
	Set loft/lie sets	$ 2.00
	Remove shaft broken in hosel	$ 4.00
	Change loft/face angle - woods	$ 8.50

This is the 1994 GolfWorks® Price List. Over the years it has been changed and refined to spell out in greater detail every type of repair. The information given in this repair price list can be used in your price list if desired without fear of copyright infringement.

THE GOLFWORKS®
REPAIR PRICE LIST

RECHROMING AND REFINISHING IRONS
Complete Refinishing of your old, nicked and battered irons.

We refinish irons to their original, new from the factory look! Send us your stainless steel or chromeplated irons—we do both! Most first time customers are amazed at the results of our refinishing as evidenced by the hundreds of complimentary letters we have received.

STAINLESS STEEL IRONS

Before

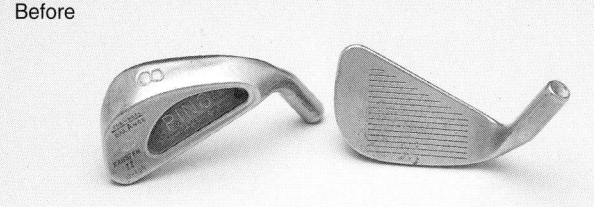

Here is what we do:
1. Check swingweight.
2. Remove head from shaft.
3. Remove nicks and buff.
4. Sandblast face.
5. Reinstall head on shaft and reswingweight.
6. Paintfill all engravings (red or black).
7. Buff ferrules to original lustre.

After - Vibratory Finish

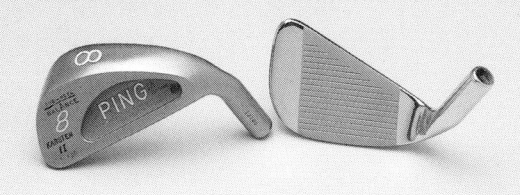

Unshafted Irons . . . . **$8.75 per club**
Shafted Irons . . . . **$14.25 per club**

After - High Polish Finish

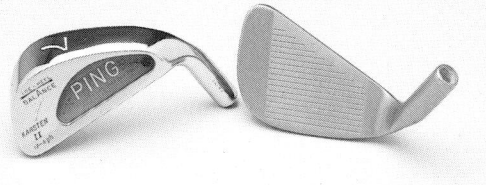

CHROMEPLATED IRONS

BEFORE

AFTER

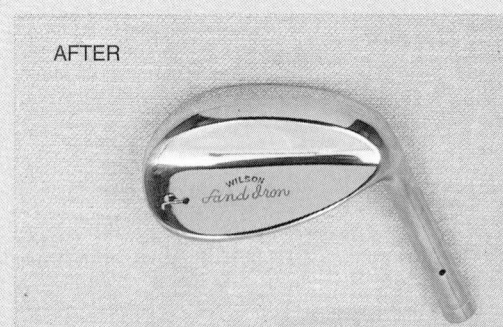

Here is what we do:
1. Check swingweight.
2. Remove head from shaft.
3. Strip off old chrome.
4. Remove nicks and buff.
5. Chromeplate and sandblast face.
6. Reinstall head on shaft and reswingweight.
7. All engravings are paintfilled (red or black).
8. Buff ferrules to original lustre.

Unshafted Irons . . . . **$12.50 per club**
Shafted Irons . . . . **$18.00 per club**
Unshafted Satin Chrome Irons $13.00 per club
Shafted Satin Chrome Irons . . $18.50 per club

SPECIAL REPAIRS OFFERED WITH REFINISHING STAINLESS STEEL OR CHROMEPLATED IRONS

Replace ferrules . . . . $ 1.75
Weld hosel cracks or holes too large to grind out . . . . $ 14.00
Weld on new hosel (specify bore) . . . . $ 23.00
Weld additional build-up . . . . $ 13.50
Custom grind to gram weight . . . . $ 6.00
Custom grind to special shape . . . . $ 6.00

ADDTIONAL NOTES FOR RECHROMING AND REFINISHING IRONS

■ We cannot remove fiberglass shafts from irons without destroying them. We can, however, install new steel or graphite shafts and grips to your specifications with the appropriate additional charge.

■ We can refinish your Ping stainless steel irons to a high polish lustre, making them quite unique and very attractive, but be sure to specify this in your instructions or they will receive the original dull vibratory Grey finish.

■ On certain heads with a clear epoxy medallion in the back of the club (such as Wilson staff heads) we cannot guarantee that these will not fall out during the chroming process.

■ Vinyl or celluloid covered shafts in older clubs are extremely difficult to remove. Occasionally they break because they are rusted internally and are brittle. If a shaft breaks we will notify you and ask if you want it replaced with a regular steel shaft and grip of your choice at an additional cost.

■ In the rechroming process, hosels are not ground down very much. The condition they arrive in is the condition in which they leave. Often hosels are very thin (or thin in spots) and new chrome will crack in these spots making them very noticeable. The only solution is to weld or replace the hosel, depending on how thin this area is. Sometimes we can identify these potential trouble spots and sometimes we cannot. This problem is fairly uncommon but deserves mentioning.

■ Ping putters are difficult to reshaft because of a ball bearing that holds the shaft in the head. Many times the only way to reshaft them is to drill up through the bottom of the sole to remove the bearing. This hole is then filled with epoxy. If you do not want us to do this, please be sure to specify in your instructions. If the shaft cannot be removed without drilling, we will return the club to you without reshafting.

■ Certain putter heads may be made of zinc, brass or other pot metals and alloys. These heads may partially dissolve during the rechroming process. We try to identify these heads before stripping, but sometimes this is impossible. *Please don't send heads of this material for rechroming as we cannot replate them.*

■ Many older clubs are covered with rust and deep pits. When grinding, a decision often must be made as to when to stop grinding -- while there are still pits or while there is still stamping. We always decide to save the stamping even though there will still be pits showing. This will retain the most value of the club. On certain models with concave backs (like the MacGregor M65), the pitting cannot fully be ground away without changing the lines and lessening the value of the club, so often the rest of the club will look like new but pitting may still be slightly evident in the concave area.

■ Welding is the most complicated iron repair. Please be aware that sometimes small pits show up after chroming. This is unavoidable.

■ We are unable to copper the faces of MacGregor Colokrom heads or ceramic faces on MacGregor CF4000 heads. We can rechome these heads and change the face to the normal sandblasted type which most people prefer due to improved durability.

■ Please adjust lofts and lies *before* sending irons in for rechroming to prevent damage to the new plating.

■ We do not offer refinishing of graphite or ceramic iron heads, nor do we offer ceramic spray coating for iron faces.

■ Pressed in tungsten weights on the back of certain irons may wear during the stripping and regrinding process. This is beyond our control and can affect the look of the weights after plating.

■ When reshafting irons or metal woods with a lighter shaft (i.e. graphite), in order to maintain the same swingweight, more head weight will be needed. There is limited space in which to add weight in a metal wood and unless there is a weight port in an iron, there is no space to add weight. In these cases, weight must be added down the shaft, so do take this into consideration when sending us this type of club to be reshafted. Please advise us if you do not want lead down the hosel and we will add lead tape to the outside of the club.

■ Many assembled irons sent to us for rechroming have lead down the hosels. When a head is removed from its shaft, weight originally put down the shaft may be lost. This weight, plus the weight sometimes lost in the rechroming process, must be replaced when the club is reassembled. We return all irons to the original swingweight by adding weight down the hosel. Please advise us if you do not want lead down the hosel and we will add lead tape to the outside of the club.

■ Swingweights can only be adjusted on completely assembled clubs.

IRON CLUB REPAIRS AND ALTERATIONS

■ **RESHAFTING irons with regripping** **$15.00**

This charge is for labor only. We install the shaft, swingweight and regrip the club. To find your exact cost, look up the shaft and grip prices in the GolfWorks® Full Line Catalog and add them to this labor charge. Be sure to add an additional $5.75 if wrapped leather is chosen.

Please let us know the shaft pattern, flex, finished length, swingweight, grip and installed grip size. (i.e. Reshaft with Dynamic Gold S300 36", Victory grip standard size, D-2 swingweight - $15.00 plus $6.00 shaft plus $1.25 grip equals $22.25.)

■ **RESHAFTING irons without regripping** **$14.00**

Reshafting charge for labor only to install a shaft without regripping. To find your exact cost, look up the shaft price in this catalog and add it to the cost of reshafting. Be sure you specify the shaft pattern, flex and finished length. *(i.e. Reshaft with Dynamic Gold S300 35" - $14.00 plus $6.00 shaft equals $20.00.)*

■ **REGRIPPING with slip-on grip** **$4.25**

Regripping charge is for the labor only to install a slip-on grip. To find your exact cost, look up the grip price in the GolfWorks® Full Line Catalog and add the grip price to the regripping charge. Be sure to specify grip desired, color and installed grip size. *(i.e. Regrip with a Victory grip installed 1/32 oversize, $1.25 grip price plus $4.25 regripping charge equals $5.50 total cost.)*

■ **REGRIPPING with wrapped leather** **$10.00**

Regripping charge for a wrapped leather grip is for the labor only (which includes underlisting). To find your exact cost look up the grip price in the GolfWorks® Full Line Catalog and add the grip price to the regripping charge. Be sure to specify grip desired, color and installed size. *(i.e. Regrip with a Neumann Maroon calf grip installed 1/64" undersize, $10.75 grip price plus $10.00 regripping charge equals $20.75 total cost.)*

GENERAL REPAIRS

Tighten loose head. . . . . $ 6.25
Repair rattle in shaft . . . . $ 14.00
Reset shaft. . . . . $ 11.00
Change length - longer or shorter (labor only - add grip price) . . . . $ 8.75
Remove broken drill bit from hosel (includes welding and refinishing) . . . . $ 30.00
Replace ferrules only . . . . $ 11.00
Electro-Etch name on head (specify location) . . . . $ 4.50
Set loft and lie (specify degrees) 1-7 irons. . . . . $ 4.50
                               8 or more irons, each. . . . . $ 4.00
Clean and condition leather wrapped grips . . . . $ 5.00
Install new iron head (labor only). . . . . $ 22.00
Wire wheel and buff rusty irons . . . . $ 8.75
Change hosel bore (specify size). . . . . $ 6.00
Remove shaft broken off flush with hosel . . . . $ 10.00

IRON BOX GROOVING SERVICES

The GolfWorks® offers precision milling of box groove score lines ("U" grooves) in your irons. We were the first to offer approved box grooving services and the high quality results of this service are in line with the latest rulings and specifications of the U.S.G.A.

Box grooves are an advantage under flyer conditions, when a lubricant becomes trapped between the clubface and the ball. This occurs commonly when hitting in wet or high grass. Compared to traditional "V" grooves, box grooves create more friction and the ball slides up the clubface less at impact. This game improvement feature can provide up to ten percent more spin to improve control, direction and will offset undesirable "flyers."

CHROMEPLATED IRONS (RIGHT-HAND ONLY)

If your irons are chromeplated it is mandatory that they are completely refinished after milling in the new box grooves. This is because milling cuts through the chromeplating and rusting will then occur. The milling process requires chromeplating first be removed, then the heads are milled, next the heads are rechromed.

Mill Box Grooves and Rechrome	1-7 Irons	8 or more
Shafted Chromeplated Iron Heads.	**$26.75** each	**$24.75** each
Unshafted Chromeplated Iron Heads	**$21.25** each	**$19.25** each
Shafted Satin Chromeplated Iron Heads	**$27.25** each	**$25.25** each
Unshafted Satin Chromeplated Iron Heads.	**$21.75** each	**$19.75** each

STAINLESS STEEL IRONS (RIGHT-HAND ONLY)

If your irons are stainless steel, it is not necessary to have a total refinishing of the iron heads after the box grooves have been milled and the head sandblasted; however, refinishing greatly enhances the club's appearance. If you want your irons box grooved and refinished, see charges below.

Mill Box Grooves and Sandblast Faces	1-7 Irons	8 or more
Shafted or Unshafted Clubs Box Grooved	**$10.00** each	**$ 8.00** each
Shafted Clubs Box Grooved and Refinished	**$22.25** each	**$20.25** each
Unshafted Clubs Box Grooved and Refinished.	**$16.75** each	**$14.75** each

METAL WOOD AND WOOD CLUB REPAIRS AND ALTERATIONS

You'll be amazed at the difference The GolfWorks® excellent repair work will make in your golf clubs. We rely on the finest in repair skills, machinery and technology to produce the highest quality results.

REFINISHING

- Wood Clubs - specify stain color. . . . . $ 39.00
- Stainless Metal Woods (sandblasted or painted) . . . . $ 26.00
- Metal/Wood Combination Head. . . . . $ 29.00
- Refurbish Display Woods (Antiques) with no insert . . . . $ 14.50

The following repairs are only done in conjunction with refinishing. To determine the total repair cost, add refinishing charges below:

- Changing swingweight by removing soleplate and adding or removing weight (woods only). . . $ 5.00
- Welding Broken Metal Wood Hosel . . . . $ 23.00
- Repair damaged face (woods only) . . . . $ 8.00
- Change face angle, loft, roll and/or bulge by filing with maximum of 2° on loft or face angle (woods only) . . . . $ 7.00
- Repair split or broken head - finish must be black (woods only). . . . . $ 21.00
- Reset backweight (woods only) . . . . $ 8.00
- Install new backweight - smaller size heads only (woods only) . . . . $ 11.00
- Install new blank soleplate with number (woods only) . . . . $ 17.50
- Repair loose weights under soleplate (woods only) . . . . $ 5.00
- Replace inserts:
  - Fiber, cycolac, pour-in-place epoxy (woods only) . . . . $ 15.00
  - Custom Inserts with Keysite, 2-color or Firing Pin (woods only) . . . . $ 20.50
  - Graphite, Aluminum or Phenolic . . . . $ 15.00

■ RESHAFTING woods or metal woods with gripping **$22.00**

Reshafting charge is for the labor only to install a shaft plus swingweighting and gripping the club. To find your exact cost, look up the shaft and grip price in the GolfWorks® catalog and add them to the cost of reshafting. Be sure to add an additional $5.75 labor charge if wrapped leather is chosen. Be sure you let us know the shaft pattern, flex, finished length, swingweight, grip and installed grip size. *(i.e. Reshaft with Dynamic Gold S300 43", Victory grip 1/32 oversize, D-2 swingweight is $22.00 plus $6.50 shaft and $1.25 grip to equal $29.75 total cost.)*

■ **RESHAFTING woods or metal woods without gripping** **$19.00**

Reshafting charge for labor only to install a shaft without grip. To find your exact cost look up the shaft price in the GolfWorks® Catalog and add it to the cost of reshafting. Be sure you let us know the shaft pattern, flex and finished length. *(i.e. Reshaft with Dynamic Gold S300 42" is $19.00 plus $6.50 shaft to equal $25.50. No grip will be installed.)*

■ **REGRIPPING with slip-on grips** . . . . **$ 4.25**

Regripping charge is for the labor only to install a slip-on grip. To find your exact cost, look up the grip price in the GolfWorks® Catalog and add the grip price to the regripping charge. Be sure to specify grip desired, color and installed size. *(i.e. Regripping with a Victory grip installed 1/64" oversize - add $1.25 grip price to $4.25 regripping charge to equal $5.50 total cost.)*

■ **REGRIPPING with wrapped leather** **$10.00**

Regripping charge is for the labor only to install a wrapped leather grip (including underlisting). To find your exact cost look up the grip price in the GolfWorks® Catalog and add the grip price to the regripping charge. Be sure to specify grip desired, color and installed size. *(i.e. Regripping with a Neumann Maroon calf grip installed 1/64" undersize - add $10.75 grip price to $10.00 regripping charge to equal $20.75 total cost.)*

GENERAL REPAIRS

- Clean and spray one coat of polyurethane* . . . . $ 8.00
- Replace nylon whipping* . . . . $ 3.25
- Replace linen whipping* . . . . $ 5.00
- Tighten loose head, reset shaft, repair rattle in shaft or repair split neck* . . . . $ 13.00
- Change hosel bore on unshafted heads, larger only (woods only) . . . . $ 9.00
- Remove shaft broken inside hosel* . . . . $ 9.50
- Change length longer or shorter (labor only - add grip price)* . . . . $ 9.00
- Reset soleplate only (includes one coat poly) (woods only) . . . . $ 16.00
- Change lie by bending shaft (±2° maximum)* . . . . $ 3.00
- Repair loose weights under soleplate (includes one coat of poly)(woods only) . . . . $ 15.00
- Refinish old wooden shaft (woods only) . . . . $ 13.00
- Install new wood or metal wood head - This price is for labor only. To find the exact cost, add the labor price to the price of the head from the GolfWorks® Catalog. We only use our heads. Be sure to specify model, finish color and swingweight.* . . . . $ 22.00
- Assemble your head, shaft and grip (includes whipping, ferrule assembly, swingweighting, reboring, trimming shaft, etc.)* . . . $ 22.00
- Metal wood swingweight adjustment . . . . $ 8.00
- Metal wood face angle and lie angle adjustment (no short hosels) . . . . $ 5.00
- Clean and condition leather wrapped grip* . . . . $ 5.00
- Install metal wood weight port . . . . $ 13.00

* Applies to both metal wood and wood heads

NOTES

_____

_____

_____

_____

_____

_____

_____

CHAPTER 31

LEARNING THROUGH THE GOLFWORKS® GOLF CLUB REPAIR AND ASSEMBLY WORKSHOPS

April of 1982 saw The GolfWorks® embark upon what has become the most successful series of golf club repair workshops held anywhere. Initially, we looked upon the club repair workshops as a short-term run to handle what was felt to be a limited number of requests by club repair enthusiasts. However, as word spread of the educational and enjoyable time had by all at The GolfWorks'® unique setting, it was soon realized that this "short term" affair would have no end. The workshop schedule has grown from eight per year in 1982, twelve in '86, 25 in '88 and to 40 in '89 and they continue to grow in number and size. Due to the success of the repair schools, many graduates demanded that additional courses be taught that would expand upon the knowledge they gained from their initial visit. We have therefore added schools that specialize in training for golf club assembly and golf club fitting.

The students have come not only from within the borders of the United States, but also from countries all over the world. A list of some of the countries represented at our workshops would include Canada, West Germany, Great Britain, South Africa, Argentina, Saudi Arabia, Italy and India. These foreign students have given the workshops an international flavor not only with their presence, but also with their stories of working conditions in their own countries. So, it is not unusual for a "local" student to come to a GolfWorks® Repair Workshop and be working along-side someone who has traveled 10,000 miles just to learn the skills of club repair.

When students arrive at The GolfWorks®, they settle into their own work environment that includes individual work stations and tools. Surrounding the work stations are all the machinery necessary to perform any steps in the golf club repair, assembly or fitting process. This includes four different sanding machines, three different bending machines, four different frequency analyzers and three different computerized swing analyzers - all to give the student a wide variety when choosing what is best for their individual club repair, fitting or assembly needs. In addition to the normal array of machines, the student is also exposed to the machinery necessary for performing the unconventional repairs — refinishing stainless irons and metal woods. Finishing off the room are tables and pegboards that hold virtually every club repair, assembly and fitting item shown in The GolfWorks® catalog. These tools, gauges and supplies are used throughout the week. Whatever the needs of the student, the workshop is set up and equipped to handle those needs.

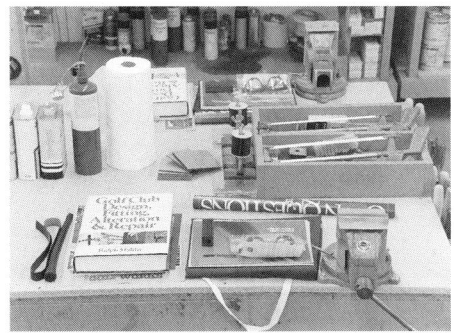

This photo shows a typical school setup.

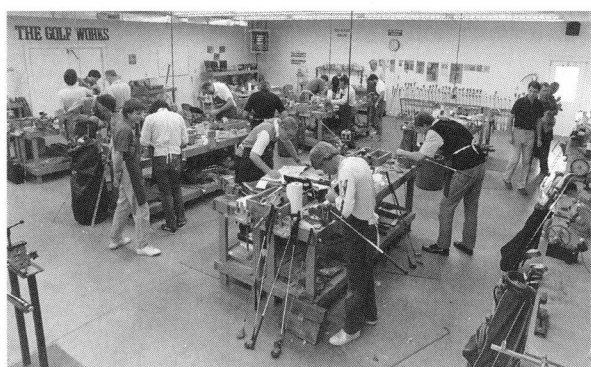

Students are seen here hard at work.

Adjacent to the workshop is an audio/visual room. Timely breaks in the work schedule enable the students to seat themselves in a comfortable setting to view movies, slides and listen to lectures that pertain to club repair, alteration, design and assembly. The students are also introduced to golf club fitting and how changes in equipment can bring about positive and negative effects in ball flight.

Our 295 yard long driving range and fitting/testing facility gets plenty of use, especially during the golf club fitting school. Students are able to hit hundreds of balls as they learn the professional techniques for fitting golf clubs to players of all skill levels. In addition, there are two fully stocked ponds on either side of the range in which students can fish when there is that rare break in the

Slide presentations and lectures are valuable for the students.

schedule. Regardless of the students prior experience in club repair, fitting or assembly; at the end of the week they leave with a well-rounded education.

These schools were not the first at which I taught club repair, assembly or fitting skills. Prior to The GolfWorks® Schools, I taught many P.G.A. Club Repair Workshops all over the United States beginning in 1974 and each one was a special treat. Everyone who attended was a winner due to the sharing of ideas, the development of new skills, the excitement of expanding one's business into fitting and club repair and the lasting acquaintances and friendships. I never left one without increasing my own knowledge of repair or fitting through this sharing.

P.G.A. golf professionals or their assistants were the only people who were eligible to attend these special schools. At one time, the workshops were taught in hotel ballrooms or large meeting rooms. This worked out surprisingly well despite many of the makeshift setups for both teaching and doing repairs. With all the flammable solvents and epoxies that were used, there were never any major accidents such as ruining the hotel carpet or starting a fire!

Shown above are two of the 1979 PGA "In-Depth Club Repair Workshops" taught by the author. The class on the top was held in Newark, Ohio at The GolfWorks® and the class on the bottom was taught in Ft. Worth, Texas at The Ben Hogan Factory.

Later, the Education Department of the P.G.A. took a giant stride forward by selecting school sites at facilities better equipped to accommodate these "Learn by Doing" Workshops. The sites used were generously offered by golf club manufacturing companies and larger club repair shops. In 1981, the first "Advanced P.G.A. Club Repair Workshop" was taught by the author at the GolfWorks® Plant in Newark, Ohio. The class was limited to sixteen students. Because this was an advanced workshop there was heavy emphasis on individual instruction and the curriculum was expanded to include an in-depth study of custom clubmaking, advanced repair techniques, fitting and club design. The schedule was grueling for the students, but hopefully rewarding both personally and financially in understanding an important part of being a golf professional.

The first "Advanced PGA Golf Club Repair Workshop" held
at The GolfWorks® in March 1981.

The advanced P.G.A. workshops evolved into the modern day club repair, fitting and assembly schools that we are now offering to all golfers. Many P.G.A. golf professionals attend these schools and by doing so, they earn six education credits which goes a long way towards meeting their minimum educational requirements. Seldom does a golf professional leave the school without commenting that it should be mandatory for all golf professionals to attend — such is the depth of knowledge that one attains here.

The P.G.A. has now further refined their educational offering and has made it mandatory that every golfer, who wishes to enter the P.G.A.'s apprentice program, must attend a nine hour, one day course on club repair and design. The P.G.A. chose The GolfWorks® to design this course and take the lead role in its instruction.

As you can see, there is a fairly long history behind the evolution of the GolfWorks® schools. We are very confident that should you decide to attend one, you will consider it to be one of the highlights in your golfing career.

CHAPTER 32

THE COMPLETE "HOW TO" ON ASSEMBLING CUSTOM WOODS, IRONS AND PUTTERS

Assembling golf clubs from components has become more and more popular because of all its advantages including ease of customizing, increased profit margins, lower inventory cost and greater satisfaction in making the clubs yourself. See Chapter 29 for a full comparison of buying retail versus buying the components at wholesale and assembling the club yourself. This chapter details the steps involved in assembling persimmon, laminated maple or graphite wood heads and assembling irons. Steps on assembling putters are at the end of this chapter. Assembling metal wood heads is detailed in Chapter 33.

Golf Wood Club Assembly

Golf wood club assembly can be broken down into two basic categories. The first is assembling woods using pro-finished heads. The other is assembling woods using pro-sanded heads. Pro-finished means the head is completely finished, including paintfilling of facelines, decals, everything except the whipping, ferrule, backscrew (when applicable) and final swingweighting. Pro-finished heads cost slightly more than pro-sanded but require far less skills and time for assembly. Pro-sanded wood heads are identical to pro-finished except for the finish, paintfilling and decals. Pro-finished and pro-sanded heads are available in either persimmon or laminated maple. Graphite heads are available only as a finished head.

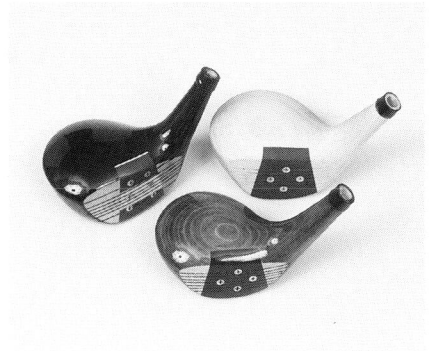

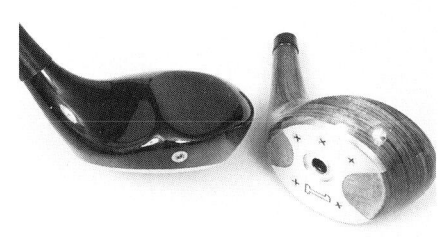

32-1 Persimmon and laminated maple wood heads are available in either pro-finished (ready for assembly) or pro-sanded (ready for assembly and finishing). The determining factors for buying these wood heads are how much time is available and whether you have the skills and desire to apply the finish. Overwhelmingly, pro-finished heads are the choice of most assemblers.

32-2 The instructions for this chapter apply not only to persimmon and laminated maple wood heads, but also to graphite and other similar "exotic" materials (excluding metal woods). If any of the following steps are pertinent to only one material it will be noted. NOTE: Graphite heads are available only as a finished head.

32-3 Most manufacturers utilize some method of swingweight adjustment after a club is finished. The GolfWorks® heads feature large weight port cavities plus medallions as well as models that access the cavity from the sole using a set screw. Some companies use a set screw that accesses the cavity from the back of the wood head. Those which must have the soleplate removed or must have weight added down the shaft are the least desirable.

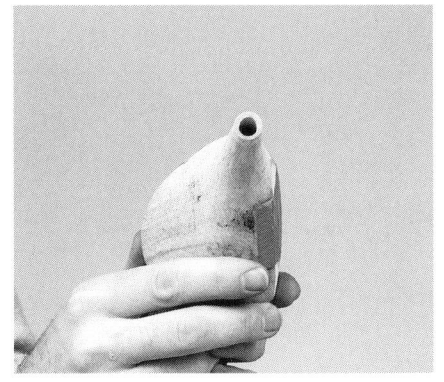

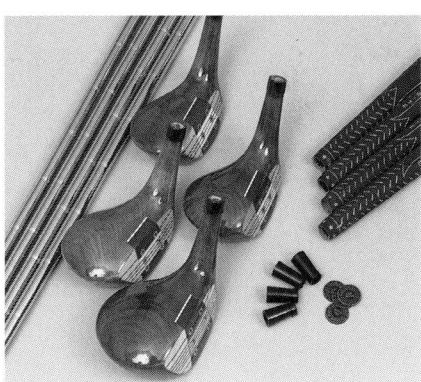

32-4 A common misconception among wood head assemblers is that the bore is off if the wood around the top of the hosel is thinner on one side. This has nothing to do with the bore and is only an indication that slightly more wood was removed on one side during the neck sanding operation. This will not affect assembly of the wood head on the shaft.

32-5 This photo shows the same club before the hosel was "turned down." From this view you can see that the hosel was perfectly bored.

32-6 On a workbench, arrange your components that you will be using. Check to make sure the shafts are identical, that the heads are without cosmetic flaws and that you have an ample supply of necessities such as epoxy, lead powder, ferrules and medallions or set screws.

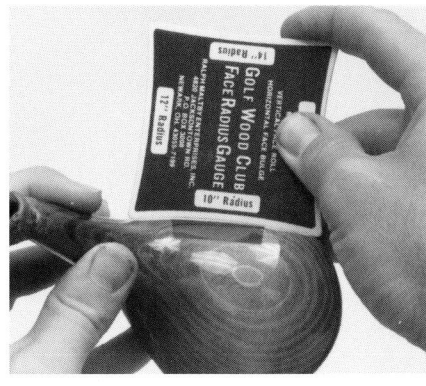

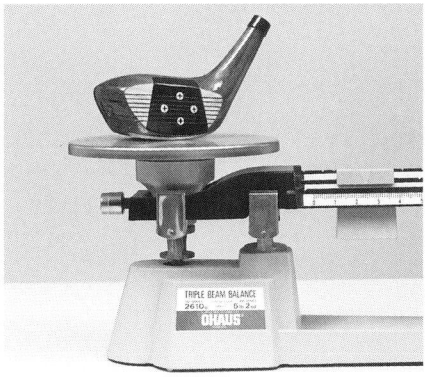

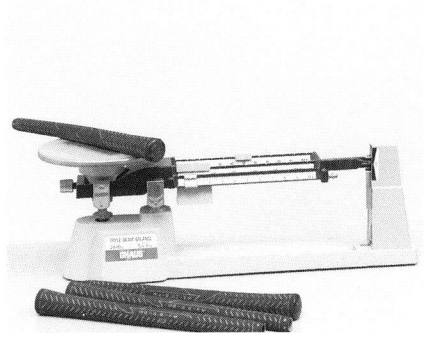

32-7 Next, check the horizontal bulge, vertical roll, loft and face angle of the head. If the specs are different from what they should be, send the finished wood head back to the manufacturer for replacement. Pro-sanded heads can be adjusted by you or also returned. See the respective chapters in this book for more information.

32-8 For checking and weighing components a gram scale, although not absolutely necessary, is a valuable tool for custom club assemblers and repairmen. Here, the head is being weighed and recorded. Tables in the back of this chapter give approximate head weights by length, grip and type of shaft to obtain a certain swingweight.

32-9 Grip weights can vary as much as ¼ to ½ ounce from specified weights. If all the grips weigh the same, the quality of the set you assemble will be enhanced. See Chapter 23 for more information on grips. Table 23-10 in Chapter 23 lists the weights of some commercially available grips. Note: Matching grip weights is also important when frequency matching a set of clubs. See Chapter 63 for more information.

357

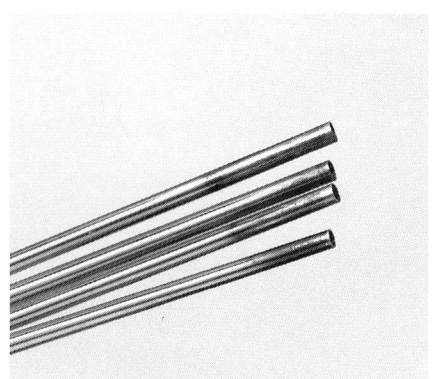

32-10 For checking bores, ferrules, fits, etc. it is handy to have some old cut off wood shaft tips in various sizes. The four shown here are .270, .277, .294 taper tip and .335 parallel tip. To identify shaft tips in our plant we used colored tape. Blue on .270, black on .277, red on .294, green on .320 and yellow on .335.

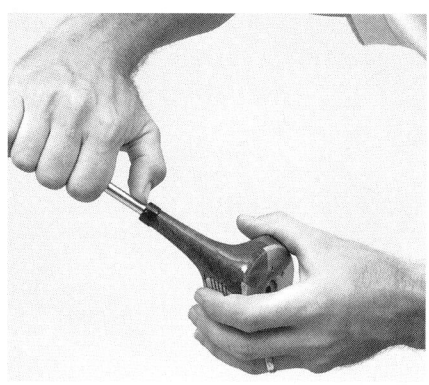

32-11 Check the hosel bore of the wood head by pushing the tip of the shaft you intend to use into the hosel until it becomes snug. Do not force fit – the hosel will split. Place your finger on the shaft even with the top of the hosel.

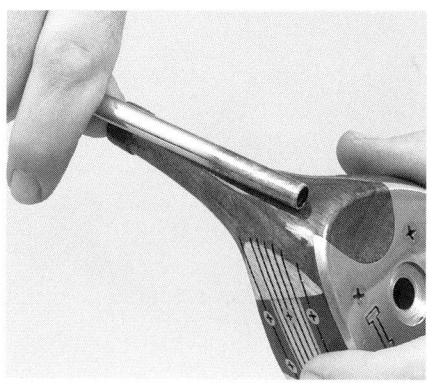

32-12 Remove the shaft and place it along the back of the hosel to check the depth of the penetration. Most blind bore heads are bored to within ¼" to ½" of the sole at the back of the heel. The correct shaft tip will penetrate to the bottom of the hosel bore.

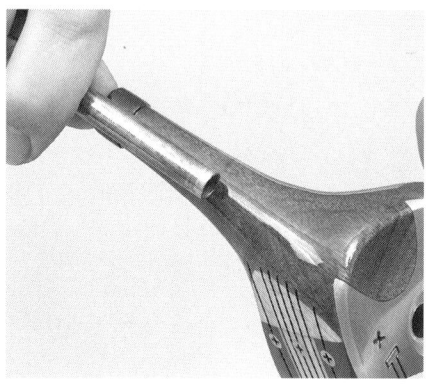

32-13 If the tip of the shaft you intend to use does not penetrate to within ½" from the back of the heel...

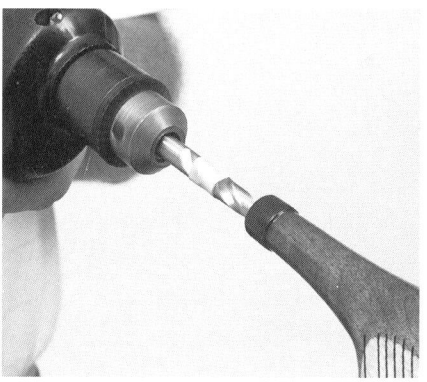

32-14 ... the hosel bore will need to be enlarged as shown in Chapter 7, photos 7-80 through 7-88. If a through-bore hosel is desired, also see photos 7-80 through 7-88. NOTE: If you decide to put a through-bore in a pro-finished head, see Chapter 16, photos 16-40 through 16-52 for finish touchup.

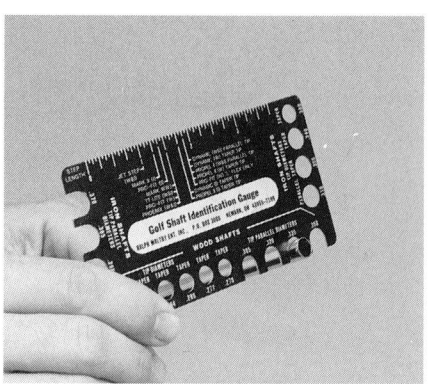

32-15 You should already know the type of shaft (Dynamic, Shadow, etc.) you are using. If not, use the Golf Shaft Identification Gauge. Instructions for its use are found in Chapter 7, photos 7-62 through 7-67. Also determine the tip size.

32-16 Once the shaft type and tip size are known, if you are using a steel shaft refer to Chapter 7, photos 7-68 through 7-79 for determining the proper back of heel to first step dimensions. This measurement is vital if you want the new shaft to perform as it was designed. When this measurement is altered, the shaft will either play more flexible or more stiff. See photos 32-87 through 32-93 for steps on cutting steel shafts.

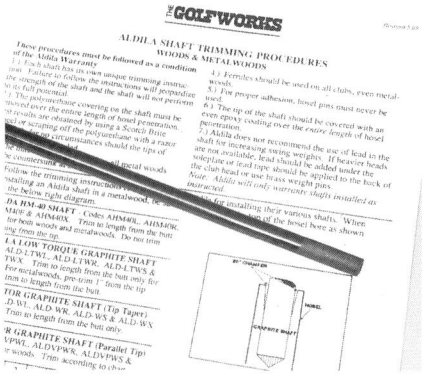

32-17 The diameters of titanium and composite shafts are not reduced along the length of the shaft through step downs, therefore, there are no back of heel to first step dimensions. Most graphite and titanium shafts have their own specific trimming instructions. These should be included with your shaft order. Please refer to these trimming instructions now. See photos 32-87 through 32-99 for steps on cutting titanium and composite shafts.

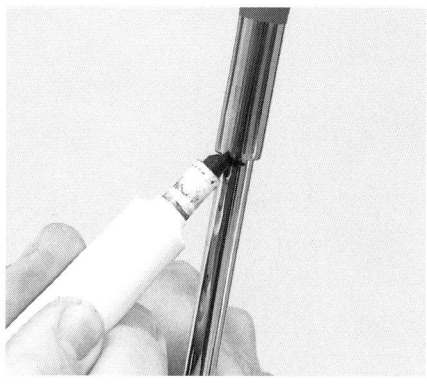

32-18 Abrading the tip of a steel or other metal shaft. Once any corrections have been made to the shaft tip, it must be abraded in order to provide a good bonding surface for the epoxy. To determine how much of the shaft tip should be abraded, install it into the hosel and mark the shaft even with the top of the hosel with a felt tip pen. Note: Make sure the shaft tip penetrated to the bottom of the hosel bore.

358

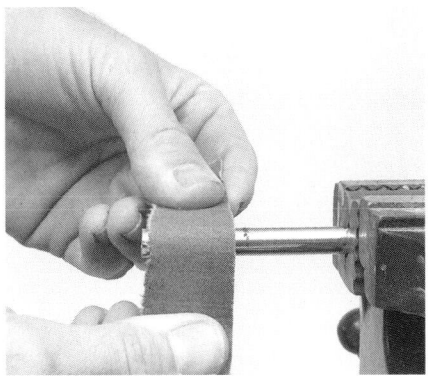

32-19 Remove the shaft from the hosel and place it in a Rubber Shaft Clamp and tighten it in your vise. Lightly sand the shaft using coarse sandpaper or emery cloth to within 1/8" of the mark. If a ferrule is being used it is recommended that the length of shaft covered by the ferrule also be abraded.

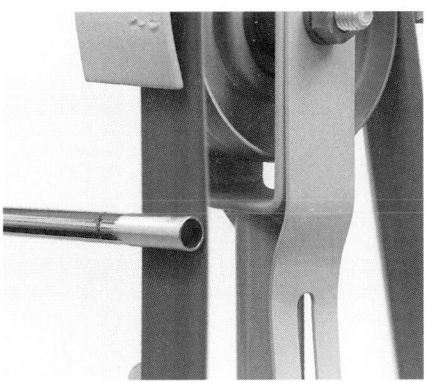

32-20 A fast alternative to hand sanding the shaft is to use a 1" x 42" or 2" x 48" Belt Sander. Lightly place the tip of the shaft against the turning belt and rotate the shaft rapidly.

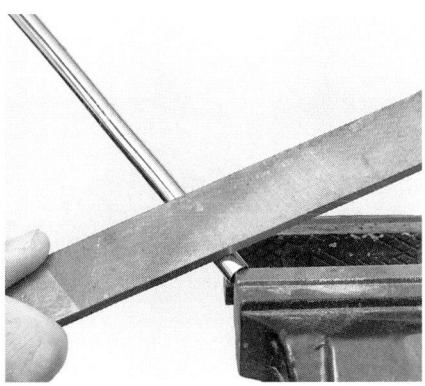

32-21 A fine file or grinding stone can also be used to abrade the metal shaft tip.

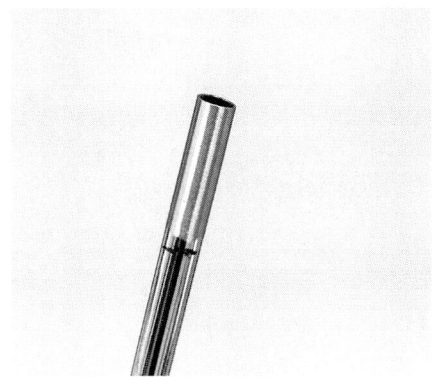

32-22 The tip of the shaft should look like this.

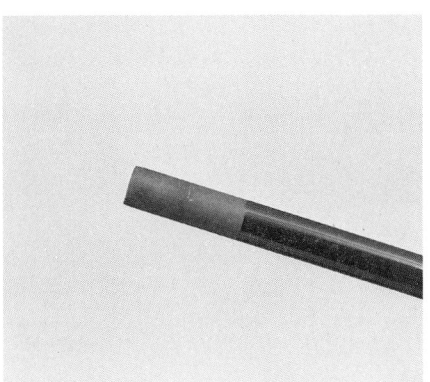

32-23 Preparing the tip of a composite shaft. The tip of composite shafts should not be abraded with a belt sander, file, etc. The polyurethane covering that portion of the shaft tip that will be installed into the hosel should be removed for good adhesion, however, the removal of more than the polyurethane coating will damage the shaft fibers.

32-24 A Scotch-Brite™ Wheel does an effective job of removing the polyurethane without damaging the fibers.

32-25 Rotate the shaft against the turning wheel until the polyurethane coating is removed. Do not pause while rotating the shaft because of the risk of cutting the fibers. Do not press too firmly. Light pressure works best. Machine set-up shows a 1/3 H.P. motor that turns at 1725 RPM.

32-26 A razor blade also works well, but is slower. Hold the razor blade perpendicular to the shaft and scrape back and forth while rotating the shaft.

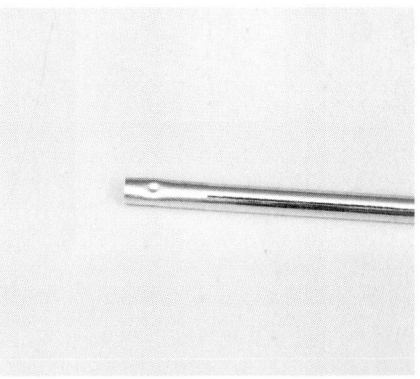

32-27 In addition to abrading the tip of the steel shaft, we also suggest the tip be "dimpled" as shown. Dimpling a steel shaft has two benefits: 1) it creates shallow depressions in the tip of the shaft that will hold the epoxy, thus creating a better bond; 2) makes the shaft tip more of an oval shape to ensure a tight fit between the shaft and the hosel bore. The fit is usually so tight that the assembler need not wait for the epoxy to dry before proceeding to the next assembly step.

32-28 At the GolfWorks®, we built this **Automatic Shaft Dimpler** which is activated by air.

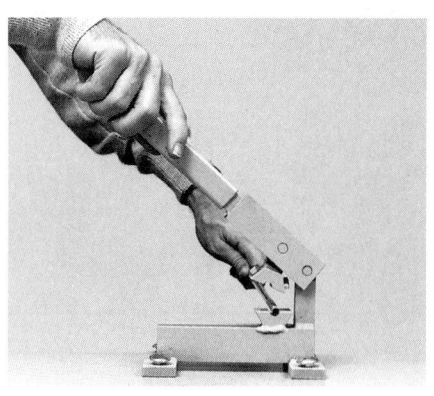

32-29 This **Whitty Shaft Dimpler** also works well. Rather than being activated by air pressure you force the dimples into the shaft. This is available from The GolfWorks®.

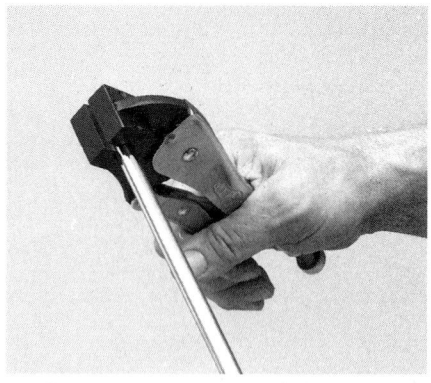

32-30 This **Hand Held Shaft Dimpler** is also available from The GolfWorks®. It is a 10" vise grip that has been adapted with a specially designed permanent attachment for dimpling steel shafts. The attachment will make four dimples with one squeeze of the handle.

32-31 Installing the ferrule. The purpose of the ferrule is to provide a smooth transition from the shaft to the larger diameter of the hosel. There are two basic types of ferrules – standard and shanked. The shanked ferrule has a lip at the top against which the whipping is started. Note: When test-fitting ferrules, always select a ferrule larger at its base than the diameter of the top of the hosel.

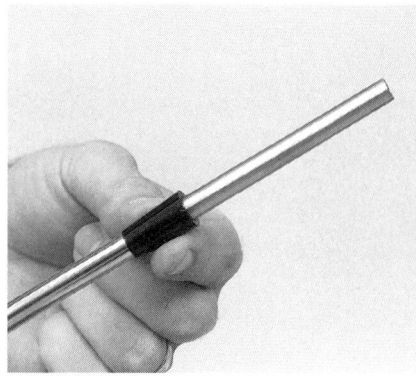

32-32 Slide the ferrule over the shaft. The ferrule should move high enough up the shaft to allow the shaft tip to penetrate to the bottom of the hosel bore.

32-33 Sometimes the ferrule will not slide on the shaft easily. In this case, place the ferrule against the mouth of a can of acetone. Turn the can upside down so the acetone runs into the ferrule but keep the other end of the ferrule covered with your finger.

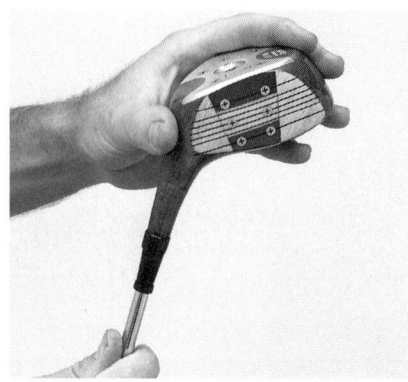

32-34 Wait 10 seconds, then quickly remove the ferrule from the can and slide the ferrule down the shaft. Immediately place the hosel over the shaft and drive the ferrule to its proper position. NOTE: Remove the shaft and check to see that the shaft tip had penetrated to the bottom of the hosel bore.

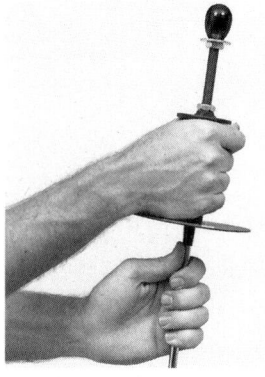

32-35 The **Ferrule Installer Tool** will accurately set an iron or wood ferrule to the proper depth. It is especially useful when a series of ferrules must be set to a consistent distance.

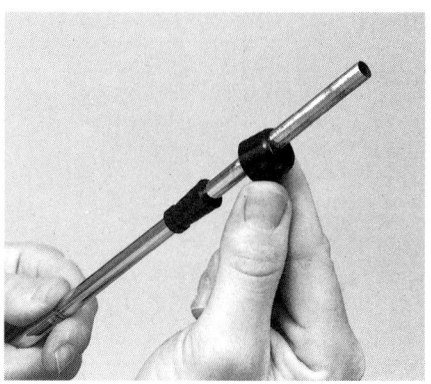

32-36 If you intend to grip the club with leather, slide the grip collar over the shaft tip now. This is much easier than trying to install it over the larger shaft butt later. Push the collar up the shaft and temporarily secure it with a piece of tape.

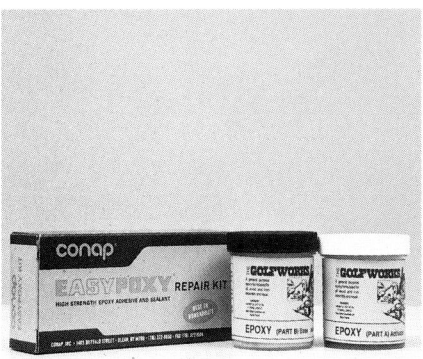

32-37 Installing the shaft. Mix a shear strength epoxy such as GolfWorks® High Strength Epoxy or Conap epoxy. NOTE: Always mix each component in the can first when possible. Read the instructions carefully so the proportion of part A and B are correct.

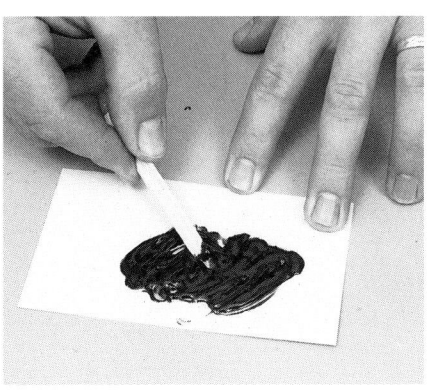

32-38 Mix part A and part B, being sure that no unmixed epoxy remains on the perimeter. A good idea is to cut up old cardboard boxes into small squares and use these for mixing pallets. Popsicle sticks, tongue depressors or an old screwdriver works well to mix the epoxy. Large volume assemblers may choose to mix the parts in a small cup.

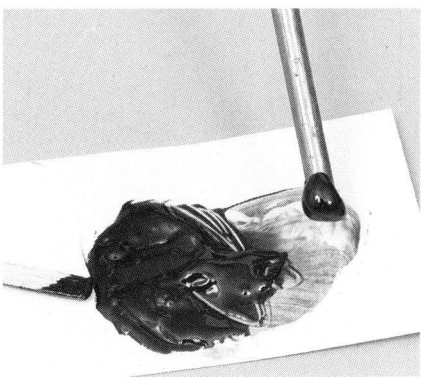

32-39 Dip the tip of the shaft into the epoxy and pick up a dab, as shown.

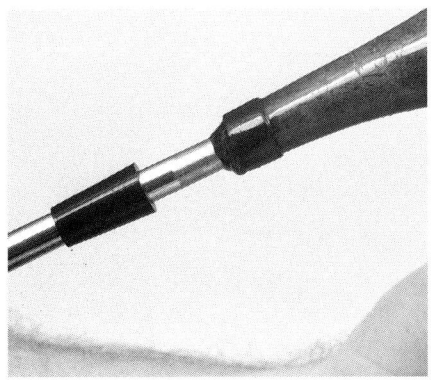

32-40 Push the shaft to the bottom of the hosel bore, simultaneously rotating the shaft. This will coat both the hosel bore and the shaft tip. The shaft tip must penetrate to the bottom of the hosel bore. If not, the shaft can break. Also, note the plastic collar supplied with every GolfWorks® head to prevent hosel splitting during assembly. Wrap 3 or 4 turns of masking tape around the hosel if there is no plastic collar on other brands.

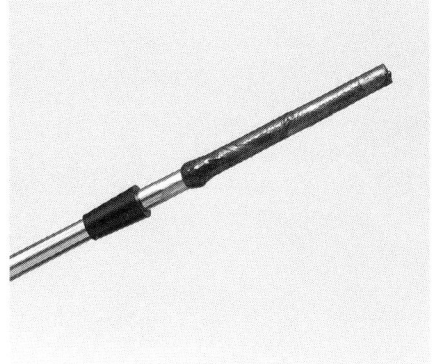

32-41 Remove the shaft from the hosel. Check to make sure the shaft is covered and, if not, apply more epoxy. This photo shows adequate epoxy coverage. Reinstall the shaft. Be sure it is firmly seated at the bottom of the bore or just pushed through in the case of a through-bore. NOTE: If the shaft has a shaft band, make sure the shaft is turned so that the band's identifying marks are facing towards the front.

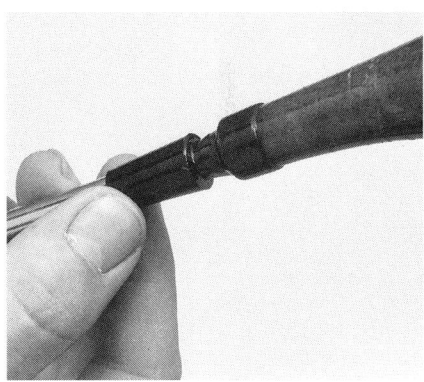

32-42 Push the ferrule against…

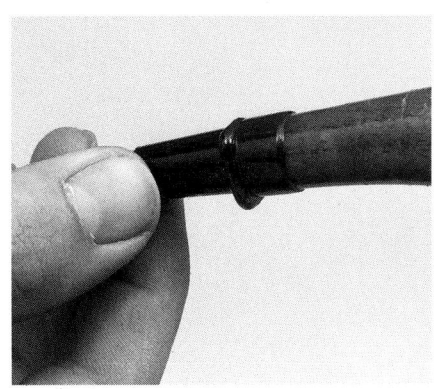

32-43 … the top of the hosel. It is not necessary to remove the excess epoxy from the hosel area. If some of the epoxy, however, has been smeared on the finish below the point that the whipping will cover, be certain to remove it by wiping. If the wood head is a "blind bore" proceed to photo 32-49. Follow photos 32-44 through 32-48 for a through-bore.

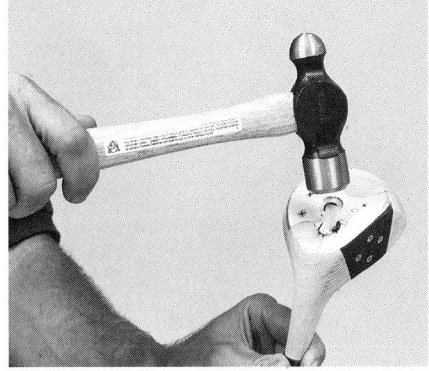

32-44 If the wood head is a "through-bore," put a dab of epoxy on the end of a tapered hardwood plug and drive it up into the end of the shaft. The diameter of the shaft will determine how deep to drive it, but ¾" is the minimum in any case. Now, allow the "through-bore" shaft assembly to cure. NOTE: The entire tip of the shaft must be showing through the sole.

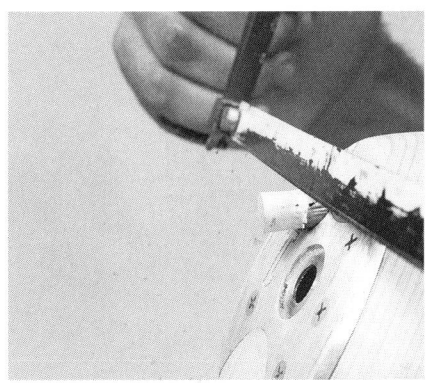

32-45 Next, break off the excess shaft plug length using a pair of pliers or saw it off with a hacksaw.

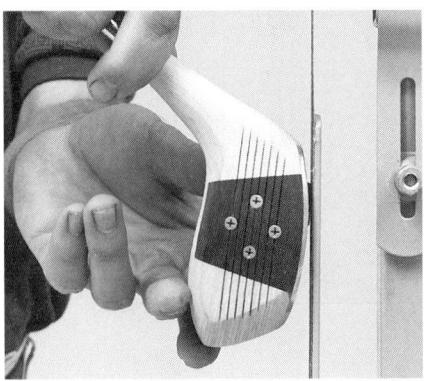

32-46 The easiest way to grind down the protruding shaft tip is with a motorized bench grinder. Be sure and hold it at the correct angle to prevent gouging the soleplate. Leave just a little bit sticking up. If you do not have a grinder, the whole operation can be done with a flat or mill file or belt sander.

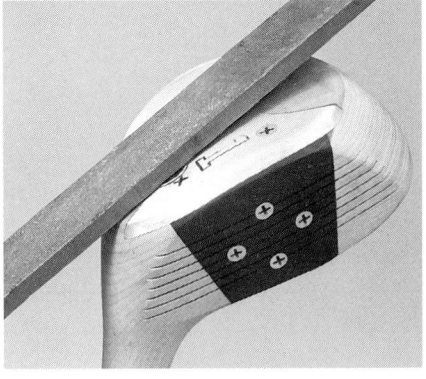

32-47 Finish blending the shaft into the soleplate using a smooth flat or smooth mill file. File strokes should be from the heel to toe to maintain the proper directional grain in the soleplate. A fine piece of emery cloth wrapped around the file will give a professional look.

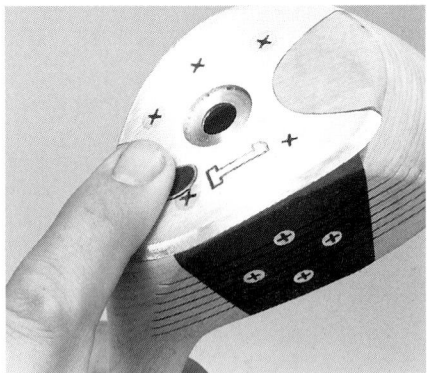

32-48 The shaft should blend in perfectly with the sole of the club and should not be felt when your finger runs across it. Obviously, this procedure should only be performed on pro-sanded heads or pro-finished heads you intend to refinish.

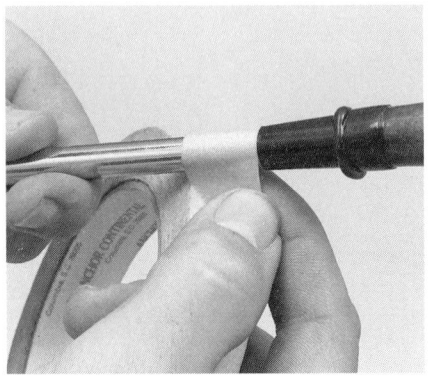

32-49 Reducing the ferrule diameter. The next step, after the epoxy hardens, will be to reduce the diameter of the ferrule so it matches the top of the hosel and tapers down to the shaft. Place a wrap of masking tape around the shaft just below the ferrule.

32-50 Place the shaft in the **Rubber Shaft Clamp** and fasten it in a vise, as shown.

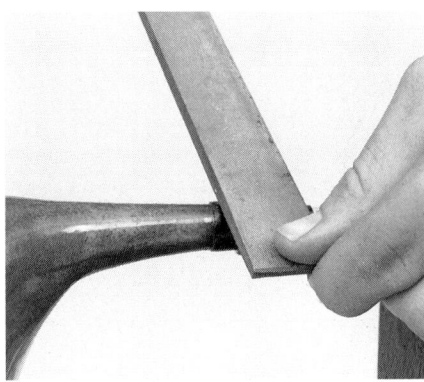

32-51 If the wood head with which you are working has a protective plastic hosel ring, lightly file it with a flat mill or fine file until…

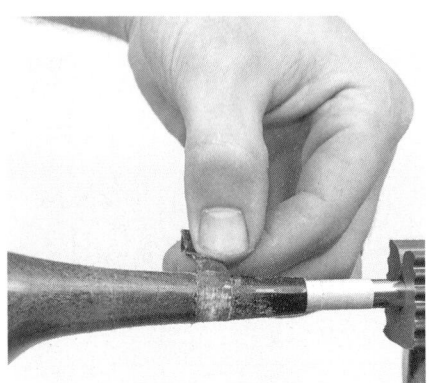

32-52 … it can easily be removed. If you had previously applied masking tape to the hosel, remove it now.

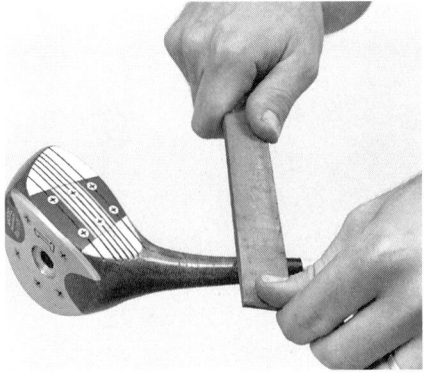

32-53 With the same file, lightly file any excess plastic and epoxy flush with the top of the hosel while …

32-54 … rotating the head.

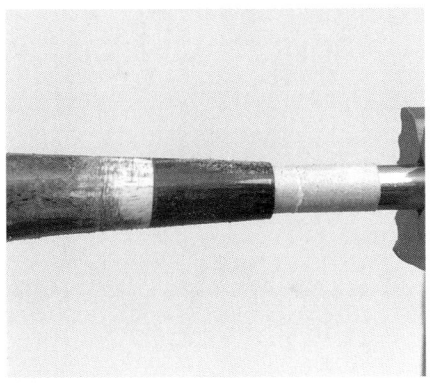

32-55 The bottom of the ferrule should look like this when finished. If the bottom of the ferrule had been smaller than the top of the hosel you would have been required to modify the already properly tapered hosel to conform with the ferrule – a highly problematic, and unnecessary, job!

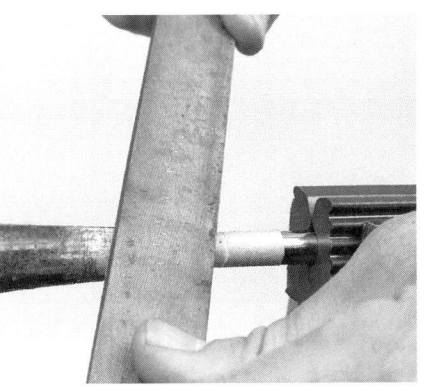

32-56 Next, reduce the diameter of the top of the ferrule until …

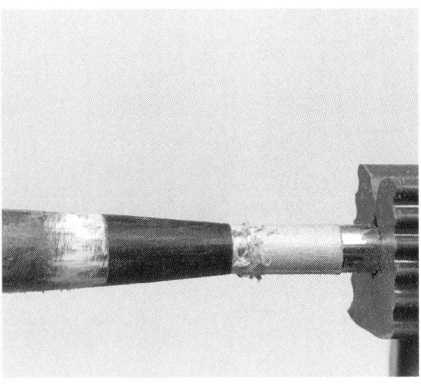

32-57 … a step no longer exists between the shaft and ferrule. There should be a uniform taper from the top to the bottom of the ferrule.

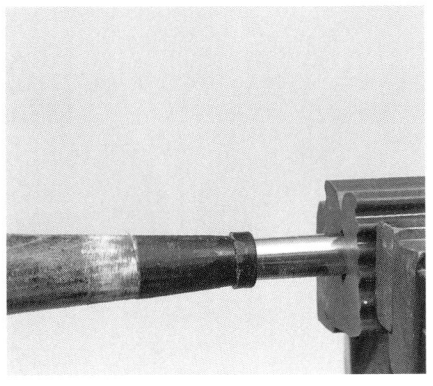

32-58 If you are using a shanked ferrule, do not file the top of the ferrule.

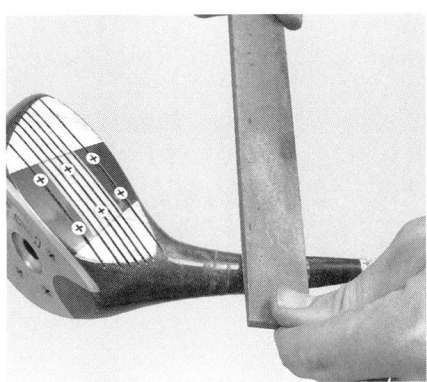

32-59 It may be necessary to lightly file the hosel if any surface irregularities (which can be caused by a polyurethane buildup) exist. Do not file below the point the whipping will cover. This is about 1" from the top of the face.

32-60 Filing usually creates flat spots, or ridges, that can be removed by lightly sanding with a strip of fine sandpaper. NOTE: If you are using a pro-sanded head, you will have more latitude when filing and sanding since you do not have to worry about scratching any finish.

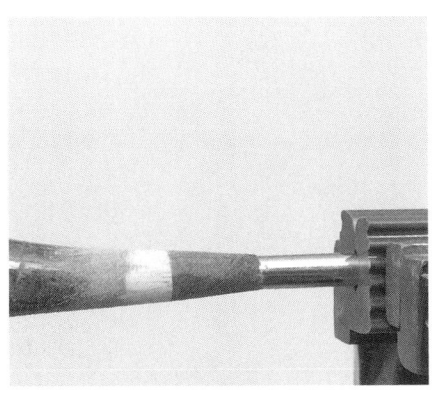

32-61 After removing the tape, the hosel should look like this. Whipping will not hide imperfections; rather, it will accentuate them. Take time to properly prepare the hosel prior to whipping.

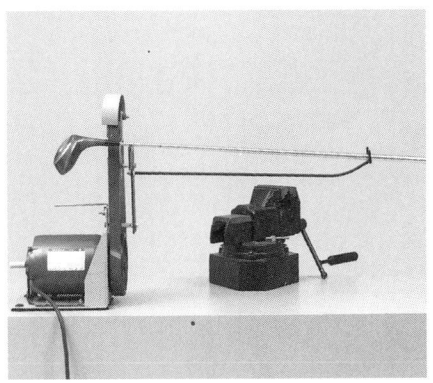

32-62 A quick alternative to filing is use of fine or medium grade sandpaper on a **1" x 42" Belt Sander.** Be careful – material is quickly removed with this method. The belt sander shown has a **Ferrule Turning Support Arm,** which makes this job much easier. Rotate the clubhead continuously and evenly until the hosel has been properly shaped.

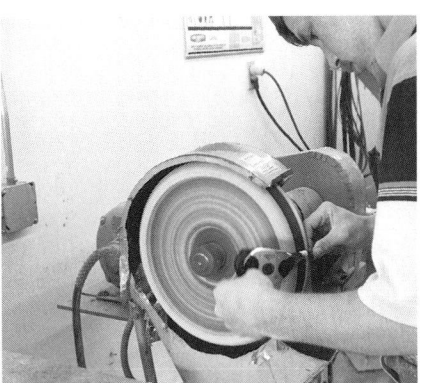

32-63 In the GolfWorks® wood assembly department we use belt sanders and a shoe wheel, as shown. Very few shoe wheels are still around but, if you can find one, they are excellent for sanding and hosel shaping.

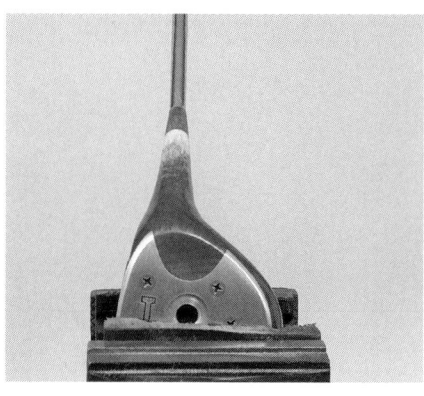

32-64 Installing a backscrew. A backscrew should always be used in persimmon and laminated maple wood heads as insurance against epoxy failure when installing steel shafts. Graphite and titanium shafts should not be backscrewed as damage will result to the shaft. Graphite or other head materials also should not be backscrewed. Position the wood head between a pair of vise pads as shown.

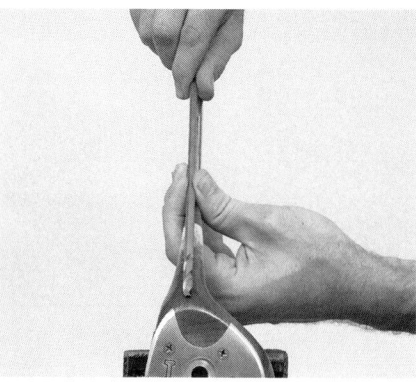

32-65 A 12" drill bit, or a straight edge, is used to help determine where the backscrew hole will be drilled. We're using a 12" x 7/32" bit. Lay the bit in line with and against the back of the shaft. Position the tip of the bit to within 5/8" of the back of the heel.

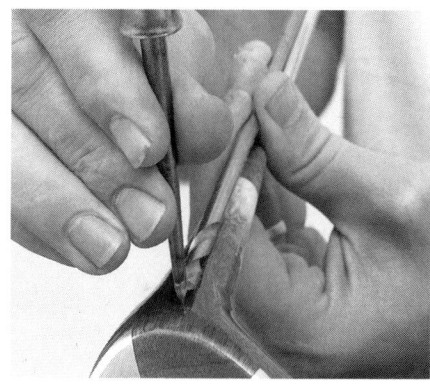

32-66 Make a small indentation in the wood just below the tip of the bit with an awl or nail. This method will always work as long as the bit or straight edge is aligned correctly with the shaft.

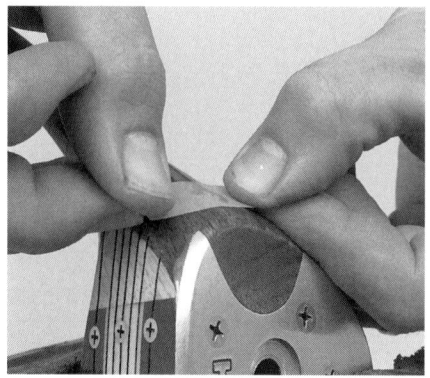

32-67 Place a strip of cellophane tape over the indentation. The tape will prevent damage to the finish when the hosel is drilled. This is not necessary for a pro-sanded head as the head will be finished as a final step.

32-68 Position an 1/8" bit in the indentation so that it is not perpendicular with the hosel but points more towards the club's sole.

32-69 Drill into the hosel until the bit encounters the shaft. Do not attempt to drill through the shaft. Instead...

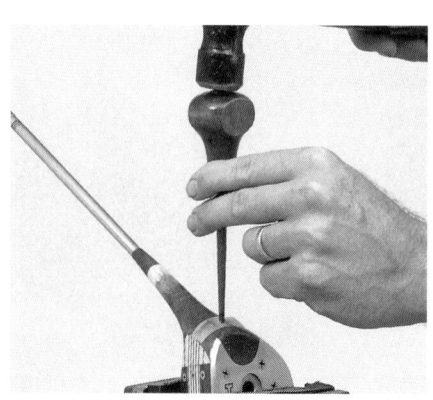

32-70 ... insert an awl into the hole and drive it through the top of the shaft. Remove the awl and ...

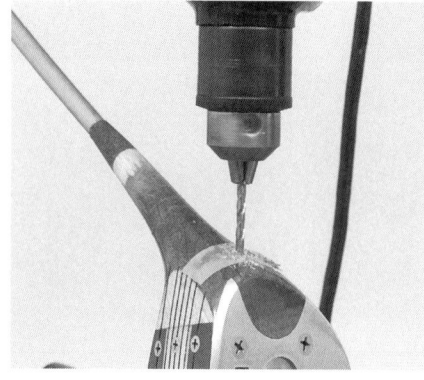

32-71 ... reinstall the 1/8" bit into the hole. Drill through the top of the shaft. Do not drill through the bottom of the shaft.

32-72 Insert the awl and drive it through the bottom of the shaft.

32-73 Reinsert the ⅛" bit into the hole and drill through the shaft into the wood below. The proper depth of the hole is 1½".

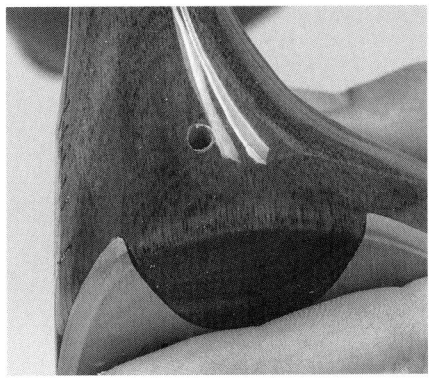

32-74 Remove the strip of tape. Your goal is to keep damage to the finish at an absolute minimum.

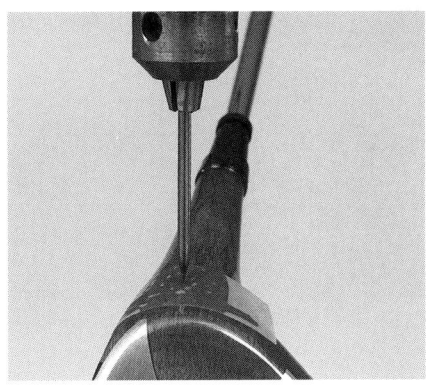

32-75 An alternative to the drill and awl method is to use an ⅛" drill blank in a drill press. This works much faster. Simply turn the drill press spindle until the drill blank quickly cuts through the wood and shaft. You may want to first pre-drill an entry hole for the drill blank with the ⅛" bit to avoid damaging the finish.

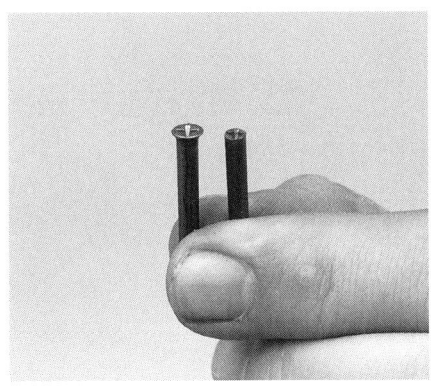

32-76 Next, select a backscrew (of the two shown, the headless backscrew is preferred) and place it in the hole. NOTE: Backscrews are a special made steel screw. (#5 x 1⅛" long with a small Phillips or Reed and Prince head.) These screws are available from club repair supplies dealers.

32-77 Lightly tap the head of the backscrew until it is flush with the surface of the hosel. If using a backscrew with a head, do not drive it any deeper into the wood.

32-78 If using a headless backscrew, drive it ⅛" below the surface of the wood with a ⅛" punch.

32-79 Mix a quick setting epoxy and fill the hole. Here we have mixed a colored paste dispersion with the epoxy, thus closely matching the color of the finish.

32-80 Do not attempt to level the epoxy even with the hosel. Instead, build a small mound and allow the epoxy to cure. Quick-setting, 5-minute epoxies work well for this.

32-81 After the epoxy hardens, remove the excess using either a file or ...

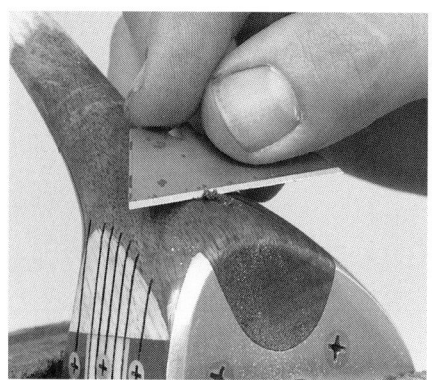

32-82 ... a sharp razor blade. Be careful not to cut the finish. If using a pro-sanded head, lightly sand the area using 150 or 220 grit sandpaper.

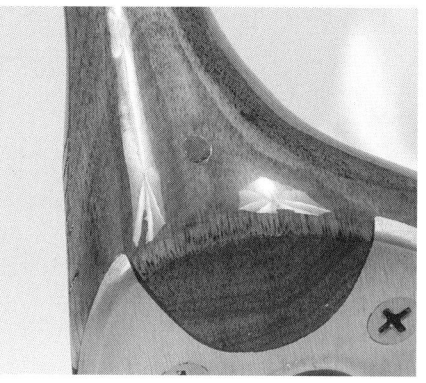

32-83 The filled backscrew hole should look like this.

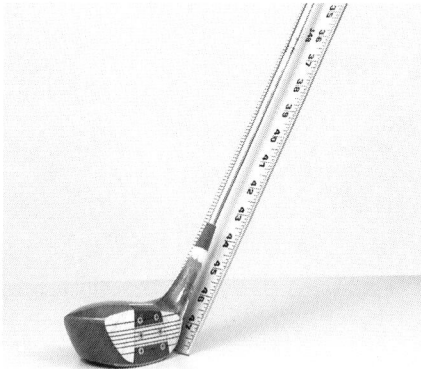

32-84 Measuring and cutting the club to length. Sole the club on the ground as shown and measure with a 48" ruler behind the club.

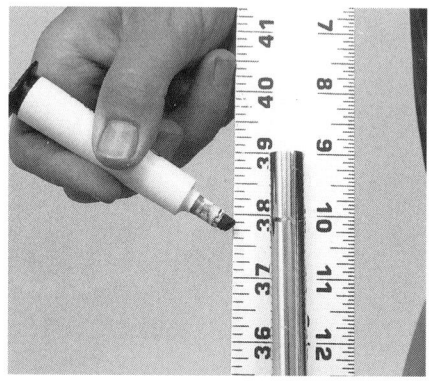

32-85 Mark the shaft using a felt tip marker or grease pencil at a point ⅛" below the desired final length (i.e., at 37⅞" if a 38" length club is desired). The grip cap will account for the ⅛" difference after the grip is installed.

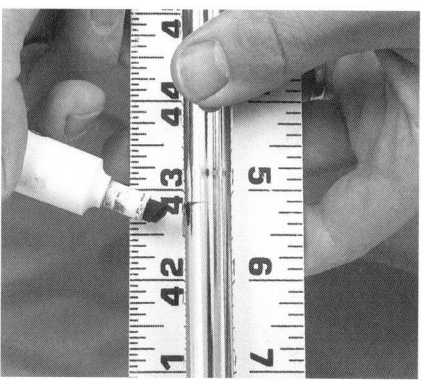

32-86 In this case the final length is to be 43" which is standard length for a driver. The mark is made ⅛" below 43" at 42⅞". See Table 32-3 for suggested wood club lengths. See Table 32-4 for iron club lengths.

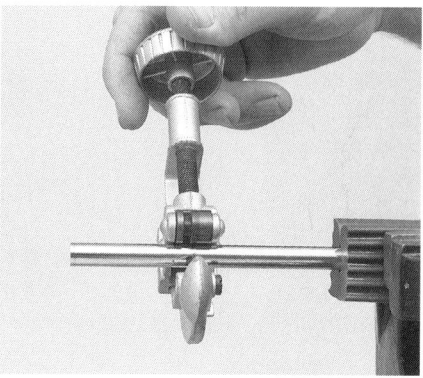

32-87 Cutting the shaft. Steel shafts are easily cut by using a **Tubing Cutter** or ...

32-88 ... a **Friction Cutoff Wheel**. When using the cutoff wheel, push the shaft firmly into the rotating wheel. NOTE: Always wear safety glasses when working around machines.

32-89 Keep pushing the shaft against the cutoff wheel until the edge of the wheel is through the shaft wall and then slowly rotate the shaft counterclockwise.

32-90 Continue turning the shaft counter-clockwise into the wheel until the shaft section comes off. A cutoff wheel also works for graphite and titanium shafts.

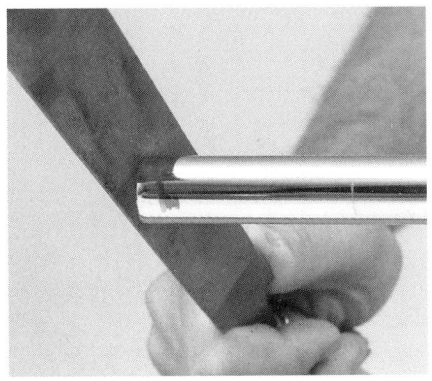

32-91 Cutting a steel or titanium shaft will usually result in a rough edge. Remove this rough edge by either lightly filing or ...

32-92 ... spinning the shaft against the wheel of a bench grinder or belt sander.

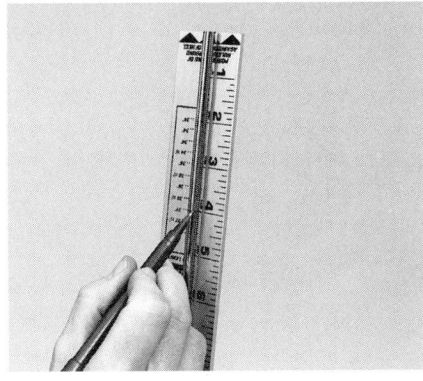

32-93 When required to cut a certain amount from the tip of the shaft, simply make the mark the appropriate distance from the tip. In the photo, 4" must be removed from the shaft tip to make it conform to the proper back of heel to first step dimension. Therefore, a mark is made exactly 4" from the tip of the shaft.

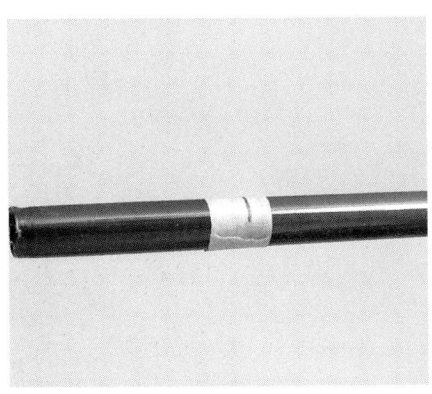

32-94 An alternative to the cutoff wheel for graphite is to cut the shaft with a common hacksaw. Place a wrapping of masking tape around the graphite shaft where you intend to make the cut. Clearly mark the tape where the cut will be made.

32-95 An important step is to first circumscribe the exterior of the shaft with the hacksaw. This step will prevent the shaft from splitting while cutting.

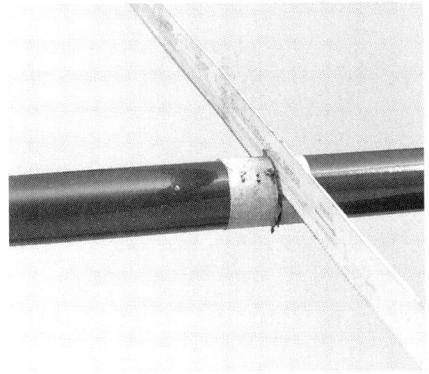

32-96 Once the shaft has been circumscribed, carefully cut into the shaft with the hacksaw.

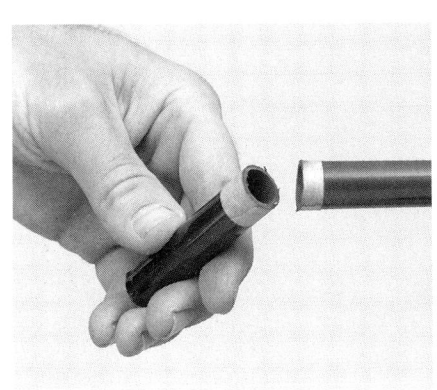

32-97 After cutting through the shaft there should not be any graphite splinters or torn pieces.

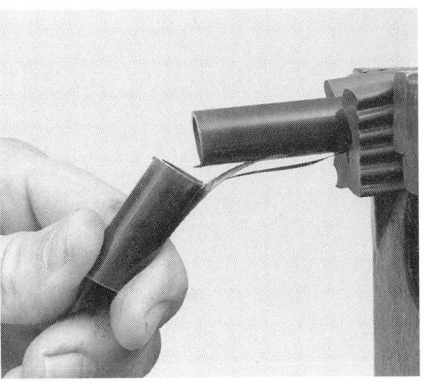

32-98 This is how a graphite shaft will usually look if the taping and circumscribing step is not followed when cutting with a hacksaw.

32-99 In addition to using the steel friction cutoff wheel, the GolfWorks® also uses this **Automatic Cutoff Saw** with a wheel. We use this on all shaft materials and it works especially well when cutting more than one shaft, as shown.

367

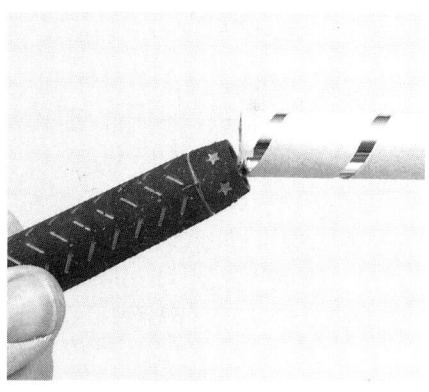

32-100 Installing the Grip. Install the grip following steps from Chapter 23. Photos 23-44 through 23-74 detail installing a rubber slip-on grip and 23-75 through 23-114 detail installing a leather wrap-on grip. NOTE: If the wood does not have a weight port, check the swingweight and adjust before installing the grip. Refer to Chapter 14 for information on swingweighting.

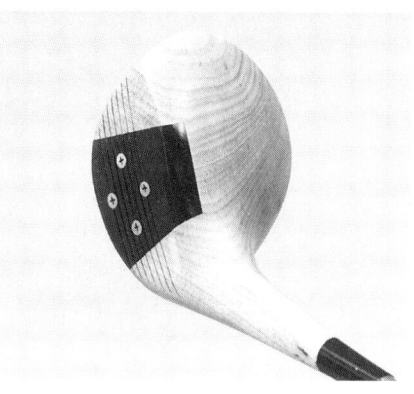

32-101 If you are assembling a pro-sanded head the club is now ready for finishing. See Chapter 1, photos 1-115 through 1-258.

32-102 Applying Whipping. See Chapter 6 for information on applying whipping to woods.

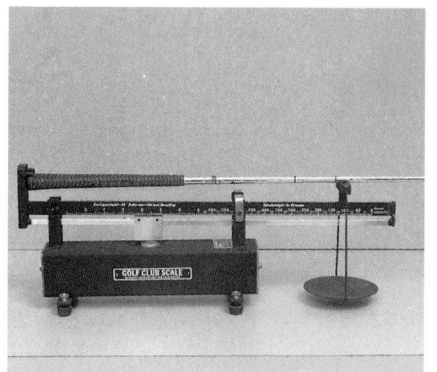

32-103 Swingweighting a Golf Club with a Weight Port. Check the club's swingweight on a swingweight scale. Because of the presence of a weight port the grip should already be installed. The following steps apply to both woods and irons. **See Chapter 33, photos 33-75 through 33-80 for swingweighting clubs without weight ports.**

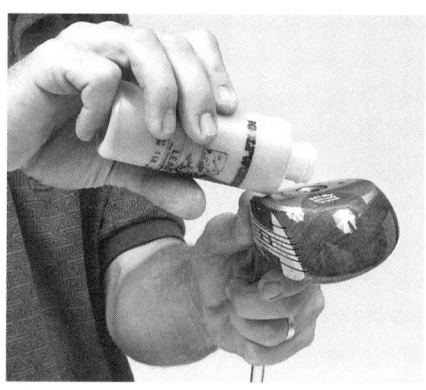

32-104 Add the appropriate amount of lead powder until the desired swingweight is achieved. The plastic medallion is practically weightless so no compensation needs to be made. If using a set screw allow for ½ point.

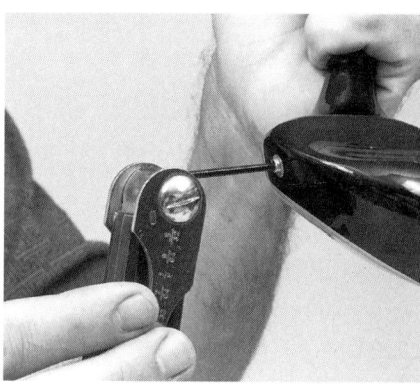

32-105 For clubs with set screws, turn in the set screw after achieving the swingweight. Do not use epoxy for this step as it is not necessary.

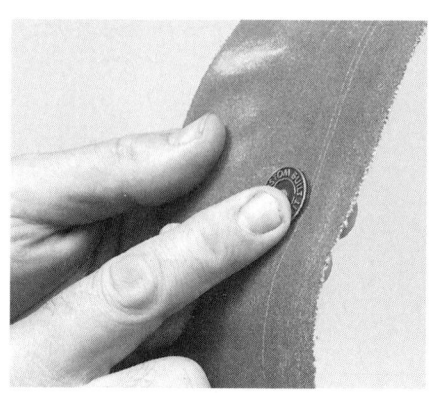

32-106 For clubs with a medallion, roughen the back and the entire outside edge of the medallion with medium or coarse sandpaper.

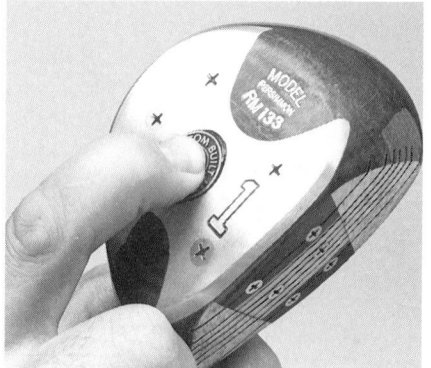

32-107 Apply epoxy to the bottom of the medallion and weight port recess. A toothpick or small stick works well to coat the entire recess with epoxy. Press the medallion into the recess. Epoxy should ooze from around the medallion. The medallion should be set at right angles to the leading edge.

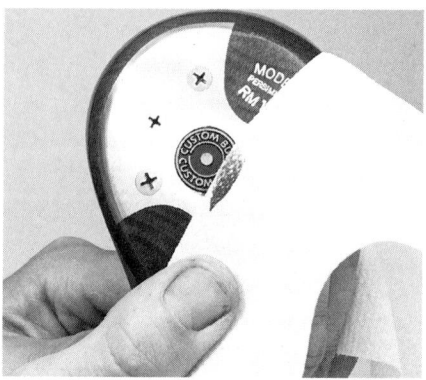

32-108 With a paper towel, wipe the excess epoxy towards the center of the medallion, filling in all gaps between the medallion and weight port. Any excess epoxy can be cleaned up with a damp naphtha rag.

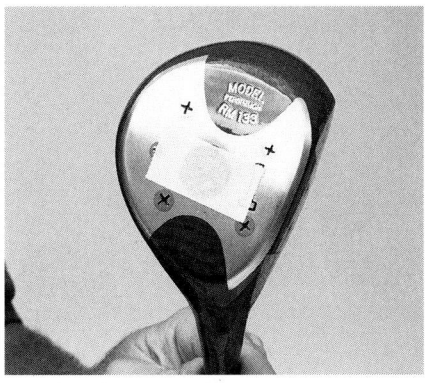

32-109 Apply tape to the medallion and sole using ⅛" or ¾" masking tape. The tape will prevent the medallion from moving while the epoxy dries.

32-110 Applying the Shaft Band. The shaft band should be positioned on a steel shaft on the second step below the bottom of the grip. This protects the band from being torn off when the club is put in the golf bag. For shafts that do not have steps, the band is installed approximately 2" below the grip.

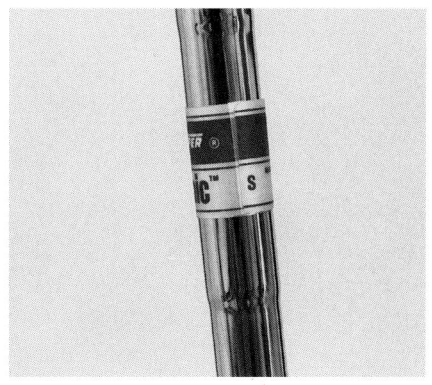

32-111 If you are using a combination flex shaft band as shown, make sure that the appropriate letter is showing after the band is wrapped around the shaft.

Golf Iron Club Assembly

It is universally agreed that golf iron club assembly is much easier than wood assembly. Also, irons heads sold for assembly are finished and ready to put on a golf shaft.

Irons heads come in a variety of materials and designs. The materials used are either stainless steel or carbon steel. Some of the more common cast stainless types are 18-8, 17-4 and 431. If a stainless head is desired I personally prefer the 17-4 and 431 type because they are better quality stainless steels than the 18-8 which tends to gray more rapidly, dings up easily while in the golf bag and has a tendency to sometimes bend during play which causes a loft and/or lie change.

Carbon steel heads are available as an investment casting or forged. Both are chromeplated which gives the head maximum durability from a discoloration, scratching and nicking standpoint only. The investment cast carbon steel head seems to incorporate all the desired qualities of both casting and forging.

Iron head designs basically fall into two categories–game improvement and traditional. Game improvement designs usually have the top of the hosels rounded and they do not require ferrules. This type of design benefits all players but especially those players who have difficulty hitting the ball in the center of the clubface. Most traditional designs have squared hosel tops that require ferrules. The traditional design may be used by those golfers who fairly consistently strike the ball on the center of the clubface.

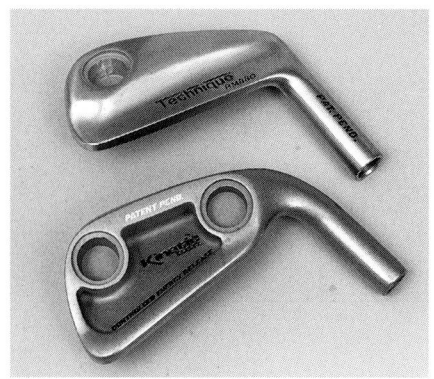

32-112 The club on the top is a traditional model while the club on the bottom is the game improvement design.

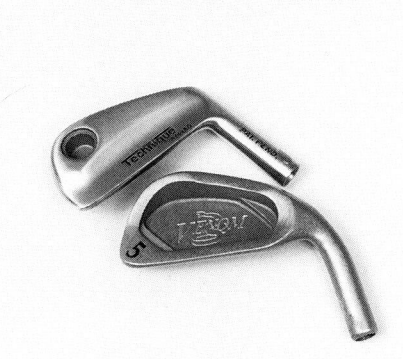

32-113 An important feature in any head manufactured for custom assembly is an adjustable weight port in the head. The weight port shown above is located low in the head and directly behind the hitting area. Clubheads with no weight ports usually require varying amounts of lead to be put down the shaft.

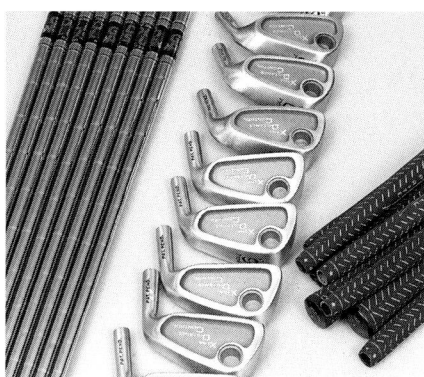

32-114 Arrange the necessary components on a workbench. Check to make sure that the shafts are identical and that the heads are without cosmetic flaws (if custom specs were requested, check to make sure they are within industry standard tolerances of ±1°). Make sure that you have an ample supply of epoxy, lead discs or powder, medallions or set screws and ferrules.

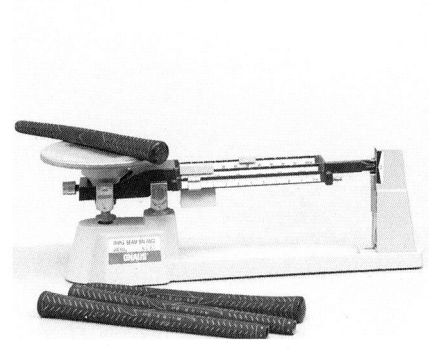

32-115 Grip weights may vary as much as ¼ to ½ an ounce from specified weights. Matched grip weights enhance the quality of the assembled set. See Chapter 23 for more information on grips. Table 23-10 in Chapter 23 lists the weights of several commercially available grips. NOTE: Matching grip weights is also important when frequency matching a set of clubs. See Chapter 63 for more information on frequency matching.

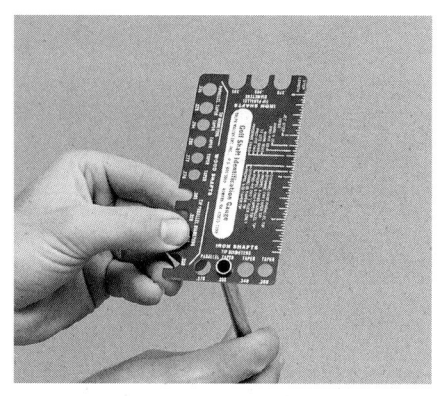

32-116 Checking the shaft tip size. Use a Golf Shaft Identification Gauge, a micrometer or vernier caliper to verify the tip size of the shaft. Virtually every shaft used for assembly will be .370".

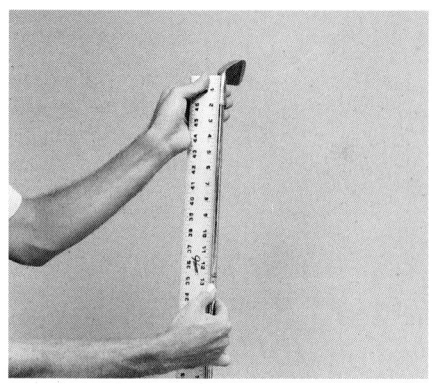

32-117 Achieving the Proper Back of Heel to First Step Dimension. For steel shaft installation, refer to Chapter 21, photos 21-85 through 21-97 for determining the proper back of heel to first step dimensions. See photos 32-87 through 32-93 in this chapter for instructions on cutting steel shafts. Once you've accomplished this, proceed to photo 32-119.

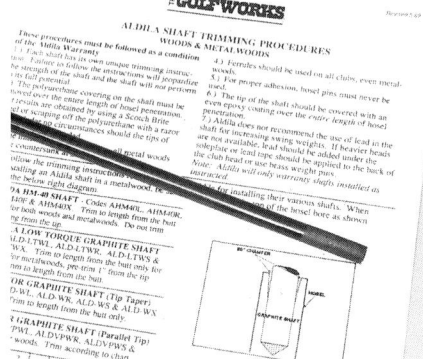

32-118 The diameter of titanium and composite shafts is not reduced along the length of the shaft, therefore, there are no back of heel to first step dimensions that can be followed. Instead, most graphite and titanium shafts have their own specific trimming instructions. These should be included with your shaft order. Please refer to these trimming instructions now. See photos 32-87 through 32-99 for steps on cutting titanium and composite shafts.

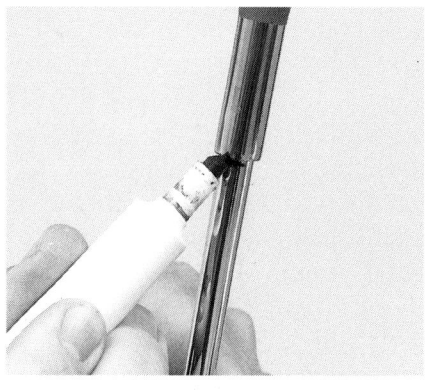

32-119 Abrading the shaft tip. After any necessary corrections have been made to the shaft tip, it must be abraded in order to provide the epoxy with a good bonding surface. To determine how much of the shaft tip should be abraded, first install it in the hosel and mark the shaft with a felt tip pen even with the top of the hosel. See photos 32-18 through 32-26 for complete instructions on abrading steel, composite and titanium shafts.

32-120 If a composite shaft is being installed, the inside hosel edge should be countersunk using an 18° or 20° countersink, as shown. The subsequent gap will be filled with epoxy which will help reduce the stress placed upon the shaft. To use, simply insert the countersink into the hosel and activate the drill until a bevel is created.

32-121 This is an 18° carbide coated steel countersink installed in a normal drill. It is very durable which makes it a good choice for the high volume user. The GolfWorks® also offers an 18° carbon steel countersink which is less expensive and is ideal for the part-time assembler.

32-122 This photo shows the inside hosel edge after countersinking. The entire job takes only a couple of seconds.

32-123 Installing a Ferrule. If the iron(s) you are assembling has a squared top hosel, a ferrule should be installed. Ferrules are available in different styles and inside diameters to match the two most common shaft tip sizes (.355" and .370"). In most cases, the shaft you will install will have a .370" tip diameter. If a ferrule is not to be installed, proceed to photo 32-129.

32-124 Sometimes the new ferrule will not easily slide on the shaft. In this case, place the ferrule against the mouth of a can of acetone and turn the can upside down so the acetone runs into the ferrule. Cover the end of the ferrule with your finger, as shown.

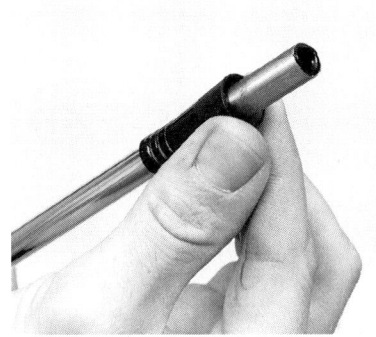

32-125 Wait 10 seconds then quickly slide the ferrule down the shaft. Immediately place the hosel over the shaft and drive the ferrule to its proper position.

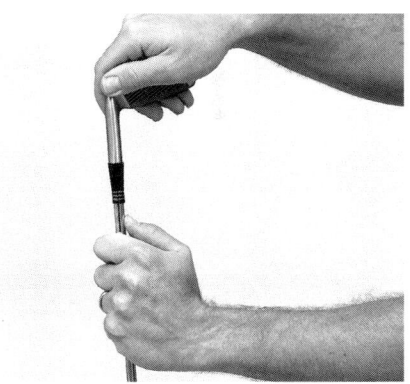

32-126 An alternative to the use of acetone is to place the hosel over the shaft and force the ferrule down the shaft by ramming the butt of the shaft against a steel plate or concrete floor. This sets the ferrule to the proper position on the shaft. After forcing the ferrule in place, remove the shaft from the hosel.

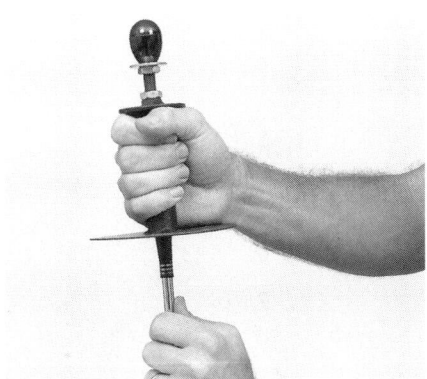

32-127 The **Ferrule Installer Tool** will accurately set an iron or wood ferrule to the proper depth and is especially helpful when a series of ferrules must be set.

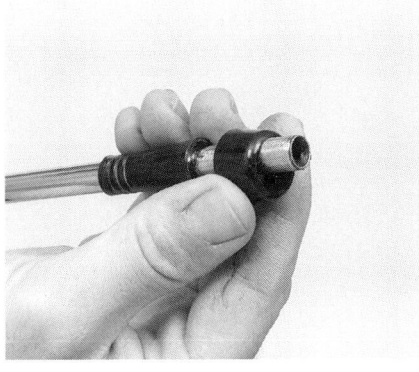

32-128 If installing a leather grip, it's a good idea to slip the grip collar over the shaft tip first rather than over the much larger shaft butt later. Push the collar up the shaft and temporarily secure it with a piece of tape.

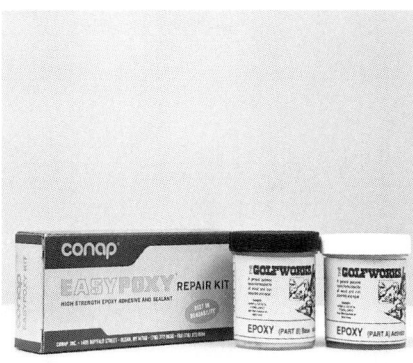

32-129 Installing the shaft. Use a shear strength epoxy such as GolfWorks® High Strength epoxy or Conap epoxy. NOTE: Always mix each component in the can first.

371

32-130 Mix the epoxies well, being sure that no unmixed epoxy remains on the perimeter. A good idea is to cut up old cardboard boxes into small squares and use these for mixing pallets. Popsicle sticks, tongue depressors or an old screwdriver work well to mix the epoxy.

32-131 Dip the tip of the shaft into the epoxy and pick up a dab, as shown.

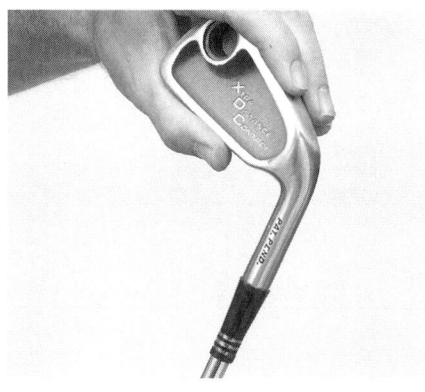

32-132 Push the shaft to the bottom of the hosel bore, simultaneously rotating the shaft. This will coat both the hosel bore and the shaft tip.

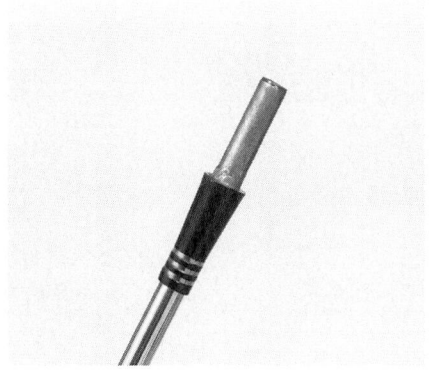

32-133 Remove the shaft from the hosel. Check to make sure the shaft is covered with epoxy and, if not, apply more. This photo shows adequate epoxy coverage.

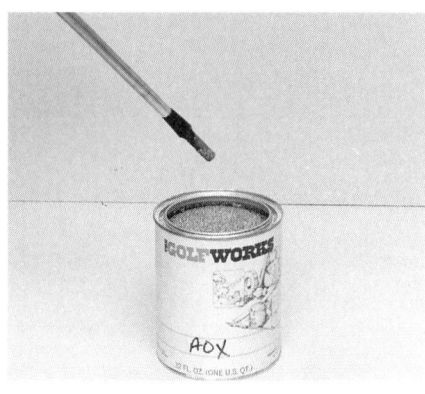

32-134 If the shaft is especially loose, insert the tip of the shaft into **Aluminum Oxide Sand.**

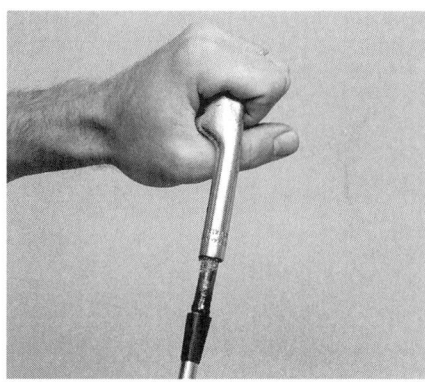

32-135 This small amount of sand will take up the excess space in the hosel.

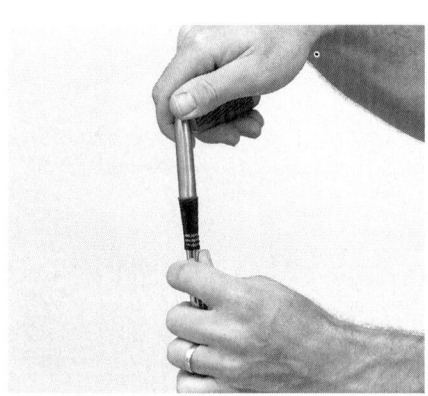

32-136 Reinstall the shaft into the hosel. NOTE: Before permanently installing the shaft, if the shaft has a shaft band, make sure the shaft is aligned so that the band's identifying marks are facing forward.

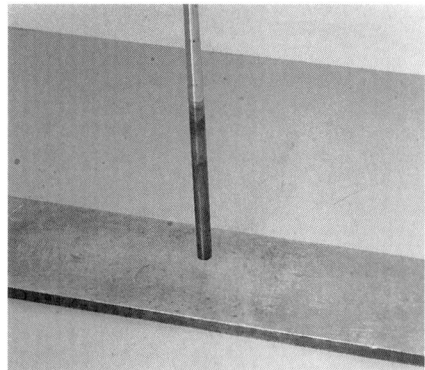

32-137 There are two good methods for driving the shaft solidly onto the head. The first, place one hand on the head and the other on the shaft and slam the shaft butt against a concrete floor or steel plate. This will seat the shaft tip to the bottom of the hosel bore.

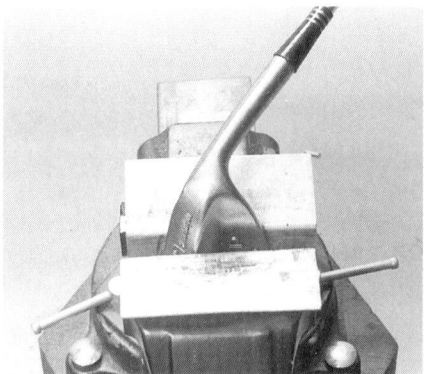

32-138 The second method uses a **Shaft Driving Plug** for "setting" the shaft into the hosel. Place a pair of aluminum or brass vise pads over the vise jaws and tighten the head securely in the vise.

32-139 Insert a **Shaft Driving Plug** in the butt end of the shaft and drive the shaft in place.

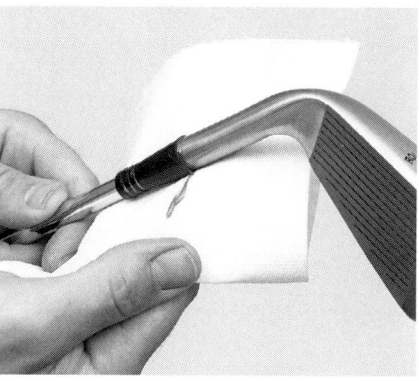

32-140 Wipe the excess epoxy from the hosel and ferrule. Also, examine the shaft for epoxy fingerprints. Many assemblers inadvertently smear epoxy over other areas of the club, and epoxy becomes more difficult to remove after curing.

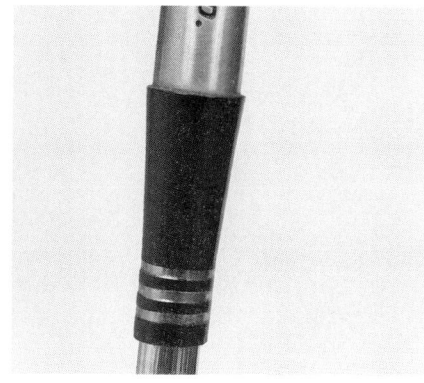

32-141 Reducing the ferrule diameter. The next step, after the epoxy cures, is to reduce the diameter of the ferrule so it matches the hosel. NOTE: If you did not install a ferrule, proceed to photo 32-150.

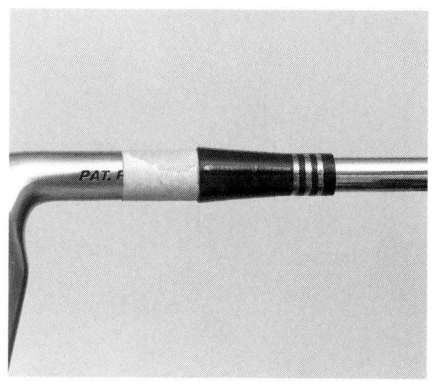

32-142 Place the shaft in a Rubber Shaft Clamp and tighten in a vise. Wrap a piece of ¾" masking tape around the hosel just below the ferrule.

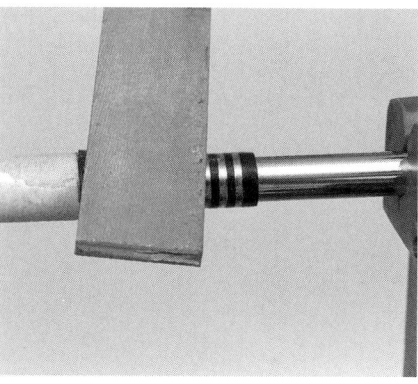

32-143 Use a flat mill or fine file and lightly file the excess plastic flush with the tape. The tape will protect the hosel from possible scratches.

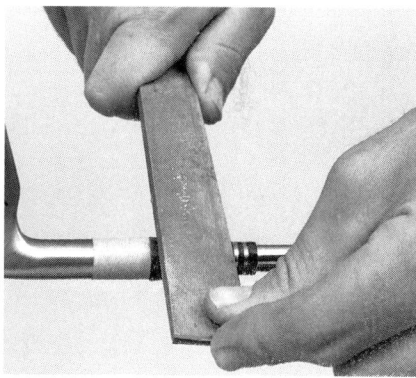

32-144 Continue to file while rotating the club. Care should be taken to ensure a proper taper in the ferrule. Carefully file the top of the ferrule to blend in the color rings flush with the ferrule. Do not file the top edge of the ferrule flush with the shaft as a definite lip should remain.

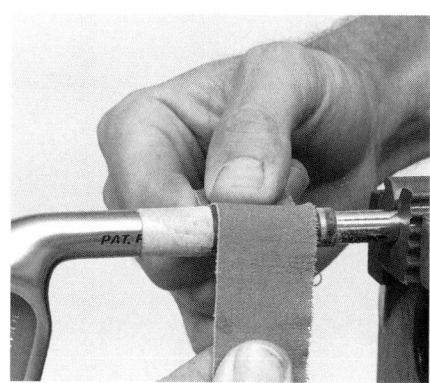

32-145 Filing will leave flat spots and ridges in the plastic. Lightly sand the ferrule with a 180 or 220 grit sandpaper.

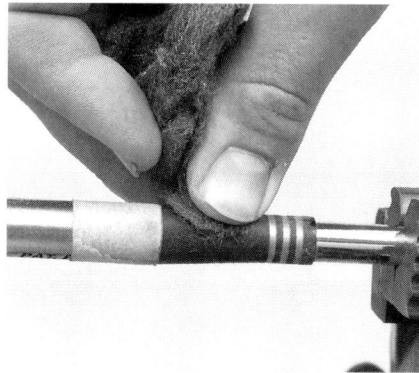

32-146 At this point, the ferrule will look rough and dull. This is normal. Rub the ferrule with 000 steel wool. This will remove some of the scratches left from the sandpaper and make the ferrule smoother. Remove the tape after steel wooling.

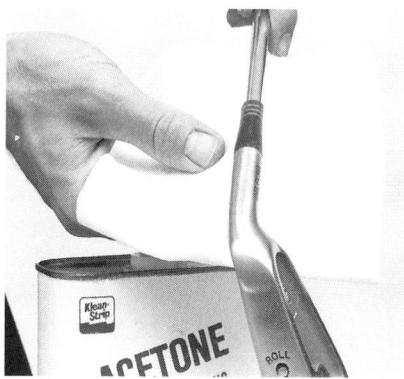

32-147 Dampen a paper towel with acetone and wipe the ferrule with the towel. Wipe lengthwise and not around the ferrule.

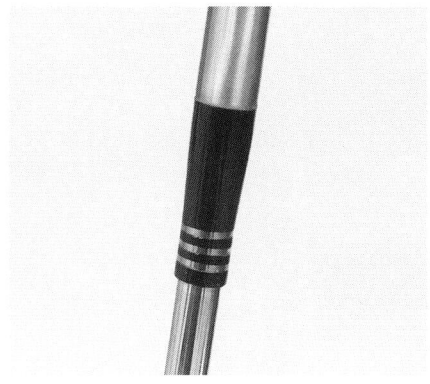

32-148 The acetone will restore the plastic ferrule to a shiny, like new appearance. Note the perfect taper from the top of the hosel to the top of the ferrule. There is an obvious step from the ferrule to the shaft, however, this is normal.

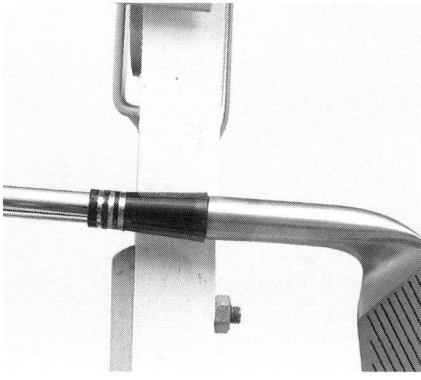

32-149 Although it is an expensive piece of equipment, a 1" x 42" belt sander/grinder with a cloth linen belt is the easiest, quickest way to get the job done and eliminates any chance of scratching the shaft or hosel. Refer to Chapter 21, photos 21-142 through 21-146 for the procedure.

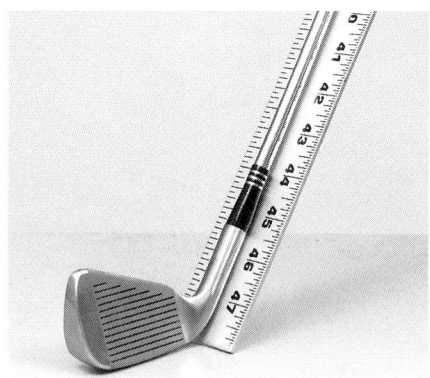

32-150 Measuring and cutting the club to length. Sole the club on the ground as shown and slide a 48" ruler behind the shaft. Refer to photos 32-85 through 32-99 in this chapter for complete steps on marking and cutting steel, titanium or graphite shafts.

32-151 Installing the grip. Determine the shaft butt size using the Grip Size and Shaft Butt Gauge. Next, verify the grip size by looking inside the mouth of the grip. Follow photos 23-44 through 23-74 for installing a slip-on rubber grip and photos 23-75 through 23-114 for installing a leather wrap-on grip. Additional information for building up grips, etc. is also detailed in Chapter 23.

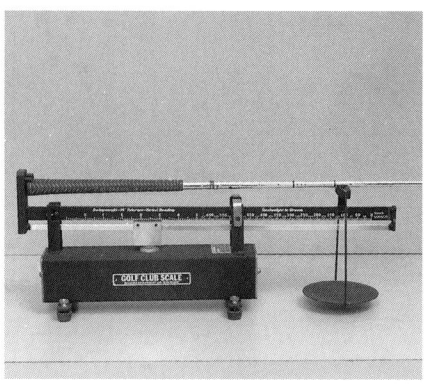

32-152 IMPORTANT NOTE: If the iron does <u>not</u> have a weight port(s), the swingweight should be checked and adjusted before installing the grip. See Chapter 33, photos 33-75 through 33-80 for clubs without weight ports. If the iron does have a weight port or set screw, photos 32-103 through 32-109 illustrate how to add weight directly to the head after gripping. Chapter 18 also details more information on swingweighting irons.

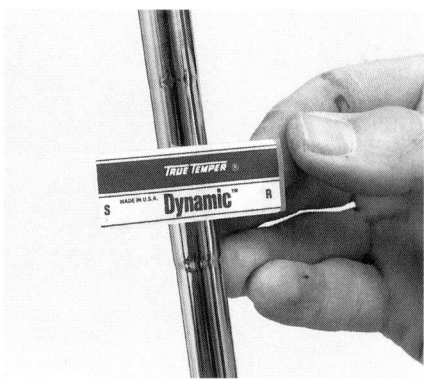

32-153 Applying the shaft band. The shaft band should be positioned on the second step below the bottom of the grip. For shafts that do not have steps, the band should be installed approximately 2" below the grip.

NOTES

_____

_____

_____

_____

_____

_____

_____

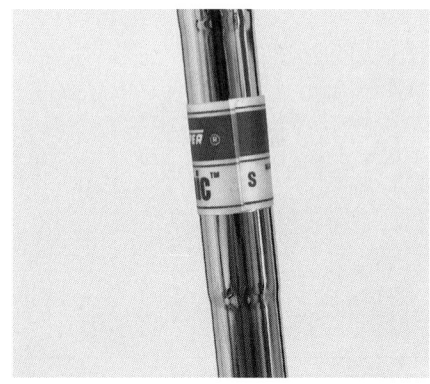

32-154 When using a combination flex shaft band, as shown, make sure the appropriate letter is showing after the band is wrapped around the shaft. After completing this step, the club(s) will be ready for play.

ADDITIONAL INFORMATION FOR ASSEMBLING WOODS AND IRONS

TABLE 32-1
Average Head Weights to Produce a D-2 Swingweight @ Standard Club Length With a Standard Size Rubber Grip and Carbon Steel Shaft

Wood Number	Club Length (Inches)	Head Weight (Ounces)	Head Weight (Grams)	[1]Average Total Weight Range (Ounces)
1	43"	6⅞	195	12⅞ to 13¼
2	42½"	7⅛	202	13⅛ to 13½
3	42"	7⅜	209	13⅜ to 13¾
4	41½"	7⅝	216	13⅝ to 14
5	41"	7⅞	223	13⅞ to 14¼
6	40½"	8⅛	230	14⅛ to 14½
7	40"	8⅜	237	14⅜ to 14¾

Iron Number	Club Length (Inches)	Head Weight (Ounces)	Head Weight (Grams)	[1]Average Total Weight Range (Ounces)
1	39½"	8	227	13⅞ to 14¼
2	39"	8¼	234	14⅛ to 14½
3	38½"	8½	241	14⅜ to 14¾
4	38"	8¾	248	14⅝ to 15
5	37½"	9	255	14⅞ to 15¼
6	37"	9¼	262	15⅛ to 15½
7	36½"	9½	269	15⅜ to 15¾
8	36"	9¾	276	15⅝ to 16
9	35½"	10	283	15⅞ to 16¼

For each ½" the club length is reduced, the head weight must be increased by ¼ ounce. Conversely, a ½" increase in club length requires a reduction of ¼ ounce in head weight.

The range of grip and shaft weight tolerances can cause a 5 swingweight difference using the head weights shown above. This points out the importance of purchasing iron heads and wood heads with an adjustable weight port properly located within the head. The head weights shown provide a good starting point in predicting a club's swingweight but can only be considered as an average.

[1] These total weights are based on medium flex carbon steel shafts. The total weights will increase slightly the stiffer the shaft flex and decrease slightly the more flexible the shaft flex.

TABLE 32-2
Comparing Total Weight, Shaft Material, Shaft Flex and Swingweight

Shaft Flex and Swingweight Range	*Driver total weight range in ounces by shaft material and type				
	3⅞ oz. Shaft Lightweight Steel	4⅛ oz. Shaft Unitized Steel	4⅜ oz. Shaft Carbon Steel	2¼ to 3¼ oz. Shaft Graphite & Titanium	3½ oz. Shaft Very Lightweight Steel
L-Ladies C6 to C8	11⅞ to 12¼	12 to 12⅜	12⅛ to 12½	11⅛ to 11½	11⅜ to 11¾
A-Flexible C9 to D1	12⅛ to 12½	12¼ to 12⅝	12⅜ to 12¾	11⅜ to 11¾	11⅝ to 12
R-Medium D1 to D3	12⅝ to 13	12¾ to 13⅛	12⅞ to 13¼	11⅝ to 12	11⅞ to 12¼
S-Stiff D2 to D4	12⅞ to 13¼	13 to 13⅜	13⅛ to 13½	11⅞ to 12¼	12⅛ to 12½
X-Extra Stiff D4 to D6	13⅛ to 13½	13¼ to 13⅝	13⅜ to 13¾	12⅛ to 12½	12⅜ to 12¾

*Based on a 43" driver length. For each ½" longer than standard driver length, subtract ¼ ounce from the weights above. Conversely, for each ½" shorter than standard driver length, add ¼ ounce to the weights above.

TABLE 32-3
Wood Club Lengths – Men's and Ladies'

Woods	Men's Standard	Ladies' Standard	Ladies' Petite
1	43"	42"	41½"
2	42½"	41½"	41"
3	42"	41"	40½"
4	41½"	40½"	40"
5	41"	40"	39½"
6	40½"	39½"	39
7	40"	39"	38½"
8	39½"	38½"	38"
9	39"	38"	37½"

The most popular length variations for men are ½" shorter or longer than standard and 1" longer than standard. The most popular length variations for ladies are ½" shorter or longer than standard. Many graphite shafted drivers are now made at lengths ½" to 2" longer than standard.

TABLE 32-4
Iron Club Lengths – Men's and Ladies'

Irons	Men's Modern Standard	Men's Traditional Standard	Ladies' Standard	[1] Ladies' Petite
1	39½"	39"	38"	37½"
2	39"	38½"	37½"	37"
3	38½"	38"	37"	36½"
4	38"	37½"	36½"	36"
5	37½"	37"	36"	35½"
6	37"	36½"	35½"	35"
7	36½"	36"	35"	34½"
8	36"	35½"	34½"	34"
9	35½"	35"	34"	33½"
PW	35½"	35"	34"	33½"
SW	35½"	35"	34"	33½"

[1] Ladies' petite is usually ½" shorter than the traditional ladies' standard length. Some companies make ladies' petite 1" shorter than ladies' standard length.

TABLE 32-5
Club Number vs. Purchased Shaft Length Combinations
(Taper Tip)

WOODS Club No.	5 Lengths	3 Lengths	1 Length	IRONS Club No.	9 Lengths	5 Lengths	3 Lengths
1	44"	44"	44"	1	39"	39"	39"
2	43½"	44"	44"	2	38½"	38"	39"
3	43"	43"	44"	3	38"	38"	39"
4	42½"	43"	44"	4	37½"	37"	37"
5	42"	42"	44"	5	37"	37"	37"
6	42"	42"	44"	6	36½"	36"	37"
7	42"	42"	44"	7	36"	36"	37"
				8	35½"	35"	35"
				9	35"	35"	35"
				PW	35"	35"	35"
				SW	35"	35"	35"

NOTE: Other combinations are also possbile depending on club length and flexibility desired.

Tools and Supplies Required for Wood and Iron Club Assembly

The following list shows the Tools and Supplies required to assemble golf clubs. Those items below that are preceded by an Asterisk (*) are not necessary if pro-finished heads will be used instead of pro-sanded heads.

Assembling woods and irons requires a minimum of space and virtually no machines. However, a couple of bench motors with attachments such as a drill chuck, buffing or steel wooling mandrels and a grinding wheel are real time savers if the volume of assembly justifies the expense. A drill press and a 1" x 42" belt sander are two other time saving machines. Actually, the only large piece of equipment needed is a good solid workbench with a vise mounted at one end. A 4" heavy duty vise is recommended vs. the light duty workshop models.

Tools Required

Face Radius Gauge
Machinist's Protractor
Grip Size and Shaft Butt Gauge
3/8" Electric Drill
.277, .294, .320 & .335 Step Drills (Woods)
.355 & .370 Step Drills (Irons)
1/8" Cobalt Drill Bit
Flat File - Smooth Cut
Mill File - Smooth Cut
File Cleaner
Wood and Felt Vise Pads (Woods)
Aluminum or Brass Vise Pads (Irons)
1/8" Pin Punch
Awl or Prick Punch
Ball Peen Hammer (12 oz.)
48" Aluminum Ruler
Tubing cutter and Spare Wheel
Razor Knife
*Face Detailing Knife
Swingweight Scale
Shaft Driving Plug
#1 & #2 Reed & Prince Screwdrivers
#1 & #2 Phillips Screwdrivers
6" Scale (Ruler)
Rubber or Vinyl Shaft Clamp
Safety Glass or Goggles
Propane Torch
Screw Heater
Stiff Bristle Brush

Optional Tools

Loft Gauges
Shaft Identification Gauge
Golf Club Gauge™
Loft and Lie Machine
Gram Scale
Unstitched Buffing Wheels
Glanz Wach
1/2" Countersink

Supplies

Shafts – Wood and Iron
Grips
Ferrules – Woods and Irons
Golf Club Epoxy
Tapered Wood Plus
Special Steel Backscrews
Masking Tape – 3/4" or 2"
Double-Coated Tape – 3/4" or 2"
China Marker or Grease Pencil
Whipping
Paper Towels or Rags
Grip Solvent
Acetone
000 Steel Wool
Brass or Aluminum Shim Stock
Grip Collars
Lead Powder, Rod or Shot
Cutting and Drilling Oil
Brass Soleplate Screws - 2 sizes
Brass Insert Screws - 2 Sizes
5 Minute Epoxy
Shaft Labels
*Decals
*Scotch Tape
*Artist's Brushes
*Alcohol - Rubbing
*Tack Rag
*Scoring Paint – Black and White
*Stains
*Fillers
*Colorcote
*Primer Sealer
*Polyurethane – Dipping or Spraying
*3" Wide Clear Tape – Soleplate
*Burlap for Wiping Filler
*2 Quart Plastic Dipping Containers
*400 Wet or Dry Sandpaper
*Lacquer Stick – Various Colors

Some Helpful Tips for Wood and Iron Club Assembly

■ Many people who purchase a custom built, custom fit set of golf clubs do not like to wait to have them built. In many cases you can use this little tip and have their clubs (wood and irons) the very next day.

Make up 2 or 3 sets of clubs with your most popular shaft type and flex. This is usually medium flex Dynamic™ shafts or medium flex TT Lite™ shafts. A stiff flex Dynamic™ set is also a good idea. Anyway, complete all the assembly steps, but do not cut the shafts to length, do not grip the clubs and do not swingweight the clubs. All of the long drying time operations have been complete and it will only take a short time to cut the clubs to length, grip and swingweight when you custom fit and sell a set of clubs.

■ If you start assembling golf clubs it is important to properly promote this new service. Place a full set of clubs on display, make up a few demo clubs in different shafts, weights, etc. Be sure and put up a sign. Don't assume people will know that you are making clubs. I heard of one clubmaker who made up buttons the staff wore that read "Ask about our Custom Made Clubs fit to you." Another ingenious method of getting customers to ask you questions is to have the whole staff wear workshop aprons. Everybody has to ask, "What are the aprons for?"

■ Figuring out exactly what components to stock can be difficult. Questions such as what insert colors or head finish colors sell best? Should I stock laminated maple, persimmon, or metal woods? Our sales experience of wood heads has shown that 70% of all heads sold by us have red inserts, 20% black inserts and 10% all other colors. Laminated and persimmon breakdown 50% each. Finish colors that are most popular are Black, Tommy Armour Mahogany and Walnut. Rosewood is gaining in popularity.

■ Look closely into making your own brand of golf clubs. A few companies have available special buttons, medallions, or you can have your own decal made. Your own brand of clubs eliminates competition because no one else has exactly the same club as you do. This can enhance your image, build brand equity and better establish yourself as a golf club authority with your customers.

PUTTER HEAD ASSEMBLY

Putter head designs fall into one of two categories: 1. The over-the-hosel model, in which the shaft fits over a hosel post that extends from the head. 2. The in-hosel model in which the shaft fits inside the hosel bore or head. Assembly steps are similar for both models.

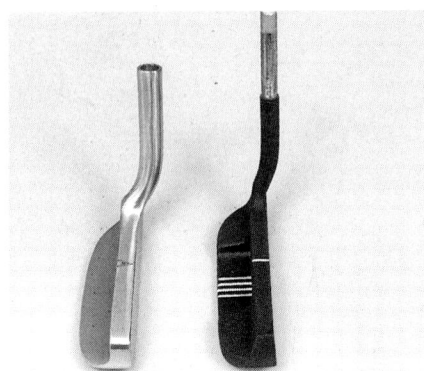

32-155 The putter on the right is an over-the-hosel design while the putter on the left is an in-hosel design. Note how a shaft would be attached to each.

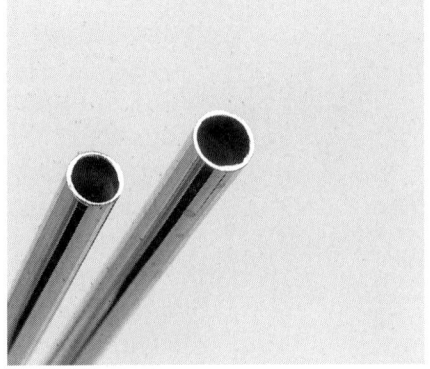

32-156 **Putter Shaft Selection.** Over-the-hosel putters often require a shaft specifically designed to fit over large hosel posts, while other over-the-hosel models can be fit with a standard .370" tip iron shaft. If you have a variety of putter shafts in stock, test several until you find one that fits. If you must order a shaft...

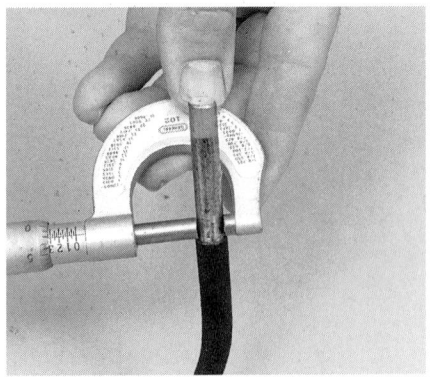

32-157 ...measure the diameter of the hosel post at its base using a micrometer or vernier calipers. If the diameter is smaller than .370", order a .370" shaft. If the diameter is from .370" to .382", True Temper's® straight taper, flared tip putter shaft (code YSTGF) will fit. If the diameter is larger than .382", True Temper's® unitized, fluted putter shaft (code UYSTG) will be a good choice.

378

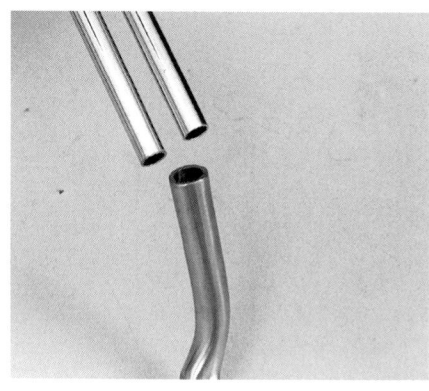

32-158 In-hosel putters commonly require either a .355" or .370" shaft. Shafts specifically designed for putters are also available with .355" tip diameters. A list of these shafts can be found in Chapter 56. True Temper's® YST or YSTG shafts are examples of putter shafts that are frequently used.

32-159 Parallel tip iron shafts (.370") are often used instead of specific putter shafts. Typically, S or R flex, parallel tip iron shafts or combination flex shafts that can be trimmed to an S flex are selected. True Temper's® UDIC, UDIS or UDIX can all be used. NOTE: Most players prefer an S flex shaft for their putters.

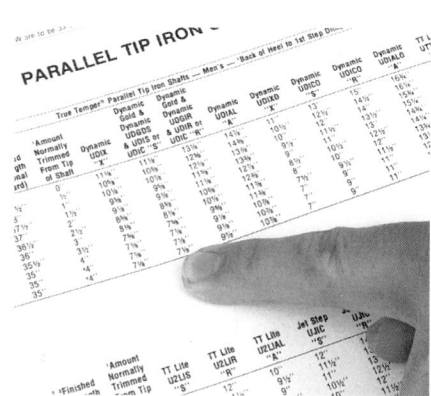

32-160 Tip Trimming Non-specific .370" Shafts for Over and In-hosel Putters. Refer to the Back of Heel to First Step Dimension Tables in Chapter 57. After locating the column head describing your shaft, scan down the column to the last measurement. This is the distance the shaft's first step down should be from the putter's heel for both in-hosel and over-hosel models. NOTE: Shafts specifically designed for putters do not require any tip trimming. Proceed to Photo 32-163.

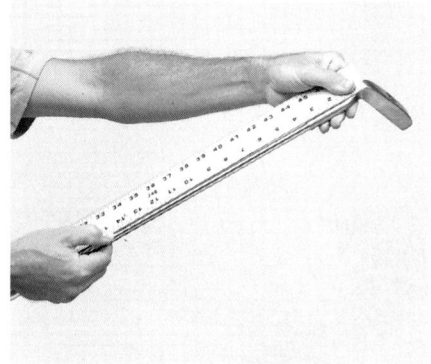

32-161 Temporarily install the putter shaft over/in the hosel as shown. Measure from the putter's heel to the first step down. In this case, we will install a UDIC shaft trimmed to the S flex. According to the Tables, the proper measurement is 7⅛"; therefore, 7⅜" will have to be trimmed from the tip of this shaft because currently the distance is 14½". Refer to photos 32-87 through 32-99 for information on shaft trimming.

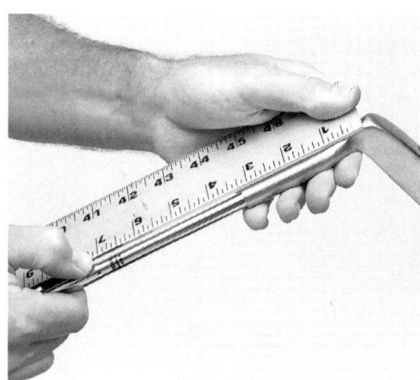

32-162 After cutting 7⅜" from the tip, the back of heel to first step dimension will be correct. If working with an in-hosel putter, proceed to photo 32-163 for shaft tip preparation. If working with an over-hosel putter, go to photo 32-167 for shaft installation.

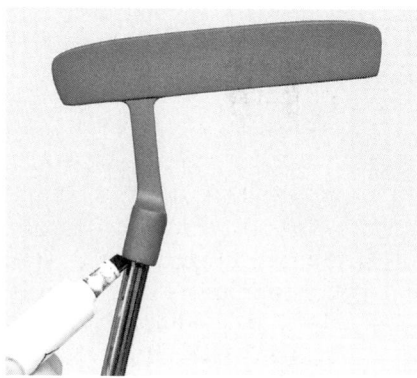

32-163 Shaft Tip Preparation. Temporarily insert the shaft into the hosel bore so that the shaft tip seats against the bottom of the hosel bore. Make a mark on the shaft even with the top of the hosel, as shown.

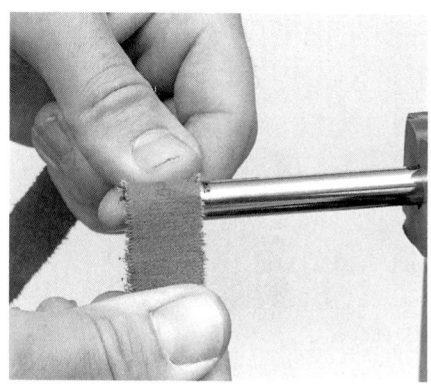

32-164 Place the tip of the shaft in a **Rubber Shaft Clamp** and tighten this in your vise. Use a strip of coarse sandpaper to sand the portion of the shaft below the mark.

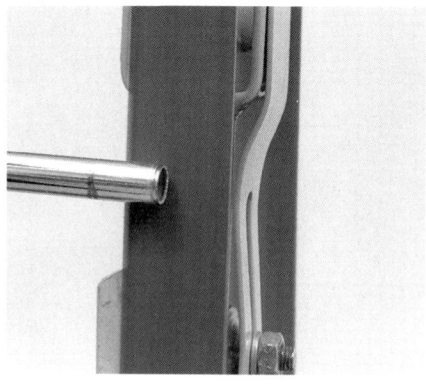

32-165 Abrade the shaft tip using a 1" x 42" **Belt Sander** as a fast alternative to hand sanding.

32-166 After abrading, the shaft tip should have a uniform "satiny" appearance. Abrading the shaft tip will ensure better adhesion between the epoxy and the shaft. If you are installing a composite shaft, refer to photos 32-23 through 32-26 for proper shaft tip preparation steps.

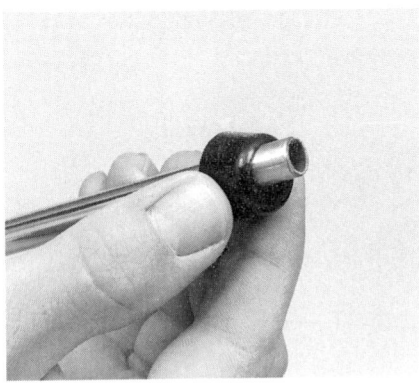

32-167 If you intend to install a leather grip, slip the grip collar over the tip of the shaft at this time. Slide the collar up the shaft and secure it with a piece of tape. NOTE: If a ferrule will be installed, refer to Photo 32-176 before proceeding to 32-168.

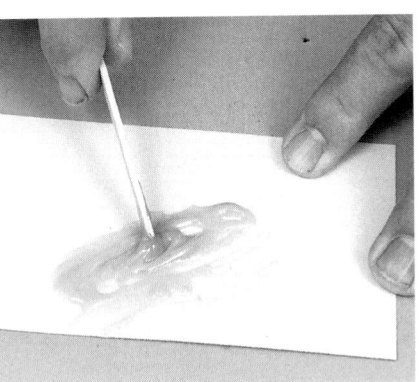

32-168 Shaft Installation. Mix a shear strength epoxy (GolfWorks® High Strength Epoxy or Conap Epoxy works well) according to directions.

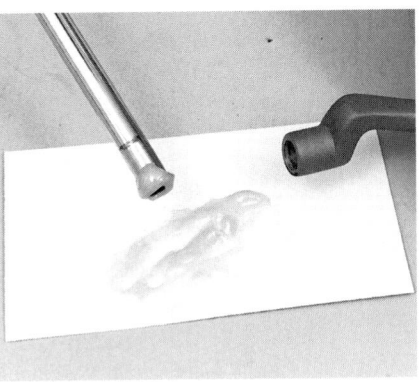

32-169 For in-hosel putters, dip the tip of the abraded shaft into the epoxy and pick up a glob of epoxy, as shown. If working with an over-hosel putter, first abrade the hosel post with a fine file or sandpaper then dip the post into the epoxy.

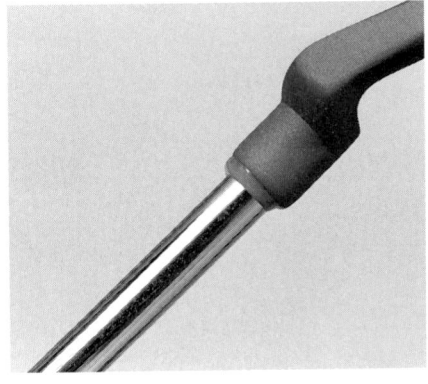

32-170 Push the epoxy coated shaft into the hosel bore of the in-hosel putter. If working with the over-hosel putter, push the hosel post into the shaft.

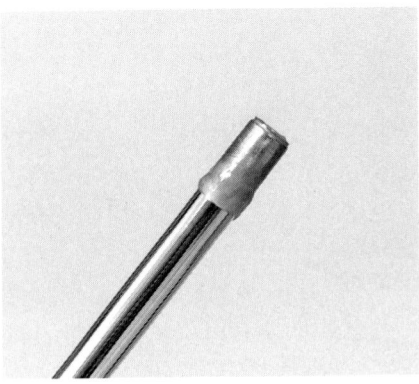

32-171 Remove the shaft from the head. Check to see that either the shaft or hosel post has been well coated with epoxy. If portions of the shaft or hosel post appear clean, apply more epoxy.

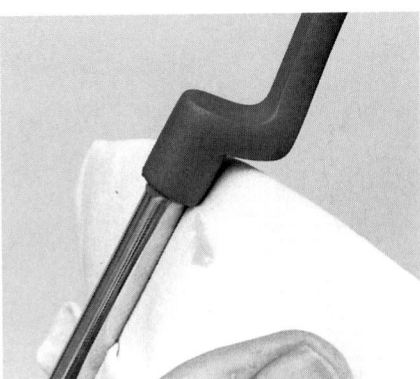

32-172 After installing the shaft into the head or the hosel post into the shaft, wipe the excess epoxy with a paper towel. Allow the epoxy to cure before cutting the putter to length as shown in Photo 32-178.

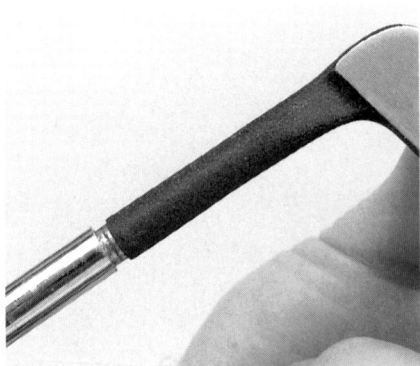

32-173 Sometimes a shaft for over-hosel putters will not slide completely over the hosel post to its base. To alleviate this problem...

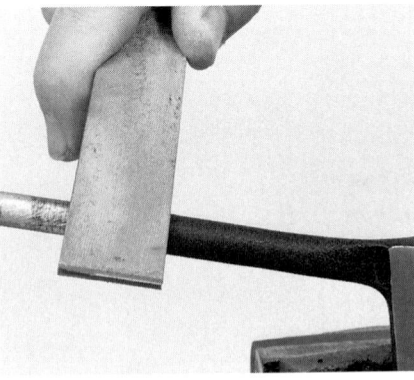

32-174 ...either reduce the diameter of the hosel post by filing or sanding or...

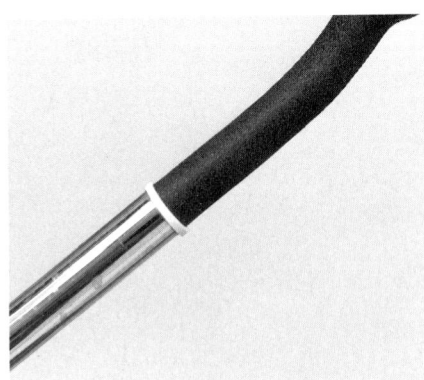

32-175 ...install a brass or plastic trim ring to take up the excess space. This can be an attractive alternative to filing. The trim ring usually will have a larger diameter than the hosel, so refer to Photos 32-141 through 32-149.

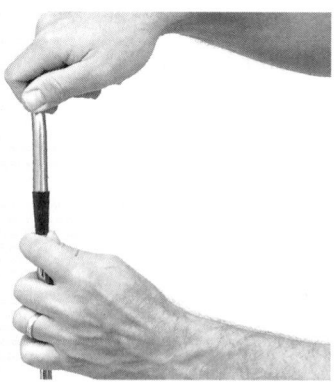

32-176 Some putters have a hosel that is flat on top, so a ferrule is required to create the proper appearance. Install the ferrule over the shaft tip prior to epoxying the shaft into the hosel. If you encounter difficulty, drive the ferrule to the proper position by tapping the hosel against the bottom of the ferrule until the shaft tip hits the bottom of the hosel bore. Wipe any epoxy that may ooze from between the ferrule and hosel.

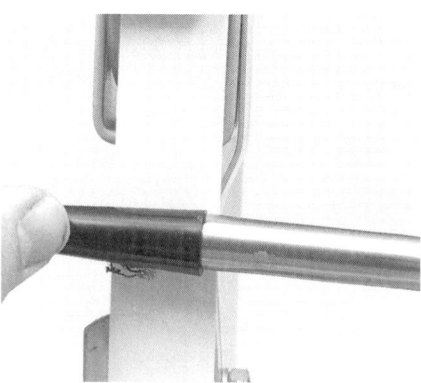

32-177 After the epoxy cures, reduce the diameter of the bottom of the ferrule to match the hosel diameter, as shown in Photos 32-141 through 32-149.

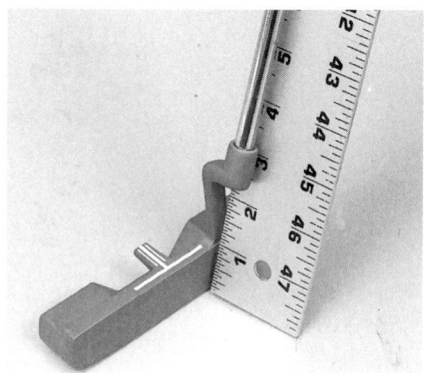

32-178 Measuring and Cutting the Putter to Length. Once the epoxy cures, measure and cut the club to length as shown in photos 32-85 through 32-99. To measure the overall length of a putter with the shaft or hosel located towards the center, place the end of the ruler in line with the shaft rather than against the putter's heel. This will give a more accurate reading.

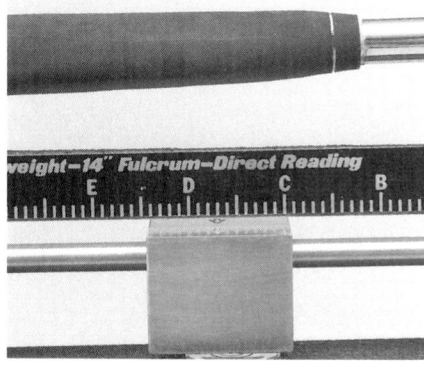

32-179 Swingweighting the Putter. Swingweight is usually not a consideration when assembling putters. However, if a specific swingweight is requested it should be calculated before the grip is installed.

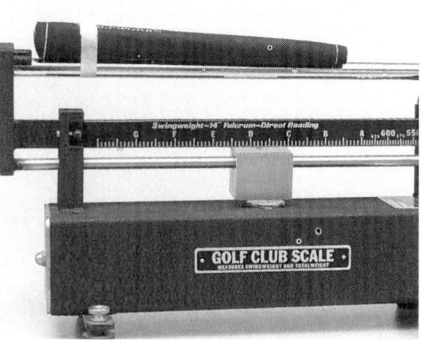

32-180 Place the putter on the swingweight scale. To get a fairly accurate idea of what the swingweight will be once the grip is installed, tape the grip to the shaft butt as shown and record the swingweight. This putter has a swingweight of C-8. Since a D-2 swingweight is desired, 4 swingweight points must be added down the shaft. Refer to Chapter 33, photos 33-75 through 33-80 for information on swingweighting.

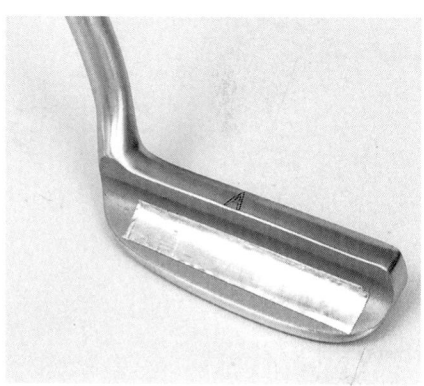

32-181 The ideal method of adding swingweight to any head is to place strips of lead tape on the back of the head. Each strip of tape 4½" long x ½" wide equals one swingweight point. Some customers resist this method because of cosmetic considerations.

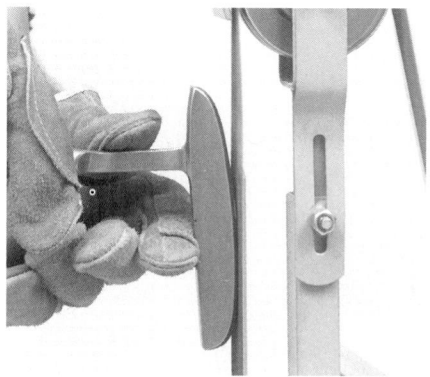

32-182 If the swingweight is too heavy, the alternatives are to either grind weight from the head using a **Belt Sander** as shown (note the use of leather gloves) or to shorten the overall length of the putter. For every ½" the putter is shortened, 3 swingweight points are lost. Grinding will leave scratches which may not be acceptable.

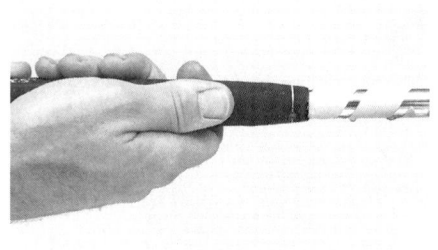

32-183 Installing the Grip. After cutting the shaft to length, and if necessary swingweighting, the putter is now ready for gripping. The procedure for gripping a putter is the same as shown in Chapter 23.

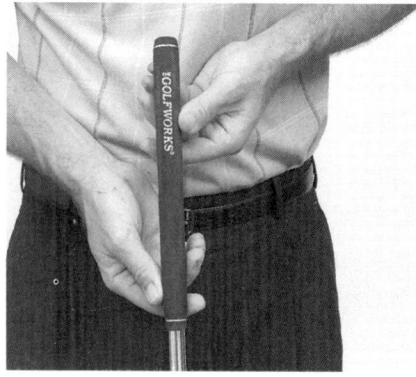

32-184 After installing the grip, place the putter in the playing position. If the grip has a flat side, be sure that side is facing towards the front unless the customer has requested otherwise. Correct grip alignment on any club is very important.

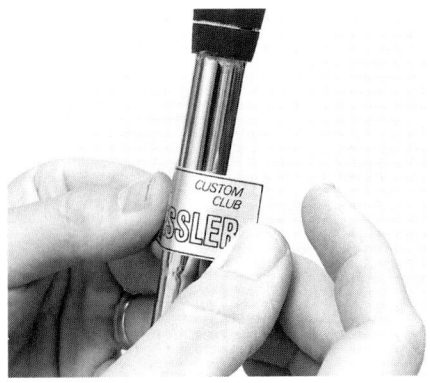

32-185 Shaft bands should be applied a couple of inches below the grip. It should be mentioned that The GolfWorks® also offers a personalized shaft band program for those who may be interested.

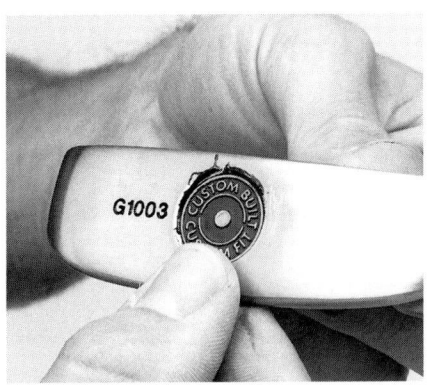

32-186 Installing a Medallion. If the putter with which you are working requires a medallion, first coat the medallion cavity with a thin layer of epoxy, then set the medallion into the cavity at right angles to the sole, as shown.

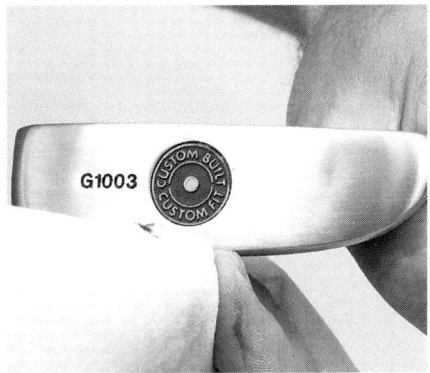

32-187 Wipe excess epoxy with a paper towel and place a strip of masking tape across the medallion to hold it in place until the epoxy dries. Place the club in an upright position and allow to cure thoroughly (usually overnight) before using it.

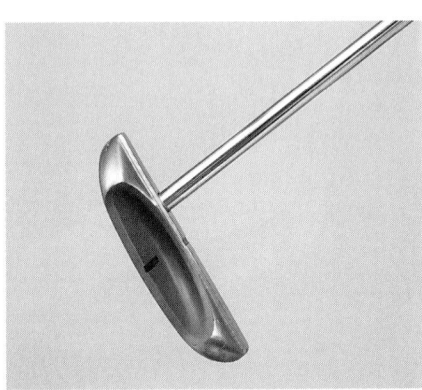

32-188 This in-hosel design, available from The GolfWorks® is specifically used for making the long putters. Assembly steps are the same as other in-hosel designs except a special long putter shaft is used.

NOTES

_____

_____

_____

_____

_____

_____

CHAPTER 33

THE COMPLETE "HOW TO" ON ASSEMBLING CUSTOM METAL WOODS

Originally, most metal woods appeared to be very similar. Now, however, metal woods are available with a variety of differing design features. For instance, the GolfWorks® Bio Mech® has two rails on the sole which are significant features because the club will have a lower center of gravity than most metal woods. This means that a ball will fly higher and shots from the rough are easier. The GolfWorks® Kinetic C.E.R. offers a classic design featuring two weight ports. Many club assemblers like the dual weight ports because they allow for a wider range of swingweight possibilities.

Besides specific design features, the overall size of metal woods is getting quite large. Metal woods are now available in mid size versions and oversized models like The GolfWorks® Out-A-Site.

Oversized models have real design benefits for the average golfer because of the added confidence inspired by the perception that they will be easier to hit. Additionally, the hosel will usually be shorter with the excess metal distributed within the walls of the head.

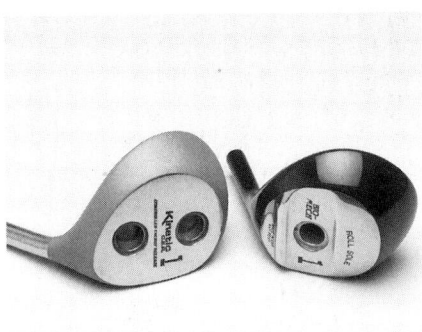

33-1 The metal wood on the right (Bio-Mech®) and the Kinetic C.E.R. are two examples of the wide variety of models available from the GolfWorks®.

33-2 Some metal woods do not require a ferrule because the top of the hosel is rounded. If the metal wood with which you are working has a squared top hosel (as shown on the club on the right), a ferrule should be installed. Purchasing metal woods that do not require a ferrule saves time because ferrules usually require time consuming modifications for a good fit. Some club assemblers, however, prefer metal woods with ferrules because of the classic appearance.

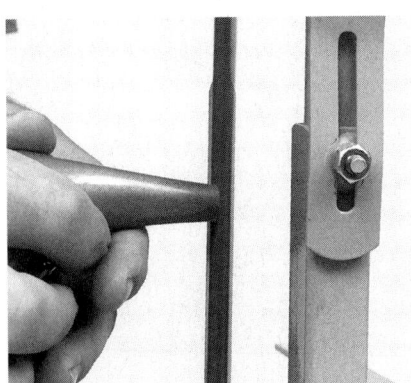

33-3 If the metal wood you are planning to assemble has a rounded top hosel and you want to install a ferrule, convert it to a squared top hosel by careful grinding. Push the top of the hosel against a grinding stone or belt sander until it is squared.

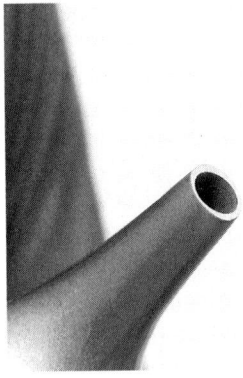

33-4 This photo shows the top of the hosel after grinding. No more than ¼" should be removed.

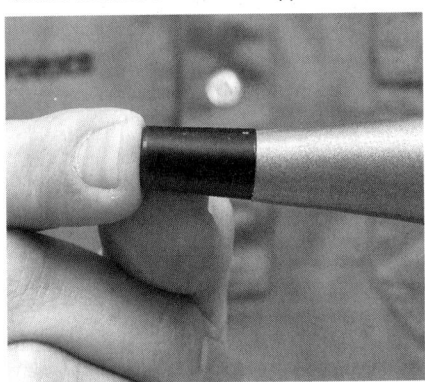

33-5 Always check the diameter of the hosel during grinding to make sure that it does not become larger than the diameter of the ferrule. This would be a real problem.

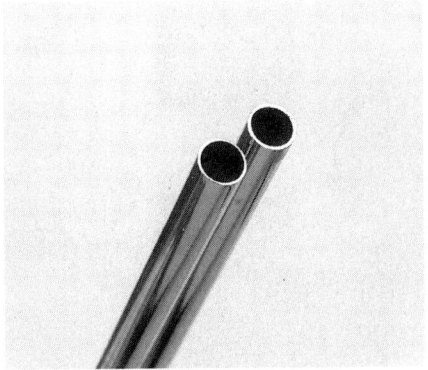

33-6 In 1987, golf shaft manufacturers designed steel shafts with thicker walls in the tip section for metal woods because some conventional parallel tip shafts would break during play. The small breakage problem was the result of stress placed on the shaft at the top of a metal wood hosel while the club was swung. When given the choice, you should choose tip reinforced shafts for metal wood assembly.

33-7 In addition, all metal woods that will be shafted with a composite shaft should have the inside hosel edge modified by countersinking with an 18° or 20° countersink. The gap between the modified hosel edge and the shaft will be filled with epoxy which will help reduce the stress placed upon the shaft. Most of the GolfWorks® metal woods already have the 20° countersunk feature (club on the right).

33-8 This is an 18° carbide coated steel countersink installed in a normal drill. It is very durable which makes it a good choice for the high volume user. The GolfWorks® also offers an 18° carbon steel countersink which is less expensive and is ideal for the part-time assembler.

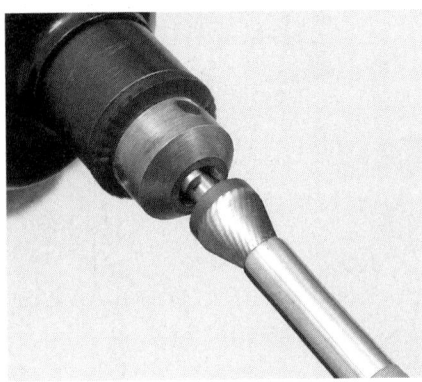

33-9 To use, simply insert the countersink into the hosel and activate the drill until a bevel is created.

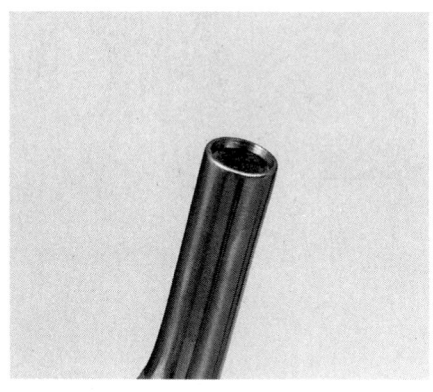

33-10 This photo shows the inside hosel edge after countersinking. The entire job takes only a couple of seconds.

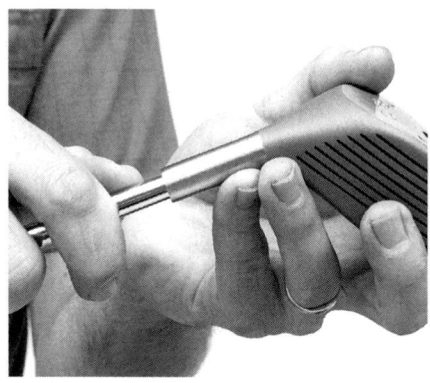

33-11 Whichever shaft you use, temporarily install it into the hosel to check the fit. Sometimes the hosel will be partially filled with foam that must be removed prior to permanent shaft installation. When temporarily installing the shaft, also check to make sure the shaft penetrates to the bottom of the hosel bore. On metal woods this is usually 1¼".

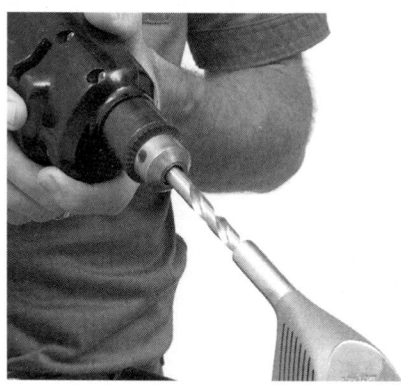

33-12 The most effective method for cleaning a hosel bore is to tighten the metal wood in a vise using a pair of vise pads. Select a letter "R" drill bit and drill into the hosel bore using an electric drill. NOTE: Most metal woods will have a thin metal "shoulder" in the hosel approximately 1½" from the top of the hosel on every club. Do not drill through this shoulder.

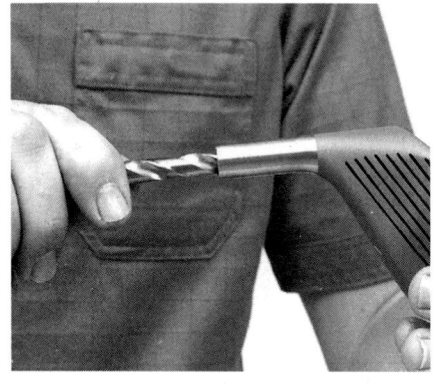

33-13 An alternative to the electric drill method is to hand turn the "R" drill into the hosel. This is slower, but you will be better able to feel the drill turning against the metal shoulder.

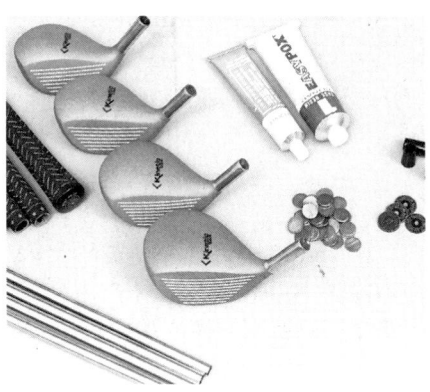

33-14 Being organized helps eliminate mistakes. Arrange the components you will be using on a work bench. Check to make sure the shafts are identical, the heads are without cosmetic flaws, and that you have an ample supply of epoxy and if necessary, lead discs or powder and medallions or set screws. If your grip inventory allows, check the weights of the grips.

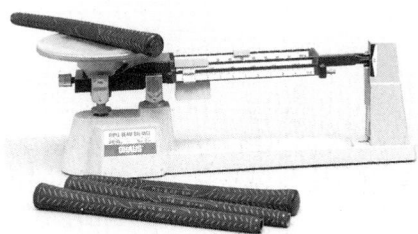

33-15 Grip weights can vary as much as ¼ to ½ ounce from specified weights. If all the grips weigh the same, the quality of the set you assemble will be enhanced.

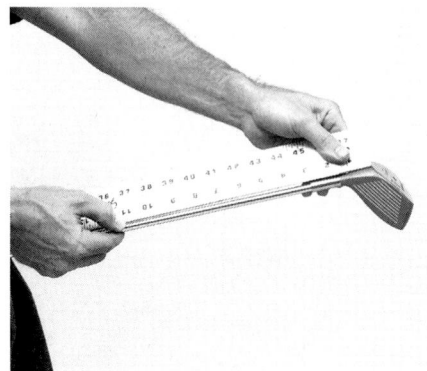

33-16 Achieving the Proper Back of Heel to First Step Dimension. After checking to see that the shaft properly fits into the hosel, refer to Chapter 7, photos 7-68 through 7-79 for information on creating the proper back of heel to first step measurement for the steel shaft you are using. This measurement is vital if you want the new shaft to perform as it was designed.

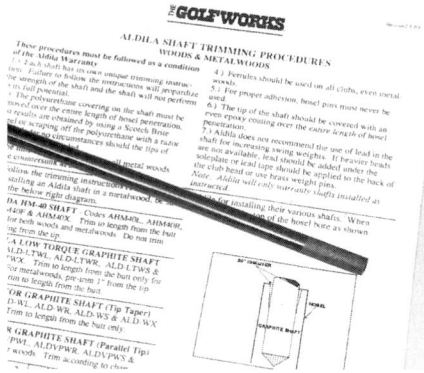

33-17 The diameters of titanium and composite shafts are not reduced along the length of the shaft through the use of steps, therefore, there are no back of heel to first step dimensions to ensure proper shaft flexibility. Instead, most composite and titanium shafts have their own specific trimming instructions. These should always be included with your shaft order. If the instructions recommend trimming from the tip, proceed with these steps now.

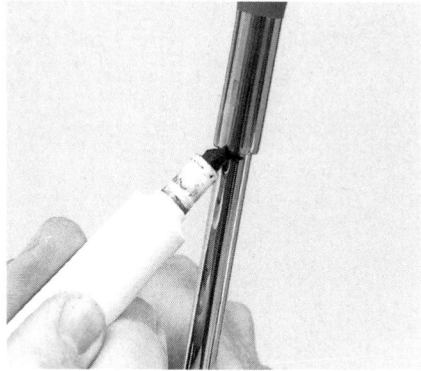

33-18 Abrading the Shaft Tip. Once any corrections have been made to the shaft tip, it must be abraded to provide the epoxy with a good bonding surface. To determine how much of the shaft tip should be abraded, insert it into the hosel, then mark the shaft with a felt tip pen even with the top of the hosel.

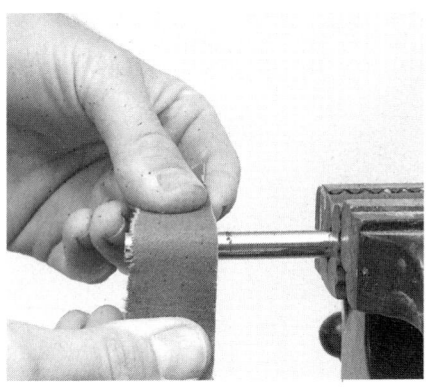

33-19 Remove the shaft from the hosel and abrade the steel or titanium shaft to within ⅛" of the mark. Place the shaft in a Rubber Shaft Clamp and tighten it in your vise. Lightly sand the shaft using coarse sandpaper or emery cloth. Refer to photo 33-23 for instructions on treating a composite shaft tip.

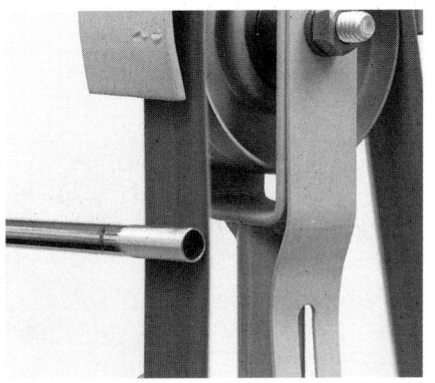

33-20 A fast alternative to hand sanding the shaft is to use a 1" x 42" or 2" x 48" Belt Sander. Lightly place the tip of the shaft against the turning belt and rotate the shaft rapidly.

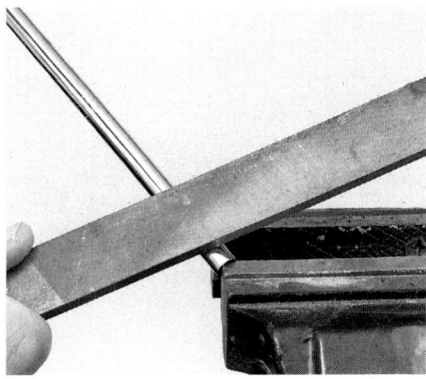

33-21 A fine file or grinding stone can also be used to abrade the titanium or steel shaft tip.

33-22 The tip of the shaft should look like this.

33-23 The shaft tip of composite shafts should not be abraded with a belt sander, file, etc. The polyurethane covering that portion of the shaft tip that will be installed into the hosel should be removed for good adhesion, however, the removal of more than the polyurethane coating will damage the shaft fibers. A Scotch-Brite™ Wheel does an effective job of removing the polyurethane without damaging the fibers.

33-24 Rotate the shaft against the turning wheel until the polyurethane coating is removed. Do not pause while rotating the shaft because of the risk of cutting the fibers. Do not press too firmly. Light pressure works best. Machine set-up shows a ⅓ H.P. motor that turns at 1725 RPM.

33-25 A razor blade also works well, but is slower. Hold the razor blade perpendicular to the shaft and scrape back and forth while rotating the shaft.

33-26 Regardless of which method is used, clean the shaft tip with a solvent to remove any oil that may be present. Oil reduces the bonding effectiveness of the epoxy.

33-27 Installing a Ferrule. If the metal wood you are using has a squared top hosel, a ferrule should be installed. Ferrules are available in different styles with various bore sizes. In most cases, the shaft you will be using will have a .335" diameter, so a ferrule with a similar inside diameter should be selected.

33-28 The recommended method of assembling graphite shafted metal woods require the use of a 20° beveled countersunk ferrule. With the ferrule countersunk at an angle of 20°, epoxy will fill in a cushion area between the top of the hosel and the bottom of the ferrule. This provides some shock absorption for the area most likely to break – the point at which the shaft flexes against the top of the hosel.

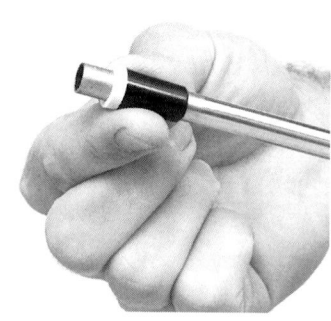

33-29 Slide the appropriate ferrule on the shaft. The ferrule should be set far enough up the shaft tip to allow the shaft to penetrate to the bottom of the hosel bore.

33-30 Sometimes the new ferrule will not slide easily on the shaft. Use this method: place the ferrule against the mouth of a can of acetone and turn the can upside down so the acetone runs into the ferrule. Keep the other end of the ferrule covered with your finger.

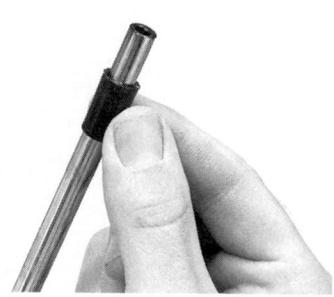

33-31 After 10 seconds, quickly remove the ferrule from the can and slide the ferrule down the shaft the appropriate distance. If the acetone is not available in the small mouth can, drop the ferrule in an open container of acetone for a few seconds and then install it.

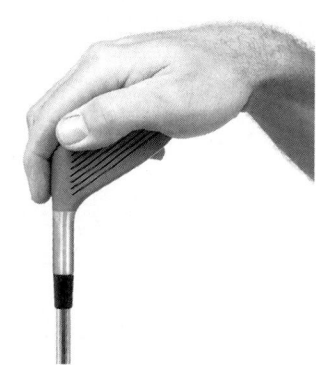

33-32 Another method is to place the hosel over the shaft and force the ferrule down the shaft. This will set the ferrule in the proper position. After forcing the ferrule in place, remove the shaft from the hosel.

33-33 Some metal woods have a squared top hosel (or if rounded it can be made square as previously shown) and the hosel tapers as well. If you are working with this type of design, you have the option of applying whipping over the ferrule and hosel. This makes the club appear more like a traditional wood.

33-34 The **Ferrule Installer Tool** will accurately set an iron or wood ferrule to the proper depth. It is especially helpful when assembling sets of clubs that demand that the ferrules be set a constant distance from the tips. Instructions for its use are sent with the tool.

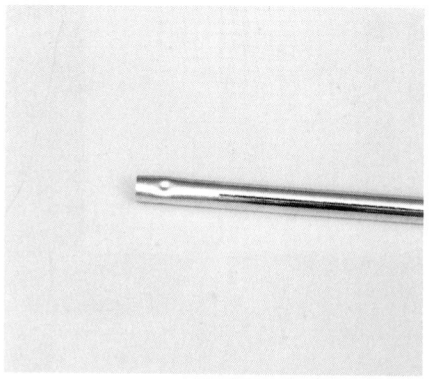

33-35 In addition to abrading the shaft tip of the steel shaft, we also suggest the tip be "dimpled" as shown. Dimpling a steel shaft has two benefits: 1) it creates shallow depressions in the tip of the shaft that will hold epoxy, thus creating a better bond; 2) makes the shaft tip more of an oval shape to ensure a tight fit between the shaft and the hosel bore. The fit is usually so tight that the assembler need not wait for the epoxy to dry before proceeding to the next assembly step.

33-36 For high volume assemblers, the **Automatic Shaft Dimpler** is a great machine to use prior to epoxying the shaft into the hosel.

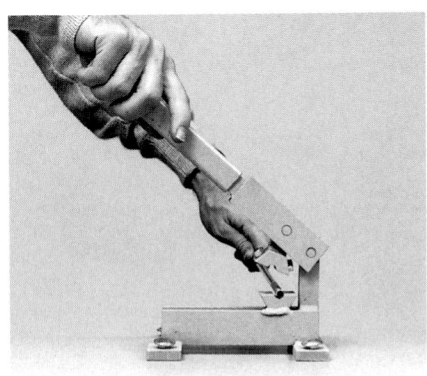

33-37 This **Whitty Shaft Dimpler** also works well. Rather than being activated by air pressure you force the dimples into the shaft.

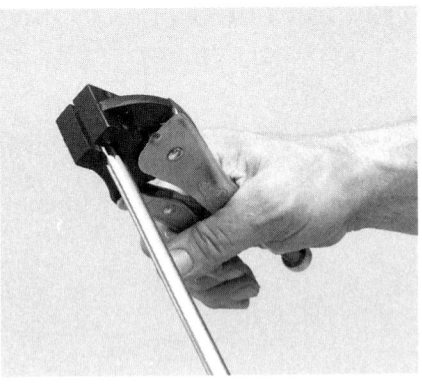

33-38 This **Hand Held Shaft Dimpler** is also available from the GolfWorks®. It is a 10" vise grip that has been adapted with a specially designed permanent attachment for dimpling steel shafts. The attachment will make four dimples with one squeeze of the hands.

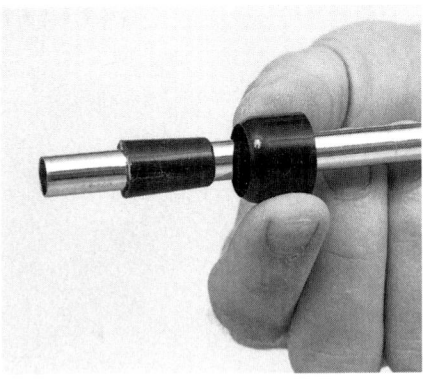

33-39 When installing a leather grip, it is much easier to slide the grip collar up the shaft from the tip section rather than trying to install it over the much larger butt section after the shaft has been installed. Secure the grip collar somewhere along the butt section with a piece of tape so that it won't slide off.

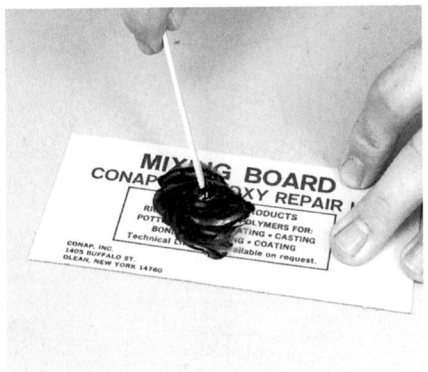

33-40 Installing the Shaft. Mix a shear strength epoxy (GolfWorks® High Strength Epoxy or Conap® Epoxy works well).

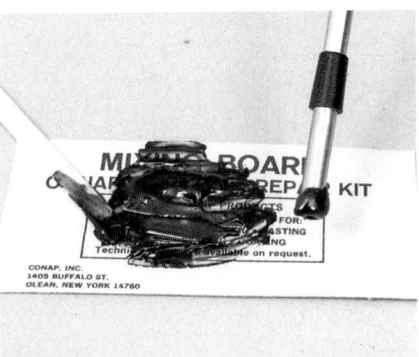

33-41 Dip the tip of the shaft into the epoxy and pick up a glob on the tip of the shaft as shown.

33-42 Insert the tip of the shaft into the metal wood hosel. Push the shaft to the bottom of the hosel bore while simultaneously rotating the shaft. This will help coat both the hosel bore and the shaft tip. Make sure the shaft tip penetrated to the bottom of the hosel bore. If not, shaft breakage can occur.

33-43 Remove the shaft from the hosel and check to make sure the shaft is well covered. If not, apply more epoxy. This photo shows adequate epoxy coverage. NOTE: If the shaft already has a shaft band, make sure the shaft is turned so that the band's identifying markings are facing towards the front before permanently setting the shaft.

33-44 Reinstall the shaft into the hosel. Place one hand on the head and the other on the shaft and hit the shaft butt against a concrete floor or steel plate. This will position the tip of the shaft to the bottom of the hosel bore and drive the ferrule (if installed) to the proper position on the shaft.

33-45 An Air Hammer is a great machine for quickly installing a shaft into a hosel. It works by placing the butt of the shaft against the activating switch which triggers the hammering action. Even shafts that are difficult to install by hand are quickly forced into the hosel.

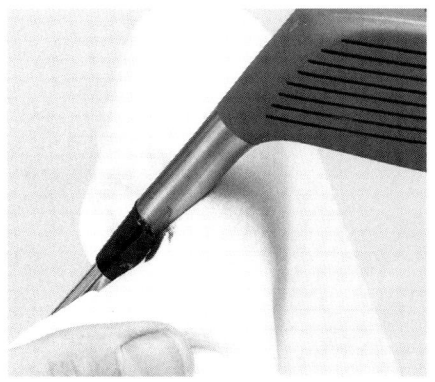

33-46 Wipe the excess epoxy from the hosel and ferrule, if one was installed. Allow the epoxy to cure before proceeding.

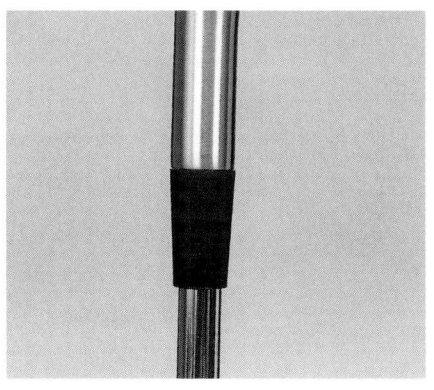

33-47 Reducing the Ferrule Diameter. After the epoxy hardens, the next step is to reduce the diameter of the ferrule so it matches the hosel's diameter. NOTE: If your metal wood does not have a ferrule installed, continue on to Photo 33-63 for cutting the club to length.

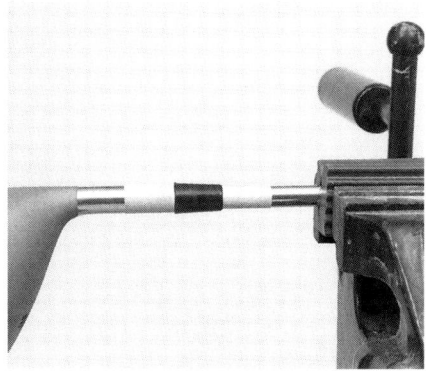

33-48 Place a **Rubber Shaft Clamp** around the shaft and tighten in a vise. Wrap a piece of ¾" masking tape around the hosel just below the ferrule then place another wrapping of tape around the shaft just above the ferrule.

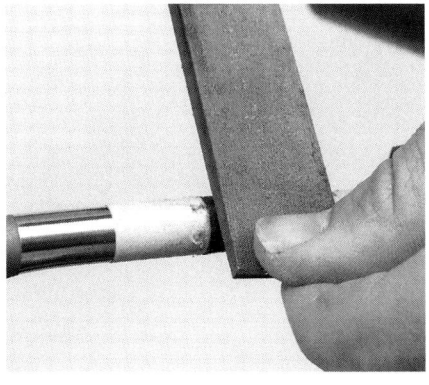

33-49 Use a flat mill or fine file and lightly file the excess plastic flush with the tape around the top of the hosel. The tape will protect the hosel from possible scratches.

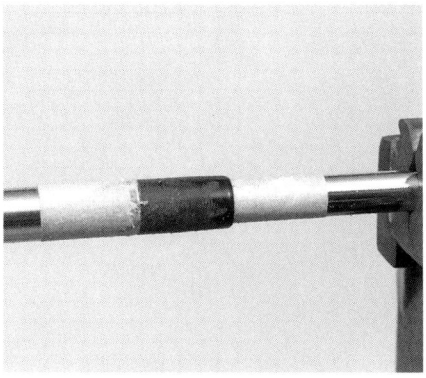

33-50 Continue filing while rotating the club. Care should be taken to ensure that the ferrule appears uniform. Do not file the top edge of the ferrule as a definite lip should remain, unless whipping is to be applied. If whipping will not be applied proceed to photo 33-53.

33-51 To prepare for whipping, file the top edge so that …

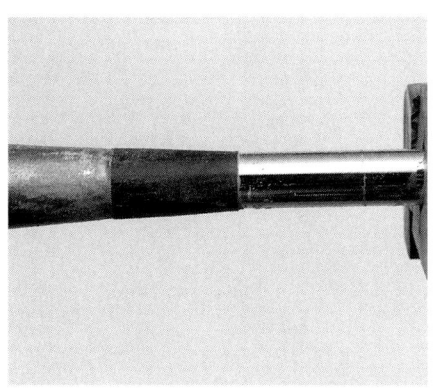

33-52 … it "feathers in" with the shaft. If properly filed, you should be able to rub your finger across the ferrule and shaft and barely feel the top edge of the ferrule. Any scratches in the hosel will be covered with whipping.

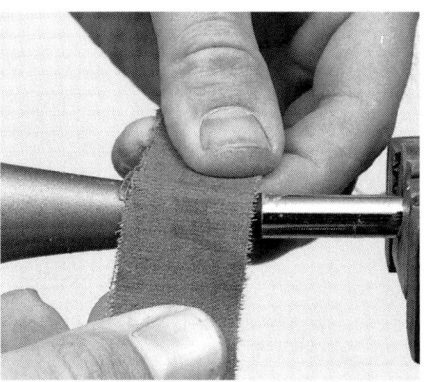

33-53 Filing will leave flat spots and ridges in the plastic. Lightly sand the ferrule with a 180 or 220 grit sandpaper. NOTE: For clubs that will be whipped, the tape should be removed prior to this step. Be careful not to sand the shaft more than ⅛" above the top of the ferrule. Remove the tape after this step on unwhipped hosels.

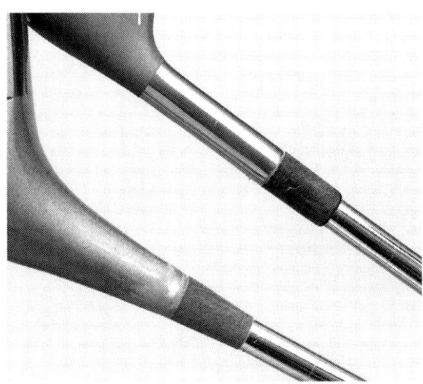

33-54 At this point, it is normal for the ferrule to look rough and dull. Because whipping is to be applied over the ferrule and hosel of the club shown on the bottom, no further smoothing is necessary. Proceed to Chapter 6 for whipping instructions. The ferrule on the club shown on the top does require further preparation.

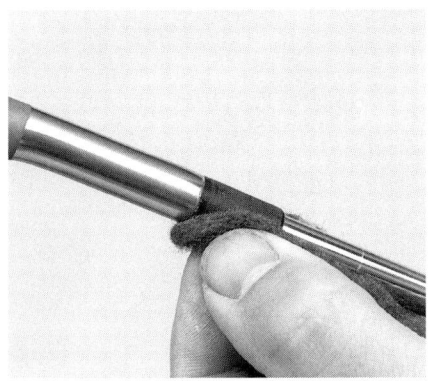

33-55 For unwhipped ferrules, rub the ferrule with 000 steel wool. This will remove scratches caused by the sandpaper and smooth the ferrule.

33-56 Wipe the ferrule with a paper towel dampened with acetone. NOTE: If a coat of finish is present on the hosel, do not allow the acetone to make contact with the hosel. Most metal woods, however, do not have a coating of finish on the hosel.

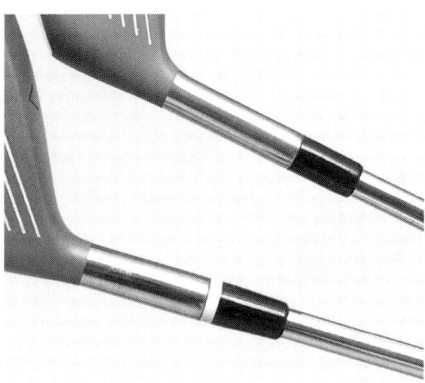

33-57 Acetone will return the plastic ferrule to a shiny, like-new condition. The ferrules shown are the two most popular styles.

33-58 A much quicker way to reduce the diameter of the ferrule is with a Belt Sander fitted with a Cloth Linen Belt. This is a non abrasive surface which removes the excess plastic through friction.

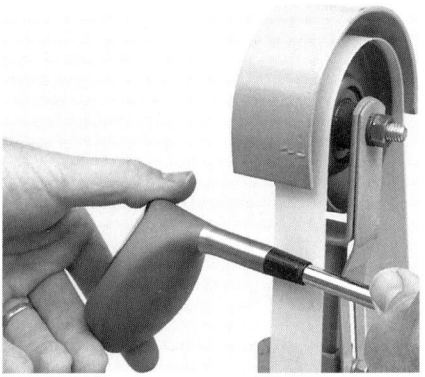

33-59 Hold the clubhead as shown and rotate the ferrule against the linen belt in...

33-60 ... a clockwise direction...

33-61 ... as shown. This is very important. Turning the clubhead in the opposite direction will burn and ruin the ferrule.

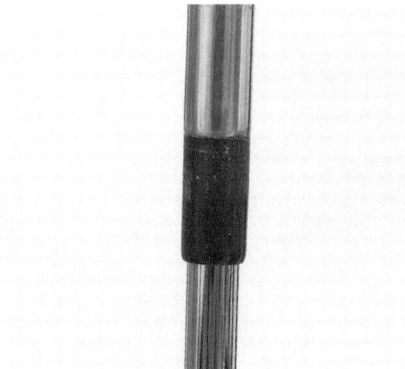

33-62 This photo shows a properly reduced ferrule. Steel wool and wipe the ferrule with an acetone dampened towel to make the ferrule look like new again. This method will also work on clubs where the ferrule must be tapered prior to whipping.

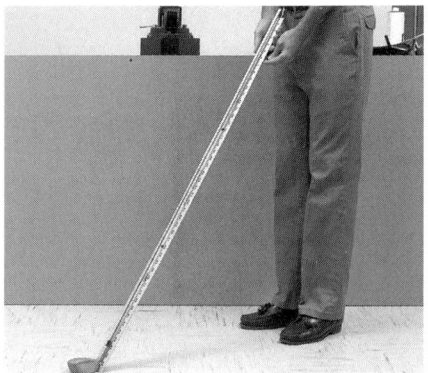

33-63 Measuring and Cutting the Club to Length. Sole the club on the ground as shown. Slide a 48" ruler behind the shaft, measure and cut the club to length as shown in Chapter 32, photos 32-85 through 32-99.

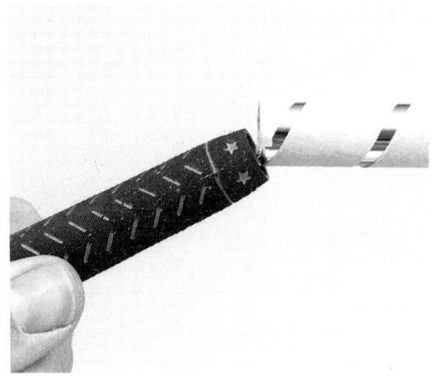

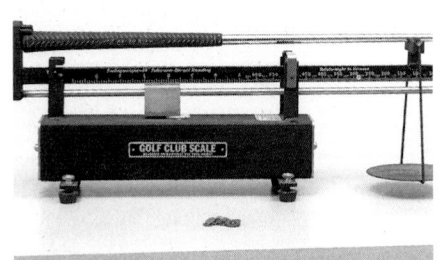

33-64 Installing the Grip. Install the grip following the steps outlined in Chapter 23. NOTE: If the metal wood does <u>not</u> have a weight port, the swingweight should be checked and adjusted before installing the grip. This is because any additional weight will have to be placed in the tip of the shaft through the shaft butt. See photos 33-75 through 33-80.

33-65 Swingweighting. For clubs with a weight port, swingweighting is done after the grip is installed. Check the club's swingweight on a swingweight scale.

33-66 Add the appropriate number of lead discs or lead powder until the desired swingweight is achieved (each lead disc is equivalent to one point). The plastic medallion that accompanies the discs is practically weightless so no compensation needs to be made. Once the swingweight has been achieved, if working with lead discs, remove the discs. If working with lead powder leave it in the cavity and proceed to photo 33-68 if installing a medallion or photo 33-74 if installing a set screw.

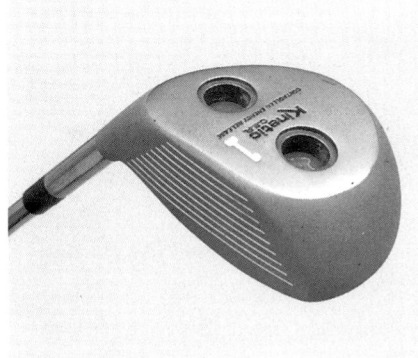

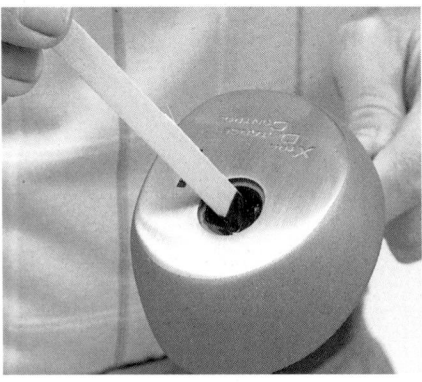

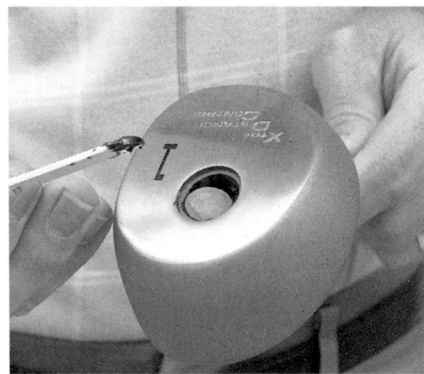

33-67 If the club has two weight ports, distribute the lead evenly unless you wish to make a marginal shift in the club's center of gravity to accommodate a golfer who tends to hit more shots out on the toe or back in the heel. For instance, if the golfer hits most shots out on the toe put all the necessary weight in the toe cavity.

33-68 Apply a glob of epoxy to the bottom and sides of the weight port.

33-69 Place the first lead disc at the bottom of the weight port. Place a glob of epoxy on top of the lead disc and place another lead disc if necessary. Continue this sequence until all the discs are installed.

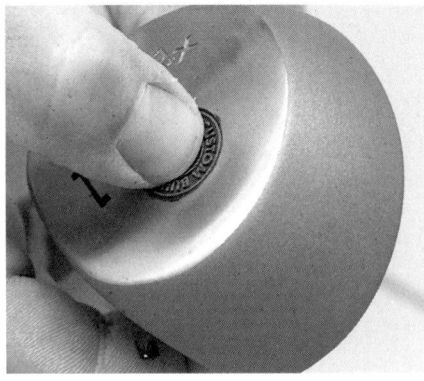

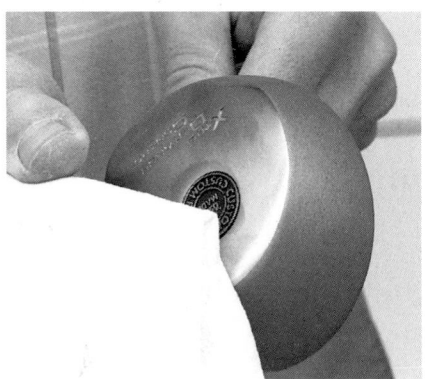

33-70 Roughen the back and the entire outside edge of the medallion with medium or coarse sandpaper.

33-71 Apply epoxy to the bottom of the medallion and weight port recess. Press the medallion into the recess. Epoxy should ooze from around the medallion. The medallion should be set at right angles to the leading edge.

33-72 With a paper towel, wipe the excess epoxy towards the center of the medallion, filling in all the gaps between the medallion and the weight port.

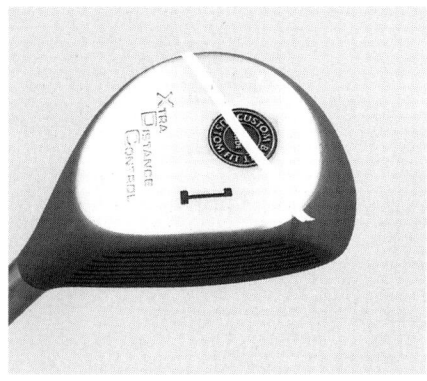

33-73 Apply tape to the medallion and sole using ⅛" or ¾" masking tape. The tape will prevent the medallion from moving while the epoxy dries.

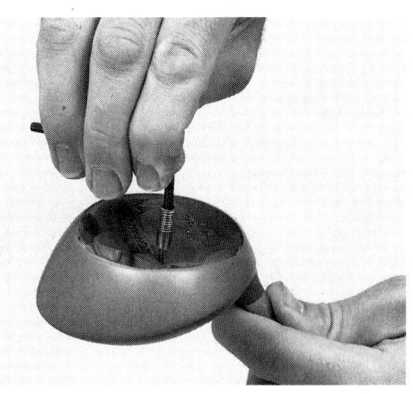

33-74 For clubs with set screws, turn in the set screw after achieving the swingweight. Do not use epoxy for this step as it is not necessary.

33-75 Swingweighting Clubs without Weight Ports. Lead rod or powder can be used to increase swingweight by placing the lead in the tip of the shaft. This is done before installing the grip. Use ³⁄₁₆" diameter lead rod for woods. Lead powder is the preferred choice of club assemblers.

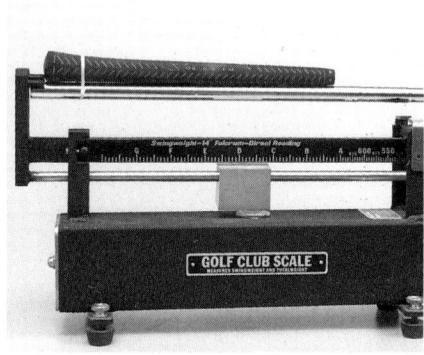

33-76 In order to compensate for the weight or the grip, you can temporarily tape it to the shaft before swingweighting, as shown. Doing this will give you an idea of the affect the grip's weight will have on the final swing-weight. Because the grip cap will extend the length of the club by ⅛", position the shaft butt ⅛" from the swingweight facing piece to compensate.

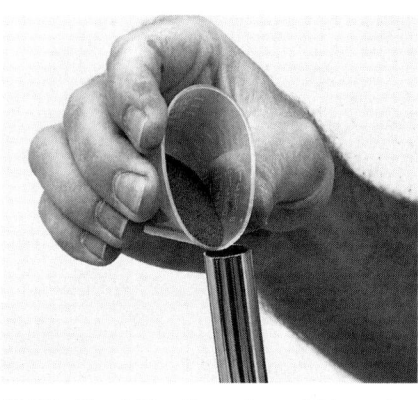

33-77 After taking the swingweight reading and determining how many points must be added, pour the lead powder down the shaft. Recheck the swingweight until the swingweight is achieved.

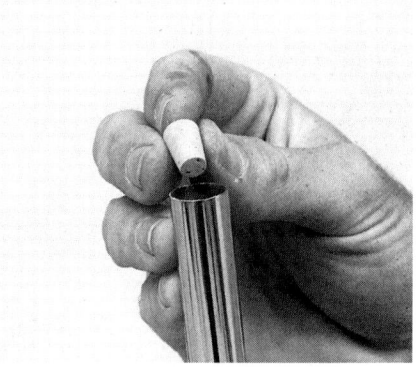

33-78 Drop a cork inside the shaft. Some assemblers place a glob of epoxy on the end of the cork before dropping it inside the shaft. This is not necessary and usually a portion of the epoxy is smeared along the side of the shaft which results in a rattle after the epoxy dries and breaks loose.

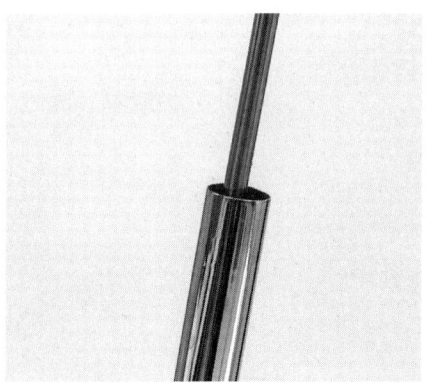

33-79 Ram the cork down the shaft with a Ramrod or the opposite end of a 47" drill bit. When finished, install the grip.

33-80 The lead rod is installed by picking up a glob of epoxy on one end and dropping the rod into the shaft. Follow-up with a cork as was previously shown. After the correct weight is achieved the grip is then installed.

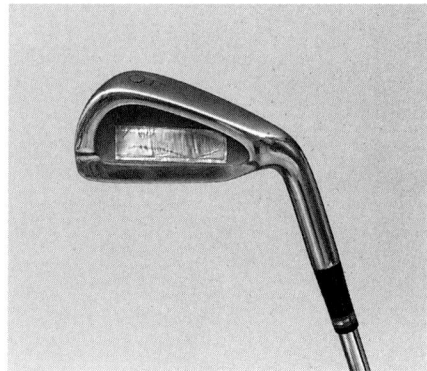

33-81 Adding lead tape to the back of an iron or wood is the best way outside of a weight port for increasing swingweight. However, most customers would frown on the addition of lead tape to a new club.

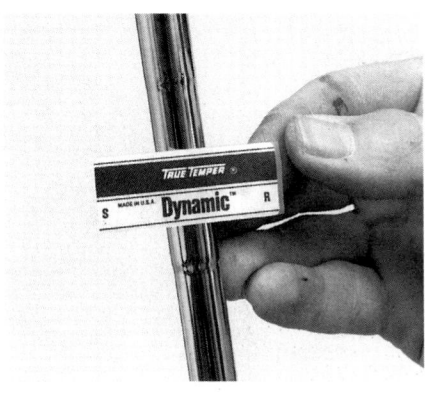

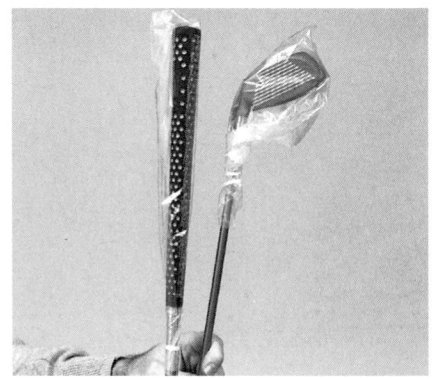

33-82 Applying the shaft band. The shaft band should be positioned on the second step below the bottom of the grip. For shafts that do not have steps, the band is installed approximately 2" below the grip.

33-83 If you are using a combination flex shaft band as shown, make sure that the appropriate letter is showing after the band is wrapped around the shaft.

33-84 It is a nice professional touch to install plastic grip and head bags before delivering the club(s) to the customer.

ADDITIONAL INFORMATION FOR ASSEMBLING METAL WOODS

TABLE 33-1 Wood Club Lengths – Men's and Ladies'			
Woods	**Men's Standard**	**Ladies' Standard**	**Ladies' Petite**
1	43"	42"	41½"
2	42½"	41½"	41"
3	42"	41"	40½"
4	41½"	40½"	40"
5	41"	40"	39½"
6	40½"	39½"	39
7	40"	39"	38½"
8	39½"	38½"	38"
9	39"	38"	37½"

The most popular length variations for men are ½" shorter or longer than standard and 1" longer than standard. The most popular length variations for ladies are ½" shorter or longer than standard. Many graphite shafted drivers are now made at lengths ½" to 2" longer than standard.

NOTES

SECTION

FIVE

GOLF WOOD CLUB DESIGN AND MANUFACTURE

CHAPTER 34

GOLF WOOD CLUB DESIGN: SPECIFICATIONS

The preciseness of various wood head specifications and their relationships determine how playable a golf wood club will be. Many people do not understand that the design of a golf wood head is very complex. Unfortunately, many manufacturers do not entirely understand either; and if they do, mass production forces many of them to produce golf clubs to such loose tolerances that it is all but impossible to obtain a close tolerance golf club by the time it is finished.

This chapter specifically concerns definitions, performance characteristics, and the important relationships that exist between face angle, loft, lie, horizontal face bulge, vertical face roll, face progression, club length, sole curvature, head weight and center of gravity of golf wood clubs. Read this entire section carefully and refer to the illustrations often because to properly fit, build, repair, discuss and understand golf wood clubs requires a complete comprehension of the design aspects and interrelationships of these important specifications. Note also that the information contained in this chapter applies to woods of all materials, including metal and graphite woods.

Building a Theoretical Driver

The easiest way to begin and understand the important relationships of wood club specifications is to first build a theoretical driver adding in each specification, one at a time, by using simple illustrations. To make this explanation as clear as possible we will start out with only a square block of wood and a list of specifications for the driver. Naturally, wood heads are not actually manufactured in this way, rather they are turned on a special type high speed copy lathe which follows a master model head shape and transfers this shape to a laminated maple or persimmon block. Metal and graphite woods also have their own unique manufacturing methods, which are explained in detail in Chapter 46. In many cases, however, the master model is originally designed and built much the same way as we will build our sample driver model, because the master model must be very accurate to transfer the correct specifications to the many wood head copies (turnings) it must make. Similarly, metal and graphite masters must also be very accurate.

To make some very basic assumptions concerning specifications for the theoretical golf wood club, assume that the club is a #1 wood (driver) with the following predetermined specifications:

Loft . . . . .11°
Lie . . . . .55°
Face Angle . . . . .2° slice (open)
Horizontal Face Bulge . . . . .10" radius
Vertical Face Roll   . . . . .10" radius
Face Progression . . . . .1³⁄₁₆"
Shaft Progression . . . . .⅞"
Sole Curvature   . . . . .6" radius
Club Length . . . . .43"
Finished Head Weight .7¼ ounces
Clubhead Center of Gravity . . . . .By Design

First start with a solid block of wood. See Figure 34-1.

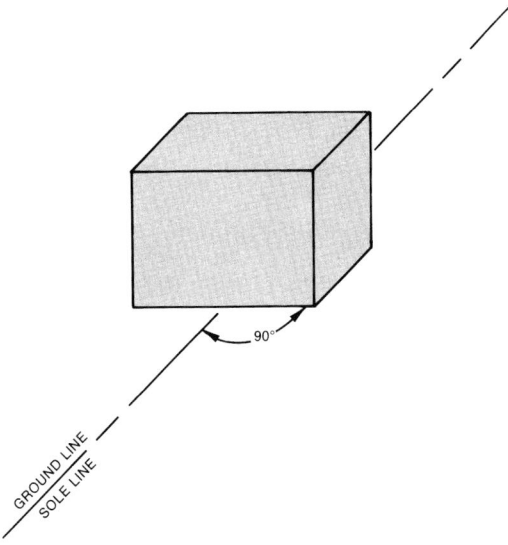

Figure 34-1

The 6" sole radius is cut into the bottom of the block. See Figure 34-2.

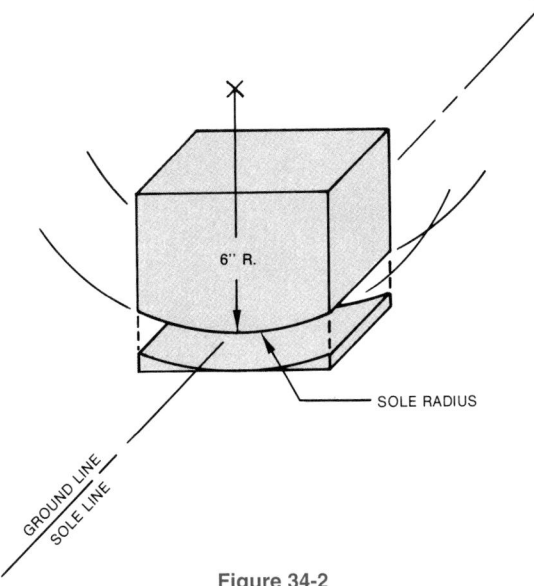

Figure 34-2

397

Next, the face angle is cut into the block. In this particular case 2° slice (open face) has been established for the face of the model. See Figure 34-3. Note that the face angle has been cut 2° open to the sole radius. The sole radius is cut perfectly square to the original block of wood. For easier understanding you can also assume that the ground line/sole line as shown in Figure 34-1 is also the intended target line.

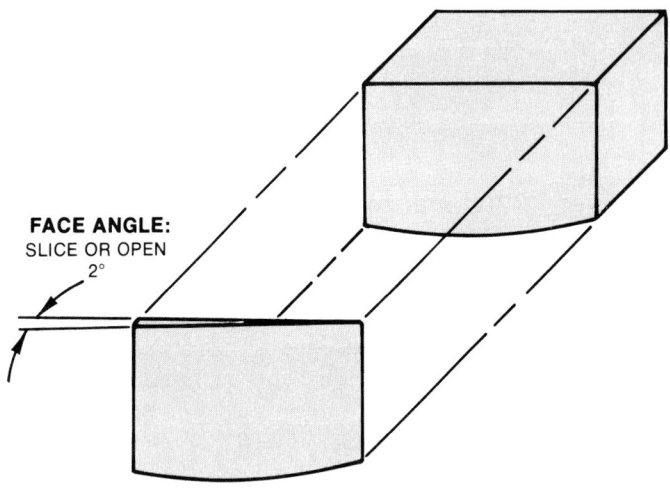

Figure 34-3

So far the wood block has a 6" sole radius and a 2° slice or open face without putting a hosel or a hole into it. Next, the excess wood will be cut away to more easily visualize how the remaining specifications will be added to the club. See Figure 34-4.

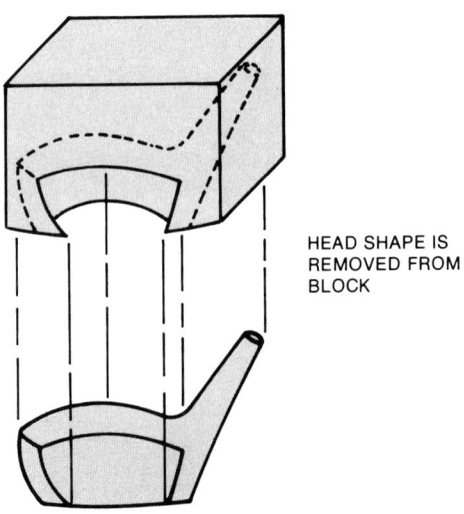

HEAD SHAPE IS REMOVED FROM BLOCK

Figure 34-4

398

The 11° loft will be established next on the driver. See Figure 34-5. Note that the loft of a wood club is defined as the angle formed by the sole and face. The loft is not measured from the bore or hosel hole as it is on irons.

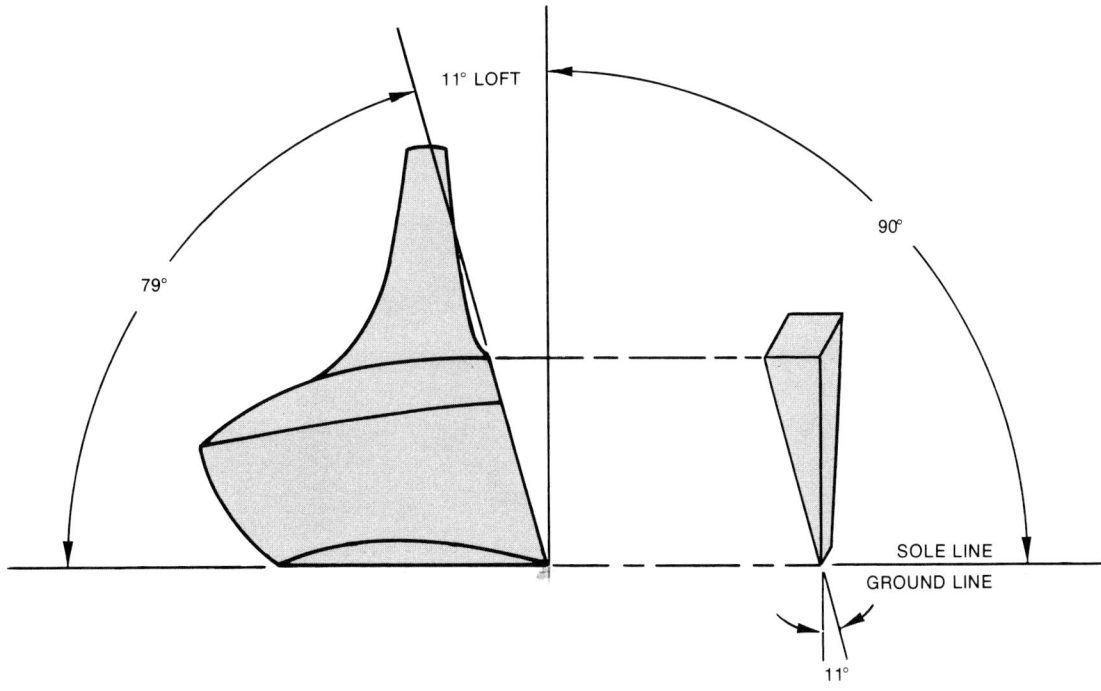

Figure 34-5

Now the 10" radius horizontal face bulge should be cut into the driver without disturbing the 11° loft. See Figure 34-6. To maintain the original 2° open or slice face, the horizontal face bulge radius is cut in perpendicular to the face and is actually 2° offset from the ground line/sole line which was established in Figure 34-1.

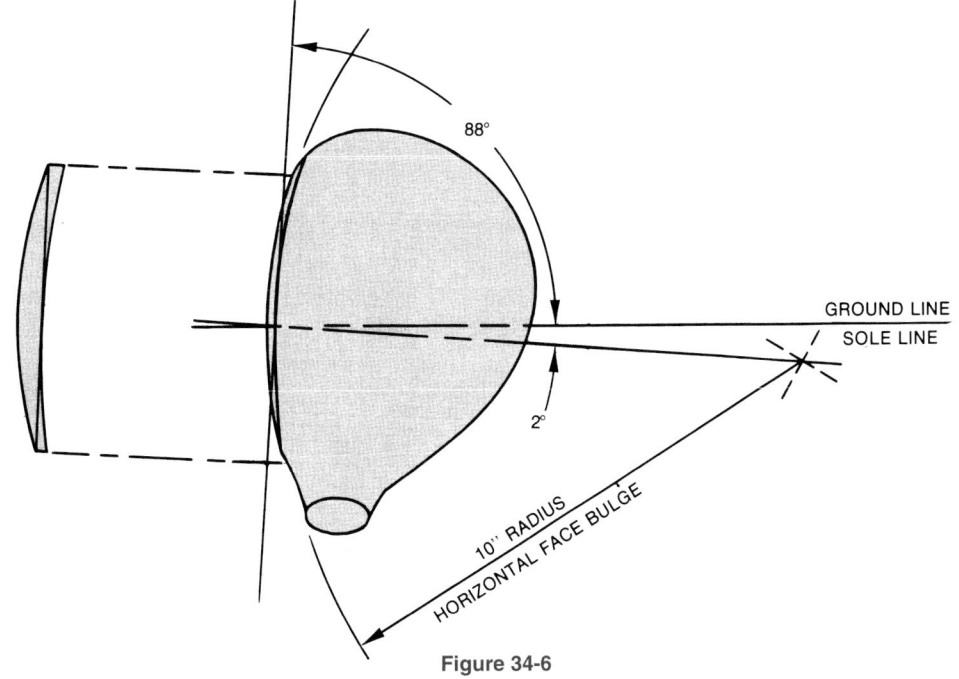

Figure 34-6

The 10" radius vertical face roll should be cut in carefully so as to not alter the 10" bulge and 11° loft. See Figure 34-7. It should be apparent that the only point on the face which has 11° loft is at ½ the vertical face height. Any point higher up the face has a greater loft angle than 11° and any point below has less than 11° loft.

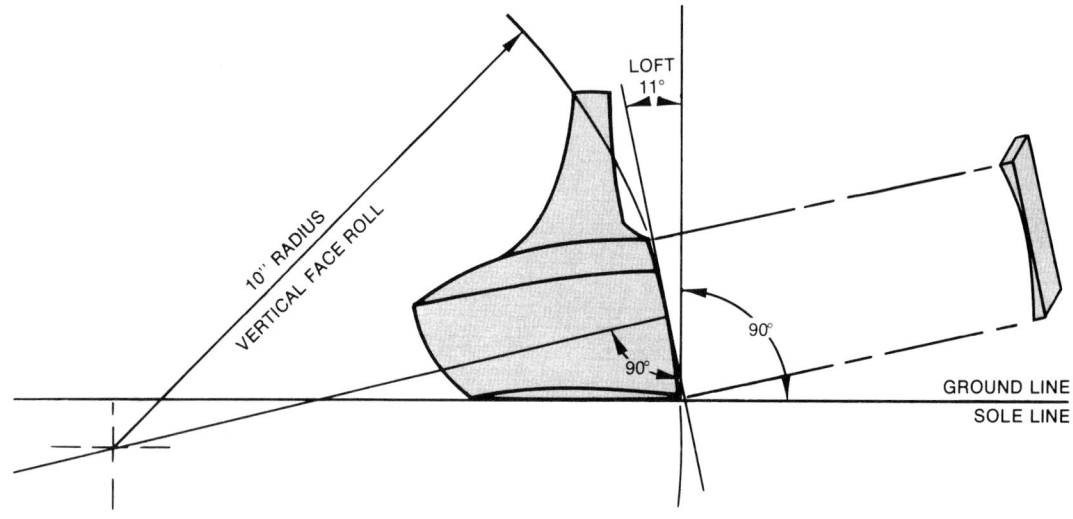

Figure 34-7

The hole must now be blind bored or through bored in the hosel. The hole will be bored in such a way as to maintain the 2° face slice while establishing the 55° lie, the 1³⁄₁₆" face progression and the ⅞" shaft progression. See Figure 34-8. The square bore/head design method of boring is used here which is explained in detail in Chapter 44.

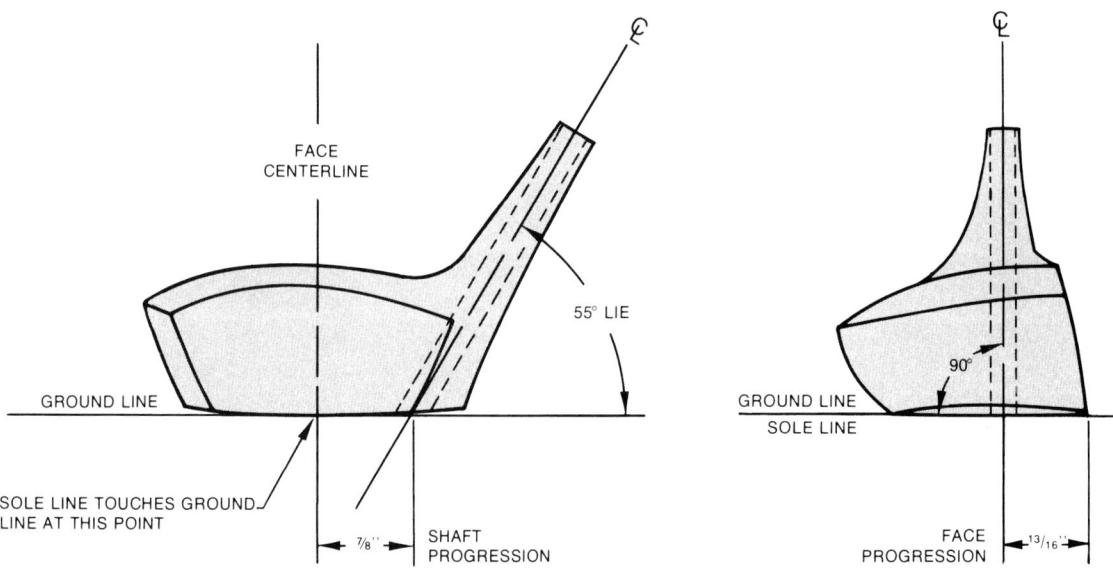

Figure 34-8

400

To best understand what has happened thus far it is recommended that a few minutes be spent studying Figure 34-9. A thorough understanding of the three views in this figure will enable the reader to look at all the specifications and better understand some of the important relationships between them.

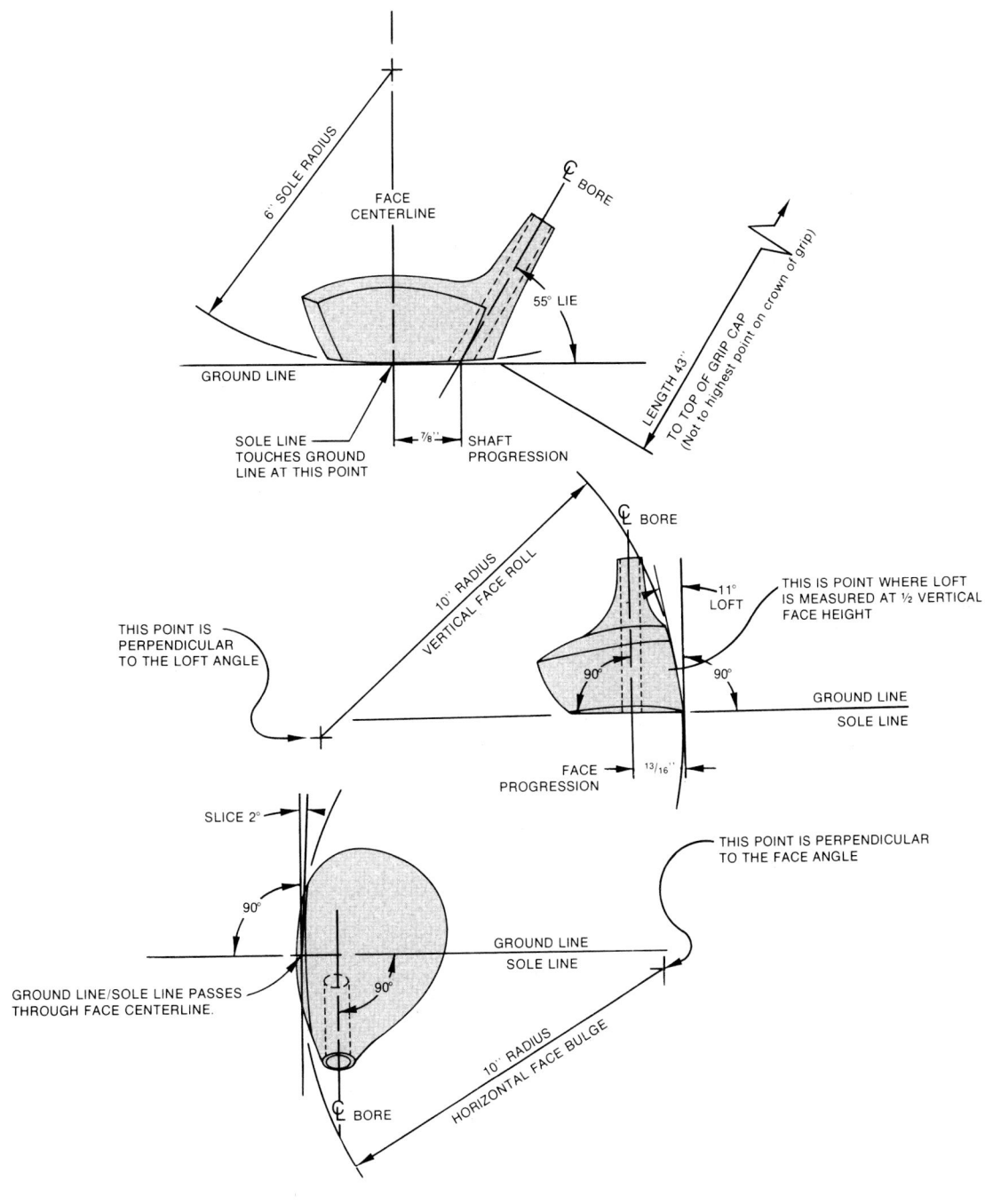

Figure 34-9

The next specification to be established for the driver is total head weight. Because this is a theoretical discussion, assume that the driver head in its present state has all the necessary components such as an insert and soleplate, but weighs only 6¾ ounces and its center of gravity just happens to be on the face centerline plane. This means that a total of ½ ounce of weight (usually lead) must be added to the head. This weight should be added in such a manner so as to maintain the center of gravity of the head as close as possible to the face centerline and also as low as possible. This can be done many ways, such as adding one ½ ounce weight in the center or two ¼ ounce weights equally distant from the face centerline. See Figure 34-10. Remember, the larger the diameter the hole, the lower the center of gravity when compared to the same amount of weight in a smaller diameter hole. The reason for this is the hole must be drilled deeper as the diameter is reduced to obtain the same cavity space. Obviously, weight is not added in this manner for a metal wood, but its total weight requirement is the same.

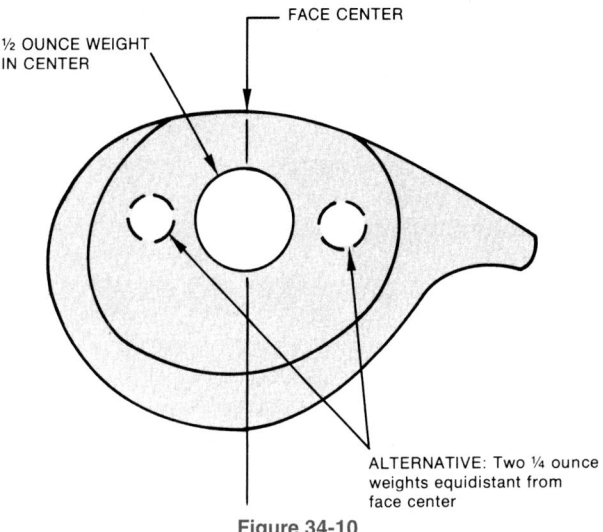

Figure 34-10

This last specification is clubhead center of gravity (or center of mass). The center of gravity location is a function of the size of the head, shape of the head, head material, density of the head and the amount and location of any added weight. The clubhead center of gravity is located inside the head and can be determined by balancing the head at any two points. It is usually easiest to balance the head on its face and also on the sole. See Figure 34-11.

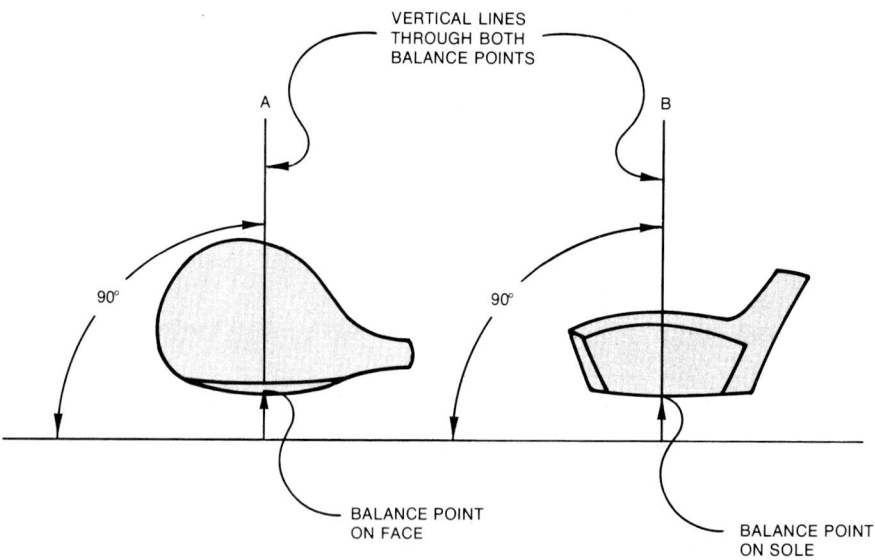

Figure 34-11

402

If two lines A & B could be extended vertically from the balance points they would intersect at some point in the head. This point of intersection is the clubhead center of gravity or center of mass. If the clubhead was balanced at ten different locations versus the two shown in Figure 34-11 all the vertical lines would still intersect at the same point. See Figure 34-12. Ideally, the center of gravity in the face plane should be as close to and as low as possible on the geometric center of the face (face centerline). See Chapter 43, **Golf Wood Club Design: Center of Gravity.**

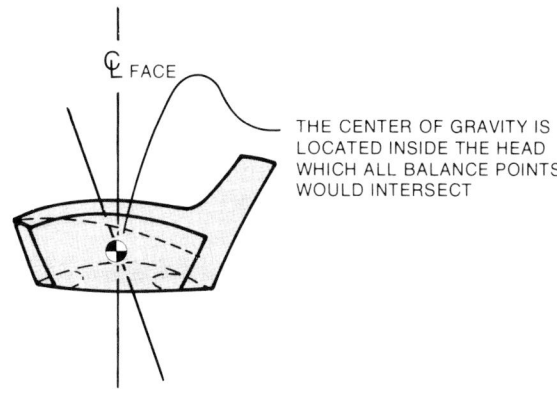

THE CENTER OF GRAVITY IS LOCATED INSIDE THE HEAD WHICH ALL BALANCE POINTS WOULD INTERSECT

Figure 34-12

Defining and Measuring Each Wood Club Specification

The next logical step in further developing a sound working knowledge of golf wood club design is to take each specification established so far and do the following:
1. Explain briefly what each specification does regarding performance.
2. Define it.
3. List all other specifications which directly affect it.
4. Give an in depth discussion where necessary to fully explain it.

The following chapters will cover each wood club specification separately. Some are quite involved and technical, while others are easier to understand and brief. Spend some time reading and studying them because they hold the key to better understanding golf wood club design.

It is also quite important that the reader takes each change in a specification on its own merit and understands that every other variable is to be considered identical for the purpose of learning cause and effect. For instance, if we are trying to determine the effect of various shaft flexes on dynamic loft we would assume to be using test clubs of identical weight, length, weight distribution, loft, face progression, lie, etc. with the only variable being the flex of the shaft.

CHAPTER 35

GOLF WOOD CLUB DESIGN: LOFT

Performance Characteristic of Loft

A determining factor concerning the angle of trajectory of the golf ball as it leaves the face.

Definition of Loft

The angle of the face to a line perpendicular to the sole of the club measured in degrees. Because most wood clubs have a vertical face roll (radius), loft is measured at a point ½ the distance of the face height on the centerline of the face. See Figure 35-1.

Other Specifications Which Affect Loft

Face Angle (hook/slice). See Figure 35-2, 35-3, 35-4 and Figure 35-5.
Face Progression. See Figure 35-8.
Head Weight Distribution. See Figure 35-9.
Vertical Face Roll. See Figure 35-10.
Shaft flex. See Figure 35-11, 35-12, 35-13 and Figure 35-14.

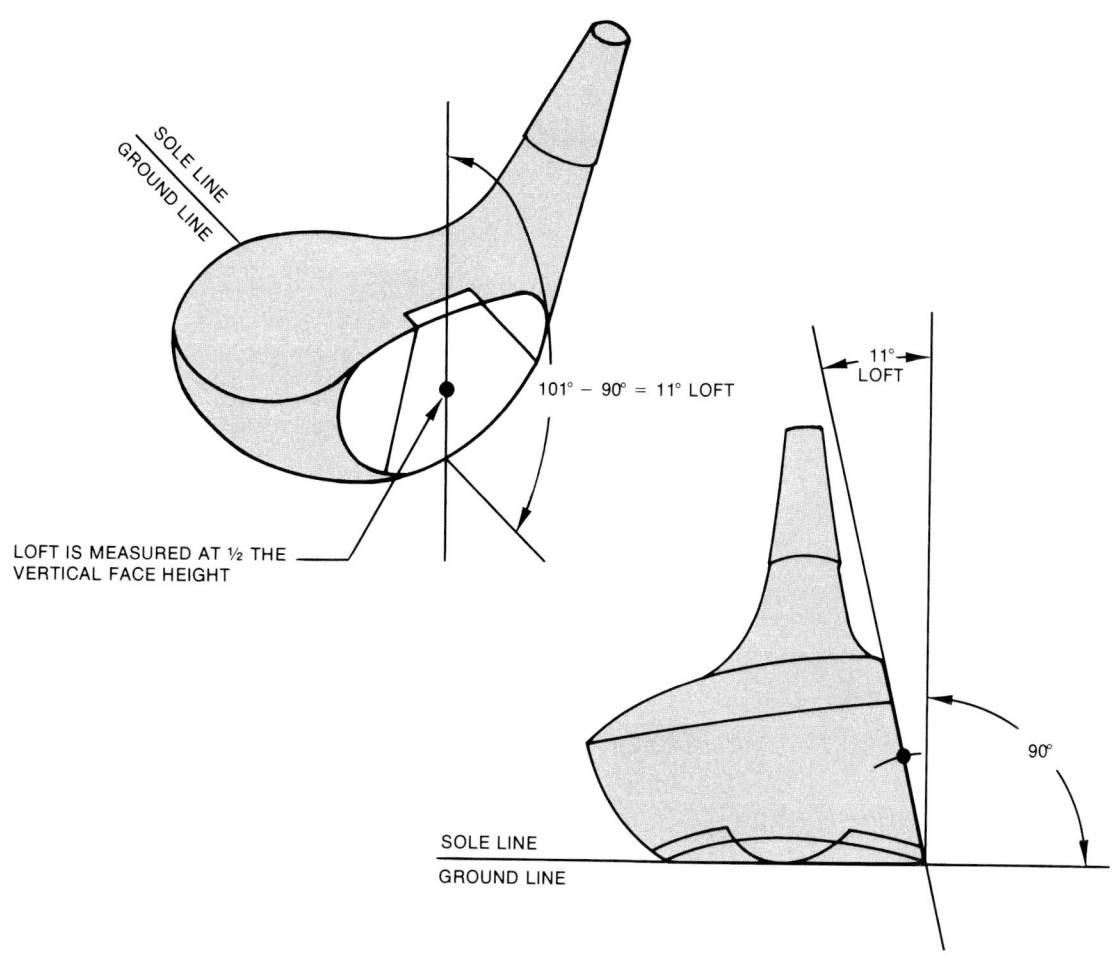

SOLE LINE
GROUND LINE

101° − 90° = 11° LOFT

LOFT IS MEASURED AT ½ THE
VERTICAL FACE HEIGHT

11°
LOFT

90°

SOLE LINE
GROUND LINE

Figure 35-1
Definition of loft

Discussion of Loft

The first and very foremost thing to understand about loft is that wood and iron lofts are measured differently. This creates a lot of confusion regarding performance, fitting and properly comparing woods and irons for relative distances in hitting the ball. Look at Figure 35-2 which illustrates these differences. An iron club's loft is the angle measured from the shaft or hosel bore to the face. A wood club's loft is the angle measured from the sole to the face less ninety degrees. The key in understanding the basics is this: wood club loft is measured without regard to the shaft or hosel bore while iron club loft is. When you measure the loft of an iron as shown in Figure 35-2 you also get the effective or real loft of that iron. However, when you measure a wood club's loft you do not get the effective or real loft of that wood unless the face angle is 0° or square.

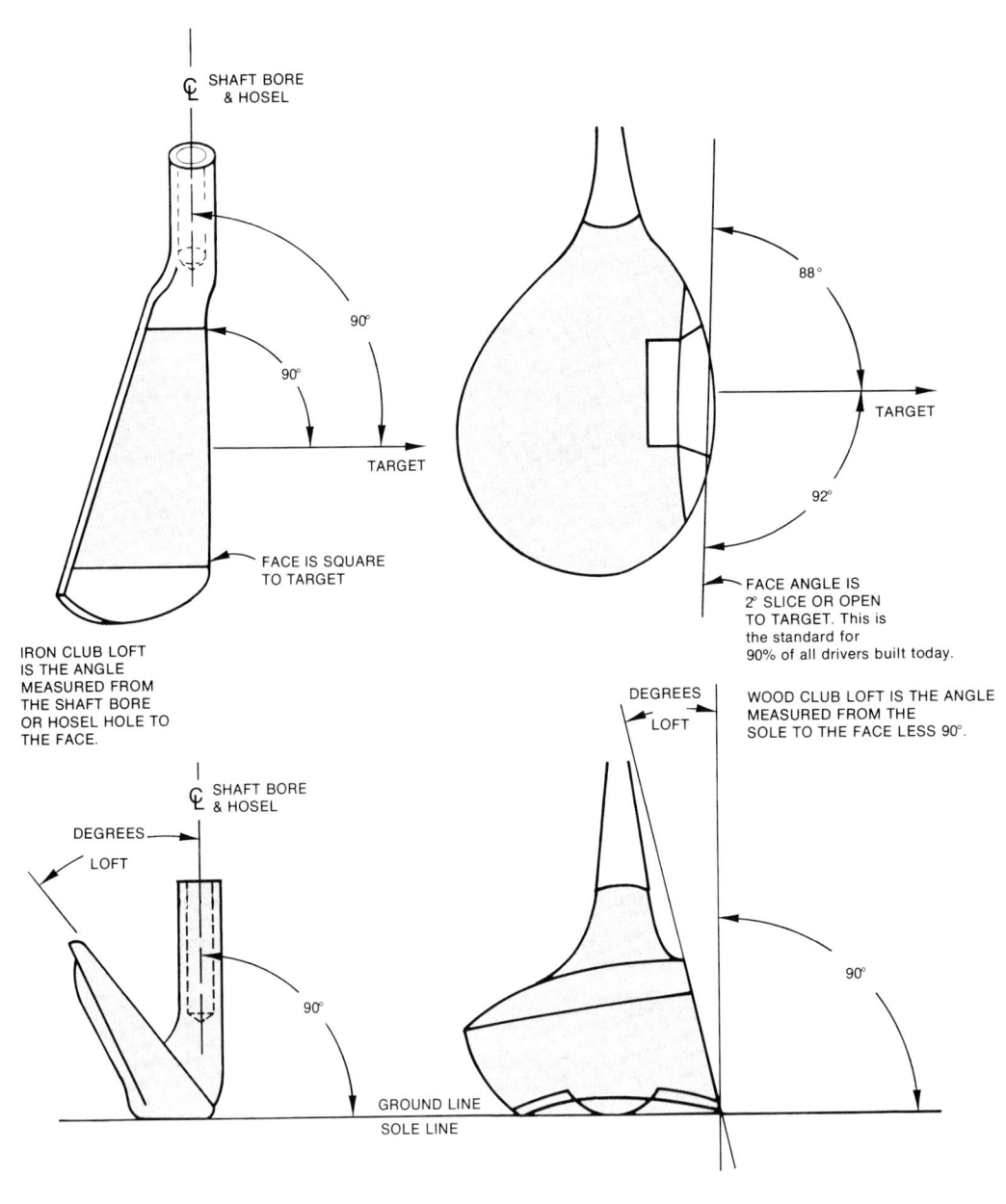

SHAFT BORE & HOSEL

90°

90°

TARGET

FACE IS SQUARE TO TARGET

IRON CLUB LOFT IS THE ANGLE MEASURED FROM THE SHAFT BORE OR HOSEL HOLE TO THE FACE.

88°

TARGET

92°

FACE ANGLE IS 2° SLICE OR OPEN TO TARGET. This is the standard for 90% of all drivers built today.

DEGREES

LOFT

WOOD CLUB LOFT IS THE ANGLE MEASURED FROM THE SOLE TO THE FACE LESS 90°.

DEGREES

LOFT

SHAFT BORE & HOSEL

90°

90°

GROUND LINE
SOLE LINE

Figure 35-2
Wood club loft is measured differently than iron club lofts

Study Figure 35-3 closely which illustrates a driver with an 11° loft and 2° slice or open face angle. Remember that a 90° angle defines any two lines as being perpendicular to each other. Lock this into your mind so the two become synonymous as you study many of the illustrations in this book.

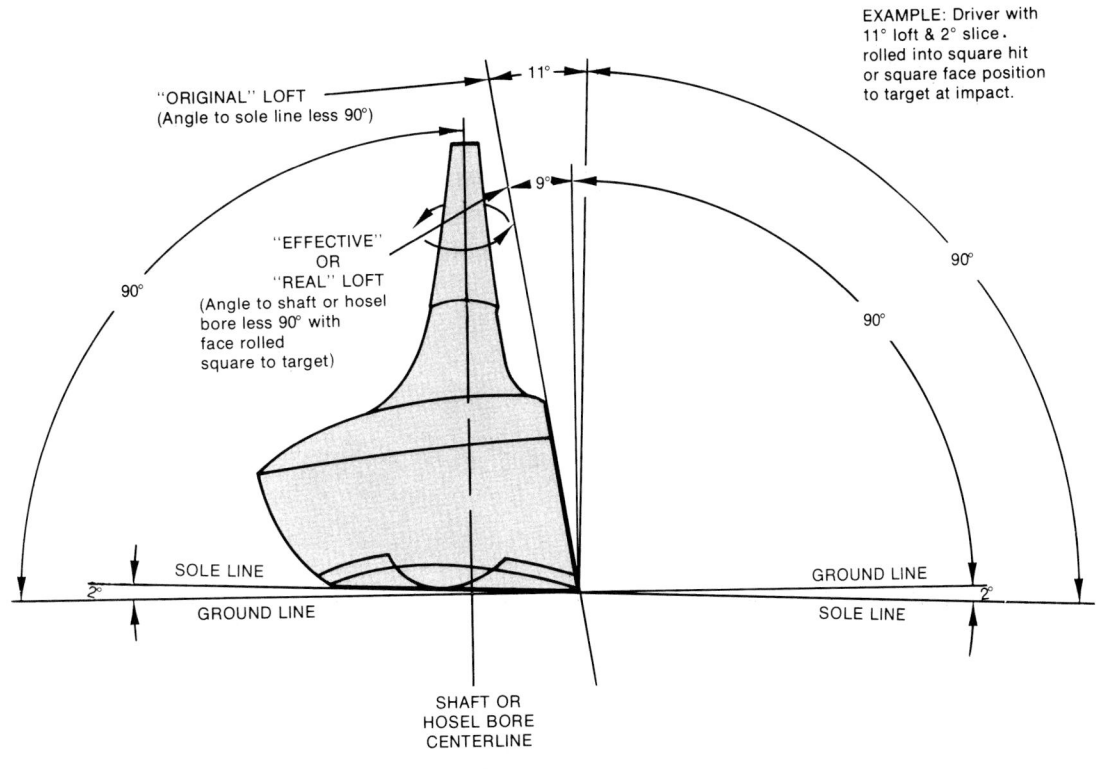

Figure 35-3
Defining "effective" or "real" loft

Next, look at Figure 35-4 which compares how both hook and slice mathematically relate to the effective or real loft. The top drawing with a 2° open or slice face angle is the same as the club shown in Figure 35-3. The bottom drawing shows a 2° closed or hook face angle. Note that the amount of the hook (2°) is added to the measured loft angle of 11° to achieve a club with a 13° effective or real loft. The top drawing with the 2° slice or open face angle is computed differently. The 2° slice is subtracted from the 11° measured loft, giving a 9° effective or real loft angle. The center drawing in Figure 35-4 is bored square, thus, whenever there is a 0° face angle the measured loft and the effective or real loft are the same. Also, if a wood club with a 0° angle and 11° loft was measured the same as an iron (from the shaft or hosel bore to the face) the loft would still be 11°. This is the only condition (0° face angle) that woods check out the same as irons using the same measuring method as is used for determining an iron's loft.

You can now see that the most important relationship that loft has is with face angle because they are directly one for one related to each other. For example, if you increase the face angle from 2° slice to 3° slice or 1° more you have also decreased the effective or real loft by 1°. (Note: Once again, the effective or real loft is the loft of the club after it is rolled into a square hit position or when the face and the shaft are both perpendicular with the intended line of flight.)

407

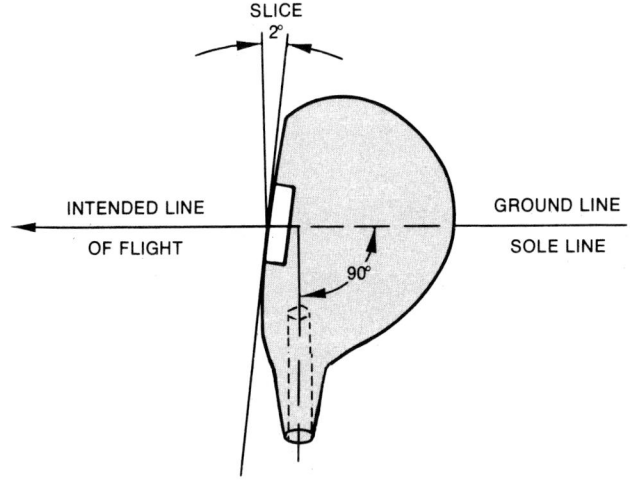

OPEN OR SLICE FACE ANGLE
11° LOFT − 2° SLICE = 9° EFFECTIVE OR REAL LOFT WITH FACE ROLLED INTO SQUARE POSITION AT IMPACT

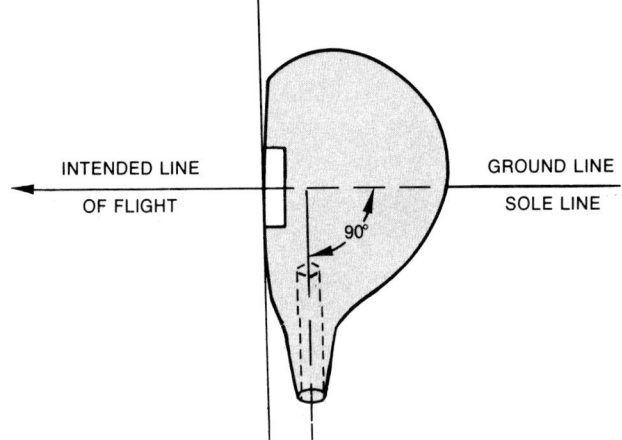

SQUARE FACE ANGLE
11° LOFT = 11° EFFECTIVE OR REAL LOFT WITH FACE IN NORMAL SQUARE POSITION AT IMPACT

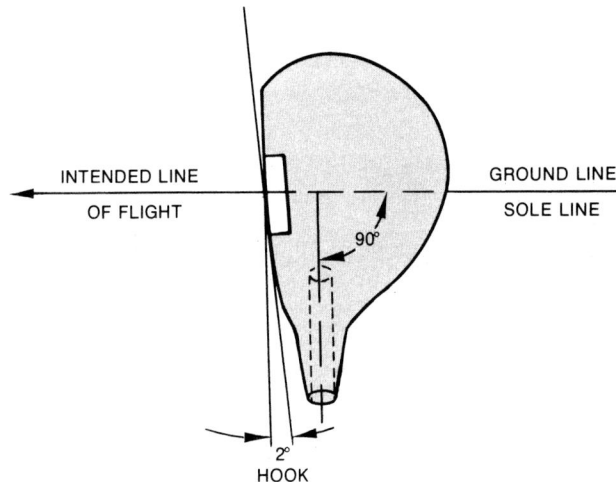

CLOSED OR HOOK FACE ANGLE
11° LOFT + 2° HOOK = 13° EFFECTIVE OR REAL LOFT WITH FACE ROLLED OPEN TO SQUARE POSITION AT IMPACT

Figure 35-4
Effect of face angle on "effective" or "real" loft (top view)

408

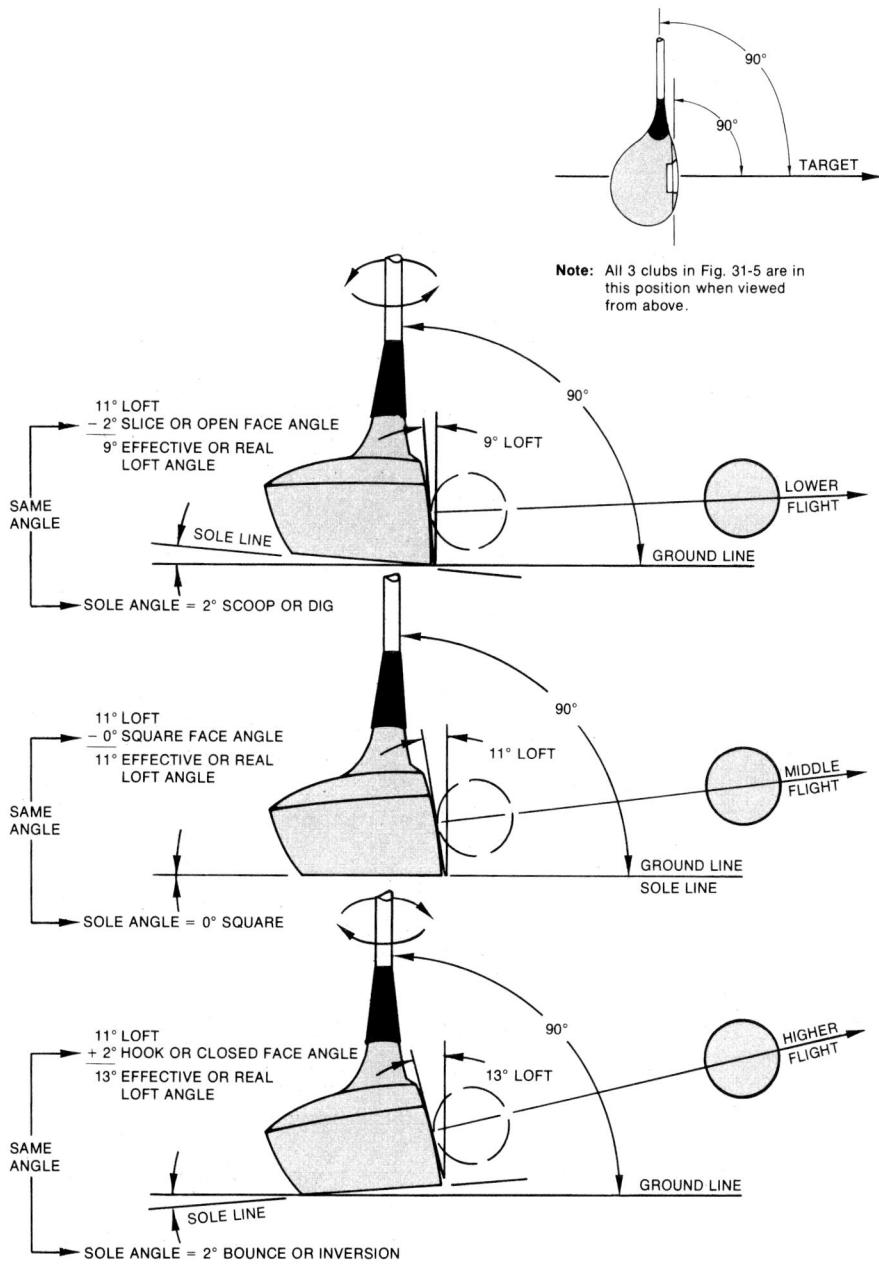

Figure 35-5
Effects of various face angles on loft and sole angle (end view)

To further understand what effective or real loft is, do this: hold any driver in the playing position without allowing the sole to touch the ground. Now, rotate the head open (slice) and rotate it closed (hook). Note that you can see more of the face (weak loft angle) in the open or slice position and less of the face (strong loft angle) in the closed or hook position. It is therefore logical to assume that to obtain a square hit on a wood club with a naturally open (slice) face, the club will have to be rolled shut to a square face position at impact, thus reducing the measured loft to what is called the "effective or real loft." Conversely, if the wood club has a naturally closed (hook) face it will have to be rolled open to a square face position at impact thus increasing the measured loft to the "effective or real loft." See Figure 35-5 for a better understanding of this. This figure also compares relative ball trajectory differences and sole angles.

It is quite important to keep in mind that we are discussing lofts from a purely mechanical standpoint and we have not as yet put in the myriad of other mechanical and dynamic influences, which could also affect the flight of the ball. Our discussion is still quite relevant and should be looked at as if a mechanical golfer with a perfect repeating swing is hitting test clubs where only one variable at a time is changed and all other specifications are exactly the same. In this manner our testing would prove out the relationships we are now discussing and will discuss throughout most of this section.

The most important wood clubs that must be controlled regarding effective or real loft at impact is the driver. This is because there is not much loft on a driver (usually 11°) and by the nature of the club alone, many golfers have trouble getting it airborne or to the proper trajectory. A rule of thumb which works well is to never allow the effective or real loft of a driver to go below 8½° for the average player and 6½° for the better player. An example of an 8½° effective or real loft would be a driver with 2½° slice (open face) with an 11° loft. Simply subtract the 2½° slice from the 11° loft and the answer is 8½° effect or real loft. Always subtract slice from loft and add hook to loft to get the effective or real loft.

Next, look at Table 35-1 for an interesting comparison of hook, slice and loft on effective or real loft.

TABLE 35-1
Driver Loft
Comparison of Hook, Slice and Loft on "Effective or Real Loft"

With Constant "Effective or Real Loft"				With Constant Measured Loft			
Hook	Slice	Driver Loft	Effective or Real Loft	Hook	Slice	Driver Loft	Effective or Real Loft
	3°	12°	9°		3°	11°	8°
	2½°	11½°	9°		2½°	11°	8½°
	2°	11°	9°		2°	11°	9°
	1½°	10½°	9°		1½°	11°	9½°
	1°	10°	9°		1°	11°	10°
	½°	9½°	9°		½°	11°	10½°
	0°	9°	9°		0°	11°	11°
½°		8½°	9°	½°		11°	11½°
1°		8°	9°	1°		11°	12°
1½°		7½°	9°	1½°		11°	12½°
2°		7°	9°	2°		11°	13°
2½°		6½°	9°	2½°		11°	13½°
3°		6°	9°	3°		11°	14°

Note: Slice is subtracted and hook is added to a wood club's loft.

TABLE 35-2
Fairway Wood's Loft Compared to Face Angle

Club Number	Loft	Face Angle	Real Loft	Difference in Real Loft
3	16°	2° Slice	14°	1°
4	19°	4° Slice	15°	
5	22°	3° Slice	19°	4°

Note: Slice is subtracted and hook is added to a wood club's loft.

Fairway woods are also manufactured to various face angles of hook and slice. This is an area where great inconsistencies can occur. Assume for a moment that you have a set of 3, 4, 5 fairway woods with the following specifications of loft and face angle as shown in Table 35-2.

It is quite common to find sets of fairway woods as shown in the example in Table 35-2. Notice the inconsistency in the differences of the real loft. Obviously the distance differences obtained with all three fairway clubs would not be consistent or in normal progressions of say ten yards. Some golfers mistakenly believe that metal wood face angles will be far more consistent due to the manufacturing process. However, a metal wood is investment cast into two pieces — the sole and a shell. The sole, with its radius shape, is then welded to the shell. If the sole shifts from its position before welding, then the face angle will be more open or more closed than intended. I have found metal wood face angles in a range from 10° hook to 10° slice even though the specified angle was 1° slice.

This brings us to one last point on this subject. When #5 woods became quite popular, many manufacturers and magazine articles indicated that a #5 wood hit the ball the same distance as a #3 iron. Anyone that plays regularly or hits practice balls knows that a #5 wood is at least equivalent to a #2 iron and in some cases a #1 iron. Look at a comparison in Table 35-3 below for an average specification #5 wood compared to an average specification #1 & #2 iron.

TABLE 35-3
Comparison of Length and Real Lofts for a #5 Wood, #1 and #2 Iron

Club Number	Std. Length	[1]Average Loft	[1]Avg. Face Angle	Real Loft
#5 wood	41"	21°	3° Slice	18°
#2 iron	39"	20°	———	20°
#1 iron	39½"	17°	———	17°

[1]Average loft and face angle was obtained by averaging specifications of the major club manufacturers.

As you can see, with its length advantage a #5 wood actually looks to be a longer hitting club than a #1 iron and in some instances, it is. However, the shaft flexibility of a #5 wood is greater than that of a #1 or #2 iron in a matched set, thus, a #5 wood will launch a golf ball in most instances at a higher trajectory than both the #1 or #2 iron.

At this point you may be wondering how to accurately gauge a wood head's face position and its effective or real loft. Several years ago there was no such device on the market. However, in an effort to standardize the golf industry and help clubmakers better understand golf club mechanics, I have developed and marketed a device called The Golf Club Gauge. This gauge will measure both woods and irons and will give you the following: loft, lie, face progression, hosel offset, face angle (hook/slice), effective lofts and all measurements such as face heights, head weight, face lengths, back height, etc. (See Photo 35-6 and 35-7.)

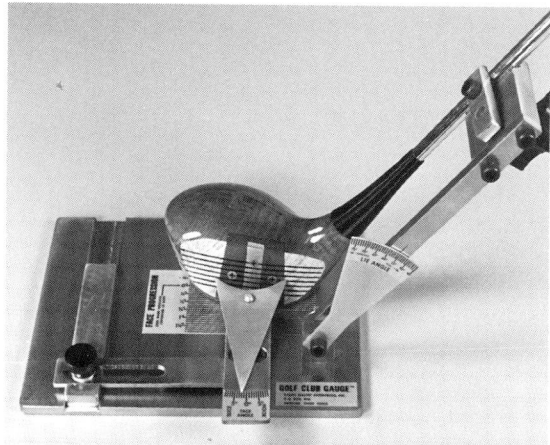

35-6
The Golf Club Gauge used for measuring
wood and iron specifications

35-7
The GolfWorks® Gauge also works great for
determining the specifications on woods with
non-traditional soles, like the ones shown.

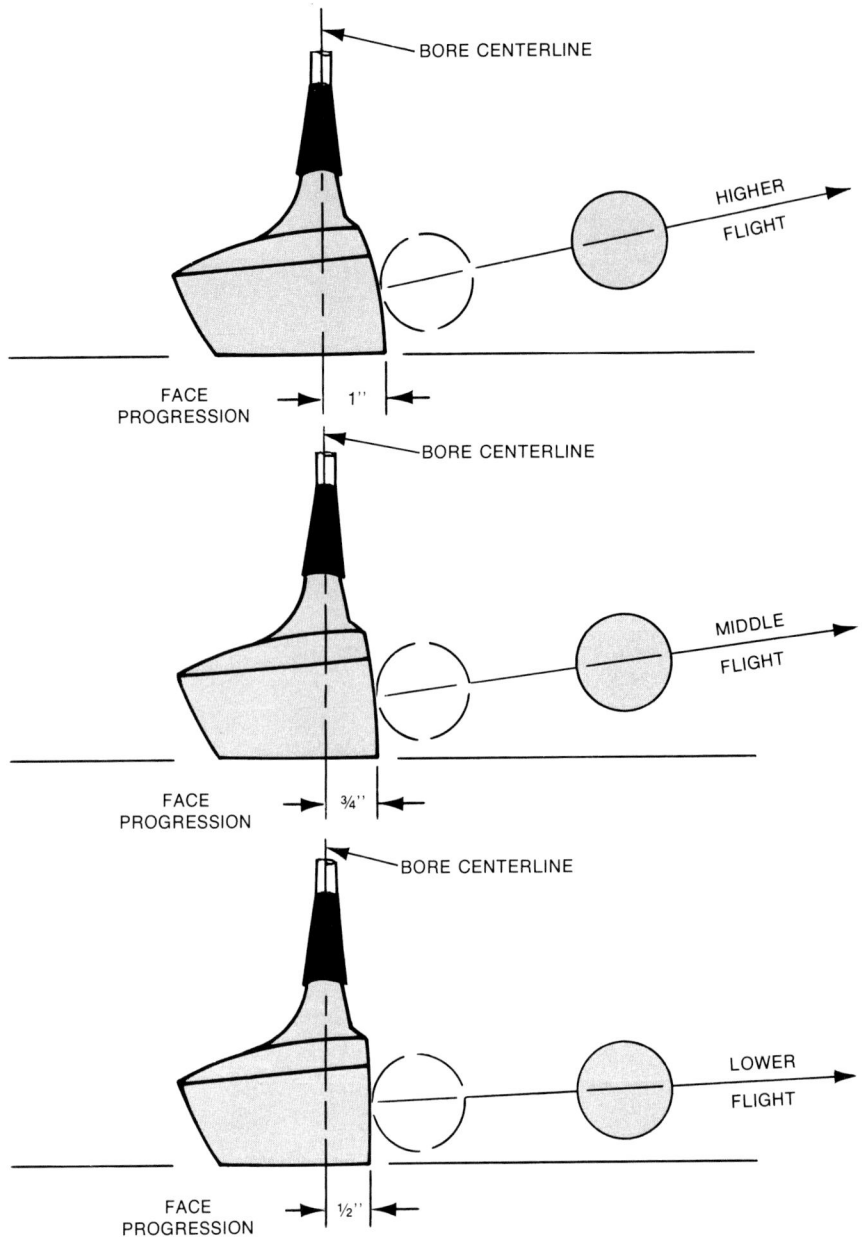

NOTE:
1. Assume all 3 clubs are identical except for face progression and each ball is struck on the same spot of the face.
2. The face progression dimensions and ball trajectories shown in this drawing are for reference and should be accepted as relative measures only.
3. Machine testing shows that increased face progression will hit the ball higher as shown above; however, keep in mind that is causes only very minor changes in trajectory and should not be considered alone as a means of noticeably changing trajectory.

Figure 35-8
Effect of face progression on loft

412

Another factor affecting the loft or trajectory of the golf ball is the location of the center of gravity in the head. See Figure 35-9. If all other variables such as loft, head weight, club length, etc. are identical; the lower the center of gravity the higher the ball will fly and the higher the center of gravity the lower the ball will fly. This, of course, assumes a constant impact location. For a more thorough understanding of center of gravity (center of mass) on ball flight and feel, see Chapter 43.

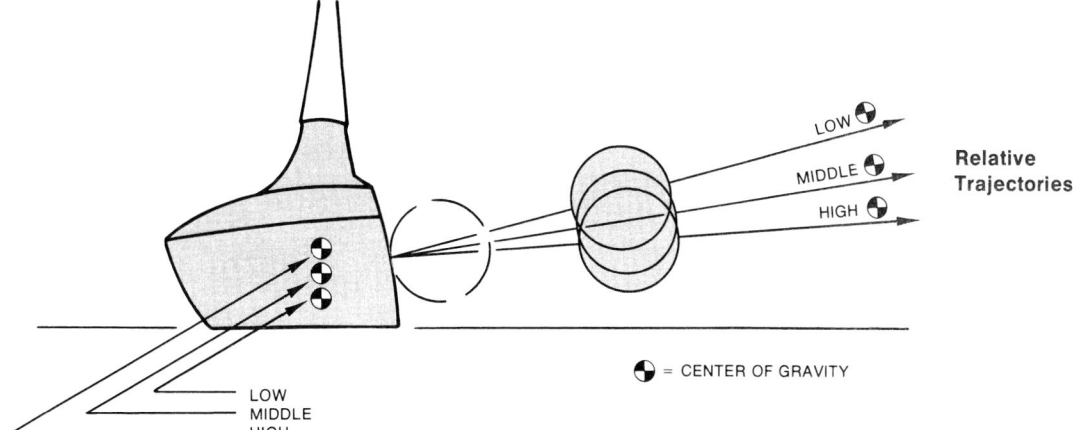

THE MORE IMPORTANT
FACTORS WHICH CONTROL
HEAD WEIGHT DISTRIBUTION

- Head Shape
- Backweights
- Soleplate Size and Material
- Density of Head Material
- Added Weight, Location, Size
  & Material

Figure 35-9
Effect of head weight distribution on loft

Vertical face roll also affects the loft of a wood club. See Figure 35-10. Forget for a moment that the club's center of gravity even exists and thus would have no effect on the shot as far as this discussion is concerned. Because a wood club has vertical face roll it has a different loft at any point vertically up and down the face. If we are discussing an 11° driver we now should know that it is only 11° loft at a point ½ of the vertical face height. See Figure 35-10. Any point above ½ of the face height has a greater loft than 11° and any point below ½ of the face height will have less loft than 11°. Chapter 41 will deal more in depth with vertical face roll.

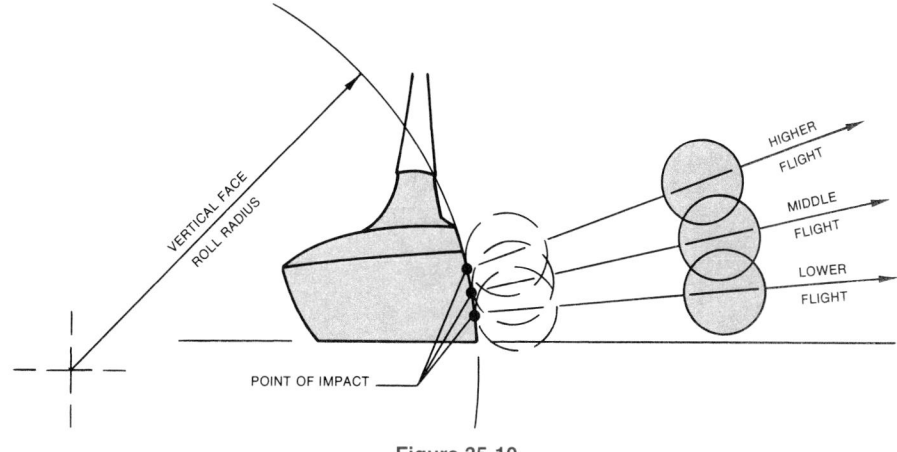

Figure 35-10
Effect of vertical face roll on loft

Shaft flexibility and shaft curve will also affect the dynamic loft or launch angle. This is a highly complex subject and will be covered in greater depth in the Golf Shaft Design Chapters; however, the explanation for Figure 35-11 will be handled here.

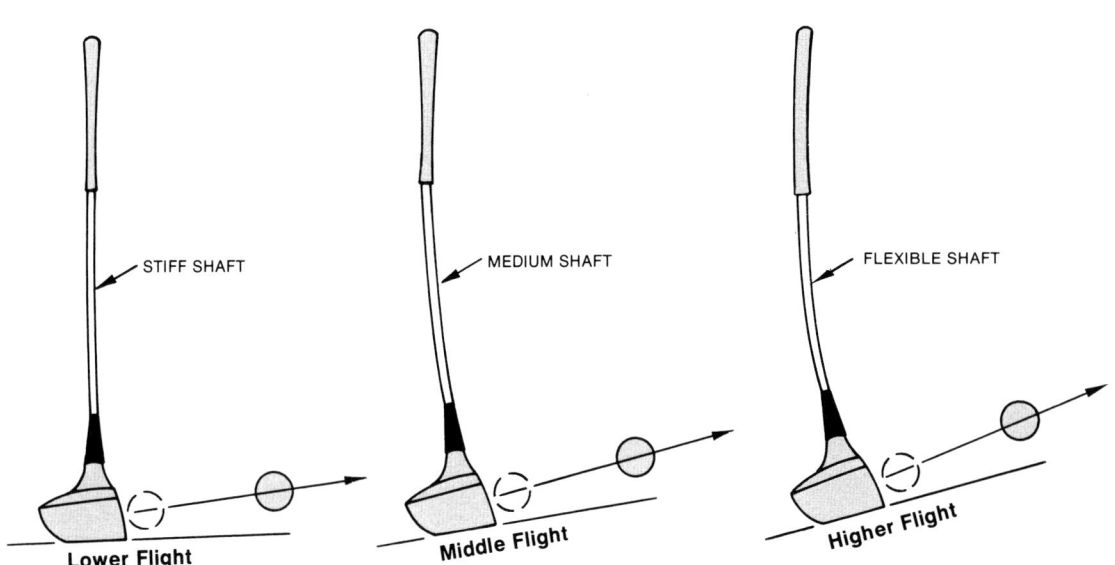

Figure 35-11
*Effect of shaft flex on loft

*Assuming all other variables on all 3 clubs except shaft flex are constant.

Much has been photographed and written about shaft flexing at impact. Many incorrect articles have stated that a properly flexed shaft for an individual will be straight or in line with the head of the club just before impact. See Figure 35-12. This is not the case and should be considered incorrect. What actually does occur can be seen in Figure 35-13. The shaft is in fact bowed forward with the head leading it just before impact. A number of photographic experts have diagnosed this as a distortion problem in some lenses, meaning that the camera lens is showing a distortion on the film due to the clubhead traveling at a faster speed than at any other point along the shaft. This of course, is true with some cameras but with very sophisticated high speed cameras Figure 35-13 has been proven to be true. Also, testing with stress and strain gauges placed on opposite sides of the shaft have verified bowed forward position. Remember, however, that during impact, the tremendous force of the ball at rest being put into motion slows the clubhead down so that it comes back in line with the shaft (shaft is straight in frontal plane) during impact, and as the ball leaves the face the clubhead is in fact lagging behind the shaft. This all occurs very rapidly in less than an inch of clubhead travel.

414

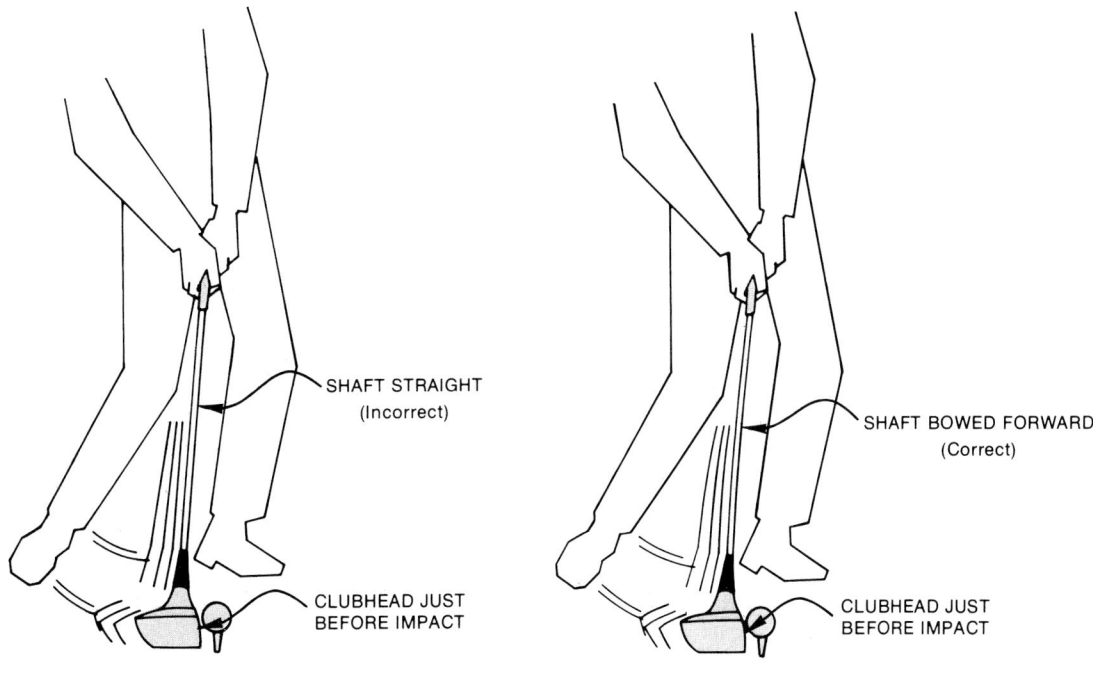

SHAFT STRAIGHT
(Incorrect)

CLUBHEAD JUST
BEFORE IMPACT

SHAFT BOWED FORWARD
(Correct)

CLUBHEAD JUST
BEFORE IMPACT

Figure 35-12   Figure 35-13

Now, let's go back to our discussion of shaft flexing and shaft curve on loft or ball launch angle. Because the clubhead is bowed ahead of the shaft at impact the dynamic loft or impact loft is increased. Assuming the only variable in our three test clubs in Figure 35-11 is shaft flex with swing speed also remaining constant; we can see that the more flexible the shaft the higher the trajectory. Most golfers at one time or another have hit balls with ladies' clubs or with flexible shafted clubs. The results are always a higher trajectory with the more flexible shafts, which confirms and also offers logical proof, in addition to photographic proof, that the head is in fact ahead of the bowed shaft at impact, thereby increasing the dynamic loft.

Remember also, that the curve of the shaft or bend point can affect dynamic loft and ball trajectory. The curve of the shaft refers to how and where maximum bending occurs in the shaft. In other words, assume that we have three shafts all stiff flex but one shaft is tip stiff and butt weak, another tip weak and butt stiff and the third in between the first two or has a mid shaft bend point. Even though all three shafts are the same relative stiffness, the tip weak shaft will hit the ball higher than the tip stiff shaft with the third in between. See Figure 35-14. The reason for this is that a tip weak shaft will have more kick or increased dynamic loft at impact than a shaft that bends higher up the shaft. Complex indeed, and the surface has only been scratched but the information presented here will give you the basic understanding required.

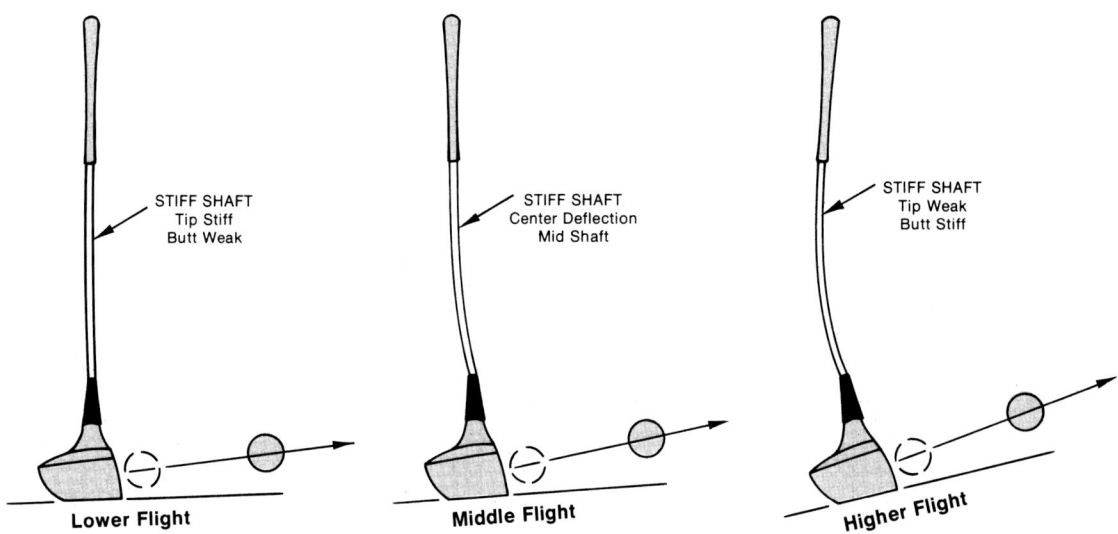

Figure 35-14
Effect of shaft curve on loft
assuming all other variables on all 3 clubs except shaft curve are constant

As you can see from this chapter, the height and trajectory a golf ball is hit is not only dependent on the actual loft of the club, but a number of other variables as well. These are very important to understand whether you are pioneering a new design, altering a club, fitting a club or just plain repairing the club.

The following table is included here as a handy reference for strong, standard and weak lofts.

	*Strong Lofts	Standard Lofts	Weak Lofts	Strong Lofts	Standard Lofts	Weak Lofts
Woods		Men's			Ladies'	
1	10°	11°	12°	11°	12°	13°
2	12°	13°	14°	13°	14°	15°
3	15°	16°	17°	16°	17°	18°
4	18°	19°	20°	19°	20°	21°
5	21°	22°	23°	22°	23°	24°
6	24°	25°	26°	25°	26°	27°
7	27°	28°	29°	28°	29°	30°
8	30°	31°	32°	31°	32°	33°
9	33°	34°	35°	34°	35°	36°

TABLE 35-4
Chart For Determining Strong, Standard and Weak Loft Specifications
Men's and Ladies' – Wood Club Lofts

* Note that metal wood standard lofts are usually the same as strong lofted woods. This is required due to the lower center of gravity location on metal woods. See Chapter 46 for a more detailed discussion.

CHAPTER 36

GOLF WOOD CLUB DESIGN: LIE

Performance Characteristic of Lie

The relationship of the clubhead to the golfer's hands at impact through the various golf club lengths. Improper lie can cause direction problems. See Figures 36-2, 36-3, 36-4 and 36-5.

Definition of Lie

The angle of the centerline of the shaft with the ground line tangent to the sole at the face centerline. See Figure 36-1.

Other Specifications Which Affect Lie

Shaft flex. See Figure 36-9.
Length. See Figure 36-10.

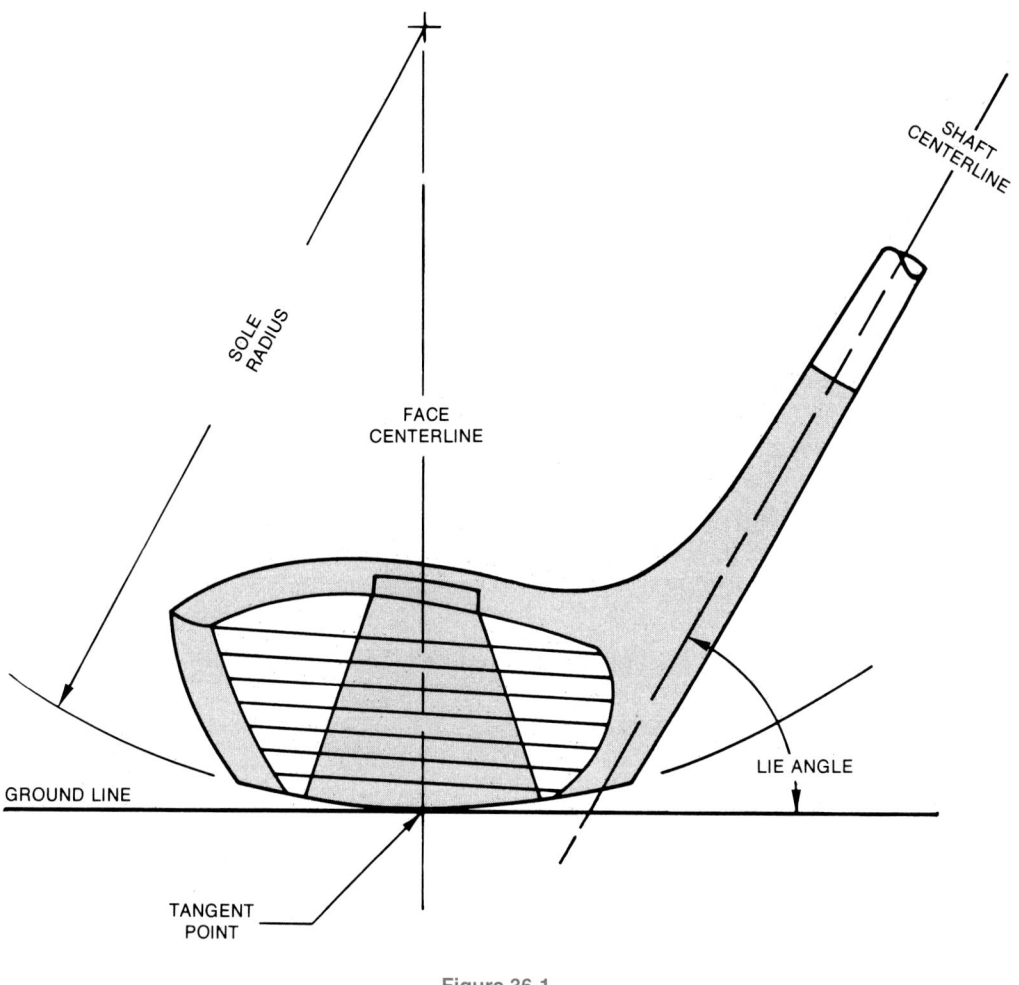

SHAFT
CENTERLINE

SOLE
RADIUS

FACE
CENTERLINE

LIE ANGLE

GROUND LINE

TANGENT
POINT

Figure 36-1
Definition of Lie

Discussion of Lie

Lie is one of the more important specifications to reckon with in the proper fitting of clubs. A discussion here concerning the technical aspects of lie will help later or when the reader gets to Chapters 64 and 65 concerning the key variables in proper fitting of golf clubs.

A good place to begin is with an explanation how an improper lie club can cause golf ball directional problems. Refer to Figure 36-2 which shows that a club with too upright a lie will have a tendency to hit the ball left and conversely too flat a lie will hit the ball right. It is important to note here that in all three drawings of Figure 36-2 that the leading edge of the clubface is perpendicular or perfectly square to the target.

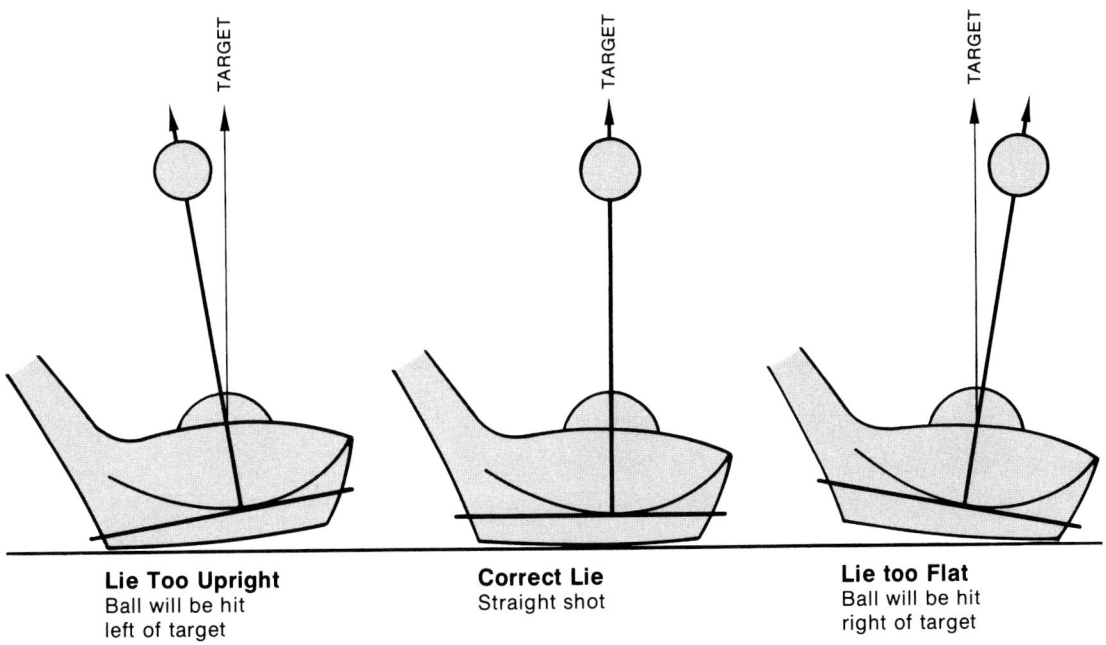

Lie Too Upright
Ball will be hit
left of target

Correct Lie
Straight shot

Lie too Flat
Ball will be hit
right of target

Figure 36-2
Improper lie can cause directional problems

The explanation on why the ball will go either left or right with too upright or too flat a lie is this: the lie of the club establishes the directional plane of the loft. If the club at impact is the same as shown under "correct lie" in Figure 36-2, the plane of the face will be perpendicular or square to the target. However, if the lie of the club at impact is too upright, the directional plane of the face will be pointing left of the target even though the leading edge of the face is aligned square to the target. The difference at impact between the proper lie and improper lie angle coupled to the amount of club-face loft is referred to as a "compound angle." This compound angle is the amount of tilt or misdirection in the face, or as the golfer sees it, the direction of ball flight. If a golf club were made with no loft (0 degrees) then improper lie would cause no directional problems because with no loft a compound angle or tilt of the face plane would not exist. To understand this better, do this: hold a #9 iron in the proper address position with the face aiming at the target. Assume this club to have 64° lie and 48° loft. Begin lowering the grip end toward the ground while keeping the leading edge of the face square with the target until the grip and shaft lie flat on the ground. At this point the club's actual lie angle is 0° because the 64° original lie angle has actually been transferred entirely into the face plane or tilt. Also, the club's actual loft angle is 0°. This means that if you were holding a #9 iron with 48° loft and could hit the ball with the club lying on the ground with the leading edge square to the target, the ball would be pulled exactly 48° left of the target or the amount of the original loft. Look closely at the club in this position and imagine the ball coming off the face. The more lofted the iron, the farther left it will go; and the less lofted the club, for example a driver, the less left it will go. See Figure 36-3. Also note that in Figure 36-3 the example club previously discussed with 0° loft shows that if no loft exists, then regardless of proper or improper lie, the ball will always go toward the target if the leading edge is square to the target.

Normally during impact, a golf ball is launched with backspin. However, the impact shown in Figure 36-3 launches a ball with counterclockwise hooking side spin, thus compounding the effect of improper lie on directional control. The shot would be a pull hook with its severity based on the amount of club loft.

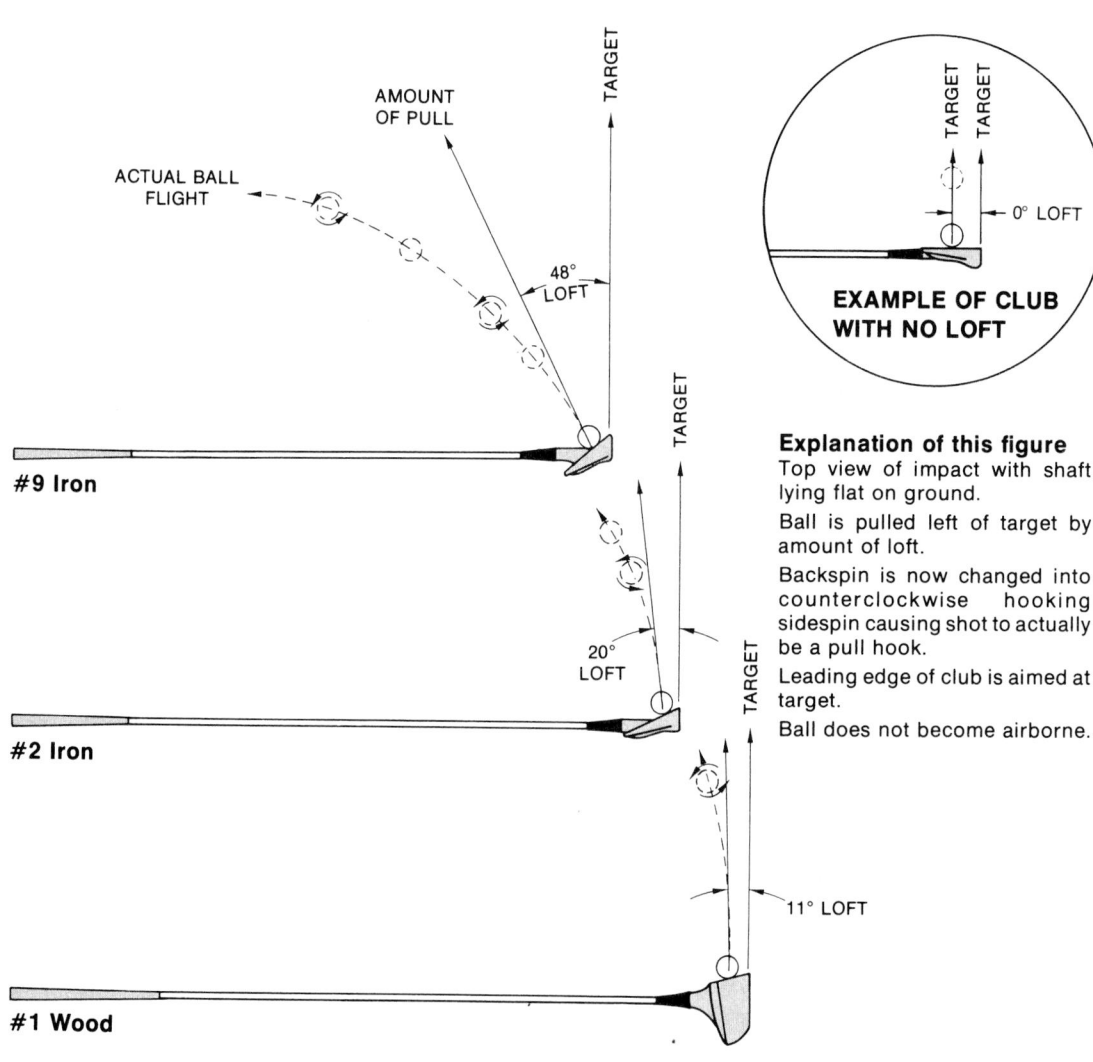

Explanation of this figure

Top view of impact with shaft lying flat on ground.

Ball is pulled left of target by amount of loft.

Backspin is now changed into counterclockwise hooking sidespin causing shot to actually be a pull hook.

Leading edge of club is aimed at target.

Ball does not become airborne.

Figure 36-3
Effect of improper lie angle on
face plane tilt vs. amount of loft

420

Let's look at an example which would better typify actual conditions of impact. Assume that you have a 115 yard #9 iron shot to a green with a bunker left. Also assume that you will execute the shot perfectly with one exception–the toe will be up at impact. This means the lie of the club is too upright for you. Here's what would happen: see Figure 36-4. With a close-up stop action we see the club at impact actually touched the ground at a point 1" rearward of the center of the face indicating that the club came through the impact zone being held at a 4° flatter lie angle than the angle to which it was actually built. Because the club was swung 4° flatter with the toe sticking up in the air 4° too upright, it can be calculated mathematically that the ball will be pulled 3° left of the actual clubhead path because the face plane is tilted in that direction. (This assumes a 48° lofted #9 iron.) On a 115 yard shot this would amount to pulling the shot left by approximately 18 feet or, as in this case, into the bunker. Also, there would be a slight hooking effect which would amount to approximately 4 more feet. This is a total of 22 feet left of target resulting from the lie being only 4° too upright at impact.

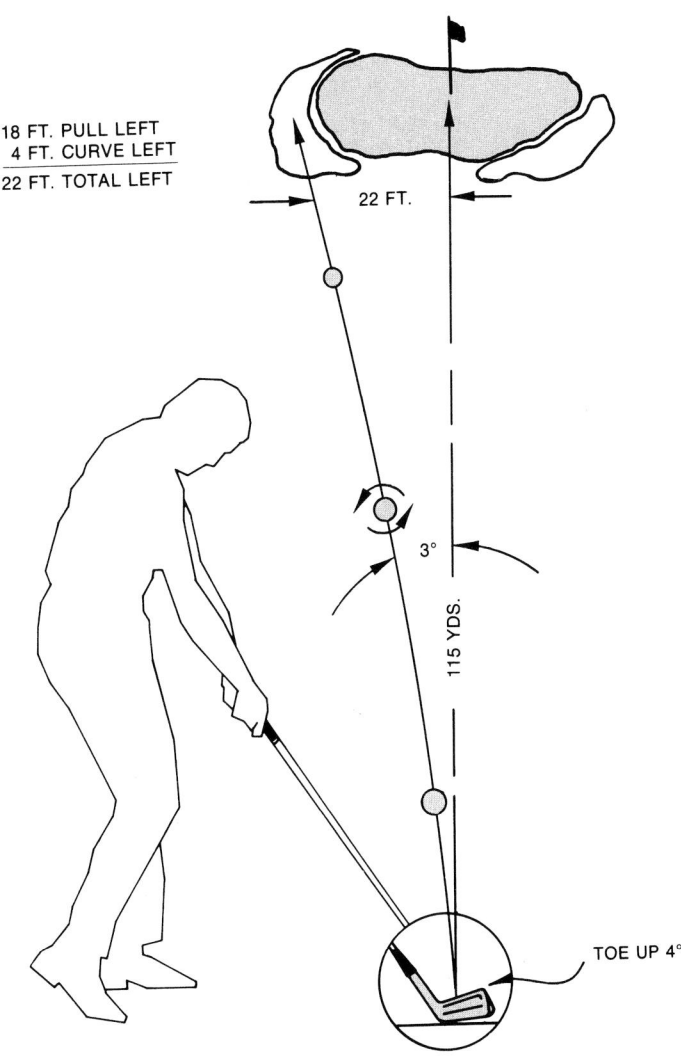

18 FT. PULL LEFT
4 FT. CURVE LEFT
22 FT. TOTAL LEFT

22 FT.

3°

115 YDS.

TOE UP 4°

Figure 36-4
Incorrect lie angle at impact—#9 iron 48° loft

421

To further the example, assume a driver is being hit with the lie 4° too upright also. Since a driver only has 10° or 11° loft compared to a #9 iron of 48° loft, the pulling effect is far less severe even though a driver hits the ball a greater distance. See Figure 36-3. With the lie of the driver 4° too upright, the ball would be pulled approximately 1° left or 11 feet. The hooking effect would only be another 2 feet for a total of 13 feet left of target. See Figure 36-5.

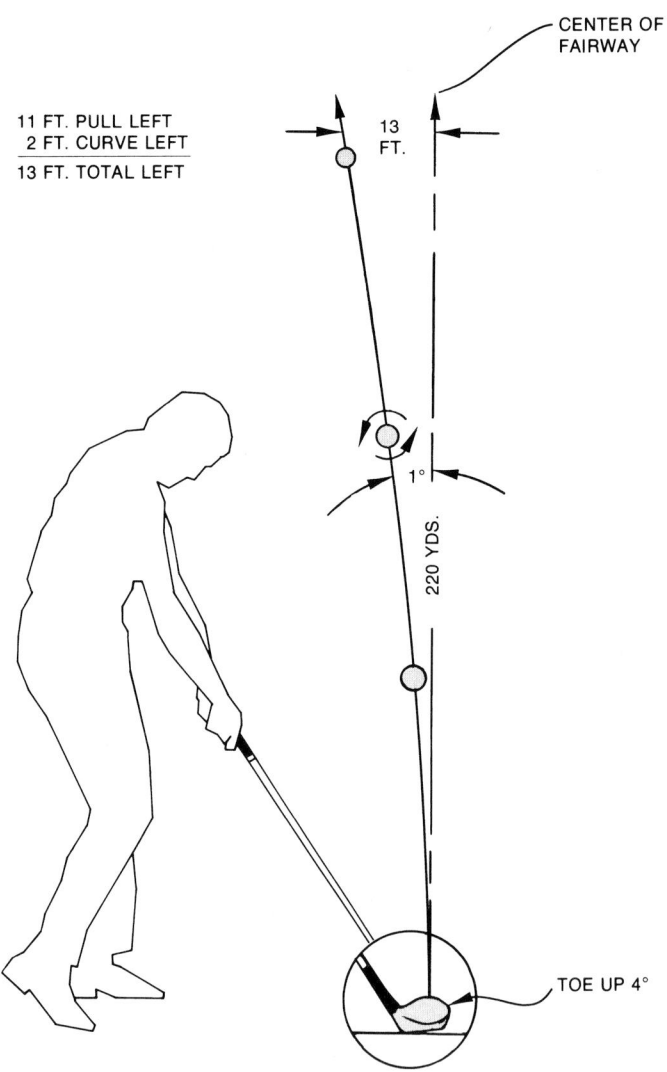

Figure 36-5
Incorrect lie angle at impact—driver 11° loft

If the reader is astute some interesting thoughts will formulate concerning lie. First, let us assume that a golfer has a set of woods and irons that are all 4° too upright. The old thinking was that since they were all off the same there would be no problem since the compensation in his swing or aim would be the same for every club. This has just been proven not to be so. We have now learned that the more lofted a club, the greater the tendency will be to hit it off line of target if the lie is consistently incorrect. Hence, the higher lofted short irons which are used for accuracy are most critical for having the proper lie. Second, if the lies on a set of woods and irons are not incrementally correct for a given golfer (i.e., assume #2 iron 1° upright, #3 iron 3° upright, #4 iron 2° flat, #3 wood 4° upright, etc.) then the problem could be even further compounded and still require a different compensating swing for each club to hit the ball at the target.

As a final word on the effect of improper lie on directional control, it has been thought and taught by many that the heel of the club digs in and the toe closes at impact. Conversely, the toe down was said to strike the ground first and open the club-face thus sending the ball to the right. This seemed fairly logical as an explanation but in fact is nothing more than myth. When using this explanation it must have been difficult to explain side hill lies when the ball would go left (ball above feet) or downhill lies when the ball would go right (ball below feet). If you think about these two types of lies, the sole of the club usually would sit properly on the ground with no chance of the toe or heel digging in. However, the ball still was hit with misdirection if the player did not properly compensate his alignment right or left of target.

The best way to understand face plane tilt caused by improper lie is to make up two special iron clubs with holes drilled in the center of the face and a shaft inserted in the hole. One of the clubs should be either a #2 or #3 iron and the other a #9 iron. Mark and center punch the middle of both faces. This should be the geometric center both vertically and horizontally on the face. Next, using a letter "T" drill, drill completely through the face, being sure the hole is drilled perpendicular to the face. See Photo 36-6. A good vise and a drill press make this much easier. The "T" drill makes the proper sized hole so a .355 taper tip shaft will slip in firmly. See Photo 36-7.

The GolfWorks® also offers a Magnetic Lie Angle Tool that easily attaches to the face of any steel iron or metal wood for quick lie demonstrations using a golfers existing clubs. See Photo 36-8.

36-6
Proper set-up for drilling hole in face of old club

36-7
Shaft is inserted in face of club to show
face plane tilt for too upright or too flat lie

423

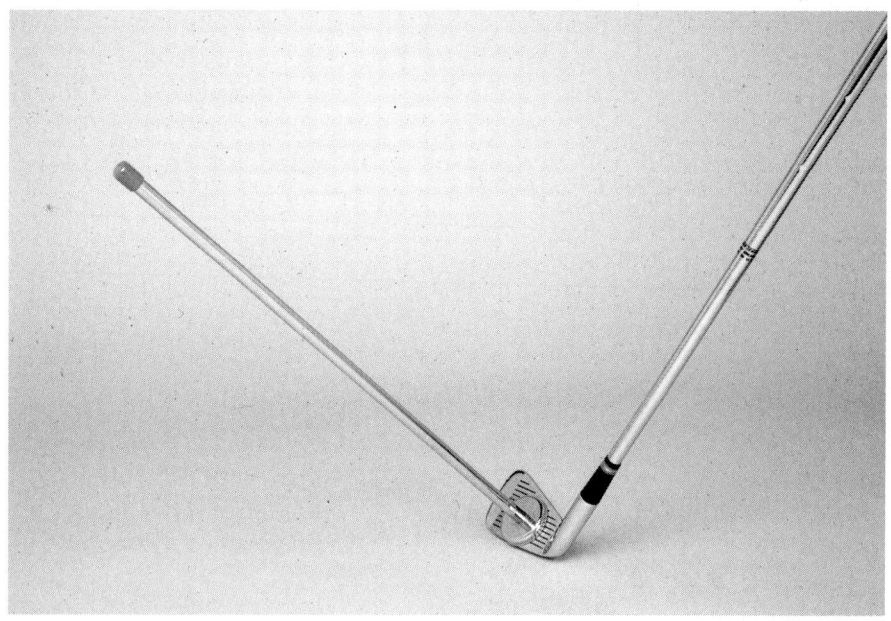

36-8
Measuring lie angle using the Magnetic Lie Angle Tool

There are two specifications which have a direct effect on lie. The first is shaft flexing. During the downswing the lie of the club is slightly flattened due to shaft flexing. See Figure 36-9. This happens because the center of mass or center of gravity of the clubhead is not in line with the centerline of the shaft. Therefore, during the downswing, centrifugal force acts through the center of gravity of the clubhead causing it to bend downward resulting in a flattening of the lie. The amount of flattening is determined by head weight, club length, head speed and shaft flex. The longer length woods will tend to be flattened slightly more than the shorter length woods. The shorter woods

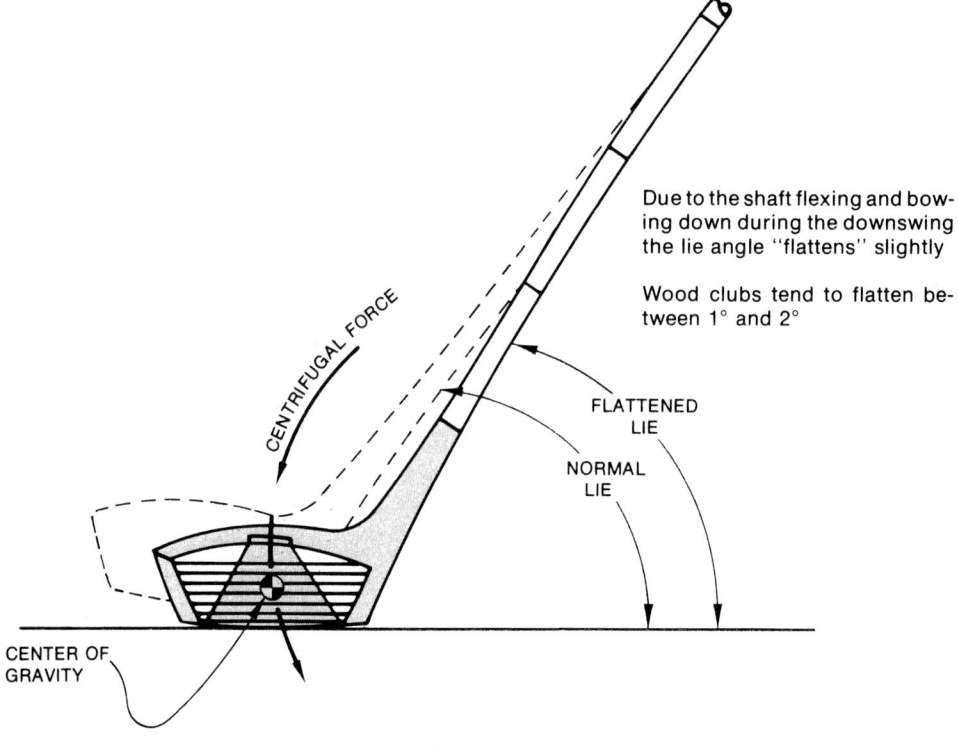

Due to the shaft flexing and bowing down during the downswing the lie angle "flattens" slightly

Wood clubs tend to flatten between 1° and 2°

CENTRIFUGAL FORCE

FLATTENED LIE

NORMAL LIE

CENTER OF GRAVITY

Figure 36-9
How centrifugal force tends to flatten the lie of a club during the downswing

424

have the heaviest heads but also have stiffer shafts to compensate and their shorter length does not allow for the higher head speeds which generate greater centrifugal force. On the other hand, the longer woods have lighter heads, more flex in the shafts, are longer in length and the head speeds are far greater than the shorter woods, generating more centrifugal force and consequently more flattening of the lie. The range of lie flattening for woods tends to be from 1° to 2°.

The second specification which has an effect on lie is club length. The longer the club, the flatter the lie must be to fit the same golfer. Also, the shorter the club, the more upright the lie must be to fit the same golfer. See Figure 36-10.

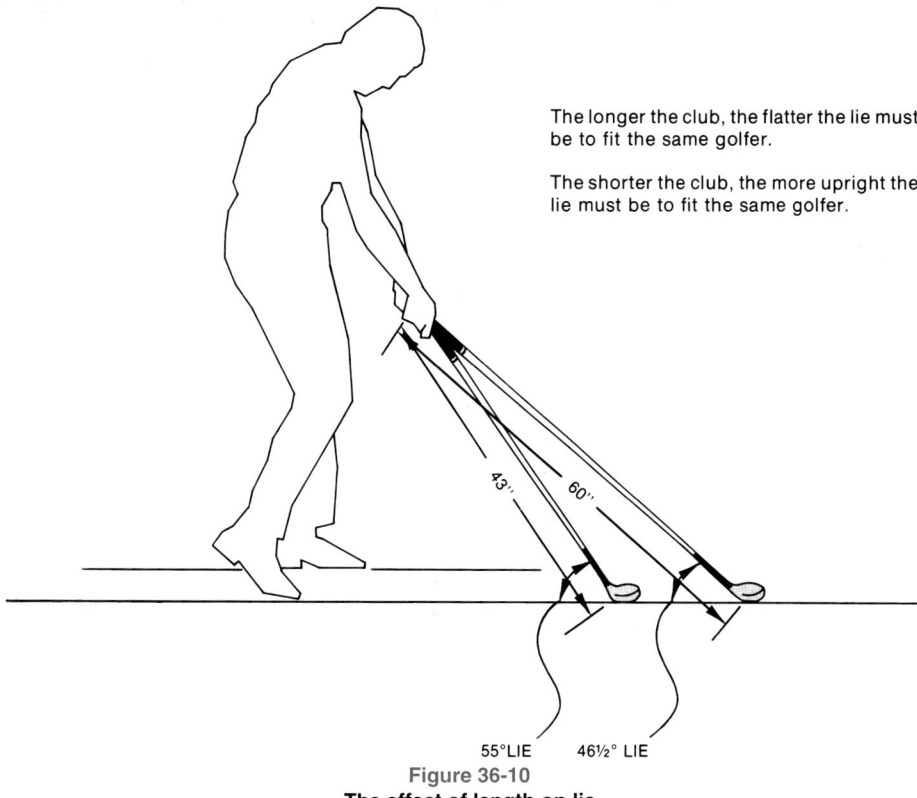

Figure 36-10
The effect of length on lie

The following table is included here as a handy reference for flat, standard and upright lies.

	Men's			**Ladies'**		
Woods	[1] **Flat Lies**	[1] **Standard Lies**	[1] **Upright Lies**	[2] **Flat Lies**	[2] **Standard Lies**	[2] **Upright Lies**
1	53°	55°	57°	51°	53°	55°
2	53½°	55½°	57½°	51½°	53½°	55½°
3	54°	56°	58°	52°	54°	56°
4	54½°	56½°	58½°	52½°	54½°	56½°
5	55°	57°	59°	53°	55°	57°
6	55½°	57½°	59½°	53½°	55½°	57½°
7	56°	58°	60°	54°	56°	58°
8	56½°	58½°	60½°	54½°	56½°	58½°
9	57°	59°	61°	55°	57°	59°

TABLE 36-1
Wood Club Lies – Men's and Ladies'

[1] Lies shown are for standard length woods (i.e., 43" driver). For each ½" added to standard length, subtract 1° in lie (flatter) and for each ½" subtracted from standard length, add 1° in lie (upright).
[2] Same as Note 1 above but based on a standard length set with a 42" driver.

CHAPTER 37

GOLF WOOD CLUB DESIGN: LENGTH

Performance Characteristic of Length
A determining factor of clubhead speed.

Definition of Length (Traditional Standard)
The distance from the back heel portion of the sole radius to the top of the grip cap. See Figure 37-1.

Other Specifications Which Affect Length
Shaft Flex. See Figure 37-5.
Sole Radius. See Figure 37-2.

Discussion of Length
Most of the specifications in the wood club design section, such as loft, lie, bulge, roll, etc., are easily defined with only one method of measurement being accepted industry-wide as the standard method. Length, however, is different, since a number of manufacturers measure using differing methods.

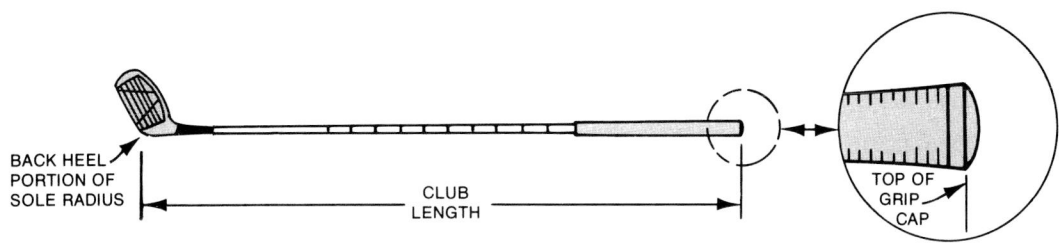

Figure 37-1
Definition of club length (Traditional Standard)

The traditional standard for measuring length is shown in Figure 37-1. It is simple to do and on the surface seems like a good quantitative and accurate method for determining a club's length. However, refer to Figure 37-2 and it can be seen that the amount of sole radius has a direct effect on two clubs that measure the same length. The greater the sole radius the longer the club will be versus less sole radius the shorter the club will be.

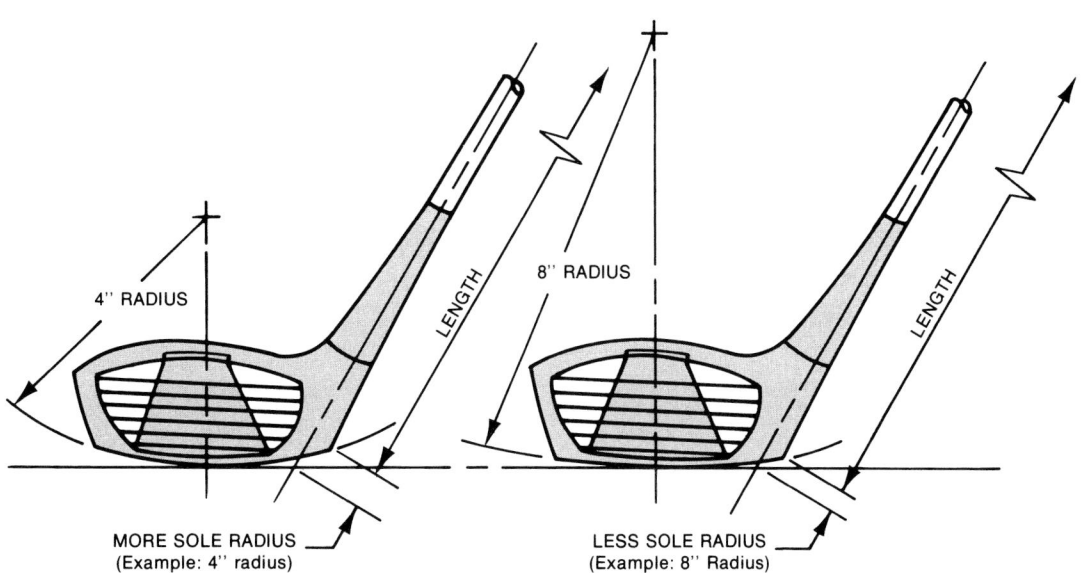

Assuming two golf clubs are the same length when measured in the traditional way, the club with more sole radius will be longer than the club with less sole radius.

Figure 37-2
Effect of sole radius on length

Remember, the terminology concerning radiuses on golf clubs can be a little misleading since more radius refers to a smaller, sharper curve and less radius refers to a more gradual, gentler curve. Hence, the smaller the number, the greater the radius. (Examples: A 4" radius is greater than an 8" radius. A club with an 8" radius horizontal face bulge has more radius than one with 10" radius.)

The best and most accurate method for measuring a golf club is shown in Figure 37-3. This method eliminates the effect of sole radius and other measuring methods. This method provides a reference whereby any two golf clubs can be compared as to their real length. It also allows for the effect that sole "rails" and irregularly shaped soles have upon club length.

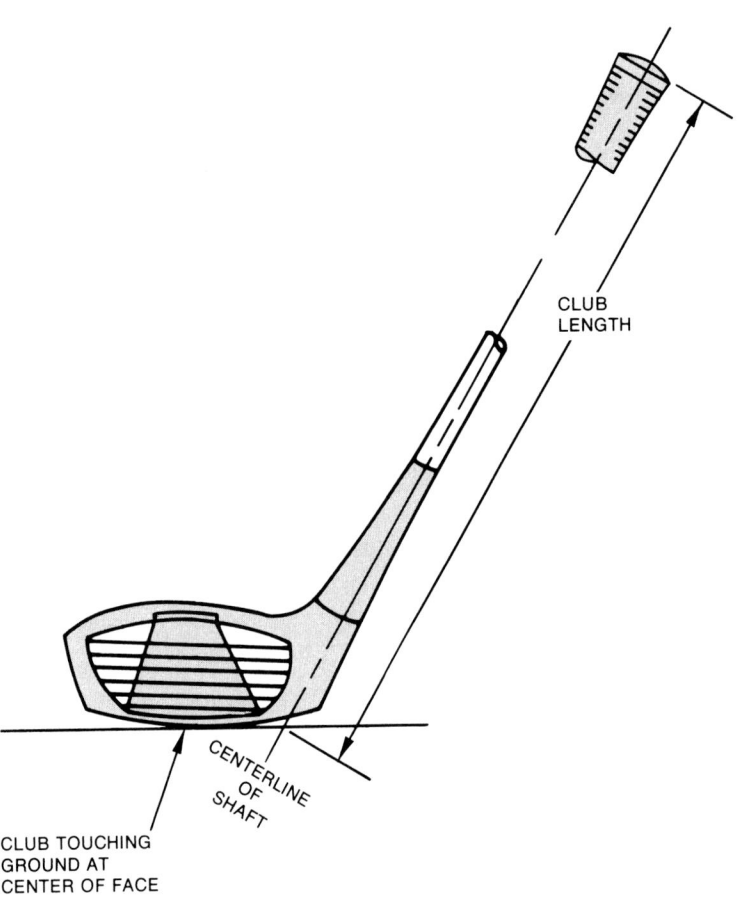

CLUB LENGTH

CENTERLINE OF SHAFT

CLUB TOUCHING GROUND AT CENTER OF FACE

Figure 37-3
Accurate method for measuring and comparing length

When manufacturing clubs using the accurate measuring method in Figure 37-3 versus the traditional standard measuring method in Figure 37-1, it is important to understand that, depending on sole radius, the traditional standard method will produce a club from ¼" to ½" longer in length than the accurate method. So, depending on the method used, club lengths can be adjusted to meet specific design objectives.

The easiest way to measure clubs using the accurate method shown in Figure 37-3 is to hold the club in the correct lie position and place a 48" rigid ruler directly behind the club and touching the heel. The grip of the club is allowed to lie against the ruler. The length of the club is read directly from the ruler where the top of the grip cap touches it. See Photo 37-4.

37-4

Another specification variable which affects the length of a club is shaft flex. See Figure 37-5.

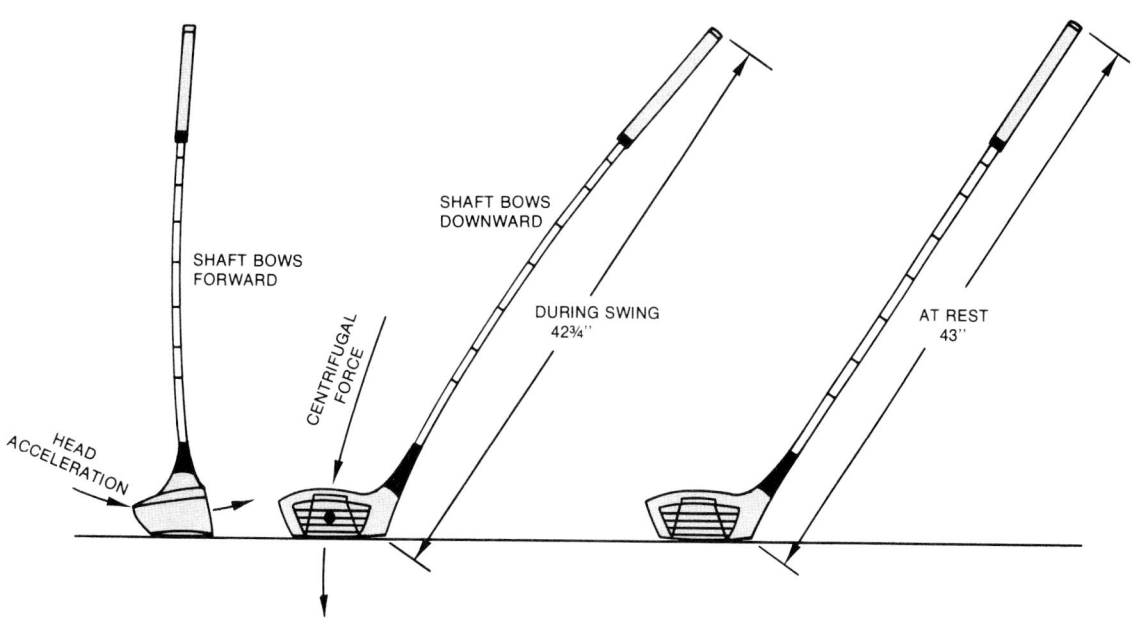

Figure 37-5
The effect of shaft flexing (bowing downward and forward) on length

A golf shaft flexes in at least two different directions during the downswing and simple logic would imply that it must shorten somewhat. The actual amount a driver would shorten was quantified on the True Temper® mechanical golfer. The tests indicated that a driver shortens approximately ¼" in length by the time it reaches impact due to shaft flexing.

The following table is included here as a handy reference for standard wood club lengths.

TABLE 37-1
Wood Club Lengths – Men's and Ladies'

Woods	Men's Standard	Ladies' Standard	Ladies' Petite
1	*43"	42"	41½"
2	42½"	41½"	41"
3	42"	41"	40½"
4	41½"	40½"	40"
5	41"	40"	39½"
6	40½"	39½"	39"
7	40"	39"	38½"
8	39½"	38½"	38"
9	39"	38"	37½"

The most popular length variations for men are ½" shorter or longer than standard and 1" longer than standard. The most popular length variations for ladies are ½" shorter or longer than standard.

*Note that some manufacturers are building certain graphite shafted drivers up to 2" longer than the listed standard. Usually the fairway woods that accompany these overlength drivers are standard length.

CHAPTER 38

GOLF WOOD CLUB DESIGN: FACE PROGRESSION

Performance Characteristic of Face Progression

A factor concerning the trajectory of the golf ball by controlling the exact moment of impact (i.e. ball will be contacted ¼" sooner by a golf club if the face progression is 1" vs. ¾"). See Figure 38-2.

Definition of Face Progression

The distance from the centerline of the shaft or hosel bore to the farthest front portion of the face on its centerline. See Figure 38-1.

Other Specifications Which Affect Face Progression

Hosel boring. See Chapter 44.

Discussion of Face Progression

Face progression is one of the many factors which controls trajectory and consequently affects the loft of a wood. It should not, however, be considered a

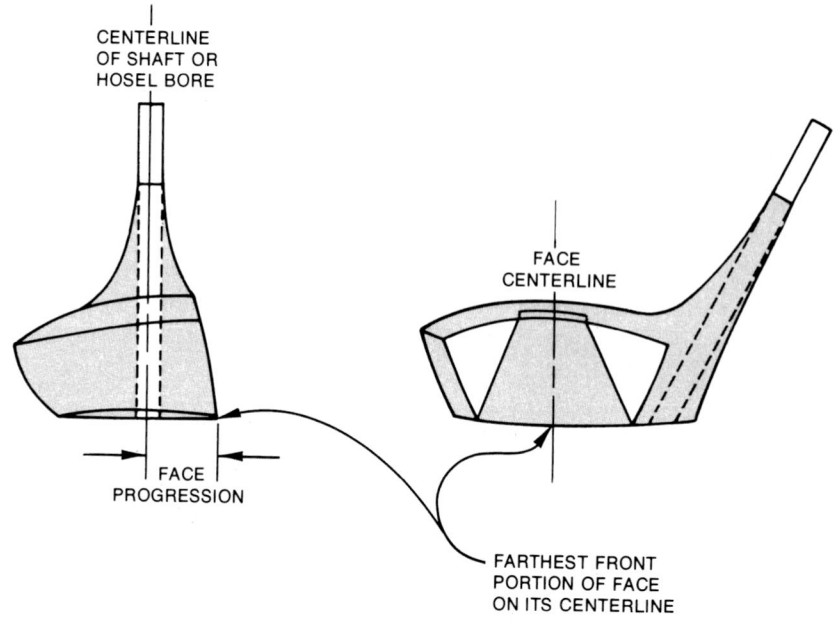

CENTERLINE
OF SHAFT OR
HOSEL BORE

FACE
CENTERLINE

FACE
PROGRESSION

FARTHEST FRONT
PORTION OF FACE
ON ITS CENTERLINE

Figure 38-1
Definition of face progression

major factor because in actual fact it requires extensive machine testing under controlled conditions to indicate ball launch trajectory differences. Face progression is a factor, but quite minor. See Figure 38-2.

The main characteristic of face progression is the visual look a golfer gets when looking down at a wood in the playing position. Many good looking wood models have been ruined by mis-boring the club with less face progression than was originally intended to be put in. When a wood head model is designed, the desired face progression dimension is built into it so that when the club is bored through the center of the hosel and properly faced, the actual face progression dimension remaining is within ±$\frac{1}{32}$" of the model. Most driver models of the past and present are designed with face progressions from $\frac{11}{16}$" to $\frac{15}{16}$". Some of the factors which are taken into consideration when determining what face progression to build into a certain model are: the final look desired, the finished neck diameter at its base, loft, the length of the whipping, bulge and roll and the length of the face from its centerline back into the heel. Of all these mentioned, the final look of the finished club is most important. Chapter 44 on hosel boring will go into greater detail on face progression's role when boring the head.

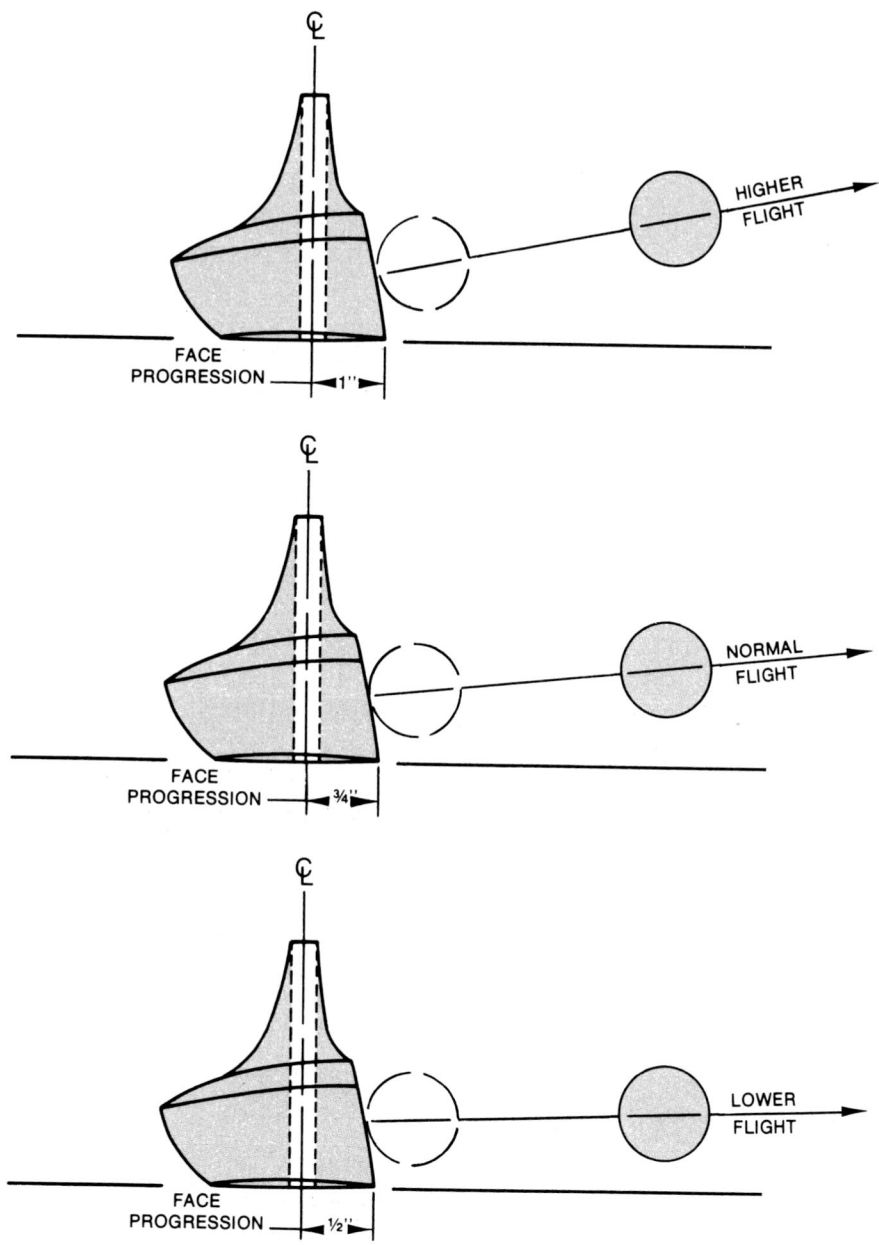

FACE PROGRESSION |◄1''►|

HIGHER FLIGHT

FACE PROGRESSION |◄¾''►|

NORMAL FLIGHT

FACE PROGRESSION |◄½''►|

LOWER FLIGHT

NOTE: 1. Assume all 3 clubs are identical except for face progression and each ball is struck on the same spot of the face.

2. The face progression dimensions and ball trajectories shown in this drawing are for reference and should be accepted as relative measures only.

Figure 38-2
Effect of face progression on loft

433

CHAPTER 39

GOLF WOOD CLUB DESIGN:
FACE ANGLE (HOOK AND SLICE)

Performance Characteristic of Face Angle
   The appearance of the face of the wood club while in the soled playing position (i.e. slice appears as an open face while hook appears as a closed face). The face angle is a controlling factor of loft and direction. See Figure 35-4.

Definition of a Face Angle
   The angle of the face to the grounded sole line with the shaft hole perpendicular to the line of flight. See Figure 39-1.

Other Specifications Which Affect Face Angle
   Shaft Flex. See Figure 39-2.
   Hosel Boring. See Chapter 44.

Discussion of Face Angle
   The face angle of the wood club is one of the more complex areas to understanding wood design. The face angle has a direct relationship on the effective or real loft of the club face at impact, the tendency to impart hooking or slicing sidespin to the ball and also the tendency to push or pull the ball from the intended line of flight. Chapter 35, **Golf Wood Club Design: Loft** and Chapter 44, **Golf Wood Club Design: Hosel Boring** give in-depth explanations of the face angle's role in both areas. These two chapters should be studied thoroughly.

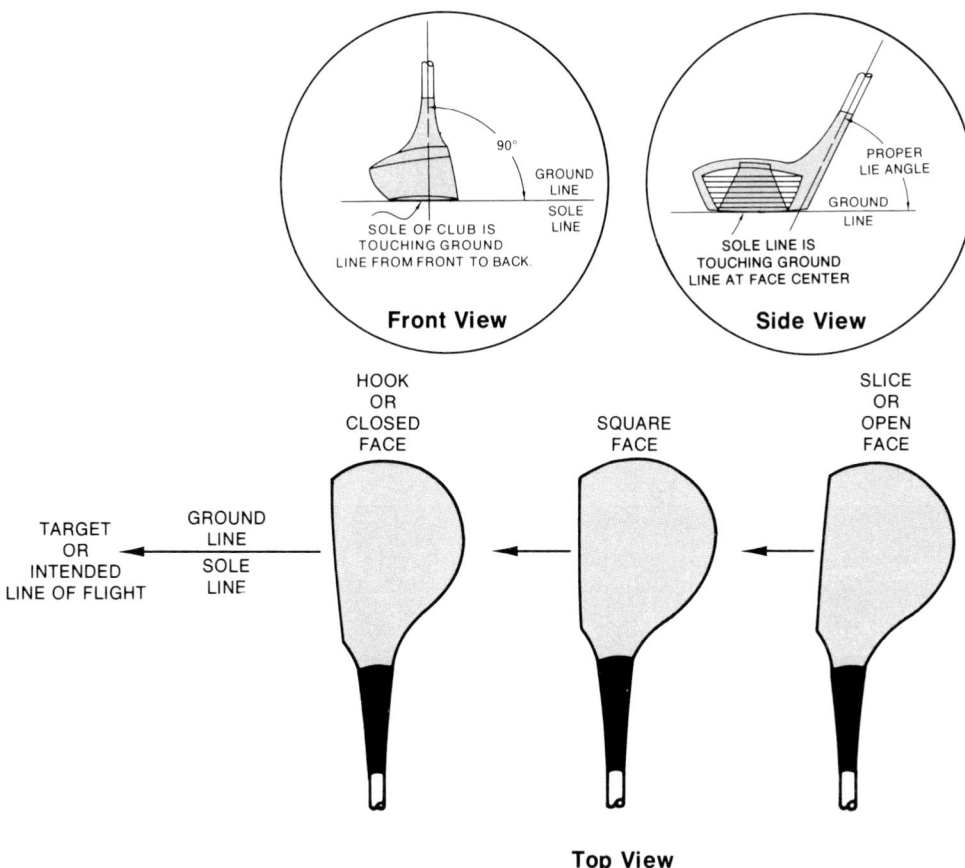

Figure 39-1
Definition of face angle

Just before impact the shaft normally flexes in a bowed forward position. This flexing action causes the face of the club to close slightly. The rule of thumb is that for each ½" the shaft bows forward, the face closes by approximately 1°. See Figure 39-2.

If you have the equipment and the inclination, a good experiment is to build up two drivers with identical specifications. Make the lengths, lofts, face angles, bulge and roll, swingweights, grip sizes, grip weights, head models, head weights and lies exactly the same. However, in one club install a parallel tip True Temper® Gold Plus "X" flex shaft (UGPWXH) and in the other install a Gold Plus "L" flex (UGPWLH). Follow the normal trimming instructions to achieve 43" and install the grip.

Now that the two test clubs have been built, hit shots with them. You should get dramatic differing results between the two clubs. The main difference, other than feel, is that the more flexible shafted club will hit the ball higher and to the left with a draw or hooking flight. The reason for this is because the increased amount of shaft flexing has closed the face more coming into impact and also has the effect of increasing the loft. Hence, a higher ball flight occurs with a tendency to go left. This experiment is proof to the controversy as to whether the head is leading the shaft or trailing the shaft coming into impact. See Figure 39-2.

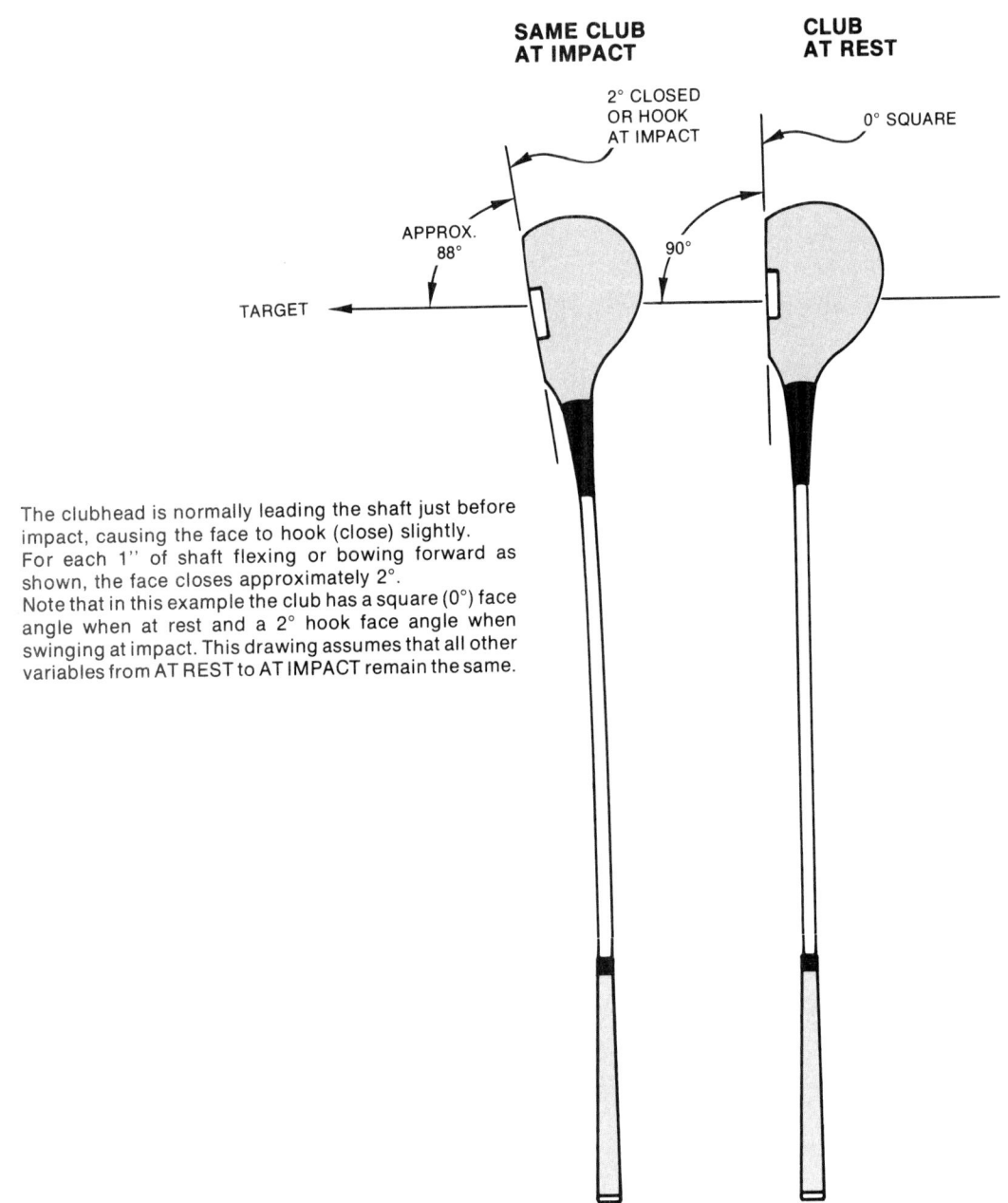

The clubhead is normally leading the shaft just before impact, causing the face to hook (close) slightly.

For each 1'' of shaft flexing or bowing forward as shown, the face closes approximately 2°.

Note that in this example the club has a square (0°) face angle when at rest and a 2° hook face angle when swinging at impact. This drawing assumes that all other variables from AT REST to AT IMPACT remain the same.

Figure 39-2
Effect of shaft flexing on face angle (hook and slice)

CHAPTER 40

GOLF WOOD CLUB DESIGN: HORIZONTAL FACE BULGE

Performance Characteristic of Bulge

The built-in correction or compensation factor which under normal circumstances at impact starts the ball farther to the right on toe shots and farther to the left on heel shots in order to compensate for ball sidespin caused by such off center hits. See Figures 40-2, 40-3, 40-4 and 40-5.

Definition of Bulge

The horizontal radius bulge of the face is measured from the heel to toe or horizontal plane of the face and is usually the same at any point vertically up and down the face. See Figure 40-1.

Other Specifications Which Affect Bulge

Clubhead Center of Gravity. See Figures 40-6 and 40-7.

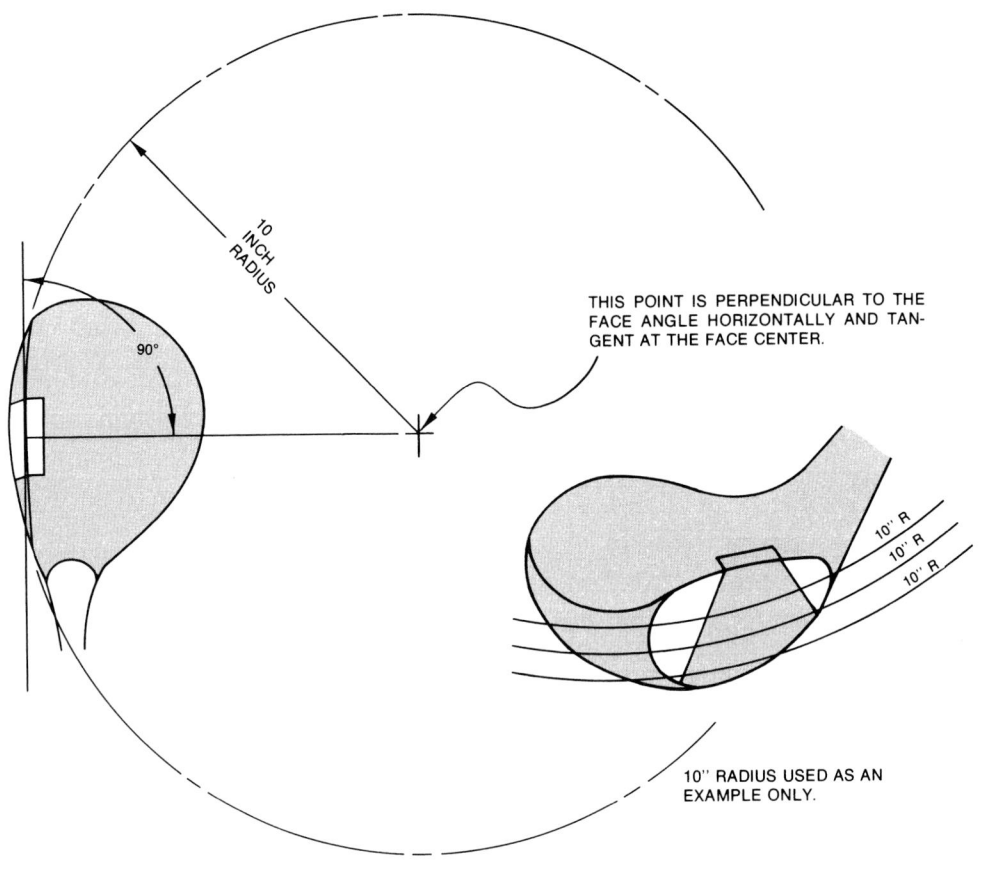

Figure 40-1
Definition of horizontal face bulge

THIS POINT IS PERPENDICULAR TO THE FACE ANGLE HORIZONTALLY AND TANGENT AT THE FACE CENTER.

10 INCH RADIUS

90°

10" R
10" R
10" R

10" RADIUS USED AS AN EXAMPLE ONLY.

Discussion of Bulge

Horizontal face bulge is one of the more misunderstood of wood club design specifications. Part of the reason is that it has two long time myths associated with it which hinder its proper understanding. The first myth is that the proper bulge either adds or reduces spin to the shot; which it does not. Its purpose is to start the ball farther to the right on toe shots and farther to the left on heel shots. Thus bulge is a correction or compensation factor for the clubhead's center of gravity which causes unwanted hooking or slicing sidespin on off-center hits. The second myth associated with bulge is that it has been thought that when a ball was struck off-center toward the toe, the clubhead rotated open by pivoting around the shaft. The clubhead does in fact open on toe shots but it rotates about the head's center of mass or center of gravity, not the axis of the shaft.

There is sort of a third myth concerning face bulge which deserves some discussion here. There have been some writings in books and articles which suggest that a face must have bulge in order to more deeply penetrate and compress the ball at impact and consequently hit it a greater distance. There have been no tests conducted on this other than my own of which I'm aware. Mechanical tests on flat faced drivers vs. 10" bulge faced drivers, otherwise as identical as possible, indicated no significant distance differences. The mechanics of physics, not to mention common sense, clearly implies that the curved face (bulge) will penetrate deeper into the ball because of less surface contact at impact vs. a flat faced club. This I do not refute. I can only report the results of the test which indicated that normal bulge on a wood club had no significant effect on overall distance and also no effect on measured ball speeds coming off the center of the clubface.

438

Assume all faces shown below are square to the target and the clubhead path is square to the target at impact. Also, all centers of gravity are in the same location.

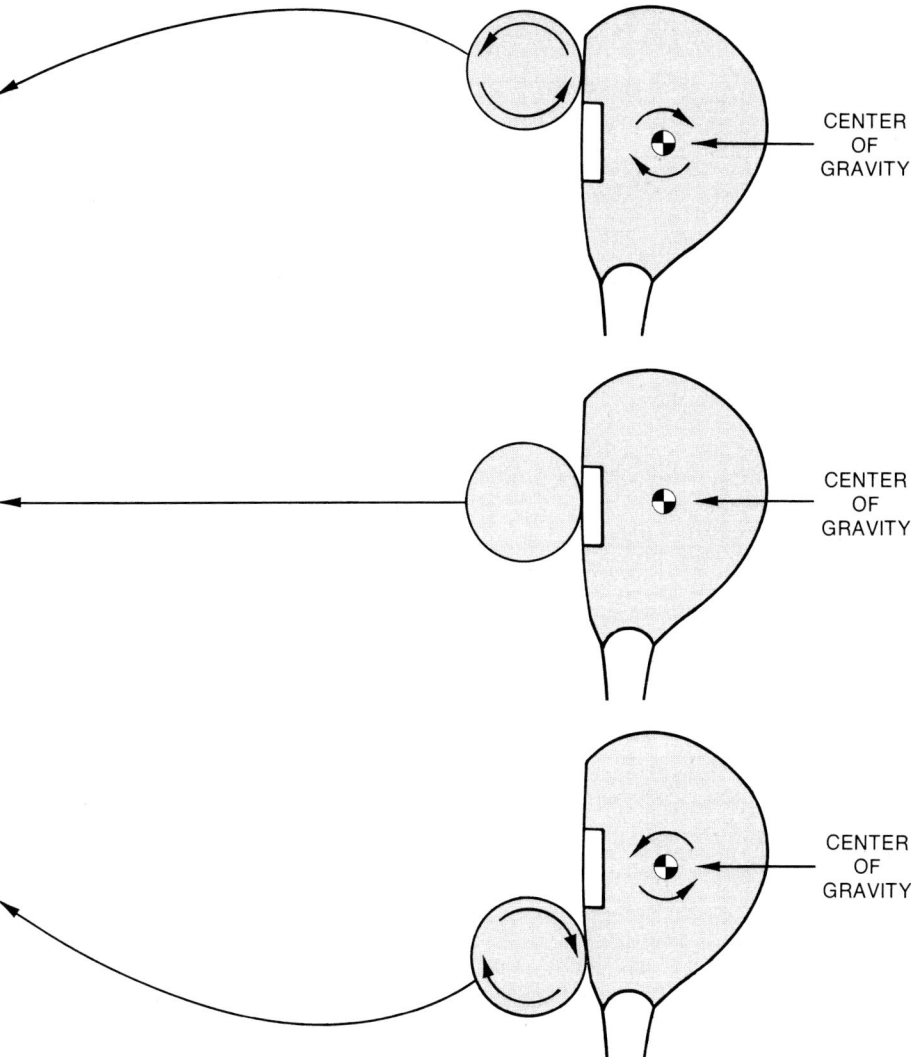

On off-center hits the clubhead is rotated about its center of gravity causing a sideways movement of point of contact. This imparts sidespin to the ball which would normally cause an undesirable hooking or slicing effect. Horizontal face bulge is the built-in correction factor which compensates for this undesirable hooking and slicing sidespin by intentionally starting the ball farther out to the right on toe shots or left on heel shots. This allows the hooking or slicing spin to bring the ball back toward the intended line of flight or target.

Figure 40-2
The correction factor of face bulge on off-center hits

The most important thing to understand about horizontal face bulge is how it works and what factor determines just how much bulge a wood needs. First, how it works. See Figure 40-2. This figure explains the basic principle of bulge. It takes a few more drawings, however, to make this even more understandable. Notice that in all 3 ball impact positions (toe, center, heel) it is assumed that the clubface is square at impact and the clubhead path is square to the target. Glance for a moment to Figure 40-3 for a definition of this.

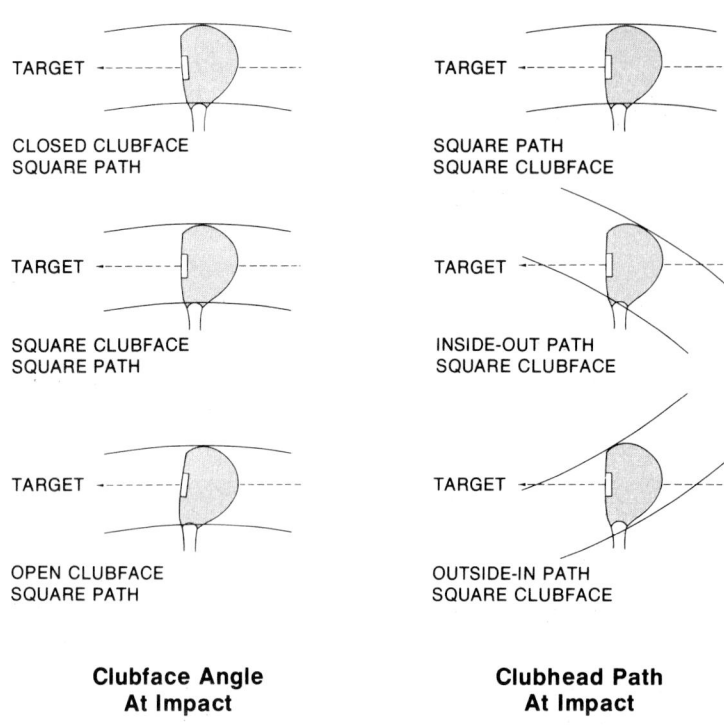

TARGET
CLOSED CLUBFACE
SQUARE PATH

TARGET
SQUARE PATH
SQUARE CLUBFACE

TARGET
SQUARE CLUBFACE
SQUARE PATH

TARGET
INSIDE-OUT PATH
SQUARE CLUBFACE

TARGET
OPEN CLUBFACE
SQUARE PATH

TARGET
OUTSIDE-IN PATH
SQUARE CLUBFACE

**Clubface Angle
At Impact**

**Clubhead Path
At Impact**

Figure 40-3
Defining clubface angle and clubhead path at impact

The reason for making these assumptions is to eliminate the many combinations of path and face angle, thus removing them as an additional factor and to concentrate on how bulge and the clubhead's center of gravity affect ball flight and spin. Look at the top illustration in Figure 40-2. The ball is struck on the toe of the clubface. At this point of ball contact the toe portion of the face is actually open because of the bulge so the initial ball direction will be started right of the target. But when the ball was hit on the toe, the force of impact knocked the toe back and allowed the heel to come forward of it. This rotating or twisting of the clubhead was around its center of mass or center of gravity. The rotating effect of the clubhead on a toe shot causes the point of ball contact on the clubface to move across the ball, imparting a counterclockwise hooking sidespin. The horizontal bulge acted as a correction or compensation factor by starting the ball right of the target to allow for the hooking effect of counterclockwise ball sidespin.

Next, study Figure 40-4. This drawing shows the effect of clubface sideways movement across the ball at impact on off-center hits. The farther back the center of gravity, the greater the radius (not bulge radius) from the center of gravity to the point of impact, hence greater sideways movement of the point of contact across the ball.

Look at the bottom drawing in Figure 40-4. The center of gravity shown here is very close to the face as it would be in an iron. Notice that there is slight if any sideways movement of the clubface across the ball. Very little sideways movement causes very little ball sidespin on toe or heel shots. So, if too much bulge is put on the face, the ball will be started on the right on a toe shot and keep on going right without enough, if any, hook to bring it back. This is exactly why irons do not have

440

any bulge. If they did, directional control problems would result on off-center hits. The U.S.G.A. permits bulge on all metal clubs, including irons, but to manufacture an iron with bulge would be a mistake, unless it was extremely broad with a rearward center of gravity.

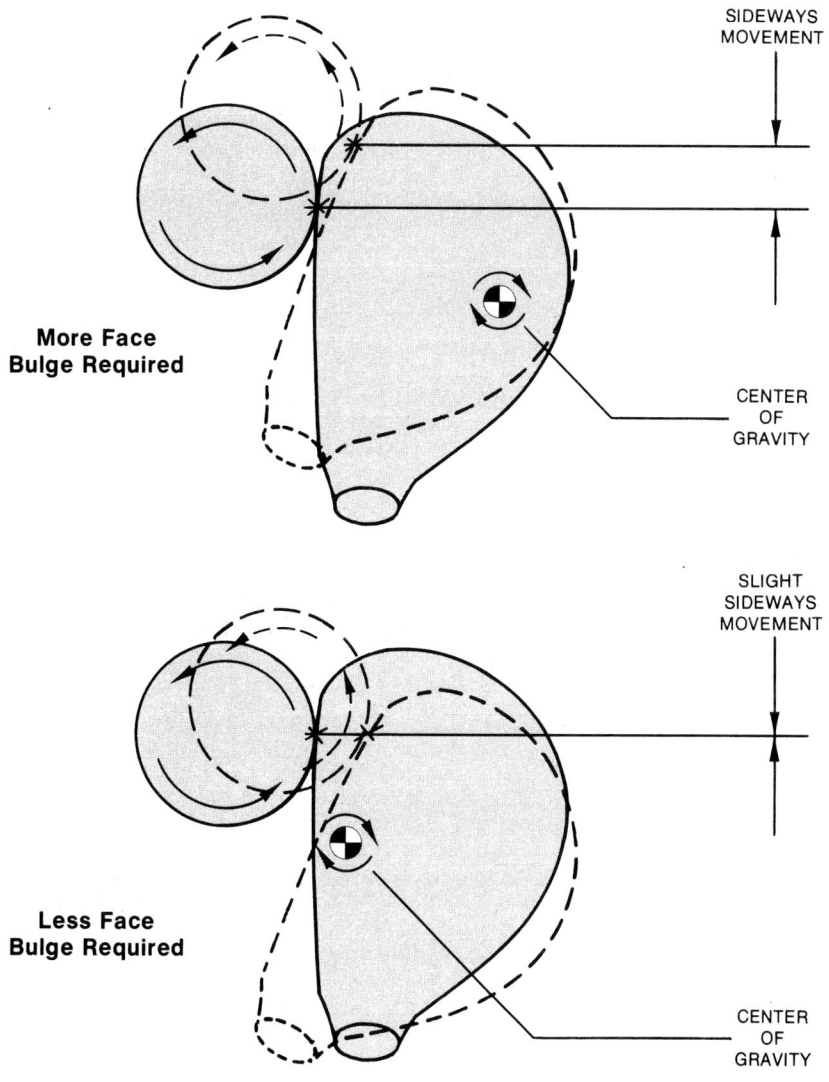

The amount of hooking or slicing spin imparted to a golf ball on off-center hits is determined by the sideways movement of point of contact across the ball as the clubhead is rotated about its center of gravity.

RESULT: The farther back the center of gravity is from the face, the more sideways movement will occur on toe shots, thus imparting more hooking spin (slice on heel shots) and requiring more horizontal face bulge to compensate. Conversely, the closer the center of gravity is to the face a lesser amount of sideways movement will occur on toe shots, thus imparting less hooking spin (slice on heel shots) and requiring less horizontal face bulge to compensate.

Figure 40-4
The center of gravity's effect on horizontal face bulge

During the previous discussion we have referred a number of times to the sideways movement of the clubface across the ball on off-center hits causing ball sidespin. During lectures I have had a few blank stares in attempting to explain how this sideways movement causes the ball to spin the way it does; in particular spinning the opposite direction of clubface movement. A good explanation is to refer to this as the "gear effect." See Figure 40-5. If the clubface and ball both had teeth, as would be the case with two gears meshed together, then rotation of one gear in a certain direction would cause the other gear to rotate in the opposite direction.

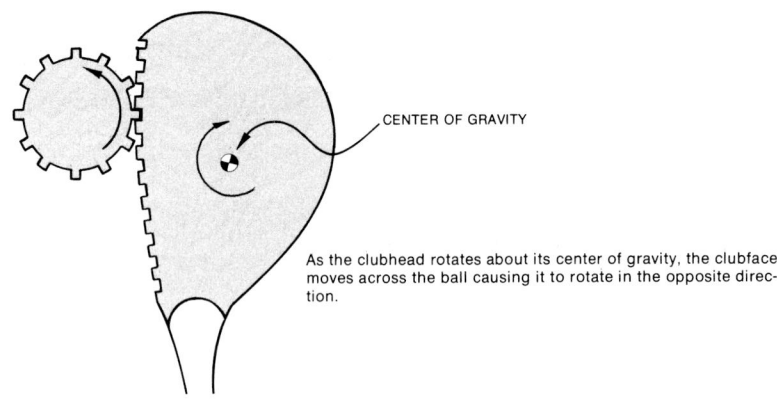

CENTER OF GRAVITY

As the clubhead rotates about its center of gravity, the clubface moves across the ball causing it to rotate in the opposite direction.

Figure 40-5
The "gear effect" during impact on off-center hits

It was mentioned earlier that the proper amount of horizontal face bulge is dependent on the clubhead's center of gravity location from front to back. A question which often arises concerning this is what happens if a club has too much bulge or too little bulge. The answer is nothing as long as the ball is always hit in the center of the clubface. But, on off-center hits the results will cause directional control problems. See Figure 40-6. Notice in the top drawing that the ball is shown going right of the target and straight. This condition would occur when the "gear effect" and the "slicing effect" negate each other. In other words, assuming a square path at impact, the toe of the club is severely radiused making it very open so a slicing spin would normally be imparted to it. However, on toe hits the "gear effect" would, as mentioned, negate this slice spin. If the bulge radius is curved more than that shown in the top drawing, then the ball could be expected to be pushed right but would also slice. Conversely, if the bulge radius is made in between that of the top drawing and middle drawing, the ball could be expected to start right and curve back towards the target but not as effectively as shown in the "correct bulge" drawing.

Next, look at Figure 40-7. The results of off-center impact when compared to Figure 40-6 are basically the same, but notice that the bulge is constant and the center of gravity locations have been changed. Also glance back at Figure 40-4 for further explanation.

The point to make here is the important relationship that exists between a wood head's center of gravity and the amount of horizontal face bulge on ball directional control only on off-center hits. This is why metal woods do not normally require as much bulge as conventional woods. Compared to a conventional wood, a metal wood's center of gravity is closer to the face. Therefore, the metal wood's face is relatively flatter. This also explains why some golfers claim that they hit their metal driver straighter than their old wood driver. The toed shot coming off the face of their old wood driver would have had a much more drastic "hook" as compared to a toed shot from their metal driver. A ball coming off the toe or heel of the metal driver will have less sidespin and will therefore not require as much bulge to send the ball off to the right or left.

442

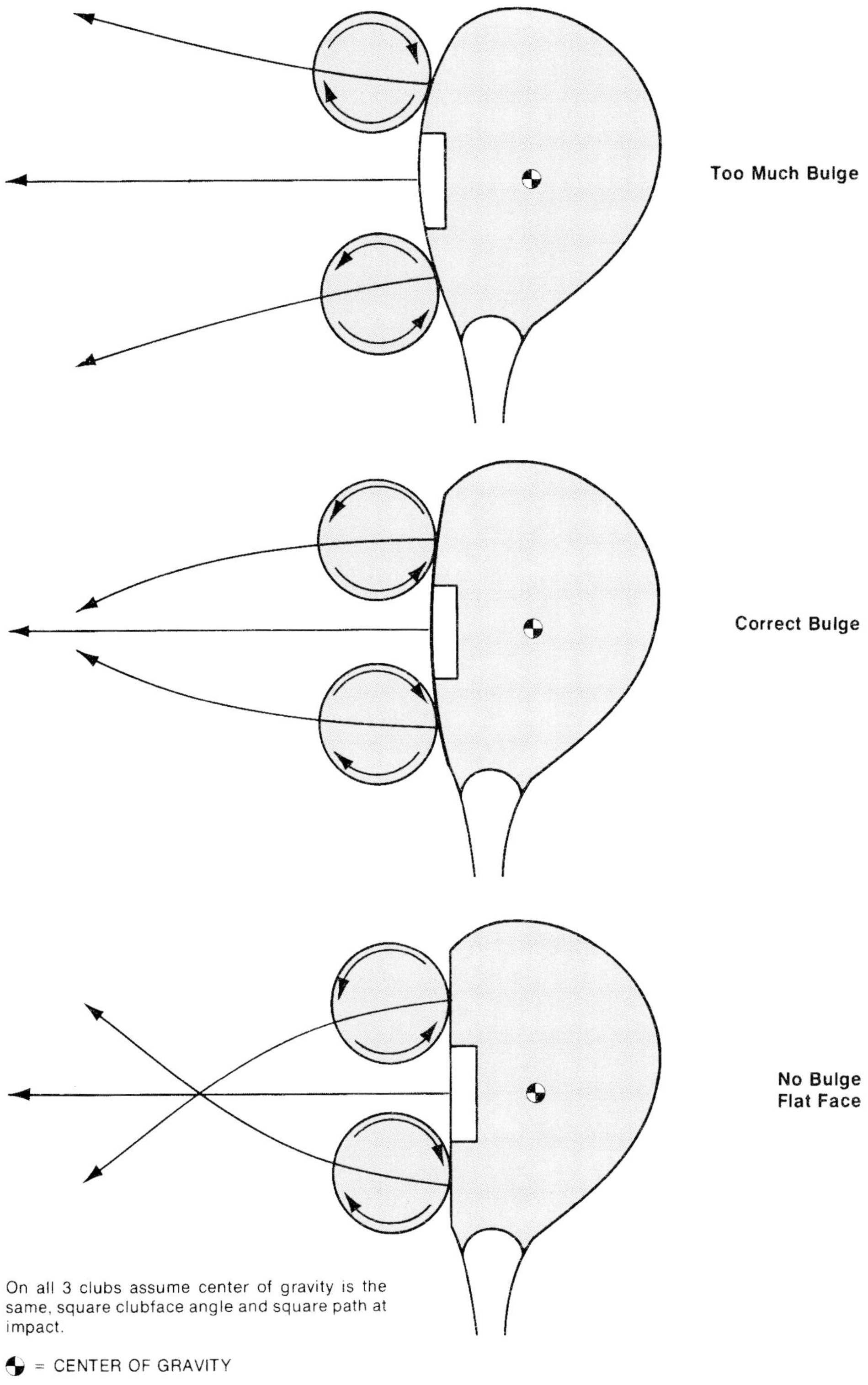
Too Much Bulge
Correct Bulge
No Bulge
Flat Face
On all 3 clubs assume center of gravity is the same, square clubface angle and square path at impact.
= CENTER OF GRAVITY

Figure 40-6
The effect of proper and improper bulge with constant center of gravity

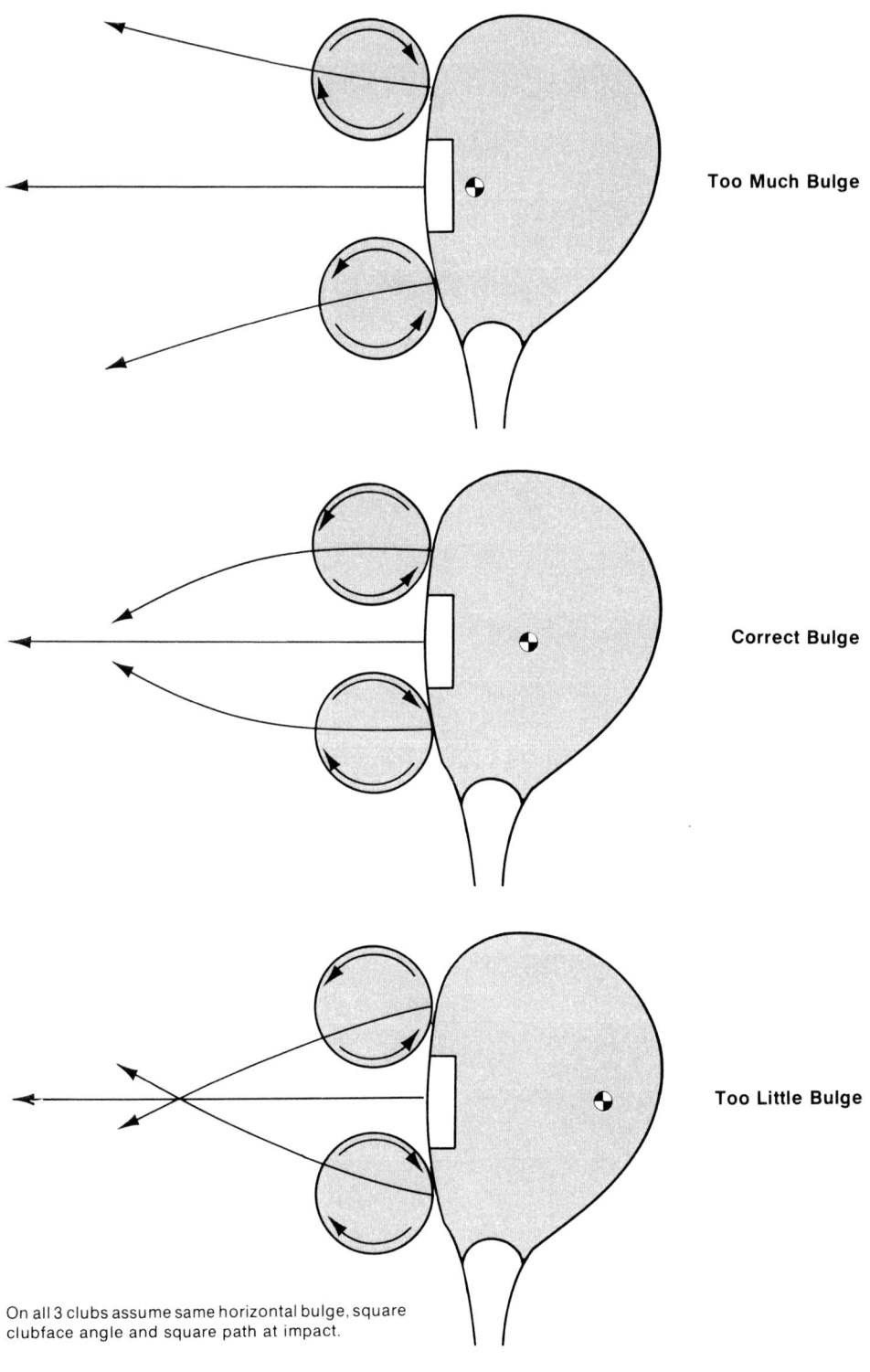

On all 3 clubs assume same horizontal bulge, square
clubface angle and square path at impact.

🌓 = CENTER OF GRAVITY

Figure 40-7
The effect of proper and improper bulge
with variable center of gravity

The following sequence photograph taken in the 1940's at the Spalding company in Chicopee, Massachusetts shows the initial counterclockwise sidespin put on the ball by an off-center toe hit using a flat faced club. See Figure 40-8. The duration of time from the first photo to the fourth is eight ten-thousandths of a second ($8/10,000$ths). A golf ball is usually only touching the face of a club for $5/10,000$ths second and as you can see by photo #4 the ball has already left the face. Both the ball and club have moved forward about $7/8$", the clubhead toe has rotated open approximately $4°$ and the ball has rotated counterclockwise approximately $4°$.

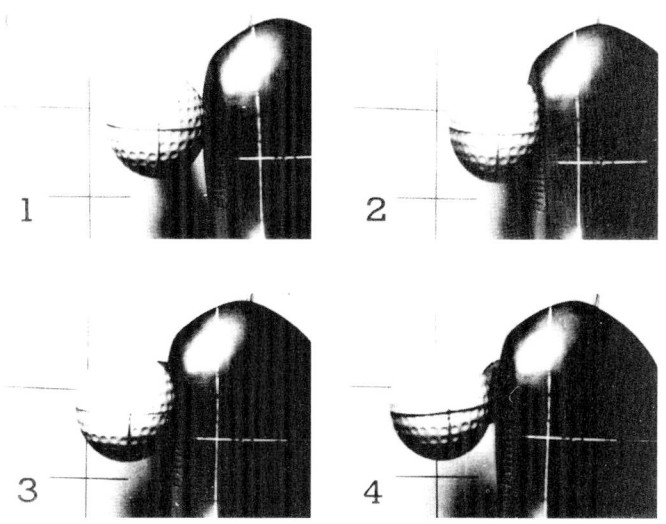

40-8
Toe shot impact sequence. Duration of time: eight ten-thousandths of a second.

Determining how much horizontal bulge to put on a face is somewhat involved with the absolute best method being to make up sample clubs and hit toe and heel shots using a mechanical golfer such as the one True Temper® developed and currently is in use by most of the major golf club companies as well as by the U.S.G.A. This is the method I have used in the past to substantiate calculations from a formula based on the distance from the face to the center of gravity along a horizontal plane. For those interested, both the formula for bulge radius and the definition of "horizontal plane of center of gravity" are shown in Figure 40-9. The reader should be cautioned that there are still other factors involved which mostly relate to the complex dynamics of impact making the formula a good starting point with the ultimate proof existing only in controlled machine testing or by using a powerful computer with sophisticated software that can duplicate the effect of ball impact. See Appendix 2 for more information on such a system used by the shaft manufacturer True Temper®.

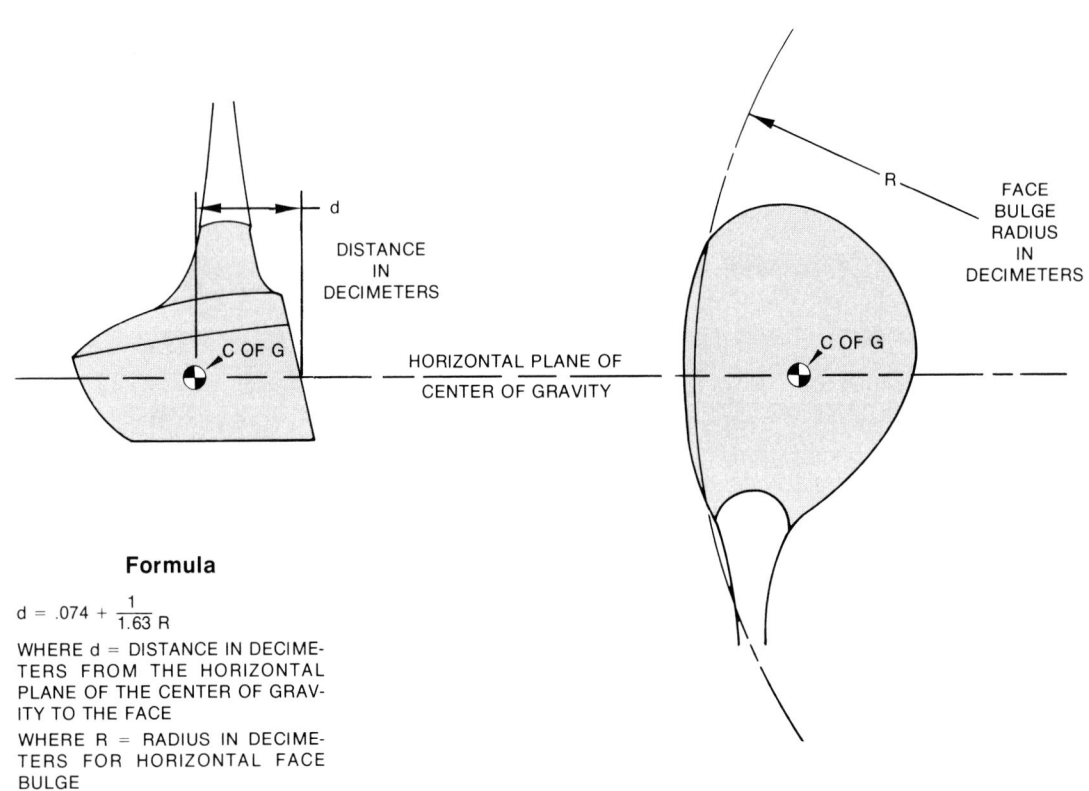

Formula

$$d = .074 + \frac{1}{1.63} R$$

WHERE d = DISTANCE IN DECIMETERS FROM THE HORIZONTAL PLANE OF THE CENTER OF GRAVITY TO THE FACE

WHERE R = RADIUS IN DECIMETERS FOR HORIZONTAL FACE BULGE

Figure 40-9
Formula and explanation for calculating face bulge radius

446

Table 40-1 has been developed to give general guidelines for determining bulge. It is interesting to note that on a driver the approximate center of gravity movement in the clubhead comparing a centerweighted to a backweighted wood is $\frac{3}{16}$" to $\frac{1}{4}$". This of course assumes two identical model wood heads that were of the same weight and density in their raw state.

TABLE 40-1
Horizontal Face Bulge — Wood Clubs

Club No.	[1]Center Weighted Clubs	[2]Fore Weighted Clubs	[3]Back Weighted Clubs
1	10" R.	11" R.	8" or 9" R.
2	12" R.	13" R.	10" or 11" R.
3	12" R.	13" R.	10" or 11" R.
4	12" R.	13" R.	10" or 11" R.
5	14" R.	15" R.	12" or 13" R.
6	14" R.	15" R.	12" or 13" R.
7	16" R.	17" R.	14" or 15" R.

Center Weighted   Fore Weighted   Back Weighted

⊕ = CENTER OF GRAVITY

[1] Center weighted clubs are weighted under the soleplate in the approximate middle of the clubhead. Drivers with an empty weight hole to reduce clubhead weight or no hole, since weight was not required are still considered center weighted as this will usually only change the center of gravity in the up and down plane and not from face to back as discussed in this table.

[2] Fore weighted clubs are either weighted in or behind the insert or use heavy inserts such as steel, brass or Gamma-Fire™. Also, foreweighted clubs sometimes have the weight hole under the soleplate drilled closer to the face.

[3] Backweighted clubs usually have less or no weight under the sole. The additional head weight is added to the back of the wood either as a brass backweight or a recessed lead backweight. Be cautioned that small recessed lead backweights or woods that are also weighted with heavy inserts should still probably be considered as center weighted.

CHAPTER 41

GOLF WOOD CLUB DESIGN: VERTICAL FACE ROLL

Performance Characteristic of Roll

A factor which directly affects loft in the vertical plane on the clubface (i.e., a ball hit high on the face will fly higher due to increased loft, a ball hit low on the face will fly lower due to decreased loft). See Figure 41-2.

Definition of Roll

The vertical radius roll of the face is measured from the top of the face to the bottom of the face in a vertical position and is the same along the face from heel to toe. See Figure 41-1.

Other Specifications Which Affect Roll

None.

Discussion of Roll

Vertical face roll has a direct relationship in a wood club to a golf ball's trajectory. Since most woods have vertical roll, the higher up the face a

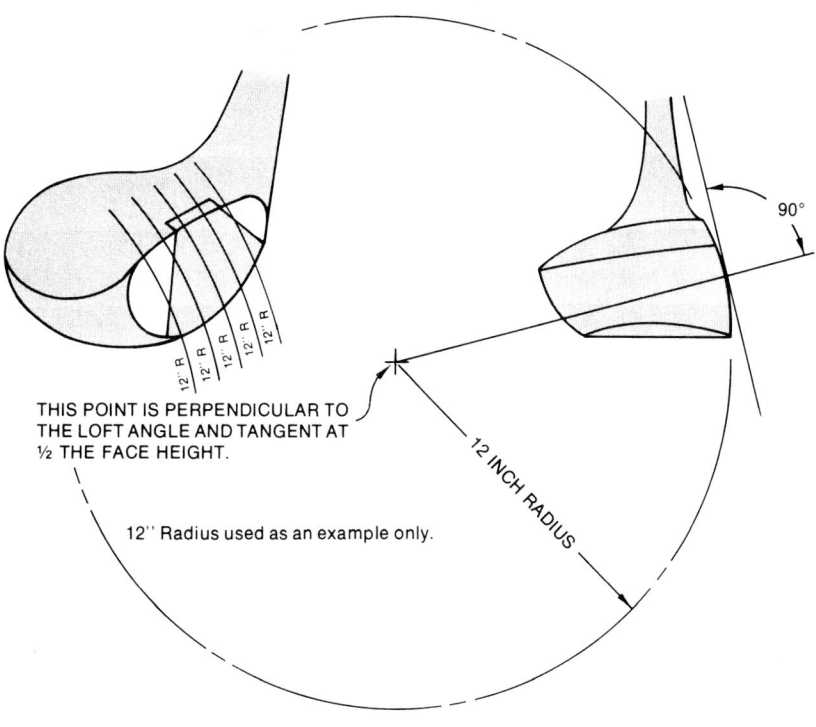

THIS POINT IS PERPENDICULAR TO
THE LOFT ANGLE AND TANGENT AT
½ THE FACE HEIGHT.

12'' Radius used as an example only.

12 INCH RADIUS

90°

12" R 12" R 12" R 12" R

Figure 41-1
Definition of vertical face roll

ball is struck the higher it will go. See Figure 41-2. The only point on the face of a wood that has the specified loft angle is a point exactly at ½ its vertical height.

Roll has an interesting history regarding wood design. It seems that when club designers found out the horizontal bulge radius really worked and most did not know why, they must have figured that the face of a club would be even better if it had some radius roll in the vertical direction also. Since that time many advertisements and catalog copy have included the words "four way face roll." Ask anyone knowledgeable in club design what roll actually does and the answer can be everything from a blank stare to a dissertation on how to orbit the club around the moon. Vertical face roll actually does the wrong thing at most vertical impact locations. It increases the trajectory of the shot on high hits and decreases the trajectory on low face hits. The main factor controlling trajectory on high and low face hits is the clubhead's center of gravity. Think about it. If a ball is struck low on the clubface, why do we want to reduce the loft even more by putting roll on the face? For the most part, we can not do anything about a low struck shot that is hit with the clubhead's center of gravity above that of the ball's which lowers trajectory, but we can reduce or eliminate roll to help correct the problem.

The biggest problem that I see is clubs made or refaced with excessive roll. We get clubs in our repair department, both old and new, where it is not uncommon to find fairways woods with 6", 7" or 8" radius vertical face roll. This is very excessive and definitely a hindrance to proper playability. We have even found some metal woods that have been designed with excessive vertical roll, demonstrating that the manufacturer did not realize the negative impact of that design feature. The problem with eliminating roll completely and making the face flat vertically is the appearance of a much stronger lofted club. It is not too bad on a fairway wood but a driver with a flat vertical face appears 1° to 2° stronger and this bothers some players who are used to a certain look. Remember, the mental part of golf on how a player perceives a certain club is very important. Wood and metal wood heads that are designed and/or manufactured by my own company all have vertical roll; however, it is reduced significantly. The woods I play with have the roll removed.

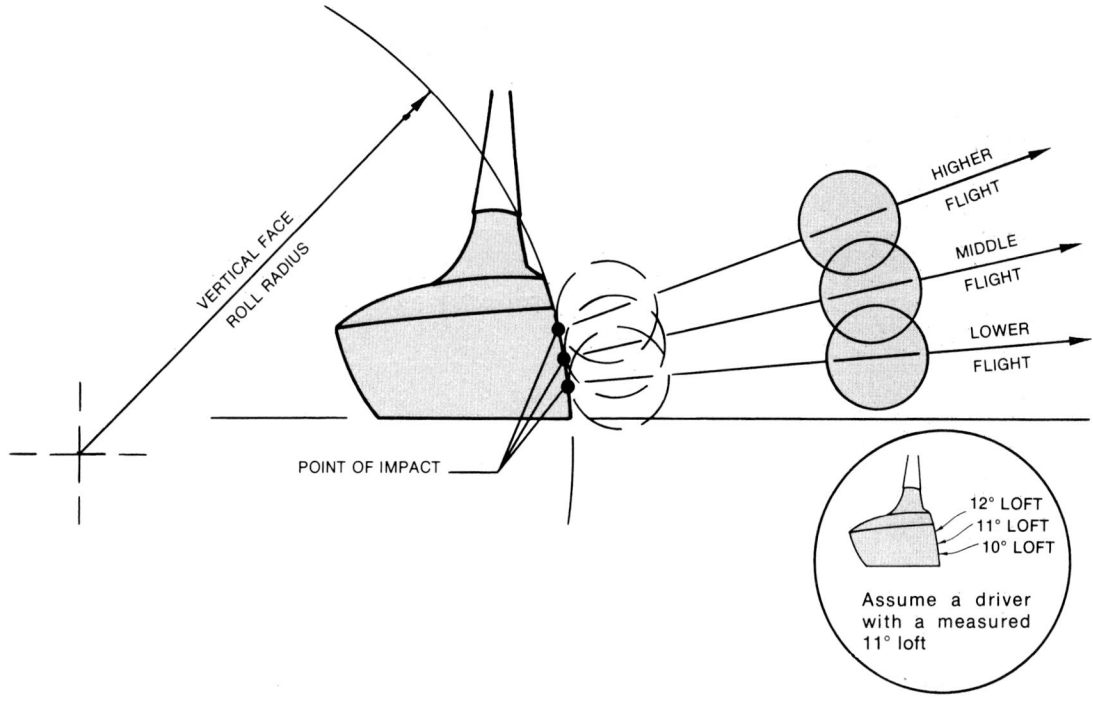

Figure 41-2
Effect of vertical face roll on loft

The following table gives the vertical face roll radiuses by club number that I recommend if some roll is desirable to obtain a traditionally accepted look. Roll can also be eliminated if desired.

TABLE 41-1
Vertical Face Roll-Wood Clubs

Club No.	Roll
1	12" Radius
2	14" Radius
3	14" Radius
4	14" Radius
5	16" Radius
6	16" Radius
7	18" Radius

CHAPTER 42

GOLF WOOD CLUB DESIGN: SOLE RADIUS AND SOLE WIDTH

Performance Characteristic of Sole Radius and Sole Width

Sole radius and sole width can have a controlling influence on the amount of ground drag and bounce through impact with the ball.

Definition of Sole Radius and Sole Width

Sole radius is the curve of the club sole in the heel to the toe direction. A golf wood club can also have a 4 way radius which includes a radius from face to back. See Figure 42-1. Sole width is that distance from the front of the face at its center to the farthest rear portion of the sole on the groundline. See Figure 42-2.

Other Specifications Which Affect Sole Radius and Sole Width

None.

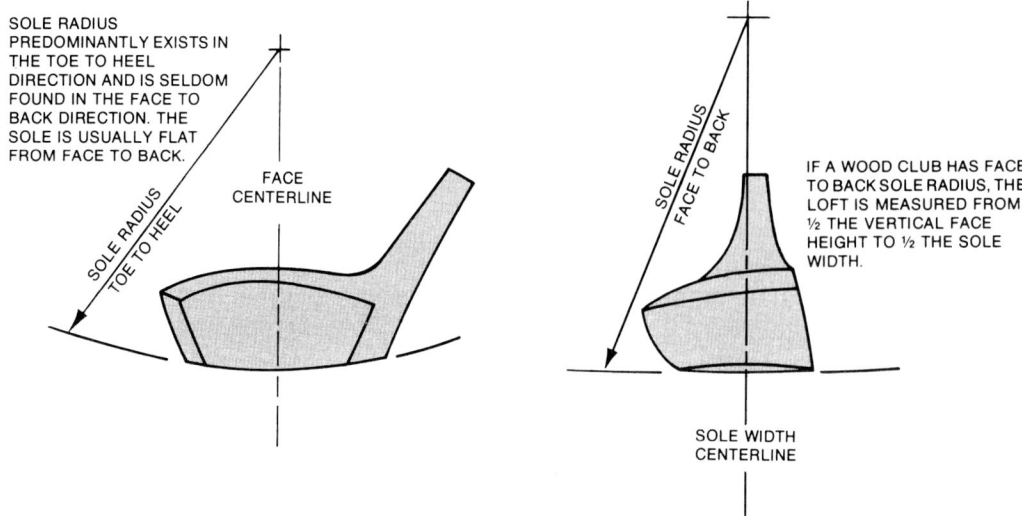

Figure 42-1
Definition of sole radius

SOLE RADIUS PREDOMINANTLY EXISTS IN THE TOE TO HEEL DIRECTION AND IS SELDOM FOUND IN THE FACE TO BACK DIRECTION. THE SOLE IS USUALLY FLAT FROM FACE TO BACK.

FACE CENTERLINE

SOLE RADIUS TOE TO HEEL

SOLE RADIUS FACE TO BACK

IF A WOOD CLUB HAS FACE TO BACK SOLE RADIUS, THE LOFT IS MEASURED FROM ½ THE VERTICAL FACE HEIGHT TO ½ THE SOLE WIDTH.

SOLE WIDTH CENTERLINE

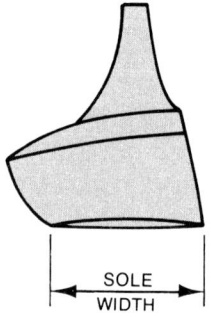

SOLE WIDTH

Figure 42-2
Definition of sole width

Discussion of Sole Radius

The sole radius from toe to heel is put on a wood club for two basic reasons. The first is that it allows for a variation in lie positions during play while still keeping the clubhead as low to the ground as possible. Assume that you are attempting to hit a fairway wood shot with the ball on an uphill lie above your feet. If the wood club has a flat sole from toe to heel, the clubhead would be sitting higher above the ball making it very difficult to hit a solid shot. See Figure 42-3. The second reason for sole radius is less resistance to ground drag coming into or at impact.

452

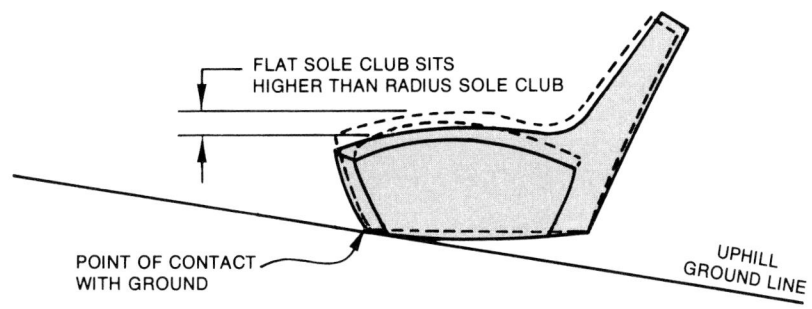

Figure 42-3
Effect of uphill (shown) and downhill lies with flat and radius soles

A club with a flat sole will have a tendency to have greater drag than a club with a radius sole if the ground is hit during or before impact since more of the sole is exposed to the ground at point of impact. It would probably be safe to say that the resultant hit from a fat shot will go farther with a radius soled club than with a flat soled club. See Figure 42-4.

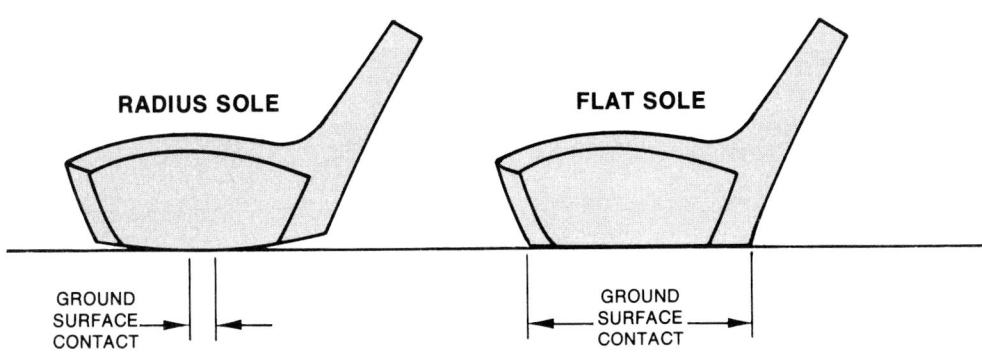

Figure 42-4
Comparison of radius and flat soles with ground surface contact

The amount of sole radius on a wood club varies with each manufacturer. Wood clubs have been produced with sole radius of 3" to 10" with the most common being a 5", 6" or 7" radius. Figure 42-5 shows each radius full scale from 3" to 10". This gives a better visual understanding showing the range from one extreme to the other.

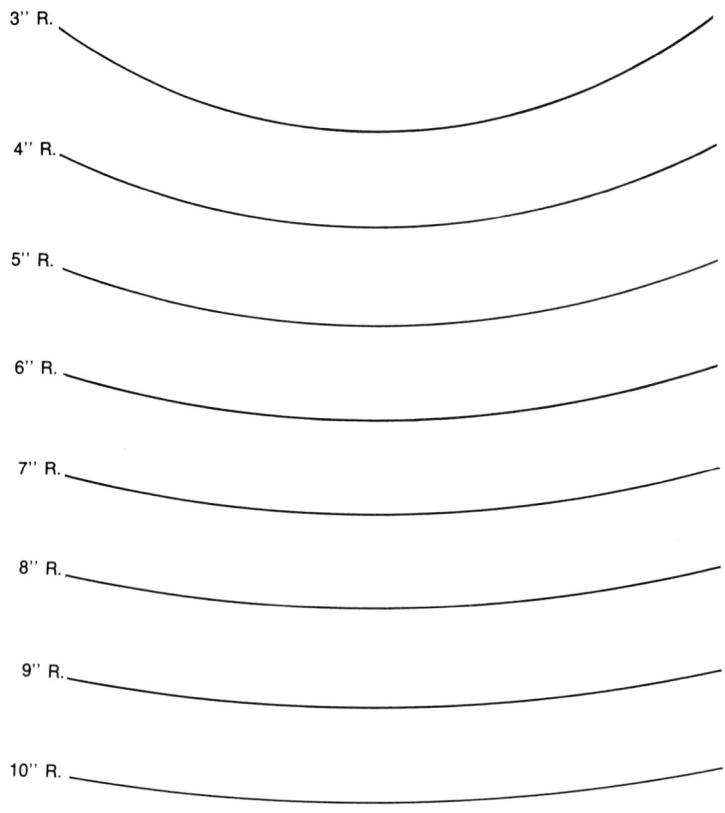

Figure 42-5
Full scale comparison of various sole radius.
5", 6" and 7" radius are the most common

Discussion of Sole Width

Take any fairway wood and set it down on a hard surface in the playing position. Now, roll the face of the club open, pretending for a moment that you intend to put some fancy cut shot swing on it. Notice that the leading edge of the sole had raised itself from the ground and the only part of the sole that is touching the ground is the extreme rear portion. This is called "sole bounce." This is a more familiar term when discussing iron clubs and in particular sand clubs, but recognize that it also exists in woods. The narrower the width of the sole, the less the leading edge will raise off the ground when rolling the face open by the same amount. Also, when the clubhead is coming into impact, the head is bowed slightly in front of the shaft. Depending on the golfer's hand position either forward, in line or rearward of the head; the sole bounce could be accentuated, thus causing thin hits. The point to make here is to avoid making the width of the sole excessive. A wood club, in particular a fairway wood, should be more playable if the sole width is on the narrow side.

When I was working at Faultless during the mid 1970's, I developed a wood called the "tunnel sole." The advertising and promotional copy on this concept mostly expounded on the tunnel reducing air drag and consequently producing greater clubhead speed with the same swing effort. Tests on True Tempers® Mechanical Golfer did in fact substantiate an increase in clubhead speed, with the tunnel sole driver versus a conventional sole. After the machine testing, I did extensive player testing with amateurs and professionals. The most important

454

characteristic that was discovered was the ease with which the fairway woods could be played. They could dig balls out of virtually any cuppy lie, and player responses indicated that with tighter lies at least one more club could be played. The reason for all the positive response was the very narrow sole width at the face center caused by the tunnel design. Sole bouncing was almost eliminated. Look at Figure 42-6 for a comparison of a conventional and a "tunnel sole" #3 wood which are both rolled open approximately 3°.

Sole radius and sole width are two design specifications which are often overlooked, but as you now realize, should be important considerations.

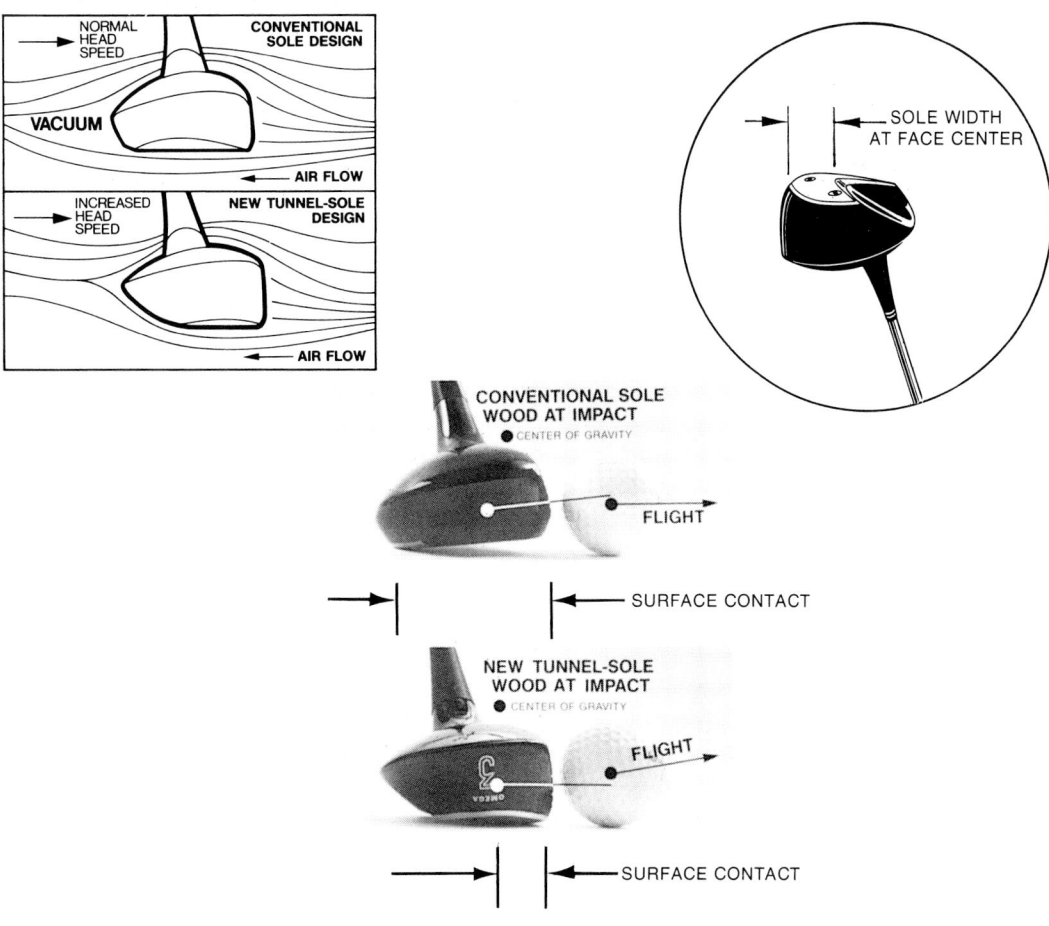

Figure 42-6
Effect of sole width on sole bounce

CHAPTER 43

GOLF WOOD CLUB DESIGN: CENTER OF GRAVITY

Performance Characteristics of Center of Gravity

A factor affecting the solidness of feel, trajectory and distance at impact between the clubhead and the golf ball. See Figure 43-2.

Definition of Center of Gravity

A point inside the clubhead determined by the vertical intersection of two or more points where the wood head balances. See Figure 43-1.

Other Specifications Which Affect Center of Gravity

Wood head shape, size and density.
Backweighting, size, location and material type.
Soleplate size, thickness and material type.
Insert size, thickness and material type.
Added tare weight, location size and material type. See Figure 43-4 and 43-5.

Discussion of Center of Gravity

The term "Center of Gravity" is usually referred to as "Center of Mass" in the scientific world. Since this term is important to understanding golf club performance it should be defined more precisely and explained more thoroughly.

When a rigid body, such as a golf wood head, is suspended by a single string, it can be observed that the string is hanging vertically. The forces of gravity on all particles of the wood head act vertically downward and have no horizontal components.

The wood head suspended by a single string assumes an orientation in which it is said to be in equilibrium. When a point of attachment of the string is changed, the hanging wood head assumes another equilibrium orientation. If the vertically hanging string could be extended straight through the wood head in each of its different points of attachment or equilibrium positions, all of the strings would be found to intersect at a common single point within the head. This common point is called the center of mass or center of gravity.

The center of gravity of an object is a point fixed relative to the object but not necessarily inside it. For example, the center of gravity of a completely assembled golf club lies outside the club. On a 43" driver it is about 12" from the sole, up the shaft and a few inches outside of the shaft. However, the components, such as the head, shaft, and grip have their individual centers of gravity inside. A golf ball is a symmetrical object, so its center of gravity is at the ball's geometrical center.

When discussing golf club performance we have to look at a wood head's center of gravity as a point located in various planes. Specifically, how high up the face is it located, is it in the face center from heel to toe and how far back is it from the face within the head? This is the reason for defining center of gravity as shown in Figure 43-1. Finding the center of gravity is easier using the balance method vs. suspending the head from a string. This will have more meaning in the discussion which follows.

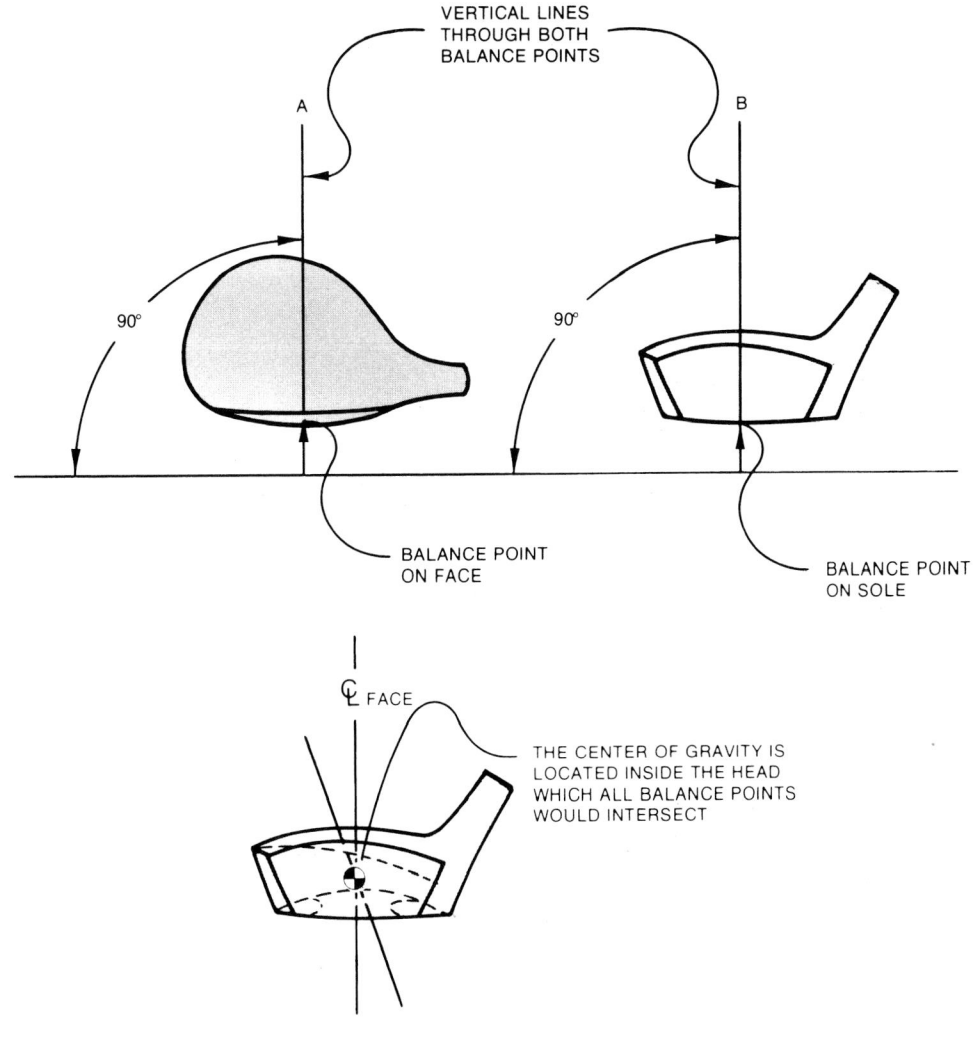

Figure 43-1
Defining wood head center of gravity

A general rule of thumb which pertains to the location of the golf club's center of gravity in the vertical plane is this: the lower the center of gravity the more solid the shot more of the time. This of course assumes that impact takes place at the center of gravity's horizontal location also. See Figure 43-2. If the center of gravity of the club-head is above that of the ball, it will produce a more unsolid shot which will tend to fly lower with less carry distance. The best example of this is trying to hit a wooden driver from the fairway. The thicker driver head has a much higher center of gravity than the fairway woods making it quite difficult to impact the ball solidly. The lesser loft of the driver compounds the problem of getting fairway shots airborne. Metal woods do not present as much of a problem because the center of gravity on a metal wood is lower than a wood of similar size and shape. In fact, players of above average ability will often use their metal driver as a fairway club. Graphite woods have a center of gravity location similar to conventional woods.

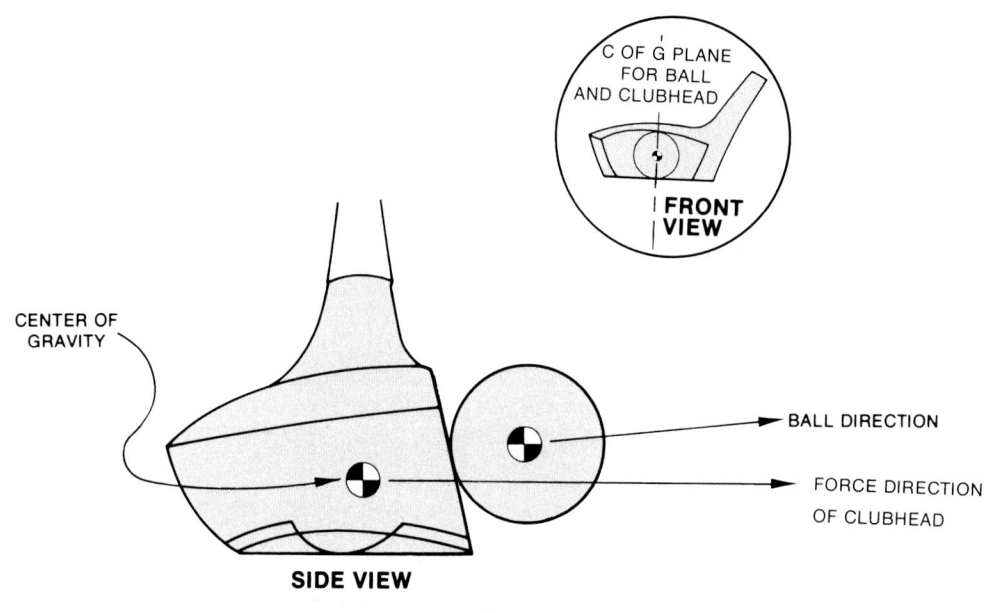

Figure 43-2
**For a solid hit, the clubhead's center of gravity must be
below or in line with the ball's center of gravity**

Another interesting area to look at is the center of gravity's effect on face angle when the club is laid across a table. The face angle being referred to here is not the hook or slice type but the angle of the face plane to vertical. Figure 43-3 shows a comparison of two clubs. One has a center of gravity close to the face and the other has a more rearward center of gravity. I have had a number of letters on this, asking which is the best way to make a club. The answer is either way. If a club is designed and built properly, the specifications which are affected by the center of gravity from face to back will be altered to make it play properly in either case. The horizontal face bulge would be different in both clubs shown in Figure 43-3. The lofts could be adjusted differently, if desired, because the farther rearward the center of gravity, the higher the shot. The two clubs shown in Figure 43-3 are in a static position which has little meaning to the dynamic forces acted upon during the swing. It is, however, a good way to compare two wood clubs to see the approximate center of gravity locations.

458

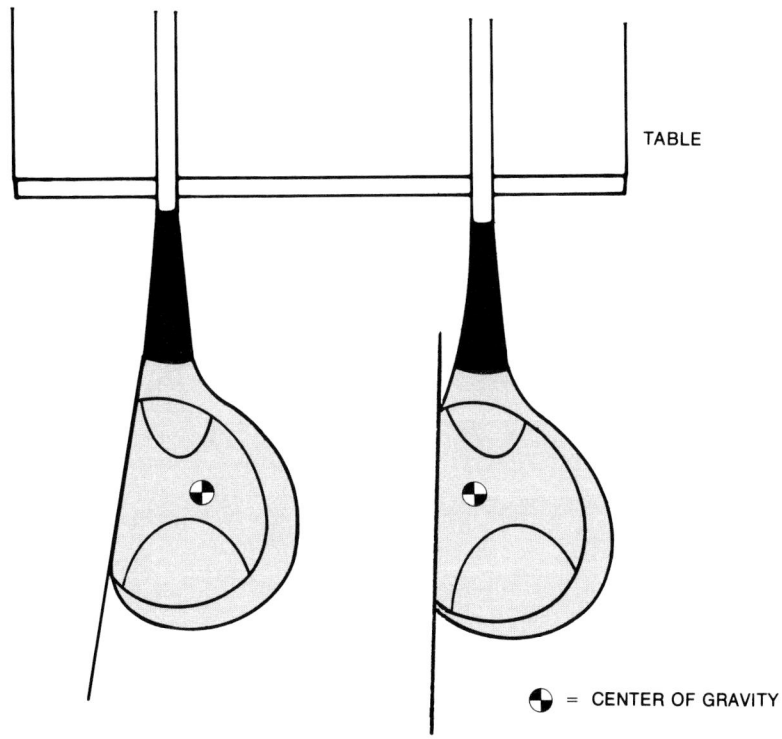

Figure 43-3
The center of gravity's effect on face angle position with the club laid across a table

One of the more abused areas in manufacturing golf clubs is adding weight down the shaft instead of under the soleplate. Weight that is properly added should be placed as low as possible, at the center of the face or equidistant on either side of the face. Adding weight down the shaft has the effect of shifting the clubhead's center of gravity toward the added weight. See Figure 43-4. Next, take a look at Figure 43-5 which shows the center of gravity shift if weight is added properly. The same problem exists with metal woods since the shaft usually penetrates the hosel by only 1½".

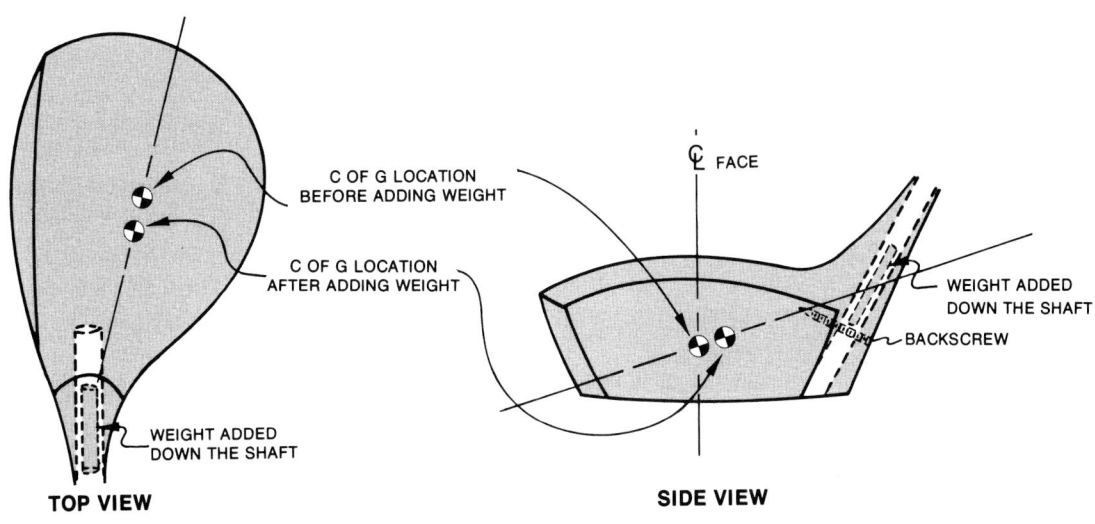

Figure 43-4
Effect of improperly adding weight down the shaft on center of gravity

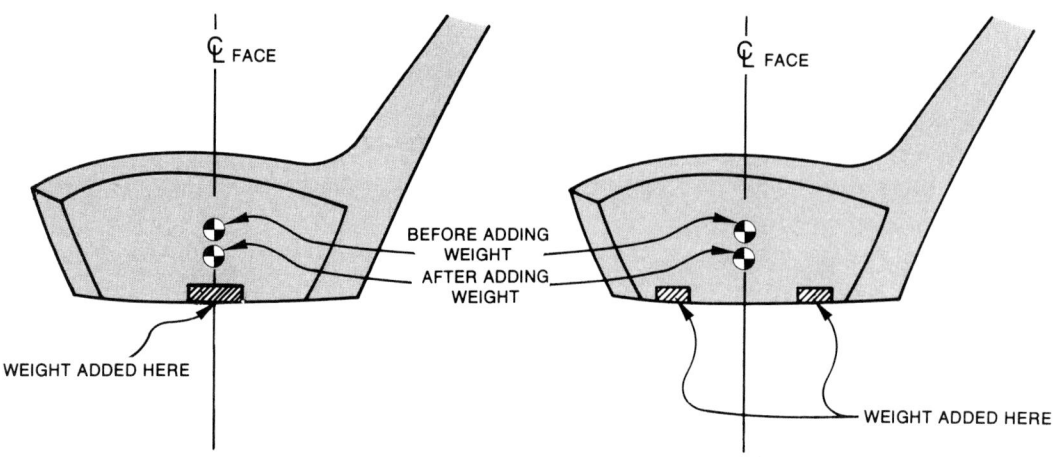

Figure 43-5
Effect of properly adding weight under the soleplate on center of gravity

Therefore, any weight added down the shaft is positioned relatively high in the hosel relative to the head. Metal woods that allow weight to be added into a cylinder directly under the sole are better designs than non-weight ported heads. Also, metal woods that have a set screw that directly accesses the hollow cavity are not very desirable because added weight tends to rattle or loosen the foam that is usually found inside.

The center of gravity's effect on performance and its relationship with other specifications is mentioned throughout the book. It explains away much of the mystery involved in club design. For example, the more recent proliferation of trouble woods which are characterized by having heavy massive cast soleplates with grooves and runners. The reason these clubs work so well is their extremely low centers of gravity caused by the heavier soleplate mass. So you see, most things can be logically explained in club design and resulting performance, but it does take away much of the exciting mystique and glamour created by advertising copy.

460

CHAPTER 44

GOLF WOOD CLUB DESIGN: HOSEL BORING

The single most important aspect of golf wood club manufacture is hosel boring. The most beautiful head shape in the world can easily be ruined if the hosel is not bored properly. Playability can also be affected dramatically since hosel boring controls many important specifications such as face angle, effective or real loft, face progression, shaft progression and lie.

In Chapter 46, **Wood Head Construction and Materials,** it was mentioned that molded ABS plastic and graphite wood heads and investment cast metal heads could be made exact from club to club with particular reference being made to boring. The hosel hole is either "molded in" or "cast in" with these materials, eliminating the need for proper fixturing to drill the bore. Although it is difficult to properly bore a wooden club, its main advantage over plastic heads and metal woods is the clubmaker's latitude in custom boring to arrive at virtually any desired specification. This fact alone will assure a place for the real wood club in the future.

It is necessary that certain terminology be defined and understood before a discussion of hosel boring can continue. Look at Figure 44-1 for a definition of face angle positions.

Hooked, or Closed Face
Square, or Straight Face
Slice, or Open Face

Also note the "front view" and "side view" sketches which define the relationship of sole to face to hosel bore (or shaft centerline).

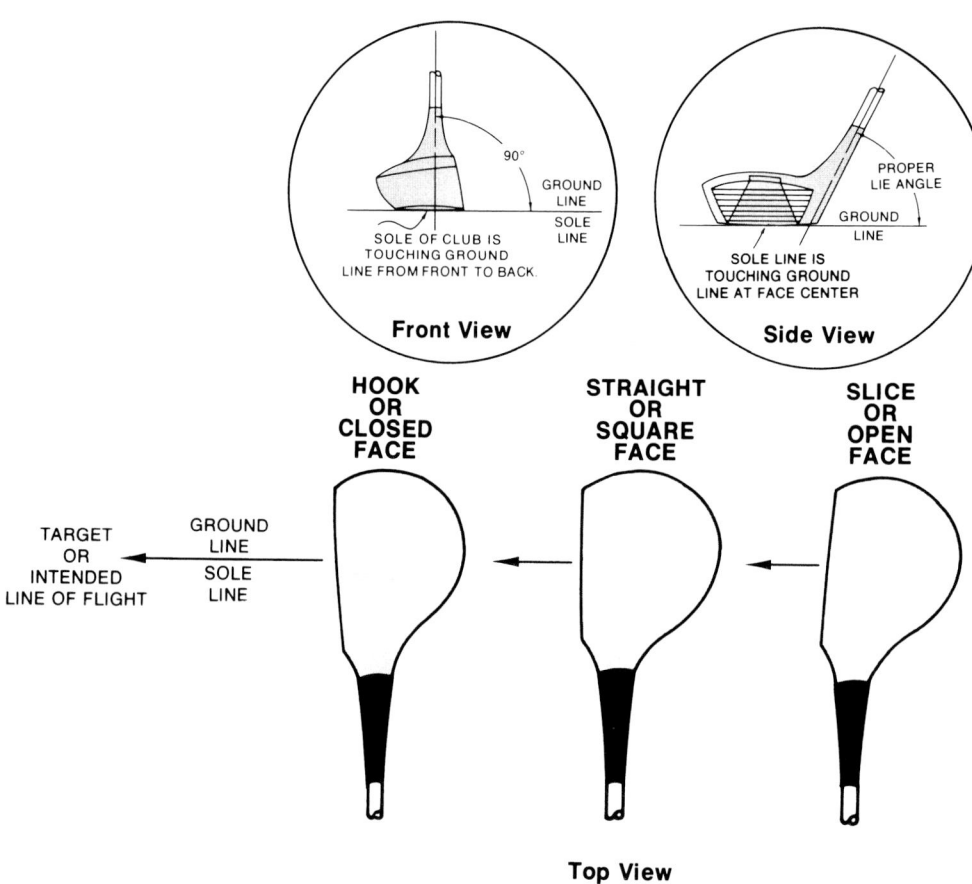

Figure 44-1
Definition of face angle positions

Other definitions that need to be reviewed are lie angle, shaft progression (Figure 44-2) and face progression (Figure 44-3). All of these specifications can be affected during the boring operation. It should now become even more apparent how complex and critical the hosel boring operation is.

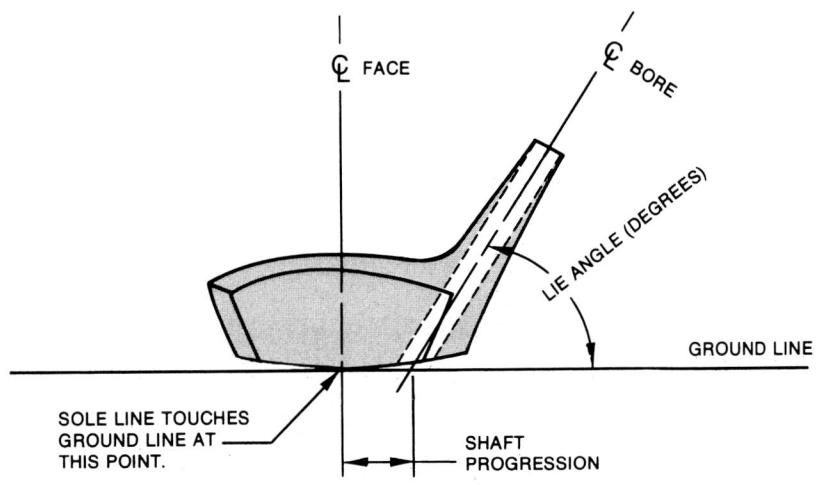

Figure 44-2
Defining lie angle and shaft progression

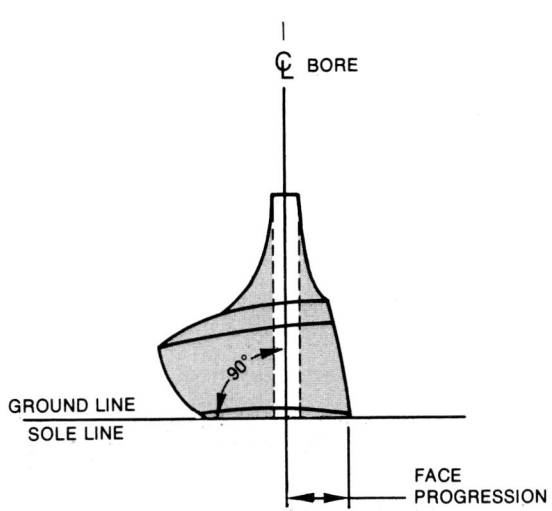

Figure 44-3
Defining face progression

The Boring Methods

There are three boring methods that can be used to derive the different face positions already discussed.

Square Bore/Head Design Method

Variable Boring Method

Combination Boring Method

These methods will be discussed in detail.

■ Square Bore/Head Design Method (Refer to Figure 44-4)

First, study Figure 44-4 thoroughly. Note that the sole line is touching the ground from the front to the back of the head. Note also that it is directed at the intended line of flight and is at a 90°, or right angle to the shaft bore. This relationship applies to all three of the face positions: open, straight and closed. This means that this method of determining a specific face position must be designed into the head master model and cannot be bored in.

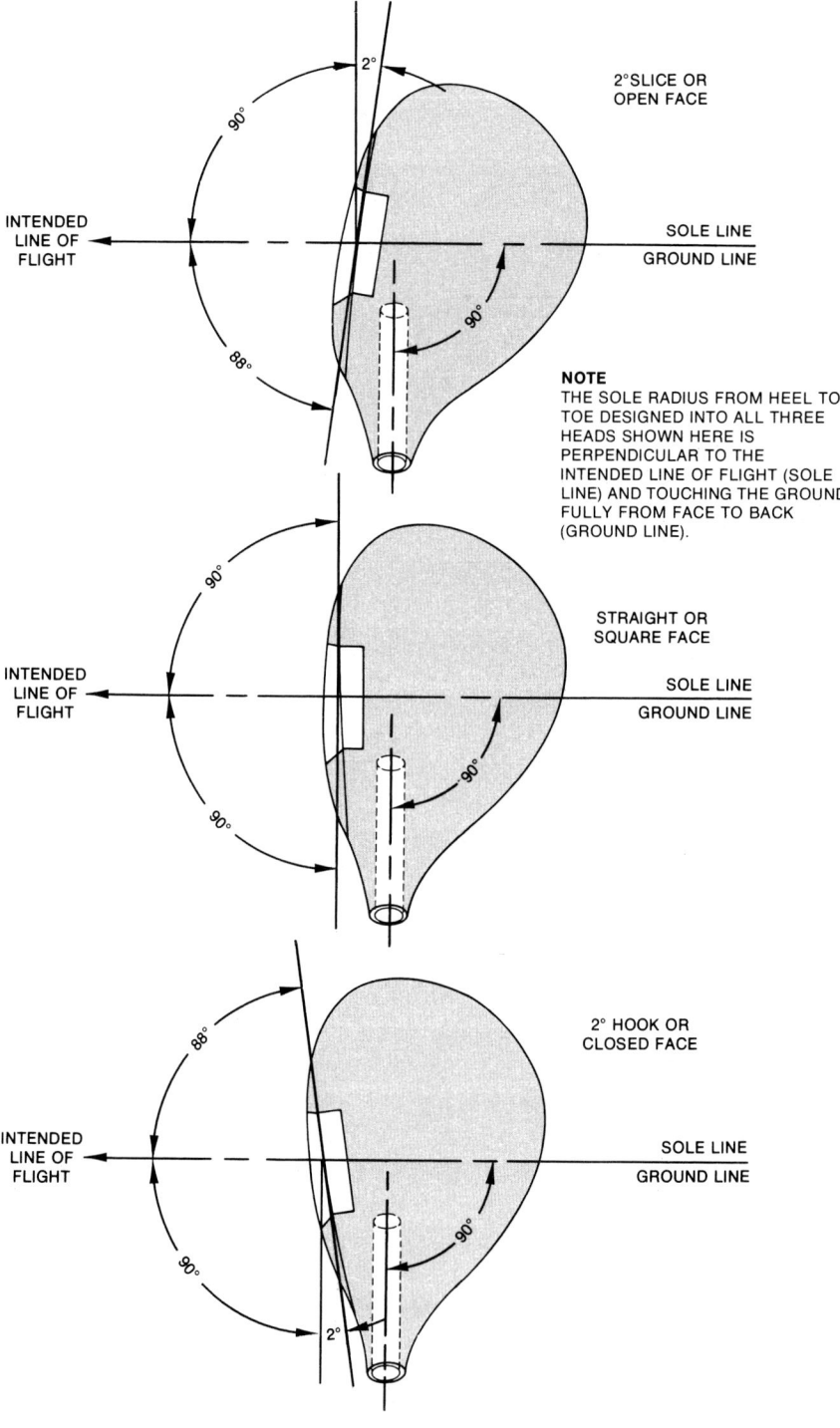

Figure 44-4
Square Bore/Head Design Method of Boring

464

This method gives the manufacturer two main advantages. First, it allows the quality control department to check incoming raw wood turnings for face position even before they are bored. This can save a company much time and expense in correcting the problem before the heads have gone too far in manufacture. Photo 44-5 shows the Golf Club Gauge™ modified to measure heads around the neck before boring. If this method of checking the head indicates that it is within specification and it is then bored exactly square or parallel through the hosel, the readings should be the same when checked on the conventional Golf Club Gauge™ which measures from the bore or shaft centerline as shown in Photo 44-6. Photo 44-7 shows a master model that I made. Notice that the upper two-thirds of the hosel is made from aluminum. It is turned to exactly ¾" diameter. This will allow each turning to be checked in the gauge around the hosel more accurately because the hosel will be perfectly round. I can also check each turning by measuring its neck diameter to make certain the head was not pantographed larger or smaller during turning. Second, the square bore/head design method allows the manufacturer to bore much quicker and more accurately because the hole is bored square to the wood hosel, thus eliminating a setup on each head to achieve the desired face position, lie angle, face progression, etc.

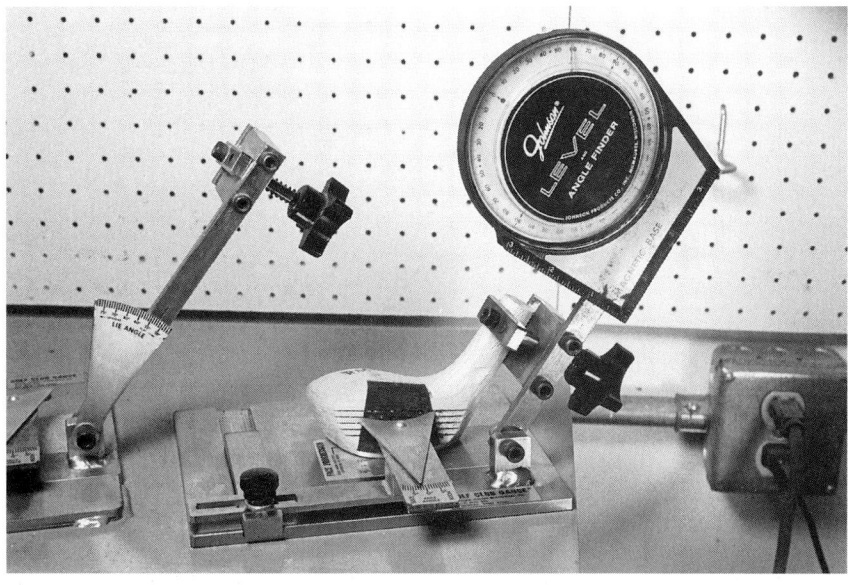

44-5
Checking face angle and lie angle before boring using the Golf Club Gauge™

This method also offers a playability advantage which the other methods do not. Because the sole line (radius) is touching the ground and is square to the shaft (90° angle) at the same time, it allows the golfer to rest the same club in different lie positions while still maintaining the same face position. Note: Take most any wood club and set it in a very upright playing position and visually note the face position. Now slowly lower the grip end to a very flat lie position. Note that the face angle probably opens significantly as the club goes from upright to flat lie positions. This means that probably the variable boring method was used because the face position is changing. This will be discussed next. Of course, the only accurate way to determine how a club was originally designed and manufactured concerning face position and its relationships, is to use the Golf Club Gauge™ or other similar device. Be cautioned that there is at least one other face angle measuring gauge, other than the Golf Club Gauge™, on the market which does not set a golf wood up properly for an accurate measurement.

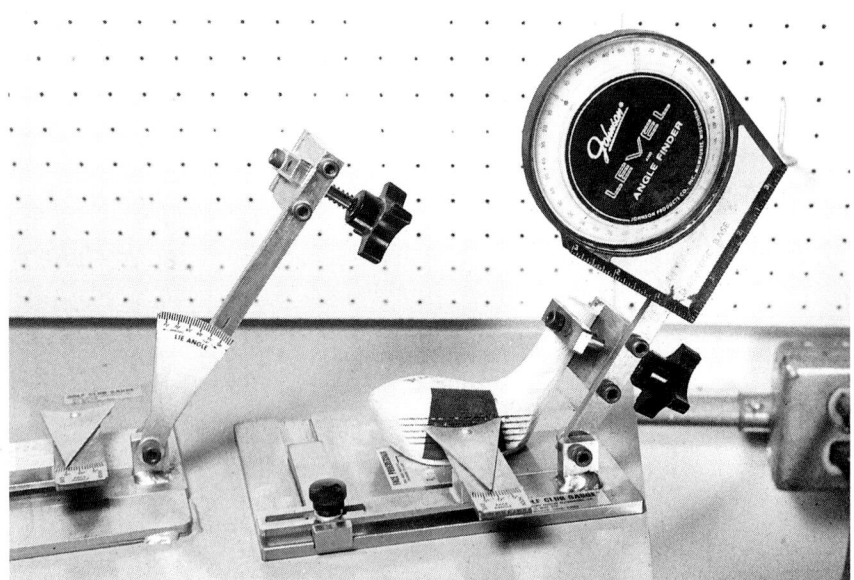

44-6
Checking face angle and lie angle after boring using the Golf Club Gauge™

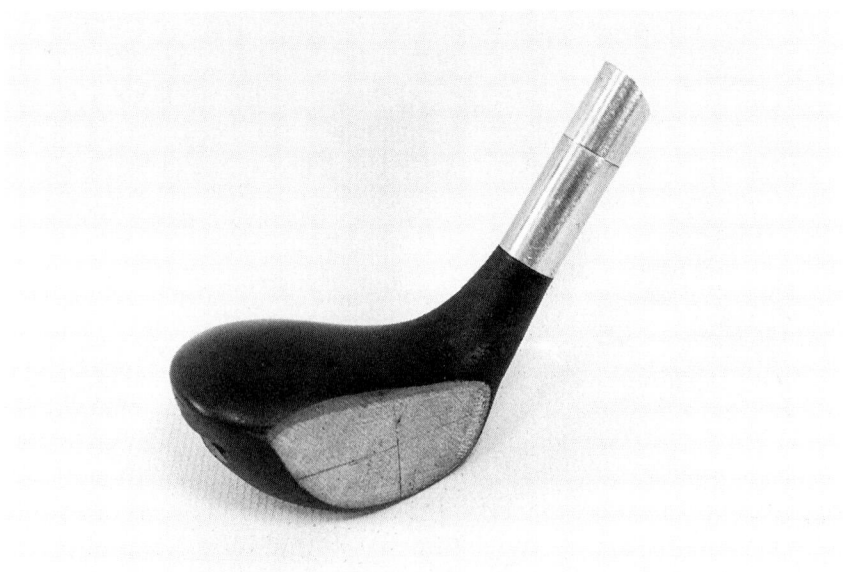

44-7
A wood head master model fitted with a ¾" diameter aluminum hosel for accuracy

■ Variable Boring Method (Refer to Figure 44-8)

It is apparent from Figure 44-8 that the main differences between the Variable Boring Method and the Square Bore/Head Design Method are:

1. The shaft hole or bore is not at 90° or right angle to the sole line where it touches the ground except in the square face position (90% of all clubs are bored open). Both boring methods are the same in the square face position only.
2. The shaft hole or bore usually will not be drilled through the center of the hosel, but rather, in most cases, at an angle to it.

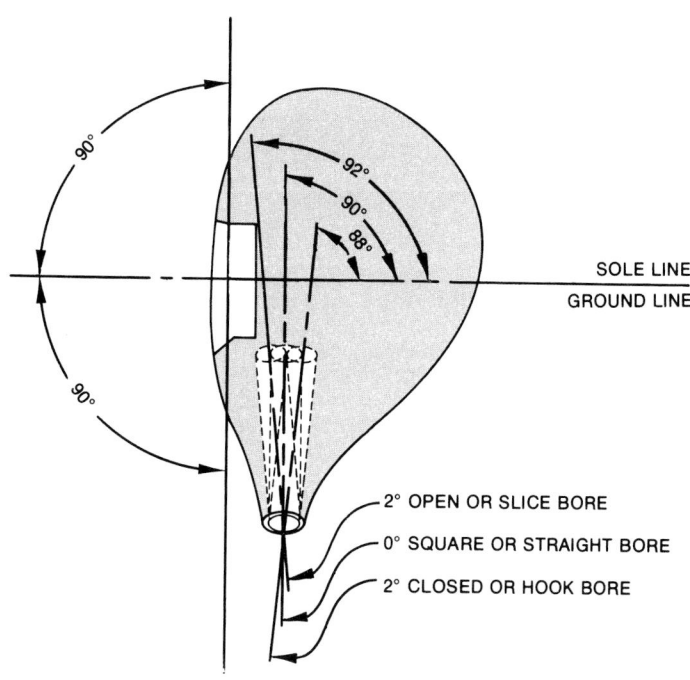

Figure 44-8
Variable boring method

The main advantage of this method is that it can be used to create special face positions such as those required on custom club orders. Also, for a one set at a time custom club shop this method would be recommended because it allows the use of virtually every turning model that is available.

When a golf wood club is bored using any other method than the Square Bore/Head Design Method, it is important to understand the finer points of just where to start the hosel hole and where it should end. Remember, after boring, the neck must be turned about the bore to give the head a flowing symmetry from the top of the hosel to where it blends at the face and head. There is also a limit on the amount a head can be hooked, opened, lie flattened or lie made more upright. This limit depends for the most part on the individual model. As a general rule of thumb the face angle can be changed plus or minus 4° from the model specification. The lie can also be changed plus or minus 4° from the model specification.

If a wood is to be bored to any specification of face angle other than its normal specification, it must be determined where to start the drill at the top of the hosel. The intention of starting the drill off center is to bore the hosel so the drill passes through its center at the hosel base. See Figure 44-9.

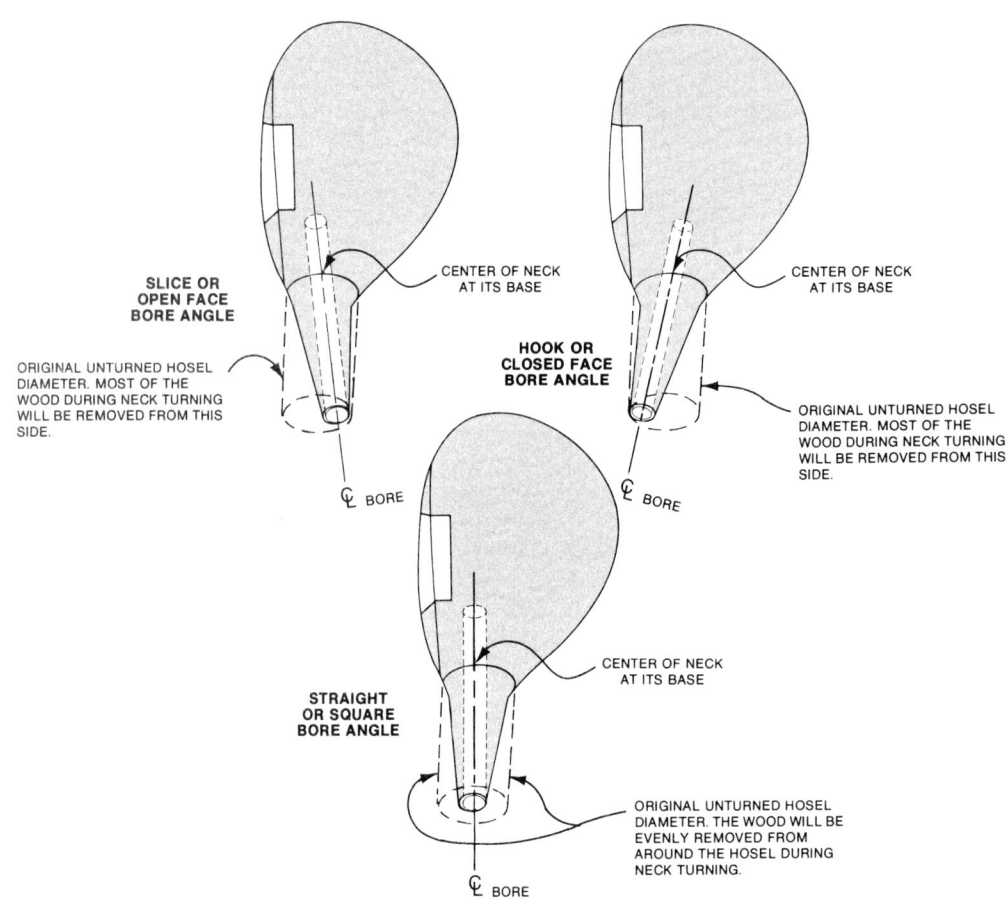

SLICE OR
OPEN FACE
BORE ANGLE

CENTER OF NECK
AT ITS BASE

ORIGINAL UNTURNED HOSEL
DIAMETER. MOST OF THE
WOOD DURING NECK TURNING
WILL BE REMOVED FROM THIS
SIDE.

℄ BORE

HOOK OR
CLOSED FACE
BORE ANGLE

CENTER OF NECK
AT ITS BASE

ORIGINAL UNTURNED HOSEL
DIAMETER. MOST OF THE
WOOD DURING NECK TURNING
WILL BE REMOVED FROM THIS
SIDE.

℄ BORE

STRAIGHT
OR SQUARE
BORE ANGLE

CENTER OF NECK
AT ITS BASE

ORIGINAL UNTURNED HOSEL
DIAMETER. THE WOOD WILL BE
EVENLY REMOVED FROM
AROUND THE HOSEL DURING
NECK TURNING.

℄ BORE

Figure 44-9
Properly locating the bore at the top of the hosel for various face angles

The same problem for centering the bore exists for changing the lie angle. See Figure 44-10 for the proper method. When both face angle and lie angle are changed from the normal model specification, then the starting point for the drill at the top of the hosel must be adjusted in a direction in between the two. See Figure 44-11. However, the maximum amount of drill movement in any one direction is reduced when boring is done in combination face angle and lie angle.

468

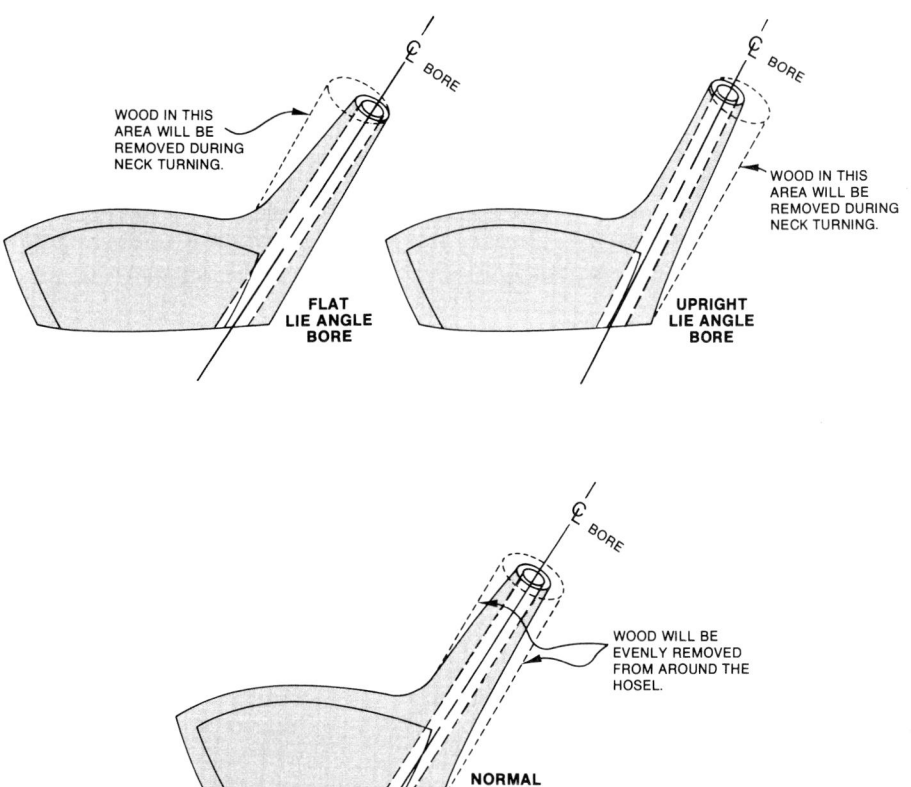

Figure 44-10
Properly locating the bore at the top of the hosel for various lie angles

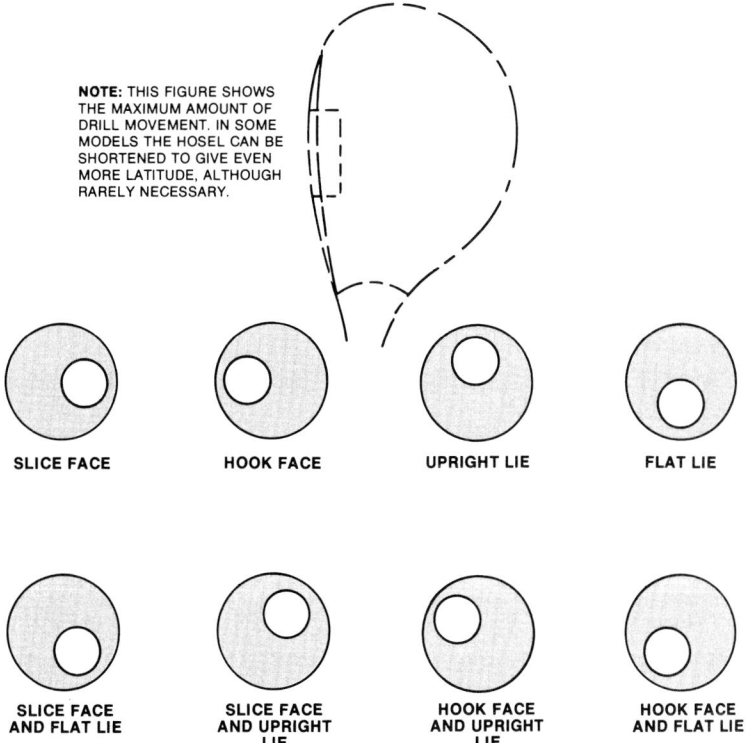

Figure 44-11
**Properly locating the bore at the top of the hosel for various
face angles and lie angles in combination**

■ Combination Boring Method (Refer to Figure 44-12)

The Combination Boring Method is as the name implies, a combination of the two previously discussed methods. If a head is of the Square Bore/Head Design type and a special face angle is required, it must be bored using the Variable Boring Method. Thus, refer to Figure 44-11 and note that the only difference between the Combination Method and the Square Bore/Head Design method is that the sole line is touching the ground but it is not pointing at the intended line of flight. (Note: The intended line of flight is always defined as an imaginary line perpendicular to the shaft.) As in the Variable Boring Method, the face will tend to open as the lie of the wood club is moved from very upright to a flat position.

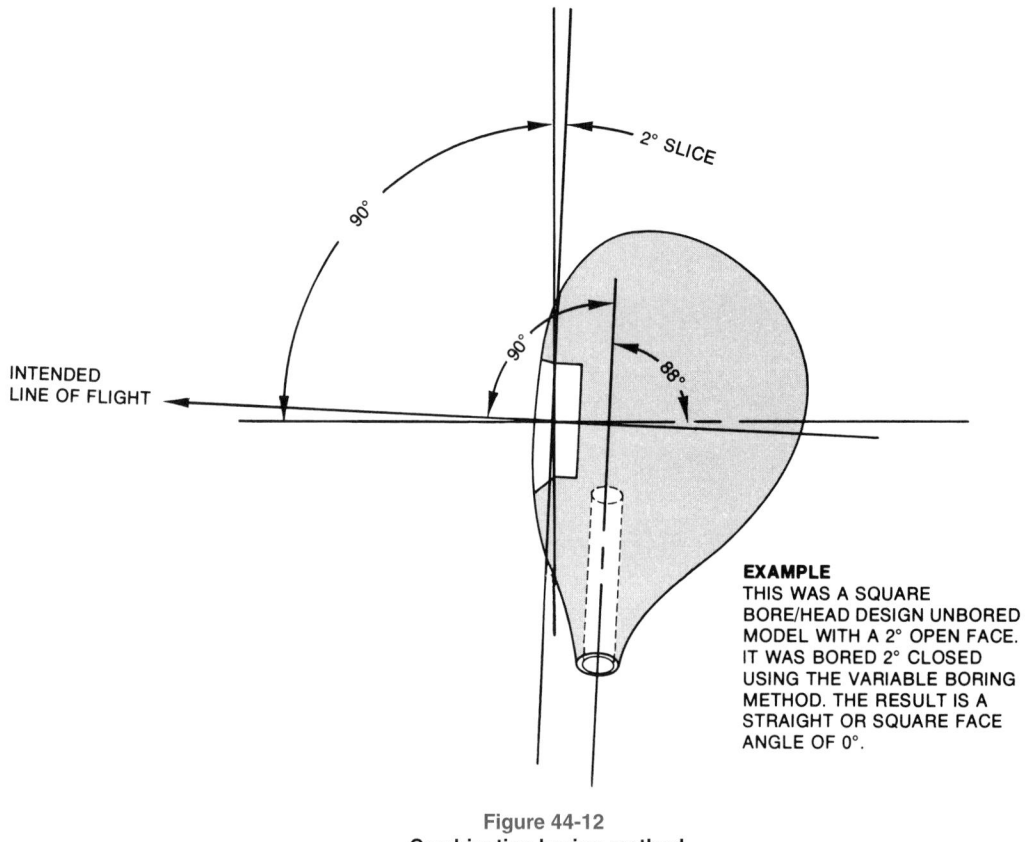

INTENDED LINE OF FLIGHT

2° SLICE

90°

90°

88°

EXAMPLE
THIS WAS A SQUARE BORE/HEAD DESIGN UNBORED MODEL WITH A 2° OPEN FACE. IT WAS BORED 2° CLOSED USING THE VARIABLE BORING METHOD. THE RESULT IS A STRAIGHT OR SQUARE FACE ANGLE OF 0°.

Figure 44-12
Combination boring method

■ Wood Head Boring Machinery

There are many different kinds of devices and machinery used in boring golf wood heads. If the proper wood head specifications can be fixtured properly, then you will get a good bore; if not, the club will probably be ruined.

Photo 44-13 and 44-14 shows the boring machinery used by The GolfWorks®. It can be quickly dialed to custom bore face angle, lie angle and face progression with close precision. It will also production bore well over 1,000 heads per day.

Each drill bit is driven by a separate 1 HP motor and is guided with a hardened drill bushing to eliminate drill wander. For blind bore drilling the right hand drill only is used. If a wood head is to be through bored, then it is drilled in both directions using one bit at the top of the hosel and another bit up through the sole. This machine has two Golf Club Gauges™ mounted to it so that every head can be checked before and after boring. Of all the wood head boring machines I have seen, none are as versatile or more accurate than this one.

44-13
The GolfWorks® wood head boring machine

44-14
A close-up of The GolfWorks® wood head boring machine in operation

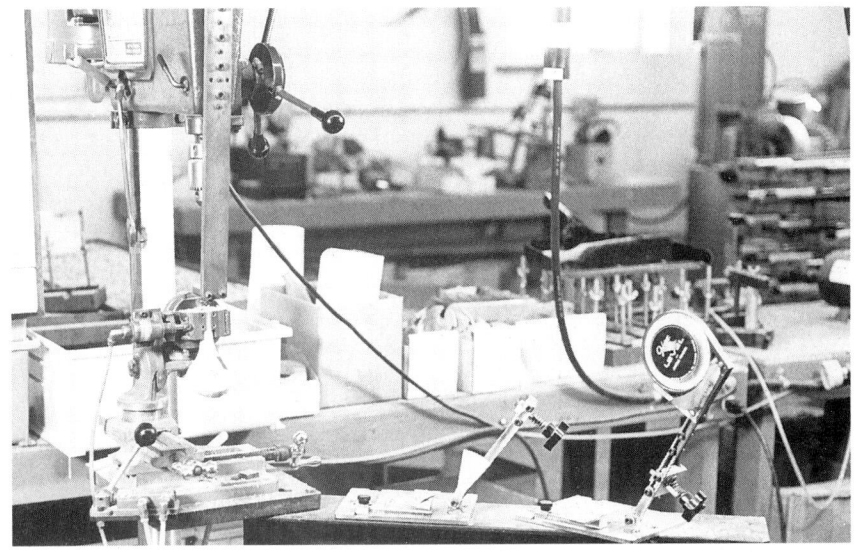

44-15
A custom wood head boring jig built by the author

Photo 44-15 shows another device for wood head boring. This machine works very well and utilizes a drill press with a 6" quill travel. It is built with a 1½" drill press vise mounted in a Rockwell® Uni-Vise which is in turn mounted on an X-Y axis compound slide table.

Bob Burns of Appleton, Wisconsin was kind enough to send me two photos of wood head boring machines that he uses. Photo 44-16 shows a drill press being used with a fixture which locates the head on its face and sole. Incidentally, Sears Craftsman® Drill Presses are popular for wood head boring because they have 6" quill travel. Many of the import drill presses will not work because they mostly have 3½" to 4" quill travels.

44-16
A drill press and fixture for boring wood heads at Bob Burns' shop

Another good device for boring is shown in Photo 44-17. This type uses a bench motor and chuck along with a linear motion fixture.

44-17
Another type wood head boring fixture

CHAPTER 45

GOLF WOOD CLUB DESIGN: SHAPE AND STYLE FEATURES

The various shape and style features of wood heads play as important a role in design as the actual loft and lie type specifications that were discussed in Chapters 34 - 43. The appearance of the golf club in the playing position relates directly to the golfer's mental attitude regarding how playable the golf club is perceived to be. Since the mental aspect of golf is such an important influencing factor in playing good golf, it is easily understood why most manufacturers strongly stress the importance of shape, style and the appearance of the club in the playing position. One of the difficulties that arise for the manufacturer is the strong opinions many golf professionals have concerning the particular shape and style golf club that is preferred. Many manufacturers recognize this fact and attempt to satisfy a larger segment of the market by offering two, three and sometimes four top grade wood head models available in different materials and shapes.

The purpose of this chapter is to define and compare some of the more important shape and style features of wood heads through illustrations. While studying these illustrations it might be interesting to compare the features of the different manufacturers' clubs and models you may have. Note how each different feature changes the appearance of the golf club in some way.

It is extremely difficult for the modelmaker to translate into words the finer subtleties of wood head shape that ultimately blend together with the more obvious shape and style features shown in this chapter to create a classic or contemporary wood head model. Experience, mastery of the clubmaker's tools, expertise in the various style features, and a feel for golf club design are all necessary.

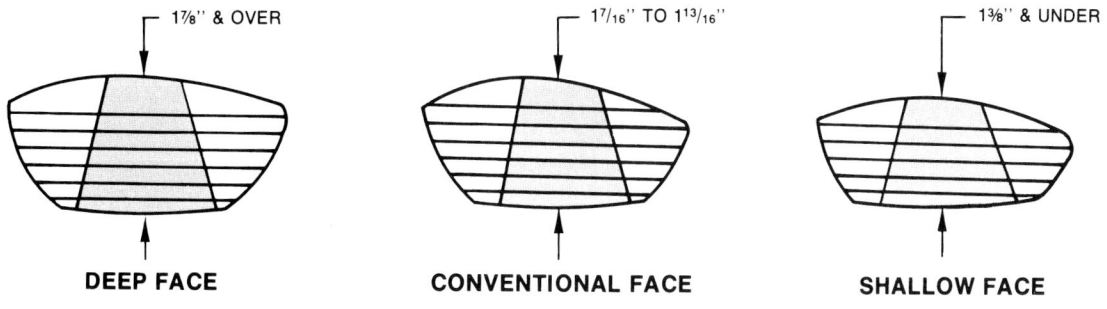

DEEP FACE
1⅞" & OVER

CONVENTIONAL FACE
1⁷/₁₆" TO 1¹³/₁₆"

SHALLOW FACE
1⅜" & UNDER

Figure 45-1
Driver face heights

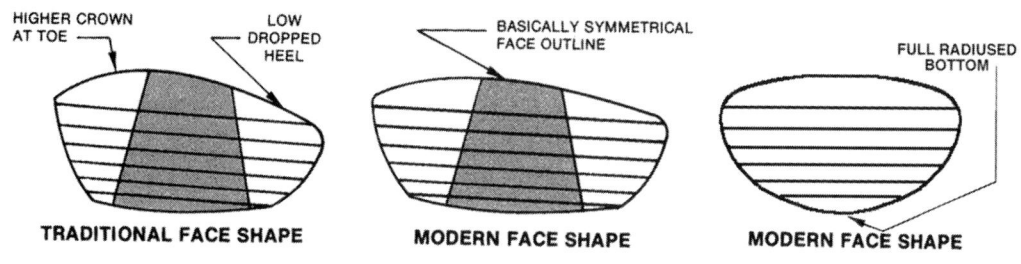

TRADITIONAL FACE SHAPE
HIGHER CROWN AT TOE
LOW DROPPED HEEL

MODERN FACE SHAPE
BASICALLY SYMMETRICAL FACE OUTLINE

MODERN FACE SHAPE
FULL RADIUSED BOTTOM

Figure 45-2
Face shapes

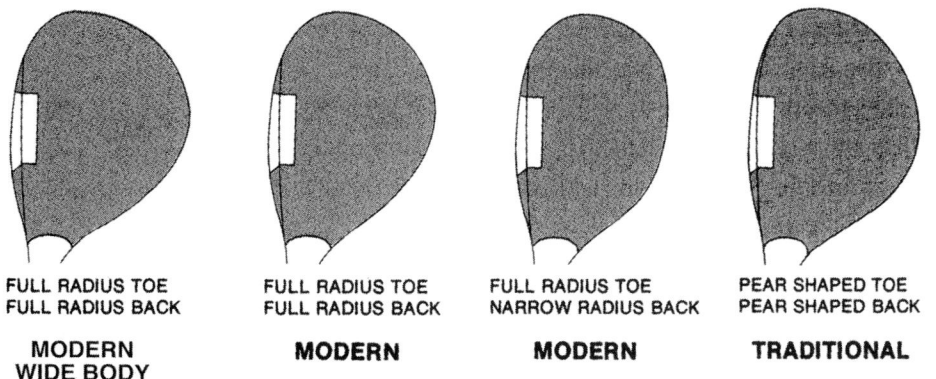

FULL RADIUS TOE
FULL RADIUS BACK

**MODERN
WIDE BODY**

FULL RADIUS TOE
FULL RADIUS BACK

MODERN

FULL RADIUS TOE
NARROW RADIUS BACK

MODERN

PEAR SHAPED TOE
PEAR SHAPED BACK

TRADITIONAL

Figure 45-3
Head shapes

475

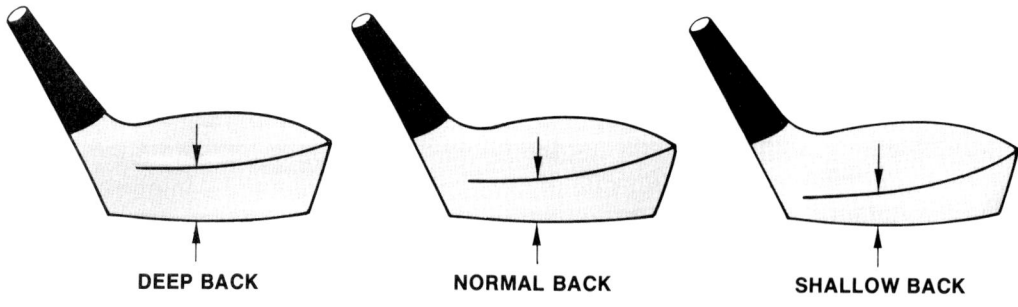

DEEP BACK   NORMAL BACK   SHALLOW BACK

Figure 45-4
Back heights

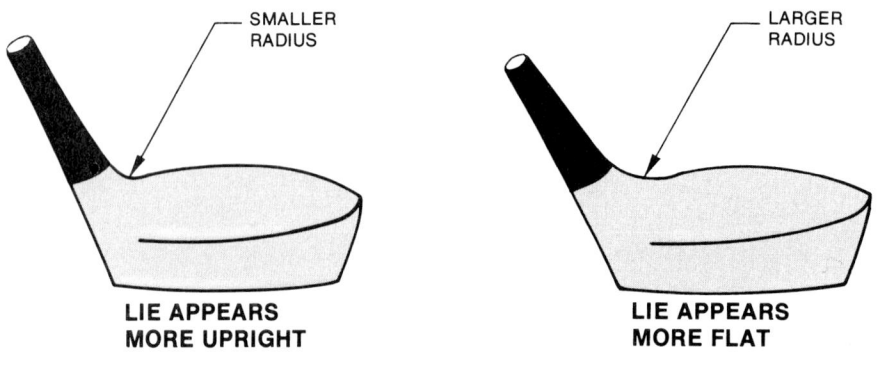

LIE APPEARS
MORE UPRIGHT   LIE APPEARS
MORE FLAT

Figure 45-5
Hosel to head radius

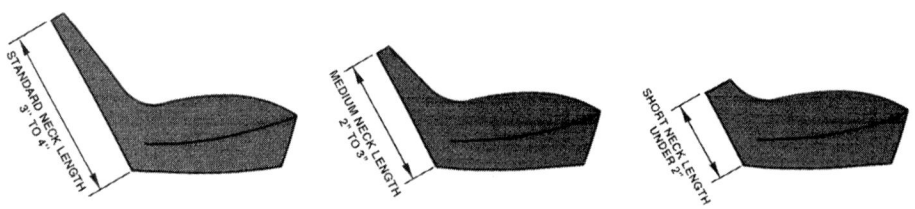

Figure 45-6
Neck length

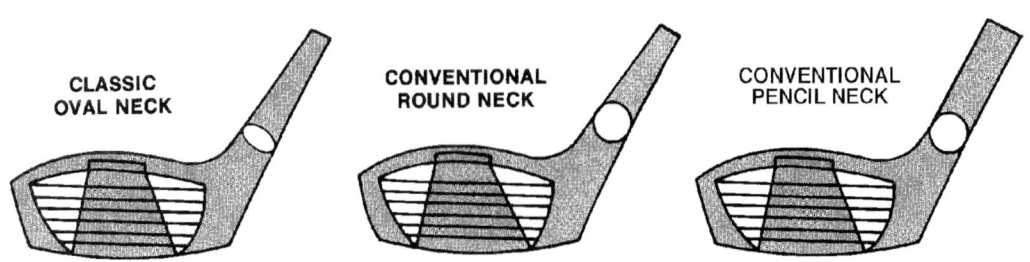

CLASSIC
OVAL NECK   CONVENTIONAL
ROUND NECK   CONVENTIONAL
PENCIL NECK

Figure 45-7
Neck shape variations

476

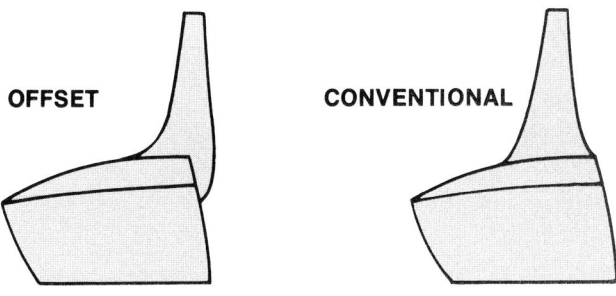

Figure 45-8
Hosel variations

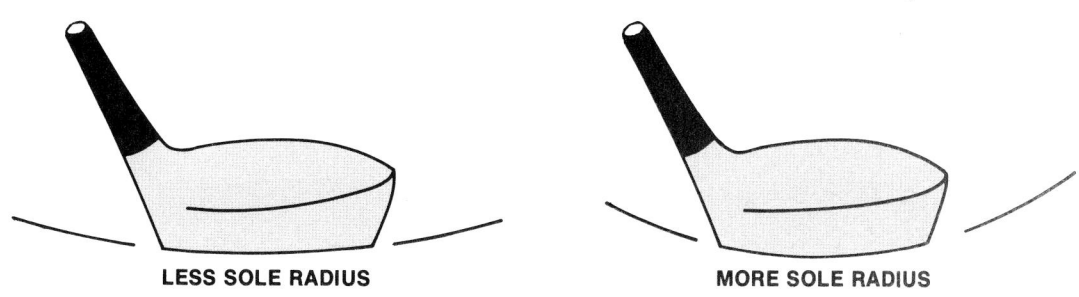

Figure 45-9
Sole radius

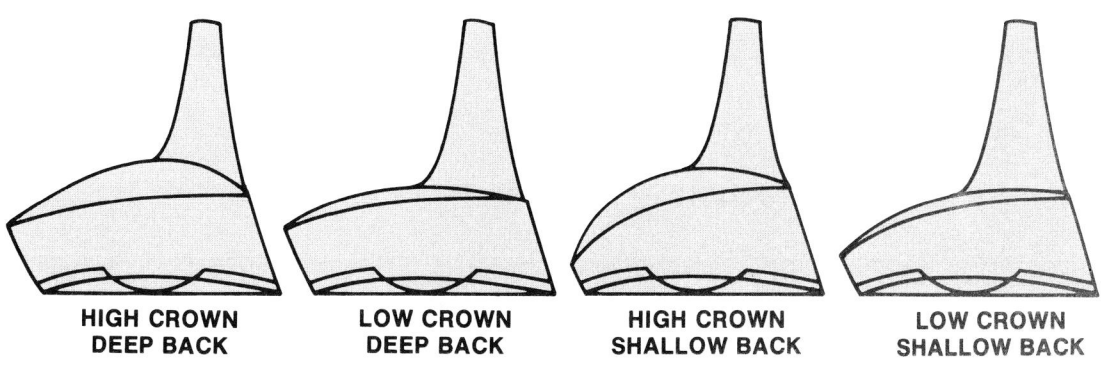

Figure 45-10
Crown and back height

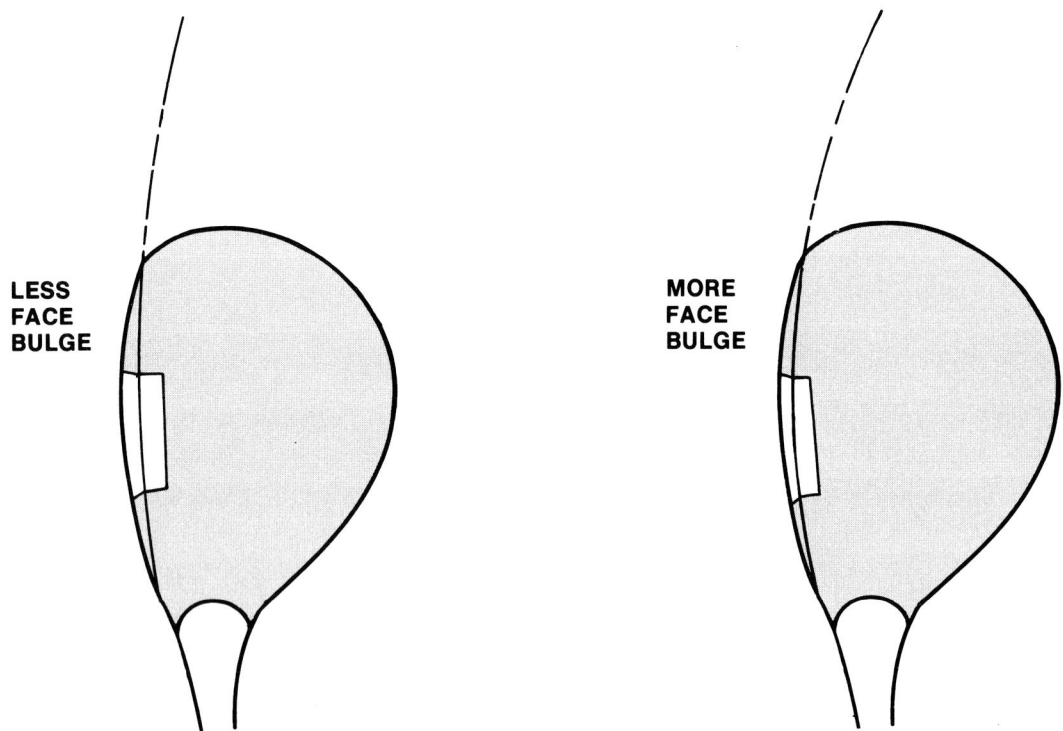

LESS FACE BULGE

MORE FACE BULGE

Figure 45-11
Face bulge

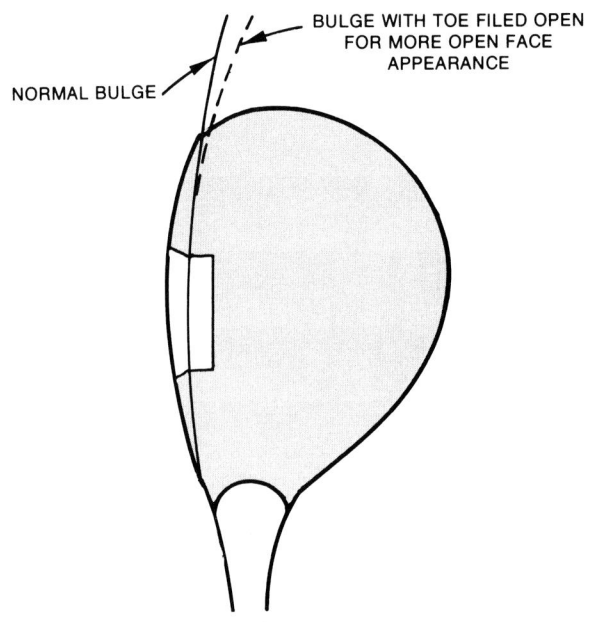

NORMAL BULGE

BULGE WITH TOE FILED OPEN
FOR MORE OPEN FACE
APPEARANCE

Figure 45-12
Open toe

478

CHAPTER 46

GOLF WOOD CLUB DESIGN: WOOD, METAL WOOD AND GRAPHITE HEAD CONSTRUCTION AND MATERIALS

Wood Head Terminology

The proper terminology and its understanding is of primary importance to any wood head discussion.

Flitch: Either a solid or laminated rough cut piece of wood which will yield more than one block. See Figure 46-1.

Block: A rough shaped piece of wood cut from a flitch which will ultimately yield one wood head. See Figure 46-1.

Head or Turning: Basically, the final clubhead shape of the block derived by turning on a special type lathe. See Figure 46-1.

Layup: The successively alternating layers of wood stacked up and bonded together to form a laminated type wood head. Layer thickness and grain direction are factors in both appearance and strength.

In Figure 46-2, the examples used are layups referred to as a 16-16-24 or a 16-16-16. The numbers indicate the thickness of each layer in inches. The grain directional layup shown in Figure 46-2 is the most common used today (two layers sidegrain, one layer edgegrain). Other layups are available and one of the more popular in recent times is one which is all sidegrain 1/16" layers bonded with a clear resin versus a dark resin. Unless this head is examined closely, it appears as if it is solid persimmon instead of laminated maple. This is especially true if the head is finished black. Photo 46-3 shows a comparison of a clear glue sidegrain layup and the dark glue alternating grain layup.

46-1
Flitch—left, block—center, head or turning—right

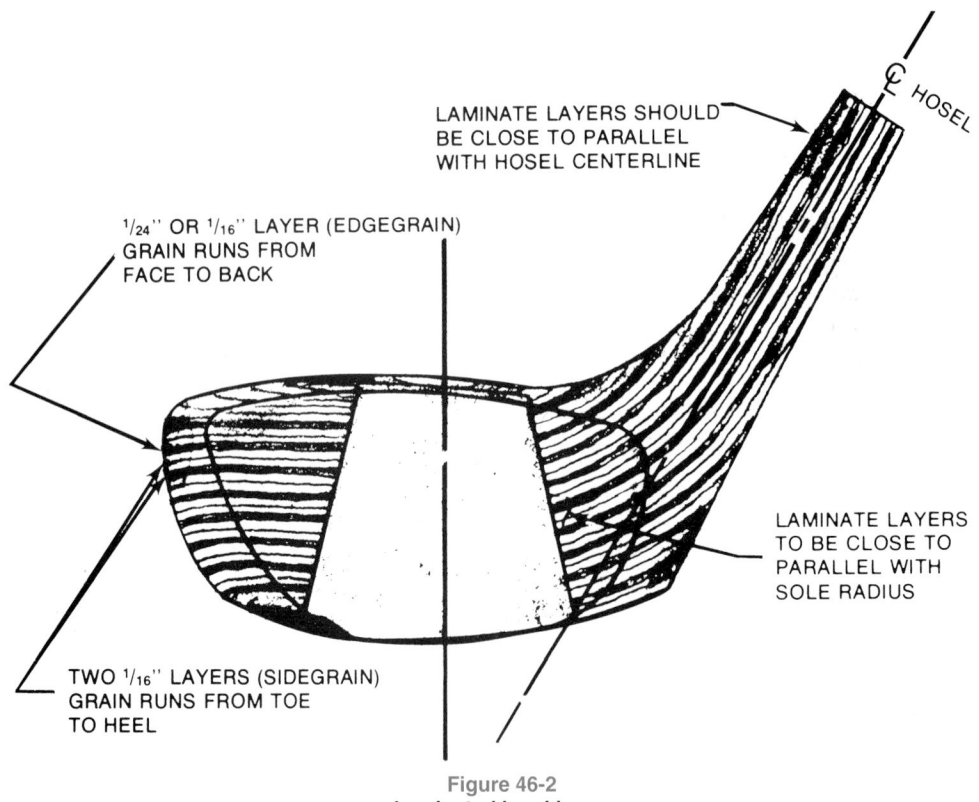

Figure 46-2
Laminated head layup

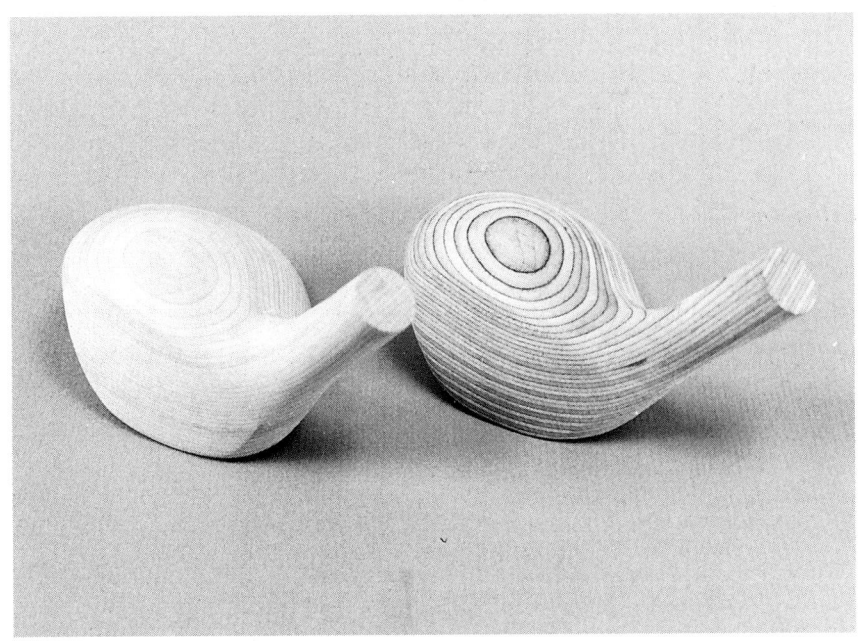

46-3
A clear glue sidegrain layup (left) compared to a dark glue alternating sidegrain, edgegrain layup

Bullseye: The smallest circle formed by the top laminated layer. It should be located as close as possible to the intersection of the hosel centerline and the face centerline. See Figure 46-4. Two factors which control the bullseye location are where the crown height of the head peaks and the block mounting hole location when the head is in the turning lathe.

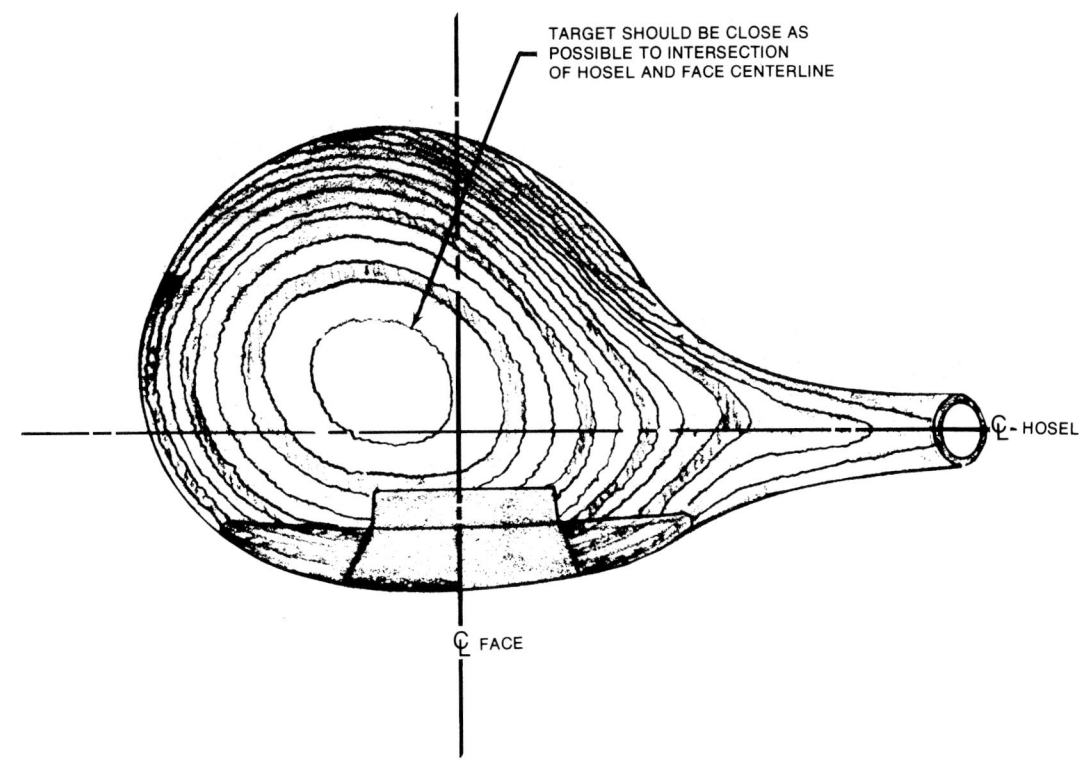

TARGET SHOULD BE CLOSE AS
POSSIBLE TO INTERSECTION
OF HOSEL AND FACE CENTERLINE

℄ - HOSEL

℄ FACE

Figure 46-4
Laminated head bullseye location

481

How a Wood Head is Made

The process of starting with a flitch and taking it to a finished turned wood head of a particular design is more complex than one might imagine. Most manufacturers buy finished turned heads of their particular model head and do not generally purchase either flitches or blocks.

A flitch can be made of either solid persimmon or of a laminated type wood, usually maple. It is marked into blocks by using a pencil and template and then each block is cut out of the flitch on a band saw.

The blocks must now be dried to remove the naturally high moisture content in wood. Drying can be accomplished in one of two ways, either by kiln drying or by radio-frequency drying. Note that prior to the 1900's, all wood heads were air dried, a process that took over two years for proper drying. Kiln drying is done in large ovens by actually baking the moisture out of the wood at elevated temperatures. This is a relatively slow process. The kiln drying process removes the moisture from the outside first and slowly works into the center of the block. Radio-frequency drying is the modern process and as the name implies, the moisture is removed electronically. This method differs from kiln drying because it removes the moisture from the center of the block first. Radio-frequency drying is much faster than kiln drying and is claimed to make a more dense, thus stronger and more stable wood head than kiln drying. A third method for wood drying has been developed in the last few years which is a variation of radio-frequency drying. This new method also uses radio frequency waves, but the process is done in a vacuum dryer. Within this chamber, atmospheric pressure is very low so the wood is not heated above 120° F. In standard radio-frequency drying, the wood becomes much hotter, and therefore somewhat more brittle.

The blocks are now trimmed and notched so that they can be held securely in the special wood head turning machines. There are a number of different types of turning machines. Some of the older models turn only one head at a time, but most machines today turn three heads at a time in less than four minutes. No matter which type of machine is used, basically they all work the same. A wood head master model, made of either wood, brass or cast iron, is held in the machine. See Figure 46-5. The blocks are then placed in the turning lathe. The machine is turned on and high speed cutters

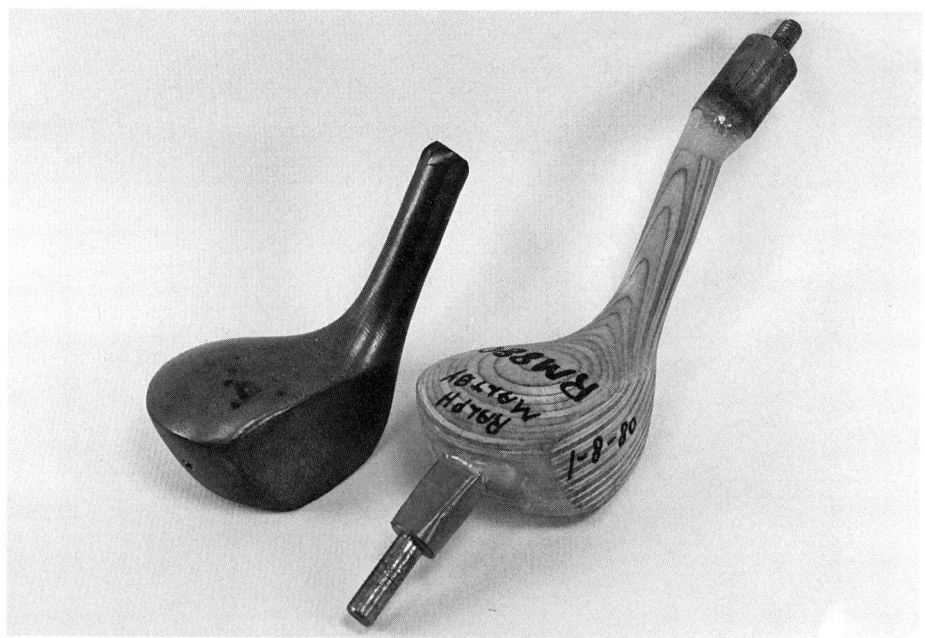

46-5
A brass metal turning master (left) and a wood turning master (right).
Both types are used in producing duplicate wood head turnings.

482

begin removing material from the blocks, duplicating exactly the shape of the master model. The duplication of the master model is accomplished by a special cam roller which is mechanically linked to the high speed cutters and traces the shape of the master model as it rotates. If needed, the turning can also be made over or undersized.

The turned wood head is now ready to begin the many operations required to make it a fully finished wood head. These operations include such things as nosing, cutting the hosel to length, moisture sealing, drilling the shaft hole, routing and installing the face insert and soleplate, tare weighting the head, sanding, facing, final weighting, applying stain, spraying clear finishing coats and applying decals.

The following photo sequence was provided by True Temper® on their manufacturing sequence for a laminated maple head from the log to the turning. True Temper®, however, no longer manufactures wood heads.

46-6
The maple log, with the bark removed, is loaded into a large lathe type machine for veneering.

46-7
A very sharp cutter blade actually peels the log continuously around its perimeter providing a thin, precise maple sheet.

46-8
The sheets of maple are cut into pieces approximately 8½" wide and 33" long and stacked. The moisture content is checked with a special tool. At this point the moisture content is quite high.

46-9
A special resin and catalyst are applied to both sides of each wood strip. The strip is then fed through this dryer which does not activate but solidifies the resin/catalyst coating. This allows the strips to be handled.

46-10

The strips of maple are stacked on top of each other to a predetermined thickness of about 38 pieces and temporarily taped together.

46-11

The stacked wood strips are called a flitch. The flitch is loaded into a radio frequency drying press.

46-12

Three operations are performed in the radio frequency drying unit. First, the mandrel closes tightly on the strips and forms them. Second, the radio waves activate the glue to cure it. Third, the moisture content of the wood is reduced to 6-8%.

46-13

The flitches are removed from the radio frequency unit.

46-14

The flitches are squared up and trimmed on a band saw.

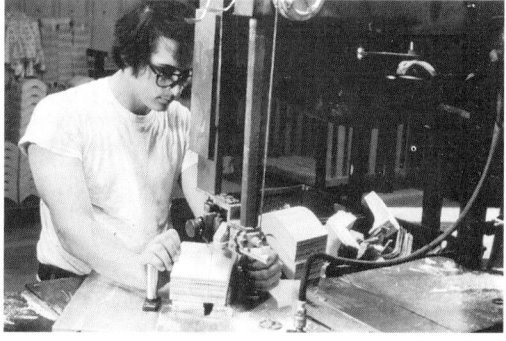

46-15

A template is used to mark the shape of the block on the flitch. A band saw is once again used to saw the flitch into blocks.

46-16

Each block is put into a machine which drills the proper mounting holes for fixturing it in the turning lathe.

46-17

The blocks now look like this. The fixturing machine drilled 2 holes in the toe area and 1 hole at the top of the hosel.

46-18

The blocks are stored in wire baskets and staged in front of the high speed turning machines seen in the background.

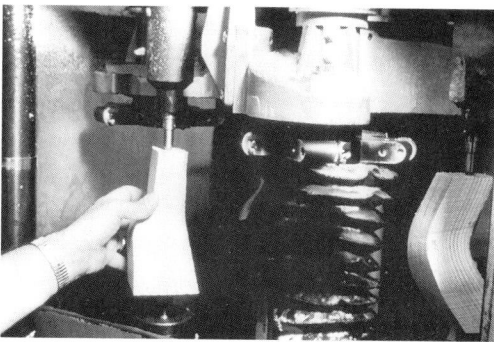

46-19

Three blocks at a time are loaded into this Richardson® turning lathe.

46-20

This photo shows the Richardson® lathe set up and ready to run. Notice the metal turning master which will be used as a guide in exactly duplicating the three blocks.

46-21

The high speed cutters have partially turned this head from the block.

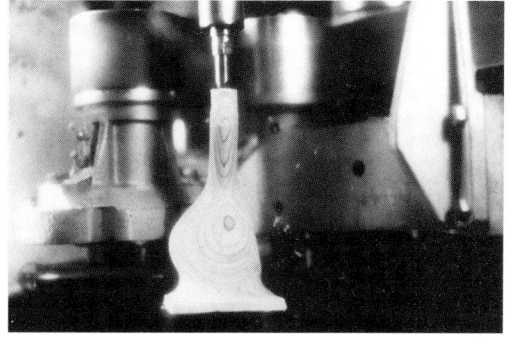

46-22
The turning is only seconds away from completion. This machine turns 3 heads in under 4 minutes.

46-23
Each head is checked for size. These machines can pantograph larger or smaller if desired.

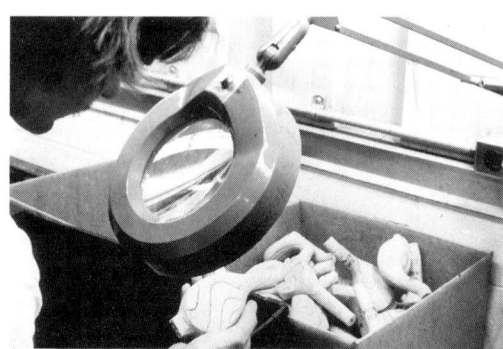

46-24
Each turned head is closely inspected for delaminations, chips or improper gluing.

Wood Head Materials

The most popular material used in wood style clubs today is stainless steel and graphite. Persimmon and laminated maple wood are still used, but comprise less than six percent of the market. ABS plastic molded heads are still used, but mostly in inexpensive sets or beginners' sets. Also, there are different types of metal woods. Some are aluminum cast or stainless steel cast with wood back insets or graphite inserts and some are stainless steel cast with no insets or inserts whatsoever. Other materials used are cobalt, titanium and lexon. The following gives general explanations of each material type.

■ Laminated Maple

Laminated heads are made from northern maple trees.
1. They are much stronger than persimmon and resist splitting, chipping, cracking and swelling.
2. Laminated woods produce a feel which is non-discernible from that of persimmon.
3. Laminated wood heads in various layups can produce striking results when finished in wood stains.
4. Top grade laminated heads are considerably less expensive than top grade persimmon heads to the golf club manufacturers.
5. Laminated heads, in the same model, will all have the same density and weigh close to the same. Persimmon wood can vary by as much as 2 ounces from head to head in the same model.

486

The biggest disadvantage of a laminated head is the resistance it gets from the traditionalist golfer in the marketplace. Persimmon was the predominant wood used in the '40s and '50s even though laminated wood was introduced as early as 1939. The traditionalist of today feels that persimmon, particularly those heads which are oil hardened, have superior hardness and density, and will unquestionably propel the golf ball longer and straighter while bestowing a mysteriously pleasant extra solid feel. Nothing could be farther from the truth.

Laminated maple heads once gained in popularity mainly because Wilson Sporting Goods adopted them in the mid 1940's for one of their major club lines. They named the laminated maple head the Strata-Bloc®. Laminated wood heads continued to gain in popularity with the other golf club manufacturers and finally overtook persimmon in the 1960's.

■ Persimmon

Persimmon wood has more mystery and myth associated with it than any other wood head material. The following explanations provide factual information on persimmon and will hopefully dispel most of the mystery and myth.

The persimmon tree is generally found in the southeastern United States. It is mostly found in wetter areas and is quite scarce. Rarely would a persimmon grove or stand of trees be found but rather they are intermittently discovered here and there. The persimmon tree is a fruit-bearing tree and in some areas the fruit is cultivated for food. The tree belongs to the ebony family which includes over 160 species. The persimmon tree is a relatively small tree rarely reaching 50 feet tall and usually around 12" diameter. A great yield of clubheads from a single tree would be 500. The sapwood is beige in color and the heartwood or center of the tree is black. The heartwood is cut out of the log and not used in wood heads.

It is often heard that the persimmon we get today is not as good as the persimmon of 10 or 20 years ago. The truth of the matter is that the persimmon is just as good but the yield from the trees is much less. Since persimmon trees are small to begin with and grow quite slowly, it takes many years for second growth; therefore, the amount of larger trees dwindles and supply is reduced.

Another area of controversy is the grain structure and density of a persimmon head. Some say a small circular grain pattern is best and others say a large circular grain or straight across grain is best. Also, it was mostly thought that a small circular grain meant that the head came from close to the middle of the tree vs. the outside of the tree. Most of this is myth, so the following will attempt to clear this up.

When identically turned persimmon heads from the same box are individually weighed, they vary considerably. Some heads are denser or heavier than others depending on the growth rate of the tree. The trees that grew slowly because of dry seasons or growing location usually produce the denser, heavier heads. The persimmon trees that have wet season or wet location growth are usually the lighter heads because they grew more rapidly. Keep in mind that dry or wet growth persimmon trees both have about 60% moisture upon cutting and they both are reduced to an average of 9% moisture after drying. Some may erroneously feel that wet season or wet location growth is associated with a wetter piece of wood, hence a heavier piece of wood, but it is not. The density or weight of a persimmon head can only be accurately measured in the raw turned head state or after the head has been nosed and the hosel cut to length. For example, the same model raw turned persimmon heads in Photo 46-25 are quite different in weight although in the photo they look basically the same. The head on the left weights 7¼ ounces and the head on the right weights 5¾ ounces. A difference of 1¾ ounces! If the two heads shown were made up into drivers, you could not determine the actual weight differences in the raw turnings.

Upon close examination, however, especially in pro-sanded heads, you would see much larger pores in the lighter head thus indicating a more open grain and more air space inside the head.

46-25
Two identical model heads. The one on the left weighs 7¼ ounces and the one on the right weighs 5¾ ounces.

Logic would seem to dictate, at this point, that the best club would be the heavier, denser head. It definitely is the stronger of the two heads. However, let's look a little closer at building two drivers from these heads. The 7¼ ounce head is far too heavy to provide a D-2 driver with a carbon steel shaft at 43" long. This head would need at least a 1" diameter by 1½" deep hole drilled in the sole to reduce the headweight. The 5¾ ounce head would need lead added into the sole area to increase its weight. Since both of these club heads are the exact same size and model, the 5¾ ounce head with lead added will have a lower center of gravity than the 7¼ ounce head. The 7¼ ounce head actually had its center of gravity raised because of the cavity. See Figure 46-26. Comparing both heads, regarding exact playability differences, would require extensive machine and player testing. It probably would have been better not bringing the point up, but at least it provides something to think about and everyone can formulate their own opinion regarding playability.

The small circular grain pattern in a persimmon head is thought to be from the center of the tree and consequently this makes the most solid, dense head. Actually, the more curved the grain the smaller in diameter the tree, say 8" to 10" and the straighter the grain (no or little curve) the larger the tree diameter (possibly up to 18"). The grain that most people refer to is formed by the annular rings of the tree. Each year of growth a tree forms one annular ring. Each annular ring is made up of a wider light area and a darker narrow area. The light part of the annular ring is the early, or spring through summer growth and the dark area is the late season or fall growth. The smaller, more curved rings that happen to line up perfectly with the farthest front tip of the toe radius produce very beautiful clubheads when finished in light stains. Their playability, however, all else being equal, would be the same as any other grained persimmon head. Besides attractiveness and tradition, the main reason wood heads are turned with the grain running edgewise into the face and parallel with the hosel is for strength. This is more critical in the smaller fairway woods. Remember, there is quite a bit of latitude in grain direction while still maintaining adequate strength. True Temper® allows approximately 30 degrees for a top grade head. Also, look closely at a head which looks like the grain is running the wrong way; upon close examination you may see that just as the grain approaches the face it turns sharply into it, producing edgegrain. Photo 46-27 shows two heads. The head on the left is a U.R. head (usable reject) because the grain turns into the face as just mentioned. Also, the grain is parallel with the hosel. Actually this head would make a very nice driver. The head on the right is an extremely dense, slow growth piece of wood from a very small tree. Note the smaller cured rings from the top of the toe back. The traditionalist would love this head and mentally would feel he has the most solid feeling wood obtainable, with probably 20 extra yards built-in. Refer back to Photo 46-25. The two heads in this photo show a more straight across grain indicating the heads came from larger trees.

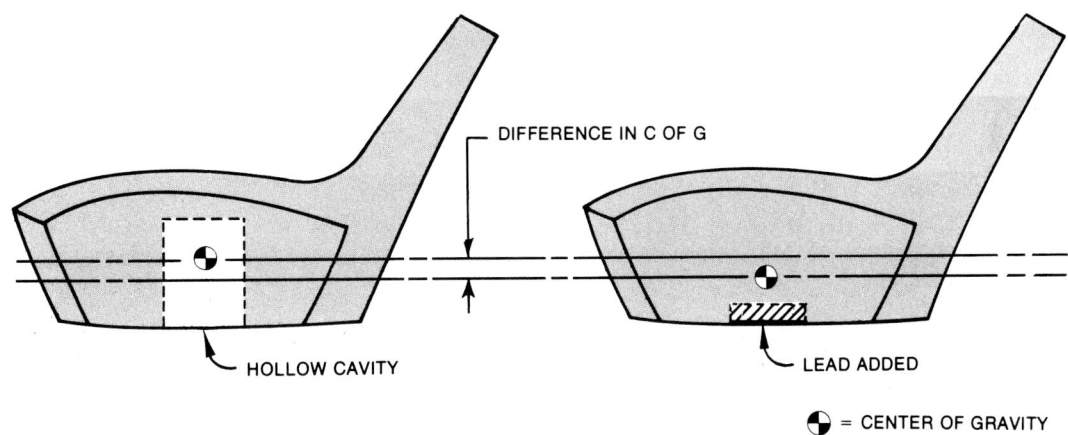

Figure 46-26
Comparing centers of gravity on different density persimmon heads

46-27
The head on the left is a U.R. (usable reject) grade head because the grain runs at a severe angle to the face. The head on the right is preferred by the traditionalist because it has a small circular grain pattern peaking at the tip of the toe. Some manufacturers will buy the U.R. heads at a reduced cost and finish them black.

489

■ Metal, Aluminum and Stainless Steel

During the last few years metal type woods have dominated the market, effectively reducing the market share of persimmon or laminated maple heads to less than ten percent. At first, metal woods were made of a combination of metal and wood and in one case, metal, wood and plastic. These designs proved to be inferior and the market has moved entirely to all metal heads with the exception that some companies have taken advantage of a U.S.G.A. rule change that now permits inserts.

The metals being used are either aluminum, stainless steel, titanium, beryllium copper and cobalt, with stainless steel being by far the most frequently used material. Metal heads made of titanium, cobalt and beryllium copper are much more expensive than stainless steel, but there is no difference in performance. It is much like distance claims made years ago between the manufacturers of persimmon and laminated maple woods — interesting argument, but not much substance behind the claims.

Metal type wood construction offers the consistency of investment casting which made this type of iron quite popular. Specifications such as loft, face angle, face progression, bulge, roll and head shape will be fairly exact from club to club. The only clubmaking skill required is proper weighting and assembly. Wood heads require a much higher skill level to produce identical clubs in the same model.

The steps involved for manufacturing a metal wood are identical with those found in Chapter 51 with one notable exception. Metal woods are cast into two different pieces: the soleplate and a hollow shell. The soleplate is welded to the shell to form the complete head. Grinding and polishing operations remove any trace of the weld mark, so it is generally not known by the average golfer that the head was made of two pieces. See Photo 46-28.

46-28
Raw metal wood casting – head and sole

The original metal woods were relatively small in size because the manufacturers were concerned with wall failure, especially in the face where ball impact occurred. However, advances in the structural design allowed for thinner walls and thus larger heads, although it is still common to take a straight edge to many metal wood faces and not a concavity or reduction in clubface bulge. Due to weight and strength demands, a clubhead can only have a certain amount of material within its walls, so there are limits to the size and shape.

Metal wood head shapes first expanded upwards with a deep-faced model introduced in 1987. Users of this head noted that the ball trajectory was significantly lower, which many attributed to the metal hardness or shaft. In fact, by virtue of the design, the deep-faced model had a higher center of gravity, more like a conventional wood head, so of course ball trajectory would be lower than the earlier shallow-faced designs. See Photo 46-29.

46-29
Shallow faced and deep faced designs

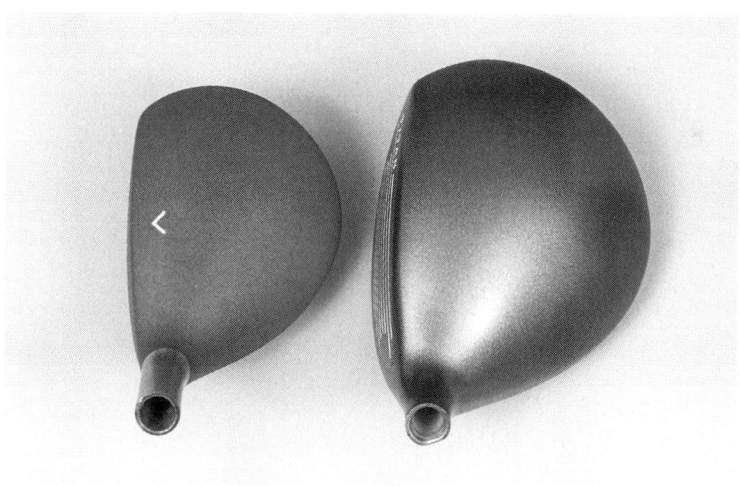

46-30
Narrow and wide body models

The next shape change was wider with the development of the "wide-body" designs, some of which touched up against the U.S.G.A. rule that limited club width by stating, "clubhead breadth must be greater than width." See Photo 46-30. By the mid-1990's, these designs dominated the market. Experimentation continues with various sole designs that incorporate rails or other protrusions and manufacturers have begun introducing models with inserts, permitted by a U.S.G.A. rule change. (See Chapter 47 for more information.)

It is impossible to say where the golf market will be in the next 5-10 years. Certainly other sophisticated materials will be tested, but it would appear that there is little chance of the metal wood being usurped by any other concept for quite awhile.

■ Graphite Heads

There are two methods for manufacturing a graphite head — injection molding and compression molding. Of the two, injection molding is most often used because it is less costly in both material and labor. However, the injection molded head is not as strong as a compression molded head and is therefore more likely to experience stress fractures and outright breakage. From a performance standpoint, golfers would not notice any difference in heads manufactured using either method.

Injection Molding

The process for manufacturing an injection molded head is similar to that of a plastic head, ABS plastic insert or even a metal wood. Pellets made of plastic and graphite are stored in large bags. Large hand scoops are used to pull the pellets from the bags and to permit the proper ratio of plastic to graphite. The pellets are poured into a large hopper and then mixed. Heat is introduced to reduce the pellets to a hot liquid which is then injected under pressure into a mold.

Sometimes the insert and soleplate are added to the mold before injection, so they become a permanent part of the head as the liquid cools and hardens around them. Thus, it is not necessary to install the insert or soleplate with epoxy and screws later. After the head cools, if the insert and soleplate are already installed, it is released from the mold and ready for finishing. Finishing requires nothing more than nominal sanding, sometimes application of an opaque colorcote and lastly the polyurethane coats. The hosel hole is already part of the head due to the appropriate sized hosel pin which was part of the mold.

If the insert and soleplate were not installed at the time of injection, the head is removed from the mold and the soleplate and insert cavity are routed with both components later installed using epoxy. Note that an insert is not always used. Sometimes a mold is designed to permit the creation of the soleplate cavity so that the routing step is not necessary. After the components are installed, the head is then finished.

Compression Molding

Compression molded heads have a much higher percentage of graphite. In fact, they should be referred to as composite heads because not only are graphite fibers used, but often other materials such as kevlar are used as well.

Long graphite fibers are accumulated in a small bundle, along with epoxy resin and filler, and then wrapped with a thin sheet of kevlar (some heads are manufactured without the kevlar wrap). The bundle is then placed between the halves of a club head mold. Heat is applied to soften the bundle and the two halves are pressed toward each other, forcing the bundle to fill every crevice of the mold with any excess forced through release points.

The mold contains a hosel pin for the hosel hole and also contains a solid mass of material in the sole area so that a cavity is created beneath what will eventually be placed a soleplate. After the head cools, it is released from the mold and the soleplate is installed. It then undergoes the same finishing process as an injection molded head.

Most compression molded heads do not have an insert as the manufacturer usually chooses to leave the entire face void of any opaque coatings so that the woven pattern produced by the kevlar and graphite fibers is exposed. The rest of the head is usually sprayed with a non-opaque colorcote to produce a finish that allows the user to see the woven pattern. Three to five coats of polyurethane are then applied.

■ Other Materials

Many other types of woods, plastics and metals have been and still are being evaluated as possible materials to be used for wood head construction. Unfortunately, most materials evaluated, especially woods and plastics, have not possessed the many qualities required to produce a head which will stand up to the tremendous stress and strains placed upon it during the swing and at impact.

Treating Wood Heads

When wood heads are received by the golf club manufacturer, the first operations that must be performed are nosing and cutting the hosel to length. These operations remove the two parts of the wood head where it was held in the turning lathe. The next operation is to treat the wood head so it will remain more stabilized regarding its moisture content. The best way to treat a wood head, particularly persimmon, is to plug up its pores. There are a number of methods and materials available for doing this.

The most common method used today for treating wood heads is to dip them in a liquid called Nelsonite®. Nelsonite® is also widely used in the furniture industry. It has a certain amount of oil in its formulation along with other ingredients. The head is dipped in Nelsonite® for a specified time, usually 30 seconds to 2½ minutes. It is then allow to dry, which varies with temperature and humidity, but the minimum time is 48 hours. As Nelsonite® dries it forms into a solid which plugs up each pore. This prevents moisture from entering the head or leaving it.

The older "oil hardened" process was made popular by MacGregor with the introduction of their 1941 woods. Oil hardening was nothing more than dipping heads in boiled linseed oil. The boiled linseed oil was not actually boiling, but rather denotes one type of linseed oil. The other common type is raw linseed oil which should not be used on wood heads. MacGregor began this linseed oil dip to prevent head swelling problems, but then soon found out that the lacquer finish would not stick to the head because of the oils. Finally, they reduced the dipping time in the oil and allowed it to dry longer which solved both problems. Oil hardening does not harden a wood head; it is just another way to reduce moisture absorption and moisture loss. It is simply amazing how this term is bandied about and the inaccurate discussions which usually follow.

Probably the best material and method ever developed for stabilizing the grain on a wood head is a resin system impregnated into the wood head using both vacuum and pressure. The heads are loaded into a sealed tank and a vacuum is pulled. Once under a vacuum, the resin is let into the tank and allowed to saturate the heads. Next, the vacuum is released and the tank is pressurized to approximately 100 pounds. The pressure is left on for 12 to 24 hours. The heads are then removed and force dried in an oven.

The biggest disadvantage to the resin impregnation system is the amount of weight it adds to larger driver models. There is no problem with fairway woods.

CHAPTER 47

GOLF WOOD CLUB DESIGN: INSERT MATERIALS

A discussion of golf club insert materials usually turns out to be a very opinionated exchange of inaccurate information. Other than testing I have done, other scientifically controlled studies of the various materials as they pertain to improved golf club performance have been limited mostly to tests conducted by the U.S.G.A. This does not mean golf club manufacturers, golf professionals and a few consumers do not have preferences, they do. Unfortunately, these preferences are usually derived from information passed along by hearsay on a pseudo-logical basis.

One such example of this would be the original fiber type inserts which were very popular in clubs of the 1940's, 50's and 60's and still enjoy some use in today's clubs. Some of the die hards still perpetuate the myth that one can "work" the ball better with woods that have fiber inserts because of their belief that the ball has a tendency to stay on the clubface a split second longer, which is untrue. If the same type of ball is used, the ball stays on all insert materials the same amount of time. Forgetting for a moment that the ball does not stay on the clubface longer, it would still be hard to assume that one can "work" the ball better with fiber inserts. The truth of the matter is that the longer a ball stays on the face, the more tendency it has to pick up additional unwanted sidespin. This is the reason that three-piece wound balata balls achieve more sidespin than two-piece surlyn balls — more of the surface of the balata ball is exposed to the clubface. Consequently, the more it tends to hook or slice. If it has no hook or slice sidespin whatsoever, "working" the ball would not even apply. Consider for a moment that the elapsed time between when a golf ball first makes contact with the clubface until the exact moment that it leaves the clubface is only approximately $5/10,000$ of a second. The golfer does not feel the hit until the ball has actually left the clubface.

The Insert's Role in Golf Club Design

There have been a number of increased distance claims made because a certain insert material is said to be so hard that more energy is applied to the ball at impact. Most of the testing I have done on inserts has been in this area of hardness and also the weights of inserts. More specifically I tested nylon, cold rolled steel, stainless steel, laminated bamboo, laminated maple, solid persimmon, cast epoxy, ABS, aluminum, phenolic and graphite inserts. These materials were made up into standard insert shapes, tested alone and mounted in golf clubs.

The first test was to mount the various materials on a solid steel plate with absolutely no deflection. An air cannon was used to fire golf balls into each material. The speed of the golf ball was measured just before impact with each insert material. The speed was also recorded after impact with each insert material. The ball speed before impact versus the ball speed after impact gives an efficiency coefficient or the amount of energy lost. These tests showed no appreciable ball velocity differences due to increased hardness of materials.

The next step was to build drivers using each of the insert materials tested in the air cannon. I made the clubs myself and took every possible measurement and recorded every specification of the finished clubs, as well as the individual components. Wherever possible, each component from club to club was identical.

The results of the testing, done on the True Temper® Mechanical Golfer were quite time consuming to analyze and plot. The test results seemed inconsistent in looking for a logical explanation of distance differences and trajectory differences. Finally, everything came together and the missing element was found. The results showed some consistency when the weight of the insert and the resulting change in the head's center of gravity were plotted against carry distance and trajectory. The heavier the insert, the lower the trajectory and the shorter the carry distance. The lighter the insert, the higher the trajectory and the greater the carry distance. The heavier the insert, the closer the clubhead center of gravity is to the face. This always has the effect of lowering the trajectory with all else being equal. Conversely, the lighter the insert, the more weight is needed under the soleplate and the farther back the center of gravity. A low and rearward center of gravity will give a higher trajectory.

The two basic functions of an insert are to be attractive and provide a more durable surface than wood in order to withstand the constant battering of the ball without denting or chipping. Wood will eventually break down from the constant abuse of impact.

Inserts can also be designed to occupy a much larger portion of the face than the traditional shaped inserts. Woods have been manufactured with full face inserts which occupy 100% of the face. See Figure 47-1. The advantage of larger inserts is greater durability on off-center hits. The main disadvantage is the non-traditional look which is important to some golfers and most better players.

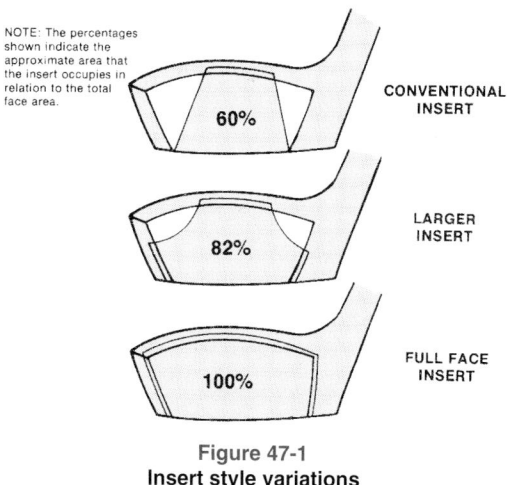

Figure 47-1
Insert style variations

Insert sizes and shapes vary quite a bit from club to club and manufacturer to manufacturer. Figure 47-2 has been included here to provide close approximations for angles and relative sizes of inserts. The inserts in the figure are drawn full scale but still can only be regarded as a starting point due to the many variables that occur during manufacture. Also, each manufacturer routs the width of the insert cavity differently depending on the face depth. A face insert installed in a driver will usually be wider at its base than the same insert installed in a fairway wood. The differences in the installed insert width at the base on drivers versus fairway woods will be less if a more vertical sided insert is used such as one with 5°. An insert with 22° of side angle will be much larger looking in a driver versus a fairway wood.

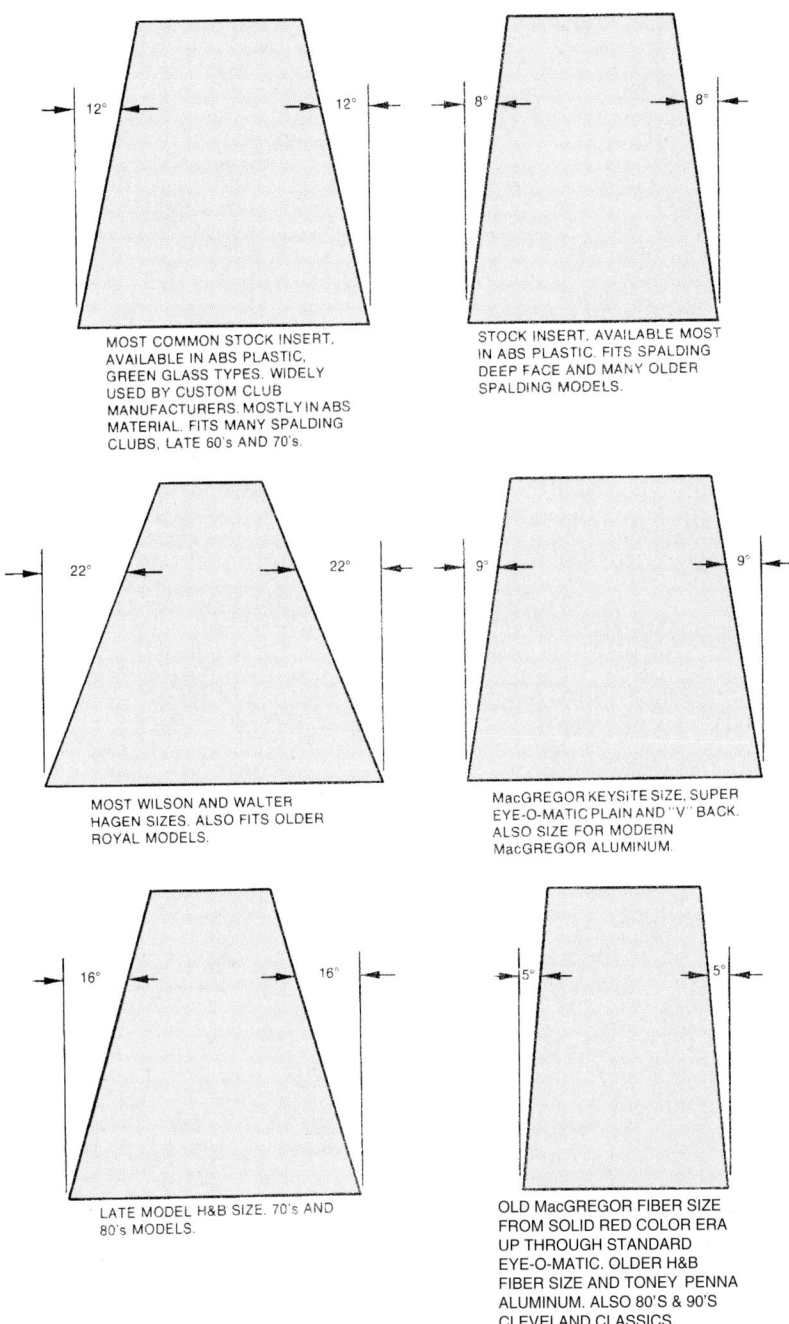

Figure 47-2
Insert size and shape variations

The Insert's Role in Metal Woods & Irons

Since 1932, the U.S.G.A. has not permitted the manufacture of irons with face inserts made of a dissimilar material from the rest of the head. Classic club collectors will recall MacGregor irons made in the 1950's and 60's with copper or black faces, but these were correctly ruled a coating or finish rather than a different insert material. Inserts, of course, are allowed on woods because the face of a wood would quickly deteriorate from ball impact without them.

However, in the early 1980's, the U.S.G.A. recognized that they had a potential problem with the golf industry's introduction of woods made with different materials. Because of the design and material changes involved, the distinction between irons and woods was blurred.

For example, new graphite irons typically had a stainless steel hosel and soleplate, around which graphite was molded to complete the head. In addition, these clubs had a reinforcing steel core behind the face with a veneer of graphite. The question was, at what point is the reinforcement of core the basic structure?

It was against this background that a rule change was proposed that permitted manufacturers to offer metal woods and irons with inserts provided, "the material and construction of the face shall not be designed or manufactured to have the effect, at impact, of a spring, or to impart significantly more spin to the ball than a standard steel face, or to have any other effect which would unduly influence the movement of the ball." This is the basis for the eventual rule change made in 1993.

The proposed rule change prompted the U.S.G.A. to conduct several tests that produced interesting results. Some of the tests confirmed findings from an extensive groove study they conducted in 1986. See Figure 47-3 for their findings involving a three-piece "balata" covered ball and a two-piece surlyn ball.

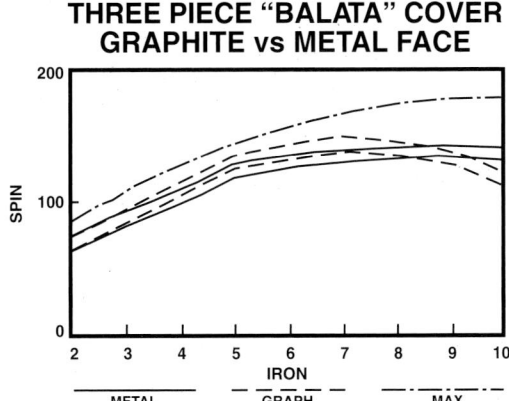

Figure 47-3

Above shows the results of using a three-piece "balata" covered ball and a two-piece surlyn ball. 1) The _dotted lines_ represent the maximum possible spin that could be achieved over the range of clubs and associated head speeds when using each ball. 2) The _dashed lines_ represent the upper and lower bounds of the spin off a graphite insert. 3) The _solid lines_ represent the upper and lower bounds of the spin off a stainless steel face.

The first conclusion is that surlyn covered balls are affected more by a graphite insert than are balata covered balls, especially for the higher lofted irons. The pitching wedge shows a fairly dramatic reduction in spin. The second conclusion is that there is a tendency for the dry graphite insert to exhibit the same phenomenon observed in the groove study test of 1986. A club with a metal face was tested by striking a ball with a thin layer of grass between the ball and club face. A slight <u>increase</u> in spin was experienced with the #2, #3 and #4 iron using surlyn balls and with the #5, #6 and #7 iron using balata balls. The differences in spin are small but interesting, since this phenomenon was contrary to popular belief.

Graphite inserts, which have a high content of plastic, filler or epoxy, have a lower coefficient of friction than do metal faces. Therefore, with a surlyn covered ball, the ball is launched at a higher angle with less backspin, much like a "flyer" shot. The decreased spin and higher launch angle produce a shot with the surlyn ball that will carry farther, up to 10 yards with a #7 iron. The increased distance is not so great with a pitching wedge due to its higher normal trajectory.

Therefore, a player using a graphite insert will hit surlyn covered balls up to 10 yards farther with the mid irons, but no measurable increase in distance will occur when using a balata ball. Graphite inserts perform like metal irons when a thin layer of grass is between the ball and the clubface at impact. This situation, depending upon the ball, might even produce a slight increase in spin for certain irons. The slight increase in spin is observable when using a #3 iron with surlyn and a #5 iron with balata. Because of the loft of drivers there is no measurable difference in spin or ball velocity with the two ball types. Therefore, when making a decision to buy a metal wood driver with an inserted face versus a standard metal wood, the choice should be for other reasons.

Insert Materials

There are a number of different materials used for inserts in golf clubs. The more common and widely used materials are listed below.

1. ABS plastic (injection molded)
2. Epoxy (precast in molds or cast in the head itself)
3. Aluminum (either sheet, bar, extrusion or casting)
4. Fiber (compressed wood fiber and bonding agent)
5. Phenolic
6. Green glass types (fiberglass and resin)
7. Graphite

There are other insert materials but they are only used in small quantities or by one manufacturer. Some of these are stainless steel (investment cast), brass, nylon, titanium, cobalt, melamine and Ligno Ferro® laminated wood inserts. New materials emerge on the market daily so rest assured that this listing is not a complete one.

■ ABS Plastic Insert Materials

This is the most popular insert type used today. The most common type of ABS material used is called Cycolac®. ABS plastics are popular for insert usage because they are very stable and relatively tough. They are also compatible with the various adhesives used to cement them into the head and also with polyurethane finishes used on today's golf wood heads.

ABS inserts are manufactured by a method known as injection molding. The ABS material is purchased in a pellet form, dumped in a hopper and injected into a multi-cavity steel mold under tremendous heat and pressure. The insert cools, solidifies and is removed from the mold. Because of the preciseness of tooling for injection molded parts, many combinations of colors and different designs are possible.

Face screws are not required to hold ABS inserts into golf heads; however, some manufacturers put them in for added assurance and decorative purposes.

■ Epoxy Insert Material

Epoxy inserts are three to four times more expensive than ABS plastic inserts because of both the raw material cost and manufacturing method. They are also a harder material and possess a slightly harder feel to the accomplished golfer than does ABS. Epoxy first became popular as a repair shop item because being a liquid it could be mixed with an activator, poured into the face cavity, allowed to cure and then it could be filed down into a new insert. This proved valuable in replacing lost or broken inserts that were otherwise not available. Later on, manufacturers used epoxy as an insert material mostly in their premium lines to add additional product differentiation from the lesser expensive models. Manufacturers who still make wood heads are now using epoxy inserts with medallions, logos or emblems cast into them and covered over with clear epoxy to enhance the cosmetics of the club. It should be noted here that ABS plastic inserts can also be made with recessed medallions with clear epoxy cast over the top for the same three dimensional effect.

Epoxy inserts are cast from a two component liquid, one component being the base and the other component being the activator. These two components are mixed in the exact proportions necessary and poured into silicon molds. After the epoxy cures they are easily removed from a mold which can be used over and over again. Epoxy inserts are also cast-in-place directly into the insert cavity. Epoxy inserts do not require screws and, in fact, should not have screws put in, even for decorative reasons as they tend to weaken the insert.

■ Fiber Inserts

Fiber inserts are rarely used in today's woods. There are a number of reasons. First, fiber is a porous material affected by moisture and temperature. These conditions can cause fiber to warp, shrink, expand and sometimes delaminate. This is why during manufacture fiber inserts should be kept in a humidity and temperature controlled environment until they are ready to be assembled. Even after the polyurethane finish has cured on the entire head, fiber inserts can be affected to the degree of actually being able to feel and see a hairline crack all around the edge of the insert, especially on the top of the insert. Secondly, fiber inserts require the use of face screws because without them the insert has a tendency to warp and ultimately break the epoxy or resin bond used to glue it in place. Thirdly, because of fiber's inherent instability causing swelling and shrinking, many owners simply send the clubs back for repair or replacement, assuming that the club is defective. The fourth reason is fiber inserts produce a club which is unquestionably inferior regarding durability with no apparent offsetting performance benefits. The main consumption of fiber inserts today is in restoration and replacement on older, classic clubs.

■ Phenolic Fiber Inserts

Phenolic inserts are made from compressed linen or cotton fibers which are bound together with a phenolic resin. These inserts are relatively new in the golf industry and are often confused with original type fiber inserts. The phenolic inserts are easily recognized by their distinctive swirl pattern which is created during the four-way roll facing process in manufacture. When putting on four-way roll, the file cuts through varying layers of impregnated cloth leaving a swirl. Almost every company today producing so-called copies of the classic woods are using this insert. It is most popular in red with a white horizontal bar through the center. This is a very durable, attractive insert and makes a good replacement for original fiber type inserts.

■ Aluminum Inserts

Aluminum has been used for some time as an insert material and is quite acceptable. Most of the aluminum materials used today are of the softer type so that they work easier in production. However, look at a few finished woods with aluminum inserts and you will usually spot one where the face bulge is not a constant radius. This is caused by the hand filing operation during manufacture which is required to set the correct bulge, roll and properly outline the face. During this operation, the file removes wood much more quickly than it does aluminum, thus a small drop-off or dip occurs on each side of the insert. Aluminum inserts usually require the use of screws because it is very difficult to get superior adhesion between aluminum and wood unless adequate preparation and roughening is done immediately before assembly. Most companies who have introduced aluminum inserts to their woods have dropped them after 1 to 2 years.

■ Green Glass Inserts (Gamma Fire)

Glass inserts were once quite popular in the 1970's and 1980's. This insert is durable and bonds exceptionally well to wood with epoxy adhesives. It is easy to cut to size and files well during facing. However, it has a tendency to dull saw blades and files very rapidly. This is caused mainly by the abrasion of the glass fibers.

Glass inserts are heavier than ABS inserts. A glass insert of the same installed size as an ABS insert is approximately 9 swingweight points heavier or slightly over ½ ounce.

To help the reader better understand the effect a heavier insert has on club design, follow this example: A customer brings a driver into the repair shop to have the ABS plastic insert replaced with a glass insert. You are told that this driver is hit by the customer with normal trajectory. The first thing you do is take out the old insert and put in a glass insert. The original swingweight of D-2 is now E-1 (9 points heavier). So, next you take off the soleplate and remove a little over ½ ounce of lead from the recess. The club will now swingweight D-2 again. However, you have shifted over 1 ounce of weight in the head. This weight has altered the clubhead's center of gravity more toward the face and higher up in the head. The net effect from this is a lower ball trajectory than before, assuming the same golfer and no specification changes other than the insert change.

■ Graphite Inserts

Using graphite as a material for inserts was a result of its success in golf shafts. A manufacturer reasoned that golfers would likely make the association that if longer drives resulted from using lightweight graphite shafts then using the same material in inserts would lengthen drives as well. However, graphite inserts are not as light as you may think. In fact, ABS plastic inserts are lighter.

Most graphite inserts sold for fitting into existing woods are manufactured by injection molding, just like plastic inserts. The smallest percentage of material composition of an injection molded graphite insert is usually graphite. Most of the material used is epoxy and filler. A liquid comprised of resin epoxy, filler and graphite fibers of various diameters is injected into a mold. After curing, the insert is released from the mold, cooled and ready for use.

Graphite inserts adhere very well to a wood head cavity and are quite durable. They are attractive due mainly to the swirl pattern created from filing. They are also frequently used to fill the entire face of some metal woods. When used in metal woods, the insert is usually cast under pressure directly into the insert cavity where it cools. This way the manufacturer can take advantage of the epoxy content to ensure good adhesion with the metal cavity.

Besides injection molding, graphite inserts are also made by compression molding. Compression molded inserts are made from a mold that contains three pieces. The upper piece contains the scoring lines, roll and bulge. The middle piece establishes the shape of the insert and the bottom piece establishes the back of the insert. The bottom piece will sometimes be marked so that the finished insert will have an irregular pattern that will better adhere to epoxy when installed into an insert cavity.

The mold is preheated to 140°C, a graphite compound containing graphite, epoxy and filler is placed into the mold and then it is covered with 2 to 3 pieces of graphite cloth. The mold is closed under great pressure, heated and 7 minutes later the insert is removed, ready to use.

SECTION

SIX

GOLF IRON CLUB DESIGN AND MANUFACTURE

CHAPTER 48

GOLF IRON CLUB DESIGN: SPECIFICATIONS

Many individual aspects of iron club design have already been discussed in Section 5, **Golf Wood Club Design and Manufacture**. The design of an iron club, however, has not been discussed as a total unit showing how each design attribute and specification interrelates with every other.

Although iron club specifications, their relationships and their effects on performance are not as complex to define and understand as those of wood clubs; they parallel one another in many instances. Even though this chapter overlaps that of wood club design, it will lead to a more thorough understanding of iron club design and ultimately total golf club design.

This chapter specifically concerns definitions, performance characteristics and the important relationships that exist between loft, lie, face progression, hosel offset, length, shaft flexing and center of gravity of golf iron clubs.

Defining and Measuring Each Iron Club Specification

As was done in the wood club design section, it is necessary to take each iron club specification and explain it using the four steps below.

1. Explain briefly what each specification does regarding performance.
2. Define it.
3. List all other specifications which directly affect it.
4. Give an in-depth discussion where necessary to fully explain it.

Loft

Performance Characteristics of Loft
A determining factor concerning the angle of trajectory of the golf ball as it leaves the face.

Definition of Loft
The angle of the face to the centerline of the hosel hole. See Figure 48-1.

Other Specifications Which Affect Loft
Face Progression. See Figure 48-4.
Center of Gravity Location (Head Weight Distribution). See Figure 48-5.
Shaft Flex. See Figure 48-9.

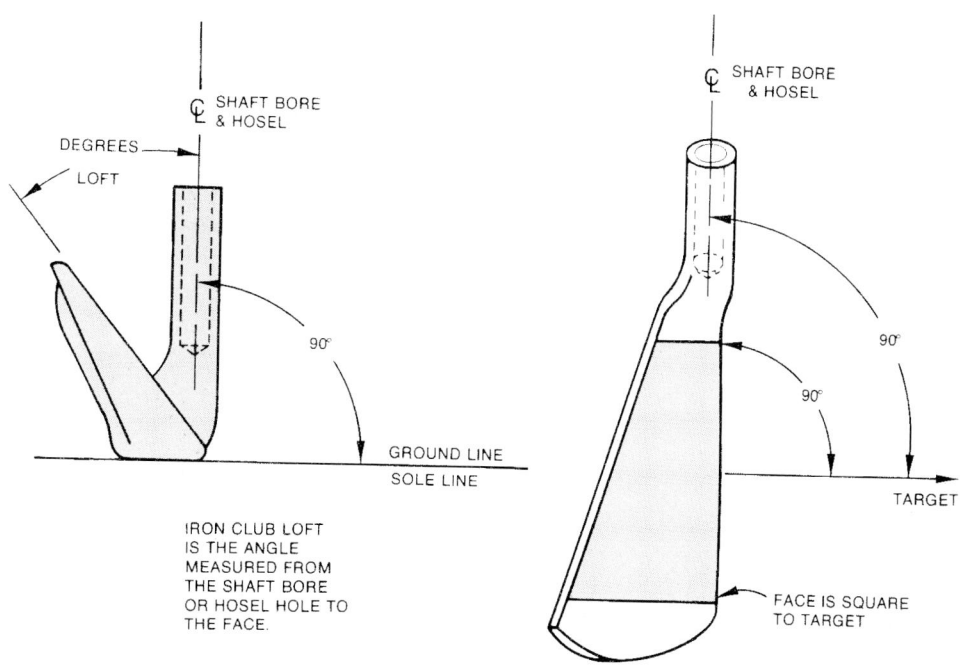

Figure 48-1
Defining loft angle

DEGREES

LOFT

℄ SHAFT BORE & HOSEL

90°

GROUND LINE
SOLE LINE

IRON CLUB LOFT
IS THE ANGLE
MEASURED FROM
THE SHAFT BORE
OR HOSEL HOLE TO
THE FACE.

℄ SHAFT BORE & HOSEL

90°

90°

TARGET

FACE IS SQUARE
TO TARGET

*Note that the loft of an iron club is measured differently than that of a wood club. Chapter 31 discusses this in detail.

Discussion of Loft

A wood club's loft is measured from a line perpendicular to the sole to the angle of the face. Although there is a simple way to measure wood club loft with an ordinary protractor or loft gauge, it is not the real or "effective loft" of that wood club. (See Chapter 35—**Golf Wood Club Design: Loft** for a more thorough explanation and understanding of "effective loft.") First, iron clubs are not measured the same as wood clubs because the sole is much narrower than that of a wood club which makes it more difficult to determine a line tangent to it. Secondly, sole designs and angles vary so much in the different makes and models that it would be impossible in most instances to obtain an accurate measurement. An example would be a manufacturer whose irons are designed with either a "bounce" sole or one which is cambered (radiused front to back). To obtain an accurate loft measurement from either of these soles with the face would require, at best, guesswork. See Figure 48-2. This is why iron lofts are measured as the angle from the centerline of the hosel to the face. This method determines the real or "effective loft" of an iron, whereas the accepted method of measuring wood club loft does not indicate real or "effective loft."

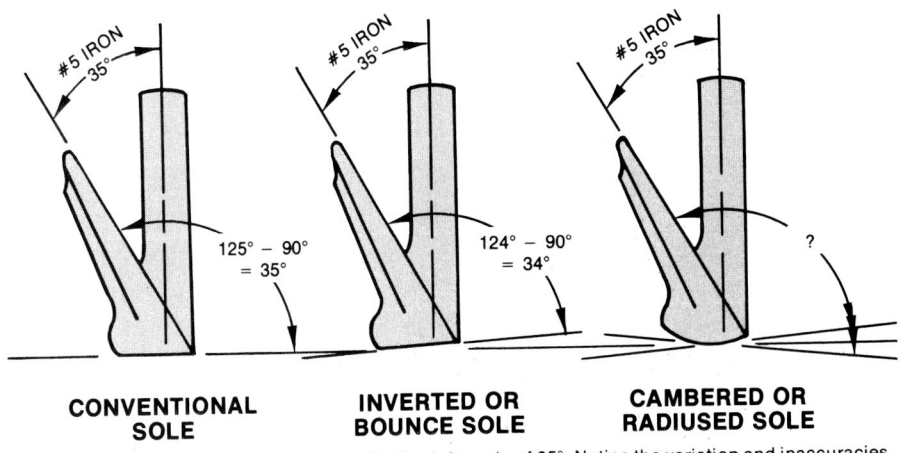

CONVENTIONAL   INVERTED OR   CAMBERED OR
SOLE   BOUNCE SOLE   RADIUSED SOLE

All #5 irons shown above have a real or effective loft angle of 35°. Notice the variation and inaccuracies
obtained when the loft angle is measured from the sole.

Figure 48-2
True or effective loft compared to sole loft

Look at Figure 48-3 and study the top drawing which shows a bounce sole. It can easily be determined that a 1° bounce exists because of the difference in readings of 35° and 34°. Now, for the interesting part of this discussion. If the iron referred to here were a wood club and measured as a wood club, it would be 34° loft with a 1° hook face! Sole inversion or bounce in any iron is the same as hook in a wood. Conversely, scoop or dig in an iron is the same as slice in a wood. This is entirely brought about by the two differing methods of measuring wood and iron lofts. Look at the bottom drawing in Figure 48-3.

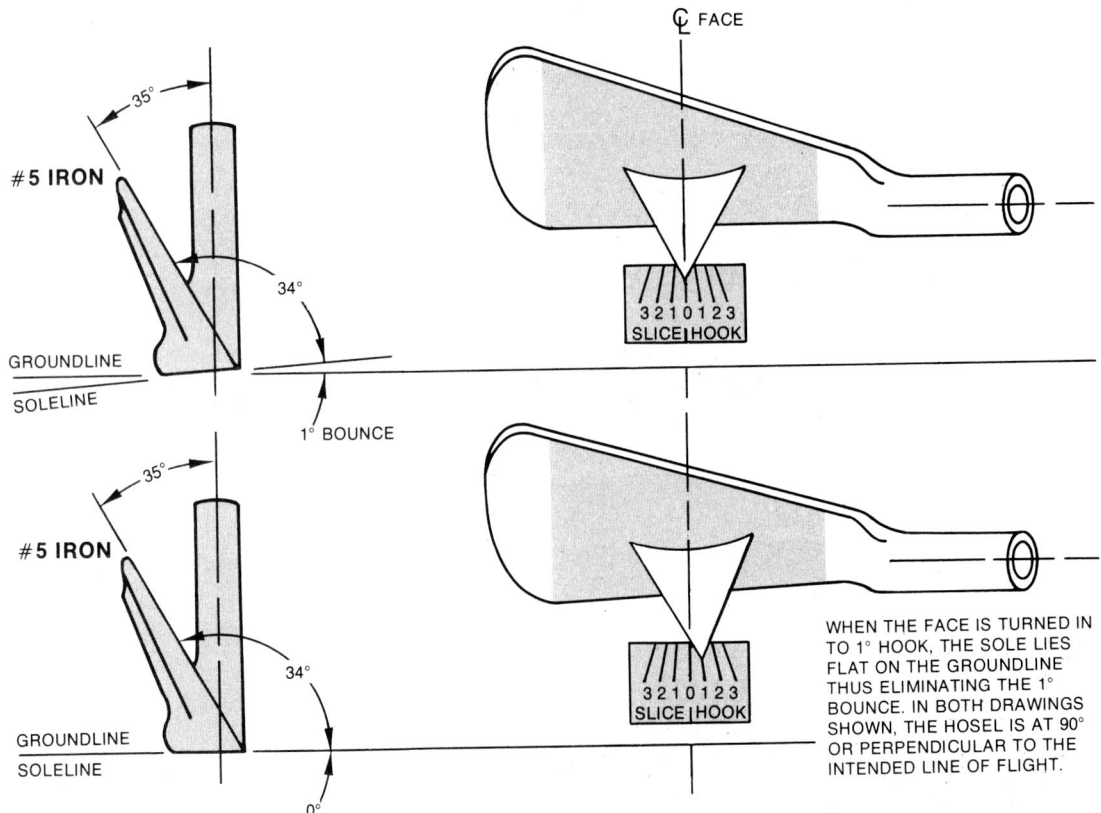

WHEN THE FACE IS TURNED IN
TO 1° HOOK, THE SOLE LIES
FLAT ON THE GROUNDLINE
THUS ELIMINATING THE 1°
BOUNCE. IN BOTH DRAWINGS
SHOWN, THE HOSEL IS AT 90°
OR PERPENDICULAR TO THE
INTENDED LINE OF FLIGHT.

Figure 48-3
Comparing sole bounce in irons to hook in woods

504

Face progression is a variable which also affects the loft of an iron. Refer to Figure 48-4. The point to mention here is that this is a minor factor in varying ball trajectory. It is a proven factor during controlled machine testing, but the differences rarely are detectable during player testing. Despite this, many players believe that irons with less face progression, and subsequently more hosel offset will hit the ball significantly higher. The reason for this misconception is that most models introduced with less face progression were game improvement designs having a lower center of gravity. For the player, less face progression was visually obvious, but the lower center of gravity was not. Therefore, the players make an incorrect assumption about the significance of face progression on ball trajectory.

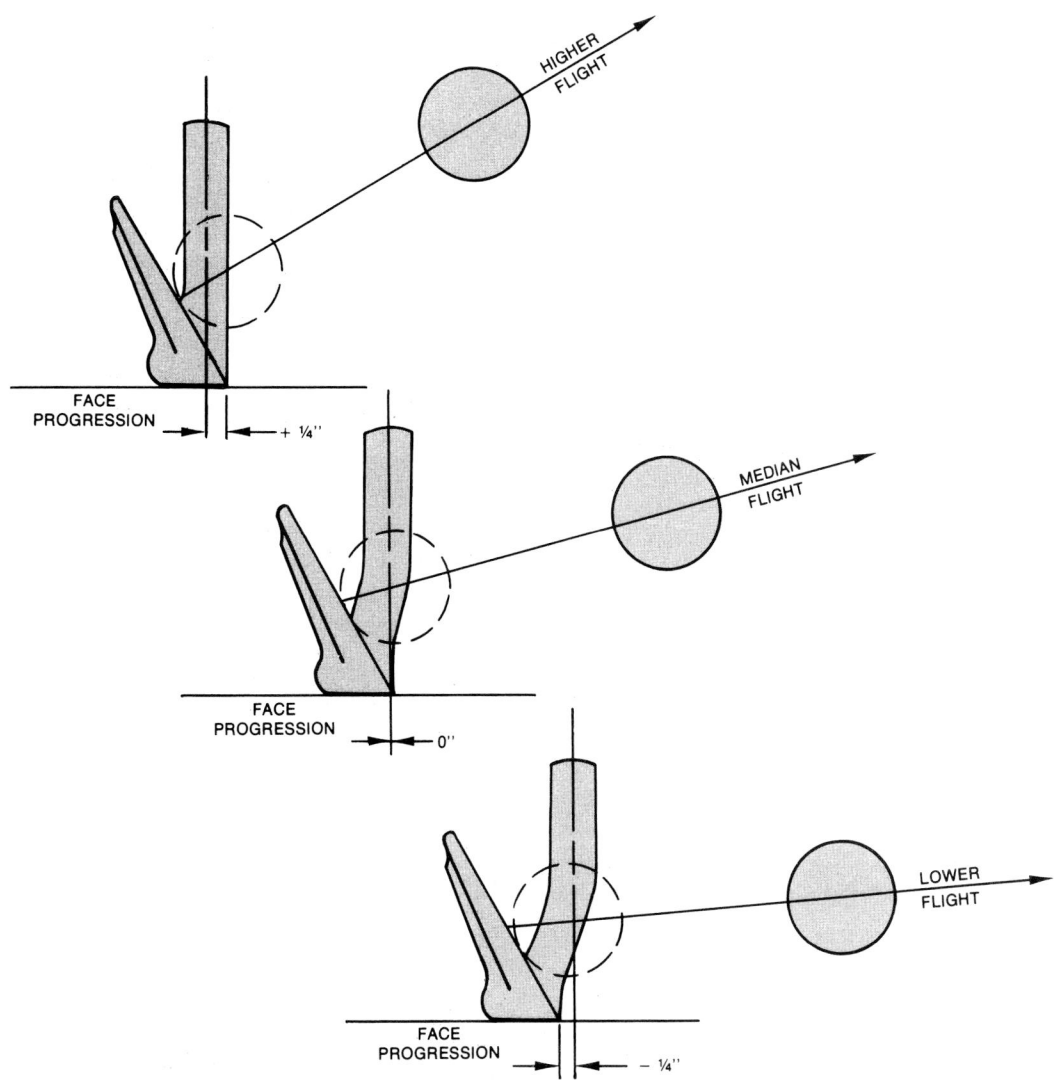

NOTE:
1. Assume all three clubs are identical except for face progression and each ball is struck on the same spot of the face.
2. The face progression dimensions and ball trajectories shown in this drawing are for reference and should be accepted as relative measures only.

Figure 48-4
Effect of face progression on loft

The location of the center of gravity in the vertical plane is one of the key variables in controlling ball trajectory. See Figure 48-5. The lower the center of gravity the higher the trajectory and the higher the center of gravity the lower the trajectory. Of course, this assumes that all other variables are constants and the impact location is at the same point on the clubface.

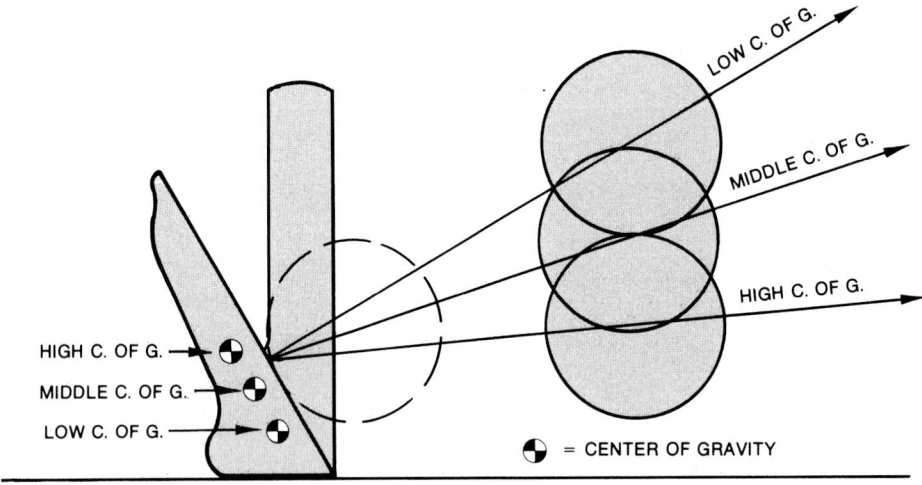

Figure 48-5
Effect of head weight distribution on loft

A number of years back, "low profile" type irons became quite popular among players who had difficulty getting the ball airborne and also hitting it solidly. The low profile irons may not be for everybody and in fact have given way to cavity back designs that share the center of gravity feature, but they do in fact work. The reason is mainly due to a more reduced center of gravity compared to conventional or larger type iron heads. See Figure 48-6. However, keep in mind that regardless of the iron head design, if the player contacts the ball in the center of the face with the iron head's center of gravity equal to or lower than that of the golf ball's center of gravity, the shot will most likely have proper trajectory and feel solid. Be cautioned not to visually compare irons or look at an iron and assume where its center of gravity is located. The head must be removed from the shaft, balanced on the face and marked because there are too many variables which control its location. Variables such as hosel length, hosel diameter, bore depth, loft angle, blade thickness, blade lengths, toe height and heel height all affect the center of gravity location.

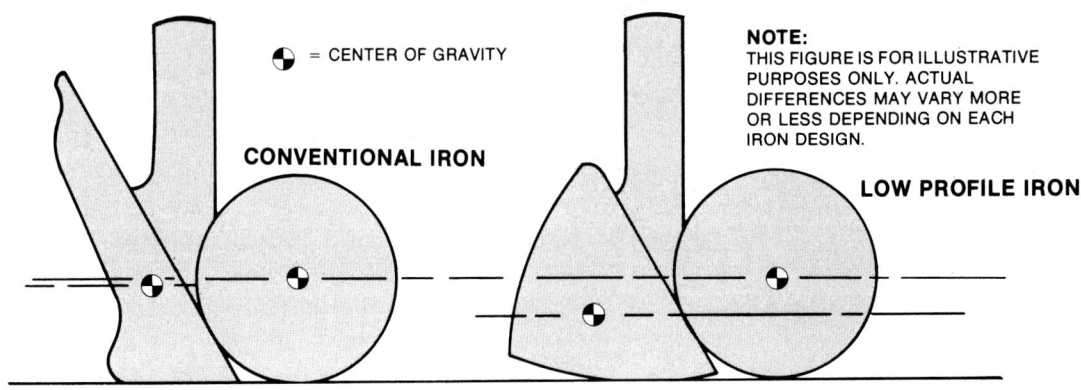

Figure 48-6
Comparing centers of gravity on conventional versus low profile irons

Because of the loft angle, each different lofted clubhead makes contact with the golf ball at different points on the face. A #9 iron, for example, will make contact with the ball lower on the face than a #2 iron. See Figure 48-7. In other words, the greater the loft angle the lower the contact point. The ball always contacts the face below the ball's center of gravity. Only an iron with a 0° loft would contact the ball in line with the ball's center of gravity.

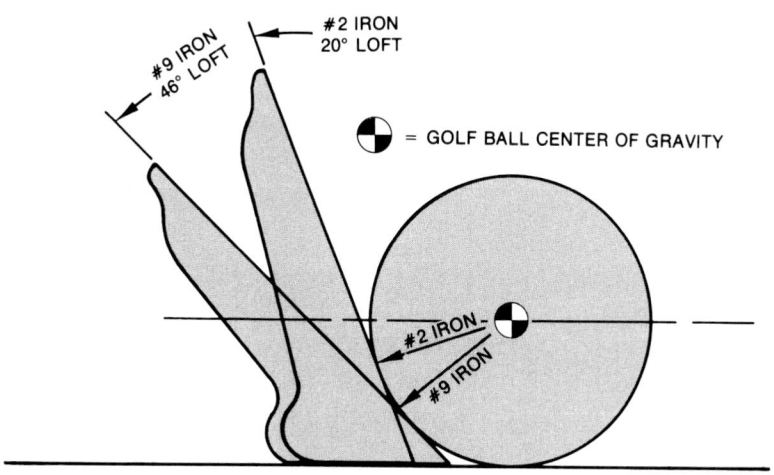

Figure 48-7
Point of contact for #2 and #9 irons

In most conventionally shaped irons the center of gravity locations for the #2 through #9 irons are about the same distance up the face from the groundline. This of course is only true if the center of gravity location is measured vertically from the groundline with the bore also perpendicular to the groundline and the face square to the intended target line. See Figure 48-8.

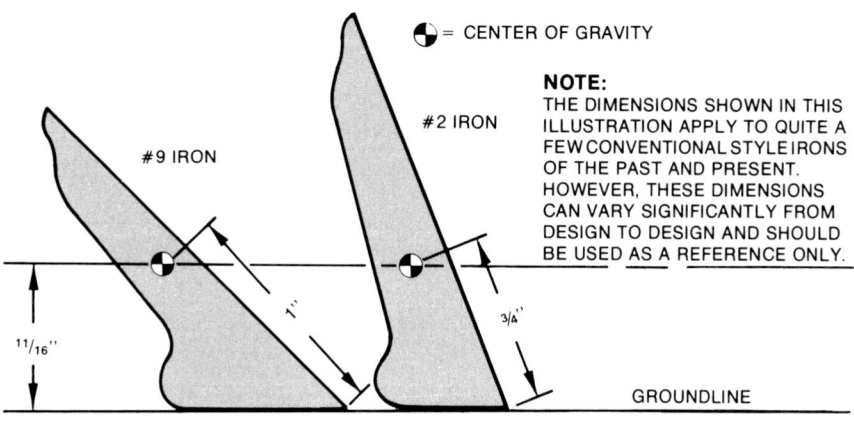

Figure 48-8
Comparing center of gravity locations of a #2 iron and a #9 iron

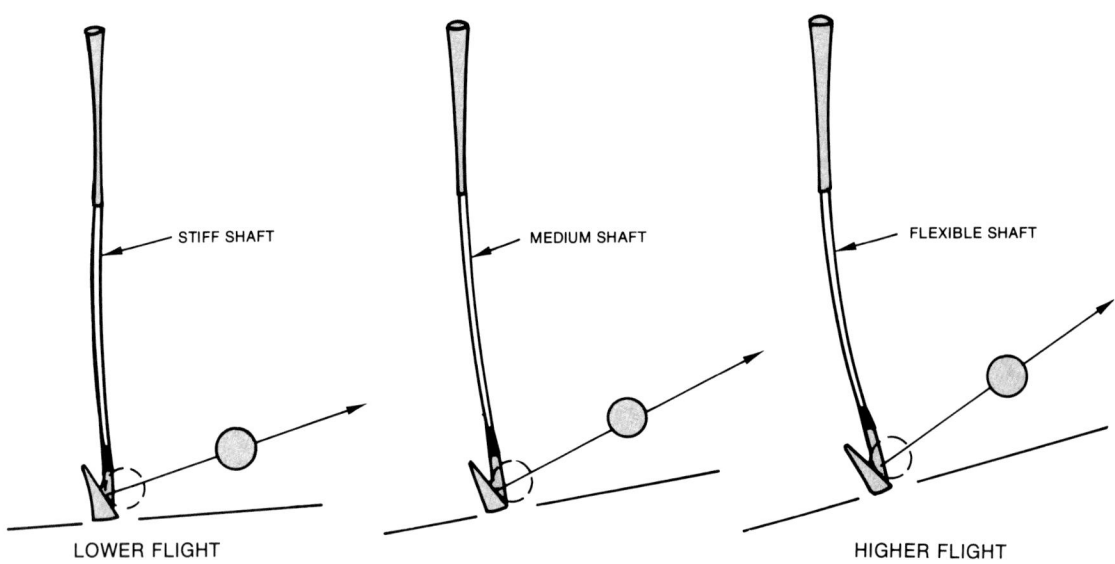

STIFF SHAFT

MEDIUM SHAFT

FLEXIBLE SHAFT

LOWER FLIGHT

HIGHER FLIGHT

Figure 48-9
*Effect of shaft flex on loft
*Assuming all other variables except shaft flex are constant

	TABLE 48-1							
	Iron Club Lofts – Men's and Ladies'							
	Men's				**Ladies'**			
Irons	**Strong Lofts**	**Modern Standard Lofts**	**Weak Lofts**	**Traditional Standard**	**Strong Lofts**	**Modern Standard Lofts**	**Weak Lofts**	**Traditional Standard**
1	15°	16°	17°	17°	–	–	–	–
2	18°	19°	20°	20°	19°	20°	22°	21°
3	21°	22°	24°	23°	22°	23°	25°	24°
4	23°	25°	28°	26°	25°	26°	28°	27°
5	26°	28°	32°	30°	28°	30°	32°	31°
6	30°	32°	36°	34°	32°	34°	36°	35°
7	34°	36°	40°	38°	36°	38°	40°	39°
8	38°	40°	44°	42°	40°	42°	44°	43°
9	42°	44°	48°	46°	44°	46°	48°	47°
PW	46°	48°	52°	50°	48°	50°	52°	51°
SW	54°	55°	56°	56°	55°	56°	58°	56°

Lie

Performance Characteristics of Lie

The relationship of the club's head to the golfer's hands at impact throughout the various golf club lengths. Improper lie can cause directional problems. See Figure 48-10.

Definition of Lie

The angle of the centerline of the shaft with the ground line tangent to the sole at the face centerline. See Figure 48-11.

Other Specifications Which Affect Lie

Shaft Flex. See Figure 48-12.
Length. See Figure 48-13.

Discussion of Lie

Chapter 36—**Golf Wood Club Design: Lie** has provided an in-depth discussion of lie pertaining to both woods and irons. Look at Figure 48-10 through 48-13 and then refer back to Chapter 36 and reread it. Lie is one of the most interesting and enlightening specifications in golf club design. It is also misunderstood and misstated by many people. Later on in this book, the golf club fitting chapters will further explain additional aspects of lie.

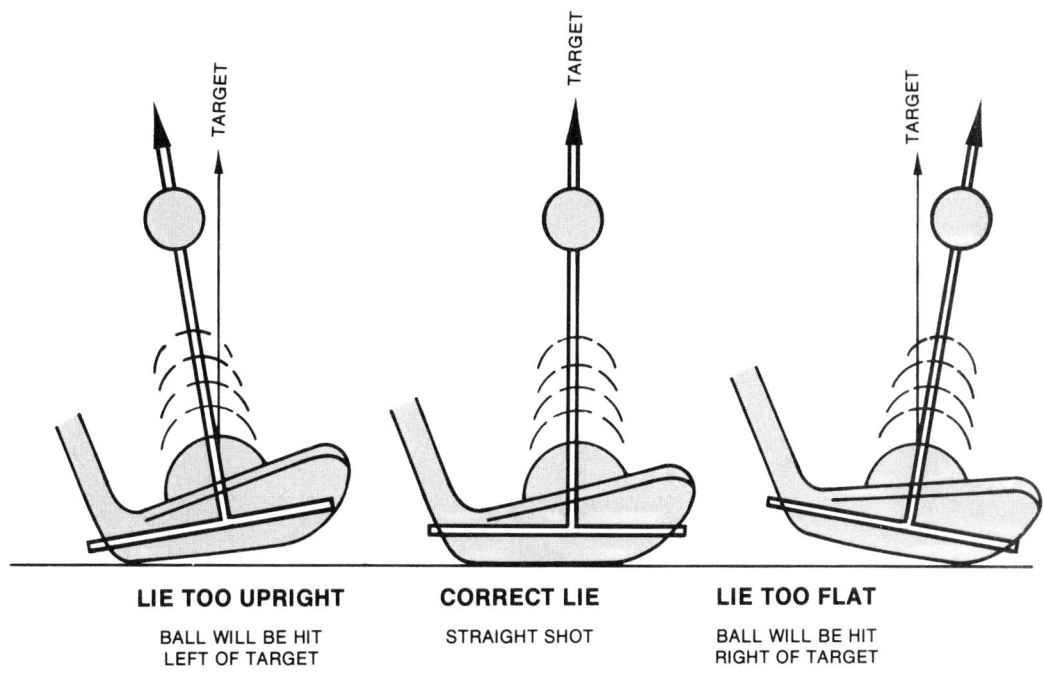

LIE TOO UPRIGHT

BALL WILL BE HIT
LEFT OF TARGET

CORRECT LIE

STRAIGHT SHOT

LIE TOO FLAT

BALL WILL BE HIT
RIGHT OF TARGET

NOTE: Even though the leading edge of the club is perpendicular to the desired direction of flight, the plane on the face of either a too upright or too flat lie club will hit the ball either left or right of the target, respectively.

Figure 48-10
Improper lie can cause directional problems

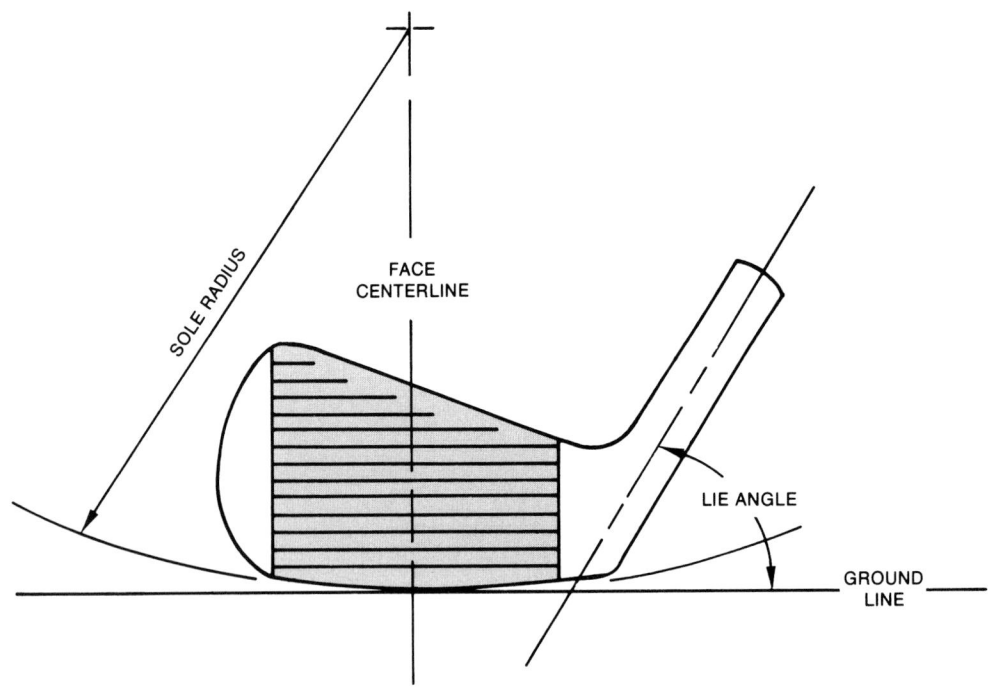

Figure 48-11
Definition of lie

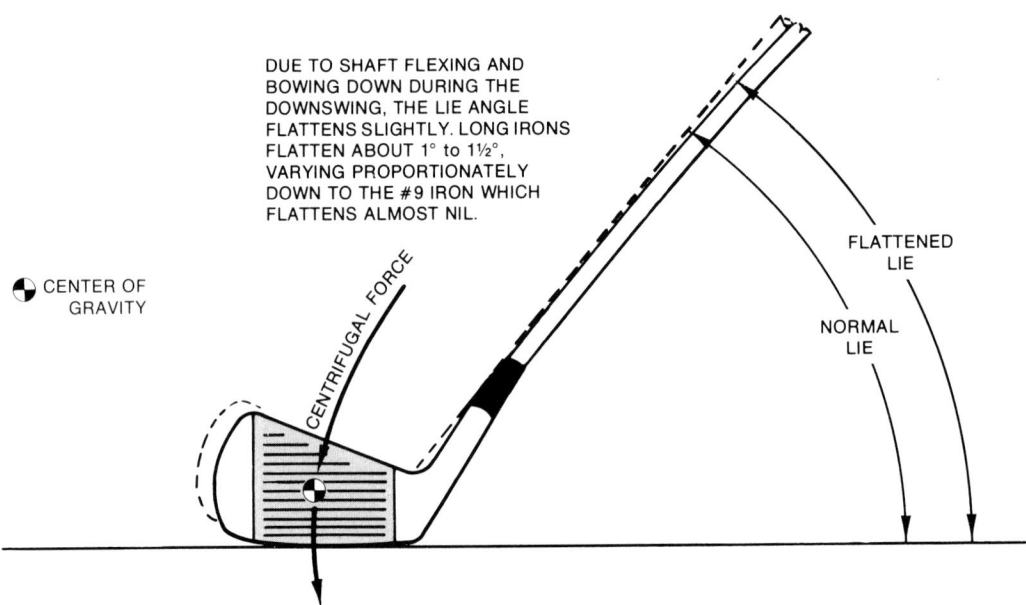

DUE TO SHAFT FLEXING AND
BOWING DOWN DURING THE
DOWNSWING, THE LIE ANGLE
FLATTENS SLIGHTLY. LONG IRONS
FLATTEN ABOUT 1° to 1½°,
VARYING PROPORTIONATELY
DOWN TO THE #9 IRON WHICH
FLATTENS ALMOST NIL.

Figure 48-12
How centrifugal force flattens the lie of a club during the downswing

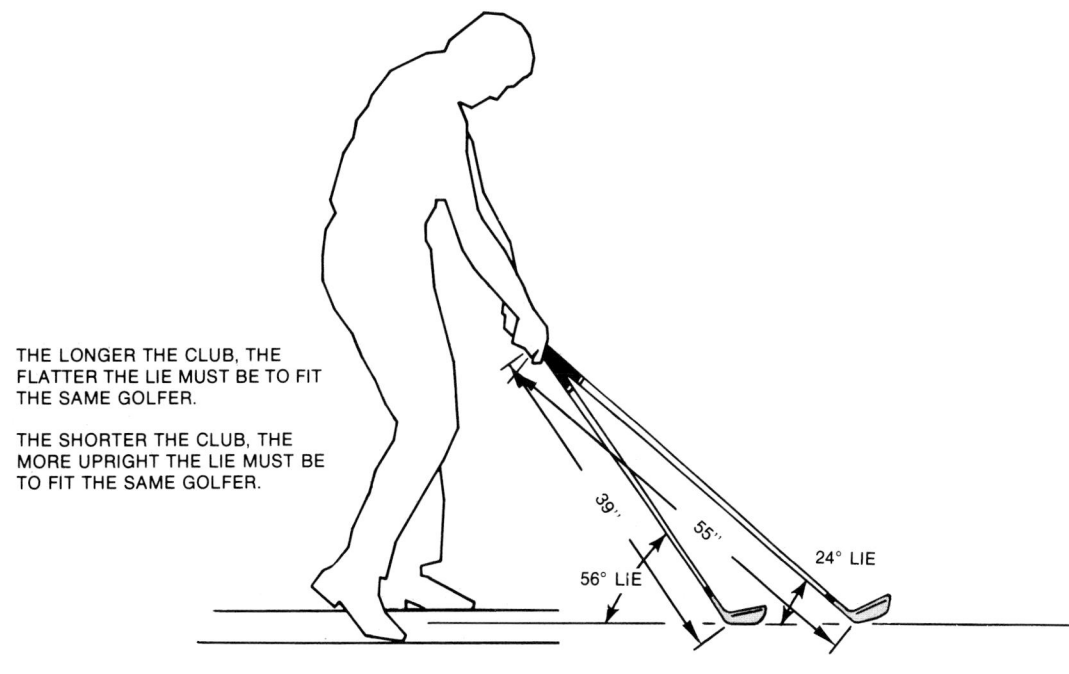

THE LONGER THE CLUB, THE FLATTER THE LIE MUST BE TO FIT THE SAME GOLFER.

THE SHORTER THE CLUB, THE MORE UPRIGHT THE LIE MUST BE TO FIT THE SAME GOLFER.

Figure 48-13
The effect of length on lie

	Men's				Ladies'		
Irons	[1] Flat Lies	[1] Standard Lies	[1] Upright Lies	[3] Modern Lies	[2] Flat Lies	[2] Standard Lies	[2] Upright Lies
1	53°	55°	57°	57°	51°	53°	55°
2	54°	56°	58°	57½°	52°	54°	56°
3	55°	57°	59°	58°	53°	55°	57°
4	56°	58°	60°	58½°	54°	56°	58°
5	57°	59°	61°	59°	55°	57°	59°
6	58°	60°	62°	59½°	56°	58°	60°
7	59°	61°	63°	60°	57°	59°	61°
8	60°	62°	64°	60½°	58°	60°	62°
9	61°	63°	65°	61°	59°	61°	63°
PW	61°	63°	65°	61°	59°	61°	63°
SW	61°	63°	65°	61°	59°	61°	63°

TABLE 48-2
Iron Club Lies – Men's and Ladies'

[1] Lies shown are for standard men's length irons (i.e., 39" #2 iron). For each ½" added to standard length, subtract 1° in lie (flatter) and for each ½" subtracted from standard length, add 1° in lie (upright).

[2] Same as Note 1 above but based on a standard length set with a 38" #2 iron.

[3] Some manufacturers have adopted this new standard in which the long irons are more upright, the mid irons standard and the short irons more flat. Ladies' lies would be 2° flatter than those listed. See the fitting chapter for more information.

Length

Performance Characteristics of Length
A determining factor of clubhead speed.

Definition of Length (Traditional Standard)
The distance from the back heel portion of the sole to the top of the grip cap. See Figure 48-14.

Other Specifications Which Affect Length
Shaft Flex. See Figure 48-15.
Sole Radius. See Figure 48-16.

Discussion of Length
Chapter 37—**Golf Wood Club Design: Length** gives an in-depth discussion of length. Most of the information given in Chapter 37 applies to irons also. Look at Figure 48-14, 15 and 16 and if you do not remember the discussion of length from Chapter 37, please reread it.

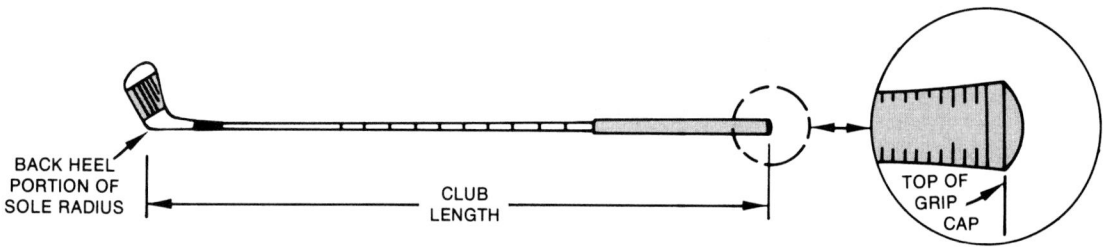

Figure 48-14
Definition of club length (traditional standard)

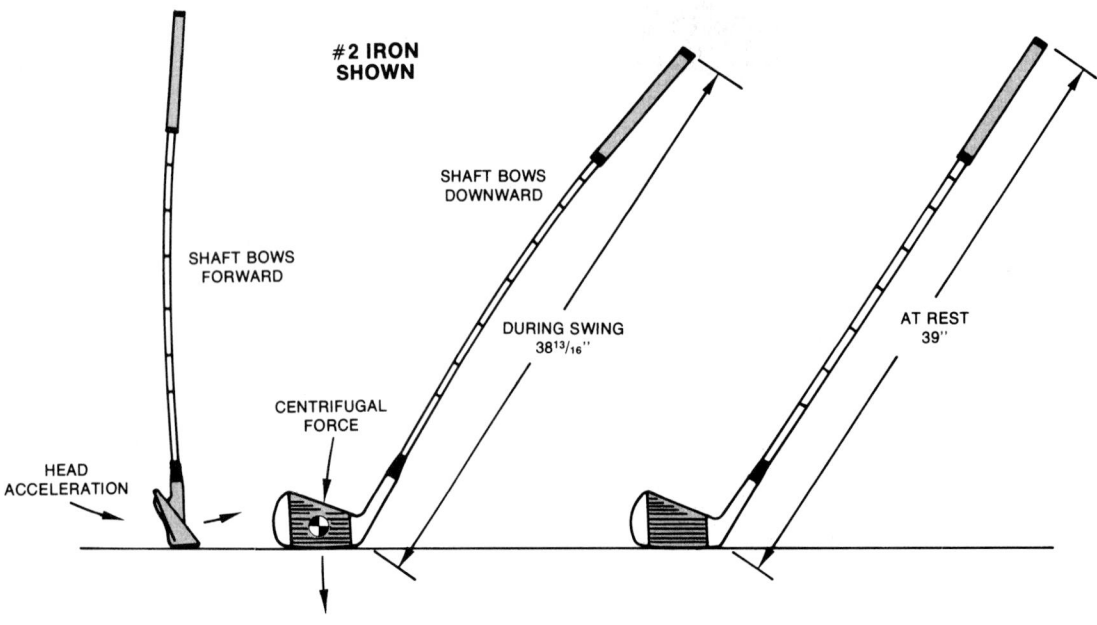

Figure 48-15
The effect of shaft flexing (bowing downward and forward) on length

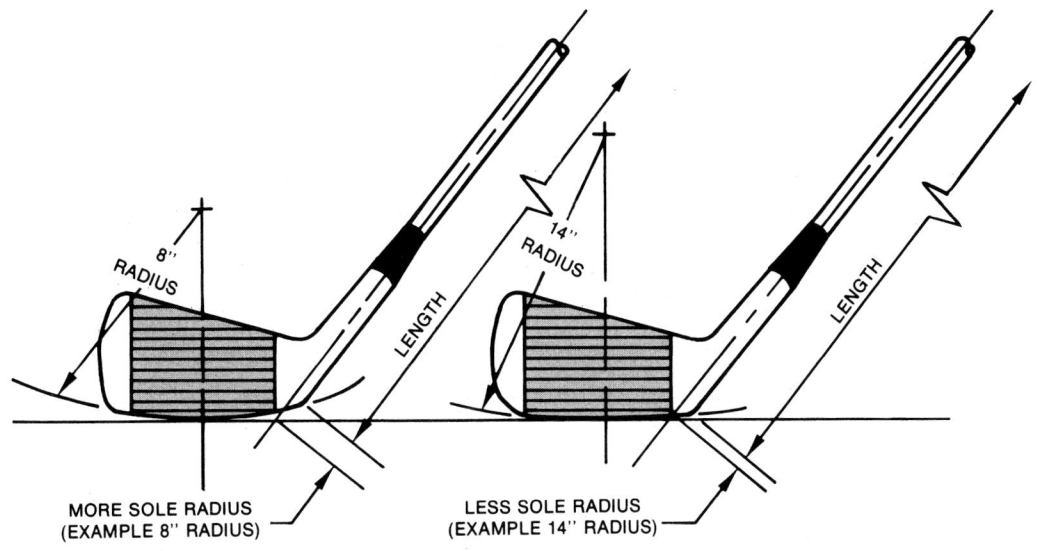

MORE SOLE RADIUS
(EXAMPLE 8" RADIUS)

LESS SOLE RADIUS
(EXAMPLE 14" RADIUS)

Assuming two golf clubs are the same length when measured in the traditional way, the club with more sole radius will be longer than the club with less sole radius.

Figure 48-16
Effect of sole radius on length

	TABLE 48-3			
	Iron Club Lengths – Men's and Ladies'			
Irons	Men's Modern Standard	Men's Traditional Standard	Ladies' Standard	[1] Ladies' Petite
1	39½"	39"	38"	37½"
2	39"	38½"	37½"	37"
3	38½"	38"	37"	36½"
4	38"	37½"	36½"	36"
5	37½"	37"	36"	35½"
6	37"	36½"	35½"	35"
7	36½"	36"	35"	34½"
8	36"	35½"	34½"	34"
9	35½"	35"	34"	33½"
PW	35½"	35"	34"	33½"
SW	35½"	35"	34"	33½"

[1]Ladies' petite is usually ½" shorter than the traditional ladies' standard length. Some companies make ladies' petite 1" shorter than ladies' standard length.

513

Face Progression or Hosel Offset

Performance Characteristic of Progression and Offset

A factor concerning the trajectory of a golf ball by altering the exact moment of impact. (i.e. the ball will be contacted ¼" sooner by a golf club if the face progression is 0" vs. -¼") See Figure 48-4.

Definition of Progression and Offset

Face Progression: The distance from the centerline of the shaft or hosel bore to the farthest front portion of the face on its centerline.

Hosel Offset: The distance from the farthest front portion of the hosel to the farthest front portion of the face on its centerline. See Figure 48-17.

Other Specifications Which Affect Face Progression or Hosel Offset

None.

Discussion of Progression and Offset

From a technical standpoint face progression is the only true measure for accurately determining the position of the face to the hosel, while hosel offset is more or less a visual determinant of this relationship. Refer to Figure 48-17 for a comparison of offset and face progression in two different hosel design irons. One iron is shaft over hosel and the other is the traditional shaft in hosel. In the address or playing position, the shaft over hosel type would not appear to have as much offset as the shaft in hosel type. However, the actual face progressions in this example would be the same in both irons if measured on proper equipment such as the Golf Club Gauge™.

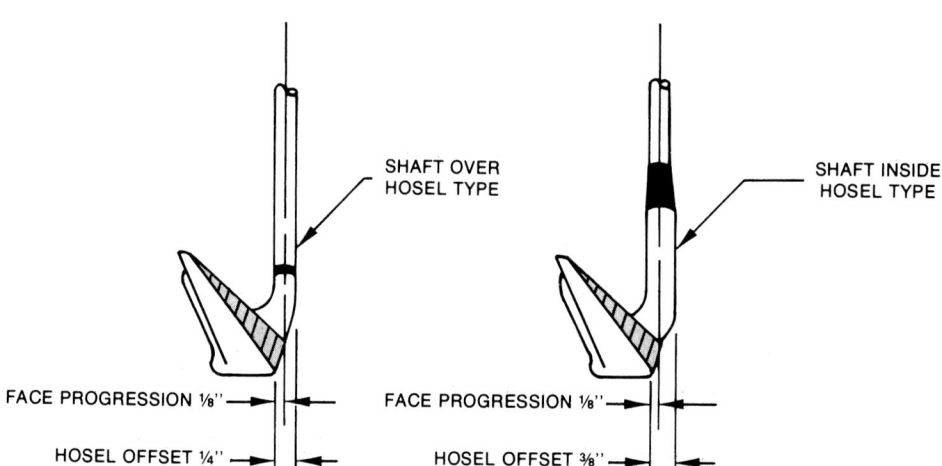

SHAFT OVER HOSEL TYPE

SHAFT INSIDE HOSEL TYPE

FACE PROGRESSION ⅛" →

FACE PROGRESSION ⅛" →

HOSEL OFFSET ¼" →

HOSEL OFFSET ⅜" →

Example Shown: Two iron clubs having the same face progression but different hosel offsets.

Figure 48-17
Definition of face progression and hosel offset

CHAPTER 49

GOLF IRON CLUB DESIGN: PITCHING AND SAND WEDGE SPECIFICATIONS

If a golfer carries a wedge or wedges in his/her golf bag, chances are that during a round more shots will be hit with the wedges than any other club in the bag with the exception of the putter. However, in most cases, the better the wedge plays the fewer the putts taken. Wedges are very important clubs and should be thoroughly understood regarding design, function and playability.

It simply amazes me at the number of golfers who play on courses which have sand traps and do not carry a sand wedge. Sand wedges, Third Wedges®, pitching wedges and dual wedges are designed to make certain shots easier. Understanding how the various design attributes of wedges correlate with why and how they work gives a valuable insight into using wedges more effectively during play.

Pitching Wedges

The family of pitching wedges includes the pitching wedge, the pitching club, #10 iron and in days of old, the "niblick" which was used for any full short shot or chip shots around the green. Pitching wedges are designed as specialty clubs and as such have different design attributes than the normal irons within a set. Some manufacturers build pitching wedges in such a manner as to perform a logical extension of one more club down from the #9 iron. This club is technically misnamed a pitching wedge and really should be called a #10 iron which is available through some manufacturers as a stock club or on a special order basis.

There is a great deal of discussion among better players, golf pros and the manufacturers as to how a pitching wedge should be designed. First, the question of swingweight is a proper topic of discussion. Should a pitching wedge designed to go with a given set of irons be lighter, the same or heavier in swingweight? It is generally agreed that a pitching wedge should be at least two swingweights and possibly four swingweights heavier than the irons within a set. However, within the last few years many of the touring pros, club pros and better amateurs have had strong feelings toward more closely matching the swingweight of the pitching wedge to that of the irons. This should not, and in all likelihood will not change the current trend of building pitching wedges heavier than the irons. The average player and most better players who do not play golf for a livelihood cannot develop the high degree of feel and touch with a pitching wedge that a golf professional can. It makes sense that to execute delicate pitch shots, the heavier clubhead can be swung more slowly and thus more accurately and will tend to give a little more distance as a result of "fat" shots because of the increased clubhead mass. This is especially true when extracting the ball from higher grass around the green. However, when hitting full pitching wedge shots, the heavier club usually cannot be hit as far because most golfers cannot swing it as fast. A pitching wedge is not designed for distance. Unfortunately, too many people judge a set of irons by how far they can hit the pitching wedge. Hitting great distances with a pitching wedge seems to denote a status level of golfing proficiency, while all the time the #9 iron is quite possibly the most underused club in the bag.

Most tour golfers today are carrying three wedges: a pitching wedge, a sand wedge and a third wedge. Apparently they feel that this is necessary to more finely develop the short stroke saving approach shot under the many varied conditions they face on the tour. This concept is also popular with good playing amateurs and now even a few touring pros and good amateurs carry four wedges. As lofts have become much stronger in the last few years, a significant loft gap has opened, usually between the pitching wedge and sand wedge. This gap is usually filled with an additional pitching wedge, weaker in loft than the other. The third wedge concept will be defined and discussed in detail later in this chapter.

Pitching wedge specifications vary greatly from manufacturer to manufacturer and model to model. See Appendix 8. The one thing to keep in mind when defining a pitching wedge versus a #10 iron is this: a #10 iron is a logical extension of one less club than the #9 iron. For instance, the #10 iron should be the same swingweight, therefore hitting distance should be incremental and in progression with the rest of the set. The blade shape and outline will be in progression with the #9 iron and the sole design will be the same and progressed in width from the #9 iron. A pitching wedge can be almost any combination of specifications shown in Figure 49-1.

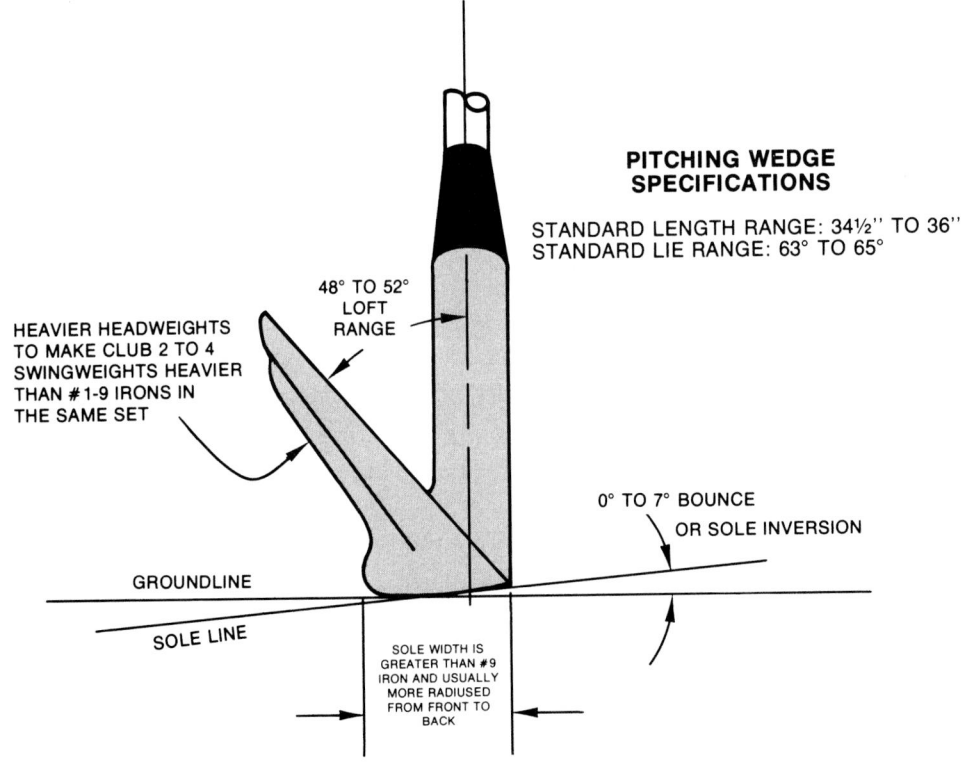

Figure 49-1
Pitching wedge specifications range and characteristics

A good habit to get into is to visually compare and determine the amount of bounce a sole has. This can apply to any wedge, either pitching, sand or dual. The importance of this will be made immediately apparent as soon as you discover a wedge that has a dig sole. This is the opposite of bounce and is obviously not good regarding playability. The main cause for this type of sole is a loft change. For instance, if a manufacturer makes their pitching wedge with a 2° bounce sole and 52° loft and the loft is changed on a loft and lie bending machine to 48° to make the wedge stronger, it will now have a 2° scoop or dig sole. See Figure 49-2.

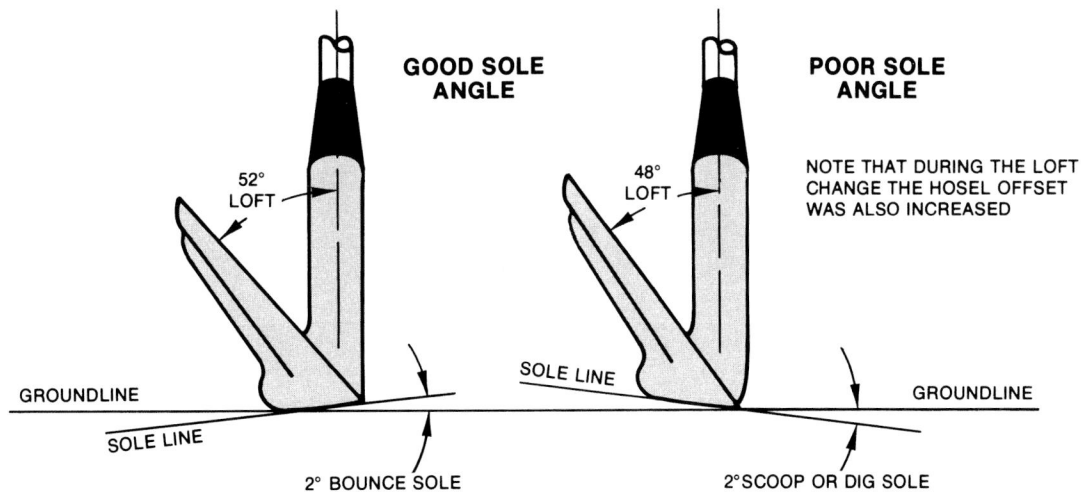

Figure 49-2
Effect of loft change on sole angle

The best way to exactly measure sole angle in degrees is on the Golf Club Gauge™. However, visually checking sole angle is fast and convenient and usually is all that is necessary. The best way to visually check sole angle is to hold the shaft of the club loosely in the fingers allowing the grip and shaft to hang vertically while you sight across the sole of the club with the toe pointing away from you. See Figure 49-3.

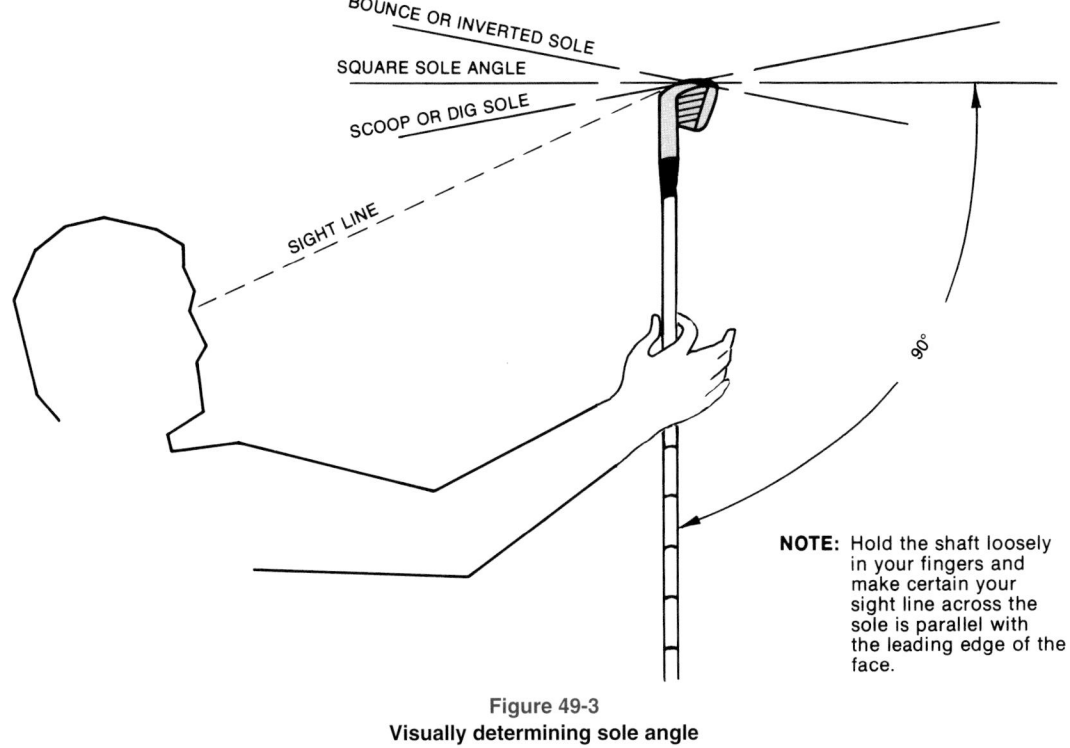

Figure 49-3
Visually determining sole angle

517

A pitching wedge with a slight amount of sole bounce is good. Some pitching wedges have no bounce, but the sole is usually more radiused from front to back; this is also good. A few pitching wedges, as already mentioned have scoop or dig soles where the leading edge of the club is lower than the trailing edge. This is not a good design because the club will have a tendency to dig into the ground thus causing a greater percentage of fat shots. The square sole angle with a radius from front to back and the bounce sole angle allow the pitching wedge head to enter the ground and immediately come back out of the ground thus eliminating the tendency for the clubhead to dig.

Sand Wedge

The family of sand wedges includes the "sand wedge," "sand club," the "#11 iron" and "niblick." In most cases the only differences are in the terminology. Sand wedges are available in an infinite number of shapes and many combinations of specifications, all of which could be correctly called any one of the names mentioned except for the niblick. One of the main problems that golfers faced in the pre-1930's era was that sand wedges were not invented yet. Thus, the trusty niblick was used to many golfers' frustration because it had a very narrow sole width and sharp leading edge which caused digging. The skill level required to extract a ball from sand with the niblick was far greater than it was with the wider, bounce sole type sand wedge first invented by Gene Sarazen in the 1940's and manufactured by the Wilson Sporting Goods Company.

Many golfers today do not have a sand wedge in their set. Regardless of golfing proficiency, a sand wedge can make most sand shots much easier and particularly so if the golfer understands how a sand wedge works. The sand wedge is designed with an inversion or "bounce" type sole which is intended to keep the clubhead from digging deeply into the sand on the downswing. The clubhead itself usually never touches the ball, but rather the sand forces the ball out as it is squeezed by the clubhead. If a sand wedge had opposite of bounce or a dig sole the clubhead would automatically dig deeper than its normal arc and would probably stop in the sand. See Figure 49-4. Other characteristics of a sand wedge are that it is more lofted than a pitching wedge and usually four to eight swingweights heavier than the set of irons. Its sole width is usually the widest of any iron in the set and is generally more radiused (cambered) from front to back and heel to toe. See Figure 49-5.

Dotted line indicates normal arc of clubhead with a "square sole."
Solid line indicates flattened arc of clubhead caused by "bounce sole" which prevents clubhead from digging in.
Heavy solid line indicates a deep digging arc of clubhead caused by scoop or dig sole.

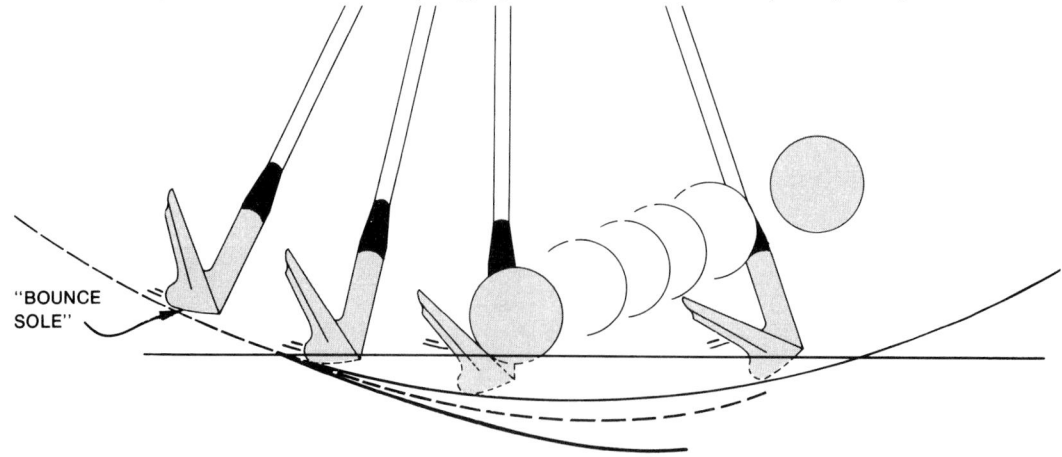

Figure 49-4
How a sand wedge works

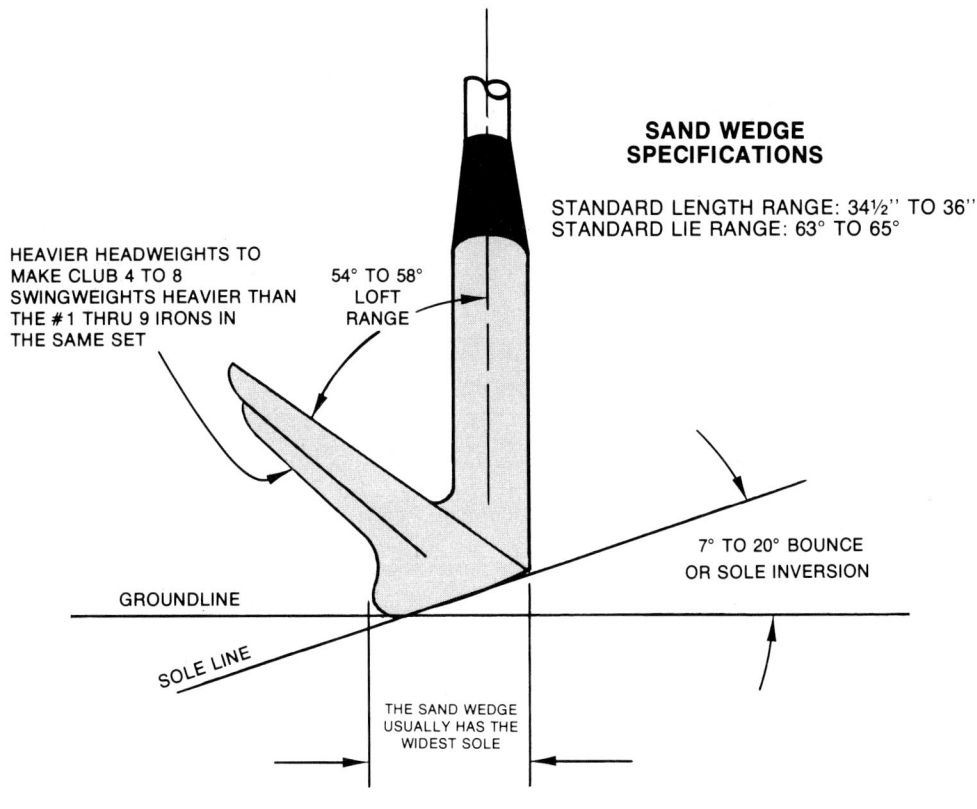

SAND WEDGE
SPECIFICATIONS

STANDARD LENGTH RANGE: 34½'' TO 36''
STANDARD LIE RANGE: 63° TO 65°

HEAVIER HEADWEIGHTS TO
MAKE CLUB 4 TO 8
SWINGWEIGHTS HEAVIER THAN
THE #1 THRU 9 IRONS IN
THE SAME SET

54° TO 58°
LOFT
RANGE

7° TO 20° BOUNCE
OR SOLE INVERSION

GROUNDLINE

SOLE LINE

THE SAND WEDGE
USUALLY HAS THE
WIDEST SOLE

Figure 49-5
Sand wedge specifications and range characteristics

A sand wedge's face is usually rolled open for most sand shots. This does two things: first, the loft is increased and the sole inversion in the swinging plane is increased thus raising the golf club's leading edge higher off the ground. To better understand this, take a sand wedge and set it on the floor in the square playing position. Now roll it open slowly and watch the leading edge of the clubface lift higher off the floor as the sole inversion or bounce is increased. Notice also that on most sand wedges the leading edge will also be raised slightly off the floor while the clubface is in the square position. This indicates that the sand wedge does in fact have an inverted or "bounce" sole. Roll the clubface slowly shut and the leading edge will drop down and touch the floor.

A technical point on sand wedge design, but a necessary one to fully understand playability, concerns the width of the sole. Assume two clubs have the same degrees of sole bounce; the wider the sole, the higher the leading edge is raised off the ground. Also, as the face is rolled open by the same amount in both clubs, the leading edge of the wider sole club will raise off the ground in even greater proportion than the narrower one. See Figure 49-6. The net effect of this statement is that the wide sole sand wedge with a lot of bounce will work well in soft, deep sand because it will not have a tendency to dig. However, it is questionable in harder, wetter or shallower sand where it may tend to "bounce" into the ball thus hitting thin shots or skulling the ball over the green.

On the other hand, a wide sole sand club with very little bounce will work well from most sand conditions and can also be played from fairway and rough around the green as long as the ball is not on bare ground.

519

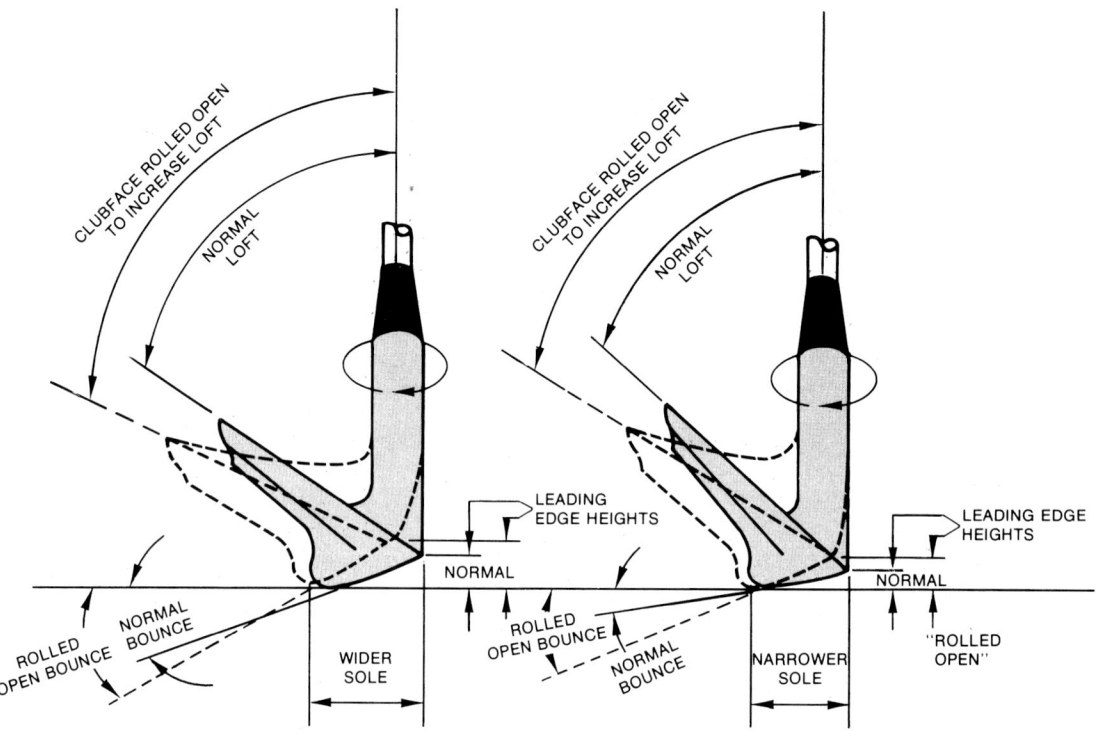

Both sand wedges above have the same loft and bounce. The sole width is the only variable. If both wedges are rolled open the same amount, notice how much higher the leading edge is raised on the wider sole sand wedge. Note that the leading edge in the normal position is also higher on the wider sole sand wedge.

Figure 49-6
Effect of sole width on leading edge height

Now you should begin to see the tradeoff of design characteristics which makes the selection process a little more difficult in determining the proper sand wedge. The sole bounce, the width of the sole and the playing conditions most frequently encountered must be considered. A number of touring pros will own more than one sand wedge and change depending if playing conditions are tight lies, hard ground, hard sand or wet, plushy conditions with fluffier sand. Some areas have gravel type sand, others have powder type sand. Study the accompanying sand wedge selection Table 49-1 and use this as a general guideline.

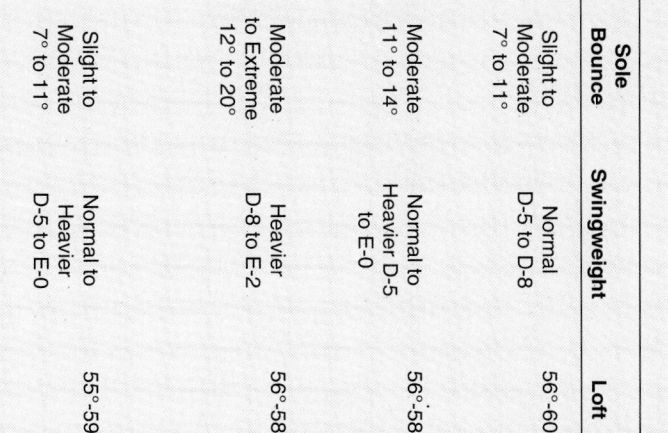

TABLE 49-1
Sand Wedge Selection Table

Width of Sole	Sole Bounce	Swingweight	Loft	Sand Conditions	Performance From Fairway	Comments
Narrow	Slight to Moderate 7° to 11°	Normal D-5 to D-8	56°-60°	Tight, packed sand, not often loosened up and shallow sand. Generally the harder sand type bunkers. Minimum bunker maintenance, rarely raked.	Best—This type sand wedge will work from most all fairway conditions and even from tight lies.	Not good in powdery sand. Fair in loose grainy sand.
Narrow to Medium	Moderate 11° to 14°	Normal to Heavier D-5 to E-0	56°-58°	Loose sand, but very grainy, slight gravel content. Rarely a buried lie. Heavy type sand, large grains, usually dark in color. Moderately raked and maintained.	Good—But bounce can cause problems if fairway conditions are hard with tighter lies.	Works better in powdery sand than in very tight packed sand.
Wide	Moderate to Extreme 12° to 20°	Heavier D-8 to E-2	56°-58°	Powdery, fine texture sand, hand or machine raked often. Buried lies not uncommon. A lot of sand in the traps, usually white in color.	Fair—Not best for fairway shots unless conditions are very plush. A narrower width sole will work better on fairways, but with a slight loss in overall sand shot ability unless skill level is high.	Will also work in loose sand, but is poorer from tight packed sand.
Medium to Wide	Slight to Moderate 7° to 11°	Normal to Heavier D-5 to E-0	55°-59°	Average sand conditions which vary quite a bit, but rarely reach the extremes of tight packed sand or fluffy powdery sand.	Good—Will work from most all fairway conditions, but a higher skill level is required on tight lies.	This sand wedge will work in most all types of sand and can be considered a good selection with a minimum of performance tradeoffs.

This chart should be used as a guide only. With all the possible weight, length, sole bounce, sole width, head shape and shaft combinations available in sand wedges today and in the past, it would be all but impossible to accurately describe each sand wedge's playing characteristics.

Dual Wedges

This type of wedge was once quite popular, but not many companies manufacture them anymore. A dual wedge is a cross between a pitching wedge and a sand wedge. It has slightly greater loft than the pitching wedge and less sole width and bounce than the sand wedge. Also, a dual wedge is usually in between the two in swingweight, but usually the same length. See Figure 49-7.

The dual wedge's purpose was to use one club for both pitching and sand shots and under many types of conditions worked quite well. However, it does not combine the best features of both a sand and pitching wedge, but rather averages them so that playability with a dual wedge from both fairway and sand are average also. A similar analogy would be to eliminate the #6 iron and #8 iron and to fill the gap you either hit a soft #7 iron or a harder #7 iron. In the case of a dual wedge, it's not hitting it harder or softer exactly, but it still does not fully replace a pitching wedge and a sand wedge under most conditions of play.

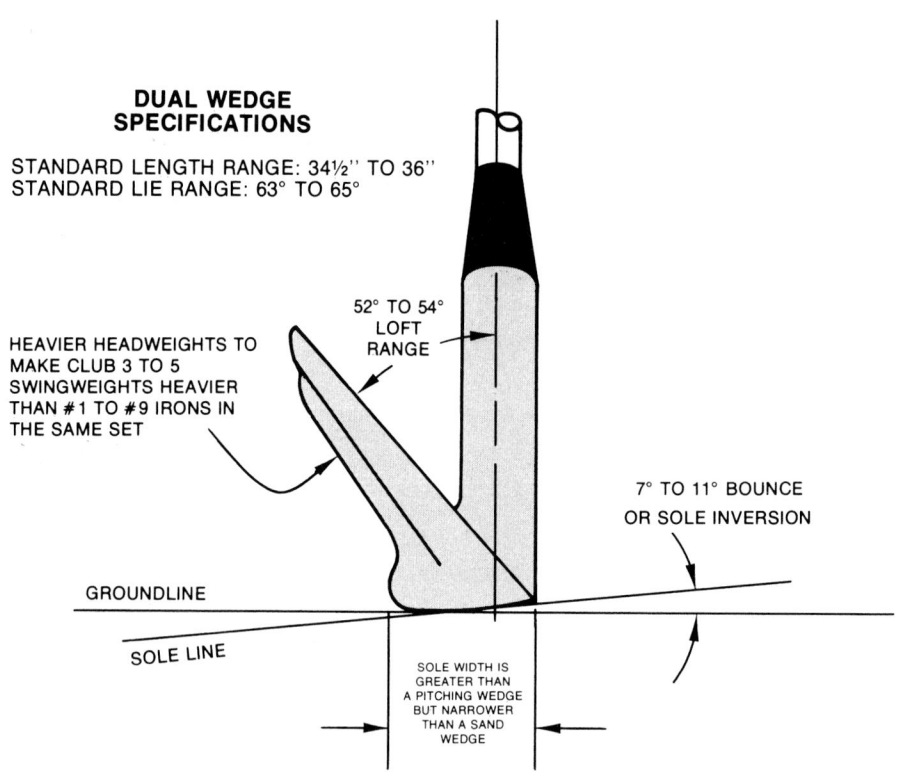

DUAL WEDGE SPECIFICATIONS

STANDARD LENGTH RANGE: 34½" TO 36"
STANDARD LIE RANGE: 63° TO 65°

52° TO 54° LOFT RANGE

HEAVIER HEADWEIGHTS TO MAKE CLUB 3 TO 5 SWINGWEIGHTS HEAVIER THAN #1 TO #9 IRONS IN THE SAME SET

7° TO 11° BOUNCE OR SOLE INVERSION

GROUNDLINE

SOLE LINE

SOLE WIDTH IS GREATER THAN A PITCHING WEDGE BUT NARROWER THAN A SAND WEDGE

Figure 49-7
Dual wedge specifications range and characteristics

522

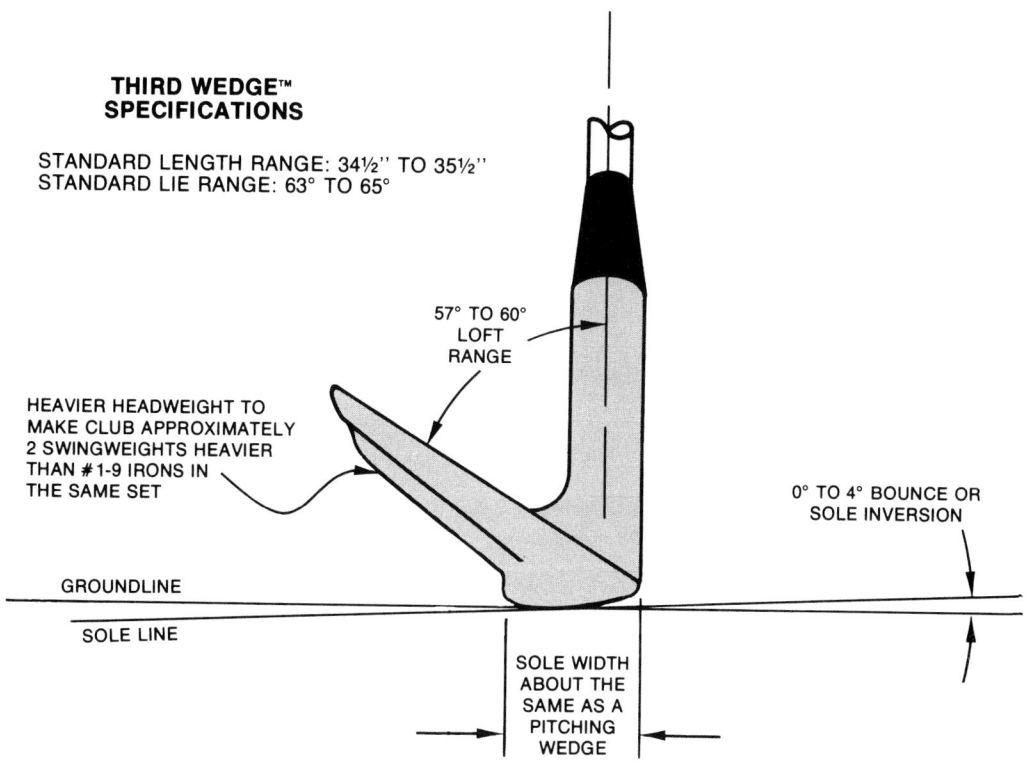

**THIRD WEDGE™
SPECIFICATIONS**

STANDARD LENGTH RANGE: 34½'' TO 35½''
STANDARD LIE RANGE: 63° TO 65°

57° TO 60°
LOFT
RANGE

HEAVIER HEADWEIGHT TO
MAKE CLUB APPROXIMATELY
2 SWINGWEIGHTS HEAVIER
THAN #1-9 IRONS IN
THE SAME SET

0° TO 4° BOUNCE OR
SOLE INVERSION

GROUNDLINE

SOLE LINE

SOLE WIDTH
ABOUT THE
SAME AS A
PITCHING
WEDGE

Figure 49-8
Third Wedge™ specifications range and characteristics

The Third Wedge®

It was mentioned earlier in this chapter that a number of tour players, club professionals and better playing amateurs have changed their set makeups to include three wedges: a pitching wedge, a sand wedge and a Third Wedge®. The Third Wedge™ can take many different forms. For some players it is another pitching wedge and for others an additional sand wedge. Its predominant form, however, seems to be as an entirely new type wedge with characteristics not often found in other wedges manufactured today or in the past.

The purpose of the Third Wedge® is to eliminate most of the compromise between selecting a proper pitching and sand wedge for varying conditions. It is designed as a short distance shot saving wedge from the fairway which will get the ball quickly up and higher into the air with increased backspin. An example is a short full shot or a chip from a tight lie over a bunker with the pin cut in close. This type of situation calls for a soft, high shot with a good amount of backspin for the ball to get close. It also requires minimal sole bounce and extra loft or being able to open the face without fear of increasing the sole bounce. This wedge has a maximum distance range of under sixty yards. It is also useful from a bunker that is very wet, has tightly packed sand or even in buried lie situations in dry, powdery sand. Figure 49-8 defines the specifications range and Third Wedge® characteristics. Note also that a new concept for wedges – the fourth wedge – was introduced in the early 90's. This wedge has similar features to the Third Wedge®, but the loft is 63°-64°, making it an option of play from 40 yards and in.

CHAPTER 50

GOLF IRON CLUB DESIGN: SHAPE AND STYLE FEATURES

A detailed discussion of every possible shape and style feature of iron clubs would be virtually impossible since the possibilities and combinations are limitless. There are a few key variables, however, which most everyone recognizes from one iron club design to another. These key variables are illustrated in this chapter. As with wood clubs, the shape and style features of an iron club have both a direct and indirect effect on how playable a golf club will be. Sole design variations and hosel offset variations are two features which affect performance directly from an actual design standpoint and indirectly from the mental standpoint regarding how playable a given golfer would perceive a certain golf club to be. For instance, if a golfer has played all his life with a set of irons which has no hosel offset whatsoever and the ball is addressed with an iron which is offset, say 5/16", which is extreme, he is likely to feel quite strongly that he cannot hit this club as well as an iron with no offset. Even if he hits a few good shots trying it out, it still can be extremely difficult to create enough confidence in this new iron to feel comfortable hitting it. Study the following figures, look at your own golf clubs or those in the golf shop and compare the differences from manufacturer to manufacturer and club to club.

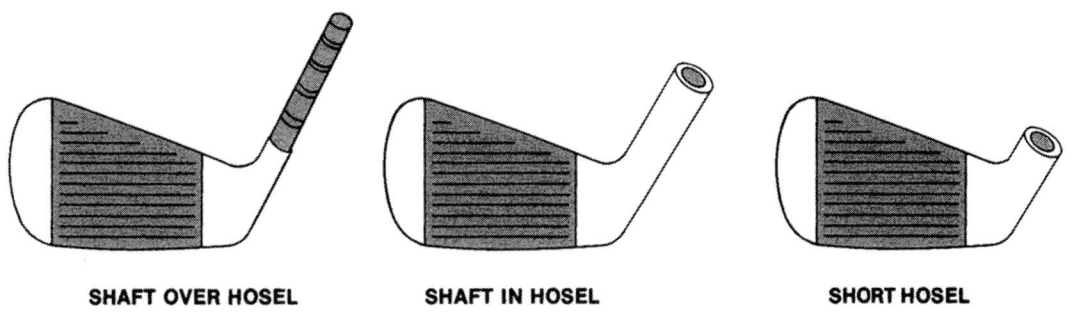

SHAFT OVER HOSEL   **SHAFT IN HOSEL**   **SHORT HOSEL**

Figure 50-1
Hosel type variations

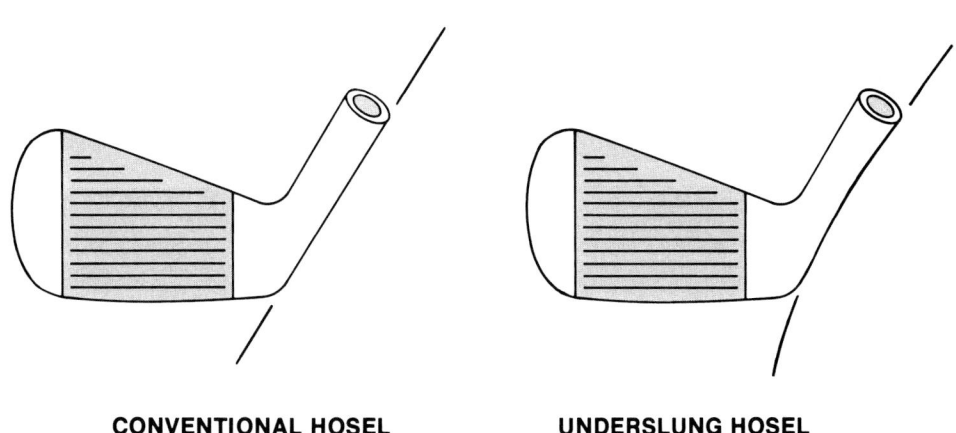

CONVENTIONAL HOSEL   **UNDERSLUNG HOSEL**

Figure 50-2
Hosel style variations

NOTE:
A BARRELED HOSEL MAKES A
ROUNDED AND BLENDED
TRANSITION FROM THE NORMAL
HOSEL DIAMETER TO THE TOP OF
THE HOSEL. THE HOSEL WALL
THICKNESS AT THE TOP IS THIN
AND DOES NOT REQUIRE A
FERRULE.

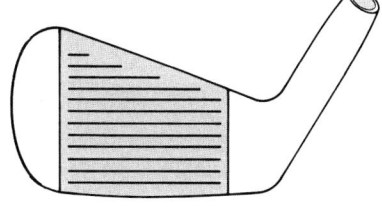

Figure 50-3
Definition of a barreled hosel

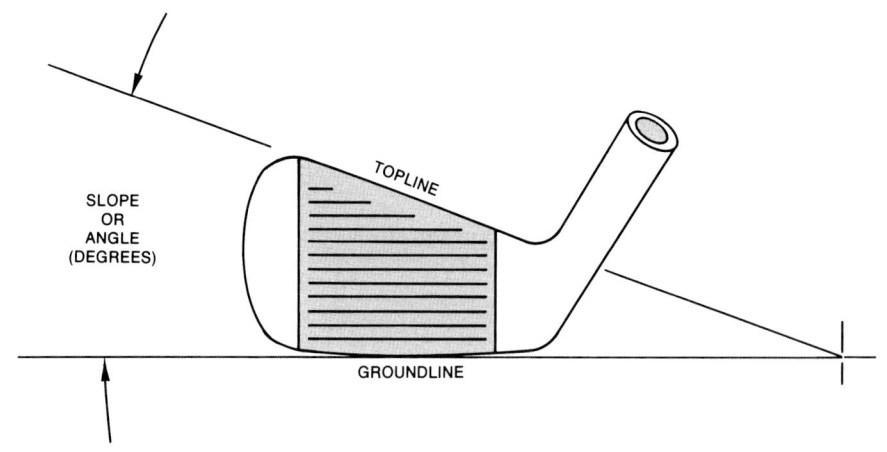

SLOPE
OR
ANGLE
(DEGREES)

TOPLINE

GROUNDLINE

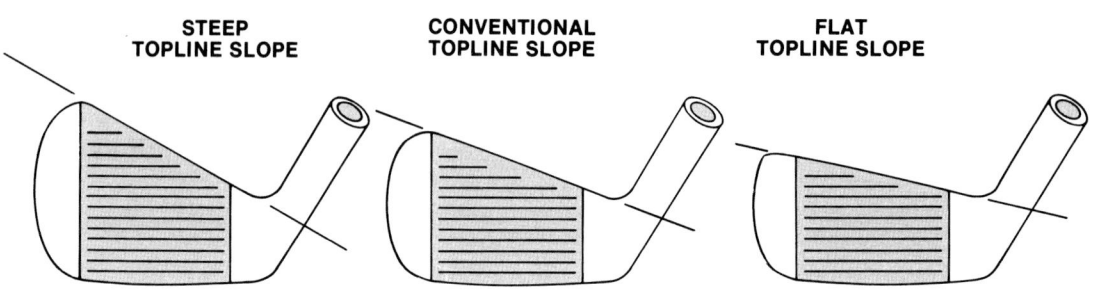

**STEEP
TOPLINE SLOPE**

**CONVENTIONAL
TOPLINE SLOPE**

**FLAT
TOPLINE SLOPE**

Figure 50-4
Topline to groundline slope definition and variations

NOTE:
SHOWN ARE THE 2 MOST COMMON
TOPLINE PROFILE VARIATIONS.
SETS HAVE BEEN MADE IN MANY
OTHER VARIATIONS ALSO,
INCLUDING CURVED TOPLINES
THROUGHOUT THE SET.

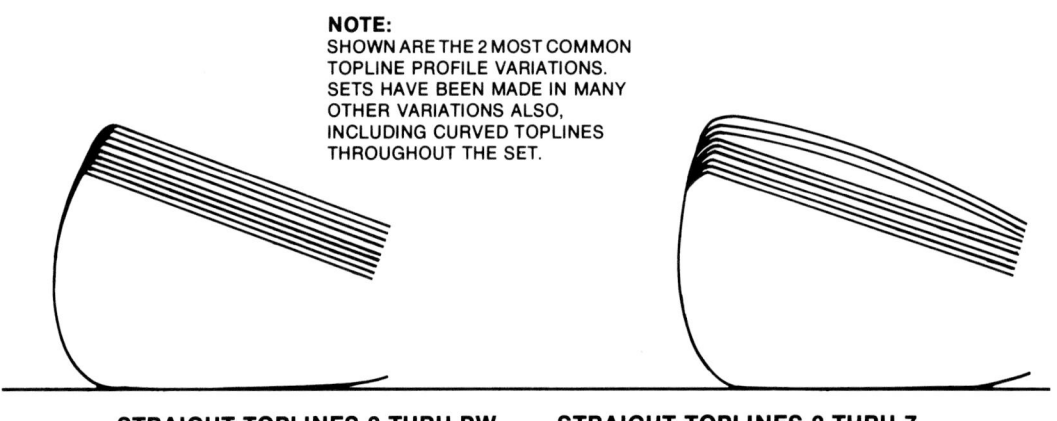

STRAIGHT TOPLINES 2 THRU PW

**STRAIGHT TOPLINES 2 THRU 7
CURVED TOPLINES 8 THRU PW**

Figure 50-5
Topline profile variations in sets of irons

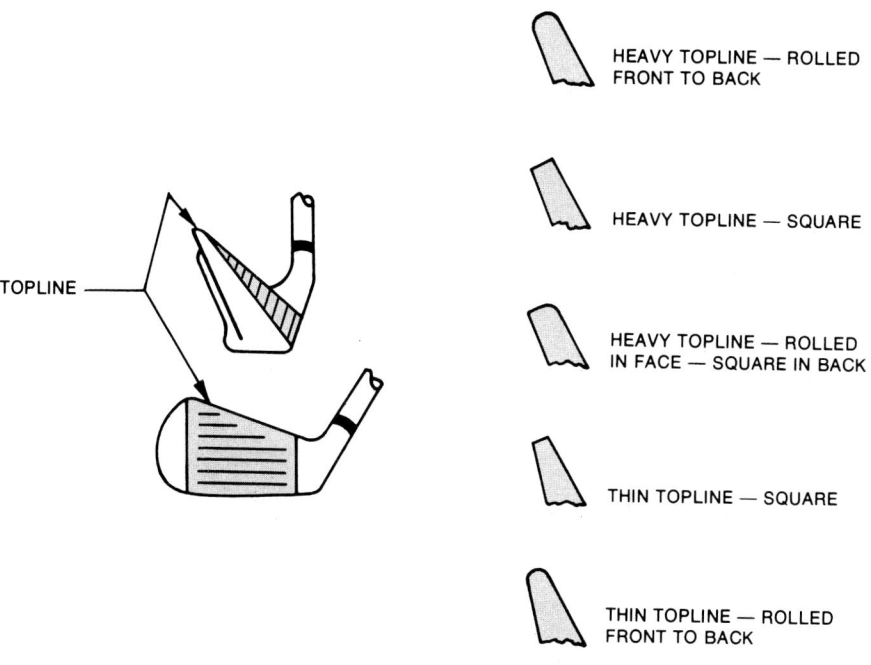

TOPLINE

HEAVY TOPLINE — ROLLED
FRONT TO BACK

HEAVY TOPLINE — SQUARE

HEAVY TOPLINE — ROLLED
IN FACE — SQUARE IN BACK

THIN TOPLINE — SQUARE

THIN TOPLINE — ROLLED
FRONT TO BACK

Figure 50-6
Topline shape and thickness variations

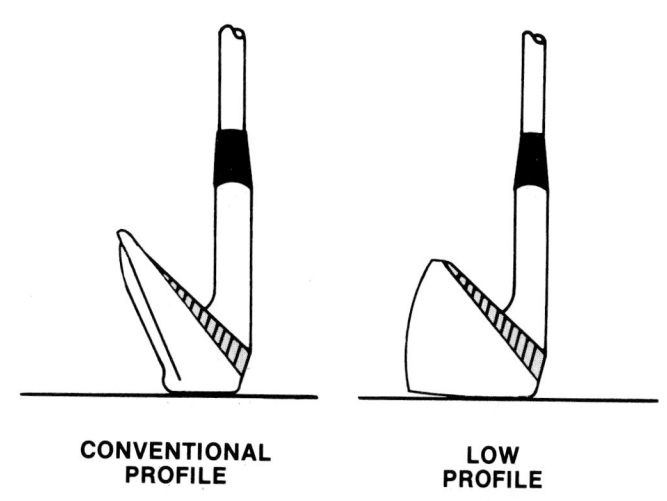

CONVENTIONAL
PROFILE

LOW
PROFILE

Figure 50-7
Profile variations

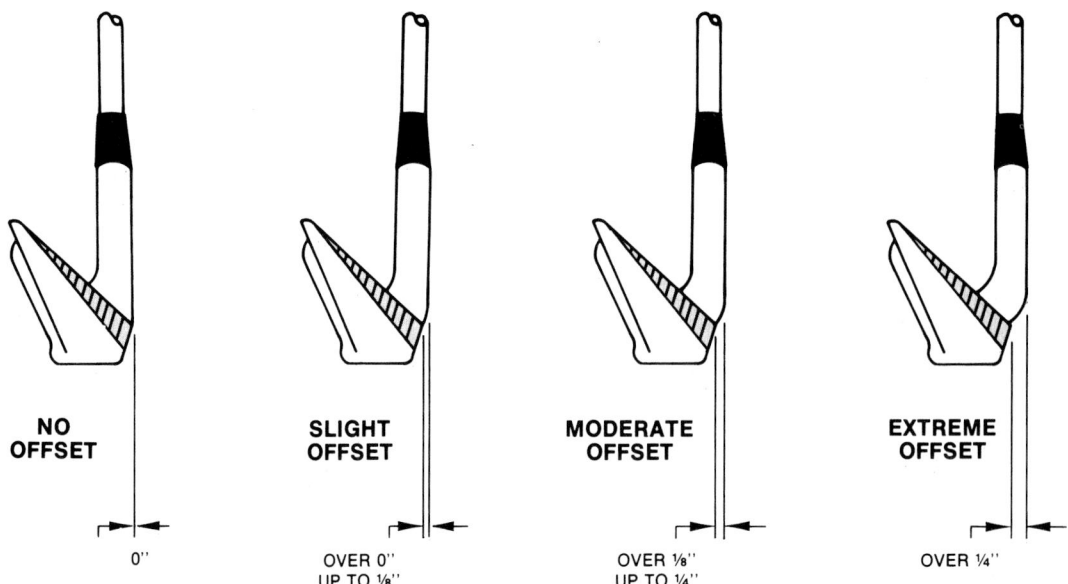

NO OFFSET	SLIGHT OFFSET	MODERATE OFFSET	EXTREME OFFSET
0''	OVER 0'' UP TO ⅛''	OVER ⅛'' UP TO ¼''	OVER ¼''

Note: It is important to remember that offset as measured above is more of a visual determinant because as has already been shown in the iron design chapters, "Face Progression" is the only accurate way of measuring the position of the hosel relative to the face.

Figure 50-8
Hosel offset variations

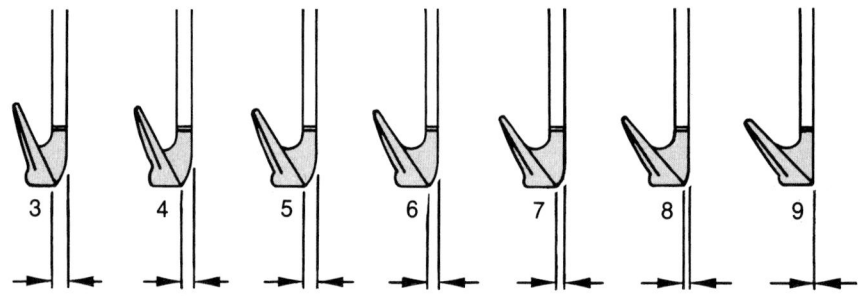

NOTE: If progressive offset is used, it is most often used as shown here. However, it has been done in reverse with the #9 iron being the most offset and the #2 or #3 with no offset.

Figure 50-9
Definition of progressive offset in a set of irons

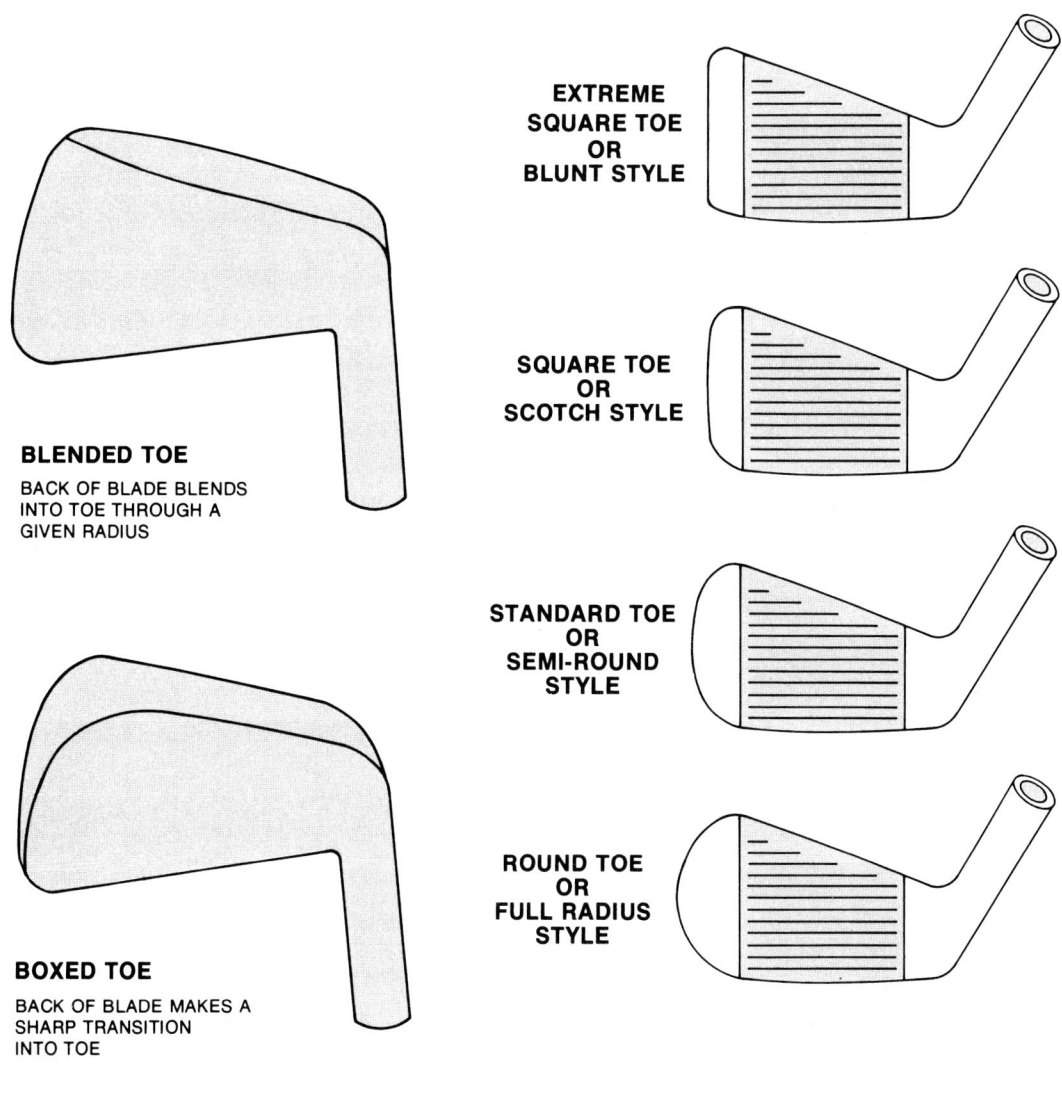

BLENDED TOE

BACK OF BLADE BLENDS
INTO TOE THROUGH A
GIVEN RADIUS

BOXED TOE

BACK OF BLADE MAKES A
SHARP TRANSITION
INTO TOE

**EXTREME
SQUARE TOE
OR
BLUNT STYLE**

**SQUARE TOE
OR
SCOTCH STYLE**

**STANDARD TOE
OR
SEMI-ROUND
STYLE**

**ROUND TOE
OR
FULL RADIUS
STYLE**

Figure 50-10
Boxed and blended toes

Figure 50-11
Toe style variations

529

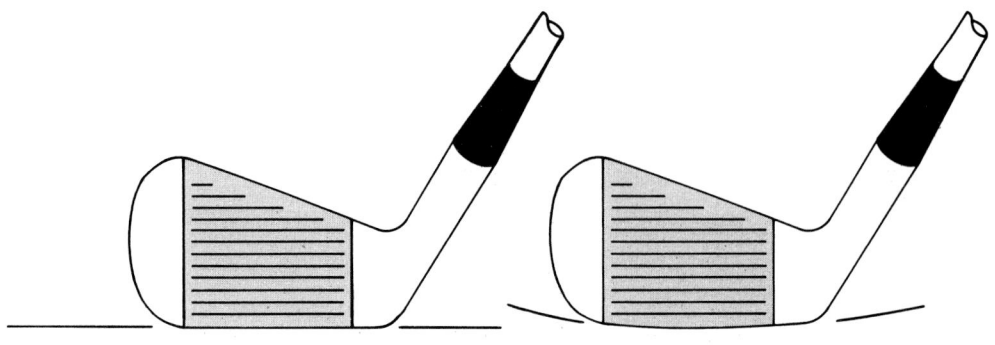

FLAT SOLE
MINIMUM OR NO SOLE
RADIUS FROM HEEL TO TOE

CAMBERED SOLE
INCREASED SOLE RADIUS
FROM HEEL TO TOE

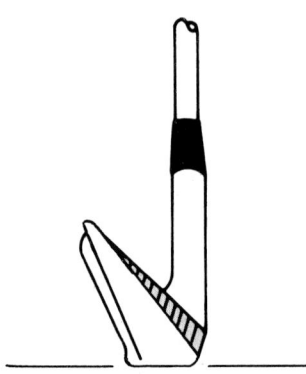

FLAT SOLE
MINIMUM OR NO SOLE RADIUS
FROM FRONT TO BACK

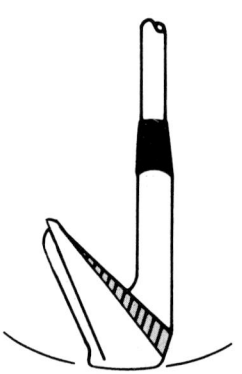

CAMBERED SOLE
INCREASED SOLE RADIUS
FROM FRONT TO BACK

Note that irons can have either 2 way camber (toe to heel radius *OR* front to back radius) or 4 way camber (heel to toe radius *and* front to back radius).

Figure 50-12
Sole variations

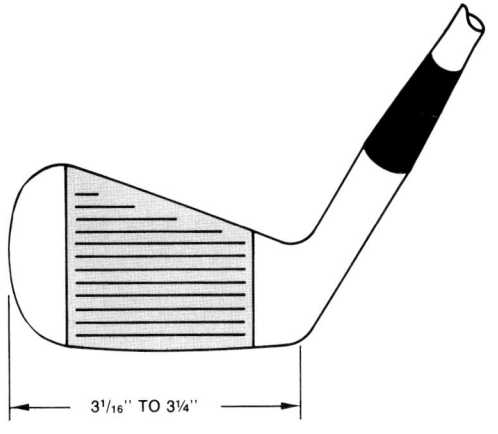

NORMAL BLADE LENGTH

$3^1/_{16}$'' TO $3^1/_4$''

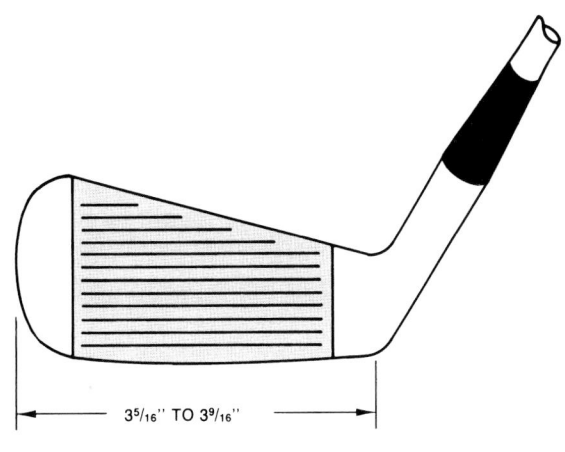

LONGER BLADE LENGTH

$3^5/_{16}$'' TO $3^9/_{16}$''

Figure 50-13
Blade length variations

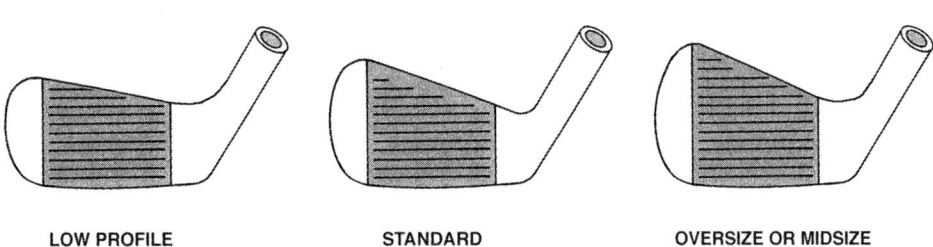

LOW PROFILE   STANDARD   OVERSIZE OR MIDSIZE

Figure 50-14
Blade size variations

CHAPTER 51

GOLF IRON CLUB DESIGN: IRON HEAD CONSTRUCTION AND MATERIALS

Up until the early 1970's, forged golf iron heads accounted for 97-99% of all iron heads made. However, the investment casting method (sometimes called the "lost wax" process) rapidly began to take over in the top grade and second grade golf club lines. At the moment, the forging method is not in danger of becoming extinct, mainly because some players still work under the misconception that there is some "feel" benefit derived from forged iron usage. But clearly, there has been a consolidation of forging manufacturing within the golf industry to the point that some OEM's (original equipment manufacturers) share their forging facilities with other manufacturers who at one time forged their own irons. A couple of manufacturers have substantial investments in capital equipment to process a forged head and have simply left a top grade forged iron head model in the line, supplemented by one or more top grade investment cast models.

There are several reasons why investment casting has assumed such a dominant position in clubhead manufacturing. The first reason is that it is much less expensive to start up a new company around investment cast golf clubs.

When forged irons dominated the market, there was a huge barrier of entry into the market because the cost of machinery to manufacture and process the forged iron was very high. All new companies now make use of foreign or domestic foundries whose principal source of business is to supply raw or finished cast iron and metal wood heads to the industry. This permits companies to invest more money into advertising to build brand recognition rather than tying it up in capital investment. A recent example of this would be Founders Club. Currently, the premier foundry that supplies many companies with their investment cast heads is Coastcast Corporation of California. They supply heads to such prominant companies as Callaway, Titleist, Tommy Armour, Maxfli and Cleveland Golf.

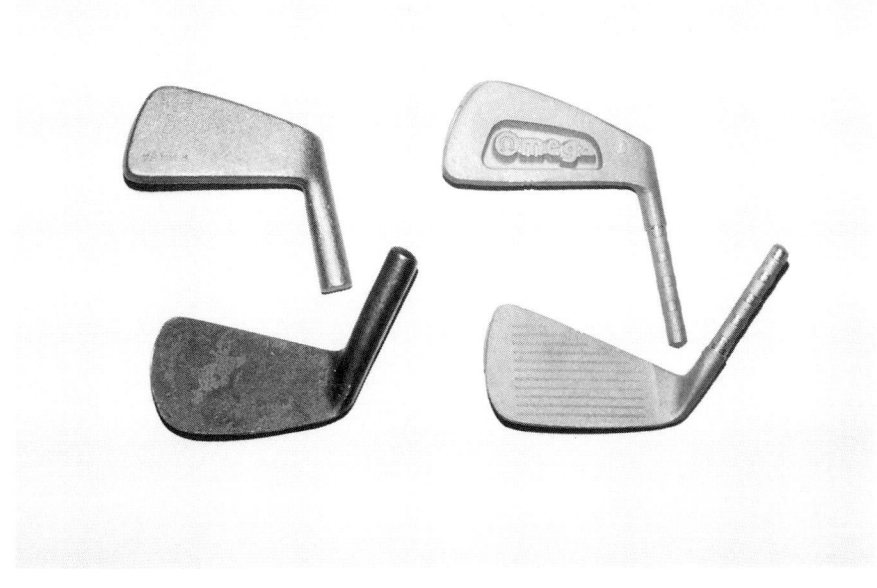

51-1
Comparison of raw forging (left) and investment cast iron heads (right)

Another reason why investment casting is so popular is it makes a wide range of head designs possible. Metal woods could not have been manufactured without investment casting and while most cavity back iron designs could be manufactured using the forging method, it would be far more expensive to do so. The Hogan company was one of the first to offer a cavity back design, the Edge, as a forging. It was a very successful model for them, but the thrust of their advertising effort was to create the impression that because it was a forging, it was better than similar cavity back investment cast clubs. This would be a very difficult argument to make to the truly knowledgeable golfer. My own testing, using identical investment cast and forged models involving touring professionals, showed no difference in performance and none of the players could identify the cast club from the forged club.

One thing seems certain. Investment casting of top grade, second grade and low-end clubs will continue to dominate the market until some new method of producing iron heads, which is either less expensive or offers stronger marketing advantages is developed.

The purpose of this chapter is to discuss the manufacturing method of both investment cast and forged iron heads, the pros and cons of each method and the different materials used in forging and castings.

Investment Casting—The Lost Wax Process

The first and most critical step in producing an investment cast iron head is to build a perfect set of iron head master models. The cast pieces produced later will be identical replicas of the master model which can include such detail as the shaft hole (if required), face lines, symbols, logos, lettering or other engravings. Next, the master models are duplicated exactly in a master female mold or cavity (also known as a metal die). The female mold is made from casting the master model in a special soft metal which exactly reproduces every detail. This female mold will be used to inject exact "wax" replicas of the master model. If a mold is cared for properly it can produce 10,000 to 12,500 waxes without being replaced. More than that and the mold becomes too worn and repairs become frequent.

Since the master model and mold making process are so very important, it is worth mentioning in greater detail. The following steps will show a method, which I feel produces an exact set of master models and ultimately exact wax reproductions from the mold. The first step to properly producing any golf club is to make engineering drawings. The drawing shown in Figure 51-2 is of a shaft over hosel assembly type that I designed and drew in the mid 1970's. The back of the iron and some notes and additional views are missing from this drawing, but it is not important for this discussion.

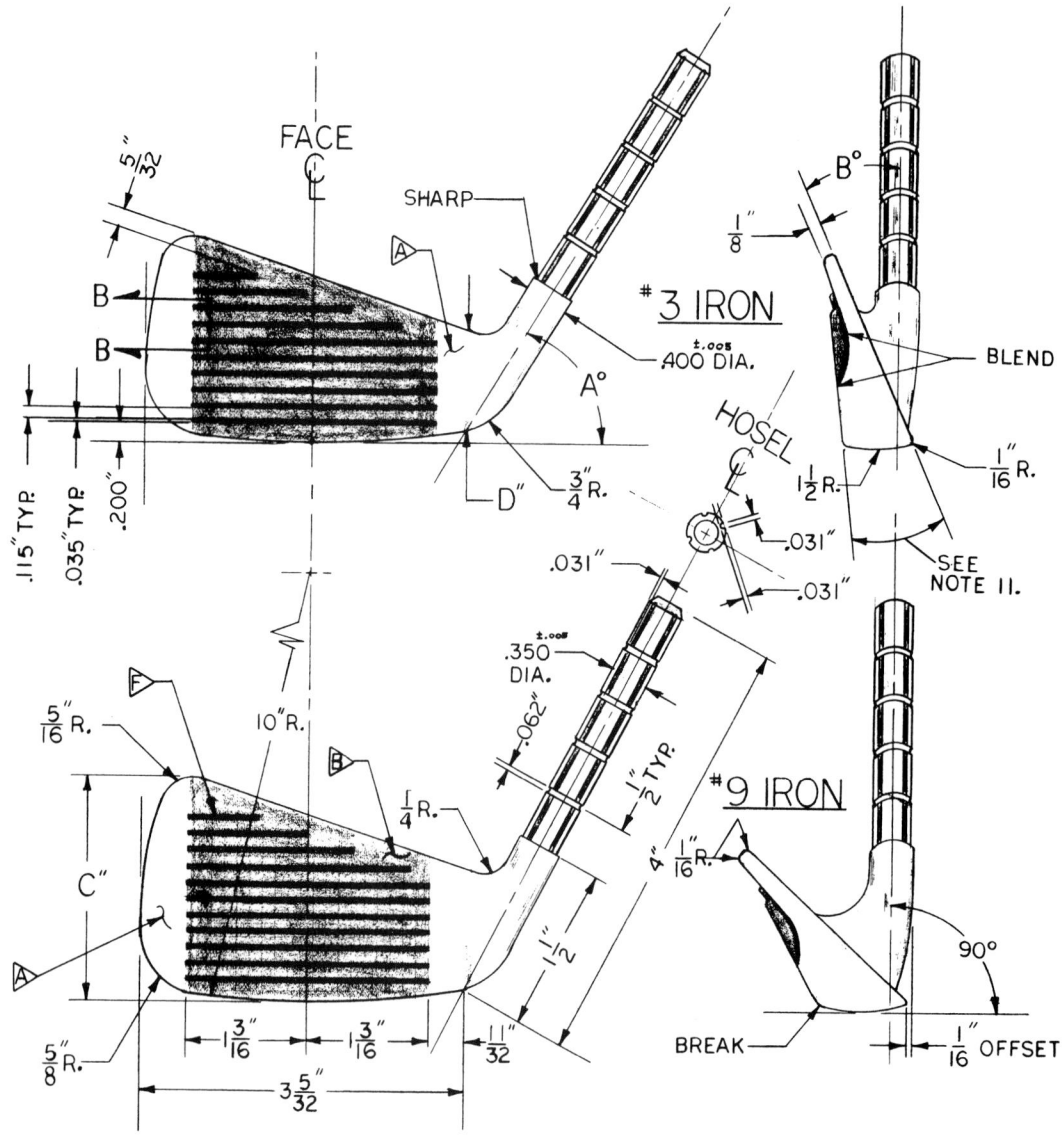

Iron No.	A° Lie	B° Loft	C" Toe Height	D" Heel Height	Finished Head Wts.
3	58°	24°	1.937	.937	261 gr.
4	59°	28°	1.968	.968	268 gr.
5	60°	32°	2.000	1.000	275 gr.
6	61°	36°	2.031	1.031	282 gr.
7	62°	40°	2.062	1.062	289 gr.
8	63°	44°	2.093	1.093	299 gr.
9	64°	48°	2.125	1.125	306 gr.
PW	64°	52°	2.125	1.125	314 gr.
SW	64°	56°	2.125	1.125	318 gr.

Figure 51-2

534

Making the Master Model

The following photos describe the master model process and show the final mold ready for operation.

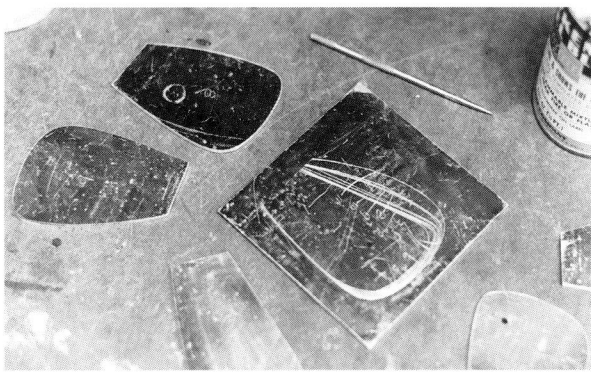

51-3
Sheet metal templates are made for each iron to exact face outlines. Notice that each template is tested for proper size progression using a scriber and a dyed piece of sheet metal.

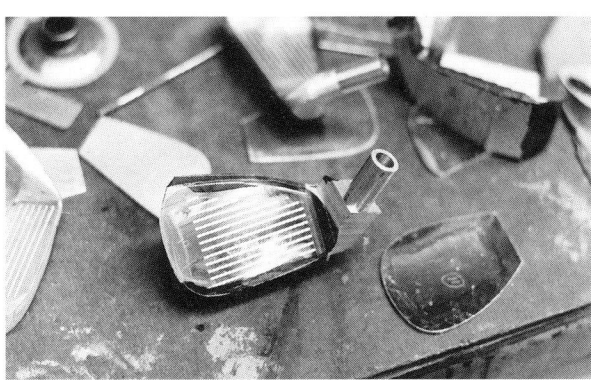

51-4
The toolmaker starts out with a solid rectangular block of aluminum or brass blank. The hosel is first precisely bored on a lathe to set the bore and offset. A special cutter in a milling machine cuts the hosel out of the block. Next, through a combination of machining and hand grinding, the loft angle is set in the master. Then, the face outline template is traced onto the master for shape reference. This template is somewhat bigger than the finished product because of casting shrinkage and polishing. The head shown in this picture is The GolfWorks® RMH #10 iron head.

51-5

The head is hand ground to the desired shape. Special attention is given, through numerous checks to the club specifications; i.e., loft, lie, offset, bounce, etc. The master must be produced to exact specifications. There are no tolerances.

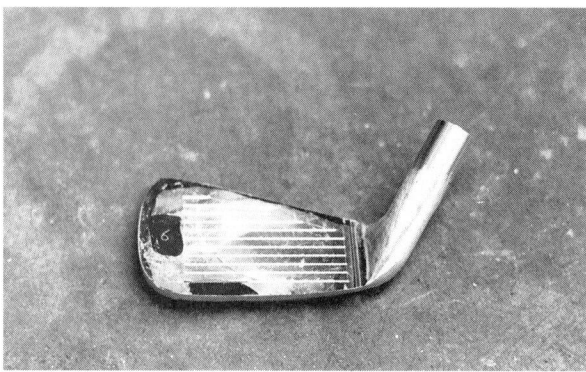

51-6

More hours of filing and shaping brings the master model to this stage. A good eye and a high degree of skill with the grinding wheel and many sizes and styles of files are necessary.

Photo courtesy of Dynamic Casting

51-7

If there is a cavity, it is precision cut in the back by either an engraving machine or EDM (Electronic Discharge Machine). An oversized template is used to cut the cavity shape.

51-8
Final filing and rubbing with emery cloth takes the master model to its final weight. The edges have all been softened, beveled and blended where necessary. The volumetric method of determining the finished head weight has been used during the master model making process to ensure the correct headweights in the finished cast heads. Lastly, any artwork logos are engraved into the master.

Photo courtesy of Dynamic Casting

51-9
The next step is to make a mold (metal die) from the master. The mold shell is made from a soft metal in two halves, as shown. The master is suspended in the cavity of the mold and molten soft metal is injected around it.

The Steps in Casting an Iron Head

Now that the master model and mold have been built, the following photos and descriptions will explain the investment casting process.

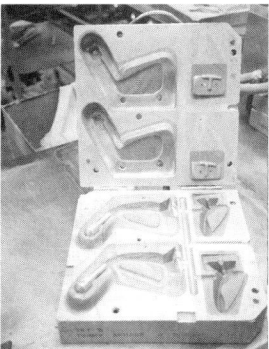

Photo courtesy of Coastcast Corp.

51-10
The two halves are separated and the master is removed. The mold is an exact negative imprint of the master. The mold must be inspected to make sure it is a perfect replica. A brass pin fits into the mold to form the hosel hole. The mold will only be used to produce wax replicas (positives) of the master.

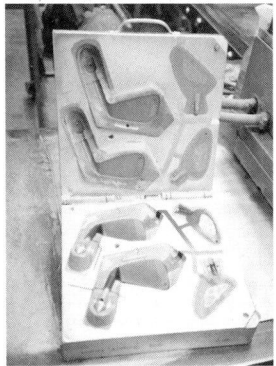

51-11

A special hot wax is injected in its liquid state into the mold and allowed to cool and solidify. The wax piece is then removed and is an exact replica (positive) of the original master. Each wax is carefully inspected for face flatness, logo and scoring line accuracy. The mold separation lines are cleaned from the wax.

51-12

A series of wax pieces are made and attached to a "tree" sometimes called a "sprue." Each sprue will usually hold 6 to 14 pieces. The number depends upon the size and complexity of the head.

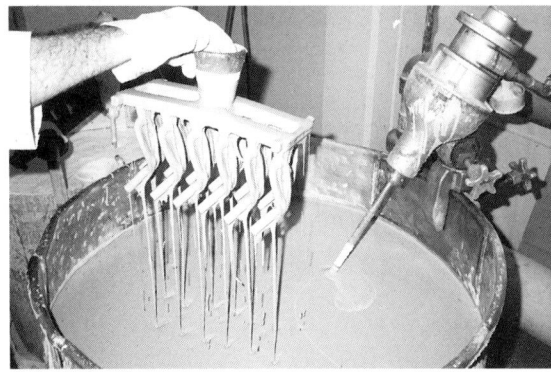

51-13

After each tree is ultrasonically cleaned, it is carefully dipped into a very fine liquid ceramic material and allowed to dry. The ceramic dipped wax trees are dried in a temperature and humidity controlled environment. Each dipping step involves alternately dipping in a liquid ceramic slurry and flour (powder). The ceramic shell is normally dried 24 hours between each of the six dips. The six dips build up a coating thick enough to allow molten steel to be poured inside. Next, the tree is heated just enough to melt the wax and allow it to completely run out, leaving behind a negative of the wax and thus the master. This is why the process is referred to as the "lost wax process." The ceramic shell is then cured in a furnace. Heating the shell prepares it and ensures a consistent flow of the molten steel.

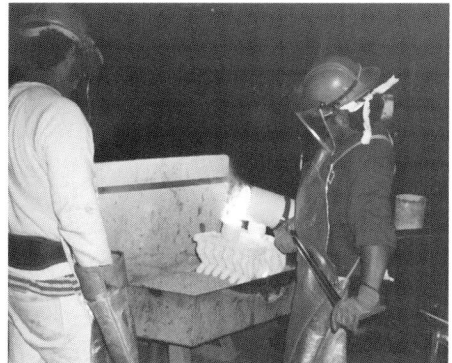

51-14
The molten metal is poured into the ceramic shell and allowed to cool. Golf iron heads are normally cast in 17-4 or 431 stainless steel. Recent technology has allowed for the casting of new exotic materials like titanium, aluminum, bronze and beryllium copper.

51-15
The ceramic is carefully broken away from the metal leaving an iron head which duplicates the original master model including face lines and engravings. The term "investment casting" comes from this last step and refers to the molten metal being invested or poured into the ceramic shell. The heads are now cut off the sprue using a friction saw, inspected for burrs, pin holes, inclusions or filled-in engravings and at this point are either accepted or rejected by quality control. The accepted heads are checked for loft and lie accuracy and adjusted if necessary.

Some investment cast iron heads are heat treated at this point. The only thing left to be done to the heads is a series of grinding, polishing and weighing operations and paintfilling the engravings before the head is ready to assemble on the shaft. At our plant in Newark, Ohio we receive raw castings and forgings from foundries located in California and overseas. We are the only "components" company that takes both cast and forged heads and performs all the grinding, polishing and cosmetic operations in house. This allows us to maintain firm control over the quality of our head finishes and specifications. All other companies simply receive already finished heads from overseas foundries and rebox them for their customers.

Forging Method

As with investment casting, a set of iron head master models must be made. However, the main difference is that master models for forgings are made oversize in certain places to allow for the many machining operations which will be required to finish them. Also, no face lines or engravings can be put into master models for forging as they would not reproduce in the forged heads.

Next, from each master model a two piece plaster casting is made. The point at which the two piece plaster casting separates will be the parting line or flash line of the forging.

Each plaster casting half is mounted on a special milling machine that traces the master model shape from the plaster casting and at the same time, mills or hogs out the duplicate shape in half of the steel forging die. This is done for each plaster casting half and thus forms both the upper and lower forging dies.

After the dies are checked and matched together, they are fastened in a forge hammer where red hot round bars of metal (usually either steel or stainless steel) are placed in the dies which come down with a tremendous force that squeezes the hot metal and forces it to take the exact shape of the upper and lower forging die. Usually more than one hit is required to fill the die completely with the metal. The head is now removed from the forging die and placed in a trimming die which removes the flashing formed at the forging die parting line or where the two dies came together. After a little grinding, touchup and sometimes a rough tumbling to remove burrs, the forging is ready to be shipped to the club manufacturer for finishing.

Briefly, the finishing operations for a forging usually includes a series of milling or broaching operations to bring the head to its approximate weight and desired shape, drilling the hosel hole, putting on face lines (scorings) with a roll die, putting in lettering and any decorations with a series of roll dies, a number of grinding, polishing and buffing operations, inspections and weighings, chromeplating and paintfilling before the iron head is ready to be assembled to the shaft.

Investment Casting—A Pro and Con Comparison

Pro

1. Virtually no mold wear as each wax master is only used once.
2. Capital investment in tooling to produce a raw head alone is lower than a forging, and only a small additional capital investment is required in equipment to finish the head.
3. This process allows for mass production of complex shapes which can be difficult with other methods.
4. Raw head is practically a finished ready to assemble component. See Figure 51-1.
5. Investment casting is adaptable to any metal which can be melted and poured.
6. Iron head weight can be very closely controlled from head to head of the same model.
7. There is no die wear because an individual shell for each golf head is built and then destroyed.

Pro (continued)

8. Loft and lie type specifications can be held accurately.
9. Relatively low per piece cost in both raw and finished head state.
10. The retail pricing on sets or individual clubs made with castings can be targeted toward the low-end, premium or any market in between.

Con

1. Some castings' loft and lie cannot be altered (bent) more than 1 or 2 degrees where other type castings can be bent as much as 4 to 6 degrees.
2. Finished cast iron heads do not lend themselves to custom grinding and shaping such as that done on special order because castings do not have the extra material and weight to remove.

Forging—A Pro and Con Comparison

Pro

1. Forging, generally speaking, can be altered (bent) considerably to obtain the desired loft and/or lie.
2. Most metals can be forged.
3. Forging orientates the grain structure of the metal in such a manner as to make it more malleable than a casting.
4. Forged irons are very versatile concerning the amount of custom grinding and shaping which can be done on special request (this would include such things as cambered soles, inversions, square toe shapes, special swingweights and shaft applications, etc.).

Con

1. Considerable mold or die wear is incurred from constant hammering during forging.

Con (continued)

2. Capital investment in tooling to produce a raw head alone is higher than with a cast head; however, a relatively large capital investment is required in equipment to finish the head.
3. Cannot produce some of the more complex shapes seen on the market today (although many irons cast today could also be forged).
4. Raw head must go through many operations to become a fully finished head. See Figure 51-1.
5. Raw forgings of the same iron head will vary as much as ½ ounce or more due to die wear and individual operator technique.
6. Loft and lie specifications vary considerably and usually must be bent into alignment.
7. Relatively high per piece cost in both raw and finished head state.
8. Retail pricing on sets or individual clubs made of forgings is in the premium market.

Conclusion

Investment casting seems to offer much more on the pro side than forgings and as such makes it very obvious why virtually the entire industry has moved into castings. The important points to consider from the manufacturing standpoint are the amount of available capital for equipment, the physical plant size, labor and skill. At the same time, the marketing organization must evaluate the market potential for a new iron such as the number of sets, gross sales, gross margins, saleable product features and product life expectancy. Then marketing should collaborate their data with manufacturing before an intelligent decision can be reached.

From the golf professional's standpoint, the pros and cons on investment cast irons and forged irons must be evaluated like anything else that would be bought and stocked in their shop. It must be determined if the particular market segment will pay the price and also how knowledgeable the golf professional must be to demonstrate and explain the product differences and advantages.

Forging and Casting Materials Used for Iron Head Manufacture

Since metallurgy is a vast and highly technical field by itself, it will suffice here to just touch the surface by discussing the basic metals and types used.

Since the two most commonly used metals in iron clubs are steel and stainless steel, it is necessary to explain how the two differ.

First, the one important characteristic common to all stainless steels is that they contain sufficient chromium to make them corrosion resistant, usually ten percent or more. This is a very basic stainless steel and usually a higher percentage (sometimes as high as thirty percent) of chromium is used along with the other elements such as nickel, molybdenum, titanium, sulfur and selenium.

Steels, on the other hand, are generally classified as having under ten percent chromium and are usually below five percent and do not possess the corrosion resistant properties of the stainless steels. This is why all steel iron heads are chromeplated.

Many of the cast iron heads on the market today have a particular stainless steel designation on them such as 17–4, 18–8. The 17–4 would mean that the stainless used for that iron was a type with seventeen percent chromium and a four percent nickel content. There seem to be at least four or five types of stainless steel currently being used for casting and a number of types used for forging. More recently, many casting manufacturers have switched to a stainless steel designated as 431 type. This stainless steel is more malleable than the 17–4 type, and allows club manufacturers the flexibility of altering lofts and lies for special requests.

There are many types of steel and stainless steel available, each with its own particular properties and cost. Both metals are used in forging and also in casting. Proper selection of a certain type for a specific application is very important.

NOTES

CHAPTER 52

GOLF IRON CLUB DESIGN: PUTTERS

The art of putting is probably the most mentally influenced part of golf. Therefore, it is not difficult to accept the fact that there are more putter designs and variations available than there are in any other segment of golf equipment. Also, each putter model has corresponding promotional literature explaining just why it happens to work better than any other putter ever made.

Here is proof of just how mental putting can be. Take a piece of wood, steel, brass, aluminum, stainless steel or any other material and fashion yourself a putter head that you like. Assemble a shaft to the head and put a grip on it. Lastly, weigh up the head until it feels right to you. Now, go out and try a few putts. I will almost guarantee that you will putt better or as good as you have ever putted in your life. The reason is that you concentrate better, have more confidence and try harder on every putt to prove and convince to yourself that this design is definitely the best ever developed. Now that your enthusiasm and confidence are at a high level you ask one of your friends to try this amazing putter while you look on. He or she too sinks putts like never before. You now begin to make a few putters because your friends all want one. Your next step is to write all the club manufacturers and tell them how fantastic your putter works, quoting your friends and saying how you can not keep up with demand. The companies at this point turn you down, so you decide to market your putter yourself. You gear up for larger production, get a few sales reps to handle the putter in other areas and eventually go out of business. First of all, the sales reps do not exactly share your degree of enthusiasm and they can not demonstrate it to every potential end user like you did and transfer your enthusiasm in as convincing a manner. I refer to this product life cycle as the "mind over putter cycle" and having worked for large club manufacturers and now having my own company, I have seen this happen numerous times. The result is usually the same, but on the other hand there have also been huge successes. I do not want to discourage anyone, but I think it is important to point out this constantly recurring phenomenon.

What Happens When a Ball is Putted?

The first thing to discuss in better understanding putter design is to explain a few facts about what happens when a ball is putted. On almost every flat surface putt, regardless of distance, the ball will skid on the grass for approximately 1/5 or twenty percent of the total distance. The ball will then roll with overspin the remaining 4/5 or eighty percent of the total distance. See Figure 52-1. The duration of impact is slightly less than that of a full drive or about 4/10,000 of a second. The direction of the putt is dictated by the path of the clubhead and the face angle at impact. The path is important and affects direction, but the face angle of the putter at impact is far more important in determining direction. See Figure 52-2.

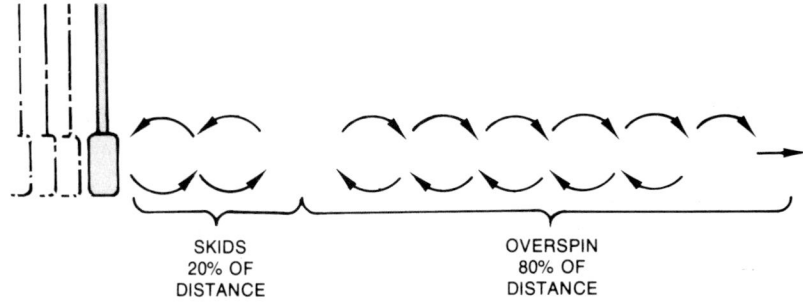

SKIDS
20% OF
DISTANCE

OVERSPIN
80% OF
DISTANCE

Figure 52-1
Ball reaction after impact with a putter

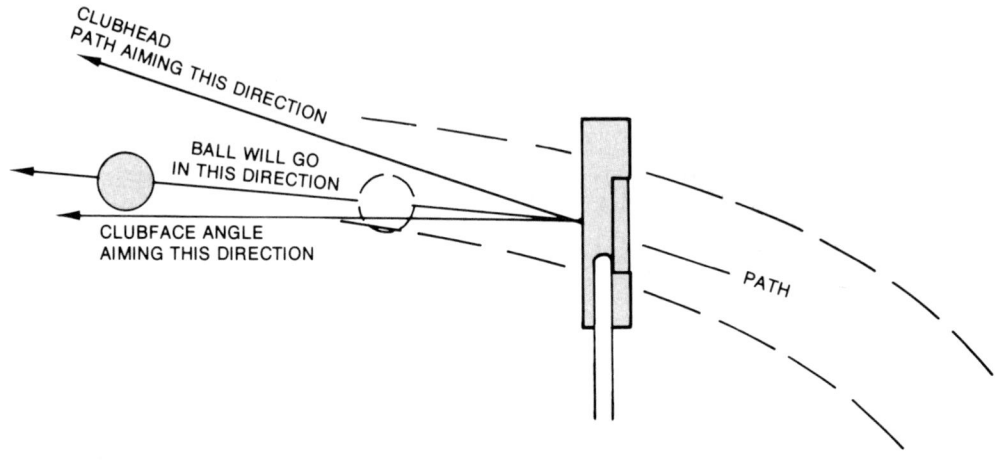

CLUBHEAD
PATH AIMING THIS DIRECTION

BALL WILL GO
IN THIS DIRECTION

CLUBFACE ANGLE
AIMING THIS DIRECTION

PATH

Figure 52-2
Path versus face angle on ball direction

If a putt is struck off-center towards the heel or toe, the ball will not travel as far as a center hit. Tests have shown that golfers strike most putts in an area 1/2" to either side of center of a 1" total width. On long putts the off-center hit range is usually greater and on short putts it is usually less. If a putt that would normally travel twenty feet is struck 1/2" from the center of gravity (which should be the center of the face or a mark on the putter) it will only travel sixteen to eighteen feet. Putters with good heel and toe weight distribution will hit putts farther on off-center hits than putters which are center weighted, but the distance will always be less than that of a center hit. If all other characteristics are equal, both putters should perform exactly the same on center hits.

If you would like to try a test of your own, do this: obtain a roll of Labelon® tape. This tape can usually be found at office supply stores and it is also available in The Golf Works® Catalog. Labelon® tape is specially laminated and when anything touches it, a visible permanent impression is recorded. Cut a piece of tape approximately 3" long and stick it to the putter face. Next, putt ten balls at a target twenty feet away. Notice that each putt leaves an imprint on the tape. Now, mark the center of the putter face on the tape and measure how far off-center you struck the ten putts. Try this at different distances and you will learn quite a bit about your putting stroke.

Finding a Putter Head's Center of Gravity or Sweet Spot

This now brings us to a very important consideration in putter design, the putter head's center of gravity. Most putters have alignment aids either on the face or on the top line. This should denote the so called "sweet spot" or center of gravity in the toe to heel direction. However, it should be pointed out that this mark is not always in the proper location. It is always a good idea to check a putter head's center of gravity and mark it with either a piece of tape or carefully cut in a shallow line using a hacksaw.

There are a number of methods in finding a putter head's center of gravity in the toe to heel direction. The best one is to remove the shaft and balance the head on its face. See Figure 52-3. Use a light pencil mark to indicate the balance point on the face. Check to see if this mark lines up closely with the mark put in at the factory.

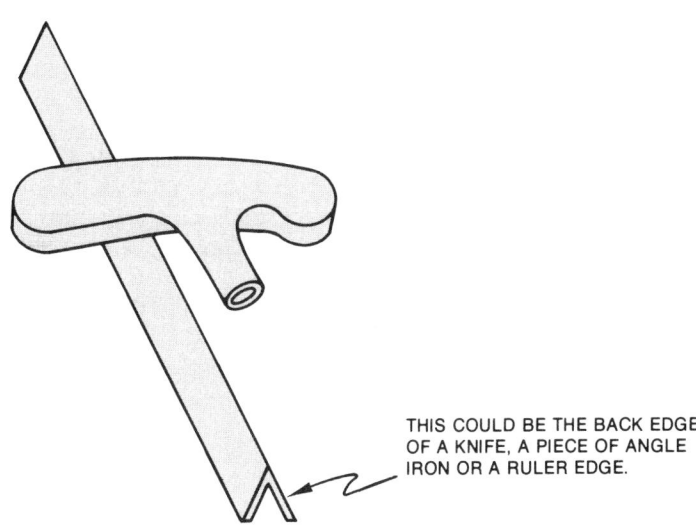

THIS COULD BE THE BACK EDGE OF A KNIFE, A PIECE OF ANGLE IRON OR A RULER EDGE.

Figure 52-3
Checking a putter head's balance point

Another method which is widely used is to hold the putter loosely between the thumb and forefinger in a hanging position and gently tap the face with the eraser end of a pencil. Keep tapping until you find the point that feels the most solid or the head resists any twisting. Mark this spot, as this is the center of gravity or sweet spot. See Figure 52-4.

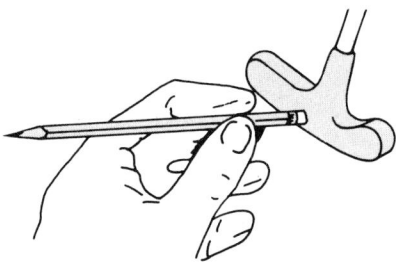

Figure 52-4
Another method for finding the putter head's balance point or sweet spot

Here's another good method for finding the sweet spot. Grasp the putter firmly in one hand about 1" up from the head while holding the face up and horizontal with the ground. Next, take a piece of Labelon® tape and lay it across the face. Now, drop a golf ball on to the face from a height of eight inches to ten inches. If the impact of the ball caused the head to twist or does not feel solid, try again. Be certain to mark an "X" through each spot left in the Labelon® tape until you finally drop the ball and get a spot that produces a solid feel with no twisting. See Figure 52-5.

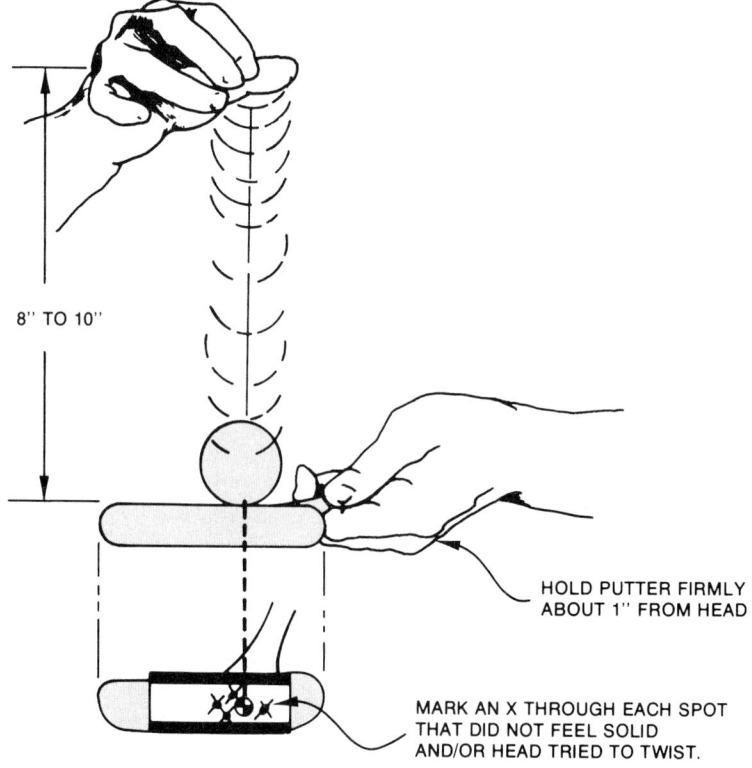

8" TO 10"

HOLD PUTTER FIRMLY
ABOUT 1" FROM HEAD

MARK AN X THROUGH EACH SPOT
THAT DID NOT FEEL SOLID
AND/OR HEAD TRIED TO TWIST.

Figure 52-5
Using Labelon® tape and a golf ball to find the putter head's balance point or sweet spot

Putter Specifications and Materials

■ Lie and Length

For the most part the lie of putters ranges from 68 degrees to 78 degrees, with the average being about 72 degrees. As with any other club, the putter should be soled directly under the sweet spot or as close to the center of the face as possible. If the putter does not sole under the sweet spot, it can be bent in the hosel area or the lower portion of the shaft.

The predominant putter lengths range from 33 inches to 36 inches, with the average men's putter length around 34 to 35 inches and the women's 33 to 34 inches. Of course, very long putters of 48" have become somewhat popular, especially among senior golfers. The lie angle for these putters is usually 78°.

■ Shafts

There are two basic theories involving putter shafts and both have support in the industry. I believe in the more prevalent one of having a stiff shaft in a putter.

The other concept of a more flexible shaft giving more action to the head is logical, but ignores the torque or twisting element in every shaft.

The stiffer shafts that give good head feel without torque are preferred over those that are so stiff that the player loses all feel of the clubhead.

■ Grip

Although many different types of putter grips are used—rubber, cork, leather and composition—the material is not as important as comfort and shape. Comfort is a main consideration, although it is my opinion that a putter grip should have a flat spot or some special shape to it. It should not be the round-type grip used on woods and irons. A flat spot down the front allows the hands to lock and square the clubface in the same manner each time. Other special shapes do this also.

Caution: Do not assume that the flat spot on the grip has been properly aligned. Sight down from the butt of the shaft to the putter head and be sure that the flat spot is at a right angle to the face.

■ Total Weight and Head Weight

Most putters have a total weight between fifteen and eighteen ounces. Generally speaking, putters with light head weights are best for faster greens, whereas putters with heavy head weights are preferable for slower greens. However, I believe the optimum head weight to be around 10¾ ounces (304.8) grams. For long putters of 48", I recommend a head weight of 14.6 ounces (414) grams.

■ Loft

It is a common misconception that putters have no loft. Not only is this idea false, but loft is an essential ingredient. When greens were not manicured as they are today, there was four to twelve degrees loft on putters. However, putters today should have between two to four degrees of loft. The reason for this has partially been explained earlier in a statement that said "when the putt is struck, the initial movement is a skidding action and then the ball begins to roll."

If there was no loft on a putter, the ball would be pinched into the ground and would then skip and bounce toward the hole. There would be less directional and distance control. Hence, the reason for loft.

■ Head Weight Distribution

Putters should have the weight located as low in the head as possible. This ensures that the center of gravity of the club is always below the center of gravity of the ball, which in turn provides a solid feel at impact.

The weight of the putter also should be distributed toward the heel and toe area versus center weighting. In the heel-and-toe weighted type putter, the more the weight is located in the heel and toe areas the better the performance on off-center hits regarding distance and directional control. Heel and toe weighting is not always obvious, but is prevalent to some degree in most models on the market today. For example: A longer putter blade length will improve heel and toe weighting.

Keep in mind also that if a putt is struck in the center of a heel and toe weighted putter and a center weighted putter with otherwise identical characteristics and specifications, the results should be identical.

■ Materials and Manufacturing Methods

The more common materials used for putter heads are: brass, aluminum, manganese bronze, zinc, steel, wood and stainless steel. Individual preferences in feel and appearance usually dictate one material choice over another. I have not conducted any tests on various material differences, but if I had to guess I would say that most of the materials listed here could not be differentiated from another in a blindfold putting test using identical putter designs.

Methods of putter head manufacture include investment casting, milling, forging, sand casting, die casting and pressed powdered metal. The cost of the tooling, production quantity, quality desired, price point, head complexity and a number of other questions must first be answered in selecting a method. One feature that I personally recommend is to use a putter with a milled face, thus guaranteeing flatness.

SECTION

SEVEN

GOLF SHAFT DESIGN, MANUFACTURE AND SPECIFICATIONS

CHAPTER 53

HOW A STEEL GOLF SHAFT IS MANUFACTURED

The first edition of "Golf Club Design, Fitting, Alteration and Repair" explained how True Temper® manufactured golf shafts in their Geneva, Ohio plant. Since the first edition was published, True Temper® moved their shaft manufacturing facility to Amory, Mississippi. Much of the process is the same with the main exception being that they now manufacture their own tubes from flat steel strip which is rolled and welded versus purchasing already made 1½" diameter steel tubes.

The following photo sequence and captions will give the reader more than a basic knowledge concerning golf shaft manufacture.

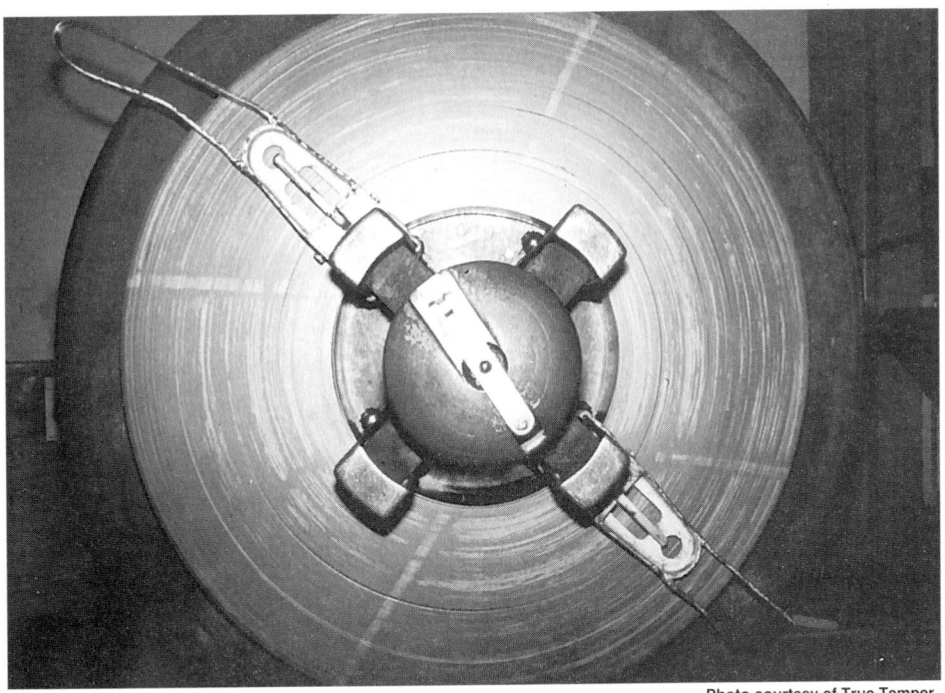

53-1
This coil of high-alloy steel strip is where a golf shaft begins. This coil weighs about 5,000 pounds and will yield approximately 15,000 finished golf shafts.

53-2
The coil of steel strip is fed through a series of rolls. Shown above, the strip is entering the first set of rolls which begin to form it into a tube.

53-3
The strip is almost formed into a tube which will be 1" in diameter with a .058" wall thickness.

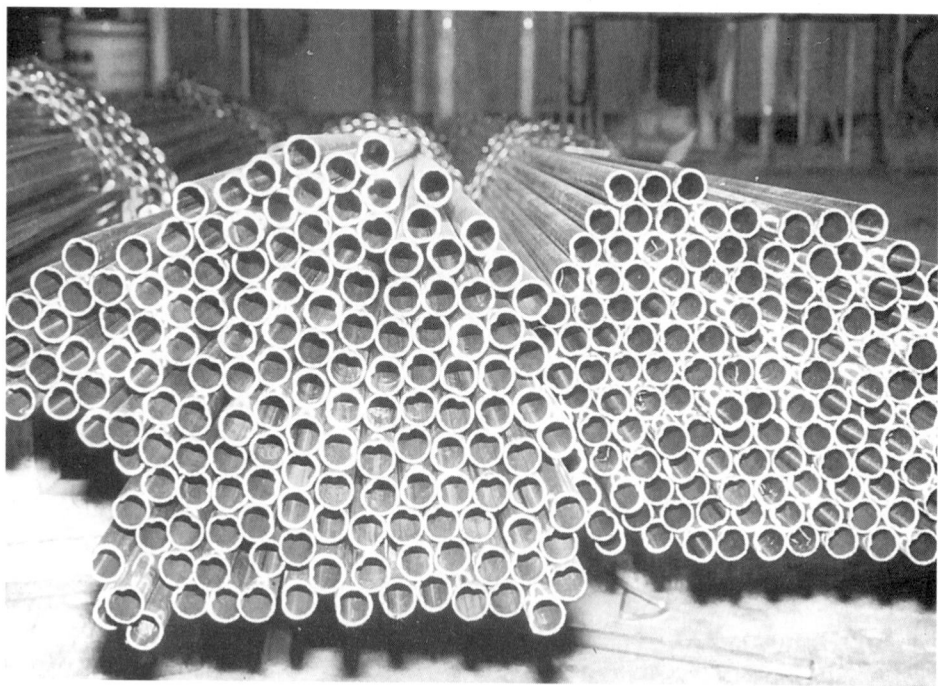

53-4
The tube is now fused together by a high frequency welding method and then cut into 18' long sections. These 18' long tubes are then coated with a lubricant and are ready to go to the next major operation which is the tube drawing operation.

53-5
The tubes are nosed or reduced at one end. This allows the tube to start through the draw bench dies which will gradually reduce the diameter and wall thickness of the tube.

53-6
The tube drawing operation is performed on giant presses called draw benches.

53-7

This is a close-up view of the tubes being inserted into ring dies which are smaller in diameter than the outside diameter of the tube. The reduced tip at one end allows the tube to start through the dies. A large ram will grab on to the reduced section of tubing and with hundreds of tons of force, pull the tube through the die to reduce its outside diameter and at the same time by using a mandrel inside the tube, reduce the wall thickness. It normally takes six to eight passes on this draw bench, each pass taking the tube down to a smaller size to achieve the final result which would be the wall thickness and butt diameter of the golf shaft.

53-8

This is a close-up of the special inside and outside dies which are used in the draw benches. A separate set of dies is required for each size reduction.

554

53-9

The most interesting fabrication process is the step tapering of the golf shafts. True Temper® was the first to introduce step tapering many years ago, and this process has now become the standard for the industry. Step tapering is accomplished in a hydraulic press that forces the golf shaft blank through a series of dies which reduces the diameters at precisely controlled points along the shaft.

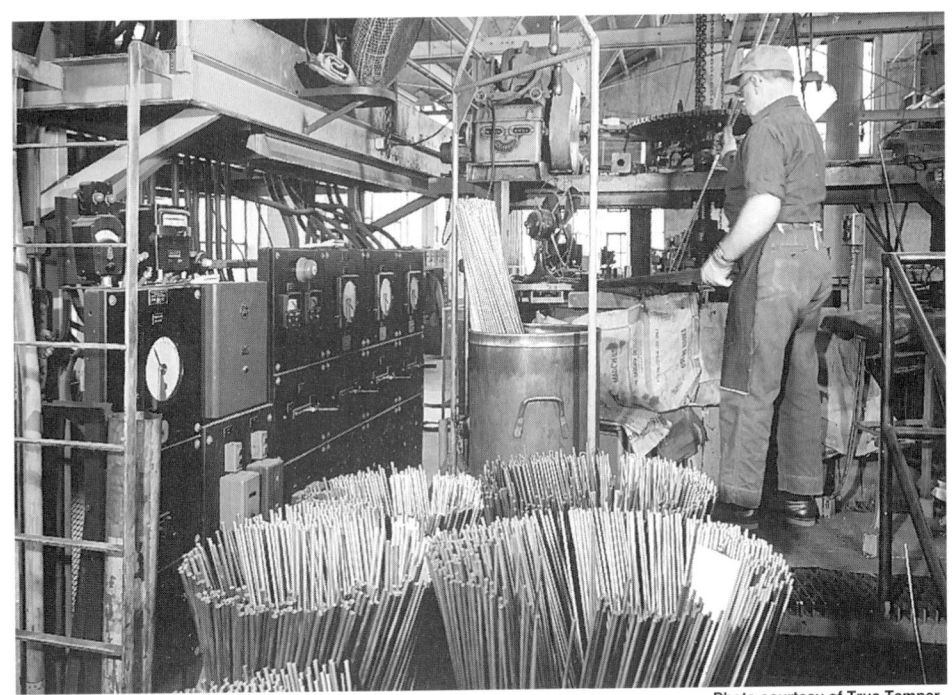

53-10

Next, and one of the most important operations is the heat treating or austempering process. Here the shafts are dropped through a small opening in the furnace which has a controlled atmosphere which maintains a temperature of approximately 1600° F. The shaft then drops through the bottom of the furnace into a molten salt quench. This process gives the shaft proper hardness and strength.

53-11

The next operation is called machine straightening. Here, a computer controlled machine spins the shaft while sensing arms detect bows or bends in the shaft. As shown above, the machine applies a load to the shaft in the area of the bend to straighten it. In addition, many shafts are also hand straightened during final inspection.

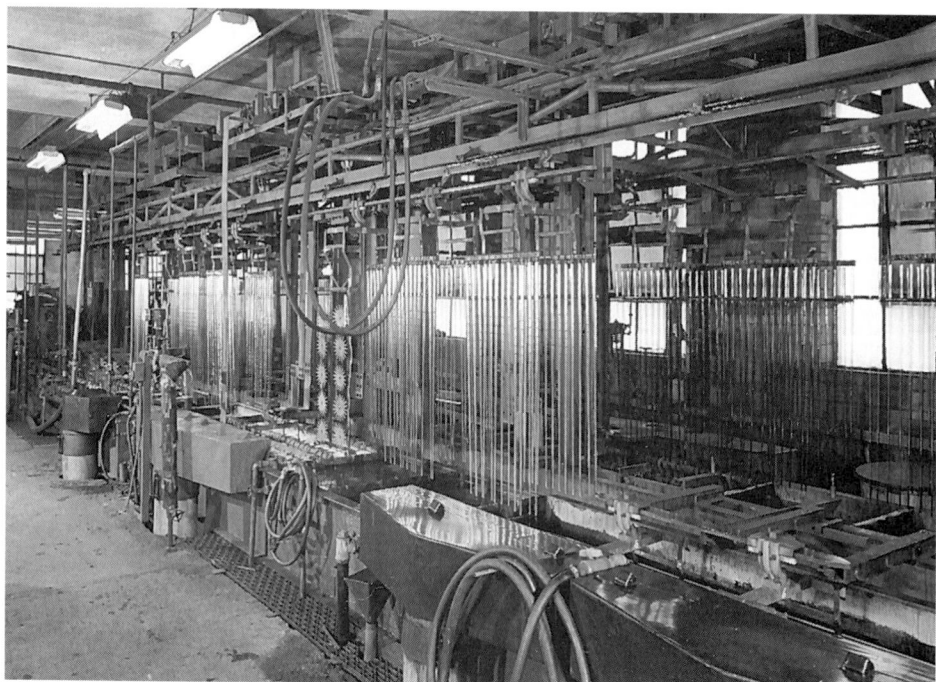

53-12

After the polishing operation, the shafts are sent to the plating room where they are subjected to several acid and water baths to remove any impurities from the metal prior to plating. Here the shafts are electrolytically plated with nickel. The nickel provides the corrosion resistance for the shaft. After the nickel plate, the shafts are then chromeplated. The chrome provides the abrasion resistance as well as a decorative appearance.

CHAPTER 54

TESTING A GOLF SHAFT FOR STRENGTH, DURABILITY AND QUALITY

When a golf pro, repair shop or a club manufacturer orders golf shafts from a shaft manufacturer they expect the shafts to have sufficient strength so they will not bend or break during play. The golf shaft manufacturers have a number of methods for testing against shaft bending and breaking. One such test is called the "Permanent Deflection Test" and indicates the steel shaft's ability to resist a permanent set or bend. On composite shafts, however, a modified three-point bend test is used to determine the bending strength at the tip of the shaft. Another test is an "Izod Impact Test" which measures the ability of a shaft to resist breaking. Following is a brief explanation of several tests used to determine strength, durability and overall quality of steel and composite shafts.

■ Permanent Deflection Test (Bending)

The tip ends of two steel shafts are inserted a few inches into two collets or holders. A certain load is applied to both shafts. This load is determined by the yield point of the metal. When the load is removed after a specified amount of time, the amount of permanent bend or deflection is accurately measured and cannot exceed certain predetermined limits. See Photo 54-1. The shaft can also be reversed and held by the butt end to measure permanent deflection. This is only necessary with certain shaft designs and is not required on all types.

Photo Courtesy of True Temper

54-1

Test device for measuring permanent steel shaft bend or deflection.

■ Izod Impact Test (Breaking)

First, the steel shaft is cut into sections approximately 4" or 5" long. Each section is then tagged for identification. Each shaft piece is then clamped in a special vise and a large hammer of a known force swings past the top of the vise breaking the shaft. The distance the hammer travels after breaking the shaft is recorded and translated into foot-pounds of force required to break the section of shaft. All of the sections of the shaft are tested and the breaking strength recorded. The minimum acceptable reading for any wood or iron shaft is generally 15 foot-pounds breaking strength as pertains to the Izod Impact Test only. See Photo 54-2.

■ Hardness

At various times during shaft manufacture, the hardness of the metal is tested. The machine which does this measures hardness by using a penetrator to indent the shaft material. The depth of the indent is measured and the hardness determined. The two more common methods for testing hardness are the Rockwell Test and the Brinell Test. See Photo 54-3.

558

Photo Courtesy of True Temper

54-2
Izod Impact Test to measure a steel shaft's resistance to breaking.

Photo Courtesy of True Temper

54-3
Measuring the hardness of the metal in a golf shaft.

559

■ Durability

A robot as well as an air cannon are used to test the durability of composite shafts. After assembling the prototype composite shafts into assembled clubs, the air cannon uses a laser sight to precisely hit the specified clubface location. The air cannon then fires golf balls at the stationary club at speeds up to 150 MPH. The club can be supported rigidly or damped depending on the test objectives. See Photo 54-4.

Before using the robot to test for composite shaft durability, the critical hit location is determined for the specific clubhead being used. The robot is then set up to strike the ball precisely on the specified clubface location. The robot can generate clubhead speeds up to 120 MPH.

Photo Courtesy of Aldila
54-4
The air cannon is used to test composite shaft durability.

■ Basic Mechanical Property Tests

Basic mechanical property tests are performed to determine the bending strength, torsional strength and impact strength of a composite shaft. First, the bending strength of the tip of the shaft is determined by a modified three-point bend test as shown in Photo 54-5. The shaft tip is first bonded into a metallic fitting which simulates the hosel of a clubhead and then is loaded until failure.

Photo 54-6 shows a composite shaft being tested for torsional strength. This is determined by clamping the butt and tip of the shaft and then applying a pure torque and recording the maximum torque at failure.

Impact strength is also tested using a modified Charpy impact test as shown in Photo 54-7. The test procedures are similar to the Izod Test for steel shafts.

Photo Courtesy of Aldila
54-5
Testing the bending strength at the tip of a composite shaft.

Photo Courtesy of Aldila
54-6
Testing the torsional strength of a composite shaft.

Photo Courtesy of Aldila
54-7
Testing the impact strength of a composite shaft.

560

■ Weighting and Final Inspection

Top grade golf shafts, regardless of steel or composites, are individually weighed to make certain they fall within the specified weight tolerances. The scale shown in Photo 54-8 is a total weight shadowgraph scale used for fast and accurate checking.

Photo Courtesy of True Temper

54-8
Total weights of golf shafts being checked on a scale.

The flex, tip diameter and butt diameter of the shaft are also inspected. In addition, composite shaft manufacturers inspect the cosmetics and surface graphite properties (i.e. straightness of fibers, surface imperfections, etc.) of the shaft.

Finally, the shafts are rolled back and forth in groups on a flat table to determine if they are perfectly straight. This is a test which anyone can perform to check a steel or composite shaft's straightness. If during this rolling operation one of the shafts "jumps," it should be checked more closely. See Photo 54-9. The shafts are now individually paper wrapped, boxed and ready for shipment.

Photo Courtesy of True Temper

54-9
Final checking of golf shafts for straightness and packing in boxes.

NOTES

CHAPTER 55

DESIGN CHARACTERISTICS OF GOLF SHAFTS

The mathematical calculations required to design a durable, properly flexed golf shaft are complicated and involved. Before computers took over these calculations, it took a mathematician hours of computations to calculate correct shaft wall thicknesses, inside and outside diameters and proper shaft flexibility versus weight. Now, after certain design variables are predetermined, computers can do the calculations in only a few minutes. Actually, golf shaft design has become so sophisticated that golf shaft manufacturers can give club manufacturers almost anything they desire. The only limitation is in material selection and legality as pertains to the U.S.G.A. Rule 4-1 which states: *The shaft shall be at least 18 inches in length. It shall be straight from the top of the grip to a point not more than 5 inches above the sole, measured along the axis of the shaft and the neck or socket. The shaft must be so designed and manufactured that at any point along its length: (i) it bends in such a way that the deflection is the same regardless of how the shaft is rotated about its longitudinal axis; and (ii) it twists the same amount in both directions.* The shaft, including any inserted plug, shall be generally circular in cross-section and shall extend to the upper end of the grip. There are certain design characteristics which golf club and shaft manufacturers must agree on. Listed on the following pages are the major design characteristics of golf shafts accompanied by an explanation of each one. Chapter 56 lists the standard specifications for golf shafts by type, pattern and manufacturer.

■ Golf Shaft Weight and Balance Point

The weight of a golf shaft and its balance point can definitely affect the feel and playing characteristics of a golf club. Steel golf shafts have the balance point (center of gravity) in the approximate middle of the shaft. The range over which the balance point can be placed in a steel shaft is one inch. Composite shafts provide a much broader range of balance points than do steel shafts. Composite shafts can be designed to have a balance point range of about four inches.

The weight and balance point of the shaft has an effect on the overall swing-weight of the finished club. Moving the center of gravity of the shaft a distance of approximately ½" will result in a one point swingweight change. This is the motive behind the development of the low balance point composite shafts. Historically, replacing a steel shaft with a composite shaft resulted in a significant swingweight reduction. For every 7 - 9 gram reduction in a shaft's weight, the swingweight would drop by one point, assuming the balance point was in the same relative place along the length of the shaft. By replacing a standard weight steel shaft with a lighter weight, low balance point composite shaft, however, will result in only a modest reduction in swingweight. Therefore, the benefits of using a lighter weight shaft are achieved without the normal sharp reduction in swingweight.

It should be pointed out that the clubhead mass and balance point have a much greater effect on the swingweight of the club. For instance, an approximate 2 gram change in clubhead mass or a 0.125" shift in the clubhead balance point can result in a 1 point swingweight change. Therefore, small changes in clubhead mass and balance point can result in major swingweight changes whereas shaft mass and balance point shifts have a minimal effect on swingweight.

The weight range or tolerance for golf shafts varies from ±¹⁄₃₂ ounce to ±³⁄₁₆ ounce depending on the shaft model and design. If a shaft has a ±³⁄₁₆ ounce tolerance, it would mean that in a case of 300, 38" regular flex steel golf shafts that have a specified weight of 4⅜ ounces, the shafts can actually vary from 4³⁄₁₆ ounces to 4⁹⁄₁₆ ounces. However, most of the shafts should be close to the specified average weight of 4⅜ ounces with only a small percentage actually reaching the extremities of the tolerance. As you can see, the weight differential between two shafts of the same length could possibly be as much as ⅜ ounce. This means that using identical components the head weight and the total weight of a manufacturing run of 50, #2 irons would vary somewhat in order that each iron will end up with the same swingweight.

Steel and titanium shafts range in weight from 105 grams to 140 grams while composite shafts can weigh as low as 50 grams. Testing has shown that the average gain in clubhead speed by going from a 120 gram shaft to a 60 gram shaft is only about 3 MPH. The reader should take any huge distance claims made by composite shaft manufacturers in their advertising with a grain of salt. While there are true cases of golfers hitting the ball 10 yards farther after switching to composite shafts, that is the exception and not the rule.

■ Golf Shaft Lengths

Golf shafts are available in many lengths. Some golf club manufacturers purchase taper tip shafts in 1" length increments and others purchase them in ½" length increments. Of course, those purchasing parallel tip shafts need only to purchase 1 shaft length for irons and 1 length for woods. Table 55-1 shows the various purchased shaft length combinations for taper tip shafts and indicates the corresponding club number to install it in.

TABLE 55-1
Club Number Versus Purchased Shaft Length Combinations (Taper Tip)

	WOODS				IRONS			
Club No.	5 Lengths	3 Lengths	1 Lengths	Club No.	9 Lengths	5 Lengths	4 Lengths	3 Lengths
1	44"	44"	44"	1	39"	39"	—	39"
2	43½"	44"	44"	2	38½"	39"	38"	39"
3	43"	43"	44"	3	38"	38"	38"	39"
4	42½"	43"	44"	4	37½"	38"	37"	37"
5	42"	42"	44"	5	37"	37"	37"	37"
6	42"	42"	44"	6	36½"	37"	36"	37"
7	42"	42"	44"	7	36"	36"	36"	37"
				8	35½"	36"	35"	35"
				9	35"	35"	35"	35"
				PW	35"	35"	35"	35"
				SW	35"	35"	35"	35"
				TW	35"	35"	35"	35"

Note: Other combinations are also possible depending on club length and flexibility desired.

■ Torsional Stiffness

Torsional stiffness is basically the shaft's resistance to twisting and is measured in degrees. The raw shaft without a grip is clamped at a specified point from the butt. A weight is suspended from a beam that is clamped to the shaft tip. The degree to which the shaft rotates with the weight is read from a digital inclinometer. Torsional stiffness of raw shafts without grips ranges from stiff at about 1° to flexible at around 6°. Also, as the length of the shaft decreases, the torsional stiffness of the shaft increases. Composite shafts have a much wider range of torsional stiffness than steel shafts. In fact, most steel shafts for woods have a torsional stiffness from 2.8° to 3.5° while irons range from 1.6° to 2.5°, which makes them moderately stiff. *Note: The torsional stiffness of an assembled club can be determined using certain torque testing machines. These readings, however, would be useful only for comparison to other assembled clubs, not for comparison with raw shafts.*

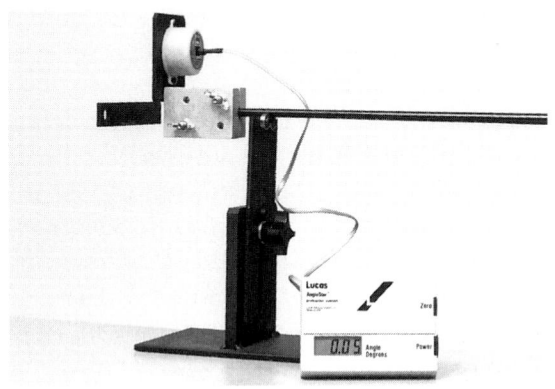

55-1
The GolfWorks® Torque Tester measures both the raw shaft and the assembled club.

■ Relative Stiffness or Bending Stiffness

Relative stiffness is defined exactly as the name implies. It is the relative measure of a shaft's flexibility as it pertains to standards set within the industry or by each individual manufacturer. The stiffness of a shaft is usually designated on a band wrapped around the shaft in one of the following ways: x-stiff, stiff, medium, flexible, ladies; A, B, C, D; X, S, M, F, L; 1, 2, 3, 4, 5 or 5, 4, 3, 2, 1. Stiffness is usually classified by natural frequency or tip deflection. Natural frequency is measured by clamping the butt end of the shaft and placing a specified weight on the tip end of the shaft. The shaft is set into oscillation by bending it a certain distance and then releasing it. Ballistic light gates are then used to measure the time interval at which the shaft passes through the gates. The natural frequency is calculated and represents the number of times or cycles the shaft passes through the light gates in a minute. The stiffer the shaft, the higher the digitally read number will be and the more flexible shaft will have a lower number. This makes sense when one considers that the stiffer shaft will vibrate at a quicker pace over a narrower range.

The most popular and most accurate method for determining the exact shaft flexibility of a given shaft is with a shaft deflection board. See Figure 55-2.

55-2
Determining a shaft's relative stiffness on a "Deflection Board."

Basically, a deflection board works like this: The butt end of the shaft is rigidly attached to a gridded board. A weight is suspended from the very tip end of the shaft causing it to bend downward. With the shaft in its flexed position a little trolley or pointer is pushed along the entire length of the shaft. At certain points along the shaft a reading is noted and recorded. These readings can be used to compare relative stiffness and curves with other shafts or to select a uniform matched set of shafts for a set of clubs. Also, there are at least two deflection boards on the market where assembled golf clubs can be checked and compared to other assembled golf clubs for comparative stiffness. Use care with this method since varying grip diameters and materials can give false readings.

It is interesting to note that two steel golf shafts of the same weight, material, length and relative stiffness can show slightly different flex curve characteristics on a deflection board. For example, Figure 55-3 shows the curve of a 44" medium flex Dynamic™ steel shaft and the curve of a 44" medium flex Pro-Fit™ steel shaft compared on a deflection board grid. They are intentionally drawn out of scale for visual comparison.

566

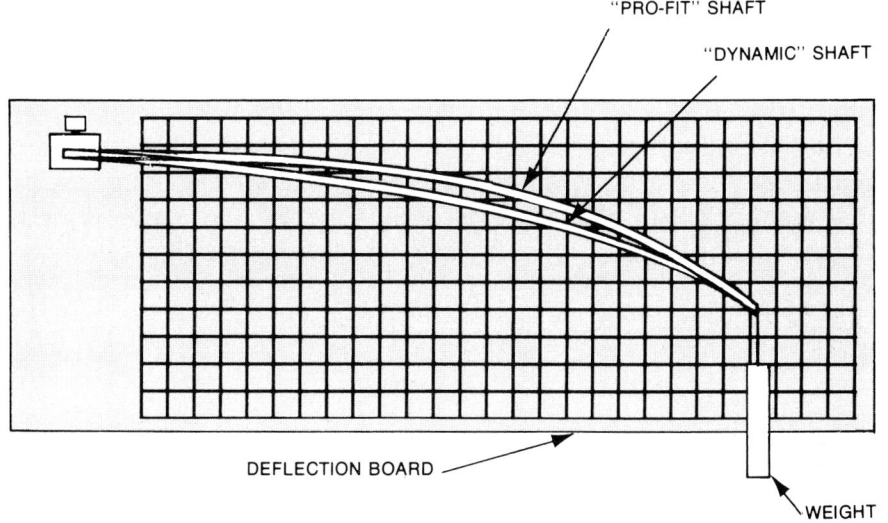

Figure 55-3
Comparing the flex curves of two "medium" steel shafts

You can see from Figure 55-3 that both shaft tips deflect to the same point, but that they have different flex curves. The Pro-Fit™ shaft is more stiff in the butt section and more flexible in the tip section. While conversely, the Dynamic™ shaft is more flexible in the butt section, but more stiff in the tip section. The better players and many touring pros seem to prefer the Dynamic™ pattern characteristics over that of most other type shafts.

Figure 55-4 shows a close-up of the trolley which runs along the shaft for plotting "curves." The best way to plot curves of two different shafts is on a piece of graph paper set up with horizontal and vertical X-Y lines. The trolley starts at the butt end of the shaft, and the corresponding horizontal and vertical position on the trolley pointer is marked on the graph paper. Each plot should represent a ½" move of the trolley until it gets to the tip end of the shaft. This is accurate, but very time consuming.

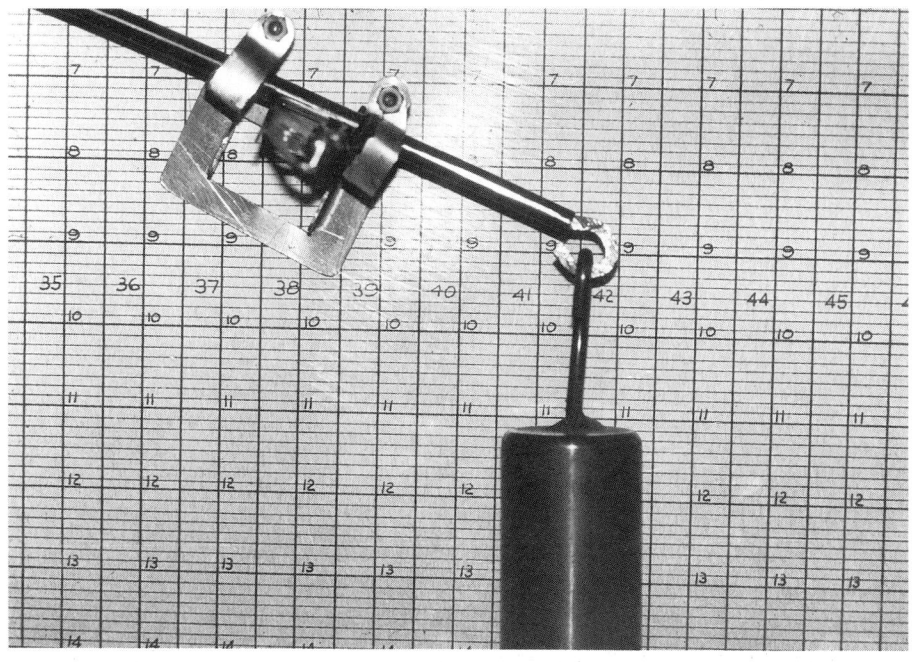

55-4
Close-up of the trolley used for determining a golf shaft's curve.
See Figure 55-2 for overall view of deflection board.

■ Relative Stiffness versus Shaft Weight

It has already been mentioned that golf shafts have plus or minus weight tolerances. Few people realize that the heavier a shaft is, the stiffer it will be when compared to the same type shaft which is lighter in weight. For example: a 44" Dynamic taper tip steel shaft (DWS) has a nominal weight of 4⅜ ounces with a tolerance of ±³⁄₁₆ ounces. On a deflection board, the lightest DWS shaft of 4³⁄₁₆ ounces will deflect at the tip end ⅝" more than a 4⁹⁄₁₆ ounce DWS shaft. Between normal flexes, ⅝" happens to correspond to the approximate standard amount of deflection. In other words, the deflection difference between a Dynamic "R" flex 44" shaft and a Dynamic "S" flex 44" shaft, both having a nominal weight of 4⅜ ounces, will be ⅝". See Figure 55-5.

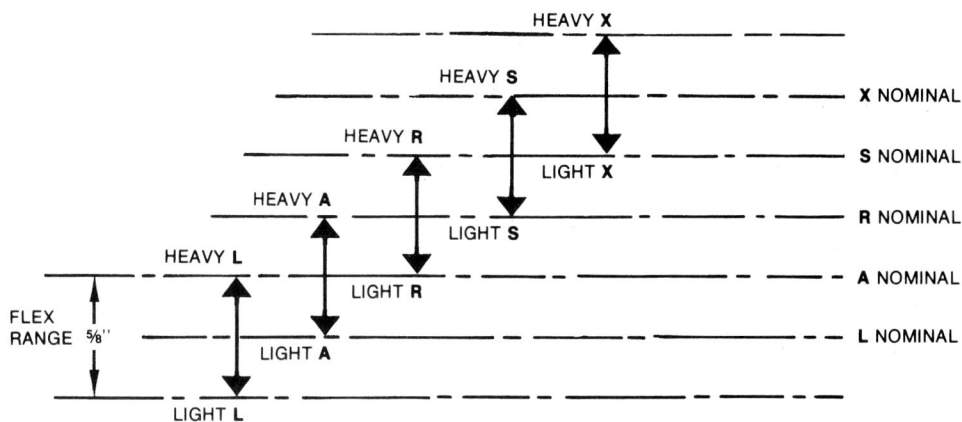

Figure 55-5
An approximate comparison of shaft flex ranges by shaft weight. Note that flex ranges overlap one another.

True Temper® introduced the Dynamic Gold™ shaft which has the exact same design characteristics of the regular Dynamic™ shaft with one exception, its weight tolerance. Dynamic Gold™ shafts have a ±¹⁄₃₂ ounce weight tolerance. This was done for the sole purpose of more closely matching flexibility within a set of clubs. The Dynamic Gold™ shaft breaks down each normal flex category into five flexes. For example, the "S" flex consists of S100, S200, S300, S400 and S500. The S100 is the lighter "S" flex shaft and is more flexible than the S500 which is the heaviest "S" flex

TABLE 55-2				
A Comparison of Flex and Weight Tolerances				
For Dynamic® and Dynamic Gold™ Shafts				
Standard Dynamic® Shaft		**Dynamic Gold™ Shaft**		
Shaft Weight & Weight Tolerance	**Standard Dynamic Flex**	**Dynamic Gold Flexes**	**Shaft Weight & Weight Tolerance**	**Flex Description**
4.50 ± ³⁄₁₆ oz.	X	X500	4.63 ± ¹⁄₃₂ oz.	Strong "X" Flex
		X400	4.56 ± ¹⁄₃₂ oz.	Firm "X" Flex
		X300	4.50 ± ¹⁄₃₂ oz.	Standard "X" Flex
		X200	4.44 ± ¹⁄₃₂ oz.	Soft "X" Flex
		X100	4.38 ± ¹⁄₃₂ oz.	Weak "X" Flex
4.37 ± ³⁄₁₆ oz.	S	S500	4.50 ± ¹⁄₃₂ oz.	Strong "S" Flex
		S400	4.43 ± ¹⁄₃₂ oz.	Firm "S" Flex
		S300	4.37 ± ¹⁄₃₂ oz.	Standard "S" Flex
		S200	4.31 ± ¹⁄₃₂ oz.	Soft "S" Flex
		S100	4.25 ± ¹⁄₃₂ oz.	Weak "S" Flex
4.37 ± ³⁄₁₆ oz.	R or T	T500	4.50 ± ¹⁄₃₂ oz.	Strong "T" Flex
		T400	4.43 ± ¹⁄₃₂ oz.	Firm "T" Flex
		T300	4.37 ± ¹⁄₃₂ oz.	Standard "T" Flex
		T200	4.31 ± ¹⁄₃₂ oz.	Soft "T" Flex
		T100	4.25 ± ¹⁄₃₂ oz.	Weak "T" Flex

shaft. In Figure 55-5 these two examples would fall at the very top range of the "S" flex (heavy "S", S500) or the very bottom range of the "S" flex (light "S", S100). Look at Table 55-2 for a complete comparison.

■ Parallel Tip versus Taper Tip Shafts

The parallel tip golf shaft was introduced in the early 1970's and became quite popular. A certain amount of confusion has always existed as to what exactly a parallel tip golf shaft is and how it compares to the traditional or conventional taper tip type of golf shaft design. The confusion increases when one reads the advertising claims that club manufacturers have used concerning the parallel tip shaft. Some manufacturers refer to it as a lightweight steel shaft while others call it a regular steel shaft. Another problem has been the use of parallel tip shafts in a set of irons and taper tip shafts of the same pattern in the woods within a set.

The first step in this discussion is to define both types of shafts. The parallel tip shaft has no tip taper, but rather the entire tip section (that portion below the last step) is a constant diameter. The reason this is done is to allow the tip section to be cut to length for each successively shorter club. With the conventional shaft, only the butt end is cut to obtain the desired shaft length. The result from all this is that by trimming parallel tip shafts mostly from the tip, only one length shaft would need to be stocked for woods and one for irons in each flex. Hence, parallel tip shafts are also referred to as unitized. With the conventional taper tip shaft, most manufacturers would buy various lengths of shafts for a set of woods and various lengths of shafts for a set of irons.

The standard weight parallel tip shaft also differs in weight compared to the standard weight taper tip shaft. The parallel tip shaft is lighter by approximately 1/16 ounce for medium flex woods (both shafts weighed at 44" for comparison) and 1/8 ounce for medium flex irons (both shafts weighed at 38" for comparison).

In the mid to late 1970's, lightweight steel parallel tip shafts were introduced. They weigh about 1/2 ounce less than standard weight parallel tip shafts. It is important to state that the lightweight parallel tip shafts did not replace the standard weight parallel tip shafts, but were an addition to this popular shaft type. A significant difference in design occurred, however, in comparing the two shafts. For example: the TT Lite™ shaft from True Temper® is made in parallel tip, but is also offered in taper tip. Regardless of the tip ordered, the shaft is still a unitized shaft. In other words, if a TT Lite™ is ordered in a 44" length with a .294 tip taper, it is made by cutting 1" from the tip of the 45" blank and reducing the tip from .335 (parallel tip) to .294 (taper tip). Therefore, if a set of TT Lite™ taper tip shafts in all lengths are ordered, each successively shorter shaft will decrease in weight by 1/10 ounce (2.8 grams). On a set of standard weight taper tip shafts, each successively shorter shaft will be the same weight. Therefore, different shaft blanks in standard weight taper tip shafts are drawn for each individual length versus one unitized blank which is tipped for each length and then tapered. Playability wise, you can be the judge by trying it. Most all of the feedback has been very favorable. TT Lite™ shafts are also used by a few tour players.

The unitized or parallel tip sizes are also different from conventional shafts. The parallel tip shaft for irons is offered with a .370 tip for inside hosel assembly and a .395 tip for outside hosel assembly. See Figure 55-6. The standard tip size for a conventional taper tip iron shaft is .355. The tip on unitized parallel tip wood shafts is .335. The taper tips on woods will be one of the following: .270, .277, .286, .294 or .320.

Figure 55-6
.370 tip for inside hosel assembly – right
.395 tip for outside hosel assembly – left

■ Lightweight Shafts versus Standard Weight Shafts

The standard weight steel golf shaft as we know it today was introduced around 1923. Then in the mid 1960's, lightweight steel golf shafts were introduced. Basically a lightweight steel golf shaft weighs about ½ ounce less than a standard weight steel shaft. Another weight reduction in steel shafts was introduced in the mid 1970's. These shafts are referred to as the very lightweight steel shafts. They include True Temper's® Gold Plus™ shafts and Brunswick's UCV-304 and Brunslite shafts. These shafts weigh approximately ¼ to ½ ounce less than lightweight steel and ¾ to 1 ounce less than standard weight steel shafts. Table 55-3 gives some shaft types, average weights and the approximate year of introduction.

The purpose of discussing lighter weight shafts versus standard weight shafts is to more fully understand their effect on head weights and total weights. Very simply stated, "The lighter the shaft, the heavier the head weight must be to obtain the same swing-weight when compared to the same club with a standard weight shaft." When most people first see or hear this statement they assume that it is a mistake. Logic seems to indicate that a lighter head weight would be required with a lighter shaft, but this is not so. The best way to explain all of this is to look at the three basic golf club components (grip, shaft and head) and see how each makes up the total golf club weight and swingweight.

TABLE 55-3			
Common Shaft Types, Weights and Characteristics			
Approx. Year Introduced	**Shaft Type**	**[1]Approx. Shaft Weight Range**	**General Shaft Characteristics**
1923	Standard Weight Tip Taper Steel Shaft	4¼ to 4½ oz.	Most popular is Dynamic step pattern –Basically the original steel shaft– Heaviest shaft – Most popular on tour.
1966	Lightweight Tip Taper Steel Shaft	3¾ to 4 oz.	Became more popular when aluminum was going out. ½ oz. lighter than original steel shaft. Same weight as aluminum.
1967	Aluminum Shaft	3¾ to 4oz.	Excellent resistance to torsion. Softer feel although relative stiffness is the same as steel. Dull appearance, larger diameter tip section. Testing indicated aluminum to be marginally longer and straighter hitting than standard weight steel and lightweight steel shafts.
1972	Standard Weight Unitized Parallel Tip Steel Shaft	4⅛ to 4¼ oz.	Very popular during last 3 to 4 years. Popularized by shaft over hosel assemblies. Weight slightly less than regular steel.
1973	Graphite Shafts	1¾ to 4 oz.	Many different manufacturers and types. Lightest weight shaft. Varying flex and torsional characteristics depending on manufacturer.
1975	Titanalloy Golf Shaft	3½ to 4 oz.	Gold in color. No stepdowns. Available for woods and irons. Has some titanium in shaft.
1975	Zirtech Titanium 3-2.5 Shaft	2½ to 3½ oz.	Comprised of 94½% titanium. In most cases as light as graphite. Company claims high strength and low torque.
1976	Very Lightweight Steel Shaft	2⅞ to 3¾ oz.	Lightest steel shafts. Very popular. Larger in diameter than other steel shafts. Made from stronger steel alloys.
1976	Large .700 Butt Dia. Steel Shafts	3¾ to 4 oz.	Same weights as lightweight steel. Larger butt diameter. Available in woods and irons.
1978	Lightweight Unitized Parallel Tip Steel Shaft	3½ to 4 oz.	Also available in tip taper but shaft is still unitized. Shaft gets very light in short irons. Good resistance to torque.

[1]The more flexible shafts are represented by the lower numbers in each weight range and the stiffer shafts by the higher numbers in each weight range. Weight ranges represent driver shafts.

First, look at Figure 55-7 and notice that with the heavier, traditional 4⅜ ounce standard weight shaft it takes approximately a 6⅞ ounce head to make a 43" driver swingweight D-2 with a total weight of 13 ounces.

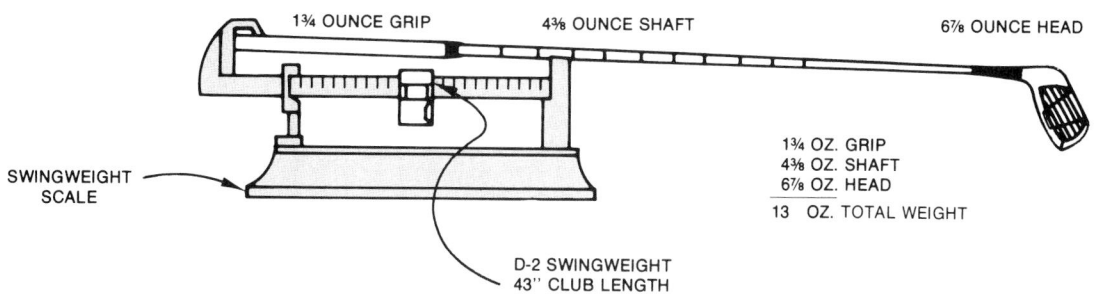

Figure 55-7
With a standard weight shaft (4⅜ oz.)

Next look at Figure 55-8 which shows the newer very light weight steel shaft of only 2⅞ ounces. Note especially that when the shaft weight is decreased that it takes a much heavier head to make the club come out the same swingweight of D-2 as in Figure 55-7. Notice also that the total weight in this example is reduced by one ounce to a total weight of 12 ounces. From the two figures you can see that the shaft decreased in weight by 1½ ounces, and the head increased in weight by ½ ounce; therefore the difference between these increases and decreases net out to a one ounce reduction in total weight (13 ounces to 12 ounces).

The seeming phenomenon which causes all of this is simply a "swingweight scale." The swingweight scale has a 12" or 14" fulcrum and measures the distribution of weight of all of the golf club's components.

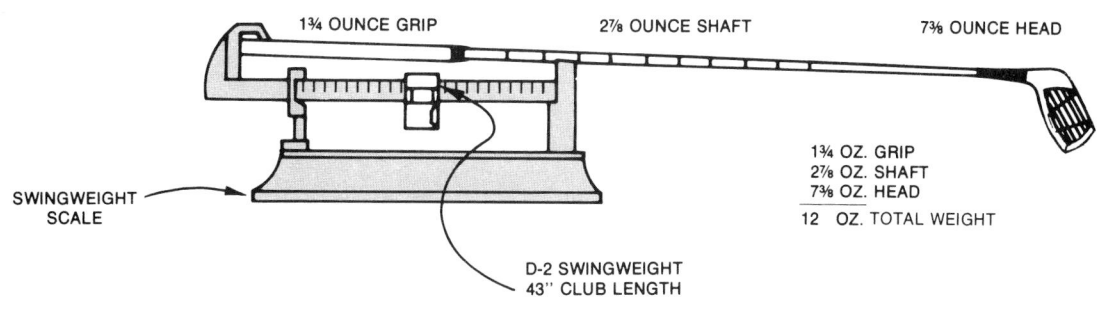

Figure 55-8
With a very light weight shaft (2⅞ oz.)

If it still makes little sense why the head must be heavier to get the same swingweight on lighter shafted clubs, look at Figure 55-9. Even though a golf shaft is larger at the butt end than the tip end, its weight is generally distributed equally in thirds over its entire length. To prove this, take a raw uncut golf shaft and balance it on your finger. It should balance very close to its middle or in the case of a 43" shaft at 21½". A few of the very light shafts have their balance points higher because the tip section has been beefed up for additional strength. Notice from Figure 55-9 that when a shaft is reduced in weight, ⅔ of the reduction is removed from that portion of the shaft which is in front of the 14" swingweight scale fulcrum. Hence, the front portion of the shaft has more of an effect on the swingweight

571

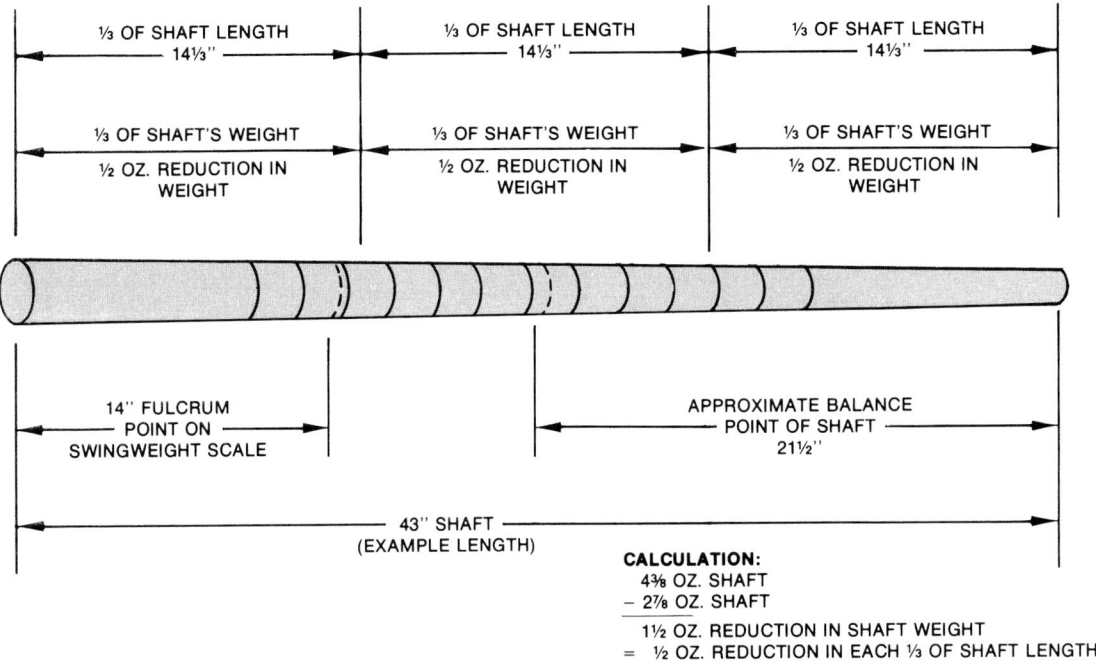

Figure 55-9
Comparing distribution of a shaft's weight to shaft length

scale than does the butt end of the shaft. It can now be reasoned that it would take a heavier head on a lighter weight shaft to make up for part of the ⅔ portion of weight removed in front of the swingweight scale fulcrum.

The lightweight shaft theory has always been expressed in terms of a lighter total weight golf club with a heavier head which can be swung faster, consequently giving greater distance. The equation used to show all this is $E = \frac{1}{2}(MV^2)$ or the more descriptive terminology as follows:

Energy applied to the ball at impact = $\frac{1}{2}\left(\begin{array}{ccc}\text{clubhead} & & \text{clubhead} \\ \text{mass} & \text{X} & \text{speed} \\ \text{weight} & & \text{squared}\end{array}\right)$

The major golf club companies have all done extensive testing as I have on the comparative distance advantages of lightweight shafts versus the heavier standard weight shafts. The testing shows that lightweight shafts do in fact have a slight distance advantage in both the mechanical golfer tests and human golfer tests. These tests were conducted with clubs of almost identical design characteristics and specifications so as to eliminate most of the variables that could give noncomparative data. It is important to understand that using lightweight golf shafts will not automatically increase the distance a ball is hit. The clubs must fit properly and they must also be built properly to take maximum advantage of the lighter shaft. Also, different materials such as graphite, titanium, etc., may react differently under different conditions and types of swings.

Another area to discuss when comparing lighter weight shafts to the older, heavier ones is the effect on shaft torque (twisting) and shaft flexibility (bending) that the heavier clubhead weight has, especially since it is usually being swung faster. Since the center of gravity of the clubhead is not in line with the axis of the shaft, forces acting on the club's center of gravity tend to bow and twist the shaft. If the relative stiffness of the lighter shaft is the same as that of the heavier shaft, the increased clubhead weight and speed will exert a greater force on the shaft which may bend or twist it to a greater degree.

Table 55-4 is provided to allow the reader to compare total weight ranges of drivers with different weight shafts. It also takes into account the flex and swingweight categories. The shaft weights listed in the heading are for general reference because most of the shafts listed change in weight as the flex category changes.

TABLE 55-4
Comparing Total Weight, Shaft Material,
Shaft Flex and Swingweight

Shaft Flex and Swingweight Range	4⅜ oz. Standard Carbon Steel	4³⁄₁₆ oz. Standard Unitized Steel	3⅞ oz. Lightweight Steel	3⅞ oz. Lightweight Unitized Steel	2⅞ to 3¾ oz. Very Lightweight Steel	2¼ to 3¼ oz. Shaft Graphite & Titanium
	¹Driver total weight range in ounces by shaft material and type					
L-Ladies C6 to C8	12⅛ to 12½	12 to 12⅜	11⅞ to 12¼	11⅞ to 12¼	11⅜ to 11¾	11⅛ to 11½
A-Flexible C9 to D1	12⅜ to 12¾	12¼ to 12⅝	12⅛ to 12½	12⅛ to 12½	11⅝ to 12	11⅜ to 11¾
R-Medium D1 to D3	12⅞ to 13¼	12¾ to 13⅛	12⅝ to 13	12⅝ to 13	11⅞ to 12¼	11⅝ to 12
S-Stiff D2 to D4	13⅛ to 13½	13 to 13⅜	12⅞ to 13¼	12⅞ to 13¼	12⅛ to 12½	11⅞ to 12¼
X-Extra Stiff D4 to D6	13⅜ to 13¾	13¼ to 13⅝	13⅛ to 13½	13⅛ to 13½	12⅜ to 12¾	12⅛ to 12½

¹Based on a 43" driver length. For each ½" longer than standard driver length, subtract ¼ ounce from the weights above. Conversely, for each ½" shorter than standard driver length, add ¼ ounce to weights above.

■ Large .700 Butt Shafts versus Conventional Butt Shafts

The large .700 butt diameter shafts were introduced in the late 1970's and have since been mostly discontinued. The probable cause for this was a lack of knowledge in the market place concerning the golf club design concept for this new shaft. The concept behind this shaft had more to do with the design feature of a reduced total weight versus simply a new type shaft. The shaft was basically the same weight as lightweight steel; however, it was designed with a larger diameter butt section or that portion inside the grip. This larger shaft diameter required a bigger hole be molded in the grip which in turn had the effect of reducing the amount of rubber in the grip and ultimately reducing the grip weight by approximately ½ ounce to ⅝ ounce. A swingweight is equivalent to approximately .07 ounces in the head of the club and approximately .14 ounces in the grip end of the club. So for every .14 ounce reduction in grip weight the same head weight will give a reading one swingweight heavier on the swingweight scale. Assuming in the large .700 butt club that the grip was reduced ½ ounce in weight meant that the same head weight would produce a reading approximately four swingweights heavier on the swingweight scale. A D-2 swingweighted club would now be D-6 if no other changes were made. However, in the case of the large .700 butt clubs, some clubmakers were striving for still lighter overall weights, so additional weight was taken out of the clubhead, which reduced the total weight of the club even further or by approximately ¾ ounce. This made the total weight of the large .700 butt driver approximately 12 ounces. See Figure 55-10.

Actually, the design effect of all this is a kind of counterbalancing in reverse. Instead of adding weight to the grip end as in normal counterbalancing which reduces swingweight, the opposite occurs; weight is removed from the grip end and swingweight is increased. In analyzing all of this from a playability standpoint, the large .700 butt shafts reduced the total weight which was all right, but the reduced headweights created less head feel and poorer directional control. This type of shaft

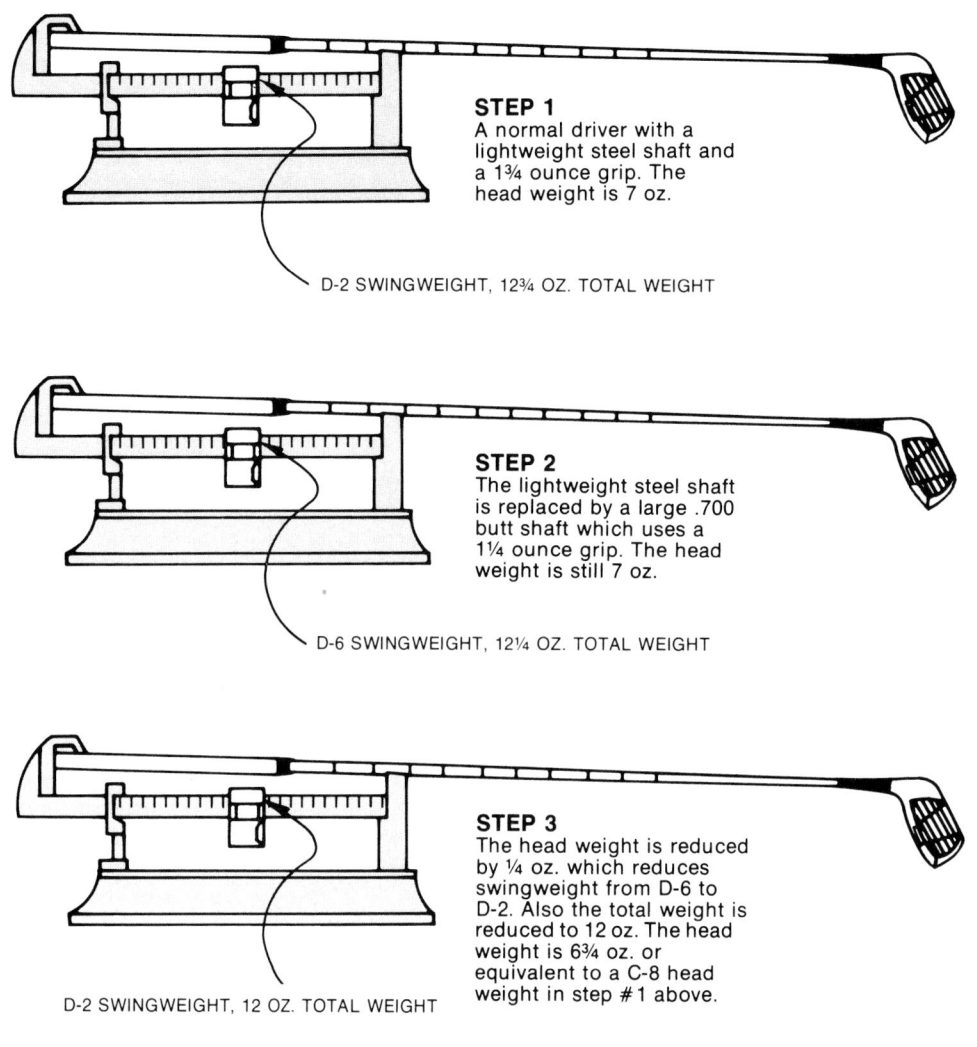

STEP 1
A normal driver with a lightweight steel shaft and a 1¾ ounce grip. The head weight is 7 oz.

D-2 SWINGWEIGHT, 12¾ OZ. TOTAL WEIGHT

STEP 2
The lightweight steel shaft is replaced by a large .700 butt shaft which uses a 1¼ ounce grip. The head weight is still 7 oz.

D-6 SWINGWEIGHT, 12¼ OZ. TOTAL WEIGHT

STEP 3
The head weight is reduced by ¼ oz. which reduces swingweight from D-6 to D-2. Also the total weight is reduced to 12 oz. The head weight is 6¾ oz. or equivalent to a C-8 head weight in step #1 above.

D-2 SWINGWEIGHT, 12 OZ. TOTAL WEIGHT

Figure 55-10
The conceptual evolution of the large .700 butt steel golf shaft

played much better if the head weights were adjusted to make the swingweight 2-4 points greater than those normally played. In other words, D-4 to D-6 swingweights were best and with the higher swingweights the total weight was still reduced. Keep in mind that a D-6 swingweight in a large butt shaft is the same headweight in a normal lightweight steel shafted club to achieve a D-2 swingweight.

■ Conclusion

The shaft has always reigned supreme in discussions about the golf club. I am sure everyone has at one time or another heard someone say that the shaft is the "heart" of the club, the single most important component. I prefer a different emphasis. The shaft is but one of the components in the overall golf club design. All of the components together along with all their attributes as they pertain to each individual club should be truly considered as the most important. The golf shaft's purpose is to bring the clubhead into the proper impact position with the most consistency, swing after swing for a given golfer. As this chapter has shown, the design characteristics of golf shafts play a major role in understanding total golf club design. See Chapter 58 for additional design characteristics pertinent to composite shafts.

CHAPTER 56

STEEL AND TITANIUM GOLF SHAFT MANUFACTURERS' PUBLISHED SPECIFICATIONS

The following specifications provide valuable information for identifying, specifying and selecting the proper golf shaft. The golf shaft manufacturers publish this data in their price lists, normally on an annual basis. The information provided here is the latest available at the time of publication.

Every club assembler should be able to identify any stock type and pattern steel golf shaft. A micrometer or vernier caliper along with a 48" ruler will work well to do this. The best way, however, is with a "Shaft Identification Gauge" developed by the author. This gauge, used in conjunction with a 48" ruler, and the "Shaft Butt Gauge," also developed by the author, will identify most shafts by type and pattern. See Figure 56-1.

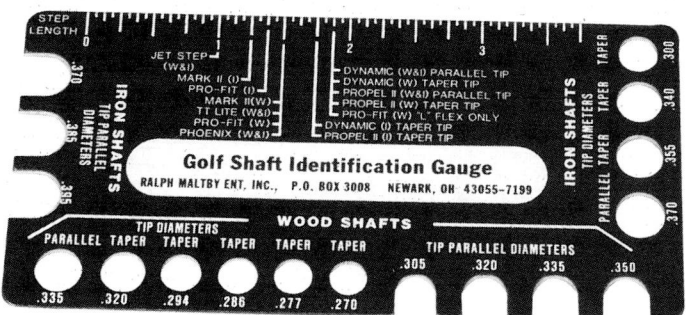

Figure 56-1
A special gauge to identify most golf shafts available from the GolfWorks®

TRUE TEMPER® STANDARD WEIGHT SHAFTS
TAPERED TIP

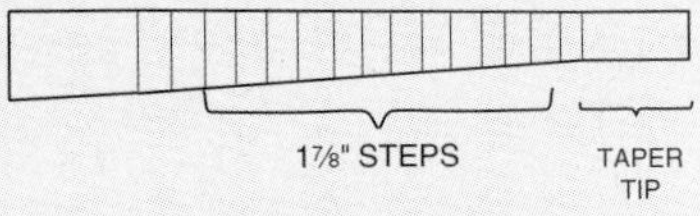

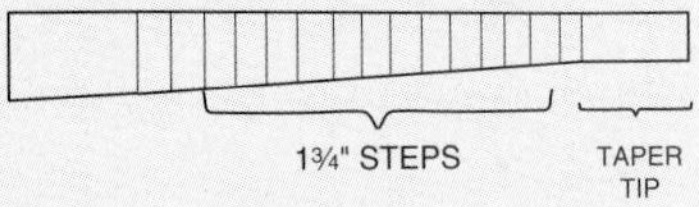

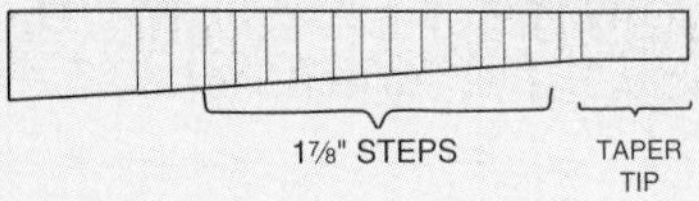

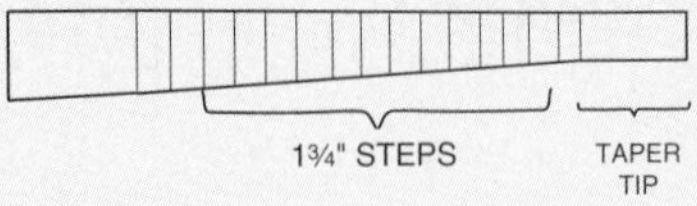

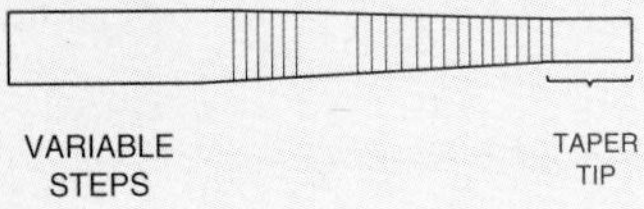

	Pattern	Flex	Butt Dia.	Tip Dia.	Tip Parallel	Length (Specify)	Nominal Weight (Ounces)	Weight Tolerance (Ounces)
DYNAMIC® WOODS	DWX	X	.620	.294	.350	42" – 45"	4.50	±⅛
	DWS	S	.620	.294	.350	42" – 45"	4.37	±⅛
1⅞" STEPS · TAPER TIP	DWT	R	.620	.277	.335	42" – 45"	4.37	±⅛
DYNAMIC® IRONS	DIX	X	.600	.355	.395	35" – 39"	4.50	±⅛
	DIS	S	.600	.355	.395	35" – 39"	4.37	±⅛
1¾" STEPS · TAPER TIP	DIT	R	.580	.355	.395	35" – 39"	4.25	±⅛
DYNAMIC GOLD™ WOODS	DGWX	X100	.620	.294	.350	42" – 45"	4.38	±.03
	DGWX	X200	.620	.294	.350	42" – 45"	4.44	±.03
	DGWX	X300	.620	.294	.350	42" – 45"	4.50	±.03
	DGWX	X400	.620	.294	.350	42" – 45"	4.56	±.03
	DGWX	X500	.620	.294	.350	42" – 45"	4.63	±.03
	DGWS	S100	.620	.294	.350	42" – 45"	4.25	±.03
	DGWS	S200	.620	.294	.350	42" – 45"	4.31	±.03
	DGWS	S300	.620	.294	.350	42" – 45"	4.37	±.03
	DGWS	S400	.620	.294	.350	42" – 45"	4.43	±.03
1⅞" STEPS · TAPER TIP	DGWS	S500	.620	.294	.350	42" – 45"	4.50	±.03
	DGWR	R100	.600	.277	.335	42" – 45"	4.25	±.03
	DGWR	R200	.600	.277	.335	42" – 45"	4.31	±.03
	DGWR	R300	.600	.277	.335	42" – 45"	4.37	±.03
	DGWR	R400	.600	.277	.335	42" – 45"	4.43	±.03
	DGWR	R500	.600	.277	.335	42" – 45"	4.50	±.03
	DGIX	X100	.600	.355	.395	35" – 39"	4.38	±.03
	DGIX	X200	.600	.355	.395	35" – 39"	4.44	±.03
	DGIX	X300	.600	.355	.395	35" – 39"	4.50	±.03
	DGIX	X400	.600	.355	.395	35" – 39"	4.56	±.03
	DGIX	X500	.600	.355	.395	35" – 39"	4.63	±.03
DYNAMIC GOLD™ IRONS	DGIS	S100	.600	.355	.395	35" – 39"	4.25	±.03
	DGIS	S200	.600	.355	.395	35" – 39"	4.31	±.03
	DGIS	S300	.600	.355	.395	35" – 39"	4.37	±.03
1¾" STEPS · TAPER TIP	DGIS	S400	.600	.355	.395	35" – 39"	4.43	±.03
	DGIS	S500	.600	.355	.395	35" – 39"	4.50	±.03
	DGIR	R100	.580	.355	.395	35" – 39"	4.13	±.03
	DGIR	R200	.580	.355	.395	35" – 39"	4.19	±.03
	DGIR	R300	.580	.355	.395	35" – 39"	4.25	±.03
	DGIR	R400	.580	.355	.395	35" – 39"	4.31	±.03
	DGIR	R500	.580	.355	.395	35" – 39"	4.37	±.03
	GPWX	X100	.620	.294	.350	42" – 44"	3.87	±.03
	GPWX	X200	.620	.294	.350	42" – 44"	3.93	±.03
GOLD PLUS® WOODS	GPWX	X300	.620	.294	.350	42" – 44"	3.99	±.03
	GPWS	S200	.610	.294	.350	42" – 44"	3.34	±.03
	GPWS	S300	.610	.294	.350	42" – 44"	3.40	±.03
VARIABLE STEPS · TAPER TIP	GPWS	S400	.610	.294	.350	42" – 44"	3.46	±.03
	GPWR	R200	.600	.294	.350	42" – 44"	3.24	±.03
	GPWR	R300	.600	.294	.350	42" – 44"	3.30	±.03
	GPWR	R400	.600	.294	.350	42" – 44"	3.36	±.03

TRUE TEMPER® STANDARD WEIGHT SHAFTS
TAPERED TIP *(cont.)*

GOLD PLUS® IRONS

VARIABLE STEPS — TAPER TIP

Pattern	Flex	Butt Dia.	Tip Dia.	Tip Parallel	Length (Specify)	Nominal Weight (Ounces)	Weight Tolerance (Ounces)
GPIX	X100	.620	.355	.395	35" – 39½"	3.87	±.03
GPIX	X200	.620	.355	.395	35" – 39½"	3.93	±.03
GPIX	X300	.620	.355	.395	35" – 39½"	3.99	±.03
GPIS	S200	.610	.355	.395	35" – 39½"	3.44	±.03
GPIS	S300	.610	.355	.395	35" – 39½"	3.50	±.03
GPIS	S400	.610	.355	.395	35" – 39½"	3.56	±.03
GPIR	R200	.600	.355	.395	35" – 39½"	3.34	±.03
GPIR	R300	.600	.355	.395	35" – 39½"	3.40	±.03
GPIR	R400	.600	.355	.395	35" – 39½"	3.46	±.03

TRUE TEMPER® LIGHTWEIGHT SHAFTS
TAPERED TIP

DYNALITE® WOODS

1½" STEPS — TAPER TIP

DYNALITE® IRONS

1¼" STEPS — TAPER TIP

DYNALITE GOLD™ WOODS

1⅞" STEPS — TAPER TIP

DYNALITE GOLD™ IRONS

1¼" STEPS — TAPER TIP

Pattern	Flex	Butt Dia.	Tip Dia.	Length (Specify)	Nominal Weight (Ounces)
LWX	X	.620	.294	42" – 45"	4.10
LWS	S	.620	.294	42" – 45"	4.00
LWR	R	.620	.294	42" – 45"	3.87
LIX	X	.600	.355	35" – 40"	4.10
LIS	S	.600	.355	35" – 40"	4.00
LIR	R	.580	.355	35" – 40"	3.87
LGWX	X100	.620	.294	42" – 45"	3.98
LGWX	X200	.620	.294	42" – 45"	4.04
LGWX	X300	.620	.294	42" – 45"	4.10
LGWS	S200	.620	.294	42" – 45"	3.94
LGWS	S300	.620	.294	42" – 45"	4.00
LGWS	S400	.620	.294	42" – 45"	4.06
LGWR	R200	.600	.294	42" – 45"	3.81
LGWR	R300	.600	.294	42" – 45"	3.87
LGWR	R400	.600	.294	42" – 45"	3.93
LGIX	X100	.600	.355	35" – 40"	3.98
LGIX	X200	.600	.355	35" – 40"	4.04
LGIX	X300	.600	.355	35" – 40"	4.10
LGIS	S200	.600	.355	35" – 40"	3.94
LGIS	S300	.600	.355	35" – 40"	4.00
LGIS	S400	.600	.355	35" – 40"	4.06
LGIR	R200	.580	.355	35" – 40"	3.81
LGIR	R300	.580	.355	35" – 40"	3.87
LGIR	R400	.580	.355	35" – 40"	3.93

TRUE TEMPER® LIGHTWEIGHT SHAFTS
TAPERED TIP *(cont.)*

	Pattern	Flex	Butt Dia.	Tip Dia.	Length (Specify)	Nominal Weight (Ounces)
DYNAMIC LITE™ WOODS	DLWX	X	.610	.294	42" – 45"	4.125
1⅞" STEPS / TAPER TIP	DLWS	S	.600	.294	42" – 45"	4.00
	DLWR	R	.600	.294	42" – 45"	3.87
DYNAMIC LITE™ IRONS	DLIX	X	.610	.355	35" – 40"	4.125
1¾" STEPS / TAPER TIP	DLIS	S	.600	.355	35" – 40"	4.00
	DLIR	R	.600	.355	35" – 40"	3.87
EXTRALITE™ WOODS AND IRONS	SDLWS	S	.600	.320	44", 43", 42"	3.40
	SDLWR	R	.600	.320	44", 43", 42"	3.30
	SDLWL	L	.580	.300	43", 42"	3.30
½" STEPS / 1" STEPS / TAPER TIP	SDLIS	S	.600	.355	35" – 39"	3.50
	SDLIR	R	.600	.355	35" – 39"	3.40
	SDLIL	L	.580	.355	34" – 38"	3.37

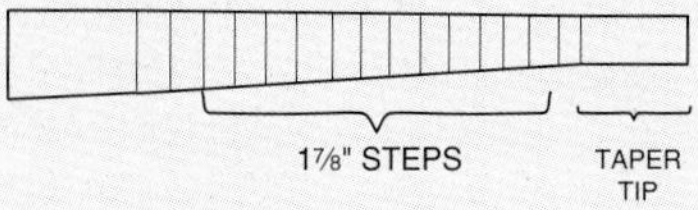

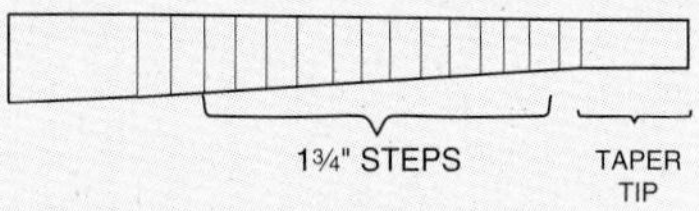

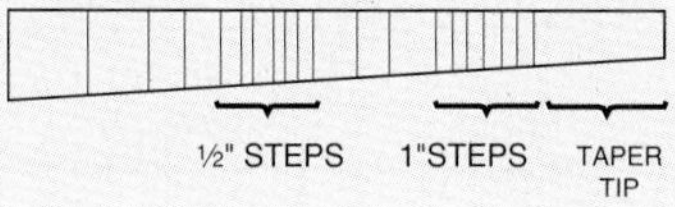

TRUE TEMPER® LIGHTWEIGHT SHAFTS
TAPERED TIP AND PARALLEL TIP

	Pattern	Flex	Butt Dia.	Tip Dia.	Length (Specify)	Nominal Weight (Ounces)	Weight Tolerance (Ounces)
TT LITE® WOODS PARALLEL TIP	U2LWAL	A&L	.580	.335	46"	4.00	±⅛
	UTTLWC	R & S	.600	.335	47"	4.31	±⅛
	UTTLWCH*	R & S	.600	.335	45"	4.25	±⅛
(*Tip reinforced)							
1½" STEPS / TAPERED TIP	2LWS	S	.620	.294	42" – 45"	4.125 @ 45"	±⅛
	2LWR	R	.620	.294	42" – 45"	4.00 @ 45"	±⅛
	2LWL	L	.580	.294	42" – 45"	3.83 @ 45"	±⅛
TT LITE® IRONS PARALLEL TIP	U2LIAL	A & L	.580	.370	40"	3.87	±⅛
	UTTLIC	R & S	.600	.370	41"	4.19	±⅛
1½" STEPS / TAPERED TIP	2LIS	S	.620	.355	35" – 39"	4.125 @ 39"	±⅛
	2LIR	R	.620	.355	35" – 39"	3.87 @ 39"	±⅛
	2LIL	L	.580	.355	34" – 38"	3.67 @ 38"	±⅛

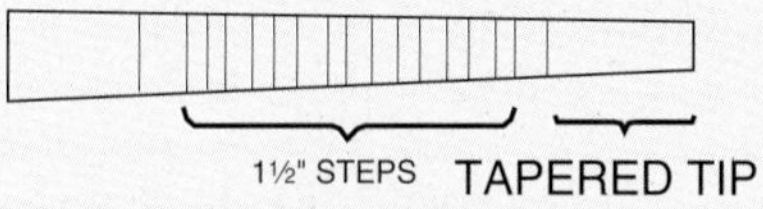

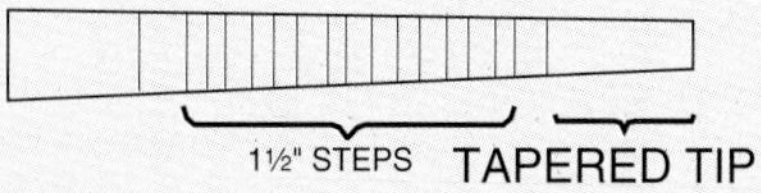

GOLF SHAFT LENGTHS
1st Quality TAPERED TIP

WOODS – All Flexes 45", 44½", 44", 43", 42½", 42"
IRONS – X-S-R-A Flexes 39", 38½", 38", 37½", 37", 36½", 36", 35½", 35"
IRONS – L Flex 38", 37½", 37", 36½", 36", 35½", 35", 34½", 34"

TRUE TEMPER® FLEX FLOW
TAPERED TIP AND PARALLEL TIP
Progressive Flex Points

1¼" STEPS • TAPER TIP

	Pattern	Flex	Butt Dia.	Tip Dia.	Length* (Specify)	Nominal Weight (Grams)	Weight Tolerance (Grams)
FLEX FLOW™ WOODS	TFFWS	S	.600	.294	41½" – 44"	110	±3
TAPERED TIP	TFFWR	R	.600	.294	41½" – 44"	106	±3
	TFFWA	A	.580	.294	41½" – 44"	106	±3
	TFFWL	L	.580	.294	41½" – 44"	106	±3
	UTFFWS	S	.600	.335	41½" – 44"	110	±3
PARALLEL TIP	UTFFWR	R	.600	.335	41½" – 44"	106	±3
	UTFFWA	A	.580	.335	41½" – 44"	106	±3
	UTFFWL	L	.580	.335	41½" – 44"	106	±3
	UTFFWSH	S	.600	.335	40½" – 43"	110	±3
PARALLEL REINFORCED TIP	UTFFWRH	R	.600	.335	40½" – 43"	106	±3
	UTFFWAH	A	.580	.335	40½" – 43"	106	±3
	UTFFWLH	L	.580	.335	40½" – 43"	106	±3
FLEX FLOW™ IRONS	TFFIS	S	.600	.355	35" – 39"	110	±3
TAPERED TIP	TFFIR	R	.600	.355	35" – 39"	106	±3
	TFFIA	A	.580	.355	35" – 39"	106	±3
	TFFIL	L	.580	.355	34½" – 38½"	106	±3
	UTFFIS	S	.600	.370	35" – 39"	110	±3
PARALLEL TIP	UTFFIR	R	.600	.370	35" – 39"	106	±3
	UTFFIA	A	.580	.370	35" – 39"	106	±3
	UTFFIL	L	.580	.370	34½" – 38½"	106	±3

*Available in ½" increments only, in both tapered and parallel tip.

Special Note: Discrete Shafts are Recommended for each Club in a Set to Achieve Best Results.

True Temper's Recommendation:

	WOODS					IRONS									
Club:	#1	#3	#4	#5	#7	#2	#3	#4	#5	#6	#7	#8	#9	PW	SW
Purchased Shaft Length in Both Parallel & Tapered Tip:	44"	43"	42½"	42"	41½"	39"	38½"	38"	37½"	37"	36½"	36"	35½"	35"	35"

Product Information on Flex Flow™ Shafts: The Flex Flow™ Shaft is designed to give each club in a set a different flex point. The Flex Flow™ Shaft provides a low flex point in the longer irons, a mid flex point in the middle irons and a higher flex point in the short irons. With woods, the driver will have the lower flex point and the fairway woods will be progressively higher in flex point location.

TRUE TEMPER® PARALLEL TIP SHAFTS

	Pattern	Flex	Butt Dia.	Parallel Tip	Length (Specify)	Nominal Weight (Ounces)	Weight Tolerance (Ounces)
DYNAMIC® WOODS	UDWX	X	.600	.335	45"	4.375	±⅛
	UDWC	R & S	.600	.335	47"	4.625	±⅛
	UDWR	R	.600	.335	45"	4.312	±⅛
	UDWS	S	.600	.335	45"	4.375	±⅛
	UDWAL	A & L	.560	.335	46"	4.375	±⅛
	UDWCH*	R & S	.600	.335	44"	4.312	±⅛

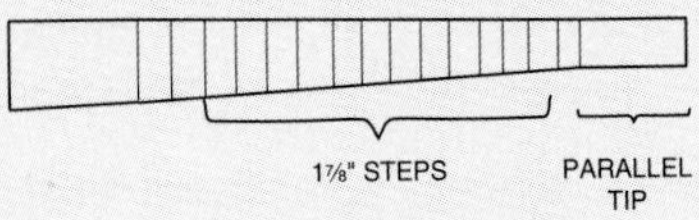

*Reinforced Tip for use in Metal Woods.

	Pattern	Flex	Butt Dia.	Parallel Tip	Length (Specify)	Nominal Weight (Ounces)	Weight Tolerance (Ounces)
DYNAMIC® IRONS	UDIX	X	.600	.370	39"	4.500	±⅛
	UDIC	R & S	.600	.370	41"	4.562	±⅛
	UDIR	R	.600	.370	39"	4.250	±⅛
	UDIS	S	.600	.370	39"	4.375	±⅛
	UDIAL	A & L	.560	.370	40"	4.312	±⅛
	UDICO	R & S	.600	.395	41"	4.562	±⅛

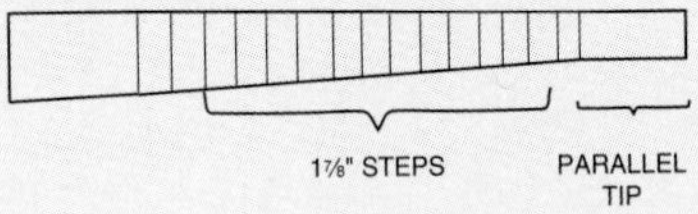

	Pattern	Flex	Butt Dia.	Parallel Tip	Length (Specify)	Nominal Weight (Ounces)	Weight Tolerance (Ounces)
DYNAMIC GOLD® WOODS	UDGWX	X100	.600	.335	45"	4.25	±.03
		X200	.600	.335	45"	4.31	±.03
		X300	.600	.335	45"	4.37	±.03
	UDGWS	S200	.600	.335	45"	4.31	±.03
		S300	.600	.335	45"	4.37	±.03
		S400	.600	.335	45"	4.43	±.03
	UDGWR	R200	.600	.335	45"	4.25	±.03
		R300	.600	.335	45"	4.31	±.03
		R400	.600	.335	45"	4.37	±.03

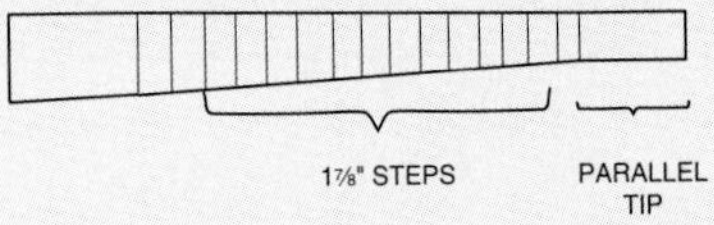

	Pattern	Flex	Butt Dia.	Parallel Tip	Length (Specify)	Nominal Weight (Ounces)	Weight Tolerance (Ounces)
DYNAMIC GOLD® IRONS	UDGIX	X100	.600	.370	40"	4.49	±.03
		X200	.600	.370	40"	4.55	±.03
		X300	.600	.370	40"	4.61	±.03
	UDGIS	S200	.600	.370	40"	4.42	±.03
		S300	.600	.370	40"	4.48	±.03
		S400	.600	.370	40"	4.54	±.03
	UDGIR	R200	.600	.370	40"	4.30	±.03
		R300	.600	.370	40"	4.36	±.03
		R400	.600	.370	40"	4.42	±.03

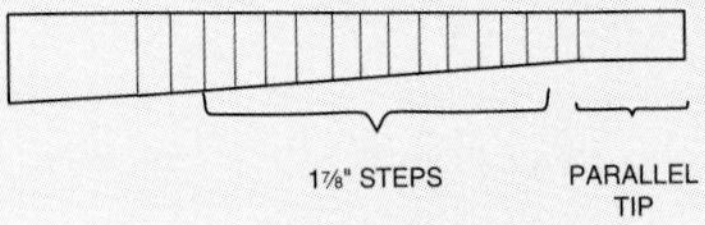

	Pattern	Flex	Butt Dia.	Parallel Tip	Length (Specify)	Nominal Weight (Ounces)	Weight Tolerance (Ounces)
GOLD PLUS™ WOODS REINFORCED TIP*	UGPWXH	X100	.620	.335	44"	3.87	±.03
		X200	.620	.335	44"	3.93	±.03
		X300	.620	.335	44"	3.99	±.03
	UGPWSH	S200	.610	.335	44"	3.72	±.03
		S300	.610	.335	44"	3.78	±.03
		S400	.610	.335	44"	3.84	±.03
	UGPWRH	R200	.610	.335	44"	3.62	±.03
		R300	.610	.335	44"	3.68	±.03
		R400	.610	.335	44"	3.74	±.03
	UGPWLH	L200	.580	.335	44"	3.31	±.03
		L300	.580	.335	44"	3.37	±.03
		L400	.580	.335	44"	3.44	±.03

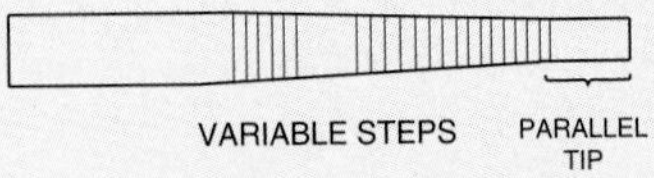

*Reinforced Tip for use in Metal Woods.

TRUE TEMPER® PARALLEL TIP SHAFTS *(cont.)*

GOLD PLUS™ IRONS

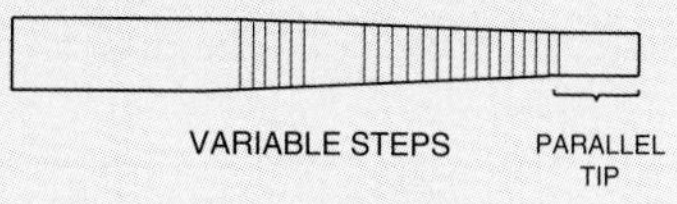

VARIABLE STEPS   PARALLEL TIP

Pattern	Flex	Butt Dia.	Parallel Tip	Length (Specify)	Nominal Weight (Ounces)	Weight Tolerance (Ounces)
UGPIX	X100	.620	.370	39½"	3.87	±.03
	X200	.620	.370	39½"	3.93	±.03
	X300	.620	.370	39½"	3.99	±.03
UGPIS	S200	.610	.370	39½"	3.69	±.03
	S300	.610	.370	39½"	3.75	±.03
	S400	.610	.370	39½"	3.81	±.03
UGPIR	R200	.600	.370	39½"	3.56	±.03
	R300	.600	.370	39½"	3.62	±.03
	R400	.600	.370	39½"	3.68	±.03
UGPIL	L200	.580	.370	39"	3.31	±.03
	L300	.580	.370	39"	3.37	±.03
	L400	.580	.370	39"	3.44	±.03

JET STEP® WOODS

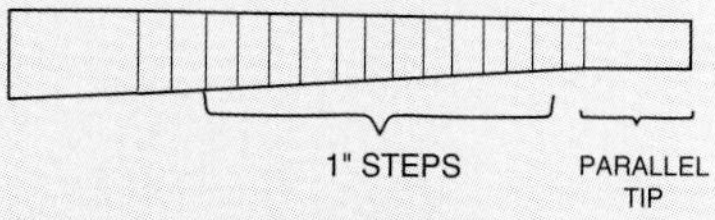

1" STEPS   PARALLEL TIP

Pattern	Flex	Butt Dia.	Parallel Tip	Length (Specify)	Nominal Weight (Ounces)	Weight Tolerance (Ounces)
UJWC	R & S	.600	.335	47"	4.625	±⅛

JET STEP® IRONS

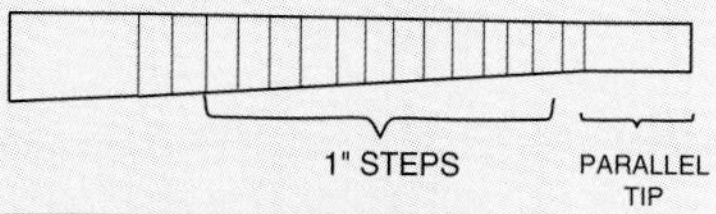

1" STEPS   PARALLEL TIP

Pattern	Flex	Butt Dia.	Parallel Tip	Length (Specify)	Nominal Weight (Ounces)	Weight Tolerance (Ounces)
UJIC	R & S	.600	.370	41"	4.562	±⅛
UJICO	R & S	.600	.395 (OTH)	41"	4.562	±⅛

PRO FIT® WOODS

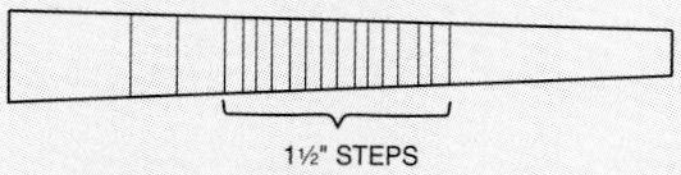

1½" STEPS

Pattern	Flex	Butt Dia.	Parallel Tip	Length (Specify)	Nominal Weight (Ounces)	Weight Tolerance (Ounces)
UPWC	R & S	.600	.335	47"	4.625	±⅛

PRO FIT® IRONS

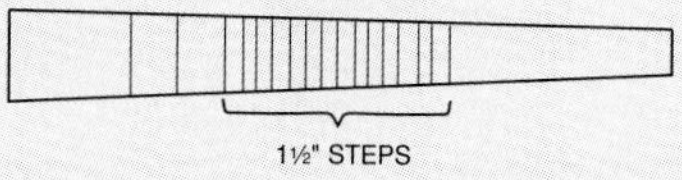

1½" STEPS

Pattern	Flex	Butt Dia.	Parallel Tip	Length (Specify)	Nominal Weight (Ounces)	Weight Tolerance (Ounces)
UPIC	R & S	.600	.370	41"	4.562	±⅛

TRUE TEMPER® LIGHTWEIGHT SHAFTS PARALLEL TIP

DYNALITE® WOODS

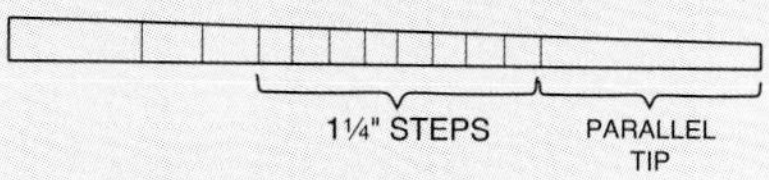

1¼" STEPS   PARALLEL TIP

Pattern	Flex	Butt Dia.	Parallel Tip	Length (Specify)	Nominal Weight (Ounces)
ULWXH*	X	.600	.335	45"	4.25
ULWCH*	R & S	.600	.335	47"	4.125
ULWAL	A & L	.580	.335	46"	3.87

*Reinforced Tip for use in Metal Woods.

DYNALITE® IRONS

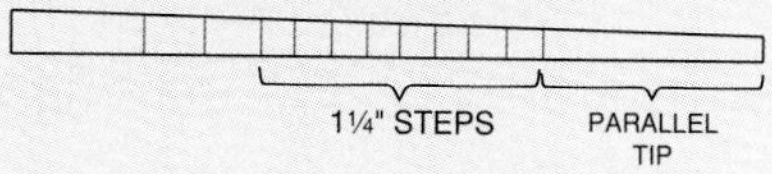

1¼" STEPS   PARALLEL TIP

Pattern	Flex	Butt Dia.	Parallel Tip	Length (Specify)	Nominal Weight (Ounces)
ULIX	X	.600	.370	40"	4.25
ULIC	R & S	.600	.370	41"	4.25
ULIAL	A & L	.580	.370	40"	3.87

TRUE TEMPER® LIGHTWEIGHT SHAFTS
PARALLEL TIP *(cont.)*

	Pattern	Flex	Butt Dia.	Parallel Tip	Length (Specify)	Nominal Weight (Ounces)
DYNALITE GOLD™ WOODS REINFORCED TIP*	ULGWXH	X100	.600	.335	45"	4.13
		X200	.600	.335	45"	4.19
		X300	.600	.335	45"	4.25
	ULGWXS	S200	.600	.335	45"	3.89
		S300	.600	.335	45"	3.95
		S400	.600	.335	45"	4.01
	ULGWRH	R200	.600	.335	45"	3.89
		R300	.600	.335	45"	3.95
		R400	.600	.335	45"	4.01

Reinforced Tip for use in Metal Woods.

	Pattern	Flex	Butt Dia.	Parallel Tip	Length (Specify)	Nominal Weight (Ounces)
DYNALITE GOLD™ IRONS	ULGIX	X100	.600	.370	40"	4.13
		X200	.600	.370	40"	4.19
		X300	.600	.370	40"	4.25
	ULGIS	S200	.600	.370	40"	4.09
		S300	.600	.370	40"	4.15
		S400	.600	.370	40"	4.21
	ULGIR	R200	.600	.370	40"	4.09
		R300	.600	.370	40"	4.15
		R400	.600	.370	40"	4.21

	Pattern	Flex	Butt Dia.	Parallel Tip	Length (Specify)	Nominal Weight (Ounces)
DYNAMIC LITE™ WOODS	UDLWS	S	.600	.335	45"	4.125
	UDLWR	R	.600	.335	45"	4.00
DYNAMIC LITE™ IRONS	UDLIS	S	.600	.370	39"	4.125
	UDLIR	R	.600	.370	39"	4.00
RELEASE™ WOODS	USLWA	A	.600	.335	45"	3.87
RELEASE™ IRONS	USLIA	A	.600	.370	40"	3.75

TRUE TEMPER® COMMERCIAL GRADE SHAFTS

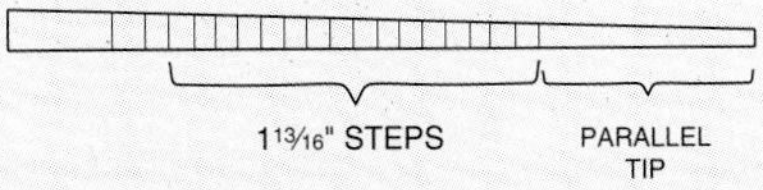

	Pattern	Flex	Butt Dia.	Parallel Tip	Length (Specify)	Nominal Weight (Ounces)	Weight Tolerance (Ounces)
COMET® WOODS							
1¹³⁄₁₆" STEPS — PARALLEL TIP	URWC	R/S	.600	.335	47"	4.51	±¼
	URWL	L	.560	.335	44"	4.30	±¼
COMET® IRONS							
1¹³⁄₁₆" STEPS — PARALLEL TIP	URIC	R/S	.600	.370	41"	4.51	±¼
	URIL	L	.560	.370	39"	4.30	±¼
JUNIOR & JUVENILE PARALLEL BUTT & TAPERED TIP							
3" STEPS	WOOD — UHSJW500		.500	.335	40"	-	-
	IRON — UHSJI500		.500	.370	37"	-	-

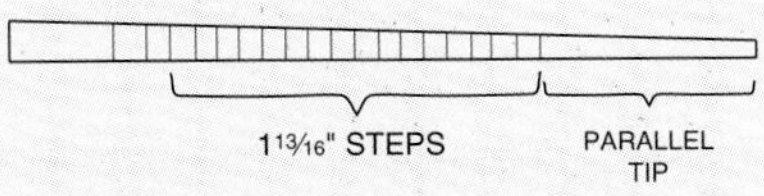

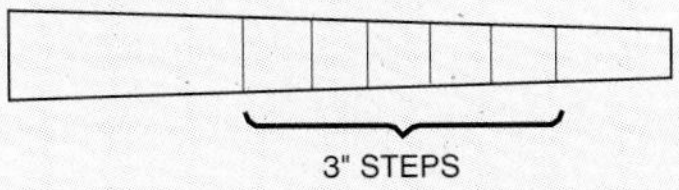

TRUE TEMPER® DISCONTINUED GOLF SHAFTS

	Pattern	Flex	Butt Dia.	Parallel Tip	Length (Specify)	Nominal Weight (Ounces)	Weight Tolerance (Ounces)
KINETIC™ WOODS (DISCONTINUED IN 1981) PARALLEL TIP	U704WC	R & S	.704-.600	.335	47"	4.375	±³⁄₁₆
1⅞" STEPS — TAPERED TIP	704WS	S	.704-.616	.294	42" – 45"	4.000	±³⁄₁₆
	704WR	R	.704-.600	.294	42" – 45"	3.875	±³⁄₁₆
KINETIC™ IRONS (DISCONTINUED IN 1981) PARALLEL TIP	U704IC	R & S	.704-.600	.370	41"	4.375	±³⁄₁₆
1¾" STEPS — TAPERED TIP	704IS	S	.704-.600	.355	35" – 39"	4.000	±³⁄₁₆
	704IR	R	.704-.560	.355	35" – 39"	3.875	±³⁄₁₆
SUPER LITE™ WOODS (DISCONTINUED IN 1980) TAPERED TIP	TTSWX	X	.620	.320	44" & 42"	3.75	±⅛
	TTSWS	S	.620	.320	44" & 42"	3.65	±⅛
	TTSWR	R	.620	.320	44" & 42"	3.55	±⅛
1½" STEPS	TTSWA	A	.580	.320	43" & 41"	3.45	±⅛
	TTSWL	L	.580	.320	43" & 41"	3.45	±⅛

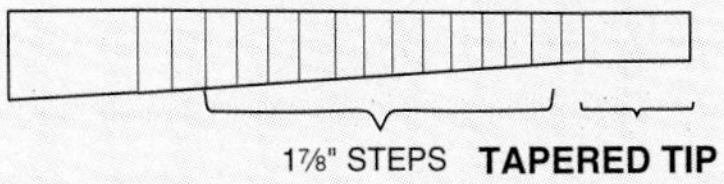

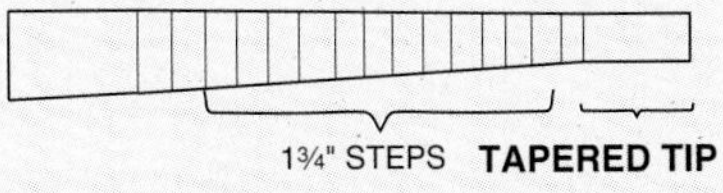

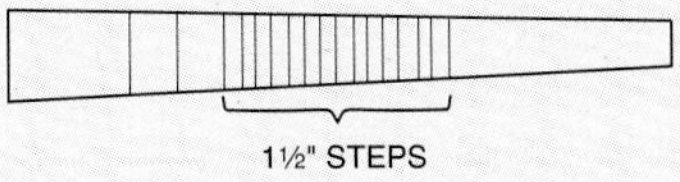

44" & 43" for Driver; 42" & 41" for Fairway Woods

TRUE TEMPER® DISCONTINUED GOLF SHAFTS *(cont.)*

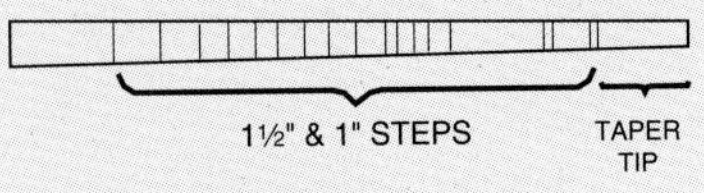

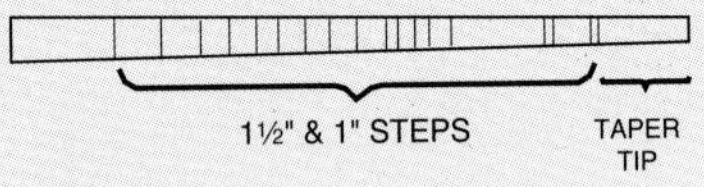

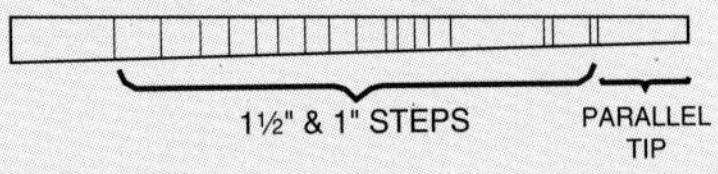

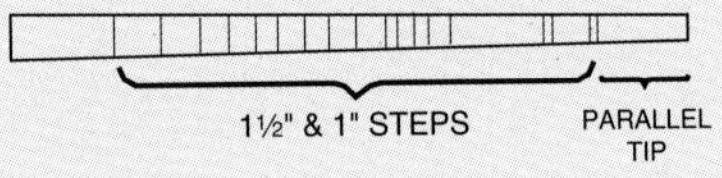

	Pattern	Flex	Butt Dia.	Parallel Tip	Length (Specify)	Nominal Weight (Ounces)	Weight Tolerance (Ounces)
CONTOUR™ WOODS 3" RECESSED SECTION IN TIP SECTION 1½" & 1" STEPS — TAPER TIP	TRWS	S	.600	.294	42" – 45"	4.250	±³/₁₆
	TRWR	R	.600	.294	42" – 45"	4.125	±³/₁₆
	TRWL	L	.560	.277	42" – 44"	4.000	±³/₁₆
CONTOUR™ IRONS 3" RECESSED SECTION IN TIP SECTION 1½" & 1" STEPS — TAPER TIP	TRIS	S	.600	.355	35" – 39"	4.125	±³/₁₆
	TRIR	R	.600	.355	35" – 39"	4.000	±³/₁₆
	TRIL	L	.560	.355	35" – 38"	3.875	±³/₁₆
CONTOUR™ WOODS 3" RECESSED SECTION IN TIP SECTION 1½" & 1" STEPS — PARALLEL TIP	UTRWS	S	.600	.335	45"	4.250	±³/₁₆
	UTRWR	R	.600	.335	45"	4.125	±³/₁₆
	UTRWL	L	.560	.335	44"	4.000	±³/₁₆
CONTOUR™ IRONS 3" RECESSED SECTION IN TIP SECTION 1½" & 1" STEPS — PARALLEL TIP	UTRIS	S	.600	.370	39"	4.125	±³/₁₆
	UTRIR	R	.600	.370	39"	4.000	±³/₁₆
	UTRIL	L	.560	.370	38"	3.875	±³/₁₆

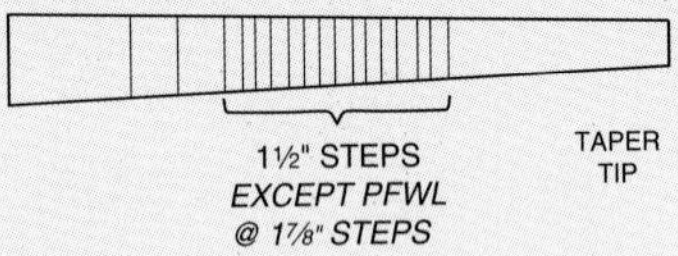

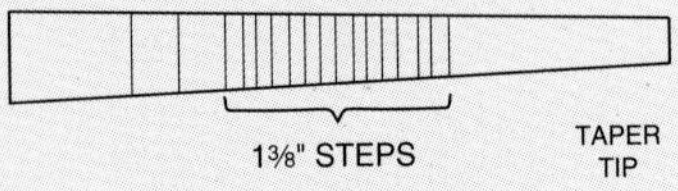

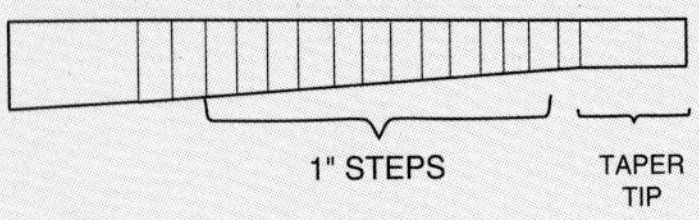

	Pattern	Flex	Butt Dia.	Tip Dia.	Tip Parallel	Length (Specify)	Nominal Weight (Ounces)	Weight Tolerance (Ounces)
PRO FIT® WOODS 1½" STEPS *EXCEPT PFWL* *@ 1⅞" STEPS* — TAPER TIP	PFWS	S	.620	.286	.340	42" – 45"	4.37	±⅛
	PFWR	R	.600	.277	.335	42" – 45"	4.37	±⅛
	PFWA	A	.580	.277	.320	42" – 45"	4.25	±⅛
	PFWL	L	.580	.270	.305	42" – 44"	4.10	±⅛
PRO FIT® IRONS 1⅜" STEPS — TAPER TIP	PFIS	S	.600	.355	.395	35" – 39"	4.37	±⅛
	PFIR	R	.580	.355	.385	35" – 39"	4.25	±⅛
	PFIA	A	.560	.355	.380	35" – 39"	4.25	±⅛
	PFIL	L	.580	.300	.335	34" – 38"	4.10	±⅛
JET STEP® WOODS 1" STEPS — TAPER TIP	JTWS	S	.620	.277	.320	42" – 45"	4.37	±⅛
	JTWR	R	.600	.277	.320	42" – 45"	4.37	±⅛

584

TRUE TEMPER® DISCONTINUED GOLF SHAFTS *(cont.)*

JET STEP® IRONS

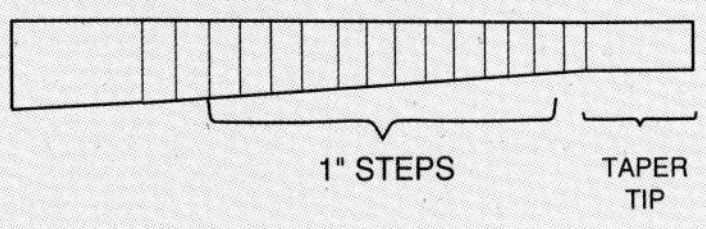

	Pattern	Flex	Butt Dia.	Tip Dia.	Tip Parallel	Length (Specify)	Nominal Weight (Ounces)	Weight Tolerance (Ounces)
	JTIS	S	.580	.355	.392	35" – 39"	4.25	±⅛
	JTIR	R	.580	.355	.380	35" – 39"	4.25	±⅛

1" STEPS — TAPER TIP

CENTURY™ WOODS

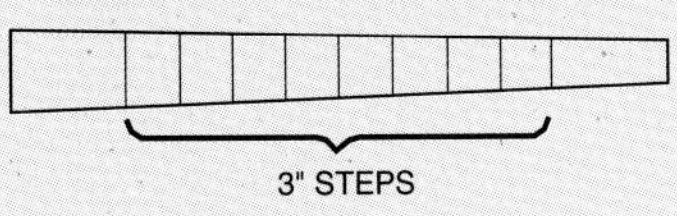

	Pattern	Flex	Butt Dia.	Parallel Tip	Length (Specify)	Nominal Weight (Ounces)	Weight Tolerance (Ounces)
PARALLEL TIP	U3W	R	.600	.335	44"	4.375	±¼
	U3WL	L	.560	.320	44"	4.250	±¼
TAPER TIP	U3WX	R	.600	.277	44"	4.375	±¼
	U3WLX	L	.560	.277	44"	4.250	±¼

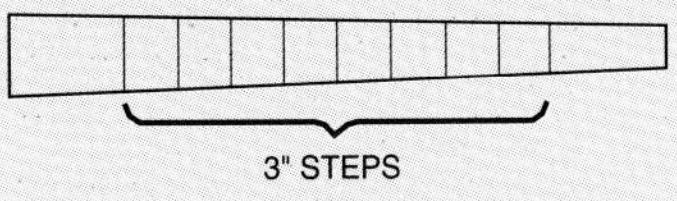

3" STEPS

CENTURY™ WOODS

	Pattern	Flex	Butt Dia.	Parallel Tip	Length (Specify)	Nominal Weight (Ounces)	Weight Tolerance (Ounces)
PARALLEL TIP	U3I	R	.600	.370	39"	4.375	±¼
	U3IL	L	.560	.320	38"	4.250	±¼
	U3ILM	I	.560	.370	38"	4.250	±¼
TAPER TIP	U3IX	R	.600	.355	39", 37", 35"	4.375	±¼
	U3ILX	L	.560	.300	38" & 36"	4.250	±¼

3" STEPS

DRIVING RANGE WOOD

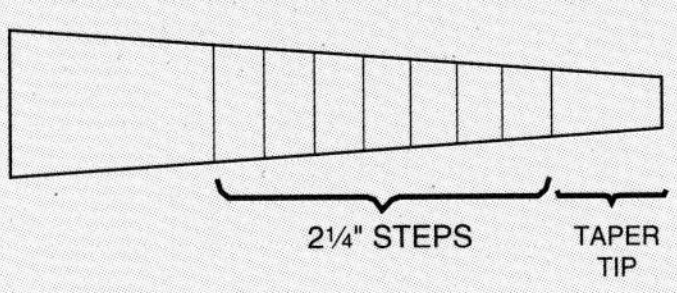

	Pattern	Flex	Butt Dia.	Parallel Tip	Length (Specify)	Nominal Weight (Ounces)	Weight Tolerance (Ounces)
	MWH	—	.600	.320	44"	5.00	±¼

2¼" STEPS — TAPER TIP

TRUE TEMPER® PUTTER SHAFTS AND BUTT EXTENSIONS

PUTTER SHAFTS

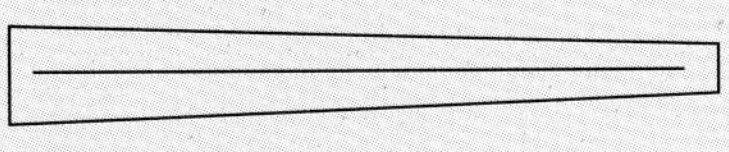

Code	Description	Butt Dia.	Tip Dia.
YST	Str. Taper	.580	.355
YSTG	Str. Taper Fluted	.580	.355
UYST	Unitized (Parallel Tip)	.580	.395
UYSTG	Unitized, Fluted (Parallel Tip)	.580	.395
UYEST	Str. Taper (Parallel Tip)	.580	.370
UDIXM	48" Parallel Tip	.600	.370
YESTF	Flared Tip, Bright Chrome	.580	N/A

NOTE: Putters are available in 35" only. Trim from the butt for shorter lengths.

BUTT EXTENSIONS

Used to increase length of shafts for longer length clubs.
Steel – Butt Size .620 - .600 - .580 - .560

|← 12" →|

Double length, cut in half

BRUNSWICK GOLF SHAFTS
TAPERED TIP AND PARALLEL TIP

	Model No.	Flex	Butt Dia.	[1]Tip Dia.	[2]Nominal Wt., Oz.
UCV-304® Wood (Chrome Vanadium Alloy) Variable Steps — Tapered Tip	6579WS (UCVWS)	S	.600	.294	3.88
	6569WR (UCVWR)	R	.600	.294	3.64
	6529WL (UCVWL)	L	.560	.286	3.60
	Lengths: S and R Flex 45", 44", 43", 42". L Flex 44", 43", 42", 41".				
UCV-304® Iron Variable Steps — Tapered Tip	6579IS (UCVIS)	S	.600	.355	3.60
	6569IR (UCVIR)	R	.580	.355	3.40
	6529IL (UCVIL)	L	.540	.355	3.60
	Lengths: S and R Flex 39", 38½", 38", 37½", 37", 36½", 36", 35½", 35". L Flex 38", 37", 36", 35".				
UCV-304® Wood (Chrome Vanadium Alloy) Variable Steps — Parallel Tip	6179WS	S	.600	.335	3.85
	6169WR	R	.600	.335	3.60
	Lengths: S and R Flex 44".				
UCV-304® Iron Variable Steps — Parallel Tip	6179IS	S	.600	.370	3.80
	6169IR	R	.600	.370	3.60
	Lengths: S and R Flex 39".				
Precision Phoenix® Woods Parallel Tip — 1½" Steps	7576WRS (UPHWRS)	R/S	.600	.335	4.25
	7556WAL (UPHWAL)	A/L	.580	.335	3.87
	Lengths: R/S Flex 47", A/L Flex 46". (Lightweight Shaft)				
Tapered Tip	7278WS (PHWS)	S	.600	.294	4.02
	7268WR ((PHWR)	R	.600	.294	3.90
	Lengths: S and R Flex 44", 43", 42½", 42". Nominal weight applies to 44" length.				
Precision Phoenix® Woods Reinforced Tip — 1½" Steps — Parallel Tip	7596WRS	R/S	.600	.335	4.25
	Lengths: R/S Flex 44". (Lightweight Shaft)				
Precision Phoenix® Irons Parallel Tip — 1½" Steps	7576IRS (UPHIR)	R/S	.600	.370	4.15
	7556IAL (UPHIAL)	A/L	.560	.370	4.00
	Lengths: R/S Flex 41", A/L Flex 40". (Lightweight Shaft)				
Tapered Tip	7278IS (PHIS)	S	.600	.355	4.00
	7268IR (PHIR)	R	.600	.355	3.87
	Lengths: S and R Flex 39", 38½", 38", 37½", 37", 36½", 36", 35½", 35". Nominal weight applies to 39" length.				

[1]Tip Diameters have a tolerance of ±.002".   [2]Weight tolerance on all shafts above is ±1/10 ounce. Standard length tolerance is ±1/16".

BRUNSWICK GOLF SHAFTS
TAPERED TIP AND PARALLEL TIP

	Model No.	Flex	Butt Dia.	[1]Tip Dia.	[2]Nominal Wt., Oz.
Precision Propel® II Woods 1⅞" Steps Parallel Tip	8076WRS (UPWC) 8056WAL (UPWAL) Lengths: R/S Flex 47", A/L Flex 46". (Standard Weight)	R/S A/L	.600 .560	.335 .335	4.60 4.40
Precision Propel® II Woods **Reinforced Tip** 1⅞" Steps Parallel Tip	8076WRS (UPWC) 8056WAL (UPWAL) Lengths: R/S Flex 47", A/L Flex 46". (Standard Weight)	R/S A/L	.600 .560	.335 .335	4.60 4.40
Precision Propel® II Irons 1⅞" Steps Parallel Tip	7876IRS (UPIC) 7856IAL (UPIAL) Lengths: R/S Flex 41", A/L Flex 40". (Standard Weight)	R/S A/L	.600 .560	.370 .370	4.58 4.30
Precision Microtaper® Woods ¾" Steps ¼" Taper Sections Parallel Tip	8176WRS 8156WAL Lengths: R/S Flex 47", A/L flex 46". (Lightweight Shaft)	R/S A/L	.600 .560	.335 .335	4.20 4.10
Precision Microtaper® Woods **Reinforced Tip** ¾" Steps ¼" Taper Sections Parallel Tip	8476WRS 8456WAL Lengths: R/S Flex 45", A/L Flex 44". (Lightweight Shaft)	R/S A/L	.600 .560	.335 .335	4.30 4.20
Precision Microtaper® Irons ¾" Steps ¼" Taper Sections Parallel Tip	8176IRS 8156IAL Lengths: R/S Flex 41", A/L Flex 40". (Lightweight Shaft)	R/S A/L	.600 .560	.370 .370	4.20 4.10

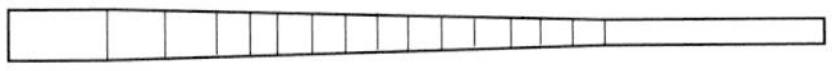

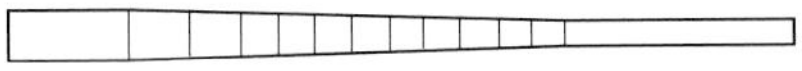

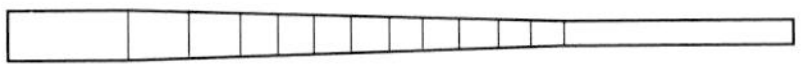

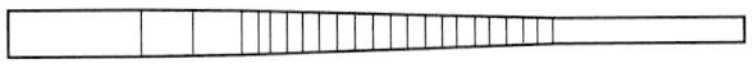

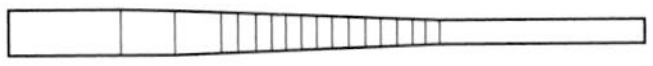

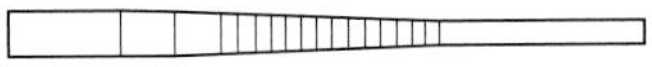

	Model No.	Flex	Butt Dia.	[1]Tip Dia.	Length	[2]Nominal Wt., Oz.
Super Champion® Woods Parallel Tip Tapered Tip 1¹³⁄₁₆" Steps	2863WR (USCWR) 2823WL (USCWL) 2663WR (SCWR) 2623WL (SCWL)	R L R L	.600 .560 .600 .560	.335 .335 .294 .294	44" 43" 44" 44"	4.30 4.20 4.30 4.30
Super Champion® Irons Parallel Tip Tapered Tip 1¹³⁄₁₆" Steps	2863IR (USCIR) 2823IL (USCIL) 2663IR (SCIR) 2623IL (SCIL)	R L R L	.600 .560 .600 .560	.370 .370 .355 .355	39" 38" 38" & 36" 38" & 36"	4.25 4.30 4.30 4.20

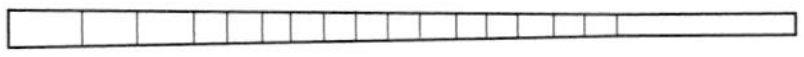

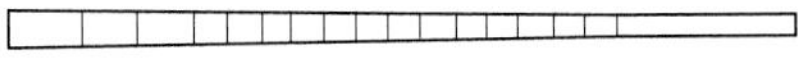

[1]Tip Diameters have a tolerance of ±.002".   [2]Weight tolerance on all shafts above is ±¹⁄₁₀ ounce. Standard length tolerance is ±¹⁄₁₆.

BRUNSWICK GOLF SHAFTS
TAPERED TIP AND PARALLEL TIP

	Model No.	Flex	Butt Dia.	[1]Tip Dia.	Length	[2]Nominal Wt., Oz.
Champion® Woods 3" Steps — Parallel Tip	2263WR (UCWR) 2223WL (UCWL)	R L	.600 .560	.335 .335	44" 44"	4.30 4.30
Champion® Irons 3" Steps — Parallel Tip	2263IR (UCIR) 2223IL (UCIL)	R L	.600 .560	.370 .370	39" 38"	4.30 4.30

	Model No.	Flex	Butt Dia.	Tip Dia.	Nominal Wt., Oz.
Precision Select - HFA® Woods (High Flex Action) 1⅞" Steps — Parallel Tip	8071LWRS 8071HWRS	R2 OR S3 R3 OR S4	.600 .600	.335 .335	4.555 4.625
	Weight tolerance .oz ± .025				
Precision Select - HFA® Irons (High Flex Action) 1⅞" Steps — Parallel Tip	7871LIRS 7871HIRS	R2 OR S3 R3 OR S4	.600 .600	.370 .370	4.555 4.605
Precision Select - MFA® Woods (Mid Flex Action) 1½" Steps — Parallel Tip	7571LWRS 7571HWRS 7551LWAL 7551HWAL	R2 OR S3 R3 OR S4 L3 A3	.600 .600 .580 .580	.335 .335 .335 .335	4.225 4.275 3.845 3.895
	Weight tolerance .oz ± .025				
Precision Select - MFA® Irons (Mid Flex Action) 1½" Steps — Parallel Tip	7571LIRS 7571HIRS 7551LIAL 7551HIAL	R2 OR S3 R3 OR S4 L3 A3	.600 .600 .560 .560	.370 .370 .370 .370	4.125 4.175 3.975 4.025
Precision Select - LFA® Woods (Low Flex Action) ¾" Steps ¼" Taper Sections — Parallel Tip	8171LWRS 8171HWRS	R2 OR S3 R3 OR S4	.600 .600	.335 .335	4.175 4.225
Precision Select - LFA® Woods (Low Flex Action) Reinforced Tip ¾" Steps ¼" Taper Sections — Parallel Tip	8471LWRS 8471HWRS 8151LWAL 8151HWAL	R2 OR S3 R3 OR S4 L3 A3	.600 .600 .560 .560	.335 .335 .335 .335	4.275 4.325 4.075 4.125

[1]Tip Diameters have a tolerance of ±.002".   [2]Weight tolerance on all shafts above is ±1/10 ounce. Standard length tolerance is ±1/16.

BRUNSWICK GOLF SHAFTS
TAPERED TIP AND PARALLEL TIP

	Model No.	Flex	Butt Dia.	Tip Dia.	Nominal Wt., Oz.
Precision Select - LFA® Irons (Low Flex Action) ¾" Steps ¼" Taper Sections — Parallel Tip	8171LIRS 8171HIRS 8151LIAL 8151HIAL	R2 OR S3 R3 OR S4 L3 A3	.600 .600 .560 .560	.370 .370 .370 .370	4.175 4.225 4.075 4.125

	Model No.	Flex	Butt Dia.	Parallel Dia.	Tapered Tip
Precision FCM® Woods Variable Steps — Parallel and Tapered Tip	WFM	3.5-8.0	.600	.335	.294
Precision FCM® Irons Variable Steps — Parallel and Tapered Tip	IFM	3.5-8.0	.600	.370	.355
Precision FCM Lite™ Woods Variable Steps — Parallel and Tapered Tip	WFML	3.5-4.0 4.1-8.0	.580 .600	.335 .335	.294 .294
Precision FCM Lite™ Irons Variable Steps — Parallel and Tapered Tip	IFML	3.5-4.0 4.1-8.0	.580 .600	.370 .370	.355 .355

BRUNSWICK GOLF PUTTER SHAFTS

	Model No.	Butt Dia.	Tip Dia.	Length
Constant Taper, Flared Tip	9493P	.580	.382 I.D.	35"
Constant Taper, Parallel Tip	9293P	.580	.370	35"
1¹³⁄₁₆" Steps, Tapered Tip	2663P	.600	.355	36"
Variable Steps, Tapered Tip	3663P	.600	.355	35"
Constant Taper, Tapered Tip	9093P	.580	.355	35"
Constant Taper, Over Fit, Parallel Tip	9693-350	.580	.395	35"

APOLLO GOLF SHAFTS
TAPERED TIP AND PARALLEL TIP

	Code	Flex	Category	Length	Butt Diam.	Tip Diam.	Nominal Weight oz.	gm.	Kickpoint
MASTERFLEX®									
Parallel Woods and Irons									
Woods	1720	R	Regular	46"	.600	.335	4.16	117.9	High
Irons	1721	R	Regular	40"	.600	.370	4.16	117.9	High
Woods	1722	S	Stiff	46"	.600	.335	4.46	126.4	High
Irons	1723	S	Stiff	40"	.600	.370	4.46	126.4	High
Woods	1724	X	Xtrastiff	46"	.600	.335	4.72	133.7	High
Irons	1726	X	Xtrastiff	40"	.600	.370	4.75	134.9	High

Weight Tolerance: ±2 g (±.07 oz.)
To achieve intermediate flexes AR flexible (I), RS Firm (III), TS Tourstiff (V) refer to Apollo Trimming Instructions.

Taper Woods and Irons

	Code	Flex	Category	Length	Butt Diam.	Tip Diam.	Nominal Weight oz.	gm.	Kickpoint
Woods	1730	R	Regular	45"-42"	.600	.294	4.07	115.4	High
Irons	1731	R	Regular	39"-35"	.600	.355	4.05	114.9	High
Woods	1732	S	Stiff	45"-42"	.600	.294	4.36	123.7	High
Irons	1733	S	Stiff	39"-35"	.600	.355	4.35	123.3	High
Woods	1734	X	Xtrastiff	45"-44"	.600	.294	4.57	129.7	High
	1735	X	Xtrastiff	43"-42"	.600	.294	4.48	127.1	High
Irons	1736	X	Xtrastiff	39"-37"	.600	.355	4.64	131.6	High
	1737	X	Xtrastiff	36½"-35"	.600	.355	4.59	130.1	HIgh

Weight Tolerance: ±2 g (±.07 oz.)
Stated nominal weights are for 45" wood and 39" iron shafts plus 43" X flex wood and 36½" X flex iron shafts.

Note: To calculate weight of other shaft lengths subtract .10 oz. (2.8 g) for woods and .06 oz. (1.7 g) for irons from nominal weights. Intermediate flexes are not available in taper tip Masterflex®.

SPECTRE
Parallel Woods and Irons

	Code	Flex	Category	Length	Butt Diam.	Tip Diam.	Nominal Weight oz.	gm.	Kickpoint
Woods	1513	R/S	Combination	47"	.600	.335	4.31	122	Mid
	1522*	R/S	Combination	44"	.600	.335	4.25	120	Mid
	1369	A/L	Combination	46"	.580	.335	4.00	113	Mid
Irons	1514	R/S	Combination	41"	.600	.370	4.19	119	Mid
	1382	A/L	Combination	40"	.580	.370	3.88	110	Mid

Weight Tolerance: ±3 g (±0.1 oz.)
*1522 recommended for metal woods.

Taper Woods and Irons

	Code	Flex	Category	Length	Butt Diam.	Tip Diam.	Nominal Weight oz.	gm.	Kickpoint
Irons	1881	S	Stiff	39"-35"	.600	.355	4.00	113.4	Mid
	1879	R	Regular	39"-35"	.600	.355	3.875	109.8	Mid
	2064	L	Ladies'	38"-35"	.580	.355	3.68	104.2	Mid

Weight Tolerance: ±3.5 g (±0.125 oz.)
Stated nominal weights are for 39" S and R flex iron and 38" L flex iron.

APOLLO GOLF SHAFTS
TAPERED TIP AND PARALLEL TIP *(cont.)*

	Code	Flex	Category	Length	Butt Diam.	Tip Diam.	Nominal Weight oz.	Nominal Weight gm.	Balance Point
PLATINUM *(formerly AP44 ELITE)*									
Parallel Woods and Irons *(High Kickpoint)*									
Woods	1890	R	Regular	45"	.600	.335	4.37	124	535
	1892	S	Stiff	45"	.600	.335	4.37	124	535
Irons	1891	R	Regular	39"	.600	.370	4.31	122	494
	1893	S	Stiff	39"	.600	.370	4.37	124	493
Taper Woods and Irons *(High Kickpoint)*									
Woods	1895	R	Regular	45-42	.600	.277	4.43	126	–
	1897	S	Stiff	45-42	.620	.294	4.37	124	–
Irons	1896	R	Regular	39-35	.580	.355	4.31	122	–
	1898	S	Stiff	39-35	.600	.355	4.37	124	–

Balance Point (mm)

Irons	Code	39"	38½"	38"	37½"	37"	36½"	36"	35½"	35"
	1896	492	485	479	472	466	459	453	447	441
	1898	488	482	476	470	464	458	452	446	441

Woods	Code	45"	44½"	44"	43½"	43"	42½"	42"		
	1895	533	527	521	515	509	503	497		
	1897	534	528	522	516	510	504	489		

Weight Tolerance: ±3 g (±0.1 oz.)
Balance point measured from the butt end. Tolerance ±5mm (±0.2 in.)

	Code	Flex	Length	Butt Diam.	Tip Diam.	Kick-Point	Nominal Weight ounces	Nominal Weight grams
AP46								
Parallel Tip Woods and Irons								
Woods	1324	R/S	46"	.600	.335	Mid	4.75	135
	1153	R	44"	.600	.335	Mid	4.38	124
	1497	L	44"	.560	.335	Mid	4.25	120
Irons	1323	R/S	40"	.600	.370	Mid	4.63	131
	1305	R	39"	.600	.370	Mid	4.38	124
	1306	L	38"	.560	.370	Mid	4.25	120
Taper Tip Woods and Irons								
Woods	1269	R	44"	.600	.277	Mid	4.38	124
Irons	1413	R	38" & 36"	.600	.355	Mid	4.19	119
JUNIOR								
Parallel Tip Wood and Iron								
Wood	1832	–	39"	.560	.335	Low	3.56	101
Iron	1833	–	36"	.560	.370	Low	3.56	101

APOLLO GOLF PARALLEL TIP SHAFTS

	Code	Flex Category	Length	Butt Diam.	Tip Diam.	Kick-Point	Nominal Weight oz.	gm.	Weight Tolerance (g)
MATCHFLEX®									
Parallel Woods and Irons									
Woods	1760	AR-Flexible	45"	.600	.335	Low	3.95	112	±2
Irons	1761	AR-Flexible	39"	.600	.370	Low	3.95	112	±2
Woods	1762	R-Regular	45"	.600	.335	Low-mid	4.10	116	±2
Irons	1763	R-Regular	39"	.600	.370	Low-mid	4.10	116	±2
Woods	1764	RS-Firm	45"	.600	.335	Hi-mid	4.25	121	±2
Irons	1765	RS-Firm	39"	.600	.370	Hi-mid	4.25	121	±2
Woods	1766	S-Stiff	45"	.600	.335	High	4.40	125	±2
Irons	1767	S-Stiff	39"	.600	.370	High	4.40	125	±2
AP44									
Woods	1083	R/S	47"	.600	.335	High	4.63	131	±3
	1537**	R/S	44"	.600	.335	High	4.31	122	±3
Irons	1085	R/S	41"	.600	.370	High	4.56	129	±3
	1084***	R/S	41"	.600	.395	High	4.56	129	±3

**1537 Recommended for metal woods.
***1084 Over the hosel.

	Code	Flex Category	Length	Butt Diam.	Tip Diam.	Kick-Point	Nominal Weight oz.	gm.	Weight Tolerance (g)
SHADOW®									
Woods	1498	R/S	47"	.600	.335	Low	4.50	127	±3
Irons	1469	R/S	41"	.600	.370	Low	4.13	117	±3
LADY SHADOW®									
Woods	1785	L	44"	.580	.335	Low	3.75	106	±3
Irons	1786	L	38"	.580	.370	Low	3.63	103	±3
SENIOR SHADOW®									
Woods	1584	A	45"	.580	.335	Low	3.75	106	±3
Irons	1585	A	39"	.580	.370	Low	3.63	103	±3
ACCULITE									
Woods	1700	R	45"	.600	.335	Low-Mid	3.56	101	±2.5
	1702	S	45"	.600	.335	Low-Mid	3.67	104	±2.5
Irons	1701	R	39"	.600	.370	Low-Mid	3.56	101	±2.5
	1703	S	39"	.600	.370	Low-Mid	3.67	104	±2.5

APOLLO GOLF PUTTER SHAFTS

	Code	Butt Diam.	Tip Diam.	Length	Shaft Pattern
Straight Taper	1211	.580	.395	35"	Plain and Flute
	1393	.580	.355	35"	Plain and Flute
	1450	.580	.355	35"	Plain
Step Formed	1390	.600	Belled	35"	3" Step and Flute
	1305	.600	.370	39"	1¹³⁄₁₆" step AP46
	1306	.560	.370	39"	1¹³⁄₁₆" step AP46
	1077	.600	.370	39"	3" step AP83
	1690	.600	.370	35"	1¼" step Hi-grip

TITANIUM SHAFT COMPANY SANDVIK
TITANIUM GOLF SHAFTS

	Flex	Butt Diam.	Tip Diam.	Length	Gram Weight	Torque
TOUR TITANIUM **Parallel Tip Woods**						
	X	.600	.335	45"	106	2.24
	R/S	.600	.335	47"	110	2.40
	A/L	.580	.335	47"	105	2.60
PRO TOUR TITANIUM **Parallel Tip Woods**						
	X	.600	.335	45"	105	2.20
	R/S	.600	.335	47"	108	2.40
	A/L	.580	.335	47"	103	2.60

	Iron Number	Flex	Butt Diam.	[1]Tip Diam.	Length	Gram Weight	Torque
TOUR TITANIUM **Parallel and Taper Tip Irons**							
	1 through 5	X	.600	.355	40"	105	1.64
	6 through wedges	X	.600	.355	37½"	98	1.64
	1 through 5	S	.600	.355	40"	105	1.68
	6 through wedges	S	.600	.355	37½"	98	1.68
	1 through 5	R	.600	.355	40"	105	1.82
	6 through wedges	R	.600	.355	37½"	98	1.76
	1 through 5	A	.600	.355	40"	105	1.90
	6 through wedges	A	.600	.355	37½"	98	1.86
	1 through 5	L	.600*	.355	40"	104	1.90
	6 through wedges	L	.600*	.355	37½"	97	1.86

[1]Also available in .370 tip for irons.
*L flex only - parallel tip shaft has .580 butt diameter.

PROPRIETARY SHAFT PATTERN IDENTIFICATION

Company	Shaft Name	Graphite or Steel	Flex Point	Weight
Ben Hogan	Apex	Steel	Low	Lightweight
	Apex Pro	Steel	Low	Standard
	Apex D	Steel	Low	Standard
	Apex Extra	Steel	Mid	Lightweight
	Vector	Steel	High	Lightweight
	Legend	Steel	Low	Lightweight
	Saber	Steel	High	Standard
	Apex	Graphite	Low	Very Lightweight
	Lady Hogan	Steel	Low	Lightweight
	Hogan Plus	Steel	Low	Lightweight
Callaway	Memphis 10	Steel	Mid	Lightweight
	RCH60	Graphite	Mid/Low (3°)	Very Lightweight
	RCH90	Graphite	Mid (3°)	Very Lightweight
	Ladies Gems	Graphite	Mid/Low (3°)	Very Lightweight
	Ladies Gems	Steel	Low	Lightweight
Cleveland Golf	Extra-Lite	Steel	Low	Lightweight
	Diamond	Graphite	Mid/High	Very Lightweight
	Square	Graphite	Mid/High	Very Lightweight
	Circle	Graphite	Mid/High	Very Lightweight
	HET	Graphite	Mid/High	Very Lightweight
Cobra	TLC	Steel	Mid	Lightweight
Daiwa	TRX-T	Graphite	High	Very Lightweight
	TRX	Graphite	Mid	Very Lightweight
	TR	Graphite	Low	Very Lightweight
Dunlop	Alta	Steel	High	Lightweight
	Maxpower	Steel	Low	Standard
	Max Lite	Steel	Mid	Lightweight
H & B	Dynasty Plus	Steel	Variable	Lightweight
	Dynasty	Steel	Mid	Very Lightweight
	Propower	Steel	Mid	Standard
	Duopower	Steel	Mid	Standard
Head Golf	Big Head	Graphite	Mid	Very Lightweight
Karsten Manufacturing	ZZ Lite	Steel	High	Lightweight
	ZZZ Lite	Steel	High	Lightweight
	K	Steel	Mid	Lightweight
	Olympic	Graphite	High	Very Lightweight
	TTT	Steel	High	Standard
	KT	Steel	Mid	Lightweight
	Microtaper	Steel	Low	Lightweight
	JZ	Steel	Mid	Lightweight
	KT-M	Steel	Mid	Lightweight
	101*	Graphite	Mid (3.4°)	Very Lightweight
	201*	Graphite	Mid (2.9°)	Very Lightweight
	301*	Graphite	Mid (2.2°)	Very Lightweight

*Note that the 101, 201 & 301 have similar characteristics except that the 201 is stiffer than the 101 and the 301 is stiffer than the 201.

Company	Shaft Name	Graphite or Steel	Flex Point	Weight
Lynx	Lynx Lite	Steel	High	Lightweight
MacGregor	Response	Steel	Mid	Very Lightweight
	Velocitized Dual Action	Steel	Low	Lightweight
	Tourney Action	Steel	High	Standard
	Microstep	Steel	Low	Standard
	Propel (1958-68)	Steel	Low	Standard
	VDA2	Steel	Low	Standard

PROPRIETARY SHAFT PATTERN IDENTIFICATION *(cont.)*

Company	Shaft Name	Graphite or Steel	Flex Point	Weight
Maxfli Golf	Alta	Steel	High	Lightweight
	Maxpower	Steel	Low	Standard
	Max Lite	Steel	Mid	Lightweight
Merit	Merit	Steel	Variable	Lightweight
Mizuno	Dynaflex 1100	Steel	Low	Lightweight
	Dynaflex 2200	Steel	Mid	Lightweight
	Dynaflex 3300	Steel	High	Lightweight
Nicklaus Golf	Nicklaus Golf	Steel	Variable	Lightweight
Northwestern	Power Kick	Steel	Low	Lightweight
	Proaction Plus	Steel	Low	Standard
	Micro Lite 400	Steel	Mid	Lightweight
Peerless	Hex Flex	Steel	High	Lightweight
	Pro-Lite	Steel	Mid	Lightweight
	Axiom-Lite	Steel	Low	Lightweight
	Palmer Lite	Steel	Low	Lightweight
	Peerless	Steel	Low	Lightweight
Pinseeker	Pin Lite	Steel	Mid	Lightweight
	Pinseeker	Graphite	Low	Very Lightweight
	MS	Graphite	Low	Very Lightweight
	Premium Gold	Graphite	Low	Very Lightweight
Ram	Reactive Rhythm	Steel	Mid	Lightweight
	Ramlite	Steel	Mid	Lightweight
Sounder	Sounder Flex	Steel	Mid	Lightweight
Top Flite	Technic	Steel	Mid	Lightweight
	Thunder Heat	Steel	Low	Standard
	Thunder Heat	Graphite	Mid	Lightweight
	XL-420	Graphite	Mid	Very Lightweight
Taylor Made	Taylite Plus	Steel	Mid	Lightweight
	Flex Twist	Graphite	Various	Lightweight/Very Lightweight
	Taylite	Steel	Mid	Lightweight
	Flex Twist Plus	Graphite	Various	Lightweight/Very Lightweight
Titleist	Power-Step	Steel	Low	Standard
	Power Flo	Steel	High	Standard
	Title-Lite II	Steel	Mid	Lightweight
	MS-209	Steel	High	Lightweight
Tommy Armour	Tour Step	Steel	High	Lightweight
	Butterfly	Steel	Mid	Lightweight
Wilson	V2	Steel	Low	Lightweight
	Aggressor	Steel	Low	Lightweight
	Dynapower	Steel	Low	Lightweight
	Counter Torque	Steel	Low	Lightweight
	Dynamic	Steel	High	Standard
	Dyna-Step	Steel	Low	Lightweight
	Firestick	Steel	Low	Lightweight
	Firestick	Graphite	Various	Lightweight/Very Lightweight
Yamaha	Paraflex	Graphite	Low	Very Lightweight

STANDARD AVAILABLE SHAFT PATTERNS

Manufacturer	Model	Flex Point	Weight	Irons	Woods	Shaft Grade
True Temper	Dynamic (Taper Tip)	High	Standard	1¾"	1⅞"	1st
True Temper	Dynamic (Parallel Tip)	High	Standard	1⅞"	1⅞"	1st
True Temper	Dynamic Gold (Taper Tip)	High	Standard	1¾"	1⅞"	1st
True Temper	Dynamic Gold (Parallel Tip)	High	Standard	1⅞"	1⅞"	1st
True Temper	Gold Plus (Taper Tip)	Mid	Lightweight	Variable	Variable	1st
True Temper	Gold Plus (Parallel Tip)	Mid	Lightweight	Variable	Variable	1st
True Temper	Dynalite (Taper Tip)	Low	Lightweight	1¼"	1½"	1st
True Temper	Dynalite (Parallel Tip)	Low	Lightweight	1¼"	1¼"	1st
True Temper	Dynalite Gold (Taper Tip)	Low	Lightweight	1¼"	1⅞"	1st
True Temper	Dynalite Gold (Parallel Tip)	Low	Lightweight	1¼"	1¼"	1st
True Temper	Dynamic Lite (Taper Tip)	High	Lightweight	1¾"	1⅞"	1st
True Temper	Dynamic Lite (Parallel Tip)	High	Lightweight	1⅞"	1⅞"	1st
True Temper	Extralite	Low	Very Lightweight	1", Random	1", Random	1st
True Temper	TT Lite	Mid	Lightweight	1½"	1½"	1st
True Temper	Flex Flow	Progressive	Lightweight	1¼"	1¼"	1st
True Temper	Jet Step (Parallel Tip)	Low	Standard	1"	1"	1st
True Temper	Pro Fit (Parallel Tip)	Mid	Standard	1½"	1½"	1st
True Temper	Comet	Mid	Standard	1¹³⁄₁₆"	1¹³⁄₁₆"	2nd
True Temper	Junior	Mid	Standard	3"	3"	2nd
True Temper (Discontinued)	Kinetic	Mid	Lightweight	1¾"	1⅞"	1st
True Temper (Discontinued)	Super Lite	Low	Lightweight	—	1½"	1st
True Temper (Discontinued)	Contour	Low	Lightweight	1½", 1"	1½", 1"	1st
True Temper (Discontinued)	Pro Fit (Taper Tip)	Mid	Standard	1⅜"	1½"	1st
True Temper (Discontinued)	Jet Step (Taper Tip)	Low	Standard	1"	1"	1st
True Temper (Discontinued)	Century	Mid	Standard	3"	3"	2nd
True Temper (Discontinued)	Driving Range	Mid	Standard	—	2¼"	1st
True Temper (Discontinued)	Rocket	Mid	Standard	1⅜"	1½"	1st
True Temper (Discontinued)	Meteor	Mid	Standard	1¼"	1¼"	2nd
True Temper (Discontinued)	325 Series	Mid	Standard	3¼"	3¼"	2nd
True Temper (Discontinued)	Classic	Mid	Standard	4"	4"	2nd
Brunswick	UCV-304	Mid	Lightweight	Variable	Variable	1st
Brunswick	Precision Phoenix	Mid	Lightweight	1½"	1½"	1st
Brunswick	Precision Propel II	High	Standard	1⅞"	1⅞"	1st
Brunswick	Precision Microtaper	Low	Lightweight	¾"	¾"	1st
Brunswick	Super Champion	Mid	Standard	1¹³⁄₁₆"	1¹³⁄₁₆"	2nd
Brunswick	Champion	Mid	Standard	3"	3"	2nd
Brunswick	Precision Select - HFA	High	Standard	1⅞"	1⅞"	1st
Brunswick	Precision Select - MFA	Mid	Lightweight	1½"	1½"	1st
Brunswick	Precision Select - LFA	Low	Lightweight	¾"	¾"	1st
Brunswick	Precision FCM	High	Lightweight	Variable	Variable	1st
Brunswick	Precision FCM Lite	High	Lightweight	Variable	Variable	1st
Brunswick (Discontinued)	Vanadium Sonic	Mid	Lightweight	Variable	Variable	1st
Brunswick (Discontinued)	Brunslite	Mid	Lightweight	Variable	Variable	1st
Apollo	Masterflex	High	Standard	Variable	Variable	1st
Apollo	Matchflex (AR)	Low	Lightweight	Variable	Variable	1st
Apollo	Matchflex (R)	Low-Mid	Lightweight	Variable	Variable	1st
Apollo	Matchflex (RS)	Mid-High	Lightweight	Variable	Variable	1st
Apollo	Matchflex (S)	High	Standard	Variable	Variable	1st
Apollo	AP44 Elite	High	Standard	1¾"	1⅞"	1st
Apollo	AP46	Mid	Standard	1¹³⁄₁₆"	1¹³⁄₁₆"	1st
Apollo	Spectre	Mid	Lightweight	1½"	1½"	1st
Apollo	AP44	High	Standard	1¾"	1⅞"	1st
Apollo	Shadow	Low	Lightweight	1⅞", ½"	1⅞", ½"	1st
Apollo	Lady Shadow	Low	Lightweight	1⅞", ½"	1⅞", ½"	1st
Apollo	Senior Shadow	Low	Lightweight	1⅞", ½"	1⅞", ½"	1st
Apollo	Acculite	Low-Mid	Lightweight	Variable	Variable	1st

1st grade shafts are usually characterized by having the most shaft steps, closer weight tolerances, a number of choices in shaft flex, a top quality scratch free chromeplating and a higher cost per shaft to the manufacturer. 2nd grade shafts usually have less shaft steps, wider weight tolerances, limited choice of shaft flex as most are available in medium flex only, chromeplating is sometimes a lesser quality and may show slight dullness and a few scratches and will cost the manufacturer less than 1st grade shafts.

CHAPTER 57

GOLF SHAFT INSTALLATION PRINCIPLES, PROCEDURES AND REFERENCE TABLES

This will be one of the most used sections in club repair because it contains most of the reference data needed to check for proper shaft installation and to properly install a golf shaft. It should be read carefully and studied thoroughly. A mastery of this information will provide the key to understanding proper shaft installation.

One of the biggest problems in checking for proper shaft installation has been the non-availability of information concerning the distance from the tip end of the shaft to the first step. In addition to this, the information has never been converted to show the proper distance from the back of the heel on both woods and irons to the first shaft step. This is the most important measurement because with everything else being equal, it is the main factor in determining just how a shaft will flex and feel.

This reference section provides shaft installation information based on what is referred to as "modern standards." For example, the modern standard for irons is a shaft in head assembly where the tip of the shaft bottoms out 1" from the back of the heel. See Figure 57-1. This standard was determined after measuring hundreds of different iron head shaft penetrations and hosel lengths in irons produced from 1940 to present. Therefore, this modern standard is an average or mean to show the predominant distance usually found from the tip of the shaft (or bottom of the hosel hole) to the back of the heel. Remember, this modern standard is being established as a benchmark and caution should be used not to draw any conclusions regarding other clubmakers or club manufacturers shaft installation procedures. In many cases there may be sound reasons for a different installation than those described in the tables in this section. Certain head designs, club lengths, head weights and test data may have dictated this. For instance, refer to Figure 57-2 to see an increasingly popular shaft to hosel assembly. Even though the shaft penetrates to the sole, the back of heel to first step dimensions discussed later in this chapter are still applicable. Also, many clubfitters, clubmakers and club repairmen are unaware of the fact that some club manufacturers purchase standard shaft types and patterns, but will change one of the specifications so the shaft is designed exactly as they want it. It may be a tip diameter change, weight change, a wall thickness change or moving the step pattern down or up. Visually the shaft may look like a standard available pattern, but it may not be. A good example to use here is the fact that some manufacturers are ordering their medium flex tip taper wood shafts in a .294 tip size so they do not have to change their head boring setup during manufacture; they now stock only one ferrule size, etc. Normally, most medium flex tip taper wood shafts have a .277 tip size.

It was far easier to determine the "modern standard" for woods. This would be a "through-bore" with the shaft tip extending ½" beyond the back portion of the heel. See Figure 57-3.

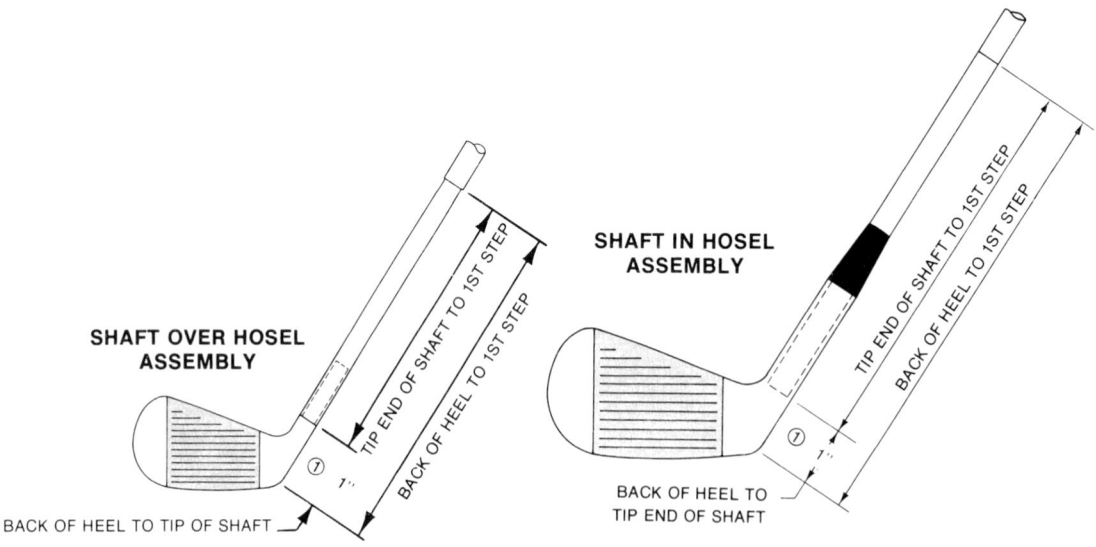

① This dimension will vary depending on hosel length and bore depth and should be calculated as shown in Fig. 53-3. The 1″ dimension is considered the traditional standard.

Figure 57-1
Iron shaft installation terminology

598

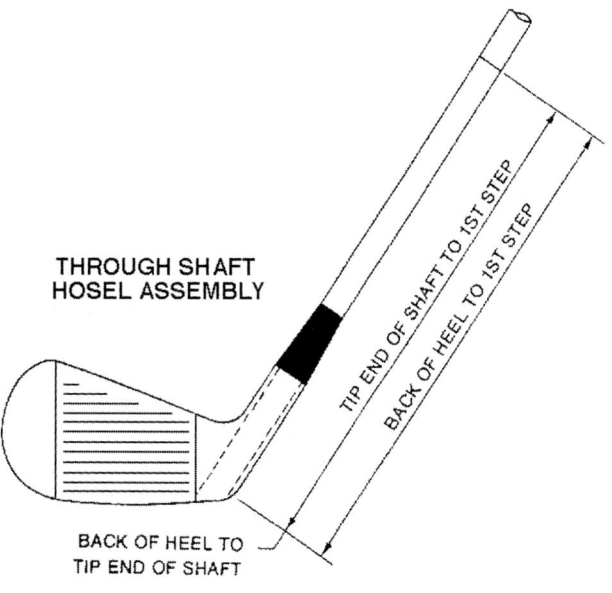

Figure 57-2
Iron shaft installation terminology

Keep in mind that with the tables in this chapter, it does not matter whether a wood is "through-bore" or "blind-bore," or what the hosel length and bore depth is on an iron. It also does not matter whether the wood or iron is made of metal, graphite, titanium or other material. The tables give the installed back of heel to first step dimensions based on the "modern standards" already discussed for woods and irons in Figure 57-1, 57-2 and 57-3. As stated earlier, this information provides a benchmark or starting point for installing a given shaft type and step pattern to the defined modern standard. Note also that composite shafts are installed using the specific instructions that accompany them. The information presented in this chapter, in most cases, does not apply to composite shafts.

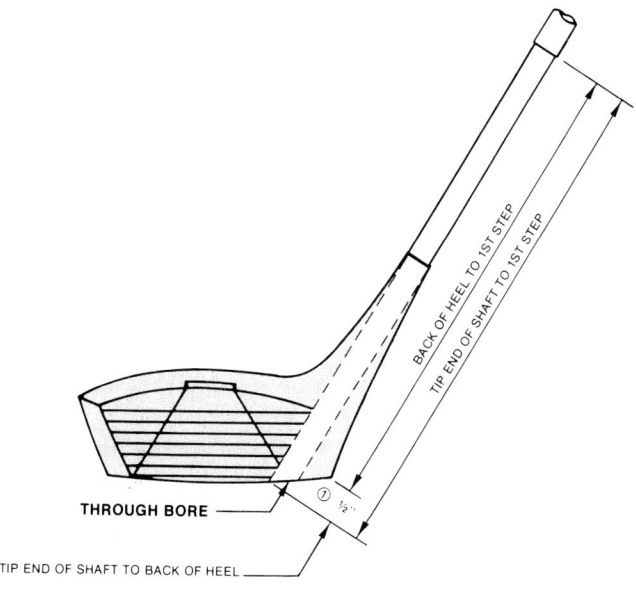

Figure 57-3
Wood shaft installation terminology

Sole Radius and Back of Heel Location

If two golf clubs of the same length were measured in the modern manner from the back of the heel to the top of the grip cap, the club with less sole radius would be shorter than the club with more sole radius.

A similar problem exists in this section concerning the back of heel to first shaft step distance. As was the case with club length, the less the sole radius, the stiffer the shaft; and the greater the sole radius, the weaker the shaft. This assumes, of course, that the first step location from the back of the heel would be the same in both clubs with either more or less sole radius. The reader should be aware of this, but in most cases the sole radiuses are quite similar from model to model and only make very slight differences. The standards in this section are based on a 6" sole radius for woods (5" and 7" radiuses make very little difference) and a 10" sole radius for irons (8" to 12" radiuses make very little difference).

Back of Heel to First Step Installation Procedure

When checking installed golf shafts according to the tables in this section, it may have been necessary to cut the tip end of the shaft shorter. I hesitate to refer to this as "tipping" because its only purpose is to adjust the tip length of the shaft so it can be installed in hosels of varying penetration and still have the desired back of heel to first step location. Depending on hosel design and bore depth, two identical golf shafts can be installed to have the same flex feel even though one of the shafts may have had ½" cut from its tip. An example of this could be a comparison between a blind-bore wood versus a through-bore wood. The blind-bore wood may need ½" cut from its tip to install with the proper back of heel to first shaft step dimension listed in the tables of this section.

There are a number of ways to predetermine before a shaft is assembled the back of heel to first step location. One method, shown in Figure 57-4 for irons and Figure

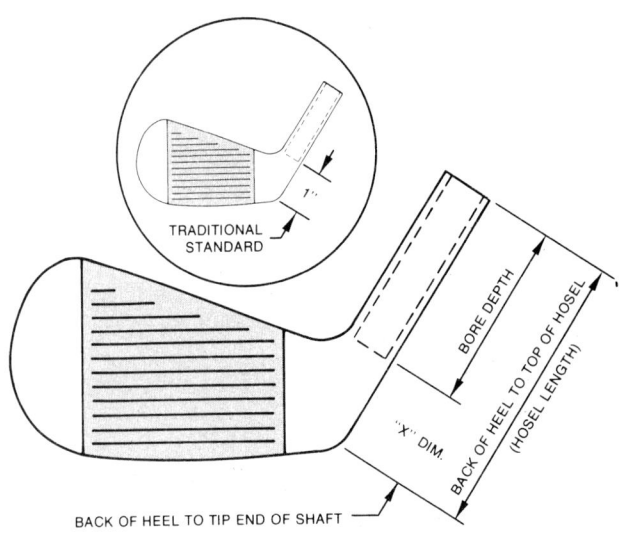

To find back of heel to tip end of shaft dimension ("X" Dim.):
A. Measure hosel length and bore depth
B. Hosel length minus bore depth = "X" Dim.
C. Example: 2¼" Hosel length minus 1¼" bore depth = 1" dimension from back of heel to tip end of shaft.

NOTE: All tables in this section are based on a 1" dimension from back of heel to tip end of shaft. This dimension is an average of most irons ever built and it is considered the traditional shaft installation standard to obtain normal flex characteristics. However, be cautioned that varying head weights, club lengths, individual head designs, etc., can affect the feel of a given shaft flex.

Figure 57-4
Calculating back of heel to tip end of shaft dimension

57-5 for woods, should be thoroughly understood. The information given thus far coupled with the tables in this section will give the reader proper procedures to check shaft installations, install new shafts or correct improper shaft installations.

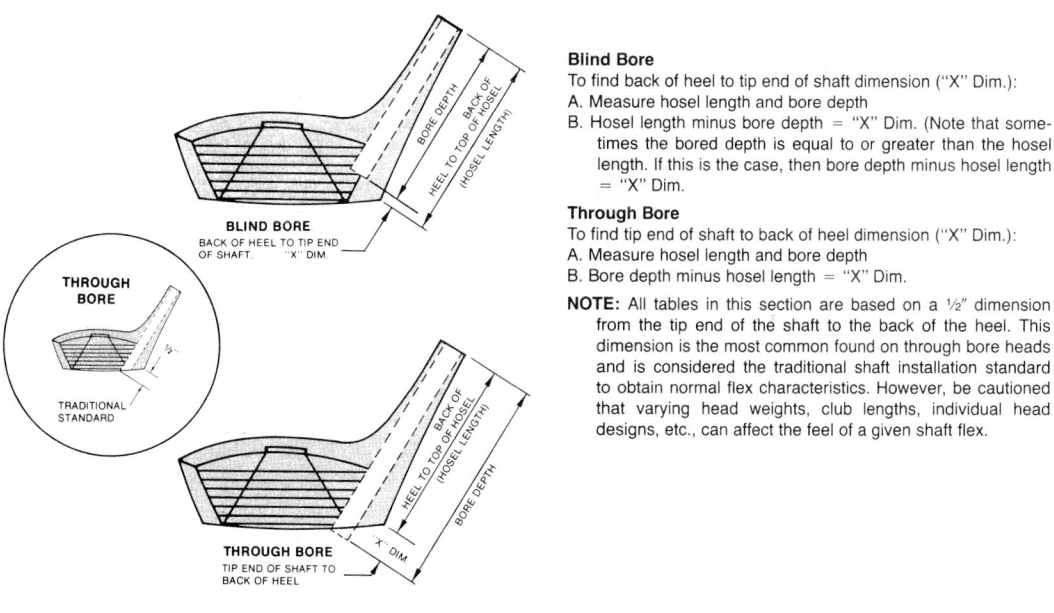

Blind Bore
To find back of heel to tip end of shaft dimension ("X" Dim.):
A. Measure hosel length and bore depth
B. Hosel length minus bore depth = "X" Dim. (Note that sometimes the bored depth is equal to or greater than the hosel length. If this is the case, then bore depth minus hosel length = "X" Dim.

Through Bore
To find tip end of shaft to back of heel dimension ("X" Dim.):
A. Measure hosel length and bore depth
B. Bore depth minus hosel length = "X" Dim.

NOTE: All tables in this section are based on a ½" dimension from the tip end of the shaft to the back of the heel. This dimension is the most common found on through bore heads and is considered the traditional shaft installation standard to obtain normal flex characteristics. However, be cautioned that varying head weights, club lengths, individual head designs, etc., can affect the feel of a given shaft flex.

Figure 57-5
Calculating back of heel to tip end of shaft dimension

Understanding Tip Taper Shaft Installations in Woods

Trimming tip taper shafts is easy to understand since they are normally only trimmed from the butt end. Therefore, unlike parallel tip shafts, tip taper shafts can usually be installed in the wood head and then cut to length. Tip taper wood shafts are either .270", .277", .286", .294" or .320" tip size with .0075 inches per inch of taper. This means that the shaft diameter gradually increases by 7½ thousandths of an inch for each inch up from the tip end. The length of the taper in the tip varies from shaft to shaft depending on the tip parallel diameter which is the parallel portion of every tip taper shaft just before the first step. See Figure 57-6.

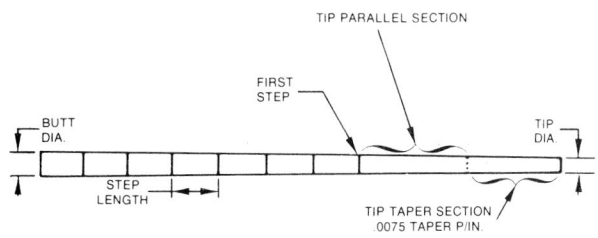

Figure 57-6
Golf shaft terminology

For example, take a 44" Dynamic® Wood Stiff (DWS 44") shaft. It has a .294" tip taper, a .350" tip parallel and an 11¼" tip length (length from tip to first step). The change in diameter from the tip (.294") to the tip parallel (.350") is .056". Divide .056" by .0075" and the answer is that this shaft has 7½" of taper and 3¾" of tip parallel (11¼" - 7½" = 3¾"). The reason for explaining this is to obtain a better understanding of changes in tip diameter if a shaft is tipped. "Tipping" refers to precutting a certain amount from the tip end of the shaft to increase its stiffness. As you can see, if a wood hosel is bored to accept a .294" tip taper shaft and you tip it, the shaft will not fit properly and the hosel must be bored out to a slightly larger size. Table 57-1 was developed to provide the tip diameters of tipped shafts and also the amount of stiffness increase.

		TABLE 57-1		
		"Tipped" Shafts, Their Stiffness Increase and New Tip Diameters		
Original Shaft Tip Size	Amount of "Tipping"	Approximate Amount of Flex Change		"Tipped" Tip Diameter
.277"	½"	+ ¼ Stiffer		.281"
.277"	1"	+ ½ Stiffer		.285"
.277"	1½"	+ ¾ Stiffer		.288"
.277"	2"	+ 1 Stiffer		.292"
.294"	½"	+ ¼ Stiffer		.298"
.294"	1"	+ ½ Stiffer		.302"
.294"	1½"	+ ¾ Stiffer		.305"
.294"	2"	+ 1 Stiffer		.309"
.320"	½"	+ ¼ Stiffer		.324"
.320"	1"	+ ½ Stiffer		.328"
.320"	1½"	+ ¾ Stiffer		.331"
.320"	2"	+ 1 Stiffer		.335"

Example: Tipping a DWS shaft (Dynamic Wood Stiff) 2" will produce a relative stiffness approximating an "X" flex in that same pattern. However, the tipped "S" shaft will be 2⁄10 ounce lighter than the standard "X" flex weight. Experimentation in actual hitting on an individual basis is the best way to confirm which may feel best or give desired performance.

An important consideration in "tipping" or for that matter when installing any wood shaft is whether or not the head is "blind" bored (shaft does not go completely through head) or "through" bored (shaft is bored completely through head). For example: if you are building two identical drivers and one is bored and shafted to within ½" of the bottom of the club and the other is bored and shafted completely through, the one that is bored through will feel one quarter flex stiffer than the blind-bored head. The reason for this is that the distance from the back of the heel to the first step is longer on the blind-bored club than the through-bored club. This is sort of an "untipped" effect. See Figure 57-7. Of course, both clubs would probably feel the same (all other specifications being the same) if the blind-bored shaft was "tipped" ½" before installation.

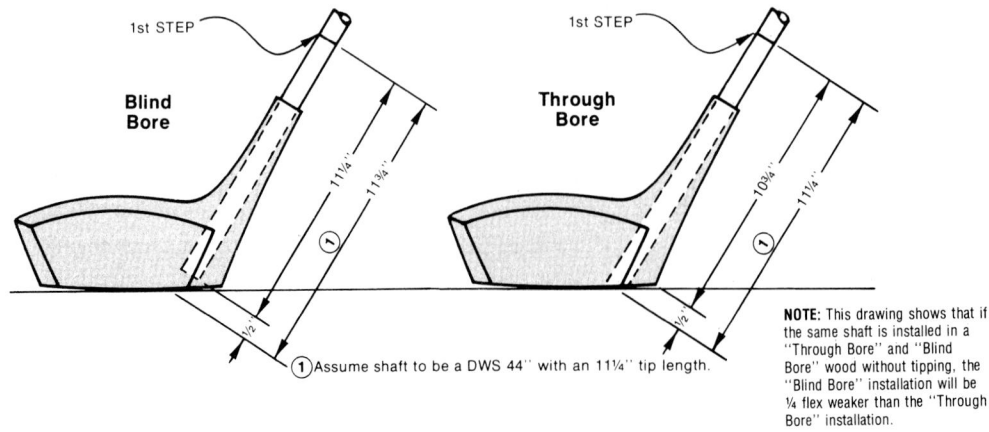

NOTE: This drawing shows that if the same shaft is installed in a "Through Bore" and "Blind Bore" wood without tipping, the "Blind Bore" installation will be ¼ flex weaker than the "Through Bore" installation.

① Assume shaft to be a DWS 44" with an 11¼" tip length.

Figure 57-7
"Through" bore and "Blind" bore effect on shaft stiffness

602

Keep in mind that "through" bored clubs play no better than "blind" bored clubs and vice-versa as long as the blind-bored club has its shaft properly installed. The main understanding to be obtained from this is to evaluate the different wood club bore types and then use the information here to make a relative playability comparison, if one exists. This is particularly useful in reshafting work.

Understanding Tip Taper Shaft Installations in Irons

As with woods, trimming tip taper shafts is easy to understand because they are also normally only trimmed from the butt end. Therefore, unlike parallel tip shafts, tip taper shafts can be installed in the iron head and then cut to length. Most all tip taper shafts have a .355" tip diameter with .0075 inches per inch of taper. This means that the shaft diameter gradually increases by 7½ thousandths of an inch for each inch away from the tip. The length of the taper in the tip varies from shaft to shaft depending on the tip parallel diameter which is the parallel portion of every tip taper shaft just before the first step. Refer back to Figure 57-6. For example, take a 39" Dynamic® Iron Stiff (DIS 39") shaft. It has a .355" diameter tip taper, a .395" diameter tip parallel and a 12" tip length (length from tip to first step). The change in diameter from the tip (.355") to the tip parallel (.395") is .040". Divide .040" by .0075" and the answer is that this shaft has 5⅓" of taper and 6⅔" of tip parallel (12" - 5⅓" = 6⅔"). Again, the reason for explaining this is to obtain a better understanding of changes in tip diameter if a shaft is tipped. "Tipping" refers to precutting a certain amount from the tip end of the shaft to increase its stiffness. As you can see, if an iron hosel is bored to accept a .355" tip taper shaft and you tip it, the shaft will not fit properly and the hosel must be bored out to a slightly larger size. Table 57-2 was developed to give you the tip diameters of tipped shafts and the proper drill bit size to use so the shaft will fit in the hosel.

Table 57-2 also shows the approximate amount a shaft stiffens when it is tipped. An important consideration in tipping, or for that matter when installing any iron shaft, is hosel length and shaft penetration. This is due to manufacturers boring irons in varying depths or designing irons with long hosels or short hosels. See Figure 57-8. In the Figure 57-8 example, the long hosel with a 1½" back of heel to shaft tip end penetration will feel more flexible than the shorter hosel with ½" back of heel to shaft tip end penetration. This of course assumes that the shafts were not tipped and that all other variables such as weight, length of club, etc. are the same.

TABLE 57-2
"Tipped" Shafts, Their Stiffness Increase and New Tip Diameters and Step Drill Sizes to Properly Install Them (For .355" Taper Tip Shafts Only)

Amount of "Tipping"	²Approximate Amount of Flex Change	"Tipped" Tip Diameter	¹1st Drill to Bottom	¹2nd Drill to Within ¾" of Bottom	¹3rd Drill Within 1" of Bottom
½"	+ ¼ Stiffer	.359"	23/64"	"U"	⅜"
1"	+ ½ Stiffer	.363"	"U"	⅜"	"V"
1½"	+ ¾ Stiffer	.366"	"U"	⅜"	"V"
2"	+ 1 Stiffer	.370"	⅜"	Not Req.	"W"

¹ Cobalt drill bits work best but high speed steel is okay. Use cutting and drilling oil during drilling. Dull drills tend to drill larger holes so some variance may occur.
² Example: Tipping a DIS shaft (Dynamic Iron Stiff) 2" will produce a relative stiffness approximating an "X" flex in that same pattern. However, the tipped "S" shaft will be ²/10 ounce lighter than the standard "X" flex weight. Experimentation in actual hitting on an individual basis is the best way to confirm which may feel best or give desired performance.

The reason for this is that the distance from the back of heel to the first step can sometimes be greater with a long hosel than it is with a short hosel strictly because of these shaft penetration differences. Notice in Figure 57-9 that a comparison is made between a long and short hosel club where both have a 1½" shaft penetration measured from the top of the hosel. The distance to the first step on one is 13½" and on the other 12½" which, if you will refer back to Table 57-2, indicates a shaft stiffness difference of ½ flex. Regardless of shaft penetration or hosel length, a shaft can usually be installed to have the same playing flex either through tipping, a change in shaft penetration or simply by using a different length shaft. This is already figured out for you in the back of heel to first step tables at the end of this section. It is a good habit to use these tables as they will provide you with far greater knowledge in understanding golf shafts in general.

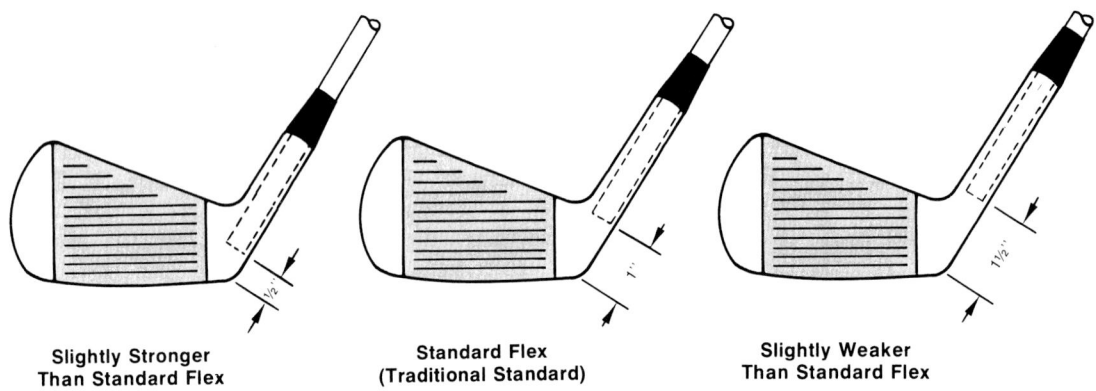

| Slightly Stronger Than Standard Flex | Standard Flex (Traditional Standard) | Slightly Weaker Than Standard Flex |

The dimension shown above is from the back of the heel to the tip of the shaft. 1″ is considered the traditional standard.

Figure 57-8
The effect of different bore depths on shaft flex

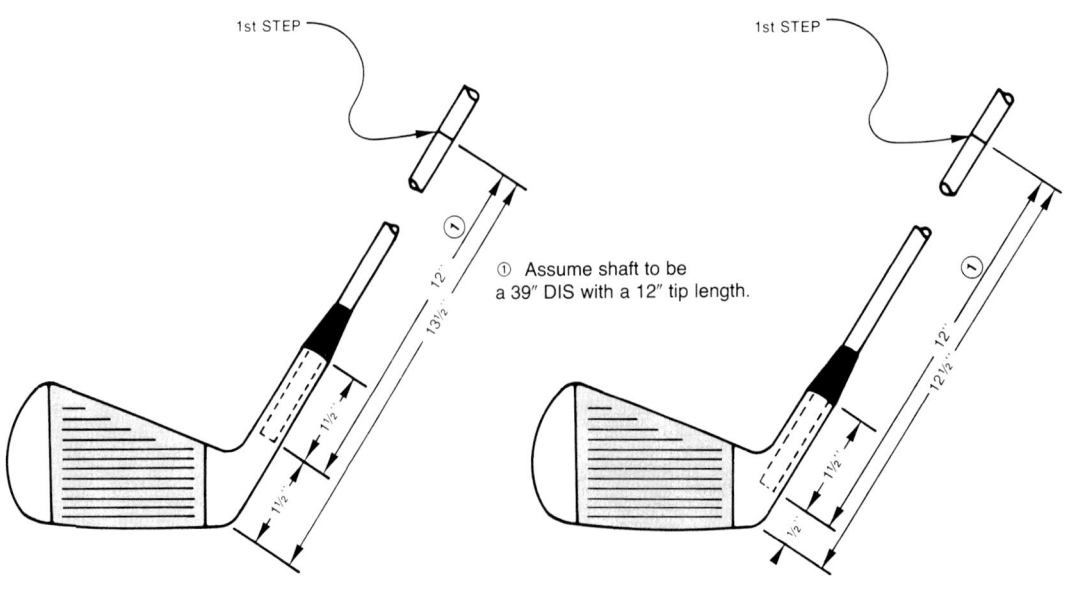

① Assume shaft to be a 39″ DIS with a 12″ tip length.

Figure 57-9
Hosel length and shaft penetration's effect on shaft stiffness

"Tipping" Tip Taper Shafts for Proper First Step Location When ½" Length Increment Shafts Are Not Available—Woods and Irons

The information presented here will be quite valuable to the repairman because it may be needed when reshafting the player's present clubs or custom assembling a set of woods and/or irons and you may not have available all the incremental shaft lengths. See Table 57-3.

TABLE 57-3 Club Number Versus Purchased Shaft Length Combinations (Taper Tip)									
WOODS				IRONS					
Club No.	5 Lengths	3 Lengths	1 Lengths	Club No.	9 Lengths	5 Lengths	4 Lengths	3 Lengths	
1	44"	44"	44"	1	39"	39"	—	39"	
2	43½"	44"	44"	2	38½"	39"	38"	39"	
3	43"	43"	44"	3	38"	38"	38"	39"	
4	42½"	43"	44"	4	37½"	38"	37"	37"	
5	42"	42"	44"	5	37"	37"	37"	37"	
6	42"	42"	44"	6	36½"	37"	36"	37"	
7	42"	42"	44"	7	36"	36"	36"	37"	
				8	35½"	36"	35"	35"	
				9	35"	35"	35"	35"	
				PW	35"	35"	35"	35"	
				SW	35"	35"	35"	35"	
				TW	35"	35"	35"	35"	

Note: Other combinations are also possible depending on club length and flexibility desired.

Tables 57-4, 57-5, 57-6 and 57-7 apply only to tip taper shafts. They provide information on tipping shafts when all of the incremental lengths are not available. The term incremental as it is used here applies to a different length uncut raw shaft made to fit each numbered wood or iron. In other words, the shafts for a full set of irons would normally be purchased in ½" incremental lengths and would usually not require any tipping to adjust the flexes.

It is also very important to understand that these tables can only provide a compromise versus using shafts in ½" increments. Experience has shown that these tables show the best way to adjust non-incremental shaft lengths, but due to so many other factors such as shaft weight changes and tip diameter changes, they should be considered as a "best bet" installation procedure.

The following tables should be used for reference and to provide a better understanding on how to install non-incremental lengths. Keep in mind, however, that the tables provided which give the back of heel to first step dimensions also apply to non-incremental lengths as well as to the incremental lengths shown in the following tables. The reason for this is simple: most all tip taper shafts are manufactured in the different lengths by changing the tip to first step distance in ½" increments. Therefore, cutting ½" from the tip of a shaft will give it the same tip to first step as if it were made in that length. The only two differences now being that the tip diameter is slightly larger (approximately four-thousandths of an inch per ½" cut from it) and the shaft weight is lighter (approximately 1.4 grams per ½" cut from the tip) than the proper incremental length shaft or those shafts purchased in ½" increments.

TABLE 57-4
Men's Tip Taper Iron Shafts
[1]Tipping Table for Proper Installation of
Incremental and Non-Incremental Uncut Shaft Lengths

Club No.	[2]Finished Club Length (Modern Standard)	Column 1		Column 2		Column 3		Column 4	
		Uncut Shaft Length	Amount of Tipping	Uncut Shaft Length	Amount of Tipping	Uncut Shaft Length	Amount of Tipping	Uncut Shaft Length	Amount of Tipping
1	39½"	39"	0"	39"	0"	39"	0"	—	
2	39"	38½"	0"	39"	½"	39"	½"	38"	0"
3	38½"	38"	0"	38"	0"	39"	1"	38"	½"
4	38"	37½"	0"	38"	½"	39"	1½"	37"	0"
5	37½"	37"	0"	37"	0"	37"	0"	37"	½"
6	37"	36½"	0"	37"	½"	37"	½"	36"	0"
7	36½"	36"	0"	36"	0"	37"	1"	36"	½"
8	36"	35½"	0"	36"	½"	37"	1½"	35"	0"
9	35½"	35"	0"	35"	0"	35"	0"	35"	½"
PW	35½"	35"	0"	35"	0"	35"	0"	35"	½"
SW	35½"	35"	0"	35"	0"	35"	0"	35"	½"

[1] This table gives standard iron shaft flexes based on a 1" dimension from back of heel to tip end of shaft when installed in a head. See Figure 57-1. Column 1 uses 9 lengths, column 2 uses 5 lengths, column 3 uses 3 lengths and column 4 uses 4 lengths. The one exception to the so-called standard flex is column 4. Many companies have used 4 lengths of shafts starting with a 38" #2 iron shaft. This can also be considered a standard, but keep in mind that on a comparative basis, a set of clubs shafted as shown in column 4 will feel about ¼ flex stiffer than those in column 1, 2 or 3.

Another point to keep in mind is this. Although column 2 and 3 show the closest way to match flex and feel to the ideal installation of column 1, it would be impossible to be perfectly exact. However, in most cases experience gained through practical application, I have found very few tour players or other accomplished players who could feel any difference. The final proof is always in actually hitting the clubs.

[2] For each ½" added to the standard club length, the shaft should be tipped an additional ½" to maintain the standard flex unless a slightly softer feel is desired. In most cases, it is doubtful that all but a highly accomplished player will feel these differences.

TABLE 57-5
Men's Tip Taper Wood Shafts
[1]Tipping Table for Proper Installation of
Incremental and Non-Incremental Uncut Shaft Lengths

Club No.	[2]Finished Club Length (Modern Standard)	Column 1		Column 2		Column 3	
		Uncut Shaft Length	Amount of Tipping	Uncut Shaft Length	Amount of Tipping	Uncut Shaft Length	Amount of Tipping
1	43"	44"	0"	44"	0"	44"	0"
2	42½"	43½"	0"	44"	½"	44"	½"
3	42"	43"	0"	43"	0"	44"	1"
4	41½"	42½"	0"	43"	½"	44"	1½"
5	41"	42"	0"	42"	0"	44"	2"
6	40½"	42"	½"	42"	½"	44"	2½"
7	40"	42"	1"	42"	1"	44"	3"

[1] This table gives standard wood shaft flexes based on a through head shaft bore which is considered the modern standard. See Figure 57-3.

[2] For each ½" added to standard club length, the shaft should be tipped an additional ½" to maintain the standard flex unless a slightly softer feel is desired. In most cases, it is doubtful that all but a highly accomplished player will feel the differences.

TABLE 57-6
Ladies' Tip Taper Iron Shafts
[1]Tipping Table for Proper Installation of
Incremental and Non-Incremental Uncut Shaft Lengths

Club No.	[2]Finished Club Length (Modern Standard)	Column 1		Column 2		Column 3	
		Uncut Shaft Length	Amount of Tipping	Uncut Shaft Length	Amount of Tipping	Uncut Shaft Length	Amount of Tipping
2	38"	38"	0"	38"	0"	38"	0"
3	37½"	37½"	0"	38"	½"	38"	½"
4	37"	37"	0"	37"	0"	38"	1"
5	36½"	36½"	0"	37"	½"	38"	1½"
6	36"	36"	0"	36"	0"	36"	0"
7	35½"	35½"	0"	36"	½"	36"	½"
8	35"	35"	0"	35"	0"	36"	1"
9	34½"	34½"	0"	35"	½"	34"	0"
PW	34½"	34½"	0"	35"	½"	34"	0"
SW	34½"	34½"	0"	35"	½"	34"	0"

[1]This table gives standard iron shaft flexes based on a 1" dimension from back of heel to tip end of shaft when installed in a head. See Figure 57-1.
[2]For each ½" added to the standard club length, the shaft should be tipped an additional ½" to maintain the standard flex unless a slightly softer feel is desired. In most cases, it is doubtful that all but a highly accomplished player will feel these differences.

TABLE 57-7
Ladies' Tip Taper Wood Shafts
[1]Tipping Table for Proper Installation of
Incremental and Non-Incremental Uncut Shaft Lengths

Club No.	[2]Finished Club Length (Modern Standard)	Column 1		Column 2		[3]Column 3	
		Uncut Shaft Length	Amount of Tipping	Uncut Shaft Length	Amount of Tipping	Uncut Shaft Length	Amount of Tipping
1	42"	43"	0"	43"	0"	44"	0"
2	41½"	42½"	0"	43"	½"	44"	½"
3	41"	42"	0"	43"	1"	44"	1"
4	40½"	42"	½"	43"	1½"	44"	1½"
5	40"	42"	1"	43"	2"	44"	2"
6	39½"	42"	1½"	43"	2½"	44"	2½"
7	39"	42"	2"	43"	3"	44"	3"

[1] This table gives standard wood shaft flexes based on a through head shaft bore which is considered the modern standard. See Figure 57-3.
[2] For each ½" added to standard club length, the shaft should be tipped an additional ½" to maintain the standard flex unless a slightly softer feel is desired. In most cases, it is doubtful that all but a highly accomplished player will feel the differences.
[3] A 44" "L" flex shaft will produce a weaker ladies' flex than the so-called modern standard. It should be noted here that this more flexible set-up will many times improve the shotmaking ability of beginning, less accomplished, non-athletic or weaker in strength women golfers.

Understanding Parallel Tip Shaft Installations – Introduction

When the unitized parallel tip shaft was first introduced by True Temper® in the early 70's, a unitized shaft trimming chart and drawing was included in their sales brochure. This method of installation gave the parallel tip shaft a firmer feel than its tip taper counterpart in the same flex and was not satisfactory.

During the latter part of the mid 70's and up to the present, True Temper® changed their recommended trimming method on unitized parallel tip shafts to more closely align the proper flex feel according to their overall shaft flex standards. See Figures 57-10 and 57-11. This "revised" method softened or weakened the flex feel of the installed shaft and more closely aligned the flex feel to that of the tip taper shaft. It should be stated here, however, that the two shafts can really never feel the same because of their significantly differing design characteristics resulting in differing club total weights and swingweights.

The method now recommended for trimming unitized parallel tip shafts is called the "Maltby Club Design" trimming method. In actuality, it is the same as True Temper's® revised trimming method of the mid 70's with one important exception.

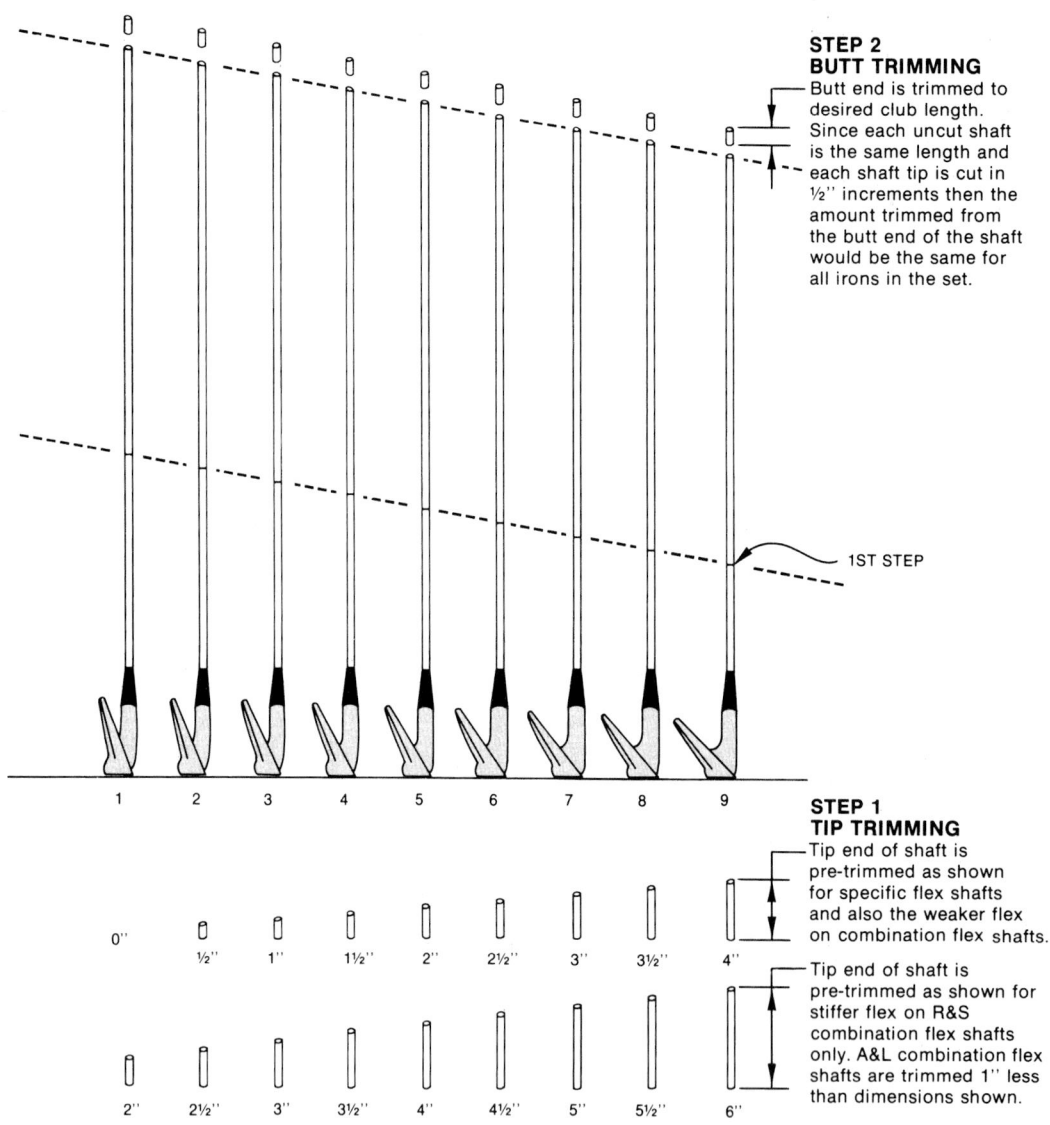

STEP 2
BUTT TRIMMING
Butt end is trimmed to desired club length. Since each uncut shaft is the same length and each shaft tip is cut in ½'' increments then the amount trimmed from the butt end of the shaft would be the same for all irons in the set.

1ST STEP

STEP 1
TIP TRIMMING
Tip end of shaft is pre-trimmed as shown for specific flex shafts and also the weaker flex on combination flex shafts.

Tip end of shaft is pre-trimmed as shown for stiffer flex on R&S combination flex shafts only. A&L combination flex shafts are trimmed 1'' less than dimensions shown.

NOTE: The True Temper Parallel Tip Shaft Trimming Method for irons was developed when the "Traditional Standard" length was followed. It was ½" shorter than the "Modern Standard" length currently used by manufacturers. If True Temper still recommended this method an additional ½" would have to be cut from the shaft tip to compensate for the added length.

Figure 57-10
Revised True Temper® Iron Parallel Tip Shaft Trimming Method

The "Maltby Club Design" method allows for the adjustment of differing shaft in-hosel penetrations. In other words, the tables that follow in this section which apply to parallel tip shafts provide back of heel to first shaft step dimensions. You simply trim the shaft tip the required amount to get the dimension shown in the back of heel to first step tables, and then trim the butt end to the desired club length.

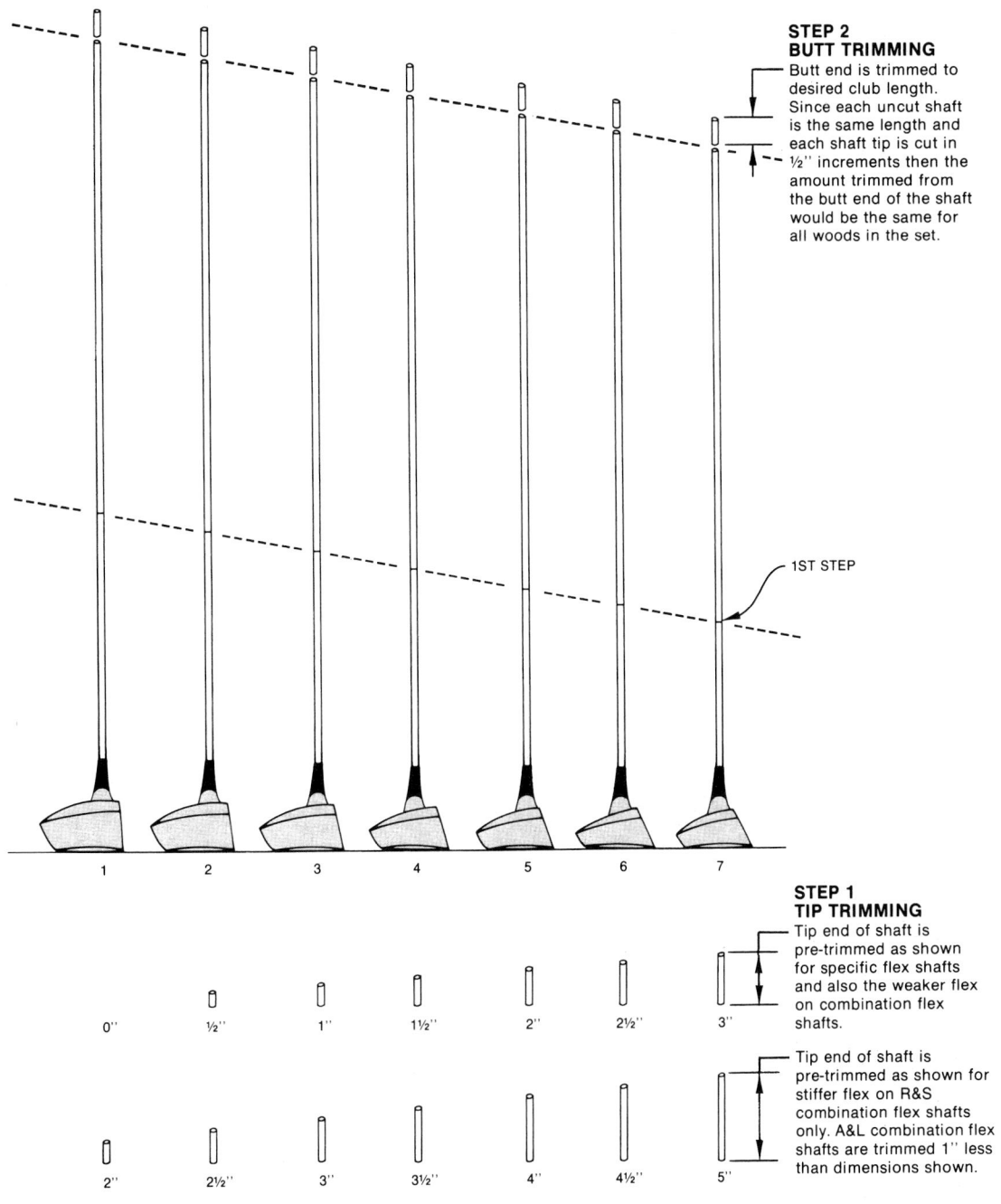

STEP 2
BUTT TRIMMING
Butt end is trimmed to desired club length. Since each uncut shaft is the same length and each shaft tip is cut in ½'' increments then the amount trimmed from the butt end of the shaft would be the same for all woods in the set.

1ST STEP

STEP 1
TIP TRIMMING
Tip end of shaft is pre-trimmed as shown for specific flex shafts and also the weaker flex on combination flex shafts.

Tip end of shaft is pre-trimmed as shown for stiffer flex on R&S combination flex shafts only. A&L combination flex shafts are trimmed 1'' less than dimensions shown.

0''   ½''   1''   1½''   2''   2½''   3''

2''   2½''   3''   3½''   4''   4½''   5''

NOTE: The True Temper Parallel Tip Shaft Trimming Method was developed when the "Traditional Standard" was followed. Since the "Modern Standard" length for woods is the same as the Traditional Standard, then the True Temper method for woods would still apply.

Figure 57-11
Revised True Temper® Wood Parallel Tip Shaft Trimming Method

One last point to aid the reader: remember earlier in this section when it was stated that the "modern standards" for shaft penetration were established at 1" from back of heel to tip of shaft in irons and through-bores on woods? Well, if you were reshafting a set of woods and irons that had these "modern standard" shaft penetrations, then the trimming dimensions as recommended by True Temper® in Figures 57-10 and 57-11 would be exactly the same as a set of shafts installed using the "Maltby Club Design" method shown in Figures 57-12 and 57-13. So you see, the "Maltby Club Design" method simply adjusts for non-modern back of heel to shaft tip dimensions to make all parallel shaft installations have a predictable flex feel.

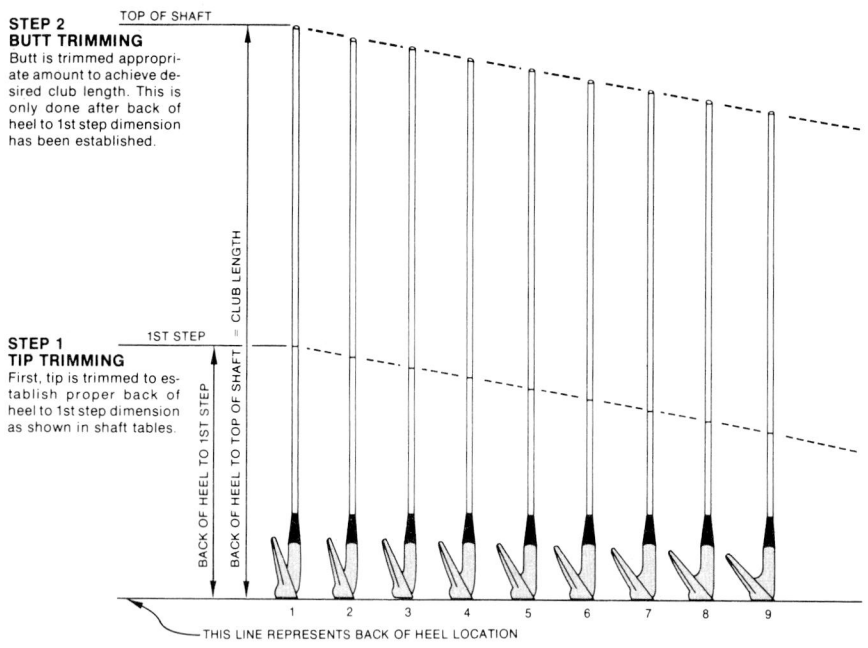

Figure 57-12
Maltby "Club Design" Iron Parallel Tip Shaft Trimming Method

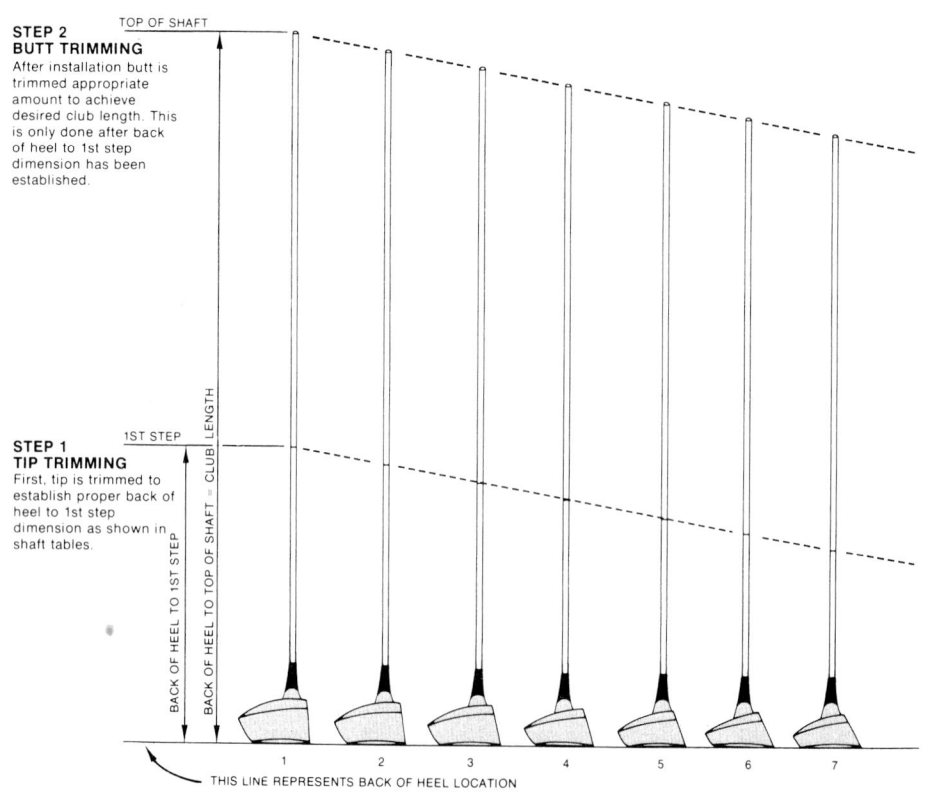

Figure 57-13
Maltby "Club Design" Wood Parallel Tip Shaft Trimming Method

These four figures, Figures 57-10 through 57-13, provide for a graphic or visual interpretation of trimming parallel tip shafts in both woods and irons. They also provide the reader with more in-depth reference information on installing parallel tip shafts in irons and woods.

610

Understanding Parallel Tip Shaft Installations in Woods

All of the steel golf shaft manufacturers have a significant line of parallel tip shafts. However, Brunswick Golf® and True Temper® are the only ones to use a fairly logical coding system whereby it is much easier to immediately identify the type of shaft. For instance, with True Temper's® system, a UDWS shaft is a "Unitized Dynamic® Wood Stiff" flex and a UDWAL is a "Unitized Dynamic® Wood Combination A or L" flex. A UJWR is a "Unitized Jet Step Wood R" flex. Unitized simply means parallel tip. This now gives you a pretty good idea of interpreting the code and understanding its meaning.

Some confusion has also existed concerning where to trim parallel tip shafts. Many parallel tip shafts are available in specific flexes such as X, S, R, A and L. The specific flex parallel tip shaft is identified by a spot of color on the butt end, usually under the grip, and also by having a .335 parallel tip. Trimming on these specific flex parallel tip shafts is quite easy and is shown in its simplest form in Table 57-8. This table represents True Temper's® recommended trimming method also shown in Figure 57-11. The only drawback to this trimming method, as has already been stated, is its disregard for shaft installation depth in the hosel such as blind-bore or through-bore type assemblies.

Trimming the "combination flex" unitized parallel tip shafts is similar to trimming "specific flex" types, but an adjustment in tip trimming is required to obtain the stiffer flex. First of all, you have to understand that a combination flex shaft such as the UDWC, which is a combination "R" or "S" flex in the Dynamic® pattern is manufactured in the weaker flex or "R" flex. In the case of the UDWC, the tip length (tip to first step) is 12½" or exactly the same as the UDWR. However, the UDWR is made 45" long, while the UDWC is 47" long. Hence, the butt section on the UDWC is lengthened by 2". So, to properly trim a UDWC shaft to make it an "R" flex, you simply pretrim the tip end by the amount shown in Table 57-9 and then trim the rest from the butt end to get the desired length for that particular wood. If you want an "S" flex from a UDWC shaft, you cut an additional 2" from the tip end and trim the butt to the desired club length. For a detailed trimming explanation on combination flex shafts, see Table 57-9 which is also shown in Figure 57-11 in a more graphic presentation.

Remember, parallel tip shafts in combination flexes do not have color coding marks on the butt end. The reason for this is quite obvious since the shaft can be made into either of the two flexes.

	TABLE 57-8	
	Trimming Chart for Specific Flex (Non-combination Flex) **Unitized Parallel Tip Wood Shafts**	
Club No.	**[1]Amount to Pretrim from Tip**	**Amount to Trim from Butt**
1	0"	
2	½"	Trim butt to obtain
3	1"	desired club lengths
4	1½"	after shaft is tipped
5	2"	and installed in head.
6	2½"	
7	3"	

[1] To obtain a weaker or stiffer flex feel, this dimension can be changed. For example, cutting an additional ½" from the tip makes the shaft ¼ flex stiffer. Conversely, leaving an additional ½" on the tip will make this shaft ¼ flex weaker or softer.

If a shaft is tipped an additional 2", it will produce the equivalent of one full flex stiffer. However, the feel of the tipped shaft to one made in the stiffer flex will usually not be the same due to different shaft weights and flex points.

TABLE 57-9

Club No.	[2] Tip Trimming for Weaker Flex	[2] Tip Trimming for Stiffer Flex	Amount to Trim from Butt
1	0"	2"	
2	½"	2½"	Trim butt to obtain
3	1"	3"	desired club lengths
4	1½"	3½"	after shaft is tipped
5	2"	4"	and installed in head.
6	2½"	4½"	
7	3"	5"	

[1] Combination flex shafts are usually identified by a "C" or "AL" in the code number. For example: UDWC is a combination "R" or "S" flex shaft and a UDWAL is a combination "A" or "L" flex.

[2] In-between flexes, stiffer flexes and weaker flexes can be obtained by tipping less or tipping more. For example: trimming the tip 1" on a driver with a UDWC shaft will give you a flex between R and S.

Understanding Parallel Tip Shaft Installations in Irons

As was stated for woods, all of the steel golf shaft manufacturers also have a significant line of parallel tip iron shafts available. Brunswick Golf® and True Temper® are the only ones that use a fairly logical coding system whereby it is much easier to immediately identify a certain type of shaft. For instance, with True Temper's® system, a UDIS shaft is a "Unitized Dynamic® Iron Stiff" flex and a UDIC is a "Unitized Dynamic® Iron Combination R or S" flex. UDICO is a "Unitized Dynamic® Iron Combination R or S Flex Over-The-Hosel." Unitized simply means parallel tip.

Some confusion has always existed concerning where to trim unitized parallel tip shafts. Many parallel tip shafts are available in specific flexes such as X, S, R, A and L. The specific flex parallel tip shaft is identified by a spot of color on the butt end and also by having a .370" parallel tip for shaft-in hosel assemblies and a .395" parallel tip for shaft-over hosel assemblies. Trimming on the specific flex parallel tip shaft is quite easy and is shown in its simplest form in Table 57-10. This table represents True Temper's® recommended trimming method which is also shown in Figure 57-10. Once again, the drawback to this trimming method is its disregard for variations in shaft installation depth. Each individual iron design may have differing dimensions from the back of the heel to the tip of the shaft, thus causing a difference in flex feel, i.e., weaker flex, standard flex or stronger flex. Refer back to Figure 57-8.

Trimming the "combination flex" unitized parallel tip shafts is similar to trimming the "specific flex" types, but an adjustment in tip trimming is required to obtain this stiffer flex. First of all, you have to understand that a combination flex shaft such as the UDIC, which is a combination "R" or "S" flex in the Dynamic® pattern, is manufactured in the weaker flex or "R" flex. In the case of the UDIC, the tip length (tip to first step) is 12⅛" or exactly the same as the UDIR. However, the UDIR is made 39" long while the UDIC is 41" long. Hence, the butt section of the UDIC is lengthened by 2". So, to properly trim a UDIC shaft to make it an "R" flex, you simply pretrim the tip end by the amount shown in Table 57-11 and then trim the rest from the butt end to get the desired length for that particular iron. If you want an "S" flex from the UDIC, you cut an additional 2" from the tip end and trim the butt for the desired club length.

For a detailed trimming explanation on combination flex shafts, see Table 57-11. Also shown in Figure 57-10 is a more graphic presentation of the same data. Remember, parallel tip shafts in combination flexes do not have a color coding mark on the butt end. The reason for this is quite obvious since the shaft can be made into either of the two flexes.

TABLE 57-10

[1] Trimming Chart for Specific Flex (Non-combination Flex)
Unitized Parallel Tip Iron Shafts

Club No.	[2] Amount to Pretrim from Tip	Amount to Trim from Butt
1	1/2"	
2	1"	Trim butt to obtain
3	1 1/2"	desired club lengths
4	2"	after shaft is tipped
5	2 1/2"	and installed in head.
6	3"	
7	3 1/2"	
8	4"	
9	4 1/2"	
PW	4 1/2"	
SW	4 1/2"	

[1] If the PW and SW are made the same length as the #9 iron then the 4 1/2" dimension applies. If, however, they are made 1/2" shorter, then 5" of tipping would apply.

[2] To obtain a weaker or stiffer flex feel, this dimension can be changed. For example, cutting an additional 1/2" from the tip makes the shaft 1/4 flex stiffer. Conversely, leaving an additional 1/2" on the tip will make this shaft 1/4 flex weaker or softer.

If a shaft is tipped an additional 2" it will produce the equivalent of one full flex stiffer. However, the feel of the tipped shaft to one made in the stiffer flex will usually not be the same due to different shaft weights and flex points.

TABLE 57-11
[1] Trimming Chart for "Combination Flex"
Unitized Parallel Tip Iron Shafts

Club No.	[2] Tip Trimming for Weaker Flex	[3] Tip Trimming for Stiffer Flex	Amount to Trim from Butt
1	1/2"	2 1/2"	
2	1"	3"	Trim butt to obtain
3	1 1/2"	3 1/2"	desired club length
4	2"	4"	after shaft is tipped
5	2 1/2"	4 1/2"	and installed in head.
6	3"	5"	
7	3 1/2"	5 1/2"	
8	4"	6"	
9	4 1/2"	6 1/2"	
PW	4 1/2"	6 1/2"	
SW	4 1/2"	6 1/2"	

[1] Combination flex shafts are usually identified by a "C" or "AL" in the code number. For example: UDIC is a combination "R" or "S" flex shaft and a UDIAL is a combination "A" or "L" flex.

[2] In-between flexes, stiffer flexes and weaker flexes can be obtained by tipping less or tipping more. For example: Trimming the tip 1" from a UDIC shaft will give you a flex between R and S.

[3] If the PW and SW are made the same length as the #9 iron then the 4 1/2" and 6 1/2" dimensions above apply. If, however, they are made 1/2" shorter than 5" and 7" of tipping respectively would apply.

Tables—Back of Heel to First Step for Wood and Iron Shafts

The back of heel to first shaft step dimensions given in the following tables were calculated by taking the tip to first step distance from the shaft manufacturer's blueprints and adjusting the dimension according to the "modern standards" shown in Figure 57-1 for irons and Figure 57-3 for woods. Each table has a corresponding footnote explanation on how the dimensions were derived and other applicable information. These tables include virtually all stock shafts available today. Every club assembler should be able to identify any stock type and pattern steel golf shaft. The best way to do this is with a "Shaft Identification Gauge" developed by the author. This gauge, used in conjunction with a 48" ruler, and the "Shaft Butt Gauge," also developed by the author, will identify most shafts by type and pattern.

One last point to reiterate: if you are checking a raw shaft for shaft tip to first step distance to determine what type shaft you have, simply subtract ½" from the actual shaft tip to first step distance and look the shaft up in the tables in this section. See Figure 57-3. (For irons add 1" to the shaft tip to first step distance. See Figure 57-1.)

Here is an example of this: suppose you are trying to identify a golf shaft which is 44" long, has a .620 butt diameter, .294 tip diameter and a .350 tip parallel section. You also determine that the distance between steps is 1⅞". Most of you will realize already that this is a Taper Tip Dynamic® shaft. However, it could be a "Stiff" or "X-Stiff" flex because both these shafts have the same dimensions we just listed. However, there is a dimension that will immediately tell us this shaft's flex. Simply measure the shaft's tip length or that dimension from the shaft tip to the first step. Let's say this shaft measures 9¼" from its tip to the first step. Next, subtract ½" from 9¼" which gives us 8¾". Turn to the "Back of Heel to First Step Dimensions" on the following pages and look up the back of heel to first step dimension for both Dynamic® "X" and Dynamic® "S" tip taper 44" wood shafts. The table shows 8¾" for an "X" flex and 10¾" for an "S" flex. So, our shaft is an "X" flex DWX 44" shaft (Dynamic® wood X-stiff, 44" long). Go ahead and practice with a few wood and iron shafts and you will see that it is quite easy to do.

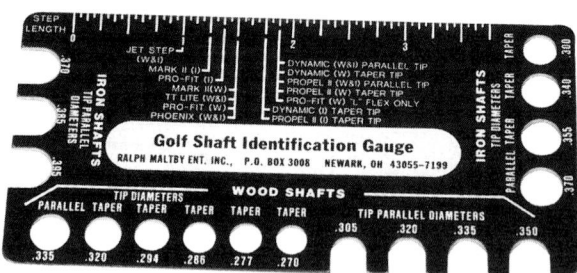

Figure 57-14
The "Golf Shaft Identification Gauge" is used to identify most golf shafts

Figure 57-15
The "Shaft Butt Gauge" will measure any size shaft butt

PARALLEL TIP IRON SHAFTS

FOOTNOTES FOR THE FOLLOWING PARALLEL TIP IRON SHAFT TABLES

[1] The following tables give standard iron shaft flexes based on a 1" dimension from back of heel to tip end of shaft when installed in a head. This is considered to most closely approximate the traditional standard assembly. See Figure 57-1. Parallel tip shafts installed in iron heads with a greater dimension than 1" may sometimes need a slight amount of additional tipping (usually ⅛" to ⅜") to make the back of heel to first step dimension conform to those below.

The back of heel to first step dimensions below were derived by taking the actual shaft manufacturer's blueprint dimensions of uncut shafts from the tip end to the first step and adding ½". Since these shafts are parallel tip and come in only one length, the blueprint tip length applies only to the #1 iron. Therefore the below first step dimensions for the #2 through #9 iron through SW were derived by subtracting an additional ½" for each successively shorter club.

[2] For each ½" added to standard club length, the shaft should be tipped an additional ½" to maintain the standard flex unless a slightly softer feel is desired. In most cases it is doubtful that all but a highly accomplished player will feel these differences. It should also be noted that most manufacturers, regardless of shaft tip to back of heel dimension, trim in ½" increments and install the shaft to the bottom of the hole. This is not necessarily wrong as individual club head designs, club lengths, head weights, etc. are all part of the overall club performance that the manufacturer may have desired and confirmed by testing.

[3] After the shaft is installed in a head with the back of heel to first step dimensions as shown below (normal installation), the finished club length is obtained by trimming from the shaft butt.

[4] For men, if the PW and SW are to be 35" long, then an additional ½" should be cut from the shaft tip (5" vs. 4½").

[5] To maintain the proper flexing characteristics in the tip area, the parallel tip Contour shaft should be tip trimmed only in ⅛" increments for each ½" reduction in club length.

[6] For ladies, if the PW and SW are to be 34" long, then an additional ½" should be cut from the shaft tip (4" vs. 3½").

PARALLEL TIP IRON SHAFTS – MEN'S
TRUE TEMPER®

Club No.	[2] [3] Finished Club Length (Modern Standard)	[1] Amount Normally Trimmed From Tip of Shaft	Dynamic UDIX "X"	Dynamic Gold & Dynamic UDGIS & UDIS or UDIC "S"	Dynamic Gold & Dynamic UDGIR & UDIR or UDIC "R"	Dynamic UDIAL "A"	Dynamic UDIXO "X"	Dynamic UDICO "S"	Dynamic UDICO "R"	Dynamic UDIALO "A"	TT Lite UTTLIC "S"	TT Lite UTTLIC "R"
1	39½"	½"	10⅝"	10⅝"	12⅝"	14⅜"	10½"	12½"	14½"	16¼"	9½"	11½"
2	39"	1"	10⅛"	10⅛"	12⅛"	13⅞"	10"	12"	14"	15¾"	9"	11"
3	38½"	1½"	9⅝"	9⅝"	11⅝"	13⅜"	9½"	11½"	13½"	15¼"	8½"	10½"
4	38"	2"	9⅛"	9⅛"	11⅛"	12⅞"	9"	11"	13"	14¾"	8"	10"
5	37½"	2½"	8⅝"	8⅝"	10⅝"	12⅜"	8½"	10½"	12½"	14¼"	7½"	9½"
6	37"	3"	8⅛"	8⅛"	10⅛"	11⅞"	8"	10"	12"	13¾"	7"	9"
7	36½"	3½"	7⅝"	7⅝"	9⅝"	11⅜"	7½"	9½"	11½"	13¼"	6½"	8½"
8	36"	4"	7⅛"	7⅛"	9⅛"	10⅞"	7"	9"	11"	12¾"	6"	8"
9	35½"	4½"	6⅝"	6⅝"	8⅝"	10⅜"	6½"	8½"	10½"	12¼"	5½"	7½"
PW	35½"	4½"	6⅝"	6⅝"	8⅝"	10⅜"	6½"	8½"	10½"	12¼"	5½"	7½"
SW	35½"	4½"	6⅝"	6⅝"	8⅝"	10⅜"	6½"	8½"	10½"	12¼"	5½"	7½"

Club No.	[2] [3] Finished Club Length (Modern Standard)	[1] Amount Normally Trimmed From Tip of Shaft	TT Lite U2LIS "S"	TT Lite U2LIR "R"	TT Lite U2LIAL "A"	Jet Step UJIC "S"	Jet Step UJIC "R"	Jet Step UJICO "S"	Jet Step UJICO "R"	[5] Contour UTRIS "S"	[5] Contour UTRIR "R"
1	39½"	½"	9½"	11½"	9½"	11½"	13½"	12½"	14½"	12⅞"	14⅜"
2	39"	1"	9"	11"	9"	11"	13"	12"	14"	12¾"	14¼"
3	38½"	1½"	8½"	10½"	8½"	10½"	12½"	11½"	13½"	12⅝"	14⅛"
4	38"	2"	8"	10"	8"	10"	12"	11"	13"	12½"	14"
5	37½"	2½"	7½"	9½"	7½"	9½"	11½"	10½"	12½"	12⅜"	13⅞"
6	37"	3"	7"	9"	7"	9"	11"	10"	12"	12¼"	13¾"
7	36½"	3½"	6½"	8½"	6½"	8½"	10½"	9½"	11½"	12⅛"	13⅝"
8	36"	4"	6"	8"	6"	8"	10"	9"	11"	12"	13½"
9	35½"	4½"	5½"	7½"	5½"	7½"	9½"	8½"	10½"	11⅞"	13⅜"
PW	35½"	4½"	5½"	7½"	5½"	7½"	9½"	8½"	10½"	11⅞"	13⅜"
SW	35½"	4½"	5½"	7½"	5½"	7½"	9½"	8½"	10½"	11⅞"	13⅜"

615

PARALLEL TIP IRON SHAFTS – MEN'S *cont.*
TRUE TEMPER®

Club No.	[2][3]Finished Club Length (Modern Standard)	[1]Amount* Normally Trimmed From Tip of Shaft	Gold Plus UGPIX "X"	Gold Plus UGPIS "S"	Gold Plus UGPIR "R"
1	39½"	0"	9"	10"	11"
2	39"	½"	8½"	9½"	10½"
3	38½"	1"	8"	9"	10"
4	38"	1½"	7½"	8½"	9½"
5	37½"	2"	7"	8"	9"
6	37"	2½"	6½"	7½"	8½"
7	36½"	3"	6"	7"	8"
8	36"	3½"	5½"	6½"	7½"
9	35½"	4"	5"	6"	7"
PW	35½"	4"	5"	6"	7"
SW	35½"	4"	5"	6"	7"

*The True Temper® Gold Plus™ has been specifically designed for Modern Standard Length golf clubs. As such, ½" less should be trimmed from the tip when compared to other shafts (UDIS, U2LIR, etc.) that were originally designed for the traditional standard length based upon a 38½" #2 iron.

Club No.	Finished Club Length (Modern Standard)	'Uncut Shaft Length for Flex Flow	Flex Flow UTFFIS "S"	Flex Flow UTFFIR "R"	Flex Flow UTFFIA "A"
2	39"	39"	10½"	11¾"	12¾"
3	38½"	38½"	10"	11¼"	12¼"
4	38"	38"	9½"	10¾"	11¾"
5	37½"	37½"	9"	10¼"	11¼"
6	37"	37"	8½"	9¾"	10¾"
7	36½"	36½"	8"	9¼"	10¼"
8	36"	36"	7½"	8¾"	9¾"
9	35½"	35½"	7"	8¼"	9¼"
PW	35½"	35"	6½"	7¾"	8¾"
SW	35½"	35"	6½"	7¾"	8¾"

*To achieve the recommended back of heel to first step dimension, be certain to choose the the recommended uncut shaft length. Tip trimming should be performed only if the same length is cut from the tip of all the shafts in the set. Failure to maintain consistent tip trimming will result in the Flex Flow's recessed section falling out of alignment.

Club No.	[2][3]Finished Club Length (Modern Standard)	Uncut Shaft Length R/S	Uncut Shaft Length A/X	Dynalite ULIX "X"	Dynalite ULIC "S"	Dynalite ULIC "R"	Dynalite ULIAL "A"	Pro-Fit UPIC "S"	Pro-Fit UPIC "R"
1	39½"	41"	40"	9½"	11"	13"	13¼"	11"	13"
2	39"	41"	40"	9"	10½"	12½"	12¾"	10½"	12½"
3	38½"	41"	40"	8½"	10"	12"	12¼"	10"	12"
4	38"	41"	40"	8"	9½"	11½"	11¾"	9½"	11½"
5	37½"	41"	40"	7½"	9"	11"	11¼"	9"	11"
6	37"	41"	40"	7"	8½"	10½"	10¾"	8½"	10½"
7	36½"	41"	40"	6½"	8"	10"	10¼"	8"	10"
8	36"	41"	40"	6"	7½"	9½"	9¾"	7½"	9½"
9	35½"	41"	40"	5½"	7"	9"	9¼"	7"	9"
PW	35½"	41"	40"	5½"	7"	9"	9¼"	7"	9"
SW	35½"	41"	40"	5½"	7"	9"	9¼"	7"	9"

PARALLEL TIP IRON SHAFTS – MEN'S *cont.*
TRUE TEMPER®

Club No.	[2,3] Finished Club Length (Modern Standard)	Uncut Shaft Length	Dynamic Lite UDLIS "S"	Dynamic Lite UDLIR "R"	Uncut Shaft Length	Dynalite Gold ULGIS "S"	Dynalite Gold ULGIR "R"	Dynalite Gold ULGIX "X"	Uncut Shaft Length	Comet URIC "S"	Comet URIC "R"
1	39½"	39"	9½"	11⅛"	40"	12"	14"	9½"	41"	11½"	13½"
2	39"	39"	9"	10⅝"	40"	11½"	13½"	9"	41"	11"	13"
3	38½"	39"	8½"	10⅛"	40"	11"	13"	8½"	41"	10½"	12½"
4	38"	39"	8"	9⅝"	40"	10½"	12½"	8"	41"	10"	12"
5	37½"	39"	7½"	9⅛"	40"	10"	12"	7½"	41"	9½"	11½"
6	37"	39"	7"	8⅝"	40"	9½"	11½"	7"	41"	9"	11"
7	36½"	39"	6½"	8⅛"	40"	9"	11"	6½"	41"	8½"	10½"
8	36"	39"	6"	7⅝"	40"	8½"	10½"	6"	41"	8"	10"
9	35½"	39"	5½"	7⅛"	40"	8"	10"	5½"	41"	7½"	9½"
PW	35½"	39"	5½"	7⅛"	40"	8"	10"	5½"	41"	7½"	9½"
SW	35½"	39"	5½"	7⅛"	40"	8"	10"	5½"	41"	7½"	9½"

PARALLEL TIP IRON SHAFTS – MEN'S
BRUNSWICK

Club No.	[2,3] Finished Club Length (Modern Standard)	[1] Amount Normally Trimmed From Tip of Shaft	Vanadium Sonic IX "X"	Vanadium Sonic IS "S"	Vanadium Sonic IR "R"	Phoenix IS "S"	Phoenix IR "R"	Phoenix IAL "A"	Microtaper UPMIC "S"	Microtaper UPMIC "R"	Microtaper UPMIAL "A"
1	39½"	½"	9⅜"	10⅞"	12⅜"	9½"	11½"	8½"	12¾"	14¾"	15¾"
2	39"	1"	8⅞"	10⅜"	11⅞"	9"	11"	8"	12¼"	14¼"	15¼"
3	38½"	1½"	8⅜"	9⅞"	11⅜"	8½"	10½"	7½"	11¾"	13¾"	14¾"
4	38"	2"	7⅞"	9⅜"	10⅞"	8"	10"	7"	11¼"	13¼"	14¼"
5	37½"	2½"	7⅜"	8⅞"	10⅜"	7½"	9½"	6½"	10¾"	12¾"	13¾"
6	37"	3"	6⅞"	8⅜"	9⅞"	7"	9"	6"	10¼"	12¼"	13¼"
7	36½"	3½"	6⅜"	7⅞"	9⅜"	6½"	8½"	5½"	9¾"	11¾"	12¾"
8	36"	4"	5⅞"	7⅜"	8⅞"	6"	8"	5"	9¼"	11¼"	12¼"
9	35½"	4½"	5⅜"	6⅞"	8⅜"	5½"	7½"	4½"	8¾"	10¾"	11¾"
PW	35½"	4½"	5⅜"	6⅞"	8⅜"	5½"	7½"	4½"	8¾"	10¾"	11¾"
SW	35½"	4½"	5⅜"	6⅞"	8⅜"	5½"	7½"	4½"	8¾"	10¾"	11¾"

Club No.	[2,3] Finished Club Length (Modern Standard)	[1] Amount Normally Trimmed From Tip of Shaft	Propel II IRS "S"	Propel II IRS "R"	Propel II IAL "A"	Mark II IR "R"	Super Champion IR "R"	Champion IR "R"
1	39½"	½"	10⅝"	12⅝"	13⅜"	12½"	13 7/16"	11½"
2	39"	1"	10⅛"	12⅛"	12⅞"	12"	12 15/16"	11"
3	38½"	1½"	9⅝"	11⅝"	12⅜"	11½"	12 7/16"	10½"
4	38"	2"	9⅛"	11⅛"	11⅞"	11"	11 15/16"	10"
5	37½"	2½"	8⅝"	10⅝"	11⅜"	10½"	11 7/16"	9½"
6	37"	3"	8⅛"	10⅛"	10⅞"	10"	10 15/16"	9"
7	36½"	3½"	7⅝"	9⅝"	10⅜"	9½"	10 7/16"	8½"
8	36"	4"	7⅛"	9⅛"	9⅞"	9"	9 15/16"	8"
9	35½"	4½"	6⅝"	8⅝"	9⅛"	8½"	9 7/16"	7½"
PW	35½"	4½"	6⅝"	8⅝"	9⅛"	8½"	9 7/16"	7½"
SW	35½"	4½"	6⅝"	8⅝"	9⅛"	8½"	9 7/16"	7½"

PARALLEL TIP IRON SHAFTS – MEN'S
APOLLO

Club No.	Finished Club Length (Modern Standard)	Amount Normally Trimmed From Tip of Shaft	[1] Matchflex 4 [2]"S"	[1] Matchflex 3 [2]"RS"	[1] Matchflex 2 [2]"R"	[1] Matchflex 1 [2]"AR"	[1][3] Torsion Matched "S"	[1][3] Torsion Matched "R"
1	39½"	½"	12"	12"	11 9/16"	13¼"	11½"	14"
2	39"	1"	11½"	11½"	11 1/16"	12¾"	Use 39" Maintain 11½"	Use 39" Maintain 14"
3	38½"	1½"	11"	11"	10 9/16"	12¼"	11½"	14"
4	38"	2"	10½"	10½"	10 1/16"	11¾"	Use 38" Maintain 11½"	Use 38" Maintain 14"
5	37½"	2½"	10"	10"	9 9/16"	11¼"	11½"	14"
6	37"	3"	9½"	9½"	9 1/16"	10¾"	Use 37" Maintain 11½"	Use 37" Maintain 14"
7	36½"	3½"	9"	9"	8 9/16"	10¼"	11½"	14"
8	36"	4"	8½"	8½"	8 1/16"	9¾"	Use 36" Maintain 11½"	Use 36" Maintain 14"
9	35½"	4½"	8"	8"	7 9/16"	9¼"	11½"	14"
PW	35½"	4½"	8"	8"	7 9/16"	9¼"	11½"	14"
SW	35½"	4½"	8"	8"	7 9/16"	9¼"	11½"	14"

[1]This table gives standard iron shaft flexes based on a 1" dimension from back of heel to tip end of shaft when installed in a head. This is considered to most closely approximate the traditional standard assembly. See Figure 57-1. Shafts installed in iron heads with a greater dimension than 1" may sometimes have to be tipped slightly (usually ⅛" to ⅜") to make the back of the heel to first step dimension conform to the above.

The back of heel to first step dimensions above were derived by taking the actual shaft manufacturer's blueprint dimensions of uncut shafts from the tip end to the first step and adding ½".

[2]"S" – Stiff   "RS" – Mid Stiff   "R" – Regular   "AR" – Flexible.

[3] All trimming to length must be from the butt end only to maintain the torsion matching properties. This applies to both parallel tip and taper tip models. For this reason, both parallel tip and taper tip shafts must be purchased in the standard 1" incremental lengths offered.

MASTERFLEX

Club No.	[1]Finished Club Length (Modern Standard)	Uncut Shaft Length	[2]Amount to Trim From Tip [3]For X, TS, S, RS and R Flexes
1	39½"	39"	0"
2	39"	39"	⅛"
3	38½"	39"	¼"
4	38"	39"	⅜"
5	37½"	39"	½"
6	37"	39"	⅝"
7	36½"	39"	¾"
8	36"	39"	⅞"
9	35½"	39"	1"
PW	35½"	39"	1"
SW	35½"	39"	1"

[1]After tip trimming and installation of shaft in head, trim butt of shaft to overall club length.

[2]For each ½" added to standard club length, the shaft should be tipped an additional ⅛" to maintain the standard flex unless a slightly softer feel is desired.

[3]"X" – Extra Stiff   "TS" – Tour Stiff   "S" – Stiff   "RS" – Mid Stiff   "R" – Regular.

Club No.	[2][3]Finished Club Length (Modern Standard)	Uncut Shaft Length S/R	Uncut Shaft Length A	Shadow "S"	Shadow "R"	Shadow "A"	AP44 "S"	AP44 "R"	AP46 "R"
1	39½"	41"	39"	12¾"	14¾"	17"	10⅝"	12⅝"	N/A
2	39"	41"	39"	12¼"	14¼"	16½"	10⅛"	12⅛"	N/A
3	38½"	41"	39"	11¾"	13¾"	16"	9⅝"	11⅝"	13 15/16"
4	38"	41"	39"	11¼"	13¼"	15½"	9⅛"	11⅛"	13 7/16"
5	37½"	41"	39"	10¾"	12¾"	15"	8⅝"	10⅝"	12 15/16"
6	37"	41"	39"	10¼"	12¼"	14½"	8⅛"	10⅛"	12 7/16"
7	36½"	41"	39"	9¾"	11¾"	14"	7⅝"	9⅝"	11 15/16"
8	36"	41"	39"	9¼"	11¼"	13½"	7⅛"	9⅛"	11 7/16"
9	35½"	41"	39"	8¾"	10¾"	13"	6⅝"	8⅝"	10 15/16"
PW	35½"	41"	39"	8¾"	10¾"	13"	6⅝"	8⅝"	10 15/16"
SW	35½"	41"	39"	8¾"	10¾"	13"	6⅝"	8⅝"	10 15/16"

PARALLEL TIP IRON SHAFTS – MEN'S *cont.*
APOLLO

Club No.	Club Length (Modern Standard)	[2][3]Finished Uncut Shaft Length R/S	A	Spectre Flex "S"	Spectre Flex "R"	Spectre Flex "A"	Uncut Shaft Length	AP46 Comb. R/S "R"	AP46 Comb. R/S "S"
1	39½"	41"	40"	9½"	11½"	9½"	40"	N/A	N/A
2	39"	41"	40"	9"	11"	9"	40"	N/A	N/A
3	38½"	41"	40"	8½"	10½"	8½"	40"	12 15/16"	10 15/16"
4	38"	41"	40"	8"	10"	8"	40"	12 7/16"	10 7/16"
5	37½"	41"	40"	7½"	9½"	7½"	40"	11 15/16"	9 15/16"
6	37"	41"	40"	7"	9"	7"	40"	11 7/16"	9 7/16"
7	36½"	41"	40"	6½"	8½"	6½"	40"	10 15/16"	8 15/16"
8	36"	41"	40"	6"	8"	6"	40"	10 7/16"	8 7/16"
9	35½"	41"	40"	5½"	7½"	5½"	40"	9 15/16"	7 15/16"
PW	35½"	41"	40"	5½"	7½"	5½"	40"	9 15/16"	7 15/16"
SW	35½"	41"	40"	5½"	7½"	5½"	40"	9 15/16"	7 15/16"

PARALLEL TIP IRON SHAFTS – LADIES'
TRUE TEMPER® AND BRUNSWICK

Club No.	[2][3]Finished Club Length (Modern Ladies' Standard)	[1]Amount Normally Trimmed From Tip of Shaft	Dynamic UDIAL "L"	Dynamic UDIALO "L"	TT Lite U2LIAL "L"	Flex Flow UTFFIL "L"	Gold Plus UGPIL "L"	[5]Contour UTRIL "L"
2	38"	½"	15⅜"	17¼"	10½"	15"	13½"	14½"
3	37½"	1"	14⅞"	16¾"	10"	14½"	13"	14⅜"
4	37"	1½"	14⅜"	16¼"	9½"	14"	12½"	14¼"
5	36½"	2"	13⅞"	15¾"	9"	13½"	12"	14⅛"
6	36"	2½"	13⅜"	15¼"	8½"	13"	11½"	14"
7	35½"	3"	12⅞"	14¾"	8"	12½"	11"	13⅞"
8	35"	3½"	12⅜"	14¼"	7½"	12"	10½"	13¾"
9	34½"	4"	11⅞"	13¾"	7"	11½"	10"	13⅝"
PW	34½"	4"	11⅞"	13¾"	7"	11"	9½"	13⅝"
SW	34½"	4"	11⅞"	13¾"	7"	11"	9½"	13⅝"

Club No.	[2][3]Finished Club Length (Modern Ladies' Standard)	[1]Amount Normally Trimmed From Tip of Shaft	Vanadium Sonic IL "L"	Phoenix IAL "L"	Propel II IAL "L"	Mark II IL "L"	Super Champion IL "L"	Champion IL "L"	Microtaper UPMIAL "L"
2	38"	½"	12½"	10½"	15⅜"	13"	16⅜"	10½"	16¾"
3	37½"	1"	12"	10"	14⅞"	12½"	15⅞"	10"	16¼"
4	37"	1½"	11½"	9½"	14⅜"	12"	15⅜"	9½"	15¾"
5	36½"	2"	11"	9"	13⅞"	11½"	14⅞"	9"	15¼"
6	36"	2½"	10½"	8½"	13⅜"	11"	14⅜"	8½"	14¾"
7	35½"	3"	10"	8"	12⅞"	10½"	13⅞"	8"	14¼"
8	35"	3½"	9½"	7½"	12⅜"	10"	13⅜"	7½"	13¾"
9	34½"	[6]4"	9"	7"	11⅞"	9½"	12⅞"	7"	13¼"
PW	34½"	[6]4"	9"	7"	11⅞"	9½"	12⅞"	7"	13¼"
SW	34½"	[6]4"	9"	7"	11⅞"	9½"	12⅞"	7"	13¼"

PARALLEL TIP IRON SHAFTS – LADIES'
TRUE TEMPER® AND APOLL0

Club No.	[2][3]Finished Club Length (Modern Ladies' Standard)	Uncut Shaft Length	Dynalite ULIAL "L"	Apollo Spectre Flex "L"	Uncut Shaft Length	Comet URIL "L"	Uncut Shaft Length	Apollo Shadow "L"	Apollo AP46 "L"
1	38½"	40"	N/A	N/A	39"	17⅜"	38"	18"	N/A
2	38"	40"	14¼"	10½"	39"	16⅞"	38"	17½"	N/A
3	37½"	40"	13¾"	10"	39"	16⅜"	38"	17"	16⅞"
4	37"	40"	13¼"	9½"	39"	15⅞"	38"	16½"	16⅜"
5	36½"	40"	12¾"	9"	39"	15⅜"	38"	16"	15⅞"
6	36"	40"	12¼"	8½"	39"	14⅞"	38"	15½"	15⅜"
7	35½"	40"	11¾"	8"	39"	14⅜"	38"	15"	14⅞"
8	35"	40"	11¼"	7½"	39"	13⅞"	38"	14½"	14⅜"
9	34½"	40"	10¾"	7"	39"	13⅜"	38"	14"	13⅞"
PW	34½"	40"	10¾"	7"	39"	13⅜"	38"	14"	13⅞"
SW	34½"	40"	10¾"	7"	39"	13⅜"	38"	14"	13⅞"

620

PARALLEL TIP WOOD SHAFTS

FOOTNOTES FOR THE FOLLOWING PARALLEL TIP WOOD SHAFT TABLES

[1]The following tables give standard wood shaft flexes based on a through head shaft bore which is considered the traditional standard assembly. Shafts installed in blind bore wood heads may sometimes need additional tipping (usually ¼" to ½") to make the back of heel to first step dimension conform to those below.

The back of heel to first step dimensions below were derived by taking the actual shaft manufacturer's blueprint dimensions of uncut shafts from the tip end to the first step and subtracting ½". The ½" is that distance from the back of the heel to the shaft tip. See Figure 57-2. Since these are parallel tip shafts which come in only one length, the blueprint tip length applies only to the driver. Therefore the above first step dimensions for the #2 through #7 woods were derived by subtracting an additional ½" for each successively shorter club.

[2]For each ½" added to standard club length, the shaft should be tipped an additional ½" to maintain the standard flex unless a slightly softer feel is desired. In most cases, it is doubtful that all but a highly accomplished player will feel these differences. It should also be noted that most manufacturers of blind bore woods simply pretrim the tip end in ½" increments and install the shaft to the bottom of the hole. This is not necessarily wrong as individual club head designs, club lengths, head weights, etc. are all part of the overall club performance that the manufacturer may have desired and confirmed by testing.

[3]After the shaft is installed in a head with the back of heel to first step dimensions as shown below (normal installation), the finished club length is obtained by trimming from the shaft butt.

[4]To maintain the proper flexing characteristics in the tip area, the parallel tip Contour shaft should be tip trimmed only to ⅛" increments for each ½" reduction in club length.

PARALLEL TIP WOOD SHAFTS – MEN'S
TRUE TEMPER®

Club No.	[2] [3]Finished Club Length (Modern Standard)	[1]Amount Normally Trimmed From Tip of Shaft	Dynamic Gold & Dynamic UDGWX & UDWX "X"	Dynamic Gold & Dynamic UDGWS & UDWS or UDWC "S"	Dynamic Gold & Dynamic UDGWR & UDWR or UDWC "R"	Dynamic UDWAL "A"	Jet Step UJWC "S"	Jet Step UJWC "R"	TT Lite U2LWS	TT Lite U2LWR
1	43"	0"	8"	10"	12"	11⅞"	10½"	12½"	11"	12½"
2	42½"	½"	7½"	9½"	11½"	11⅜"	10"	12"	10½"	12"
3	42"	1"	7"	9"	11"	10⅞"	9½"	11½"	10"	11½"
4	41½"	1½"	6½"	8½"	10½"	10⅜"	9"	11"	9½"	11"
5	41"	2"	6"	8"	10"	9⅞"	8½"	10½"	9"	10½"
6	40½"	2½"	5½"	7½"	9½"	9⅜"	8"	10"	8½"	10"
7	40"	3"	5"	7"	9"	8⅞"	7½"	9½"	8"	9½"

Club No.	[2] [3]Finished Club Length (Modern Standard)	[1]Amount Normally Trimmed From Tip of Shaft	TT Lite U2LWAL "A"	TT Lite UTTLWC "S"	TT Lite UTTLWC "R"	*Gold Plus UGPWXH "X"	*Gold Plus UGPWSH "S"	*Gold Plus UGPWRH "R"	[4]Contour UTRWS	[4]Contour UTRWR
1	43"	0"	12"	10"	12"	5¼"	6¾"	7½"	11"	13"
2	42½"	½"	11½"	9½"	11½"	4¾"	6¼"	7"	10⅞"	12⅞"
3	42"	1"	11"	9"	11"	4¼"	5¾"	6½"	10¾"	12¾"
4	41½"	1½"	10½"	8½"	10½"	3¾"	5¼"	6"	10⅝"	12⅝"
5	41"	2"	10"	8"	10"	3¼"	4¾"	5½"	10½"	12½"
6	40½"	2½"	9½"	7½"	9½"	–	4¼"	5"	10⅜"	12⅜"
7	40"	3"	9"	7"	9"	–	3¾"	4½"	10¼"	12¼"

*True Temper® Gold Plus shafts were originally designed for metal woods but can also be used in conventional woods. However, the tip section length of the "X" and "S" flex are too short for proper installation into conventional higher lofted fairway woods having normal hosel lengths. To accommodate this, the recommended back of heel to first step dimensions may be increased by 1". This will yield an in-between flex that can be countered by reducing swingweight by 4 points.

PARALLEL TIP WOOD SHAFTS – MEN'S *cont.*
TRUE TEMPER®

Club No.	Finished Club Length (Modern Standard)	*Uncut Shaft Length for Flex Flow	Flex Flow UTFFWS "S"	Flex Flow UTFFWR "R"	Flex Flow UTFFWA "A"
1	43"	44"	7¾"	9¼"	11½"
2	42½"	44"	7¼"	8¾"	11"
3	42"	43"	6¾"	8¼"	10½"
4	41½"	42½"	6¼"	7¾"	10"
5	41"	42"	5¾"	7¼"	9½"
6	40½"	41½"	5¼"	6¾"	9"
7	40"	41½"	4¾"	6¼"	8½"

*To achieve the recommended back of heel to first step dimension, be certain to choose the recommended Uncut Shaft Length. Tip trimming should be performed only if the same length is cut from the tip of all the shafts in the set. If consistent tip trimming is not maintained, then the Flex Flow's recessed section will fall out of alignment.

Club No.	2 3 Finished Club Length (Modern Standard)	Uncut Shaft Length R/S	Uncut Shaft Length A	Uncut Shaft Length X	Dynalite ULWXH "X"	Dynalite ULWCH "S"	Dynalite ULWCH "R"	Dynalite ULWAL "A"	Pro-Fit UPWC "S"	Pro-Fit UPWC "R"
1	43"	47"	46"	45"	7½"	9"	11"	12½"	10"	12"
2	42½"	47"	46"	45"	7"	8½"	10½"	12"	9½"	11½"
3	42"	47"	46"	45"	6½"	8"	10"	11½"	9"	11"
4	4½"	47"	46"	45"	6"	7½"	9½"	11"	8½"	10½"
5	41"	47"	46"	45"	5½"	7"	9"	10½"	8"	10"
6	40½"	47"	46"	45"	5"	6½"	8½"	10"	7½"	9½"
7	40"	47"	46"	45"	4½"	6"	8"	9½"	7"	9"

Club No.	2 3 Finished Club Length (Modern Standard)	Uncut Shaft Length	Dynamic Lite UDLWS "S"	Dynamic Lite UDLWR "R"	Dynalite Gold ULGWSH "S"	Dynalite Gold ULGWRH "R"	Dynalite Gold ULGWXH "X"
1	43"	45"	9½"	10½"	9"	11"	7½"
2	42½"	45"	9"	10"	8½"	10½"	7"
3	42"	45"	8½"	9½"	8"	10"	6½"
4	41½"	45"	8"	9"	7½"	9½"	6"
5	41"	45"	7½"	8½"	7"	9"	5½"
6	40½"	45"	7"	8"	6½"	8½"	5"
7	40"	45"	6½"	7½"	6"	8"	5"

PARALLEL TIP WOOD SHAFTS – MEN'S
TRUE TEMPER® AND APOLL0

Club No.	[2][3] Finished Club Length (Modern Standard)	Uncut Shaft Length	Comet URWC "S"	Comet URWC "R"	Apollo Shadow "S"	Apollo Shadow "R"	Uncut Shaft Length	Apollo Shadow "A"
1	43"	47"	9"	11"	13⅝"	15⅝"	45"	15⅞"
3	42"	47"	8"	10"	12⅝"	14⅝"	45"	14⅞"
5	41"	47"	7"	9"	11⅝"	13⅝"	45"	13⅞"
7	40"	47"	6"	8"	10⅝"	12⅝"	45"	12⅞"

Club No.	[2][3] Finished Club Length (Modern Standard)	Uncut Shaft Length R/S	Uncut Shaft Length A	AP44 "S"	AP44 "R"	Spectre Flex "S"	Spectre Flex "R"	Spectre Flex "A"
1	43"	47"	46"	9½"	10½"	10½"	11½"	12"
3	42"	47"	46"	8½"	9½"	9½"	10½"	11"
4	41½"	47"	46"	8"	9"	9"	10"	10½"
5	41"	47"	46"	7½"	8½"	8½"	9½"	10"
7	40"	47"	46"	6½"	7½"	7½"	8½"	9"

APOLLO

Club No.	[2][3] Finished Club Length (Modern Standard)	Uncut Shaft Length	AP46 Comb. R/S "R"	AP46 Comb. R/S "S"	Uncut Shaft Length	AP46 "R"
1	43"	46"	12¼"	10¼"	44"	9¹⁵⁄₁₆"
2	42½"	46"	11¾"	9¾"	44"	9⁷⁄₁₆"
3	42"	46"	11¼"	9¼"	44"	8¹⁵⁄₁₆"
4	41½"	46"	10¾"	8¾"	44"	8⁷⁄₁₆"
5	41"	46"	10¼"	8¼"	44"	7¹⁵⁄₁₆"
6	40½"	46"	9¾"	7¾"	44"	7⁷⁄₁₆"
7	40"	46"	9¼"	7¼"	44"	6¹⁵⁄₁₆"

Club No.	[2][3] Finished Club Length (Modern Standard)	[1] Amount Normally Trimmed From Tip of Shaft	[1] Matchflex 4 [2](S)	[1] Matchflex 3 [2](RS)	[1] Matchflex 2 [2](R)	[1] Matchflex 1 [2](AR)	Uncut Shaft Length For Torsion Matched	[3] Torsion Matched "S"	[3] Torsion Matched "R"
1	43"	0"	12¾"	9¾"	13⁸⁄₁₀"	13¼"	44"	11"	13"
2	42½"	½"	12¼"	9¼"	13³⁄₁₀"	12¾"	44"	Use 44" Maintain 11"	Use 44" Maintain 13"
3	42"	1"	11¾"	8¾"	12⁸⁄₁₀"	12¼"	43"	11"	13"
4	41½"	1½"	11¼"	8¼"	12³⁄₁₀"	11¾"	43"	Use 43" Maintain 11"	Use 44" Maintain 13"
5	41"	2"	10¾"	7¾"	11⁸⁄₁₀"	11¼"	42"	11"	13"
6	40½"	2½"	10¼"	7¼"	11³⁄₁₀"	10¾"	42"	11"	13"
7	40"	3"	9¾"	6¾"	10⁸⁄₁₀"	10¼"	42"	11"	13"

[1]This table gives standard wood shaft flexes based on a through head shaft bore which is considered the traditional standard assembly. Shafts installed in blind bore wood heads may sometimes have to be tipped slightly (usually ¼" to ½") to make the back of heel to first step dimension conform to the above.

The back of heel to first step dimensions above were derived by taking the actual shaft manufacturer's dimensions of uncut shafts from the tip end to the first step and subtracting ½". The ½" is that distance from the back of the heel to the shaft tip. See Figure 57-2.

[2]"S" – Stiff   "RS" – Mid Stiff   "R" – Regular   "AR" – Flexible

[3]All trimming to length must be from the butt end only to maintain the torsion matching properties. This applies to both parallel tip and taper tip models. For this reason, both parallel tip and taper tip shafts must be purchased in the standard 1" incremental lengths offered.

APOLLO

Club No.	Finished Club Length (Modern Standard)	Amount Normally Trimmed From Tip of Shaft	Masterflex VI [2](X)	Masterflex V [2](TS)	Masterflex IV [2](S)	Masterflex III [2](RS)	Masterflex II [2](R)
1	43"	0"	13$\frac{1}{10}$"	13$\frac{9}{16}$"	12½"	12½"	12$\frac{3}{10}$"
2	42½"	½"	12$\frac{6}{10}$"	13$\frac{1}{16}$"	12"	12"	11$\frac{8}{10}$"
3	42"	1"	12$\frac{1}{10}$"	12$\frac{9}{16}$"	11½"	11½"	11$\frac{3}{10}$"
4	41½"	1½"	11$\frac{6}{10}$"	12$\frac{1}{16}$"	11"	11"	10$\frac{8}{10}$"
5	41"	2"	11$\frac{1}{10}$"	11$\frac{9}{16}$"	10½"	10½"	10$\frac{3}{10}$"
6	40½"	2½"	10$\frac{6}{10}$"	11$\frac{1}{16}$"	10"	10"	9$\frac{8}{10}$"
7	40"	3"	10$\frac{1}{10}$"	10$\frac{9}{16}$"	9½"	9½"	9$\frac{3}{10}$"

[1] This table gives standard wood shaft flexes based on a through head shaft bore which is considered the traditional standard assembly. Shafts installed in blind bore wood heads may sometimes have to be tipped slightly (usually ¼" to ½") to make the back of heel to first step dimension conform to the above.

The back of heel to first step dimensions above were derived by taking the actual shaft manufacturer's dimensions of uncut shafts from the tip end to the first step and subtracting ½". The ½" is that distance from the back of the heel to the shaft tip. See Figure 57-2.

[2] "X" – Extra Stiff   "TS" – Tour Stiff   "S" – Stiff   "RS" – Mid Stiff   "R" – Regular

PARALLEL TIP WOOD SHAFTS – MEN'S
BRUNSWICK

Club No.	[2][3] Finished Club Length (Modern Standard)	[1] Amount Normally Trimmed From Tip of Shaft	Vanadium Sonic WX "X"	Vanadium Sonic WS "S"	Vanadium Sonic WR "R"	Phoenix WS "S"	Phoenix WR "R"	Phoenix WAL "A"	Microtaper UPMWC "S"	Microtaper UPMWC "R"
1	43"	0"	8½"	10¼"	12"	11"	12½"	11"	11¾"	13¾"
2	42½"	½"	8"	9¾"	11½"	10½"	12"	10½"	11¼"	13¼"
3	42"	1"	7½"	9¼"	11"	10"	11½"	10"	10¾"	12¾"
4	41½"	1½"	7"	8¾"	10½"	9½"	11"	9½"	10¼"	12¼"
5	41"	2"	6½"	8¼"	10"	9"	10½"	9"	9¾"	11¾"
6	40½"	2½"	6"	7¾"	9½"	8½"	10"	8½"	9¼"	11¼"
7	40"	3"	5½"	7¼"	9"	8"	9½"	8"	8¾"	10¾"

Club No.	[2][3] Finished Club Length (Modern Standard)	[1] Amount Normally Trimmed From Tip of Shaft	Microtaper UPMWAL "A"	Propel II WRS "S"	Propel II WRS "R"	Propel II WAL "A"	Mark II WR "R"	Super Champion WR "R"	Champion WR "R"
1	43"	0"	14¾"	10"	12"	10⅞"	10½"	9$\frac{15}{16}$"	9½"
2	42½"	½"	14¼"	9½"	11½"	10⅜"	10"	9$\frac{7}{16}$"	9"
3	42"	1"	13¾"	9"	11"	9⅞"	9½"	8$\frac{15}{16}$"	8½"
4	41½"	1½"	13¼"	8½"	10½"	9⅜"	9"	8$\frac{7}{16}$"	8"
5	41"	2"	12¾"	8"	10"	8⅞"	8½"	7$\frac{15}{16}$"	7½"
6	40½"	2½"	12¼"	7½"	9½"	8⅜"	8"	7$\frac{7}{16}$"	7"
7	40"	3"	11¾"	7"	9"	7⅞"	7½"	6$\frac{15}{16}$"	6½"

Club No.	[2][3] Finished Club Length (Modern Standard)	Precision FM & FW Amount to Trim From Tip For All Flexes
1	43"	0"
2	42½"	1$\frac{1}{16}$"
3	42"	1⅜"
4	41½"	2$\frac{1}{16}$"
5	41"	2¾"
6	40½"	3$\frac{7}{16}$"
7	40"	4⅛"

PARALLEL TIP WOOD SHAFTS – LADIES'
TRUE TEMPER® AND APOLLO

Club No.	[2][3]Finished Club Length (Modern Standard)	Uncut Shaft Length	Comet URWL "L"	Apollo Shadow "L"	Uncut Shaft Length	Apollo Spectre Flex "L"
1	42"	44"	16¾"	16½"	46"	13"
3	41"	44"	15¾"	15½"	46"	12"
4	40½"	44"	15¼"	15"	46"	11½"
5	40"	44"	14¾"	14½"	46"	11"
7	39"	44"	13¾"	13½"	46"	10"

Club No.	[2][3]Finished Club Length (Modern Standard)	Uncut Shaft Length	Dynalite ULWAL "L"	Uncut Shaft Length	Apollo AP46 "L"
1	42"	46"	13½"	44"	15¹⁵⁄₁₆"
2	41½"	46"	13"	44"	15⁷⁄₁₆"
3	41"	46"	12½"	44"	14¹⁵⁄₁₆"
4	40½"	46"	12"	44"	14⁷⁄₁₆"
5	40"	46"	11½"	44"	13¹⁵⁄₁₆"
6	39½"	46"	11"	44"	13⁷⁄₁₆"
7	39"	46"	10½"	44"	12¹⁵⁄₁₆"

TRUE TEMPER® AND BRUNSWICK

Club No.	[2][3]Finished Club Length (Modern Standard)	[1]Amount Normally Trimmed From Tip of Shaft	Dynamic UDWAL "L"	TT Lite U2LWAL "L"	Gold Plus UGPWLH "L"	[4]Contour UTRWL "L"	*Uncut Shaft Length For Flex Flow	Flex Flow UTFFWL "L"
1	42"	0"	12⅞"	13"	11"	13½"	44"	11½"
2	41½"	½"	12⅜"	12½"	10½"	13⅜"	44"	11"
3	41"	1"	11⅞"	12"	10"	13¼"	43"	10½"
4	40½"	1½"	11⅜"	11½"	9½"	13⅛"	42½	10"
5	40"	2"	10⅞"	11"	9"	13"	42"	9½"
6	39½"	2½"	10⅜"	10½"	8½"	12⅞"	41½"	9"
7	39"	3"	9⅞"	10"	8"	12¾"	41½"	8½"

*To achieve the recommended back of heel to first step dimension for the Flex Flow, be certain to choose the recommended Uncut Shaft Length. Tip trimming should be performed only if the same length is cut from the tip of all shafts in the set. Failure to maintain consistent tip trimming will result in the Flex Flow's recessed section falling out of alignment.

Club No.	[2][3]Finished Club Length (Modern Standard)	[1]Amount Normally Trimmed From Tip of Shaft	Vanadium Sonic WL "L"	Phoenix WAL "L"	Propel II WAL "L"	Mark II WL "L"	Super Champion WL "L"	Champion WL "L"	Microtaper UPMWAL "L"
1	42"	0"	12¼"	13"	12⅞"	12"	16¾"	15½"	15¾"
2	41½"	½"	11¾"	12½"	12⅜"	11½"	16¼"	15"	15¼"
3	41"	1"	11¼"	12"	11⅞"	11"	15¾"	14½"	14¾"
4	40½"	1½"	10¾"	11½"	11⅜"	10½"	15¼"	14"	14¼"
5	40"	2"	10¼"	11"	10⅞"	10"	14¾"	13½"	13¾"
6	39½"	2½"	9¾"	10½"	10⅜"	9½"	14¼"	13"	13¼"
7	39"	3"	9¼"	10"	9⅞"	9"	13¾"	12½"	12¾"

METAL WOOD REINFORCED PARALLEL TIP SHAFTS – MEN'S & LADIES'
TRUE TEMPER®

Club No.	Finished Club Length (Modern Standard)	Uncut Shaft Length	Dynamic UDWCH or UDWRH "R"	Dynamic UDWCH or UDWSH "S"	TT Lite UTTLWCH "R"	TT Lite UTTLWCH "S"	TT Lite U2LWRH "R"	TT Lite U2LWSH "S"	Gold Plus UGPWXH "X"	Gold Plus UGPWSH "S"	Gold Plus UGPWRH "R"	Gold Plus UGPWLH (Use Ladies' Standard Club Length)
1	43"	43"	10½"	8½"	11½"	9½"	12"	10"	5¼"	6¾"	7½"	11"
2	42½"	43"	10"	8"	11"	9"	11½"	9½"	4¾"	6¼"	7"	10½"
3	42"	43"	9½"	7½"	10½"	8½"	11"	9"	4¼"	5¾"	6½"	10"
4	41½"	43"	9"	7"	10"	8"	10½"	8½"	3¾"	5¼"	6"	9½"
5	41"	43"	8½"	6½"	9½"	7½"	10"	8"	3¼"	4¾"	5½"	9"
6	40½"	43"	8"	6"	9"	7"	9½"	7½"	–	4¼"	5"	8½"
7	40"	43"	7½"	5½"	8½"	6½"	9"	7"	–	3¾"	4½"	8"

Club No.	Finished Club Length (Modern Standard)	4Contour UTRWS	4Contour UTRWR	4Contour UTRWL "L"	Uncut Shaft Length for Flex Flow	Flex Flow UTFFWSH "S"	Flex Flow UTFFWRH "R"	Flex Flow UTFFWLH (Use Ladies' Standard Club Length)
1	43"	9"	11"	11½"	43"	8¼"	9¾"	11½"
2	42½"	8⅞"	10⅞"	11⅜"	43"	7¾"	9¼"	11"
3	42"	8¾"	10¾"	11¼"	42"	7¼"	8¾"	10½"
4	41½"	8⅝"	10⅝"	11⅛"	41½"	6¾"	8¼"	10"
5	41"	8½"	10½"	11"	41"	6¼"	7¾"	9½"
6	40½"	8⅜"	10⅜"	10⅞"	40½"	5¾"	7¼"	9"
7	40"	8¼"	10¼"	10¾"	40½"	5¼"	6¾"	8½"

TAPER TIP IRON SHAFTS – MEN'S

FOOTNOTES FOR THE FOLLOWING TAPER TIP IRON SHAFT TABLES

[1]The following tables give standard iron shaft flexes based on a 1" dimension from back of heel to tip end of shaft when installed in a head. This is considered to most closely approximate the traditional standard assembly. See Figure 57-1. Shafts installed in iron heads with a greater dimension than 1" may sometimes have to be tipped slightly (usually ⅛" to ⅜") to make the back of heel to first step dimension conform.

The back of heel to first step dimension below were derived by taking the actual shaft manufacturer's blueprint dimensions of uncut shafts from the tip end to the first step and adding ½".

[2]For each ½" added to standard club length, the shaft should be tipped an additional ½" to maintain the standard flex unless a slightly softer feel is desired. In most cases, it is doubtful that all but a highly accomplished player will feel these differences. Some golf club manufacturers' models will not conform exactly to those dimensions given in the tables below. This is not necessarily wrong as individual club head designs, club lengths, head weights, etc. are all part of the overall club performance that the manufacturer may have desired and confirmed by testing.

[3]If the PW and the SW are to be 35" long, the 35" uncut shaft can be tipped ½", then, subtract ½" from the back of heel to first step dimensions shown in the tables below for the PW and SW only.

[4]Each individual shaft length is not available in every pattern shaft.

[5]"X" – Extra Stiff   "TS" – Tour Stiff   "S" – Stiff   "RS" – Mid Stiff   "R" – Regular

TAPER TIP IRON SHAFTS – MEN'S
TRUE TEMPER®

Club No.	[2]Finished Club Length (Modern Standard)	Uncut Shaft Length	Dynamic & Dynamic Gold DIX & DGIX	Dynamic & Dynamic Gold DIS & DGIS	Dynamic & Dynamic Gold DIT & DGIT	Dynamic DIA
1	39½"	39"	10½"	12½"	15¼"	16¼"
2	39"	38½"	10"	12"	14¾"	15¾"
3	38½"	38"	9½"	11½"	14¼"	15¼"
4	38"	37½"	9"	11"	13¾"	14¾"
5	37½"	37"	8½"	10½"	13¼"	14¼"
6	37"	36½"	8"	10"	12¾"	13¾"
7	36½"	36"	7½"	9½"	12¼"	13¼"
8	36"	35½"	7"	9"	11¾"	12¾"
9	35½"	35"	6½"	8½"	11¼"	12¼"
PW	35½"	[3]35"	6½"	8½"	11¼"	12¼"
SW	35½"	[3]35"	6½"	8½"	11¼"	12¼"

Club No.	[2]Finished Club Length (Modern Standard)	Uncut Shaft Length	Pro-Fit PFIS	Pro-Fit PFIR	Pro-Fit PFIA	Jet Step JTIS	*Dynamic NDIS (Modified) GolfWorks®
1	39½"	39"	15⅛"	14⅞"	16⅜"	15"	16¼"
2	39"	38½"	14⅝"	14⅜"	15⅞"	14½"	15¾"
3	38½"	38"	14⅛"	13⅞"	15⅜"	14"	15¼"
4	38"	37½"	13⅝"	13⅜"	14⅞"	13½"	14¾"
5	37½"	37"	13⅛"	12⅞"	14⅜"	13"	14¼"
6	37"	36½"	12⅝"	12⅜"	13⅞"	12½"	13¾"
7	36½"	36"	12⅛"	11⅞"	13⅜"	12"	13¼"
8	36"	35½"	11⅝"	11⅜"	12⅞"	11½"	12¾"
9	35½"	35"	11⅛"	10⅞"	12⅛"	11"	12¼"
PW	35½"	[3]35"	11⅛"	10⅞"	12⅛"	11"	12¼"
SW	35½"	[3]35"	11⅛"	10⅞"	12⅛"	11"	12¼"

*NDIS is the True Temper® code designation for "New Dynamic Iron Stiff." This shaft was developed many years ago by True Temper®. The shaft, however, was thought to be too flexible by touring professionals and better players so the above modified version was developed in the early 1960's to have a firmer feel. It is a special order shaft and is usually only available in 3 or 5 lengths and not in ½" increments. The above tables shows proper tipping for these lengths. Regardless of the lengths used, the distance shown above from the back of the heel to the first step would apply for a standard flex. Tour players and harder hitting, lower handicap players usually prefer this shaft tipped ½" to 1½".

TAPER TIP IRON SHAFTS – MEN'S *cont.*
TRUE TEMPER®

Club No.	[2]Finished Club Length (Modern Standard)	Uncut Shaft Length	Jet Step JTIR	Contour TRIS	Contour TRIR	TT Lite 2LIS	TT Lite 2LIR	TT Lite 2LIA	Extralite SLIS	Extralite SLIR
1	39½"	39"	16"	12½"	14"	9½"	11½"	9½"	11"	13"
2	39"	38½"	15½"	12"	13½"	9"	11"	9"	10½"	12½"
3	38½"	38"	15"	11½"	13"	8½"	10½"	8½"	10"	12"
4	38"	37½"	14½"	11"	12½"	8"	10"	8"	9½"	11½"
5	37½"	37"	14"	10½"	12"	7½"	9½"	7½"	9"	11"
6	37"	36½"	13½"	10"	11½"	7"	9"	7"	8½"	10½"
7	36½"	36"	13"	9½"	11"	6½"	8½"	6½"	8"	10"
8	36"	35½"	12½"	9"	10½"	6"	8"	6"	7½"	9½"
9	35½"	35"	12"	8½"	10"	5½"	7½"	5½"	7"	9"
PW	35½"	[3]35"	12"	8½"	10"	5½"	7½"	5½"	7"	9"
SW	35½"	[3]35"	12"	8½"	10"	5½"	7½"	5½"	7"	9"

Club No.	[2]Finished Club Length (Modern Standard)	Uncut Shaft Length	Gold Plus GPIX "X"	Gold Plus GPIS "S"	Gold Plus GPIR "R"
1	39½"	39½"	10½"	11"	12½"
2	39"	39"	10"	10½"	12"
3	38½"	38½"	9½"	10"	11½"
4	38"	38"	9"	9½"	11"
5	37½"	37½"	8½"	9"	10½"
6	37"	37"	8"	8½"	10"
7	36½"	36½"	7½"	8"	9½"
8	36"	36"	7"	7½"	9"
9	35½"	35½"	6½"	7"	8½"
PW	35½"	35½"	6½"	7"	8½"
SW	35½"	35½"	6½"	7"	8½"

Club No.	[2]Finished Club Length (Modern Standard)	*Uncut Shaft Length	Flex Flow TFFIS "S"	Flex Flow TFFIR "R"	Flex Flow TFFIA "A"
2	39"	39"	11¾"	13"	14"
3	38½"	38½"	11¼"	12½"	13½"
4	38"	38"	10¾"	12"	13"
5	37½"	37½"	10¼"	11½"	12½"
6	37"	37"	9¾"	11"	12"
7	36½"	36½"	9¼"	10½"	11½"
8	36"	36"	8¾"	10"	11"
9	35½"	35½"	8¼"	9½"	10½"
PW	35½"	35"	7¾"	9"	10"
SW	35½"	35"	7¾"	9"	10"

*To achieve the recommended back of heel to first step dimension, be certain to choose the recommended uncut shaft length. Tip trimming should be performed only if the same length is cut from the tips of all the shafts in the set. Failure to maintain consistent tip trimming will result in the Flex Flow's recessed section falling out of alignment.

TAPER TIP IRON SHAFTS – MEN'S *cont.*
TRUE TEMPER®

Club No.	[2]Finished Club Length (Modern Standard)	Uncut Shaft Length	Dynalite LIX "X"	Dynalite LIS "S"	Dynalite LIR "R"	Dynamic Lite DLIX "X"	Dynamic Lite DLIS "S"	Dynamic Lite DLIR "R"	Dynalite Gold LIX "X"	Dynalite Gold LIS "S"	Dynalite Gold LIR "R"
1	39½"	39"	13"	15"	16"	11½"	12"	14½"	13"	15"	16"
2	39"	38½"	12½"	14½"	15½"	11"	11½"	14"	12½"	14½"	15½"
3	38½"	38"	12"	14"	15"	10½"	11"	13½"	12"	14"	15"
4	38"	37½"	11½"	13½"	14½"	10"	10½"	13"	11½"	13½"	14½"
5	37½"	37"	11"	13"	14"	9½"	10"	12½"	11"	13"	14"
6	37"	36½"	10½"	12½"	13½"	9"	9½"	12"	10½"	12½"	13½"
7	36½"	36"	10"	12"	13"	8½"	9"	11½"	10"	12"	13"
8	36"	35½"	9½"	11½"	12½"	8"	8½"	11"	9½"	11½"	12½"
9	35½"	35"	9"	11"	12"	7½"	8"	10½"	9"	11"	12"
PW	35½"	35"	9"	11"	12"	7½"	8"	10½"	9"	11"	12"
SW	35½"	35"	9"	11"	12"	7½"	8"	10½"	9"	11"	12"

TAPER TIP IRON SHAFTS – MEN'S
BRUNSWICK

Club No.	[2]Finished Club Length (Modern Standard)	[4]Uncut Shaft Length	Propel II IX "X"	Propel II IS "S"	Propel II IR "R"	Propel II IA "A"	Mark II IR "R"	Super Champion IR "R"
1	39½"	39"	Tip 39" to 10½"	12½"	14"	16¼"	–	–
2	39"	38½"	10"	12"	13½"	15¾"	–	–
3	38½"	38"	Tip 38" to 9½"	11½"	13"	15¼"	12"	12¹⁵⁄₁₆"
4	38"	37½"	9"	11"	12½"	14¾"	–	–
5	37½"	37"	Tip 37" to 8½"	10½"	12"	14¼"	–	–
6	37"	36½"	8"	10"	11½"	13¾"	–	–
7	36½"	36"	Tip 36" to 7½"	9½"	11"	13¼"	10"	10¹⁵⁄₁₆"
8	36"	35½"	7"	9"	10½"	12¾"	–	–
9	35½"	35"	6½"	8½"	10"	12¼"	–	–
PW	35½"	[3]35"	6½"	8½"	10"	12¼"	–	–
SW	35½"	[3]35"	6½"	8½"	10"	12¼"	–	–

Club No.	[2]Finished Club Length (Modern Standard)	Uncut Shaft Length	Bruns Lite IV "V"	UCV-304 IX "X"	UCV-304 IS "S"	UCV-304 IR "R"	Phoenix IS "S"	Phoenix IR "R"
1	39½"	39"	12¾"	Tip 39" to 11½"	13½"	14½"	9½"	11½"
2	39"	38½"	12¼"	11"	13"	14"	9"	11"
3	38½"	38"	11¾"	Tip 38" to 10½"	12½"	13½"	8½"	10½"
4	38"	37½"	11¼"	10"	12"	13"	8"	10"
5	37½"	37"	10¾"	Tip 37" to 9½"	11½"	12½"	7½"	9½"
6	37"	36½"	10¼"	9"	11"	12"	7"	9"
7	36½"	36"	9¾"	Tip 36" to 8½"	10½"	11½"	6½"	8½"
8	36"	35½"	9¼"	8"	10"	11"	6"	8"
9	35½"	35"	8¾"	7½"	9½"	10½"	5½"	7½"
PW	35½"	[3]35"	8¾"	7½"	9½"	10½"	5½"	7½"
SW	35½"	[3]35"	8¾"	7½"	9½"	10½"	5½"	7½"

TAPER TIP IRON SHAFTS – MEN'S
APOLLO

Club No.	[2]Finished Club Length (Modern Standard)	Uncut Shaft Length	Masterflex VI [5]"X"	Masterflex V [5]"TS"	Masterflex IV [5]"S"	Masterflex III [5]"RS"	Masterflex III [5]"R"
1	39½"	39"	11¾"	12¼"	12 9/10"	13"	13 2/10"
2	39"	38½"	11¼"	11¾"	12 4/10"	12½"	12 7/10"
3	38½"	38"	10¾"	11¼"	11 9/10"	12"	12 2/10"
4	38"	37½"	10¼"	10¾"	11 4/10"	11½"	11 7/10"
5	37½"	37"	9¾"	10¼"	10 9/10"	11"	11 2/10"
6	37"	36½"	9¼"	9¾"	10 4/10"	10½"	10 7/10"
7	36½"	36"	8¾"	9¼"	9 9/10"	10"	10 2/10"
8	36"	35½"	8¼"	8¾"	9 4/10"	9½"	9 7/10"
9	35½"	35"	7¾"	8¼"	8 9/10"	9"	9 2/10"
PW	35½"	35"	7¾"	8¼"	8 9/10"	9"	9 2/10"
SW	35½"	35"	7¾"	8¼"	8 9/10"	9"	9 2/10"

TAPER TIP IRON SHAFTS – LADIES'
TRUE TEMPER® & BRUNSWICK

Club No.	[2]Finished Club Length (Modern Standard)	Uncut Shaft Length	Pro-Fit PFIL	Control TRIL	TT Lite 2LIL	Extralite SLIL	Flex Flow TFFIL "L"
2	38"	38"	12"	13½"	10½"	14"	15"
3	37½"	37½"	11½"	13"	10"	13½"	14½"
4	37"	37"	11"	12½"	9½"	13"	14"
5	36½"	36½"	10½"	12"	9"	12½"	13½"
6	36"	36"	10"	11½"	8½"	12"	13"
7	35½"	35½"	9½"	11"	8"	11½"	12½"
8	35"	35"	9"	10½"	7½"	11"	12"
9	34½"	34½"	8½"	10"	7"	10½"	11½"
PW	34½"	34½"	8½"	10"	7"	10½"	11"
SW	34½"	34½"	8½"	10"	7"	10½"	11"

Club No.	[2]Finished Club Length (Modern Standard)	[4]Uncut Shaft Length	UCV-304 IL "L"	Phoenix IL "L"	Super Champion IL "L"	Champion IL "L"
2	38"	38"	13½"	11"	13"	11"
3	37½"	38"	Tip 38" to 13"	Tip 38" to 10½"	–	–
4	37"	37"	12½"	10"	–	–
5	36½"	37"	Tip 37" to 12"	Tip 37" to 9½"	–	–
6	36"	36"	11½"	9"	11"	9"
7	35½"	36"	Tip 36" to 11"	Tip 36" to 8½"	–	–
8	35"	35"	10½"	8"	–	–
9	34½"	35"	Tip 35" to 10"	Tip 35" to 7½"	–	–
PW	34½"	35"	Tip 35" to 10"	Tip 35" to 7½"	–	–
SW	34½"	35"	Tip 35" to 10"	Tip 35" to 7½"	–	–

TAPER TIP WOOD SHAFTS – MEN'S

FOOTNOTES FOR THE FOLLOWING TAPER TIP WOOD SHAFT TABLES

[1]The following tables give standard wood shaft flexes based on a through head shaft bore which is considered the traditional standard assembly. Shafts installed in blind bore wood heads may sometimes have to be tipped slightly (usually ¼" to ½") to make the back of heel to first step dimension conform.

The back of heel to first step dimensions below were derived by taking the actual shaft manufacturer's dimensions of uncut shafts from the tip end to the first step and subtracting ½". The ½" is that distance from the back of the heel to the shaft tip. See Figure 57-2.

[2]For each ½" added to standard club length, the shaft should be tipped an additional ½" to maintain the standard flex unless a slightly softer feel is desired. In most cases it is doubtful that all but a highly accomplished player will feel these differences. It should also be noted that most manufacturers of blind bore woods simply install the shaft to the bottom of the hole and do not tip it. This is not necessarily wrong as individual club head designs, club lengths, head weights, etc. are all part of the overall club performance that the manufacturer may have desired and confirmed by testing.

[3]The contour shaft has a recessed section in its tip which is a constant distance from the tip for all available lengths. Therefore, if the shaft is tipped, this recessed section woud vary up and down in relation to the back of the heel.

[4]Each individual shaft length is not available in every pattern shaft.

[5]The Bruns Lite™ shaft is made with a constant tip length. The various raw uncut shaft lengths are made by shortening the butt length by the appropriate amount. If a #2 wood is desired, use a 44" shaft and install in the normal manner, maintaining the 8½" distance from the back of the heel to the first step. Trim to overall club length from the butt.

[6]The UCV-304® shaft is made similar in design to the Bruns Lite™. Read note 5. The UCV-304® shaft is also available in a 45" length.

[7]Mark II and Super Champion can be tipped ½" for each successively shorter club.

[8]The UCV-304® "L" flex is made with a constant tip length. The various raw uncut shaft lengths are made by shortening the butt length by the appropriate amount. Use the uncut shaft lengths shown below and install in the normal manner, maintaining the 7½" distance from the back of the heel to the first step. Trim to overall club length from the butt.

[9]"X" – Extra Stiff   "TS" – Tour Stiff   "S" – Stiff   "RS" – Mid Stiff   "R" – Regular

TAPER TIP WOOD SHAFTS – MEN'S
TRUE TEMPER®

Club No.	[2]Finished Club Length (Modern Standard)	[4]Uncut Shaft Length	Dynamic & Dynamic Gold DWX & DGWX	Dynamic & Dynamic Gold DWS & DGWS	Dynamic & Dynamic Gold DWT & DGWT	Dynamic DWA	Jet Step JTWS	Jet Step JTWR	Pro-Fit PFWS	Pro-Fit PFWR
1	43"	44"	8¾"	10¾"	9½"	9½"	10"	11½"	11½"	11¼"
2	42½"	43½"	8¼"	10¼"	9"	9"	9½"	11"	11"	10¾"
3	42"	43"	7¾"	9¾"	8½"	8½"	9"	10½"	10½"	10¼"
4	41½"	42½"	7¼"	9¼"	8"	8"	8½"	10"	10"	9¾"
5	41"	42"	6¾"	8¾"	7½"	7½"	8"	9½"	9½"	9¼"
6	40½"	42"	Tip 42" to 6¼"	Tip 42" to 8¼"	Tip 42" to 7"	Tip 42" to 7"	Tip 42" to 7½"	Tip 42" to 9"	Tip 42" to 9"	Tip 42" to 8¾"
7	40"	42"	Tip 42" to 5¾"	Tip 42" to 7¾"	Tip 42" to 6½"	Tip 42" to 6½"	Tip 42" to 7"	Tip 42" to 8½"	Tip 42" to 8½"	Tip 42" to 8¼"

Club No.	[2]Finished Club Length (Modern Standard)	[4]Uncut Shaft Length	Pro-Fit PFWA	[3]Contour TRWS	[3]Contour TRWR	TT Lite 2LWS	TT Lite 2LWR	TT Lite 2LWA	Extralite SLWS	Extralite SLWR
1	43"	44"	10⅞"	10½"	12"	10"	11½"	11"	10½"	12½"
2	42½"	43½"	10⅜"	Use 44" @ 10½"	Use 44" @ 12"	9½"	11"	10½"	Tip 44" to 10"	Tip 44" to 12"
3	42"	43"	9⅞"	9½"	11"	9"	10½"	10"	9½"	11½"
4	41½"	42½"	9⅜"	Use 43" @ 9½"	Use 43" @ 11"	8½"	10"	9½"	Tip 43" to 9"	Tip 43" to 11"
5	41"	42"	8⅞"	8½"	10"	8"	9½"	9"	8½"	10½"
6	40½"	42"	Tip 42" to 8⅜"	Use 42" @ 8½"	Use 42" @ 10"	Tip 42" to 7½"	Tip 42" to 9"	Tip 42" to 8½"	Tip 42" to 8"	Tip 42" to 10"
7	40"	42"	Tip 42" to 7⅞"	Use 42" @ 8½"	Use 42" @ 10"	Tip 42" to 7"	Tip 42" to 8½"	Tip 42" to 8"	Tip 42" to 7½"	Tip 42" to 9½"

Club No.	[2]Finished Club Length (Modern Standard)	Uncut Shaft Length	Gold Plus GPWX "X"	Gold Plus GPWS "S"	Gold Plus GPWR "R"
1	43"	44"	7"	7"	8½"
2	42½"	43½"	6½"	6½"	8"
3	42"	43"	6"	6"	7½"
4	41½"	42½"	5½"	5½"	7"
5	41"	42"	5"	5"	6½"
6	40½"	42"	4½"	4½"	6"
7	40"	42"	4"	4"	5½"

TAPER TIP WOOD SHAFTS – MEN'S *cont.*
TRUE TEMPER®

Club No.	[2]Finished Club Length (Modern Standard)	*Uncut Shaft Length For Flex Flow	Flex Flow TFFWS "S"	Flex Flow TFFWR "R"	Flex Flow TFFWA "A"	Uncut Shaft Length For NDWS	[1]Dynamic NDWS
1	43"	44"	9"	10½"	11½"	44"	11⅜"
2	42½"	43½"	8½"	10"	11"	44"	10⅞"
3	42"	43"	8"	9½"	10½"	44"	10⅜"
4	41½"	42½"	7½"	9"	10"	44"	9⅞"
5	41"	42"	7"	8½"	9½"	44"	9⅜"
6	40½"	41½"	6½"	8"	9"	44"	8⅞"
7	40"	41½"	6½"	8"	9"	44"	8⅜"

[1]NDWS is the True Temper® code designation for "New Dynamic Wood stiff." This shaft was actually developed in 1946. It is a special order shaft and is usually available from suppliers in only the 44" length. For tour players and exceptionally hard hitting low handicap players, the driver shaft is usually tipped from ½" to 1½".
[2]For each ½" added to standard club length, the shaft should be tipped ½" to maintain the standard flex, unless a slightly softer flex is desired.
*To achieve the recommended back of heel to first step dimension, be certain to choose the recommended Uncut Shaft Length. Tip trimming should be performed only if the same length is cut from the tips of all the shafts in the set. Failure to maintain consistent tip trimming will result in the Flex Flow's recessed section falling out of alignment.

Club No.	[2]Finished Club Length (Modern Standard)	Uncut Shaft Length	Dynalite LWX "X"	Dynalite LWS "S"	Dynalite LWR "R"	Dynamic Lite DLWX "X"	Dynamic Lite DLWS "S"	Dynamic Lite DLWR "R"	Dynalite Gold LWX "X"	Dynalite Gold LWS "S"	Dynalite Gold LWR "R"
1	43"	44"	9¾"	11¾"	13¾"	10½"	10¾"	10¼"	9¾"	12"	12"
2	42½"	43½"	9¼"	11¼"	13¼"	10"	10¼"	9¾"	9¼"	11½"	11½"
3	42"	43"	8¾"	10¾"	12¾"	9½"	9¾"	9¼"	8¾"	11"	11"
4	41½"	42½"	8¼"	10¼"	12¼"	9"	9¼"	8¾"	8¼"	10½"	10½"
5	41"	42"	7¾"	9¾"	11¾"	8½"	8¾"	8¼"	7¾"	10"	10"
6	40½"	42"	7¼"	9¼"	11¼"	8"	8¼"	7¾"	7¼"	9½"	9½"
7	40"	42"	6¾"	8¾"	10¾"	7½"	7¾"	7¼"	6¾"	9"	9"

TAPER TIP WOOD SHAFTS – MEN'S
BRUNSWICK

Club No.	[2]Finished Club Length (Modern Standard)	[4]Uncut Shaft Length	[5]Bruns Lite IV "V"	[6]UCV-304 WE "X"	[6]UCV-304 WS "S"	[6]UCV-304 WS "R"	Phoenix WS "S"	Phoenix WR "R"
1	43"	44"	8½"	8¼"	9½"	10½"	10"	11½"
2	42½"	43½"	Use 44" Maintain 8½"	Use 44" Maintain 8¼"	Use 44" Maintain 9½"	Use 44" Maintain 10½"	Tip 44" to 9½"	Tip 44" to 11"
3	42"	43"	8½"	8¼"	9½"	10½"	9"	10½"
4	41½"	42½"	8½"	Use 43" Maintain 8¼"	Use 43" Maintain 9½"	Use 43" Maintain 10½"	8½"	10"
5	41"	42"	8½"	8¼"	9½"	10½"	8"	9½"
6	40½"	42"	8½"	Use 42" Maintain 8¼"	Use 42" Maintain 9½"	Use 42" Maintain 10½"	Tip 42" to 7½"	Tip 42" to 9"
7	40"	42"	8½"	Use 42" Maintain 8¼"	Use 42" Maintain 9½"	Use 42" Maintain 10½"	Tip 42" to 7"	Tip 42" to 8½"

TAPER TIP WOOD SHAFTS – MEN'S *cont.*
BRUNSWICK

Club No.	[2]Finished Club Length (Modern Standard)	[4]Uncut Shaft Length	Propel II WX "X"	Propel II WS "S"	Propel II WR "R"	Propel II WA "A"	[7]Mark II WR "R"	[7]Super Champion WR "R"
1	43"	44"	8¾"	9¾"	8½"	10⅞"	12"	9¹⁵⁄₁₆"
2	42½"	43½"	Tip 44" to 8¼"	Tip 44" to 9¼"	Tip 44" to 8"	Tip 44" to 10⅜"	–	–
3	42"	43"	7¾"	8¾"	7½"	9⅞"	–	–
4	41½"	42½"	Tip 43" to 7¼"	8¼"	7"	9⅜"	–	–
5	41"	42"	6¾"	7¾"	6½"	8⅞"	–	–
6	40½"	42"	Tip 42" to 6¼"	Tip 42" to 7¼"	Tip 42" to 6"	Tip 42" to 8⅜"	–	–
7	40"	42"	Tip 42" to 5¾"	Tip 42" to 6¾"	Tip 42" to 5½"	Tip 42" to 7⅞"	–	–

TAPER TIP WOOD SHAFTS – MEN'S
APOLLO

Club No.	[2]Finished Club Length (Modern Standard)	[4]Uncut Shaft Length	Masterflex VI [9]"VI"	Masterflex V [9]"TS"	Masterflex IV [9]"S"	Masterflex III [9]"RS"	Masterflex II [9]"S"
1	43"	44"	13¹⁄₁₀"	13⁹⁄₁₆"	12½"	12½"	12³⁄₁₀"
2	42½"	43½"	12⁶⁄₁₀"	13¹⁄₁₆"	12"	12"	11⁸⁄₁₀"
3	42"	43"	12¹⁄₁₀"	12⁹⁄₁₆"	11½"	11½"	11³⁄₁₀"
4	41½"	42½"	11⁶⁄₁₀"	12¹⁄₁₆"	11"	11"	10⁸⁄₁₀"
5	41"	42"	11¹⁄₁₀"	11⁹⁄₁₆"	10½"	10½"	10³⁄₁₀"
6	40½"	41½"	10⁶⁄₁₀"	11¹⁄₁₆"	10"	10"	9⁸⁄₁₀"
7	40"	41"	10¹⁄₁₀"	10⁹⁄₁₆"	9½"	9½"	9³⁄₁₀"

TAPER TIP WOOD SHAFTS – LADIES'
TRUE TEMPER® & BRUNSWICK

Club No.	[2]Finished Club Length (Modern Standard)	[4]Uncut Shaft Length	Pro-Fit PFWL or DWL	[3]Contour TRWL	TT Lite 2LWL	Extralite SLWL	Uncut Shaft Length For Flex Flow	Flex Flow TFFWL "L"
1	42"	43"	8½"	12½"	12"	14"	44"	13½"
2	41½"	42½"	8"	Use 43" @ 12½"	11½"	Use 43" Tip to 13½"	43½"	13"
3	41"	42"	7½"	11½"	11"	13"	43"	12½"
4	40½"	42"	Use 43" Tip to 7"	Use 42" @ 11½"	Use 42" Tip to 10½"	Use 42" Tip to 12½"	42½"	12"
5	40"	42"	Use 42" Tip to 6½"	Use 42" @ 11½"	Use 42" Tip to 10"	Use 42" Tip to 12"	42"	11½"
6	39½"	42"	Use 42" Tip to 6"	Use 42" @ 11½"	Use 42" Tip to 9½"	Use 42" Tip to 11½"	41½"	11"
7	39"	42"	Use 42" Tip to 5½"	Use 42" @ 11½"	Use 42" Tip to 9"	Use 42" Tip to 11"	41½"	11"

Club No.	[2]Finished Club Length (Modern Standard)	[4]Uncut Shaft Length	[8]UCV-304 WL "L"	Phoenix WL "L"	Super Champion WL "L"	Champion WL "L"
1	42"	44"	7½"	13"	Use 43" Maintain 14¹⁵⁄₁₆"	15½"
2	41½"	44"	Use 44" Maintain 7½"	Tip 44" to 12½"	Tip 43" to 14⁷⁄₁₆"	Tip 44" to 15"
3	41"	43"	7½"	12"	Tip 43" to 13¹⁵⁄₁₆"	Tip 44" to 14½"
4	40½"	43"	Use 43" Maintain 7½"	Tip 43" to 11½"	Tip 43" to 13⁷⁄₁₆"	Tip 44" to 14"
5	40"	42"	7½"	11"	Tip 43" to 12¹⁵⁄₁₆"	Tip 44" to 13½"
6	39½"	42"	Use 42" Maintain 7½"	Tip 43" to 10½"	–	–
7	39"	41"	7½"	Tip 43" to 10"	–	–

CHAPTER 58

THE GRAPHITE SHAFT: DESIGN & MANUFACTURE

The graphite golf shaft (now commonly referred to as composite) was first introduced to the golfing world at the January, 1973 PGA Merchandise Show, which is held in Florida each year. The graphite shafts were sold by two companies–Shakespeare and a familiar name, Aldila, which was then known as Aldila Precision Golf, Inc.

While the industry was in its infancy, very few complete sets of graphite shafted clubs were sold mainly because of their high cost. Woods sold for about $100.00 each and irons sold for about $80.00 each. Today there is a considerable gap between the highest and lowest priced graphite shafted clubs. Currently, a graphite shaft can be purchased at a cost between $7.00 and $115.00, which has a huge impact on the selling price of the assembled club.

A lot of confusion over graphite shafts still exists with consumers, golf professionals and even the golf club manufacturers. The confusion begins with the evolutionary changing of shaft specifications and design characteristics by many of the graphite shaft manufacturers who are trying to improve their product and thus obtain the competitive edge in performance and also in advertising claims. Adding to the confusion is the proliferation of composite shaft manufacturers and a blizzard of new shaft offerings–each proclaiming itself to most benefit specific target markets (i.e., low handicap players, seniors, ladies, players who hit the ball too low, etc.). The confusion over graphite shafts is similar to the confusion over golf ball performance claims with the exception that golf professionals have had more experience with golf balls and have in most cases weeded out the non-performers from the performers and they basically understand golf balls better. PGA tour professionals have access to and experiment with all the high-end, high performance shafts available through the repair vans located at the various tournaments. Their experimentation has also weeded out the non-performers for players possessing their unique playing characteristics, but this leaves hundreds of other shafts to which the average golfer cannot practically access in sufficient numbers to do their own performance testing.

The graphite shaft has carved out a significant share of the market. As of 1993, approximately 60% of all golfers have at least one graphite shaft in their woods and 13% have graphite shafts in their irons. The percentage of graphite shaft usage on the tour is marginally higher for the woods but significantly higher for the irons; up to 24%! There is every reason to believe that the percentage of graphite shaft usage among consumers will continue to increase throughout the late 1990's.

■ What is a Composite Shaft and How is it Made?

A composite shaft is made using the sheet wrapped method or filament wound method. The sheet wrapped method is a very labor intensive operation for even the most technically sophisticated companies.

For most composite companies, the manufacturing process begins with the purchase of rolls of "prepreg," which is preimpregnated carbon fibers with epoxy resin. These rolls of prepreg are purchased from companies like BP Chemicals, Hercules, Mitsubishi Rayon or several other sources. Two companies, Grafalloy and Aldila are currently making their own prepreg.

Prepreg is made by pulling graphite strands from large spools. The strands are passed through a resin solution, cured to the proper consistency and wound into rolls. See Photos 58-1 and 58-2. Each graphite strand is comprised of 3,000 to 12,000 individual crystalline carbon fibers which are held together by epoxy. The crystalline carbon fibers are created from rayon, polyacrylonitrile (also known as PAN) or a type of pitch. The pitch is a residue left from the distillation of coal and petroleum products. Of these three materials or precursors, PAN and pitch are the most frequently used due to the strength of the carbon fibers they produce. The crystalline carbon fibers are formed by spinning the precursors at temperatures around 1400°F in an inert environment. They are further heat treated to strength and weight properties at temperatures approaching 6000°F. The extreme heat burns off everything but the carbon content of the precursors.

The differences in the carbon products from these two precursors lie in their final properties and therefore their individual applications. The amount of carbon available in a pitch-based fiber is more than is available in a PAN-based fiber. However, in order to make the higher strength pitched-based fiber, the manufacturing process results in a fiber that is more brittle and not as elastic. This is why PAN-based crystalline carbon fibers are used in most cases.

The graphite fibers are rated according to their modulus. Modulus is an indication of how much a material will deform when stressed. The four common ratings are low, intermediate, high and ultra high modulus. Higher modulus graphite has a higher resistance to deformity because the carbon atoms lie closer together to form a stronger bond. The development of higher modulus graphite has increased the strength of composite shafts and has put in question the need for boron as a tip reinforcement material. One way that stiffer torsional characteristics are attained is by increasing the modulus of the graphite in those layers that are responsible for the parameter. Higher modulus shafts cost more money because you are getting a shaft comprised of a higher strength, harder to make material. Higher modulus in general, or lower torque in particular, are major contributors to higher costs.

An analogous situation to prepreg would be fiberglass boats which are made from glass fibers laid in place in a mold, impregnated with an activated polyester or epoxy resin, allowed to cure and removed from the mold. As with the fiberglass boats, the ratio of carbon fibers to epoxy resin is important. Too much resin to fiber ratio will make the prepreg too brittle, and too little resin to fiber ratio will make the prepreg too weak. The proper ratio of resin to carbon fiber is very important in satisfying the strength requirements of the composite shaft.

The prepreg is cut into sections or plys. The plys are cut at various angles, from 90° down to 45° sides. See Photo 58-3. They are cut at different angles principally to influence the degree of torsional stiffness the shaft has been designed to have. The plys are placed on a special paper that has an adhesive backing to which the plys will adhere. Only those plys having the same angled sides are placed on the same paper. Plys with 90° sides are placed on one paper, 70° sides on another and so on. The combination of plys and paper is called a "swatch." See Photo 58-4. Each swatch is then cut lengthwise producing long tapered "flags" that, of course, contain fibers running in the same direction. See Photo 58-5. The paper backing is removed and the flags are ready to be rolled around tapered steel mandrels. These mandrels differ in profile and radius. For instance, if a heavier weight composite shaft was required, the mandrel would have a smaller diameter so more flags could be wrapped around it to bring it up to the desired outside diameter, ultimately creating a heavier weight shaft. Very lightweight shafts are made by starting with a larger diameter mandrel so that few flags will be wrapped around it.

The mandrel is placed lengthwise along a flag and the flag wrapped around it by hand or with the help of a rolling press. See Photo 58-6. The flag is wide enough to require that the mandrel be rolled more than one full revolution. A rolling press ensures an appropriate amount of tension and pressure is applied to achieve a tight wrapping, without voids. Alternately, flags having straight and angled plys are wrapped around the mandrel.

Graphite shaft manufacturing of the early 1970's basically followed the same procedure. There was however, one big difference. The carbon fibers within the flags were always running parallel with the edge of the flag. This resulted in them always running vertically, up and down the shaft which is what caused the very low torsional stiffness.

Often included in the roll-up procedure is a smaller sheet of material called boron. See Photo 58-7. The amount of boron used in composite shafts varies widely as it can run the length of the shaft or be placed only in the tip section. The boron piece is referred to as an insert and is included in the roll-up procedure. Boron, as it is found in composite shafts, is a series of tungsten wires with boron deposited on the exterior of the wires. Boron prevents breakage of the shaft due to its resistance to bending. In the tip section of the shaft this is very important due to the stress placed in this area during the golf swing.

After the appropriate number of flags have been wrapped around the mandrel it is wrapped in cellophane and placed in an oven. See Photo 58-8. The heat causes the cellophane to shrink and the mandrel to expand, which further eliminates the presence of voids in the shaft. The cellophane is removed, as is the mandrel and the shaft is then cut to the desired length. The tip of the shaft is sanded to make it a constant diameter (unitized) and then the rest of the shaft is sanded to remove imperfections and irregularities. See Photo 58-9. Sanding can alter the flex of the shaft so they are checked for flex afterwards. See Photo 58-10. The shafts are then cleaned and coats of special polyurethane are applied. See Photos 58-11 through 58-13. The shafts are examined for finish flaws, butt and tip diameters are checked, along with the flex and torque. See Photo 58-14. They are then ready for use.

The filament wound shaft was introduced principally because the sheet wrapped shaft did not perform very well when placed in a frequency analyzer to check for flex. This is not necessarily bad, it only means that the wrapped shaft tended to wobble in an analyzer, producing inconsistent results. A filament wound shaft is made by wrapping a steel mandrel with several layers of composite tape. See Photo 58-15. Several shafts are then placed in a special unit that holds each shaft at the tip and butt. A strand of fiber is started at the end of each shaft and the shafts rotate as the machine moves back and forth, following a computerized pattern. See Photo 58-16. The angle at which the strands are applied can vary from 5° to 90°, depending upon the design specifications. As the angle varies, torsional stiffness and flex are altered. The shafts are finished using the same method as that used for wrapped shafts.

636

58-1
A prepreg creel which holds spools of graphite strands. The strands are pulled between epoxy coated sheets, heated and compressed.

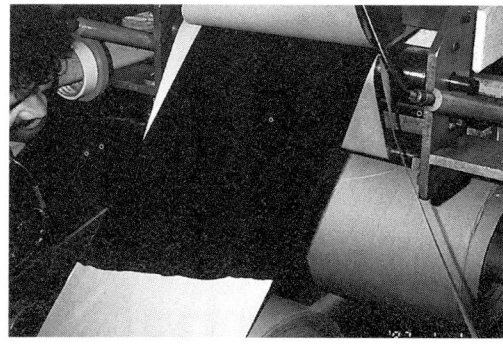

58-2
Out comes the pre-impregnated carbon fiber with epoxy binding agent. It will be rolled up in large rolls and kept in cold storage for later use.

58-3
The prepreg is brought out of storage and cut into short pieces called plys. The prepreg is cut at 45° to 90° angles.

58-4
The plys with identical angled sides are located to the same adhesion backed paper. These are called swatches.

58-5
The swatches are placed on die boards which have razor sharp rails. A press forces the rails through the swatch creating long, tapered pieces called flags.

58-6
A steel mandrel is selected for each different shaft type. The mandrels differ in profile and radius. The flags are wrapped around the mandrel under intense pressure, using a rolling press.

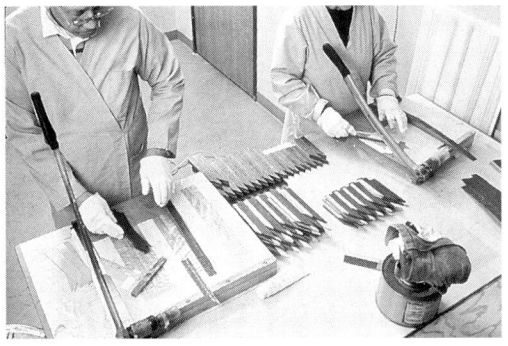

58-7

The narrow pieces being separated are boron inserts. In this case, a single insert 6" long is wrapped around the mandrel after several flags have already been rolled.

58-8

Before being cured in an oven by baking, each shaft is wrapped in cellophane. The cellophane contracts during the curing porcess, compressing the graphite fibers and resin together. The shafts are baked around the mandrel for 30 minutes at 180° Fahrenheit.

58-9

The cellophane and mandrel are removed and then the tip is ground, usually to make a unitized tip. The butt is also ground as is the rest of the shaft.

58-10

Every shaft is weighed and the flex is checked. Each shaft is designed for a specific flex, however, sanding can sometimes make a shaft more flexible than it was intended.

58-11

The shafts are cleaned and the paint and/or finish is then applied. Here, an electrostatic sprayer applies a consistent coat of finish. This is an area in which there has been marked improvement in recent years. Seldom do you see the finish or paint wear through in the tip section, which used to happen frequently.

58-12

The coatings can also be applied using this interesting device called a squeegy. Finish is held in the canister and the shaft is pulled through the squeegy controlling the thickness of the coat on the shaft.

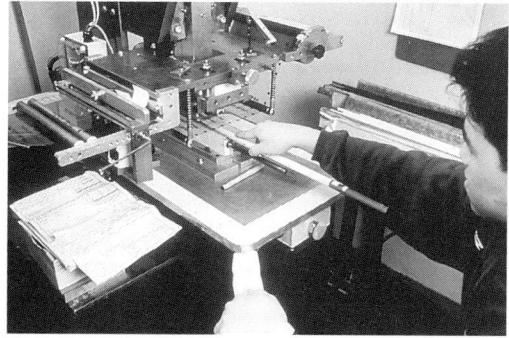

58-13
Shaft markings are applied using heat transfer decals or silk screening, as shown.

58-14
The finish is examined for flaws and the shafts are final checked for flex, straightness and torsional stiffness. They are then ready for shipment.

58-15
The **filament wound** shaft is made by first wrapping prepreg tape around a tapered steel mandrel. Two layers of tape are usually applied.

58-16
The tape wrapped mandrel is placed in a rack with other mandrels. A filament winding machine follows a computerized course as it moves back and forth, with occasional pauses, while the mandrels are rotating.

■ The Effect of the Graphite Shaft on Golf Club Design and Fitting

When graphite was first introduced, it rode the crest of highly exaggerated distance claims of 20 to 50 additional yards. These claims were published in magazine articles and never actually denied by the graphite shaft manufacturers. They cannot be blamed entirely because the feedback they received from over-zealous owners of graphite shafted drivers seemed to indicate that, in fact, graphite shafted drivers were knocking the ball out of sight. When the dust had finally settled and both the golf equipment and the graphite shaft manufacturers had obtained enough data from actual controlled player and machine tests, the results were somewhat different than the original claims. The test results indicated that most graphite shaft drivers were only marginally longer than steel shafted drivers. The term "marginally" translated into approximately 2.5 to 3.5 yards longer or 1 to 1½% increased distance. Not all of the graphite shafted clubs performed this well. In certain cases some were shorter than steel shafted clubs. This points up again that graphite shaft selection should be done by actually trying the product and asking knowledgeable individuals for their opinions and any supporting data that may be available. It should also be noted that many of the distance claims made in the early 90's were justified but only because the players were using graphite shafted drivers that were 1" to 2" longer than the clubs to which they were being compared.

In theory, the graphite shaft offers many interesting possibilities concerning total golf club design. At one time or another, everyone has heard the definition of the ideal golf shaft being one which would weigh nothing and be comprised only of a force field linking the grip to the clubhead. This may not take into consideration all of the design criteria necessary to make a playable golf club (See Appendix 7, The Myths of Golf) but it is the proper approach to additional distance through increased clubhead velocity. The theory to all of this is that by reducing shaft weight more weight can be added to the clubhead and because the golf club is still lighter overall in total weight, the clubhead could be swung faster through the hitting zone with more mass at the end of the shaft. (See Chapter 55, Design Characteristics of Golf Shafts.) The graphite shaft, in part, supports this theory. It is from 1½ to 2½ ounces lighter in weight than steel golf shafts and from ½ to 2 ounces lighter than the new very light or lightweight steel shafts. Each manufacturer of graphite shafts produces to their own different weight specifications, but generally speaking, a "stiff" flex graphite shaft would weigh an average of 2.8 ounces compared to a "stiff" standard weight steel shaft of approximately 4.3 ounces. An increased differential in shaft weight can be expected as the shafts become more flexible. For comparative purposes, based only on averages and not specifically relating to any given manufacturer's shaft, look at the following chart and compare the before and after differences of a steel shaft driver which has been reshafted with a graphite shaft. Both shafts have their center of mass in the middle.

It is important to understand what has happened to the original swingweight and total weight of the club. As already mentioned, the graphite shaft is approximately 1½ to 2 ounces lighter in weight than a standard weight steel golf shaft; therefore, when a steel shaft is replaced in a clubhead with a graphite shaft, the club's static or total weight is decreased substantially. The exact amount of the decrease in total weight is the difference in shaft weights, or from 1½ to 2 ounces. This reduction in total club weight changes the club's weight distribution to the extent of reducing the swingweight by 6 to 8 points.

	Steel Shafted Driver	Graphite Shafted Driver	Difference
Shaft Weight (ounces)	4.3	2.8	-1.5
Head Weight (ounces)	7.0	7.0	Same
Grip Weight	1.8	1.8	Same
Total Weight	13.1	11.6	-1.5
Swingweight	D-2	C-4	-8 Swingweights

The question now arises as to how much weight, if any, should be added to the clubhead. This is a very difficult question to answer because there are a number of different types of graphite shafts currently available and each has its own performance attributes. It is generally agreed that a good starting place would be to add ⅜ ounce to the clubhead, which is the equivalent of approximately 5 to 6 swingweights. This will still allow for a golf club with a much reduced total weight even though the swingweight is almost increased to where it was originally. A number of stronger players seem to prefer increasing the swingweight significantly higher than that of the original steel shaft. The point is that some weight should be added to the head and then begin experimenting by adding lead tape to the clubhead until the desired feel and performance is attained.

Regarding the length of graphite shafted clubs, it seems that when graphite first came out the promoters only made their test and sample drivers in 44" (1" longer than standard) lengths to obtain greater clubhead speeds and thus hopefully attempt to prove the exaggerated claims of 30 extra yards. This additional 1" in length has in some cases been assumed to be necessary if you switch from steel to graphite, but this is simply not so. Generally speaking, when switching to graphite, you should not change the length of your club(s) other than that to which you are accustomed or fits you best. The same fitting rules apply to graphite that apply to other shafts. (See Chapter 65, The Key Variables in Proper Fitting of Golf Clubs.)

Regarding the proper flex in fitting graphite shafts, the same flex specifications vary from manufacturer to manufacturer. Our testing shows identical flexes indicated on the shaft band will be more or less flexible depending on the manufacturer. Keep in mind, however, that the graphite shaft makers do change their specifications from time to time and also that some shaft brands are quite different from others. For example, graphite shafts are available in different flex points. In other words if three graphite shafts are available in different flex stiffness but one had a high flex point, one a mid flex point and the other a low flex point, they would all feel different in identical clubs. Generally speaking, the higher flex point or bend point shaft will feel stiffer than the low flex point shaft. Therefore, it may be possible to use the same flex shaft in graphite as would be used in steel if the graphite shaft had a high flex point. Once again, experimentation by actual hitting is the best way to judge this.

Originally, graphite shaft manufacturers supported two different theories regarding the amount of torque that a graphite shaft should or should not have. A few manufacturers elected to design their shafts with a low resistance to radial torque and other manufacturers designed theirs with a high resistance to radial torque with a few manufacturers staying somewhere in between. The shafts with the higher resistance to radial torque more closely approximate the torque characteristics of the long accepted steel shaft. Torque in a golf shaft can be defined as the amount of rotational twist in the shaft that occurs during the swing. Torque can be measured accurately in a golf shaft on either a static or electronic test device both of which clamp one end of the shaft securely and applies a known force to twist the shaft at the other end. The amount of twisting is measured in degrees. Although this measurement is accurate, it should only be considered relative when compared with other shafts of like flex and length. The dynamic torque characteristics of golf shafts vary significantly when different weight heads are swung at different head speeds by different golfers.

Theory would suggest that a golf shaft should have enough built-in resistance to torque to minimize ball dispersion and maximize clubhead feel at impact. This would support that faction of graphite manufacturers who have designed their shafts with a higher resistance to torque or one which is closer to that of steel. Some of the basic parameters inherent in the design of a golf club and ultimately how it is used to hit a golf ball support this statement as follows: The axis of the shaft and the center of gravity of the clubhead are not in line with each other; therefore, when a golf club is swung, forces acting through the center of gravity of the clubhead tend to generate a twist in the shaft. The amount of twist in the shaft will vary according to swing speed, head weight and distribution of that weight. In theory, a shaft with a low resistance to torque will not be very consistent regarding accuracy for the golfer who does not possess a smooth accelerating clubhead speed, shot after shot. The tour player or better golfer has a better chance to adjust to this type of shaft because of his/her constancy and smoothness.

NOTES

CHAPTER 59

GRAPHITE (COMPOSITE) GOLF SHAFT SPECIFICATIONS BY MANUFACTURER

There have been quite a number of graphite shaft manufacturers since graphite was first introduced in 1973. Some lasted only a few months and others a number of years. By 1985, the graphite shaft industry in the United States had basically been reduced to two manufacturers, Aldila and Grafalloy. Due to the increasing demand, however, the manufacturers ranks have again swollen. All of the major steel shaft companies (True Temper®, Brunswick Golf and Apollo) began producing quality graphite shafts beginning in 1989. Following is a list of all the manufacturers whose graphite shaft specifications are detailed in this chapter. This list is not all-inclusive, however, it represents the vast majority of the market share. The information provided here is the latest available from the manufacturers at the time of publication. This information will prove valuable for identifying, specifying and selecting the proper golf shaft.

Graphite Shaft Manufacturers
Grafalloy®
Aldila®
True Temper®
Apollo Golf, Inc.
Brunswick Golf®
Carbon Fiber Products, Inc.
Fiber-Speed™ International
Paragon Sports
Swix®
Arcal Golf Systems, Inc.
Easton®
Rapport Composites™
Unifiber
Fenwick® Golf
United Sports Technologies, Inc. (UST®)

1994 GRAFALLOY® GRAPHITE SHAFT SPECIFICATIONS – WOODS

Model	Color	Flex	Tip Dia.	Butt Dia.	Taper Tip or Parallel	Length	Weight Grams	Ozs.	Nominal Torque	Flex Point
CLASSIC	Silver/Black	L/A	.335	.590	Parallel	46"	84	2.96	4.5	Mid
	Silver/Black	R/S	.335	.600	Parallel	46"	88	3.10	4.5	Mid
LADY CLASSIC	Fuchsia/White or Lavender	L	.335	.580	Parallel	43"	70	2.47	5.0	Low
SENIOR CLASSIC	Black/Gray	A	.335	.595	Parallel	44"	84	2.96	4.3	Low
	Black/Gray	R	.335	.600	Parallel	44"	86	3.03	4.3	Low
M29 ATTACK*	Black/Red	L	.335	.580	Parallel	45"	76	2.68	4.0	Mid
	Black/Red	A	.335	.590	Parallel	45"	84	2.96	4.0	Mid
	Black/Red	R	.335	.600	Parallel	45"	86	3.03	4.0	Mid
	Black/Red	S	.335	.600	Parallel	45"	88	3.10	4.0	Mid
PRO M54*	Black/Blue	R	.335	.600	Parallel	45"	90	3.17	3.0	High
	Black/Blue	S	.335	.600	Parallel	45"	92	3.24	3.0	High
	Black/Blue	X	.335	.600	Parallel	45"	94	3.31	3.0	High
PRO M66*	Black/Bronze	R	.335	.600	Parallel	45"	96	3.38	2.2	High
	Black/Bronze	S	.335	.600	Parallel	45"	98	3.45	2.2	High
	Black/Bronze	X	.335	.600	Parallel	45"	100	3.52	2.2	High
VHM M90*	Black/Burgundy	R	.335	.610	Parallel	45"	90	3.17	1.8	High
	Black/Burgundy	S	.335	.610	Parallel	45"	92	3.24	1.8	High
	Black/Burgundy	X	.335	.610	Parallel	45"	94	3.31	1.8	High
VHM M90 LITE*	Burgundy	R	.335	.610	Parallel	44"	74	2.61	1.8	High
	Burgundy	S	.335	.610	Parallel	44"	76	2.68	1.8	High
NITRO FLEX*	Black/Gold	Nitro	.335	.600	Parallel	45"	90	3.17	2.4	Mid
FILAMENT WOUND										
ASW245	Green	R	.335	.600	Parallel	45"	85	3.00	3.5	Mid
ASW255	Green	S	.335	.600	Parallel	45"	85	3.00	3.0	Mid

*The tips of these shafts are reinforced with Boron and are designed for metal woods.

1994 GRAFALLOY® GRAPHITE SHAFT SPECIFICATIONS – IRONS

Model	Color	Flex	Tip Dia.	Butt Dia.	Taper Tip or Parallel	Length	Weight Grams	Ozs.	Nominal Torque	Flex Point
CLASSIC	Silver/Black	L/A	.370	.590	Parallel	41"	82	2.89	4.0	Mid
	Silver/Black	R/S	.370	.600	Parallel	41"	86	3.03	4.0	Mid
LADY CLASSIC	Fuchsia/White or Lavender	L	.370	.580	Parallel	39"	70	2.47	5.0	Low
SENIOR CLASSIC	Black/Gray	A	.370	.595	Parallel	39"	80	2.82	4.0	Low
	Black/Gray	R	.370	.600	Parallel	39"	82	2.89	4.0	Low
M29 ATTACK	Black/Red	L/A	.370	.580	Parallel	41"	86	3.03	3.0	Mid
	Black/Red	R/S	.370	.600	Parallel	41"	90	3.17	3.0	Mid
	Black/Red	R	.355	.600	Taper	40"	86	3.03	3.0	Mid
	Black/Red	S	.355	.600	Taper	40"	90	3.17	3.0	Mid

1994 GRAFALLOY® GRAPHITE SHAFT
SPECIFICATIONS – IRONS *(cont.)*

Model	Color	Flex	Tip Dia.	Butt Dia.	Taper Tip or Parallel	Length	Weight Grams	Ozs.	Nominal Torque	Flex Point
PRO M54	Black/Blue	R	.370	.600	Parallel	40"	90	3.17	2.0	High
	Black/Blue	S	.370	.600	Parallel	40"	92	3.24	2.0	High
	Black/Blue	X	.370	.600	Parallel	40"	94	3.31	2.0	High
NITRO FLEX	Black	Nitro	.370	.600	Parallel	40"	82	2.89	2.2	Mid
	Black	Nitro	.355	.600	Taper	40"	85	3.00	2.2	Mid
FILAMENT WOUND										
ASI290	Green	R	.370	.600	Parallel	40"	80	2.82	2.5	Mid
ASI305	Green	S	.370	.600	Parallel	40"	80	2.82	2.5	Mid
LBP SERIES										
LBP29	Black	R	.370	.600	Parallel	40"	90	3.17	3.0	Low
	Black	S	.370	.600	Parallel	40"	90	3.17	3.0	Low
	Black	R	.355	.600	Taper	40"	90	3.17	3.0	Low
	Black	S	.355	.600	Taper	40"	90	3.17	3.0	Low
LBP54	Black	R	.370	.600	Parallel	40"	92	3.24	2.0	Low
	Black	S	.370	.600	Parallel	40"	92	3.24	2.0	Low
	Black	R	.355	.600	Taper	40"	92	3.24	2.0	Low
	Black	S	.355	.600	Taper	40"	92	3.24	2.0	Low
PUTTER										
P29	Black	Putter	.370	.600	Parallel	36"	75		3.0	-

1994 ALDILA® GRAPHITE SHAFT
SPECIFICATIONS – WOODS

Model	Color	Flex	Tip Dia.	Butt Dia.	Taper Tip or Parallel	Length	Weight Grams	Ozs.	Nominal Torque	Flex Point
HM-55	Light	Regular	.335	.615	Parallel	44"	107	3.77	1.6	High
	Golden	Firm	.335	.620	Parallel	44"	107	3.77	1.6	High
	Pearl	Strong	.335	.620	Parallel	44"	107	3.77	1.6	High
HM-50 TGw	Brown	Firm	.335	.620	Parallel	44"	106	3.74	1.9	Mid
	Metallic	Strong	.335	.620	Parallel	44"	106	3.74	1.9	Mid
HM-50	Platinum	Regular	.335	.615	Parallel	44"	106	3.74	1.9	Mid
	Pearl	Firm	.335	.620	Parallel	44"	106	3.74	1.9	Mid
		Strong	.335	.620	Parallel	44"	106	3.74	1.9	Mid
HM-40	Golden	Light	.335	.615	Parallel	44"	95	3.35	2.2	Mid
	Pearl	Regular	.335	.615	Parallel	44"	97	3.42	2.2	Mid
		Firm	.335	.615	Parallel	44"	98	3.46	2.2	Mid
		Strong	.335	.615	Parallel	44"	98	3.46	2.2	Mid
		Firm	.335	.630	Parallel	46"	104	3.67	2.2	Mid
		Strong	.335	.630	Parallel	46"	104	3.67	2.2	Mid

1994 ALDILA® GRAPHITE SHAFT
SPECIFICATIONS – WOODS *(cont.)*

Model	Color	Flex	Tip Dia.	Butt Dia.	Taper Tip or Parallel	Length	Weight Grams	Ozs.	Nominal Torque	Flex Point
HM-35	Bronze	Light	.335	.610	Parallel	44"	86	3.03	3.9	Mid
	Pearl	Regular	.335	.610	Parallel	44"	90	3.17	3.1	Mid
		Firm	.335	.610	Parallel	44"	89	3.14	3.1	Mid
		Strong	.335	.620	Parallel	44"	94	3.32	3.1	Mid
		Regular	.335	.615	Parallel	46"	92	3.24	3.1	Mid
		Firm	.335	.615	Parallel	46"	91	3.21	3.1	Mid
		Strong	.335	.620	Parallel	46"	96	3.39	3.1	Mid
HM-35 B.T.	Bronze	Regular	.335	.610	Parallel	44½"	87	3.07	3.9	Mid
	Pearl	Firm	.335	.610	Parallel	44½"	90	3.17	3.1	Mid
		Strong	.335	.610	Parallel	44½"	89	3.14	3.1	Mid
HM-30	Satin	Ex. Light	.335	.580	Parallel	44"	78	2.75	3.6	Mid
	Taupe	Light	.335	.580	Parallel	44"	80	2.82	3.6	Mid
		Regular	.335	.605	Parallel	44"	87	3.07	3.6	Mid
		Firm	.335	.605	Parallel	44"	91	3.21	3.6	Mid
ASD SERIES (FILAMENT WOUND)										
ASD 2.6	Black	Firm	.335	.604	Parallel	45"	90	3.17	2.6	Mid
ASD 3.2	*(with center fade)*	Regular	.335	.610	Parallel	45"	96	3.39	3.2	Mid
SUPERLITE SERIES										
HM-40 SL	Metallic	Firm	.335	.605	Parallel	44"	82	2.89	2.8	Low
	Brown	Firm	.335	.605	Parallel	45"	84	2.96	2.8	Low
HM-35 Superlite	Satin Sand Grey	Regular	.335	.575	Parallel	44"	71	2.50	3.7	Low
HM-30 Superlite	Metallic Sand Grey	Regular	.335	.605	Parallel	44"	62	2.19	7.0	Low
HM-30 Superlite Ladies	Satin Grey	Light	.335	.595	Parallel	44"	59	2.08	7.0	Low
LOW TORQUE SERIES										
Low Torque 2.5	Satin	Regular	.335	.610	Parallel	45"	115	4.03	2.5	Mid
	Black	Firm	.335	.610	Parallel	45"	118	4.15	2.5	Mid
		Strong	.335	.610	Parallel	45"	120	4.23	2.5	Mid
Low Torque 4.0	Satin	Ex. Light	.335	.586	Parallel	44"	74	2.61	4.0	Low
	Black	Light	.335	.586	Parallel	44"	87	3.07	4.0	Low
		A/L	.335	.588	Parallel	46"	90	3.17	4.0	Low
		Regular	.335	.611	Parallel	44"	89	3.14	4.0	Low
		R/F	.335	.611	Parallel	46"	94	3.32	4.0	Low
		Firm	.335	.615	Parallel	44"	92	3.24	4.0	Low
		Strong	.335	.623	Parallel	44"	96	3.39	4.0	Low
Low Torque 5.0	Satin	Ex. Light	.335	.607	Parallel	44"	71	2.50	5.0	Low
	Black	Light	.335	.615	Parallel	44"	75	2.65	5.0	Low
		Regular	.335	.620	Parallel	44"	77	2.71	5.0	Low
		Firm	.335	.620	Parallel	44"	80	2.82	5.0	Low
Low Torque 5.0	Satin	Light	.320	.607	Taper	44"	75	2.65	5.0	Low
	Black	Regular	.320	.615	Taper	44"	77	2.71	5.0	Low
		Firm	.320	.615	Taper	44"	80	2.82	5.0	Low
Low Torque Ladies	Satin Green	XL	.335	.586	Parallel	44"	74	2.57	4.0	Low

1994 ALDILA® GRAPHITE SHAFT
SPECIFICATIONS – IRONS

Model	Color	Flex	Tip Dia.	Butt Dia.	Taper Tip or Parallel	Length	Weight Grams	Weight Ozs.	Nominal Torque	Flex Point
HM-55	Light	Regular	.370	.610	Parallel	39"	97	3.42	1.4	High
	Golden	Firm	.370	.620	Parallel	39"	100	3.53	1.4	High
	Pearl	Strong	.370	.620	Parallel	39"	104	3.67	1.4	High
HM-50 TGi	Brown	Regular	.370	.620	Parallel	39"	112	3.92	1.6	Mid
	Metallic	Firm	.370	.620	Parallel	39"	112	3.92	1.6	Mid
		Strong	.370	.620	Parallel	39"	115	4.06	1.6	Mid
HM-50	Platinum	Regular	.370	.610	Parallel	39"	97	3.42	1.6	Mid
	Pearl	Firm	.370	.620	Parallel	39"	104	3.67	1.6	Mid
		Strong	.370	.620	Parallel	39"	107	3.77	1.6	Mid
HM-40	Golden	Light	.370	.600	Parallel	39"	85	3.00	2.0	Mid
	Pearl	Regular	.370	.610	Parallel	39"	90	3.17	2.0	Mid
		Firm	.370	.616	Parallel	39"	93	3.28	2.0	Mid
		Strong	.370	.625	Parallel	39"	96	3.39	2.0	Mid
HM-35	Bronze	Light	.370	.590	Parallel	39"	75	2.65	3.0	Mid
	Pearl	Regular	.370	.590	Parallel	39"	75	2.65	3.0	Mid
		Firm	.370	.590	Parallel	39"	75	2.65	3.0	Mid
		Strong	.370	.600	Parallel	39"	84	2.96	3.0	Mid
HM-30	Satin	Ex. Light	.370	.575	Parallel	39"	76	2.68	3.6	Mid
	Taupe	Light	.370	.585	Parallel	39"	78	2.75	3.6	Mid
		Regular	.370	.590	Parallel	39"	82	2.89	3.6	Mid
		Firm	.370	.600	Parallel	39"	86	3.03	3.6	Mid
ASD SERIES (FILAMENT WOUND)										
ASD 2.0 TGi	Metallic	Firm	.370	.620	Parallel	40"	120	4.23	2.0	Mid
	Brown	Strong	.370	.620	Parallel	40"	122	4.30	2.0	Mid
ASD 2.5	Black	Regular	.370	.620	Parallel	41"	100	3.53	2.5	Mid
	(w/center fade)	Firm	.370	.620	Parallel	41"	98	3.46	2.5	Mid
HM-30 Superlite	Metallic Sand Grey	Regular	.370	.600	Parallel	39"	69	2.43	6.0	Low
HM-30 Ladies Superlite	Satin Grey	Light	.370	.590	Parallel	39"	66	2.33	6.0	Low
LOW TORQUE SERIES										
Low Torque 2.5	Satin	Regular	.355	.600	Taper	39"	107	3.77	2.5	Mid
	Black	Firm	.355	.600	Taper	39"	111	3.88	2.5	Mid
		Strong	.355	.600	Taper	39"	115	4.03	2.5	Mid
Low Torque 2.5	Satin	Regular	.370	.600	Parallel	39"	107	3.77	2.5	Mid
	Black	Firm	.370	.600	Parallel	39"	111	3.88	2.5	Mid
		Strong	.370	.600	Parallel	39"	115	4.03	2.5	MId
Low Torque 4.0	Satin	Ex. Light	.370	.580	Parallel	39"	66	2.33	4.0	Low
	Black	Light	.370	.580	Parallel	39"	69	2.43	4.0	Low
		A/L	.370	.580	Parallel	41"	72	2.54	4.0	Low
		Regular	.370	.590	Parallel	39"	72	2.54	4.0	Low
		R/F	.370	.595	Parallel	41"	80	2.82	4.0	Low
		Firm	.370	.600	Parallel	39"	74	2.61	4.0	Low
		Strong	.370	.610	Parallel	39"	78	2.75	4.0	Low

1994 ALDILA® GRAPHITE SHAFT
SPECIFICATIONS – IRONS *(cont.)*

Model	Color	Flex	Tip Dia.	Butt Dia.	Taper Tip or Parallel	Length	Weight Grams	Weight Ozs.	Nominal Torque	Flex Point
Low Torque 5.0	Satin Black	Ex. Light	.370	.580	Parallel	39"	70	2.46	5.0	Low
		Light	.370	.600	Parallel	39"	73	2.57	5.0	Low
		Regular	.370	.588	Parallel	39"	79	2.79	5.0	Low
		Firm	.370	.588	Parallel	39"	81	2.85	5.0	Low
		Strong	.370	.588	Parallel	39"	81	2.85	5.0	Low
Low Torque 5.0	Satin Black	Light	.355	.593	Taper	39"	76	2.68	5.0	Low
		Regular	.355	.581	Taper	39"	81	2.85	5.0	Low
		Firm	.355	.581	Taper	39"	82	2.89	5.0	Low
Low Torque Ladies	Satin Green	XL	.370	.580	Parallel	39"	66	2.33	4.0	Low

1994 ALDILA® GRAPHITE SHAFT
SPECIFICATIONS – PUTTERS

Model	Color	Flex	Tip Dia.	Butt Dia.	Taper Tip or Parallel	Length	Weight Grams	Weight Ozs.	Nominal Torque	Flex Point
HM-40	Golden Pearl	Firm	.355	.590	Taper	36"	73	2.57	2.1	—
HM-30 I.H.	Satin Taupe	–	.370	.615	Parallel	36"	58	2.05		
			.370	.600	Parallel	34"	54	1.90		
			.355	.605	Taper	36"	58	2.05		
			.355	.590	Taper	34"	54	1.90		
HM-30 O.H.	Satin Taupe	–	.299 I.D. .378 O.D.	.585		35"	58	2.05		

1994 TRUE TEMPER® GRAPHITE SHAFT
SPECIFICATIONS – WOODS

Model	Code	Flex	Tip Dia.	Taper Tip or Parallel	Butt Dia.	Length	Weight Grams	Weight Ozs.	Nominal Torque
BLACK GOLD™	UCBHWX	X100, 200, 300	.335	Parallel	.600	45"	95	3.35	2.9
	UCBHWS	S200, 300, 400	.335	Parallel	.600	45"	91	3.21	3.0
	UCBHWR	R200, 300, 400	.335	Parallel	.600	45"	90	3.17	3.1
	TCBHWX	X100, 200, 300	.294	Taper	.600	43" – 45"	92	3.25	3.2
	TCBHWS	S200, 300, 400	.294	Taper	.600	43" – 45"	92	3.25	3.3
	TCBHWR	R200, 300, 400	.294	Taper	.600	43" – 45"	91	3.21	3.5
MODULUS EV-40™	UEV5WX	X	.335	Parallel	.600	45"	95	3.35	4.6
	UEV5WS	S	.335	Parallel	.600	45"	94	3.52	4.6
	UEV5WR	R	.335	Parallel	.600	45"	90	3.17	4.7
BLACK GOLD TOUR™	UBGTWXF	X100, 400	.335	Parallel	.600	45"	98	3.46	2.3
	UBGTWSF	S400	.335	Parallel	.600	45"	97	3.42	2.3

1994 TRUE TEMPER® GRAPHITE SHAFT
SPECIFICATIONS – WOODS *(cont.)*

Model	Code	Flex	Tip Dia.	Taper Tip or Parallel	Butt Dia.	Length	Weight Grams	Weight Ozs.	Nominal Torque
DYNAMIC® GRAPHITE	UDYNTWX	TOUR X	.335	Parallel	.600	45"	107	3.77	3.5
	UDYNTWS	TOUR S	.335	Parallel	.600	45"	105	3.70	3.5
	UDYNTWR	TOUR R	.335	Parallel	.600	45"	103	3.63	3.6
	UDYNWX	X	.335	Parallel	.600	45"	83	2.93	3.7
	UDYNWS	S	.335	Parallel	.600	45"	81	2.85	3.7
	UDYNWR	R	.335	Parallel	.600	45"	79	2.78	3.7
EI-70™	EI7WS	S	.294	Taper	.580	43" – 45"	79	2.79	3.7
	EI7WR	R	.294	Taper	.580	43" – 45"	77	2.72	3.8
	UEI7WX	X	.335	Parallel	.580	45"	83	2.93	3.3
	UEI7WS	S	.335	Parallel	.580	45"	79	2.79	3.3
	UEI7WR	R	.335	Parallel	.580	45"	77	2.72	3.5
	UEI7TWX	TOUR X	.335	Parallel	.600	45"	89	3.14	3.3
	UEI7TWS	TOUR S	.335	Parallel	.600	45"	88	3.10	3.3
EI-70 HIGH IMPACT™	UEI7WXH	X	.335	Parallel	.580	45"	85	3.00	3.1
	UEI7WSH	S	.335	Parallel	.580	45"	83	2.93	3.2
	UEI7WRH	R	.335	Parallel	.580	45"	78	2.75	3.3
COMMAND™	UVWS	S	.335	Parallel	.600	45"	99	3.49	3.9
	UVWR	R	.335	Parallel	.600	45"	97	3.42	4.0
COMMAND LITE™	UV3WS	S	.335	Parallel	.600	45"	84	2.96	4.2
	UV3WR	R	.335	Parallel	.600	45"	83	2.93	4.2

1994 TRUE TEMPER® GRAPHITE SHAFT
SPECIFICATIONS – FOR SENIORS & LADIES – WOODS

Model	Code	Flex	Tip Dia.	Taper Tip or Parallel	Butt Dia.	Length	Weight Grams	Weight Ozs.	Nominal Torque
EI-60 SENIORS™	UEI6WA	-	.335	Parallel	.580	45"	74	2.40	5.0
COMMAND SENIORS™	UVWA	-	.335	Parallel	.600	45"	95	3.35	5.0
COMMAND LITE SENIORS™	UV3WA	-	.335	Parallel	.600	45"	80	2.82	5.0
EI-60 LADIES™	UEI6WL	-	.335	Parallel	.580	44"	68	2.40	5.0
COMMAND LADIES™	UVWL	-	.335	Parallel	.580	44"	90	3.17	5.0
COMMAND LITE LADIES™	UV3WA	-	.335	Parallel	.580	44"	75	2.65	4.5
DYNAMIC® GRAPHITE	UDYNWA	Seniors	.335	Parallel	.600	45"	83	2.93	4.3
	UDYNWL	Ladies	.335	Parallel	.580	45"	79	2.78	4.3

1994 TRUE TEMPER® GRAPHITE SHAFT SPECIFICATIONS – IRONS

Model	Code	Flex	Tip Dia.	Taper Tip or Parallel	Butt Dia.	Length	Weight Grams	Ozs.	Nominal Torque
BLACK GOLD™	UCBHIX	X100, 200, 300	.370	Parallel	.600	40"	93	3.28	1.9
	UCBHIS	S200, 300, 400	.370	Parallel	.600	40"	93	3.28	2.0
	UCBHIR	R200, 300, 400	.370	Parallel	.600	40"	90	3.17	2.1
	TCBHIX	X100, 200, 300	.355	Taper	.600	35½" – 40"	94	3.31	2.5
	TCBHIS	S200, 300, 400	.355	Taper	.600	35½" – 40"	94	3.31	2.5
	TCBHIR	R200, 300, 400	.355	Taper	.600	35½" – 40"	93	3.28	3.0
MODULUS EV-40™	UEV5IX	X	.370	Parallel	.600	40"	94	3.32	3.1
	UEV5IS	S	.370	Parallel	.600	40"	91	3.21	3.1
	UEV5IR	R	.370	Parallel	.600	40"	90	3.17	3.2
DYNAMIC®	DYNTIX	TOUR X	.355	Taper	.600	35½" – 40"	110	3.88	2.0
	DYNTIS	TOUR S	.355	Taper	.600	35½" – 40"	108	3.81	2.0
	DYNTIR	TOUR R	.355	Taper	.600	35½" – 40"	105	3.70	2.0
	DYNIX	X	.355	Taper	.600	35½" – 40"	85	3.00	3.3
	DYNIS	S	.355	Taper	.600	35½" – 40"	82	2.89	3.3
	DYNIR	R	.355	Taper	.600	35½" – 40"	80	2.82	3.3
	UDYNTIX	TOUR X	.370	Parallel	.600	35½" – 40"	110	3.88	2.0
	UDYNTIX	TOUR S	.370	Parallel	.600	35½" – 40"	108	3.81	2.0
	UDYNTIR	TOUR R	.370	Parallel	.600	35½" – 40"	105	3.70	2.0
	UDYNIX	X	.370	Parallel	.600	35½" – 40"	85	3.00	3.3
	UDYNIS	S	.370	Parallel	.600	35½" – 40"	82	2.89	3.3
	UDYNIR	R	.370	Parallel	.600	35½" – 40"	80	2.82	3.3
EI-70™	EI7IS	S	.355	Taper	.580	35½ – 40"	78	2.75	2.5
	EI7IR	R	.355	Taper	.580	35½" – 40"	77	2.72	2.5
	UEI7IX	X	.370	Parallel	.580	40"	83	2.93	2.5
	UEI7IS	S	.370	Parallel	.580	40"	78	2.75	2.6
	UEI7IR	R	.370	Parallel	.580	40"	77	2.72	2.6
	EI7TIX	TOUR X	.355	Taper	.600	35½" – 40"	93	3.28	2.5
	EI7TIS	TOUR S	.355	Taper	.600	35½" – 40"	93	3.28	2.5
	UEI7TIX	TOUR X	.370	Parallel	.600	40"	93	3.28	1.9
	UEI7TIS	TOUR S	.370	Parallel	.600	40"	93	3.28	2.0
COMMAND™	UVIS	S	.370	Parallel	.600	40"	99	3.49	2.8
	UVIR	R	.370	Parallel	.600	40"	97	3.42	3.0
COMMAND LITE™	UV3IS	S	.370	Parallel	.600	40"	91	3.21	3.3
	UV3IR	R	.370	Parallel	.600	40"	88	3.10	3.5

1994 TRUE TEMPER® GRAPHITE SHAFT SPECIFICATIONS – FOR SENIORS & LADIES – IRONS

Model	Code	Flex	Tip Dia.	Taper Tip or Parallel	Butt Dia.	Length	Weight Grams	Ozs.	Nominal Torque
EI-60 SENIORS™	UEI6IA	-	.370	Parallel	.600	40"	79	2.79	3.5
COMMAND SENIORS™	UVIA	-	.370	Parallel	.600	40"	93	3.28	4.0
COMMAND LITE SENIORS™	UV3IA	-	.370	Parallel	.600	40"	85	3.00	4.0
EI-60 LADIES™	UEI6IL	-	.370	Parallel	.580	38"	75	2.65	3.5
COMMAND LADIES™	UVIL	-	.370	Parallel	.580	38"	90	3.17	3.5

650

1994 TRUE TEMPER® GRAPHITE SHAFT
SPECIFICATIONS – FOR SENIORS & LADIES – IRONS *(cont.)*

Model	Code	Flex	Tip Dia.	Taper Tip or Parallel	Butt Dia.	Length	Weight Grams	Weight Ozs.	Nominal Torque
COMMAND LITE LADIES™	UV3IA	-	.370	Parallel	.580	38"	80	2.82	3.5
DYNAMIC®	DYNIA	Seniors	.355	Taper	.600	35½" – 40"	78	2.75	3.5
	DYNIL	Ladies	.355	Taper	.580	35½" – 39"	78	2.75	3.6
	UDYNIA	Seniors	.370	Parallel	.600	35½" – 40"	78	2.75	3.5
	UDYNIL	Ladies	.370	Parallel	.580	35½" – 39"	78	2.75	3.6

1994 APOLLO GRAPHITE SHAFT
SPECIFICATIONS – WOODS

Model	Flex	Tip Dia.	Taper Tip or Parallel	Butt Dia.	Length	Weight Grams	Weight Tolerance (g)	Nominal Torque
BORON TOURLINE	R	.335	Parallel	.600	45"	96	±2	4.0
	S	.335	Parallel	.605	45"	98	±2	4.0
	X	.335	Parallel	.605	45"	100	±2	4.0
G100 SHADOW	S	.335	Parallel	.600	45"	83	±1.5	5.0
	R	.335	Parallel	.600	45"	80	±1.5	5.0
SHADOW FLX	A	.335	Parallel	.600	45"	72	±1.5	5.0
LADY SHADOW	L	.335	Parallel	.580	45"	76	±1.5	5.0
SENIOR SHADOW	A	.335	Parallel	.580	45"	79	±1.5	5.0
HMF LOW TORQUE	S	.335	Parallel	.610	45"	96	±2	2.5
	R	.335	Parallel	.610	45"	92	±2	2.5
SEAMLESS CO-WOUND	S	.335	Parallel	.600	45"	89	±2	3.5
	R	.335	Parallel	.600	45"	79	±2	4.0

1994 APOLLO GRAPHITE SHAFT
SPECIFICATIONS – IRONS

Model	Flex	Tip Dia.	Taper Tip or Parallel	Butt Dia.	Length	Weight Grams	Weight Tolerance (g)	Nominal Torque
BORON TOURLINE	R	.370	Parallel	.600	39"	80	±2	3.5
	S	.370	Parallel	.600	39"	85	±2	3.5
	X	.370	Parallel	.610	39"	90	±2	3.5
G100 SHADOW	S	.355	Taper	.600	39"	78	±1.5	4.0
	R	.355	Taper	.600	39"	73	±1.5	4.0
LADY SHADOW	L	.370	Parallel	.580	39"	69	±1.5	4.0
SENIOR SHADOW	A	.370	Parallel	.580	39"	70	±1.5	4.0
HMF LOW TORQUE	S	.370	Parallel	.600	39"	83	±2	2.5
	R	.370	Parallel	.605	39"	79	±2	2.5
SEAMLESS CO-WOUND	S	.370	Parallel	.600	39"	85	±2	3.5
	R	.370	Parallel	.600	39"	81	±2	4.0

1994 BRUNSWICK GRAPHITE SHAFT SPECIFICATIONS – WOODS

Model	Code	FCM Level	Tip Dia.	Taper Tip or Parallel	Butt Dia.	Length	Weight		Nominal Torque
							Grams	Ounces	
PRECISION FIBREMATRIX	WFX	4.5	.335	Parallel	.600	45½"	75	2.65	3.75
	WFX	5.5	.335	Parallel	.600	45½"	76	2.68	3.75
	WFX	6.5	.335	Parallel	.600	45½"	78	2.75	3.75
	WFX	7.0	.335	Parallel	.600	45½"	80	2.82	3.75
	WFX	7.5	.335	Parallel	.600	45½"	82	2.89	3.75
FIBREMATCH®	WFMPC	3.5	.335	Parallel	.580	45"	82	2.90	2.8
	WFMPC	4.5	.335	Parallel	.600	45"	89	3.15	2.8
	WFMPC	5.5	.335	Parallel	.600	45"	91	3.20	2.8
	WFMPC	6.5	.335	Parallel	.600	45"	91	3.20	2.8
	WFMPC	7.0	.335	Parallel	.600	45"	91	3.20	2.8
	WFMPC	7.5	.335	Parallel	.600	45"	91	3.20	2.8

Model	Code	Flex	Tip Dia.	Taper Tip or Parallel	Butt Dia.	Length	Weight		Nominal Torque
							Grams	Ounces	
MARK II®	MARK-W12	S	.335	Parallel	.600	45"	89	3.14	5.5
	MARK-W11	R	.335	Parallel	.600	45"	83	2.93	5.5
	MARK-W10	L	.335	Parallel	.600	45"	72	2.54	6.0

1994 BRUNSWICK GRAPHITE SHAFT SPECIFICATIONS – IRONS

Model	Code	FCM Level	Tip Dia.	Taper Tip or Parallel	Butt Dia.	Length	Weight		Nominal Torque
							Grams	Ounces	
FIBREMATCH®	IFMPC	3.5	.370	Parallel	.580	39"	83	2.93	-
	IFMPC	4.5	.370	Parallel	.600	39"	89	3.16	-
	IFMPC	5.5	.370	Parallel	.600	39"	91	3.23	-
	IFMPC	6.5	.370	Parallel	.600	39"	91	3.23	-
	IFMPC	7.0	.370	Parallel	.600	39"	91	3.23	-
	IFMPC	7.5	.370	Parallel	.600	39"	91	3.23	-

Model	Code	Flex	Tip Dia.	Taper Tip or Parallel	Butt Dia.	Length	Weight		Nominal Torque
							Grams	Ounces	
MARK II®	MARK-I12	S	.370	Parallel	.600	39"	83	2.93	3.5
	MARK-I11	R	.370	Parallel	.600	39"	77	2.72	3.5
	MARK-I10	L	.370	Parallel	.600	39"	70	2.47	6.0

1994 CARBON FIBER COMPOSITE SHAFT SPECIFICATIONS – WOODS & IRONS

Model	Shafts	Flex	Tip Dia.	Taper Tip or Parallel	Butt Dia.	Length	Weight Grams	Nominal Torque	Flex Point
CFP-57	Woods	X,S,R,	.335	Parallel	.590	45"	90	3.5	Mid
	Irons		.370	Parallel	.590	42"	83	2.5	Mid
			.355	Taper	.590	42"	83	2.5	Mid
CFP57LF	Woods	S,R,L	.335	Parallel	.590	45"	89	2.5	Low
	Irons		.370	Parallel	.590	45"	82	2.0	Low
			.355	Taper	.590	42"	82	2.0	Low
NOVUS II	Woods	X, S, R, L, Light, XLight	.335	Parallel	.590	46"	90	4.5	Mid
	Irons		.370	Parallel	.590	42"	80	3.5	Mid
			.355	Taper	.590	42"	80	3.5	Mid
A/C	Woods	X, S, R, L, Light, XLight	.335	Parallel	.590	44"	72	6.5	Low
	Irons		.370	Parallel	.585	39"	64	5.5	Low
			.355	Taper	.585	39"	64	5.5	Low
A/C+	Woods	50+ Swing Speed 60+ Swing Speed	.335	Parallel	.590	43"	77	6.0	Low
	Irons		.370	Parallel	.585	38"	66	5.5	Low
NOVUS II+	Woods	70+ Swing Speed	.335	Parallel	.590	45"	90	4.5	Mid
	Irons		.370	Parallel	.585	41"	80	3.5	Mid
NOVUS III	Woods	80+ Swing Speed 90+ Swing Speed	.335	Parallel	.590	44"	90	3.2	Mid
	Irons		.370	Parallel	.585	41"	80	2.8	Mid
NOVUS III+	Woods	80+ Swing Speed 90+ Swing Speed	.335	Parallel	.590	44"	90	3.2	Mid
	Irons		.370	Parallel	.585	41"	80	2.8	Mid
PUTTERS	Standard		.370/.355	-	.590	36"	70	-	-
	X-Long in hosel		.370/.355	-	.600	54"	105	-	-
	X-Long over hosel		.315 int./dia.	-	-	54"	100	-	-

1994 FIBER-SPEED™ FIBERGLASS SHAFT SPECIFICATIONS – WOODS & IRONS

Model	Flex	Tip Dia.	Taper Tip or Parallel	Butt Dia.	Length	Weight Grams
WOODS						
FSW-100	Flexible	.335	Parallel	.620	45"	80
FSW-200	Medium	.335	Parallel	.620	45"	89
FSW-300	Firm	.335	Parallel	.620	45"	98
TP-4000	Firmer	.335	Parallel	.620	45"	86
IRONS						
FSI-100	Flexible	.370	Parallel	.620	40"	86
FSI-200	Medium	.370	Parallel	.620	40"	86
FSI-300	Firm	.370	Parallel	.620	40"	86
TP-4000	Firmer	.370	Parallel	.620	40"	86

1994 PARAGON GRAPHITE SHAFT SPECIFICATIONS – WOODS & IRONS

Model	Shafts	Color	Flex	Tip Dia.	Taper Tip or Parallel	Butt Dia.	Length	Weight Grams	Nominal Torque	Kick Point
MIRAGE 2001	Woods		R	.335	Parallel	.610	45"	88	2.5	-
		Charcoal	S	.335	Parallel	.612	45"	90	2.5	-
			X	.335	Parallel	.614	45"	92	2.5	-
LITE TOUCH	Woods		R	.335	Parallel	.600	46"	69	5.8	-
			A	.335	Parallel	.600	46"	63	5.8	-
		Steel Blue	L	.335	Parallel	.600	46"	63	5.8	-
	Irons		R	.370	Parallel	.600	40"	63	5.0	-
			A	.370	Parallel	.600	40"	58	5.0	-
			L	.370	Parallel	.600	40"	58	5.0	-
PARA-SONIC	Woods	Matte Green	S	.335	Parallel	.610	45"	96	3.5	-
		Matte Gold	R	.335	Parallel	.612	45"	94	3.5	-
		Gloss Black								
	Irons	Black/Silver	S	.370	Parallel	.612	39"	86	3.0	-
			R	.370	Parallel	.622	39"	82	3.0	-
LOW TORQUE	Woods	Gloss Black	S	.335	Parallel	.600	45"	86	5.5	Low
		Matte Black	R	.335	Parallel	.600	45"	82	5.5	Low
		Gray Metallic	L	.335	Parallel	.600	45"	78	6.0	Low
		Gold								
		Black Cherry								
	Irons	Blue Metallic	S	.370	Parallel	.600	39"	88	3.5	Low
		Lavender (L only)	R	.370	Parallel	.600	39"	82	3.5	Low
		Black/Silver	L	.370	Parallel	.600	39"	78	3.5	Low
		Purple/Pink (L only)								
FIBERSONIC 2.0	Woods		S	.335	Parallel	.610	45"	111	2.0	High
		Champagne/	X	.335	Parallel	.610	45"	113	2.0	High
		Charcoal								
	Irons		S	.370	Parallel	.610	39"	94	2.0	High
			X	.370	Parallel	.610	39"	99	2.0	High
FIBERSONIC 2.8	Woods		R	.335	Parallel	.600	45"	96	2.8	Mid
			S	.335	Parallel	.600	45"	99	2.8	Mid
		Gold/Black								
	Irons		R	.370	Parallel	.600	39"	80	2.8	Mid
			S	.370	Parallel	.600	39"	85	2.8	Mid
FIBERSONIC 3.5	Woods		A	.335	Parallel	.600	45"	85	3.5	Low
			R	.335	Parallel	.600	45"	89	3.5	Low
		Gold/Burgundy								
	Irons		A	.370	Parallel	.600	39"	82	3.5	Low
			R	.370	Parallel	.600	39"	85	3.5	Low
DUAL KICK SYSTEM	Woods		S	.335	Parallel	.600	45"	95	3.5	Dual
			R	.335	Parallel	.600	45"	93	3.5	Dual
			AA	.370	Parallel	.600	45"	91	3.5	Dual
		Charcoal								
	Irons		S	.370	Parallel	.620	39"	92	2.5	Dual
			R	.370	Parallel	.620	39"	88	2.5	Dual
			AA	.370	Parallel	.620	39"	86	2.5	Dual

1994 SWIX® GRAPHITE SHAFT
SPECIFICATIONS – WOODS & IRONS

Model	Shafts	Flex	Tip Dia.	Taper Tip or Parallel	Butt Dia.	Length	Weight Grams	Weight Ounces	Nominal Torque	Flex Point
PERFORMA™ LITE	Woods	L,A,R	.335	Parallel	.580	45"	64	2.26	5.0	Mid
	Irons	L,A,R	.370	Parallel	.575	41"	67	2.36	3.3	Mid
PERFORMA™ 80	Woods	L,A,R	.335	Parallel	.585	45"	76	2.68	4.3	Mid
PERFORMA™ 90	Woods	A,R,S	.335	Parallel	.590	45"	78	2.75	3.1	Mid
	Irons	R,S	.370	Parallel	.600	41"	88	3.10	2.7	Mid
PERFORMA™ 100	Woods	R,S,X	.335	Parallel	.600	45"	86	3.03	2.6	Mid
	Irons	R,S	.370	Parallel	.608	41"	94	3.32	2.1	Mid
PERFORMA™ 100+	Woods	R,S,X	.335	Parallel	.605	45"	95	3.35	1.9	Mid

1994 ARCAL SYSTEM FLEX® GRAPHITE SHAFT
SPECIFICATIONS – WOODS & IRONS

Model	Shafts	Pattern	Flex	Tip Dia.	Taper Tip or Parallel	Butt Dia.	Length	Weight Grams	Nominal Torque
K2 TOUR 55	Woods	K2TWXA	X	.335	Parallel	.614	45"	98	2.6
		K2TWSA	S	.335	Parallel	.614	45"	98	2.6
K2 PRO	Woods	K2PWXA	X	.335	Parallel	.624	45"	104	3.6
		K2PWSA	S	.335	Parallel	.624	45"	100	3.6
		K2PWRA	R	.335	Parallel	.612	45"	96	3.6
	Irons	K2PISA	S	.370	Parallel	.600	39"	91	3.0
		K2PIRA	R	.370	Parallel	.600	39"	86	3.0
K3 COMBINATION	Woods	K3WCA	R/S	.335	Parallel	.606	46"	94	4.7
	Irons	K3ICA	R/S	.370	Parallel	.602	40"	94	4.0
K4 COMBINATION	Woods	K4WC	R/S	.335	Parallel	.618	46"	95	5.5
	Irons	K4IC	R/S	.370	Parallel	.622	40"	95	4.5
K4SL	Woods	K4SLW1	A	.335	Parallel	.600	44"	83	6.5
	Irons	K4SLI1	A	.370	Parallel	.600	39"	86	5.0
KLADY	Woods	KLADYW1	L	.335	Parallel	.580	43"	70	7.5
	Irons	KLADYI1	L	.370	Parallel	.580	38"	70	5.5

1994 EASTON® ALUMINUM SHAFT
SPECIFICATIONS – WOODS & IRONS

Model	Shafts	Color	Flex	Tip Dia.	Taper Tip or Parallel	Butt Dia.	Length	Weight Grams	Ounces	Nominal Torque
TOUR	Woods	Black	R,S	.335	Parallel	.600	44"	111	3.92	2.5
	Irons	Black	R,S	.370	Parallel	.600	39"	107	3.77	2.5
SENIORS	Woods	Gold	A,R	.335	Parallel	.600	44"	102	3.60	3.0
	Irons	Gold	A,R	.370	Parallel	.600	39"	99	3.48	2.5
LADIES	Woods	Red	L,A	.335	Parallel	.580	44"	99	3.50	3.5
	Irons	Red	L,A	.370	Parallel	.580	39"	96	3.37	3.0

1994 EASTON® ALUMINUM CARBON SHAFT
SPECIFICATIONS – WOODS & IRONS

Model	Shafts	Color	Flex	Tip Dia.	Taper Tip or Parallel	Butt Dia.	Length	Weight Grams	Ounces	Nominal Torque
TOUR	Woods	Black	R,S,X	.335	Parallel	.600	44"	100	3.53	3.0
	Irons	Black	R,S,X	.370	Parallel	.600	39"	104	3.67	2.5
COMPETITOR	Woods	Silver	A,R,S	.335	Parallel	.600	44"	76	2.68	4.5
	Irons	Silver	A,R,S	.370	Parallel	.600	39"	94	3.32	3.0
SENIORS	Woods	Blue	A,R	.335	Parallel	.600	44"	76	2.68	4.5
	Irons	Blue	A,R	.370	Parallel	.600	39"	94	3.32	3.0
LADIES	Woods	Yellow	L,A	.335	Parallel	.580	44"	76	2.68	5.5
	Irons	Yellow	L,A	.370	Parallel	.580	39"	80	2.82	3.5

1994 RAPPORT COMPOSITES™ GRAPHITE SHAFT SPECIFICATIONS – WOODS

Model	Code	Color	Flex	Tip Dia.	Taper Tip or Parallel	Butt Dia.	Length	Weight Grams	Nominal Torque
HYPERFLEX TOUR	HT95WX	Blackberry	X	.335	Parallel	.620	45"	96	2.8
	HT95WS		S	.335	Parallel	.620	45"	92	2.8
	HT95WR		R	.335	Parallel	.620	45"	88	2.8
HYPERFLEX PLUS	HP85WX	Copper Mist	X	.335	Parallel	.620	45"	95	3.5
	HP85WS		S	.335	Parallel	.620	45"	91	3.5
	HP85WR		R	.335	Parallel	.620	45"	87	3.5
HYPERFLEX	HF62WS	Sandy Champagne	S	.335	Parallel	.610	45"	89	4.5
	HF62WR		R	.335	Parallel	.610	45"	87	4.5
	HF62WA		A	.335	Parallel	.610	45"	85	4.5
RECOIL XLT	XL90WN	Emerald	Recoil	.335	Parallel	.610	45"	85	2.8
SCEPTRE ULTRALITE	SU86WR	Black Sable	R	.335	Parallel	.600	45"	75	4.5
	SU86WA		A	.335	Parallel	.600	45"	75	4.5
SYNSOR R/S	SR61WC	Lite Jadestone	R/S	.335	Parallel	.610	46"	86	4.5
SYNSOR	SR61WS	Lite Jadestone	S	.335	Parallel	.610	45"	87	5.0
	SR61WR		R	.335	Parallel	.610	45"	83	5.0
	SR61WA		A	.335	Parallel	.610	45"	80	5.0
	SR61WL	Blue Firemist	L	.335	Parallel	.610	45"	75	5.0
ADVENT II	AT52WR	Pewter	R	.335	Parallel	.610	45"	89	6.5
	AT52WA		A	.335	Parallel	.600	45"	87	6.5
	AT52WL	Platinum	L	.335	Parallel	.600	45"	86	6.5
ADVENT	AT50WR	Pewter	R	.335	Parallel	.620	45"	89	7.0
	AT50WA		A	.335	Parallel	.620	45"	87	7.0
	AT50WL	Platinum	L	.335	Parallel	.620	45"	85	7.0
ORACLE SGS PLUS	O262WX	Clear Raven Black	X	.335	Parallel	.600	45"	98	3.5
	O262WS		S	.335	Parallel	.600	45"	96	3.5
	O262WR		R	.335	Parallel	.600	45"	94	3.5
ORACLE SGS	O261WS	Clear Slate Gray	S	.335	Parallel	.580	45"	88	4.5
	O261WR		R	.335	Parallel	.580	45"	86	4.5
	O261WA		A	.335	Parallel	.580	45"	84	4.5
	O261WL		L	.335	Parallel	.580	45"	82	4.5
LADY SCEPTRE	LS83WL	Amethyst	L	.335	Parallel	.600	45"	78	4.0

1994 RAPPORT COMPOSITES™ GRAPHITE SHAFT SPECIFICATIONS – IRONS

Model	Code	Color	Flex	Tip Dia.	Taper Tip or Parallel	Butt Dia.	Length	Weight Grams	Nominal Torque
HYPERFLEX TOUR	HT95IX	Blackberry	X	.370	Parallel	.610	39"	91	2.2
	HT95IS		S	.370	Parallel	.610	39"	87	2.2
	HT95IR		R	.370	Parallel	.610	39"	83	2.2
HYPERFLEX PLUS	HP85IX	Copper Mist	X	.370	Parallel	.610	39"	91	3.0
	HP85IS		S	.370	Parallel	.610	39"	87	3.0
	HP85IR		R	.370	Parallel	.610	39"	83	3.0
HYPERFLEX	HF62IS	Sandy Champagne	S	.370	Parallel	.610	39"	87	3.5
	HF62IR		R	.370	Parallel	.610	39"	85	3.5
	HF62IA		A	.370	Parallel	.610	39"	83	3.5
RECOIL XLT	XL90IN	Emerald	Recoil	.370	Parallel	.610	39"	83	1.9
SCEPTRE ULTRALITE	SU86IR	Black Sable	R	.370	Parallel	.590	39"	73	3.5
	SU86IA		A	.370	Parallel	.590	39"	73	3.5
SYNSOR R/S	SR61IC	Lite Jadestone	R/S	.370	Parallel	.600	41"	84	3.5
SYNSOR	SR61IS	Lite Jadestone	S	.370	Parallel	.610	39"	85	4.0
	SR61IR		R	.370	Parallel	.610	39"	80	4.0
	SR61IA		A	.370	Parallel	.610	39"	76	4.0
	SR61IL	Blue Firemist	L	.370	Parallel	.610	39"	72	4.0
ADVENT	AT50IR	Pewter	R	.370	Parallel	.610	39"	87	6.0
	AT50IA		A	.370	Parallel	.610	39"	85	6.0
	AT50IL	Platinum	L	.370	Parallel	.610	39"	83	6.0
ORACLE SGS PLUS	O262IX	Clear Raven Black	X	.370	Parallel	.580	39"	78	3.2
	O262IS		S	.370	Parallel	.580	39"	76	3.2
	O262IR		R	.370	Parallel	.580	39"	75	3.2
ORACLE SGS	O261IS	Clear Slate Gray	S	.370	Parallel	.580	39"	86	3.5
	O261IR		R	.370	Parallel	.580	39"	84	3.5
	O261IA		A	.370	Parallel	.580	39"	82	3.5
	O261IL		L	.370	Parallel	.580	39"	80	3.5
LADY SCEPTRE	LS83IL	Amethyst	L	.370	Parallel	.580	39"	72	3.0
TOUR PROFILE	T190IX	Graphite	X	.370	Parallel	.610	39"	88	2.0
	T190IS		S	.370	Parallel	.600	39"	84	2.0
	T190IR		R	.370	Parallel	.600	39"	82	2.0
	T190IX-T	Graphite	X	.355	Taper	.610	39"	88	2.0
	T190IS-T		S	.355	Taper	.600	39"	84	2.0
	T190IR-T		R	.355	Taper	.600	39"	82	2.0

1994 UNIFIBER GRAPHITE SHAFT
SPECIFICATIONS – WOODS & IRONS

Model	Shafts	Flexes	Tip Dia.	Taper Tip or Parallel	Butt Dia.	Length	Weight Grams	Nominal Torque	Flex Point
T-25	Woods	L,A,R	.335	Parallel	.600	44"	73	5.2	Low
	Irons	L,A,R	.370	Parallel	.598	39"	69	3.7	Low
T-30	Woods	L,A,R,S	.335	Parallel	.605	44"	85	4.5	Low
	Irons	L,A,R,S	.370	Parallel	.600	39"	76	3.0	Low
T-30 LADY	Woods	L	.335	Parallel	.605	44"	85	5.0	Low
	Irons	L	.370	Parallel	.605	39"	72	4.3	Low
T-30 SENIOR	Woods	A	.335	Parallel	.605	44"	85	5.0	Low
	Irons	A	.370	Parallel	.605	39"	76	4.3	Low
T-40	Woods	R,S	.335	Parallel	.605	45"	84	4.0	Mid
	Irons	R,S	.370	Parallel	.605	39"	92	3.1	Mid
TB-40	Woods	R,S	.335	Parallel	.605	45"	84	3.5	Mid
T-45	Woods	R,S	.335	Parallel	.605	45"	84	3.5	High
	Irons	R,S	.370	Parallel	.605	39"	92	3.1	High
T-50	Woods	R,S,X	.335	Parallel	.600	45"	90	2.5	High
	Irons	R,S	.370	Parallel	.605	39"	90	2.6	High
UFX	Woods	S,X,XX	.335	Parallel	.620	45"	115	1.9	High
L.C.G. TOUR	Tip Heavy Irons	A,R,S	.370	Parallel	.605	39"	85	3.5	Mid-High
UNIFIBER LITE	Woods	A,R,S	.335	Parallel	.600	45"	65	4.1	Mid
BIG RED	Woods	S,X	.335	Parallel	.620	60"	144	2.5 @ 44"	Mid
UNIFLEX	Woods	Uniflex	.335	Parallel	.605	45"	84	2.4	Mid
CFT FILAMENT WOUND	Woods	R,S	.335	Parallel	.605	45"	86	3.5	Mid
	Irons	R,S	.370	Parallel	.605	39"	91	2.5	Mid
UNIFIBER PT	Putter	-	.370	Parallel	.605	35"	75	-	-

1994 FENWICK® GRAPHITE SHAFT
SPECIFICATIONS – WOODS & IRONS

Model	Code	Flex	Tip Dia.	Butt Dia.	Weight Grams	Nominal Torque
WORLD CLASS™ Tapered Woods, 45"						
	GS2	A	.300	.600	92	3.2
	GS3	R	.300	.600	93	3.0
	GS4	S	.300	.600	94	3.0
	GS5	X	.300	.600	96	2.9
WORLD CLASS™ Tapered Irons, 40"						
	GS240	A	.355	.600	90	2.0
	GS340	R	.355	.600	92	1.9
	GS440	S	.355	.600	94	1.8
	GS540	X	.355	.600	96	1.6

1994 FENWICK® GRAPHITE SHAFT
SPECIFICATIONS – WOODS & IRONS *(cont.)*

Model	Code	Flex	Tip Dia.	Butt Dia.	Weight Grams	Nominal Torque
WORLD CLASS™ Tapered Irons, 37"	GS237	A	.355	.600	84	1.9
	GS337	R	.355	.600	86	1.8
	GS437	S	.355	.600	87	1.7
	GS537	X	.355	.600	89	1.6
WORLD CLASS™ & BIOLINE Parallel Woods, 45"	GS1P	L	.335	.600	95	3.0
	GS2P	A	.335	.600	97	2.8
	GS3P	R	.335	.600	98	2.6
	GS4P	S	.335	.600	100	2.5
	GS5P	X	.335	.600	103	2.4
WORLD CLASS™ & BIOLINE Parallel Irons, 40"	GS240	A	.370	.600	94	1.8
	GS340	R	.370	.600	95	1.7
	GS440	S	.370	.600	97	1.6
	GS540	X	.370	.600	102	1.5
WORLD CLASS™ & BIOLINE Parallel Irons, 37"	GS237	A	.370	.600	85	1.7
	GS337	R	.370	.600	87	1.6
	GS437	S	.370	.600	88	1.5
	GS537	X	.370	.600	91	1.4

Model	Code	Flex	Tip Dia.	Butt Dia.	Weight Grams	Nominal Torque	Kick Point
MEN'S AEROFLEX Parallel Woods, 45"	AF-2P	A	.335	.600	85	4.3	Lower 1/3
	AF-3P	R	.335	.600	96	3.0	Mid
	AF-4P	R/S	.335	.600	98	3.0	Mid
	AF-45P	S	.335	.600	98	2.8	Mid
MEN'S AEROFLEX Parallel Irons	AF-340	R	.370	.600	90	2.2	Mid
	AF-440	R/S	.370	.600	93	2.1	Mid
	AF-337	R	.370	.600	85	2.2	Mid
	AF-437	R/S	.370	.600	88	2.1	Mid
	Length: 340 & 440 = 40" for #1 - 5 irons; 337 & 437 = 37" for #6 - wedges.						
LADY AEROFLEX™ Parallel Woods, 44"	AF-1PL	L	.335	.600	70	4.3	Lower 1/3
	AF-2PL	R	.335	.600	75	4.1	Lower 1/3
BIO-MAG™ Parallel Woods, 45"	BMG-2P	A	.335	.620	80	3.9	Low
	BMG-3P	R	.335	.620	80	3.2	Mid
	BMG-4P	S	.335	.620	80	2.9	Mid
AEROSTAR Parallel Woods, 44"	AS-1P	L	.335	.600	70	4.6	Low
	AS-3P	R	.335	.600	75	4.4	Low
	AS-4P	S	.335	.600	80	4.0	Mid/Low
AEROSTAR Parallel Irons, 39"	AS139	L	.370	.600	68	4.0	Low
	AS339	R	.370	.600	68	3.8	Low
	AS439	S	.370	.600	78	3.4	Mid/Low
AEROFIRE™	ASE-9P	A	.335	.600	71	5.4	Low
BIO-SENSE™ Putter, 37"	BPS-10P	-	.370	.580	50	7.0	-

660

1994 UST® GRAPHITE SHAFT
SPECIFICATIONS – WOODS & IRONS

Model	Shafts	Flexes	Tip Dia.	Butt Dia.	Taper Tip or Parallel	Length	Weight Grams	Nominal Torque	Flex Point
COMPETITION SERIES *TOUR WEIGHT™*	Woods	R,S,X	.335	.600	Parallel	45"	100-105	3.3-3.0	Mid
	Irons	R,S,X	.370	.600	Parallel	40"	115	2.4	High
	Irons	R,S,X	.355	.600	Taper	40"-35½"	115-105	2.2	High
9200	Woods	R,S,X	.335	.600	Parallel	45"	87-97	3.5	Mid
6600 M-40	Woods	R,S,X	.335	.620	Parallel	45"	90-94	3.0	High
6600 M-40 BORE-THROUGH	Woods	R,S,X	.335	.620	Parallel	46"	95-98	3.0	High
660 M-40	Irons	R,S,X	.370	.610	Parallel	40"	85-90	2.4	High
660T M-40	Irons	R,S,X	.355	.610	Taper	40"-35½"	88-94	2.2	High
ULTRA LIGHT SERIES **4200**	Woods	R,S	.335	.600	Parallel	46"	63-68	5.0	Mid
EASYFLEX™ SERIES **6010E**	Woods	*soft* R	.335	.580	Parallel	45"	83	4.3	Low
601E	Irons	*soft* R	.370	.580	Parallel	40"	83	3.5	Low
LADY EASYFLEX™ **6010L**	Woods	Ladies	.335	.580	Parallel	44"	80	4.5	Low
601L	Irons	Ladies	.370	.580	Parallel	39"	78	4.0	Low
6400 SERIES **6400F (Fade)**	Woods	R,S	.335	.600	Parallel	45"	92/94	4.0	Mid
6400	Woods	R,S	.335	.600	Parallel	45"	92/94	4.0	Mid
640	Irons	R,S	.370	.600	Parallel	40"	84/85	3.4	Mid
640T	Irons	R,S	.355	.600	Taper	40"-35½"	92/94	3.0	Mid
6200 SERIES **6200**	Woods	A/L	.335	.570	Parallel	46"	86	5.4	Mid
	Woods	R/S	.335	.590	Parallel	46"	87	5.4	Mid
620	Irons	A/L	.370	.570	Parallel	42"	89	3.5	Mid
	Irons	R/S	.370	.590	Parallel	42"	94	3.5	Mid

PROPRIETARY SHAFT PATTERN IDENTIFICATION

Company	Shaft Name	Graphite or Steel	Flex Point	Weight
Ben Hogan	Apex	Steel	Low	Lightweight
	Apex Pro	Steel	Low	Standard
	Apex D	Steel	Low	Standard
	Apex Extra	Steel	Mid	Lightweight
	Vector	Steel	High	Lightweight
	Legend	Steel	Low	Lightweight
	Saber	Steel	High	Standard
	Apex	Graphite	Low	Very Lightweight
	Lady Hogan	Steel	Low	Lightweight
	Hogan Plus	Steel	Low	Lightweight
Callaway	Memphis 10	Steel	Mid	Lightweight
	RCH60	Graphite	Mid/Low (3°)	Very Lightweight
	RCH90	Graphite	Mid (3°)	Very Lightweight
	Ladies Gems	Graphite	Mid/Low (3°)	Very Lightweight
	Ladies Gems	Steel	Low	Lightweight
Cleveland Golf	Extra-Lite	Steel	Low	Lightweight
	Diamond	Graphite	Mid/High	Very Lightweight
	Square	Graphite	Mid/High	Very Lightweight
	Circle	Graphite	Mid/High	Very Lightweight
	HET	Graphite	Mid/High	Very Lightweight
Cobra	TLC	Steel	Mid	Lightweight
Daiwa	TRX-T	Graphite	High	Very Lightweight
	TRX	Graphite	Mid	Very Lightweight
	TR	Graphite	Low	Very Lightweight
Dunlop	Alta	Steel	High	Lightweight
	Maxpower	Steel	Low	Standard
	Max Lite	Steel	Mid	Lightweight
H & B	Dynasty Plus	Steel	Variable	Lightweight
	Dynasty	Steel	Mid	Very Lightweight
	Propower	Steel	Mid	Standard
	Duopower	Steel	Mid	Standard
Head Golf	Big Head	Graphite	Mid	Very Lightweight
Karsten Manufacturing	ZZ Lite	Steel	High	Lightweight
	ZZZ Lite	Steel	High	Lightweight
	K	Steel	Mid	Lightweight
	Olympic	Graphite	High	Very Lightweight
	TTT	Steel	High	Standard
	KT	Steel	Mid	Lightweight
	Microtaper	Steel	Low	Lightweight
	JZ	Steel	Mid	Lightweight
	KT-M	Steel	Mid	Lightweight
	101*	Graphite	Mid (3.4°)	Very Lightweight
	201*	Graphite	Mid (2.9°)	Very Lightweight
	301*	Graphite	Mid (2.2°)	Very Lightweight

*Note that the 101, 201 & 301 have similar characteristics except that the 201 is stiffer than the 101 and the 301 is stiffer than the 201.

Company	Shaft Name	Graphite or Steel	Flex Point	Weight
Lynx	Lynx Lite	Steel	High	Lightweight
MacGregor	Response	Steel	Mid	Very Lightweight
	Velocitized Dual Action	Steel	Low	Lightweight
	Tourney Action	Steel	High	Standard
	Microstep	Steel	Low	Standard
	Propel (1958-68)	Steel	Low	Standard
	VDA2	Steel	Low	Standard

PROPRIETARY SHAFT PATTERN IDENTIFICATION *(cont.)*

Company	Shaft Name	Graphite or Steel	Flex Point	Weight
Maxfli Golf	Alta	Steel	High	Lightweight
	Maxpower	Steel	Low	Standard
	Max Lite	Steel	Mid	Lightweight
Merit	Merit	Steel	Variable	Lightweight
Mizuno	Dynaflex 1100	Steel	Low	Lightweight
	Dynaflex 2200	Steel	Mid	Lightweight
	Dynaflex 3300	Steel	High	Lightweight
Nicklaus Golf	Nicklaus Golf	Steel	Variable	Lightweight
Northwestern	Power Kick	Steel	Low	Lightweight
	Proaction Plus	Steel	Low	Standard
	Micro Lite 400	Steel	Mid	Lightweight
Peerless	Hex Flex	Steel	High	Lightweight
	Pro-Lite	Steel	Mid	Lightweight
	Axiom-Lite	Steel	Low	Lightweight
	Palmer Lite	Steel	Low	Lightweight
	Peerless	Steel	Low	Lightweight
Pinseeker	Pin Lite	Steel	Mid	Lightweight
	Pinseeker	Graphite	Low	Very Lightweight
	MS	Graphite	Low	Very Lightweight
	Premium Gold	Graphite	Low	Very Lightweight
Ram	Reactive Rhythm	Steel	Mid	Lightweight
	Ramlite	Steel	Mid	Lightweight
Sounder	Sounder Flex	Steel	Mid	Lightweight
Top Flite	Technic	Steel	Mid	Lightweight
	Thunder Heat	Steel	Low	Standard
	Thunder Heat	Graphite	Mid	Lightweight
	XL-420	Graphite	Mid	Very Lightweight
Taylor Made	Taylite Plus	Steel	Mid	Lightweight
	Flex Twist	Graphite	Various	Lightweight/Very Lightweight
	Taylite	Steel	Mid	Lightweight
	Flex Twist Plus	Graphite	Various	Lightweight/Very Lightweight
Titleist	Power-Step	Steel	Low	Standard
	Power Flo	Steel	High	Standard
	Title-Lite II	Steel	Mid	Lightweight
	MS-209	Steel	High	Lightweight
Tommy Armour	Tour Step	Steel	High	Lightweight
	Butterfly	Steel	Mid	Lightweight
Wilson	V2	Steel	Low	Lightweight
	Aggressor	Steel	Low	Lightweight
	Dynapower	Steel	Low	Lightweight
	Counter Torque	Steel	Low	Lightweight
	Dynamic	Steel	High	Standard
	Dyna-Step	Steel	Low	Lightweight
	Firestick	Steel	Low	Lightweight
	Firestick	Graphite	Various	Lightweight/Very Lightweight
Yamaha	Paraflex	Graphite	Low	Very Lightweight

CHAPTER 60

MEASURING THE TORQUE OF A GOLF SHAFT

Shaft torque is defined as a shaft's resistance to twisting along its longitudinal axis. To better understand the torque specification, select an assembled golf club and place one hand around the clubhead and the other hand around the grip. Twist the two components in opposite directions. The resistance to twist that you feel is a measurable feature. Some golf clubs that you could select would have a shaft that would permit you to twist the shaft a significant degree while there are other shafts that would permit very little twisting.

Torque in a golf shaft has an impact upon the angle of the clubface at impact and how the club reacts when ball impact occurs. Torque also affects the feel of the golf club in a player's hands and can therefore influence the player's acceptance of the entire golf club.

As club assemblers become more aware of the importance of torque in a golf shaft, the need to be able to measure this specification increases. The GolfWorks® Digital Shaft Torque Tester is the only unit that permits the club assembler to measure torque on a raw shaft and one that is already assembled. You can therefore ask a customer to select his/her favorite club, measure the torque (as well as the frequency as demonstrated in Chapter 63) and then build another club or a set of clubs based upon the measured torque specification. Keep in mind that trimming will affect the torque. The more the shaft has been trimmed from the tip, the more the torque will decrease. Conversely, the more the shaft is trimmed from the butt the less the torque will decrease.

Please note that the reading from an assembled club will not be the same as it would be for the same shaft if it were unassembled. However, from your own personal experience and testing, you can develop your own chart that will permit you to select raw shafts that have similar torque characteristics to a shaft that is already in an assembled club.

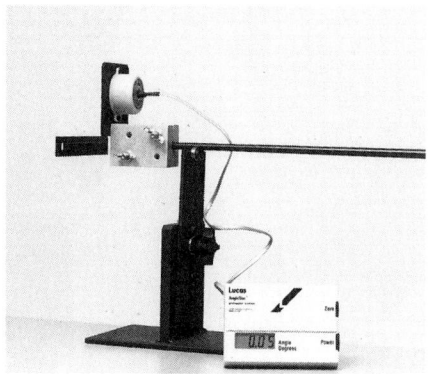

60-1 The GolfWorks® **Digital Shaft Torque Tester** will measure the torque on a set of shafts or on an assembled club. NOTE: Because the methods for measuring torque varies with each manufacturer, the torque values may not be comparable to specifications provided by the shaft manufacturers.

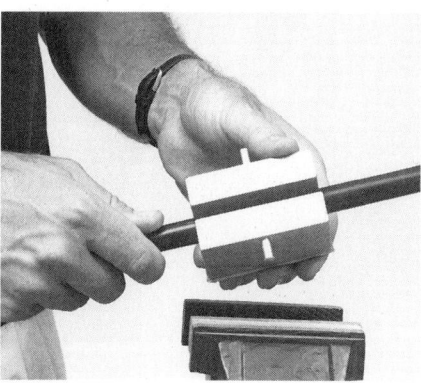

60-2 To test the torque of a shaft only. Tighten the butt end of the shaft in the **shaft butt clamp** so the shaft is 32" on woods and 28" for irons from the end of the **shaft butt clamp** nearest the tip to the shaft tip. Place into a vise so the shaft is horizontal and tighten.

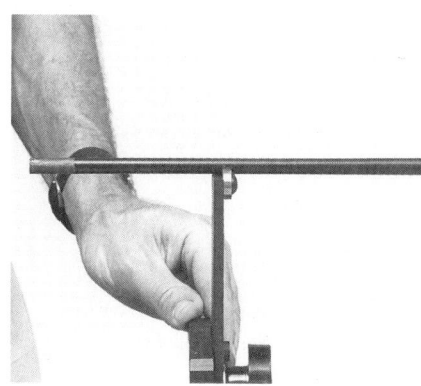

60-3 Position the **rolling device** so the rollers just touch the shaft 4" from the tip.

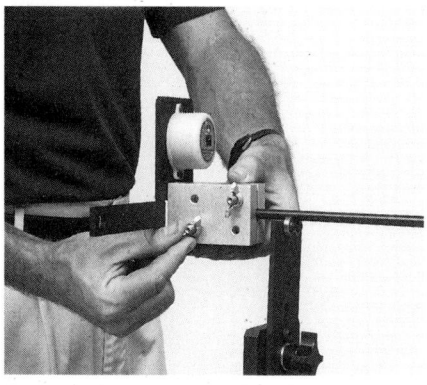

60-4 Attach the **clamping component** of the **Lucas Angle Star** to the shaft. The tip of the shaft should be even with the back of the clamp. Finger tighten the wing nut.

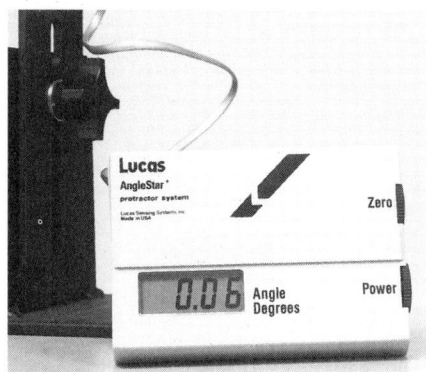

60-5 Plug in the electronic gauge. Turn the unit on. Gently adjust the **clamping component** of the **Lucas Angle Star** to get a reading below 1° and firmly tighten the wing nuts.

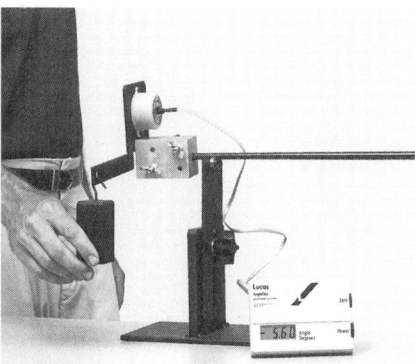

60-6 Hang the weight on either end of the **Tip Torquing Device**. Record the reading as digitally displayed.

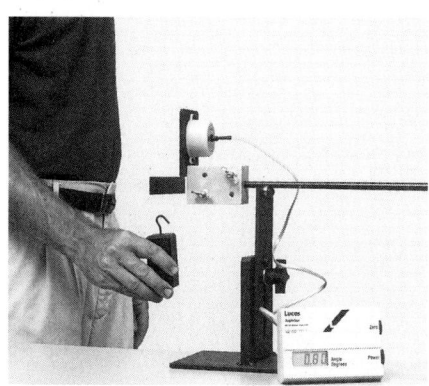

60-7 After recording the first reading, remove the weight and take a second reading. Subtract this second reading from the first reading. If both readings are positive, subtract to determine the degree of torque; if both readings are negative, subtract; if one reading is negative and one is positive, add.

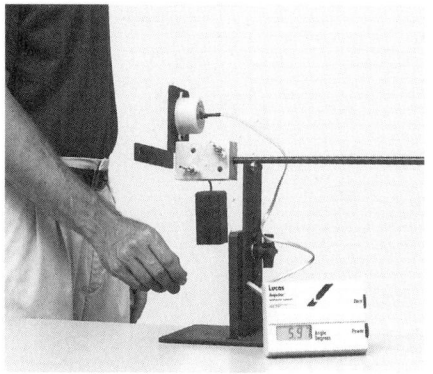

60-8 Next, hang the weight on the opposite end of the **Tip Torquing Device** and record the reading.

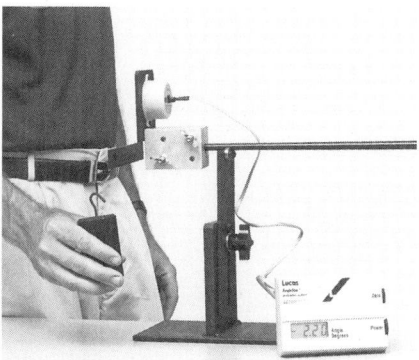

60-9 Remove the weight and take a second reading. Subtract the second reading from the first reading. Finally, average the torque measured in this step and the torque measured in Photo 60-7 to obtain the final torque measurement for the shaft. **NOTE: The final reading in degrees is always positive... there is no such thing as a negative torque.**

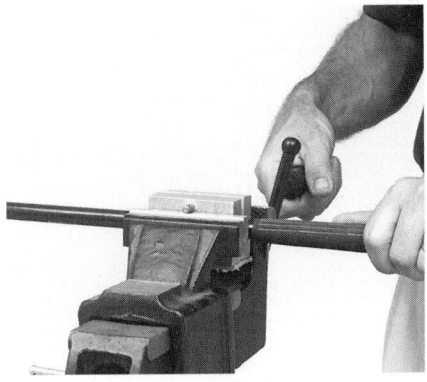

60-10 The shaft torque of an assembled club can be tested for comparison purposes only with another club. The actual torque of a shaft within an assembled club cannot be obtained, however, by measuring two assembled clubs, it can be determined which club has more torque and approximate degrees of torque can be established. To begin, clamp the butt end of the shaft just below the grip with the **shaft butt clamp.**

60-11 Adjust the rollers on the **rolling device** 4" from the top of the ferrule (or hosel if no ferrule is present).

60-12 Remove the wing nuts and separate the **clamping unit**. Place one half of the **clamping unit** against the shaft so it is resting against the top of the ferrule (or hosel if no ferrule is present). Place the other half of the **clamping unit** over the shaft and retighten the wing nuts. Make the appropriate adjustment to achieve a reading less than 1°.

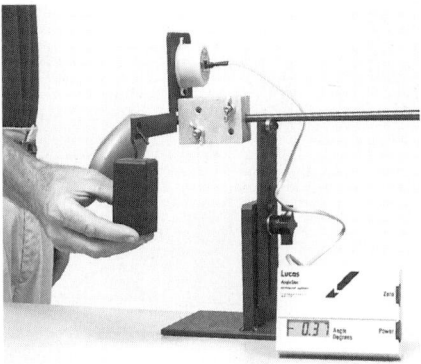

60-13 Follow Photos 60-6 through 60-9 to obtain the final torque measurement.

NOTES

SECTION

EIGHT

GOLF CLUB BALANCING AND MATCHING METHODS AND PROCEDURES

CHAPTER 61

SWINGWEIGHT METHOD

Although it's been in existence for more than fifty years, swingweight is probably one of the most misunderstood and most commonly written about aspects of golf club design. While there have been some good articles written about swingweight, many have been incomplete and somewhat confusing. Over the years, swingweight has increased in complexity with the introduction of newly designed scales, and a number of claims concerning special balancing methods. Swingweight can be more easily understood if specific examples are used to prove the relationships that exist and their effects on one another as part of the total golf club design.

■ Definition of Swingweight

This is where much of the misunderstanding about swingweight begins. There have been so many definitions written which are partially wrong, partially correct. The simple, correct non-technical definition of swingweight is: the measurement of a golf club's weight distribution about a fulcrum point which is established at a specified distance from the grip end of the club. This still does not pin swingweight down to an exact definition. For an exact definition we need to know which of the two different swingweight scale fulcrum points were used, 12" on the Official Scale or 14" on the Prorythmic Scale, Lorythmic Scale, Ping Scale, Hogan Scale, Shadowgraph, Golfsmith Scale and The GolfWorks® Scale.

■ History of Swingweight

The first swingweight scale was invented by Robert Adams of Waban, Massachusetts in the early 1920's. The first man to recognize the potential of such a scale was Kenneth Smith. He used this scale in the manufacture of golf clubs and he was also the supplier and in later years, the manufacturer of this original swingweight scale. In the early years the scale was manufactured by the Howe Scale Company in Massachusetts. The swingweight scale was called the Lorythmic Scale and was characterized by a 14" dimension from the grip end stop to the fulcrum point. It also had arbitrary swingweight values assigned to its scale which we call today a "Direct Reading Scale" (D-1, D-2, E-0, etc.).

Apparently as time went on, Kenneth Smith recognized a few deficiencies in the Lorythmic Scale. In the late 1940's he introduced another scale of his invention called the Official Swingweight Scale. This scale differed from the Lorythmic Scale as follows:

1. The Official Scale was designed with a 12" dimension from the grip end stop to the fulcrum point as compared to the Lorythmic Scale with a 14" dimension to the fulcrum. See Figure 61-1. This change was said to eliminate the correction factor of swingweighting irons two swingweights lighter than woods on the Lorythmic Scale. According to Kenneth Smith, most pros had generally agreed that this was necessary when using the Lorythmic Scale to maintain a sameness of feel between the woods and irons. The intent of the Official Scale was to make a slight adjustment of 2" on the fulcrum point (12" versus 14") thus allowing both woods and irons to be swing-weighted the same and consequently feel the same. The puzzling part and inconsistency in this logic is that the Lorythmic Scale is still almost exclusively used by golf club manufacturers, and I know of no one's swingweighting irons two points less than woods.

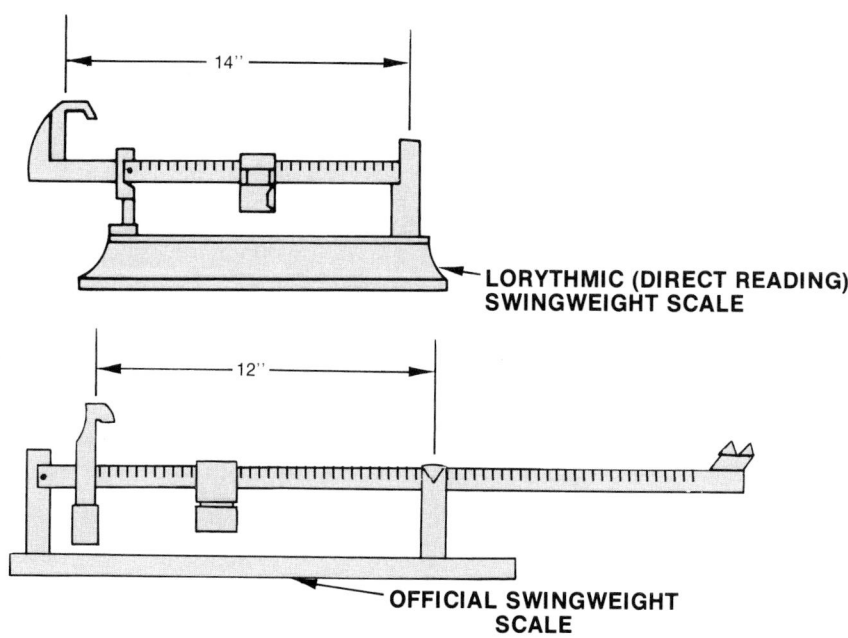

Figure 61-1
"Official" versus "Lorythmic" fulcrum distance

669

2. The Official Scale does not read swingweight with the traditional symbol which characterize the Lorythmic Scale such as E-1, D-0, etc. The Official Scale measures swingweight as a direct reading in ounces such as 20.0, 20.3, 20.5. This ounce reading is simply the amount of weight required to counterbalance the club horizontally from a 12" fulcrum point. See Figure 61-2.

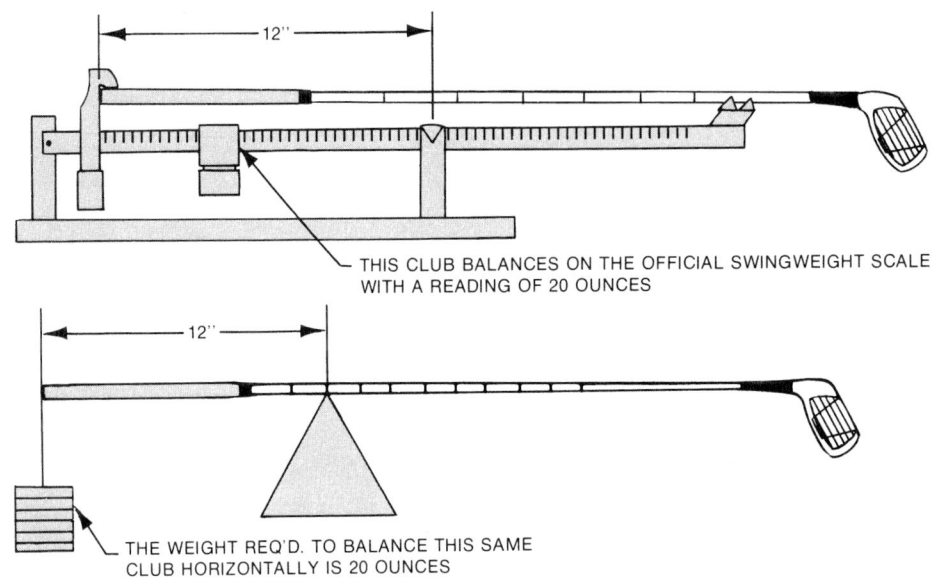

THIS CLUB BALANCES ON THE OFFICIAL SWINGWEIGHT SCALE WITH A READING OF 20 OUNCES

THE WEIGHT REQ'D. TO BALANCE THIS SAME CLUB HORIZONTALLY IS 20 OUNCES

Figure 61-2
Defining the direct ounce reading on the "Official Scale"

3. The Official Scale will also measure a golf club's total weight in ounces or grams whereas the original Lorythmic Scale only measures swingweight.

After the Official Scale, Kenneth Smith added still another type of swingweight scale. This one, called the Prorythmic Scale, turned out to be a logical extension of both the Lorythmic and the Official Swingweight Scales. The Prorythmic Scale incorporated the total weight feature of the Official Scale in ounces and grams and the direct reading feature of the Lorythmic Scale (E-1, D-0, D-1). This scale was designed to utilize the 14" dimension from grip end stop to fulcrum point which is the same as the Lorythmic Swingweight Scale.

As mentioned earlier, most manufacturers use the Lorythmic Scale as purchased from Kenneth Smith. However, a number of manufacturers have found that this particular design creates two problems in manufacturing golf clubs. First, when a golf club is placed on the scale an operator must slide a weight back and forth to get the scale to balance. When it finally does begin to balance, the scale arm is usually bounding up and down so that it takes a while to dampen or come to a complete stop, thus making this a relatively slow process to check the swingweight of a golf club in mass production.

Second, use of the Lorythmic Scale requires that the operator use his own judgment as to whether or not the scale is balancing in its exact middle position. As a result, a number of manufacturers have worked with various scale companies to develop special swingweight scales which overcome the above problems. These scales still use the same principle of determining swingweight and give the same reading as the Lorythmic Scale. The most popular production scale of this type is the Shadowgraph Direct Reading Swingweight Scale manufactured by the Franklin Electric Company. It is widely used in the golf industry. See Photo 61-3. Also, Photos 61-4 through 61-12 describe different types of swingweight scales.

670

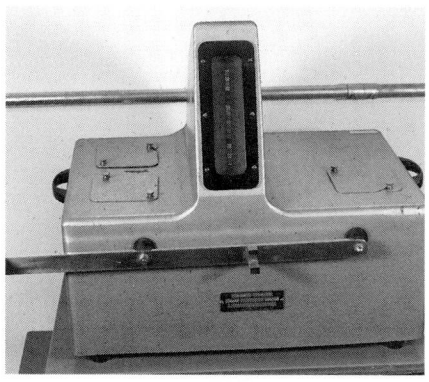

61-3

The Shadowgraph Swingweight Scale.
This is an electronic scale which measures swingweight only. It is Lorythmic (D0, D1, D2, etc.) and is designed for production use because of its rapid dampening characteristic. 14" fulcrum.

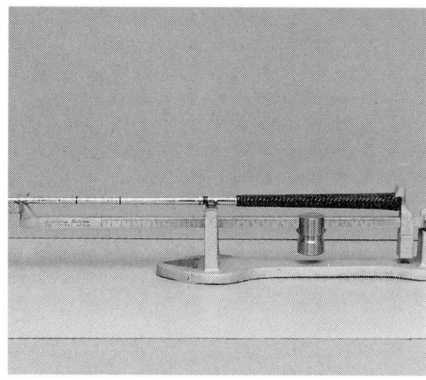

61-4

The Official Swingweight Scale measures in ounces (20.3, 20.4, 20.5, etc.) and total weight in ounces and grams. A conversion chart is used with this scale to convert readings to Lorythmic units. 12" fulcrum. The name is a misnomer as virtually every manufacturer uses the Lorythmic reading type scales with 14" fulcrums.

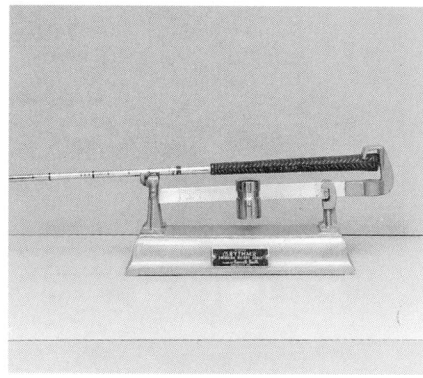

61-5

The Lorythmic Swingweight Scale measures swingweight only in Lorythmic units (D0, D1, D2, etc.). This is the original swingweight scale developed in the late 1920's. 14" fulcrum.

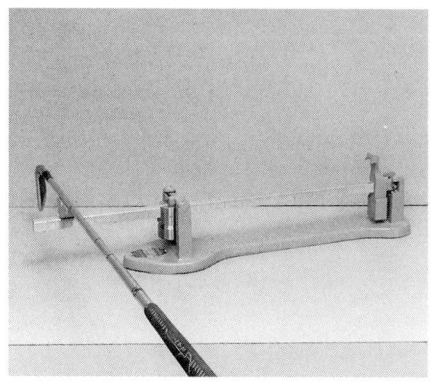

61-6

The Prorythmic Swingweight Scale measures swingweight in Lorythmic units (D0, D1, D2, etc.) and total weight in ounces and grams. 14" fulcrum. This photo shows total weight being measured.

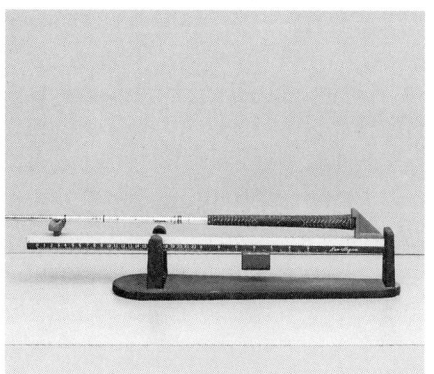

61-7

The Ben Hogan Co. Swingweight Scale measures swingweight in Lorythmic units (D0, D1, D2, etc.) and total weight in ounces and grams. 14" fulcrum.

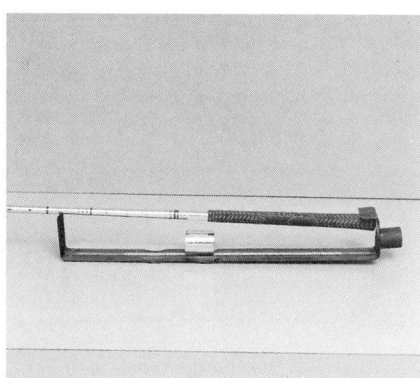

61-8

The Ping Swingweight Scale measures swingweight in Lorythmic units (D0, D1, D2, etc.) and total weight in ounces. 14" fulcrum.

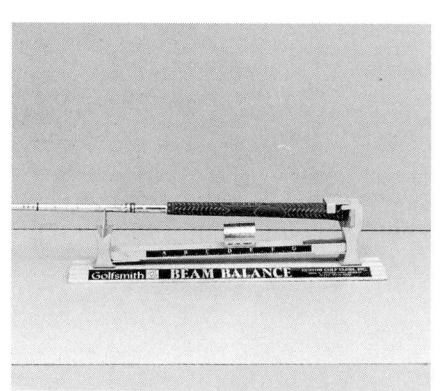

61-9

The Golfsmith Swingweight Scale measures swingweight only. Measures in Lorythmic units (D0, D1, D2, etc.). 14" fulcrum.

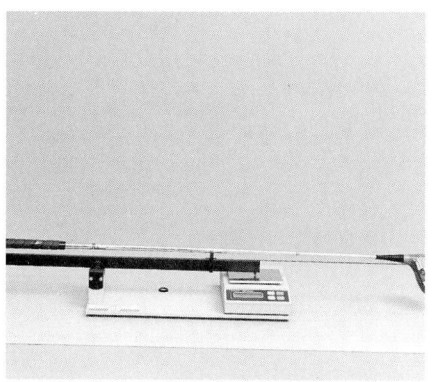

61-10

The O'Haus Electronic Swingweight Scale. This scale measures swingweight in Lorythmic units (D0, D1, D2, etc.) and total weight in ounces or grams. 14" fulcrum.

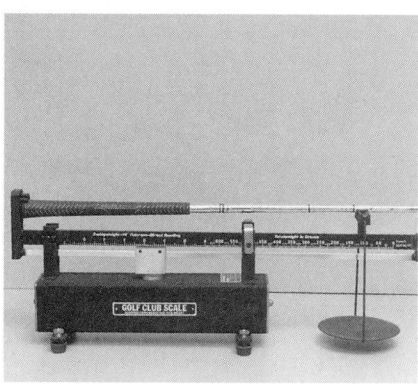

61-11

The GolfWorks® Swingweight Scale measures swingweight in Lorythmic units (D0, D1, D2, etc.) and total weight in ounces and grams. 14" fulcum. The scale also has a tray for weighing individual components during club assembly.

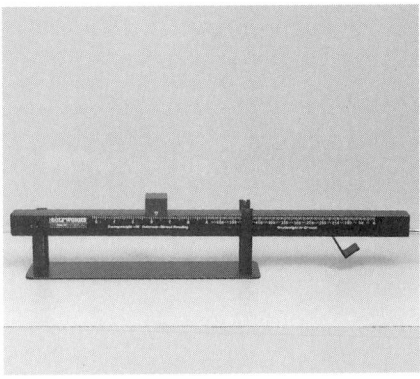

61-12
The GolfWorks® Low Cost Swingweight Scale measures swingweight in Lorythmic units (D0, D1, D2, etc.) and total weight in ounces and grams. 14" fulcrum.

■ Converting Official Swingweight Scale Readings to Lorythmic Swingweight Scale Readings

Swingweight has already been defined earlier in this chapter, but for the sake of clarity and exactness it will be defined again for the appropriate type swingweight scale:

Scale Type	Definition
14" Fulcrum Direct Reading (Lorythmic type)	The measurement of a golf club's weight distribution about a point 14" from the grip end of the club.
12" Fulcrum Ounces Reading (Official Scale)	The measurement of a golf club's weight distribution about a point 12" from the grip end of the club.

Most manufacturers today use the Lorythmic Scale to measure swingweight; however, many golf professionals and repair shops measure swingweight on the Official Scale. Naturally, much confusion is created simply because each of these different type swingweight scales do not always correlate and provide identical readings from the same golf club.

To be able to understand how the Lorythmic (14" fulcrum) and the Official (12" fulcrum) Scales relate we must first understand the mechanics of what swingweight measures. Swingweight should actually be expressed in units called "inch-ounces." Swingweight is a function of a portion of the golf club's length in inches, determined by its balance point, and its total weight in ounces multiplied together. When you multiply inches and ounces the product is called "inch-ounces." Figure 61-13 shows a simple method of determining swingweight in this manner by simply multiplying the total weight of the club times the distance in inches between a point 12 inches from the grip end of the club and the point at which the golf club balances. Also, note that Figure 61-13 shows a conversion chart whereby the Official Scale inch-ounce reading can be converted to a Lorythmic type reading (E-0, D-1, D-2).

The main problem with accurately converting Official Scale readings to Lorythmic readings is that the conversion chart is based on standard weight steel shafts and does not take into consideration the lighter weight shafts available today, which in turn build clubs of lighter overall weights. There have been some conversion charts worked out which also utilize the golf club's total weight to give a more accurate conversion from Official to Lorythmic. However, in all of the writings done on Lorythmic versus Official, including my own in the past, one very important question has not been asked: Why does the golf industry need a 12" fulcrum swingweight scale? The answer in my opinion is quite simple. There is no need for a 12" fulcrum swingweight scale. The following facts should speak for themselves.

1. The golf club manufacturers build golf clubs on 14" fulcrum swingweight scales. They never converted to the 12" fulcrum Official Scale after its introduction in the 1940's.

2. Irons are not swingweighted two points lighter than woods when they are built on the 14" fulcrum scale.

3. In all my years in the golf industry I have never heard any golf professionals, tour players or amateurs tell me that they preferred their irons swingweighted two points less than their woods for sameness of feel. There may be a number of golfers who do play with irons lighter in swingweight than their woods, but no general consensus exists. Since this fact was the main premise for the Official Swingweight Scale's existence, it does not seem to be justified. The Official Swingweight Scales' popularity with golf professionals and repair shops was its ability to measure a golf club's total weight in ounces or grams and this gave it a dual purpose. Now, as seen in Figures 61-3 through 61-12 there are a number of 14" fulcrum direct reading swingweight scales that also measure a golf club's total weight in ounces and grams.

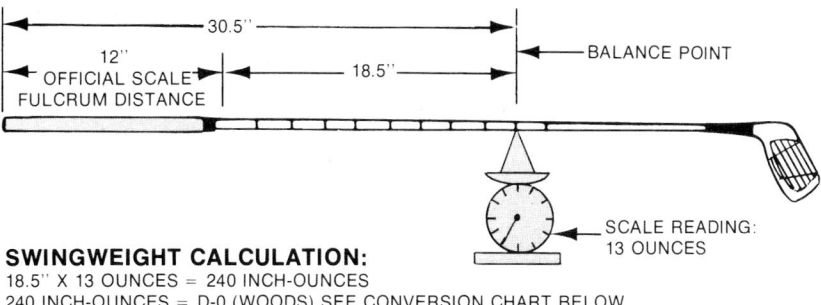

SWINGWEIGHT CALCULATION:
18.5" X 13 OUNCES = 240 INCH-OUNCES
240 INCH-OUNCES = D-0 (WOODS) SEE CONVERSION CHART BELOW

LORYTHMIC SWINGWEIGHT (14" FULCRUM)

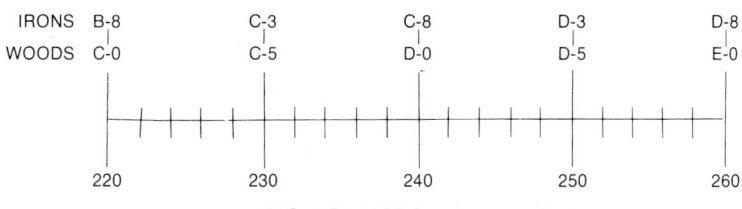

The 12" Fulcrum Inch-Ounce Conversion Figures above were derived by multiplying the Official Scale Ounce Reading from a Standard Swingweight Conversion Chart times the 12" Fulcrum Distance. EXAMPLE: A scale reading of 20 ounces (D-0) X 12" = 240 inch-ounces. Every 2 inch-ounces equals 1 swingweight or .166 ounces X 12" fulcrum. .166 ounces is the counterbalance weight being measured by the Official Scale for each swingweight.

Figure 61-13
Swingweight Principle and Conversion (12" Fulcrum
Inch-ounces to 14" Fulcrum Direct Reading Lorythmic)

■ Converting 14" Fulcrum Inch-Ounces to Lorythmic Readings

Basically, this is the same procedure shown in Figure 61-13 with the main exception being that the fulcrum is 14" and not 12". This procedure and conversion chart are shown here for those who wish to calculate the Lorythmic direct reading swingweights (D-0, D-1, E-0, etc.) without the use of a swingweight scale. See Figure 61-14.

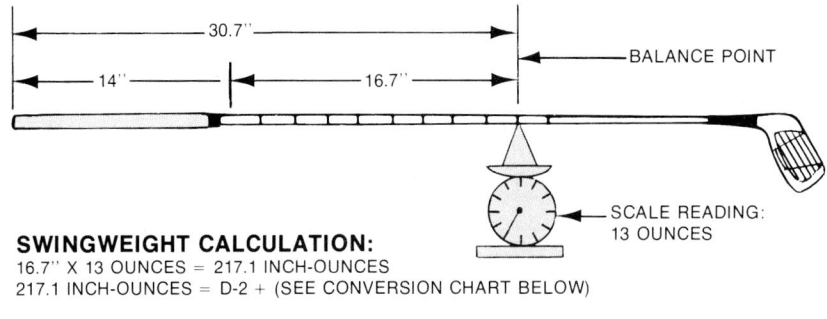

SWINGWEIGHT CALCULATION:
16.7" X 13 OUNCES = 217.1 INCH-OUNCES
217.1 INCH-OUNCES = D-2 + (SEE CONVERSION CHART BELOW)

LORYTHMIC SWINGWEIGHT (14" FULCRUM)

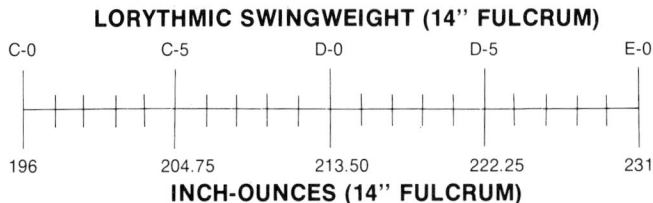

INCH-OUNCES (14" FULCRUM)

The 14" Fulcrum Inch-ounce Conversion Figures above were derived by multiplying 14 ounces (the amount of weight required to counterbalance a club at C-0) times the 14" Fulcrum Distance. Each swingweight equals 1¾ Inch-ounces and also equals ⅛ ounce of counterbalancing weight to change the swingweight by 1.
⅛ Ounce X 14" = 1¾ Inch-ounces.

Figure 61-14
Swingweight Principle and Conversion (14" Fulcrum
Inch-ounces to 14" Fulcrum Direct Reading Lorythmic)

■ Summary

The Official Scale is more sensitive than the Lorythmic Scale when measuring swingweight of long and short length clubs with different weight distributions and total weights. Consequently, when checking known Lorythmic swingweights on the Official Scale it will usually be found during conversion that wood clubs will swingweight slightly more than iron clubs. This generally confirms the intent of Kenneth Smith in developing the Official Scale which was to swingweight woods and irons the same on the Official Scale and have the woods measure approximately two swingweights heavier than irons on the Lorythmic Scale.

Table 61-1 provides a conversion chart for Official Scale and Lorythmic Scale readings. It is not always accurate. The reason is that club lengths, shaft weights, grip weights and head weights from set to set and club to club vary, making a conversion table of this type theoretical or approximate at best. When actually converting or checking Lorythmic Swingweights on the Official Balance Scale, allow for a variation within a set of up to three swingweights, although it should usually be less. Some manufacturers adjust swingweight in the butt end or under the grip by adding weights thus increasing the total golf club weight while obtaining the desired swingweight. This will usually tend to make the conversion spread greater than usual, especially in the shorter irons.

It is the author's opinion that the Official Swingweight Scale has limited practical application other than its ability to measure total weight in ounces and grams. The most practical type of swingweight scales and those which would surely eliminate much of the confusion in converting swingweights is the Prorythmic Type 14" Fulcrum Direct Reading Scales which also measure total weight. The following list indicates this type of scale and the manufacturer.

Prorythmic Swingweight Scale . . . . Kenneth Smith Golf Co.
Ping Swingweight Scale . . . . Karsten Manufacturing Co.
Ben Hogan Swingweight Scale. . . . . Ben Hogan Co.
The Golf Works® Swingweight Scale . . . . Ralph Maltby Enterprises Inc.

TABLE 61-1
Swingweight Conversion Chart
Official Swingweight Scale vs. Lorythmic Swingweight Scale

Official Swingweight Scale Reading	Lorythmic Scale Swingweight		Official Swingweight Scale Reading	Lorythmic Scale Swingweight	
	Woods	Irons		Woods	Irons
18.33	C0	B8	20.00	D0	C8
18.4	0.4	8.4	20.05	0.3	8.3
18.45	0.7	8.7	20.1	0.6	8.6
			20.15	0.9	8.9
18.5	C1	B9	20.17	D1	C9
18.55	1.3	9.3			
18.6	1.6	9.6	20.2	1.2	9.2
			20.25	1.5	9.5
18.65	C2	C0	20.3	1.8	9.8
18.7	2.2	0.2	20.33	D2	D0
18.75	2.5	0.5			
18.8	2.8	0.8	20.35	2.1	0.1
			20.4	2.4	0.4
18.83	C3	C1	20.45	2.7	0.7
18.85	3.1	1.1	20.5	D3	D1
18.9	3.4	1.4			
18.95	3.7	1.7	20.55	3.3	1.3
			20.6	3.6	1.6
19.00	C4	C2	20.65	D4	D2
19.05	4.3	2.3			
19.1	4.6	2.6	20.7	4.2	2.2
19.15	4.9	2.9	20.75	4.5	2.5
			20.8	4.8	2.8
19.17	C5	C3	20.83	D5	D3
19.2	5.2	3.2			
19.25	5.5	3.5	20.85	5.1	3.1
19.3	5.8	3.8	20.9	5.4	3.4
			20.95	5.7	3.7
19.33	C6	C4	21.00	D6	D4
19.35	6.1	4.1			
19.4	6.4	4.4	21.05	6.3	4.3
19.45	6.7	4.7	21.1	6.6	4.6
			21.15	6.9	4.9
19.5	C7	C5	21.17	D7	D5
19.55	7.3	5.3			
19.6	7.6	5.6	21.2	7.2	5.2
19.65	7.9	5.9	21.25	7.5	5.5
			21.3	7.8	5.8
19.66	C8	C6	21.33	D8	D6
19.7	8.2	6.2			
19.75	8.5	6.5	21.35	8.1	6.1
19.8	8.8	6.8	21.4	8.4	6.4
			21.45	8.7	6.7
19.83	C9	C7	21.5	D9	D7
19.85	9.1	7.1			
19.9	9.4	7.4	21.55	9.3	7.3
19.95	9.7	7.7	21.6	9.6	7.6
			21.65	9.9	7.9
			21.66	E0	D8

NOTE: The above conversion chart is not accurate for all weights of clubs. Variations in shafts, club lengths and grips can affect the conversion. This conversion chart has been accepted and used as a standard means of obtaining Lorythmic designations from ounce readings.

CHAPTER 62

THE RELATIONSHIP OF SWINGWEIGHT TO A GOLF CLUB'S TOTAL WEIGHT

Since the swingweight scale has been in existence, the entire validity of swingweighting's advantages, if any, have been questioned. Good, bad or indifferent one fact remains, matched swingweights within a set have been accepted in the market and connote a higher quality, better balanced set of golf clubs to the consumer. It has only been recently that some manufacturers have marketed their top quality pro-line golf clubs using only a total weight balancing concept or frequency matching (See Chapter 63) and not swingweighting. But, since swingweighting is still the most accepted golf club balancing method presently employed and is a feature of most golf clubs being played today, a discussion of the relationship of swingweight to total weight is important to understanding golf club design principles.

The one specification that swingweighting affects most is a golf club's total weight. Always remember that total golf club weight alone has no effect on swingweight, but how a golf club's total weight is distributed determines the balance of that golf club and its swingweight.

To use an example that will clarify these seemingly conflicting statements: Assume that a driver has a total weight of 13 ounces and a swingweight of D-2, and it is desired to make this same driver weigh 13¾ ounces and not change its swingweight. Can it be done? Sure, it is easy if you know how to fool swingweight scales. Figure 62-1 shows how to do this by taking the 13 ounce driver and adding ½ ounce weight in the grip end and ¼ ounce in the head thus increasing the total weight by ¾ ounce while maintaining the D-2 swingweight. This is called "counterbalancing" and requires approximately twice as much weight added to the grip end to counterbalance half as much weight added to the head to maintain the same swingweight. This 2:1 weight ratio of adding weight to the grip and head ends of the club is a "Rule of Thumb" approximation which applies to both woods and iron. The swingweight scale is fooled because the golf club's balance point is moved closer to the grip end of the club by redistributing the added weight in such a manner as to maintain the present swingweight. Most manufacturers today do not counterbalance to adjust swingweight because they cannot maintain relatively even increments of total weight from club to club within a set. Swingweighting by adding weight only to the head is the most accepted method thus allowing for a relatively even total weight increment from club to club within each set. This club to club total weight increment can be closely controlled if the components such as grips, shafts and head are individually selected by weight and balance.

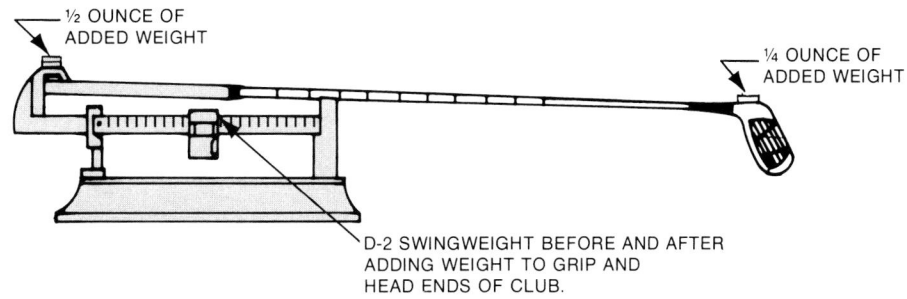

ORIGINAL DRIVER 13 OUNCES + ¾ OUNCE OF WEIGHT ADDED = 13¾ OUNCES TOTAL WEIGHT.

Figure 62-1
Increasing total weight without changing swingweight

Another point to discuss is the total weight relationship of the driver through the #9 iron within the same set. The driver is the lightest club and the #9 iron should be the heaviest (assuming no pitching wedge or sand wedge). The swingweight scale is directly responsible for this. In order for a set of clubs to have the same swingweight, as each club gets shorter more weight must be added to the head to maintain the same swingweight or balance. Since the individual components such as grips and shafts vary in weight due to manufacturing tolerances and different types and styles, it is impossible to give the exact incremental difference in total weight between say a #5 and #6 iron. But, again as a "Rule of Thumb" the difference is approximately ³⁄₁₆ to ¼ ounce decrease in total weight as each succeeding club is longer by ½". Table 62-1 is included to show the average weight specifications of woods and irons with medium flex standard weight steel shafts, rubber grips and a D-2 swingweight.

TABLE 62-1	
Total Weight Comparison of a Set of Woods and Irons	
Woods	**[1]Total Weight (ounces)**
1	13⅛
2	13⅜
3	13⅝
4	13⅞
5	14⅛
6	14⅜
7	14⅝
Irons	
1	14⅝
2	14⅞
3	15⅛
4	15⅜
5	15⅝
6	15⅞
7	16⅛
8	16⅜
9	16⅝

[1]Average total weights of woods and irons with rubber grips, medium flex standard weight steel shafts, standard lengths and D-2 swingweights.

As was pointed out earlier, swingweighting is the most accepted golf club balancing method currently being used and it is also one that is often abused. Swingweighting like anything else, can be done poorly or well. Swingweighting alone is not the ultimate answer in correctly matching a set of clubs for sameness of feel. It does seem logical, however, that some method of selecting individual components could be utilized with swingweighting to at least insure a more uniform set of specifications and ultimately better feel from club to club within a given set. Some of the things that can be done to improve club balance and feel are:

Grips: Since grips of the same style and size can vary as much as 5/16 ounce, they should be sorted by weight. Grips of the same weight and size should be used within a set of golf clubs. If for instance the lightest and heaviest weight grips within the 5/16 ounce tolerance range were interchanged on the same golf club, the swingweight could vary by as much as 2½ points. (Within the golf industry, points refer to individual swingweights.)

Shafts: Shafts of the same flex, type, material and length can vary as much as 3/8 ounce. Since weight has a direct effect on a shaft's flexibility and the club's total weight, each shaft should be checked and sorted by weight. Also, the use of a deflection board or frequency analyzer would allow more accurate sorting so that shafts of the same relative stiffness could be matched to those within a close weight range to be used within a set. A shaft's weight distribution can also vary from shaft to shaft thus causing a slight change in its balance point and ultimately affecting head weight and total weight. Shafts could also be balanced and sorted to provide more consistency.

Heads: Head weights should be of a relatively even increment from club to club within a set. If weight must be added to make swingweight, it should be added in such a way that it does not alter the center of gravity of the clubhead. Adding weight down the shaft shifts the center of gravity rearward and higher up the face.

Lengths: Finished lengths of golf clubs within a set should be of exact increments. Shaft installation should be done with consistent hosel penetrations and correct first step alignments. (See Chapters 7, 21 and 57)

There is no absolute proof that any of this will improve the playability or the sameness of feel from club to club, swing after swing. Having built a number of clubs for better players, conducted many different tests with touring pros and studied the mechanics of golf clubs for several years, I believe that this is the best way to match clubs at the present time. As you will see, it is basically the same as frequency matching which is explained in Chapter 63. Frequency matching adds a final element because swingweighting and component weight matching are static measurements and golf clubs are dynamically used implements.

CHAPTER 63

FREQUENCY METHOD

The term "frequency" when referring to golf clubs has been written about and talked about for many years. However, in the last several years it has been used by more and more golf club manufacturers. For some manufacturers, the term "frequency" makes good advertising copy and for others it is used in an attempt to build a better set of golf clubs. However, most manufacturers who offer frequency matched clubs are using shafts from the shaft manufacturer, Brunswick, who owns the patent for the "slope line" frequency method.

■ What is frequency?

The terminology used when referring to "frequency" is somewhat varied, but it all means basically the same thing. Terms such as frequency matched, frequency of vibration, swing flex ratings and frequency method are some of the terms used. Frequency is defined simply as a method of dynamically determining the stiffness feel of a golf club. There are three basic factors which influence this stiffness feel:

1. Overall club length
2. Head weight and distribution of weight
3. Shaft stiffness, weight and distribution of weight

It is easier to understand frequency with a brief discussion of these three factors.

First, if any golf club is lengthened, it will feel more flexible than it was originally if no adjustment is made to compensate for the heavier swingweight. Conversely, shortening a golf club makes it feel stiffer if no adjustment is made to compensate for the lighter swingweight.

Second, adding weight to the head of a golf club will make that club feel more flexible and removing weight from the head will make it feel stiffer. The distribution of weight within a head is another factor in stiffness feel although usually not as predominant as simply adding or removing weight. For example, assume a driver has a swingweight of D-2, but six swingweights of lead are inside the tip of the shaft. If the lead was removed from the shaft tip and put under the soleplate in the middle of the face, the weight distribution within the head would be changed causing a slightly more flexible club feel. It may not be noticeable to human sensitivity, but a frequency measuring device would pick this up easily. Another good example of a head weight distribution change would be to take any iron in a set and flatten its lie by 5°. If the iron was a D-2 swingweight originally, it is now a D-3 and in terms of frequency measurement, the club has been reduced by approximately three cycles per minute. It is also more flexible in feel. This occurs because by flattening the lie, the golf club's head weight is moved farther away from the hands.

Third, the stiffer flex a given golf shaft, the stiffer the club will feel. Also, when referring to the same type, material and pattern golf shaft, the heavier the shaft the stiffer the feel and the lighter the shaft and the more flexible the feel. An example of this would be a 4⅜ ounce standard weight Dynamic steel shaft with a weight tolerance of +³⁄₁₆ ounce. The lighter 4³⁄₁₆ ounce shaft will be a full flex weaker than the 4⁹⁄₁₆ ounce heavier shaft when the full weight tolerance range of ⅜ ounce is encountered.

■ How is Frequency Measured?

The frequency of a golf club or a set of golf clubs is measured in vibration cycles as a function of time. The units are usually referred to as "cycles per second" or more commonly in the golf industry, "cycles per minute." Each cycle of vibrational frequency is described in Figure 63-1.

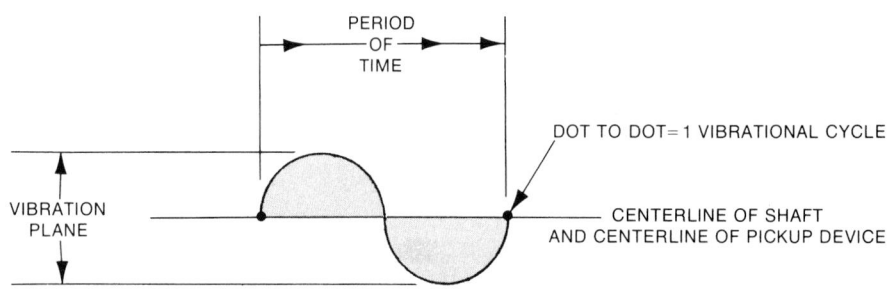

Figure 63-1
Definition of 1 vibrational cycle

There are many different methods of determining frequency and many frequency measuring machines are commercially available. See Photos 63-7 through 63-23 for instructions on using a Brunswick frequency analyzer which is used by most manufacturers. It uses a pick-off light in conjunction with a photo cell and reads out the results on a frequency calibrated oscilloscope. Some manufacturers use True Temper's® frequency machine which uses a phototransistor and electronic logic circuitry hooked up to a universal counter. See Photos 63-2 and 63-3. The machine works like this: A golf club is rigidly fastened by the butt end of the shaft. The head end is pulled down to a certain point and released. While the club is vibrating up and down, the phototransistors are picking up the impulses, relaying these impulses through the logic control and displaying them on the universal counter readout. The #9 iron shown in the True Temper® machine in Photos 63-2 and 63-3 had a reading of 5.83 cycles per second or when multiplied by 60 gives a reading of 349.8 cycles per minute. The GolfWorks® also offers a quality frequency analyzer which is used by many club assemblers and repairmen. Note that most composite shafts cannot be frequency matched due to the sheet wrapped method of manufacturing which is the prevalent composite shaft manufacturing method. The filament winding method was developed specifically to permit frequency matching. See Chapter 58 for more information.

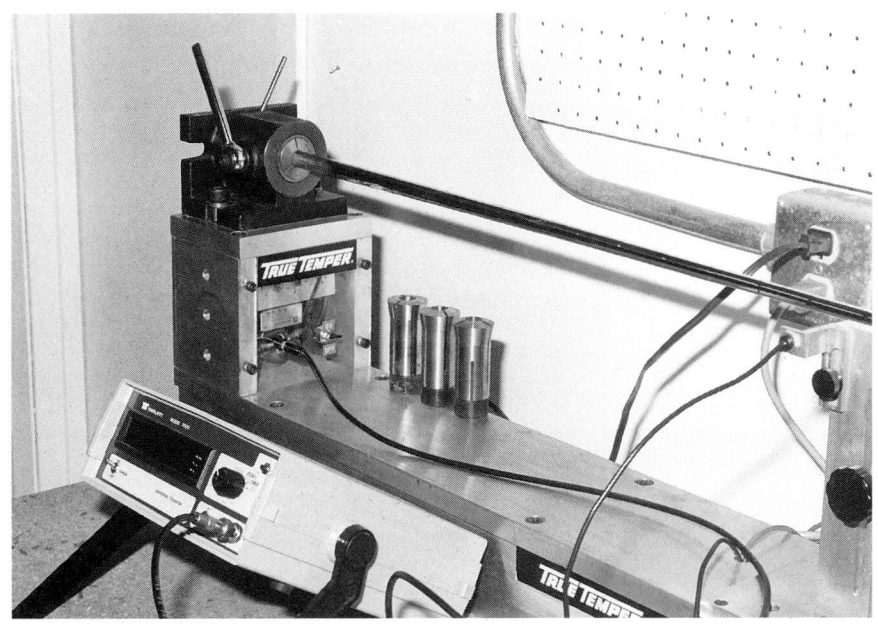

63-2

The True Temper® frequency machine is shown above. The machine is sturdily built
of aluminum plate and utilizes a standard 5C collet bench fixture and a separate
collet for each shaft butt size to insure solid butt clampings.

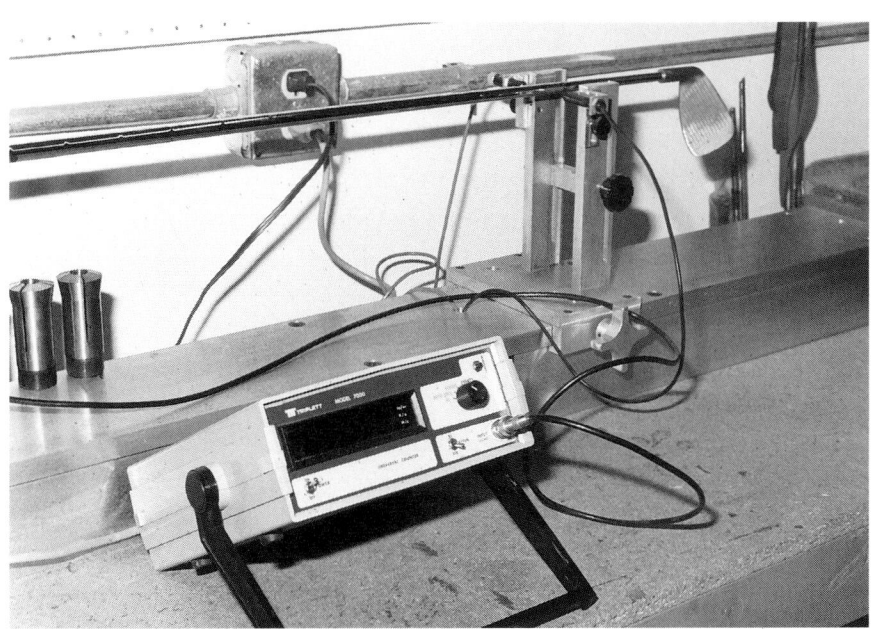

63-3

Another view of the True Temper® machine showing the phototransistor pick-off
light assembly. The frequency is displayed on an electronic universal counter
attached to the machine's logic module.

■ The Frequency Method of Golf Club Matching

The first step in understanding the matching of golf clubs by measuring their frequency or stiffness feel is to develop a chart whereby an entire set of woods or irons or both can be plotted and visually compared. See Figure 63-4. This would be a good chart to use when building golf clubs from components, checking out an existing set of clubs or comparing one set to another.

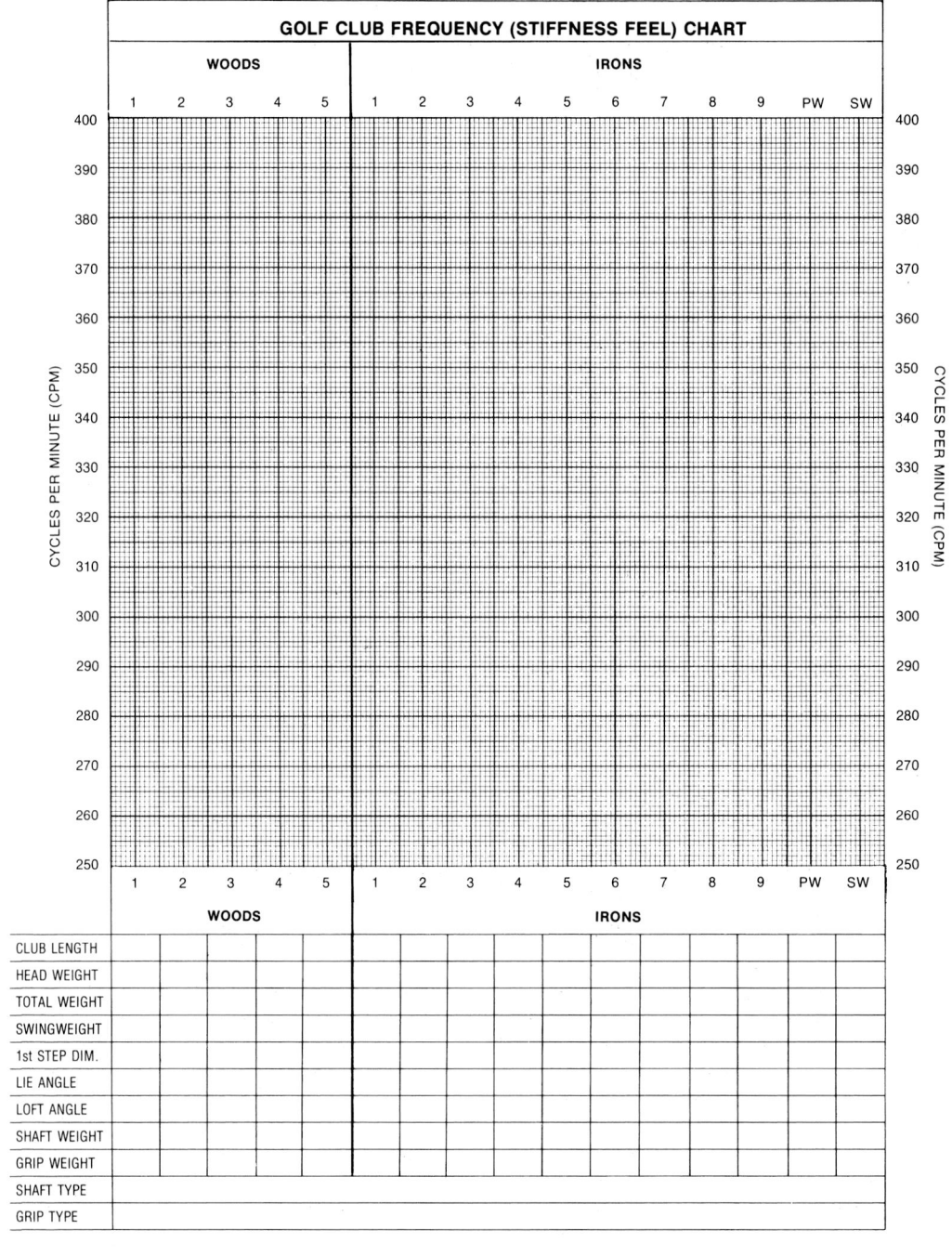

63-4
A chart to plot and compare the frequency of a set of golf clubs

There are a number of different methods currently in use to frequency match a set of golf clubs. However, the method shown below is a logical extension of component weight and specification matching and if done properly as explained in Chapter 62 and the listing followed at the bottom of Figure 63-4, a frequency machine is not absolutely necessary. If all the components are carefully weighed, matched and assembled, the set should come out very close to being matched when checked on a frequency machine. The frequency machine does add the element of set to set comparisons and allows matching a lost or favorite club, but the point to make is anyone can build frequency matched golf clubs. See Photos 63-7 through 63-23 for instructions on using the Brunswick frequency analyzer to frequency match a set of clubs.

The method of frequency or stiffness feel matching being discussed here is one where the differences between the frequencies of successive clubs within a set are the same. For example: Assume a set of irons and woods are built by carefully weighing, sorting and assembling components. Next, the irons and woods are checked in a frequency machine. Assume the following readings:

Iron	Frequency (Cycles per minute)	Differences In Frequency
3	309.5	—
4	317.0	7.5
5	324.5	7.5
6	332.0	7.5
7	339.5	7.5
8	347.0	7.5
9	354.5	7.5

Wood	Frequency (Cycles per minute)	Differences In Frequency
1	265.0	—
3	277.0	12.0
4	283.0	6.0
5	289.0	6.0

Figure 63-5 shows the golf club frequency for this set of woods and irons completely filled out.

Figure 63-6 shows a set of woods and irons that are not frequency matched. This figure also shows the factors of length, stiffness and head weight and how changes in these three factors change the frequency cycles per minute either up or down.

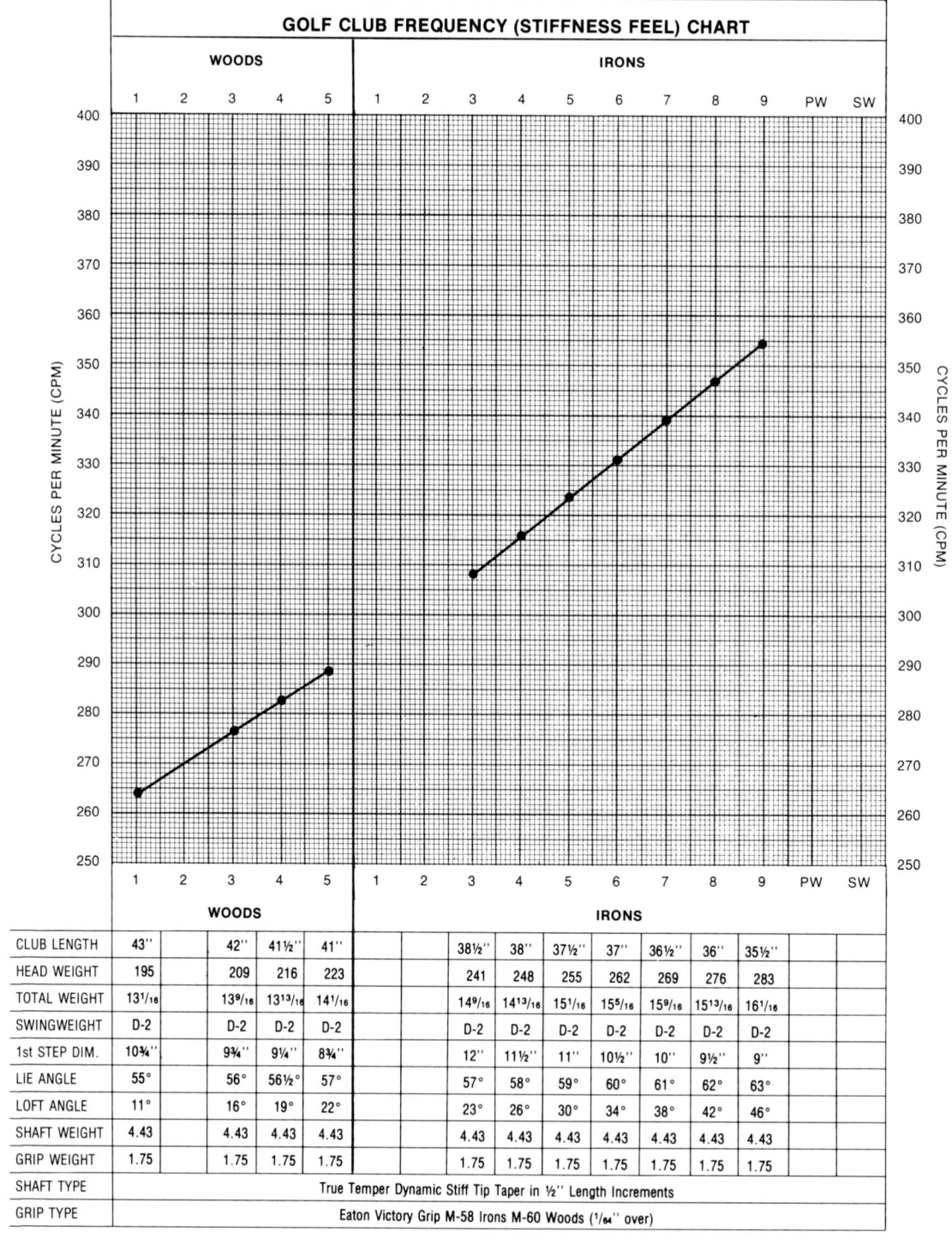

Figure 63-5
A frequency matched set of woods and irons (examples for reference only).

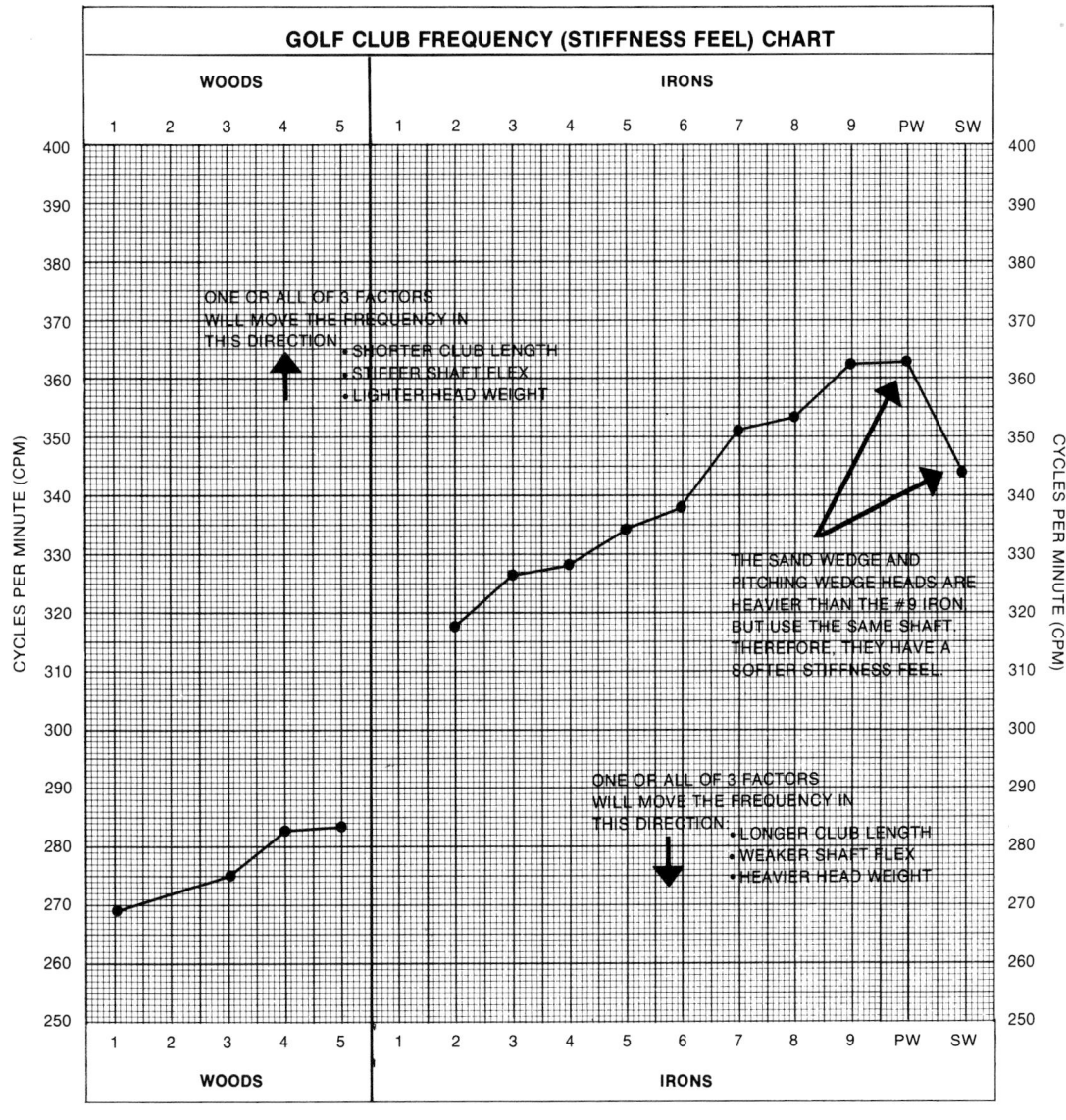

Figure 63-6
A set of golf clubs as they would probably plot if they were not frequency matched

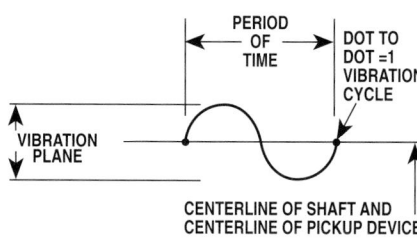

Definition of 1 vibration cycle.

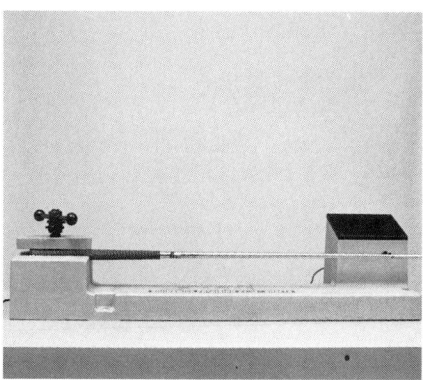

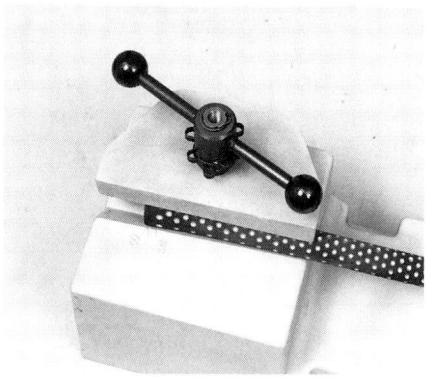

63-7 The frequency of a golf club or a set of golf clubs is measured in vibration cycles as a function of time. The units are usually referred to as "cycles per second" or more commonly in the golf industry, "cycles per minute." Each cycle of vibrational frequency is described above.

63-8 A frequency analyzer is a machine that provides the user with digital readings that demonstrate the precise flexibility of a golf shaft. This Brunswick Frequency Analyzer is very popular. It incorporates the traditional phototransistor pick-off light assembly in a "tower" that measures shaft vibration cycles and displays the information on an electronic universal counter.

63-9 Commonly, an analyzer works by first fastening the butt end of the golf shaft, with or without the grip, in a special clamping unit.

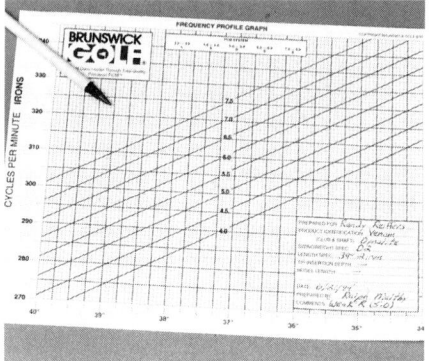

63-10 The tip of the shaft, with or without the head, is drawn down a distance and released. As the shaft vibrates back and forth, the impulses are measured...

63-11 ...and the results read out on a frequency calibrated oscilloscope. Generally, the higher the displayed number, the stiffer the shaft flex because a stiff shaft will vibrate at a quicker pace over the same distance as a more flexible shaft.

63-12 The analyzer will usually have a frequency chart, an example of which is shown above. As the frequency of each club is determined, the results are plotted on the chart. The chart enables the user to determine the exact flex of each shaft and how consistent they are throughout a set.

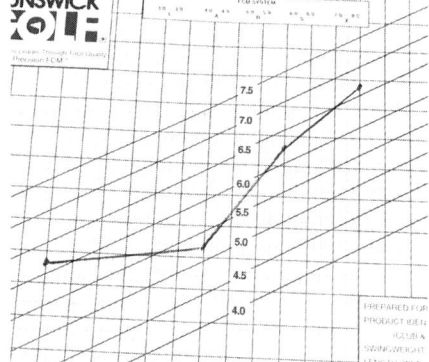

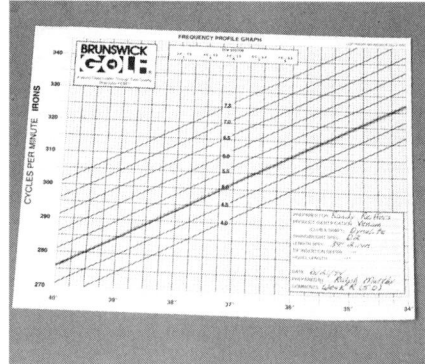

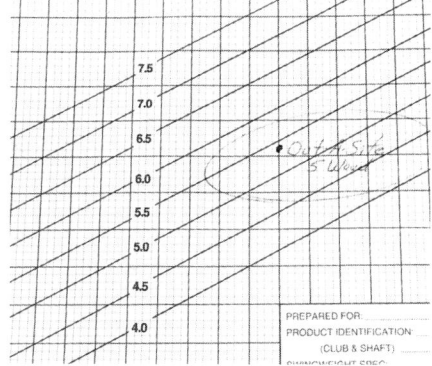

63-13 If the numbers plotted on the chart do not fall in a relatively straight line, as shown, then the flex of the shafts within the set are inconsistent, making it more difficult for the user to hit consistent shots with each of the clubs.

63-14 Joe Braly of Brunswick Golf developed the slope line frequency matching system. Brunswick owns the patent right for golf clubs manufactured on a constant slope line frequency, which is generally considered the best method for matching a set of clubs.

63-15 Another way in which the analyzer can be used is to select a golfer's favorite club from a set. After determining the frequency, compare the number to the chart. Whichever flex the number corresponds, an entire set can be built around that identical flex.

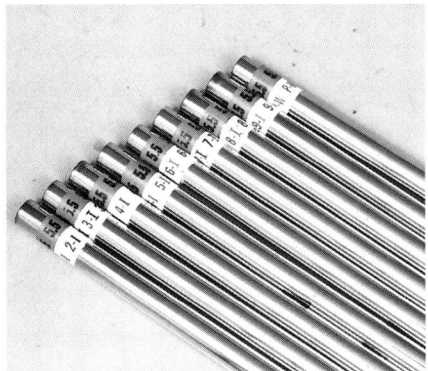

63-16 For instance, if the number corresponds to the 5.5 regular flex, then a full set of Brunswick Precision FM 5.5 flex shafts can be installed, thus duplicating the feel in the golfer's favorite club throughout the set.

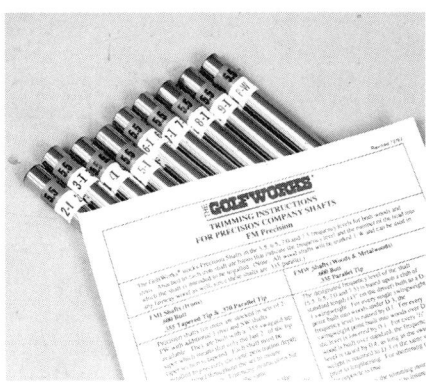

63-17 Since the Precision FM shafts are already frequency matched, you simply have to follow precise assembly steps to ensure the assembled golf clubs remain frequency matched. Frequency matched shafts by themselves do not guarantee a frequency matched set of clubs unless the following steps are followed.

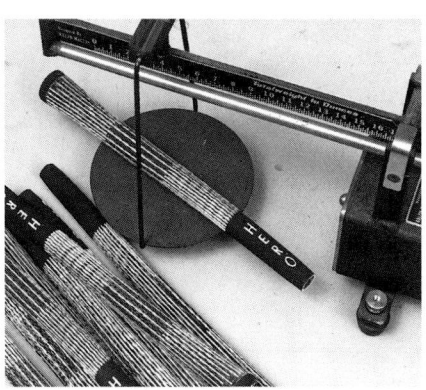

63-18 First, the grips must be weight sorted so they are all the same weight. The GolfWorks® Swingweight Scale, as shown, has a weight tray to achieve this step.

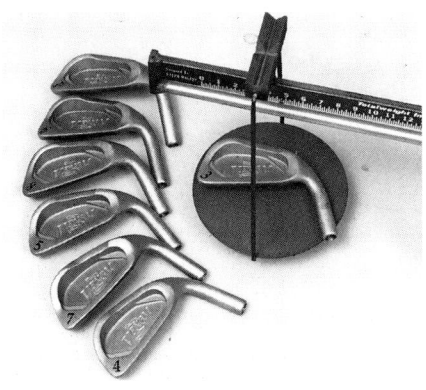

63-19 If you are assembling the shafts into heads that do not have weight ports, as those shown here, it is necessary to weight sort them. Table 63-1 lists standard head weights to be matched. The table assumes the set, or individual club, will otherwise be assembled to standard specifications. If different, make note of the footnotes that accompany the table.

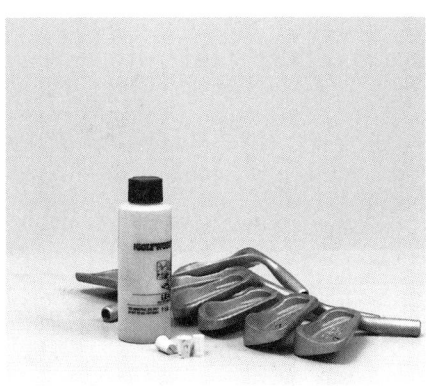

63-20 Failure to weight sort the heads will result in unmatched swingweights after assembly which will invalidate the advantages of frequency matched shafts. If weight is added down the shaft to create matching swingweights, then you have again negatively impacted the concept and the set would not be truly frequency matched. Lead tape applied to the back of the heads, however, is acceptable.

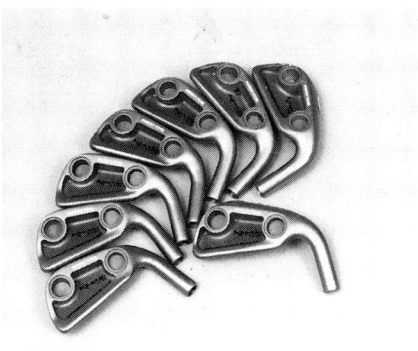

63-21 If using heads that allow weight to be added directly to them, like the type shown, then you may wait until the swingweighting step to add any additional weight. Weight added directly to the head, through weight ports, ensures maintenance of the concept.

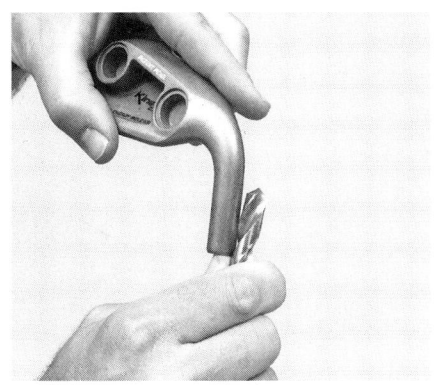

63-22 Lastly, the hosel bore depth must be consistent through the set of irons or woods. If the bore depths vary, then an adjustment must be made by drilling to make them consistent.

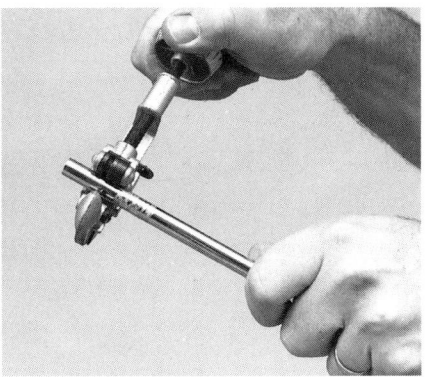

63-23 Having achieved grips of equal weight, heads of equal weight (or the valid means to make them so after assembly) and consistent hosel bore depths throughout the set, you are ready for assembly. Proceed with normal assembly steps following instructions that accompany the shafts. In certain cases, you may be required to trim some material from the shaft tip prior to assembly but this will be clearly stated in the instructions.

NOTES

_____

_____

_____

_____

_____

_____

_____

_____

_____

_____

_____

ADDITIONAL INFORMATION ON FREQUENCY MATCHING

TABLE 63-1
Recommended Head Weights (Grams) – Woods and Irons

Iron #	[1]Standard weight	[2]Lightweight	[3]Very Lightweight	[4]Super Lightweight	Wood #	[1]Standard weight	[2]Lightweight	[3]Very Lightweight	[4]Super Lightweight
1	231	233	235	237	1	206	208	210	212
2	238	240	242	244	3	216	218	220	222
3	245	247	249	251	4	221	223	225	227
4	252	254	256	258	5	226	228	230	232
5	259	261	263	265	6	231	233	235	237
6	266	268	270	272	7	236	238	240	242
7	273	275	277	279					
8	280	282	284	286					
9	287	289	291	293					
10	294	296	298	300					
11	294	296	298	300					

[1]Shaft used to test this weight category was a 130 gram True Temper Dynamic iron and wood shaft. Other shafts falling in this weight category would be True Temper's Dynamic Gold, Pro Fit, Comet and Jet Step; Brunswick's Propel II; Apollo's Masterflex and AP44.

[2]Shaft used in this category was the True Temper 120 gram TT Lite. Other shafts with a similar weight would be True Temper's Dynamic LIte, Dynalite and Dynalite Gold; Brunswick's Precision FM, Microtaper and Phoenix; Apollo's Shadow, Spectre and Matchflex.

[3]Shaft used in this category was the 106 gram True Temper Gold Plus. Other shafts with a similar weight would be True Temper's Extralite and Brunswick's UCV-304.

[4]Shaft used in this category was the 96 gram Aldila HM40. Other graphite shafts, too numerous to list here, fall in this weight category.

Refer to Appendix 3 for a complete listing of various shaft weights. Roughly, for every 10 gram decrease in shaft weight from the weights listed in this table there would be a required 2 gram increase in head weight.

NOTES:

a) Tables based upon standard length (39" - #2 iron, 35" - 10 & 11 iron, 43" - Driver), standard grip weight (50 grams) and D2 swingweight.

b) For every ½" increase in length, to maintain the same swingweight, the clubhead weight should decrease by 6 grams. The opposite is true of a ½" decrease in length.

TABLE 63-2
Incremental Tipping Impact on CPM*– Woods and Irons

	Woods					Irons			
Amount Tipped	Steel	Lightweight Steel	Very Lightweight Steel	Graphite	Amount Tipped	Steel	Lightweight Steel	Very Lightweight Steel	Graphite
¼"	+3	+4	+1	+2	¼"	+2.5	+4	+1.5	+3
½"	+4	+5	+1	+3	½"	+5	+8	+3	+5
1"	+5	+5	+2	+6	1"	+10	+13	+6	+11
2"	+10	+6	+5	+13	2"	+20	+17	+12	+21

*CPM = Cycles Per Minute. All numbers are in cpm.

NOTES:

a) **This table is to be used as a general guide only.** The 4 shafts tested: Dynamic, Dynalite, Gold Plus and HM40 provided results that will not be duplicated on all shafts. Special tipping consideration must be given to graphite shafts since effect on cpm (cycles per minute) varies greatly among available shafts.

b) Check the trimming instructions that accompany graphite shafts to determine if tip trimming is acceptable. Some graphite shaft manufacturers will void their warranties if specific tip trimming is exceeded.

The assembler will note that cpm readings do not always increase at a consistent rate. This is due to a variety of variables including difference in materials, material distribution, wall thickness, diameters, etc.

TABLE 63-3
Weight Increase Effect on CPM (Cycles Per Minute)

Weight Increase	Wood	Iron
+2 grams	-1	-1
+4 grams	-2	-2
+6 grams	-3	-3
+8 grams	-4	-4

■ Conclusion

The frequency machine shown in this chapter measures a golf club without its grip. In this chapter and in the previous chapter, I stressed the importance of also weight sorting grips to build matched golf clubs. The reason for this is to maintain the golf club's center of gravity or balance point in proper relation to the other clubs in the set. This in turn will maintain more closely matched swingweights in addition to matched frequencies.

It is very important to realize the frequency machines, like swingweight scales can be fooled quite easily and just because a set of clubs is so-called frequency matched, it does not mean the set is better than any other set. I am convinced that when done properly, frequency matching adds another element to golf club balancing and matching technology.

Remember, using the three variables of club length, shaft stiffness and head weight there are a myriad of differing combinations of the three which will produce exactly the same frequency. If a club is to be matched to a certain frequency, all of its other specifications must also be closely matched.

NOTES

NOTES

SECTION NINE

GOLF CLUB FITTING

CHAPTER 64

CUSTOM FITTING GOLF CLUBS TO THE INDIVIDUAL

Properly fitting golf clubs to the individual golfer requires a thorough understanding of all aspects of golf club design. Forming the basis for this understanding has been one of the primary goals in writing this book. In each chapter the reader can gain valuable knowledge on the mechanics of golf clubs regardless of whether the chapter specifically applies to design, alteration or repair. Knowing and understanding the mechanics of golf clubs does not imply that one can automatically fit an individual with the best possible clubs, although it certainly should give new perspectives to it.

Most important in the proper fitting of golf clubs is how knowledgeable the golf professional or other qualified person is regarding the swing itself, and then being able to translate each of the golfer's individual characteristics into proper equipment selection. The complications in proper fitting arise from matching the many possible combinations of golf clubs available, with a particular golfer's swing and physical characteristics. To further complicate fitting, the golfer's potential must be evaluated from the standpoint of how his/her clubs will fit later, should the desire or ability to substantially improve their golf game occur.

Who Needs Custom Fitting?

The obvious answer to this would be everybody, but to be more realistic there are certain golfers who would reap increased golfing pleasure by having their golf equipment custom tailored to fit them correctly.

The first type would be the golfer who is playing with clubs that are not in correct adjustment. This could mean that the club's specifications have changed over a period of time, such as a wood club picking up moisture and consequently swinging too heavy, or a set of clubs with specifications which were not incrementally correct from the start. An example of incorrect specifications could refer to iron head lofts and lies not properly set and checked during manufacture. As a matter of fact, an educated guess would place the percentage of incorrectly set lofts and lies at over 70% of all golf equipment being played today.

The second type of golfer who would benefit from custom fit clubs would be one with unusual physical characteristics such as short or long fingers, extremely tall height with short arms or short height with long arms. Many of the golfers falling into this category have adjusted their golf game to their equipment rather than have the equipment adjusted to their golf game.

The third type of golfer would be one that has some kind of consistent, undesirable playing characteristic that is predictable and usually firmly rooted in the golfer's mental approach to the game. This would include golfers who have a golfing history of doing some things consistently wrong such as hitting the ball too high or too low, hooking or slicing, or pushing or pulling the ball to only name a few of the more common characteristics.

The last type of golfer is the very low handicap or scratch golfer who more or less knows what he/she likes and feels comfortable with, but who would benefit with the expert assistance of a skilled golf professional or possibly someone that is trained in this area.

Recommending New Golf Clubs or Altering Present Golf Clubs

Fitting of golf clubs breaks down into two basic classifications; recommending new equipment or altering the individual's present equipment. In most instances, a golfer seeking advice on equipment from their golf professional would be far better off buying it new. The reason is that usually the golfer has an incomplete, outdated or non-matched set of clubs and it would be economically unsound to put a lot of money into extensive alterations and repairs. With the rapid technological strides equipment manufacturers are improving golf club designs and manufacturing methods, a golfer would do well to consider new clubs if only from this standpoint. However, new clubs are expensive and if the golfer has a strong reason for not wanting to buy new clubs and the present clubs are satisfactory for alteration, there is nothing wrong with approaching the correct fit problem within this parameter.

Custom-Built or Stock Golf Clubs

The golf professional must decide whether or not a particular golfer needs specially made custom-built clubs or whether the manufacturer's so-called "stock" clubs will do. Some specifications of stock clubs can be altered by the golf professional if the proper equipment is available. Changing lofts and lies of iron clubs and increasing grip sizes are two of the more common alterations done on stock clubs. If the golf professional determines that a number of alterations to stock clubs are required, it would be far better to custom order the clubs through one of the manufacturers or custom club shops. The time and expense would be prohibitive for the golf professional to radically change new, stock golf clubs that are in inventory.

The time required to get custom-built golf clubs is a real problem to the golf professional. It can take anywhere from 6 to 14 weeks to get custom clubs and most golfers are unwilling to wait that long. When a customer's clubs do not come in on time, which is often the case, the customer first blames the golf professional when in fact the manufacturer is at fault. Six to twelve or even fourteen weeks delivery time on custom club orders must be reduced to four weeks or less from receipt of order.

A solution to quicker delivery of custom club orders is to assemble golf clubs from an inventory of components on hand. Section 4 of this book provides complete information on getting started in custom clubmaking and assembling.

Ideas, Facts and Thoughts on Improving Clubfitting Methods

There are a number of approaches to the problem of correctly fitting golf clubs to the individual, and some methods are better than others. Regardless, the approach to custom club fitting should be logical, mechanically sound and ultimately produce the best possible results. Basically, this requires that the golf professional spend a few minutes with the individual in learning about the golf clubs that are presently being used, the physical requirements and limitations, the swing and personal preferences on both brand and desired specifications.

The following statements and ideas are intended to help in developing a sound approach and your own successful method of club fitting.

1. Five ways to improve your game.
Think about it. What are the ways to improve at golf? They are:
1. Professional Swing Instruction
2. Properly Fit, Quality Equipment
3. Practice
4. Play
5. Positive Attitude

These are very good points to keep in mind and to pass along to those individuals who come to you for club fitting and/or instruction that want to know what else it takes to improve their games.

2. The squarer the hit, the more solid the feel.
If we could be so basic as to pick only one goal to accomplish in club fitting and teaching the swing, it would be squareness of hit. If you as a player, clubfitter and/or teacher would think about every swing correction or change and every club fitting recommendation in regards to accomplishing a more square hit, you will be more successful. Sure, there is a lot more to teaching the swing and club fitting than this, but by working toward "squareness of hit" you uncomplicate the approach taken by working sort of backwards from the hit in regards to ball cause and effect. You have read in the design chapters of this book many things that cause a more square hit. Virtually every club fitting variable will have some effect on this with some obviously having a greater effect than others. If you work toward squareness of hit, the results will be greater distance and better accuracy. If we start out with our goal to just hit the ball farther and straighter, we put the proverbial cart before the horse and waste a lot of time – besides making things more complicated. However, when we look at all elements of the swing and the 11 clubfitting variables in trying to achieve a more square and consequently a more solid hit; we place the horse in front of the cart and our task is much easier by more accurately defining the problem.

Here is what a more square hit will accomplish:
1. The squarer the hit the more energy is applied to the ball, resulting in greater distance.
2. The squarer the hit the less curve on the ball, usually resulting in a straighter hit.
3. The squarer the hit the greater amount of backspin with each different lofted club, usually resulting in better bite through reduced roll.
4. The squarer the hit the more solid the feel at impact.

Here are the factors at impact which create square or unsquare hits:
1. Clubhead path (outside in, square or inside out).
2. Clubface angle (open, square or closed).
3. Clubhead speed (accelerating rate, decelerating rate, faster or slower).
4. Angle of attack (arc angle of clubhead vertically as it descends into the impact area).
5. Face impact location (toe, center or heel hit).

And here are a few of the specific equipment variables which have an effect on squareness of hit:
1. Clubface Angle
2. Lie Angle
3. Loft Angle
4. Clubhead Center of Gravity Location
5. Shaft Flex, Material, Weight and Flex Point
6. Club Length
7. Swingweight and Total Weight
8. Grip Size

694

One of the more interesting and challenging aspects of club fitting is to be able to relate all the appropriate equipment variables above into creating a more square hit while at the same time separating out and correcting any faulty swing elements. I think it can now be more easily accepted that if you achieve a more square hit everything else from solidness of feel, to greater distance, to better accuracy falls automatically and neatly into place.

3. The Main Differences Between Good Players and Other Players Ball Striking

The main differences between good players and other players are:

1. Good players consistently hit the ball on or near the center of the clubface.
2. Good players can control the clubface angle and clubhead path during the swing.
3. Good players strike the ball with the clubhead in a descending arc with the center of gravity of the clubhead equal to or lower than that of the center of gravity of the ball.
4. Good players accelerate the clubhead at an accelerating rate coming into impact.
5. Good players have confidence in their ball striking and golfing abilities in general, usually as a result of practice.

4. Measuring a Golfers Present Equipment

The specifications of the golfer's present equipment are often overlooked in the fitting process. Checking and recording basic information on a golfer's present clubs should be a primary consideration in understanding the golfer and the golfer's game better and in recommending new equipment or alterations to the present set. This can either be a spot check of specifications or a complete analysis by filling out a chart similar to the one shown below. Pads of these forms are available from The GolfWorks®. Also, a more in-depth approach to measuring a player's clubs can be found in "The Complete Golf Club Fitting Plan" by Ralph Maltby.

Specifications	Woods				Irons									
	1	3	4	5	2	3	4	5	6	7	8	9	PW	SC
1. Swingweight														
2. Total Weight														
3. Length														
4. Loft														
5. Lie														
6. Shaft Flex														
7. Shaft Material														
8. Grip Diameter														
9. Bulge					Notes:									
10. Roll														
11. Face Angle														

5. Hitting Actual Clubs on the Golf Range

The main portion of fitting clubs should be done on the lesson tee where the golfer could possibly try out different shaft flexes and swingweights while being watched and analyzed by the professional. The golfer should not be limited only to hitting clubs within a narrow range in shaft stiffness such as a medium and stiff flex shaft, but rather should be encouraged to also hit a flexible and an extra stiff flex shaft. This will allow the golfer to more fully understand the effects of shaft flex on both feel and performance by actually experiencing the results.

6. Golfer's Preferences

Admittedly, the psychological uplift of having clubs fitted to the individual is very important, and usually whatever the golf professional recommends is accepted. Most golfers do not have a brand preference. However, if they do have a preference, this must be considered in the decision making process as it will have a direct bearing on how the customer perceives their new clubs. Also, cosmetics of the clubs such as finish, color and insert color are very important to most golfers. The point is that all of the golfer's preferences should be discussed and considered before making final recommendations.

7. Keep a Record

A record should be kept on each golfer's specifications after fitting. The record should also include dates and any other pertinent comments which could be of value at some future date.

8. Use a Custom Fitting Chart

Some manufacturers with custom clubmaking facilities and some custom clubmakers use special order blanks to ensure that they get all the information they need on a custom order. It is a good idea to try and obtain a few of these from each manufacturer who has them, as it will be more convenient when ordering. At the end of Chapter 65, a universal custom fitting chart is shown. This chart is available in pad form from The GolfWorks®.

9. The Proper Facilities and Equipment

It is very difficult if not impossible to properly fit golf clubs and recommend equipment changes if the golf professional does not have the proper facilities and equipment. The following list outlines the basics which a good facility should have: (See Appendix 2 for The GolfWorks® Fitting Center).

Hitting area: • Outdoor driving range or hitting net

Measuring Equipment:
• Calipers or a grip gauge for measuring grip sizes
• Protractor or loft gauges for measuring wood club lofts
• Golf Shaft Identification Gauge
• Swingweight Scale that also measures total weight (14" fulcrum)
• Weight checker - a thin steel rod to check for any weight added inside the shaft tip of woods and irons
• Loft and lie machine for irons
• Bulge and roll gauge for wood faces
• 48" long rigid measuring stick
• Shaft deflection board
• Golf Club Gauge for measuring face angles and other wood club specifications

Fitting Equipment:
• Sample clubs on hand in different shaft flexes, swingweights, lengths, lies and face angles
• Sample grip sizes ($\frac{1}{64}$" over and undersize, $\frac{1}{32}$" oversize, $\frac{1}{16}$" oversize and standard size) in both men's and ladies' sizes.
• $\frac{3}{4}$" x 4' x 4' plywood board for fitting lie (painted green is best)
• Lead tape
• Shaft Bending Block for changing lies and face angles on woods

Conclusion

Whether a golfer wants their clubs altered for a perfect fit, custom-made or stock, the advice of a knowledgeable person who utilizes the proper fitting aids is advisable before purchasing any set of clubs. This person can look at the clubs, check that the relationship between clubs is correct, check the shafts for relative stiffness and the grip for fit. A few unplayable clubs get on the market each year and you don't want to be stuck with them. It is nice to have clubs that look beautiful, but beauty is only skin deep. It is the dimensions of the clubs which make them a help or hindrance to your game.

NOTES

CHAPTER 65

THE KEY VARIABLES IN PROPER FITTING OF GOLF CLUBS

When a golf professional analyzes an individual golfer to determine the best fitting golf clubs for that golfer, more than just the obvious variables of shaft flex, club length, loft, lie, swingweight, total weight, wood club facing and grip size must be determined. The golf professional should also evaluate other variable factors such as the set makeup, grip material, shaft material and perhaps even head design. If the golfer has a preference or opinion on any of these variables they should be taken into account before any final decisions are made. No variable is more important than another. To do a club fitting job properly, all of the variables used by the clubmaker should be determined and specified. Much of the information on club fitting available to golf professionals and golfers today indicates that there are only from 5 to 7 club fitting variables which need to be determined, when in fact, there are eleven variables in club fitting, each as important as the other. They are:

1. **Loft**
2. **Lie**
3. **Shaft Flex**
4. **Club Length**
5. **Grip Size**
6. **Swingweight and Total Weight**
7. **Clubhead Design**
8. **Face Angle of Woods (Open, Square, Closed)**
9. **Shaft Material Selection**
10. **Grip Material Selection**
11. **Set Makeup**

The golf professional today must become as knowledgeable as possible to understand the changes in golf club design, the new materials available for the construction of golf clubs and some of the basic methods used to manufacture golf clubs. The burden is being placed more and more on the golf professional to thoroughly understand all the design attributes of golf clubs when fitting and selling them and how each translates into some performance benefit to satisfy a golfer's individual needs.

The total weight of a golf club would be a case in point to discuss here. In the past, clubmakers, not the golf professional, determined total weight as a result of which specifications and components were used. Shaft flex, shaft material, grip type, club length and swingweight are the key variables which determine total weight. Today, the golf professional should be able to recommend a total weight range for an individual golfer as part of the club fitting process. The advent of graphite and very light steel shafts makes a club's total weight more important because of the shaft's extreme lightness which can have a drastic effect on reducing the total weight to a point where the club will not perform satisfactorily unless in the hands of an extremely skilled golfer.

The discussion which follows on each of the 11 variables for proper fitting is not in order of importance because each variable should be considered as important as any other. When playing golf, a golfer does not care whether or not the shaft flex is more important than swingweight or vice versa. The golfer is simply trying to execute a particular kind of shot, with a particular type of club, using a particular type swing, and that everything about the golfer's clubs are right for his/her game.

1. LOFT
(Reference: See Chapters 10, 12, 19, 34, 35, 39, 41, 48, 49, 52, Appendices 1, 8.) See Figure 65-1.

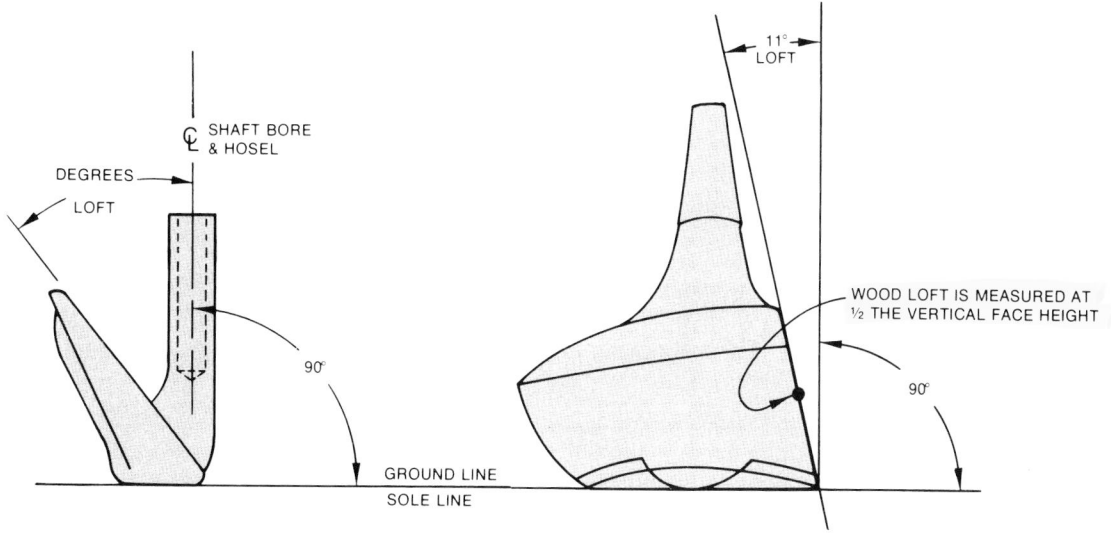

Note that the loft of an iron club is measured differently than that of a wood club. Chapter 35 discusses this in detail.

Figure 65-1
Defining loft

When loft is discussed as a fitting variable, it is more in reference to the resultant ball trajectory than it is to the physical loft angle of the golf club. The reason for this is that while loft angle is a definite factor in controlling ball trajectory, it is only one of many factors which do so. Some of the others which also influence the trajectory of a golf ball are shaft flex, center of gravity location in the head, lie angle, face progression of woods, hosel offset of irons, club length, face angle of woods and the face roll of wood clubs. Ideally, when fitting someone, the loft angle and these other important factors should be thoroughly evaluated as a combined affect on determining ball trajectory. In most cases, the best approach is to achieve what would be considered normal ball trajectory, not too high or not too low. This will maximize average carry against and with the wind, provide adequate backspin to hold iron shots that land on the green and give some roll on shots which land in the fairway. Once again, everything in golf club design and fitting is some form of a trade-off. There are many trade-off combinations possible to achieve normal ball trajectories, and the knowledgeable clubfitter will be analyzing these trade-offs to accomplish two other important playing characteristics as follows. The first is solidness of hit which translates into more distance, and the other is directional control or accuracy. Take a few moments to study Table 65-1 to get a basic knowledge of how each trajectory variable relates to performance.

Table 65-1

Fitting Table — Trajectory Variables in Woods and Irons

Loft Angle
1. Increase loft; Ball flies higher — more backspin — less roll
2. Decrease loft; Ball flies lower — less backspin — more roll

Center of Gravity (C. of G.)
1. Lower C. of G.; Ball flies higher — more backspin — less roll — usually more solid hits
2. Raise C. of G.; Ball flies lower — less backspin — more roll — usually fewer solid hits

Shaft Flex
1. Too flexible shafts; Ball flies higher — more backspin — less roll — less accuracy
2. Too stiff shafts; Ball flies lower — less backspin — more roll — more accuracy

Face Roll (Woods)
1. Too much roll; Inconsistent trajectories
2. Very little or no roll; Consistent trajectories

Face Angle (Woods)
1. Face too open; Slicing tendency, or if hits are straight the trajectory is lower
2. Face too closed; Hooking tendency, or if hits are straight the trajectory is higher

Club Length
1. Clubs too long; Sometimes higher trajectory due to increased shaft flexibility, poorer directional control, many unsolid hits
2. Clubs too short; Sometimes lower trajectory due to decreased shaft flexibility, better directional control, mostly solid hits

Face Progression
1. More face progression; Ball flies slightly higher
2. Less face progression; Ball flies slightly lower

Hosel Offset
1. More offset; Ball flies slightly lower
2. Less offset; Ball flies slightly higher

Lie Angle
1. Too upright at impact (toe up); Ball flies lower — ball is pulled left and curves left
2. Too flat at impact (toe down); Ball flies lower — ball is pushed right and curves right

Table 65-1 outlined the important variables which control or affect golf ball trajectory. Now it is time to make a number of statements which will help us to utilize this knowledge in better fitting someone to ball trajectory. As was stated earlier, in most cases, the ideal situation would be to make a fitting recommendation that would result in "normal ball trajectory." Of course, there can also be situations when a higher or lower than normal trajectory is desired, but this would mainly apply to low handicappers and golf professionals who have a specific reason to do so.

Figure 65-2 provides an illustration showing various ball trajectories in relation to relative distance, backspin and roll. Again, from a fitting and playability standpoint, the lower the ball trajectory on any given club, the harder that club is to hit. This is something to always keep in mind because club fitting is a method whereby you are trying to make any club easier to hit with accuracy. The lower the trajectory in any shot simply means that the ball will be struck less obliquely and will be compressed more by the clubface. The more the golf ball is compressed by the clubface, the more important it is to hit the ball on the clubhead's center of gravity and not toward the toe or heel. Any shot off-center on a lower trajectory will feel more unsolid and will lose more distance than a shot with a higher trajectory. Let's assume, for example, that a #1 iron hits a ball 1" toward the toe and let's also assume a #9 iron hits a ball 1" toward the toe. Which club do you think will feel more unsolid, the #1 iron or the #9 iron? Of course, we all know the #1 iron will feel very unsolid on a toe shot and will lose a lot of distance. The #9 iron, however, will still feel quite solid with very little distance loss. The reason for this is the #1 iron applies far greater energy to the ball at impact (compresses it more) than does the #9 iron (ball is compressed very little). The ball impacting with the #1 iron on the toe tends to twist the clubhead far greater than the #9 iron shot on the toe. Because of this, far more energy is lost during impact with a #1 iron versus a #9 iron. The ball is compressed so little on the #9 iron that very little clubhead twisting occurs and a much higher percentage of energy is transferred to the ball. Hence, the #9 iron does not feel that bad on a toe hit and the resulting shot will probably be quite acceptable. It is exactly the same comparison to a lesser degree when using the same club and altering its loft angle. If you decrease the loft, the ball will fly lower and will be compressed more by the face at impact. Conversely, if you increase the loft, the ball will fly higher and will be compressed less by the face at impact. The greater the club's loft and resulting higher trajectory, the more solid the hit more of the time on off-center hits. There is no difference in solidness of feel on face center hits between the various loft angles, only trajectory differences.

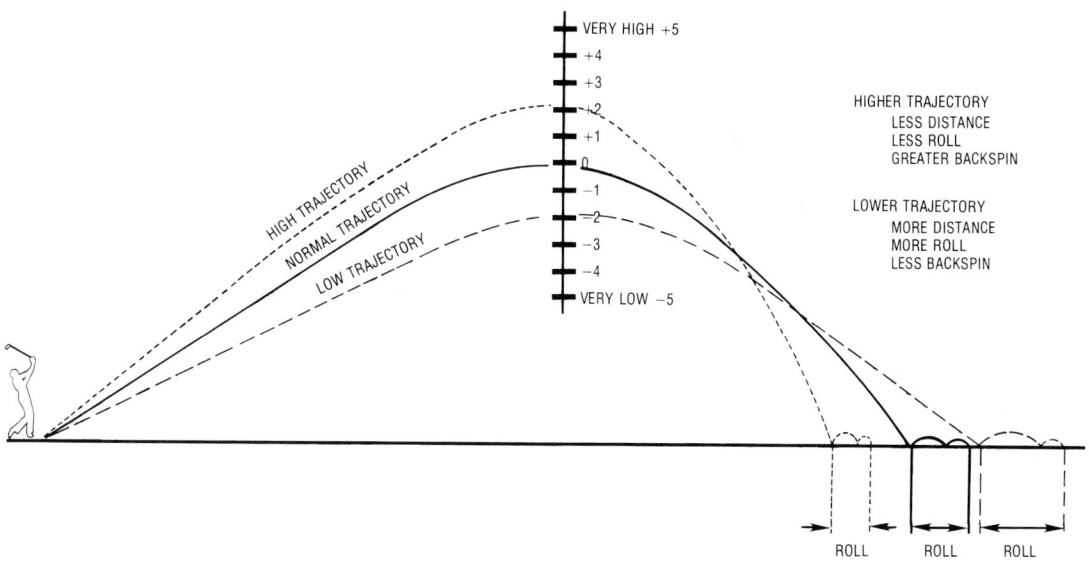

Figure 65-2
Effect of trajectory on distance, backspin and roll

A conclusion which is easy to draw from all of this is to hit the ball as high as possible. This is obviously not a good solution because the fitting trade-off is a significant loss in distance. So, we are right back where we started from and that is to try and achieve normal ball trajectories during the fitting process. The information provided thus far has given us the knowledge to deal with the many club specifications and fitting variables that can and do affect ball trajectory.

Use the following explanations when increasing and decreasing loft for a rule-of-thumb comparison on performance.
• Increasing the loft of any club:
  1. Lessens the force applied to the ball by the clubhead because of the increased obliqueness of the hit. Easier to hit and more solid hits more of the time.
  2. Increases the amount of backspin applied to the ball.
  3. Increases the trajectory or height of the ball.
  4. Reduces the amount of roll after the ball lands.
  5. Usually reduces the distance.

- Decreasing the loft of any club:
  1. Increases the force applied to the ball by the clubhead because of reducing the obliqueness of the hit. Harder to hit and less solid hits more of the time.
  2. Reduces the amount of backspin applied to the ball.
  3. Decreases the trajectory or height of the ball.
  4. Increases the amount of roll after the ball lands.
  5. Usually increases distance.

Tables 65-2 and 65-3 below give recommended lofts for strong (less lofted), standard (normal lofted) and weak (more lofted) woods and irons for men and ladies. There can be many possible combinations when recommending proper lofts in both woods and irons for a specific golfer. For example, since a driver is a very individual club and usually the more difficult club to hit properly, a logical recommendation to a certain golfer for a set of woods could be to use a weak lofted driver (12°) and a strong lofted set of fairway woods.

TABLE 65-2
Chart For Determining Strong, Standard and Weak Loft Specifications
Men's and Ladies' – Wood Club Lofts

	Men's			Ladies'		
Woods	Strong Lofts	Standard Lofts	Weak Lofts	Strong Lofts	Standard Lofts	Weak Lofts
1	10°	11°	12°	11°	12°	13°
2	12°	13°	14°	13°	14°	15°
3	15°	16°	17°	16°	17°	18°
4	18°	19°	20°	19°	20°	21°
5	21°	22°	23°	22°	23°	24°
6	24°	25°	26°	25°	26°	27°
7	27°	28°	29°	28°	29°	30°
8	30°	31°	32°	31°	32°	33°
9	33°	34°	35°	34°	35°	36°

TABLE 65-3
Iron Club Lofts – Men's and Ladies'

	Men's				Ladies'			
Irons	Strong Lofts	Modern Standard Lofts	Weak Lofts	Traditional Standard	Strong Lofts	Modern Standard Lofts	Weak Lofts	Traditional Standard
1	15°	15°	17°	17°	–	–	–	–
2	18°	18°	20°	20°	19°	20°	22°	21°
3	21°	21°	24°	23°	22°	23°	25°	24°
4	23°	24°	28°	26°	25°	26°	28°	27°
5	27°	28°	32°	30°	29°	30°	32°	31°
6	31°	32°	36°	34°	33°	34°	36°	35°
7	35°	36°	40°	38°	37°	38°	40°	39°
8	39°	40°	44°	42°	41°	42°	44°	43°
9	43°	44°	48°	46°	45°	46°	48°	47°
PW	47°	48°	52°	50°	49°	50°	52°	51°
SW	54°	55°	56°	56°	55°	56°	58°	56°

2. LIE

(Reference: See Chapters 11, 19, 34, 36, 48, 49, 52, Appendices 1, 8.) See Figure 65-3.

Improper lie angle on clubs will more than likely cause directional control problems for the golfer. Clubs with too upright a lie will have a tendency to pull the ball left of the target and will also increase the possibility of imparting a hooking spin to the ball. Conversely, clubs with a lie that is too flat for a golfer will have a tendency to push the ball right of the target and will increase the possibility of imparting a slicing spin to the ball. It is possible to hit the ball straight with improper lie clubs, but this means that the golfer has compensated for this by adjusting his/her swing and/or aim to the club's lie. The club's lie is not adjusted to the golfer's personal swing and physical stature.

The correct lie angle is one of the most important specifications to check for in the proper fitting of golf clubs. Consider this: most everyone realizes lie angle at impact has a direct effect on ball direction, but this isn't the full story. The lie angle at impact also helps to determine solidness of feel, distance, amount of backspin, trajectory and the amount of ball roll. If the lie angle is not correct for a golfer he/she must compensate for all or some of these variables in each and every shot. The problem is, the golfer usually does not know he or she is unconsciously correcting for improper lie thus making the game of golf much more difficult.

A thorough understanding of fitting lie angle and understanding exactly what it does is one of the fitting variables which can make immediate and often dramatic improvements in someone's golf game. It seems that whenever a player is having problems with their clubs, most clubfitters automatically start thinking "shaft" when in actuality nine out of ten times the problem is somewhere else. Do not overlook lie angle; it could save a lot of needless troubleshooting work!

The "lie angle" is defined as the angle made between the shaft and clubhead. See Figure 65-3. For most of us, this is a static measurement put in by the club designer and takes on very little significance in defining it. However, look again at Figure 65-3 because this is exactly how both a wood and iron should look at impact if the lie angle is correct for a given golfer. You must understand this definition in fitting lie because you will no doubt need to make decisions when actually fitting lie angle as to which way or how much to alter the club to make the lie angle correct for a given player.

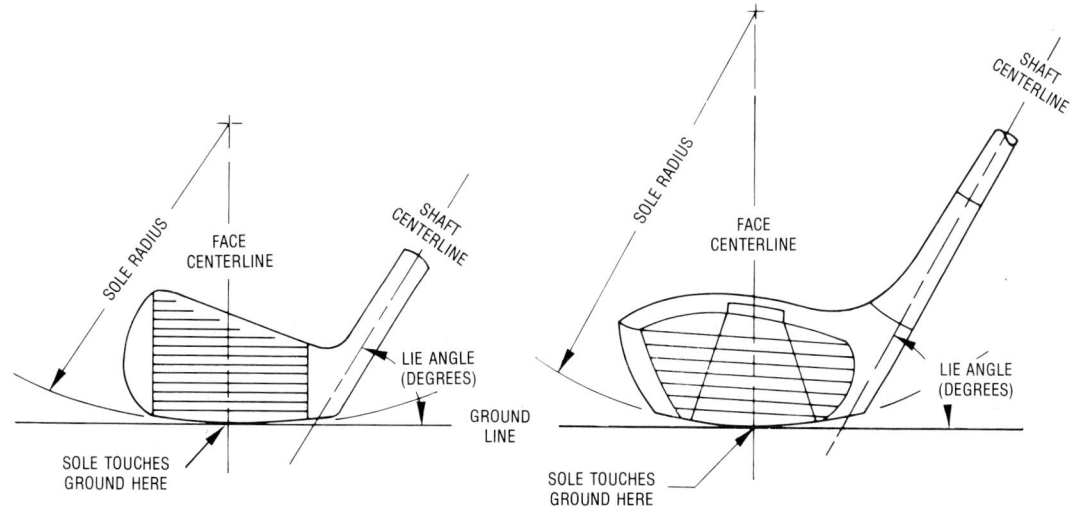

Figure 65-3
Defining lie

The following is an explanation of how an improper lie angle can cause golf ball directional problems. Refer to Figure 65-4 which shows that a wood or iron with too upright a lie will have a tendency to hit the ball left of target, and conversely too flat a lie will hit the ball right of target. It is important to note here that in all three drawings of Figure 65-4 the leading edge of the clubface is perpendicular or perfectly square to the target.

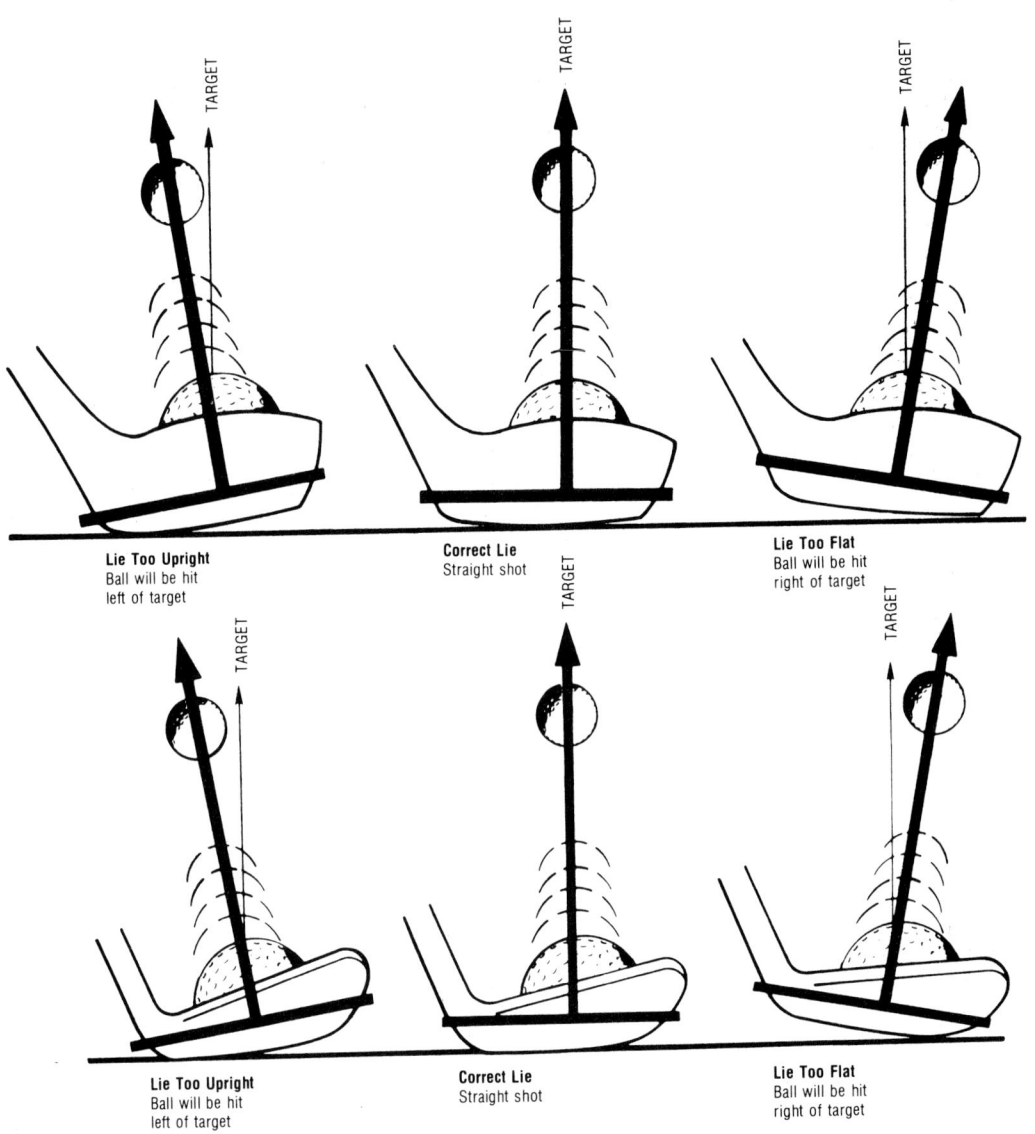

NOTE: Even though the leading edge of the club is perpendicular to the desired direction of flight, the plane on the face of either a too upright or too flat lie club will hit the ball either left or right of the target, respectively.

Figure 65-4
Improper lie can cause directional problems in both woods and irons

The explanation of why the ball will go either left or right with too upright or too flat a lie is this: The lie of the club establishes the directional plane of the loft. If the club at impact is the same as shown under "correct lie" in Figure 65-4, the plane of the face will be perpendicular or square to the target. However, if the lie of the club at impact is too upright, the directional plane of the face will be pointing left of the target or tilted left even though the leading edge of the face is aligned square to the target. The difference at impact between the proper and improper lie angle and also the amount of clubface loft is referred to as a "compound angle." This compound angle is the amount of tilt or misdirection in the face, or as the golfer sees it, the initial

704

direction of ball flight. If a golf club were made with no loft (0 degrees) then improper lie would cause no directional problems because with no loft a compound angle or tilt of the face plane would not exist. To understand this better, do this: hold a #9 iron in the proper address position with the face aiming at the target. Assume this club to have 64° lie and 48° loft. Begin lowering the grip end toward the ground while keeping the leading edge of the face square with the target until the grip and shaft lie flat against the ground. At this point, the club's actual lie angle in the playing position is 0° because 64° original lie angle has actually been transferred entirely into the tilt of the face plane. In addition, the club's actual loft angle in the playing position is also 0° because no amount of vertical loft exists to get the ball airborne. This means that if you were holding a #9 iron with 48° loft and could hit the ball with the club shaft lying flat against the ground and the leading edge square to the target, the ball would be pulled exactly 48° left of the target or the amount of the built-in club loft. Look closely at the iron in this position and imagine the ball coming off the face. The more lofted the iron, the farther left it will go; and the less lofted the club, for example a driver, the less left it will go. See Figure 65-5. Also note that in Figure 65-5 there is an example of a club with no loft or 0° loft. This shows that if no loft exists; then regardless of the proper or improper lie, the ball will always go toward the target if the leading edge of the clubface is pointed square to the target. This points out that putters have minimal directional control problems when the lie is improper because putters usually only have between 1° and 4° loft.

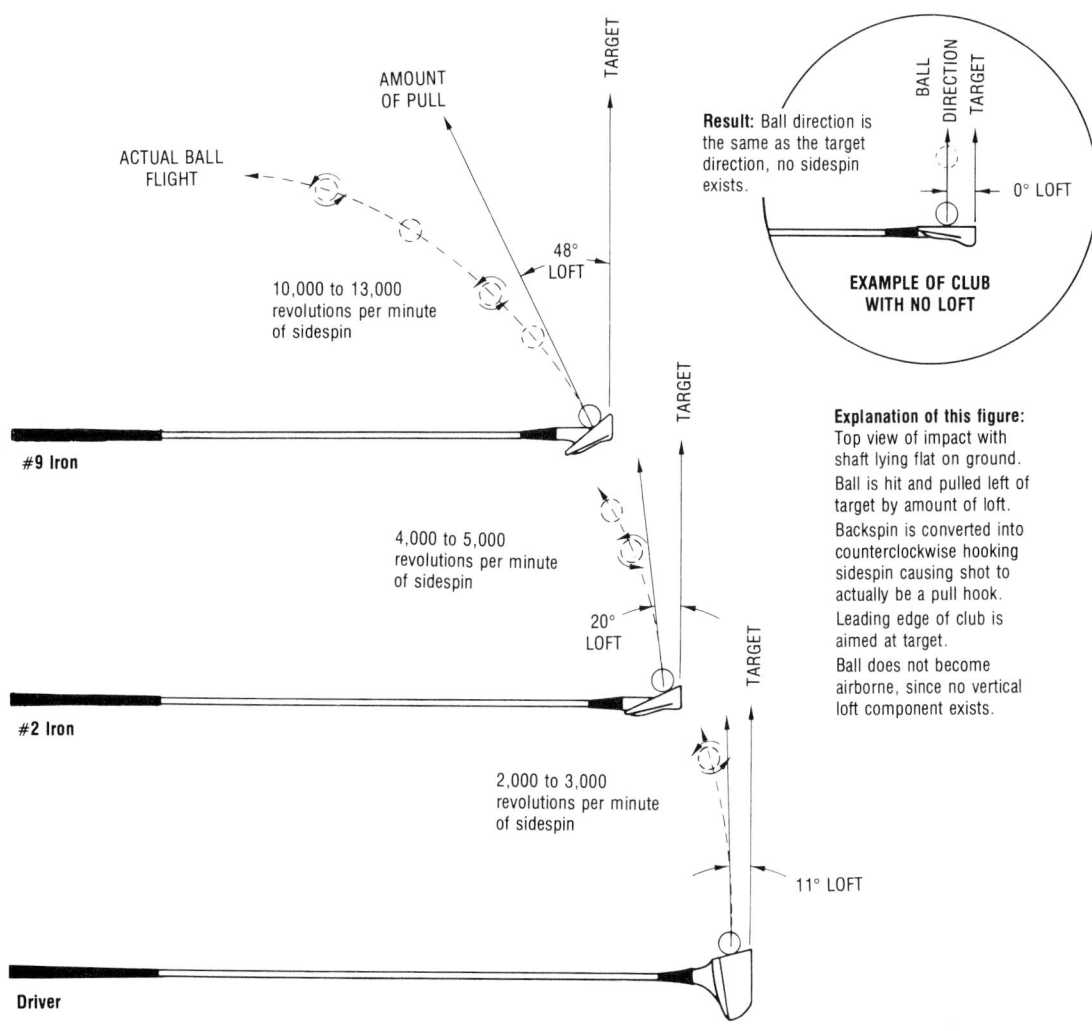

Figure 65-5
Effect of improper lie angle on face plane tilt versus amount of loft

Normally during impact, a golf ball is launched with backspin. However, the impact shown in Figure 65-5 for the #9 iron, #2 iron and driver, will launch the ball with counterclockwise hooking sidespin only, thus compounding the effect of improper lie on directional control. The resulting shot would be a pull hook with its severity based on the amount of club loft. To illustrate this severity, let's look at the #9 iron shot more closely. First, as already stated the ball is pulled 48° left of the target or by the amount of the club's loft. Also, a #9 iron normally generates some 10,000 to 13,000 revolutions per minute of backspin. Couple this 48° pull left with the extremely high amount of pure counterclockwise hooking sidespin (converted from backspin) and you can easily visualize how severe the ball will start left and curve left in this example.

Next, let's look at the driver example in Figure 65-5. The driver pulls the ball 11° left of the target. Because of its reduced loft angle, only 2,000 to 3,000 revolutions per minute of hooking sidespin is produced resulting in far less severity of pull hook versus the #9 iron example.

So you now understand, the amount of loft is a primary consideration when fitting lie from club to club. From an accuracy standpoint, proper lie is far more critical in the higher lofted clubs versus the less lofted clubs such as the long irons and driver. However, from an overall playability standpoint the lie angle should be adjusted properly in all clubs of the set.

Let's look at some examples which would better typify actual conditions of impact. First, assume that you have a 115 yard #9 iron shot to the green with a bunker left. The pin is positioned 15 feet from the left edge of the green. Also, assume that you will execute the shot perfectly with one exception: the toe will be up 4° at impact. This means the lie of the club is adjusted too upright for you. Here is what would happen. See Figure 65-6. With a close-up, stop action film, we see the club at impact actually touches the ground at a point 1" rearward of the center of the face, indicating on most irons that the club came through the impact zone with the player holding the club 4° flatter in lie angle than the lie angle actually built into the club. Because the club was swung 4° flatter, this causes the toe of the club to stick up in the air 4° which is too upright for this player. It can be calculated mathematically that the ball will be pulled 3° left of the target because the face plane is tilted by 3° in that direction. (This assumes a 48° lofted #9 iron.) On a 115 yard shot, this would amount to pulling the shot left by approximately 18 feet or, as in this case, into the bunker. Also, there would be a slight hooking effect from sidespin which would amount to an additional 4 feet left. This shot is a pull hook resulting in the ball landing 22 feet left of the target from the lie being only 4° too upright at impact. Imagine a pull hook 22 feet left of the target even though the clubhead path and face angle at impact were square to the target. The player made a perfect swing, but the improperly fit lie angle made it into a poor shot.

To further the example, assume a driver is also being hit with the lie 4° too upright for the player. Since a driver only has a 10° or 11° loft compared to a #9 iron with 48° loft, the pulling effect is far less severe even though the driver hits the ball a much greater distance. Refer back to Figure 65-5. With the lie of the driver 4° too upright, the ball would be pulled approximately 1° left of the target or only 11 feet. The hooking effect from sidespin would only be another 2 feet causing the ball to land 13 feet left of the middle of the fairway. See Figure 65-7.

An astute reader will start to formulate some interesting thoughts concerning lie. First, let us assume that the golfer has a set of woods and irons that are all 4° too upright at impact. The old thinking was that since the lies were all off by the same amount, there would be no problem because the player could adjust his/her swing and/or aim by compensating the same amount for every club. This has just been proven not to be so. We have now learned that the more lofted a club, the greater the tendency will be to hit it off target line if all the lies are consistently incorrect. Hence, the higher lofted short irons which are used for accuracy are the most critical for having the proper lie. Second, if the lies on a set of woods and irons are not incrementally correct for a given golfer (i.e., assume #2 iron, 1° upright; #3 iron, 3° upright; #4 iron, 2° flat; #3 wood, 4° upright, etc.) then the problem could be even further compounded and would still require a different compensating swing for each club to hit the ball with any consistency at the target.

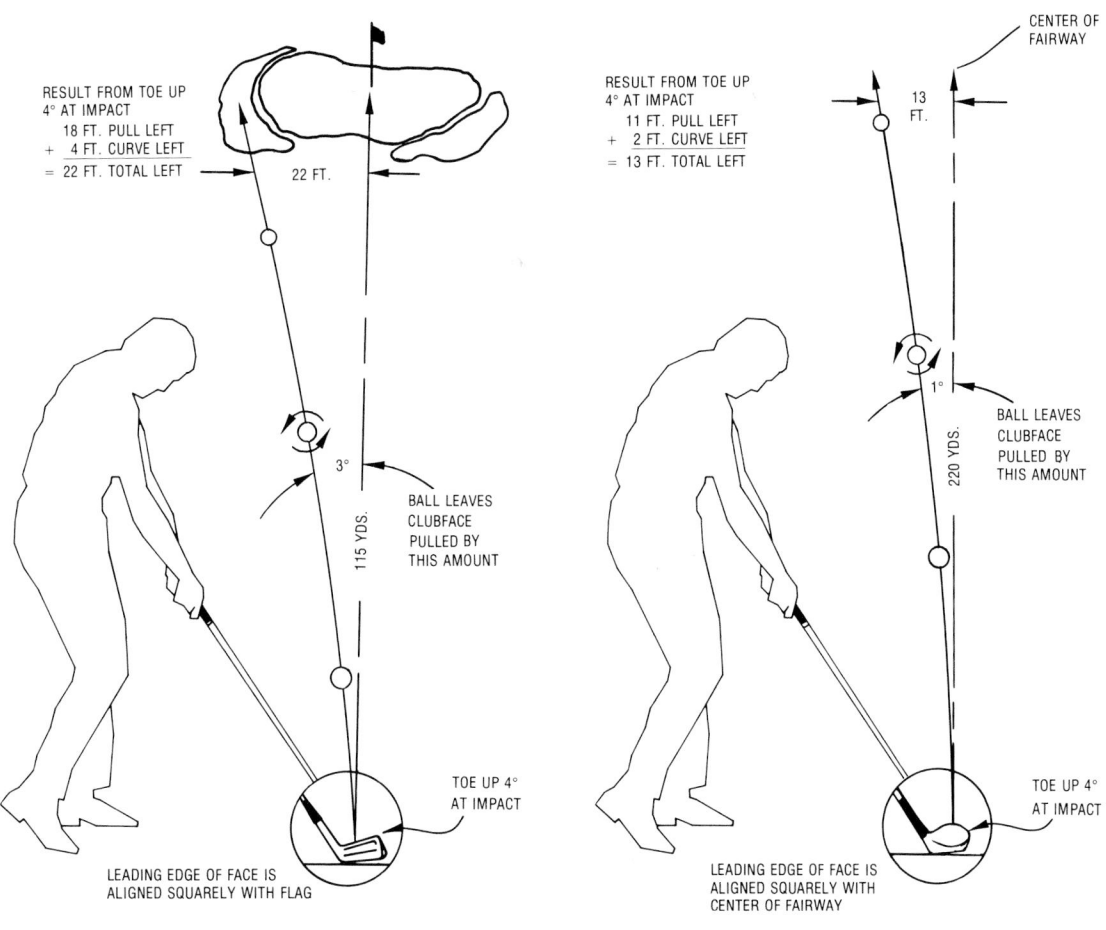

Figure 65-6
Incorrect lie angle at impact — #9 iron 48° loft

Figure 65-7
Incorrect lie angle at impact — driver 11° loft

Next, let's discuss lie angle even further and explore its relationship with trajectory, backspin, ground roll, distance and solidness of feel. First of all, if the clubhead is at the proper lie angle during impact, the resultant shot will fly at the target (assume a square clubface and clubhead path for this discussion), provide maximum ball trajectory for each given loft angle, provide the proper incremental distance for each loft angle, generate maximum backspin and minimize ground roll while also providing the player the most solid feeling at impact.

For a comparison of this, let us go back to the example shown in Figure 65-6 where the toe of a #9 iron was too upright for the player at impact by 4°. In this example, the clubhead is actually contacting the ball with more of a glancing blow due to the tilted face plane which will impact some hooking sidespin along with mostly backspin resulting in a slightly more unsolid feeling at impact. This is not too severe on a #9 iron, but far more noticeable on a long iron.

IMPORTANT GENERAL NOTE: Any time the ball is hit with a glancing blow, even in the face center on the sweetspot, a reduction in the amount of energy or force applied to the ball results.

The less loft a club has, the greater this energy loss at impact. From a teaching standpoint, the golf instructor should work toward square contact at impact regarding clubhead path and clubface angle as a means of hitting the ball more solidly and resulting in greater distance. Quite possibly a 2° open face angle at impact coupled with a 4° inside-out path will result in the ball landing on the middle of the green, but it lands there by starting to the right and then hooking left while in flight (face angle closed to clubhead path). During the fitting process, be cognizant of those players, both high and low handicap, that have significant swing angle differences between clubhead path and clubface angle. If the player is hitting a club with the proper lie, the shape of the shot (initial ball direction and curve) will be the best indicator as to this problem which should be corrected by working on the player's swing. The difference between clubface angle and clubhead path during any swing should not be greater in either direction by more than 2°. Also, neither angle should be greater than 2° open or closed (clubface angle) and 2° inside-out or outside-in (clubhead path) in relation to the target.

Now let's get back to our #9 iron example in Figure 65-6. The trajectory will be reduced due to the face plane tilt which causes the backspin to be less resulting in greater ground roll after landing. So, you begin to see the compounding effect on play that an improper lie angle can cause. It should also be quite evident that while the pushing and pulling effect or directional control is more severe with the more lofted clubs, the unsolidness of feel and energy loss at impact is greater on the less lofted clubs.

There are two specifications which have a direct affect on lie. The first to talk about is shaft flexing. During the downswing, the lie of the club is slightly flattened due to shaft flexing. See Figure 65-8. This happens because the center of mass or center of gravity of the clubhead is not in line with the centerline of the shaft. Therefore, during the downswing, centrifugal force acts through the center of gravity of the clubhead causing it to bend downward resulting in a flattening of the lie. The exact amount of flattening is determined by head weight, club length, head speed and shaft flex. However, a good rule of thumb is that the longer length club will tend to flatten more than the shorter length clubs. The shorter clubs have the heaviest heads, but they also have stiffer shafts to compensate. Also, their shorter length does not allow for the higher clubhead speeds which generate greater centrifugal force. On the other hand, the longer clubs have lighter heads, more flex in the shafts, longer lengths and clubhead speeds far greater than the shorter clubs. This creates more centrifugal force and consequently increased flattening of the lie. The range of lie flattening for woods tends to be from 1° to 2° and for irons from 0° to 1½°.

The second specification which has an effect on lie is club length. The longer the club, the flatter the lie must be to fit the same golfer. Also, the shorter the club, the more upright the lie must be to fit the same golfer. See Figure 65-9 for an example using both woods and irons.

There are a number of methods that can be used to determine the proper lie angle for a given player; however, all but one can be inaccurate to some degree and require more skill and guesswork. The best way to fit lie angle, particularly with irons and fairway woods, is to use a 4' x 4' plywood board (¾" or ⅝" thickness is best, although ½" thick will work), and actually hit shots off the board. See Figure 65-10.

Due to the shaft flexing and bowing down during the downswing the lie angle "flattens" slightly

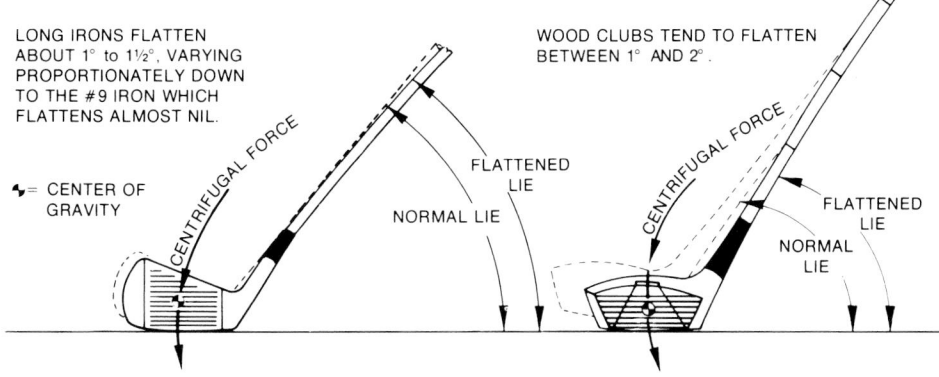

Figure 65-8
How centrifugal force tends to flatten the lie of a club during the downswing

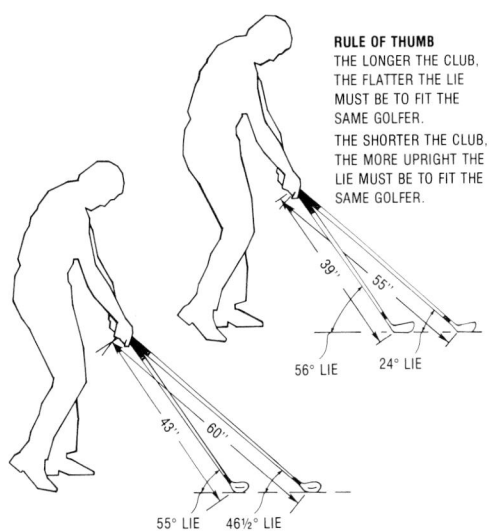

Figure 65-9
The effect of length on lie

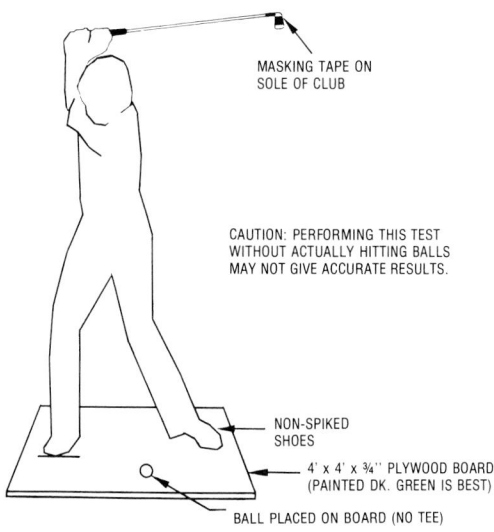

Figure 65-10
Checking for proper lie angle: The Plywood Board Method

The following procedure best describes this method: first, start with a #9 iron and place a piece of ½" or ¾" wide masking tape lengthwise on its sole in the toe to heel direction. Next, place a golf ball on the board and have the player hit a few shots being sure to actually hit the sole of the iron on the board. The golfer should not be wearing spiked shoes. The tape on the sole of the club will have a mark on it in the area where it touched the plywood board during impact with the golf ball. If the mark on the sole is located at the middle of the face, the lie is correct. If the mark is toward the toe, the club is too flat for that particular golfer; and if the mark is toward the heel, the club is too upright for that particular golfer. See Figure 65-11.

One note to make regarding the size of the mark: rarely will you get a very small concise mark. Usually the mark will look like a blotch on the tape, but this in no way compromises the accuracy of this method. Simply measure to the center or visually determine the center of the mark and not this location from the center of the face. The center of the mark will accurately show the exact face plane tilt of the clubhead at impact. Refer to Figure 65-12 for a "How To" example of interpreting the sole mark.

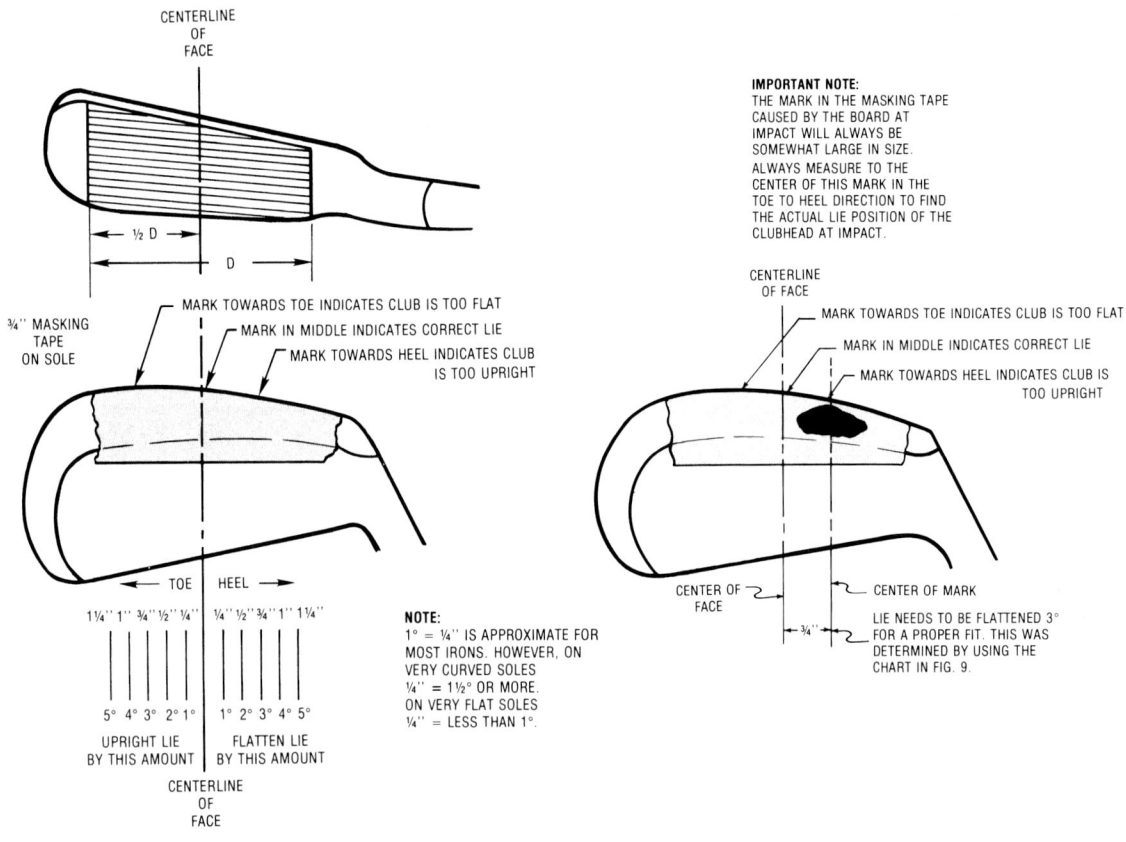

Figure 65-11
How to interpret lie angle using the Plywood Board Method of fitting

Figure 65-12
Interpreting the exact location of the actual sole mark when fitting lie using the Plywood Board Method

This procedure can be repeated using a middle iron and a long iron and then compared with the results for the #9 iron. If everything is done correctly, the remaining clubs can be adjusted on a loft and lie machine and fit proportionately in between the ones that were actually checked. If desired, each iron in the set can be checked and adjusted by hitting from the board.

A very important precaution using the "Plywood Board Method" is in order here: **You must actually hit a real golf ball off the board to get accurate results. Simply swinging a club without a golf ball or hitting whiffle balls will provide erroneous data.** You do not swing the same when you are not hitting a real golf ball. It is okay, however, to hit real balls into a net versus out on the range when using this method.

Lastly, the plywood board will not scratch or cause damage to the sole of the golf club. However, it may take a few shots to get used to the idea of hitting off the board. At The GolfWorks® our lie angle fitting boards are painted with grass green enamel for two reasons: One is to achieve an outdoor grassy look and the other is to cause a small mark of green paint to mark the sole during the test, thus eliminating the use of masking tape. Pick your own method, but be sure to actually hit real golf balls.

Fairway woods can also be checked using the "Plywood Board Method." Put one piece of ¾" masking tape on the front of the soleplate and another on the rear of the soleplate in the heel to toe direction. Hit a few balls from the board and look for the mark location on either piece of tape.

The reason that the "Plywood Board" method works best is that it eliminates all of the dynamic forces and individual golfer swing peculiarities that are inherent in other methods of fitting lie. For instance, a popularly accepted method to check lie is to first have a golfer assume his normal address position with a certain club. Next, using two pieces of paper, slip one under the toe and the other under the heel as far as they will go toward the center of the club. A point halfway in between the two pieces of paper is the address lie position. This method is certainly better than no method at all, but it does not take into account the bowing down of the shaft during the downswing and the change in hand position from address to impact which varies with every golfer. Since this book came out in 1974, I have done extensive fitting of lie and discovered that most every player from amateur to tour player comes through impact with the actual lie of the club 2° to 4° flatter than it was in the address position. Up to 2° of this is caused by the bowing down of the shaft. The other 1° to 3° is caused by a more upright change in the player's hand position from address to impact. See Figure 65-13. (Note: The 1° to 3° more upright hand position of the player causes the clubhead to come through impact 1° to 3° flatter.)

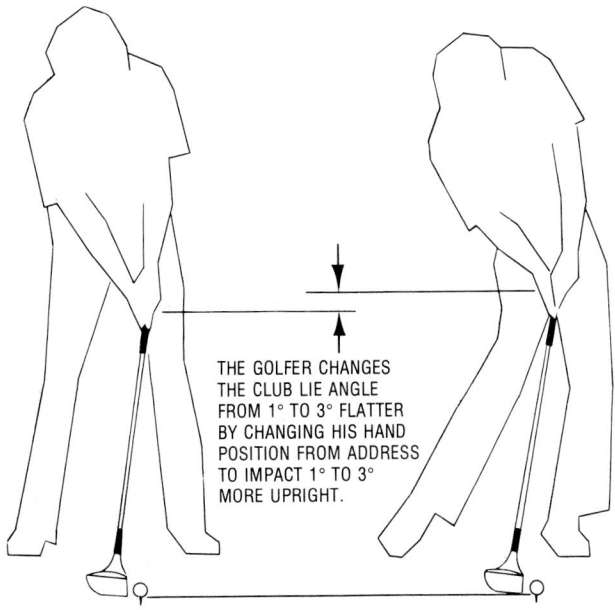

THE GOLFER CHANGES THE CLUB LIE ANGLE FROM 1° TO 3° FLATTER BY CHANGING HIS HAND POSITION FROM ADDRESS TO IMPACT 1° TO 3° MORE UPRIGHT.

Figure 65-13
Hand position change from address to impact

The driver lie cannot easily be checked on the plywood board, and it is recommended to use the method previously mentioned using two pieces of paper while the golfer assumes the address position. Proper lie angle is less critical on the less lofted clubs regarding directional control, but it is still an important factor in the solidness of the hit. The driver has less loft than all the other clubs in the bag with the exception of the putter. Because of the greater amount of shaft flexing and the change in hand positions from address to impact, it is recommended that a proper lie driver sit ½" to 1" rearward (¾" is a good starting point) of the face center in the address position. See Figure 65-14.

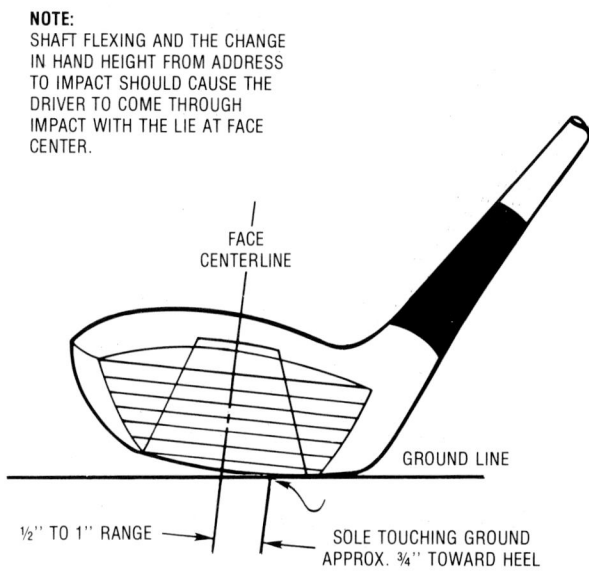

NOTE:
SHAFT FLEXING AND THE CHANGE IN HAND HEIGHT FROM ADDRESS TO IMPACT SHOULD CAUSE THE DRIVER TO COME THROUGH IMPACT WITH THE LIE AT FACE CENTER.

FACE CENTERLINE

GROUND LINE

½" TO 1" RANGE

SOLE TOUCHING GROUND APPROX. ¾" TOWARD HEEL

Figure 65-14
A driver with the proper lie angle in the address position

Sometimes, it is virtually impossible to fit lie using the plywood board and tape method. If this is the case, the following "Address Position Method" has been devised to compensate as much as possible for the variables of shaft bowing and hand height changes by assuming some averages. This method has a few trade-offs when compared to the "Plywood Board Method," but it will be fairly accurate for fitting lie and should give good results.

First, determine the face center location on each iron by measuring the face scoring width and dividing this in half. See Figure 65-15. Put a light pencil mark at the bottom of the face to indicate the face center position. Now, again measuring from the face center, make a light pencil mark on each iron as shown in the chart in Figure 65-15. This will determine the point on each iron that should be touching the ground in the address position if the lie is correct. Since the #9 iron flattens almost nil, the initial ⅜" rearward compensates about 1½° for an average hand height increase and each ¹⁄₁₆" added for every iron thereafter compensates for the amount of shaft flexing or clubhead bowing down which increases from the #9 to the #1 iron.

Next, start with either a #2 or #9 iron and have the golfer get comfortable in the address position by waggling the club a number of times and finally setting it down in position on the floor.

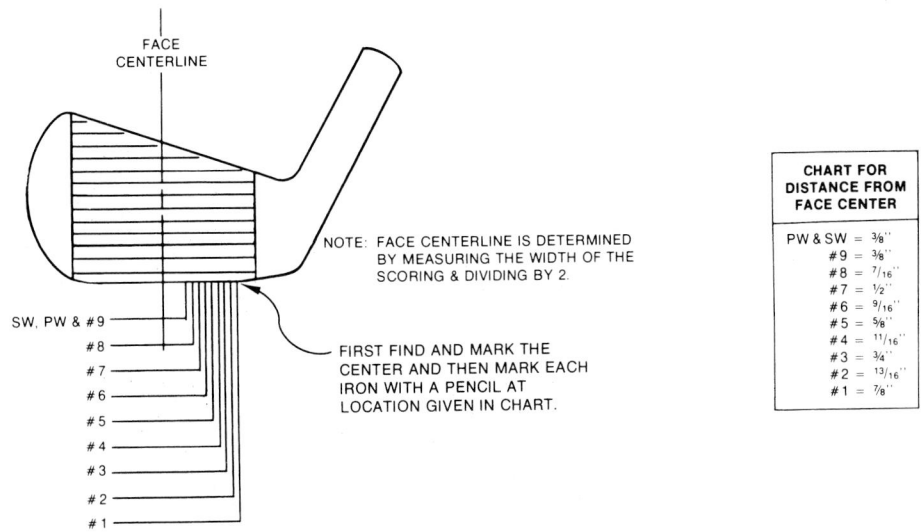

FACE
CENTERLINE

NOTE: FACE CENTERLINE IS DETERMINED
BY MEASURING THE WIDTH OF THE
SCORING & DIVIDING BY 2.

SW, PW & #9
#8
#7
#6
#5
#4
#3
#2
#1

FIRST FIND AND MARK THE
CENTER AND THEN MARK EACH
IRON WITH A PENCIL AT
LOCATION GIVEN IN CHART.

**CHART FOR
DISTANCE FROM
FACE CENTER**

PW & SW	= 3/8''
#9	= 3/8''
#8	= 7/16''
#7	= 1/2''
#6	= 9/16''
#5	= 5/8''
#4	= 11/16''
#3	= 3/4''
#2	= 13/16''
#1	= 7/8''

Figure 65-15
Determining the proper lie position for each iron using the Address Position Method of fitting lie angle

Now, have the player hold this position while you take two small pieces of paper (business cards work well) and slide one in from the toe as far as it will go and the other in from the heel as far as it will go. Exactly in between the gap of these two pieces of paper is where the club is actually touching the ground. Visually you can determine if the lie is too upright (papers indicate golf club is touching ground rearward of the pencil mark); lie is too flat (papers indicate golf club is touching ground forward of the pencil mark); or lie is correct (papers indicate golf club is touching ground at exact point of the pencil mark). See Figure 65-16.

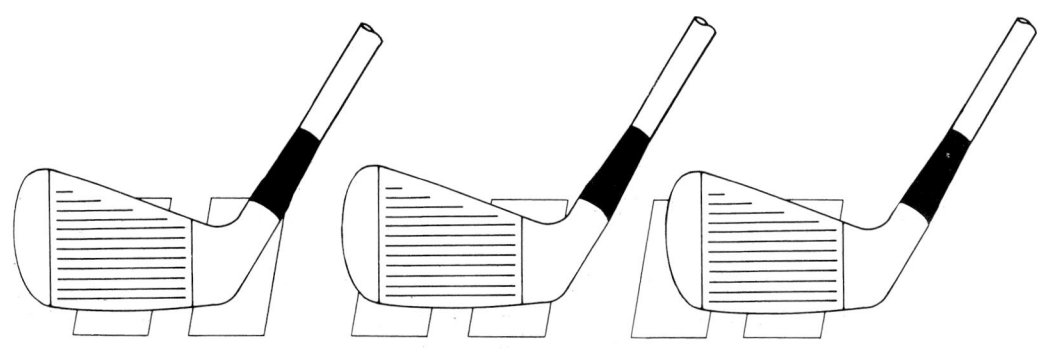

Figure 65-16
Method for determining exactly where the club is touching the ground in the address position

The club should now be put in a loft and lie bending machine and the lie adjusted accordingly. Remember to always record the loft and lie readings before and after bending the hosel. This is extremely important to have and keep for reference purposes. The driver and fairway wood lie should be fit in exactly the same manner as just described by using the range shown in Figure 65-14.

The best visual aid to have when discussing the importance of lie is an old iron with a hole drilled in its face. Chapter 36 shows how to do this in Photos 36-6 and 36-7. A golf shaft is inserted into the drilled face hole to show how the plane of the face tilts either right or left if the lie is too flat or too upright. This device can also be used in teaching, to explain why a ball usually does not fly straight on uphill and sidehill lies. It is best to make up two of these clubs, one should be a #9 or #8 iron and the other a #2 or #3 iron. In this manner, it is easier to explain the greater misdirection that can occur in the high lofted irons versus the less lofted irons if the lie is not correct.

Many books, articles and people have passed on the myth that an iron with too upright a lie will cause the heel of the club to dig in and the toe to close at impact causing the ball to be pulled left of the intended line. Conversely, when the toe is down on clubs with too flat a lie angle, it was said the toe struck the ground first and opened the clubface, thus sending the ball to the right. This seemed fairly logical as an explanation and is still widely accepted, but in fact is nothing more than a myth. When using this false explanation, it must have been difficult to explain sidehill lies when the ball would go left (ball above the feet) or downhill lies when the ball would go right (ball below feet). If you think about these two types of lies, the sole of the club usually would sit properly on the ground with no chance of the toe or heel digging in. However, the ball still was hit with misdirection if the player did not properly compensate his/her alignment right or left of the target.

So, the heel or toe cannot possibly dig in enough to cause poor ball direction, and we all know now that the face plane is actually tilted to cause this when the lie angle is not correct for a given player.

Here is something to think about and be aware of during fitting. There are a number of players who have a tendency to pull their short irons left of the green and push their long irons to the right. At least one golf company recognized this and came out with a set of irons a few years back with each iron from the long irons to the short irons having a different horizontal weight location in an effort to solve this problem. The irons incidentally were a good design, had good weight distribution and played quite well; but they only solved the pulling and pushing problem in the advertising copy and not on the golf course.

Others that recognize and try to solve this long standing problem usually suggest that the shaft is either too stiff or too flexible for the player. In actuality, the culprit is the lie angle. If a set of clubs are built with progressive 1° lie angle increments from the #1 iron down to the #9 iron, chances are the short irons will end up too upright for the individual and the long irons too flat. This section on fitting lie has already explained that too upright a lie causes the ball to be pulled left and too flat a lie causes the ball to be pushed right. This is why fitting lie angle to the individual is necessary on every set of clubs made. You certainly cannot blame the manufacturers that most people need to have the lie adjusted to fit them correctly and that a so-called standard lie is only a good starting point. As a further explanation, the 1° progressive increments between clubs would work if each different length club did not flatten in lie differently during the swing resulting from shaft flexing. Remember, the longer clubs tend to flatten more and the shorter clubs less.

This information is worth pointing out because it helps tremendously in troubleshooting a common fitting problem of players pulling their short irons and pushing their long irons. The Fitting Score Card, explained further on in Variable #11 "Set Makeup," should easily point out this problem when it is analyzed.

Tables 65-4 and 65-5 give the recommended angles for sets of golf clubs with flat, standard and upright lies for both men and women. Compare this table with each manufacturer's lie specification in Appendix 8.

TABLE 65-4
Wood Club Lies – Men's and Ladies'

Woods	Men's			Ladies'		
	[1] Flat Lies	[1] Standard Lies	[1] Upright Lies	[2] Flat Lies	[2] Standard Lies	[2] Upright Lies
1	53°	55°	57°	51°	53°	55°
2	53½°	55½°	57½°	51½°	53½°	55½°
3	54°	56°	58°	52°	54°	56°
4	54½°	56½°	58½°	52½°	54½°	56½°
5	55°	57°	59°	53°	55°	57°
6	55½°	57½°	59½°	53½°	55½°	57½°
7	56°	58°	60°	54°	56°	58°
8	56½°	58½°	60½°	54½°	56½°	58½°
9	57°	59°	61°	55°	57°	59°

[1] Lies shown are for standard length woods (i.e., 43" driver). For each ½" added to standard length, subtract 1° in lie (flatter) and for each ½" subtracted from standard length, add 1° in lie (upright).
[2] Same as Note 1 above but based on a standard length set with a 42" driver.

TABLE 65-5
Iron Club Lies – Men's and Ladies'

Woods	Men's			Ladies'		
	[1] Flat Lies	[1] Standard Lies	[1] Upright Lies	[2] Flat Lies	[2] Standard Lies	[2] Upright Lies
1	53°	55°	57°	51°	53°	55°
2	54°	56°	58°	52°	54°	56°
3	55°	57°	59°	53°	55°	57°
4	56°	58°	60°	54°	56°	58°
5	57°	59°	61°	55°	57°	59°
6	58°	60°	62°	56°	58°	60°
7	59°	61°	63°	57°	59°	61°
8	60°	62°	64°	58°	60°	62°
9	61°	63°	65°	59°	61°	63°
PW	61°	63°	65°	59°	61°	63°
SW	61°	63°	65°	59°	61°	63°

[1] Lies shown are for standard men's length irons (i.e., 39" #2 iron). For each ½" added to standard length, subtract 1° in lie (flatter) and for each ½" subtracted from standard length, add 1° in lie (upright).
[2] Same as Note 1 above but based on a standard length set with a 38" #2 iron.

3. SHAFT FLEX

(Reference: Chapters 7, 21, 24, 36, 37, 48, 49, 52, 55, 56, 57, 58, 63, Appendices 1, 2.)

A golf shaft has three important elements which you must consider during fitting. They are:

1. Shaft flex or relative stiffness.
2. Material and weight.
3. Pattern, curve, flex point or bend point.

The first element, shaft flex or relative stiffness, is a relative measure of stiffness or resistance to bending when comparing one shaft to another. The second element, material or weight of the shaft is a factor in determining the weight distribution of the club required to obtain a certain swingweight. The third element, pattern or flex point is a key determinant in where the shaft will bend most during the swing such as in the tip area, middle of the shaft, or in the butt area of the shaft. This element, to some degree, helps control ball trajectory, directional control and gives the player a certain swing "feel." The point to fully understand here is that all three elements are important to proper shaft fitting and each interrelates with the other to determine the remaining club specifications in the club fitting process.

When using these three elements of fitting golf shafts, the clubfitter should keep in mind what is actually trying to be solved for the player. This solution is based on the golf shaft's main purpose in the golf club. The golf shaft's purpose is to bring the clubhead into the proper impact position with predictable repeatability, swing after swing for a given golfer. To do this the golf club must have the proper shaft stiffness, shaft flex point and shaft weight to complement both the golfer's ability and the golf club's other specifications of head weight, loft, lie, total weight, length and grip size.

Now that we know the three important elements of fitting golf shafts and the shaft's main purpose in a golf club, we need to discuss the five important elements of playability that shafts influence. They are:

1. Trajectory.
2. Solidness of feel.
3. Consistency of hit.
4. Directional control.
5. Clubhead speed.

If you can properly analyze a player by: 1) using the three elements to properly fit golf shafts, 2) the five elements of playability, 3) the ball's flight pattern and trajectory, and then make a proper shaft recommendation; you will have satisfied the golf shaft's purpose of repeatability swing after swing.

In many articles, books and discussions, the golf shaft is often considered to be the most important variable of the eleven fitting variables. Actually it should only be considered as just one of the eleven fitting variables. The shaft is important; however, it is but one of the components and specifications in the overall golf club design. All of the components and specifications together, along with all their combined attributes as they pertain to each individual club and each individual golfer should all be considered as most important.

When a golfer swings a club, he/she gets some sort of a feel sensation. This sensation is basically undefinable because it would be different with each particular player's swing. But we can discuss the characteristics of a golf club that cause this feel so we understand it better during club fitting. In Chapter 62, frequency matching is thoroughly discussed. In this discussion, it was pointed out that there are three basic specifications on a golf club which affect its frequency (cycles per minute) or a better term "flex feel." They are:

1. Shaft flex
2. Head weight
3. Club length

These three specifications should always be kept in mind during the fitting of golf shafts. Change any one of these three specifications and you change the other two, either actually or by player feel during the swing. Let's use an example here to show how you should think during the fitting of golf shafts.

The player has clubs which are determined to be too short by 1"; otherwise you have determined that the clubs fit fine. If new clubs are made 1" longer, the shafts will feel at least ½ flex more flexible due to the added length combined with a higher swingspeed. The flex feel change occurs even though the head weight was properly reduced in the new clubs to maintain the same swingweight as the player's original clubs. As a note of interest here, the higher swingspeed is a result of two factors. The first factor is the longer club and the second is the reduced total weight of the club.

There are a number of solutions to be looked at with this example and they are:

- The shaft could have been tipped 1" to regain the approximate original flex feel.
- A more tip stiff shaft (higher kick point) could have been used in the same flex.
- A more tip flexible shaft (lower kick point) could have been used in a stiffer flex.
- The head weight and consequently the swingweight could be reduced 2 or 3 points lighter than original (example: original D-2 now D-0 or C-9). This will make the shaft feel more stiff.

Keep in mind that the three specifications we have just discussed — shaft flex, head weight and club length — affect the swing feel or flex feel from a golf club specifications standpoint only. The final element to toss in here is the golfer's physical swing characteristics which will give an entirely different flex feel for this club than that of another player. We all know this to be true because most of us swing differently; it is just a matter of always relating this back to shaft flex, head weight and club length, so we firmly keep these club factors in mind during club fitting.

Next, let us again list the three elements of golf shafts which should always be taken into consideration during shaft fitting.

1. Shaft flex
2. Material and weight
3. Pattern or flex point

Also, proper fitting of golf shafts can be made much easier if the analysis includes the five steps which follow:

Step 1. Distance the ball is hit or player's clubhead speed

Step 2. Trajectory in reference to normal, low or high

Step 3. Directional control of shot

Step 4. Consistency of shot

Step 5. Player comments on solidness of feel

Let us take a look at these steps one at a time.

• Step 1. Distance the ball is hit or player's clubhead speed.

This is the main step in selecting the proper shaft flexibility such as X-Stiff, Stiff, Medium, Flexible or Ladies. This is relatively easy to do because it is best based on a player's distance carry with his driver or his measured swingspeed. Be cautioned, however, that when using swingspeed, there are numerous swing computers on the market that measure and give swingspeeds differently. Unless you know the exact correlation of swingspeed on your machine versus actual swingspeed, it may be best to use carry distance. Also, most golf professionals and skilled players can usually look at a player hitting balls and tell what flex shaft is needed. Table 65-6 provides general carry distance and swingspeeds by shaft flex. Note also that throughout our discussions, swingspeed and clubhead speed have the same meaning.

TABLE 65-6

Shaft Flex Selection by Distance and Swingspeed

Shaft Flex	Type of Golfer	Carry Distance of Drivers
L-Ladies	Average women golfers — young juniors	160 yards or less
A-Flexible	Senior golfers and stronger women — swingspeed 60 mph +	160 yards to 185 yards
R-Medium	Used by the majority of golfers who possess average swingspeed and strength of many women golf professionals — swingspeed 75 mph +	175 yards to 220 yards
S-Stiff	Used by scratch and low handicap amateurs, most golf professionals and strong players who lack control — swingspeed 95 mph +	210 yards to 250 yards
X-Extra Stiff	Used only by few of the stronger touring professionals who need this extra control because of extremely fast clubhead speeds — swingspeed 115 mph +	240 yards and over

The best method of actually fitting and convincing the golfer which shaft flex suits best is to have the golfer hit clubs equipped with different flex shafts. Which shafts you choose to use in your test clubs depends on many factors. The golfer should, however, experience hitting balls with all flexes and in particular with the extremes of shaft flex such as a flexible shaft (A) and an extra-stiff (X). Then, after doing this, the golfer should hit again with the shaft flex which best fits. This will enable the golfer to better understand the role of shaft flex in hitting a golf ball and reinforce the rationale in the clubfitter's recommendation. Besides the various shaft flexes in test clubs, you should also have some different material types to try such as very lightweight steel and possibly graphite. If it is determined that a player should be using a shaft flex which is between the available flexes shown in the table or in the test clubs, the shaft can be tipped. Tipping refers to trimming a shaft from the tip end to stiffen it rather than trimming it from the butt end as is usually done to obtain proper club length. Tipping a shaft 1" will usually obtain a flex that is in between. Now let's look at Steps 2, 3 and 4 and discuss them.

- **Step 2. Trajectory in reference to normal, low and high**
- **Step 3. Directional control of shot**
- **Step 4. Consistency of shot**

It is necessary for a person who fits clubs to understand what a normal ball trajectory should look like from the driver to the #9 iron. This is an important fitting consideration because normal trajectory maximizes carry distance on the driver and provides predictable incremental distance differences on the rest of the clubs. There are a number of golf club characteristics and specifications which help control trajectory and all have been discussed in great detail in the other fitting variables booklets. The golf shaft is, however, an important variable in fitting because the flexing of the golf shaft during the swing can cause inconsistencies in trajectory and, for that matter, directional control.

If we have already picked the proper shaft flex for the player, this leaves material and weight and also the pattern or flex point of the shaft still to consider. The material and weight of the shaft affect other club specifications such as head weight and total weight, which as previously mentioned, affect the swing feel or flex feel of the shaft. These combinations are limitless and are best determined by hitting specific test clubs with different shaft types and head designs to narrow down the decision. The shaft pattern or flex point can be fit and determined in much the same manner, but we can make a more rational recommendation in this area by watching closely as the player hits balls. Again, if we have previously selected the correct shaft flex and the player is hitting the ball too high, we can recommend a more tip stiff (high flex point) shaft. The Dynamic® pattern shaft would be a good example of a high flex point shaft and the Pro-Fit® pattern shaft would be a good example of a low flex point shaft.

Finally, let's discuss the last step:

• **Step 5. Player comments on solidness of feel.**

When hitting test clubs and possibly alternating back and forth with the player's present clubs, ask for any player comments. These comments can be quite valuable and particularly so if they are referring to solidness of feel as perceived by the player. If you use the player's comments in relation to the actual shot just hit, it will be easier to determine what shaft is hit best and also feels best.

So, in the final analysis to sum up proper shaft fitting: you are trying to get the player to hit the ball with a normal trajectory, good consistency and directional control, while at the same time providing a solid feeling golf club to the player. This not only applies to fitting golf shafts, but fitting golf clubs in general. I think that one of the best tips I can give in clubfitting is to first "lock in" as well as you can in determining all the other clubfitting variables, and then fit the proper shaft to the specific clubs and the specific player. Finally, after fitting clubs in this sequence, go back and make any other adjustments if necessary.

The following Golf Club Troubleshooting Guide has been developed to aid the clubfitter in fitting golf clubs and it is particularly helpful in fitting golf shafts. Keep in mind that this is a golf club troubleshooting guide and that in all six causes listed in the guide, the player may also have a swing problem in which the solution may be to take a lesson and practice.

GOLF CLUB TROUBLESHOOTING GUIDE

If You Do This...	A Possible Solution Could Be...	
Hook or Pull the Ball	• Open face angle to more slice (Woods) • Use a more tip stiff shaft • Check for proper club length • Increase swingweight	• Use a stiffer flex shaft • Check for too upright a lie • Check for too small a grip
Slice or Push the Ball	• Use a more flexible shaft • Check for too flat a lie • Decrease swingweight • Close face angle to more hook (Woods)	• Use a more tip weak shaft • Check for proper club length • Check for too large a grip • Check for weight in grip end of club
Hit Ball Too High	• Decrease loft • Use a more tip stiff shaft • Check for excessive face roll (Woods) • Check for excessive hook in face angle (Woods)	• Use a stiffer shaft • Check for proper club length • Use a deeper faced club • Check for backweighted club
Hit Ball Too Low	• Increase loft • Use a more tip weak shaft • Use a shallow faced club • Use backweighted woods	• Use a more flexible shaft • Check for proper club length • Check for excessive slice in face angle (Woods)
Accuracy Generally Inconsistent In Both Directions	• Shaft too flexible • Swingweight too heavy or too light • Check for proper club length • Check for weight in grip end of club	• Use a more tip stiff shaft • Check all lie angles • Check for proper grip size
Unsolid Feeling During the Shot	• Swingweight too light • Shaft too stiff • Check for proper club length • Check for weight in grip end of club • Possibly improper designed clubhead	• Total weight too light • Use a more tip weak shaft • Check for excessive weight down shaft • Check all lie angles
Loss of Distance	• Swingweight too heavy • Trajectory too high (Irons) • Shaft too stiff • Use a lighter overall weight shaft • Check for proper club length • Check all loft angles	• Total weight too heavy • Trajectory too high or low (Woods) • Use a more tip weak shaft • Check for too large a grip • Check for excessive face roll (Woods)

Finally, the following additional guide has been prepared to reference directly the situation of too stiff or too flexible a shaft for the golfer.

GOLF SHAFT TROUBLESHOOTING GUIDE

Shaft Problem	Possible Causes
Shaft flex too stiff or kick point too high for the golfer	• Lower than normal ball trajectory • Unsolid feeling at impact on all but the exact dead center hits, boardy feeling • Consistently pushing the ball to the right or slicing • Loss of distance
Shaft flex too flexible or kick point too low for the golfer	• Higher than normal ball trajectory • Poor directional control, usually excessive hooking resulting from the face closing before impact • Whippy feeling • Loss of distance

The following discussion of shaft flex and flex point versus clubhead acceleration falls in the "for what it's worth" department because it will probably not be fully understood by everyone. It is, however, important in explaining generally why we have golf shafts that have their maximum point of deflection (flex point) in various locations in differing shaft types.

Although only a rule of thumb and not true in all cases due to various clubhead designs, club lengths, head weights, etc., it is usually said that tip stiff shafts (high flex point) are generally for better players and tip flexible shafts (low flex point) are for less skilled players. It is not recommended to use this criteria in the actual fitting of golf shafts, but rather to fit shafts as already explained using distance, trajectory, direction control, feel, etc. Still, in many cases, the less skilled player will fit into mid or low flex point shafts that are usually lighter in weight. The purpose for bringing this up is to give a general explanation for why this occurs.

First of all, better players tend to hit the ball more often in the middle of the face. This produces a solid shot and coupled with a tip stiff shaft (which has less torque in the tip than a tip flexible shaft), they will hit the ball consistently straighter more of the time. Also, most good players can achieve normal trajectories from the tip stiff shafts because they accelerate at an accelerating rate coming into impact with the ball.

Here is what I mean: Let's say that two players have the exact same swingspeed of 105 mph and they both fit into a stiff flex shaft. Both players hit the exact same test club with a stiff flex, tip stiff shaft, but the better player hits the ball on a normal trajectory and the less skilled player hits the ball much lower. Why does this happen? The reason is the difference in the two players' swingspeed rates of acceleration which is caused by where each player releases or uncocks their wrists on the downswing. This causes the clubhead to accelerate at an accelerating rate coming into impact. This is usually referred to as a "late release." Conversely, the less skilled player may have a tendency to release quite early during the downswing causing the clubhead to accelerate at a decelerating rate coming into impact. This "early release" is sometimes called "swinging from the top." When you watch tour players hit balls, they seem to do it effortlessly and they also appear to be swinging slower. Actually, they are not swinging slower, but swinging faster as caused by their very late wrist releases before impact.

A phrase you will often hear teachers use, or for that matter, announcers at golf tournaments is: "He isn't accelerating through the ball." Or they may say: "He is decelerating coming into impact." Well, the idea is correct, but the terminology is not. All players accelerate the clubhead during a normal full swing coming into impact. But as we just pointed out, some accelerate at an accelerating rate and others accelerate at a decelerating rate. Let's explain further.

Suppose from a dead stop we accelerate a powerful sports car to 105 mph with the gas pedal all the way to the floor. The car is always accelerating and it is doing so at an accelerating rate, meaning it is always picking up greater amounts of speed over equal time intervals. Now suppose we take the same sports car and once again put the gas pedal to the floor; but as the car accelerates past 90 mph, we let up on the gas pedal slightly and very slowly back it off. So, we are still accelerating to 105 mph, but instead of accelerating at an accelerating rate as was the case with the pedal to the floor, we are now still accelerating, but it is at a decelerating rate. The car is always accelerating or going faster, but the rate is different, meaning we are picking up lesser and lesser amounts of speed over equal time intervals.

Now, back to fitting golf shafts. The key point here is not whether the player is good or less skilled or even downright poor, but for this given swingspeed, where does the golfer release on the downswing. Once again, the trajectory of the shot will be the final determinant of whether or not a player can handle a low, mid or high flex point shaft with a certain relative stiffness in a certain golf club. Also, remember that certain clubhead designs perform very well with high flex point shafts for average to poor players. It's the entire golf club and how it feels and performs that really counts.

Relative stiffness or shaft flex is defined exactly as the name implies. It is the relative measure of a shaft's flexibility as it pertains to standards set within the industry or by each individual manufacturer. The stiffness of a shaft is usually designated on a band wrapped around the shaft in one of the following ways: X-Stiff, Stiff, Medium, Flexible; Ladies: A, B, C, D; X, S, M, A, L; 1, 2, 3, 4, 5 or 5, 4, 3, 2, 1. A shaft's relative stiffness can be measured by using a deflection board or a frequency machine. Figure 65-17 shows how a deflection board works.

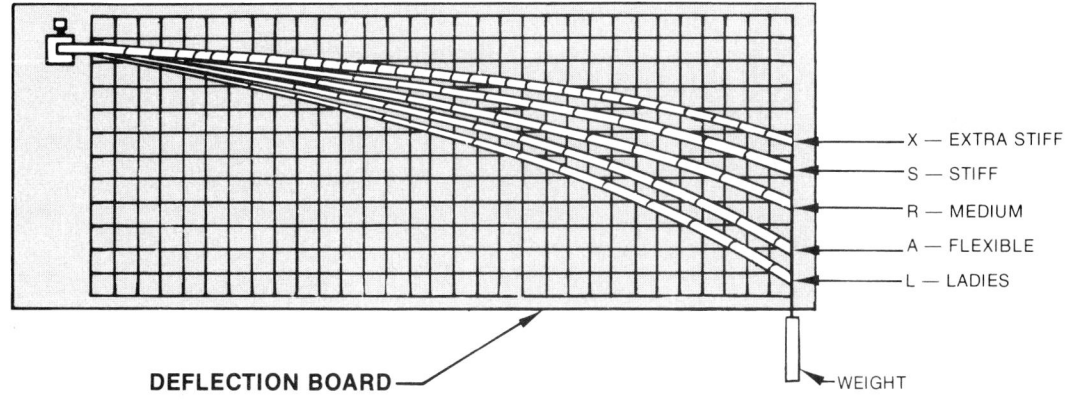

X — EXTRA STIFF
S — STIFF
R — MEDIUM
A — FLEXIBLE
L — LADIES

DEFLECTION BOARD

WEIGHT

Figure 65-17
Defining relative stiffness on a deflection board

Basically, a deflection board works like this: The butt end of the shaft is rigidly attached to a gridded board. A weight is suspended from the very tip end of the shaft causing it to bend downward. With the shaft in its flexed position, a little trolley or pointer is pushed along the entire length of the shaft. At certain points along the shaft a reading is noted and recorded. These readings can be used to compare relative stiffness and curves with other shafts or to select a uniform matched set of shafts for a set of clubs. Also, there are at least two deflection boards on the market where assembled golf clubs can be checked and compared to other assembled golf clubs for comparative stiffness. Use care with this method since varying grip diameters and materials will give false readings.

The word "shaft curve" was just mentioned and it needs to be defined along with "flex point" as the two are directly related and for our purposes can be used interchangeably. As a matter of fact, all the terms used to define a shaft's flex point have the same meaning. Some of these terms are: pattern, curve, kick point and bend point. Look at Figure 65-18 which shows the direct relationship of a shaft's "curve" and the proper "flex point" terminology. Keep in mind that not all high flex point shafts have their flex point in the same exact location as other high flex point shafts. The same holds true for mid and low flex point shafts. This is only a relative term for the approximate location where maximum bending occurs in the shaft.

Flex Point or Shaft Curve Comparison

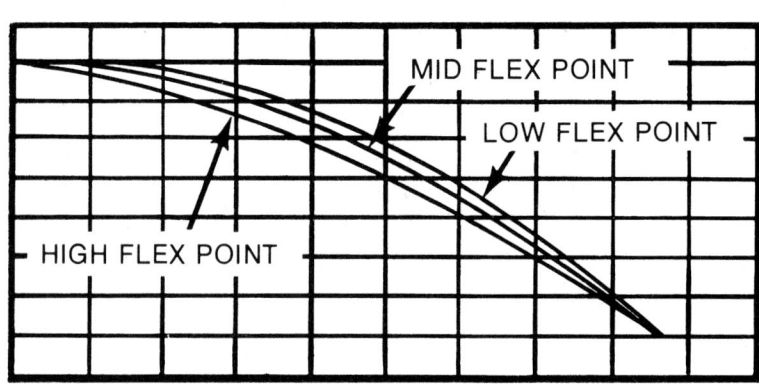

Figure 65-18
Defining flex point and curve

Now, take a look at Figure 65-19 which defines "flex point."

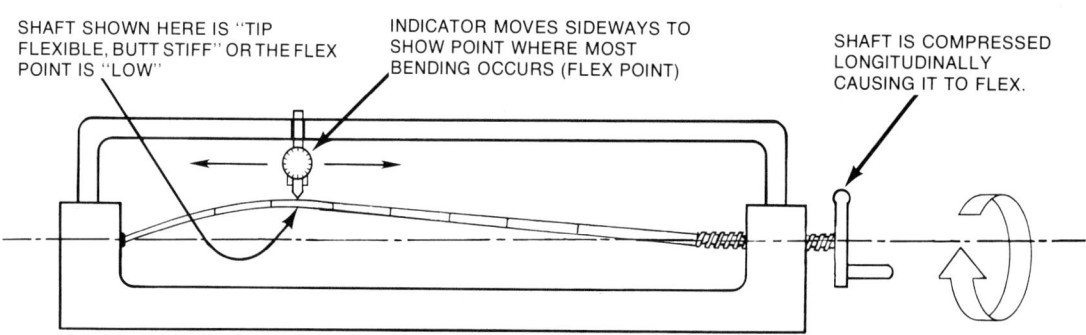

Figure 65-19
Defining flex point, bend point, kick point and curve of a golf shaft. All terms are defined the same, but flex point is the best term to use.

As already explained, two steel golf shafts of the same weight, material, length and relative stiffness can have slightly different flex point or flex curve characteristics on a deflection board. For example, Figure 65-20 shows the curve of a 44" medium flex Dynamic® steel shaft and the curve of a 44" medium flex Pro-Fit® steel shaft compared on a deflection board grid. They are intentionally drawn out of scale for visual comparison.

722

It can be seen in Figure 65-20 that both shaft tips deflect to the same medium shaft flex point, but that they have different curves of flex points. The Pro-Fit® shaft is more stiff in the butt section and more flexible in the tip section. While conversely, the Dynamic® shaft is more flexible in the butt section, but more stiff in the tip section. Hard hitting average players, better players and many touring pros who generate higher clubhead speeds seem to prefer the tip stiff Dynamic® or Dynamic Gold™ pattern characteristics for feel and control over that of most other type shafts.

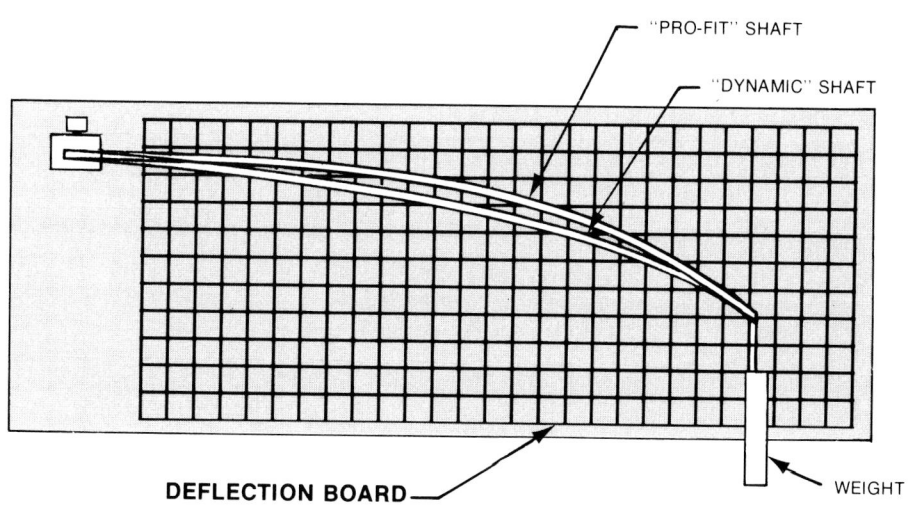

Figure 65-20
Comparing the flex points and curves of two "medium flex" steel shafts

Because better players prefer Dynamic® shafts, a certain mystique has developed among all players thinking this must be the shaft for everybody. Manufacturers build many of their clubs with Dynamic® or Dynamic Gold™ shafts because of consumer demand through imitation of the better player when in fact many average golfers would benefit more from mid or low flex point shafts such as the Pro-Fit® or the even more weak tip (very low flex point) Jet Step® pattern. Weak tip or low flex point shafts in general will hit the ball higher, feel a little more solid on off-center hits and have a feel that is slightly more flexible than stiff tip or high flex point shafts because of the increased tip action (flexing) during the swing. Of course, however, since everything in fitting is some form of a trade-off, the more tip flexible a shaft is, the less accuracy it will have. This is a marginal point and not as bad as it sounds since you are usually trading off for the best attributes to improve play. Again, this is what fitting is all about.

A general guideline to golf shaft patterns, types and their various flex points can be found in Table 65-7 and Table 65-8. Notice that some of the shafts listed are no longer available, but they do exist in many clubs that players are using today.

The following chart has been included to help eliminate any confusion as to the related terminology when talking about high, mid or low "flex points."

Flexpoint		Equivalent Terminology
HIGH	=	Tip stiff, butt flexible
MID	=	Tip, center and butt area bend about the same
LOW	=	Tip flexible, butt stiff

TABLE 65-7
Shaft Pattern, Type and Flex Point Comparisons

DYNAMIC — Tip stiff, butt flexible shaft. Should not be used by players who have difficulty getting the ball airborne. Most popular of all shaft patterns. Available in Extra-Stiff (X), Stiff (S), Medium (T), Flexible (A) and Ladies' (L) flexes. Also available in standard weight tip taper and parallel tip. (True Temper)

DYNAMIC GOLD — Same as Dynamic above but manufactured to very close weight tolerances. Used on tour. Allows a set of clubs to be more closely balanced and matched by frequency. Available in 15 flexes, 5 in "X," 5 in "S" and 5 in "T." Available in standard weight tip taper and parallel tip. (True Temper)

PRO FIT — Tip flexible, butt stiff shaft with more kick in the tip than Dynamic. Allows the average player to get a more solid feel on off-center hits and higher trajectory than Dynamic. Available in Stiff (S), Medium (R) and Ladies' (L) flexes. Available in standard weight taper tip and parallel tip. (True Temper)

JET STEP — More tip flexible than Pro-Fit pattern. Butt is stiff. This shaft allows a less accomplished player to achieve good feel and best trajectory if the player has any problems getting the ball up in the air. Available in Stiff (S) and Medium (R) flexes. Available in standard weight parallel tip. Taper Tip discontinued. (True Temper)

NDWS (FOR WOODS) AND NDIS (FOR IRONS) — Only available in "Stiff" flex. Used on tour. Designed for exceptionally hard hitters and low handicaps. Gives excellent release, feel and control. Tip and center stiff, butt flexible. Scratch and professional players usually tip this shaft ½" to 1½". Available in standard weight tip taper only. (True Temper)

TT LITE — A semi-tip stiff shaft in lightweight steel. Excellent steel shaft for those desiring a light overall weight golf club. S, R, A and L flexes. Available in tip taper and parallel tip. (True Temper)

CONTOUR — Discontinued. Very tip flexible, butt stiff. Shaft is made for average players desiring solid feel and ease in getting the ball airborne. Forgiving shaft on off-center hits. S, R and L flexes. ⅛ ounce lighter than standard weight steel shafts. Available in tip taper and parallel tip. (True Temper)

KINETIC — Dropped in 1981-82 but some shafts still around. Mid to intermediate flex point. .700 butt shaft designed to use a very light grip along with a standard weight head to produce a club in the very light total weight range. If you use this shaft, swingweights must be D-4 or higher for good ball control and solid feel. Available in Stiff (S) and Medium (R) flexes. Lightweight steel shaft available in tip taper and parallel tip. (True Temper)

EXTRALITE — Semi-tip and butt stiff with mid-shaft flexibility. It is one of the lightest steel shafts available at approximately 3⁷⁄₁₆ ounces. Available in R, S and L flexes in tip taper only. (True Temper)

FLEX FLOW — Bend points vary from the long irons to the short irons, i.e., long irons have a low bend point, mid irons a mid bend point and short irons a high bend point. A good shaft for the middle to higher handicap. It is a lightweight steel shaft available in Stiff (S), Medium (R) and Ladies' (L) flexes. Available in taper tip and parallel tip. (True Temper)

GOLD PLUS — A lightweight mid bend point steel shaft designed for the average player. Available in X, S, R and L flex in taper tip and parallel tip. (True Temper)

DYNALITE — A low bend point shaft with a soft tip for higher ball trajectories. Lightweight steel shaft available in taper tip and parallel tip. (True Temper)

RELEASE — This lightweight steel shaft was designed specifically for golfers with slow swing tempos. Available in A flex and parallel tip only. (True Temper)

PROPEL II — Tip stiff, butt flexible shaft. Should not be used by players who have difficulty getting the ball airborne. Most popular type of shaft pattern. Available in X, S, R and L flexes. Available in parallel tip. Taper Tip discontinued. (Brunswick Golf)

PHOENIX — More tip flexible than Propel II pattern. Butt is stiff. This shaft allows a less accomplished player to achieve good feel and best trajectory if he has any problems getting the ball up in the air. Available in S, R, A and L flexes. Lightweight steel shaft available in tip taper and parallel tip. (Brunswick Golf)

UCV-304 — This shaft is semi-tip and butt stiff with its deflection point or flexibility mid shaft. A series of 2", ¾" and ½" steps generate this mid shaft flexibility and give excellent torque control. S, R and L flexes. Very lightweight steel shafts weigh approximately 3⁷⁄₁₆ ounces and available in taper tip and parallel tip. (Brunswick Golf)

PROPEL MICROTAPER — A low bend point tip flexible shaft. Generally used by medium to higher handicappers, however, preferred by some better players who like its feel. Available in S, R, A and L flexes. A lightweight steel shaft in parallel tip. (Brunswick Golf)

PRECISION SHAFT — Popular among better playing amateurs and professionals. Very predominant on tour. A frequency matched shaft that is slightly lighter than standard weight steel shafts. It is considered a tip stiff type shaft. Available in FM (frequency matched) levels of stiffness from FM 3.5 to FM 8.0. The higher numbers are stiffest. FM 7.5 is the average level for a professional and FM 6.0 is average for an amateur. Available in tip taper and parallel tip in irons and woods. (Brunswick Golf)

AP44 — Tip stiff, butt flexible shaft. Should not be used by players who have difficulty getting the ball airborne. Most popular type of shaft pattern. Available in S and R flexes. Available in standard weight parallel tip. Taper Tip discontinued. (Apollo)

SHADOW — A low bend point game improvement lightweight steel shaft to help higher handicap players achieve greater height and distance. Available in S, R, A and L flex, parallel tip only. (Apollo)

SPECTRE — This lightweight, medium bend point steel shaft is designed for the average player with a slower swing. Available in S, R, A and L flex. Available in taper tip and parallel tip. (Apollo)

PRO M54 — Heavier weight graphite shaft that is tip stiff, butt flexible and has a high bend point. Better for stronger golfers and low handicapper. Flexes available in R, S and X for woods and irons. Available in parallel tip. (Grafalloy)

CLASSIC— Graphite shaft that has its flex point in the middle. Best for average golfers, strong seniors and strong women. Very lightweight, available in parallel tip. (Grafalloy)

LOW TORQUE 2.5 — For the mid to low handicap players. Heavier weight graphite with a mid bend point and lower torque. Available in strong, firm and regular flex. Taper tip and parallel tip. (Aldila)

LOW TORQUE 5.0 AND 4.0 — Very lightweight, soft tip graphite shaft with a low bend point to benefit the middle to high handicap players. Available in firm, regular, light and extra light flexes in parallel tip only. (Aldila)

BLACK GOLD — Lightweight mid bend point frequency matched graphite shaft designed for the mid to low handicap players. Available in X, S and R flex. Parallel tip only. (True Temper)

COMMAND — Lightweight graphite shaft with a mid bend point and a medium firm tip. Designed for average players. Available in S or R flex in parallel tip only. (True Temper)

M29 ATTACK — This mid bend point graphite shaft is designed for the above average golfer. Available in S, R, A and L flex, parallel tip only. (Grafalloy)

TABLE 65-8
Flex Point Comparisons by Shaft Weight
(Steel and Graphite)

Company	Shaft Name	Graphite or Steel	Flex Point	Weight	Company	Shaft Name	Graphite or Steel	Flex Point	Weight
Aldila	HM-55	Graphite	High	Lightweight	**Carbon Fiber**	CFP-57	Carbon Fiber	Mid	Lightweight
	HM-50 TGw	Graphite	Mid	Heavier Weight		CFP57LF	Carbon Fiber	Low	Lightweight
	HM-50	Graphite	Mid	Lightweight		Novus II	Carbon Fiber	Mid	Lightweight
	HM-40	Graphite	Mid	Lightweight		A/C	Carbon Fiber	Low	Very Lightweight
	HM-35	Graphite	Mid	Lightweight		Novus III	Carbon Fiber	Mid	Lightweight
	HM-35 BT	Graphite	Mid	Lightweight					
	HM-30	Graphite	Mid	Lightweight	**Cleveland Golf**	Extra-Lite	Steel	Low	Lightweight
	ASD Filament Wound	Graphite	Mid	Lightweight		Diamond	Graphite	Mid/High	Very Lightweight
	HM-40 Superlite	Graphite	Low	Very Lightweight		Square	Graphite	Mid/High	Very Lightweight
	HM-35 Superlite	Graphite	Low	Very Lightweight		Circle	Graphite	Mid/High	Very Lightweight
	HM-30 Superlite	Graphite	Low	Very Lightweight		HET	Graphite	Mid/High	Very Lightweight
	HM-30 Superlite Ladies	Graphite	Low	Very Lightweight					
	Low Torque 2.5	Graphite	Mid	Heavier Weight	**Cobra**	TLC	Steel	Mid	Lightweight
	Low Torque 4.0	Graphite	Low	Very Lightweight					
	Low Torque 5.0	Graphite	Low	Very Lightweight	**Daiwa**	TRX-T	Graphite	High	Very Lightweight
	Low Torque Ladies	Graphite	Low	Very Lightweight		TRX	Graphite	Mid	Very Lightweight
						TR	Graphite	Low	Very Lightweight
Apollo	Masterflex	Steel	High	Standard					
	Matchflex (AR)	Steel	Low	Lightweight	**Dunlop**	Alta	Steel	High	Lightweight
	Matchflex (R)	Steel	Low/Mid	Lightweight		Maxpower	Steel	Low	Standard
	Matchflex (RS)	Steel	Mid/High	Lightweight		Max Lite	Steel	Mid	Lightweight
	Matchflex (S)	Steel	High	Standard					
	AP44 Elite	Steel	High	Standard	**Fenwick**	World Class	Graphite	Variable	Lightweight
	AP46	Steel	Mid	Standard		Bioline	Graphite	Variable	Lightweight
	Spectre	Steel	Mid	Lightweight		Aerostar	Graphite	Low	Lightweight
	AP44	Steel	High	Standard		Biomag	Graphite	Mid	Lightweight
	Shadow	Steel	Low	Lightweight		Aerofire	Graphite	Low	Lightweight
	Lady Shadow	Steel	Low	Lightweight		Aeroflex	Graphite	Mid	Lightweight
	Senior Shadow	Steel	Low	Lightweight					
	Acculite	Steel	Low/Mid	Lightweight	**GolfWorks**	FlexMaster	Graphite	Mid	Lightweight
	Boron Tourline	Graphite	High	Lightweight		TournamentMaster	Graphite	High	Heavier Weight
	G100 Shadow	Graphite	Low/Mid	Lightweight		DistanceMaster	Graphite	Mid	Lightweight
	Shadow FLX	Graphite	Low	Lightweight		Lady DistanceMaster	Graphite	Low	Lightweight
	Lady Shadow	Graphite	Low	Lightweight		LiteMaster	Graphite	Low	Very Lightweight
	Senior Shadow	Graphite	Low	Lightweight		PerformanceMaster	Graphite	Mid	Lightweight
	HMF Low Torque	Graphite	Low/Mid	Lightweight		Senior Success System	Graphite	Low	Lightweight
	Seamless Co-wound	Graphite	Mid	Very Lightweight		JuniorMaster	Graphite	Low	Lightweight
					Grafalloy	Classic	Graphite	Mid	Lightweight
Arcal System Flex	K2 Tour 55	Graphite	Mid	Lightweight		Lady Classic	Graphite	Low	Lightweight
	K2 Pro	Graphite	Low	Lightweight		Senior Classic	Graphite	Low	Lightweight
	K3 Combination	Graphite	Low	Lightweight		M29 Attack	Graphite	Mid	Lightweight
	K4 Combination	Graphite	Low	Lightweight		Pro M54	Graphite	High	Heavier Weight
	K4SL	Graphite	Low	Lightweight		Pro M66	Graphite	High	Lightweight
	KLADY	Graphite	Low	Very Lightweight		VHM M90	Graphite	High	Heavier Weight
						VHM M90 Lite	Graphite	High	Very Lightweight
Ben Hogan	Apex	Steel	Low	Lightweight		Nitro Flex	Graphite	Mid	Lightweight
	Apex Pro	Steel	Low	Standard		Filament Wound	Graphite	Mid	Lightweight
	Apex D	Steel	Low	Standard		LBP Series	Graphite	Low	Heavier Weight
	Apex Extra	Steel	Mid	Lightweight					
	Vector	Steel	High	Lightweight	**H & B**	Dynasty Plus	Steel	Variable	Lightweight
	Legend	Steel	Low	Lightweight		Dynasty	Steel	Mid	Very Lightweight
	Saber	Steel	High	Standard		Propower	Steel	Mid	Standard
	Apex	Graphite	Low	Very Lightweight		Duopower	Steel	Mid	Standard
	Lady Hogan	Steel	Low	Lightweight					
	Hogan Plus	Steel	Low	Lightweight	**Head Golf**	Big Head	Graphite	Mid	Very Lightweight
Brunswick Golf	UCV-304	Steel	Mid	Lightweight	**Karsten**	ZZ Lite	Steel	High	Lightweight
	Phoenix	Steel	Mid	Lightweight	**Manufacturing**	ZZZ Lite	Steel	High	Lightweight
	Propell II	Steel	High	Standard		K	Steel	Mid	Lightweight
	Microtaper	Steel	Low	Lightweight		Olympic	Graphite	High	Very Lightweight
	Super Champion	Steel	Mid	Standard		TTT	Steel	High	Standard
	Champion	Steel	Mid	Standard		KT	Steel	Mid	Lightweight
	HFA	Steel	High	Standard		Microtaper	Steel	Low	Lightweight
	MFA	Steel	Mid	Lightweight		JZ	Steel	Mid	Lightweight
	LFA	Steel	Low	Lightweight		KT-M	Steel	Mid	Lightweight
	Precision FCM	Steel	High	Lightweight		101**	Graphite	Mid (3.4°)	Very Lightweight
	Precision FCM Lite	Steel	High	Lightweight		201**	Graphite	Mid (2.9°)	Very Lightweight
	Vanadium Sonic*	Steel	Mid	Lightweight		301**	Graphite	Mid (2.2°)	Very Lightweight
	Brunslite*	Steel	Mid	Lightweight		**Note that the 101, 201 & 301 have similar characteristics except that the 201 is stiffer			
	Fibrematrix	Graphite	Mid	Lightweight		than the 101 and the 301 is stiffer than the 201.*			
	Fibrematch	Graphite	Mid	Lightweight					
	Mark II	Graphite	Mid	Lightweight	**Lynx**	Lynx Lite	Steel	High	Lightweight
	Denotes Discontinued								
					MacGregor	Response	Steel	Mid	Very Lightweight
Callaway	Memphis 10	Steel	Mid	Lightweight		Velocitized Dual Action	Steel	Low	Lightweight
	RCH60	Graphite	Mid/Low	Very Lightweight		Tourney Action	Steel	High	Standard
	RCH90	Graphite	Mid	Very Lightweight		Microstep	Steel	Low	Standard
	Ladies Gems	Graphite	Mid/Low	Very Lightweight		Propel (1958-68)	Steel	Low	Standard
	Ladies Gems	Steel	Low	Lightweight		VDA2	Steel	Low	Standard

... CONTINUED ON NEXT PAGE ...

TABLE 65-8 Cont.
Flex Point Comparisons by Shaft Weight
(Steel and Graphite)

Company	Shaft Name	Graphite or Steel	Flex Point	Weight
Maxfli Golf	Alta	Steel	High	Lightweight
	Maxpower	Steel	Low	Standard
	Max Lite	Steel	Mid	Lightweight
Merit	Merit	Steel	Variable	Lightweight
Mizuno	Dynaflex 1100	Steel	Low	Lightweight
	Dynaflex 2200	Steel	Mid	Lightweight
	Dynaflex 3300	Steel	High	Lightweight
Nicklaus Golf	Nicklaus Golf	Steel	Variable	Lightweight
Northwestern	Power Kick	Steel	Low	Lightweight
	Proaction Plus	Steel	Low	Standard
	Micro Lite 400	Steel	Mid	Lightweight
Paragon	Mirage 2001	Graphite	Mid	Lightweight
	Lite Touch	Graphite	Low	Very Lightweight
	Para-Sonic	Graphite	Mid	Lightweight
	Low Torque	Graphite	Mid/Low	Lightweight
	Fibersonic 2.0	Graphite	High	Heavier Weight
	Fibersonic 2.8	Graphite	Mid	Lightweight
	Fibersonic 3.5	Graphite	Low	Lightweight
	Dual Kick System	Graphite	Dual	Lightweight
Peerless	Hex Flex	Steel	High	Lightweight
	Pro-Lite	Steel	Mid	Lightweight
	Axiom-Lite	Steel	Low	Lightweight
	Palmer Lite	Steel	Low	Lightweight
	Peerless	Steel	Low	Lightweight
Pinseeker	Pin Lite	Steel	Mid	Lightweight
	Pinseeker	Graphite	Low	Very Lightweight
	MS	Graphite	Low	Very Lightweight
	Premium Gold	Graphite	Low	Very Lightweight
Ram	Reactive Rhythm	Steel	Mid	Lightweight
	Ramlite	Steel	Mid	Lightweight
Rapport	Hyperflex Tour	Graphite	High	Lightweight
	Hyperflex Plus	Graphite	Mid	Lightweight
	Hyperflex	Graphite	Mid	Lightweight
	Recoil XLT	Graphite	Variable	Lightweight
	Sceptre Ultralite	Graphite	Low	Lightweight
	Synsor R/S	Graphite	Low	Lightweight
	Synsor	Graphite	Low	Lightweight
	Advent II	Graphite	Low	Lightweight
	Advent	Graphite	Low	Lightweight
	Oracle SGS Plus Filament Wound	Graphite	Mid	Lightweight
	Oracle SGS Filament Wound	Graphite	Mid	Lightweight
	Lady Sceptre	Graphite	Low	Very Lightweight
Sounder	Sounder Flex	Steel	Mid	Lightweight
Swix	Performa Lite	Graphite	Mid	Very Lightweight
	Perfoma 80	Graphite	Mid	Lightweight
	Perfoma 90	Graphite	Mid	Lightweight
	Perfoma 100	Graphite	Mid	Lightweight
Top Flite	Technic	Steel	Mid	Lightweight
	Thunder Heat	Steel	Low	Standard
	Thunder Heat	Graphite	Mid	Lightweight
	XL-420	Graphite	Mid	Very Lightweight
Taylor Made	Taylite Plus	Steel	Mid	Lightweight
	Flex Twist	Graphite	Various	Very Lightweigh
	Taylite	Steel	Mid	Lightweight
	Flex Twist Plus	Graphite	Various	Very Lightweight
True Temper	Dynamic	Steel	High	Standard
	Dynamic Gold	Steel	High	Standard
	Gold Plus	Steel	Mid	Lightweight
	Dynalite	Steel	Low	Lightweight
	Dynalite Gold	Steel	Low	Lightweight
	Dynamic Lite	Steel	High	Lightweight
	Extralite	Steel	Low	Very Lightweight
	TT Lite	Steel	Mid	Lightweight
True Temper cont.	Flex Flow	Steel	Progressive	Lightweight
	Jet Step	Steel	Low	Standard
	Pro Fit	Steel	Mid	Standard
	Comet	Steel	Mid	Standard
	Junior	Steel	Mid	Standard
	Kinetic*	Steel	Mid	Lightweight
	Super Lite*	Steel	Low	Lightweight
	Contour*	Steel	Low	Lightweight
	Century*	Steel	Mid	Standard
	Driving Range*	Steel	Mid	Standard
	Rocket*	Steel	Mid	Standard
	Meteor*	Steel	Mid	Standard
	325 Series*	Steel	Mid	Standard
	Classic*	Steel	Mid	Standard
	Black Gold	Graphite	Mid	Lightweight
	Modulus EV-40	Graphite	Mid	Lightweight
	Black Gold Tour	Graphite	High	Lightweight
	Dynamic Graphite	Graphite	Mid	Lightweight
	Dynamic Tour	Graphite	Mid	Heavier Weight
	EI-70	Graphite	Mid	Very Lightweight
	EI-70 High Impact	Graphite	Mid	Very Lightweight
	Command	Graphite	Mid	Lightweight
	Command Lite	Graphite	Low	Lightweight
	EI-60 Seniors	Graphite	Low	Lightweight
	Command Seniors	Graphite	Low	Lightweight
	Command Lite Seniors	Graphite	Low	Lightweight
	EI-60 Ladies	Graphite	Low	Very Lightweight
	Command Ladies	Graphite	Low	Lightweight
	Command Lite Ladies	Graphite	Low	Lightweight
	Denotes Discontinued			
Titleist	Power Step	Steel	Low	Standard
	Power Flo	Steel	High	Standard
	Title-Lite II	Steel	Mid	Lightweight
	MS-209	Steel	High	Lightweight
Tommy Armour	Tour Step	Steel	High	Lightweight
	Butterfly	Steel	Mid	Lightweight
Unifiber	T-25	Graphite	Low	Very Lightweight
	T-30	Graphite	Low	Lightweight
	T-30 Lady	Graphite	Low	Lightweight
	T-30 Senior	Graphite	Low	Lightweight
	T-40	Graphite	Mid/High	Lightweight
	TB-40	Graphite	Mid	Lightweight
	T-45	Graphite	High	Lightweight
	T-50	Graphite	High	Lightweight
	UFX	Graphite	High	Heavier Weight
	LCG Tour	Graphite	Mid/High	Llightweight
	Unifiber Lite	Graphite	Mid	Very Lightweight
	Big Red	Graphite	Mid	Heavier Weight
	Uniflex	Graphite	Mid	Lightweight
	CFT Filament Wound	Graphite	Mid	Lightweight
Wilson	V2	Steel	Low	Lightweight
	Aggressor	Steel	Low	Lightweight
	Dynapower	Steel	Low	Lightweight
	Counter Torque	Steel	Low	Lightweight
	Dynamic	Steel	High	Standard
	Dyna-Step	Steel	Low	Lightweight
	Firestick	Steel	Low	Lightweight
	Firestick	Graphite	Various	Very Lightweight
UST	Tour Weight	Graphite	High	Heavier Weight
	6600	Graphite	High	Lightweight
	6600 Bore-through	Graphite	High	Lightweight
	660	Graphite	High	Lightweight
	Easy Flex	Graphite	Low	Lightweight
	Lady Easy Flex	Graphite	Low	Lightweight
	6200	Graphite	Mid	Lightweight
	6400	Graphite	Mid	Lightweight
	640	Graphite	Mid	Lightweight
	Ultra Light	Graphite	Mid	Very Lightweight
Yamaha	Paraflex	Graphite	Low	Very Lightweight

4. Club Length
(Reference: Chapters 24, 37, 48, 49, 52, Appendix 8.)

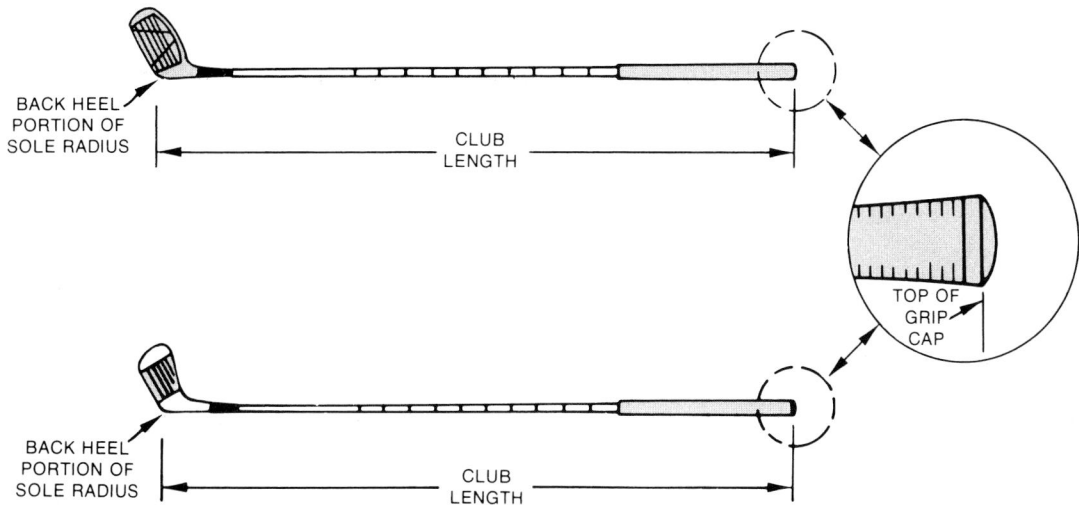

Figure 65-21
Definition of club length (modern standard measuring method)

Determining the proper length of a club for a given golfer is one fitting variable that has been misunderstood and abused. This is particularly true when a chart is used that determines the proper club length for an upright individual by measuring from fingertips or knuckles to the floor as shown in Figure 65-22.

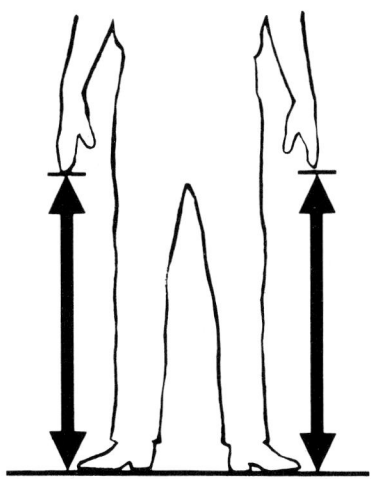

Figure 65-22
Incorrect method of fitting length

This type of measurement does not take into consideration a golfer's playing ability or posture while in the address position. It has absolutely nothing to do with fitting proper club length and as such should be abolished. This also includes the specially marked rulers used to measure club length in this same manner.

While it would be easier for all of us to fit length using this method, it simply does not utilize enough information or even the proper information to make a correct fitting decision on proper club length. Unfortunately, fitting length properly can require some experimenting, quite a bit of reasoning, a little deductive logic and some good old-fashioned horse sense.

One of the first things that must be overcome in the golfer's mind, if not in your own mind, is the preconceived notion that taller golfers automatically need longer clubs and shorter players automatically need shorter clubs. You now have to become a psychologist because many golfers coming to you to be fit have certain expectations, usually preconceived by reading golf articles, books and listening to other golfers telling them what they need. You can almost hear them now. "D-3 clubs are too heavy and wear me out by the end of a round" and "D-1 gives me no head feel." "I know D-2 is perfect." "I have larger hands and need a really big grip." "I will only play with persimmon wood heads." "The Dynamic® shaft is the best shaft made. I heard a tour player say this and so that's the shaft I want." The list goes on and on, but back to fitting club length with some rules and examples.

Tall golfers do not necessarily need longer clubs nor short golfers shorter clubs. Length, in all but very unusual circumstances, should be determined by what the golfer feels comfortable and confident with. More importantly, a golfer's playing ability and athletic coordination are the key factors. For example, a tall golfer, say 6'3" with an 18 or higher handicap who has a hard time hitting the ball solid and on the center of the clubface, may be better off with standard length clubs. On the other hand, a shorter golfer — say 5'6" tall who has a 6 handicap, hits the ball mostly straight with solid face center hits may want to try ½" to 1" longer than standard clubs to obtain more distance by increasing clubhead speed. Generally speaking, almost any length golf club can be fit to any height golfer as long as the lie angle is correct for that particular club length and golfer's hand height at impact. See Figure 65-23.

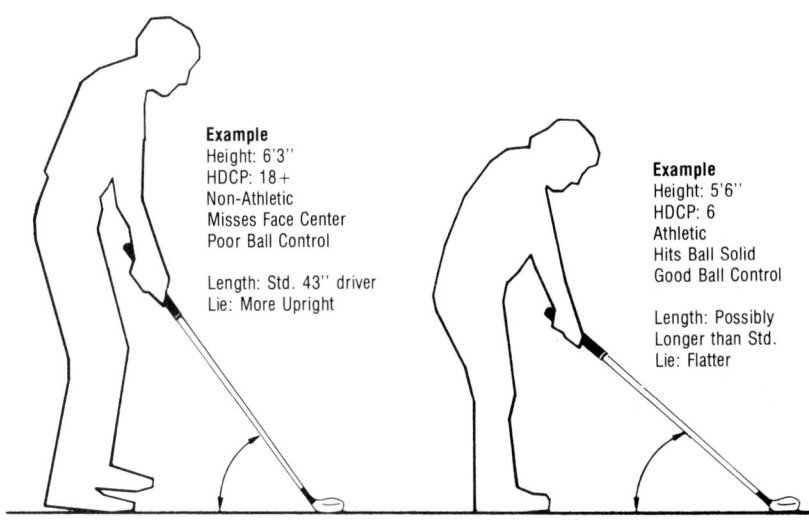

Example
Height: 6'3"
HDCP: 18+
Non-Athletic
Misses Face Center
Poor Ball Control

Length: Std. 43" driver
Lie: More Upright

Example
Height: 5'6"
HDCP: 6
Athletic
Hits Ball Solid
Good Ball Control

Length: Possibly
Longer than Std.
Lie: Flatter

Figure 65-23
A high-handicap, tall golfer (left) is better off with standard length or possibly shorter driver and an upright lie, whereas a good short player (right) can possibly control a longer than standard length driver with a flatter lie.

Listed below are the fitting variables which are directly affected when a longer or shorter club is fit to an individual.

Lie — As a general rule, the longer the club is than standard, the flatter the lie must be, and the shorter the club is than standard, the more upright the lie. This, of course, does not take into account each and every situation. However, it is important to remember that for almost any height golfer, any length of clubs, whether longer or shorter than standard, can be made to fit properly through an adjustment in the lie angle. See Figure 65-24.

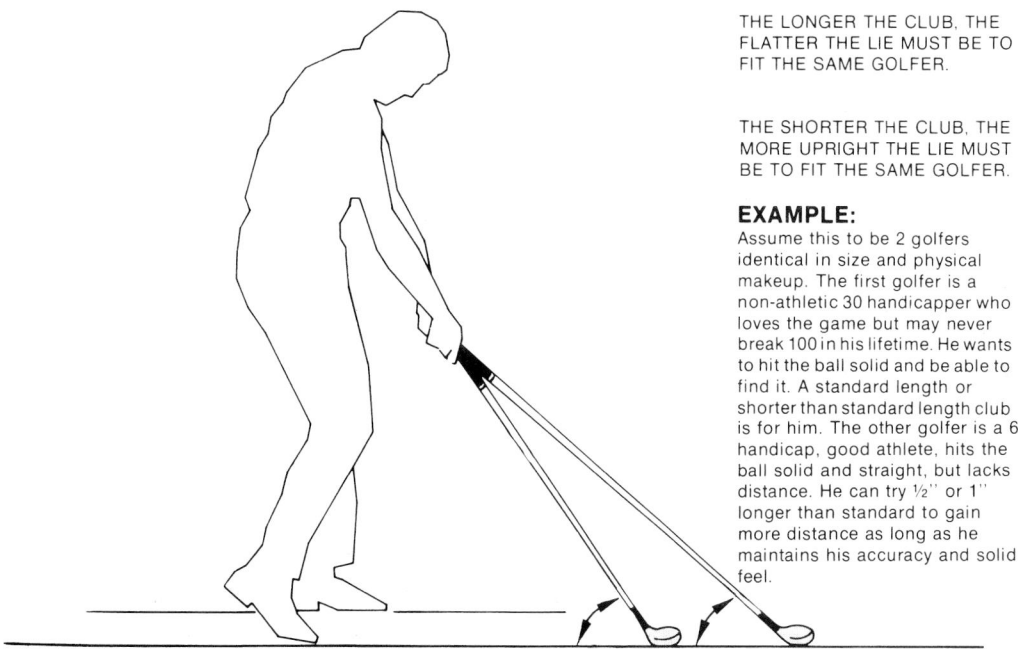

THE LONGER THE CLUB, THE FLATTER THE LIE MUST BE TO FIT THE SAME GOLFER.

THE SHORTER THE CLUB, THE MORE UPRIGHT THE LIE MUST BE TO FIT THE SAME GOLFER.

EXAMPLE:
Assume this to be 2 golfers identical in size and physical makeup. The first golfer is a non-athletic 30 handicapper who loves the game but may never break 100 in his lifetime. He wants to hit the ball solid and be able to find it. A standard length or shorter than standard length club is for him. The other golfer is a 6 handicap, good athlete, hits the ball solid and straight, but lacks distance. He can try ½" or 1" longer than standard to gain more distance as long as he maintains his accuracy and solid feel.

Figure 65-24
Determining length by player ability and adjusting that length by a change in lie angle.

Shaft Flex — A given shaft flex tends to feel more flexible as a club is lengthened and more stiff as a club is shortened. Therefore, a change in club length may require a change or alteration in shaft flex.

Swingweight and Total Weight — The same swingweight on a longer than standard club will produce a club lighter in total weight and conversely, the same swingweight on a shorter than standard club will produce a club heavier in total weight.

It is not a fallacy that increased club length will usually result in greater distance; however, there is one very important, often overlooked criterion — the ball must be hit on the center of the clubface. The longer the club, the harder it is to hit the ball on the center of the clubface and the distance lost from off-center hits is quite significant.

An average golfer who often misses the center of the clubface will usually get greater distance by playing with clubs shorter than are now being played or even shorter than standard. This seeming phenomenon occurs because the player now hits the ball on or near the center of the clubface more often than he/she could with harder-to-hit longer clubs. Remember, for each ½" you hit a ball away from the center of the clubface, your distance will decrease by 5% on a #5 iron and 7% on a driver; so a would-be 220 yard drive hit 1" out on the toe of the driver will probably turn out to be a 189 yard drive (less 14%) and require at least three clubs longer to hit the ball on the green. See Figure 65-25. A rule of thumb here is to fit the longest clubs in which a player has confidence, without sacrificing accuracy or solid feel.

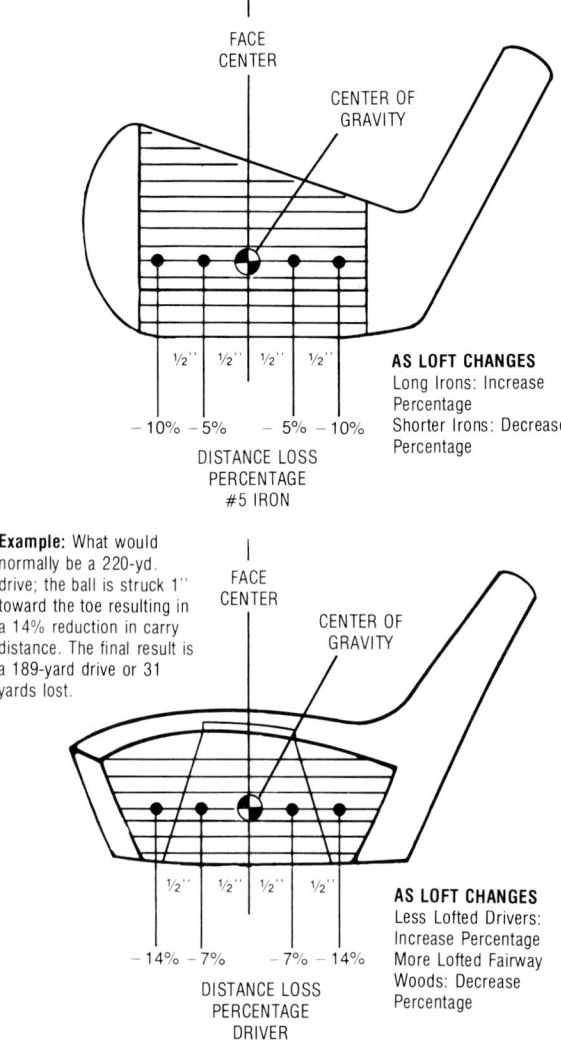

FACE CENTER

CENTER OF GRAVITY

½'' | ½'' | ½'' | ½''

−10% −5% −5% −10%

DISTANCE LOSS PERCENTAGE #5 IRON

AS LOFT CHANGES
Long Irons: Increase Percentage
Shorter Irons: Decrease Percentage

Example: What would normally be a 220-yd. drive; the ball is struck 1'' toward the toe resulting in a 14% reduction in carry distance. The final result is a 189-yard drive or 31 yards lost.

FACE CENTER

CENTER OF GRAVITY

½'' | ½'' | ½'' | ½''

−14% −7% −7% −14%

DISTANCE LOSS PERCENTAGE DRIVER

AS LOFT CHANGES
Less Lofted Drivers: Increase Percentage
More Lofted Fairway Woods: Decrease Percentage

Figure 65-25
Approximate loss of distance for off-center hits

Here is an example which may help to firmly implant some club length fitting rules. This is a rather extreme example, but it hopefully will help you when considering the pros and cons of longer and shorter clubs.

Let's assume we have two drivers, one is 24" long (two feet) and the other is 72" long (six feet). If we took both drivers out on the practice tee and hit them, what would happen? See Figure 65-26. First of all, we would have to hit the 24" long club from our knees. It should be very easy to hit the ball consistently in the center of the clubface. The ball should fly relatively straight and every hit should land in the fairway. The distance hit, however, will be a lot shorter because of the significantly reduced clubhead speed of the shorter length club. Most all shots would feel very solid and this club could be played quite well by a beginner, even if they had little athletic or golfing ability. Venturing out on the golf course with this club would probably turn out to be a mistake and would surely cause most players to place undue wear and tear on their fairway woods and wedges to get to the green.

Now let's give the 72" driver a try. This club is definitely long drive contest material, but after a few shots we can see that an extremely high golfing skill level coupled with significant athletic ability is required to simply hit the ball in

This club is very simple to hit on the center of the face consistently, but distance is quite short. It is very accurate and never misses the fairway.

This club is the hardest to hit on the center of the face, but when you do, it is quite long hitting. It is also the poorest for directional control and will seldom land in the fairway.

Figure 65-26
Club length versus accuracy and distance. An extreme example to prove a point.

the center of the clubface. Adequate directional control is non-existent for three main reasons: First, the longer club; second, missing the center of the face often and having very little control over clubhead path and face angle; third, the shaft is quite flexible and whippy at this long length. Hitting the ball solid with any consistency is also a problem. However, when everything does come together with perfect rhythm and timing, the resultant hit can go an astonishingly long distance. Imagine the clubhead speed and consequently the amount of energy that can be generated at impact. Now, would you go out and play with this club? Certainly not, it is far too difficult to control. I have always found it interesting to look at the driver lengths used by players on the professional golf tour. The average length is 43½" with many 43" and 44" drivers. It is quite rare to find a 44½" driver on the tour. My 6'4" next-door neighbor, who took up the game of golf five years ago, was fitted by someone using the fingertip to floor method and is now playing 2" longer than standard woods and irons. He cannot hit his driver, 3 wood or 4 wood, so he tees off with his #5 wood boasting that he hits it as far as most people hit their drivers. This is quite possibly true and I am sure you are saying to yourself, I can help this person.

A rule of thumb: Longer clubs are harder to hit because maximum energy can only be transferred from the clubhead to the ball if the ball is struck on the center of the face or the clubhead's center of gravity in the heel to toe direction. Any off-center hit causes the clubhead to twist and impart less energy to the ball; hence distance loss, an unsolid feeling and usually poorer directional control.

General Fitting Tips and Notes on Club Length

• Any length golf club can be fit to any height golfer by changing the lie angle.

• A golfer's ability, not height, is the main determinant in properly fitting club length.

• Be cautious about fitting clubs more than ½" longer than standard, especially the driver.

• Club length is a trade-off between distance and accuracy. There is no place on a score card to write down a 280 yard drive only the total number of shots. Accuracy is the more important of the two if you have to make a choice.

• The trade-off on playing with longer clubs to achieve more distance is usually more frequent off-center hits and less accuracy.

• Use the longest clubs possible and maintain player confidence, but do not sacrifice feel and accuracy. This statement is a mouthful and applies more to woods than irons and mostly to the driver.

• On very tall players of poor ability, it may be necessary to fit standard length woods with longer than standard length irons, particularly because the short irons may not reach the ground in a normal address position. Try not to sacrifice improper posture for proper length. This would usually turn out to be a poor trade-off.

• Sets of irons and their lengths are different than sets of woods and their lengths. It is not necessary to change both together either longer or shorter during fitting. Treat wood sets and iron sets separately in the fitting process and evaluate each golfer individually as to his or her club length requirements.

• The longer a club the harder it is to hit.

• The longer a club with less loft, the harder it is to hit.

• The longer a club with less loft and a stiffer shaft, the harder it is to hit.

• When fitting length to average and poorer players, always have them hit a "Hero type driver" for performance comparisons. A Hero driver is a test club ½" shorter than standard, 0° face angle, 11° loft with a lightweight steel shaft in a slightly heavier swingweight of say D-4 with a ¹⁄₆₄" oversize grip. This driver simply has all the specifications that make a club easier to hit.

• For good playing senior golfers who have lost distance, try ½" longer club lengths and very light steel shafts with a D-0 or less swingweight.

• More women golfers fit into ladies' petite club lengths versus standard ladies' club lengths. (Ladies' petite is 1½" shorter than men's standard length and ½" shorter than ladies' standard length.)

• The performance characteristic of club length is that it is a controlling factor of clubhead speed.

• If an existing club is lengthened ½" with a butt extension, the swingweight will increase by approximately 3 points, the total weight will increase ³⁄₁₆ to ¼ ounce, the shaft will feel ½ flex more flexible and the lie will appear 1° more upright to the same player.

• If a club is ordered ½" longer than standard, in general you should: specify the swingweight desired and tip the shaft ½" to obtain the same flex feel. The total weight will be ³⁄₁₆ to ¼ ounce lighter and the lie should be specified 1° flatter.

• On any new set of woods and irons, lay the clubs flat and in order across a table with the soles of the clubs matching. Looking at the grip end visually and compare that the length difference between each club is the same from club to club. Also, compare the first step locations on each shaft for this same consistency.

• A nifty trick: Hit 3 or 4 shots with either a wood or an iron in the normal manner. Next, put 3 swingweights of lead tape on the club and hit 3 or 4 more balls while choking down ½" from where the club is normally held. This will provide a fairly good feel test of the same club at the same swingweight but in two different playing lengths.

The following tables give standard lengths of woods and irons for both men and ladies.

TABLE 65-9
Custom Fitting Table — Wood Club Lengths

Woods	Men's Standard	Ladies' Standard	Ladies' Petite
1	*43"	42"	41½"
2	42½"	41½"	41"
3	42"	41"	40½"
4	41½"	40½"	40"
5	41"	40"	39½"
6	40½"	39½"	39"
7	40"	39"	38½"
8	39½"	38½"	38"
9	39"	38"	37½"

The most popular length variations for men are ½" shorter or longer than standard and 1" longer than standard. The most popular length variations for ladies are ½" shorter or longer than standard.

*Note that some manufacturers are building certain graphite shafted drivers up to 2" longer than the listed standard. Usually the fairway woods that accompany these overlength drivers are standard length.

TABLE 65-10
Iron Club Lengths – Men's and Ladies'

Irons	Men's Modern Standard	Men's Traditional Standard	Ladies' Standard	[1] Ladies' Petite
1	39½"	39"	38"	37½"
2	39"	38½"	37½"	37"
3	38½"	38"	37"	36½"
4	38"	37½"	36½"	36"
5	37½"	37"	36"	35½"
6	37"	36½"	35½"	35"
7	36½"	36"	35"	34½"
8	36"	35½"	34½"	34"
9	35½"	35"	34"	33½"
PW	35½"	35"	34"	33½"
SW	35½"	35"	34"	33½"

[1]Ladies' petite is usually ½" shorter than the traditional ladies' standard length. Some companies make ladies' petite 1" shorter than ladies' standard length.

5. Grip Size
(Reference: Chapter 23.)

The grip provides the golfer the only physical contact with the golf club. The size of the grip under both hands and the material it is made of gives the golfer a certain grip feel. This grip feel can enhance how the golfer mentally perceives the club or it may detract from it. One of the main problems I have discovered is that most golfers are not aware of poorly transmitted grip feel. This can be caused by too small a grip, too large a grip or in most cases, a slick or hardened worn-out grip. Strangely enough, sometimes the size is correct and the grip is new, but the player may not have experienced the various other grip material types which may be liked better than his or her present grips.

As a general rule, the majority of golfers are only aware of two things regarding grips: they are made of either rubber or leather. A very important grip consideration in which very little consumer awareness exists is regarding grip size and shape. Golfers as a whole are not aware that grips can be installed in different sizes, either ribbed or round, arthritic or non-arthritic and also that different variations of grip size are possible under the left hand versus under the right hand. This is why it is vitally important in club fitting to have available different sample grip sizes for men and women and also samples of arthritic grips, round grips and grips of varying materials.

Grip size can be measured using a number of different gauges. Some people prefer a standard micrometer or vernier caliper to obtain decimal type readings and then they refer to grip size Table 65-11 and 65-12 to check the actual designated size.

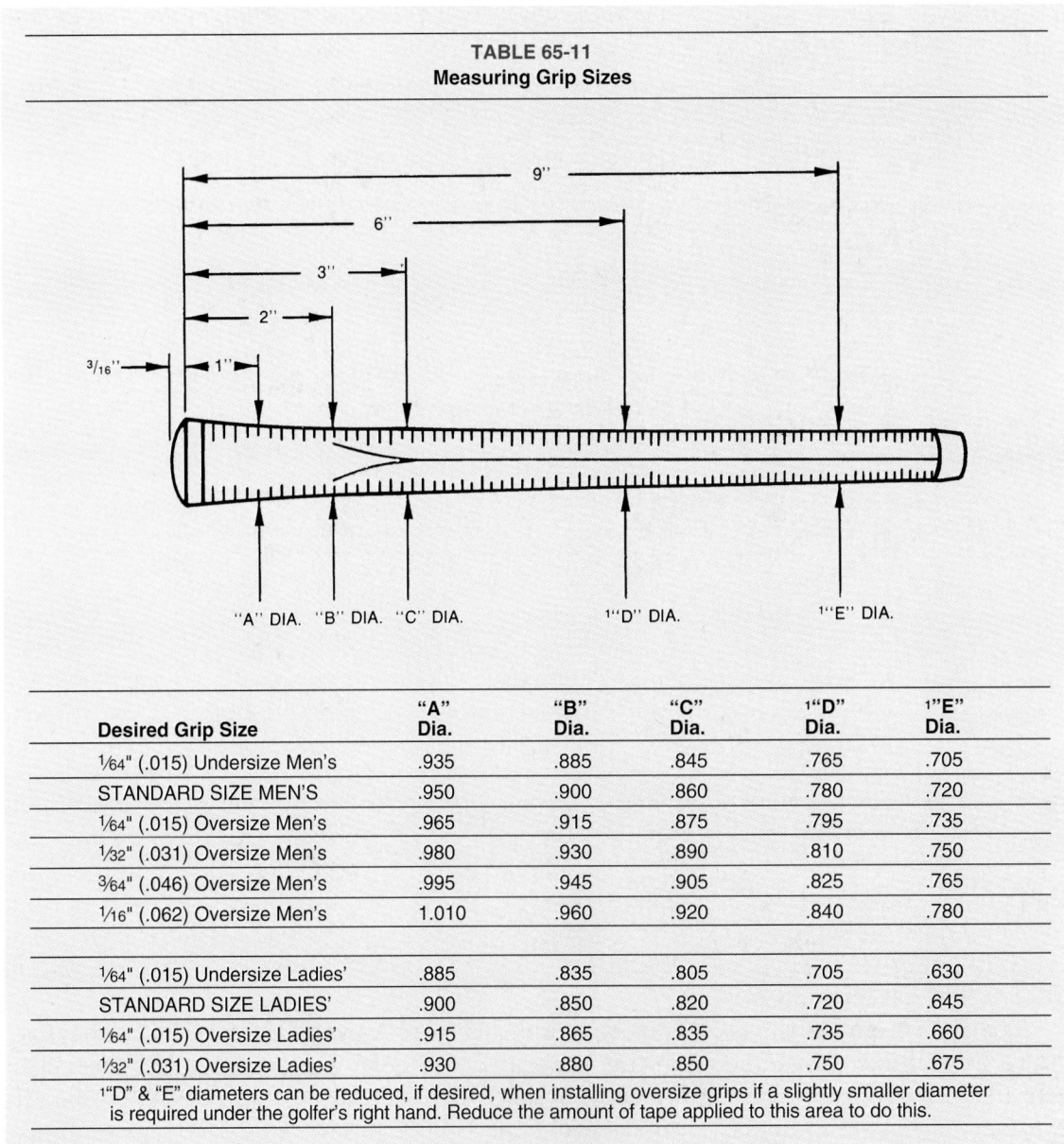

TABLE 65-11
Measuring Grip Sizes

Desired Grip Size	"A" Dia.	"B" Dia.	"C" Dia.	1"D" Dia.	1"E" Dia.
1/64" (.015) Undersize Men's	.935	.885	.845	.765	.705
STANDARD SIZE MEN'S	.950	.900	.860	.780	.720
1/64" (.015) Oversize Men's	.965	.915	.875	.795	.735
1/32" (.031) Oversize Men's	.980	.930	.890	.810	.750
3/64" (.046) Oversize Men's	.995	.945	.905	.825	.765
1/16" (.062) Oversize Men's	1.010	.960	.920	.840	.780
1/64" (.015) Undersize Ladies'	.885	.835	.805	.705	.630
STANDARD SIZE LADIES'	.900	.850	.820	.720	.645
1/64" (.015) Oversize Ladies'	.915	.865	.835	.735	.660
1/32" (.031) Oversize Ladies'	.930	.880	.850	.750	.675

1"D" & "E" diameters can be reduced, if desired, when installing oversize grips if a slightly smaller diameter is required under the golfer's right hand. Reduce the amount of tape applied to this area to do this.

TABLE 65-12
Grip Size Table @ 2" Down From Top of Grip

Designation	Relative Size	Measurement @ 2" Down From Top of Grip "B" Diameter	
		Men's Diameter	Ladies' Diameter
Extra Large	1/16" oversize	.960"	.910"
Very Large	3/64" oversize	.945"	.895"
Large	1/32" oversize	.930"	.880"
Slightly Larger	1/64" oversize	.915"	.865"
Average	Standard Size	.900"	.850"
Slightly Smaller	1/64 " undersize	.885"	.835"
Very Small	1/32" undersize	.870"	.820"

Since the 2" dimension down from the grip cap is located under the middle of the golfer's left hand, it has been traditionally designated as the best place to check grip size. See Figure 65-27. However, in the case of special grip size build-ups, such as increasing size under the right hand, it is necessary to check other positions up or down the grip as required.

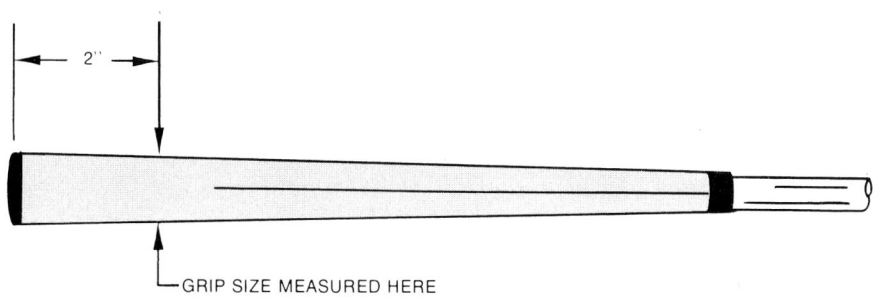

2"

GRIP SIZE MEASURED HERE

Figure 65-27

A special grip size gauge has been developed which makes it quite easy and fast to accurately check grip size. It is very easy to use, has no moving parts and does not require a machinist's knowledge to read grip size. Also, it can be comfortably carried in a pocket for convenient use. Figure 65-28 shows how this gauge works in measuring a grip's size at 2" down from the grip cap. This particular grip gauge is made by The GolfWorks® and comes with complete instructions.

The proper grip size should give the golfer a comfortable feeling at address, positive control during the swing and should not inhibit wrist action as the clubhead moves into the impact zone.

A grip which is too large for a particular golfer could do the following:
• Decrease clubhead feel.
• Inhibit wrist action by not allowing the golfer's wrists to roll properly before impact causing the ball to be pushed to the right.
• Cause the golfer to "choke" down on the grip where it is smaller in diameter and thus feels better. This reduces swing speed by effectively shortening the club.

A grip which is too small for a particular golfer could do the following:
• The clubhead may twist at impact because the golfer cannot get a firm hold on the club.

• The golfer may squeeze too tightly to "hold on" to the club, thus inhibiting his wrist action before impact.

• If the player holds the club with normal grip pressure he may now have "overactive" wrist movement causing the ball to be pulled left of the target.

• Cause the golfer to hold the club too far out on the end where the grip is larger, thus increasing the golfer's chances of "losing" the club at the top of the backswing and reducing ball control.

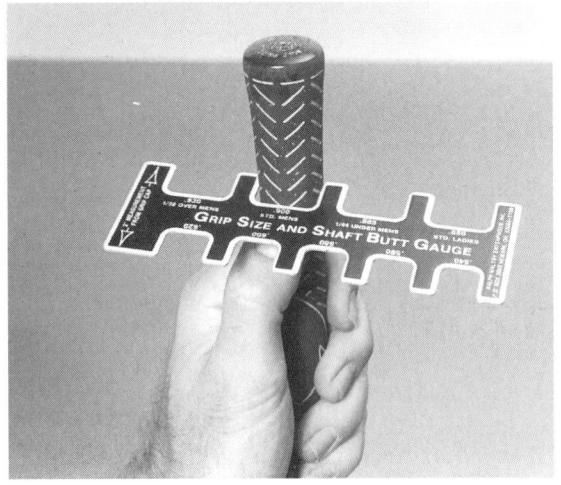 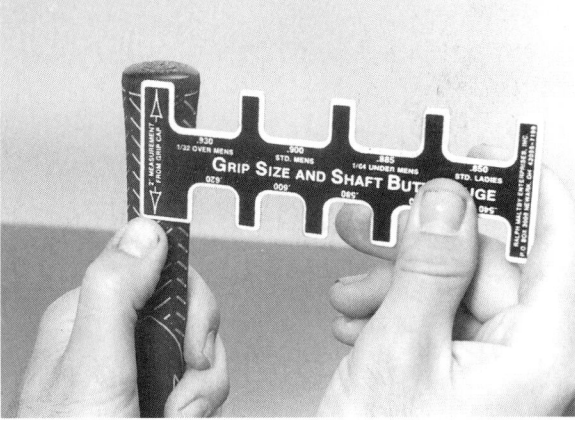

The grip size can be checked with a special grip size and shaft butt gauge. Slip gauge on the grip and slide gauge up the grip until it stops. Mark the spot with your thumb, slip gauge off of grip and…

…use end of gauge for measurement. This gauge measures grip size at 2" from end of the grip. One of the various grip gauge openings will allow it to slide up the grip, but will stop it 2" from the top. The actual size of the grip is found at that opening.

Figure 65-28
Using the Grip Size Gauge

The best way to fit a golfer to proper grip size is to have some sample grip sizes mounted on cut-off shaft butt sections. It is best to pick one of the popular styles such as the black/green Victory grip and make up all sample sizes using this grip. Be sure and mark the shaft at the bottom of the grip with the proper grip size designation. This can be done using "Dymo-tape," stick-on office labels or better yet, inexpensive grip size shaft bands available through The GolfWorks®. When you make up the sample grip sizes be sure to take your time and do it accurately.

The minimum number of grip sizes to have in both men's and ladies' grips are listed below. Figure 65-29 shows what they should look like when you're finished.

Ideally, there are a number of additional grip sizes, types and styles which can also be mounted on shaft butt sections to further aid in grip fitting. The following is a listing and explanation on each.

• **Extremely large and extremely small grip sizes.**

These grip sizes are used for two purposes. First, it is an excellent way to demonstrate the effect of too large or too small a grip on normal wrist action during the swing. Secondly, it provides a radical grip feel extreme for the player when alternately gripping the two sizes. Both of these purposes can be combined into one main club fitting point which is: The golfer is convinced through a visual demonstration of the importance of proper grip size.

The extremely large grip should be almost baseball bat handle size. It is made by first installing a rubber grip (such as a Victory Jumbo) to a very large size on a shaft butt section and then wrapping a leather grip strip on top of it.

736

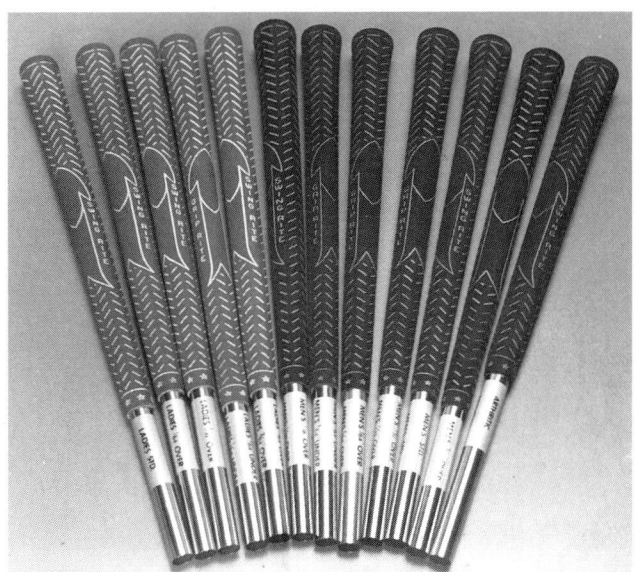

Figure 65-29
Men's and Ladies' grip size samples including an Arthritic grip

The extremely small grip size can be more easily made by simply wrapping a leather grip strip against the bare metal of a shaft butt section. Figure 65-30 shows what these grip samples should look like.

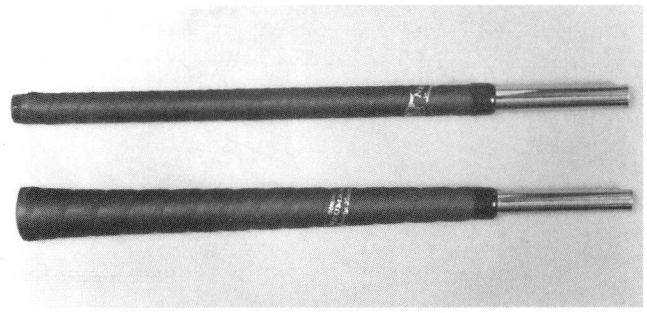

Figure 65-30
Extremes in grip size

To properly demonstrate the large and small grip extremes, do this: first, have the golfer grip the extremely large grip, hold it out in front of him and rapidly pronate and supinate (roll) the wrists while holding the grip in this position. Next, have the golfer do exactly the same thing with the very small grip. He should easily feel how much harder it is to roll the wrists open and closed with the larger grip versus the smaller grip. For an even better demonstration, repeat this same procedure, but now ask the person to grip each end of the grips quite tight. This shows that increasing the grip pressure will further reduce the already restricted wrist roll with the large grip and will also reduce somewhat the excessive wrist roll with the small grip. See Figure 65-31.

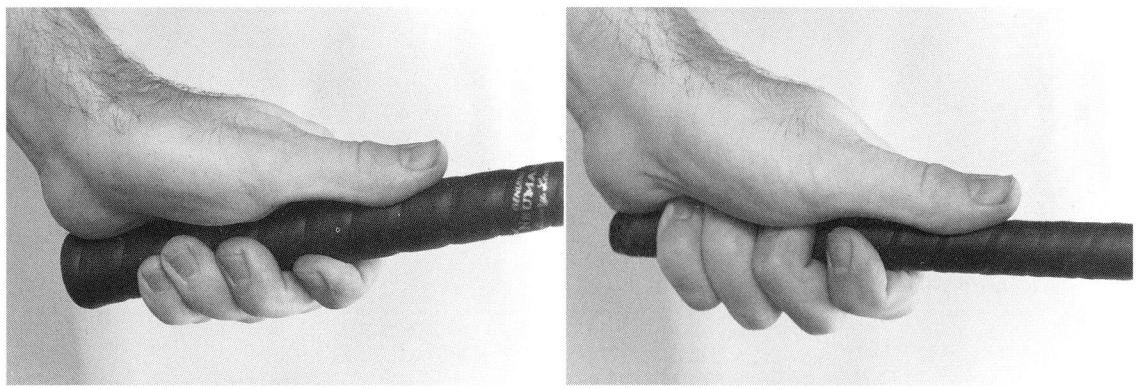

Figure 65-31
Proper position to demonstrate the effect of too large and too small a grip on normal wrist roll

Rule of thumb: Too large a grip reduces normal wrist roll and generally causes a pushed shot. Too small a grip increases the possibility of a very active wrist roll which can cause erratic directional control, but mostly results in a pulled shot.

• **Round Grip**

Mount a round style grip on a shaft butt section to men's standard size. It is not necessary to make up various sizes as this is only used to show the player what a round grip feels like compared to the more popular ribbed grip.

• **Rubber and Cord Grip**

Mount one of your most popular cord grips to a shaft butt section in men's standard size so players can see how a rubber and cord grip feel compared to all rubber grips and/or leather grips.

• **Leather Grip**

It is best here to mount a Neumann® black calf grip in men's standard size. This is a premium calf strip that is popular with those tour players who prefer leather. This grip is quite expensive, but it is considered the best feeling and tackiest leather grip made. A player can now compare this grip with rubber grips and the rubber/cord combination grip.

• **Arthritic Grip**

Pick your most popular arthritic grip and mount it on a shaft butt section. The two best grips to choose from are the Tacki-Mac® arthritic and the Eaton® Jumbo Victory grip.

• **Putter Grips**

This is entirely up to you, but I would recommend three popular styles of your choosing in rubber and one in wrapped leather, or slip-on leather. My own recommendation would be Eaton's® Pro-Only Putter and Eaton's® Golf Pride Putter, Tacki-Mac's® Paddle Putter Grip in black or tan and a Neumann® black or burgundy calf leather strip wrapped over an Eaton® Pro-Only shape rubber underlisting.

How to Best Fit Grip Size

Grip size cannot be properly fit by tracing the player's hand on a sheet of paper or by utilizing golf glove size. Agreed, this information is better than no information at all because it does give some indication of the player's hand size. This method was originally developed in an attempt to appear logical and quantitative in calculating proper grip size for a mail-in fitting form. In the real world, however, these methods will only work in some cases, mainly because of the variations in posture, hand height and wrist angle of golfers in the address position.

Here is an example that will explain this reasoning. Let's assume that two players have exactly the same size hands, wear the same size glove and they currently play with exactly the same size grip. The first player holds the club flat at address very similar to Lanny Wadkins and the other player holds the club more upright at address, very similar to David Graham.

Let us momentarily stop our example at this point and explain how proper grip size is best determined and then we will conclude the example to prove that our two players probably could not be fit to proper grip size by tracing their hand on a piece of paper or using their glove sizes.

The best way to fit grip size is to have the golfer take his normal grip on the club in the playing position. Next, remove the right hand only from the club (left hand for left-handed golfers) and with the left hand remaining in the same gripped position, bring the club up so that the finger tips of the left hand are visible. If the fingertips dig into the palm, the grip size is too small. If the fingertips barely touch or just miss touching the heel portion of the palm, the grip size is correct. If the fingertips are separated more than ⅛" from the heel portion of the palm, then the grip size is too large. See Figure 65-32.

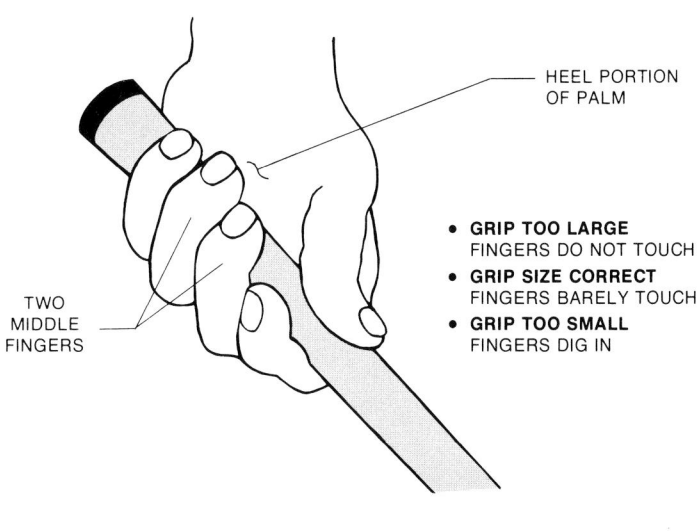

Figure 65-32
Determining proper grip size

Now back to our example: If we fit grip size to both players using the aforementioned method, we would find that the relative grip size would appear to be smaller when checking the player who held the club quite flat and the relative grip size would appear larger when checking the player who held the club very upright. The reason for this is when a club is held quite flat in the address position, the grip lies more square across the player's left hand making it feel smaller and indicate smaller when checking grip size. However, when the same club is held very upright in the address position, the grip lies at more of a slanted angle across the left hand making it feel larger and indicating a larger grip when checking grip size. A good way to prove this is to try this example yourself using the same grip size and holding the club extremely flat and then extremely upright. First, hold the club very flat in the address position with a normal grip. Drop off your right hand, bring the club up so you can see the middle fingers of the left hand. Now open your left hand while keeping it pressed against the grip. It should appear to you as shown in Figure 65-33.

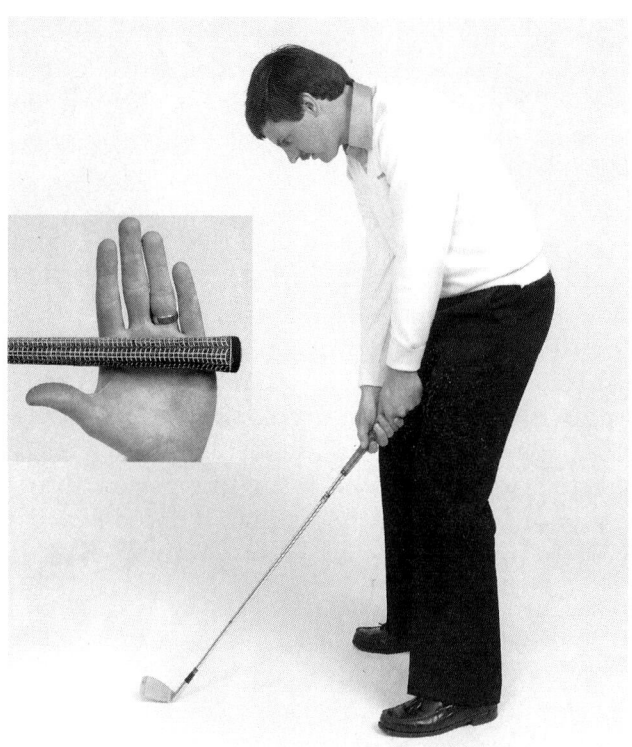

Figure 65-33
A flat address position causes the grip to cross the left hand squarely

Next, hold the club very upright in the address position. Drop off your right hand, bring the club up so you can see the two middle fingers of the left hand. Now open your left hand while keeping it once again pressed against the grip. It should appear to you as shown in Figure 65-34.

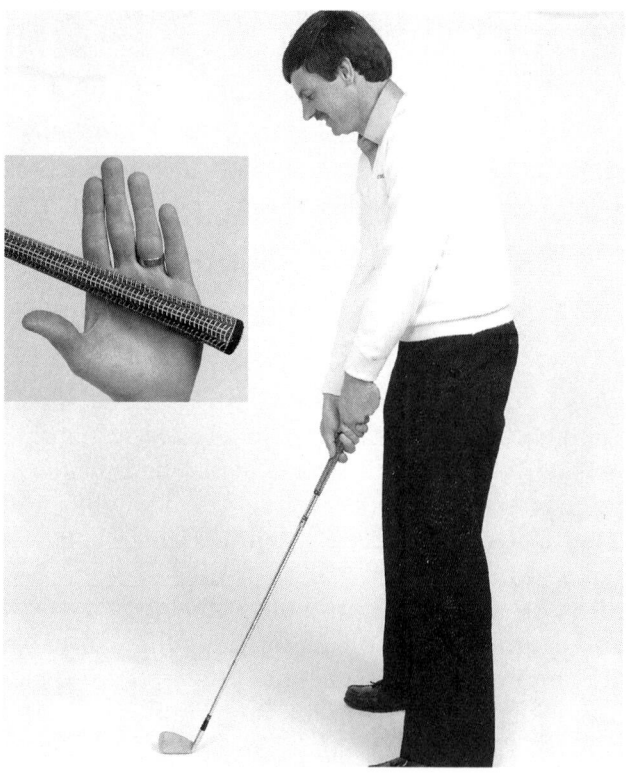

Figure 65-34
A very upright address position causes the grip to cross the left hand at an angle

Of course, most golfers will fall somewhere in between the extremes of this example, but you can now see why it is important to fit grip size physically to the person.

Here are a few additional tips to take into consideration when fitting grip size:

• Better players may tend to have strong opinions on a specific grip size they prefer. This does complicate the grip fitting process, but I have found that a better player's mental feeling toward his preferred grip size can overcome the fact that the grip is actually too large or too small for him as ascertained through the fitting process.

• If a player has abnormally large hands and fitting indicates a much larger grip than 1/16" oversize, try at first to compromise to a slightly smaller grip or one that is no more than 1/16" oversize. Players have successfully played with very large grips, but the problem that occurs is associated with the balance of the club. A very large grip counterbalances the club at its grip end and significantly raises the total weight while lowering the swingweight. This is discussed more fully in the latter portion of this section.

If during fitting of grip size, it was determined that the grip size was too small and sample grip sizes are not available; then proceed as follows to determine the proper grip size increase. This is a good alternative method to fitting grip size.

First, obtain some Gauzetex™ tape available in sporting goods stores, drug stores and many pro shops. Select a club and wrap the grip carefully with one layer of tape, butting it edge to edge and not overlapping it. See Figure 65-35. Now, repeat the left-hand fingertip and palm grip size test to check for proper size. If the grip is still too small, proceed with another layer of Gauzetex™ and keep repeating the process until the grip is the proper size. Refer to Table 65-13 for converting layers of tape to increased grip sizes. Remember, if the golfer has extremely large hands it is still recommended not to exceed 1/16" oversize without first trying one club regripped in this manner. It is important to understand that using Gauzetex™ tape to build-up the grip is temporary for fitting purposes only to determine which grip size would be best for the player.

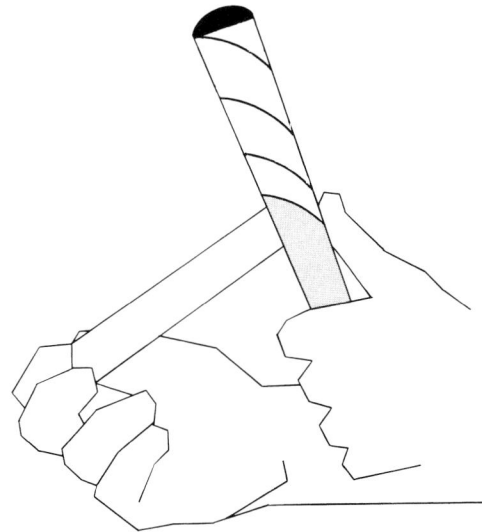

Figure 65-35
Using Gauzetex® tape to temporarily increase grip size

TABLE 65-13

Gauzetex™ Tape Wrapping Information Over Grips

Butted Layers of Tape	Decimal Equivalent	Amount Oversize
1	.010"	+ 1/64"
2	.020"	
3	.030"	+ 1/32"
4	.040"	+ 3/64"
5	.050"	
6	.060"	+ 1/16"

If it is determined that the present grip size is too large and sample grip sizes are not available, use this method for finding out how much smaller the grip should be. For every ½" a golfer chokes down on the grip from his normal gripping location, he is feeling a 1/64" reduction in grip size. Choking down 1" is equivalent to a 1/32" reduction in grip size. Refer to Table 65-14 for grip size equivalents when choking down.

TABLE 65-14
Grip Size Equivalent When Choking Down

Amount of Chokedown	Amount Undersize
½"	- 1/64"
1"	- 1/32"
1½"	- 3/64"
2"	- 1/16"

There are many men and women golfers who suffer from varying degrees of arthritis in their hands and do not realize that some help can be provided by arthritic type grips. Arthritic grips are generally designed to feel softer and install to a much larger size under both the right hand and left hand of the player. The softer feel and larger size of the arthritic grip allows it to be more easily held during the swing while exerting a lesser amount of hand pressure than normally would be required.

The two most popular grips used for arthritic purposes are the Tacki-Mac® black arthritic grip and the Eaton® Jumbo Victory grip. The Eaton® grip is made in a ribbed or air cushion core to create a very soft feel. The Tacki-Mac® arthritic grip gets its soft feel from thousands of small ribs or fins encircling the outside of the grip.

There are also a number of other grip types and styles which can be "built up" to arthritic size proportions and will work quite well. Keep in mind that there are varying degrees of discomfort in an arthritic player's hands and as a general rule you should only make the grip large enough to solve that player's arthritic problem. This is definitely another one of the many trade-offs in club fitting: you intentionally fit oversize grips to a player to solve a physical gripping problem. When you do this, it is sometimes important to adjust the players swing or his grip on the club to overcome any possibility that he may push shots to the right.

Quite a few players on the tour and low handicappers prefer round grips or those without a rib reminder on the underneath side. Some players install ribbed grips and file the rib off after the grip is installed. However, the majority of players simply install grips that do not have reminder ribs. Tacki-Mac® makes their grips without ribs and Eaton® offers the round grip variation in some models of their popular rubber Victory, all velvet cord, all cord and rubber underlistings, which are available in round or ribbed styles.

If a player has ribs on his grips and prefers a round type, the ribs can be removed using a medium cut wood file (not a rasp) by carefully filing off rubber along the rib until the grip is round.

Keep in mind that the reminder rib is highly recommended for those golfers who have difficulty in aligning the clubface to the target or who are generally inconsistent in gripping each club the same way. Of course, for the reminder rib style grip to work properly, it must be installed correctly. This is something that should always be checked.

The tour players and low handicappers that play with round grips, prefer to square the clubface to the target visually with no outside influence from a rib in the grip. Also, they can open or close the clubface for special shots without changing the feel of the grip in their hands as would be the case when the reminder rib would be repositioned for these special shots.

Here is something to try that I have found to work very well. Try it on at least one of your own clubs first, or you can experiment on a few players to prove this concept to yourself.

Grips are produced in a taper from the top to the bottom. For many players the grip size, which is much smaller under the right hand, is too small. This causes some players a number of possible problems such as: the grip may feel uncomfortably small or thin in the right hand. The player may unconsciously regrip with the thumb and forefinger of the right hand either before or during the swing. This causes directional control problems.

If a problem exists, a way to solve it is to fit proper grip size in the normal manner and then during installation, build up the grip an additional $\frac{1}{32}$" larger in diameter under the right hand only portion of the grip. This will still be a legal grip to U.S.G.A. rules as long as the grip continues at the same or a decreasing diameter from top to bottom which it should.

During grip size fitting and later during grip installation you should be very cognizant of the grip size under the right hand. We already mentioned that grips are manufactured in a certain taper from top to bottom. However, after installation of the same grip on many different types of golf shafts, it will be found that the taper and consequently the various diameters of the grip along its length will vary. This is caused by the differing shaft butt lengths, step locations and the step lengths which all contribute to the final taper of the installed grip.

There are two main points to reinforce here: first, the installed grip diameter under the left hand is very consistent in size from shaft to shaft in differing types and lengths of the same butt diameter shaft. The right hand size, however, will vary considerably and should always be checked. Secondly, building up the right hand only portion of the grip $\frac{1}{32}$" larger than the standard taper may improve consistency of play and at least warrants a trial since I have found this to work very well.

6. Swingweight and Total Weight
(Reference: Chapters 14, 18, 23, 24, 49, 52, 55, 61, 62 and 63.) See Figure 65-36.

Swingweight and total weight are two fitting variables that interrelate and are best determined for a proper fit when they are analyzed along with a number of other fitting variables. Club length, shaft flex, shaft material, shaft bend point and clubhead design are the other interrelated fitting variables which should be considered.

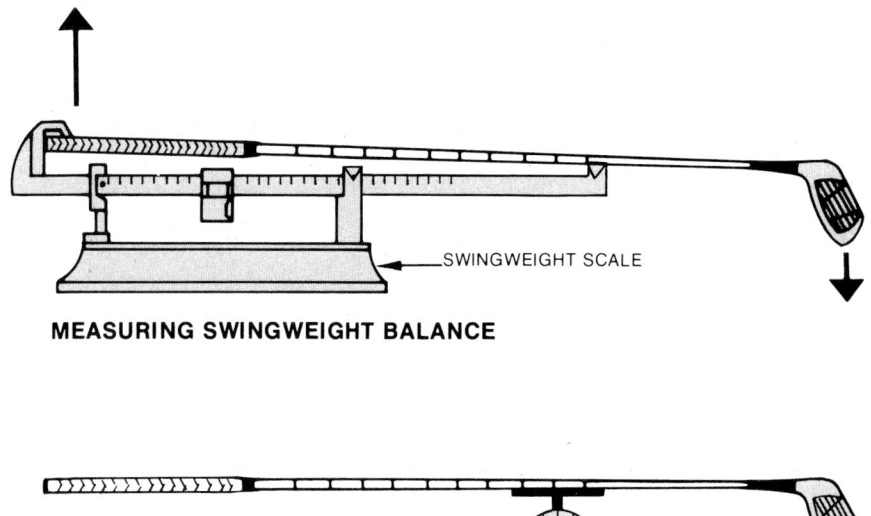

MEASURING SWINGWEIGHT BALANCE

SWINGWEIGHT SCALE

STANDARD WEIGHING SCALE

MEASURING TOTAL WEIGHT

Figure 65-36
Measuring swingweight and total weight

A discussion of swingweight and total weight as they only relate to the "How to Fit" category would not provide enough information to make a knowledgeable fitting recommendation. The following discussion will help bring these interrelated fitting variables together and help the clubfitter make a more knowledgeable recommendation.

The swingweight of a club is simply and accurately described as a measurement of a golf club's weight distribution, or to put it another way, the weight relationship of grip, shaft and head. The amount of weight equivalent to a swingweight in a golf club is quite small (.065 ounces for woods and .07 ounces for irons) and even the finest players in the world cannot tell two clubs apart by feel that differ by only one swingweight.

The swinging balance of a club, which should be considered as both a factor of the club's swingweight and total weight, should be such that it provides the golfer with the best chance of properly timing the hit. Therefore, swingweight and total weight together are important factors in obtaining the proper ball trajectory, directional control, feel and general playability of the club.

Fitting a golfer with the correct swingweight and total weight golf clubs relies heavily on the selection of shaft flex, shaft material, grip size, grip material and club length. Each of these components has a direct effect on the total weight and swinging balance of the club.

In most cases, swingweight and not total weight should be specified when fitting clubs. The reason is that total weight will be determined by individual component selection and the club's length. The only other variable factor left in determining total weight would be to specify the desired swingweight which would determine the proper head weight. So, head weight, each individual component and club length determine the total weight of a golf club. This is assuming that the club is swing-weighted by added weight only to the head and not counterbalanced in the grip end.

744

Counterbalancing is a method whereby the total weight can be increased as much as desired while still maintaining the same swingweight. This is generally not recommended as it destroys the natural balance of the club and only tends to "fool the swingweight scale" and not the golfer.

Table 65-15 below gives the recommended swingweight range by shaft flex and should be used as a general guide in selecting swingweight. If swingweights are specified other than in these recommended ranges, it should most likely be for a low handicap player, golf professional or a golfer with an unusual physical characteristic.

TABLE 65-15
Swingweight Range by Shaft Flex

Shaft Flex Designation	[1] Recommended Swingweight Range	Average
L-Ladies	C-4 to D-0	C-7
A-Flexible	C-7 to D-3	D-0
R-Medium	C-9 to D-5	D-2
S-Stiff	D-0 to D-6	D-3
X-Extra Stiff	D-1 to D-8	D-5

[1] Range is based on standard length clubs (i.e. 43" driver and 39" #2 iron). For each ½" longer than standard length club, swingweight range should be reduced by 1 swingweight. Conversely, for each ½" shorter than standard length club, swingweight range should be increased by 1 swingweight.

A good method to use when fitting swingweight on a certain club is to use lead tape to increase head weight for test hitting purposes. Another way is to tape a penny or a dime on the head which is equivalent to a one swingweight increase. A quarter taped to the head equals a three swingweight increase. The old statement of adding a dollar bill to the head of the club as an analogy for a one swingweight increase is not correct since a dollar bill is equal to less than ½ of a swingweight.

Another experiment that can be tried is to take a driver, say it is a D-2 swingweight, and have the player swing it 8 to 9 times with his eyes closed. Next, have him choke down ½" and swing the club 8 to 9 more times with his eyes closed. Choking down ½" is equivalent to a swing feel difference of approximately 3 swingweights less or making it feel like a C-9. Remember that the total weight does not change during this experiment, but the feel will certainly be different. A variation of this test with the eyes open using both a wood and an iron is to hit 3 or 4 balls while gripping the club in the normal manner. Assume that this club is a D-2 swingweight. Next, put the equivalent of three swingweights of lead tape on the club and have the player hit 3 or 4 more balls while choking down ½". This will give a fairly good feel test of the same club at the same swingweight, but in two different playing lengths. The only disadvantage to this is the grip size is usually too small for the player while choking down.

Another method used to vary the actual club swingweight up or down is to make up two or three test #5 irons or use the special adjustable swingweight #5 iron manufactured by The GolfWorks®. This club has a wide adjustment range and has proven to be a valuable swingweight fitting aid because it keeps most other variables the same while the player only experiences changes in swingweight feel. See Figure 65-37.

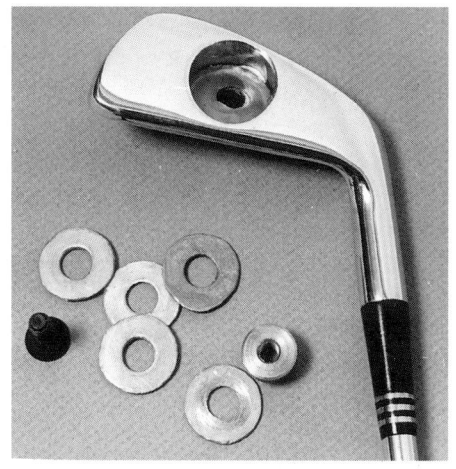 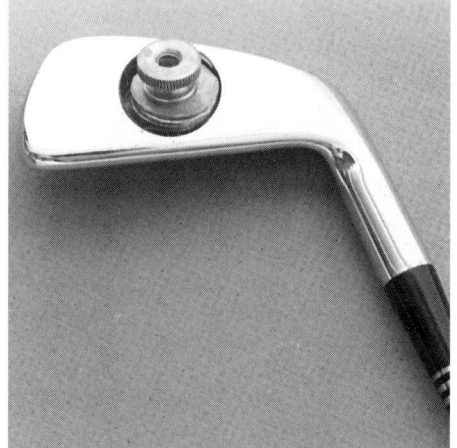

Figure 65-37
The GolfWorks® Adjustable Swingweight #5 Iron

As you can see, there are a number of ways to test for a golfer's perceived feel of various swingweights and total weights while actually hitting balls. During this hitting process, note any player comments, his/her shot pattern and trajectory differences. More specifically, the purpose of all this is to devise a method whereby feel, distance, trajectory, accuracy and golfer comments can be evaluated to fit the golfer to the best length and swingweight for a certain design wood and iron.

Even though it is recommended that only swingweight be specified, the proficient clubfitter should know approximately what the total weight range would be. Table 65-16 has been included to show the total weight range of drivers only, by shaft flex, swingweight and shaft material. The table should be used for relative comparison purposes, and it can also help in specifying swingweight and shaft materials even though only driver weight ranges are compared.

TABLE 65-16
Comparing Total Weight, Shaft Material, Shaft Flex and Swingweight

Shaft Flex and Swingweight Range	*Driver total weight range in ounces by shaft material and type				
	3⅞ oz. Shaft Lightweight Steel	4⅛ oz. Shaft Unitized Steel	4⅜ oz. Shaft Carbon Steel	2¼ to 3¼ oz. Shaft Graphite & Titanium	3½ oz. Shaft Very Lightweight Steel
L-Ladies C6 to C8	11⅞ to 12¼	12 to 12⅜	12⅛ to 12½	11⅛ to 11½	11⅜ to 11¾
A-Flexible C9 to D1	12⅛ to 12½	12¼ to 12⅝	12⅜ to 12¾	11⅜ to 11¾	11⅝ to 12
R-Medium D1 to D3	12⅝ to 13	12¾ to 13⅛	12⅞ to 13¼	11⅝ to 12	11⅞ to 12¼
S-Stiff D2 to D4	12⅞ to 13¼	13 to 13⅜	13⅛ to 13½	11⅞ to 12¼	12⅛ to 12½
X-Extra Stiff D4 to D6	13⅛ to 13½	13¼ to 13⅝	13⅜ to 13¾	12⅛ to 12½	12⅜ to 12¾

*Based on a 43" driver length. For each ½" longer than standard driver length, subtract ¼ ounce from the weights above. Conversely, for each ½" shorter than standard driver length, add ¼ ounce to the weights above.

The following are some rules and tips on fitting and understanding swingweight and total weight.

• The heavier the head weight the slower the club will be swung, resulting in less distance and more accuracy.

• The lighter the head weight, the faster the club will be swung, resulting in more distance and less accuracy.

In the proper fitting of overall weight, swingweight and club length, these are important trade-offs to consider. Would you sacrifice ten yards distance for greater accuracy (if the player already hits the ball straight, the answer is "no") or would you sacrifice accuracy for ten yards greater distance (if the player already hits the ball straight, the answer is "yes"). So, depending on each individual player, the fitting decision can usually be reasoned out as to the best way to approach this fitting trade-off. Take a look at Figure 65-38. Study it for a few minutes and try to relate the fitting of swingweight and total weight to finding the optimum trade-off point for best distance with accuracy; or, saying it another way and meaning the same, the best accuracy with distance.

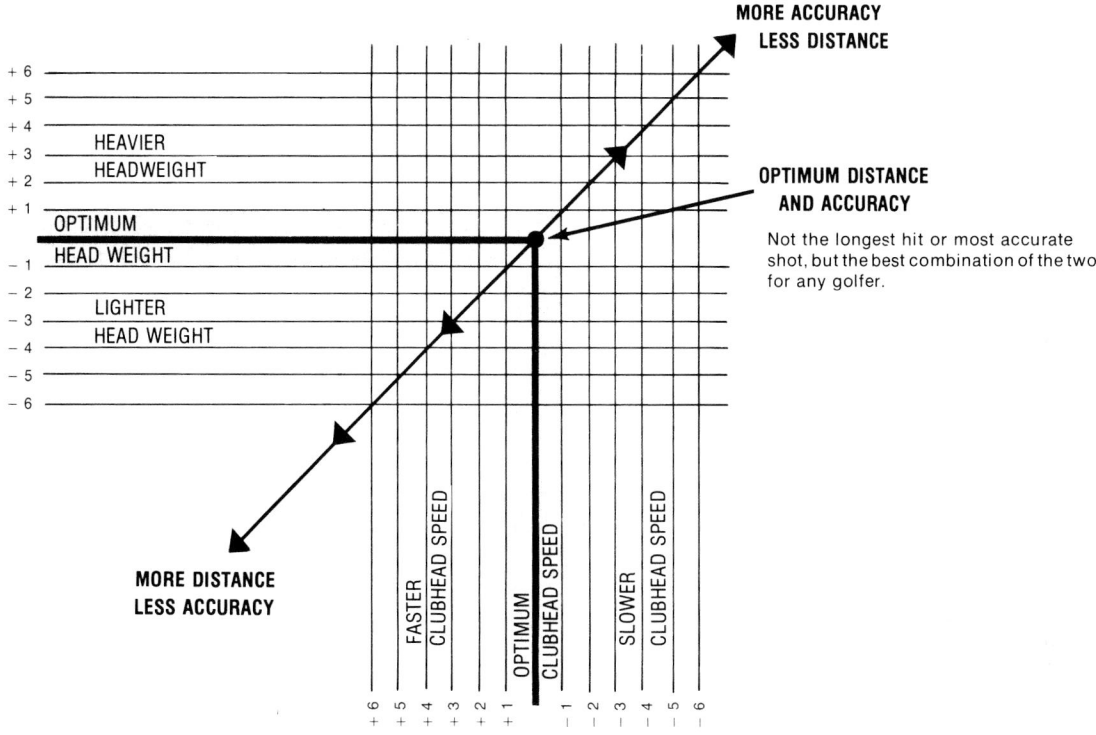

Figure 65-38
Optimum trade-off point for distance versus accuracy

Here is a handy little reference chart that can help in analyzing what change in head weight, if any, will be required if one of the four variables listed in the chart is changed from a so-called standard. See Figure 65-39.

THE 4 VARIABLES	
1. Weight of the Shaft	3. Weight of the Grip
2. Length of the Club	4. Size of the Grip

	Variable Specification	Relative Change In Head Weight Required
1.	Standard weight shaft	NONE
	Lightweight shaft	Heavier
	Very lightweight shaft	Much Heavier
2.	Longer club length	Lighter
	Shorter club length	Heavier
3.	Standard weight grip	NONE
	Lightweight grip	Lighter
	Heavy grip	Heavier
4.	Oversize grip	Heavier
	Undersize grip	Lighter (sometimes)

Figure 65-39
The 4 Variables that affect head weight change

The following test club can be made up by you to prove a certain point or it can be used as an adjustable swingweight test driver. The specific point to prove here is that in a properly done test, golfers cannot with any statistical consistency feel the difference in a one swingweight point change either up or down. They will, however, usually pick out a two swingweight point change.

The test club is easy to make. You simply put enough lead tape on the sole of a D-0 driver to bring it up to D-4, but be sure you put the tape on in one swingweight increments. First, start off with the club at D-2 and have the golfer hit a few balls or take a few swings. Next, after each sequence of hitting or swinging, change the swingweight up or down by one or two swingweights or just pretend to change it. Do not tell the player which way you changed the swingweight and do not let the player see the bottom of the club. Each time ask if the club feels lighter, heavier or the same and record the answer. Do this at least ten times (20 is better) and compare the answers against the actual changes made. Remember, with this test we are proving that players will not be able to feel a one swingweight change. However, we are not saying that a one swingweight change will not affect performance; to the contrary, .07 ounces (one swingweight) moving around 100 mph at impact will definitely do something different. I wish that I could outline a procedure that could be developed to offer a more simplified approach to fitting swingweight and total weight, but it does not exist.

My best recommendation is to master the information in this section and other related sections and then let your judgment and expertise be your guide. Test clubs will prove to help the most in properly fitting this variable. The best recommendation I can give you is not to stray too far from the traditionally accepted swingweight ranges unless you are changing some other directly related fitting variable as mentioned in Figure 65-39 that will have a direct bearing on swingweight or total weight. There certainly has not been any substantiated data at this point in time to suggest that radical changes in swingweight will provide increased distance, feel and accuracy benefits to the general golfing population.

7. Clubhead Design
(Reference: Chapters 34 through 52, Appendices 1, 7 and 8.) See Figure 65-40.

It is important to understand the effect of various clubhead designs on performance and be able to recommend specific types, shapes and styles of heads during the fitting process that could help the player overcome certain problem areas of the game. Most manufacturers of either assembled clubs or component heads offer two or three different head design types to choose from. Also, some of the manufacturers with custom club departments offer many other head styles and shapes ranging from the traditional to the modern.

The relative performance attributes of a given clubhead design type can be compared in Table 65-17 which should be thoroughly studied and referred to often. Remember that this table is for comparisons and should be used when discussing the basic clubhead design types in relative performance terms only. Before actually recommending a specific clubhead design type for a given individual, it would be most beneficial to have the individual hit shots with a similar or the exact clubhead design type to be certain that the golfer can personally adjust to this change and obtain the performance desired.

The center of gravity's effect on performance and its relationship with other specifications is far reaching. It explains away much of the mystery and consequently myth involved in club design. Center of gravity sounds like a complicated area to understand; but just the contrary, it is very straightforward and quite simple. It is interesting to note the relationship of center of gravity to so many other golf club specifications in both woods and irons. A basic knowledge and understanding of a golf club's center of gravity and its effect on ball flight and feel will yield far better results in the fitting process. Also, it is always best to explain to someone why one club differs from another in terms other than simply saying they have a different appearance.

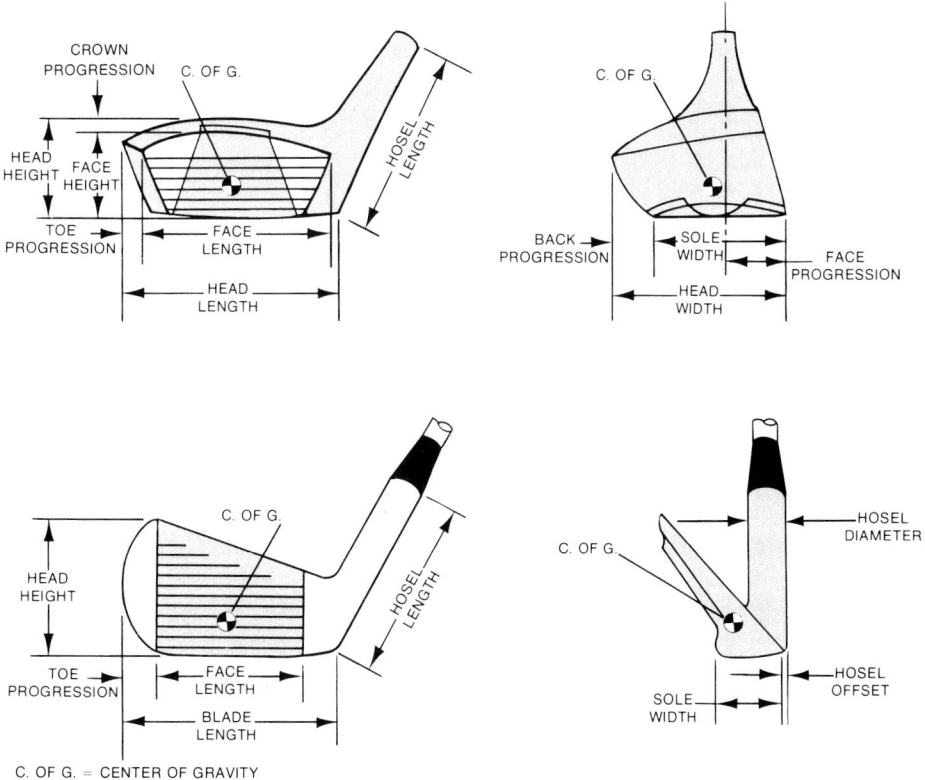

Figure 65-40
Head Design Variables

Generally speaking, the performance characteristic of a clubhead's center of gravity could best be described as a factor affecting the solidness of feel, trajectory and distance at impact between the clubhead and golf ball. Since the center of gravity is affected by mostly two factors — namely, the shape and weight distribution of the clubhead — it would be best to point out the specific characteristics which help determine its location in both woods and irons. Regarding woods, the following characteristics affect center of gravity:
- Wood head or metal wood shape, size and its material density
- Backweighting, size, shape, location and its material density
- Soleplate size, shape, thickness and its material density
- Insert size, shape, thickness and its material density
- Added weighting location, size, shape and its material density
For irons, the following characteristics affect center of gravity:
- Iron head shape, size and its material density
- Added weighting, location, size, shape and its material density
Specifically read Chapter 43 Golf Wood Club Design: Center of Gravity for a further explanation.

A general rule of thumb which pertains to the location of the golf club's center of gravity in the vertical plane is this: the lower the center of gravity, the more solid the shot more of the time. This, of course, assumes that impact also takes place at the center of gravity's horizontal location which is usually located at the face center. If the center of gravity of the clubhead is above that of the ball at impact, it will produce a more unsolid shot which will tend to fly lower with less carry distance. The best example of this is trying to hit a conventional driver from the fairway. The thicker

Table 65-17
Fitting Table — Clubhead Design Types, Woods and Irons

Clubhead Design Type	Clubhead Design Attribute	Applies to: Woods	Applies to: Irons	Relative Performance Change	Reason	Comments
Traditional or Conventional	• Standard to deeper heads • Mostly center weighted • Some iron models called "Muscleback"	X	X	• Ball can tend to fly lower on deep head types. • Less forgiving on off-center and thin hits.	• Center of gravity of clubhead raised due to deeper conventional style head • Most of weight is concentrated in center of club resulting in more head twisting on off-center hits.	• If jumbo woods are desired, loft should be increased; (i.e. 2" face depth driver should have a 12° minimum loft). • Very deep faced sets of irons should have lofts increased if normal trajectories are desired. • This category of club can also be called "Classic" and is used mostly by low handicap and professional golfers.
Low Profile	• Shallower heads • Wide Soles	X	X	• Ball will tend to fly higher. • Long irons easier to hit.	• Center of gravity of clubhead lowered due to head thickness in sole area.	• Shallower woods can have lofts decreased slightly to achieve normal trajectories.
Perimeter Weighted and Narrow Sole Hollow Irons	• Heel, Toe, Sole Weighting • Usually Cavity Back Design	X		• Better chance of straight hits and more solid feel from off-center shots.	• Higher moment of inertia (resistance to head twisting on off-center hits) due to better heel to toe weight distribution. • Center of gravity usually lowers. • Increased hitting area along heel to toe axis of blade.	• Longer blade lengths on iron clubs have gained in popularity; however, the extremely long blades of the early to mid 70's have been shortened to a length in between traditional and long. The longer blade length improves heel/toe weight distribution. • Conventional shaped hollow irons with normal sole widths have perimeter weighted iron playing characteristics.
Wide Sole Hollow Irons and Metal Woods	• Heel, Toe, Sole Weighting and Backweighting Effect	X	X	• Best chance of straight hits and more solid feel from off-center shots.	• Higher moment of inertia (resistance to head twisting on off-center hits) due to better heel to toe weight distribution. • Center of gravity usually lower. • Increased hitting area along heel to toe axis of blade.	• The wide sole hollow irons are the most forgiving on off-center hits regarding distance, directional control and solidness of feel. • Hollow irons complement metal woods in playability. • The only disadvantage is that some traditional players do not like the look of wide soled clubs in the playing position. • Hollow irons have a very similar sound to hitting conventional irons.
Offset Metal Woods and Some Models of All Design Types of Irons	• Offset Hosels (Offset is defined as the distance from the very front of hosel to the front of the face at the leading edge.)	X	X	• The more offset the easier to hit the ball more solidly. • The more offset the lower the ball trajectory only if loft and center of gravity are the same.	• The offset forces the golfer's hands ahead of the ball thus giving more chance to hit down and through. • The offset reduces the face progression thus producing marginally lower ball trajectory.	• Basically 4 variations of offset irons available: 1. No offset at all in set. (Front of hosel is in line with face leading edge.) 2. Each iron is offset the same amount. 3. Progressive offset — most offset on #9 iron, least on #1 iron. 4. Progressive offset — most offset on #1 iron, least on #9 iron. (If progressive offset is used, this is the most desirable method.) • Metal woods with offsets have a low center of gravity thus trajectories are normal to slightly higher.
Backweighted Woods	• Usually Brass Backweight but sometimes Recessed Lead in Back of Wood	X		• Ball tends to fly higher, usually by 1° to 2° unless loft or center of gravity is adjusted.	• Center of gravity moved farther back in clubhead thus causing loft to be increased as back of wood turns down before impact.	• Brass backweighted woods generally have increased face bulge which is necessary to maintain ball directional control because head slides more sideways on off-center hits, the farther back the center of gravity.
Foreweighted Woods	• Usually Tungsten, Lead or Very Heavy Insert in Face of Wood	X		• Ball tends to fly lower by ½° unless loft or center of gravity is adjusted.	• Center of gravity moved farther forward than normal causing loft to slightly decrease at impact when compared to conventional weighted wood.	• Heavy insert foreweighted woods generally have slightly reduced face bulge which is necessary to maintain ball directional control because head slides less sideways on off-center hits, the closer the center of gravity is to the face.
Thick, Heavy Soleweighting (Includes many Metal Woods)	• Soleplates with V's, Runners and Other Very Thick Types	X		• Ball is easier to hit from tight or deep grass lies. • Ball tends to fly higher.	• Center of gravity is effectively lowered by heavy weight mass on sole of wood.	• It is now easier to get center of gravity of clubhead below center of gravity of ball at impact. • Center of gravity on some of these clubs is lowered by as much as ⅜".

driver head has a much higher center of gravity than the fairway woods, making it quite difficult to impact the ball solidly. The lesser loft of the driver compounds the problem of getting fairway shots airborne. Most hollow metal wood drivers, on the other hand, have relatively low centers of gravity and excellent toe, heel weight distribution compared to wooden drivers resulting in the less skilled player having a much better chance of hitting this type club from the fairway. The toe, heel weighting also provides for a more solid hit on any off-center hits. Another good example of easier-to-get-airborne clubs are the so-called "trouble clubs" usually characterized by having very thick, heavy cast soleplates with deep runners and grooves. Again, the success of these trouble clubs in easily extricating balls from deep rough or tighter than normal lies is simply explained by their very low centers of gravity as compared to conventional clubs. On top of this, add in adequate loft and heavier head weights and all the ingredients are built-in for a very easy-to-hit golf club.

Regarding any iron or wood club design, an important point needs to be made. If a player contacts the ball in the center of the face with the golf club's center of gravity equal to or lower than the golf ball's center of gravity, the shot will most likely have the proper shape in trajectory and a solid feel. Picking a clubhead design type is one of the things fitting is all about. The right clubs for a particular golfer may not only be those that perform and feel best, but clubs also that possess acceptable trade-offs. Everything in golf club design and fitting is some form of a trade-off and this coupled with understanding the swing, separates good clubfitters from great ones.

Although visually comparing different golf club design types will give some approximation as to the relative location of the center of gravity, be cautioned that the only accurate comparison is to remove the head from the shaft and balance it as previously shown. The reason for this is the many variables which can control the center of gravity's location. Variables such as hosel length, hosel diameter, bore depth, loft angle, blade thickness, blade lengths, toe height and heel height and weight added down the shaft will all affect the center of gravity location.

Clubhead design is a fairly large and all encompassing fitting variable to discuss. Using the information here, coupled with your own experiences in hitting the many design types, provides a sound basis for making recommendations during fitting. By far the biggest fitting benefit today is the numerous new game improvement head designs that are currently on the market. Be sure you spend time on the practice tee comparing each of these new design types with the older designs; read all the hype in product brochures, catalogs and ads; quiz the salesmen; and then form your own opinions. Finally, be sure to further substantiate or raise doubt to your opinions by finding out what other golfers say about them.

8. Face Angle of Woods
(Reference: Chapters 12, 35, 39, 44, Appendix 1.) See Figure 65-41.

This discussion on face angle of woods is actually much more than the title suggests. Since face angle is one of the factors which has a direct bearing on ball directional control; it is necessary in this section to get deeply involved in its relationship with another factor in ball directional control, namely clubhead path. This knowledge is necessary to understanding an important part of the ball flight laws. It certainly can give new insight into teaching and club fitting and is actually quite simple to master. This section will be one of the more interesting of the fitting variables to learn. Much of it, particularly the face angle/clubhead path discussions can also apply to an iron club at impact. The iron club applications are more "teaching" than "club fitting" oriented, but the end purpose is the same and that is to hit the ball solidly with accuracy.

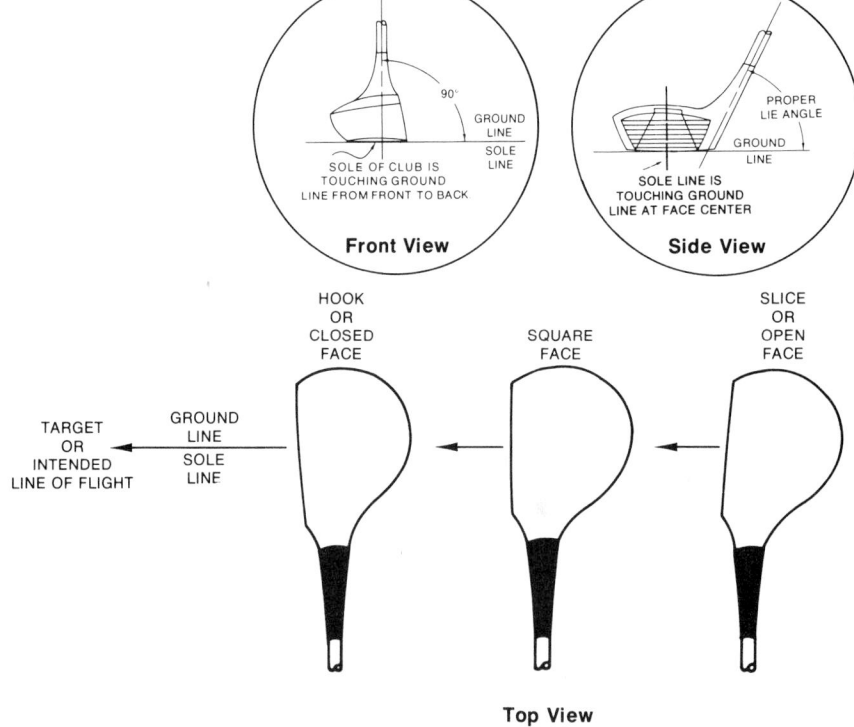

Front View

Side View

Top View

Figure 65-41
Definition of face angle

We have already learned in the Golf Club Design section that wood club lofts are measured differently than iron club lofts. Because of this difference, wood clubs have face angles which are either open, square or closed. If the face angle is either open or closed then we must perform a calculation to determine the real or effective loft of that wood. Iron club lofts on the other hand are always measured with the face square to the target so no face angle other than square can exist. But irons have something woods do not have and that is either bounce or scoop sole angles. Herein lies our problem because hook or a closed face in a wood is the same as bounce in the sole of an iron; and slice or an open face in a wood is the same as scoop or dig in the sole of an iron. Because of this major difference in measuring woods versus iron loft, too little understanding exists regarding a wood club's face angle. Also, it is difficult for some manufacturers to accurately control face angle during manufacture, and since most people do not have equipment to measure it or understand other ways to check it, they simply ignore it and possibly cause one more golfer to say, "I just can't hit this driver or these woods!"

Face angle in woods, when thoroughly understood and properly fit is one variable which can make a significant and immediate difference in playability. This section will teach you all about face angle by using a gradual building block process of explanation. But first, before going on, it is highly recommended that you make sure you have already read Chapters 35, 39 and 44.

A very simple definition of face angle would be the appearance of the face direction of a wood club while in the soled playing position. If the face appears to be aiming left of the target, it is said to be a closed or hook face. If the face appears to point at the target, it is said to be a square face. If the face appears to be aiming right of the target, it is said to be an open or slice face. Figure 65-41 illustrates these three face positions.

The more technical definition of face angle in Figure 65-41 is as follows: The angle of the face to the intended target line with the sole of the club grounded and the hosel bore or shaft also perpendicular to the target line.

The best way to measure the exact face angle in degrees is to use a special gauge made for this purpose. The Golf Club Gauge™ manufactured by The GolfWorks® will do this plus measure every other specification of a wood or iron club. Figure 65-42 shows a driver being measured that has a 2° open face angle and 55° lie angle.

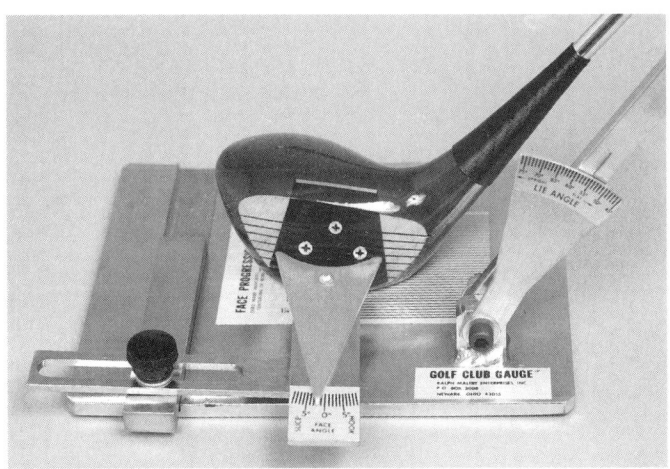

Figure 65-42
Using The Golf Club Gauge™ to measure face angle

The serious clubfitter should strongly consider having a golf club gauge. It eliminates guesswork and allows you to calculate exactly the effective or real loft of any wood club. Also, it elevates your status as a qualified clubfitter when you place a customer's club in it and actually show what is either right or wrong with it.

Does face angle appear the same to the player as the measured face angle? No. A wood club's face angle appears to the player to be approximately 2° more hooked or closed than it actually measures on an accurate gauge such as The Golf Club Gauge™. This seeming phenomenon is caused by a number of things which create a sort of optical illusion. The angle of the left eye to the clubface with the right eye to the clubface is about a 2° angle. Also, one eye usually has dominance over the other. It is not hard to see that an illusion could and does occur when you couple this with the fact that woods are usually placed slightly forward in the stance and the difficulty a player has in focusing on the shaft simultaneously to that of the clubface angle.

The first point to get out of all this is that when a golf club appears perfectly square in the playing or address position, it will probably measure between 1½° to 2½° open in an accurate face angle gauge. So, manufacturers who build clubs to appear square in the playing position are actually boring the clubs from 1½° to 2½° open. There is absolutely nothing wrong with this, but we need to fully understand it in club fitting. Another way of restating our last statement is to say that those few manufacturers who build woods which always appear slightly hooked in the playing position are probably boring their heads to an actual 0° face angle.

Take my word for a moment that clubs tend to appear 2° more closed or hooked in the playing position than they really are and try this experiment: select any driver which appears to have a square face angle while in the playing position. Next, lean the driver up against a wall with the clubhead sitting on a hard floor and the club's sole touching the floor near the clubhead's face center. Walk around in front of the club standing opposite the toe, approximately eight feet away. Now look at the face angle once again in relation to the shaft. The face will now visually appear open and not square like it did while being held in the playing or address position. As previously stated, from the playing position, most golfers will visually determine the face angle to be 2° more hooked than it actually is; or a 2° slice or open face will appear square, a 0° square face will appear 2° hooked and a 2° hooked face will appear 4° hooked. However, simply reverse the position of viewing the face angle by standing in front of the club which is leaning against a wall and the face angle will now appear as it actually would measure in a face angle gauge. Look at Figure 65-43 which illustrates how to conduct this face angle experiment.

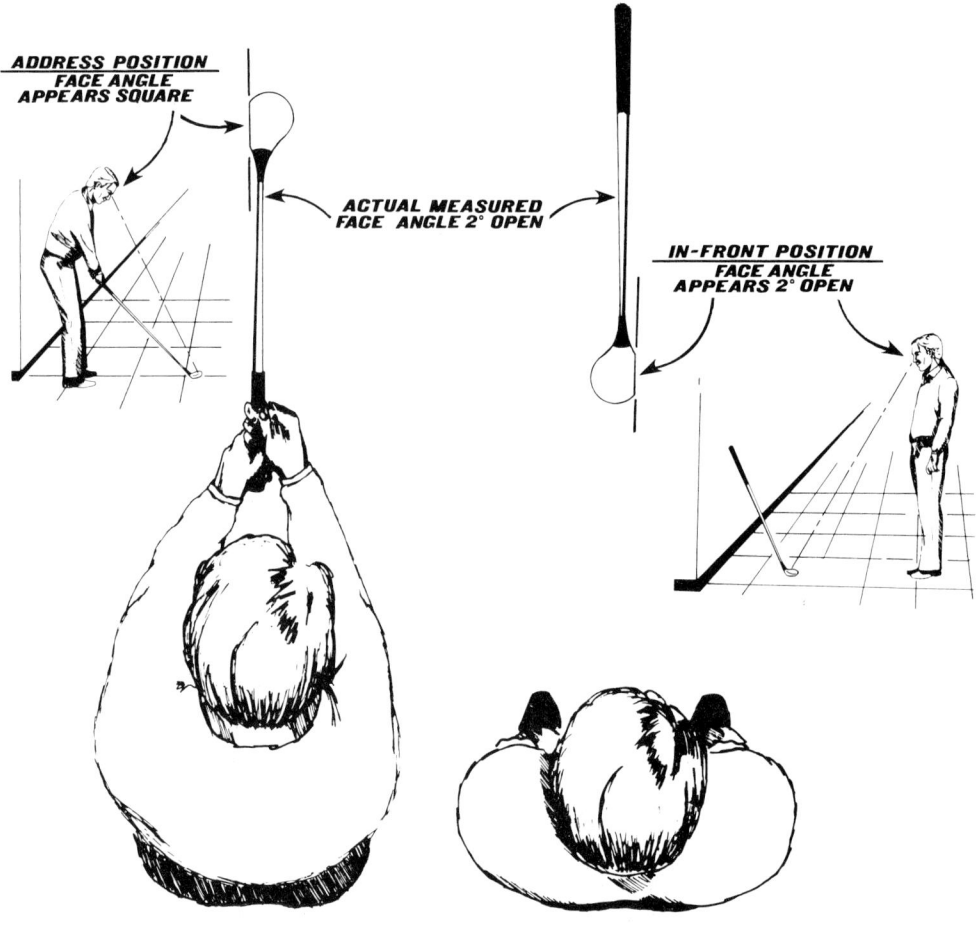

Figure 65-43
Comparing face angle in the address position and in-front position

Finally, one last way to prove the point concerning face angle illusion has to do with "teaching." Many golf professionals have found that during teaching they keep telling their students to "get the clubface square to the target." The student responds that he/she feels the clubface is square to the target. The golf professional indicates that the face looks open to him. The point is that the golf professional giving the lesson is viewing the student's target alignment from opposite the toe and the student sees the face alignment from the address position. There is approximately a 2° visual difference in face angle alignment between what the instructor sees and what the pupil is seeing.

754

Thus far, our building block explanations should have provided a basic insight into understanding what face angle is and how to recognize the three basic positions of hook (closed), square and open (slice) face angles.

Now it's time to discuss one of the primary outside influences on face angle, the shaft flex or more aptly stated shaft flexing. Because the clubhead is traveling faster than any other point along the club and it is accelerating coming into impact with the ball, the shaft normally flexes in a bowed forward position. This flexing action causes the face of the club to close slightly. The rule of thumb is that for each ½" the shaft bows forward, the face closes by approximately 1°. A properly flexed driver for most individuals will cause the face to close between 1° and 2°. See Figure 65-44.

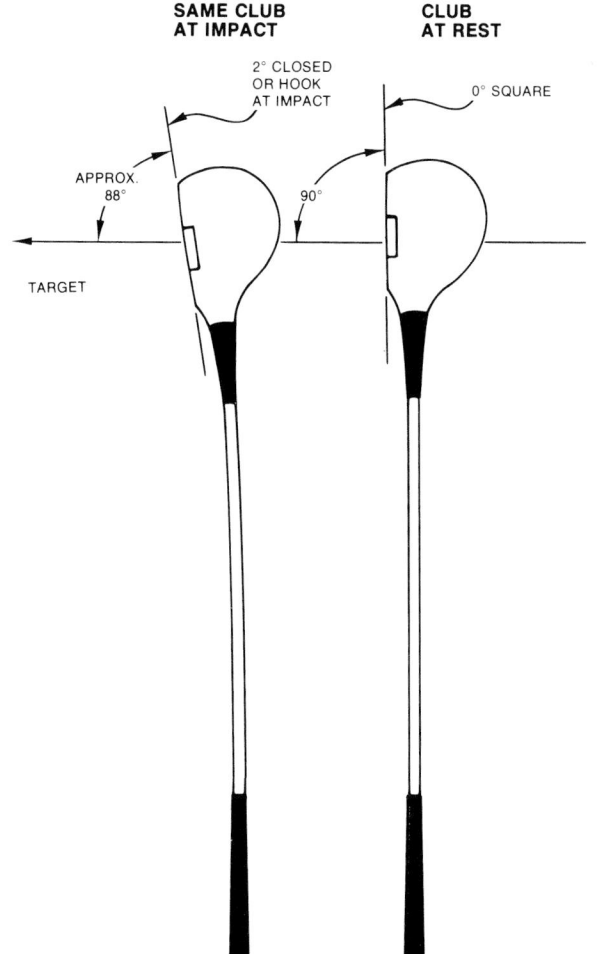

- The clubhead is normally leading the shaft just before impact, causing the face to hook (close) slightly.

- For each 1" of shaft flexing or bowing forward as shown, the face closes approximately 2°.

- **NOTE:** In this example the club has a square (0°) face angle when at rest and a 2° hook face angle when swinging at impact. This drawing assumes that all other variables from AT REST to AT IMPACT remain the same.

- This drawing is a good example why a 0° square face angle helps a golfer with a slicing tendency. Since most drivers built today and in the past have 2° open face angles you can see that at best the face will square with the target before impact. This, however, is not enough "compensation" for a slicer who hits the ball with the clubface open to the club path.

Figure 65-44
Effect of shaft flexing on face angle (hook and slice)

Here is another good experiment to try which will prove to you that the clubhead is in fact closed and leading the shaft at impact. If you don't already have them, some sample drivers and #5 irons should be made up in various shaft flexes for comparative shaft fitting purposes. If you have these clubs, select an "L" flex driver and an "X" flex driver for our experiment. It is best to have all other specifications the same in each test club so only the shaft flexes are being compared. Next, hit some shots with the "L" or ladies' flex driver. This club should tend to be hit higher and to the left with possibly a draw or hooking flight. This is caused by the face closing and the loft increasing due to excessive shaft flexing coming into impact. Now hit the "X" flex or extra-stiff shafted driver. This club should tend to fly lower and straighter or even have a slight pushing tendency. This is caused by a lack of shaft flexing that causes little or no increase in loft and does not close the face at impact. This experiment is proof to the controversy as to whether the head is leading the shaft, in-line or trailing the shaft coming into impact.

A good rule of thumb in fitting face angle is this: if the player is hitting the correct flex shaft, then ignore the shaft flex effect on face angle and fit face angle solely based on ball directional flight and curve. However, if you feel the person has the wrong shaft flex, you cannot fit face angle until you first select the proper shaft and also preferably the proper club length and clubhead weight.

"Let the ball flight be your guide in club fitting."

This is one of the most important statements in club fitting and also in teaching. Regardless of the player's golf club specifications or swing characteristics, the flight of the ball tells all and never lies. There are many variables in equipment and also in the swing which creates a certain ball flight and the good clubfitter/teacher learns to separate the two and work independently in each area if necessary, to solve any problems.

The objective of this discussion is to provide a mastery of two of the three factors which control a golf ball's initial direction leaving the clubface and then, whether or not it will fly straight, curve left or curve right. The two factors to discuss here are clubface angle and clubhead path. The third factor which is centeredness of hit or impact location can be easily determined using stick on face impact decals. For the sake of our discussion, clubface angle will be talked about in reference to the target as being square to, open to or closed to the target at impact. Clubhead path will also be referenced to the same target as being square to, inside out or outside in to the target.

Take a look at Figure 65-45 for one example of clubface angle to clubhead path and the resultant initial ball direction and its curving flight path. The ball is hit on the face center in all our examples shown, as it is not a factor in ball directional control. Notice in this illustration that the clubface angle is square to the target at impact, but the clubhead path is rather severe from inside to outside. Keep in mind that whenever an angle or a difference exists between clubface angle and clubhead path at impact, (in other words, they are not the same and the angle is not 0°) a sideways ball spin component will occur (either hooking or slicing sidespin). Figure 65-45 shows a large angle difference between the clubhead path and the clubface angle; hence a lot of counter-clockwise hooking sidespin is applied to the ball. Here is a more accurate explanation of what happened at impact in Figure 65-45. First of all, the initial ball flight direction is right of target. Notice that the ball's direction does not equally divide the angle between clubface angle and path direction, but rather it favors the clubface angle. The reason for this is the clubface angle is a more important influencing factor than the clubhead's path regarding initial ball direction only. If a percentage could be applied to this, the clubface angle would be about 60% to 70% cause of initial ball direction and clubhead path the remaining 30% to 40%. The resultant ball spin in this example, as already stated, is a very severe hooking sidespin. Since the driver usually only generates ¼ to ⅕ as much backspin as a #9 iron, the hooking sidespin component on this driver shot would comprise a much larger percentage of the total amount of backspin revolutions versus if the same shot occurred on a #9 iron. The sidespin applied to the #9 iron would represent a much smaller percentage when compared to the total backspin revolutions, thus resulting in a less severe hooking tendency. See Figure 65-46. Remember, the greater the backspin (caused by a greater amount of loft), the straighter the ball will fly when compared to the identical clubface angle and clubhead path angles in a less lofted golf club such as a driver.

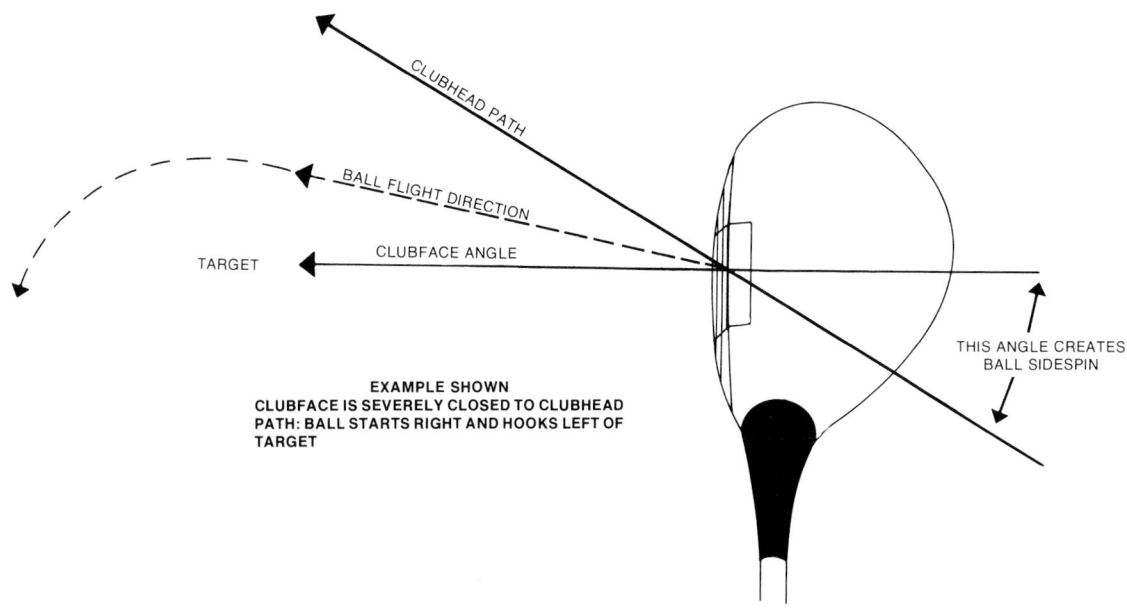

Figure 65-45
An example of clubhead path and clubface angle at impact

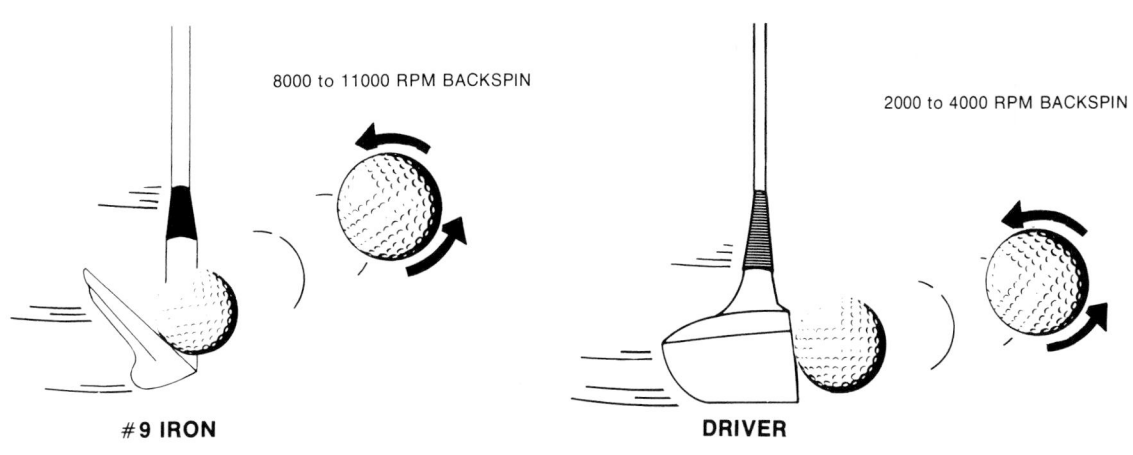

Figure 65-46
Average amounts of backspin: driver versus #9 iron

It is important to note that there are only three possible conditions that can possibly exist on a centered hit at impact regarding clubface angle and clubhead path. They are:

1. Clubface open to the path: Ball curves right
2. Clubface square to the path: Ball flies straight
3. Clubface closed to the path: Ball curves left

Figure 65-47 shows examples of some conditions of these variables at impact. The three drawings on the left show varying clubface angles with a constant path, and the three drawings on the right show varying clubhead paths with a constant face angle. Notice, however, that in all six drawings only our three possible conditions exist.

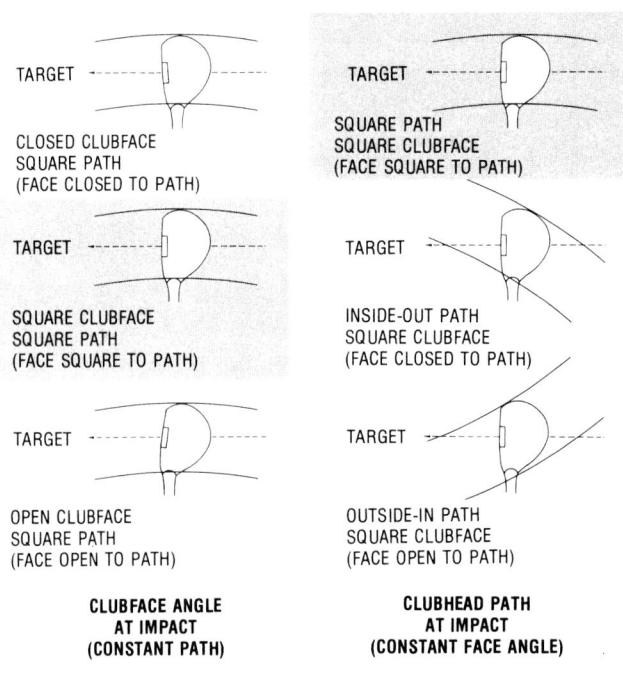

CLUBFACE ANGLE
AT IMPACT
(CONSTANT PATH)

CLUBHEAD PATH
AT IMPACT
(CONSTANT FACE ANGLE)

Figure 65-47
Defining clubface angle and clubhead path at impact

It is generally agreed that the three conditions of a centered hit at impact: 1. Clubface square to path; 2. Clubface open to path; and 3. Clubface closed to path will generate nine distinctive and identifiable flight patterns in reference to ball directional control. These flight patterns are listed in Figure 65-48 to allow the clubfitter a means of accurate ball flight notetaking while hitting balls on the range during the fitting process. The best way to put Figure 65-48 to work for you on the range is to first note the initial ball direction in relation to the target. This indicates the general position of the clubface relative to the target as follows:

1. If the ball flies straight — either at the target or right or left of it — then the clubface is square to the clubhead path and both the clubface and clubhead path are pointing exactly at the line of ball flight.

2. If the ball curves left, use this rule of thumb: On a slight curve left or a draw, the clubface angle will be pointed slightly left of the initial ball direction off the clubface. On a more severe curve left or a hook, the clubface will be pointing more to the left of the initial ball direction off the clubface. See Figure 65-49 which illustrates this example.

3. If the ball curves right, use this rule of thumb: On a slight curve right or a fade, the clubface angle will be pointing slightly right of the initial ball direction off the clubface. On a more severe curve right or a slice, the clubface will be pointing more to the right of the initial ball direction off the clubface. This information helps to determine how much, if any, face angle correction will be needed in either an equipment alteration or change or possibly a swing correction.

758

4. Just so we don't ignore it, keep in mind that during this hitting process, you will be using some means to determine exactly where the ball contacts the face. This can be as simple as an impact marking decal applied to the clubface or having the golfer swing through a swing analyzer computer which provides this valuable information.

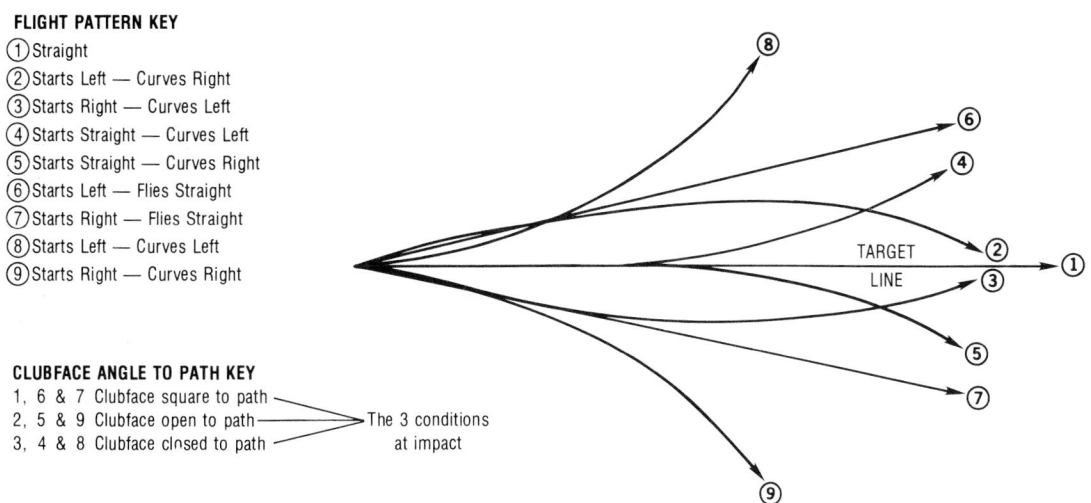

FLIGHT PATTERN KEY
① Straight
② Starts Left — Curves Right
③ Starts Right — Curves Left
④ Starts Straight — Curves Left
⑤ Starts Straight — Curves Right
⑥ Starts Left — Flies Straight
⑦ Starts Right — Flies Straight
⑧ Starts Left — Curves Left
⑨ Starts Right — Curves Right

CLUBFACE ANGLE TO PATH KEY
1, 6 & 7 Clubface square to path ———┐
2, 5 & 9 Clubface open to path ———————→ The 3 conditions
3, 4 & 8 Clubface closed to path ———┘   at impact

Figure 65-48
Ball flight relationships to clubface angle and clubhead path (The nine ball flight possibilities)

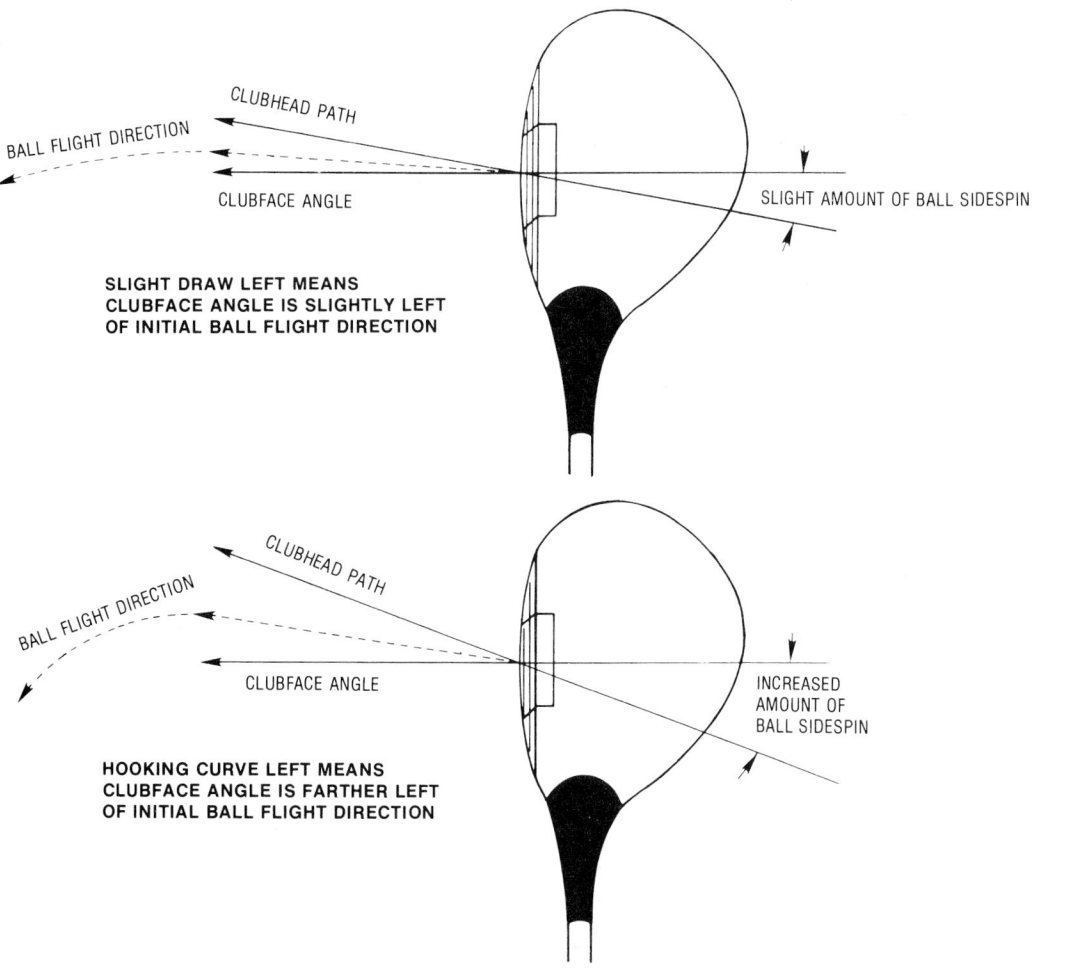

CLUBHEAD PATH
BALL FLIGHT DIRECTION
CLUBFACE ANGLE
SLIGHT AMOUNT OF BALL SIDESPIN

**SLIGHT DRAW LEFT MEANS
CLUBFACE ANGLE IS SLIGHTLY LEFT
OF INITIAL BALL FLIGHT DIRECTION**

CLUBHEAD PATH
BALL FLIGHT DIRECTION
CLUBFACE ANGLE
INCREASED AMOUNT OF BALL SIDESPIN

**HOOKING CURVE LEFT MEANS
CLUBFACE ANGLE IS FARTHER LEFT
OF INITIAL BALL FLIGHT DIRECTION**

Figure 65-49
Interpreting where the clubface is pointing versus the amount of ball curve

Once you have determined the relative position of the face by using initial ball direction coupled with the amount of curve to the ball, it is then simple to approximate the angle between the clubface and path. Use Table 65-18 as a reference to determine this.

TABLE 65-18 Clubface Angle and Clubhead Path versus Ball Curve		
Clubface Angle to Clubhead Path	=	Flight Characteristic
Clubface Open to Path 6°	=	Severe Slicing
Clubface Open to Path 4°	=	Slicing
Clubface Open to Path 2°	=	Fade
Clubface Square to Path 0°	=	Straight Flight
Clubface Closed to Path 2°	=	Draw
Clubface Closed to Path 4°	=	Hooking
Clubface Closed to Path 6°	=	Severe Hooking

Here is another rule of thumb that should be used in club fitting to separate equipment recommendations from recommended changes in the golf swing itself. Since we are all now aware that ball flight regarding curve and direction are a function of the equipment and the swing, we need a guideline to separate the two. More specifically, how do we decide on an equipment change versus taking lessons to hit the ball more straight and at the target? I feel the best criteria to use is whenever the clubface angle and clubhead path exceed 3° then a lesson is in order. The only exceptions to this are when obvious problems of a significant magnitude exist in the player's equipment. One that immediately comes to mind is someone playing with a shaft two flexes too flexible, an excessively heavy or light head weight or most commonly, a wood club with an excessively open face which will be discussed next.

The Effect of Excessively Open Face Angles
We have all heard about a golfer who cannot hit his/her driver for whatever reasons, but hits fairway woods and irons relatively solid and mostly straight. Usually, the problem is diagnosed as "too stiff a shaft" in the driver. But, is this the real problem? If the club happens to have the correct flex shaft for this particular golfer and if he/she hits this shaft fine in the fairway woods and irons, "Why would it be too stiff only in the driver?" Shaft stiffness is usually not the problem in this all too common occurrence. The problem is usually an excessively open face angle or a severe slice face. Let's use an example to better understand this. Assume the driver in question has 11° loft, which is usually standard on most drivers, but it has been improperly bored or somehow built with a 6° open or slice face angle. See Figure 65-50. We have already learned how to calculate the real or effective loft of a wood club in Chapter 35 **Golf Wood Club Design: Loft** by simply adding hook degrees to the measured loft degrees, or as in this case, by subtracting the slice degrees from the measured loft degrees. So, 11° loft minus 6° slice or open face equals 5° real or effective loft at impact. Of course, this calculation would apply only if we rolled the clubface into alignment with the target, thereby reducing the loft exactly by the 6° open face angle to achieve a straight hit. This is quite easy to do, but it does not leave enough loft in most cases to get the ball airborne on a "normal" trajectory. Now, the question to ask is, "Will most average golfers know enough to take a driver with too open a face and roll it closed so they can attempt to hit it straight?" The answer is "no." First of all, the club does not appear all that open to the player. Remember, from the

address side this club will appear only about 4° open — not too bad. But, if we walked around in front of this driver and viewed it from the toe side, it would appear very open. This incidentally is the best way to easily detect a club with an excessively open face angle. Now, back to our example. Since the player will probably not adjust the face angle to a more closed position, he/she will simply place the club behind the ball, swing and hit it. The result will, in most cases, be a drive which starts right and fades or slices right. Here is why: Assume also that this player generates a very consistent and good clubhead path of 2° inside-out. You should now be able to calculate that a clubface at impact which is 6° open, coupled with a clubhead path 2° inside-out, will cause the face to be open to the path by 4°. This results in the ball starting right of the target 4° and slicing farther right. See Figure 65-51 for an example of this. The astute reader is also probably factoring in the effect of shaft flexing in closing the clubface from 1° to 2° at impact which definitely is a factor. However, for this part of our discussion it is best to let face angle and path stand on their own so as not to confuse the issue, but always keep this point in mind.

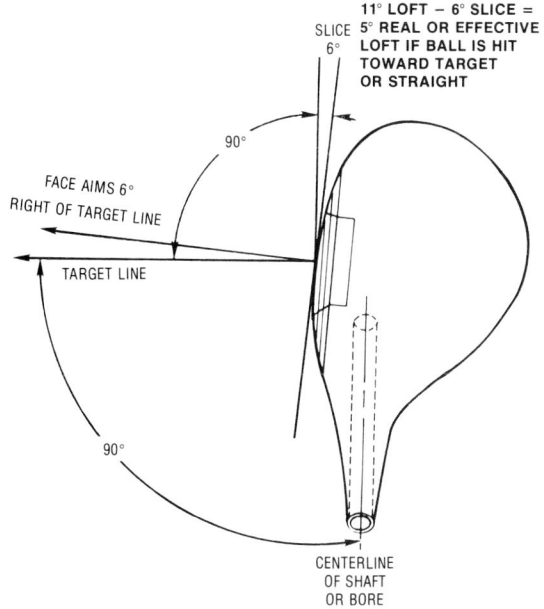

Figure 65-50
A driver with a 6° open or slice face and 11° loft

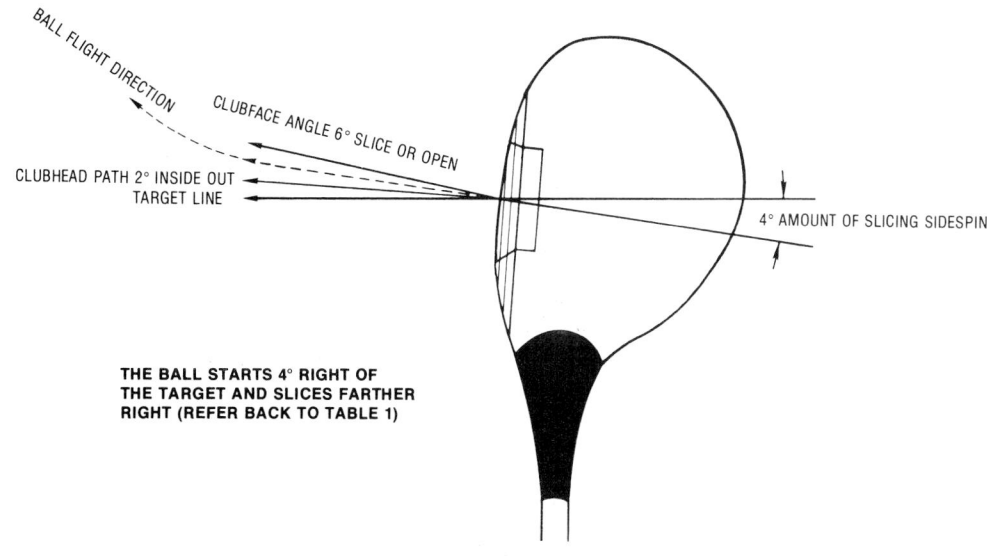

Figure 65-51

The face angle on fairway woods is also important regarding trajectory and directional control, but not as critical as it is on the driver. The reason for this is the increased amount of loft on fairway woods versus the driver. A #3 wood, for example, with a 6° open or slice face angle and 16° loft will end up with 9° real or effective loft at impact in the square hit position. Although this would not make a good #3 wood for most players, at least the club could possibly be hit solid, even though it would fly quite low and be difficult to hit from any sort of a tight lie. The driver previously mentioned with a 6° open or slice face that ended up with 5° real or effective loft would be almost impossible to play with. Remember, the less the loft, the more the ball is compressed on the clubface. The more the ball is compressed on the clubface, the more unforgiving the shot on off-center hits regarding solidness of feel, distance and directional control. All this is relative and mostly varies by the amount of real or effective loft at impact, which as we know, is directly affected by the face angle.

Try this fun type of demonstration that eliminates clubhead path. It actually allows the player to hit the ball with greater accuracy, although the procedure is illegal by U.S.G.A. rules. Why are we doing it then? Because it is a good teacher in further understanding clubface angle versus clubhead path. Here is how it works:

Have you ever heard of a player actually teeing a ball up inside a paper cup and hitting it? Or, have you ever heard of someone applying a greasy substance called "No Slice" to their clubface or the ball? Or finally, have you ever seen a golf tee with a flap built into its back which is positioned between the clubface and the ball? All three of these products have one common characteristic and that is: something is put between the ball and the clubface at impact. See Figure 65-52. What does this do? Quite simply, it eliminates the effect of clubhead path on the shot. It eliminates path because now any resulting angle difference between clubface angle and clubhead path cannot apply any sidespin to the ball. This happens because the face never touches the ball directly. The only factor now remaining at impact that controls ball direction is clubface angle. Wouldn't it be nice to always hit the ball straight and only worry about the clubface angle at impact and completely forget about clubhead path and any resulting sidespins? What an easy game this would be! This is why the following U.S.G.A. Rules apply to both clubs and balls.

Rule 4. Clubs
4-3. Foreign Material
No foreign material shall be applied to the clubface for the purpose of influencing the movement of the ball. Penalty for Breach of Rule 4-3 — Disqualification.

Rule 5. The Ball
5-2. Foreign Material Prohibited
No foreign material shall be applied to a ball for the purpose of changing its playing characteristics. Penalty for Breach of Rule 5-2 — Disqualification.

Since no one wants to grease up their clubfaces and the special tee illustrated in Figure 65-52 is hard to find, go ahead and try this with a paper cup. It is one more teaching/club fitting aid to show students the importance of club face angle and clubhead path and what it feels like to hit the ball without sidespin. Also, since this demonstration isolates face angle, it is a great visual club fitting aid as to where the face angle is actually aiming at impact without the complications of figuring in the clubhead path.

As your fitting skills and experiences increase, you will undoubtedly find that more average golfers will do much better with drivers that are bored to an actual 0° face angle. This is even more factual anytime the player curves the ball from left to right or imparts slicing spin. Unfortunately, as stated earlier, most manufacturers, but not all, build drivers to appear square in the playing position by actually making the face angles 1½° to 2½° open or slice. This so-called standard face angle does in fact work quite well with many players, but don't overlook making up a few test drivers with 0° face angles and differing shaft flexes. This will assure you of a higher success rate in at least fitting the correct driver face angle and shaft combination.

The following table provides terminology references and a ball flight generalization of the various face angles and types.

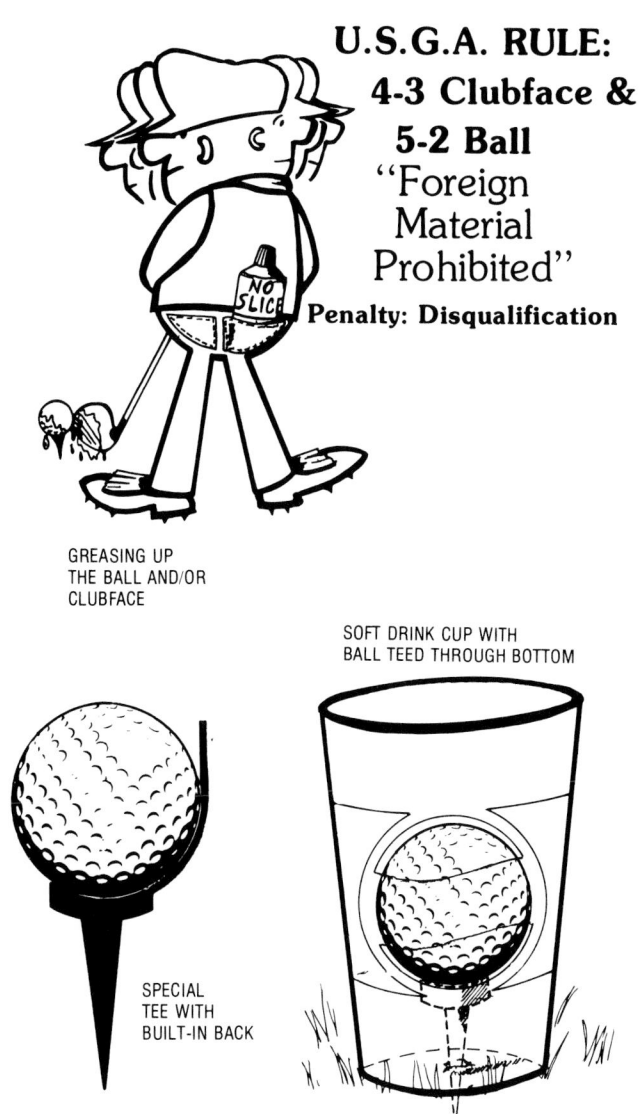

U.S.G.A. RULE:
4-3 Clubface &
5-2 Ball
"Foreign Material Prohibited"
Penalty: Disqualification

GREASING UP
THE BALL AND/OR
CLUBFACE

SOFT DRINK CUP WITH
BALL TEED THROUGH BOTTOM

SPECIAL
TEE WITH
BUILT-IN BACK

Figure 65-52
The U.S.G.A. says, "Foreign material shall not be applied to the ball and/or clubface."

	TABLE 65-19	
	Custom Fitting Table — Face Angle of Wood Clubs	
Face Angle	**Relative Directional Tendency of Shot (Based on Square Face Producing a Straight Shot)**	**Relative Ball Trajectory**
Open	Prounounced Slice or Push	Lower
Slightly Open	Slight Slice or Push	Slightly Lower
Square	Square Hit	Normal
Slightly Closed	Slight Hook or Pull	Slightly Higher
Closed	Pronounced Hook or Pull	Higher

9. Shaft Material Selection

(Reference: Chapters 7, 8, 21, 54, 55, 56, 57, 58, Appendices 1,2.)

Shaft material selection is one of mostly individual preference, although it can have considerable effects on the performance of the golf club. Unfortunately, different shaft materials are in and out of vogue almost as fast as women's and men's fashions and cause a considerable amount of confusion to both golf professionals and golfers.

Table 65-20 has been developed to indicate the general comparative physical and playing characteristics of the various shaft material types.

TABLE 65-20
Custom Fitting Table — Common Shaft Material Types and Characteristics

Approx. Year Introduced	Shaft Type	[1] Approx. Shaft Weight Range	General Shaft Characteristics
1923	Standard Weight Tip Taper Steel Shaft	4¼ to 4½ oz.	Most popular is Dynamic step pattern — Basically the original steel shaft — Heaviest shaft — Most popular on tour.
1966	Lightweight Tip Taper Steel Shaft	3¾ to 4 oz.	Became more popular when aluminum was going out. ½ oz. lighter than original steel shaft. Same weight as aluminum.
1967	Aluminum Shaft	3¾ to 4 oz.	Excellent resistance to torsion. Softer feel although relative stiffness is the same as steel. Dull appearance, larger diameter tip section. Testing indicated aluminum to be marginally longer and straighter hitting than standard weight steel and lightweight steel shafts.
1972	Standard Weight Unitized Parallel Tip Steel Shaft	4⅛ to 4¼ oz.	Very popular during last 3 to 4 years. Popularized by shaft over hosel assemblies. Weight slightly less than regular steel.
1973	Graphite Shafts	2¼ to 3¼ oz.	Many different manufacturers and types. Lightest weight shafts. Varying flex and torsional characteristics depending on manufacturer.
1975	Titanalloy Golf Shaft	3½ to 4 oz.	Gold in color. No stepdowns. Available for woods and irons. Has some titanium in shaft.
1975	Zirtech Titanium 3-2.5 Shaft	2½ to 3½ oz.	Comprised of 94½% titanium. In most cases as light as graphite. Company claims high strength and low torque.
1976	Very Lightweight Steel Shaft	2⅞ to 3¾ oz.	Lightest steel shafts. Very popular. Larger in diameter than other steel shafts. Made from stronger steel alloys.
1976	Large .700 Butt Dia. Steel Shafts	3¾ to 4 oz.	Same weights as lightweight steel. Larger butt diameter. Available in woods and irons.
1978	Lightweight Unitized Parallel Tip Steel Shaft	3½ to 4 oz.	Also available in tip taper but shaft is still unitized. Shaft gets very light in short irons. Good resistance to torque.

[1] The more flexible shafts are represented by the lower numbers in each weight range and the stiffer shafts by the higher numbers in each weight range. Weight ranges represent driver shafts.

10. Grip Material Selection

(Reference: Chapter 23.)

Grip material selection depends entirely on personal preference. Each material type comes in a variety of different shapes, colors, lengths and styles to further confuse the golfer's decision. Each type of grip, however, does have certain general characteristics. During recent years rubber type grips have probably accounted for 95% of all the grips sold, and leather type grips the remaining 5%. The one exception to this sales breakdown would be on the men's professional golf tour where it is estimated rubber and leather grips each comprise about 90% and 10% respectively of this small, but highly influential market segment. It should also be noted that professional golfers prefer supple calf leather grips over the less expensive cowhide leather grips.

Grip Material	Most Common Types	Pro	Con
	TABLE 65-21		
	Custom Fitting Table — Grip Material Selection		
Rubber	• Solid Rubber • Rubber and Cork • Rubber, Cork and Cord • Rubber and Kraton	• Good all weather grips • Excellent general durability • Inexpensive • Easy to install	• Cord grip can be harsh on hands not accustomed to this type grip • Some softer compounds wear easily
Leather	• Wound-wrap on • Wound-slip on • Panel-slip on	• Leather grips are more tacky than rubber if kept in good condition giving excellent control	• Leather tends to get slippery if not kept dry • Leather grips tend to wear out quickest unless cleaned and treated with leather conditioner occasionally • Usually costlier
Comment • Rubber or leather grips available with or without rib reminders in 10" or 11" lengths.			

11. Set Makeup Selection

Selecting the proper set makeup for any given golfer is probably one of the easier, although often overlooked, steps toward an improved and more enjoyable game of golf. The ruling body of golf, The United States Golf Association (U.S.G.A.) limits a golfer to carrying no more than 14 clubs during a round of golf. So, why not play with the 14 clubs that will do the most good? Just because manufacturers offer stock sets a certain way, and because traditionally everybody that ever played well had to carry a #2 iron should not limit or influence the choice of how a set should be made up for a certain golfer. This is one area where golf club manufacturers have been taking a long hard look during the last 15 years or so and have made changes in their standard set offerings of stock clubs. For example, #2 irons have almost disappeared from most stock men's sets; more and more ladies' wood sets are being offered 1, 3, 5, 7 or 1, 5, 7 as standard makeup; and men's #6 and #7 woods are being offered by a number of manufacturers.

Probably the biggest change to occur in the search for the ideal set makeup has been the recent trend of club manufacturers to offer individual specialty clubs such as special drivers, higher numbered fairway woods, heavy sole-weighted fairway woods, numerous wedges and special driving irons. The list goes on and on, but the point is that manufacturers realize the large market that exists for individual specialty clubs that usually play easier and can solve many golfers' individual shotmaking problems by simply altering their set makeup.

There are some golfers that play with a set makeup which most of us would consider extreme. At almost every golf course you can find someone who plays with only a bagful of woods and the opposite extreme of the player who carries only irons. Also, out there somewhere is a player with a conventional set of irons #2 through sand wedge with each and every club stamped with the number 7. It seems this player was tired of letting his playing partners figure out which club he was hitting, so he simply had them all stamped #7. This is a true story because I had this set made for a customer when I worked at Spalding.

■ Finding the Correct Set Makeup

Finding the correct set makeup for a golfer relies on a number of factors and also some trial and error. The purpose of discussing set makeup here is to provide some "food for thought" by giving general methods of approaching the fitting of set makeup and by providing recommended set makeups by a player's ability and the shaft flex used. Keep in mind that the possible combinations of set makeup for any specific type golfer can and will vary dramatically. The intent of any set makeup categorized in this section is to simply provide some food for thought and a possible starting point. However, before getting more deeply involved in discussions of specific set makeups, it would be best to describe those areas which can help you the most in fitting set makeup to an individual.

• Personal Interview (See miscellaneous fitting information at the end of this chapter.)

During the personal interview with the customer, you will be asking information about favorite clubs, wants, goals and preferences and physical limitations. This area should provide quite a bit of information on how this person perceives the clubs he/she now plays, and what is mentally perceived as clubs that would be easier to hit, along with mental attitude toward the driver, fairway woods, long irons, mid-irons, short irons, wedges and putter.

• Fitting Scorecard (See miscellaneous fitting information at the end of this chapter)

The Fitting Scorecard allows the golfer to chart every shot hit during a specified number of rounds. This helps to determine the frequency of each club's use, which clubs are actually hit good or bad and which club is missing that could benefit this particular golfer. The Fitting Scorecard more easily quantifies the abilities of the player on a specific type of golf course. His strengths and weaknesses with each type club are more easily uncovered if more than one Fitting Scorecard is analyzed.

• Hitting Results Evaluation Worksheet (See miscellaneous fitting information at the end of this chapter.)

In completing the Hitting Results Worksheet you are actually on the practice range hitting balls using the player's present clubs and certain test clubs. This is the best way to confirm which clubs or group of clubs the player hits best or worst and overall mental attitude toward these groups of clubs. Actually observing the trajectory, shape of the shot and overall distances hit by the various wood and iron categories can be the biggest help in recommending additional wood clubs versus iron clubs or vice versa.

■ Using the Fitting Scorecard

The Fitting Scorecard is a great help in fitting set makeup and as such is treated here in more detail. The golfer begins by filling out one, or preferably more of the Fitting Scorecards as shown in Figure 65-53. Spend a few minutes studying this score card to get a feel for how this player went around the course. Be sure to read the instructions at the bottom of the scorecard to understand the meaning of "squares" and/or "circles" around some of the X's.

Keep in mind that when analyzing the Fitting Scorecard for possible set makeup changes, additional factors must also be weighted. The type of course played most often, conditions of play and the strengths and weaknesses of the individual's game must be taken into consideration.

For example, using the golfer in Figure 65-53, assume play is on a course where summer rules are almost always in effect and the ball does not sit up particularly well on the fairways. The par 5 holes are not reachable in two and there are no par 3's or par 4's, which normally require a #3 wood shot. Switching the #3 wood to a #4 wood may help in consistency of fairway wood play both in better trajectory and more solid hits.

Further assume that this player's #2 and #3 irons are usually not hit with any consistency, but his fairway wood play in general is quite satisfactory. It may be wise to drop both the #2 and #3 irons in favor of a more lofted #6 and/or #7 wood, a utility type wood with a heavy soleplate or a metal wood.

Also, if only 5, 6 or 7 greens are hit in regulation, it may be wise to add another wedge. This player did hit a respectable 10 greens in regulation this day. Remember, the better the chipping and wedge play, the fewer putts usually required. This alone has made the "Third Wedge" or high lofted wedge concept very popular with all caliber of players.

To sum up this example, the player started with a driver, #3 and #5 wood, #2 through #9 irons, pitching wedge, sand wedge and putter. It has now been recommended to try a driver, #4, #5 and either a #6 and/or #7 wood (or utility wood), #3 or #4 through #9 irons, pitching wedge, sand wedge, putter and possibly a third wedge. As you can see, it is quite difficult using the Fitting Scorecard alone as a single source for fitting set makeup. However, add to this the aforementioned "Personal Interview" information and the "Hitting Results Evaluation" from the driving range and you would have no trouble in being more confident about recommending any set makeup changes.

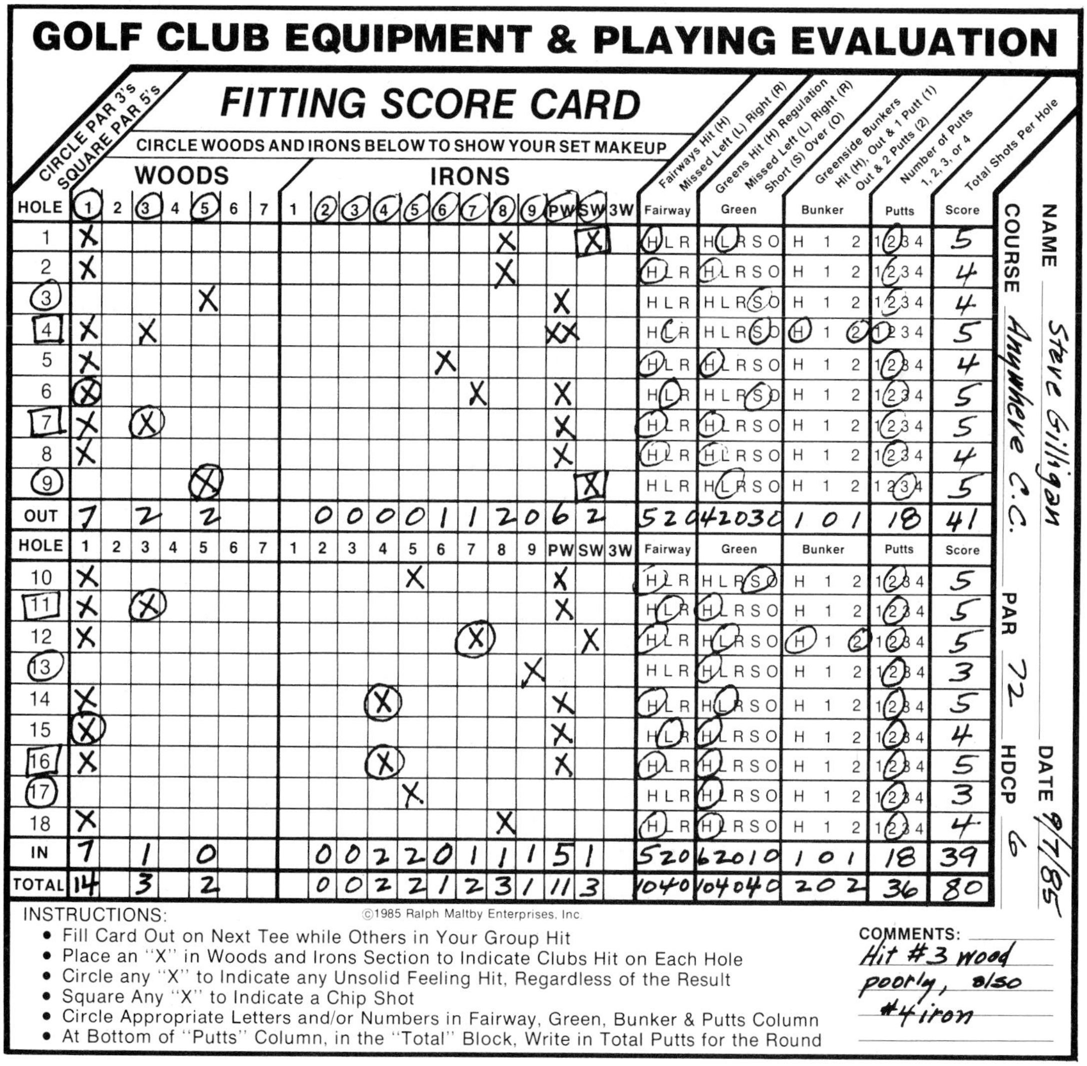

GOLF CLUB EQUIPMENT & PLAYING EVALUATION

FITTING SCORE CARD

CIRCLE WOODS AND IRONS BELOW TO SHOW YOUR SET MAKEUP

CIRCLE PAR 3s / SQUARE PAR 5s

Fairways Hit (H) / Missed Left (L) Right (R) / Greens Hit (H) Regulation / Missed Left (L) Right (R) / Short (S) Over (O) / Greenside Bunkers / Hit (H), Out & 1 Putt (1) / Out & 2 Putts (2) / Number of Putts 1, 2, 3, or 4 / Total Shots Per Hole

NAME: Steve Gilligan
COURSE: Anywhere C.C.
PAR 72 HDCP 6
DATE 9/7/85

HOLE	WOODS 1	2	3	4	5	6	7	IRONS 1	2	3	4	5	6	7	8	9	PW	SW	3W	Fairway	Green	Bunker	Putts	Score
1	X														X				X	H L R	H L R S O	H 1 2	1 2 3 4	5
2	X														X					H L R	H L R S O	H 1 2	1 2 3 4	4
(3)				X														X		H L R	H L R S O	H 1 2	1 2 3 4	4
[4]	X	X															X X			H L R	H L R S O	H 1 2	1 2 3 4	5
5	X											X								H L R	H L R S O	H 1 2	1 2 3 4	4
6	X													X			X			H L R	H L R S O	H 1 2	1 2 3 4	5
[7]	X	X															X			H L R	H L R S O	H 1 2	1 2 3 4	5
8	X																X			H L R	H L R S O	H 1 2	1 2 3 4	4
(9)				X															X	H L R	H L R S O	H 1 2	1 2 3 4	5
OUT	7	2		2				0	0	0	0	1	1	2	0	6	2			5 2 0 4	2 0 3 0	1 0 1	18	41
10	X										X						X			H L R	H L R S O	H 1 2	1 2 3 4	5
[11]	X	X															X			H L R	H L R S O	H 1 2	1 2 3 4	5
12	X													X				X		H L R	H L R S O	H 1 2	1 2 3 4	5
(13)															X					H L R	H L R S O	H 1 2	1 2 3 4	3
14	X											X					X			H L R	H L R S O	H 1 2	1 2 3 4	5
15	X																X			H L R	H L R S O	H 1 2	1 2 3 4	4
[16]	X											X					X			H L R	H L R S O	H 1 2	1 2 3 4	5
(17)											X									H L R	H L R S O	H 1 2	1 2 3 4	3
18	X														X					H L R	H L R S O	H 1 2	1 2 3 4	4
IN	7	1		0				0	0	2	2	0	1	1	1	5	1			5 2 0 6	2 0 1 0	1 0 1	18	39
TOTAL	14	3		2				0	0	2	2	1	2	3	1	11	3			10 4 0 10	4 0 4 0	2 0 2	36	80

©1985 Ralph Maltby Enterprises, Inc.

INSTRUCTIONS:
- Fill Card Out on Next Tee while Others in Your Group Hit
- Place an "X" in Woods and Irons Section to Indicate Clubs Hit on Each Hole
- Circle any "X" to Indicate any Unsolid Feeling Hit, Regardless of the Result
- Square Any "X" to Indicate a Chip Shot
- Circle Appropriate Letters and/or Numbers in Fairway, Green, Bunker & Putts Column
- At Bottom of "Putts" Column, in the "Total" Block, Write in Total Putts for the Round

COMMENTS: Hit #3 wood poorly, also #4 iron

Figure 65-53
Using the Fitting Scorecard for set makeup

767

■ Understanding Distance Equivalency of Woods and Irons

One of the more common recommendations in changing a player's set makeup regards the swapping of fairway woods for long irons or the not so common swapping of long irons for fairway woods. Table 65-22 provides the distance equivalency comparisons as they really should be and not how they have been written about in past books and magazine articles. For example, I can remember years back when #5 woods were just beginning to become popular. It seemed as though every publication at the time compared the #5 wood to the #3 iron. Anyone who has gone out on a practice range to compare these two clubs will find that the #5 wood in most every case will carry the ball 10 to 20 yards longer than a #3 iron. In actuality, a #5 wood is closer to a #2 iron and sometimes even a #1 iron in distance equivalency.

TABLE 65-22
[1] Wood versus Iron Distance Equivalency — A General Guide

#4 Wood	=	#1 Iron
#5 Wood	=	#1 or #2 Iron
#6 Wood	=	#2 or #3 Iron
#7 Wood	=	#3 or #4 Iron
#8 Wood	=	#4 or #5 Iron
#9 Wood	=	#5 or #6 Iron
#10 Wood	=	#6 or #7 Iron

[1] Wood trajectory is usually higher with more backspin and less roll versus iron trajectory in those equivalents shown above.

As a general rule, here is what you should look at when comparing fairway woods versus irons of the same distance equivalency as shown in Table 65-22. The fairway woods are longer in length than the comparable irons by approximately 1½" to 2". The lofts of the wood and iron equivalents are basically the same after the slice or open face angle of the woods is subtracted from the standard loft to obtain the real loft.

The total weight of the comparable fairway wood is approximately ¼ to ⅜ ounce lighter than the iron, but the head weight of the wood is ½ to ⅝ ounce lighter than the iron. The shaft flex of the wood is approximately ½ flex more flexible feeling. The result of all this is that equivalent distance fairway woods versus irons will launch the ball higher in trajectory with greater distance, greater backspin and less roll. The fairway woods will feel more solid on off-center hits because of the increased shaft flexibility and the farther back from the face location of the center of gravity. The fairway woods will generate higher clubhead speeds due to their lighter total weight, head weight and longer length. They will, however, be harder to hit consistently on face center due to the 1½" to 2" longer club lengths and for this same reason they will tend to be less accurate than the irons. The reader should see now that once again we are faced with a trade-off in fitting.

Here is an example that may help. We have all watched a tournament on television where the player hits a #1 iron off the tee on a tricky hole because it demands increased accuracy. This works well for the tour player because he can hit the #1 iron solid and long and can best utilize its better accuracy. But, for most of us, the fairway wood off the tee is probably much easier to hit solid and we can achieve good distance with acceptable accuracy. Remember, if you simply cannot hit a #1 iron, what good is the fact that it is more accurate than an equivalent fairway wood that you can hit? This is one of the fitting trade-offs that makes good common sense. However, a proper fitting analysis of set makeup should provide a recommendation that maximizes these trade-offs to achieve increased playability. This is what fitting is all about.

■ Myth: The #6 and #7 Woods Are Only For Women and Senior Golfers

Many golfers of average ability fear that if they replace their long irons with the more lofted woods, they will become the butt of humor among their playing partners. The truth is that even a number of pros on the PGA Tour now carry the #6 and #7 utility woods for use in tight situations.

The #6 and #7 woods are good replacements for the #2 and #3 irons. It will be easier to hit long approach shots from the rough or fairway, bring the ball in on a higher trajectory, hold the green better and feel more solid to hit more of the time.

Also, golfers who in the past might have bounced a #3 iron up onto the green can now place a #7 wood shot softly on the putting surface, carrying all bunkers and other hazards. The biggest disadvantage of replacing a long iron with a lofted wood is evident only in those instances when a golfer must hit a low shot under the limb of a tree or possibly in situations that demand a low punch shot. All golfers should at least have the opportunity to hit some practice shots with #6 and #7 woods to see how they perform. In this regard, the #6 and/or #7 wood should be included in your arsenal of fitting test clubs.

Finally, Table 65-23 gives my personal recommendations for set makeups by both shaft flex and player ability. This table is only intended as a general guide for set makeup recommendations. Many golf professionals and others have strong feelings on what set makeups they personally recommend to a given golfer; however, the point to make here is not to overlook this important part of proper fitting and give it all the consideration necessary. For many players, this can be the easiest and fastest way to a lower handicap and more enjoyable golf.

TABLE 65-23
Set Makeup Selection Guide

Shaft Flex	Player Category	General Golfing Ability	[1][2] Set Makeup [4] Woods	Irons	No. of Clubs/Set
L(Ladies)	Ladies &	18 Hdcp. or Less	1, 3, 5, 7	3-9, PW, SW & P	
	Weak	Over 18 Hdcp.	1, 3, 4, 5, 7	4-9, PW, SW & P	14
	Senior	Over 18 Hdcp. (alternative)	1, 3, 5, 6, 7, 8	5-9, PW, SW & P	
A(Flexible)	Ladies,	18 Hdcp. or Less	1, 3, 5, 6 (or 7)	3-9, PW, SW & P	
	Men &	Over 18 Hdcp.	1, 3, 4, 5, 7	4-9, PW, SW & P	14
	Seniors	Over 18 Hdcp. (alternative)	1, 3, 5, 6, 7, 8	5-9, PW, SW & P	
R(Medium)	Ladies,	14 Hdcp. or Less	1, 3, 4, 5	3-9, PW, SW & P	
	Men &	15-24 Hdcp.	1, 3, 5, 7	3-9, PW, SW & P	14
	Seniors	Over 24 Hdcp.	1, 3, 4, 5, 7	4-9, PW, SW & P	
S(Stiff)	Men &	10 Hdcp. or Less	1, 3, 4 (or 5)	[3]2-9, PW, SW & P	
	Stronger	11-18 Hdcp.	1, 3, 4, 5 (or 7)	3-9, PW, SW & P	14
	Seniors	Over 18 Hdcp.	1, 3, 5 , 7	3-9, PW, SW & P	
X(Extra Stiff)	Men	10 Hdcp. or Less	1, 3, 4 (or 5)	[3]2-9, PW, SW & P	14

[1] A third wedge can be added by dropping #3 or #4 wood or longest iron in set.

[2] A utility or trouble wood can be substituted for #5 or #7 wood or longest iron in set.

[3] A #1 iron could replace #2 iron or #3 wood or #4 wood.

[4] A wooden driver can be accompanied by metal wood fairways.

■ Miscellaneous Fitting Information

The following information provides the clubfitter with additional thoughts and methods to better fit an individual. Every clubfitter must develop their own methods with which they are comfortable and have achieved fitting successes. For those that are further interested in thoroughly understanding clubfitting; it is recommended that a copy of Ralph Maltby's "The Complete Golf Club Fitting Plan" be obtained from The GolfWorks® or the Professional Golfers Association of America. At the end of this section, the "Fitting Worksheet" from the aforementioned book has been reproduced along with a "Fitting Scorecard" so the reader can actually walk through the 4 step fitting process. While the "Fitting Worksheet" is quite easy to fill out, the advanced analysis of the data requires some practice. "The Complete Golf Club Fitting Plan" book explains this in great detail. Extra "Fitting Worksheets" and "Fitting Scorecards" are available individually from The GolfWorks®.

■ Fitting Drivers

It has been said many times that golf is simply a game of "distance and direction." Probably the one club this statement applies to most is the driver because it is the longest hitting club in the bag and, consequently, if it is hit off line any misdirection is magnified by the distance.

A properly fit driver will enable the player not only to hit the ball long, but accurately as well. It builds a feeling of confidence and control and ultimately leads to better scoring.

The driver is critical to good golf because it is the one club that sets up everything else. A good, long or well-placed drive makes a better approach shot which in turn may make for an easier putt.

For most players, their better playing and scoring rounds probably occurred when they were driving the ball well and putting decently. This usually happens because it is easier to hit greens from fairways or at least be closer to the green for an easier chip and possibly a one putt.

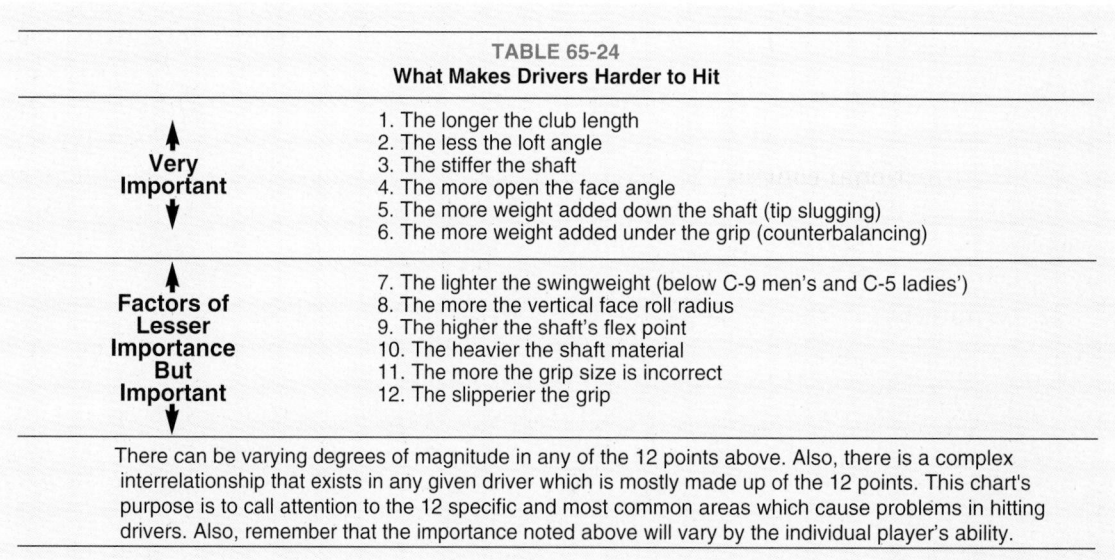

	TABLE 65-24 What Makes Drivers Harder to Hit	
Very Important ↑↓	1. The longer the club length 2. The less the loft angle 3. The stiffer the shaft 4. The more open the face angle 5. The more weight added down the shaft (tip slugging) 6. The more weight added under the grip (counterbalancing)
Factors of Lesser Importance But Important ↑↓	7. The lighter the swingweight (below C-9 men's and C-5 ladies') 8. The more the vertical face roll radius 9. The higher the shaft's flex point 10. The heavier the shaft material 11. The more the grip size is incorrect 12. The slipperier the grip

There can be varying degrees of magnitude in any of the 12 points above. Also, there is a complex interrelationship that exists in any given driver which is mostly made up of the 12 points. This chart's purpose is to call attention to the 12 specific and most common areas which cause problems in hitting drivers. Also, remember that the importance noted above will vary by the individual player's ability.

Many people experience problems with their driver and become resolved to the fact that they will be hitting a #3 wood off the tee for the rest of their golfing lives. Obviously, this need not be the case if we follow some simple rules and logically look at fitting drivers by starting off with those attributes (See Table 65-24) which make drivers harder to hit.

■ Building A Driver Which Is Very Easy to Hit

Each year I used to do approximately 15 to 20 seminars for the Professional Golfers' Association of America. I have been doing these continuously since 1973. The presentations include subjects on golf club repair, golf club design and fitting. During the seminars, the subject always comes up regarding fitting drivers to those individuals who have abandoned the club in favor of a fairway wood off the tee. The explanation I use as to what makes drivers harder to hit is shown in Table 65-24. I then ask all students to take out a pencil and paper and write down the specifications of a special driver to be used in fitting. This driver is called the "Hero" driver because it can be hit by almost anyone and it makes you, the clubfitter, a hero when someone who normally cannot hit a driver hits this hero down the middle of the fairway long and with a solid feel.

■ The Hero Driver Background Information

As we all know, there are many golfers in this world who cannot hit their drivers. They hit their #3, #4 and #5 woods straight. They hit their irons straight. But every time they attempt to hit their driver, the ball starts right and usually slices right. There are many causes for this and most are equipment-related. This is an especially true statement if clubs within the set other than the driver tend to be hit solid and relatively straight. The usual diagnosis for the above mentioned problem is that the shaft in the driver is too stiff. While this can contribute significantly to this condition, it is usually not the major part of the problem. The culprit is usually an excessively open face angle (slice face). The industry standard is approximately two degrees open or slice facing on a driver which incidentally makes the club appear perfectly square in the playing position. Face angles of 3 degrees, 4 degrees or 5 degrees open are not at all uncommon in mass-produced clubs and are not easily detectable without special measuring gauges. This type of facing will cause the face angle at impact to be open to the clubhead path resulting in the ball starting right and fading or slicing right. Obviously this is not a good situation.

Besides the shaft being too stiff and/or the face being too open or slice, the driver length also may be too long. Simply put, the longer a club the harder it is to hit. Can you hit the ball on the center of the face more often with a driver length three feet long or six feet long? The three foot long club will win everytime. It will hit the ball more solid, straighter and more consistently at the target versus the six foot long club which will be hit all over the face, produce many unsolid hits, give poor consistency and erratic directional control. However, catch this six foot long club on the center of the face and it will go much farther than the three foot long club because of the much higher clubhead speed generated with the longer club. Another way of stating that longer clubs are harder to hit is simply this: maximum energy from the clubhead to the ball at impact can only be obtained if you hit the ball on the center of the clubface. Any off-center hit causes the clubhead to twist and impart less energy to the ball, hence loss of distance and a more unsolid feeling.

Another problem with drivers is the amount of real or effective loft. A rule of thumb is: the less the loft, the harder the club is to hit. Why? This is because the less the loft, the more the face will compress the golf ball; and the more the face compresses the ball, the more important it is to hit the ball on the face center. Question: Do you lose more distance on a toe shot with a #1 iron or a #9 iron? Also, which feels worse? Answer: #1 iron. A toe shot 1" forward of face center using a #1 iron will lose 12% of the total distance versus a shot hit on the face center. A #9 iron hit 1" forward of face center will only lose 5% of the total distance versus a shot hit on the face center.

So you can see, a driver is harder to hit on the center of the face because it is the longest club in the bag (longer clubs are harder to hit) and when you do hit it, you better hit it on the center of the face or you will lose a significant amount of distance from the off-center hit. Rule: The less the loft, the harder a club is to hit.

As you can see, this is a very technical and somewhat confusing subject, but definitely fun to talk about because this is what fitting is all about. First, you determine the appropriate trade-offs for a specific ability player, then you use all your skills to make a club or recommend a club which is easier to hit and lands the ball more consistently in the fairway.

■ The Hero Diver Specifications

This driver is nothing more than a club which utilizes every corrective fitting tip, specification or component thrown into one club to make it extremely easy to hit for anyone having trouble hitting the driver. It is definitely an average golfer type club, which means it fits most of the people playing golf today. The most important aspect of this driver is that it works nearly every time. You can try it yourself, but it works best when you simply hand it to someone who is having driver problems. Remember, however, not to divulge the specifications until some time later, if at all, because this club will not be perceived as a macho driver and we all know how important it is to perceive a club properly and eliminate any common mental hang-ups which are particularly prevalent in the sport of golf. Most everybody wants to emulate the touring pro and play with the same equipment. Isn't it great for a player to tell his playing partners he has "a classic shape oil hardened persimmon driver with low center portion of the tree density, fiber inserts for working the ball, 2" tipped Dynamic® Gold X100 shaft, ½" longer than standard driver length, strong 10 degree loft…" Sounds great, but only a handful of skilled players can hit this driver. The majority of us certainly cannot.

The following specifications are the ones I give to each PGA class so that they can build a "hero" driver to use in fitting drivers to average players:

Driver Head
• Standard size laminated maple or persimmon head.
• Any insert you desire.
• 0 degree face angle. (Will appear slightly hooked in the playing position. More importantly, this will correct equipment-induced error of face open to path for players with slicing problems.)
•11 degree loft. (Because of 0 degree face angle, you actually have 2 degrees more effective loft than with a conventional 11 degree driver loft and 2 degree open or slice face.)
• 56 degree lie. (Lie is 1 degree more upright than standard because club is ½" short. Actually, a 56 degree lie would be the standard lie for a 42½" driver.)

Optional Metal Wood Head
• If you also want to make up one of these clubs with a metal wood head, it will work just fine. Because low center of gravity metal woods hit the ball higher, a 10 or 11 degree loft will work okay. The .335 bore on most metal woods will accept a U2LWR parallel tip TT Lite shaft. After assembly, bend it slightly at the top of the hosel to close the face to 0 degrees if the metal wood head you are working with is not already 0 degrees square.

Shaft
• True Temper® TT Lite in medium flex (TT Lite has a mid to low flex point and is ½ ounce lighter than a conventional steel shaft thus allowing a lighter total weight golf club with a heavier head weight). The True Temper® Flex Flow and Dynalite shafts or Brunswick Golf's® UCV-304 shaft works great also, but all are more expensive. The Jet Step shaft is a moderately priced shaft that will also work.
• Install the shaft properly and cut to an overall club length of 42½". The reduction

in swingspeed for an average golfer is more than compensated for by:

1. Making it easier to hit the ball on the center of the clubface.
2. Giving the player more confidence.
3. Having more balls landing in the fairway since accuracy is improved.

Initially during fitting, it is most important not to tell the player that the club is shorter than standard.

Grip:
• Eaton® Victory or any other good rubber grip. Install ¹⁄₆₄" oversize under left hand and ¹⁄₃₂" oversize under right hand. (Eighty percent of all men players use too small a grip and most have the much too small grip under the right hand which causes inadvertent regripping during swing.)

Assembly Tips:
• Final weight this club only under the soleplate with no weight added down the shaft.
• Swingweight D-4. (This will give good clubhead feel, control and accuracy with a ½" short driver.) If you substitute a True Temper® Extralite or Brunswick UCV-304 shaft, change the swingweight to D-2 since these very light shafts require a heavier head weight to equal the same swingweight as a heavier shaft requires.

MEN'S HERO DRIVER SPECIFICATIONS SUMMARY

HEAD:
MATERIAL: Persimmon, Laminated Maple or Metal Wood
LOFT: 11° (10° is okay for metal woods)
LIE: 56°
FACE ANGLE: 0° Square
BULGE AND ROLL RADIUS: 10" Radius Bulge, 12" Radius Roll

SHAFT:
MATERIAL: TT Lite, Jet Step or Flex Flow (lightweight steel)
FLEX: Medium
FLEX POINT: Mid to Low (TT Lite is mid; Jet Step & Flex Flow are low)

GRIP:
MATERIAL: Victory or other good rubber grip
SIZE: ¹⁄₆₄" oversize under left hand, ¹⁄₃₂" oversize under right hand

ASSEMBLY:
CLUB LENGTH: 42½"
SWINGWEIGHT: D-4
NOTE: No weight added in shaft tip

LADIES' HERO DRIVER SPECIFICATIONS SUMMARY

HEAD:
MATERIAL: Persimmon, Laminated Maple or Metal Wood
LOFT: 12°
LIE: 54°
FACE ANGLE: 1° Hook
BULGE AND ROLL RADIUS: 10" Radius Bulge, 12" Radius Roll

SHAFT:
MATERIAL: TT Lite or Flex Flow (lightweight steel)
FLEX: Ladies'
FLEX POINT: Mid to Low (TT Lite is mid; Flex Flow is low)

GRIP:
MATERIAL: Victory or other good rubber grip
SIZE: ¹⁄₆₄" oversize under left hand, ¹⁄₃₂" oversize under right hand

ASSEMBLY:
CLUB LENGTH: 41½"
SWINGWEIGHT: C-9
NOTE: No weight added in shaft tip

■ Expected Results Using the Hero Driver

First of all, I am not advocating shorter golf clubs for people. This driver utilizes all the special specifications and component combinations I can think of to make it easy to hit, feel solid and go straighter. Use it as a fitting tool to prove to yourself and your customers that a driver can be made easier to hit. It will also help you to isolate certain problems in fitting a particular person or in solving problems of your own.

Keep in mind that the Hero Driver is a starting point. Start by hitting this ultimate game improvement driver and then make recommendations based on what the golfer can effectively handle. For example: Let's say we are working with a fairly good player who just cannot hit the driver. In checking, we find that the driver has a 5 degree open or slice face angle, but all the other specifications are quite close. During the hitting evaluation, we let the player hit the Hero Driver. He obviously will hit it very well. Does this mean that we should recommend those exact Hero Driver specs to him? Probably not. First of all, it is apparent why he can hit the Hero Driver better than his own driver. The 5 degree more closed face on the Hero now allows him to hit the club straighter, more solidly and with proper trajectory.

Next, it was determined from the face impact location testing that this player hits the ball near the face center, so a 43" driver length can be easily handled. Also, the player swings fast enough to fit into an "S" flex, but likes the TT Lite shaft in our Hero Driver test club. So, we spec out a TT Lite "S" flex shaft. This player has large hands and fits into a $\frac{1}{32}$" oversize grip under the left hand. He did, however, like the feel of our Hero grip, especially under the right hand. So, we can try $\frac{1}{32}$" oversize under the left hand and $\frac{3}{64}$" oversize under the right hand in keeping with our Hero club concept. Finally, we would probably specify the swingweight to be D-2 due to the length change from 42½" to 43". The lie angle would be changed to 55 degrees also because of the length change. This example shows how to best use the Hero Driver as a fitting tool.

Again, the hero is a very good starting point and for many golfers may not need any adjustments. The point is, use it and analyze its effect on a player's ability to hit the ball, and how the club complements a player's individual attributes and abilities.

■ Building Drivers for Distance

Building a driver to hit the ball farther for virtually any golfer is quite easy if you stick to the facts and shy away from all the myths and promises that golf club advertisements make. There are basically two main ingredients to increase distance: 1) Increase the club's length and, 2) Lighten the head weight. Of course, to come up with the magic long driver for you, the other fitting variables need strong consideration because these same two ingredients for added distance are also the same ones for hitting the ball more crooked, less solid and generally more inconsistent.

We have mentioned throughout the fitting material in this book that the goal in fitting is an acceptable compromise between distance and direction. This applies mostly to the driver because it is such an important determinant in the outcome of each round of golf. Many times you will have someone come in for a fitting with their main goal to gain back lost distance. This fitting goal is much easier to achieve if the player's present equipment does not come close to fitting properly. However, if the person has good, properly fitting equipment already and they want more distance; then we must work to increase the club's length and to lighten the head weight. It should be apparent that this approach will not produce acceptable trade-offs in distance and direction for everyone; but, with good, practical club fitting knowledge on your part, you can achieve success with many golfers. It's definitely worth a try. Having a few longer and lighter driver test clubs made up will quickly prove whether it will work or not.

■ Fitting Putter Length and Lie Angle

The lie angle of most putters ranges from 68 degrees to 78 degrees, with the average being about 72 degrees. Keep in mind that any putter lie angle which exceeds 80 degrees is illegal according to U.S.G.A. Rule 4-1b. At address, the putter should be touching the ground at a point directly under the sweet spot or as close to the center of the face as possible. If the putter does not sole in this manner, it can be bent in the hosel area or the lower portion of the shaft to adjust its lie.

Most putter lengths range from 32 inches to 36 inches, with the average men's putter length around 34 or 35 inches and the women's 33 to 34 inches. Table 65-25 has been developed to provide an average putter length and length range by player height category.

Height Category	Length Range	Average Length
TABLE 65-25		
[1] **Putter Length by Height Category**		
Shorter Women	30"-32"	31"
Average Women	32"-34"	33"
Taller Women	34"-36"	35"
Shorter Men	32"-35"	33½"
Average Men	34"-36"	35"
Taller Men	35"-37"	36½"

[1] This table should be used for reference only.

The best way to fit proper putter length and lie angle is to use the Putter Fitter Tool, available through The GolfWorks®. The Putter Fitter works like this: the player addresses the putt and places his hands on the Putter Fitter in a manner in which he is comfortable with the length. During this procedure you must make sure the player is in the proper posture position and proper lie position. Figure 65-54 shows how to do this. Note the importance of placing the player in the correct putting position. Do

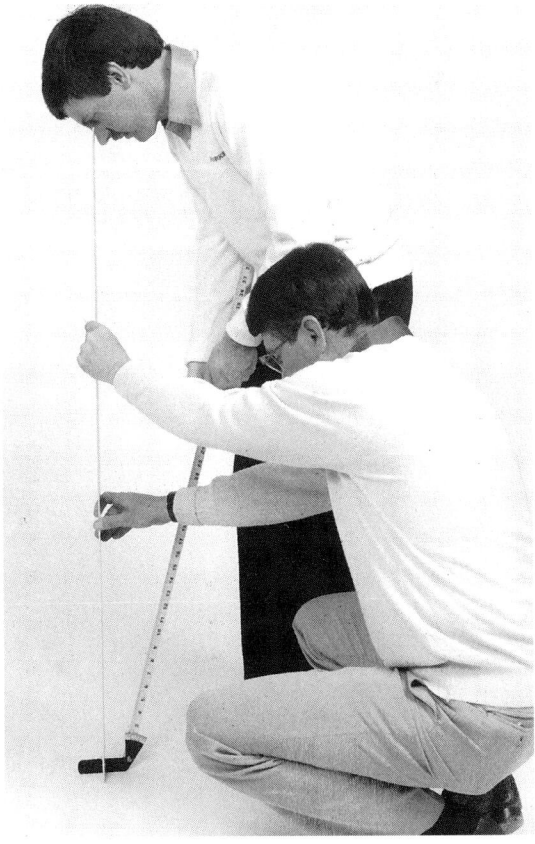

Figure 65-54
Using the Putter Fitter with the player in the proper putting position

not overlook eye position over the ball, hand position, elbows, etc. Next, read the correct putter length from the Putter Fitter shaft a point ½" above the top of the left hand (for right-handed golfers). Now, simply press the Putter Fitter's adjustable head flush against the floor or putting surface and read off the lie angle. Finally, it is a simple matter of picking out the correct putter and possibly altering the length and/or lie angle according to the putter fitter results.

■ Fitting Wedges

The number of different kinds of wedges on the market far outnumber the different iron club designs available. As a matter of fact, wedges are only second to putters in varieties available. Also, there are a number of wedge classifications, each having its own particular characteristics. Because of all this, it is important to thoroughly study wedges.

If a golfer carries a wedge or wedges in his/her bag, chances are that during a round more shots will be hit with the wedges than any other club in the bag, with the exception of the putter, However, in most all cases, the better the wedge play, the fewer the putts taken. The wedges are very important clubs and should be thoroughly understood regarding design, function, playability and proper fitting.

It simply amazes me at the number of golfers who play on courses which have sand traps and yet they do not carry a sand wedge. Sand wedges, pitching wedges, dual wedges and Third Wedges™ are designed to make certain shots easier. Understanding the various design attributes of wedges, along with why and how they work, gives a valuable insight into fitting wedges and using them more effectively during play.

■ Tips for Fitting Seniors

Generally when fitting average senior golfers, you will be confronted with a changing game pattern. Usually, as result of lost distance off the tee, it is not possible to get home in regulation on many holes. This puts more emphasis on the short game and putting, while throughout this change the handicap has been creeping upward. The questions are: "What can be done?" and "Where do we start?" There is nothing magic here. All of the fitting skills we have been learning apply here as well. However, there are some specific areas that can be looked into which hopefully will give positive results.

The first area to look at is how to hit the tee shot farther. We have discussed this subject thoroughly already. However, for this discussion let us ignore all the fitting details and make a few recommendations. I will give you the recommendations that have generally worked best for me and it is then your job to make sure the club or clubs fit properly for each individual case.

Assuming a fairly smooth swing, here are some specifications for a driver which should gain back at least ten or maybe fifteen yards distance. The key to this club is to use the True Temper® Release shaft or the Dynalite shaft in the proper flex. These are very light, do most of their bending near the tip area, have very little torque and are quite forgiving on off-center hits.

Driver for Seniors:
• Length: 43½" long (try 44" if it stays in the fairway and feels solid 90% of the time)
• Lie: Standard (depending on length)
• Loft: 11 degrees
• Face angle: 0 degrees square
• Shaft: True Temper® Release or Dynalite in the proper flex
• Grip: Victory or any good rubber grip fit to the player's hand size. Make grip slightly larger under the right hand.
• Swingweight: C-8 or C-9

Because of the fact that many seniors no longer hit as many greens as they once did, a set makeup change may be in order. Look at the possibility of carrying three wedges. Consider strongly eliminating the #2 and #3 irons in favor of more lofted woods. Look at the heavy soleplated trouble woods and also metal woods. The game improvement type head designs coupled with game improvement type golf shafts will usually help the most.

The point is, analyze the particular senior's game very closely. Use the Fitting Scorecards on two or maybe three rounds of golf. There are ways to help, but it takes some investigating and experimenting to find all of them.

■ Tips for Fitting Women

There are basically two common problems that the clubfitter will encounter when fitting women. First, most women play with golf clubs which are too long for them and in some cases also too heavy. Secondly, most women do not play with a set makeup which will maximize their scoring ability. Possibly, the set makeup problem exists because husbands go out and buy their wives a set of clubs with no regard for proper fitting. Women need to be fit also.

Here are some additional but general observations that should help:
• Use game improvement golf clubs with heel, toe and sole weighting.
• Make sure all woods have face angles square or hooked slightly.
• Consider ladies' petite golf club lengths which are usually ½" shorter than ladies' standard.
• Fit women with a good quality putter in proper length and lie. Putter should be heel to toe weighted.
• Consider irons with a set-makeup starting with the #5 or #4 iron.

Of course, all of this is very general and was derived from my own fitting experience. The point is, do not overlook anything that makes a golf club easier to hit and may possibly lower one's score.

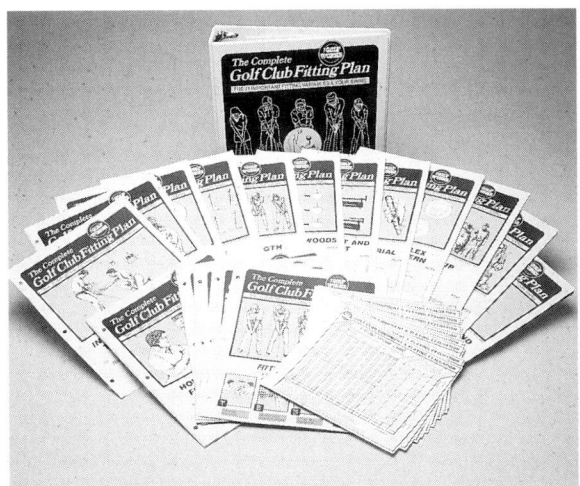

For more information on fitting, Ralph Maltby's
***The Complete Golf Club Fitting Plan* is available**
from the GolfWorks®.

PERSONAL INTERVIEW

STATISTICS

1. Height _____ ft. _____ in.
2. Weight _____ lbs.
3. Age _____ yrs.
4. Male _____ Female _____
5. Right Hand Golfer _____
6. Left Hand Golfer _____
7. Number of years playing golf _____ yrs.
8. Current Handicap _____
9. Handicap is going up _____
10. Handicap is going down _____
11. What is your average score _____
12. Highest score previous 12 months _____
13. Lowest score previous 12 months _____
14. Average number rounds per month during season _____
15. Have you ever taken lessons? ☐ Yes ☐ No
16. Have you taken lessons during the last year ☐ Yes ☐ No
17. Do you hit practice balls before playing?
    ☐ Regularly ☐ Never ☐ Sometimes
18. Do you hit practice putts before playing?
    ☐ Regularly ☐ Never ☐ Sometimes
19. Do you ever hit practice balls just to practice?
    ☐ Regularly ☐ Never ☐ Sometimes
20. Do you ever practice putting just to practice?
    ☐ Regularly ☐ Never ☐ Sometimes
    General comments on practicing: _____

PHYSICAL LIMITATIONS

21. Do you have any physical pain when you swing?
    ☐ Yes ☐ No
    If yes, explain _____
    Is it ☐ Permanent ☐ Temporary ☐ Recurring
22. If you have arthritis, does it affect your grip at any time from address through the swing?
    ☐ Yes ☐ No ☐ Not Applicable
23. Do you have any other physical limitations that affect your swing? ☐ Yes ☐ No
    If yes, explain _____

PLAYING CHARACTERISTICS

24. When you hit a poor drive, do you have a specific tendency to: (Answer more than one if necessary)
    ☐ Top it   ☐ Push it right
    ☐ Sky it   ☐ Slice it right
    ☐ Hit it very low   ☐ Straight but unsolid hit
    ☐ Pull it left   ☐ Very inconsistent
    ☐ Hook it left   ☐ Don't know
25. What is your confidence level with your driver?
    ☐ Very confident   ☐ Some confidence
    ☐ Have confidence   ☐ No confidence
26. What do you think of your driver length? (i.e. club length 43'', 43½'', etc.)
    ☐ Too long   ☐ Length OK
    ☐ Too short   ☐ Don't know

27. How does the weight of your driver feel to you?
    ☐ Too heavy   ☐ Weight OK
    ☐ Too light   ☐ Don't know
28. When you hit a poor iron shot, do you have a specific tendency to: (Answer more than one if necessary)
    ☐ Top it   ☐ Push it right
    ☐ Sky it   ☐ Slice it right
    ☐ Hit it very low   ☐ Straight but unsolid hit
    ☐ Pull it left   ☐ Very inconsistent
    ☐ Hook it left   ☐ Don't know
29. When hitting a long or mid iron approach shot to the green is your tendency more often than not to:
    ☐ Hit the Green
    ☐ On line but short of the green
    ☐ On line but over the green
    ☐ Left of the green
    ☐ Right of the green
    ☐ Be very inconsistent
    ☐ Don't know
30. When hitting a short iron (#8, 9 or any wedge) approach shot to the green is your tendency more often than not to:
    ☐ Hit the green
    ☐ On line but short of the green
    ☐ On line but over the green
    ☐ Left of the green
    ☐ Right of the green
    ☐ Be very inconsistent
    ☐ Don't know
31. What is the longest iron you hit with confidence?
    ☐ #1 iron   ☐ #4 iron
    ☐ #2 iron   ☐ #5 iron
    ☐ #3 iron   ☐ Don't know
32. How does the weight of your irons feel to you?
    ☐ Too heavy   ☐ Weight OK
    ☐ Too light   ☐ Don't know
33. How well can you get out of a bunker around the green?
    ☐ No problem with sand play
    ☐ Out and on the green 95% of the time
    ☐ Usually out and on the green
    ☐ Usually stay in bunker
    ☐ Usually hit over the green
    ☐ Very inconsistent
    ☐ Don't know
34. What is your confidence level regarding bunker play?
    ☐ Very confident   ☐ Some confidence
    ☐ Have confidence   ☐ No confidence
35. Do you have one or more favorite clubs that you have complete confidence in? ☐ Yes ☐ No
    Please list 1. _____
               2. _____
               3. _____

GOALS, WANTS & PREFERENCES

36. My immediate goal in golf is:
    ☐ I'll spend a lot of time and energy to improve as rapidly as possible
    ☐ I'll spend a reasonable amount of time and effort to improve
    ☐ I can spend very little time but want to improve my game
    ☐ I just want to find out if my equipment is right for me

37. My future goal regarding my handicap is to be:
- ☐ A scratch handicap (72)
- ☐ A low handicap 1-8 (73-82)
- ☐ A middle handicap 9-15 (83-89)
- ☐ An average golfer 16-22 (90-98)
- ☐ Don't know

38. From your own point of view, check off any personal wants that apply: (Check as many as you like, but only if you feel you have a problem in that area)
- ☐ I want to hit the ball higher
- ☐ I want to hit the ball lower
- ☐ I want to stop slicing the ball
- ☐ I want to stop pushing the ball
- ☐ I want to stop hooking the ball
- ☐ I want to stop pulling the ball
- ☐ I want to hit the ball straighter
- ☐ I want to hit the ball longer
- ☐ I want to drive the ball with more consistency
- ☐ I want to be able to hit long irons
- ☐ I want to hit my short irons with more accuracy
- ☐ I want to putt better
- ☐ I want to get the ball up & down around greens

- ☐ I want to be a better bunker player
- ☐ Any other wants, explain _____

39. Do you have a preference in the type of wood heads you play?
- ☐ Persimmon wood heads ☐ Metal wood heads
- ☐ Laminated Maple wood heads ☐ Graphite wood heads
- ☐ No preference

40. Do you have a preference in the type of iron heads you play?
- ☐ Forged iron heads ☐ Graphite iron heads
- ☐ Cast iron heads ☐ No preference

41. Do you have a preference in grip materials?
- ☐ Rubber ☐ Leather
- ☐ Rubber and cord combination ☐ No preference

42. Do you have a preference in shaft materials?
- ☐ Steel ☐ Titanium
- ☐ Lightweight steel ☐ Stainless steel
- ☐ Very lightweight steel ☐ Other composites
- ☐ Graphite ☐ No preference

PERSONAL INTERVIEW SUMMARY

STATISTICS

You are a **(8)** _____ handicap and your game is **(9,10)** *improving, getting worse, staying the same.* You play an average of **(14)** _____ rounds per month and before playing you **(17)** *regularly, never, sometimes* hit practice balls and **(18)** *regularly, never, sometimes* hit practice putts. At other times you **(19)** *regularly, never, sometimes* hit practice balls on the range and you **(20)** *regularly, never, sometimes* practice your putting.

PHYSICAL LIMITATIONS

You **(21)** *do, do not* have physical limitations that affect your swing or game. **(21)** *If yes, explain:* _____

PLAYING CHARACTERISTICS

You perceive your own game and your equipment in the following manner. First, when you hit a poor drive you tend to **(24)** _____ and when you hit a poor iron shot you tend to **(28)** _____ . More specifically, when you hit a long or mid iron shot to the green your tendency is to **(29)** _____ and when hitting a short iron approach shot to the green your tendency is to **(30)** _____ . When you hit a bunker around the green you **(33)** _____ and you **(34)** _____ confidence in your bunker play. You have **(25)** _____ confidence in your driver and you also feel its length is **(26)** _____ and its weight is **(27)** _____ . The longest iron in your bag that you hit with confidence is your **(31)** _____ and you think that the weight of your irons regarding your own feel is **(32)** _____ . You **(33)** *do, do not* have a favorite club that you have complete confidence in. **(35)** *List:* _____ .

GOALS, WANTS & PREFERENCES

The professional golf club fitting plan will evaluate your present equipment and swing and make a specific equipment fitting recommendation. From this, you intend as a main immediate goal to **(36)** _____

_____ .

Your future goal regarding your handicap level is to be **(37)** _____ .

In general, you feel the following areas of your game need improving. You want to:
(38)
- ☐ Hit the ball higher
- ☐ Hit the ball lower
- ☐ Stop slicing the ball
- ☐ Stop pushing the ball
- ☐ Stop hooking the ball
- ☐ Stop pulling the ball
- ☐ Hit the ball straighter
- ☐ Hit the ball longer
- ☐ Drive with more consistency
- ☐ Hit long irons better
- ☐ Hit short irons with more accuracy
- ☐ Putt better
- ☐ Get up and down around greens
- ☐ Be a better bunker player
- ☐ Other, *explain* _____

In recognizing that many different types of equipment can be properly fit to most individuals, you have, to some degree certain equipment preferences. You prefer **(39)** _____ wood heads, **(40)** _____ iron heads, **(41)** _____ grips and **(42)** _____ shafts.

COMMENTS ON PERSONAL INTERVIEW

_____

_____

_____

PRESENT GOLF CLUB EVALUATION

ABBREVIATION KEY   STR. = Straight   − = Undersize   RT. = Right   BNCE. = Bounce Sole
FOR THIS PAGE   + = Oversize   SQ. = Square   LT. = Left   DIG = Dig or Scoop Sole

COMMENTS	SPECIFICATION		WOODS							IRONS											
		1	2	3	4	5	6	7	1	2	3	4	5	6	7	8	9	PW	SW	3W
1	Mfgr., Brand, Approx. Year Set Makeup																			
2	Swingweight	1	2	3	4	5	6	7	1	2	3	4	5	6	7	8	9	P	S	T
3	Total Weight — Actual / Diff.	1	2	3	4	5	6	7	1	2	3	4	5	6	7	8	9	P	S	T
4	Club Length — Spec. / Actual / Diff.	1	2	3	4	5	6	7	1	2	3	4	5	6	7	8	9	P	S	T
5	Loft Angle — Spec. / Actual / Diff.	1	2	3	4	5	6	7	1	2	3	4	5	6	7	8	9	P	S	T
6	Lie Angle — Spec. / Actual / Diff.	1	2	3	4	5	6	7	1	2	3	4	5	6	7	8	9	P	S	T
7	Shaft Pattern, Flex, Material																			
8	Shaft — Heel to 1st Step Check																			
9	Shaft Straightness Check	STR. BENT	STR. BENT	STR. BENT	STR. BENT	STR. BENT	STR. BENT	STR. BENT	STR. BENT	STR. BENT	STR. BENT	STR. BENT	STR. BENT	STR. BENT	STR. BENT	STR. BENT	STR. BENT	STR. BENT	STR. BENT	STR. BENT
10	Shaft Tip Slugging Check	NONE YES	NONE YES	NONE YES	NONE YES	NONE YES	NONE YES	NONE YES	NONE YES	NONE YES	NONE YES	NONE YES	NONE YES	NONE YES	NONE YES	NONE YES	NONE YES	NONE YES	NONE YES	NONE YES
11	Grip Style, Material																			
12	Grip Size	+ STD. −	+ STD. −	+ STD. −	+ STD. −	+ STD. −	+ STD. −	+ STD. −	+ STD. −	+ STD. −	+ STD. −	+ STD. −	+ STD. −	+ STD. −	+ STD. −	+ STD. −	+ STD. −	+ STD. −	+ STD. −	+ STD. −
13	Grip Counterbalance Check	NONE YES	NONE YES	NONE YES	NONE YES	NONE YES	NONE YES	NONE YES	NONE YES	NONE YES	NONE YES	NONE YES	NONE YES	NONE YES	NONE YES	NONE YES	NONE YES	NONE YES	NONE YES	NONE YES
14	Grip Alignment Check	SQ. RT. LT.	SQ. RT. LT.	SQ. RT. LT.	SQ. RT. LT.	SQ. RT. LT.	SQ. RT. LT.	SQ. RT. LT.	SQ. RT. LT.	SQ. RT. LT.	SQ. RT. LT.	SQ. RT. LT.	SQ. RT. LT.	SQ. RT. LT.	SQ. RT. LT.	SQ. RT. LT.	SQ. RT. LT.	SQ. RT. LT.	SQ. RT. LT.	SQ. RT. LT.
15	Irons — Sole Angle Check								OK BNCE. DIG	OK BNCE. DIG	OK BNCE. DIG	OK BNCE. DIG	OK BNCE. DIG	OK BNCE. DIG	OK BNCE. DIG	OK BNCE. DIG	OK BNCE. DIG	OK BNCE. DIG	OK BNCE. DIG	OK BNCE. DIG
16	Woods — Face Angle	1	2	3	4	5	6	7												
17	Woods — Bulge Radius	1	2	3	4	5	6	7												
18	Woods — Roll Radius	1	2	3	4	5	6	7												

GENERAL CONDITION AND EVALUATION: _____

_____

_____

_____

PUTTER EVALUATION	Mfgr., Brand, Year	Swingweight	Total Weight	Club Length	Loft	Lie	Shaft Straightness Check	Grip Alignment Check	Comments: _____
							STR. BENT	SQ. RT. LT.	

780

STEP 3

HITTING RESULTS EVALUATION

It is best to start by using the player's present golf clubs; and then after this initial evaluation, sample or test golf clubs may be hit and compared.

1 FACE IMPACT LOCATION GRID

Procedure: Use impact transfer decals on face of Driver and #5 Iron, 10 hits recommended. Place X's on drawings in proper grid indicating location of each hit.

Start with present #5 Iron and Driver. Optional grid drawings are for any optional test clubs.

Comments: _____
_____
_____
_____
_____

#5 IRON

Present #5 Iron   Test #5 Iron

DRIVER

Club Description   Club Description

Present Driver   Test Driver

Club Description   Club Description

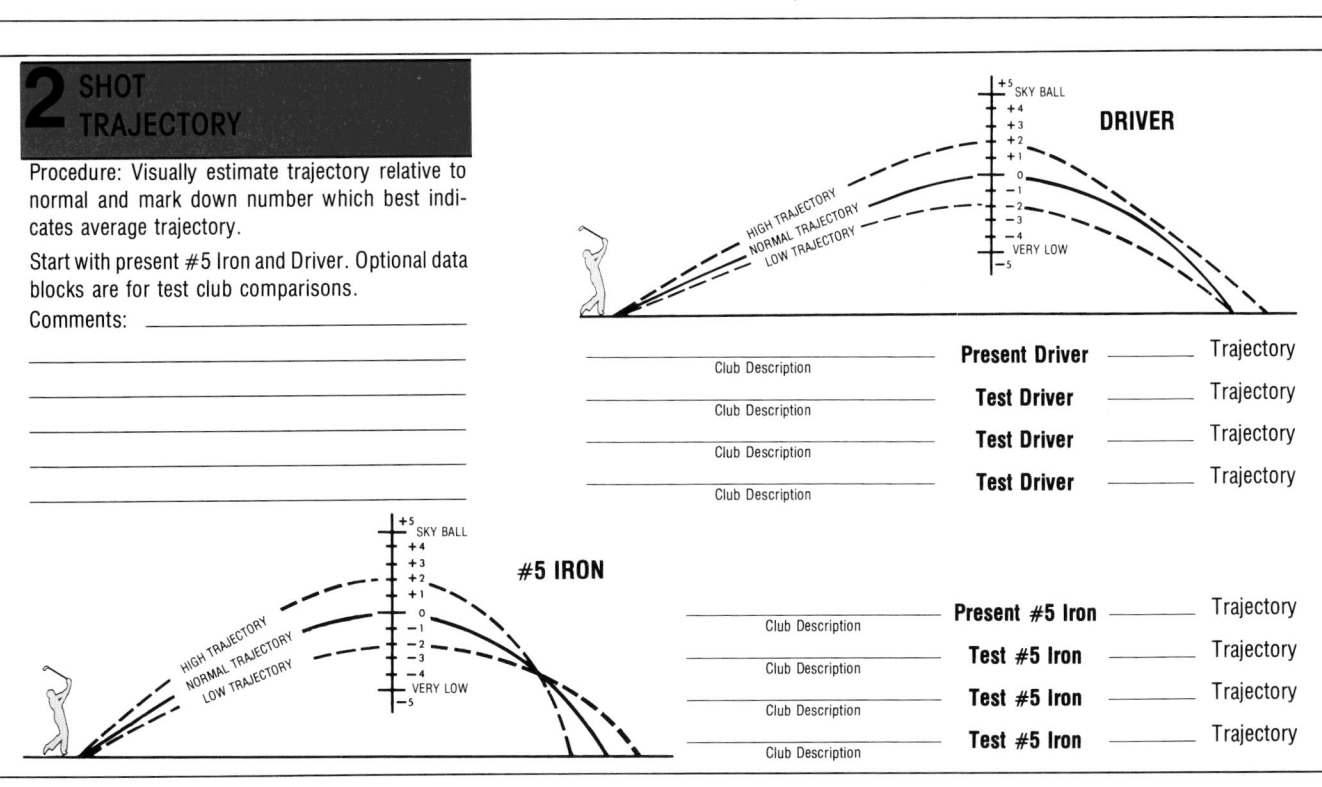

2 SHOT TRAJECTORY

Procedure: Visually estimate trajectory relative to normal and mark down number which best indicates average trajectory.

Start with present #5 Iron and Driver. Optional data blocks are for test club comparisons.

Comments: _____
_____
_____
_____
_____
_____
_____

DRIVER

+5 SKY BALL / +4 / +3 / +2 / +1 / 0 / −1 / −2 / −3 / −4 VERY LOW / −5

HIGH TRAJECTORY / NORMAL TRAJECTORY / LOW TRAJECTORY

Club Description	Present Driver	_____	Trajectory
Club Description	Test Driver	_____	Trajectory
Club Description	Test Driver	_____	Trajectory
Club Description	Test Driver	_____	Trajectory

#5 IRON

+5 SKY BALL / +4 / +3 / +2 / +1 / 0 / −1 / −2 / −3 / −4 VERY LOW / −5

HIGH TRAJECTORY / NORMAL TRAJECTORY / LOW TRAJECTORY

Club Description	Present #5 Iron	_____	Trajectory
Club Description	Test #5 Iron	_____	Trajectory
Club Description	Test #5 Iron	_____	Trajectory
Club Description	Test #5 Iron	_____	Trajectory

3 CARRY DISTANCE

Procedure: Estimate carry against the average distance most players hit a Driver and a #5 Iron.

Start with present #5 Iron and Driver.

Comments: _____
_____
_____
_____

	Driver	#5 Iron	Driver	#5 Iron	Driver	#5 Iron	Driver	#5 Iron
Very Long								
Long								
Longer Than Avg.								
Average								
Shorter Than Avg.								
Short								
Very Short								
	PRESENT CLUBS		**TEST CLUBS**		**TEST CLUBS**		**TEST CLUBS**	
	Driver Description		Driver Description		Driver Description		Driver Description	
	#5 Iron Description		#5 Iron Description		#5 Iron Description		#5 Iron Description	

4 DIRECTIONAL CONTROL FLIGHT PATTERN

Procedure: Hit each of the categories of clubs listed below and circle the appropriate number next to it to best indicate the ball's flight. Use X's to indicate test clubs.

Hit the present clubs first and then any test clubs.

Comments: _____

Category	Flight Pattern								
Driver	1	2	3	4	5	6	7	8	9
Fairway Woods	1	2	3	4	5	6	7	8	9
Long Irons	1	2	3	4	5	6	7	8	9
Mid Irons	1	2	3	4	5	6	7	8	9
Short Irons	1	2	3	4	5	6	7	8	9

FLIGHT PATTERN KEY

(1) Straight
(2) Starts Left — Curves Right
(3) Starts Right — Curves Left
(4) Starts Straight — Curves Left
(5) Starts Straight — Curves Right

(6) Starts Left — Flies Straight
(7) Starts Right — Flies Straight
(8) Starts Right — Curves Left
(9) Starts Right — Curves Right

Target Line

5 LIE ANGLE TEST AT IMPACT

Procedure: Use a plywood board or hard rubber range mat and non-spiked shoes. Place a strip of ¾'' masking tape on sole as shown. Note: Always measure to the center of the mark after each hit. Write the actual club number hit on the drawing above the appropriate arrow.

Testing a long, middle and short iron is recommended, such as a #3, 6, 9 Iron. If desired, all Irons can be tested. Also, this procedure works well on fairway woods.

Comments: _____

IRONS — Proper Fit Lie Angles

1	2	3	4	5	6	7	8	9	P	S	T

WOODS — Proper Fit Lie Angles

1	2	3	4	5	6	7

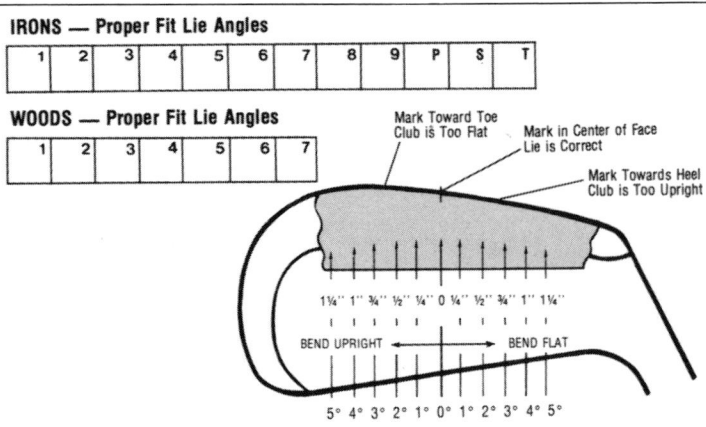

Mark Toward Toe Club is Too Flat
Mark in Center of Face Lie is Correct
Mark Towards Heel Club is Too Upright

1¼'' 1'' ¾'' ½'' ¼'' 0 ¼'' ½'' ¾'' 1'' 1¼''

BEND UPRIGHT ← → BEND FLAT

5° 4° 3° 2° 1° 0° 1° 2° 3° 4° 5°

6 HOW WELL WERE THE FOLLOWING CATEGORIES OF CLUBS HIT

Procedure: Rate clubs on a scale of 1-10 as shown. Circle appropriate number for player's present clubs. Use X's for any test clubs.

	Poor				Average				Excellent	
Driver	1	2	3	4	5	6	7	8	9	10
Fairway Woods	1	2	3	4	5	6	7	8	9	10
Long Irons (1, 2, 3)	1	2	3	4	5	6	7	8	9	10
Mid Irons (5, 6, 7)	1	2	3	4	5	6	7	8	9	10
Short Irons (8, 9, PW)	1	2	3	4	5	6	7	8	9	10

7 PRELIMINARY NOTES ON POSSIBLE HITTING PROBLEM AREAS USING PRESENT CLUBS

____ Lofts Too Weak   ____ Lofts Too Strong
____ Lie Too Flat   ____ Lie Too Upright
____ Grips Too Large   ____ Grips Too Small
____ Shafts Too Flexible   ____ Shafts Too Stiff
____ Clubs Too Long   ____ Clubs Too Short
____ Clubs Too Heavy   ____ Clubs Too Light
____ Woods: Too Much Slice   ____ Woods: Too Much Hook

Other: _____

8 GRIP SIZE FITTING

Procedure: Use the various grip size samples beginning with standard size. Check grip size at two middle fingers and palm.

MEN'S   LADIES'   GRIP SIZE _____

Comments: _____

9 LESSONS RECOMMENDATION

The hitting results have indicated that to maximize this fitting evaluation golf lessons are recommended in the following area(s). (Example — Grip, Setup & Posture, Swing, etc.)

____ Yes   ____ No

Comments: _____

10 NOTES OR CONCLUSIONS ON HITTING EVALUATION

_____
_____

11 PUTTER CHECK ON PUTTING GREEN OR ARTIFICIAL SURFACE

Procedure: Check for proper length, lie, loft and head weight.

Comments: _____

FITTING RECOMMENDATION

DATE _____ CUSTOMER NAME _____ FILLED OUT BY _____

1 CLUB HEAD DESIGN

- ☐ Model or Brand — Irons _____
- ☐ Model or Brand — Woods _____
- ☐ Stain Color _____ ☐ Insert Color and Type _____
- Club Head Notes: _____

2 LOFT

Woods
- ☐ Strong 1°
- ☐ Standard
- ☐ Weak 1°
- ☐ Other _____

Irons
- ☐ Strong 2°
- ☐ Strong 1°
- ☐ Standard
- ☐ Weak 1°
- ☐ Weak 2°
- ☐ Other _____

3 LIE

Woods
- ☐ Flat 2°
- ☐ Flat 1°
- ☐ Standard
- ☐ Upright 1°
- ☐ Upright 2°
- ☐ Other _____

Irons
- ☐ Flat 2°
- ☐ Flat 1°
- ☐ Standard
- ☐ Upright 1°
- ☐ Upright 2°
- ☐ Other _____

4 CLUB LENGTH

Woods
- ☐ Standard (43" men's #1)
  (42" ladies' #1)
- ☐ ½" longer
- ☐ 1" longer
- ☐ ½" shorter
- ☐ Other _____

Irons
- ☐ Standard (39" men's #2)
  (37½" ladies #3)
- ☐ ½" longer
- ☐ 1" longer
- ☐ ½" shorter
- ☐ Other _____

5 FACE ANGLE — WOODS

- ☐ Open (2° Slice)
- ☐ Slightly Open (1° Slice)
- ☐ Square (0°)
- ☐ Slightly Closed (1° Hook)
- ☐ Closed (2° Hook)
- ☐ Other _____

Bulge and Roll Notes: ___

Facing Notes: _____

6 SWINGWEIGHT & TOTAL WEIGHT

SW Woods _____
Specify

SW Irons _____
Specify

Notes on Total Weight: _____

7 GRIP SIZE

- ☐ 1/16" oversize
- ☐ 3/64" oversize
- ☐ 1/32" oversize
- ☐ 1/64" oversize
- ☐ Standard
- ☐ 1/64" undersize
- ☐ Special Arthritic
- ☐ Other _____

Grip Core Size Notes: ___

8 GRIP MATERIAL & SIZE

- ☐ Rubber
- ☐ Rubber and Cord
- ☐ Leather
- ☐ Model _____
- ☐ Color _____

Grip Notes: _____

9 SHAFT FLEX

- ☐ L-Ladies'
- ☐ A-Flexible
- ☐ R-Medium
- ☐ S-Stiff
- ☐ X-Extra Stiff
- ☐ Other _____

☐ Tipping Amount _____

10 SHAFT MATERIAL & PATTERN

- ☐ Steel
- ☐ Lt. Wt. Steel
- ☐ Very Lt. Wt. Steel
- ☐ Graphite
- ☐ Other _____

PATTERN
- ☐ Dynamic
- ☐ Dynamic Gold
- ☐ FM Precision
- ☐ Jet Step
- ☐ Pro-Fit
- ☐ TT Lite
- ☐ Extralite
- ☐ Flex-Flow
- ☐ UCV-304
- ☐ Microtaper
- ☐ ND
- ☐ Other _____

11 SET MAKEUP

Woods 1 2 3 4 5 6 7 8 9 10 11 12 13 14 15
☐ ☐ ☐ ☐ ☐ ☐ ☐ ☐ ☐ ☐ ☐ ☐ ☐ ☐ ☐

Irons 1 2 3 4 5 6 7 8 9 PW SW 3W
☐ ☐ ☐ ☐ ☐ ☐ ☐ ☐ ☐ ☐ ☐ ☐

- ☐ Men's Right Hand
- ☐ Men's Left Hand
- ☐ Ladies' Right Hand
- ☐ Ladies' Left Hand

ADDITIONAL COMMENTS AND RECOMMENDATIONS — FITTING OR SWING

_____
_____
_____
_____

PUTTER RECOMMENDATION

1 CLUB HEAD DESIGN

Model, Brand or Type
_____
_____
_____

2 LOFT

- ☐ Strong 1°
- ☐ Standard
- ☐ Weak 1°
- ☐ Other _____

3 LIE

- ☐ Flat 2°
- ☐ Flat 1°
- ☐ Standard
- ☐ Upright 1°
- ☐ Upright 2°
- ☐ Other _____

4 LENGTH

- ☐ 32"
- ☐ 33"
- ☐ 34"
- ☐ 35"
- ☐ 36"
- ☐ Other _____

5 GRIP TYPE & MODEL

- ☐ Rubber
- ☐ Leather
Model _____

6 SWINGWEIGHT OR TOTAL WEIGHT

_____
(Specify)
Comments: _____
_____
_____
_____

Additional Putter Information: _____

GOLF CLUB EQUIPMENT & PLAYING EVALUATION

FITTING SCORE CARD

THE GOLF WORKS

CIRCLE PAR 3's
SQUARE PAR 5's

CIRCLE WOODS AND IRONS BELOW TO SHOW YOUR SET MAKEUP

Fairways Hit (H) / Missed Left (L) Right (R)
Greens Hit (H) Regulation / Missed Left (L) Right (R) / Short (S) Over (O)
Greenside Bunkers / Hit (H), Out & 1 Putt (1) / Out & 2 Putts (2)
Number of Putts / 1, 2, 3, or 4
Total Shots Per Hole

HOLE	WOODS 1	2	3	4	5	6	7	IRONS 1	2	3	4	5	6	7	8	9	PW	SW	3W	Fairway	Green	Bunker	Putts	Score
1																				H L R	H L R S O	H 1 2	1 2 3 4	
2																				H L R	H L R S O	H 1 2	1 2 3 4	
3																				H L R	H L R S O	H 1 2	1 2 3 4	
4																				H L R	H L R S O	H 1 2	1 2 3 4	
5																				H L R	H L R S O	H 1 2	1 2 3 4	
6																				H L R	H L R S O	H 1 2	1 2 3 4	
7																				H L R	H L R S O	H 1 2	1 2 3 4	
8																				H L R	H L R S O	H 1 2	1 2 3 4	
9																				H L R	H L R S O	H 1 2	1 2 3 4	
OUT																								
HOLE	1	2	3	4	5	6	7	1	2	3	4	5	6	7	8	9	PW	SW	3W	Fairway	Green	Bunker	Putts	Score
10																				H L R	H L R S O	H 1 2	1 2 3 4	
11																				H L R	H L R S O	H 1 2	1 2 3 4	
12																				H L R	H L R S O	H 1 2	1 2 3 4	
13																				H L R	H L R S O	H 1 2	1 2 3 4	
14																				H L R	H L R S O	H 1 2	1 2 3 4	
15																				H L R	H L R S O	H 1 2	1 2 3 4	
16																				H L R	H L R S O	H 1 2	1 2 3 4	
17																				H L R	H L R S O	H 1 2	1 2 3 4	
18																				H L R	H L R S O	H 1 2	1 2 3 4	
IN																								
TOTAL																								

NAME
COURSE
PAR
HDCP
DATE

©1985 Ralph Maltby Enterprises, Inc.

INSTRUCTIONS:
- Fill Card Out on Next Tee while Others in Your Group Hit
- Place an "X" in Woods and Irons Section to Indicate Clubs Hit on Each Hole
- Circle any "X" to Indicate any Unsolid Feeling Hit, Regardless of the Result
- Square Any "X" to Indicate a Chip Shot
- Circle Appropriate Letters and/or Numbers in Fairway, Green, Bunker & Putts Column
- At Bottom of "Putts" Column, in the "Total" Block, Write in Total Putts for the Round

COMMENTS: _____

CHAPTER 66

FITTING JUNIORS

Junior golf has been promoted heavily during the last fifteen years or so and consequently great numbers of boys and girls have taken up golf. The ultimate success of this program is to increase the number of future golfers and thereby increase the total golf market size. So, it would seem that getting juniors started in golf is half the battle and keeping them interested is the other half. Certainly, one of the important aspects to prolong interest is being able to create player successes early in their involvement with golf. It goes without saying that a proper environment with a qualified instructor/motivator is one key ingredient, but there is also another that is often overlooked — proper equipment. We are not talking about expensive custom made golf clubs as a necessity for a proper introduction to golf, but we are talking about using a little common sense. The information presented here will help guarantee success in hitting the ball somewhat straight and more importantly getting it airborne most every time.

Very little has been researched and written on the proper fitting of golf clubs for junior golfers. I began in 1978 collecting and researching information that would provide the much needed background data to allow for a more knowledgeable approach to this problem. Some of the data that was collected and organized appeared in a condensed form in Golf Magazine and also in the "Clubs for Kids" brochure published by the Professional Golfer's Association of America.

The information presented here is very complete and provides quite a bit of reference material, tips, hints and procedures for fitting juniors. Most of the material is in table form and has been developed for various uses. Tables 66-1, 66-2 and 66-3 provide complete in-depth reference data for fitting, cutting down or assembling clubs for junior boys and girls ages five through eighteen. Because Tables 66-1, 66-2 and 66-3 are so complete, it takes a few minutes to look up the required information, so Tables 66-4 and 66-5 were developed as "Quick Reference" charts. These two tables are very easy to use and provide the same data as Tables 66-1, 66-2 and 66-3, but are not as complete. For most club-fitting you will find that Tables 66-4 and 66-5 will be used most often. For "cutting down" and assembling clubs for juniors, the data from Tables 66-1, 66-2 and 66-3 will need to be used.

It is important to note that in Tables 66-1, 66-2 and 66-3 there are a number of footnote reference numbers. The footnotes explain in-depth the specific areas in the tables which may need additional amplification. Take some time to thoroughly study this material and it will provide a much better insight into those areas which are most important in junior clubfitting. Finally, always keep in mind that most all of the fitting rules and the other fitting information presented throughout the book also apply to fitting juniors.

■ Footnotes to Fitting Tables 66-1, 66-2 and 66-3 for Juniors

[1] Source: National Center for Health Statistics

[2] It is extremely important to understand that one cannot fit golf clubs to juniors using these tables unless other factors are also taken into consideration and certain adjustments made. Heights and weights listed by age group are national averages and cannot possibly take into account those individuals with larger or smaller bone structures that help to make up those averages.

The following guidelines and factors are intended to provide a basis for determining the proper length, shaft flex, swingweight range and set make-up in fitting clubs for boys and girls between the ages of 5 and 18.

Determine the junior's height. This factor will most importantly determine the length of clubs that he or she should probably be using. Notice that club length is also indicated by a length range to accommodate shorter or taller heights by age group.

Determine the junior's weight and age. These two factors usually give an indication of strength (i.e., the heavier the stronger, and the older the stronger). This will help determine what shaft flex and swingweight range that best fits the youth, although for 12 years old and younger the more flexible the shaft the better.

Natural athletic ability and coordination are other factors that must be considered as the youth gets older (usually 12 and beyond). As an example: the faster he or she can swing the clubhead and consistently hit the ball near the center of the clubhead (solid hit) will also help in determining shaft flex, swingweight and the longest length of club that can be handled while still maintaining this consistency of hit and good directional control. Keep in mind that the longer the club, the stiffer the shaft and the less the loft, the harder the club is to hit. Conversely, the shorter the club, the more flexible the shaft, and the greater the loft, the easier the club is to hit. This applies to all golfers as well.

The reasons are as follows:
- The longer the club, the more ability is required to hit the ball on the center of the clubface more of the time.
- The stiffer the shaft, the more unforgiving it is (in terms of feel and distance) on off center hits. In other words, it feels less solid and more clunky. A stiffer shaft will tend to hit the ball lower at slower swing speeds; however, a stiff shaft will hit the ball straighter than a shaft with more flex. The lower trajectory and feel aspects explain the problems associated with cutting adult clubs down for juniors.
- The less the loft angle (strong loft), the greater will be the penetration of the clubface into the ball; hence, higher head speeds are required to adequately compress it and a more exact center hit is required to provide a solid feel.

[3] The weight range column from age 5 through 13 lists only total weight and not swingweight. The reason for this is that the proper clubhead weight and length are not sufficient in most cases to obtain known swingweight values from golf club swingweight scales. Conversely, the total weight is not shown for ages 14 through 18 because of the great number of different type shafts that are available, each affecting total weight significantly.

[4] The "Age Equalization Factor" is simply defined as utilizing the increased lofts of the #1, #2, #3, #4 and #5 woods in combination with the length which best applies to that age group. The reason for it is to help a beginning or younger golfer to build confidence and enjoyment in the game. By fitting golf clubs to them that will get the ball airborne

TABLE 66-1
[2] Fitting Junior Boys by Age, Average Height and Average Weight

[1] Boy's Age	[1] Boy's Avg. Height		[1] Boy's Avg. Weight	Driving Wood				#5 Iron	
				Average Length	Length Range	Loft	[3] Weight Range	Average Length	Length Range
5	44"	(3'8")	37 lbs.	31"	30" - 32"	5 wood 23°	12 to 12½ oz. Total weight	27"	26" - 28"
6	46"	(3'10")	41 lbs.	31"	30" - 32"	5 wood 23°	12 to 12½ oz. Total weight	27"	26" - 28"
7	48"	(4')	47 lbs.	31"	30" - 32"	5 wood 23°	12 to 12½ oz. Total weight	27"	26" - 28"
8	49"	(4'1")	53 lbs.	35"	32½" - 37"	4 wood 20°	11½ - 12 oz. Total Weight	30½"	28½" - 32"
9	51"	(4'3")	60 lbs.	35"	32½" - 37"	4 wood 20°	11½ - 12 oz. Total Weight	30½"	28½" - 32"
10	53"	(4'5")	67 lbs.	35"	32½" - 37"	4 wood 20°	11½ - 12 oz. Total Weight	30½"	28½" - 32"
11	55"	(4'7")	73 lbs.	39"	38" - 40½"	3 wood 17°	11 to 11½ oz. Total Weight	33½"	32½" - 34½"
12	57½"	(4'9½")	83 lbs.	39"	38" - 40½"	3 wood 17°	11 to 11½ oz. Total Weight	33½"	32½" - 34½"
13	60"	(5')	94 lbs.	39"	38" - 40½"	3 wood 17°	11 to 11½ oz. Total Weight	33½"	32½" - 34½"
14	63¼"	(5'3¼")	109 lbs.	41½"	40½" - 42"	2 wood 14°	C-6 to D-0 Swingweight	36"	35" - 36½"
15	65¾"	(5'5¾")	124 lbs.	41½"	40½" - 42"	2 wood 14°	C-6 to D-0 Swingweight	36"	35" - 36½"
16	67¾"	(5'7¾")	134 lbs.	41½"	40½" - 42"	2 wood 14°	C-6 to D-0 Swingweight	36"	35" - 36½"
17	69"	(5'9")	142 lbs.	43"	42½" - 43½"	Driver 12°	C-9 to D-3 Swingweight	37"	36½" - 37½"
18	70"	(5'10")	149 lbs.	43"	42½" - 43½"	Driver 12°	C-9 to D-3 Swingweight	37"	36½" - 37½"

TABLE 66-1 Continued

[1] Boy's Age	Putter		Recommended Set Make-up	Shaft Flex Equivalent	Avg. Grip Size @ 2" Down From Butt	Avg. Grip Size Equivalent Terminology	Grip Size Range @ 2" Down from Butt
	Average Length	Length Range					
5	25"	24" - 26"	5 wood 5, 9 irons & P	L (Ladies')	.820"	1/32" under Ladies'	.805" - .835"
6	25"	24" - 26"	5 wood 5, 9 irons & P	L (Ladies')	.820"	1/32" under Ladies'	.805" - .835"
7	25"	24" - 26"	5 wood 5, 9 irons & P	L (Ladies')	.820"	1/32" under Ladies'	.805" - .835"
8	28½"	26½" - 30"	4 wood 5, 7, 9 irons & P	L (Ladies')	.835"	1/64" under Ladies'	.820" - .850"
9	28½"	26½" - 30"	4 wood 5, 7, 9 irons & P	L (Ladies')	.835"	1/64" under Ladies'	.820" - .850"
10	28½"	26½" - 30"	4 wood 5, 7, 9 irons & P	L (Ladies')	.835"	1/64" under Ladies'	.820" - .850"
11	31½"	30½" - 32"	3, 5 woods 3, 5, 7, 9 irons & P	L (Ladies')	.850"	Sandard Ladies'	.835" - .880"
12	31½"	30½" - 32"	3, 5 woods 3, 5, 7, 9 irons & P	L (Ladies')	.850"	Sandard Ladies'	.835" - .880"
13	31½"	30½" - 32"	3, 5 woods 3, 5, 7, 9 irons & P	L or A (Ladies' or Flexible)	.850"	Sandard Ladies'	.835" - .880"
14	33½"	32½" - 34"	2, 4, 5 woods 3 - 9 irons, PW, SW & P	A (Flexible)	.885"	1/64" under Men's	.850" - .900"
15	33½"	32½" - 34"	2, 4, 5 woods 3 - 9 irons, PW, SW & P	A (Flexible)	.885"	1/64" under Men's	.850" - .900"
16	33½"	32½" - 34"	2, 4, 5 woods 3 - 9 irons, PW, SW & P	A (Flexible)	.885"	1/64" under Men's	.850" - .900"
17	35"	34" - 36"	1, 3, 4, 5 woods 3 - 9 irons, PW, SW & P	R or S (Med. or Stiff)	.900"	Standard Men's	.885" - .930"
18	35"	34" - 36"	1, 3, 4, 5 woods 3 - 9 irons, PW, SW & P	R or S (Med. or Stiff)	.900"	Standard Men's	.885" - .930"

TABLE 66-2
[2]Fitting Junior Girls by Age, Average Height and Average Weight

[1]Girl's Age	[1]Girl's Avg. Height		[1]Girl's Avg. Weight	Driving Wood				#5 Iron	
				Average Length	Length Range	Loft	[3]Weight Range	Average Length	Length Range
5	43½"	(3'7½")	37 lbs.	31"	30" - 32"	5 wood 23°	12 to 12½ oz. Total weight	27"	26" - 28"
6	45½"	(3'9½")	41 lbs.	31"	30" - 32"	5 wood 23°	12 to 12½ oz. Total weight	27"	26" - 28"
7	47½"	(3'11½")	48 lbs.	31"	30" - 32"	5 wood 23°	12 to 12½ oz. Total weight	27"	26" - 28"
8	48½"	(4'½")	52 lbs.	35"	32½" - 37"	4 wood 20°	11½ - 12 oz. Total Weight	30½"	28½" - 32"
9	50¾"	(4'2¾")	61 lbs.	35"	32½" - 37"	4 wood 20°	11½ - 12 oz. Total Weight	30½"	28½" - 32"
10	53"	(4'5")	69 lbs.	35"	32½" - 37"	4 wood 20°	11½ - 12 oz. Total Weight	30½"	28½" - 32"
11	55¾"	(4'7¾")	77 lbs.	39"	38" - 40½"	3 wood 17°	11 to 11½ oz. Total Weight	33½"	32½" - 34½"
12	58"	(4'10")	87 lbs.	39"	38" - 40½"	3 wood 17°	11 to 11½ oz. Total Weight	33½"	32½" - 34½"
13	61"	(5'1")	103 lbs.	39"	38" - 40½"	3 wood 17°	11 to 11½ oz. Total Weight	33½"	32½" - 34½"
14	63"	(5'3")	110 lbs.	40"	39" - 41"	2 wood 15°	C-2 to C-5 Swingweight	34½"	34" - 35"
15	63¾"	(5'3¾")	118 lbs.	40"	39" - 41"	2 wood 15°	C-2 to C-5 Swingweight	34½"	34" - 35"
16	64"	(5'4")	124 lbs.	40"	39" - 41"	2 wood 15°	C-2 to C-5 Swingweight	34½"	34" - 35"
17	64"	(5'4")	127 lbs.	41½"	41" - 42½"	Driver 13°	C-5 to C-9 Swingweight	35½"	35" - 36½"
18	64"	(5'4")	127 lbs.	41½"	41" - 42½"	Driver 13°	C-5 to C-9 Swingweight	35½"	35" - 36½"

TABLE 66-2 Continued

[1]Girl's Age	Putter		Recommended Set Make-up	Shaft Flex Equivalent	Avg. Grip Size @ 2" Down From Butt	Avg. Grip Size Equivalent Terminology	Grip Size Range @ 2" Down from Butt
	Average Length	Length Range					
5	25"	24" - 26"	5 wood 5, 9 irons & P	L (Ladies')	.820"	1/32" under Ladies'	.805" - .835"
6	25"	24" - 26"	5 wood 5, 9 irons & P	L (Ladies')	.820"	1/32" under Ladies'	.805" - .835"
7	25"	24" - 26"	5 wood 5, 9 irons & P	L (Ladies')	.820"	1/32" under Ladies'	.805" - .835"
8	28½"	26½" - 30"	4 wood 5, 7, 9 irons & P	L (Ladies')	.835"	1/64" under Ladies'	.820" - .850"
9	28½"	26½" - 30"	4 wood 5, 7, 9 irons & P	L (Ladies')	.835"	1/64" under Ladies'	.820" - .850"
10	28½"	26½" - 30"	4 wood 5, 7, 9 irons & P	L (Ladies')	.835"	1/64" under Ladies'	.820" - .850"
11	31½"	30½" - 32"	3, 5 woods 5, 7, 9 irons & P	L (Ladies')	.835"	1/64" under Ladies'	.820" - .850"
12	31½"	30½" - 32"	3, 5 woods 3, 5, 7, 9 irons & P	L (Ladies')	.835"	1/64" under Ladies'	.820" - .850"
13	31½"	30½" - 32"	3, 5 woods 3, 5, 7, 9 irons & P	L or A (Ladies' or Flexible)	.835"	1/64" under Ladies'	.820" - .850"
14	32½"	32" - 33"	2, 4, 7 woods 3 - 9 irons, PW, SW & P	L (Ladies')	.850"	1/64" under Ladies'	.820" - .850"
15	32½"	32" - 33"	2, 4, 7 woods 3 - 9 irons, PW, SW & P	L (Ladies')	.850"	Standard Ladies'	.835" - .880"
16	32½"	32" - 33"	2, 4, 7 woods 3 - 9 irons, PW, SW & P	L (Ladies')	.850"	Standard Ladies'	.835" - .880"
17	33½"	33" - 34½"	1, 3, 5, 7 woods 3 - 9 irons, PW, SW & P	L (Ladies')	.850"	Standard Ladies'	.835" - .880"
18	33½"	33" - 34½"	1, 3, 5, 7 woods 3 - 9 irons, PW, SW & P	L (Ladies')	.850"	Standard Ladies'	.835" - .880"

The darker shaded portion above indicates that these specifications are the same as for boys.

TABLE 66-3
²Wood Club Length, Loft & Set Make-up by Age Group

¹Boy's Age Group	Driver 12° Loft	#2 Wood 14°Loft	#3 Wood 17° Loft	#4 Wood 20° Loft	#5 Wood 23° Loft	¹Girl's Age Group	Driver 13° Loft	#2 Wood 15° Loft	#3 Wood 18° Loft	#4 Wood 21° Loft	#5 Wood 24° Loft	#7 Wood 30° Loft
5-6-7					31"							
8-9-10					35"							
11-12-13			39"		37½"							
14-15-16		41½"		40½"	40"	14-15-16			40"		39"	37½"
17-18	43"		42"	41½"	41"	17-18	41½"		40½"		39½"	38½"

⁴Age Equalization Factor

Girl's age groups for 5-6-7, 8-9-10 and 11-12-13 are not shown because they are the same as the boy's age groups.

TABLE 66-3 Continued
²Iron Club Length, Loft & Set Make-up by Age Group

¹Boy's Age Group	#3 Iron 24° Loft	#4 Iron 28°Loft	#5 Iron 32° Loft	#6 Iron 36° Loft	#7 Iron 40° Loft	#8 Iron 44° Loft	#9 Iron 48° Loft	PW 52° Loft	SW 56° Loft	Putter 1°- 4° Loft	No. of Clubs In Set
5-6-7			27"				25"			25"	4
8-9-10			30½"		29½"		28½"			28½"	5
11-12-13	34½"		33½"		32½"		31½"			31½"	7
14-15-16	37"	36½"	36"	35½"	35"	34½"	34"	34"	34"	34"	13
17-18	38"	37½"	37"	36½"	36"	35½"	35"	35"	35"	35"	14

¹Girl's Age Group	#3 Iron 25° Loft	#4 Iron 29°Loft	#5 Iron 33° Loft	#6 Iron 37° Loft	#7 Iron 41° Loft	#8 Iron 45° Loft	#9 Iron 49° Loft	PW 53° Loft	SW 57° Loft	Putter 1°- 4° Loft	No. of Clubs In Set
14-15-16	35½"	35"	34½"	34"	33½"	33"	32½"	32½"	32½"	32½"	13
17-18	36½"	36"	35½"	35"	34½"	34"	33½"	33½"	33½"	33½"	14

Girl's age groups for 5-6-7, 8-9-10 and 11-12-13 are not shown because they are the same as the boy's age groups.

more of the time and enable them to hit the ball in the center of the clubface, both of these goals will be realized.

The astute observer will also note that the relationship of length between the woods and the irons has not been changed. In other words, if all the lengths of all the clubs not listed on the chart were filled in, the length difference between the #5 wood and #3 iron would in every case be 3" as it is in most traditional standard men's and ladies' sets.

■ Example for Using the Fitting Tables for Juniors

A boy is ten years old, weighs 94 pounds and is 5'1" tall. He is athletic, stronger than the average 12 year old and has above average coordination. His height indicates an average driver length of 35"; however, because of his heavier weight, added height, strength and good coordination, he should probably be fitted in the 11-12-13 year old bracket. Also, instead of a set make-up consisting of a #4 wood, #5, #7 and a #9 iron and putter, he should use a set make-up of #3 and a #5 wood, #3, #5, #7 and a #9 iron and putter. An alternative to this would be to stay with the #4 wood, #5, #7 and #9 iron and putter, but change the individual club specifications of weight, length and grip size to those of the 11-12-13 year old bracket. This may be desired if the boy is a beginner and it is questionable as to his immediate interest, or if there are financial considerations in favor of the fewer number of clubs.

One area which has not been mentioned thus far is lie. Because of significant differences in juniors' heights and address positions, it was determined that lie should be fit according to normal methods. It has already been shown how important lie is regarding directional control; however, when fitting the under 12 age groups, lie is not nearly as important as proper length, loft, grip size and weight. A beginning junior just wants to hit the ball and have it fly in the air. The interest of the junior, his or her willingness to improve and practice are all factors in determining just how far one goes in the entire fitting process.

TABLE 66-4
Boys & Girls Quick Reference General Fitting Chart

Age, Height & Weight Range	Boys and/or Girls	Driving Wood Length & Loft Range	#5 Iron Length Range & Average	Putter Length Range & Average	Driving Wood Weight Range & Average	Grip Size Range @ 2" Down From Butt	Recommended Set Make-up For Playing
5-7 Years 44" - 48" 37 - 47 lbs.	Boys & Girls	30" - 32" 20° - 23° (#5 wood)	26" - 28" 27"	24" - 26" 25"	12 - 12½ oz. 12¼ oz.	.805" - .835" 1/32" under Ladies' size	#5 wood, 5, 9 iron & P
8-10 Years 49" - 53" 53 - 69 lbs.	Boys & Girls	32½" - 37" 17° - 19° (#4 wood)	28½" - 32" 30½"	26½" - 30" 28½"	11½ - 12 oz. 11¾ oz.	.820" - .850" 1/64" under Ladies' size	#4 wood, 5, 7, 9 iron & P
11-13 Years 55" - 61" 73 - 103 lbs.	Boys & Girls	37½" - 40" 14° - 16° (#3 wood)	32½" - 34½" 33½"	30½" - 32" 31½"	11 - 11½ oz. 11¼ oz.	.835" - .880" Standard Ladies' size	#3, 5 woods, 3, 5, 7, 9 irons & P
14-16 Years 63" - 68" 109 - 134 lbs.	Boys	40½" - 42" 11° - 13° (#1 or #2 wood)	35" - 36½" 36"	32½" - 34" 33½"	C-6 to D-0 C-8	.850" - .900" 1/64" under Men's size	#1 or 2, 4, 5 woods, 3 - 9 irons, PW, SW & P
14-16 Years 63" - 64" 118 - 127 lbs.	Girls	39" - 41" 13° - 15° (#2 or #3 wood)	34" - 35" 34½"	32" - 33" 32½"	C-2 to C-5 C-4	.835" - .880" Standard Ladies' size	#2 or 3, 4, 7 woods, 3 - 9 irons, PW, SW & P
17-18 Years 69" - 70" 142 - 149 lbs.	Boys	42½" - 43½" 11° - 12° (#1 wood)	36½" - 37½" 37"	34" - 36" 35"	C-9 to D-3 D-1	.885" - .930" Standard Men's size	#1, 3, 4, 5 woods, 3 - 9 irons, PW, SW & P
17-18 Years 64" 124 - 127 lbs.	Girls	41" - 42½" 13° - 14° (#1 or #2 wood)	35" - 36½" 35½"	33" - 34½" 33½"	C-5 to C-9 C-7	.835" - .880" Standard Ladies' size	#1, 3, 5, 7 woods 3 - 9 irons PW, SW & P

TABLE 66-5
Boys & Girls Quick Reference Club Length Chart by Age Group

Age Group	Boys and/or Girls	WOODS Measured by Inches						IRONS Measured by Inches										
		1	2	3	4	5	7	2	3	4	5	6	7	8	9	PW	SW	P
5-7	Both					31	30				27	26½	26	25½	25	25	25	25
8-10	Both				35	34½	33½				30½	30	29½	29	28½	28½	28½	28½
11-13	Both			38½	38	37½	36½	34½	34	33½	33	32½	32	31½	31½	31½	31½	
14-16	Boys		41½	41	40½	40	39	36½	36	35½	35	34½	34	33½	33½	33½	33½	
14-16	Girls		40	39½	39	38½	37½	35½	35	34½	34	33½	33	32½	32½	32½	32½	
17-18	Boys	43	42½	42	41½	41	40	38½	38	37½	37	36½	36	35½	35	35	35	35
17-18	Girls	41½	41	40½	40	39½	38½	36½	36	35½	35	34½	34	33½	33½	33½	33½	

APPENDICES

APPENDIX 1

WHAT HAPPENS WHEN AN AVERAGE GOLFER HITS A DRIVE?

Very few golfers realize exactly what happens when they step up on the tee, pull out their driver and smack the golf ball down the fairway. It is quite interesting to look at a few of the more common actions and reactions of the hit because it shows how little control a golfer has over the shot once he/she has passed a certain point on the downswing. After reading this section, one should be able to appreciate the many variables of golf club design and better understand how they relate to performance.

■ The Backswing

The logical starting place to begin is with the backswing. As the golfer begins his takeaway, the clubhead does not immediately start to move backwards because its total mass is at rest and resists being put into motion. This resistance causes the shaft to bend or flex slightly resulting in the head lagging behind the shaft. See Figure A1-1. The head remains in a following or lagging position through the remainder of the backswing.

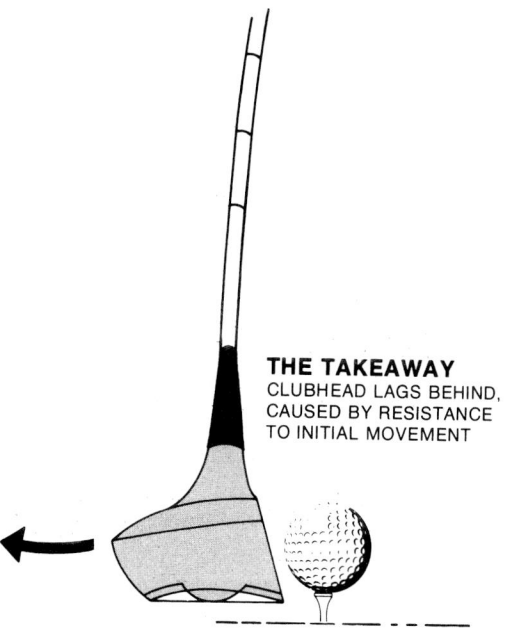

THE TAKEAWAY
CLUBHEAD LAGS BEHIND,
CAUSED BY RESISTANCE
TO INITIAL MOVEMENT

Figure A1-1

■ The Downswing

The clubhead will now reverse its direction at the very top of the backswing to begin the downswing. The clubhead mass again resists movement causing the shaft to flex in the opposite direction of the takeaway, thus leaving the clubhead again in a lagging position or following the shaft on the downswing. However, because the clubhead is on the end of the shaft during the downward acceleration, it accelerates more quickly than any point along the shaft, thus causing the clubhead to catch up with the shaft and pass it. Now the clubhead is not lagging the shaft, but rather leading ahead of the shaft as it approaches impact with the golf ball. See Figure A1-2.

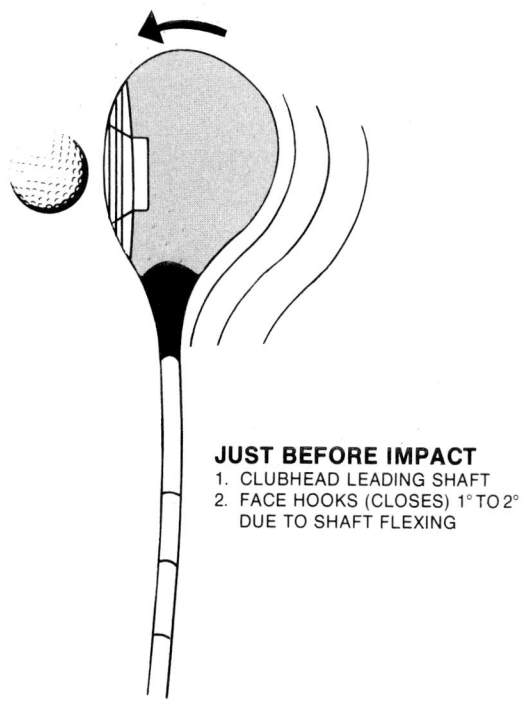

JUST BEFORE IMPACT
1. CLUBHEAD LEADING SHAFT
2. FACE HOOKS (CLOSES) 1° TO 2°
   DUE TO SHAFT FLEXING

Figure A1-2

The fact that the clubhead is leading the shaft before and up to impact shows that the clubhead is more or less a free wheeling object. Its total stored up energy to be applied to the golf ball at impact is almost solely dependent on the clubhead mass itself and its velocity. More specifically, E (energy applied to ball) = ½ [M (clubhead mass) x V2 (clubhead velocity squared)].

Before impact takes place there are at least three other things happening to the golf club during the downswing. First, because the head is leading the shaft, the flexing forward causes the clubface to hook (close) slightly. Each 1" of shaft flexing causes the face to close approximately 2 degrees. See Figure A1-2. Second, as already discussed the shaft is flexed so as to have the clubhead leading it. It is also flexing in another plane causing the lie of the golf club to flatten slightly. This happens because the center of mass or center of gravity of the clubhead is not in line with the centerline of the shaft. Therefore, during the downswing the centrifugal force acts through the center of gravity of the clubhead causing it to bend downward resulting in a flattening of the lie, usually one degree to two degrees maximum depending on the shaft flex and head speed. See Figure A1-3. Third, elapsed time from the very top of the backswing to just

THE DOWNSWING

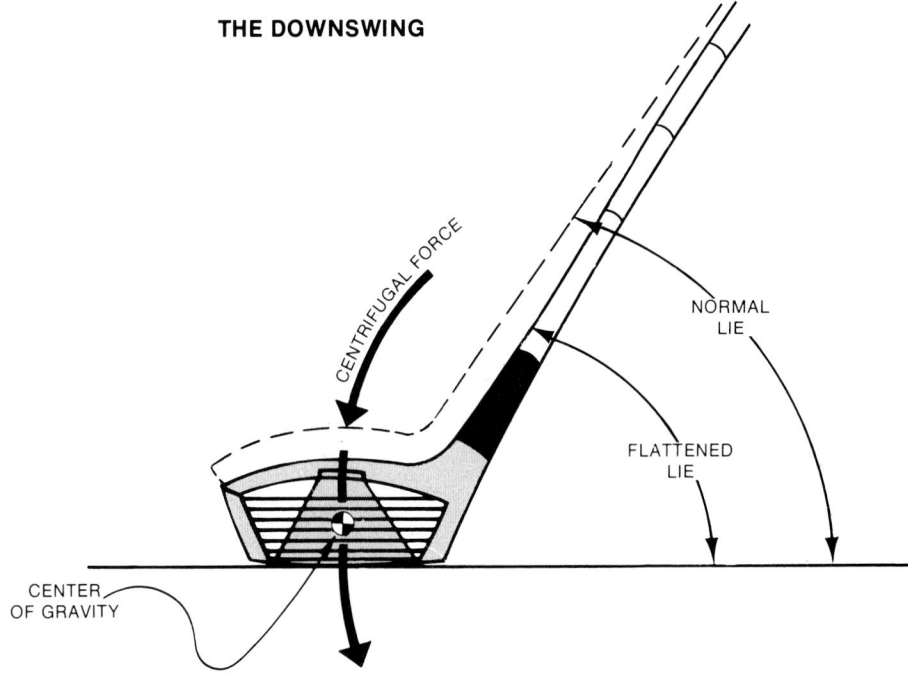

Figure A1-3

before impact with the golf ball takes approximately ⅕ of a second. During this short time an average adult male golfer will generate a head speed of approximately 100 M.P.H. (depending upon which computerized swing analyzer is used). See Figure A1-4. Men players on the pro tour range from approximately 115 to 135 M.P.H. with the average around 124 M.P.H. A touring pro who could swing a driver 132 M.P.H. would send the ball off at approximately 177 M.P.H. and the resultant carry would be about 280 yards.

Women tour pros range from 85 M.P.H. to over 120 M.P.H. The average would be estimated at 105 M.P.H. In tests conducted with junior girls (10-12 year olds) using a 38½" driver, clubhead speeds ranged from 35 M.P.H. to 65 M.P.H. with the average being around 50 M.P.H.

■ Impact

The total duration of impact from the time the clubhead first contacts the ball

794

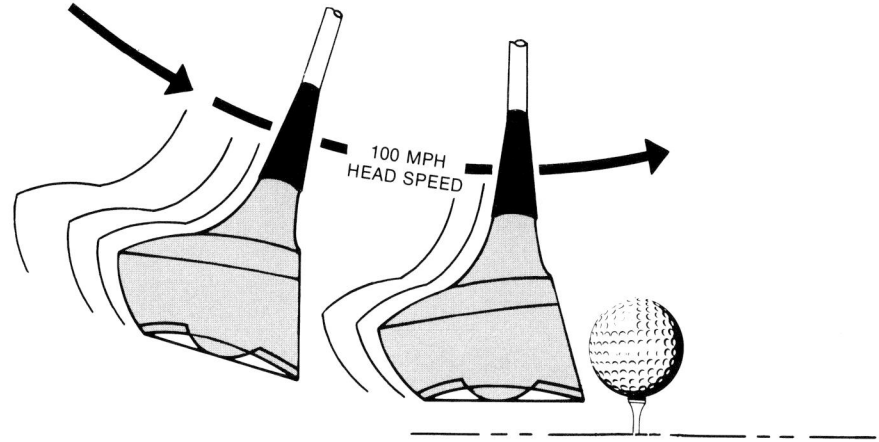

Figure A1-4

until the ball leaves the clubface takes only $^5/_{10,000}$ of a second. During this time the clubhead travels a total distance of ¾" to 1". See Figure A1-5.

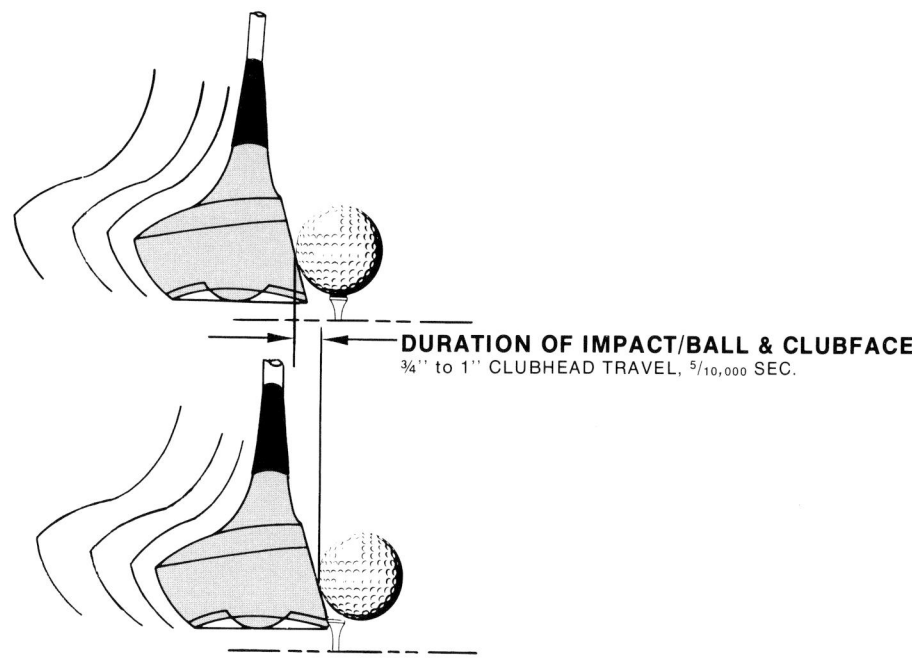

DURATION OF IMPACT/BALL & CLUBFACE
¾" to 1" CLUBHEAD TRAVEL, $^5/_{10,000}$ SEC.

Figure A1-5

The maximum force (energy applied to the ball) at impact approaches 2,000 pounds, or one ton and causes the clubface to compress the golf ball fifteen to thirty percent of its original diameter. See Figure A1-6.

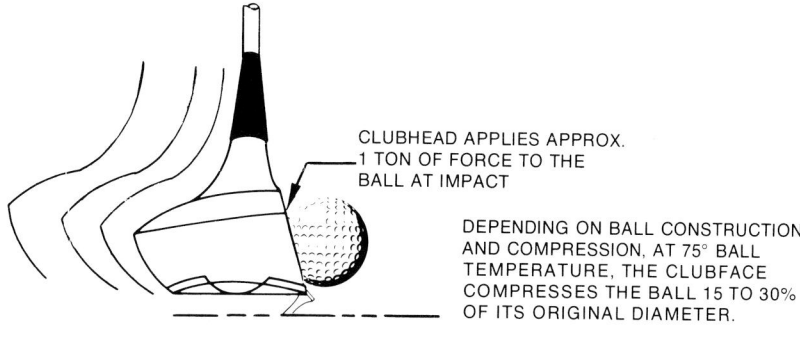

CLUBHEAD APPLIES APPROX. 1 TON OF FORCE TO THE BALL AT IMPACT

DEPENDING ON BALL CONSTRUCTION AND COMPRESSION, AT 75° BALL TEMPERATURE, THE CLUBFACE COMPRESSES THE BALL 15 TO 30% OF ITS ORIGINAL DIAMETER.

Figure A1-6

During impact of clubface and ball, the clubhead speed slows to approximately 82 M.P.H. and the ball leaves the clubface at about 135 M.P.H., spinning backwards between 3,000 and 4,000 revolutions per minute. See Figure A1-7.

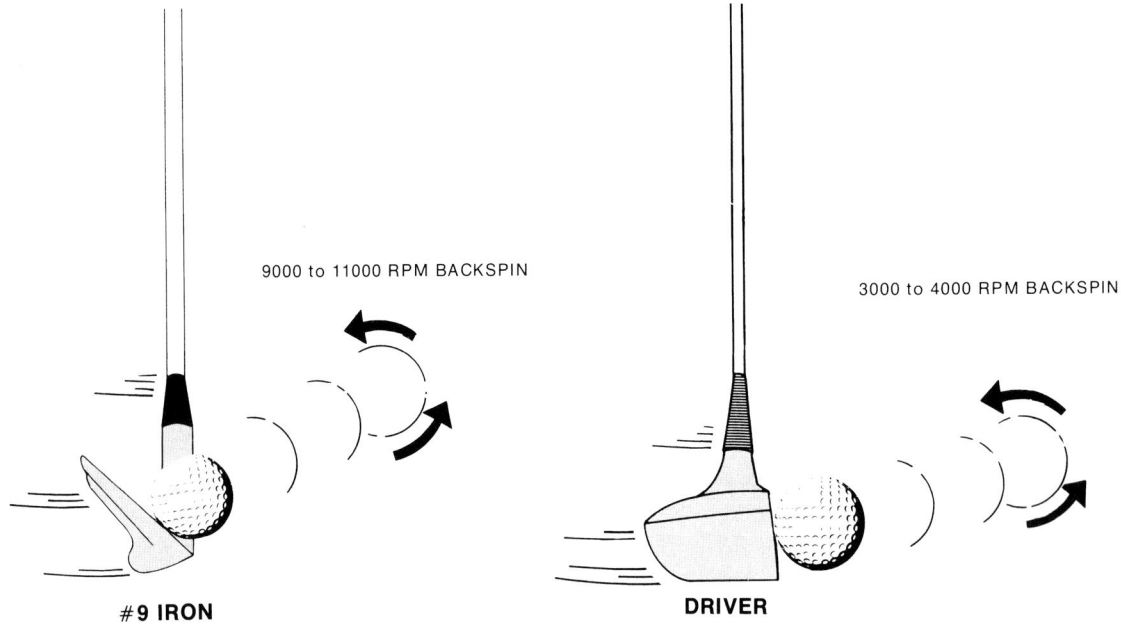

9000 to 11000 RPM BACKSPIN

3000 to 4000 RPM BACKSPIN

#9 IRON

DRIVER

Figure A1-7

Collision of clubface and ball has also caused the shaft to flex backwards so that once again the clubhead is lagging behind the shaft instead of leading the shaft as it was when approaching impact.

During any golf shot, the golfer gets a certain sensation of feel at the exact moment the clubface strikes the ball. Right? Wrong! The golfer does in fact feel the hit, but because of the time required for the impact to travel through the clubhead, up the shaft, into the golfer's hands and register with the brain, the golf ball is already 10" to 12" from the clubface and in flight. So the golfer does not feel the hit when it actually takes place; rather it is felt when it has already left the clubface. See Figure A1-8. In addition, the centrifugal force exerted downward and pulling on the golfer's hands at impact is the equivalent of 40 to 60 pounds. See Figure A1-9.

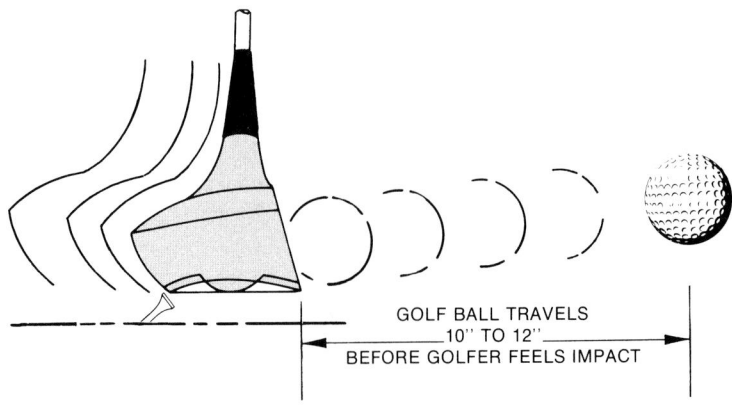

GOLF BALL TRAVELS
10" TO 12"
BEFORE GOLFER FEELS IMPACT

Figure A1-8

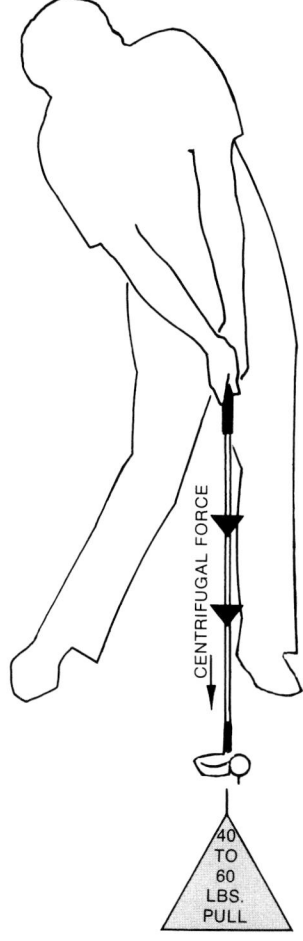

Figure A1-9

Another interesting fact of impact is that the direction the ball initially travels is a result of two factors, the clubface angle at impact and the clubhead path. The face angle, however, is the more important influencing factor of the two. See Figure A1-10.

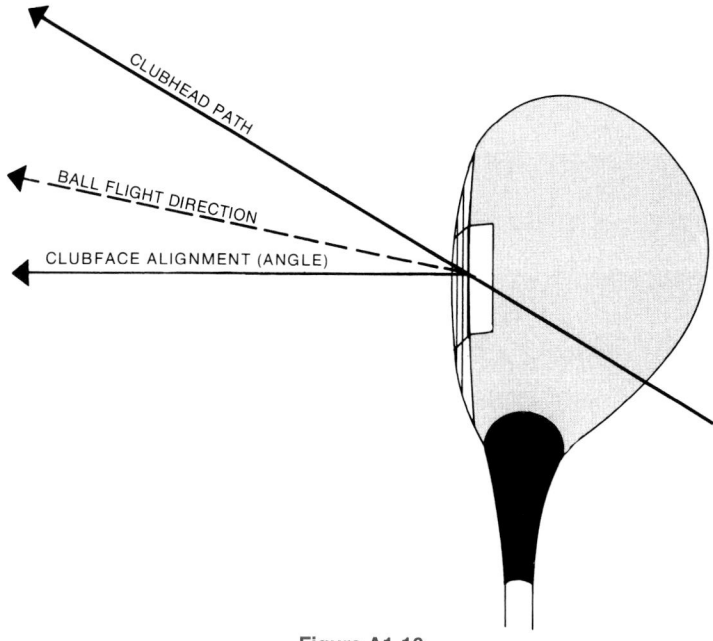

Figure A1-10

■ The Followthrough

Thus far during the swing the clubhead has been alternately lagging behind and leading the shaft as it flexed. As was mentioned, the clubhead has assumed a lagging position as a result of the impact with the ball which slowed down the clubhead enough to allow the shaft to catch up and flex in the opposite direction. Now during the followthrough up to the point where the clubhead reaches approximately waist high; the clubhead alternately leads ahead of and lags behind the shaft as it flexes. From the time of impact to the waist high position, this occurs at least three times. It can be assumed that this constant flexing of the shaft causing alternating positions of the clubhead from impact on is one of the more important factors which determine the feel of a shot. Because the word "feel" as a golfer utilizes it is so vague; it is impossible to segment and understand all the factors that determine it. However, after reading this section it should be easier to understand some of the more meaningful variables which must contribute to feel.

The following photographic sequence shows a well known tour professional hitting a stiff flex Dynamic shafted #3 iron. A special camera was used to shoot this sequence at 64 frames per second. Note the different shaft flexing in each frame.

APPENDIX 2

METHODS USED TO OBTAIN GOLF CLUB PERFORMANCE DATA

Since the first golf club was made, man has devised hundreds of ways to change or improve it. To substantiate this, spend some time and look through the patents which have been filed on golf club innovations during the last 70 or 80 years. The impression one gets after reviewing these patents is that most innovations today are not really new at all, but refinements of old ideas. It should be noted, however, that without today's technological advances in manufacturing processes, raw materials, sophisticated testing equipment and a more refined understanding of the mechanics of golf clubs, that golf club improvements would not have advanced to where they are now.

When a new design or innovation does occur, it requires that a well thought out product development and testing program be coupled with the marketing objectives, to insure adequate planning for a successful new product introduction into the market.

A few of the items that must be considered in new club planning are:
1. Will the club be legal according to United States Golf Association rules (USGA)?
2. What particular market segment will this new club satisfy? Specifically, who will buy it, where will they buy it and why will they buy it?
3. Can it be manufactured and if so, exactly how much will it cost to produce?
4. Through which channel or channels of distribution will it be sold?
5. What inherent marketing advantages does this club possess over competitors and can it be successfully marketed.
6. What inherent performance advantages does this club have over other golf clubs and **how can it be proven?**

The last statement, **How can it be proven?**, is the basis for this section.

■ Obtaining Golf Club Performance Data

There are basically four ways to measure the performance characteristics of a golf club as a complete unit including shaft, grip and head in its finished state.

1. Machine testing using True Temper's mechanical golfer.
2. Computer evaluation that duplicates dynamic performance.
3. Player testing using amateurs, golf professionals and touring golf professionals.
4. Bio-mechanical analysis using all types of golfers, high speed photographic equipment and computers programmed to interpret the information.

■ True Temper's® Mechanical Golfer (See Photo A2-1)

One of the most significant developments in golf club testing equipment is the mechanical golfer developed by True Temper Corporation in collaboration with Battelle Memorial Institute of Columbus, Ohio. The research and development program took

Photo Courtesy True Temper

A2-1
A multiple exposure photograph showing how the mechanical golfer duplicates the swing of a golfer to the extent of uncocking the wrists and rolling the wrists at the precise moment for a perfectly timed shot.

two years and a cost of more than $250,000 to complete. True Temper recognized the need for such a machine for several reasons. A sophisticated testing device was needed to determine performance characteristics of new golf shaft materials and designs. A way to prove or disprove the many claims that both golf club manufacturers and golf shaft manufacturers made concerning certain shafts was also needed. Because True Temper used to manufacture wood heads, the machine was of much value in testing durability and design characteristics. True Temper wanted to learn more about total golf club performance by examining and comparing the traditional, benchmark proven designs with the new innovations being marketed. Here, True Temper agreed to work in conjunction with the golf club manufacturers by allowing them to use the machine for testing. It should be mentioned here that True Temper requires that golf club companies test only clubs of their own manufacture and that golf club companies agree not to use the results for advertising purposes outside their own company. This policy has somewhat broken down during the past few years because True Temper agreed to build and sell mechanical golfers, identical to the original one, for other golf club manufacturers and organizations. Some of the mechanical golfers in existence are owned by the following companies and organizations: True Temper, Ben Hogan Co., Maxfli, United States Golf Association, Titleist, Wilson, Tommy Armour, Spalding and Callaway.

It is interesting how the mechanical golfer was developed. A number of action films were made of a representative group of golf pros and low handicap amateur golfers. By analyzing swing similarities and differences, the engineers were able to plot and graph a typical professional swing.

A computer program was developed from this to measure the force inputs of the entire swing and thus determine a man's capabilities and the requirements of the golf club. This computer program supplied sufficient data on the geometry of the swing to make possible the design of the simulated professional swing. A series of throttling valves vary the pressure to the single air cylinder during the swinging of the club to synchronize with the golfer's application of body power and wrist action. See Photo A2-2.

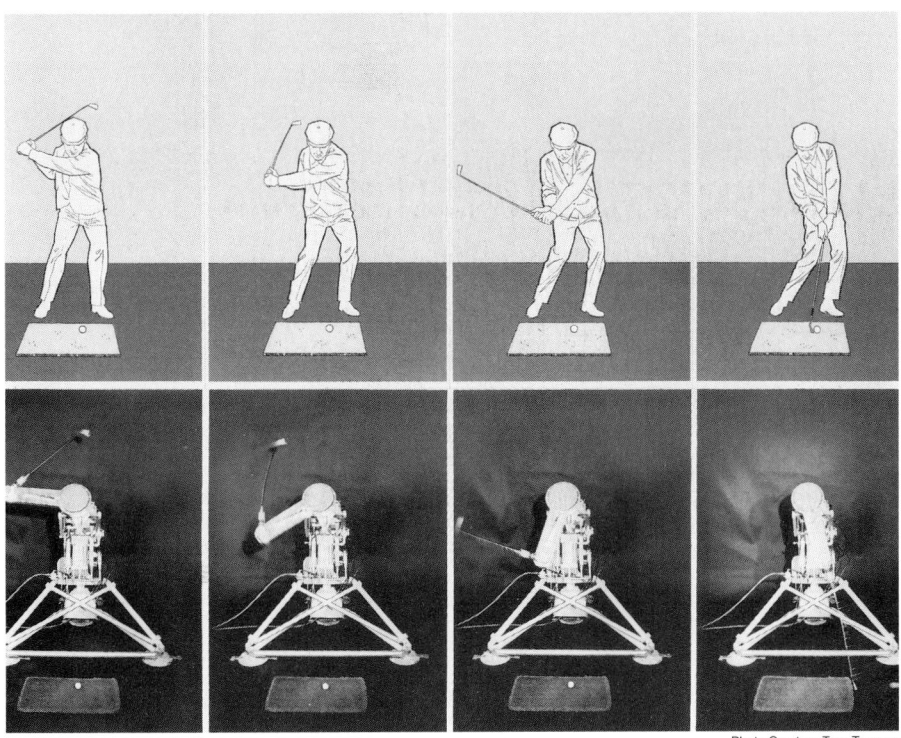

Photo Courtesy True Temper

A2-2
A multiple sequence photograph showing how the True Temper® mechanical golfer
duplicates the essential movements of a human swing.

The machine is powered by air pressure and accurately simulates a human golf swing from the point where a golfer starts the power application of his swing (from the top). It can use any club from driver to pitching wedge, hitting from a tee or off the turf. The machine can hit a golf ball with a repeatable velocity within plus or minus ½%. This eliminates the human factors of fatigue and changes in the swing.

To further insure scientific accuracy, the machine features a ball placement device or tee which permits accurate ball placement, both vertically and horizontally. This means that hit after hit will be struck on the exact same spot of the clubface.

The machine also has timing lights positioned just before the impact zone to electronically measure the exact clubhead speed.

A high speed camera can be attached to the machine to take accurately timed pictures of the ball and clubhead in any position. For example, the ball can be so marked that the pictures can be used to determine ball velocity, ball spin and ball flight direction. See Photo A2-3.

A2-3
This is a high speed photograph of a marked ball. Ball velocity, spin and flight angle can be determined from the photograph. Duration of the photographic sequence above is 8/10,000 of a second.

■ Obtaining Golf Club Performance Data from the Mechanical Golfer

The questions of how a golf club test is conducted and how the results are analyzed is an important discussion if one is to fully realize some of the dynamic interrelationships of golf club variables. Each golf club test must be individually tailored to meet certain criteria and answer specific questions. Because of this, each test is varied considerably regarding sample sizes, significance levels, and types of data. However, for this discussion, these points are rather insignificant. We are mainly concerned with the key, non-variable parts of every golf club test and how it is conducted.

First, whenever golf club tests are planned, it is important that control clubs be added into the test. These clubs provide the benchmark from which the actual test results of the other clubs will be compared. All test golf clubs must have every pertinent specification recorded. Some must be recorded during the assembly of the club and the other specifications taken from the finished club. Below is a list of the information usually needed:

Club Model	Finished Total Length
Club Weight	Swingweight
Grip Weight	Total Weight
Shaft Deflection Board Reading	Face Angle (Hook, Square, Slice)
Shaft Weight Uncut	Loft
Shaft Weight Cut	Lie
Shaft Flex Designation	Face Progression
Frequency	Horizontal Bulge
Shaft Material	Vertical Roll
Finished Head Weight	Finished Head Center of Gravity (3 planes)

Note that in the above static golf club test data some specifications apply only to wood clubs. Also, the golf balls used in any golf club test should be marked for identification and the pertinent data listed below recorded about each ball.

Ball Type	Size
Ball Number	Weight
Construction Type	Coefficient
Compression (if applicable)	Initial Velocity

The control club is now mounted in the mechanical golfer. The swing pressure (regulated air pressure input) is determined. Rule of thumb measurements are that an input setting of 120 pounds air pressure equals approximately 160 feet-per-second clubhead speed with a driver. Of course, the clubhead speed of successively shorter length clubs (#3 wood, #4 wood, #6 iron) would be much less since the constant input of 120 pounds air pressure cannot generate the same clubhead speeds on shorter clubs. The 160 feet-per-second corresponds to that of the average touring professional's driver head speed. A speed of 140 to 145 feet-per-second would correspond to the average driver head speed of amateur golfers with an 18 handicap or less.

The next step is to hit a few practice shots and adjust the machine so that it is hitting the balls down the middle of the gridded field. With this done and the first run ready to begin, the following data is recorded:

Club Test #1

Machine Swing Angle	Club Description
Height	Ball Type
Start Position	Humidity
Swing Pressure	Wind Direction
Brake Pressure	Wind Velocity
Align Position	Temperature
Hit Position	

Each test ball in order is now hit out onto the gridded field. As each ball is hit, the clubhead speed is measured on an electronic digital readout unit and is recorded by the operator on a data sheet. At the same time, spotters in the field are recording exact ball carry, total ball roll and deviation from the center of the grid. Another spotter, working with the operator at the machine, is recording pertinent information concerning trajectory variances and comparisons, hooking and slicing. At first glance it may seem quite easy to draw some definite conclusions by simply averaging the hits of each club and comparing them to see which club was the longest hitting and/or the most accurate. Surprisingly, this is only a part of the total picture because in many instances these tests are being conducted on a particular golf club to determine the optimum specifications at which it performs best. Of course, there has been no definition as to what this test was to accomplish, and while it is true that each test would have its own criteria for evaluating the data, it would be noteworthy to look at the more common ways of going about such an evaluation of the data.

■ Methods of Analyzing Golf Club Data

1. Golf ball carry distance — average and range.
2. Golf ball total distance (includes roll) — average and range.
3. Golf ball deviation from range centerline — average and range.
4. Head speed at impact versus golf ball carry distance — graph.
5. Head speed at impact versus golf club total weight — graph.
6. Head speed at impact versus golf clubhead weight — graph.
7. Head speed at impact versus cut shaft weight — graph.
8. Head speed at impact versus swingweight — graph.
9. Golf ball carry distance versus golf club total weight — graph.
10. Golf ball carry distance versus golf clubhead weight — graph.
11. Golf ball carry distance versus cut shaft weight — graph.
12. Golf ball carry distance versus swingweight — graph.

It should now be apparent what kind of information would be generated from this cross reference of data, and how enlightening it could be if analyzed and used correctly.

The most important thing to remember is that although the True Temper machine is a sound, scientifically designed device, it cannot duplicate a human golf swing 100 percent. Even if it could, it would not apply to all the different types of golfers. The machine is designed to simulate an ideal swing with amazing repeatability. No golf club test conducted on the True Temper mechanical golfer should be considered complete until a similar supporting test is conducted with human golfers.

■ Computer Evaluation

The performance of a new model is still usually evaluated using a mechanical golfer and player testing by the major manufacturers. However, a new step utilizing a powerful computer with sophisticated software has been introduced in order to provide the manufacturer with performance data at an earlier stage – the test itself being conducted entirely within the computer. This is important because it reduces the cost of taking a new design to the market, especially for innovative models, as explained later.

As was the case with the mechanical golfer, True Temper® is also the leader in the development of this impressive new tool and makes it available as a free service to its major customers. Among those companies having already taken advantage of this service are Callaway with the Big Bertha iron and Maxfli with their VHL design.

The evaluation of a head using a computer is usually performed in one of two ways. The first method is to break the head down into hundreds of disconnected, finite elements through a process known as discretization, and then use a large computer and a finite element software package to determine how the head will respond to various ball impact velocities and positions. So precise are the results from this test that actual mechanical testing using a real club and balls only duplicates the results generated by the computer.

The second method, which is used by True Temper®, provides more accurate results in only one day versus the several weeks or months it may take using the first method. Using the clubhead design sample from the manufacturer, the head is modeled as an "equivalent mass system" in the computer. This model behaves the same dynamically as the discretized head in the first method. The only drawback to the equivalent mass model has been an inability to accurately measure the inertia dyadic of a clubhead. However, True Temper® successfully overcame that drawback and is able to present to the manufacturer a set of results that makes actual ball striking for the same results unnecessary.

The procedure for modeling a clubhead begins with making basic physical measurements and then applying engineering principles to produce a useful model. The mass of the clubhead is the first measurement made and is done using a digital scale with an accuracy of a tenth of a gram. Next, the center of gravity relative to the hosel exit is located using an analytical type balance developed by True Temper® as shown in Figure A2-4. The coordinate system used is shown in Figure A2-5. The clubhead is attached to a bar that rests on a pivot. By sliding the weight on the other side of the pivot until the bar is perfectly horizontal the head center of gravity location can then be calculated by summing moments about the pivot.

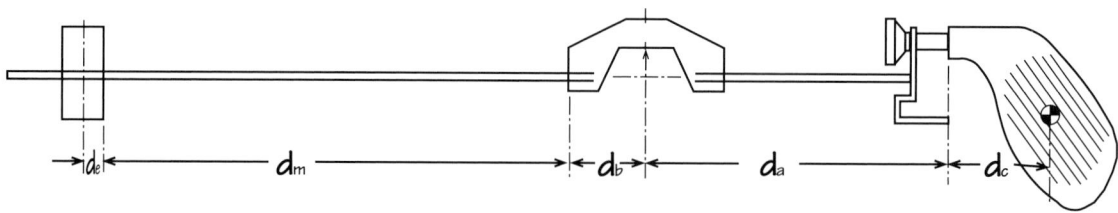

Figure A2-4

Following the mass measurement and locating the center of gravity, the inertia dyadic of the clubhead is determined, which is a representation of the inertia properties of a clubhead. Moment of inertia is a measure of an objects resistance to twist. The resistance of the clubhead to twisting by off-center shots is an important game improvement feature of the cavity-back designs which push material to the perimeter. Every object has what are called its three principal axes of inertia. These axes form a coordinate system with its origin at the center of gravity of the object, or in this case, the clubhead. When the inertia dyadic is found about the clubhead's principal axes we have what is referred to as the "central principal inertia dyadic."

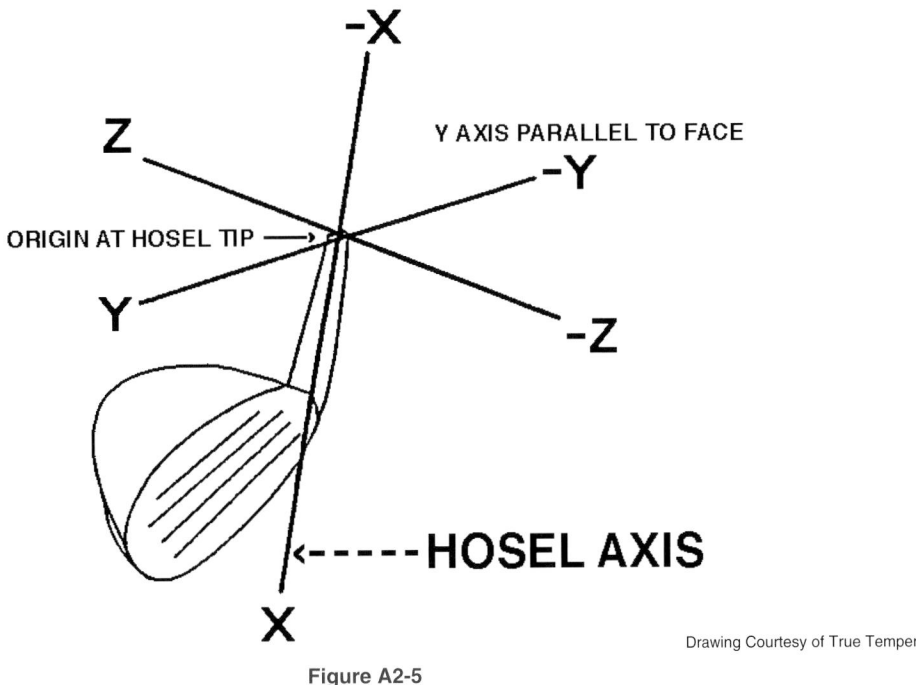

Drawing Courtesy of True Temper

Figure A2-5

The next step is to develop the equivalent mass system. This is done by dividing the mass of the clubhead by 6 and placing 6 "lumped masses" on the three principal axes as shown in Figure A2-6. Each axis will have two lumped masses – one on each side of, and equal distance from, the center of gravity. These are positioned at a distance from the center of gravity such that the moments of inertia about these three axes are the same as that of the clubhead.

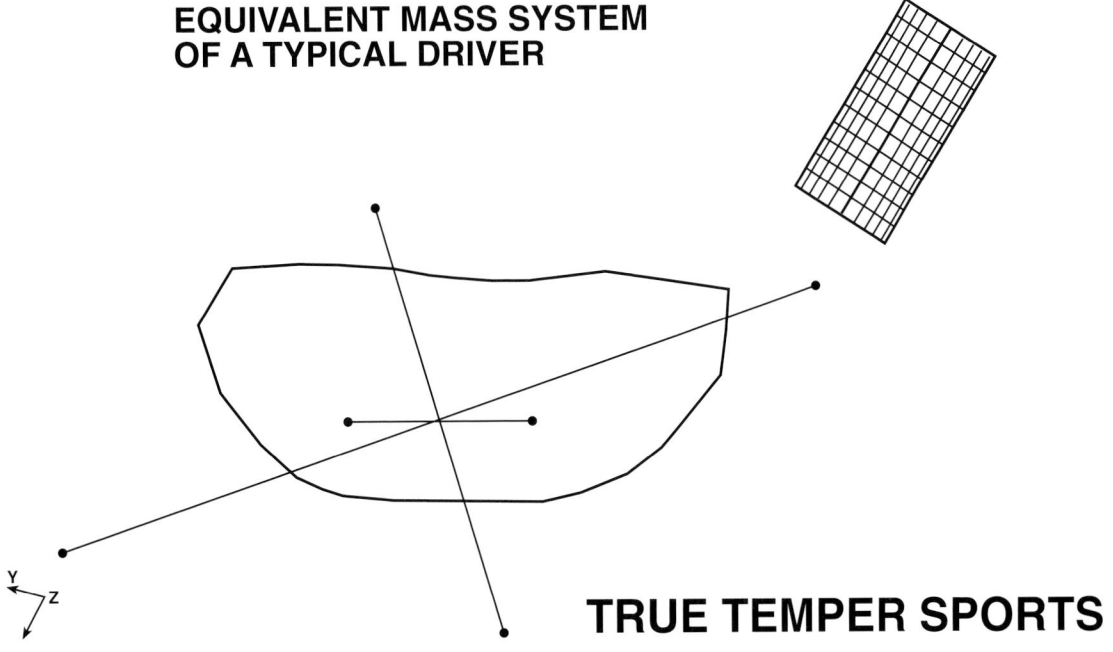

EQUIVALENT MASS SYSTEM OF A TYPICAL DRIVER

TRUE TEMPER SPORTS

Drawing Courtesy of True Temper

Figure A2-6

The final step is to measure the face and include it in the model so that it can be "hit" with a ball in the computer. After putting the equivalent mass model into the computer the head can be hit any place on the face and at any velocity. By doing this, ball spins, ball velocities and ball flight characteristics can be calculated. Where the ball lands can even be accurately predicted.

The impulse profile graphs shown in Figures A2-7 and A2-8 show the amount the ball velocity decays over the surface of the clubface of a persimmon wood driver and a metal wood driver as impact occurs at different points. Looking at Figure A2-8, a swing which results in a 100 M.P.H. ball velocity at the sweet spot would only produce an 82 M.P.H. ball velocity if hit in the extreme high toe region – a significant loss of distance.

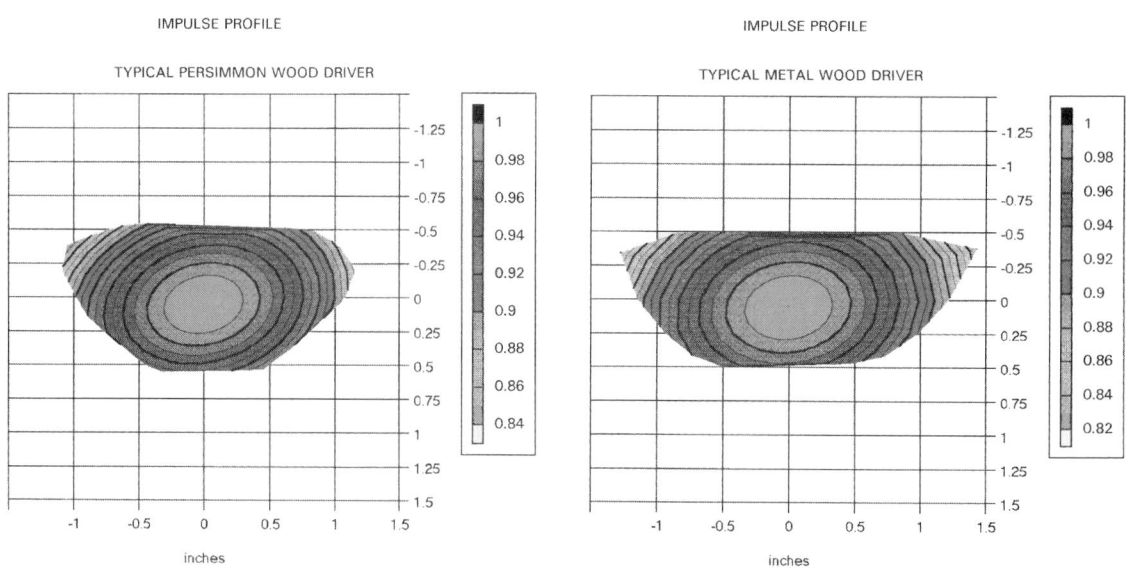

Figure A2-7

Figure A2-8

Each ring represents an increasing loss of ball velocity. When provided to the club manufacturer, each ring is presented in a different color, which readily illustrates the loss of velocity. In this comparison of two drivers, the metal wood has a slightly larger "sweetspot" than the persimmon driver. More significant though is how much more velocity is lost on an impact 1" out on the toe of the persimmon driver as compared to the metal driver. An oversized metal driver would have exhibited an even greater discrepancy.

Given this information, the head designers working for a specific manufacturer will retreat to their office and do one of two things: make subtle design changes to their model for retesting to enhance the computer generated data or, decide the design submitted to True Temper® is good and begin limited production of models for machine and player testing.

■ Player Testing

Player testing, as referred to here, pertains to controlled conditions for obtaining golf club data (or golf ball data) by using human golfers. The sample may be designed to include any one or combination of the following.

Golf Touring Professionals
Golf Professionals at Clubs
Low Handicap Amateurs
Middle Handicap Amateurs
High Handicap Amateurs

Many of the same basic procedures used in machine testing apply here such as utilizing control clubs and recording all the important data concerning the physical attributes of the test clubs and balls. If at all possible, players should not know exactly what the test is to prove. Also, the differences in the test clubs or balls should be disguised so as not to be recognizable by the players, such as marking out golf ball brand names during a competitive ball test. This procedure tends to help eliminate any built in bias that could occur. Because human golfers are not as accurate as the mechanical golfer, it is usually necessary that at least three spotters be in the field. Two helpers are usually at the tee with the golfer, one to make sure the proper test club and ball are being hit, and the other to either tape record or write down the golfer's pertinent comments concerning each hit. These comments will be used as valuable cross reference information later when compared with the actual plotted distance charts.

If required, player testing can also include the use of high speed photography, both still and motion, and the use of stroboscopic photography to gain additional information. See Photo A2-9 and Photo A2-10.

Player test results must be analyzed differently from machine test results simply because there is not as much analytical information available with player testing. However, for any golf club manufacturer to introduce new golf clubs or balls into the market without extensive player testing to substantiate the machine testing, could be suicide. Remember, the mechanical golfer never bought a set of golf clubs or a golf ball and never will.

A2-9
Stroboscopic picture of player using a wood club.

A2-10
Stroboscopic picture of player using an iron club.

■ The GolfWorks® Player Testing and Fitting Center

The GolfWorks® has a combination testing and fitting facility which employs the proper principles and techniques already mentioned. We now have over 300 test clubs located in a permanent building on our private driving range and we are adding to the arsenal of clubs constantly. See Photo A2-11 and Photo A2-12.

A2-11
Outside view of the testing and fitting facility located at The GolfWorks®.

808

A2-12
Inside view of The GolfWorks® testing and fitting facility, looking out on the
300 yard long x 100 yard wide private driving range.

The building measures 20 feet wide x 24 feet long x 12 feet high at the ceiling. It has one 16 feet wide x 10 feet high overhead door facing the range. An additional building was added in 1989 so that we could expand our testing and club fitting capabilities. The new building added 2,600 square feet. The floor is 4" concrete covered with green grass-like outdoor carpet. Construction is the pole type with steel outside walls and roof. The building is insulated and temperature controlled. In 1979, the total construction cost was under $7,000 for the original building.

The testing and fitting buildings contain just about everything to properly analyze a player and make equipment adjustments or recommendations. During golf club tests, the equipment is available for double checking specifications and analyzing differences from one club to another. The major equipment in the building includes the following. See Photo A2-13.

> Golfer Swing Analyzers (Sportech)
> 3 Frequency Machines
> Shaft Deflection Board
> Loft and Lie Machine
> Swingweight Scale, Golf Club Gauge and other measuring equipment
> 2 - 9 x 12 Driving Range Nets and Stands
> 4' x 4' x ¾" Plywood Board for Lie Check
> Video Recording and Playback Equipment
> Fitting, Teaching and Playing Aids
> Sony Caddy Cam
> Graph Check Camera

Some of the test clubs are re-makes of those that I used years back to prove certain points or dispel myths concerning golf clubs. They are kept around for those skeptics that want to prove it to themselves. A complete listing would require too much space here, but listed below are some of the more interesting test clubs we have on hand.

Persimmon versus Laminated: Eight identical golf clubs, 4 of which are persimmon and 4 laminated maple. All other specifications are the same. The faces are painted black so that the player cannot visually tell which club is which. The test is designed for those that feel persimmon is superior in playability to laminated maple. So far, no one has ever picked one over the other in all the testing I have done.

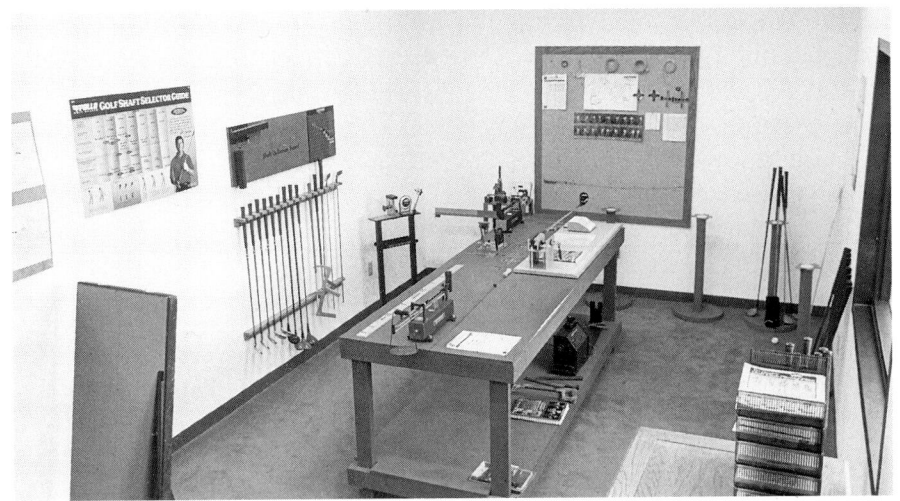

A2-13
View of the club measuring and evaluation room.

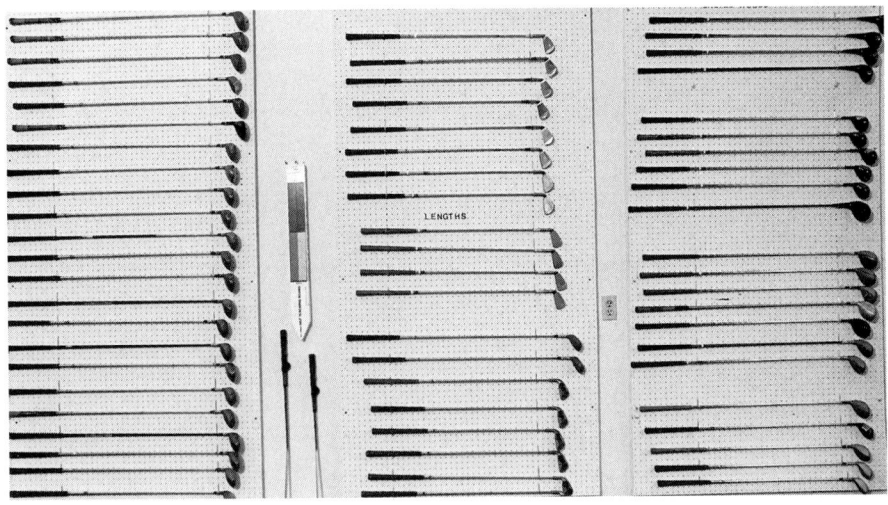

A2-14
Some of the test and fitting clubs used at The GolfWorks®.

Facelines versus No Facelines: Sets of both woods and irons have been made up without any face lines whatsoever. This test is designed to show that facelines do not cause backspin.

Changeable Swingweight from D0-D4: This club is made to a D0 and has 4 strips of lead tape stuck to the sole, each equivalent to a swingweight. The club is used to show players that in a properly conducted test, they cannot tell the difference in a 1 swingweight change, but will notice a 2 swingweight change.

Extremes in Grip Size: One leather grip is mounted close to baseball bat size and the other is wound around a bare shaft with no underlisting. This test accentuates the playability difference in too large or too small grip sizes.

Investment Cast Stainless Steel versus Forged Mild Steel Irons: Two complete sets of identically designed iron heads with only the head materials being different. This test is designed to dispel the myth that investment cast stainless steel heads feel harder, hit fliers and generate less backspin than forged mild steel heads.

Woods With and Without Backweights: We have two complete sets of woods, #1 through #7. One set is fitted with brass backweights and the other set without brass backweights. The result of this test is backweighted clubs will launch the ball from 1° to 2° higher than non-backweighted clubs of identical specifications.

Flat Faced Woods versus Horizontal Bulge Faced Woods: This test shows the importance of bulge in woods regarding directional control on off-center hits.

■ Swing Computers and Player Testing

There are only a few manufacturers of electronic swing analyzer type computers on the market. The reason probably being that they require a large amount of development capital and the market size is not large at the higher prices associated with this type equipment. At The GolfWorks® Testing and Fitting Center, the Sportech and Golf Tek Swing Analyzers are used.

A2-15
The Sportech Swing Analyzer in the foreground and one of our hitting nets in the background.

The Sportech Swing Analyzer is a special-purpose electronic computer that measures and displays the important characteristics of the golf swing by tracking the movement of the clubhead in the impact area. The flight path and carry distance of the golf ball are also calculated and displayed. An array of light sensors are precisely positioned in the base of the machine and a light source is mounted above. This optoelectronic system tracks the moving clubhead and the data is processed in a computer that gives an

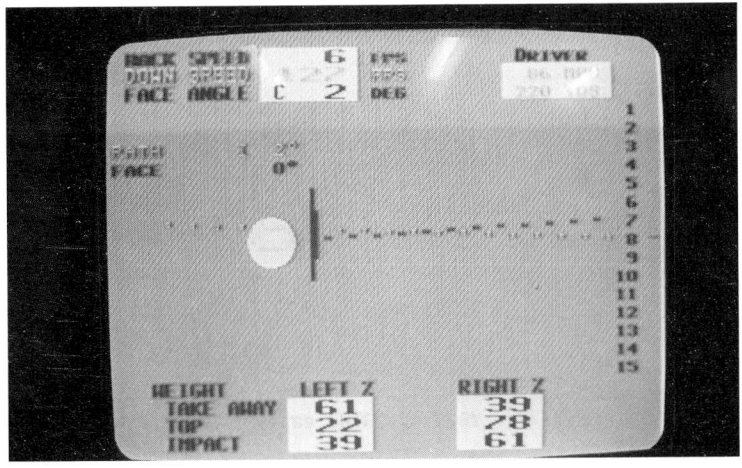

A2-16
A closeup of the display board for the Sportech Swing Analyzer.

instant readout of the results of the swing. See Photo A2-16 which shows the display board layout for the Sportech model.

The computer analyzes the following:

Clubhead Path *(also referred to as swingpath)* —

> The clubhead is tracked from approximately 4 inches before impact to about 2 inches after impact. The computer determines whether the path is straight, inside-out or outside-in and calculates the angle of this path in degrees with respect to the target line. (Target line is the imaginary line from ball to target.)

Backswing Path —

> A dotted line indicates the direction that the clubhead travels as it is moved away from the ball. The take away speed is measured in feet per second.

Clubface Angle —

> The computer determines the degree to which the clubface is open, closed or square at impact and calculates the angle of the clubface with respect to square to the open target line. It also calculates the angle of the face relative to the clubhead path.

Clubhead Speed —

> Clubhead velocity or speed, is measured over the last 1.3" prior to impact and displayed in both miles per hour (MPH) and feet per second (FPS).

Impact —

> The point of impact, in a horizontal plane, between ball and clubface is measured and displayed by positioning a ball on the screen relative to where impact occurred.

Ball Carry —

> The approximate distance the ball will carry in the air is displayed in yards. This calculation is made by measuring the clubhead speed and allowing for the club used, i.e., driver, 3 iron, etc.

Weight —

> How your weight is distributed over your left and right foot is calculated at address, top of swing and impact.

■ Ball Impact Analysis

The Sportech Swing Analyzer will print the results of a specific swing or the average of several swings. This provides the clubfitter with a profile of impact data that is useful for determining the right specification mix for the golfer.

A glance at the print-out reveals that the player's average take away is to the inside as denoted by the arrow track. The downswing is from outside-in at a 4° angle from square. The face is 6° closed relative to the clubhead path. Therefore, the ball will start left of center and then curve farther to the left due to the counter-clockwise sidespin imparted to the ball. Ball impact occurs on the heel which will offset somewhat the hooking sidespin due to the gear effect. The speed at which the clubhead is traveling at impact is 76 MPH with a carry distance of 193 yards. This speed is a little below the average male golfer, for this machine. Refer to the fitting portion of this book to see how this information can be used to determine the right set of clubs.

The other interesting feature of this swing analyzer is the weight distribution at the three positions. The majority of the players weight is on the left side at address. The weight is transferred to the right side but still has what most PGA Professionals feel is too much weight on the left side at the top of the swing. The player does have a good transfer to the left side at impact.

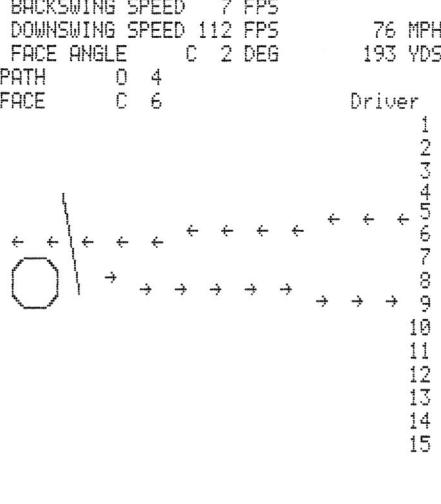

```
                    GOLF SWING ANALYZER

              (parentheses denote assignments)

          BACKSWING SPEED   7 FPS
          DOWNSWING SPEED 112 FPS           76 MPH
            FACE ANGLE      C  2 DEG        193 YDS
          PATH       O  4
          FACE       C  6                  Driver
                                              1
                                              2
                                              3
                                              4
                                  ← ← ←     5
          ← ←\← ← ←   ← ← ←             ←  6
          ○   \                               7
              \→                             8
                 → → → → → →   → → →     9
                                             10
                                             11
                                             12
                                             13
                                             14
                                             15



          WEIGHT DIST  LEFT %     RIGHT %
              TAKE AWAY  67         33
              TOP        29         71
              IMPACT     92          8
```

Figure A2-17
Printout from the Sportech Golf Swing Analyzer.

■ Bio-mechanical Analysis

Machine testing and player testing have both been discussed and the reader should have a good idea of the benefits and limitations of each method.

The main limitation of the mechanical golfer is that it represents only one type of swing and it cannot react to feel, nor can it give any player comments. However, the machine's main advantage is that it eliminates many of the variables inherent in player testing.

The main limitation of player testing is that the test environment cannot be as tightly controlled as that of the machine. This particularly refers to incomplete analytical data and player bias which enters into the tests, usually unknowingly. A plus factor is that player testing allows for player comments concerning feel, product aesthetics and playability as perceived by that particular golfer.

All this is leading up to a discussion of a method to obtain golf club performance data that eliminates many of the limitations of both machine testing and player testing. This method is known as bio-mechanical analysis. Technically speaking, it is the field of study known as Kinesiology, or the study of the principles of mechanics and anatomy in relation to human movement. Although this method has not been widely used in the golf field until recently, it has been widely used in other sports for both improving an athlete's performance and also for improving the equipment used.

To illustrate bio-mechanics, assume a golfer is hitting a drive. During this entire process there is an infinite amount of variables which directly affect the manner in which the golf ball leaves the clubface. These variables include the entire human body as a link system made up of different length, weight and shape segments. Each one of these segments also has a center of gravity and radius of gyration, which are factors to be used in calculating the various force measurements. Other variables are the components and specifications of the golf club and ball. All this data is obtained by special methods and fed into a computer utilizing a specially developed program which determines the instantaneous angular velocities, accelerations, moments of force and the percentage contribution to the total moment of each segment at any position of the swing. These measurements can be made as many times during the swing as necessary to adequately analyze a golf drive. In summary, bio-mechanical analysis applies the laws of physics and mechanics to both the golf club and ball used, and also applies them to the individual motions of the various segments of the human body during the swing.

■ Obtaining Golf Club Performance Data Through Bio-mechanical Analysis

Again, as with both machine testing and player testing, control clubs or control balls are used and all important data is recorded.

Data for bio-mechanical analysis is obtained from high speed motion pictures taken while the golfer is hitting. Cameras can be placed above, behind or to the side of the golfer as he swings depending on what type of data is required. Cameras can also be placed in all positions simultaneously if necessary. This photography session is most important and basic to the analysis. The cameras can be quite complex and expensive and usually range from a capability of 64 frames per second up to 5,000 frames per seconds. The camera which is used to take up to 5,000 frames per second is electrically motor driven and consumes a full 100 foot roll of film just to capture the sequence from the top of the backswing through the impact zone.

During the filming, each ball hit is recorded for distance, roll and accuracy on a gridded field as was also done in player and machine testing. This data is recorded in such a way as to correspond to the filming of each hit. Player comments are also recorded for future correlation with both film and the hitting results.

A recent improvement in bio-mechanics has been through the use of the computer and newly developed accessories. What once took as long as 20 hours of manual calculations with a slide rule can now be done in one minute or less with the computer when analyzing complex body motions. Some of the many measurements which can be obtained from the use of the computer coupled with this special equipment are listed below.

1. Position of maximum deceleration of each body segment.
2. The extent of the muscle action at each joint.
3. The extent of contribution of each body segment to the total motion.
4. Clubhead velocities before and after impact.
5. Ball velocity and spin.
6. Initial angle of trajectory.
7. Calculation of the striking mass.
8. Selected moment of inertial measurements.
9. Magnitude of shaft deflection.

■ How the Data Can Be Valuable

Bio-mechanical analysis can be applied to three basic areas relative to golf.

First, it can help determine what a particular golfer is doing wrong and help to isolate the portion of the body that causes the wrong movement. With present methods, this would be quite costly.

As an example of bio-mechanical analysis of body motion during the golf swing, assume that a particular golfer was accelerating their upper arm segment too fast causing their wrists to uncock early during the downswing. The ultimate result is a slow head speed at impact. If the analysis shows this, it can also show that if the golfer slows down his upper arm segment his wrists would uncock at the correct place to achieve maximum acceleration of the hands and ultimately resulting in maximizing the clubhead speed at impact. The system could be followed through at a later date after the problem is corrected to see how much the golfer had improved.

Second, bio-mechanics can also provide the types of information required to further understand golf club design and advance technology still further regarding the optimum golf club design.

As an example, during the swing a significant amount of shaft flexing takes place which affects not only the exact timing of the hit but also the effective loft of the club at impact, the effective lie of the club at impact, and also the effective face angle of the club at impact. By knowing the exact dynamics of shaft flexing, as shown by bio-mechanical analysis, can help determine the correct specifications of a club for a given force input to get the maximum benefit from the hit.

Third, and most important, bio-mechanics can satisfactorily relate the optimum golf club and ball to a given type of golfer. Here again, the combinations of possibilities are limitless when coupling a human to a particular golf club design that suits them best. For example, assume that a golfer wanted to determine the exact stiffness of shaft required. Possibly, a more flexible shaft is needed because the golfer has weak wrists, or a stiffer shaft is needed because the golfer has strong wrists and can generate adequate clubhead speed. To determine this exactly would require the use of bio-mechanical analysis since so many other variables exist both in the human and in the golf club. Weak or strong wrists cannot stand alone as the only variable relating to the choice of shaft flexes, but it is an important one.

NOTES

ACETONE — A clear, flammable chemical liquid used to soften and shine the plastic trim parts of golf clubs. Acetone can also completely dissolve most plastic parts if left in contact for too long a time.

ANALINE DYE STAINS — Water or alcohol soluble stains which have the ability to penetrate deep into hardwoods.

ANGLE OF ATTACK — The degree of descent of the clubhead approaching the ball just prior to impact.

AWL — A small pointed tool similar to an ice pick used for making small holes. Also called a prick punch.

BACKSCREW — A special steel screw used to secure the shaft to the wood head. It is installed in the back of the hosel, through the shaft and into the head.

BACKSPIN — The backward rotation of a golf ball in flight around a horizontal axis.

BACKWEIGHT(ING) — An amount of weight added to the rear portion of a wood club designed to move the center of gravity back in the clubhead; normally done by attaching preformed brass or steel pieces to the rear of the wood head, or by pouring lead into a rear cavity.

BELL PLUG — Found on older clubs, this is the hardwood plug driven into the butt end of the shaft to provide the proper tapered shaft for the top of a leather grip. It also served as a base on which to secure the grip and cap.

BLADE — The head of an iron club.

BLADE LENGTH — The distance from the forward most portion of the toe to the heel portion of the hosel radius.

BLENDED TOE — A type of iron head design where the back of the blade rounds into the toe through a given radius.

BLOCK — A rough 'L' shaped piece of wood cut from a flitch which will yield one raw wood head.

BORING — The drilling of the hole in the neck of a clubhead into which the shaft will fit. This determines the lie, face progression and face angle of the head.

BORON — A high strength, high modulus lightweight filament that is 5 times the strength of steel and twice the stiffness. Used as one of several material types in composite shaft designs. Boron influences flex point but primarily is used to add strength to the tip area.

BOUNCE (OR INVERSION) — When the trailing edge of the sole is below the leading edge of the sole in the square hit position.

BOXED TOE — A type of iron head design where the back of the blade makes a sharp transition into the toe.

BULGE — The horizontal curvature on the face of a wood head, expressed in inches of radius.

BULLSEYE — The smallest full circle formed by the top layer on a laminated wood head.

BUTT SECTION — The larger end or grip end of a golf shaft. The butt section can be measured from the last step to the butt end.

CALIPER — A tool used to measure diameters of grips, shaft sections, etc.

CAMBER — Referred to also as a rocker sole, radiused sole, 2 way and 4 way roll. The radius curve in the sole of an iron club, whether from toe to heel, or leading edge to trailing edge, or both. Hence, 2 way and 4 way radius.

COLLAR SHRINKER — An electric element used to reduce the size of trim collars by heating. This only works on certain trim collars made from a material capable of being shrunk under heat.

COLORCOTE — A paint used to cover the grain of a wood head during finishing thus giving an opaque look. Colorcotes can also be obtained in "see through" or non-opaque paints.

COMPOSITE — A combination of materials comprised of a base material and some type of adhesive to bind them together. Can come in a variety of forms ranging from fibers, particles or layers. Also, the principal term used to describe shafts made of more than one material.

CORRUGATION — *See Scoring.*

COUNTERSINK — (noun) A cone shaped tool used to enlarge the top part of a hole so that the head of a screw will fit flush with the surface. (verb) To modify a sharp edge such as found inside a hosel.

COUNTERBALANCING — Reducing the club's swingweight by adding weight to the grip end. Total weight increases and swingweight decreases.

CROWN — The highest point of the top radius of a wood head.

CYCOLAC — An injection molded plastic used for face inserts in wood clubs.

DECALS — Transfers or designs made from lacquer or enamel silkscreened on a special paper. Decals are usually applied to wood clubs and are available in water soluble or reverse image types which require a special solvent.

DEEP FACE — Wood heads that have a face height of 1⅞" or higher. Any wood head with a face height greater than standard.

DEFLECTION BOARD — A tool used to measure and compare the bending of one shaft to another. The butt end of the shaft is clamped and a 7 pound weight is hung from the tip end to create a bend or curve in the shaft. Readings are taken along the shaft and compared to readings taken from other shafts.

DELAMINATION — The separation of the layers of a laminated wood head or insert.

DIG — *See Scoop.*

DOWEL — A round wooden rod, usually ⅝" diameter, inserted into the butt end of a shaft for lengthening woods or irons.

DRAW KNIFE — A knife with a handle at each end used to remove old grips and underlistings.

DRILL REAMER — A tapered drill bit which is used to both enlarge and deepen a tapered bore hole.

DYNAMIC FITTING — Method of fitting golf clubs in which fitting decisions are made based upon ball striking tests. Gained credibility following the printing of Ralph Maltby's book, "The Complete Golf Club Fitting Plan."

EFFECTIVE LOFT (Also Real Loft) — The loft of a wood club when it is rolled into the square (0°) face angle position. Also the loft of a wood club when the face and shaft centerline are both perpendicular to target line.

END SCREW — A small screw, usually brass, installed through the bottom of through bore shafts that serves as a second locking screw. Seen usually on pre-1960 through-bored woods.

EPOXY — A two part resin used for adhesion, coating, casting, etc. It is mixed by combining a base and activator together causing an exothermic reaction to create a very strong bond.

FACE — The outlined or defined hitting surface of a wood or iron club.

FACE ANGLE — The angle of the face of a wood club to the grounded sole line with the shaft hole perpendicular to the line of flight.

FACE CENTERLINE — An imaginary line which bisects the head of a club in the exact geometric center of the face or insert.

FACE DEPTH — The measurement of the height of the face of a wood head or iron head on its centerline. Noted as either shallow, normal or deep.

FACE PROGRESSION — Measurement of the distance from the centerline of the shaft or hosel bore to the front leading portion of the clubface in both woods and irons.

FERRULE — A tapered plastic sleeve which forms a smooth transition from the top of the hosel to the shaft.

FILAMENT WINDING — The process for manufacturing a seamless composite shaft with continuous resin-impregnated "yarns" of graphite wound around a mandrel in a pre-determined pattern from tip to butt, forming a shaft.

FIRING PIN — A circular piece of metal installed in the center of some types of inserts. Usually aluminum or brass.

FIRST STEP — The first formed and defined visual transition to increased diameter in a golf shaft.

FLANGE — Term describing the elongation of the trailing edge of an iron club or putter.

FLAT LIE — The lie angle is more level or horizontal than the standard.

FLEX — The bending action of the shaft as it relates to the speed of the golfers swing. A designation given to shafts to denote the degree to which they bend against industry standards.

FLEX POINT *(Also known as "Kick-Point")* — The location on the shaft where the bend is the greatest.

FLITCH — A solid or laminated rough piece of wood which will yield blocks and ultimately raw turned wood heads.

FLUTED SHAFT — A steel shaft that has channels formed vertically (longitudinally) in the shaft usually near the tip end.

FORCE FIT SHAFT — A tip taper wood or iron shaft to a tapered hosel head assembly.

FOREWEIGHTING(ING) — Locating weight in the face area of a club, done to bring the center of gravity forward in the clubhead. Usually done through installation of heavier insert material.

FORGING — One of the processes for forming iron heads. A metal bar is placed between two halves of a die and hammered under pressure into the rough shape of an iron head.

431 — A type of stainless steel used to make investment cast iron heads.

GATE — The buildup of metal on a raw investment cast iron or metal wood head that indicates where the metal was poured into the mold. Usually found on the bottom radius of the toe.

GATING — The grinding off of the excess metal left from the raw casting on the toe of an investment cast iron or metal wood head.

GOLF CLUB NAME TERMINOLOGY

Driver — Name given to the #1 wood.
Brassie — Older name given to a #2 wood.
Spoon — Older name given to the #3 wood.
Cleek — Older name given to the #4 wood.
Baffy — Older name given to the #5 wood.
Driving Iron — Older name given to the #1 iron.
Mid Iron — Older name given to the #2 iron.
Mid Mashie — Older name given to the #3 iron.

Mashie Iron — Older name given to the #4 iron.
Mashie — Older name given to the #5 iron.
Spade Mashie — Older name given to the #6 iron.
Mashie Niblick — Older name given to the #7 iron.
Lofter — *See Pitcher.* Older name given to the #8 iron.
Niblick — Older name given to the #9 iron.
Pitching Wedge — More of modern era iron club used to approach the green and for chipping.
Sand Wedge — An iron club used from sand or pitching from around the green.
Putter — The club designed for use on greens to stroke the ball into the hole.

GRAPHITE — A pure carbon mineral made into fibers, mixed with a resin and formed into a golf shaft. It is known for its very light weight and high strength.

GRAPHITE COMPOSITE — A golf shaft made of a low percentage of carbon graphite and a higher percentage of another material such as fiberglass.

GRIP MATERIAL — The substance from which any grip is made. The most common types are rubber, rubber and cork, rubber and cord, kraton and rubber and leather.

GRIT — The degree of coarseness of abrasive cloth or paper denoted by a number. The larger the number, the finer the grit or coarseness.

GROUND LINE — An imaginary line running from the clubface to back and perpendicular to the shaft centerline.

HEAD WIDTH — In a wood head, the distance from the farthest forward point of the leading edge to the farthest rear point of the back line.

HEEL — The lower back area of the hosel where the sole meets it.

HEEL/TOE WEIGHTING — Process of weight distribution whereby weight is relocated from the center of a wood or iron equally to the toe and heel. This process does not change the center of gravity but does improve off-center hits by putting more mass in these areas.

HOSEL *(Also called the Neck)* — Portion of wood or iron head that receives the shaft.

HOSEL OFFSET — The distance from the farthest front portion of the hosel to the farthest front portion of the leading edge at the face center.

IMPULSE PROFILE — Color computer generated graph demonstrating the loss of ball velocity for ball impacts from various points of the clubface.

INLAY — 1) Another term for an insert. 2) The wood or epoxy section set into the heads of some models of metal woods.

INSERT — A piece of material placed into a routed cavity in the face of a wood head, designed to improve the durability of the face from impact between the ball and clubhead. Also, used mainly as a decorative piece on metal woods and irons.

INSERT MATERIALS — Cycolac, epoxy, vulcanized fiber, aluminum, wood, radiated fiberglass, graphite, melamine, titanium, brass, phenolic laminate and acrylics.

INVESTMENT CASTING *(Also known as the "Lost Wax" process)* — A method of accurately producing iron heads, some soleplates and metal woods. A mold is made, and a wax is cast from the mold. This wax is dipped several times in a ceramic slurry or mixture which then hardens. The slurry is heated and the wax melts out (lost wax). Molten metal is poured into the slurry shell (invested) and allowed to cool.

KICK-POINT — *See Flex Point.*

KILN DRYING — The removal of moisture from wood by baking at elevated temperatures over a period of time.

LAMINATED — A type of wood head made by gluing thin strips of maple together.

LAYUP — The layup is the type of lamination in a wood head. Layups can be either edgegrain or sidegrain or a combination of both. Layup also refers to the various thicknesses of each layer of wood in a laminated head.

LENGTH - CLUB — The distance from the heel portion of the sole radius to the top of the grip cap. This definition is the traditional method.

LIE — The angle of the centerline of the shaft with the ground line, tangent to the sole at the centerline of the face.

LOCKING SCREW — *See Backscrew.*

LOFT - IRON — The angle of the face on its centerline to the centerline of the hosel bore, measured in degrees.

LOFT - WOOD — The angle of the face on its centerline to a line perpendicular to the sole line measured in degrees. Loft is then read at a point ½ the distance of the face height.

LORYTHMIC SCALE — A type of swingweight scale measuring swingweight about a fulcrum point 14" down from the top of grip. Measurements are in the direct letter/number swingweight designation such as D0, D1, D2.

LOST WAX — *See Investment Casting.*

LOW PROFILE — Iron heads whose face heights are lower than the average.

MASKING — 1. The application of a lacquer or varnish to the face of a wood club to prevent stain from bleeding onto the face. 2. Covering the face and soleplate surfaces with tape prior to application of colorcote.

MASTER MODEL — The exact replica of a particular wood or iron head from which all the other heads will be copied.

MIRACLE TAPE *(Also known as "2 Way Tape")* — A tape which is coated on both surfaces with adhesive. Used for grip installation.

MODULUS — The amount a material will deform when stressed. (i.e., High modulus graphite has a higher resistance to deformity (bending) because the carbon atoms lie closer together to form a stronger bond.

MOLDS — In the investment casting procedure, a 2 part cavity which exactly reproduces the iron or metal wood head by injecting wax into it.

MOMENT OF INERTIA — Measure of an object's resistance to twisting.

MORTITE — A non-hardening putty material used to build a dam around the insert cavity of a wood head before pouring the epoxy insert.

NECK — *See Hosel.*

NOSING — The removal of that portion of wood left on the toe by the holding locations of the turning machine.

OFFICIAL SCALE — A type of swingweight scale that bases its measurements about a fulcrum point 12" down from the grip end. Swingweight measurements are in direct ounce readings such as 20.3, 20.5, etc.

OFFSET *(Also called Hosel Offset)* — The distance from the farthest front portion of the hosel to the farthest front portion of the leading edge of the clubface.

OVERALL WEIGHT *(Also called Static Weight, Total Weight and Dead Weight)* — The measurement in grams or ounces of a golf club's actual weight.

PERIMETER WEIGHTING — Process of weighting a club whereby most of the weight is placed in the toe, heel and sole of the head rather than the center.

PERSIMMON — A type of hardwood tree from which some wood heads are made. The tree is native to parts of North America and the Far East. A persimmon tree is in the ebony family.

PHILLIPS HEAD — A type of screw with crossed slots on the head. The corresponding screwdriver has four ridges tapering to a blunt tip. *Note: Not to be confused with a Reed and Prince type. (Frearson)*

PREPREG — Shortened term for "preimpregnated carbon fiber." Available as a sheet or tape made up of composite fibers with epoxy resin acting as a binding agent.

PRORYTHMIC SCALE — A type of swingweight scale basing its measurement on a 14" fulcrum, but also giving total weight readings in ounces and grams.

RADIO-FREQUENCY DRYING — The removal of moisture from a wood head using electronic radio waves. This method dries the wood from the center out and is the fastest method of moisture removal.

RADIUSED SOLE — *See Camber.*

RAKE — The alternate flaring out of the cutting teeth of a hacksaw blade. This must be filed off before the hacksaw blade may be used for cutting scoring lines on woods. The word is also used by some manufacturers to describe a bounce sole.

REAMER — A tapered cutting tool usually having straight cutting flutes, which is used to enlarge or clean out a tapered hosel bore.

REED AND PRINCE — A type of screw head with crossed slots. The matching screwdriver is recognized by four ridges tapering to a sharp tip. Note: Not to be confused with a Phillips head.

REGISTRATION NUMBER *(Also called Recording Number)* — A number or series of letters and numbers stamped on the back, sole or neck of woods and irons, indicating either the model style or partial specifications of the club. A decal is also sometimes used on woods.

RIND — Used on antique clubs, these were strips of coarse cloth or wool wrapped around the shaft under the leather grip to serve as the underlisting.

ROLL — The vertical curvature or radius built from crown to sole on the face of a wood head.

SANDING CONE — A padded cone which attaches to a motor. It is covered with abrasive paper and used to remove finish and sand wood heads.

SCARE — In antique wood clubs, the area of the neck where the shaft and head are spliced together.

SCOOP (Also called Dig) — The sole angle of an iron where the leading edge is lower than the trailing edge when the face is square to the target, and the hosel or bore is perpendicular to the target.

SCORING (Also called Corrugation) — The lines cut, stamped or cast into the face of wood, metal wood or iron head.

SCORING SAW — A special hacksaw used to cut the scoring lines in the face of a wood head. The blade is altered to remove the rake of the cutting teeth, thus giving a proper width cut.

SCOTCH TOE — A type of iron head design where the toe is somewhat square in its appearance as opposed to being rounded.

SCREW-IN SHAFTS — A type of iron shaft with a threaded tip which is designed to screw into a threaded hosel securing the head to the shaft.

SET MAKEUP — The particular complement of golf clubs in any set which by U.S.G.A. Rules cannot exceed 14 clubs.

17-4 — A type of stainless steel used in the manufacture of investment cast iron heads, denoting 17% chromium and 4% nickel in the steel composition.

SHAFT BEND POINT — The point of maximum deflection during the bending of a shaft.

SHAFT CENTERLINE — An imaginary line running down the exact center of the shaft, through the hosel and touching the ground.

SHAFT CLAMP — A rubber or vinyl jaw designed to hold the shaft firmly in a vise without damaging it.

SHAFT CURVE — The deflected curve of a shaft when its stiffness is being plotted on a deflection board. The curve indicates some of the bending or deflection properties of a shaft.

SHAFT FLEX — A comparative measurement of a shaft's resistance to bending or deflection under a given stress and load. Flex can be measured on a shaft deflection board and divided into the 5 shaft flexes: L, A, R, S and X.

SHAFT FREQUENCY — The measurement of the rate of oscillations of a given flex shaft at a given head weight and club length.

SHAFT IN HOSEL — Type of head to shaft assembly where the shaft fits inside the hosel.

SHAFT OVER HOSEL — Type of head to shaft assembly in which the shaft fits over the hosel. *(Irons or putters only)*

SHAFT STEP PATTERNS — The length and arrangement of the shaft's diameter changes (step downs) which indicate the flex characteristics of the shaft. Examples are ProFit, Jet Step, Dynamic and Propel II.

SHALLOW FACE — Wood heads that have a face height of 1⅜" or less. Any wood head with a face height less than standard.

SHEATHING — A cellulose acetate material that is cut into strips to make grip collars or whipping collars. It was predominantly used on older clubs.

SHIM — A small, thin piece of paper or metal that is installed between the shaft and hosel to tighten the head to the shaft during installation.

SLOPE ANGLE — The angle created by the intersection of the top line and sole line in an iron head.

SOLE — The bottom of a wood or iron head that would normally touch the ground.

SOLE ANGLE — The angle created in the sole of an iron between the sole line (front to back) and the ground. The three sole angles are bounce, square and scoop.

SOLE INVERSION — *See Bounce.*

SOLE LINE — With the clubhead in the proper lie and playing position, this is the line of contact of sole to ground running from the leading to trailing edge.

SOLEPLATE — The metal part attached to the bottom of wood heads to prevent wear on the bottom of the head. Another primary function of the plate is to increase the weight of the head. Soleplate materials are usually aluminum, brass, zinc and steel.

SOLE RADIUS — The amount of curvature of the sole of a wood or iron head, as measured from toe to heel. Usually ranges from four to eight inches of radius.

SOLE WEIGHTING — Distributing the weight on a wood or iron head as low in the head as it can be placed. This process is usually associated with low profile clubs and heavy soleplated woods.

SQUARE BORE METHOD — The method of drilling the hole for the shaft that results in the center line of the hosel being perpendicular to the sole line for any face angle.

STATIC FITTING — Method of fitting golf clubs using charts or rulers. Seldom do players actually hit shots.

STATIC WEIGHT — *See Total Weight.*

STEEL WOOL — Long fine fibers of steel joined together into pad or ribbon form and used as a light abrasive for leveling, polishing or cleaning.

STEP DRILLING — Making or enlarging the bore hole on a clubhead to receive a tapered shaft by using a series of three progressively larger drill bits to simulate the taper.

STEP PATTERN — The order and lengths of the individual steps in a golf shaft which are used to indicate shaft model or brand name.

STEP-TAPERING — In the manufacture of steel golf shafts, the procedure of progressively reducing the tube's diameter from butt to tip by squeezing the shaft down through a series of step dies.

STRONG (LOFT) — Less loft than is the standard for any given club.

SWINGWEIGHT — A measurement which indicates the weight distribution of a golf club about a fixed fulcrum point. It is expressed by a letter/number combination (A1, B2, C3, D1, etc.) or an ounce measurement (20.3, 20.5, etc.).

TACK-RAG — A cloth treated with a sticky compound which is used to pick up dirt and dust particles from a wood head prior to finish application.

TARGET LINE — An imaginary line drawn from the ball or clubface directly to the target.

TIP PARALLEL SECTION — The constant diameter of a golf shaft just below the first step down.

TIP SECTION — That part of a shaft from the tip end to the first step.

TIP TAPER SHAFT — A golf shaft with a tapering of its diameter in the tip section. This tapering is at a rate of .0075" per inch.

TOE — The point farthest outward of the clubhead on a wood or ironhead.

TOP LINE — The top of an iron head where the face and the back meet. This line can be sharp, blunt or rounded in shape.

TORQUE — The amount of rotational twist that occurs in a golf shaft during the swing.

TRAJECTORY — The pattern or shape of the flight of a golf ball with respect to its height and direction.

TWO COMPONENT POLYURETHANE — A type of polyurethane with an epoxy resin component commonly used on metal woods.

UNDERLISTING *(Also called a Listing)* — The form placed on the grip section of a shaft which serves as the foundation for the shape and size of a leather grip.

UNITIZED SHAFT *(Also called a Parallel Tip Shaft)* — A type of shaft in which the outside diameter of the shaft from the tip to the first step remains constant or is parallel.

UPRIGHT — When the lie angle is more erect or vertical than the standard.

VARIABLE BORE METHOD — The method of drilling the hole for the shaft that results in the center line of the hosel not being perpendicular to the sole line, except for the boring of a 0° face angle.

VENT HOLE — The hole in the cap end of a rubber grip or underlisting designed to release air pressure built up during grip installation.

VISE PADS — Padded holders used to secure and protect a wood head while being held in a vise.

WEAK — Term indicating more loft than is the standard for any given club.

WHIPPING — The string wrapping which covers the neck of a wood club. Made of braided nylon or monofilament nylon in modern era clubs. Made of linen, waxed linen or pitch tar linen in old era clubs.

WOOD FILLER — A thick, pasty substance used to fill the pores of a wood head prior to finish application.

DEFINITION NOTES

NOTES

APPENDIX 4

UNITED STATES GOLF ASSOCIATION RULES GOVERNING GOLF CLUB AND BALL DESIGN

The following Rules of Golf, which apply to golf equipment, have been reprinted through the courtesy of the United States Golf Association. (1993)

Clubs and the Ball

The United States Golf Association and the Royal and Ancient Golf Club of St. Andrews reserve the right to change the Rules and make and change the interpretations relating to clubs, balls and other implements at any time.

Rule 4. Clubs

If there may be any reasonable basis for doubt as to whether a club which is to be manufactured conforms with Rule 4 and Appendix II, the manufacturer should submit a sample to the United States Golf Association for a ruling, such sample to become its property for reference purposes. If a manufacturer fails to do so, he assumes the risk of a ruling that the club does not conform with the Rules of Golf.

A player in doubt as to the conformity of a club should consult the United States Golf Association.

4-1. Form and Make of Clubs

A club is an implement designed to be used for striking the ball.

A putter is a club designed primarily for use on the putting green.

The player's clubs shall conform with the provisions of this Rule and with the specifications and interpretations set forth in Appendix II.

a. GENERAL

The club shall be composed of a shaft and a head. All parts of the club shall be fixed so that the club is one unit. The club shall not be designed to be adjustable except for weight. The club shall not be substantially different from the traditional and customary form and make.

b. SHAFT

The shaft shall be generally straight, with the same bending and twisting properties in any direction, and shall be attached to the clubhead at the heel either directly or through a single plain neck or socket. A putter shaft may be attached to any point in the head.

c. GRIP

The grip consists of that part of the shaft designed to be held by the player and any material added to it for the purpose of obtaining a firm hold. The grip shall be substantially straight and plain in form and shall not be molded for any part of the hands.

d. CLUBHEAD

The distance from the heel to the toe of the clubhead shall be greater than the distance from the face to the back. The clubhead shall be generally plain in shape.

The clubhead shall have only one face designed for striking the ball, except that a putter may have two such faces if their characteristics are the same, they are opposite each other and the loft of each is the same and does not exceed 10 degrees.

e. CLUB FACE

The face shall not have any degree of concavity and, in relation to the ball, shall be hard and rigid. It shall be generally smooth except for such markings as are permitted by Appendix II.

f. WEAR

A club which conforms with Rule 4-1 when new is deemed to conform after wear through normal use. Any part of a club which has been purposely altered is regarded as new and must conform, in the altered state, with the Rules.

CLUBS

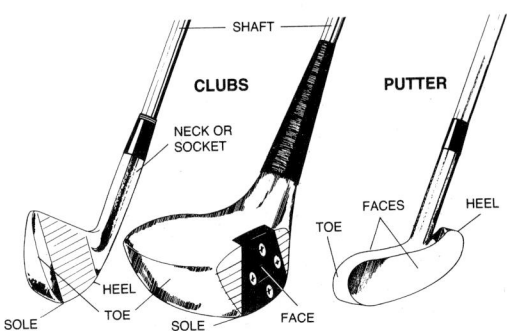

824

g. DAMAGE

If a player's club ceases to conform with Rule 4-1 because of damage sustained in the normal course of play, the player may:

(i) use the club in its damaged state, but only for the remainder of the stipulated round during which such damage was sustained; or

(ii) without unduly delaying play, repair it.

A club which ceases to conform because of damage sustained other than in the normal course of play shall not subsequently be used during the round.

(Damage changing playing characteristics of club — see Rule 4-2.)

(Damage rendering the club unfit for play — see Rule 4-4a.)

4-2. Playing Characteristics Changed

During a stipulated round, the playing characteristics of a club shall not be purposely changed by adjustment or any other means.

If the playing characteristics of a player's club are changed during a round because of damage sustained in the normal course of play, the player may:

(i) use the club in its altered state; or

(ii) without unduly delaying play, repair it.

If the playing characteristics of player's club are changed because of damage sustained other than in the normal course of play, the club shall not subsequently be used during the round.

Damage to a club which occurred prior to a round may be repaired during the round, provided the playing characteristics are not changed and play is not unduly delayed.

4-3. Foreign Material

No foreign material shall be applied to the club face for the purpose of influencing the movement of the ball.

Penalty for Breach of Rule 4-1, -2 or -3:
Disqualification.

Appendices II and III

Any design in a club or ball which is not covered by Rules 4 and 5 and Appendices II and III, or which might significantly change the nature of the game, will be ruled on by the United States Golf Association and the Royal and Ancient Golf Club of St. Andrews.

Note: Equipment approved for use or marketed prior to January 1, 1988 which conformed to the Rules in effect in 1987 but does not conform to the 1988 and subsequent Rules may be used until December 31, 1995, thereafter all equipment must conform to the current Rules.

Appendix II
Design of Clubs

Rule 4-1 prescribes general regulations for the design of clubs. The following paragraphs, which provide some detailed specifications and clarify how Rule 4-1 is interpreted, should be read in conjunction with this Rule.

4-1a. General

ADJUSTABILITY — Exception for Putters

Clubs other than putters shall not be designed to be adjustable except for weight.

Some other forms of adjustability are permitted in the design of a putter, provided that:

(i) the adjustment cannot be readily made;

(ii) all adjustable parts are firmly fixed and there is no reasonable likelihood of them working loose during a round; and

(iii) all configurations of adjustment conform with the Rules.

The disqualification penalty for purposely changing the playing characteristics of a club during a stipulated round (Rule 4-2) applies to all clubs, including a putter.

Note: It is recommended that all putters with adjustable parts be submitted to the United States Golf Association for a ruling.

4-1b. Shaft

GENERALLY STRAIGHT

The shaft shall be at least 18 inches (457 mm) in length. It shall be straight from the top of the grip to a point not more than 5 inches (127 mm) above the sole, measured along the axis of the shaft and the neck or socket.

BENDING AND TWISTING PROPERTIES

The shaft must be so designed and manufactured that at any point along its length:

(i) it bends in such a way that the deflection is the same regardless of how the shaft is rotated about its longitudinal axis; and

(ii) it twists the same amount in both directions.

ATTACHMENT TO CLUBHEAD

The neck or socket must not be more than 5 inches (127 mm) in length, measured from the top of the neck or socket to the sole along its axis. The shaft and the neck or socket must remain in line with the heel, or with a point to the right or left of the heel, when the club is viewed in the address position. The distance between the axis of the shaft or the neck or socket and the back of the heel must not exceed .625 inches (16 mm).

Exception for Putters: The shaft or neck or socket of a putter may be fixed at any point in the head and need not remain in line with the heel. The axis of the shaft from the top to a point not more than 5 inches (127 mm) above the sole must diverge from the vertical in the toe-heel plane by at least 10 degrees when the club is in its normal address position.

4-1c. Grip

(i) For clubs other than putters the grip must be generally circular in cross-section, except that a continuous, straight, slightly raised rib may be incorporated along the full length of the grip.

(ii) A putter grip may have a non-circular cross-section, provided the cross-section has no concavity and remains generally similar throughout the length of the grip.

(iii) The grip may be tapered, but must not have any bulge or waist.

(iv) For clubs other than putters, the axis of the grip must coincide with the axis of the shaft.

(v) The cross sectional dimension of a grip measured in any direction shall not exceed 1.75 inches (45 mm).

(vi) A putter may have more than one grip, provided each is circular in cross-section and the axis of each coincides with the axis of the shaft.

Note: Putters approved for use or marketed prior to January 1, 1992 which are in breach of clause (vi) may be used until December 31, 1992.

GRIPS

CLUB GRIP CIRCULAR

PUTTER GRIP FLAT SIDE (Permitted on putters only)

4-1d. Clubhead

DIMENSIONS

The dimensions of a clubhead (see diagram) are measured with the clubhead in its normal address position, on horizontal lines between vertical projections of the outermost points of (i) the heel and the toe and (ii) the face and the back. If the outermost point of the heel is not clearly defined, it is deemed to be .625 inches (16 mm) above the horizontal plane on which the club is resting in its normal address position.

PLAIN IN SHAPE

The clubhead shall be generally plain in shape. All parts shall be rigid, structural in nature and functional.

Features such as holes through the head, windows or transparencies, or appendages to the main body of the head such as plates, rods or fins for the purpose of meeting dimensional specifications for aiming or for any other purpose are not permitted. Exceptions may be made for putters.

Any furrows in or runners on the sole shall not extend into the face.

4-1e. Club Face

GENERAL

Except for specified markings, the surface roughness must not exceed that of decorative sandblasting. Markings must not have sharp edges or raised lips, as determined by a finger test. The material and construction of the face shall not be designed or manufactured to have the effect at impact of a spring, or to impart significantly more spin to the ball than a standard steel face, or to have any other effect which would unduly influence the movement of the ball.

IMPACT AREA MARKINGS

Markings within the area where impact is intended (the "impact area") are governed by the following:

(i) *Grooves.* A series of straight grooves with diverging sides and symmetrical cross-section may be used. (See diagram.) The width and cross-section must be generally consistent across the face of the club and along the length of the grooves. Any rounding of groove edges shall be in the form of a radius which does not exceed .020 inches (.5 mm). The width of the groove shall not exceed .035 inches (.9 mm), using the 30 degree method of measurement on file with the United States Golf Association. The distance between edges of adjacent grooves must not be less than three times the width of a groove and not less than .075 inches (1.9 mm). The depth of a groove must not exceed .020 inches (.5 mm).

GROOVES

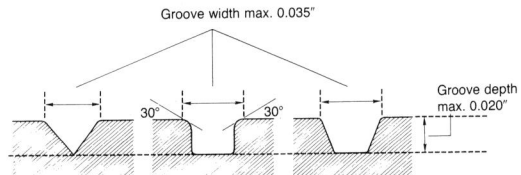

EXAMPLES OF PERMISSIBLE GROOVE CROSS-SECTIONS

(ii) *Punch Marks.* Punch marks may be used. The area of any such mark must not exceed .0044 square inches (2.8 sq. mm). A mark must not be closer to an adjacent mark than .168 (4.3 mm), measured from center to center. The depth of a punch mark must not exceed .040 inches (1.0 mm). If punch marks are used in combination with grooves, a punch mark may not be closer to a groove than .168 inches (4.3 mm), measured from center to center.

DECORATIVE MARKINGS

The center of the impact area may be indicated by a design within the boundary of a square whose sides are .375 inches (9.5 mm) in length. Such a design must not unduly influence the movement of the ball. Decorative markings are permitted outside the impact area.

NON-METALLIC CLUB FACE MARKINGS

The above specifications do not apply to clubs on which the impact area of the face is non-metallic and whose loft angle is 24 degrees or less, but markings which could unduly influence the movement of the ball are prohibited. Clubs with this type of face and a loft angle exceeding 24 degrees may have grooves of maximum width .040 inches (1.0 mm) and maximum depth 1½ times the groove width, but must otherwise conform to the markings specifications above.

PUTTER FACE MARKINGS

The specifications above with regard to clubface markings do not apply to putters.

Appendix III
The Ball

a. WEIGHT

The weight of the ball shall not be greater than 1.620 ounces avoirdupois (45.93 gm).

b. SIZE

The diameter of the ball shall be not less than 1.680 inches (42.67 mm). This specification will be satisfied if, under its own weight, a ball falls through a 1.680 inches diameter ring gauge in fewer than 25 out of 100 randomly selected positions, the test being carried out at a temperature of 23°±1°C.

c. SPHERICAL SYMMETRY

The ball must not be designed, manufactured or intentionally modified to have flight properties which differ from those of a spherically symmetrical ball.

Furthermore, the ball will not conform to the Rules of Golf if it fails to satisfy the performance specifications outlined below:

As described in procedures on file at the United States Golf Association, each ball type will be tested using 40 balls of that type, in 20 pairs. One ball of each pair will be launched spinning about one specified axis; the other ball of each pair will be launched spinning about a different, but also specified axis. Differences in carry and time of flight between the two balls of each pair will be recorded. If the mean of the differences in carry is greater than 3.0 yards, and that value is significant at the 5% level, OR if the mean of the differences in time of flight is greater than .20 seconds, and that value is significant at the 5% level, the ball type will not conform to the Rules of Golf.

Note: Methods of determining whether a ball performs as if it were generally spherically symmetrical may be subject to change as instrumentation becomes available to measure other properties accurately, such as the aerodynamic coefficient of lift, coefficient of drag and moment of inertia.

d. INITIAL VELOCITY

The velocity of the ball shall not be greater than 250 feet (76.2 m) per second when measured on apparatus approved by the United States Golf Association. A maximum tolerance of 2% will be allowed. The temperature of the ball when tested shall be 23°±1°C.

e. OVERALL DISTANCE STANDARD

A brand of golf ball, when tested on apparatus approved by the U.S.G.A. on the outdoor range at the U.S.G.A. Headquarters under the conditions set forth in the Overall Distance Standard for golf balls on file with the U.S.G.A., shall not cover an average distance in carry and roll exceeding 280 yards plus a tolerance of 6%. Note: The 6% tolerance will be reduced to a minimum of 4% as test techniques are improved.

APPENDIX 5

GOLF CLUB MANUFACTURERS' NAME AND ADDRESS LISTING

Accuform Golf International, Inc.
8933 Western Way Bldg. 4, Suite 12
Jacksonville FL 32256
800/668-7873

Aldila, Inc.
15822 Bernardo Center Dr.
San Diego CA 92127
800/854-2786

All American Golf Sales, Inc.
112 East Van Buren St.
Joliet IL 60432
800/621-5811

Allied Golf Co.
4538 West Fullerton Ave.
Chicago IL 60639
800/877-5346

Bel Air Golf Company
235 East Gardena Blvd.
Gardena CA 90248
800/824-3707

Callaway Golf
2285 Rutherford Rd.
Carlsbad CA 92008-8815
800/228-2767

Cleveland Golf Company, Inc.
5630 Cerritos Ave.
Cypress CA 90630
800/999-6263

Cobra Golf Inc., II
1812 Aston Ave.
Carlsbad CA 92008
800/BAFFLER

Confidence Golf Co.
2858 Walnut Hill Lane
Dallas TX 75229
800/421-1833

Ray Cook Golf Company
1396 Poinsettia Ave.
Vista CA 92083
800/531-7252

Otey Crisman Golf Company
201 Faulk Ave.
Selma AL 36703
800/633-2575

Daiwa Corporation - Golf Division
7421 Chapman Ave.
Garden Grove CA 92641
800/736-GOLF

Delta Golf Co.
2901 W. Montrose Ave.
Chicago IL 60618
800/767-3953

Foot-Joy (Titleist & Foot-Joy
Worldwide)
PO Box 965
Fairhaven MA 02719-0965
800/225-8500

Golf Design USA
14535 Firestone Blvd.
La Mirada CA 90638
800/854-6148

GolfWorks®
4820 Jacksontown Rd.
PO Box 3008
Newark OH 43058-3008
800/848-8358

H & B / Powerbilt
PO Box 35700
200 W. Broadway Ave.
Louisville KY 40232
800/282-2287

Ben Hogan Co.
8000 Villa Park Dr.
Richmond VA 23228
800/227-3290

Karsten Manufacturing Corp.
2201 W. Desert Cove
Phoenix AZ 85029
800/528-0650

Kenneth Smith Inc.
12931 W. 71st St.
Shawnee KS 66216
800/234-8968

Lynx Golf Inc.
16017 East Valley Blvd.
City of Industy CA 91749
800/233-5969

MacGregor Golf Co., Inc.
1601 South Slappey Blvd.
Albany GA 31708
800/841-4358

Maruman Golf USA, Inc.
5870 Oakbrook Parkway, Suite B
Norcross GA 30093
800/533-2716

Matzie Golf Co., Inc.
112 Penn St.
El Segundo CA 90245
800/722-7125

Mizuno Corporation of America
5125 Peachtree Ind. Blvd.
Norcross GA 30092
800/333-7888

Northwestern Golf Co.
4701 North Ravenswood Ave.
Chicago IL 60640
800/621-5156

Odyssey Sports, Inc.
1945 Camino Vida Roble
Suite "L"
Carlsbad CA 92008
800/487-5664

Ofer Custom Swing-Fit Golf Clubs
3621 Middle Branch Ave. NE
Canton OH 44705
800/477-7893

Old Master
65 North Congress St.
PO Box 379
York SC 29745
800/332-6853

Orlimar Golf Co., Inc.
25673 Nickel Place
Hayward CA 94545
800/833-4266

Pinseeker Golf Corp.
3502 South Susan St.
Santa Ana CA 92704
800/824-4656

Joe Powell Golf, Inc.
1781 Barber Rd.
Sarasota FL 34240
800/237-4660

ProGroup Inc.
6201 Mountain View Rd.
Ooltewah TN 37363
800/735-6300

Ram Golf Corp.
2020 Indian Boundary Dr.
Melrose Park IL 60160
800/833-4653

Ryobi-Toski Corp.
160 Essex St.
PO Box 576
Newark OH 43055
800/848-2075

Slazenger Golf, USA
PO Box 7259
Greenville SC 29611
800/766-2615

Spalding Sports Worldwide
425 Meadow St.
Chicopee MA 01021
800/438-4025

Square Two Golf Co.
18 Gloria Lane
Fairfield NJ 07004
800/526-2250

Taylor Made Golf Co.
2371 Cosmos Court
Carlsbad CA 92009
800/456-8633

Stan Thompson Golf Club Co.
2616 Temple Heights Dr.
Oceanside CA 92056
800/959-5900

Titleist and Foot-Joy Worldwide
PO Box 965
Fairhaven MA 02719-0965
800/225-8500

Tommy Armour Golf Co.
8350 N. Lehigh Ave.
Morton Grove IL 60053
800/723-4653

Tru-Ex Golf Co.
890 Warrington Ave.
Redwood City CA 94063
800/348-7839

Wilson Sporting Goods Co.
8700 W. Bryn Mawr Ave., 3 North
Chicago IL 60631
800/622-0444

Yamaha Motor Manufacturing Corp.
1000 Highway 34 East
Newnan GA 30265
404/254-4150

Yonex Corp.
3520 Challenger St.
Torrance Ca 90503
800/992-9461

APPENDIX 6

HELPFUL TABLES, CHARTS, DATA AND REFERENCE INFORMATION

This appendix includes information which is most often used or difficult to find for the golf club repairman. Since weights and measures are used in both fitting and club repair, some basic metric conversions are also provided.

■ Calculating Pulley Size and Belt Length

Many times it is necessary to set up a motorized piece of equipment that should run at a certain speed. Also, it may be necessary to find out the RPM of a machine that has been previously set up.

First, to determine what size pulley is required:

When stepping up or reducing speed with pulleys, four factors are involved. [1]Motor RPM, [2]Drive pulley diameter, [3]Driven pulley diameter and [4]Driven pulley shaft RPM. Assume that 3 out of 4 of the above factors are known and the drive pulley diameter must be calculated.

This is the way to do it:

First, write down the driven pulley diameter and the driven pulley shaft RPM (the RPM can be actual or the desired RPM, in either case it is a known). Next, multiply the driven pulley diameter times the actual or desired driven shaft RPM. Divide this result by the motor RPM. The answer is the drive pulley diameter required.

For example: A belt sander has a 2½" pulley attached to its shaft (driven pulley). The belt sander should run at 1400 RPM (driven pulley shaft RPM). The motor turns at 1725 RPM (Motor RPM). What size pulley should be put on the motor (drive pulley)?

$$\frac{[4]\text{Driven Pulley Shaft RPM x }[3]\text{Driven Pulley Diameter}}{[1]\text{Motor RPM}} = [2]\text{Drive Pulley Diameter}$$

$$\frac{1400 \text{ RPM x } 2\frac{1}{2}"}{1725 \text{ RPM}} = \frac{3500}{1725} = 2.02 \text{ or a 2" Diameter Pulley}$$

To solve the above formula for other knowns and unknowns use the appropriate formula below:

$$\frac{1 \times 2}{4} = 3 \qquad \frac{1 \times 2}{3} = 4 \qquad \frac{3 \times 4}{2} = 1$$

The "V" belt length can now be determined mathematically as follows: Add the diameters in inches of both pulleys and multiply this result by 1.57. To this result add twice the distance, in inches, between the centers of the two shafts. Example: Assume the two pulleys in the belt sander example above are 14" apart from center of shaft to center of shaft. The formula and calculation would be as follows:

(1st Pulley Diam. = 2nd Pulley Diam. x 1.57) + Shaft Ctr. to Ctr. Dim. x 2 = Approx. "V" Belt Length

2" + 2½" = 4½"

4½" x 1.57 = 7.065"

14" + 14" = 28"

7.065" + 28" = 35.065" or a 35" Approximate Length "V" Belt

■ Comparative Grades of Abrasive

The proper use of abrasives is very important in golf club repair. It is also important to have available a cross reference table to compare abrasives which are identified or marked using different terminology such as 120 grit, 000 grade or medium grit. See Table A6-1.

■ Metric Equivalents

The meter is the basic unit of measuring length in the metric system. A meter is 39.37 inches long or 3.37 inches longer than a yard. A meter can be divided into 100 centimeters and 1000 millimeters.

"Mass" is the more common term for "weight" in the metric system, but using the term "weight" is still acceptable. The kilogram is the basic metric system term for measuring mass. It is slightly more than 2 pounds. 1800 kilograms equal a metric ton and ⅟₁₀₀₀ kilogram equals 1 gram.

Volume measurements in the metric system use the liter as a basic unit. A liter is slightly larger than a quart. ⅟₁₀₀₀ of a liter is referred to as a milliliter.

Temperature in the metric system is measured in degrees Celsius versus degrees Fahrenheit. Unlike Fahrenheit degrees, Celsius degrees use 0° for the freezing point of water and 100° for the boiling point of water. Degrees centigrade is another term for Celsius. See Table A6-2.

TABLE A6-1 Comparative Grades of Abrasive		
Grit	"O" Symbols	Simplified Markings
600	None	Super fine
500	None	
400	10/0	Extra fine
360	None	
320	9/0	
280	8/0	Very fine
240	7/0	
220	6/0	
180	00000	Fine
150	0000	
120	000	Medium
100	00	
80	0	
60	½	Coarse
50	1	
40	1½	
36	2	Very coarse
30	2½	

The following tables will help in making conversions *from* metric and *to* metric.

TABLE A6-2
To Convert To Metric

To Convert From:	To:	Multiply By:
LENGTH		
inches	millimeters	25.40
inches	centimeters	2.54
inches	meters	.025
feet	centimeters	30.48
yards	meters	.914
AREA		
square inches	square centimeters	6.452
square feet	square meters	.093
square yards	square meters	.836
MASS		
ounces	grams	28.35
pounds	kilograms	.454
VOLUME		
fluid ounces	milliliters	29.574
pints	liters	.473
quarts	liters	.946
gallons	liters	3.785
TEMPERATURE		
Fahrenheit	Celsius (centigrade)	5/9 after subtracting 32

TABLE A6-3
To Convert From Metric

To Convert From:	To:	Multiply By:
LENGTH		
millimeters	inches	.039
centimeters	inches	.394
meters	inches	39.37
meters	feet	3.281
meters	yards	1.094
AREA		
square centimeters	square inches	.155
square meters	square feet	10.765
square meters	square yards	1.196
MASS		
grams	ounces	.035
kilograms	pounds	2.205
VOLUME		
milliliters	fluid ounces	.034
liters	pints	2.113
liters	quarts	1.057
liters	gallons	.264
TEMPERATURE		
Celsius (centigrade)	Fahrenheit	9/5 and then add 32

■ Drill Bit Sharpening Information

As furnished from manufacturers most twist drills are machine ground. This insures uniform drilling and wear, which results in maximum drill life. A large percentage of drill failure can be directly attributed to improper point grinding. It is important that care be exercised when regrinding drill points. The following figures illustrate proper and improper grinding of drill points.

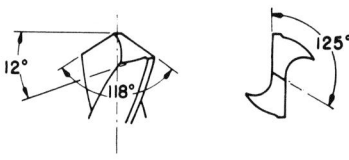

Figure A6-1
Illustrates a drill properly ground. Lip angles and lengths are equal, resulting in a central chisel. The chisel angle and lip relief are correct.

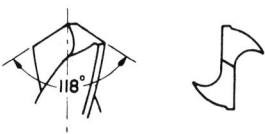

Figure A6-2
Illustrates a drill ground off-center, resulting in uneven lip lengths, and even though the lip angles are correct the chisel is not in the middle of the drill. Such a drill will tend to walk on initial penetration. Rapid drill breakdown and oversize holes will result.

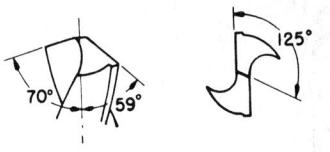

Figure A6-3
Illustrates a drill with central chisel edge, but unequal lip angles. Such a drill allows all the cutting to be done by one lip, resulting in premature breakdown.

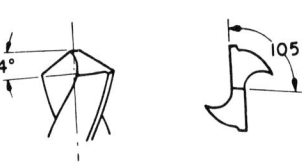

Figure A6-4
Illustrates a drill with insufficient clearance and improper chisel angle. Drills ground in this manner require abnormal high thrust, and rapidly wear.

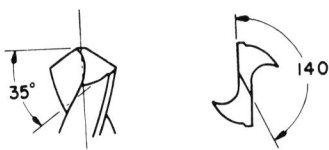

Figure A6-5
Illustrates a drill ground with excessive lip relief and too great a chisel angle. Drills ground in this manner will chip readily and cut an oversize hole.

832

Outer Corners Break Down
Cutting speed too high — Hard spots in material — No cutting compound at drill point — Flutes clogged with chips

Cutting Lips Chip
Too much feed — Lip relief too great

Drill Breaks
Point improperly ground — Feed too heavy — Drill is dull — Flutes clogged with chips

Drill Breaks When Drilling Brass or Wood
Flutes clogged with chips

Drill Will Not Enter Work
Drill is dull — Lip relief too small — Too heavy a web

Hole Rough
Point improperly ground or dull — No cutting compound at drill point — Improper cutting compound — Feed too great

Hole Oversize
Unequal angle or length of the cutting edges — or both

Large Chip Coming Out of One Flute, Small Chip Out of Other Flute
Point improperly ground, one lip doing all the cutting

■ Decimal Equivalents, Letter Sizes and Number Sizes of Drills

This information is used constantly in any type of shop work, and club repair is no exception. Check with your local hardware store or industrial supply house and try to obtain a large chart similar to the one reproduced here. The chart should be hung on the wall or above the bench for handy reference.

DECIMAL EQUIVALENTS

1/64	.0156	17/64	.2656	33/64	.5156	49/64	.7656
1/32	.0312	9/32	.2812	17/32	.5312	25/32	.7812
3/64	.0468	19/64	.2968	35/64	.5468	51/64	.7968
1/16	.0625	5/16	.3125	9/16	.5625	13/16	.8125
5/64	.0781	21/64	.3281	37/64	.5781	53/64	.8281
3/32	.0937	11/32	.3437	19/32	.5937	27/32	.8437
7/64	.1093	23/64	.3593	39/64	.6093	55/64	.8593
1/8	.125	3/8	.375	5/8	.625	7/8	.875
9/64	.1406	25/64	.3906	41/64	.6406	57/64	.8906
5/32	.1562	13/32	.4062	21/32	.6562	29/32	.9062
11/64	.1718	27/64	.4218	43/64	.6718	59/64	.9218
3/16	.1875	7/16	.4375	11/16	.6875	15/16	.9375
13/64	.2031	29/64	.4531	45/64	.7031	61/64	.9531
7/32	.2187	15/32	.4687	23/32	.7187	31/32	.9687
15/64	.2343	31/64	.4843	47/64	.7343	63/64	.9843
1/4	.25	1/2	.5	3/4	.75	1	1

DRILL SIZES

Letter Sizes	Drill Diameter Inches	Wire Gage Sizes	Drill Diameter Inches	Wire Gage Sizes	Drill Diameter Inches	Wire Gage Sizes	Drill Diameter Inches
Z	0.413	1	0.2280	28	0.1405	55	0.0520
Y	0.404	2	0.2210	29	0.1360	56	0.0465
X	0.397	3	0.2130	30	0.1285	57	0.0430
W	0.386	4	0.2090	31	0.1200	58	0.0420
V	0.377	5	0.2055	32	0.1160	59	0.0410
U	0.368	6	0.2040	33	0.1130	60	0.0400
T	0.358	7	0.2010	34	0.1110	61	0.0390
S	0.348	8	0.1990	35	0.1100	62	0.0380
R	0.339	9	0.1960	36	0.1065	63	0.0370
Q	0.332	10	0.1935	37	0.1040	64	0.0360
P	0.323	11	0.1910	38	0.1015	65	0.0350
O	0.316	12	0.1890	39	0.0995	66	0.0330
N	0.302	13	0.1850	40	0.0980	67	0.0320
M	0.295	14	0.1820	41	0.0960	68	0.0310
L	0.290	15	0.1800	42	0.0935	69	0.0292
K	0.281	16	0.1770	43	0.0890	70	0.0280
J	0.277	17	0.1730	44	0.0860	71	0.0260
I	0.272	18	0.1695	45	0.0820	72	0.0250
H	0.266	19	0.1660	46	0.0810	73	0.0240
G	0.261	20	0.1610	47	0.0785	74	0.0225
F	0.257	21	0.1590	48	0.0760	75	0.0210
E	0.250	22	0.1570	49	0.0730	76	0.0200
D	0.246	23	0.1540	50	0.0700	77	0.0180
C	0.242	24	0.1520	51	0.0670	78	0.0160
B	0.238	25	0.1495	52	0.0635	79	0.0145
A	0.234	26	0.1470	53	0.0595	80	0.0135
		27	0.1440	54	0.0550		

NOTES

APPENDIX 7

THE MYTHS OF GOLF

One of the main purposes of this book is to bring golf club technology and its understanding up-to-date. Throughout this book, each chapter either directly or indirectly dispels some passed-along inaccuracy or myth related to golf equipment.

Because empirical testing of golf equipment is a relatively recent phenomenon, what with the advent of swing machines, computers and sophisticated high speed cameras, much of what has been accepted as truth can now be labeled as myth.

In this appendix are listed a number of the more common and a few of the not so common myths that have been passed along and handed down over the years.

■ A Dollar Bill Equals One Swingweight

When describing swingweight, I'm sure you have heard someone say that if a dollar bill is laid across the clubhead that the weight of the dollar bill would be equivalent to increasing the swingweight by one. I too believed this and used the analogy many times when I first started into club repair to explain a swingweight change to a customer. Not until writing my first book did I actually lay a dollar bill on a head and found out that it is equivalent to slightly less than ½ of a swingweight. A dime is actually equivalent in weight to 1 swingweight which is approximately .07 ounces.

Another test concerning swingweight which may be of interest is that even the finest players in the world cannot tell the difference if the swingweight is increased or decreased by 1. However, they can detect changes of 2 swingweights or more.

You can conduct this test on your own the same way I did. Find a driver (any club will work, but most golfers are more finicky about drivers) that is a D-0 swingweight. Put enough lead tape on the sole of the club to bring it up to D-4 swingweight, but be sure you put the tape on in 1 swingweight increments so you can later take it off and put it back on in 1 swingweight increments. First, start off with the club at D-2 and have the golfer hit a few balls or take a few swings. Next, after each sequence of hitting or swinging, change the swingweight up or down by 1 or 2 swingweights or just pretend to change it. Do not tell the golfer which way you went and do not let him see the bottom of the club. Each time ask if the club feels lighter, heavier or the same and record the comments. Do this at least ten times (twenty is better) and compare the comments against the actual changes made. I think you will find the results interesting.

■ Golf Shafts Lose Their Stiffness

It has long been thought by many that over a period of time a golf shaft through constant flexing will tend to lose its stiffness and become weaker. Exhaustive tests have been performed by club manufacturers and golf shaft manufacturers only to find out that the shaft does not lose its stiffness. Of course, if a shaft is rusted or pitted or has been bent, it is certainly suspect to some form of a physical change, meaning its flex characteristics may have been altered. Due to sloppy manufacturing, some low quality graphite shafts may lose stiffness but this is rare.

■ #5 Iron Has The Most Backspin

A number of years ago a very prominent professional tour golfer made the statement that a properly struck #5 iron generated the greatest amount of backspin and would bite better than any other club. Obviously, this is not so as the #6 iron will generate more backspin than the #5 and so will the #7, and #8 and so on. Simply, the greater the loft, the more the backspin.

■ Face Grooves Create Backspin

During a business school, one for P.G.A. apprentices, I was delivering my standard opening remarks, one part of which is to go through 6 or 7 of the most common myths of golf. A student raised his hand and asked me if I would actually play with a set of clubs that had no face lines since I had just remarked that face lines do not create or improve backspin. I answered yes, but admitted that up until now I had only conducted a number of hitting tests but had not actually played with them. So, I built myself a complete set of irons #1 through pitching wedge with no face lines. I did not play with any other irons for two years and during that time my handicap went from 6 to 5. Admittedly, I did get a few disbelieving stares and comments like, "How can you make the ball stop with those irons?" The irons were always well received after a round when they went into the club cleaning area.

Basically, here is how backspin is generated. Coming into impact, the clubhead is moving forward or near parallel with the ground. This is the direction of the clubhead's force which is a product of the clubhead mass times acceleration or speed. At impact, the ball is struck by the face of the club which has a certain loft angle. Backspin is created by the difference in the angle the ball is launched (loft plane) to that of the force direction of the clubhead. The greater this difference (more loft) the greater the amount of backspin. See Figure A7-1. It was once thought that backspin was created by the ball rolling up the face during impact, but high speed photography has disproved this under dry impact conditions. Since a golf ball is only in contact with the face of the club for about $5/10,000$ths of a second, it has little time to roll up the face. A #9 iron shot will generate approximately 8,000 to 10,000 revolutions per minute of backspin and a driver will generate approximately 2,000 to 4,000 revolutions per minute of backspin.

The U.S.G.A. confirmed all this at the conclusion of their exhaustive groove studies in the mid 1980's. Of course, when a lubricant, like grass or moisture, is trapped between the ball and clubface at impact, the ball does skid up the face. The ball leaves the clubface at a higher launch angle and with less backspin than under dry conditions creating a "flyer" type shot. But again, it is not the grooves that create the backspin – only exerting some influence under "flyer" like conditions.

The next logical question is, why does the U.S.G.A. and R & A have a rule governing the face lines on all irons regardless of loft and woods with more than 24 degrees of loft. In 1921 Jock Hutchison won the British Open using a set of irons with very wide

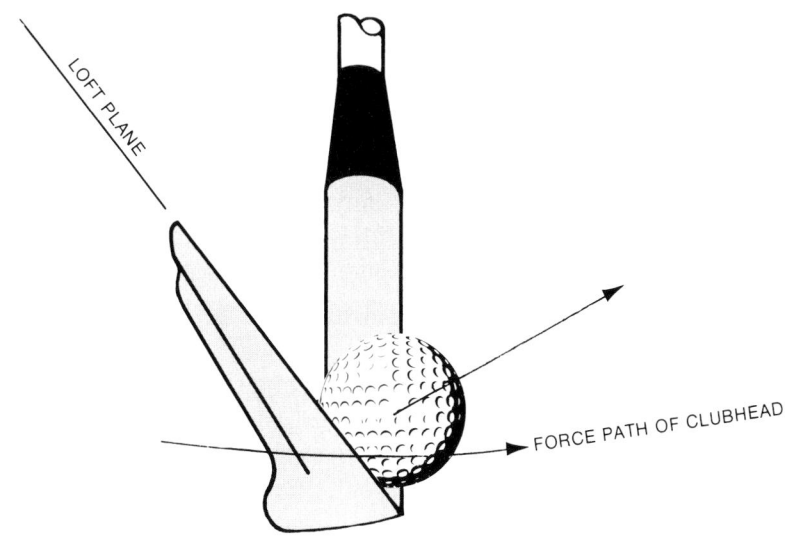

Figure A7-1
How backspin is created: The ball does not roll up the clubface to generate backspin from friction with the grooves as once thought. Backspin is created by the angle difference between the force path of the clubhead and the loft plane.

and deep face lines. The Royal and Ancient (R & A) immediately banned any clubs with this type of face. Because of this victory, however, most of the U.S. golf club manufacturers immediately came out with their own respective models with deep and wide grooves. Spalding came out with the "Dedstop," MacGregor the "Bakspin," and Wilson the "Bacspin" models. Three years later in 1924, the United States Golf Association concurred with the R & A rule limiting the width, depth and the amount of scoring because of their belief of improved shot control and greater bite on the greens. The old wide grooved irons are good collectors items.

■ Bulge Reduces Sidespin

A myth which has appeared in golf club advertising in the past is that the proper horizontal face bulge radius will reduce the amount of slicing or hooking sidespin on off-center hits. This is simply not so. The horizontal bulge actually hits the ball farther to the right on toe shots and farther to the left on heel shots. Hitting the ball farther off line is done to compensate for the hooking spin (counterclockwise rotation) applied on toe shots and the slicing spin (clockwise rotation) applied on heel shots. The reason that hooking and slicing spins occur on off-center hits is that the clubhead at impact rotates about is own center of mass which is located in line with the center of the clubface. During this slight rotation, the clubface slides across the ball and imparts sidespin. When a ball is hit on the center of the clubface, no twisting or clubhead rotation occurs; therefore no sidespin is imparted, only backspin.

It is interesting to note here that a ball impacted ½" on either side of the center of the clubface will lose approximately 7% distance. A ball hit 1" on either side of the face center will lose approximately 14% distance (slightly less percentage on metal woods). This distance loss is caused by a dissipation of energy transfer at impact when the center of mass of the clubhead does not line up with the center of mass of the golf ball and the aforementioned resultant clubhead rotation occurs. Chapter 40 provides an in depth discussion on this subject.

■ Topspin (Overspin) Creates More Ball Roll

How many times have you heard someone say that they hit that one with a lot of overspin or topspin because the ball rolled quite a distance on the ground after it landed. Actually, if a ball could be hit with any overspin whatsoever, it would immediately dive to the ground and roll, thus dramatically reducing distance. Only backspin can create the aerodynamic qualities which keep a ball airborne. The reason for this myth's evolution is probably in the fact that not every shot with the same club has the same amount of backspin and trajectory. For instance, a hooking shot hit low off the clubface will have far less backspin than a straight shot hit high or in the middle of the face. The hooking ball loses some of the backspin because it also has a certain amount of counterclockwise hooking sidespin and coupled with a low hit on the clubface generates less backspin and consequently more roll.

■ Persimmon Feels More Solid Than Laminated Maple

Many people feel that persimmon wood is noticeably more solid feeling at impact when compared with laminated maple. I was involved in this interesting controversy back in the days when I was employed by one of the major golf companies. We were concerned with feedback from golfers that nothing felt as solid, nor could anything replace the feel of persimmon. A test was set up with 10 drivers, all made to be as identical as possible. Five were made of persimmon wood and five laminated maple wood with a great deal of care taken in the selection of components, weights, lengths, etc. Also, the faces were all painted black, and each club was identified with a different mark on its sole. Both touring professionals and amateurs participated in the test. The results showed that no one could come close to picking out the persimmon drivers from the laminated maple drivers. In actuality, the solid feel of a certain golf club, be it persimmon or laminated maple, is accomplished by proper head design, center of gravity location, proper interrelationships of specifications and proper assembly of components. Chapter 46 provides additional information on persimmon and laminated maple woods.

■ Oil Hardening Hardens a Wood Head

The words "oil hardened" seem to connote a wood head that is made harder by soaking it in oil, the most popular of which is boiled linseed oil or Nelsonite. The purpose of the oil soaking or Nelsoniting process has always been to better seal the larger pores on persimmon so that it will not lose or pick up moisture as easily as it would if it were not treated. The wood grain is also stabilized better and hopefully, with care, the club should last a little longer and not change in swingweight during wet or dry seasons. The head is not hardened, and even if it were, increasing the hardness would have absolutely no effect on increasing distance.

■ Forged Irons Have a Softer Feel Than Cast Irons

Many players seem to think that forged clubs which are made of a mild carbon steel have a much softer, more controllable feel at impact. It is felt that the ball stays on the face of the club longer and therefore will leave the clubface with extra backspin and bite better when it hits the green. Many of these same players feel that cast clubs made of stainless steel are quite hard feeling and the ball shoots off the clubface with less backspin. They mostly criticize the hard feel of cast clubs compared to the soft feel of forged mild steel.

All of this is untrue and has been perpetuated by preconceived notions handed down from player to player during the last twenty years or when cast clubs were first introduced.

When cast stainless golf clubs first hit the market enmasse, most of them were significantly different from the so-called traditional and classic designs. Some had cavity backs, longer blade lengths, heel and toe weighting, sole weighting, perimeter weighting, high toes and shallow heels and some even had a shaft over hosel assembly as compared to the conventional shaft in hosel assembly.

Most professionals and better playing amateurs at the time were playing with conventional forged irons, mostly center weighted varieties (usually called muscle back) with a normal shaft in hosel assembly. When they hit shots with these new cast clubs, they immediately noticed differences in feel. The ball also seemed to fly higher. The feel and trajectory differences were caused by the different weight distributions, the shaft over hosel assemblies which utilized a completely different shaft type, and also there was the negative mental aspect of this new non-traditional appearing iron design.

During the last few years, there have been a number of tests conducted where identical twin sets of forged and cast irons have been made up and compared by golf professionals, good amateurs and others. They hit shots with each type and were asked if they could feel or notice any differences. The results showed conclusively that in identically designed heads, not even the finest players in the world can tell any difference.

■ Face Screws Produce a More Solid Hit

I know we have all heard the expression "That shot felt solid, I hit it on the screws." This should be taken more as a cliché and not fact. The truth is, a wood club can be made to perform the same with or without face insert screws and feel just as solid.

Face screws were put in woods back in the days when adhesives were not as good as they are today and the screws actually held the insert in the head. Today, if screws are used in the face, they are put in mostly for traditional or cosmetic reasons although they certainly will provide additional holding of the insert to the head should the glue bond fail.

■ A Big Head is a Heavy Head

Large headed drivers often make golfers wary. People have been conditioned over the years to associate size with weight. I have often heard players complain that they "can't get that big head through the hitting area." Some golfers even complain of fatigue after 18 holes of playing with a big headed driver. Actually, the size of the driver is irrelevant to its weight. Generally speaking, the headweight on a 43" driver with a Dynamic Gold taper tip shaft, rubber grip and a swingweight of D-2 will be approximately 7 ounces, regardless of the size or shape of the head, and the overall weight of the club will be around 13¼ ounces. This is because a large block may be drilled to reduce the weight, whereas lead could be added to a cavity underneath the soleplate on a smaller, more compact driver head to make it heavier. Also, wide body metal drivers that are 44" to 45" long with a steel shaft will usually have a lighter head weight. The reason for this is that the increase in length also increases the swingweight (1" ≈ 6 points). The manufacturer actually reduces the 7 ounce head to create a swingweight that stays in the D5 to D6 range.

■ The Ideal Golf Shaft is Weightless

It's been stated in more than one publication that the ideal golf shaft would be weightless, thus allowing for more mass in the clubhead. Although there is no practical way to disprove the theory, logic says that a shaft of absolutely no weight would require an exceptionally heavy head weight to bring the club to a swingweight of D-2; in fact, so heavy would the head be that no golfer could swing it. If the head weight were reduced, the overall weight would be approximately 8½ to 9 ounces. Then the club would be so light that the golfer would be able to exert very little directional control on shots. Certainly, greater distance would be a result, but it would be at the expense of accuracy. The opposite is true of a very heavy shaft. It would give the golfer increased control, but rob him of distance because of the loss of clubhead speed. This is not to say that the lightweight shafts now on the market are not perfectly fine. It is rather the extremely light weight or hypothetical weightless shaft that is less than ideal.

■ Tall People Need Longer Clubs; Short People Need Shorter Clubs

Tall golfers do not necessarily need longer clubs and short golfers shorter clubs. Length, in all but very unusual circumstances should be determined by what the golfer feels comfortable and confident with. More importantly, a golfer's playing ability and athletic coordination are key factors. For example, a tall golfer, say 6'3" with an 18 or higher handicap who has a hard time hitting the ball solid and on the center of the clubface, may be better off with standard length clubs. On the other hand, a shorter golfer — say 5'6" tall who has a 6 handicap hits the ball straight with solid face center hits — may want to try ½" to 1" longer than standard clubs to obtain more distance that is felt to be lacking. Generally speaking, almost any length golf club can be fit to any height golfer as long as the lie angle is correct for that particular club length and golfer's hand height at impact.

It is not a fallacy that increased club length will usually result in greater distance, however, there is one very important, often overlooked criteria, which is the ball must be hit on the center of the clubface. The longer the club, the harder it is to hit the ball on the center of the clubface and the distance loss from off-center hits is quite significant. Chapter 65 provides additional information on fitting golf club length.

■ A Harder Insert Hits the Ball Farther

Although inserts of various degrees of hardness will certainly produce different sounds at impact and transmit different "feels;" tests have shown that insert hardness has no significant effect on the initial velocity of the golf ball off the clubface. In other words, an extremely hard insert on a driver will compress the golf ball no more than a softer, more resilient type. As a matter of record, clubs with no inserts have performed favorably under all conditions. On the other hand, the weight of the insert material does have some effect on overall distance and trajectory. Inserts of different materials can vary as much as three-fourths of an ounce. This weight difference means that a club with a heavy insert will be more foreweighted with the center of gravity also being higher on the face than a club with a light insert. Clubs with the heavier inserts usually require little or no lead under the soleplate, whereas those with light inserts tend to be sole-weighted. The lofts on both clubs being equal, the foreweighted club with the higher center of gravity will tend to produce a lower trajectory and thus, more roll. Consequently, some additional distance can result. Chapter 47 provides an in-depth discussion of various insert materials and their role in club design.

■ The #7 Wood is For Women and Seniors

Many golfers of average ability fear that if they replace their long irons with the more lofted woods, they'll become the butt of humor among their playing partners. The truth is that even a number of pros on the PGA Tour carry these utility woods for use in tight situations in major tournaments.

The #7 wood is a good replacement for the #3 iron. It will be easier to hit long approach shots from the rough and fairway, bring the ball in on a higher trajectory, hold the green better and feel more solid to hit more of the time.

Also, golfers who in the past might have run a #3-iron up to the green can place a #7 wood shot softly on the putting surface, carrying all bunkers and other hazards. The disadvantage of replacing a long iron with a lofted wood is evident only in those instances when a golfer must hit a low shot under the limb of a tree or possibly in situations that demand a low punch shot.

■ The Line on the Top of a Putter is the Sweet Spot

Many golfers are under the impression that putter manufacturers place the line on top of their putters exactly above the sweet spot. In my testing, I've found that usually in better than 50 percent of the putters I scrutinized, the sweet spot has been closer to the heel than indicated by the alignment aid. Obviously, this position does not help the golfer who stands up to the ball with the line directly behind it, believing that this is the logical position of the sweet spot. Chapter 52 shows how to find a putter head's center of gravity or sweet spot.

■ Putters Have No Loft

Not only is this idea false, but loft is an essential ingredient. When greens were not manicured as they are today, there was admittedly more loft on putters. However, even now, there should be between one and four degrees of loft. The reason for this is really quite simple. When the putt is struck, the initial movement is a skidding action. The ball may even take one or two revolutions backwards before it begins to roll. At times the ball may skid as much as 20 percent of the distance of the putt. If there was no loft on the putter, the ball would be pinched into the turf and would then skip and bounce toward the hole. There would be less control and accuracy. Chapter 52 provides additional information on what happens when a ball is putted.

■ The Higher a Golf Ball Bounces, the Farther It Can Be Hit

It is a common occurrence to see someone comparing two different golf balls by dropping them from a certain height and seeing which ball bounces the highest. It is then assumed that the ball which bounced higher can probably be hit farther. This, of course, is usually not true.

The bounce test can be very deceiving as to distance potential. The reason for this is that when a clubhead at impact exerts a pressure of some 2,000 pounds upon the golf ball, it compresses the ball and causes it to rebound forward at a great initial velocity. This is not the case when a golf ball is bounced on a hard surface because there is minimal compression, a few pounds at best. So, the bounce test obviously is not a test of a ball's compression or resiliency. See Figure A7-2. What may sometimes make the more

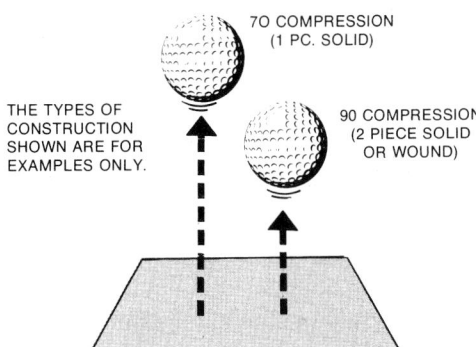

70 COMPRESSION
(1 PC. SOLID)

90 COMPRESSION
(2 PIECE SOLID
OR WOUND)

THE TYPES OF
CONSTRUCTION
SHOWN ARE FOR
EXAMPLES ONLY.

Figure A7-2
Although the ball on the left bounces higher, the other ball has a higher compression and may be hit farther

inexpensive ball bounce higher is simply that its efficiency (coefficient of restitution) is greater when less force is applied. However, in many cases, this same ball will decrease rapidly in efficiency as the force becomes even greater, such as that of impact with the clubface. This does not mean that those players who swing easy at the ball should switch to inexpensive, one piece solid-type balls. Impact between the ball and clubhead exerts a force far greater and will compress the ball much more than the bounce test.

■ You Can't "Work" a Ball with a Metal Wood

I've heard several touring professionals make this comment and it is simply not true. To "work" the ball means to make the ball go right to left or, left to right. If you are an average golfer, your tee shots still slice or hook as much as they used to if you have switched to a metal wood. The degree to which a ball hooks or slices is determined by the direction in which the clubhead is traveling and the angle at which the clubface is pointing for an on-center shot. It does not matter if the club is made of steel, persimmon or graphite.

It is true that off-center shots go marginally straighter from a metal wood because of the weight distribution to the periphery of the head. Golf professionals, however, do not base their claim upon the results of mis-hit shots.

Conclusion

One area we cannot fail to overlook in any of our discussions of golf equipment myths is the player's mental attitude. During a number of the player tests I conducted it was proved conclusively to the participant, and many were well known tour players and better golfers, that they could not detect a certain difference which they previously had felt they could. However, in some instances, player's final parting comments would be something to the effect that he would still only play with clubs that had this or that. The mind, we are all aware, has a strong influence over our golf games and we must respect its power by feeling comfortable with how we mentally perceive golf equipment whether it is myth or fact.

NOTES

APPENDIX 8

GOLF CLUB MANUFACTURERS' PUBLISHED LENGTH, LOFT AND LIE SPECIFICATIONS

This reference material includes most manufacturers' standard specifications and will save time in comparing, checking or resetting lofts, lies and lengths of both men's and ladies' woods and irons.

The information here includes the original published loft, lie and length specifications from the 1974 and 1982 editions of Golf Club Design, Fitting, Alteration and Repair, as well as specifications published in the 1986 edition of The Complete Golf Club Fitting Plan, and it also includes the latest available specifications from the golf club manufacturers. In this manner, as additional editions of this book are published in the future, the historical information will expand using these easy-to-use reference tables.

The specifications were derived from the latest manufacturers' published data or obtained from phone calls to the companies. In some cases, manufacturers do not make this information available or they have recently stopped publishing part or all of this information. If this was the case, the latest published specifications were used.

Listed in the manufacturers' name column is the model year for which the data applies. Remember manufacturers' specifications are not often changed, thus making the data valid for a number of years. Since most manufacturers' standard specifications of loft, lie and length apply to 90% to 100% of the models they offer, the information here is mostly listed by manufacturer; however, many individual models are also listed.

It is very interesting to study and compare the specifications from manufacturer to manufacturer listed here.

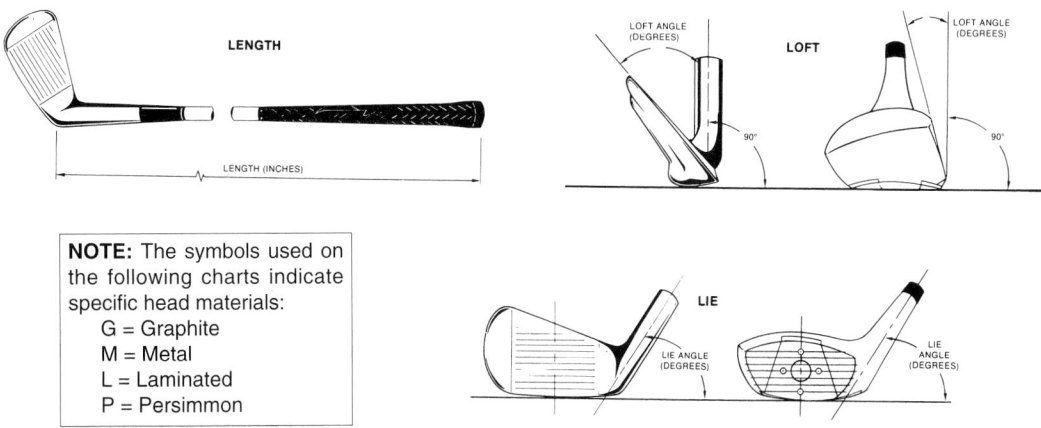

NOTE: The symbols used on the following charts indicate specific head materials:
- G = Graphite
- M = Metal
- L = Laminated
- P = Persimmon

LENGTH — MEN'S

GOLF CLUB MANUFACTURERS' STANDARD SPECIFICATIONS — DATA FROM 1974 DESIGN BOOK

Mfgr. & Year Specs. Published	#1 Wood	#2 Wood	#3 Wood	#4 Wood	#5 Wood	#2 Iron	#3 Iron	#4 Iron	#5 Iron	#6 Iron	#7 Iron	#8 Iron	#9 Iron	Pitch Wedge	Sand Wedge
Acushnet (1973)	43	43	42½	42	41¾	38¾	38¼	37¾	37¼	36½	36¾	36¼	35¾	35¼	35¼
Dunlop (1973)	48⅜	42⅞	42⅜	41⅞	41⅝	38½	38	37½	37	36½	36	35¾	35½	35	35
Faultless (1974)	43	42½	42	41½	41	38½	38	37½	37	36½	36	35½	35	35	35
H & B (1973)	43	42½	42	41½	41½	38½	38	37½	37	36½	36	35½	35	35	35
MacGregor (1972)	43	42¾	42½	42	42	38½	38	37½	37	36½	36	35¾	35½	35	35
Northwestern (1973)	43	42½	42	41½	41	38½	38	37½	37	36½	36	35½	35	35	35
P.G.A. (1972)	43	42½	42	41½	41¼	38½	38	37½	37	36½	36	35¾	35½	35	35
First Flight (1974)	43	42½	42	41½	41	38½	38	37½	37	36½	36	35½	35	35	35
Pro-Dyn (1974)	43	—	42	41½	41¼	38½	38	37½	37	36½	36	35½	35	35	35
Ram (1973)	43	—	42	41½	41	38½	38	37½	37	36½	36	35½	35	35	35
Royal (1974)	43	42½	42	41½	41¼	38½	38	37½	37	36½	36	35½	35	35	35
Spalding (1974)	43	42 9/16	42⅛	41 11/16	41¼	38⅝	38 3/16	37¾	37 5/16	36⅞	36 7/16	36	35 9/16	35⅛	34⅝
Hagen (1974)	43	42½	42	41½	41¼	38½	38	37½	37	36½	36¼	35¾	35¼	35	35
Wilson (1974)	43	42½	42	41½	41¼	38½	38	37½	37	36½	36¼	35¾	35¼	35¼	35¼

LOFT — MEN'S

GOLF CLUB MANUFACTURERS' STANDARD SPECIFICATIONS — DATA FROM 1974 DESIGN BOOK

Mfgr. & Year Specs. Published	#1 Wood	#2 Wood	#3 Wood	#4 Wood	#5 Wood	#2 Iron	#3 Iron	#4 Iron	#5 Iron	#6 Iron	#7 Iron	#8 Iron	#9 Iron	Pitch Wedge	Sand Wedge
Acushnet (1973)	11	14	17	20	22	22	25	28	31	35	39	43	47	51	55
Dunlop (1973)	11	14	17	19	22	21	24	28	32	36	40	44	48	52	56
Faultless (1974)	12	—	15	18	21	20	24	28	32	36	40	44	48	52	56
H & B (1973)	11	13	16	19	21	20	24	28	32	36	40	44	48	52	58
MacGregor (1972)	11	13	15½	18½	22	22	25	28	32	36	38½	43	45	49	56
Northwestern (1973)	11	14	16	19	22	21	24	27	31	35	39	43	47	51	55
P.G.A. (1972)	11	14	17	20	22	21	23	26	29	33	37	41	45	50	54
First Flight (1974)	12½	14	17	20	23	21	24	27	31	35	39	43	47	51	55
Pro-Dyn (1974)	12	—	16½	19½	22½	21	24	27	30	34	38	42	46	51	57
Ram (1973)	11	—	16.5	19.2	22	21	24.3	27.8	31.5	35.3	39.2	43.3	47.5	51.6	56.7
Royal (1974)	11	14	17	19	21	21	24	27	31	35	39	43	47	51	57
Spalding (1974)	11	13	16	19	22	20	23	27	31	35	39	43	47	52	58
Hagen (1974)	11	16	17	19	21	21	24	27	31	35	39	43	47	51	55
Wilson (1974)	11	14	16	19	21	21	24	27	31	35	39	43	47	51	55

LIE — MEN'S

GOLF CLUB MANUFACTURERS' STANDARD SPECIFICATIONS — DATA FROM 1974 DESIGN BOOK

Mfgr. & Year Specs. Published	#1 Wood	#2 Wood	#3 Wood	#4 Wood	#5 Wood	#2 Iron	#3 Iron	#4 Iron	#5 Iron	#6 Iron	#7 Iron	#8 Iron	#9 Iron	Pitch Wedge	Sand Wedge
Acushnet (1973)	54	54	55	56	56	57	58	59	60	61	62	63	63	64	64
Dunlop (1973)	55	55	56	56	57	58	59	60	61	62	63	64	65	65	64
Faultless (1974)	54	54½	55	55½	56	57	58	59	60	61	62	63	64	64	64
H & B (1973)	55	55	56	57	57	57	58	59	60	61	62	63	64	64	64
MacGregor (1972)	53	53	54	54½	54½	58	59	60	60½	61	62	62	62	62	63
Northwestern (1973)	53	53½	54	54½	55	58	59	60	61	62	63	64	65	65	65
P.G.A. (1972)	54	54	55	55	55	58	59	60	61	61½	62	62½	63	63	63
First Flight (1974)	54	54	55	56	56	57	58	59	60	61	62	63	63	63	63
Pro-Dyn (1974)	54	—	55	55	55	57	58	59	60	61	62	63	63	64	64
Ram (1973)	54	—	55.6	56	56.3	56.7	57.5	58.2	59	60	60.9	61.7	62.6	62.6	62.6
Royal (1974)	56	56	57	57	57	56	57	58	59	60	61	62	62	63	63
Spalding (1974)	56	—	56¾	57	57¼	58½	58¾	59¼	59¾	60¼	60½	61¼	62	63	63
Hagen (1974)	56	56	57	57	57	57	58	59	60	61	62	63	63	64	64
Wilson (1974)	55	55	55½	56	56	57	58	59	60	61	62	63	63	64	64

MEN'S — LATE 1970's & EARLY 1980's

LENGTH — MEN'S

GOLF CLUB MANUFACTURERS STANDARD SPECIFICATIONS

Mfgr. & Year Specs. Published		#1 Wood	#2 Wood	#3 Wood	#4 Wood	#5 Wood	#6 Wood	#7 Wood	#1 Iron	#2 Iron	#3 Iron	#4 Iron	#5 Iron	#6 Iron	#7 Iron	#8 Iron	#9 Iron	Pitch Wedge	Sand Wedge
Ajay Double Eagle	(1977)	43	—	42	41½	41	—	—	—	38½	38	37½	37	36½	36	35½	35	35	35
Browning	(1980)	43	—	42	41½	41	—	—	39½	39	38½	38	37½	37	36½	36	35½	35½	—
Cobra Low Profile	(1982)	—	—	—	—	—	—	—	39½	39	38½	38	37½	37	36½	36	35½	35¼	35
Cobra Premier Iron	(1982)	—	—	—	—	—	—	—	39½	39	38½	38	37½	37	36½	36	35½	35¼	35
Cobra Tour Model	(1982)	—	—	—	—	—	—	—	39½	39	38½	38	37½	37	36½	36	35½	35½	35¼
Confidence	(1977)	43	—	42	41½	41	—	—	39	38½	38	37½	37	36½	36	35½	35	35	35
Dunlop Australian Blade	(1978)	—	—	—	—	—	—	—	39½	39	38½	38	37½	37	36½	36	35½	35	35
Dunlop Maxfli Woods	(1978)	43⅜	42⅞	42⅜	41⅜	41⅛	—	41⅛	39½	39	38½	38	37½	37	36½	36	35½	35	35
Walter Hagen The Haig	(1982)	43	42½	42	41½	41¼	—	41	—	39	38½	38	37½	37	36¾	36¼	35¾	35½	35½
Hogan Apex	(1978)	43¼	—	42¼	41¾	41¼	—	—	39¾	39¼	38¾	38½	37¾	37¼	36¾	36¼	35¾	35½	—
Hogan Director	(1978)	43¼	—	42¼	41¾	41¼	—	—	—	39¼	38¾	38¼	37¾	37¼	36¾	36¼	35¾	35½	—
Hogan Medallion	(1978)	43¼	—	42¼	41¾	41¼	—	—	—	39¼	38¾	38¼	37¾	37¼	36¾	36¼	35¾	35½	—
Hogan Producer	(1978)	43¼	42¾	42¼	41¾	41¼	—	40¼	—	39¼	38¾	38¼	37¾	37¼	36¾	36¼	35¾	35½	—
MacGregor M693 Woods	(1982)	43¼	—	42¾	42¾	42¼	—	—	—	—	—	—	—	—	—	—	—	—	—
MacGregor M85 Woods	(1982)	43¼	—	42¾	42¼	41¼	—	—	—	—	—	—	—	—	—	—	—	—	—
MacGregor MT Woods/Irons	(1982)	43¼	—	42¾	42¼	42¼	—	—	39¾	39¼	38¾	38¼	37¾	37¼	36¾	36½	36¼	35¾	35¾
MacGregor MCX Woods/Irons	(1982)	43¼	—	42¾	42¼	42¼	—	42¼	—	39¼	38¾	38¼	37¾	37¼	36¾	36½	36¼	36	35¾
MacGregor Limited Edition	(1982)	43¼	—	42¾	42¼	42¼	—	—	39¾	39¼	38¾	38¼	37¾	37¼	36¾	36½	36¼	35¾	35¾
Northwestern	(1982)	43	42½	42	41½	41	—	40	39	38½	38	37½	37	36½	36	35½	35	35	35
P.G.A. Emblem	(1982)	43¼	—	42¼	41¾	41¼	—	40¾	—	38½	38	37½	37	36½	36	35½	35	35	35
P.G.A. Tommy Armour	(1982)	43½	—	42½	42	41¾	—	—	39½	39	38½	38	37½	37	36½	36	35½	35	35
P.G.A. Performer	(1982)	43¼	—	42¼	41¾	41¼	—	40¾	—	39	38½	38	37½	37	36½	36	35½	35½	35½
P.G.A. Concept LCG	(1982)	43	—	42	41½	41¼	—	40¾	—	38½	38 1/16	37⅝	37 3/16	36¾	36 5/16	35⅞	35 7/16	35	35
P.G.A. Ryder Cup II	(1982)	43	—	42	41½	41¼	—	40¾	—	39	38½	38	37½	37	36½	36	35½	35	35
Pedersen	(1978)	43	42¾	42¼	42	41½	—	41	39	38½	38	37½	37	36½	36	35½	35	35	35
Toney Penna	(1980)	43	—	42½	42	41½	—	—	39½	39	38½	38	37½	37	36½	36	35½	35	35
Penna Driver Model JS	(1980)	43	—	—	—	—	—	—	—	—	—	—	—	—	—	—	—	—	—
Penna Driver Model I	(1980)	43	—	—	—	—	—	—	—	—	—	—	—	—	—	—	—	—	—

GOLF CLUB MANUFACTURERS STANDARD SPECIFICATIONS

Mfgr. & Year Specs. Published		#1 Wood	#2 Wood	#3 Wood	#4 Wood	#5 Wood	#6 Wood	#7 Wood	#1 Iron	#2 Iron	#3 Iron	#4 Iron	#5 Iron	#6 Iron	#7 Iron	#8 Iron	#9 Iron	Pitch Wedge	Sand Wedge
Penna Driver Model 2 + 65	(1980)	43	—	—	—	—	—	—	—	—	—	—	—	—	—	—	—	—	—
Penna Driver Model 12	(1980)	43	—	—	—	—	—	—	—	—	—	—	—	—	—	—	—	—	—
Pinseeker (Length only)	(1978)	43	42½	42	41½	41¼	—	—	39½	39	38½	38	37½	37	36½	36	35½	35½	35¼
PowerBilt/All	(1982)	43	42½	42	41½	41½	—	—	39½	39	38½	38	37½	37	36½	36	35½	35½	35½
Pro-Dyn	(1977)	43	—	42	41½	41	—	40½	39	38½	38	37½	37	36½	36	35½	35	35	35
Pro Group	(1982)	43	42½	42	41½	41	—	—	39½	39	38½	38	37½	37	36½	36	35½	35½	—
Ram Accubar	(1982)	43½	—	42½	42	41½	—	—	—	39	38½	38	37½	37	36½	36	35½	35½	35½
Ram Golden Ram, Tour Grind	(1982)	43½	—	43	42½	42	—	—	39½	39	38½	38	37½	37	36½	36	35½	35½	35½
Rawlings RXP	(1980)	43	—	42	41½	41	—	—	—	39	38½	38	37½	37	36½	36	35½	35½	35½
Royal Edge	(1978)	43½	—	42½	42	41¾	—	—	—	39	38½	38	37½	37	36½	36	35½	35	35
Royal Impact	(1978)	43½	—	42½	42	41¾	—	41	—	39	38½	38	37½	37	36½	36	35½	35	35
Sigma Tiger Shark	(1982)	41½	—	41	—	40½	—	40	—	—	37¼	37	36¾	36½	36¼	36	35¾	35½	35⅛
Slotline	(1982)	43	—	42	41½	41	—	—	39½	39	38½	38	37½	37	36½	36	35½	35¼	35⅛
Spalding Elite	(1982)	43¼	—	42¼	41¾	41¼	—	—	39½	39	38½	38	37½	37	36½	36	35½	35	35
Spalding XL4	(1982)	43¼	—	42¼	41¾	41¼	—	—	39½	39	38½	38	37½	37	36½	36	35½	35	35
Spalding Top Flite	(1982)	43¼	—	42¼	41¾	41¼	—	—	39½	39	38½	38	37½	37	36½	36	35½	35	35
Spalding Executive	(1982)	43	—	42⅛	41 11/16	41¼	—	—	39 1/16	38⅝	38 3/16	37¾	37 5/16	36⅞	36 7/16	36	35 9/16	35⅛	34 11/16
Square Z	(1978)	43	—	42	41½	41	—	—	—	39	38½	38	37½	37	36½	36	35½	35½	35½
Taylor Made Golf	(1982)	43	—	42	41½	41	—	41	39½	39	38½	38	37½	37	36½	36	35½	35½	35½
Titleist Pro 100	(1976)	43	43	42½	42	41¾	—	—	39½	39	38½	38	37½	37	36½	36	35½	35½	—
Titleist AC-108	(1976)	43	43	42½	42	41¾	—	—	—	38¾	38¼	37¾	37¼	36⅞	36½	36	35½	35¼	35¼
Unique	(1982)	43	—	42	41½	41	—	—	39½	39	38½	38	37½	37	36½	36	35½	35½	35½
Wilson Staff	(1982)	43	42½	42	41½	41¼	—	41	39	38½	38	37½	37	36½	36¼	35¾	35¼	35	35
Wilson Aggressor	(1982)	43	42½	42	41½	41¼	—	41	39	38½	38	37½	37	36½	36¼	35¾	35¼	35	35
Wilson X-31	(1982)	43	42½	42	41½	41¼	—	41	—	39	38½	38	37½	37	36½	36	35½	35	35
Wilson 1200 GE	(1982)	43	42½	42	41½	41¼	—	41	—	39	38½	38	37½	37	36½	36	35½	35	35½
Wilson Reflex	(1982)	43	42½	42	41½	41¼	—	41	—	39	38½	38	37½	37	36¾	36¼	35¾	35	35½
Stan Thompson	(1982)	43	43	42½	42	41½	—	41	—	39	38½	38	37½	37	36½	36	35½	35½	35½

LOFT — MEN'S

GOLF CLUB MANUFACTURERS STANDARD SPECIFICATIONS

Mfgr. & Year Specs. Published		#1 Wood	#2 Wood	#3 Wood	#4 Wood	#5 Wood	#6 Wood	#7 Wood	#1 Iron	#2 Iron	#3 Iron	#4 Iron	#5 Iron	#6 Iron	#7 Iron	#8 Iron	#9 Iron	Pitch Wedge	Sand Wedge
Ajay Double Eagle	(1977)	11	—	16	19	21	—	—	—	21	24	27	31	35	39	43	47	51	55
Browning	(1980)	11	—	16	19	22	—	—	17	20	23	26	29	32	36	40	44	49	—
Cobra Low Profile	(1982)	—	—	—	—	—	—	—	17	20	23	26	29	32	36	40	44	48	55
Cobra Premier Iron	(1982)	—	—	—	—	—	—	—	17	19	22	25	29	33	37	41	45	49	56
Cobra Tour Model	(1982)	11	14	16	19	22	—	—	17	19	22	25	29	33	37	41	45	49	56
Confidence	(1977)	11	—	17	19	21	—	—	17	20	23	26	29	33	37	41	45	49	54
Dunlop Australian Blade	(1978)	—	—	—	—	—	—	—	17	20	23	27	31	35	39	42	47	51	57
Dunlop Maxfli	(1978)	11	14	16	19	22	—	28	17	20	23	27	31	35	39	42	47	51	57
Walter Hagen The Haig	(1982)	11	14	16	19	21	—	25	17	20	23	26	30	34	38	42	46	50	55
Hogan Apex	(1978)	10½	—	15½	18½	21½	—	—	—	19½	23	26½	30	33½	37	41	45	50	—
Hogan Director	(1978)	11	—	17	19	21½	—	—	—	19½	23	26½	30	33½	37	41	45	50	—
Hogan Medallion	(1978)	11½	—	17	19	21½	—	—	—	19½	23	26½	30	33½	37	41	45	50	—
Hogan Producer	(1978)	12	15	17	19	21½	—	25½	—	19½	23	26½	30	33½	37	41	45	50	—
MacGregor M693 Woods	(1982)	10	—	15	18	21	—	—	—	—	—	—	—	—	—	—	—	—	—
MacGregor M85 Woods	(1982)	—	—	15½	18½	22	—	—	—	—	—	—	—	—	—	—	—	—	—
MacGregor MT Woods/Irons	(1982)	10	—	15	18	21	—	—	17	20	23	26	29	33	37	41	46	51	56
MacGregor MCX Woods/Irons	(1982)	12	—	15½	18½	22	—	24½	—	18	21	24	27	31	36	40	44	48	55
MacGregor Limited Edition	(1982)	10	—	15	18	21	—	—	17	20	23	26	29½	33	37	41	45	51	55
Northwestern	(1982)	11	13	16	19	21	—	24	17	20	23	27	31	35	39	43	47	51	56
P.G.A. Emblem	(1982)	12	—	17	20	22	—	25	—	19	22	25	28½	32	36	40	44	48	55
P.G.A. Tommy Armour	(1982)	11	—	16	19	21	—	—	18	20	23	26	29	32	36	40	44	49	56
P.G.A. Performer	(1982)	12	—	17	20	22	—	25	—	19	22	25	28½	32	36	40	44	48	55
P.G.A. Concept LCG	(1982)	12	—	17	20	22	—	25	—	20	23	26	30	34	38	42	46	51	56
P.G.A. Ryder Cup II	(1982)	12	—	17	20	22	—	25	—	21	23	26	29	33	36	39	42	47	54
Pedersen	(1978)	11½	15	18	21	24	—	29	18	20	23	26	30	34	38	42	46	50	55
Toney Penna	(1980)	11	—	15	18	21	—	—	13	15	18	21	25	28	31	34	37	42	47
Penna Driver Model JS	(1980)	11	—	—	—	—	—	—	—	—	—	—	—	—	—	—	—	—	—
Penna Driver Model I	(1980)	9½	—	—	—	—	—	—	—	—	—	—	—	—	—	—	—	—	—

GOLF CLUB MANUFACTURERS STANDARD SPECIFICATIONS

Mfgr. & Year Specs. Published		#1 Wood	#2 Wood	#3 Wood	#4 Wood	#5 Wood	#6 Wood	#7 Wood	#1 Iron	#2 Iron	#3 Iron	#4 Iron	#5 Iron	#6 Iron	#7 Iron	#8 Iron	#9 Iron	Pitch Wedge	Sand Wedge
Penna Driver Model 2 + 65	(1980)	11	—	—	—	—	—	—	—	—	—	—	—	—	—	—	—	—	—
Penna Driver Model 12	(1980)	12	—	—	—	—	—	—	—	—	—	—	—	—	—	—	—	—	—
PowerBilt/All	(1982)	11	14	17	20	22	—	—	18	20	24	28	32	35	38	41	44	50	56
Pro-Dyn	(1977)	12	—	16½	19½	22½	—	28	18	21	24	27	30	34	38	42	46	51	57
Pro Group	(1982)	11½	14	17	20	23	—	—	18	21	24	27	30	34	38	41	45	49	—
Ram Accubar	(1982)	11	—	16¼	19¼	22	—	—	—	19½	23.2	27	30.5	34.2	37	42	45.8	49.5	55.5
Ram Golden Ram, Tour Grind	(1982)	11	—	16	19	22	—	—	16	19.5	23	26.5	30	33.5	37	41	45	49	55
Rawlings RXP	(1980)	11	—	17	20	23	—	—	—	19	23	27	30	35	39	43	47	51	56
Royal Edge	(1978)	12	—	17	20	22	—	—	—	21	23	26	29	33	37	41	45	50	54
Royal Impact	(1978)	12	—	17	20	22	—	26	—	19	22	25	29	33	37	41	45	49	55
Slotline	(1982)	11	—	16	19	22	—	—	17	20	23	26	29	32	36	40	44	49	56
Spalding Elite	(1982)	12	—	16	18	20	—	—	17	19	22	25	29	33	37	41	45	49	54
Spalding XL4	(1982)	12	—	16	18	20	—	—	17	19	22	25	28	32	36	40	44	48	54
Spalding Top Flite	(1982)	11	—	16	18	20	—	—	17	19	22	26	30	34	38	41	46	49	56
Spalding Executive	(1982)	12	—	17	20	23	—	—	17½	19½	22½	26	30	34	38	41½	46½	52	58
Square 2	(1978)	11	—	16	19	22	—	—	—	20	23	26	29	32	35³/10	38⁹/10	43	49	55
Taylor Made Golf	(1982)	9½	—	19	21	23	—	27	18	21	24	27	30	33	37	41	45	49	57
Titleist Pro 100	(1976)	11	14	17	20	22	—	—	19	21	24	27	30	33	36	40	44	48	—
Titleist AC-108	(1976)	11	14	17	20	22	—	—	—	22	25	28	30	33½	36	40	43	47	55
Unique	(1982)	11	—	16	19	22	—	—	17	20	23	26	29	33	37	41	45	50	57
Wilson Staff	(1982)	11	14	16	19	21	—	25	17	20	23	26	30	34	38	42	46	50	55
Wilson Aggressor	(1982)	12	—	16	19	21	—	25	—	20	23	26	30	34	38	42	46	50	55
Wilson X-31	(1982)	12	14	16	19	21	—	26	—	20	23	26	30	34	38	42	46	50	55
Wilson 1200 GE	(1982)	11	14	16	19	21	—	25	—	20	23	26	30	34	38	42	46	50	55
Wilson Reflex	(1982)	11	14	16	19	21	—	25	—	20	23	26	30	34	38	42	46	50	55
Stan Thompson	(1982)	11	14	17	20	23	—	29	—	21	24	27	30	34	38	42	46	51	56

LIE — MEN'S

GOLF CLUB MANUFACTURERS STANDARD SPECIFICATIONS

Mfgr. & Year Specs. Published		#1 Wood	#2 Wood	#3 Wood	#4 Wood	#5 Wood	#6 Wood	#7 Wood	#1 Iron	#2 Iron	#3 Iron	#4 Iron	#5 Iron	#6 Iron	#7 Iron	#8 Iron	#9 Iron	Pitch Wedge	Sand Wedge
Ajay Double Eagle	(1977)	55	—	55½	55¾	56	—	—	—	57	58	59	60	61	62	63	63	64	64
Browning	(1980)	55	—	56	57	57	—	—	56½	57	58	59	60	61	62	63	64	64	—
Cobra Low Profile	(1982)	—	—	—	—	—	—	—	56½	57	58	59	60	61	62	63	63	64	64
Cobra Premier Iron	(1982)	—	—	—	—	—	—	—	56	57	58	59	60	61	62	63	64	64	64
Cobra Tour Model	(1982)	54	54	54½	55	55	—	—	56	57	58	59	60	61	62	63	64	64	64
Confidence	(1977)	54	—	55	55	55	—	—	56	56	57	58	59	60	61	62	62	63	63
Dunlop Australian Blade	(1978)	—	—	—	—	—	—	—	56	57	58	59	60	61	62	63	64	65	65
Dunlop Maxfli Woods	(1978)	55	55	56	56	57	—	57	56	57	58	59	60	61	62	63	64	65	65
Walter Hagen The Haig	(1982)	55	55	56	57	57	—	57	—	57	58	59	60	61	62	63	63	64	65
Hogan Apex	(1978)	55½	—	57	57	58	—	—	—	57	58	59	60	61	62	62½	63	64½	—
Hogan Director	(1978)	55½	—	57	57	58	—	—	—	57	58	59	60	61	62	62½	63	64½	—
Hogan Medallion	(1978)	55½	—	57	57	58	—	—	—	57	58	59	60	61	62	62½	63	64½	—
Hogan Producer	(1978)	55½	56	57	57	58	—	59	—	56½	57½	58½	59½	60½	61½	62	62½	64	—
MacGregor M693 Woods	(1982)	54	—	55	56	56	—	—	—	—	—	—	—	—	—	—	—	—	—
MacGregor M85 Woods	(1982)	54	—	55	56	56	—	—	—	—	—	—	—	—	—	—	—	—	—
MacGregor MT Woods/Irons	(1982)	54	—	55	56	56	—	—	58	59	60	61	62	63	63	64	64	64	65
MacGregor MCX Woods/Irons	(1982)	54	—	55	56	56	—	57	—	58	59	60	61	61½	62	62½	63	63½	65
MacGregor Limited Edition	(1982)	55	—	55½	56½	56½	—	—	59	59½	60	60½	61	61½	62½	62½	63½	65	66
Northwestern	(1982)	55	55¼	55½	55¾	56	—	56½	55	56	57	58	59	60	61	62	63	63	63
P.G.A. Emblem	(1982)	54	—	55	55	56	—	—	—	57	58	59	60	60½	61	62	63	64	64
P.G.A. Tommy Armour	(1982)	54	—	55	55	55	—	—	57	57	58	59	60	60½	61	62	63	64	64
P.G.A. Performer	(1982)	54	—	55	55	56	—	—	—	56½	57½	58½	59½	60	61	62	63	64	64
P.G.A. Concept LCG	(1982)	54	—	55	55	56	—	56	—	58	59	60	60½	61	62	63	63	64	64
P.G.A. Ryder Cup II	(1982)	54	—	55	55	55	—	56	—	58	59	60	61	61½	62	62½	63	63	63
Pedersen	(1978)	56	56½	57	57½	58	—	58	56	57	58	59	60	61	62	63	64	64	64
Toney Penna/All	(1980)	54	—	56	57	58	—	—	56	56½	56½	57	58	59	59½	60	60½	61	61
Penna Driver Model JS	(1980)	54	—	—	—	—	—	—	—	—	—	—	—	—	—	—	—	—	—
Penna Driver Model I	(1980)	54	—	—	—	—	—	—	—	—	—	—	—	—	—	—	—	—	—

GOLF CLUB MANUFACTURERS STANDARD SPECIFICATIONS

Mfgr. & Year Specs. Published		#1 Wood	#2 Wood	#3 Wood	#4 Wood	#5 Wood	#6 Wood	#7 Wood	#1 Iron	#2 Iron	#3 Iron	#4 Iron	#5 Iron	#6 Iron	#7 Iron	#8 Iron	#9 Iron	Pitch Wedge	Sand Wedge
Penna Driver Model 2 + 65	(1980)	54	—	—	—	—	—	—	—	—	—	—	—	—	—	—	—	—	—
Penna Driver Model 12	(1980)	54	—	—	—	—	—	—	—	—	—	—	—	—	—	—	—	—	—
PowerBilt/All	(1982)	55	55	56	57	57	—	—	56	57	58	59	60	61	62	63	64	64	64
Pro-Dyn	(1977)	54	—	55	55	55	—	55	56	57	58	59	60	61	62	63	63	64	64
Pro Group	(1982)	54	54	55	56	—	—	—	57	57	58	59	60	61	61	62	62	63	—
Ram Accubar	(1982)	55	—	56	56½	57	—	—	—	57½	58	58½	59	60	61	62	63	63	63
Ram Golden Ram, Tour Grind	(1982)	55	—	56	56½	57	—	—	56½	57½	58½	59½	60½	61½	62½	63½	64½	65½	65½
Rawlings RXP	(1980)	56	—	57	58	58	—	—	—	57	58	59	60	61	62	63	64	64	64
Royal Edge	(1978)	54	—	55	55	55	—	—	—	57	58	59	60	60½	61	61½	62	62	62
Royal Impact	(1978)	54	—	55	55	55	—	56	—	58	59	60	61	62	63	64	64	64	64
Slotline	(1982)	55	—	56	57	57	—	—	56½	57	58	59	60	61	62	63	64	64	64
Spalding Elite	(1982)	54½	—	54¾	55¼	55¾	—	—	57¾	58¼	58¾	59¼	59¾	60¼	60¾	61¼	62	63	63
Spalding Executive	(1982)	55	—	55¼	55½	56	—	—	58¼	58¼	58¾	59¼	59¾	60¼	61	61¾	62¼	63	63
Spalding Top Flite	(1982)	54	—	54½	55	55½	—	—	58	58	59¼	59¾	60	60¾	61	61¾	62½	63½	63½
Spalding XL4	(1982)	55	—	55½	56	56½	—	—	57¾	58¼	58¾	59¼	59¾	60¼	60¾	61¼	62	63	63
Square 2	(1978)	55	—	56	56½	57	—	—	—	58	59	60	61	62	62½	63	63½	63½	63½
Taylor Made Golf	(1982)	54	—	55	55	55	—	55	56	57	58	59	60	61	62	63	64	64	64
Titleist Pro 100	(1976)	54	54	55	56	56	—	—	56	57	58	59	60	61	62	63	63	64	—
Titleist AC-108	(1976)	54	54	55	56	56	—	—	—	57	58	59	60	61	62	63	63	64	64
Unique	(1982)	55	—	55½	56	56½	—	—	58	58	59	60	61	62	63	64	65	65	65
Wilson Staff	(1982)	—	—	—	—	—	—	—	56	57	58	59	60	60	61	62	62	63	64
Wilson Aggressor	(1982)	55	55	56	57	57	—	57	—	56	57	58	59	60	61	62	62	63	64
Wilson X-31	(1982)	54	54	55	56	56	—	56	—	57	58	59	60	60	61	62	62	63	64
Wilson 1200 GE	(1982)	54	54	55	56	56	—	56	—	57	58	59	60	60	61	62	62	63	64
Wilson Reflex	(1982)	54	54	55	56	56	—	56	—	57	58	59	60	61	62	63	63	64	65
Stan Thompson	(1982)	54	54	55	56	57	—	58	—	57	58	59	60	61	62	63	64	64	64

CUSTOM MFGR.'S — MEN'S — LATE 1970's & EARLY 1980's

LENGTH, LOFT & LIE — MEN'S

GOLF CLUB MANUFACTURERS STANDARD SPECIFICATIONS

Mfgr. & Year Specs. Published		#1 Wood	#2 Wood	#3 Wood	#4 Wood	#5 Wood	#6 Wood	#7 Wood	#1 Iron	#2 Iron	#3 Iron	#4 Iron	#5 Iron	#6 Iron	#7 Iron	#8 Iron	#9 Iron	Pitch Wedge	Sand Wedge
Length:																			
Mario Cesario	(1982)	43	42½	42	41½	41	—	40	39	38½	38	37½	37	36½	36	35½	35	35	35
Bert Dargie	(1982)	43	42½	42	41½	41	—	40	39	38½	38	37½	37	36½	36	35½	35	35	35
George Izett	(1982)	43	43	42	41½	41	—	40	39½	39	38½	38	37½	37	36½	36	35½	35½	35½
Irving King	(1982)	43	42½	42	41½	41	—	—	—	38½	38	37½	37	36½	36	35½	35	35	35
Louisville Golf	(1982)	43	42½	42	41½	41	—	40	—	38½	38	37½	37	36½	36	35½	35	35	35
Ralph Maltby	(1982)	43	42½	42	41½	41	40½	40	39½	39	38½	38	37½	37	36½	36	35½	35½	35½
John Ofer	(1982)	43	42½	42	41½	41	41	41	—	39	38½	38	37½	37	36⅝	36¼	35¾	35½	35½
Orlimar	(1982)	43	42¾	42	41½	41	—	—	39¾	39¼	38¾	38¼	37¾	37¼	36¾	36¼	35¾	35½	35½
Kenneth Smith	(1979)	43	42½	42	41½	41	—	39½	39	38½	38	37½	37	36½	36	35½	35	34½	34½
Bob Toski	(1982)	43	42½	42	41½	41	—	40	39½	39	38½	38	37½	37	36½	36	35½	35½	35½
Loft:																			
Mario Cesario	(1982)	11	13	16	19	22	—	28	17	20	24	28	32	36	40	44	48	52	58
Bert Dargie	(1982)	11	13	16	19	22	—	28	18	21	24	27	31	35	39	43	47	51	55
George Izett	(1982)	10	13	16	19	22	—	28	17	20	22½	25	27½	30	32½	35	37½	40	42½
Irving King	(1982)	11	13	16	19	21	—	—	—	20	24	28	32	36	40	44	48	52	56
Louisville Golf	(1982)	10½	13	16	19	22	—	28	—	20	23	26	30	34	38	42	46	50	55
Ralph Maltby	(1982)	11	13	16	19	22	25	28	17	20	23	26	30	34	38	42	46	50	56
John Ofer	(1982)	10½	13	16	19	22	25	27	—	20	23	26	30	34	38	42	46	50	55
Orlimar	(1982)	11	14	17	20	23	—	—	16	19	22	25½	29	33	37	41	45	50	58
Kenneth Smith	(1979)	11	14	17	20	23	—	29	17	20	23	27	31	35	39	43	47	51	56
Bob Toski	(1982)	12	15	18	20	22	—	27	22	24	26½	29	31½	35	38½	41½	45	48½	51½
Lie:																			
Mario Cesario	(1982)	54	55	56	57	57	—	57	56	57	58	59	60	61	62	63	64	65	65
Bert Dargie	(1982)	54	54	55	56	56	—	57	57	58	59	60	61	62	63	64	64	65	65
George Izett	(1982)	55	55	56	57	58	—	59	56	57	58	59	60	61	62	63	64	64	64
Irving King	(1982)	55	55½	56	56½	57	—	—	—	57	58	59	60	61	62	63	64	64	64
Louisville Golf	(1982)	55	55	56	57	57	—	58	—	55	56	57	58	59	60	61	61	62	62
Ralph Maltby	(1982)	55	55½	56	56½	57	57½	58	55	56	57	58	59	60	61	62	63	63	63
John Ofer	(1982)	55	55	57	57	57	57	57	—	57	58	59	60	60	61	62	62	63	65
Orlimar, Pers. (Lam. 1° Flatter)	(1982)	56	56¼	56¾	57	57¼	—	—	58¼	58¼	58¾	59¼	59¾	60¼	60½	61¼	62	62¼	62½
Kenneth Smith	(1979)	54	55	56	57	58	—	60	56	57	58	59	60	61	62	63	64	64	64
Bob Toski, Cast (Forged 1° Upright)	(1982)	54	54	55	56	57	—	57	56½	57	57½	58	58½	60	61	61½	62	63	63

MEN'S — MID 1980's

LENGTH — MEN'S

GOLF CLUB MANUFACTURERS STANDARD SPECIFICATIONS

Mfgr. & Year Specs. Published		#1 Wood	#2 Wood	#3 Wood	#4 Wood	#5 Wood	#6 Wood	#7 Wood	#1 Iron	#2 Iron	#3 Iron	#4 Iron	#5 Iron	#6 Iron	#7 Iron	#8 Iron	#9 Iron	Pitch Wedge	Sand Wedge
Armour Golf T-Line BC	(1986)	43¼	—	42¼	41¾	41¼	—	40¾	39½	39	38½	38	37½	37	36½	36	35½	35½	35½
Browning 440	(1986)	43	—	42	41½	41	—	41	—	39	38½	38	37½	37	36½	36	35½	35½	35½
Browning Automatic	(1986)	43	—	42	41½	41	—	41	—	39	38½	38	37½	37	36½	36	35½	35½	35½
Daiwa Exceler	(1986)	43¼	—	42¼	41¾	41¼	—	40¾	—	39	38½	38	37½	37	36½	36	35½	35½	35½
Dunlop 357	(1986)	43⅜	—	42⅜	—	41⅝	—	41⅛	39½	39	38½	38	37½	37	36½	36	35½	35½	35½
The GolfWorks® Bio-Mech	(1986)	43	42½	42	41½	41	40½	40	39½	39	38½	38	37½	37	36½	36	35½	35½	35½
The GolfWorks® RMH	(1986)	43	42½	42	41½	41	40½	40	39½	39	38½	38	37½	37	36½	36	35½	35½	35½
H & B All	(1986)	43	—	42	41½	41½	—	—	—	39	38½	38	37½	37	36½	36	35½	35½	35½
Hogan Apex	(1986)	43¼	—	42¼	41¾	41¼	—	—	—	39¼	38¾	38¼	37¾	37¼	36¾	36¼	35¾	35½	35
Hogan Radial	(1986)	43¼	—	42¼	41¾	41¼	—	—	—	39	38½	38	37½	37	36½	36	35½	35¼	35¼
Lynx - Parallax	(1986)	43	—	42	41½	41	—	40	39½	39	38½	38	37½	37	36½	36	35½	35½	35¼
Lynx - Liberty	(1986)	43	—	42	41½	41	—	40	—	39	38½	38	37½	37	36½	36	35½	35½	35¼
MacGregor Muirfield	(1986)	43½	—	42¾	42¼	41¾	—	—	39¾	39¼	38¾	38¼	37¾	37¼	36¾	36½	36¼	35¾	35¾
MacGregor CG1800	(1986)	43½	—	42¾	42¼	41¾	—	—	39¾	39¼	38¾	38¼	37¾	37¼	36¾	36½	36¼	35¾	35¾
Mizuno MS-5	(1986)	43¼	—	42¾	42½	42	—	—	39¾	39¼	38¾	38¼	37¾	37¼	36¾	36½	36¼	36	35¾
Mizuno MS-4	(1986)	43¼	—	42¾	42½	42	—	—	39¾	39	38¾	38¼	37¾	37¼	36¾	36½	36¼	36	35¾
Northwestern 241 Tour	(1986)	43	—	42	41½	41	—	—	39	38½	38	37½	37	36½	36	35½	35	35	35
Northwestern 865GR	(1986)	43	—	42	41½	41	—	—	39	38½	38	37½	37	36½	36	35½	35	35	35
Northwestern 965	(1986)	43	—	42	42½	41	—	—	39	38½	38	37½	37	36½	36	35½	35	35	35
Penna Golf Original	(1986)	43	—	42½	42	41	—	—	—	39	38½	38	37½	37	36½	36	35½	35	35
Penna Golf Innovater	(1986)	43	—	42½	42	41	—	—	—	39	38½	38	37½	37	36½	36	35½	35	35
Pinseeker Fireball	(1986)	43	—	42	41½	41¼	41	—	39½	39	38½	38	37½	37	36½	36	35½	35½	35½
Pinseeker Olympian	(1986)	43	—	42	41½	41¼	41	—	39½	39	38½	38	37½	37	36½	36	35½	35½	35½
Pro Group Axiom	(1986)	43	—	42	41¾	41½	—	41¼	39½	39	38½	38	37½	37	36½	36	35½	35½	35½
Pro Group Peerless	(1986)	43	—	42	41¾	41½	—	41¼	39½	39	38½	38	37½	37	36½	36	35½	35½	35½
Ram Tour Grind	(1986)	43¼	—	42¼	41¾	41¼	—	—	39½	39	38½	38	37½	37	36½	36	35½	35½	35
Ram Accubar	(1986)	43¼	—	42¼	41¾	41¼	—	—	—	39	38½	38	37½	37	36½	36	35½	35½	35
Spalding Cannon	(1986)	43	—	42	41½	41	—	40	—	39	38½	38	37½	37	36½	36	35½	35½	35½
Spalding Executive	(1986)	43	—	42	41½	41	—	40	—	38⅝	38⅛	37⅝	37⅛	36⅝	36⅛	35⅝	35⅛	35⅛	35⅛
Taylor Metalwoods	(1986)	43	—	42	41½	41	41	41	—	—	—	—	—	—	—	—	—	—	—
Taylor Technician	(1986)	42½	—	41¾	41½	41	—	—	38½	38⅛	37¾	37⅜	37	36⅝	36⅛	35¾	35¼	35	35
Taylor Iron Cleek	(1986)	—	—	—	—	—	—	—	39½	39	38½	38	37½	37	36½	36	35½	35½	35½
Taylor Tour Preferred	(1986)	—	—	—	—	—	—	—	39½	39	38½	38	37½	37	36½	36	35½	35½	35½
Titleist Tour Model	(1985)	43	—	42½	42	41¾	—	—	39½	39	38½	38	37½	37	36⅝	36¼	35⅞	35½	35½
Titleist Pinnacle	(1985)	43	—	42½	—	41¾	—	—	—	38¾	38¼	37¾	37¼	36¾	36⅜	36	35⅝	35¼	35
Wilson Aggressor	(1984)	43	—	42	41½	41¼	—	41	—	38½	38	37½	37	36½	36¼	35¾	35¼	35	35
Wilson Staff	(1986)	43	—	42	41½	41¼	41	41	—	39	38½	38	37½	37	36½	36	35½	35	35
Wilson 1200LT	(1986)	43	—	42	41½	41¼	41	41	—	39	38½	38	37½	37	36½	36	35½	35	35
Wilson 1200GE	(1986)	43	—	42	41½	41¼	41	41	—	39	38½	38	37½	37	36½	36	35½	35	35
Yahama Spada	(1986)	43½	—	42½	42	41½	—	—	—	—	—	—	—	—	—	—	—	—	—
Yamaha Y-45	(1986)	43½	—	42½	42	41½	—	—	—	—	—	—	—	—	—	—	—	—	—
Yamaha ST-30	(1986)	—	—	—	—	—	—	—	39½	39	38½	38	37½	37	36½	36	35½	35	35
Yamaha EX-22	(1986)	—	—	—	—	—	—	—	39½	39	38½	38	37½	37	36½	36	35½	35	35

MEN'S — MID 1980's

LOFT — MEN'S

GOLF CLUB MANUFACTURERS STANDARD SPECIFICATIONS

Mfgr. & Year Specs. Published		#1 Wood	#2 Wood	#3 Wood	#4 Wood	#5 Wood	#6 Wood	#7 Wood	#1 Iron	#2 Iron	#3 Iron	#4 Iron	#5 Iron	#6 Iron	#7 Iron	#8 Iron	#9 Iron	Pitch Wedge	Sand Wedge
Armour Golf T-Line BC	(1986)	10	—	12½	18½	21½	—	24½	16	18½	21½	25	28½	32½	36½	40½	44½	49	52
Browning 440	(1986)	10	—	16	19	22	—	25	—	21	24	27	30	34	38	42	46	50	56
Browning Automatic	(1986)	10	—	16	19	22	—	25	—	21	24	27	30	34	38	42	46	50	56
Daiwa Exceler	(1986)	11½	—	16½	19	21	—	25	—	17	19	22	25	29	33	37	41	45	50
Dunlop 357	(1986)	12	—	15	—	20	—	23	15	18	21	24	28	32	36	40	44	50	55
The GolfWorks® Bio-Mech	(1986)	11	13	16	19	22	25	28	17	19	22	25	29	33	37	41	45	49	55
The GolfWorks® RMH	(1986)	11	13	16	19	22	25	28	17	20	23	26	30	34	38	42	46	50	56
H & B All	(1986)	11	—	17	20	22	—	—	—	20	24	28	32	35	38	41	44	50	56
Hogan Apex	(1986)	10½	—	15	17½	21	—	—	—	19½	23	26½	30	33½	37	41	45	49	—
Hogan Radial	(1986)	10½	—	15	17½	21	—	—	—	19½	23	26½	30	33½	37	41	45	49	—
Lynx - Parallax	(1986)	10	—	17	20	23	—	26	16	19	22	25	29	33	37	41	45	49	57
Lynx - Liberty	(1986)	11	—	16	19	22	—	26	—	19	22	25	29	33	37	41	45	49	57
MacGregor Muirfield	(1986)	10	—	14	17	21	—	—	18	20	23	26	29	33	37	41	45	50	56
MacGregor CG1800	(1986)	13	—	16	19	21½	—	—	16	18	21	24	27½	32	37	41	45	50½	57
Mizuno MS-5	(1986)	10½	—	16	19	22	—	—	16	18	21	25	29	33	37	41	45	50	56
Mizuno MS-4	(1986)	11	—	16	19	22	—	—	16	18	21	25	29	33	37	41	45	50	56
Northwestern 241 Tour	(1986)	10	—	15	18	20	—	—	16	19	22	26	30	34	38	42	46	50	52
Northwestern 865GR	(1986)	10	—	15	18	20	—	—	16	19	22	26	30	34	38	42	46	50	52
Northwestern 965	(1986)	10	—	15	18	20	—	—	16	19	22	26	30	34	38	42	46	50	52
Penna Golf Original	(1986)	11	—	15	18	21	—	—	—	20	23	27	31	35	39	43	47	51	56
Penna Golf Innovator	(1986)	9½	—	15	18	21	—	—	—	20½	23	26	28½	31½	36	39	43	48	56
Pinseeker Fireball	(1986)	9	—	15	20	—	—	25	—	17	20	24	27	31	35	39	44	49	56
Pinseeker Olympian	(1986)	9	—	15	—	21	—	—	16	18	21	24	27	31	35	39	44	49	56
Pro Group Axiom	(1986)	12½	—	16	19	21	—	25	19	22	24	27	29	32	36	40	44	48	54
Pro Group Peerless	(1986)	10½	—	16	19	21	—	25	17	20	23	27	31	35	38	42	46	51	56
Ram Tour Grind	(1986)	11	—	16	19	22	—	—	16	19½	23	26½	30	33½	37	41	45	49	55
Ram Accubar	(1986)	12	—	17	—	22	—	26	—	17½	23½	27	30½	34½	37	42	46	50	55
Spalding Cannon	(1986)	11	—	16	—	21	—	26	17	19	22	25	28	32	36	40	45	50	—
Spalding Executive	(1986)	12	—	16	—	21	—	—	17½	19½	22	26	30	34	38	41½	46½	52	—
Taylor Metalwoods	(1986)	10	—	17	20	23	25	27½	—	—	—	—	—	—	—	—	—	—	—
Taylor Technician	(1986)	10	—	17	20	23	25	27½	16	19	22	25	28	32	36	40	44	48	54
Taylor Iron Cleek	(1986)	—	—	—	—	—	—	—	16	18	21	25	29	33	37	41	45	50	—
Taylor Tour Preferred	(1986)	—	—	—	—	—	—	—	16	19	22	25	29	33	37	41	45	49	55
Titleist Tour Model	(1985)	10½	—	16	19	22	—	—	18	20	23	26	30	33	37	41	45	49	54
Titleist Pinnacle	(1985)	12	—	17	—	23	—	—	—	19	22	26	30	33	36	40	44	48	55
Wilson Aggressor	(1984)	12	—	16	19	21	—	25	—	20	23	26	30	34	38	42	46	50	55
Wilson Staff	(1986)	12	—	16	19	21	—	—	—	20	23	26	30	34	38	42	46	50	55
Wilson 1200LT	(1986)	12	—	16	19	21	—	—	—	20	23	26	30	34	38	42	46	50	55
Wilson 1200GE	(1986)	12	—	16	19	21	—	—	—	19	22	25	29	33	37	41	45	49	54
Yahama Spada	(1986)	10½	—	16½	19	21½	—	—	—	—	—	—	—	—	—	—	—	—	—
Yamaha Y-45	(1986)	11	—	15	18	21	—	—	—	—	—	—	—	—	—	—	—	—	—
Yamaha ST-30	(1986)	—	—	—	—	—	—	—	19	21	24	27	31	35	39	43	47	51	56
Yamaha EX-22	(1986)	—	—	—	—	—	—	—	—	—	23	26	29	32	36	40	45	50	58

MEN'S — MID 1980's

LIE — MEN'S

GOLF CLUB MANUFACTURERS STANDARD SPECIFICATIONS

Mfgr. & Year Specs. Published		#1 Wood	#2 Wood	#3 Wood	#4 Wood	#5 Wood	#6 Wood	#7 Wood	#1 Iron	#2 Iron	#3 Iron	#4 Iron	#5 Iron	#6 Iron	#7 Iron	#8 Iron	#9 Iron	Pitch Wedge	Sand Wedge
Armour Golf T-Line BC	(1986)	55	—	55	55½	56	—	56½	56	56¾	57¾	58¾	59¾	60¾	61¾	62¾	63¾	63¾	63¾
Browning 440	(1986)	55	—	56	57	57	—	57	—	57	58	59	60	61	62	63	64	64	64
Browning Automatic	(1986)	55	—	56	57	57	—	57	—	57	58	59	60	61	62	63	64	64	64
Daiwa Exceler	(1986)	54	—	55	56	56	—	56	—	57	58	59	60	61	62	63	64	64	64
Dunlop 357	(1986)	55	—	55½	—	56½	—	57	57	58	59	60	61	62	63	64	65	65	65
The GolfWorks® Bio-Mech	(1986)	55	55½	56	56½	57	57½	58	58	58½	59	59½	60	60½	61	61½	62	63	63
The GolfWorks® RMH	(1986)	55	55½	56	56½	57	57½	58	55	56	57	58	59	60	61	62	63	63	63
H & B All	(1986)	55	—	56	57	57	—	—	—	57	58	59	60	61	62	63	64	64	64
Hogan Apex	(1986)	55	—	56	56	57	—	—	—	57	58	59	60	61	62	62½	63	63½	—
Hogan Radial	(1986)	55	—	56	56	57	—	—	—	57	58	59	60	61	62	63	63½	64	—
Lynx - Parallax	(1986)	54	—	55	56	57	—	58	57	57	58	59	60	61	62	63	64	64	64
Lynx - Liberty	(1986)	55	—	56	56	57	—	58	—	57	58	59	60	61	62	63	64	64	64
MacGregor Muirfield	(1986)	55	—	56	56½	56½	—	—	57	57½	58	59	60	60½	61	61½	62	63	63
MacGregor CG1800	(1986)	55	—	56	56	56	—	—	57	57½	58	59	60	60½	61	61½	62	63	63
Mizuno MS-5	(1986)	55	—	56	56½	57	—	—	56	57	58	59	60	60½	61	62	63	63	63
Mizuno MS-4	(1986)	55	—	56	56½	57	—	—	56	57	58	59	60	60½	61	62	63	63	63
Northwestern 241 Tour	(1986)	55	—	55½	55¾	56	—	—	55	56	57	58	59	60	61	62	63	63	63
Northwestern 865GR	(1986)	55	—	55½	55¾	56	—	—	55	56	57	58	59	60	61	62	63	63	63
Northwestern 965	(1986)	55	—	55½	55¾	56	—	—	55	56	57	58	59	60	61	62	63	63	63
Penna Golf Original	(1986)	55	—	56	56	57	—	—	—	58	58½	59	59½	60	60½	61	61½	61½	61½
Penna Golf Innovator	(1986)	55	—	56	56	57	—	—	—	58	59	59½	60	61	61½	62½	63	63½	61
Pinseeker Fireball	(1986)	54	—	55	55½	55½	—	—	55	56	57	58	59	60	61	62	63	63	63
Pinseeker Olympian	(1986)	54	—	55	55½	55½	—	—	55	56	57	58	59	60	61	62	63	63	63
Pro Group Axiom	(1986)	55½	—	56	57	57	—	58	56	56	57	58	59	60	61	62	63	63	64
Pro Group Peerless	(1986)	54½	—	55	56	56	—	—	56	56	57	58	59	60	61	62	63	63	64
Ram Tour Grind	(1986)	55	—	56	56½	57	—	—	55½	57½	58	59½	60½	61½	62½	63½	64½	65½	65½
Ram Accubar	(1986)	55	—	56	—	57	—	58	—	57½	58	58½	59	60	61	62	63	63	64
Spalding Cannon	(1986)	55	—	55½	—	56	—	56½	58	58½	59	59½	60	60½	61	61½	62	63	—
Spalding Executive	(1986)	55	—	55½	—	56	—	—	58¼	58¼	58¾	59¼	59¾	60¼	61	61¾	62¼	63	—
Taylor Metalwoods	(1986)	54	—	55	55	55	55	55	—	—	—	—	—	—	—	—	—	—	—
Taylor Technician	(1986)	54	—	55	55	55	55	55	57½	58¼	59	59¾	60½	61¼	62	63	63	64	64
Taylor Iron Cleek	(1986)	—	—	—	—	—	—	—	56½	57	58	59	60	61	62	63	64	64	—
Taylor Tour Preferred	(1986)	—	—	—	—	—	—	—	56½	57	58	59	60	61	62	63	64	64	—
Titleist Tour Model	(1985)	54	—	55	56	56	—	—	56	57	58	59	60	61	62	63	63	64	64
Titleist Pinnacle	(1985)	54	—	56	—	57	—	—	—	57	58	59	59	60	61	61	62	62	64
Wilson Aggressor	(1984)	55	—	56	57	57	57	—	—	56	57	58	59	60	61	62	62	63	64
Wilson Staff	(1986)	54	—	55	56	56	56	—	—	57	58	59	60	60	61	62	62	63	64
Wilson 1200LT	(1986)	55	—	56	57	57	—	—	—	57	58	59	60	60	61	62	62	63	64
Wilson 1200GE	(1986)	54	—	55	56	56	56	—	—	57	58	59	60	60	61	62	62	63	64
Yahama Spada	(1986)	55	—	56	56½	57	—	—	—	—	—	—	—	—	—	—	—	—	—
Yamaha Y-45	(1986)	55	—	56	56½	57	—	—	—	—	—	—	—	—	—	—	—	—	—
Yamaha ST-30	(1986)	—	—	—	—	—	—	—	57	57	58	59	60	61	62	63	63½	64	64
Yamaha EX-22	(1986)	—	—	—	—	—	—	—	—	—	58	58½	59	60	61	62	63	63½	64

CUSTOM MFGR.'S — MEN'S — MID 1980's

LENGTH — MEN'S

GOLF CLUB MANUFACTURERS STANDARD SPECIFICATIONS

Mfgr. & Year Specs. Published		#1 Wood	#2 Wood	#3 Wood	#4 Wood	#5 Wood	#6 Wood	#7 Wood	#1 Iron	#2 Iron	#3 Iron	#4 Iron	#5 Iron	#6 Iron	#7 Iron	#8 Iron	#9 Iron	Pitch Wedge	Sand Wedge
Length:																			
Mario Cesario	(1986)	43	42½	42	41½	41	—	40	39	38½	38	37½	37	36½	36	35½	35	35	35
Cobra	(1986)	43	42¾	42½	42	41½	41¼	41	39½	39	38½	38	37½	37	36½	36	35½	35½	35¼
Bert Dargie	(1982)	43	42½	42	41½	41	—	40	39	38½	38	37½	37	36½	36	35½	35	35	35
The GolfWorks®	(1986)	43	42½	42	41½	41	40½	40	39½	39	38½	38	37½	37	36½	36	35½	35½	35½
George Izett	(1986)	43	43	42	41½	41	—	40	39½	39	38½	38	37½	37	36½	36	35½	35½	35½
Irving King	(1982)	43	42½	42	41½	41	—	—	—	38½	38	37½	37	36½	36	35½	35	35	35
Louisville Golf	(1986)	43	42½	42	41½	41	—	40	39½	39	38½	38	37½	37	36½	36	35½	35½	35½
John Ofer	(1986)	43	42½	42	41½	41	41	41	—	39	38½	38	37½	37	36⅝	36¼	35¾	35½	35½
Orlimar	(1982)	43	42¾	42	41½	41	—	—	39¾	39¼	38¾	38¼	37¾	37¼	36¾	36¼	35¾	35½	35½
Pederson	(1986)	43	42¾	42¼	42	41½	41	40½	39	38½	38	37½	37	36½	36	35½	35	35	35
Kenneth Smith	(1986)	43	42½	42	41½	41	—	39½	39	38½	38	37½	37	36½	36	35½	35	34½	34½
Bob Toski	(1986)	43	42½	42	41½	41	—	40	39½	39	38½	38	37½	37	36½	36	35½	35½	35½

LOFT — MEN'S

GOLF CLUB MANUFACTURERS STANDARD SPECIFICATIONS

Mfgr. & Year Specs. Published		#1 Wood	#2 Wood	#3 Wood	#4 Wood	#5 Wood	#6 Wood	#7 Wood	#1 Iron	#2 Iron	#3 Iron	#4 Iron	#5 Iron	#6 Iron	#7 Iron	#8 Iron	#9 Iron	Pitch Wedge	Sand Wedge
Loft:																			
Mario Cesario	(1986)	11	13	16	19	22	—	28	17	20	24	28	32	36	40	44	48	52	58
Cobra	(1986)	10	14	16	19	22	25	27	17	20	23	27	31	36	40	44	48	52	56
Bert Dargie	(1982)	11	13	16	19	22	—	28	18	21	24	27	31	35	39	43	47	51	55
The GolfWorks®	(1986)	11	13	16	19	22	25	28	17	20	23	26	30	34	38	42	46	50	56
George Izett	(1986)	10	13	16	19	22	—	28	17	20	22½	25	27½	30	32½	35	37½	40	42½
Irving King	(1982)	11	13	16	19	21	—	—	—	20	24	28	32	36	40	44	48	52	56
Louisville Golf	(1986)	11	13½	16	18½	21½	24	26½	17	20	23	26	29	33	37	41	45	50	55
John Ofer	(1986)	10½	13	16	19	22	25	27	—	20	23	26	30	34	38	42	46	50	55
Orlimar	(1982)	11	14	17	20	23	—	—	16	19	22	25½	29	33	37	41	45	50	58
Pederson	(1986)	11	13	16	19	22	24	26	18	22	23	26	30	34	38	42	46	50	55
Kenneth Smith	(1986)	11	14	17	20	23	—	29	17	20	23	27	31	35	39	43	47	51	56
Bob Toski	(1986)	12	15	18	20	22	—	27	22	24	26½	29	31½	35	38½	41½	45	48½	51½

LIE — MEN'S

GOLF CLUB MANUFACTURERS STANDARD SPECIFICATIONS

Mfgr. & Year Specs. Published		#1 Wood	#2 Wood	#3 Wood	#4 Wood	#5 Wood	#6 Wood	#7 Wood	#1 Iron	#2 Iron	#3 Iron	#4 Iron	#5 Iron	#6 Iron	#7 Iron	#8 Iron	#9 Iron	Pitch Wedge	Sand Wedge
Lie:																			
Mario Cesario	(1986)	54	55	56	57	57	—	57	56	57	58	59	60	61	62	63	64	65	65
Cobra	(1986)	54	54	55	55½	56	55	55½	57	57½	58	59	59½	60	61	62	63	63	64
Bert Dargie	(1982)	54	54	55	56	56	—	57	57	58	59	60	61	62	63	64	64	65	65
The GolfWorks®	(1986)	55	55½	56	56½	57	57½	58	55	56	57	58	59	60	61	62	63	63	63
George Izett	(1986)	55	55	56	57	58	—	59	56	57	58	59	60	61	62	63	64	64	64
Irving King	(1982)	55	55½	56	56½	57	—	—	—	57	58	59	60	61	62	63	64	64	64
Louisville Golf	(1986)	55	55½	56	56½	57	57½	58	56	57	58	59	60	61	62	63	64	64	64
John Ofer	(1986)	55	55	57	57	57	57	57	—	57	58	59	60	60	61	62	62	63	63
Orlimar	(1982)	56	56¼	56¾	57	57¼	—	—	58¼	58¼	58¾	59¼	59¾	60¼	60½	61¼	62	62¼	62½
Pederson	(1986)	54	54½	55	56	56½	57	57½	56	57	58	59	60	61	62	63	64	64	64
Kenneth Smith	(1986)	54	55	56	57	58	—	60	56	57	58	59	60	61	62	63	64	64	64
Bob Toski	(1986)	54	54	55	56	57	57	57	56½	57	57½	58	58½	60	61	61½	62	63	63

MEN'S — LATE 1980's

LENGTH — MEN'S

GOLF CLUB MANUFACTURERS STANDARD SPECIFICATIONS — DURING PERIOD OF 1985 TO 1990

Mfg. & Model ■	#1 Wood	#2 Wood	#3 Wood	#4 Wood	#5 Wood	#6 Wood	#7 Wood	#1 Iron	#2 Iron	#3 Iron	#4 Iron	#5 Iron	#6 Iron	#7 Iron	#8 Iron	#9 Iron	Pitch Wedge	Sand Wedge
Accuform (all)	43	42½	42	41½	41	—	40	39½	39	38½	38	37½	37	36½	36	35½	35½	35
Browning 440 Gold	43	—	42	—	41	—	—	39½	39	38½	38	37½	37	36½	36	35½	35½	35½
Browning Pinache	43	—	42	—	41	—	—	39½	39	38½	38	37½	37	36½	36	35½	35½	35½
Browning Automatic	43	—	42	41½	41	—	41	—	39	38½	38	37½	37	36½	36	35½	35½	35½
Browning Tour Class	43	—	42	41½	41	—	—	—	—	38½	38	37½	37	36½	36	35½	35½	35½
Browning Maxim	43	42½	42	41½	41	—	41	—	39	38½	38	37½	37	36½	36	35½	35½	35½
Browning 440	43	—	42	41½	41	—	41	—	39	38½	38	37½	37	36½	36	35½	35½	35½
Browning System 350	43	—	42	41½	41	—	—	39½	39	38½	38	37½	37	36½	36	35½	35½	35½
Browning 440 Plus	43	42½	42	41½	41	—	41	—	39	38½	38	37½	37	36½	36	35½	35½	35½
Browning Premier	43	—	42	—	41	—	—	39½	39	38½	38	37½	37	36½	36	35½	35½	35½
Browning Mirage (L.)	43	—	42	—	41	—	—	—	39	38½	38	37½	37	36½	36	35½	35½	35½
Callaway Bobby Jones Comm.	43	—	42	—	41	40½	—	39½	39	38½	38	37½	37	36½	36	35½	35	34½
Callaway Bobby Jones	43½	—	42½	42	41½	—	41	40	39½	39	38½	38	37½	37	36½	36	35½	35
Callaway Classic	43½	—	42½	42	41½	—	41											
Callaway S2H2	43½	—	42½	—	41½	—	—	40	39½	39	38½	38	37½	37	36½	36	35½	35
Cleveland Classics Tour Action 588	43¼	42½	42	41½	41	—	—	39½	39	38½	38	37½	37	36½	36	35½	35¼	35
Cleveland Classics TC 15	43¼	42½	42	41½	41	—	—											
Cleveland Classics RC85	43¼	—	42	41½	41	—	—											
Cleveland Classics TA289	43¼	—	42	41½	41	40	40											
Cleveland Classics Tour Action 588 (P.)								39½	39	38½	38	37½	37	36½	36	35½	35⅛	
Cleveland Classics 10th Anni. Woods	43¼	—	42	41½	41	—	—											
Cobra Baffler Steel Classic	43	—	42	—	41½	—	41½	40	40	39½	39	38½	38	37½	36	36	36½	36¼
Cobra Traditional Baffler Blade								39½	39	38½	38	37½	37	36	36	35½	35½	35¼
Cobra Baffler*	42½	42¼	42	41¾	41½	41¼	41											
Cobra Long Tom	46																	
Daiwa Lite Touch (G.)	43¼	—	42¼	41¾	41¼	—	40¾		39	38½	38	36½	37	36½	36	35½	35½	35½
Daiwa SRX3 (P.)	43¼	—	42¼	41¾	41¼	—	40¾		39	38½	38	36½	37	36½	36	35½	35½	35½
Daiwa Hi-Trac (L.)	43¼	—	42¼	41¾	41¼	—	40¾		39	38½	38	36½	37	36½	36	35½	35½	35½
Daiwa Chairman (P.)	43¼	—	42¼	41¾	41¼	—	40¾		39	38½	38	36½	37	36½	36	35½	35½	35½
Daiwa Ballistic II (M.)	43¼	—	42¼	41¾	41¼	—	40¾											
Daiwa Monodyne								39½	39	38½	38	37½	37	36½	36	35½	35½	35½
Daiwa Advisor								39½	39	38½	38	37½	37	36½	36	35½	35½	35½
Daiwa DB-561	43¼	—	42¼	41¾	41¼	—	—											
Daiwa DB-591	43¼	—	42¼	41¾	41¼	—	—											
Daiwa Exceler	43¼	—	42¼	41¾	41¼	—	40¾											
Daiwa Exceler BPT	43¼	—	42¼	41¾	41¼	—	40¾											
Daiwa DB-611 (P.)	43½	—	42½	42	41½	—	—											
Daiwa DB-612 (P.)	43½	—	42½	42	41½	—	—											
Dunlop Maxfli DP 30								39½	39	38½	38	37½	37	36½	36	35½	35½	35½
Dunlop Seve Ballesteros (P.)	43¼	—	42¼	41¾	—	—	—	39½	39	38½	38	37½	37	36½	36	35½	35½	35½
Dunlop Maxfli 901 (P.)	43¼	—	42¼	41¾	41¼	—	—											

■ G. = Graphite M. = Metal L. = Laminated P. = Persimmon *Woods also available as #8-40¾, #9-40½, #11-40¼, #13-40 and TS-41½

MEN'S — LATE 1980's

LENGTH — MEN'S

GOLF CLUB MANUFACTURERS STANDARD SPECIFICATIONS — DURING PERIOD OF 1985 TO 1990

Mfg. & Model	#1 Wood	#2 Wood	#3 Wood	#4 Wood	#5 Wood	#6 Wood	#7 Wood	#1 Iron	#2 Iron	#3 Iron	#4 Iron	#5 Iron	#6 Iron	#7 Iron	#8 Iron	#9 Iron	Pitch Wedge	Sand Wedge
Dunlop Maxfli 357 MP (M.)	43¼	—	42½	—	41¾	—	41¼	39¾	39¼	38¾	38¼	37¾	37¼	36¾	36¼	35¾	35¾	35¾
Dunlop Maxfli Tour Limited	43¼	—	42½	—	41¾	—	41¼	39¾	39¼	38¾	38¼	37¾	37¼	36¾	36¼	35¾	35¾	35¾
Dunlop Black Missile (G.)	43	—	42	—	41¼	—	—	—	—	39	38½	38	37½	37	36½	36	35½	35½
Dunlop Maxfli Pro. Special (P.)	43	—	42	41½	40	—	—	39½	39	38½	38	37½	37	36½	36	35½	35½	35½
Dunlop Red Max (M.)	43	—	42	—	41	—	—	39¾	39¼	38¾	38¼	37¾	37¼	36¾	36¼	35¾	35¼	35
Dunlop Maxfli Tour Limited (M.)	43¼	—	42¼	—	41½	—	41	39¾	39¼	38¾	38¼	37¾	37¼	36¾	36¼	35¾	35¾	35¾
Dunlop Maxfli Missile (G.)	43	—	42	—	41¼	—	—	—	—	39	38½	38	37½	37	36½	36	35½	35½
Dunlop Power Max (M.)	43	—	42	—	41¼	—	—	—	—	38½	38	37½	37	36½	36	35½	35½	35½
GolfWorks® Kinetic	43	—	42	—	41	—	40	39½	39	38½	38	37½	37	36½	36	35½	35½	35½
GolfWorks® Technique	43	—	42	41½	41	—	—	39½	39	38½	38	37½	37	36½	36	35½	35½	35½
GolfWorks® Bio Mech (M.)	43	—	42	—	41	—	40	39½	39	38½	38	37½	37	36½	36	35½	35½	35½
GolfWorks® XDC	43	—	42	—	41	—	40	39½	39	38½	38	37½	37	36½	36	35½	35½	35½
GolfWorks® Commander	43	—	42	41½	41	—	—	39½	39	38½	38	37½	37	36½	36	35½	35½	35½
GolfWorks® Tandem	43	—	42	41½	41	—	40	39½	39	38½	38	37½	37	36½	36	35½	35½	35½
GolfWorks® RMH	—	—	—	—	—	—	—	39½	39	38½	38	37½	37	36½	36	35½	35½	35½
GolfWorks® Hero Plus	43	—	42	41½	41	—	40	39½	39	38½	38	37½	37	36½	36	35½	35½	35½
GolfWorks® Bio Mech (L.)*	43	42½	42	41½	41	40½	40											
GolfWorks® Accu-Weight	43	—	42	—	41	—	40	—	—	38½	38	37½	37	36½	36	35½	35½	35½
H & B/Power Bilt Citation (P.)	43	42½	42	41½	41½	41	41											
H & B/Power Bilt Citation (L.)	43	42½	42	41½	41½	41	41											
H & B/Power Bilt TPS								39½	39	38½	38	37½	37	36½	36	35½	35½	35½
H & B/Power Bilt TPS (M.)	43	42½	42	41½	41½	—	41											
H & B/Power Bilt Grand Slam (L.)	43	—	42	41½	41½	—	41											
H & B/Power Bilt Grand Slam (M.)	43	—	42	—	41½	—	41											
H & B/Power Bilt Citation Plus	43	42½	42	41½	41½	41	41											
H & B/Power Bilt Scotch Blade								39½	39	38½	38	37½	37	36½	36	35½	35½	35½
H & B/Power Bilt Citation Forged								39½	39	38½	38	37½	37	36½	36	35½	35½	35½
H & B/Power Bilt Citation Cast								39½	39	38½	38	37½	37	36½	36	35½	35½	35½
H & B/Power Bilt Propower								39½	39	38½	38	37½	37	36½	36	35½	35½	35½
Walter Hagen Haig Ultra	43	—	42	41½	41½	—	—	39½	39	38½	38	37½	37	36½	36	35½	35	35
Hogan Apex	43¼	—	42¼	41¾	41¼	—	—	39¾	39¼	38¾	38¼	37¾	37¼	36¾	36¼	35¾	35½	35
Hogan Radial	43¼	—	42¼	41¾	41¼	—	—	—	39	38½	38	37½	37	36½	36	35½	35½	35¼
Hogan Magnum								39¼	38¾	38¼	38	37¾	37½	37¼	36¾	36¼	35¾	35¼
Hogan Series 56	43¼	42¾	42¼	41¾	41¼	—	40¼											
Hogan Series 56 (G.)	43¼	42¾	42¼	41¾	41¼													
Hogan Saber	41¾																	
Hogan Companion	42	41¾	41½	41	40½	—	39½											
Hogan Apex PC								—	39¼	38¾	38¼	37¾	37¼	36¾	36¼	35¾	35½	
Hogan Edge Irons								39¾	39¼	38¾	38¼	37¾	37¼	36¾	36¼	35¾	35½	35
Hogan 56 (Carbon Woods)	43¼	42¾	42¼	41¾	41¼	—	—											
Hogan Magnum Plus (Woods)	43¼	—	42¼	—	41¼	—	—											
Hogan Magnum Plus (Irons)								39¼	38¾	38¼	38	37¾	37½	37¼	36¾	36¼	35¾	35¼

*Bio Mech (L.) woods are also available as 8-39½, 9-39, 10-38½, 11-38, 12-37½.

MEN'S — LATE 1980's

LENGTH — MEN'S

GOLF CLUB MANUFACTURERS STANDARD SPECIFICATIONS — DURING PERIOD OF 1985 TO 1990

Mfg. & Model	#1 Wood	#2 Wood	#3 Wood	#4 Wood	#5 Wood	#6 Wood	#7 Wood	#1 Iron	#2 Iron	#3 Iron	#4 Iron	#5 Iron	#6 Iron	#7 Iron	#8 Iron	#9 Iron	Pitch Wedge	Sand Wedge
Louisville Golf Air Dried Class.50's (P.)	43	42½	42	41½	41	—	40	—	39	38½	38	37½	37	36½	36	35½	35½	35½
Louisville Golf Level Four	43	—	42	41½	41	—	40	—	39	38½	38	37½	37	36½	36	35½	35½	35½
Louisville Golf Personal Model	43	—	42	41½	41	—	40	—	39	38½	38	37½	37	36½	36	35½	35½	35½
Louisville Golf Natural Lite	43	—	42	41½	41	—	40	—	39	38½	38	37½	37	36½	36	35½	35½	35½
Louisville Golf MWH Metalwood	43	—	42	41½	41	—	40											
Lynx Predator G (M.)	43	—	42	—	41	—	40½	39½	39	38½	38	37½	37	36½	36	35½	35¼	35
Lynx Silver Lynx (G.)	43	—	42	—	41	—	—	—	39	38½	38	37½	37	36½	36	35½	35½	35¼
Lynx Radius (M.)								39½	39	38½	38	37½	37	36½	36	35½	35½	35¼
Lynx USA	43	42½	42½	42	41½	41	40½	39½	39	38½	38	37½	37	36½	36	35½	35½	35¼
Lynx Liberty (L.)	43	—	42	41½	41	—	40	—	39	38½	38	37½	37	36½	36	35½	35½	35¼
Lynx Old Parallax (M.)	43	—	42	41½	41	—	40	39½	39	38½	38	37½	37	36½	36	35½	35½	35¼
Lynx Parallax Offset (M.)	43	—	42	—	41	—	40½											
Lynx Classic	43	—	42	—	41													
Lynx Super Predator (M.)	43	42½	42	41½	41	—	40	39½	39	38½	38	37½	37	36½	36	35½	35½	35¼
MacGregor Nicklaus Muirfield (P.)	43½	—	42¾	42¼	41¾	—	—	39¾	39¼	38¾	38¼	37¾	37¼	36¾	36½	36¼	35¾	35¾
MacGregor CG1800 (L.)	43½	—	42¾	42¼	41¾	—	—	39¾	39¼	38¾	38¼	37¾	37¼	36¾	36½	36¼	35¾	35¾
Maruman Sole M210	43½																	
Maruman Sole MSL71	42																	
Maruman Verity	43½	—	42½	—	41½	—	—	—	—	39	38½	38	37½	37	36½	36	35½	35½
Maruman Tap 18	43½	—	42½	42	41½	—	—	—	39½	39	38½	38	37½	37	36½	36	35½	—
Maruman DCA Kevlar	50/47	—	45	44	43	—	—	—	—	39	38½	38	37½	37	36½	36	35½	35
Maruman Dangan 303	43½	—	42½	42	41½	42	40½											
Maruman Conductor (Metal)	43½																	
Maruman Conductor (Carbon)	43	—	42½	—	41½													
Mizuno Altron (G.)	43¼	—	42	—	41¼	—	40¼	—	39¼	38¾	38¼	37¾	37¼	36¾	36¼	36	35¾	35¾
Mizuno Black Turbo II	43¼	—	42	41½	41	—	—	—	39¼	38¾	38¼	37¾	37¼	36¾	36½	36¼	36	—
Mizuno MST	43¼	43*	42¼	41¾	41¼	—	41¼	39¾	39¼	38¾	38¼	37¾	37¼	36¾	36¼	36	35¾	35¾
Miquno MGC-35	43¼	—	42¼	—	41¾	—	—	39¾	39¼	38¾	38¼	37¾	37¼	36¾	36½	36¼	36	36
Mizuno MS-8 Pro Forge	43¼	—	42¾	42¼	42	—	—	40	39½	39	38½	38	37½	37	36¾	36½	36¼	36
Mizuno MS-9 Pro Forge								39¾	39¼	38¾	38¼	37¾	37¼	36¾	36¼	36	35¾	35¾
Mizuno Black Turbo (G.)*	43¼	—	42¼	41¾	41¼	40¾	40¼											
Mizuno Turbo Pro (G.)	43½	—	42½	42	—	—	—											
Mizuno Turbo EL (G.)	43¼	—	42¼	41¾	41¼	—	—											
Mizuno Turbo LX (G.)	43¼	—	42¼	41¾	41¼	—	—											
Mizuno Cimarron (P.)	43½	—	43	42½	42¼	—	—											
Mizuno Cimarron (M.)	43¼	—	42¼	41¾	41½	—	—											
Mizuno MS-4 (M.)	43½	—	43	42½	41¼	—	—	39¾	39	38¾	38¼	37¾	37¼	36¾	36½	36¼	36	35¾
Mizuno MS-5 (P.)	43½	—	43	42½	41¼	—	—	39¾	39	38¾	38¼	37¾	37¼	36¾	36½	36¼	36	35¾
Mizuno MS-3 (M.)	43½	—	43	42½	41¼	—	—	39¾	39¼	38¾	38¼	37¾	37¼	36¾	36½	36¼	36	35¾
Mizuno Champion Flag (Maple)	43¼	—	42¼	41¾	41¼	—	41¼	—	—	38½	38	37½	37	36½	36	35½	35	35
Mizuno Silver Cup (Maple)	43½	—	42¼	—	41¾	—	—	—	—	38¾	38¼	37¾	37¼	36¾	36¼	35¾	35¼	35¼
Mizuno Silver Cups (M.)	43¼	—	42¼	—	41¼	—	—	—	—	39	38½	38	37½	37	36½	36	35¾	35¾

*1½ Wood

GOLF CLUB MANUFACTURERS STANDARD SPECIFICATIONS — DURING PERIOD OF 1985 TO 1990

Mfg. & Model	#1 Wood	#2 Wood	#3 Wood	#4 Wood	#5 Wood	#6 Wood	#7 Wood	#1 Iron	#2 Iron	#3 Iron	#4 Iron	#5 Iron	#6 Iron	#7 Iron	#8 Iron	#9 Iron	Pitch Wedge	Sand Wedge
Mizuno MS-7	43½	—	43	—	42½	—	—											
Mizuno MS-7 Pro Forge								40	39½	39	38½	38	37½	37	36¾	36½	36¼	36
Mizuno Pro Original	43¼	—	42¾	42½	42	—	—											
Mizuno Wings	43¼	—	42¼	—	41¼	—	—	—	39¼	38¾	38¼	37¾	37¼	36¾	36¼	36	35¾	35¾
Mizuno SPL	43	—	42½	—	41¾	—	—	—	39¼	38¾	37¾	37¼	36¾	36½	36½	36¼	36	35½
Mizuno Trump	43¼	—	42¼	—	41¼	—	—	—	39¼	38¾	38¼	37¾	37¼	36¾	36¼	36	35¾	35¾
Mizuno MSX	43¼	—	42¼	41¾	41¼	—	—											
Mizuno Turbo PC	43½/44	—	42½	42	41½	—	—											
Mizuno Altron SE90	43¼	—	42¼	—	41¼	—	—	39¾	39¼	38¾	38¼	37¾	37¼	36¾	36¼	36	35¾	35¾
Northwestern De Vicenzo 241 Tour (P.)	43	—	42	41½	41	—	—											
Northwestern Weiskopf 865 GR (G.)	43	—	42	—	41	—	—											
Northwestern 965 Limited Edition (P.)	43	—	42	—	41	—	—	39½	39	38½	38	37½	37	36½	36	35½	35½	35½
Northwestern Thunderbird (M.)	43	—	42	41½	41	—	—											
Northwestern Thunderbird II								39½	39	38½	38	37½	37	36½	36	35½	35½	35½
Northwestern Dyna-Tour (M.)	43	—	42	—	41	—	—	39½	39	38½	38	37½	37	36½	36	35½	35½	35½
Northwestern Gold Signature (L.)	43	—	42	—	41	—	—	—	—	38½	38	37½	37	36½	36	35½	35½	35½
Northwestern Hubert Green Tour II (M.)	43	—	42	—	41	—	—	—	39	38½	38	37½	37	36½	36	35½	35½	35½
Northwestern Weiskopf 360CS (M.)	43	—	42	—	41	—	—	—	—	38½	38	37½	37	36½	36	35½	35½	35½
Northwestern Pro Classic (M.)	43	—	42	—	41	—	—	39½	39	38½	38	37½	37	36½	36	35½	35½	35½
Northwestern Team Player (G.)	43	—	42	—	41	—	—	—	39	38½	38	37½	37	36½	36	35½	35½	35½
Northwestern Team Player (P.)	43	—	42	—	41	—	—	—	39	38½	38	37½	37	36½	36	35½	35½	35½
Northwestern Weiskopf Dyna-Tour (M.)	43	—	42	—	41	—	—	—	39	38½	38	37½	37	36½	36	35½	35	35
Northwestern Hubert Green RS (M.)	43	—	42	—	41	—	—	—	39	38½	38	37½	37	36½	36	35½	35	35
Northwestern Hubert Green 300 CS (M.)	43	—	42	—	41	—	—	—	—	38½	38	37½	37	36½	36	35½	35	35
Northwestern Weiskopf Pro Classic (M.)	43	—	42	41½	41	—	—	39½	39	38½	38	37½	37	36½	36	35½	35	35
Northwestern Hubert Green Ultimate (M.)	43	—	42	—	41	—	—	—	—	38½	38	37½	37	36½	36	35½	35	35
Northwestern Gary Player GP270 (M.)	43	—	42	—	41	—	—	—	—	38½	38	37½	37	36½	36	35½	35½	35½
Northwestern Tour Select II (L.)	43	—	42	—	41	—	—	—	—	38½	38	37½	37	36½	36	35½	35½	35½
Northwestern Weisk. Promaster Plus (M.)	43	—	42	—	41	—	—	—	—	38½	38	37½	37	36½	36	35½	35½	35½
Toney Penna Model 1 Driver (3-7 Fairways)*	43½	—	42½	42	41½	—	41½											
Toney Penna Jupiter Slugger	43																	
Toney Penna Model 12	43																	
Toney Penna 59	43																	
Toney Penna Model 65	43																	
Toney Penna Model 65 LH	43																	
Toney Penna Natural	43																	
Toney Penna Model 75	43																	
Toney Penna Model 85	43																	
Toney Penna Avenger	43	—	42½	—	41½	—	—	—	39	38½	38	37½	37	36½	36	35½	35	35
Toney Penna TP80	43	42¼	42	—	—	—												
Toney Penna True Site II	43	—	42½	—	41½	—	—	—	39	38½	38	37½	37	36½	36	35½	35	35

*One set of fairway woods was available to match most of the Toney Penna Drivers.

LENGTH — MEN'S

MEN'S — LATE 1980's

LENGTH — MEN'S

GOLF CLUB MANUFACTURERS STANDARD SPECIFICATIONS — DURING PERIOD OF 1985 TO 1990

Mfg. & Model	#1 Wood	#2 Wood	#3 Wood	#4 Wood	#5 Wood	#6 Wood	#7 Wood	#1 Iron	#2 Iron	#3 Iron	#4 Iron	#5 Iron	#6 Iron	#7 Iron	#8 Iron	#9 Iron	Pitch Wedge	Sand Wedge
Toney Penna* Beryllium Copper 8°	43½																	
Toney Penna Beryllium Copper 10°	43																	
Toney Penna Cobalt 8°	43½	—	42½	—	41½													
Toney Penna Cobalt 10°	43																	
Toney Penna Metalwood (Grey)	43																	
Toney Penna Metalwood (Black)	43																	
Toney Penna Original (Forged)								—	39	38½	38	37½	37	36½	36	35½	35	35
Toney Penna Stainless Cast								—	39	38½	38	37½	37	36½	36	35½	35	35
Toney Penna Tru Site Cast								—	39	38½	38	37½	37	36½	36	35½	35	35
Toney Penna Super Blade Cast								—	39	38½	38	37½	37	36½	36	35½	35	35
Toney Penna USA Forged								—	39	38½	38	37½	37	36½	36	35½	35	35
Pinseeker Bombshell								39½	39	38½	38	37½	37	36½	36	35½	35½	35¼
Pinseeker Bombshell II	43	1½=43	42	4½=41½	—	—	Bullet 41	39½	39	38½	38	37½	37	36½	36	35½	35½	35¼
Pinseeker Tri-Mar.	43	42½	42	—	41¼	—	—	—										
Pinseeker Rebound II	43	—	42	41½	41¼	—	—	—	39	38½	38	37½	37	36½	36	35½	35½	35¼
Pinseeker Classic Persimmon	43	—	42	41½	41¼	—	—											
Pinseeker INS Woods & Irons	43	—	42	41¼	—	—	—											
Pinseeker TPW Irons								39½	39	38½	38	37½	37	36½	36	35½	35½	35¼
Pinseeker 350 Series	43	—	42	41½	41¼	—	41											
Pinseeker 350 ORS								39½	39	38½	38	37½	37	36½	36	35½	35½	35¼
Pro Group Peerless (P.)	43	—	42	41¾	41½	—	41¼	39½	39	38½	38	37½	37	36½	36	35½	35½	35½
Pro Group Axiom (P.)	43	—	42	41¾	41¼	—	41	39½	39	38½	38	37½	37	36½	36	35½	35½	35½
Ram Tour Series Steelwoods	43¼	—	42¼	41¾	41¼	41	41											
Ram Tour Grind	43¼	—	42¼	41¾	41¼	—	—	39¾	39¼	38¾	38¼	37¾	37¼	36¾	36¼	35¾	35½	35¼
Ram Tour Grind Axial	43	—	42	41½	41	—	—	39½	39	38½	38	37½	37	36½	36	35½	35¼	35
Ram Laser X-2	43¼	—	42¼	—	41	—	40	39¾	39¼	38¾	38¼	37¾	37¼	36¾	36¼	35¼	35½	35¼
Ram Custom 800 Series	43	—	42	—	41	—	40¾											
Ram Laser X-2 (G.)	43¼	—	42¼	41¾	41¼	—	41	—	39¼	38¾	38¼	37¾	37¼	36¾	36¼	35¾	35½	35¼
Ram Accubar	43	—	42	—	41	—	40¾	—	39	38½	38	37½	37	36½	36	35½	35¼	35
Ram Laser FX Forged	43½	—	42½	42	41½	—	—	40	39½	39	38½	38	37½	37	36½	36	35¾	35½
Ram Laser FX Bore Thru	43½	—	42½	42	41½	—	—	40	39½	39	38½	38	37½	37	36½	36	35¾	35½
Rawlings Toney Penna Model 89 Driver	43½																	
Rawlings Toney Penna Model TPIX Driver	43½																	
Rawlings Toney Penna Special Edition II Driver	43½																	
Rawlings Toney Penna 79 Driver	43½																	
Rawlings Toney Penna Special Edition II	43½	—	42½	42	41½	—	—											
Rawlings Toney Penna Steelwoods	43½	—	42½	42	41½	—	—											
Slazenger Crown Sterling	43½	—	42½	42	41½	—	41	39¾	39¼	38¾	38¼	37¾	37¼	36¾	36¼	35¾	35¾	35½
Slazenger Royal Panther	43½	—	42½	—	42	—	41½	39½	39	38½	38	37½	37	36½	36	35½	35½	35½
Slazenger Crown Limited	43½	—	42½	42	41½	—	—	39½	39	38½	38	37½	37	36½	36	35½	35½	35½
Slazenger Royal Panther BC								39½	39	38½	38	37½	37	36½	36	35½	35½	35½

*One set of fairway woods was available to match most of the Toney Penna Drivers.

MEN'S — LATE 1980's

LENGTH — MEN'S

GOLF CLUB MANUFACTURERS STANDARD SPECIFICATIONS — DURING PERIOD OF 1985 TO 1990

Mfg. & Model	#1 Wood	#2 Wood	#3 Wood	#4 Wood	#5 Wood	#6 Wood	#7 Wood	#1 Iron	#2 Iron	#3 Iron	#4 Iron	#5 Iron	#6 Iron	#7 Iron	#8 Iron	#9 Iron	Pitch Wedge	Sand Wedge
Sounder Triad Graphite	43	—	42	—	41	—	40½	39½	39	38½	38	37½	37	36½	36	35½	35	35
Sounder Triad	43	—	42	—	41	—	40½	39½	39	38½	38	37½	37	36½	36	35½	35	35
Sounder Tour Limited	43	—	42	41½	41	—	—	39½	39	38½	38	37½	37	36½	36	35½	35	35
Sounder Star	43	42½	42	—	41	—	40½	39½	39	38½	38	37½	37	36½	36	35½	35	35
Sounder Silver Star	43	42½	42	—	41	—	40½	39½	39	38½	38	37½	37	36½	36	35½	35	35
Sounder Triad Laminated	43	—	42	—	41	—	40½	39½	39	38½	38	37½	37	36½	36	35½	35	35
Sounder Excalibar	43	—	42	—	41	—	—	39½	39	38½	38	37½	37	36½	36	35½	35	35
Sounder Tour Star	43	—	42	41½	41	—	40	39½	39	38½	38	37½	37	36½	36	35½	35	35
Spalding Tour Edition (M.)	43							39½	39	38½	38	37½	37	36½	36	35½	35	35
Spalding Tour Edition (L.)	43¼	42¾	42¼	41¾	—	—	—	39½	39	38½	38	37½	37	36½	36	35½	35	35
Spalding Tour Edition Custom Crafted (P.)	43¼	42¾	42¼	41¾	—	—	—	39½	39	38½	38	37½	37	36½	36	35½	35	35
Spalding Tour Edition Executive (M.) XE	43	—	42	41½	41	—	40	41½	40½	39½							35	
Spalding Tour Edition Executive (L.)	43	—	42	41 11/16	—	—	40¾	—	38⅝	38⅛	37⅝	37⅛	36⅝	36⅛	35⅝	35⅛	35⅛	35⅛
Spalding Cannon (M.)	43	—	42	41½	41	—	40	—	39	38½	38	37½	37	36½	36	35½	35½	35½
Spalding Top Flite XL4	43¼	—	—	41¾	—	—	—	39½	39	38½	38	37½	37	36½	36	35½	35	35
Spalding Tour Edition (P.)	43¼	42¾	42¼	41¾	41¼	—	—	39½	39	38½	38	37½	37	36½	36	35½	35	35
Spalding Executive (M.)	43						40¾	39 1/16		38 3/16								34 11/16
Spalding Top Flite XL Beryllium Copper	43	—	42¼	—	41½	—	—											
Square Two Sabre II	43	42½	42	41½	41	—	40	39½	39	38½	38	37½	37	36½	36	35½	35½	35½
Square Two PCX	43	—	42	41½	41	—	40	39½	39	38½	38	37½	37	36½	36	35½	35½	35½
Square Two Forged								39½	39	38½	38	37½	37	36½	36	35½	35½	35½
Square Two Persimmon	43	42½	42	41½	41													
Taylor Made Tour Preferred								39½	39	38½	38	37½	37	36½	36	35½	35½	35½
Taylor Made Tour Preferred (M.)	43	42½	42	41½	41													
Taylor Made Pittsburgh Persimmon	43	—	42	41½	41	—	41											
Taylor Made Tour Cleek	—	—	41½	41½	41	41	—											
Taylor Made Iron Cleek								39½	39	38½	38	37½	37	36½	36	35½	35½	—
Titleist Tour Model	43	—	42½	42	41	—	—	39½	39	38½	38	37½	37	36⅝	36¼	35⅞	35½	35½
Titleist Metalwood	43	—	42½	—	41¾	—	—											
Titleist DTR								—	39⅛	38⅝	38⅛	37⅝	37⅛	36⅝	36⅛	35¾	35½	35¼
Titleist Graphite	43	—	42½	42	41¼	—	—											
Titleist Pinnacle (L.)	42½	—	42	—	41¼	—	—	39¼	38¾	38¼	37¾	37¼	36¾	36¼	36	35⅝	35¼	35
Titleist Box Blade								—	39	38½	38	37½	37	36⅝	36¼	35⅞	35½	35¼
Tommy Armour Silver Scot 986 Tour	43¼	—	42¼	41¾	41½	—	—	39½	39	38½	38	37½	37	36½	36	35½	35¼	35
Tommy Armour Golden Scot	43	—	42	—	41	—	—	39½	39	38½	38	37½	37	36½	36	35½	35½	35½
Tommy Armour Silver Scot 845's								39½	39	38½	38	37½	37	36½	36	35½	35½	35½
Tommy Armour T-Line B/C	43¼	—	42¼	41¾	41¼	—	40¾	39½	39	38½	38	37½	37	36½	36	35½	35½	35½
Tommy Armour T-Line	43¼	—	42¼	41¾	41¼	—	40¾	39½	39	38½	38	37½	37	36½	36	35½	35	35
Tommy Armour Concept 2 (1987-89)	43¼	—	42¼	41¾	41¼	—	40¾	—	39	38½	38	37½	37	36½	36	35½	35¼	35½
Tommy Armour Emblem	43¼	—	42¼	41¾	41¼	—	40¾	—	38½	38	37½	37	36½	36	35½	35	35	35
Tommy Armour Cameron	43¼	—	42¼	41¾	41¼	—	—	39½	39	38½	38	37½	37	36½	36	35½	35	35
Tommy Armour Silver Scot 835's	43	—	42	41½	41	—	40½											

MEN'S — LATE 1980's

LENGTH — MEN'S

GOLF CLUB MANUFACTURERS STANDARD SPECIFICATIONS — DURING PERIOD OF 1985 TO 1990

Mfg. & Model	#1 Wood	#2 Wood	#3 Wood	#4 Wood	#5 Wood	#6 Wood	#7 Wood	#1 Iron	#2 Iron	#3 Iron	#4 Iron	#5 Iron	#6 Iron	#7 Iron	#8 Iron	#9 Iron	Pitch Wedge	Sand Wedge
Tommy Armour EQL	41	—	41	—	41	—	41	37	37	37	37	37	37	37	37	37	37	37
Tommy Armour Concept 2 (1990)	43¼	—	42¼	—	41¼	—	—	—	39	38½	38	37½	37	36½	36	35½	35	35
Wilson 1200 Gear Effect (M.)	43	—	42	41½	41¼	—	41	—	39	38½	38	37½	37	36½	36	35½	35	35
Wilson Staff Metal	43	42½	42	41½	41¼	—	—	—	39½	39	38½	38	37½	37	36½	35½	35	35
Wilson Ultra	43	—	42	41½	41¼	—	—											
Wilson Staff	43	—	42	41½	41¼	—	—	39½	39	38½	38	37½	37	36½	36	35½	35	35
Wilson 1200 Gear Effect (L.)	43	—	42	41½	41¼	—	—	39½	39	38½	38	37½	37	36½	36	35½	35	35
Wilson Staff Gooseneck (M.)								39½	39	38½	38	37½	37	36½	36	35½	35	35
Wilson X31	43	—	42	41½	41¼	—	—	—	39	38½	38	37½	37	36½	36	35½	35	35
Wilson 1200 LT	43¼	—	42	41½	41¼	41	41	—	39	38½	38	37½	37	36½	36	35½	35	35
Wilson Turfrider								—	39	38½	38	37½	37	36½	36	35½	35	35
Yamaha C-200	43½	—	42½	42	41½	—	—											
Yamaha C-300	43½	—	42½	42	41½	—	—											
Yamaha C-500 Driver	43½																	
Yamaha FD 20 Irons								—	—	38½	38	37½	37	36½	36	35½	35	35
Yamaha EX-Gold (1988)	43½	—	42½	—	41½	—	—											
Yamaha SX-Pro Driver	43½																	
Yamaha Hal Sutton Persimmon	43½																	
Yamaha The Secret III								—	—	38½	38	37½	37	36½	36	35½	35½	35
Yamaha EAM10								—	—	38½	38	37½	37	36½	36	35½	35½	35
Yamaha FOS (1990)	44	—	43	—	42	—	—	—	—	38½	38	37½	37	36½	36	35½	35½	35
Yamaha Secret	43½	—	42½	42	41½	—	—											
Yamaha Pro Driver	43½																	
Yamaha Super Driver	45																	
Yamaha DR Driver	43½																	
Yamaha EX Gold (1990)								—	—	38½	38	37½	37	36½	36	35½	35½	35
Yamaha Metrix Metal	43½	—	42½	—	41½	—	—											
Yamaha FOS (1989)	43½	—	42½	—	41½	—	—											
Yamaha Accurace								—	—	38½	38	37½	37	36½	36	35½	35½	35
Yamaha SX-25								—	—	38½	38	37½	37	36½	36	35½	35½	35
Yamaha X200	43½	—	42½	42	41½	—	41											
Yamaha X300	43½	—	42½	42	41½	—	41											
Yamaha The Secret	43½	—	42½	42	41½	—	—	—	—	38½	38	37½	37	36½	36	35½	35½	35
Yamaha W602	43½	—	42½	—	41½	—	—											
Yamaha SX25	43½	—	42½	42	41½	—	—	—	—	38½								
Yonex Boronwood (G.)	43¼	—	42¼	41¾	41¼	—	—	—	—	38½	38	37½	37	36½	36	35½	35	35
Yonex Carbonex II (G.)	43¼	—	42¼	41¾	41¼	—	—	—	—	38½	38	37½	37	36½	36	35½	35	35
Yonex Carbonex 22 (G.)	43¼	—	42¼	41¾	41¼	—	—											
Yonex Tournament SP								—	39	38½	38	37½	37	36½	36	35½	35	35
Yonex Graphlex	43¼	—	42¼	41¾	41¼	—	—	—	—	38½	38	37½	37	36½	36	35½	35	35
Yonex ADX100	45	—	43	42½	42	—	—											
Yonex ADX200	45	—	43	42½	42	—	—	—	39½	39	38½	38	37½	37	36½	36	35½	

MEN'S — LATE 1980's

LOFT — MEN'S

GOLF CLUB MANUFACTURERS STANDARD SPECIFICATIONS — DURING PERIOD OF 1985 TO 1990

Mfg. & Model	#1 Wood	#2 Wood	#3 Wood	#4 Wood	#5 Wood	#6 Wood	#7 Wood	#1 Iron	#2 Iron	#3 Iron	#4 Iron	#5 Iron	#6 Iron	#7 Iron	#8 Iron	#9 Iron	Pitch Wedge	Sand Wedge
Accuform (all)	9/11	13	16	19	22	—	28	17	20	23	27	31½	34½	38½	42½	46½	51½	56
Browning 440 Gold	8/10	—	15	—	21	—	26	17	20	23	26	29	32	36	40	44	49	54
Browning Pinache	♥	—	15	—	21	—	—	16	18	21	24	28	32	36	40	44	50	55
Browning Automatic	10	—	16	19	22	—	25	—	21	24	27	30	34	38	42	46	50	56
Browning Tour Class	11	—	16	19	22	—	—	—	—	23	26	29	33	37	41	45	49	55
Browning Maxim	10	13	16	19	21	—	25	—	21	24	27	30	34	38	42	46	50	56
Browning 440	10	—	16	19	22	—	25	—	21	24	27	30	34	38	42	46	50	56
Browning System 350	11	—	16	19	22	—	—	17	20	23	26	29	32	36	40	44	49	56
Browning 440 Plus	11	13	16	19	22	—	27	—	21	24	27	30	34	38	42	46	50	56
Browning Premier	♣	—	15	—	21	—	—	18	21	24	27	30	34	38	42	46	50	56
Browning Mirage (L.)	9/11	—	16	—	22	—	26	—	18	21	24	27	30	34	38	42	46	56
Callaway Bobby Jones Comm.	11	17	—	—	20	24	—	17	20	23	26	29	33	37	41	46	51	56
Callaway Bobby Jones	♠	—	14½	17¾	21¾	—	24¾	17	20	23	26	29	33	37	41	46	51	56
Callaway Classic	10½	—	16	19	21	—	—											
Callaway S2H2	♦	—	15	18	21	—	24	17	20	23	26	29	33	37	41	46	51	56
Cleveland Classics Tour Action 588	10	13	15	18	21	—	—	17	20	23	26	29	33	37	41	45	49	56
Cleveland Classics TC 15	10	13	15	18	21	—	—											
Cleveland Classics RC85	10	—	15	18	21	—	—											
Cleveland Classics TA289	9/11	—	13/15	17	19	21	23											
Cleveland Classics Tour Action 588 (P.)	9/11	—	15½	17½	20	—	25	17	19	22	25	28	32	36	40	44	49	—
Cleveland Classics 10th Anni. Woods	10	—	15	18	21	—	—											
Cobra Baffler Steel Classics	★	—	16	—	19	—	23											
Cobra Traditional Baffler Blade								15	18	21	24	28	32	36	40	44	48	—
Cobra Baffler*	13	15	17	20	23	25	27											
Cobra Long Tom	9																	
Daiwa Lite Touch (G.)	12	—	16	19	21	—	25	—	18	21	24	28	32	36	41	46	51	57
Daiwa SRX3 (P.)	12	—	16	19	21	—	—	—	18	21	24	28	32	36	41	46	51	57
Daiwa Hi-Trac (L.)	12	—	16	19	21	—	—	—	18	21	24	28	32	36	41	46	51	57
Daiwa Chairman (P.)	12	—	16	19	21	—	—	—	18	21	24	28	32	36	41	46	51	57
Daiwa Ballistic II (M.)	9/11½	—	15½	17½	20	—	25											
Daiwa Monodyne								17	19	22	25	29	33	37	41	45	50	55
Daiwa Advisor								17	19	22	25	29	33	37	41	45	50	55
Daiwa DB-561	11	—	16	19	21	—	—											
Daiwa DB-591	11	—	16	19	21	—	—											
Daiwa Exceler	11½	—	16½	19	21	—	25											
Daiwa Exceler BPT	11½	—	16½	19	21	—	25											
Daiwa DB-611 (P.)	11	—	16	19	21	—	—											
Daiwa DB-612 (P.)	11	—	16	19	21	—	—											
Dunlop Maxfli DP 30								15	18	21	24	28	32	36	40	44	50	55
Dunlop Seve Ballesteros (P.)	10½	—	17	19	—	—	—	15	18	21	24	28	32	36	40	44	50	55
Dunlop Maxfli 901 (P.)	10½	—	17	19	22	—	—											

♥-8/10,12 ♣-8.5/10.5 ♦-8,9½,10½,12 ★-9½,10½,12 ♠-10¼,12¼

*Woods also available as #8-29, #9-31, #11-33, #13-35 and TS-20

LOFT — MEN'S

GOLF CLUB MANUFACTURERS STANDARD SPECIFICATIONS — DURING PERIOD OF 1985 TO 1990

Mfg. & Model	#1 Wood	#2 Wood	#3 Wood	#4 Wood	#5 Wood	#6 Wood	#7 Wood	#1 Iron	#2 Iron	#3 Iron	#4 Iron	#5 Iron	#6 Iron	#7 Iron	#8 Iron	#9 Iron	Pitch Wedge	Sand Wedge
Dunlop Maxfli 357 (M.)	11	—	15	—	20	—	23	14	17	20	24	28	32	36	40	44	49	55
Dunlop Black Missile	12	—	17	—	23	—	—	—	—	19	23	27	31	35	39	43	47	51
Dunlop Maxfli Pro. Spec. (P.)	9½	—	15	18	21	—	—	15	18	21	25	29	33	37	41	45	50	56
Dunlop Maxfli Tour Limited (M.)	♥	—	15	17	20	—	23	15	18	21	24	28	32	36	40	44	50	55
Dunlop Maxfli Missile (G.)	12	—	17	—	23	—	—	—	—	19	23	27	31	35	39	43	47	51
Dunlop Power Max (M.)	12	—	17	—	22	—	—	—	—	23	27	31	35	39	43	47	51	56
GolfWorks® Kinetic	11	—	16	—	21	—	27	16	18	21	24	28	32	36	40	44	48	55
GolfWorks® Technique	11	—	16	19	22	—	—	17	20	23	26	29	33	37	41	45	50	55
GolfWorks® Bio Mech (M.)	11	—	16	—	22	—	28	17	19	22	25	29	33	37	41	45	49	55
GolfWorks® XDC	10	—	16	—	22	—	28	—	—	23	25	28	32	36	40	44	48	55
GolfWorks® Commander	9½	—	15	18	21	—	—	15	17	20	23	27	31	35	39	43	48	55
GolfWorks® Tandem	♣	—	16	19	22	—	28	16	18	21	24	29	32	36	40	44	48	55
GolfWorks® RMH								17	20	23	26	30	34	38	42	46	50	56
GolfWorks® Hero Plus	♣	—	16	19	22	—	28	16	18	21	24	28	32	36	40	44	48	54
GolfWorks® Bio Mech* (L.)	11	13	16	19	21	24	27											
GolfWorks® Accu-Weight	10	—	16	—	22	—	28	—	—	22	25	28	32	36	40	44	48	55
H & B/Power Bilt Citation (P.)	11	14	17	20	22	24	26											
H & B/Power Bilt Citation (L.)	11	14	17	20	22	24	26											
H & B/Power Bilt TPS								18	19	22	26	29	32	35	39	43	48	54
H & B/Power Bilt TPS (M.)	7½	12	16	19	22	—	24											
H & B/Power Bilt Grand Slam (L.)	11	—	17	20	22	—	26											
H & B/Power Bilt Grand Slam (M.)	11	—	16	—	22	—	26											
H & B/Power Bilt Citation Plus	11	14	17	20	22	24	26											
H & B/Power Bilt Scotch Blade								18	20	24	28	32	35	38	41	44	50	56
H & B/Power Bilt Citation Forged								18	20	24	28	32	35	38	41	44	50	56
H & B/Power Bilt Citation Cast								18	20	24	28	32	35	38	41	44	50	56
H & B/Power Bilt Propower								18	20	24	28	32	35	38	41	44	50	56
Walter Hagen Haig Ultra	11	—	16	19	21			18	20	23	26	30	34	38	42	46	50	55
Hogan Apex	11/10	—	15½	18½	21½			17½	19½	23	26½	30	33½	37	41	45	49	56
Hogan Radial	10½	—	15	17½	21			—	19½	23	26½	30	33½	37	41	45	49	—
Hogan Magnum								16½	18½	22	25½	29	32½	36	40	44	48	55
Hogan Series 56	†						24½											
Hogan Series 56 (G.)	12/10	13	15½	18½	21½													
Hogan Saber	13½																	
Hogan Companion	13	15	17	19	21½		25½											
Hogan Apex PC								19½	23	26½	30	33½	37	41	45	49		
Hogan Edge (Irons)								15½	17½	21	24½	28	31½	35	39	43	47	55
Hogan 56 (Carbon Woods)	12/10	—	15½	18½	21½													
Hogan Magnum Plus (Woods)	12	—	16	—	22													
Hogan Magnum Plus (Irons)								16½	18½	22	25½	29	32½	36	40	44	48	55

♥ -8.5/9.5/10.5/12   ♣ -8/10/12   *Woods also available in 8-30, 9-33, 10-36, 11-39, 12-42   †Hogan Series 56 is available in 12, 10, 9½, 7½ degree lofts

LOFT — MEN'S

GOLF CLUB MANUFACTURERS STANDARD SPECIFICATIONS — DURING PERIOD OF 1985 TO 1990

Mfg. & Model	#1 Wood	#2 Wood	#3 Wood	#4 Wood	#5 Wood	#6 Wood	#7 Wood	#1 Iron	#2 Iron	#3 Iron	#4 Iron	#5 Iron	#6 Iron	#7 Iron	#8 Iron	#9 Iron	Pitch Wedge	Sand Wedge
Louisville Golf Air Dried Class. 50's (P.)	11	13½	16	18½	21½	–	26½	–	20	23	26	30	34	38	42	46	50	55
Louisville Golf Level Four	11	–	16	18½	21½	–	26½	–	20	23	26	30	34	38	42	46	50	55
Louisville Golf Personal Model	11	–	16	18½	21½	–	26½	–	20	23	26	30	34	38	42	46	50	55
Louisville Golf Natural Lite	11	–	16	18½	21½	–	26½	–	20	23	26	30	34	38	42	46	50	55
Louisville Golf MWH Metalwood	11	–	16	18½	21½	–	26½											
Lynx Predador G (M.)	10	–	15	–	20	–	25	14	17	20	23	27	31	35	39	43	47	55
Lynx Silver Lynx (G.)	11	–	16	–	22	–	–	–	19	22	25	29	33	37	41	45	49	57
Lynx Radius (M.)								17	19	22	25	29	33	37	41	45	49	56
Lynx USA								17	19	22	25	29	33	37	41	45	49	57
Lynx Liberty (L.)	11	–	16	19	22	–	26	–	19	22	25	29	33	37	41	45	49	57
Lynx Paralax (M.)	7/11	–	17	20	23	–	26	14	17	20	23	26	29	33	37	41	46	55
Lynx Parallax Offset (M.)	9	–	15	–	21	–	25											
Lynx Classic	11	–	16	–	19	–	–											
Lynx Super Predator (M.)	9/10	12	15	18	21	–	25	17	19	22	25	29	33	37	41	45	49	57
MacGregor Nicklaus Muirfield (P.)	10	–	14	17	21	–	–	18	20	23	26	29	33	37	41	45	50	56
MacGregor CG1800 (L.)	13	–	16	19	21½	–	–	16	18	21	24	27½	32	37	41	45	50½	57
Maruman Sole M210	11	–	16	18½	21	–	–											
Maruman Sole MSL71	14	–	18½	–	23½	–	–											
Maruman Verity	10½	–	17	–	23	–	–											
Maruman Tap 18	11/12	–	16	–	18½	–	21	–	19	22	25	28	31	34	38	43	48	56
Maruman DCA Kevlar	10½	–	16	19	22	–	–	–	–	22	25	28	31	34	38	43	48	56
Maruman Dangan 303	10/12	–	17	20	23	25	27											
Maruman Conductor (Metal)	9/10½	–	16	19	22	–	–											
Maruman Conductor (Carbon)	10½																	
Mizuno Altron (G.)	11	–	15	–	21	–	–	–	18	21	24	27	30	34	38	42	47	54
Mizuno Black Turbo II	11	–	16	19	22	–	–	–	20	22	25	28	32	36	40	44	48	–
Mizuno MST	♦	13	15	18	21	–	27	15	18	21	24	27	31	35	39	43	48	55
Mizuno MCG-35	10	–	16	–	21	–	–	16	18	20	22	25	28	32	36	40	44	55
Mizuno MS-8 Pro Forge	10	–	15	18	21	–	–	15	18	21	24	27	30	34	38	42	47	54
Mizuno MS-9 Pro Forge								16	18	21	24	27½	31	35	39	43	47	54
Mizuno Black Turbo (G.)	12	–	17	20	23	26	30	34										
Mizuno Turbo Pro (G.)	7/9	–	16	19	–	–	–											
Mizuno Turbo EL (G.)	11½	–	16	19	22	–	–											
Mizuno Turbo LX (G.)	11	–	16	19	21	–	–											
Mizuno Cimarron (P.)	11½	–	17	20	23	–	–											
Mizuno Cimarron (M.)	12	–	16	19	22	–	–	–	20	23	26	30	34	38	42	47	52	56
Mizuno MS-4 (M.)	11	–	16	19	22	–	–	–	18	21	24	27	31	35	39	43	48	56
Mizuno MS-5 (P.)	10½	–	16	19	22	–	–	–	18	21	25	29	33	37	41	45	50	56
Mizuno MS-3 (M.)	10	–	15	18	21	–	–	–	18	21	24	27	31	35	39	43	48	56
Mizuno Champion Flag (Maple)	11	–	16	19	22	–	25	–	–	23	26	29	33	37	41	45	50	56
Mizuno Silver Cup (Maple)	12	–	17	–	21	–	–	–	–	23	26	29	33	37	41	45	50	56
Mizuno Silver Cup (M.)	12	–	17	–	22	–	–	–	–	23	26	29	33	37	41	45	50	56

♦ -7/9/11

MEN'S — LATE 1980's

LOFT — MEN'S

GOLF CLUB MANUFACTURERS STANDARD SPECIFICATIONS — DURING PERIOD OF 1985 TO 1990

Mfg. & Model	#1 Wood	#2 Wood	#3 Wood	#4 Wood	#5 Wood	#6 Wood	#7 Wood	#1 Iron	#2 Iron	#3 Iron	#4 Iron	#5 Iron	#6 Iron	#7 Iron	#8 Iron	#9 Iron	Pitch Wedge	Sand Wedge
Mizuno MS-7	11	—	15	—	21	—	—	16	18	21	25	29	33	37	41	45	50	56
Mizuno MS-7 Pro Forge																		
Mizuno Pro Original	10	—	15	18	21	—	—	—										
Mizuno Wings	12	—	15	18	20	—	—	—	18	21	24	27	30	34	38	42	47	54
Mizuno SPL	11	—	16	—	22	—	—	—	21	24	27	30	33	36	39	42	46	56
Mizuno Trump	11	—	16	—	22	—	—	—	18	21	24	27	30	34	38	42	47	54
Mizuno MSX	9/11	—	15	18	21	—	—											
Mizuno Turbo PC	11	—	16	19	22	—	—											
Mizuno Altron SE 90	11	—	15	—	21	—	—	15	18	21	24	27	30	34	38	42	47	54
Northwestern E Vicenzo 241 Tour (P.)	11	—	6	19	21	—	—											
Northwestern Weiskopf 865 GR (G.)	11	—	16	—	21	—	—											
Northwestern 965 Limited Edition (P.)	11	—	16	—	21	—	—	17	20	23	27	31	35	39	43	47	51	56
Northwestern Thunderbird (M.)	11	—	16	19	21	—	—	17	20	23	27	31	35	39	43	47	51	56
Northwestern Thunderbird II								17	20	23	27	31	35	39	43	47	51	56
Northwestern Dyna-Tour (M.)	11	—	16	—	21	—	—	—	20	23	27	31	35	39	43	47	51	56
Northwestern Gold Signature (L.)	11	—	16	—	21	—	—	—	—	23	27	31	35	39	43	47	51	56
Northwestern Hubert Green Tour II (M.)	11	—	16	—	21	—	—	—	20	23	27	31	35	39	43	47	51	56
Northwestern Weiskopf 360CS (M.)	11	—	16	—	21	—	—	—	—	23	27	31	35	39	43	47	51	56
Northwestern Pro Classic (M.)	11	—	16	19	21	—	—	17	20	23	27	31	35	39	43	47	51	56
Northwestern Team Player (G.)	11	—	16	—	21	—	—	—	20	23	27	31	35	39	43	47	51	56
Northwestern Team Player (P.)	11	—	16	—	21	—	—	—	20	23	27	31	35	39	43	47	51	56
Northwestern Weiskopf Dyna-Tour (M.)	11	—	16	—	21	—	—	—	20	23	27	31	35	39	43	47	51	56
Northwestern Hubert Green RS (M.)	11	—	16	—	21	—	—	—	20	23	27	31	35	39	43	47	51	56
Northwestern Hubert Green 300 CS (M.)	11	—	16	—	21	—	—	—	—	23	27	31	35	39	43	47	51	56
Northwestern Weiskopf Pro Classic (M.)	11	—	16	19	21	—	—	17	20	23	27	31	35	39	43	47	51	56
Northwestern Hubert Green Ultimate (M.)	11	—	16	—	21	—	—	—	—	23	27	31	35	39	43	47	51	56
Northwestern Gary Player GP270 (M.)	11	—	16	—	21	—	—	—	—	23	27	31	35	39	43	47	51	56
Northwestern Tour Select II (L.)	11	—	16	—	21	—	—	—	—	23	27	31	35	39	43	47	51	56
Northwestern Weiskopf Promaster Plus (M.)	11	—	16	—	21	—	—	—	—	23	27	31	35	39	43	47	51	56
Toney Penna Avenger (1986)	—	—	15	—	21	—	—											
Toney Penna Model 1 Driver (3-7 Fairways)*	9½	—	15	18	21	—	24											
Toney Penna Jupiter Slugger	11																	
Toney Penna Model 12	12																	
Toney Penna Model 59	9½																	
Toney Penna Model 65	11																	
Toney Penna Model 65 LH	11																	
Toney Penna Natural	11																	
Toney Penna Model 75 Woods	11	—	15	18	21	—	—											
Toney Penna Model 85	11																	
Toney Penna Avenger (1989-90)	10½	—	17	—	22	—	—											
Toney Penna TP80	—	—	15	18	21	—	—											
Toney Penna True Site	10½	—	17	18	22	—	—											

*One set of fairway woods was available to match most of the Toney Penna Drivers.

LOFT — MEN'S

GOLF CLUB MANUFACTURERS STANDARD SPECIFICATIONS — DURING PERIOD OF 1985 TO 1990

Mfg. & Model	#1 Wood	#2 Wood	#3 Wood	#4 Wood	#5 Wood	#6 Wood	#7 Wood	#1 Iron	#2 Iron	#3 Iron	#4 Iron	#5 Iron	#6 Iron	#7 Iron	#8 Iron	#9 Iron	Pitch Wedge	Sand Wedge
Toney Penna* Beryllium Copper 8°	8	–	15	18	21	–	–											
Toney Penna Beryllium Copper 10°	10	–	15	18	21	–	–											
Toney Penna Cobalt 8°	8	–	15	–	21	–	–											
Toney Penna Cobalt 10°	10	–	15	–	21–	–	–											
Toney Penna Metalwood (Grey)	8	–	15	18	21	–	–											
Toney Penna Metalwood (Black)	10	–	15	18	21	–	–											
Toney Penna Original (Forged)								17	20	23	26	30	34	38	42	46	50	55
Toney Penna Stainless Cast								–	20	23	27	31	35	43	47	51	56	
Toney Penna Tru Site Cast								–	20	23	27	31	35	39	43	46	51	57
Toney Penna Super Blade Cast								–	20	23	27	31	35	39	43	46	51	57
Toney Penna USA Forged								–	18	21	24	28	32	36	40	44	48	53
Pinseeker Bombshell II	9	11	15	20	–	–	25											
Pinseeker Tri-Mar.	10	12	16	–	21	–	25											
Pinseeker Rebound II	12	16	19	–	22	–	–											
Pinseeker 350 Series	11	–	16	19	22	–	28											
Pro Group Peerless (P.)	10½	–	16	19	21	–	25	17	20	23	27	31	35	38	42	46	51	56
Pro Group Axiom (P.)	12½	–	16	19	21	–	25	19	22	24	27	29	32	36	40	44	48	54
¹Ram Tour Series Steelwoods	9,10½	–	16	19	22	24	27											
Ram Tour Grind	10	–	16	19	21	–	–	15	18	21	24	27	31	35	39	43	47	54
Ram Tour Grind Axial	11	–	16	19	21	–	–	15	18	21¼	24½	27½	31	35½	40	44	48	55
Ram Laser X-2	11	–	17	–	–	22	27	15	18	21	24	27	31	35	39	43	47	54
Ram Custom 800 Series	9,11	–	16	19	21	–	–											
Ram Laser X-2 (G.)	11	–	17	19½	22	–	27	–	18	21	24	27	31	35	39	43	47	54
Ram Accubar	11	–	16	–	22	–	27	19	19	22¼	25½	28½	32	36½	41	45	49	55
Ram Laser FX Forged	9,10½	–	13	16	19	–	–	16½	19½	22	25	28	32	35½	39½	43	47	54
Ram Laser FX Bore Thru	9,10½	–	13	16	19	–	–	16½	19½	22	25	28	32	35½	39½	43	47	54
Rawlings Toney Penna Model 89 Driver	9½																	
Rawlings Toney Penna Model TPIX Driver	10																	
Rawlings Toney Penna Special Edition II Driver	10																	
Rawlings Toney Penna 79 Driver	11																	
Rawlings Toney Penna Special Edition II	–	–	13	–	21	–	–											
Rawlings Toney Penna Steelwoods	–	–	13	–	21	–	–											
Slazenger Crown Sterling	8-12	–	13,15	18	21	–	24	17	20	23	26	30	34	38	42	46	49	♦
Slazenger Royal Panther	10	–	17	–	22	–	26	18	21	24	27	30	33	37	41	45	49	55
Slazenger Crown Limited	9-11	–	16	19	21	–	–	17	20	23	26	30	34	38	42	46	49	55,58
Slazenger Royal Panther BC								18	21	24	27	29	32	36	40	44	48	54
Sounder Tour Star	10	–	16	18½	21½	–	25	16	18	22	26	30	34	38	42	46	50	55,58
Sounder Triad Graphite	10	–	16	–	21	–	25	15	17	20	24	28	32	36	40	44	48	54,58
Sounder Triad	10	–	16	–	21	–	25	15	16	20	24	28	32	36	40	44	48	54,58
Sounder Tour Limited	10	–	16	18½	21½	–	–	16	18	22	26	30	34	38	42	46	50	55,—

*One set of fairway woods was available to match most of the Toney Penna Drivers. ♦-55,58,60

¹Beginning in 1988, Ram Clubs were available in a variety of custom lie angles & loft angles.

MEN'S — LATE 1980's

LOFT — MEN'S

GOLF CLUB MANUFACTURERS STANDARD SPECIFICATIONS — DURING PERIOD OF 1985 TO 1990

Mfg. & Model	#1 Wood	#2 Wood	#3 Wood	#4 Wood	#5 Wood	#6 Wood	#7 Wood	#1 Iron	#2 Iron	#3 Iron	#4 Iron	#5 Iron	#6 Iron	#7 Iron	#8 Iron	#9 Iron	Pitch Wedge	Sand Wedge
Sounder Star	11	13	16	—	21	—	25	15	17	21	25	29	33	37	41	45	49	55,—
Sounder Silver Star	11	13	16	—	21	—	25	15	17	21	25	29	33	37	41	45	49	55,—
Sounder Triad Laminated	10	—	16	—	21	—	25	15	17	20	24	28	32	36	40	44	48	54,58
Sounder Excalibar	11	—	16	—	21	—	—	16	18	22	26	30	34	38	42	46	50	55,—
Spalding Tour Edition Executive (L.)	12	—	16	—	21	—	—	17½	19½	22	26	30	34	38	41½	46½	52	—
Spalding Cannon (M.)	11	—	16	—	21	—	26	17	19	22	25	28	32	36	40	45	50	—
Spalding Tour Edition (P.)	11	13	16	19	22	—	—	17	19	22	25	28	32	36	40	45	50	55
Spalding Top Flite XL Beryllium Copper	11	—	16	—	21	—	—											
Square Two Sabre II	11	13½	16	19	22	—	26½	17	20	23	26	29	32	35½	39	43	49	56
Square Two PCX	10	—	16	19	22	—	27	16	19	22	25	28	31	35	39	43	48	55
Square Two Forged								16	19	22	25	28	31	35	39	43	48	54
Square Two Persimmon	11	13½	16	19	22	—	—	17	19	22	25	29	33	37	41	45	50	56
Taylor Made Tour Preferred																		
Taylor Made Tour Preferred (M.)	—	12	15	18	21	—	—											
Taylor Made Pittsburgh Persimmon	—	—	17	20	23	—	27½											
Taylor Made Tour Cleek	—	—	16	19	24	27	—											
Taylor Made Iron Cleek								16	18	21	25	29	33	37	41	45	50	—
Titleist Tour Model	10½	—	16	19	22	—	—	18	20	23	26	30	33	37	41	45	49	54
Titleist Metalwood	12	—	17	—	23	—	—											
Titleist DTR	12	—	16	19	22	—	—	—	20	23	26	30	33	37	41	45	49	54
Titleist Graphite	12	—	16	19	22	—	—											
Titleist Pinnacle (L.)	12	—	15	—	18	—	—	17	19	22	26	30	36	40	44	49	54	54
Titleist Box Blade								—	19	22	26	30	33	36	40	44	49	54
Tommy Armour Silver Scot 986 Tour	11	—	16	19	21	—	—	17	20	23	26½	30	33½	37	41	45	50	55
Tommy Armour Golden Scot	♥	—	15½	—	21½	—	—	16	18	21	24½	28	32	36	40	44	48	56
Tommy Armour Silver Scot 845's								16	18	21	24½	28	32	36	40	44	48	56
Tommy Armour T-Line B/C	—	—	15½	18½	21½	—	25	16	18½	21½	25	28½	32½	36½	40½	44½	49	56
Tommy Armour T-Line	—	—	15½	18½	21½	—	25	16	18½	21½	25	28½	32½	36½	40½	44½	49	56
Tommy Armour Concept 2 (1987-89)	12	—	17	20	22	—	25	—	19	22	25	28½	32	36	40	44	48	55
Tommy Armour Emblem	12	—	17	20	22	—	25	—	19	22	25	28½	32	36	40	44	48	55
Tommy Armour Cameron	11	—	16	19	21	—	—	17	20	23	26	29	33	37	41	45	50	56
Tommy Armour Silver Scot 835's	—	—	—	18½	21½	—	25½											
Tommy Armour EQL	—	—	14	—	19½	—	24	16	18	21	24½	28	32	36	40	44	48	56
Tommy Armour Concept 2 (1990)	11½	—	15½	—	23	—	—	—	19	22	25	28½	32	36	40	44	48	55

♥ 9¼ & 10½ lofts available

LOFT — MEN'S

GOLF CLUB MANUFACTURERS STANDARD SPECIFICATIONS — DURING PERIOD OF 1985 TO 1990

Mfg. & Model	#1 Wood	#2 Wood	#3 Wood	#4 Wood	#5 Wood	#6 Wood	#7 Wood	#1 Iron	#2 Iron	#3 Iron	#4 Iron	#5 Iron	#6 Iron	#7 Iron	#8 Iron	#9 Iron	Pitch Wedge	Sand Wedge
Wilson 1200 Gear Effect (M.)	11	–	14	17	20	–	24										–	–
Wilson Staff Metal	7/10	12	15	18	21	–	–											
Wilson Ultra	♦	–	13/15	17	20/24	–	–											
Wilson Staff	11	–	16	19	21			18	20	23	26	30	34	38	42	46	50	55
Wilson 1200 Gear Effect (L.)	12	–	16	19	21			17	19	21	24	28	32	36	40	44	49	54
Wilson Staff Gooseneck (M.)								17	19	22	25	28	32	36	40	44	48	53
Wilson X31	11	–	16	19	21			–	19	21	24	28	32	36	40	44	49	54
Wilson 1200 LT	12	–	16	19	21			–	20	23	26	30	34	38	42	46	50	55
Wilson Turfrider								–	20	23	26	30	34	38	42	46	50	55
Yamaha C-200	10	12	15	18	21	–	–											
Yamaha C-300	9/10	–	15	18	21	–	–											
Yamaha C-500 Driver	9/11																	
Yamaha FD 20 Irons								–	–	23	26	30	34	38	42	46	50	56
Yamaha Image Irons								–	–	–	26	30	34	38	42	46	50	56
Yamaha FOS (1990)	10	–	17	–	23	–	–	–	21	23	26	29	32	36	40	45	50	56
Yamaha Secret	10/12	–	14/17	–	23	–	–											
Yamaha Pro Driver	♦																	
Yamaha Super Driver	10																	
Yamaha DR Driver	12																	
Yamaha EX Gold																		
Yamaha Metrix Metal	10	–	17	–	23	–	–	–	18	20	23	27	31	35	39	43	47	52
Yamaha FOS (1989)	10	–	17	–	23	–	–											
Yamaha Accurace								–	20	23	26	30	34	38	42	46	51	56
Yamaha AR-1	12																	
Yamaha SX-25								19	22	24	27	31	35	39	43	47	51	58
Yamaha X200	10	–	14/17	20	23	–	26	–	20	22	25	28	31	34	37	40	49	57
Yamaha X300	8½	–	14/17	20	23	–	26											
Yamaha The Secret																		
Yamaha W602	11	–	17	–	23	–	–	–	18	21	24	28	32	36	40	44	48	53
Yamaha SX25																		
Yonex Boronwood (G.)	9/11	–	18	21	24	–	–	–	18	21	24	28	32	36	40	44	48	53
Yonex Carbonex II (G.)	9/11	–	18	21	24	–	–	–	–	21	24	27	31	35	39	43	47	52
Yonex Tournament SP								–	–	21	24	27	31	35	39	45	47	52
Yonex Graphlex	11½	–	17	20	23	–	–	–	20	23	26	29	33	37	41	45	52	58
Yonex ADX100	9/11	–	16	19	22	–	–	–	–	22	25	28	32	36	40	44	50	58
Yonex ADX200	9/11	–	16	19	22	–	–	–	17	20	23	27	31	35	39	43	52	–

♦ -7/9/11   ♦ -7½/8½

MEN'S — LATE 1980's

LIE — MEN'S

GOLF CLUB MANUFACTURERS STANDARD SPECIFICATIONS — DURING PERIOD OF 1985 TO 1990

Mfg. & Model	#1 Wood	#2 Wood	#3 Wood	#4 Wood	#5 Wood	#6 Wood	#7 Wood	#1 Iron	#2 Iron	#3 Iron	#4 Iron	#5 Iron	#6 Iron	#7 Iron	#8 Iron	#9 Iron	Pitch Wedge	Sand Wedge
Accuform (all)	52	53	54	55	56	–	58	56	57	58	59	60	61	62	63	64	64	65
Browning 440 Gold	55	–	56	–	57	–	57	56½	57	58	59	60	61	62	63	64	64	64
Browning Pinache	55	–	56	–	57	–	–	56	57	58	59	60	61	62	63	64	64	64
Browning Automatic	55	–	56	57	57	–	57	–	–	58	59	60	61	62	63	64	64	64
Browning Tour Class	55	–	56	57	57	–	–	–	57	58	59	60	61	62	63	64	64	64
Browning Maxim	55	–	56	56	56	–	56	–	57	58	59	60	61	62	63	64	64	64
Browning 440	55	–	56	57	57	–	57	–	57	58	59	60	61	62	63	64	64	64
Browning System 350	55	–	56	57	57	–	–	56½	57	58	59	60	61	62	63	64	64	64
Browning 440 Plus	55	55	56	57	57	–	57	–	57	58	59	60	61	62	63	64	64	64
Browning Premier	55	–	56	–	57	–	–	56	57	58	59	60	61	62	63	64	64	64
Browning Mirage (L.)	55	–	56	–	57	–	57	–	57	58	59	60	61	62	63	64	64	64
Callaway Bobby Jones Commemorative	55	–	55½	–	56½	–	57	56	57	58	59	60	61	62	63	64	64	64
Callaway Bobby Jones	55	–	55½	56	56½	–	57½	56	57	58	59	60	61	62	63	64	64	65
Callaway Classic	55	–	55½	56	56½	–	–	56	57	58	59	60	61	62	63	64	64	65
Callaway S2H2	55	–	55½	56	56½	–	57½	56	57	58	59	60	61	62	63	64	64	
Cleveland Classics Tour. Action 588	56	56	57	57	58	–	–	56	57	58	59	60	61	62	63	64	64	65
Cleveland Classics TC 15	56	56	57	57	58	–	–											
Cleveland Classics RC85	56	–	57	57	58	–	–											
Cleveland Classics TA289	56	–	57	57	58	58	58											
Cleveland Classics Tour Action 588 (P.)	56	56	57	57	58	–	57½	56	56	57	58	59	60	61	62	63	64	64
Cleveland Classics 10th Anniversary Woods	55	–	55½	–	56	–	56	55	56	57	58	59	60	61	62	63	64	–
Cobra Baffler Steel Classic					56	–	56											
Cobra Traditional Baffler Blade								58½	59	59½	60	60½	61	61½	62	63	63	63
Cobra Baffler*	54	54½	55	55	55	55½	55½											
Daiwa Lite Touch (G.)	55	–	56	56	57	–	57	55	57	58	59	60	61	62	63	64	64	64
Daiwa SRX3 (P.)	54	–	55	56	56	–	–	–	57	58	59	60	61	62	63	64	64	64
Daiwa Hi-Trac (L.)	54	–	55	56	56	–	–	–	57	58	59	60	61	62	63	64	64	64
Daiwa Chairman (P.)	54	–	55	56	56	–	57	–	57	58	59	60	61	62	63	64	64	64
Daiwa Ballistic II (M.)	54½	–	55	56	57	–	57	–	57	58	59	60	61	62	63	64	64	64
Daiwa Monodyne								56	57	58	59	60	61	62	63	64	64	64
Daiwa Advisor								56	57	58	59	60	61	62	63	64	64	64
Daiwa DB-561	54	–	55	56	56	–	–											
Daiwa DB-591	54	–	55	56	56	–	–											
Daiwa Exceler	55	–	56	56	57	–	57											
Daiwa Exceler BPT	55	–	56	56	57	–	57											
Daiwa DB-611 (P.)	54	–	55	56	56	–	–											
Daiwa DB-612 (P.)	54	–	55	56	56	–	–											
Dunlop Maxfli DP 30																		
Dunlop Seve Ballesteros (P.)	55	–	56	57	–	–	–	57	57½	58	58½	59	59½	60	60½	61	61½	62
Dunlop Maxfli 901 (P.)	5	–	56	57	57	–	–	57	57½	58	58½	59	59½	60	60½	61	61½	62
Dunlop Maxfli 357 (M.)	55	–	55½	–	56½	–	57	57	57½	58	58½	59	59½	60	60½	61	61½	62

*Woods also available as #8-56, #9-56, #11-56½, #13-56½ and TS-55

MEN'S — LATE 1980's

LIE — MEN'S

GOLF CLUB MANUFACTURERS STANDARD SPECIFICATIONS — DURING PERIOD OF 1985 TO 1990

Mfg. & Model	#1 Wood	#2 Wood	#3 Wood	#4 Wood	#5 Wood	#6 Wood	#7 Wood	#1 Iron	#2 Iron	#3 Iron	#4 Iron	#5 Iron	#6 Iron	#7 Iron	#8 Iron	#9 Iron	Pitch Wedge	Sand Wedge
Dunlop Black Missile (G.)	56	—	57	—	58	—	—	—	—	58½	59	59½	60	61	61½	62	62½	63
Dunlop Maxfli Professional Special (P.)	55	—	57	57	57	—	—	57	57½	58	58½	59	60	61	62	62½	62½	63
Dunlop Maxfli Tour Limited (M.)	55	—	55½	56	56½	—	57	57	58	59	60	61	62	63	64	65	65	65
Dunlop Maxfli Missile (G.)	56	—	57	—	58	—	—	—	—	58½	59	59½	60	61	61½	62	62½	63
Dunlop Power Max (M.)	55	—	56	—	57	—	—	—	—	57	58	59	60	61	62	63	63	63
GolfWorks® Kinetic	55	—	56	—	58	—	58	58	58½	59	59½	60	60½	61	61½	62	63	63
GolfWorks® Technique	55	—	56	56½	57	—	—	56	57	58	59	60	61	62	63	64	64	64
GolfWorks® Bio-Mech (M.)	55	—	56	—	57	—	58	58	58½	59	59½	60	60½	61	61½	62	63	63
GolfWorks® XDC	55	—	56	—	57	—	58	—	—	59	59½	60	60½	61	61½	62	63	63
GolfWorks® Commander	55	—	56	56½	57	—	—	56	57	58	59	60	61	62	63	64	64	64
GolfWorks® Tandem	55	—	56	56½	57	—	58	58	58½	59	59½	60	60½	61	61½	62	63	63
GolfWorks® RMH								55	56	57	58	59	60	61	62	63	63	63
GolfWorks® Hero Plus	55	—	56	56½	57	—	58	58	58½	59	59½	60	60½	61	61½	62	63	63
GolfWorks® Bio-Mech (L.)*	55	55½	56	56½	57	57½	58											
GolfWorks® Accu-Weight	55	—	56	—	57	—	58	—	—	59	59½	60	60½	61	61½	62	63	63
H & B/Power Bilt Citation (P.)	55	55	56	57	57	57	57											
H & B/Power Bilt Citation (L.)	55	55	56	57	57	57	57											
H & B/Power Bilt TPS								56	57	58	59	60	61	62	63	64	64	64
H & B/Power Bilt TPS (M.)	55	55	56	57	57	—	57											
H & B/Power Bilt Grand Slam (L.)	55	—	56	57	57	—	57											
H & B/Power Bilt Grand Slam (M.)	55	—	56	—	57	—	58											
H & B/Power Bilt Citation Plus	55	55	56	57	57	57	57											
H & B/Power Bilt Scotch Blade								56	56	57	58	59	60	61	62	63	63	63
H & B/Power Bilt Citation Forged								56	56	57	58	59	60	61	62	63	63	63
H & B/Power Bilt Citation Cast								56	57	58	59	60	61	62	63	64	64	64
H & B/Power Bilt Propower								56	57	58	59	60	61	62	63	64	64	64
Walter Hagen Haig Ultra	55	—	56	57	57	—	—	56	57	58	59	60	60	61	62	62	63	64
Hogan Apex	55	—	56	57	58	—	—	56	57	58	59	60	61	62	62½	63	63½	65
Hogan Radial	55	—	56	56	57	—	—	—	57	58	59	60	61	62	63	63½	64	—
Hogan Magnum								56	57	58	59	60	61	62	63	63½	64	65
Hogan Series 56	55	55½	56	56½	57	—	57½											
Hogan Series 56 (G.)	55	55½	56	56½	57	—	—											
Hogan Saber	55																	
Hogan Companion	55½	56	57	57	58	—	59											
Hogan Apex PC								—	57	58	59	60	61	62	62½	63	63½	—
Hogan Edge (Irons)								56	57	58	59	60	61	62	62½	63	63½	65
Hogan 56 (Carbon Woods)	55	55½	56	56½	57	—	—											
Hogan Magnum Plus (Woods)	55	—	56	—	57	—	—											
Hogan Magnum Plus (Irons)								56	57	58	59	60	61	62	63	63½	64	65

*Additional GolfWorks® Bio-Mech (L.) woods available 8-58½, 9-59, 10-59½, 11-60, 12-60½

MEN'S — LATE 1980's

LIE — MEN'S

GOLF CLUB MANUFACTURERS STANDARD SPECIFICATIONS — DURING PERIOD OF 1985 TO 1990

Mfg. & Model	#1 Wood	#2 Wood	#3 Wood	#4 Wood	#5 Wood	#6 Wood	#7 Wood	#1 Iron	#2 Iron	#3 Iron	#4 Iron	#5 Iron	#6 Iron	#7 Iron	#8 Iron	#9 Iron	Pitch Wedge	Sand Wedge
Louisville Golf Air Dried Class. 50's (P.)	55	55½	56	56½	57	—	58	—	57	58	59	60	61	62	63	64	64	64
Louisville Golf Level Four	55	—	56	56½	57	—	58	—	57	58	59	60	61	62	63	64	64	64
Louisville Golf Personal Model	55	—	56	56½	57	—	58	—	55	56	57	58	59	60	61	61	62	62
Louisville Natural Lite	55	—	56	56½	57	—	58	—	57	58	59	60	61	62	63	64	64	64
Louisville Golf MWH Metalwood	55	—	56	56½	57	—	58											
Lynx Predator G (M.)	55	—	55	—	56	—	57	57	57	58	59	60	61	62	63	64	64	64
Lynx Silver Lynx (G.)	54	—	55	—	56	—	—	—	57	58	59	60	61	62	63	64	64	64
Lynx Radius (M.)								57	57	58	59	60	61	62	63	64	64	64
Lynx USA								57	57	58	59	60	61	62	63	64	64	64
Lynx Liberty (L.)	55	—	56	56	57	—	58	—	57	58	59	60	61	62	63	64	64	64
Lynx Parallax (M.)	54½	—	55½	56½	57½	—	58½	57	57	58	59	60	61	62	63	64	64	64
Lynx Parallax Offset (M.)	54½	—	55	—	56	—	57											
Lynx Classic	54	—	55	—	56	—	—											
Lynx Super Predator (M.)	54	54½	55	56	56	—	56	57	57	58	59	60	61	62	63	64	64	64
MacGregor Nicklaus Muirfield (P.)	55	—	56	56½	56½	—	—	57	57½	58	59	60	60½	61	61½	62	63	63
MacGregor CG1800 (L.)	55	—	56	56	56	—	—	57	57½	58	59	60	60½	61	61½	62	63	63
Maruman Sole M210	55½	—	57	58	58½	—	—											
Maruman Sole MSL71	56	—	58	—	58½	—	—											
Maruman Verity	55½	—	57½	—	59½	—	—	—	—	59	60	61	61½	62	62½	63	63½	63½
Maruman Tap 18	♥	—	57	58	58½	—	—	—	57	58	59	60	61	61½	62	63	63	—
Maruman DCA Kevlar	56	—	56	57	58	—	—	—	—	59	60	60½	61	61½	62	62½	63	63
Maruman Dangan 303	55	—	57	57½	57½	58	58											
Maruman Conductor (Metal)	53½	—	55	56	56½	—	—											
Mizuno Altron (G.)	54½	—	55½	—	56½	—	57	—	—	58	59	60	60½	61	62	63	63½	63½
Mizuno Black Turbo II	56	—	57	57½	58	—	—	—	59	59½	60	60½	61	61½	62	62½	62½	—
Mizuno MST	54½	55	55½	56	56½	—	56½	56	57	58	59	60	60½	61	61½	62	62½	62½
Mizuno MCG-35	55½	—	58	—	59	—	—	56	56½	57	58	59	60	61	61½	62	62½	63
Mizuno MS-8 Pro Forge	55	—	56	56½	57	—	—	56	57	58	59	60	61	61½	62	63	64	64
Mizuno Black Turbo (G.)	55	—	56	56½	57	57½	58	58½										
Mizuno Turbo Pro (G.)	55	—	58	58½	—	—	—											
Mizuno Turbo EL (G.)	55	—	56	56½	57	—	—											
Mizuno Turbo LX (G.)	55	—	56	56½	56½	—	—											
Mizuno Cimarron (P.)	55	—	56	56½	57	—	—											
Mizuno Cimarron (M.)	54	—	55	55½	56	—	—	—	57	58	59	60	61	61½	62	63	64	64
Mizuno MS-4 (M.)	55½	—	56	56½	57	—	—	56	57	58	59	60	60½	61	62	63	63½	63½
Mizuno MS-5 (P.)	55	—	56	56½	57	—	—	56	57	58	59	60	60½	61	62	63	63	63
Mizuno MS-3 (M.)	55	—	56	56	57	—	—	56	57	58	59	60	61	61½	62	63	64	64
Mizuno Champion Flag (Maple)	55	—	56	56½	57	—	58	—	—	58	59	60	60½	61	62	63	63	63
Mizuno Silver Cup (Maple)	55	—	56	—	56½	—	—	—	—	58	59	60	60½	61	62	63	63	63
Mizuno Silver Cup (M.)	56	—	57	—	58	—	—	—	—	58	59	60	60½	61	62	63	63	64

♥ —55/55½

MEN'S — LATE 1980's

LIE — MEN'S

GOLF CLUB MANUFACTURERS STANDARD SPECIFICATIONS — DURING PERIOD OF 1985 TO 1990

Mfg. & Model	#1 Wood	#2 Wood	#3 Wood	#4 Wood	#5 Wood	#6 Wood	#7 Wood	#1 Iron	#2 Iron	#3 Iron	#4 Iron	#5 Iron	#6 Iron	#7 Iron	#8 Iron	#9 Iron	Pitch Wedge	Sand Wedge
Mizuno MS-7	55	—	56	—	57	—	—											
Mizuno MS-7 Pro Forge								56	57	58	59	60	60½	61	62	63	63	64
Mizuno Pro Original	56	—	57	57½	58	—	—											
Mizuno Wings	55	—	55½	—	56½	—	—	—	57	58	59	60	61	61½	62	63	64	64
Mizuno SPL	55½	—	56	—	57	—	—	—	58½	59	59½	60	60½	61	61½	62	62½	63½
Mizuno Trump	56	—	57	—	58	—	—	—	57	58	59	60	61	61½	62	63	64	64
Mizuno MSX	55	—	56	56½	57	—	—											
Mizuno Turbo PC	55	—	56	56½	57	—	—											
Mizuno Altron SE 90	54½	—	55½	—	56½	—	—	56	57	58	59	60	61	61½	62	63	64	64
Northwestern De Vicenzo 241 Tour (P.)	55	—	55½	55¾	56	—	—											
Northwestern Weiskopf 865 GR (G.)	55	—	55½	—	56	—	—											
Northwestern 965 Limeted Editon (P.)	55	—	55½	—	56	—		55	56	57	58	59	60	61	62	63	63	63
Northwestern Thunderbird (M.)	55	—	55½	55½	56	—	—											
Northwestern Thunderbird II								55	56	57	58	59	60	61	62	63	63	63
Northwestern Dyna-tour (M.)	55	—	55½	—	56	—	—	55	56	57	58	59	60	61	62	63	63	63
Northwestern Gold Signature (L.)	55	—	55½	—	56	—	—	—	—	57	58	59	60	61	62	63	63	63
Northwestern Hubert Green Tour II (M.)	55	—	55½	—	56	—	—	—	56	57	58	58	60	61	62	63	63	63
Northwestern Weiskopf 360CS (M.)	55	—	55½	—	56	—	—											
Northwestern Pro Classic (M.)	55	—	55½	55¾	56	—	—	55	56	57	58	59	60	61	62	63	63	63
Northwestern Team Player (G.)	55	—	55½	—	56	—	—	—	56	57	58	59	60	61	62	63	63	63
Northwestern Team Player (P.)	55	—	55½	—	56	—	—	—	56	57	58	59	60	61	62	63	63	63
Northwestern Weiskopf Dyna-Tour (M.)	55	—	55½	—	56	—	—	—	56	57	58	59	60	61	62	63	63	63
Northwestern Hubert Green RS (M.)	55	—	55½	—	56	—	—	—	56	57	58	59	60	61	62	63	63	63
Northwestern Hubert Green 300 CS (M.)	55	—	55½	—	56	—	—	—	—	57	58	59	60	61	62	63	63	63
Northwestern Weiskopf Pro Classic (M.)	55	—	55½	55¾	56	—	—	55	56	57	58	59	60	61	62	63	63	63
Northwestern Hubert Green Ultimate (M.)	55	—	55½	—	56	—	—	—	—	57	58	59	60	61	62	63	63	63
Northwestern Gary Player GP270 (M.)	55	—	55½	—	56	—	—	—	—	57	58	59	60	61	62	63	63	63
Northwestern Tour Select II (L.)	55	—	55½	—	56	—	—	—	—	57	58	59	60	61	62	63	63	63
Northwestern Weiskopf Promaster Plus (M.)	55	—	55½	—	56	—	—	—	—	57	58	59	60	61	62	63	63	63
Toney Penna Avenger (1986)	55	—	56	—	57	—	—											
Toney Penna Model 75 Woods	55	—	56	56	57	—	—											
Toney Penna Model 1 Driver*	55	—	56	56½	57	—	58											
Toney Penna Jupiter Slugger	55																	
Toney Penna Model 12	55																	
Toney Penna Model 59	55																	
Toney Penna Model 65 LH	55																	
Toney Penna Natural	55																	
Toney Penna Model 75	55																	
Toney Penna Model 85	55																	
Toney Penna Avenger (1989-90)	55							—	56	56	57½	58	59	60	60½	61	61	61
Toney Penna TP80	55	—	56	56	57	—	—											
Toney Penna True Site II	55								56	56	57½	58	59	60	60½	61	61	61

*One set of fairway woods was available to match most of the Toney Penna Drivers.

MEN'S — LATE 1980's

LIE — MEN'S

GOLF CLUB MANUFACTURERS STANDARD SPECIFICATIONS — DURING PERIOD OF 1985 TO 1990

Mfg. & Model	#1 Wood	#2 Wood	#3 Wood	#4 Wood	#5 Wood	#6 Wood	#7 Wood	#1 Iron	#2 Iron	#3 Iron	#4 Iron	#5 Iron	#6 Iron	#7 Iron	#8 Iron	#9 Iron	Pitch Wedge	Sand Wedge
Toney Penna Beryllium Copper 8°	55																	
Toney Penna Beryllium Copper 10°	55																	
Toney Penna Cobalt 8°	55																	
Toney Penna Cobalt 10°	55																	
Toney Penna Metalwood (Grey)	55																	
Toney Penna Metalwood (Black)	55																	
Toney Penna Original (Forged)	55								56	56	57½	58	59	60	60½	61	61	61
Toney Penna Stainless Cast	55								56	56	57½	58	59	60	60½	61	61	61
Toney Penna Tru Site Cast	55								56	56	57½	58	59	60	60½	61	61	61
Toney Penna Super Blade Cast	55								56	56	57½	58	59	60	60½	61	61	61
Toney Penna USA Forged	55								56	56	57½	58	59	60	60½	61	61	61
Pro Group Peerless (P.)	54½	—	55	56	56	—	—	56	56	57	58	59	60	61	62	63	63	64
Pro Group Axium (P.)	55½	—	56	57	57	—	—	56	56	57	58	59	60	61	62	63	63	64
Ram Tour Series Steelwoods	57	—	58	58½	59	59	59											
Ram Tour Grind	56	—	57	57½	58	—	—	58	58½	59	60	61	62	62½	63	63½	64	64½
Ram Tour Grind Axial	56	—	57	57½	58	—	—	58	58½	59	60	61	62	62½	63	63½	64	64½
Ram Laser X-2	56	—	57	—	58	—	58	58	58½	59	60	61	62	62½	63	63½	64	64½
Ram Custom 800 Series	56	—	57	57½	58	—	—											
Ram Laser X-2 (G.)	56	—	57	57½	58	—	58	—	58½	59	60	61	62	62½	63	63½	64	64½
Ram Accubar	55	—	56	—	57	—	57	—	58½	59	60	61	62	62½	63	63½	64	64½
Ram Laser FX Forged	57	—	58	58½	59	—	—	58	58½	59	60	61	62	62½	63	63½	64	64½
Ram Laser FX Bore Thru	57	—	58	58½	59	—	—	58	58½	59	60	61	62	62½	63	63½	64	64½
Rawlings Toney Penna Model 89 Driver	55																	
Rwalings Toney Penna Model TPIX Driver	55																	
Rawlings Toney Penna Special Edition II Driver	55																	
Rawlings Toney Penna 79 Driver	55																	
Rawlings Toney Penna Special Edition II	55	—	56	56	57	—	—											
Rawlings Toney Penna Steelwoods	55	—	56	56	57	—	—											
Slazenger Crown Sterling	55	—	55½	56	56½	—	57	56	57	58	59	60	61	62	63	64	64	64
Slazenger Royal Panther	55	—	56	—	57	—	58	56	57	58	59	60	61	62	63	64	64	64
Slazenger Crown Limited	55	—	56	57	57	—	—	56	57	58	59	60	61	62	63	64	64	64
Slazenger Royal Panther BC								56	57	58	59	60	61	62	63	64	64	64
Sounder Tour Star	55	—	56	56½	57	—	58	56	57	58	59	60	61	62	63	63½	63½	63½
Sounder Triad Graphite	55	—	56	—	57	—	57	55	56	57	58	59	60	61	62	63	63	63
Sounder Triad	55	—	56	56½	57	—	—	56	57	58	59	60	61	62	63	63	63	63
Sounder Tour Limited	55	—	56	56½	57	—	57	56	57	58	59	60	61	62	63	63½	63½	63½

MEN'S — LATE 1980's

LIE — MEN'S

GOLF CLUB MANUFACTURERS STANDARD SPECIFICATIONS — DURING PERIOD OF 1985 TO 1990

Mfg. & Model	#1 Wood	#2 Wood	#3 Wood	#4 Wood	#5 Wood	#6 Wood	#7 Wood	#1 Iron	#2 Iron	#3 Iron	#4 Iron	#5 Iron	#6 Iron	#7 Iron	#8 Iron	#9 Iron	Pitch Wedge	Sand Wedge
Sounder Star.	55	55½	56	–	57	–	57	56	57	58	59	60	61	62	63	63½	63½	63½
Sounder Silver Star	55	55½	56	–	57	–	57	56	57	58	59	60	61	62	63	63½	63½	63½
Sounder Triad Laminated	55	–	56	–	57	–	57	55	56	57	58	59	60	61	62	63	63	63
Sounder Excalibar	55	–	56	–	57	–	–	56	57	58	59	60	61	62	63	63½	63½	63½
Spalding Tour Edition Exec. (L.)	55	–	55½	–	56	–	–	58¼	58¼	58¾	59¼	59¾	60¼	61	61¾	62¼	63	–
Spalding Cannon (M.)	55	–	55½	–	56	–	52½	58	58½	59	59½	60	60½	61	61½	62	63	–
Square Two Sabre II	55	55½	56	56½	57	–	58	55	56	57	58	59	60	61	62	63	63	63
Square Two PCX	55	–	55	56	56	–	57	55	56	57	58	59	60	61	62	63	63	63
Square Two Forged	55	–	–	–	–	–	–	55	56	57	58	59	60	61	62	63	63	63
Square Two Persimmon	55	55½	56	56½	57	–	–	56	57	58	59	60	61	62	63	64	64	64
Taylor Made Tour Preferred	54	55	55	55½	56	–	–											
Taylor Made Tour Preferred (M.)	54	–	55	55	56	–	–											
Taylor Made Pittsburgh Persimmon	54	–	55	55	55	–	55											
Taylor Made Tour Cleek	–	–	55	55	55	55	–											
Taylor Made Iron Cleek	54	–	55	56	56	–	–	56½	57	58	59	60	61	62	63	64	64	–
Titleist Tour Made	54	–	55	56	56	–	–	56	57	58	59	60	61	62	63	63½	63	62
Titleist Metalwood	54	–	55	–	56	–	–											
Titleist DTR	54	–	55	56	56	–	–	–	57	58	59	60	61	62	62	62	63	–
Titleist Graphite	54	–	55	56	56	–	–											
Titleist Pinnacle (L.)	54	–	55	–	55	–	–	56	57	58	59	60	61	62	62	62	62	62
Titleist Box Blade	–	–	55	55	56	–	–	–	57	58	59	60	62	62	62	63	63	64
Tommy Armour Silver Scot 986 Tour	54	–	55	55	55	–	–	56	57	58	59	60	60½	61	61½	62	63	64
Tommy Armour Golden Scot	54	–	55	55	56	–	–	56½	57½	58½	59½	60	61	61½	62	63	63	63
Tommy Armour Silver Scot 845's	54	–	55	55	56	–	56	56½	57½	58½	59½	60	61	61½	62	62½	63	63
Tommy Armour T-Line B/C	54	–	55	56	56	–	56	56	56¾	57¾	58¾	59¾	60¾	61¾	62¾	63¾	63¾	64
Tommy Armour T-Line	54	–	55	56	56	–	56	56	56¾	57¾	58¾	59¾	60¾	61¾	62¾	63¾	63¾	64
Tommy Armour Concept 2 (1987-89)	54	–	55	55	56	–	56	–	56½	57½	58½	59½	60	61	62	63	64	64
Tommy Armour Emblem	54	–	55	55	56	–	56	–	57	58	59	60	61	61	62	63	63	64
Tommy Armour Cameron	54	–	55	55	55	–	–	56	56	57	58	59	60	61	62	63	63	64
Tommy Armour Silver Scot 835's	54	–	55	55½	56	–	56½											
Tommy Armour EQL	56	–	56	–	56	–	56	61	61	61	61	61	61	61	61	61	61	61
Tommy Armour Concept 2 (1990)	55	–	56	–	57	–	–	–	56½	57½	58½	59½	60	61	62	63	64	64

LIE — MEN'S

GOLF CLUB MANUFACTURERS STANDARD SPECIFICATIONS — DURING PERIOD OF 1985 TO 1990

Mfg. & Model	#1 Wood	#2 Wood	#3 Wood	#4 Wood	#5 Wood	#6 Wood	#7 Wood	#1 Iron	#2 Iron	#3 Iron	#4 Iron	#5 Iron	#6 Iron	#7 Iron	#8 Iron	#9 Iron	Pitch Wedge	Sand Wedge
Wilson 1200 Gear Effect (M.)	54	—	55	55	56	—	56											
Wilson Staff Metal	54	55	55	55	56	—	—											
Wilson Ultra	54	—	55	55	56	—	—											
Wilson Staff	55	—	56	57	57	—	—	56	57	58	59	60	60	61	62	62	63	64
Wilson 1200 Gear Effect (L.)	55	—	56	57	57	—	—	56	57	58	59	60	60	61	62	62	63	64
Wilson Staff Gooseneck (M.)								56	57	58	59	60	60	61	62	62	63	64
Wilson X31	55	—	56	57	57	—	—	—	57	58	59	60	60	61	62	62	63	64
Wilson 1200 LT	55	—	56	57	57	—	—	—	57	58	59	60	60	61	62	62	63	64
Wilson Turfrider								—	57	58	59	60	60	61	62	62	63	64
Yamaha C-200	55	1½=54	56	56½	57		—											
Yamaha C-300	55	—	56	56½	57		—											
Yamaha C-500 Driver	55																	
Yamaha FD 29 Irons								—	—	57	58	59	60	61	62	63	64	64
Yamaha Image Irons								—	—	—	58	59	60	61	62	63	64	64
Yamaha EX-Gold (1988)	55	—	55½	—	56	—	—											
Yamaha SX-Pro Driver	55																	
Yamaha Hal Sutton Persimmon	55																	
Yamaha The Secret III								—	58½	59	59½	60	60½	61	61½	62	63	63
Yamaha XAM10								—	—	59	59½	60	60½	61	61½	62	63	63
Yamaha FOS (1990)	55	—	55	—	56	—	—											
Yamaha Secret	54/55	—	55	55½	56	—	—											
Yamaha Pro Driver	55																	
Yamaha Super Driver	55																	
Yamaha DR Driver	54																	
Yamaha EX Gold (1990)								—	56	57	58	59	60	61	62	62½	63	63
Yamaha Metrix Metal	43½	—	42½	—	41½	—	—											
Yamaha FOS (1989)	43½	—	42½	—	41½	—	—											
Yamaha Accurace								—	57	58	59	60	60½	61	61½	62	63	63
Yamaha SX-25								57	57	58	59	60	61	62	63	63½	64	64
Yamaha X200	55	55	56	56½	57	—	57½											
Yamaha X300	55	—	56	56½	57	—	57½											
Yamaha The Secret	55	—	56	56½	57	—	—	—	58½	59	59½	60	60½	61	61½	62	63	64
Yamaha W602	55	—	56	—	57	—	—											
Yamaha SX25								—	57	58	59	60	61	62	63	63½	64	64
Yonex Boronwood (G.)	56	—	57	57½	58	—	—	—	—	57	58	59	60	61	62	63	64	64
Yonex Carbonex II (G.)	56	—	57	57½	58	—	—	—	—	57	58	59	60	61	62	63	64	64
Yonex Carbonex 22 (G.)	56	—	57	57½	58	—	—	—	—	57	58	59	60	61	62	63	64	64
Yonex Tournament SP								—	56	57	58	59	60	61	62	63	64	64
Yonex Graphlex	56	—	57	57½	58	—	—	—	—	58	59	60	61	62	63	64	64	64
Yonex ADX100	53	—	56	56½	57	—	—											
Yonex ADX200	56	—	57	57½	58	—	—	—	56	57	58	59	60	61	62	63	64	—

MEN'S — LENGTH, LOFT & LIE —
— FILL IN YOUR OWN TO KEEP UPDATED

GOLF CLUB MANUFACTURERS STANDARD OR CUSTOM SPECIFICATIONS

Manufacturer & Model	Year Specs. Published	#1 Wood	#2 Wood	#3 Wood	#4 Wood	#5 Wood	#6 Wood	#7 Wood	#1 Iron	#2 Iron	#3 Iron	#4 Iron	#5 Iron	#6 Iron	#7 Iron	#8 Iron	#9 Iron	Pitch Wedge	Sand Wedge	Third Wedge
Length:																				
Loft:																				
Lie:																				

874

LADIES' — EARLY & MID 1970's

LENGTH — LADIES'

GOLF CLUB MANUFACTURERS' STANDARD SPECIFICATIONS — DATA FROM 1974 DESIGN BOOK

Mfgr. & Year Specs. Published	#1 Wood	#2 Wood	#3 Wood	#4 Wood	#5 Wood	#2 Iron	#3 Iron	#4 Iron	#5 Iron	#6 Iron	#7 Iron	#8 Iron	#9 Iron	Pitch Wedge	Sand Wedge
Length:															
Acushnet (1973)	41½	41½	41	40½	40¼	37½	37	36½	36	35½	35¼	35	34½	34½	34½
Dunlop (1973)	42	41½	41	40½	40¼	37½	37	36½	36	35½	35	34¾	34½	34	34
Faultless (1974)	42	—	41	40½	40	—	37½	37	36½	36	35½	35	34½	34½	34½
MacGregor (1972)	42	41¾	41½	41	41	38	37½	37	36½	36	35½	35¼	35	34½	34½
P.G.A. (1972)	42	41½	41	40½	40	—	37½	37	36½	36	35½	35¼	35	34½	34½
Ram (1973)	41½	41	40½	40	39	37½	37	36½	36	35½	35	34½	34	34	34
Royal (1974)	42	—	41½	41	40½	—	—	—	—	—	—	—	—	—	—
Spalding (1974)	42	41⁹/₁₆	41⅛	40¹¹/₁₆	40¼	37⅝	37³/₁₆	36¾	36⁵/₁₆	35⅞	35⁷/₁₆	35	34⁹/₁₆	34⅛	33⅝

LOFT — LADIES'

GOLF CLUB MANUFACTURERS' STANDARD SPECIFICATIONS — DATA FROM 1974 DESIGN BOOK

Mfgr. & Year Specs. Published	#1 Wood	#2 Wood	#3 Wood	#4 Wood	#5 Wood	#2 Iron	#3 Iron	#4 Iron	#5 Iron	#6 Iron	#7 Iron	#8 Iron	#9 Iron	Pitch Wedge	Sand Wedge
Loft															
Acushnet (1973)	12	15	18	21	23	21	24	27	31	35	39	43	47	51	55
Dunlop (1973)	12	15	17	19	22	20	22½	26½	30½	34½	38½	42½	46½	50½	56
Faultless (1974)	12	—	17	20	23	—	24	28	32	36	40	44	48	52	56
MacGregor (1972)	12	15	18	20	23	22	25	28	32	36	38½	43	45	50	55
P.G.A. (1972)	13	15	18	20	22	—	23	26	29	33	37	41	45	50	54
Ram (1973)	12.5	14	16.5	19.2	22	21	24.3	27.8	31.5	35.3	39.2	43.3	47.5	56.6	56.7
Royal (1974)	12	—	17	20	22	—	24	27	31	35	39	43	47	51	57
Spalding (1974)	13	—	19	—	22	20	23	27	31	35	39	43	47	52	58

LIE — LADIES'

GOLF CLUB MANUFACTURERS' STANDARD SPECIFICATIONS — DATA FROM 1974 DESIGN BOOK

Mfgr. & Year Specs. Published	#1 Wood	#2 Wood	#3 Wood	#4 Wood	#5 Wood	#2 Iron	#3 Iron	#4 Iron	#5 Iron	#6 Iron	#7 Iron	#8 Iron	#9 Iron	Pitch Wedge	Sand Wedge
Lie:															
Acushnet (1973)	54	54	55	56	56	57	58	59	60	61	62	63	63	64	64
Dunlop (1973)	55	55	56	56	57	58	59	60	61	62	63	64	65	65	64
Faultless (1974)	54	—	55	55½	56	—	57	58	59	60	61	62	63	63	63
MacGregor (1972)	53	53	53½	54½	54	58	59	60	60½	61	62	62	62	64	65
P.G.A. (1972)	54	54	55	55	55	—	59	60	61	61½	62	62½	63	63	63
Ram (1973)	55.5	55.8	56	56.5	57	57.6	58.4	59.1	60	61	61.9	62.6	63.5	63.5	63.5
Royal (1974)	56	—	57	57	57	—	58	59	60	61	62	63	63	64	64
Spalding (1974)	55	—	56	—	56½	58½	58¾	59¼	59¾	60¼	60½	61¼	62	63	63

NOTE: Some manufacturers who publish men's specifications do not publish ladies' specifications.

LADIES' — LATE 1970's & EARLY 1980's

LENGTH — LADIES'

GOLF CLUB MANUFACTURERS STANDARD SPECIFICATIONS

Mfgr. & Year Specs. Published		#1 Wood	#2 Wood	#3 Wood	#4 Wood	#5 Wood	#6 Wood	#7 Wood	#1 Iron	#2 Iron	#3 Iron	#4 Iron	#5 Iron	#6 Iron	#7 Iron	#8 Iron	#9 Iron	Pitch Wedge	Sand Wedge
Ajay Double Eagle	(1977)	42	—	41	40½	40	—	—	—	—	37	36½	36	36½	35	34½	34	34	34
Browning	(1980)	42	41	40½	40	—	—	—	38½	38	37½	37	36½	36	35½	35	34½	34½	—
Cobra Ladies' Low Profile	(1982)	—	—	—	—	—	—	—	38½	38	37½	37	36½	36	35½	35	34½	34½	34
Confidence	(1977)	42	—	41	40½	40	—	—	—	38	37½	37	36½	36	35½	35	34½	34½	34½
Dunlop	(1978)	42	—	41	40½	40¼	—	—	—	38	37½	37	36½	36	35½	35	34½	34	34
Walter Hagen AM-Lady	(1979)	41	—	40½	40	39¾	—	39½	—	37	36½	36	35½	35	34¾	34½	33¾	-33½	33½
Walter Hagen Onyx	(1979)	42	—	41½	41	40¾	—	40½	—	38	37½	37	36½	36	35¾	35¼	34¾	34½	34½
Walter Hagen Lady Ultra	(1979)	42	—	41½	41	40¾	—	40½	—	38	37½	37	36½	36	35¾	35¼	34¾	34½	34½
Hogan Champion Woods	(1978)	42	—	41½	41	40½	—	39½	—	—	—	—	—	—	—	—	—	—	—
Hogan Medallion Irons	(1978)	—	—	—	—	—	—	—	—	38	37½	37	36½	36	35½	35	34½	34¼	—
Hogan Director Irons	(1978)	—	—	—	—	—	—	—	—	38	37½	37	36½	36	35½	35	34½	34¼	—
MacGregor Finesse	(1982)	42¼	—	41¾	41½	41½	—	41¼	—	—	37¾	37¼	36¾	36¼	35¾	35½	35¼	34¾	34¾
P.G.A. Butterfly	(1982)	41½	—	40½	40	39½	—	39	—	—	37^{1}/$_{16}$	36⅝	36^{3}/$_{16}$	35¾	35^{5}/$_{16}$	34⅞	34^{7}/$_{16}$	34	34
P.G.A. Lady Ryder Cup II	(1982)	42	—	41	40½	40	—	39	—	—	37½	37	36½	36	35½	35	34½	34	34
Pedersen	(1978)	41½	—	40¾	40½	40	—	39½	38	37½	37	36½	36	35½	35	34½	34	34	34
Pinseeker (Length only)	(1978)	42	—	41½	41	40½	—	40	—	38	37½	37	36½	36	35½	35	34½	34½	34½
Pro-Dyn	(1977)	42	—	41	40½	40	—	39½	38	37½	37	36½	36	35½	35	34½	34	34	34
Pro Group	(1982)	42	—	41	40½	40	—	39	—	—	37½	37	36½	36	35½	35	34½	34½	34½
Royal	(1978)	42	—	41	40½	40	—	39	—	—	37½	37	36½	36	35½	35	34½	34½	34½
Spalding Ladies' Executive	(1982)	42	—	41⅛	—	40¼	—	39⅜	—	—	37^{3}/$_{16}$	36¾	36^{5}/$_{16}$	35⅞	35^{7}/$_{16}$	35	34^{9}/$_{16}$	34⅛	33^{11}/$_{16}$
Taylor Made Golf	(1982)	41½	—	40½	40	39½	—	39½	38½	38	37½	37	36½	36	35½	35	34½	34½	34½
Unique	(1982)	42	—	41	40½	40	—	39	38½	38	37½	37	36½	36	35½	35	34½	34½	34½
Wilson Berg Staff	(1982)	42	—	41½	41	40¾	—	40½	—	38	37½	37	36½	36	35¾	35¼	34¾	34½	34½
Wilson Tiara	(1982)	41½	—	40½	—	39½	—	38½	—	—	37	36½	36	35½	35¼	34¾	34¼	34*	
Stan Thompson	(1982)	42	42	41½	41	40½	—	40	—	37½	37	36½	36	35½	35	34½	34	34	34

*Dual Wedge Only

LOFT — LADIES'

GOLF CLUB MANUFACTURERS STANDARD SPECIFICATIONS

Mfgr. & Year Specs. Published		#1 Wood	#2 Wood	#3 Wood	#4 Wood	#5 Wood	#6 Wood	#7 Wood	#1 Iron	#2 Iron	#3 Iron	#4 Iron	#5 Iron	#6 Iron	#7 Iron	#8 Iron	#9 Iron	Pitch Wedge	Sand Wedge
Ajay Double Eagle	(1977)	11	—	16	19	21	—	—	—	—	24	27	31	35	39	43	47	51	55
Browning	(1980)	14	18	21	24	—	—	—	17	20	23	26	29	32	36	40	44	49	—
Cobra Low Profile	(1982)	—	—	—	—	—	—	—	17	20	23	26	29	32	36	40	44	48	55
Confidence	(1977)	13	—	18	20	22	—	—	—	20	23	26	29	33	37	41	45	49	54
Dunlop	(1978)	13	—	16	19	22	—	—	—	20	23	27	31	35	39	43	47	51	57
Hagen AM-Lady	(1979)	13	—	19	22	25	—	31	—	—	24	27	31	35	39	43	47	51	55
Hagen Onyx	(1979)	14	—	17	20	22	—	26	—	—	25	28	31	35	39	43	47	51	55
Hagen Lady Ultra	(1979)	14	—	17	20	22	—	26	—	—	24	27	31	35	39	43	47	51	55
Hogan Champion	(1978)	13	—	17	19	21½	—	25½	—	—	—	—	—	—	—	—	—	—	—
Hogan Medallion	(1978)	—	—	—	—	—	—	—	—	19½	23	26½	30	33½	37	41	45	50	—
Hogan Director	(1978)	—	—	—	—	—	—	—	—	19½	23	26½	30	33½	37	41	45	50	—
MacGregor Finesse	(1982)	12½	—	15½	18½	22	—	30	—	—	23	25	29	33	37	41	44	51	57
P.G.A. Butterfly	(1982)	13	—	17	20	22	—	25	—	—	23	26	29	33	37	41	45	52	57
P.G.A. Lady Ryder Cup II	(1982)	13	—	18	20	22	—	26	—	—	23	26	29	33	36	39	42	47	54
Pedersen	(1978)	13	—	18	21	24	—	29	18	20	23	26	30	34	38	42	46	50	55
Pro-Dyn	(1977)	13	—	18	20	22½	—	28	18	21	24	27	30	34	38	42	46	51	57
Pro Group	(1982)	14	—	18	21	24	—	27	—	—	24	27	31	35	39	43	47	51	—
Royal	(1978)	13	—	18	20	22	—	26	—	—	23	26	29	33	37	41	45	49	56
Spalding Ladies' Executive	(1982)	13	—	18	—	24	—	29	—	—	22½	26	30	34	38	41½	46½	52	58
Taylor Made Golf	(1982)	12	—	19	21	23	—	27	18	21	24	27	30	33	37	41	45	49	57
Unique	(1982)	13	—	16	19	22	—	28	17	20	23	26	29	33	37	41	45	50	57
Wilson Berg Staff	(1982)	13	—	17	20	22	—	26	—	20	23	26	30	34	38	42	46	50	55
Wilson Tiara	(1982)	14	—	18	—	23	—	27	—	20	23	26	30	34	38	42	46	50	55
Stan Thompson	(1982)	12	15	18	21	24	—	30	—	21	24	27	30	34	38	42	46	51	56

LIE — LADIES'

GOLF CLUB MANUFACTURERS STANDARD SPECIFICATIONS

Mfgr. & Year Specs. Published		#1 Wood	#2 Wood	#3 Wood	#4 Wood	#5 Wood	#6 Wood	#7 Wood	#1 Iron	#2 Iron	#3 Iron	#4 Iron	#5 Iron	#6 Iron	#7 Iron	#8 Iron	#9 Iron	Pitch Wedge	Sand Wedge
Ajay Double Eagle	(1977)	55	—	55½	55¾	56	—	—	—	—	58	59	60	61	62	63	63	64	64
Browning	(1982)	55	56	57	57	—	—	—	56½	57	58	59	60	61	62	63	64	64	—
Cobra Low Profile	(1982)	—	—	—	—	—	—	—	56½	57	58	59	60	61	62	63	64	64	64
Confidence	(1977)	54	—	55	55	55	—	—	—	57	58	59	60	61	62	63	63	64	64
Dunlop	(1978)	55	—	56	56	57	—	—	—	57	58	59	60	61	62	63	64	64	65
Hagen AM-Lady	(1979)	55	—	56	57	57	—	57	—	—	58	59	60	61	62	63	64	64	64
Hagen Onyx	(1979)	55	—	56	57	57	—	57	—	—	58	59	60	61	62	63	64	64	64
Hagen Lady Ultra	(1979)	55	—	56	57	57	—	57	—	—	58	59	60	61	62	63	64	64	64
Hogan Champion	(1978)	55½	—	57	57	58	—	58	—	—	—	—	—	—	—	—	—	—	—
Hogan Medallion Irons	(1978)	—	—	—	—	—	—	—	—	57	58	59	60	61	62	62½	63	64½	—
Hogan Director Irons	(1978)	—	—	—	—	—	—	—	—	57	58	59	60	61	62	62½	63	64½	—
MacGregor Finesse	(1982)	54	—	55	56	56	—	58	—	—	59	59½	60	61	62	62½	63	63	65
P.G.A. Butterfly	(1982)	53	—	54	54	55	—	55	—	—	58	59	60	60½	61	61½	62	62½	63
P.G.A. Lady Ryder Cup II	(1982)	54	—	55	55	56	—	56	—	—	59	60	61	61½	62	62½	63	63	63
Pedersen	(1978)	56	—	57	57½	58	—	58	56	57	58	59	60	61	62	63	64	64	64
Pro-Dyn	(1977)	54	—	55	55	55	—	55	56	57	58	59	60	61	62	63	63	64	64
Pro Group	(1982)	54	—	55	56	56	—	56	—	—	58	59	60	61	62	63	64	64	—
Royal	(1978)	54	—	55	55	55	—	56	—	—	58	59	60	61	62	63	63	64	64
Spalding Ladies' Executive	(1982)	55	—	55½	—	56	—	56½	—	—	58¾	59¼	59¾	60¼	61	61¾	62¼	63	63
Taylor Made Golf	(1982)	54	—		55	55	—	55	56	57	58	59	60	61	62	63	64	64	64
Unique	(1982)	55	—	55½	56	56½	—	57½	58	58	59	60	61	62	63	64	65	65	65
Wilson Berg Staff	(1982)	54	—	55	56	56	—	56	—	57	58	59	60	60	61	62	62	63	64
Wilson Tiara	(1982)	54	—	55	—	56	—	56	—	—	57	58	59	60	61	62	62	64	Dual Wedge
Stan Thompson	(1982)	54	54	55	56	57	—	58	—	57	58	59	60	61	62	63	64	64	64

CUSTOM MFGR.'S — LADIES' —

LIE — LADIES'

GOLF CLUB MANUFACTURERS STANDARD SPECIFICATIONS

Mfgr. & Year Specs. Published		#1 Wood	#2 Wood	#3 Wood	#4 Wood	#5 Wood	#6 Wood	#7 Wood	#1 Iron	#2 Iron	#3 Iron	#4 Iron	#5 Iron	#6 Iron	#7 Iron	#8 Iron	#9 Iron	Pitch Wedge	Sand Wedge
Length:																			
Mario Cesario	(1982)	42	41½	41	40½	40	—	39	—	37½	37	36½	36	35½	35	34½	34	34	34
Bert Dargie	(1982)	42	41½	41	40½	40	—	—	38	37½	37	36½	36	35½	35	34½	34	34	34
George Izett	(1982)	42	42	41	40½	40	—	39	—	38	37½	37	36½	36	35½	35	34½	34½	34½
Irving King	(1982)	42	41½	41	40½	40	—	39	—	37½	37	36½	36	35½	35	34½	34	34	34
Louisville Golf	(1982)	41½	41	40½	40	39½	—	39	—	37½	37	36½	36	35½	35	34½	34	34	34
Ralph Maltby	(1982)	42	—	41	40½	40	39½	39	38½	38	37½	37	36½	36	35½	35	34½	34½	34½
John Ofer	(1982)	42	—	41½	41	41	40	40	—	—	37½	37	36½	35¾	35⅝	35¼	34¾	34½	34½
Orlimar	(1982)	42	41¾	41	40½	40	—	39	38¾	38¼	37¾	37¼	36¾	36¼	35¾	35¼	34¾	34½	34½
Kenneth Smith	(1979)	41½	41	40½	40	39½	—	38	38	37½	37	36½	36	35½	35	34½	34	33½	33½
Bob Toski	(1982)	42	41½	41	40½	40	—	39	38½	38	37½	37	36½	36	35½	35	34½	34½	34½
Loft:																			
Mario Cesario	(1982)	12½	14	17	20	23	—	29	—	20	24	28	32	36	40	44	48	52	56
Bert Dargie	(1982)	11	13	16	19	22	—	—	18	21	24	27	31	35	39	43	47	51	55
George Izett	(1982)	12	14	16	19	22	—	—	—	20	22½	25	27½	30	32½	35	37½	40	42½
Louisville Golf	(1982)	12	14	16	19	22	—	28	—	20	23	26	30	34	38	42	46	50	55
Ralph Maltby	(1982)	13	—	17	20	23	26	29	17	20	23	26	30	34	38	42	46	50	56
John Ofer	(1982)	13	—	17	20	22	25	27	—	—	24	27	31	35	39	43	47	51	56
Orlimar	(1982)	13	14½	18½	21½	24½	—	31	16	19	22	25½	29	33	37	41	45	50	58
Kenneth Smith	(1979)	12	15	18	21	24	—	30	18	21	24	28	32	36	40	44	48	52	57
Bob Toski	(1982)	13	15	18	20	22	—	27	22	24	26½	29	31½	35	38½	41½	45	48½	51½
Lie:																			
Mario Cesario	(1982)	53	54	56	56	56	—	56	—	56	57	58	59	60	61	62	63	64	64
Bert Dargie	(1982)	54	54	55	56	56	—	—	57	58	59	60	61	62	63	64	64	65	65
George Izett	(1982)	53	53	54	55	56	—	57	—	56	57	58	59	60	61	62	63	63	63
Irving King	(1982)	55	55½	56	56½	57	—	58	—	57	58	59	60	61	62	63	64	64	64
Louisville Golf	(1982)	54	54	55	56	56	—	57	—	54	55	56	57	58	59	60	60	61	61
Ralph Maltby	(1982)	53	—	54	54½	55	55½	56	55	56	57	58	59	60	61	62	63	63	63
John Ofer	(1982)	54	—	55	56	56	56	56	—	—	57	58	59	59	60	61	61	62	63
Kenneth Smith	(1979)	53	54	55	56	57	—	59	56	57	58	59	60	61	62	63	64	64	64
Bob Toski	(1982)	53	53	54	55	56	—	56	56½	57	57½	58	58½	60	61	61½	62	63	63

LENGTH — LADIES'

Mfgr. & Year Specs. Published		GOLF CLUB MANUFACTURERS STANDARD SPECIFICATIONS																	
		#1 Wood	#2 Wood	#3 Wood	#4 Wood	#5 Wood	#6 Wood	#7 Wood	#1 Iron	#2 Iron	#3 Iron	#4 Iron	#5 Iron	#6 Iron	#7 Iron	#8 Iron	#9 Iron	Pitch Wedge	Sand Wedge
Armour Golf BC	(1986)	42	—	41	40½	40	—	39½	—	—	37¾	37¼	36¾	36¼	35¾	35¼	34¾	34¾	34¾
Browning 440	(1986)	42	—	41	—	40	—	39½	—	38	37½	37	36½	36	35½	35	34½	34½	34½
Daiwa Exceler	(1986)	42	—	41	40½	40	—	39½	—	—	37½	37	36½	36	35½	35	34½	34½	34½
H & B All	(1986)	41½	—	40½	40	40	—	39½	—	—	37	36½	36	35½	35	34½	34	34	34
Lynx - Tigress SP	(1986)	42	—	41	—	40	—	39	—	—	37½	37	36½	36	35½	35	34½	34½	34½
MacGregor L. Finesse	(1986)	42½	—	41¾	41¼	40¾	—	—	—	—	37¾	37¼	36¾	36¼	35¾	35½	35¼	34¾	34¾
Mizuno Quad	(1986)	42	—	41½	—	40¾	—	—	—	—	37½	37	36½	36	35½	35¼	35	34¾	34½
Northwestern Micro-Lite	(1986)	42	—	41	40½	40	—	—	—	—	37	36½	36	35½	35	34½	34	34	34
Penna Golf Original	(1986)	42	—	41½	41	40	—	—	—	—	37½	37	36½	36	35½	35	34½	34	34
Pinseeker Fireball	(1986)	42	—	41	40½	40½	40	—	—	38	37½	37	36½	36	35½	35	34½	34½	34½
Pro Group Axiom	(1986)	42	—	41	40¾	40½	—	40¼	—	—	37½	37	36½	36	35½	35	34½	34½	34¼
Ram Patty Sheehan	(1986)	42	—	41	—	40	—	40	—	—	38	37½	37	36½	36	35½	35	34½	34½
Spalding Cannon	(1986)	42	—	41¼	—	40½	—	39¾	—	—	37½	37	36½	36	35½	35	34½	34	—
Taylor Metal	(1986)	42	—	41	40½	40	—	—	—	—	—	—	—	—	—	—	—	—	—
Taylor Technician	(1986)	41½	—	40¾	—	40	—	—	37½	37½	36¾	36⅜	36	35⅝	35¼	34¾	34¼	34	34
Taylor Iron Cleek	(1986)	—	—	—	—	—	—	—	38½	38	37½	37	36½	36	35½	35	34½	34½	—
Titleist Titlette	(1985)	42	—	41½	—	40¾	—	—	—	—	—	37	36½	36	35⅝	35¼	34⅞	34½	—
Wilson Patty Berg	(1986)	42	—	41½	41	40¾	—	40½	—	—	37½	37	36½	36	35½	35	34½	34	34
Wilson Tiara	(1986)	41½	—	40½	40	39½	—	38½	—	—	37½	37	36½	36	35½	35	34½	34	34
Yamaha C-100	(1986)	42¼	—	41	40½	40	—	—	—	—	—	—	—	—	—	—	—	—	—
Yamaha Image	(1986)	—	—	—	—	—	—	—	—	—	37½	37	36½	36	35½	35	34½	34	34

LOFT — LADIES'

Mfgr. & Year Specs. Published		GOLF CLUB MANUFACTURERS STANDARD SPECIFICATIONS																	
		#1 Wood	#2 Wood	#3 Wood	#4 Wood	#5 Wood	#6 Wood	#7 Wood	#1 Iron	#2 Iron	#3 Iron	#4 Iron	#5 Iron	#6 Iron	#7 Iron	#8 Iron	#9 Iron	Pitch Wedge	Sand Wedge
Armour Golf BC	(1986)	12½	—	15½	18½	21½	—	25	—	—	21½	25	28½	32½	36½	40½	44½	49	52
Browning 440	(1986)	13	—	19	—	22	—	25	—	21	24	27	30	34	38	42	45	50	56
Daiwa Exceler	(1986)	14	—	16½	19	21	—	25	—	17	19	22	25	29	33	37	41	45	50
H & B All	(1986)	14	—	20	22	24	—	27	—	—	24	28	32	35	38	41	44	50	56
Lynx - Tigress SP	(1986)	12	—	16	—	22	—	26	—	—	22	25	29	33	37	41	45	44	56
MacGregor L. Finesse	(1986)	15½	—	18	22	25½	—	—	—	—	23	26	29	33	37	41	45	50	56
Mizuno Quad	(1986)	11½	—	17	—	23	—	—	—	—	21	24	27	30	34	38	42	47	54
Northwestern Micro-Lite	(1986)	11	—	15	18	20	—	—	—	—	22	26	30	34	38	42	46	50	52
Penna Golf Original	(1986)	11	—	15	18	21	—	—	—	—	23	27	31	35	39	43	47	51	56
Pinseeker Fireball	(1986)	11	—	15	20	—	—	25	—	—	20	24	27	31	35	39	44	49	56
Pro Group Axiom	(1986)	12½	—	16	19	21	—	25	—	22	24	27	29	32	36	40	44	48	54
Ram Patty Sheehan	(1986)	13	—	17	—	22	—	26	—	—	23½	27	30½	34½	37	42	46	50	55
Spalding Cannon	(1986)	13	—	16	21	26	—	—	—	—	22	25	28	32	36	40	44	48	—
Taylor Metal	(1986)	12	—	17	20	23	25	27½	—	—	—	—	—	—	—	—	—	—	—

LADIES' — MID 1980's

LOFT — LADIES' (cont.)

GOLF CLUB MANUFACTURERS STANDARD SPECIFICATIONS

Mfgr. & Year Specs. Published	Year	#1 Wood	#2 Wood	#3 Wood	#4 Wood	#5 Wood	#6 Wood	#7 Wood	#1 Iron	#2 Iron	#3 Iron	#4 Iron	#5 Iron	#6 Iron	#7 Iron	#8 Iron	#9 Iron	Pitch Wedge	Sand Wedge
Taylor Technician	(1986)	12	—	17	20	23	25	27½	16	19	22	25	28	32	36	40	44	48	54
Taylor Iron Cleek	(1986)	—	—	—	—	—	—	—	16	18	21	25	29	33	37	41	45	50	—
Titleist Titlette	(1985)	12	—	16	—	21	—	—	—	—	—	26	30	34	38	42	46	53	—
Wilson Patty Berg	(1986)	13	—	17	20	22	—	26	—	—	23	26	30	34	38	42	46	50	55
Wilson Tiara	(1986)	14	—	18	—	23	—	27	—	—	23	26	30	34	38	42	46	50	55
Yamaha C-100	(1986)	14	—	19	22	25	—	—	—	—	—	—	—	—	—	—	—	—	—
Yamaha Image	(1986)	—	—	—	—	—	—	—	—	—	—	26	30	34	38	42	46	50	56

LIE — LADIES'

GOLF CLUB MANUFACTURERS STANDARD SPECIFICATIONS

Mfgr. & Year Specs. Published	Year	#1 Wood	#2 Wood	#3 Wood	#4 Wood	#5 Wood	#6 Wood	#7 Wood	#1 Iron	#2 Iron	#3 Iron	#4 Iron	#5 Iron	#6 Iron	#7 Iron	#8 Iron	#9 Iron	Pitch Wedge	Sand Wedge
Armour Golf BC	(1986)	54	—	55	55½	56	—	56½	—	—	57¾	58¾	59¾	60¾	61¾	62¾	63¾	63¾	63¾
Browning 440	(1986)	55	—	57	—	57	57	57	—	57	58	59	60	61	62	63	64	64	64
Daiwa Exceler	(1986)	54	—	55	56	56	—	56	—	—	58	59	60	60	61	62	62	63	64
H & B All	(1986)	55	—	57	57	57	—	—	—	—	58	59	60	61	62	63	64	64	64
Lynx - Tigress SP	(1986)	55	—	56	—	56½	—	57	—	—	58	59	60	61	62	63	64	64	64
MacGregor L. Finesse	(1986)	56	—	57	57	57	—	—	—	—	58	59	60	60½	61	61½	62	63	63
Mizuno Quad	(1986)	55	—	56	—	57	—	—	—	—	58	59	60	61	61½	62	63	64	64
Northwestern Micro-Lite	(1986)	55	—	55½	55¾	56	—	—	—	—	57	58	59	60	61	62	63	63	63
Penna Golf Original	(1986)	55	—	56	56	57	—	—	—	—	58½	59	59½	60	60½	61	61½	61½	61½
Pinseeker Fireball	(1986)	54	—	55	55½	55½	—	—	—	—	57	58	59	60	61	62	63	63	63
Pro Group Axiom	(1986)	55½	—	56	57	57	—	—	—	—	57	58	59	60	61	62	63	63	64
Ram Patty Sheehan	(1986)	55½	—	56½	—	57½	—	58½	—	—	58	58½	59	60	61	62	63	63	64
Spalding Cannon	(1986)	55	—	55½	—	56	—	56½	—	—	58¾	59¼	59¾	60¼	60¾	61¼	62	63	—
Taylor Metal	(1986)	54	—	55	55	55	55	55	—	—	—	—	—	—	—	—	—	—	—
Taylor Technician	(1986)	54	—	55	55	55	55	55	57½	58¼	59	59¾	60½	61¼	62	63	63	64	64
Taylor Iron Cleek	(1986)	—	—	—	—	—	—	—	56½	57	58	59	60	61	62	63	64	64	—
Titleist Titlette	(1985)	54	—	55	—	57	—	—	—	—	—	59	60	60	61	62	63	63	63
Wilson Patty Berg	(1986)	54	—	55	56	56	56	—	—	—	58	59	60	60	61	62	62	63	64
Wilson Tiara	(1986)	54	—	55	56	56	56	—	—	—	57	58	59	60	61	62	62	—	—
Yamaha C-100	(1986)	52	—	53	53½	54	—	—	—	—	—	—	—	—	—	—	—	—	—
Yamaha Image	(1986)	—	—	—	—	—	—	—	—	—	—	58	59	60	61	62	63	64	64

CUSTOM MFGR.'S — LADIES' — MID 1980's

LENGTH — LADIES'

GOLF CLUB MANUFACTURERS STANDARD SPECIFICATIONS

Mfgr. & Year Specs. Published		#1 Wood	#2 Wood	#3 Wood	#4 Wood	#5 Wood	#6 Wood	#7 Wood	#1 Iron	#2 Iron	#3 Iron	#4 Iron	#5 Iron	#6 Iron	#7 Iron	#8 Iron	#9 Iron	Pitch Wedge	Sand Wedge
Length: Mario Cesario	(1986)	42	41½	41	40½	40	—	39	—	37½	37	36½	36	35½	35	34½	34	34	34
Cobra	(1986)	42	41¾	41½	41	40½	40¼	40	38½	38	37½	37	36½	36	35½	35	34½	34½	34½
Bert Dargie	(1982)	42	41½	41	40½	40	—	—	38	37½	37	36½	36	35½	35	34½	34	34	34
The GolfWorks®	(1986)	42	—	41	40½	40	39½	39	38½	38	37½	37	36½	36	35½	35	34½	34½	34½
George Izett	(1986)	42	42	41	40½	40	—	39	—	38	37½	37	36½	36	35½	35	34½	34½	34½
Irving King	(1982)	42	41½	41	40½	40	—	39	—	37½	37	36½	36	35½	35	34½	34	34	34
Louisville Golf	(1986)	42	41½	41	40½	40	39½	39	38½	38	37½	37	36½	36	35½	35	34½	34½	34½
John Ofer	(1986)	42	—	41½	41	41	40	40	—	—	37½	37	36½	35¾	35⅝	35¼	34¾	34½	34½
Orlimar	(1982)	42	41¾	41	40½	40	—	39	38¾	38¼	37¾	37¼	36¾	36¼	35¾	35¼	34¾	34½	34½
Pederson	(1986)	41½	41¼	40¾	40½	40	39½	39	38	37½	37	36½	36	35½	35	34½	34	34	34
Kenneth Smith	(1986)	41½	41	40½	40	39½	—	38	38	37½	37	36½	36	35½	35	34½	34	33½	33½
Bob Toski	(1986)	42	41½	41	40½	40	—	39	38½	38	37½	37	36½	36	35½	35	34½	34½	34½

LOFT — LADIES'

GOLF CLUB MANUFACTURERS STANDARD SPECIFICATIONS

Mfgr. & Year Specs. Published		#1 Wood	#2 Wood	#3 Wood	#4 Wood	#5 Wood	#6 Wood	#7 Wood	#1 Iron	#2 Iron	#3 Iron	#4 Iron	#5 Iron	#6 Iron	#7 Iron	#8 Iron	#9 Iron	Pitch Wedge	Sand Wedge
Loft: Mario Cesario	(1986)	12½	14	17	20	23	—	29	—	20	24	28	32	36	40	44	48	52	56
Cobra	(1986)	11	14	16	19	22	25	27	17	20	23	27	31	36	40	44	48	52	56
Bert Dargie	(1982)	11	13	16	19	22	—	—	18	21	24	27	31	35	39	43	47	51	55
The GolfWorks®	(1986)	13	—	17	20	23	26	29	17	20	23	26	30	34	38	42	46	50	56
George Izett	(1986)	12	14	16	19	22	—	—	—	20	22½	25	27½	30	32½	35	37½	40	42½
Louisville Golf	(1986)	12	14½	17	19½	22½	25	27½	18	21	24	27	30	34	38	42	46	51	56
John Ofer	(1986)	13	—	17	20	22	25	27	—	—	24	27	31	35	39	43	47	51	56
Orlimar	(1982)	13	14½	18½	21½	24½	—	31	16	19	22	25½	29	33	37	41	45	50	58
Pederson	(1986)	12	13	16	19	22	24	26	18	20	23	26	30	34	38	42	46	50	55
Kenneth Smith	(1986)	12	15	18	21	24	—	30	18	21	24	28	32	36	40	44	48	52	57
Bob Toski	(1986)	13	15	18	20	22	—	27	22	24	26½	29	31½	35	38½	41½	45	48½	51½

LIE — LADIES'

GOLF CLUB MANUFACTURERS STANDARD SPECIFICATIONS

Mfgr. & Year Specs. Published		#1 Wood	#2 Wood	#3 Wood	#4 Wood	#5 Wood	#6 Wood	#7 Wood	#1 Iron	#2 Iron	#3 Iron	#4 Iron	#5 Iron	#6 Iron	#7 Iron	#8 Iron	#9 Iron	Pitch Wedge	Sand Wedge
Lie: Mario Cesario	(1986)	53	54	56	56	56	—	56	—	56	57	58	59	60	61	62	63	64	64
Cobra	(1986)	54	54	55	55½	56	55	55½	57	57½	58	59	59½	60	61	62	63	63	64
Bert Dargie	(1982)	54	54	55	56	56	—	—	57	58	59	60	61	62	63	64	64	65	65
The GolfWorks®	(1986)	53	—	54	54½	55	55½	56	55	56	57	58	59	60	61	62	63	63	63
George Izett	(1986)	53	53	54	55	56	—	57	—	56	57	58	59	60	61	62	63	63	63
Irving King	(1986)	55	55½	56	56½	57	—	58	—	57	58	59	60	61	62	63	64	64	64
Louisville Golf	(1986)	54	54½	55	55½	56	56½	57	55	56	57	58	59	60	61	62	63	63	63
John Ofer	(1986)	54	—	55	56	56	56	56	—	—	57	58	59	59	60	61	61	62	63
Pederson	(1986)	53	53½	54	55	55½	56	56½	55	56	57	58	59	60	61	62	63	63	63
Kenneth Smith	(1986)	53	54	55	56	57	—	59	56	57	58	59	60	61	62	63	64	64	64
Bob Toski	(1986)	53	53	54	55	56	—	56	56½	57	57½	58	58½	60	61	61½	62	63	63

LADIES' — LATE 1980's

LENGTH — LADIES'

GOLF CLUB MANUFACTURERS STANDARD SPECIFICATIONS — DURING PERIOD OF 1985 TO 1990

Mfg. & Model	#1 Wood	#2 Wood	#3 Wood	#4 Wood	#5 Wood	#6 Wood	#7 Wood	#1 Iron	#2 Iron	#3 Iron	#4 Iron	#5 Iron	#6 Iron	#7 Iron	#8 Iron	#9 Iron	Pitch Wedge	Sand Wedge
Browning 440 Gold	42	—	41	—	40	—	40	38½	38	37½	37	36½	36	35½	35	34½	34½	34½
Browning Premier	42	—	41	—	40	—	—	38½	38	37½	37	36½	36	35½	35	34½	34½	34½
Browning Panache	42	—	41	—	40	—	—	38½	38	37½	37	36½	36	35½	35	34½	34½	34½
Browning Maxim	42	—	41	40½	40	—	39½	—	38	37½	37	36½	36	35½	35	34½	34½	34½
Browning System 350	42	—	41	40½	40	—	—	38½	38	37½	37	36½	36	35½	35	34½	34½	34½
Browning Lady 440	42	—	41	40½	40	—	40	—	38	37½	37	36½	36	35½	35	34½	34½	34½
Browning TLC	42	—	41	—	40	—	40	—	—	37½	37	36½	36	35½	35	34½	34½	34½
Cobra Steel Classics (M.)	42	—	41	—	40½	—	40											
Cobra Baffler Blade Irons								38½	38	37½	37	36½	36	35½	35	34½	34½	34¼
Daiwa Lady Lite Touch (G.)	41½	—	40½	40	39½	—	39	—	—	37½	37	36½	36	35½	35	34½	34½	34½
Daiwa Lady Exceler	41½	—	40½	40	39½	—	39	—	—	37½	37	36½	36	35½	35	34½	34½	34½
Daiwa Escala	41½	—	40½	40	39½	—	39	—	—	37½	37	36½	36	35½	35	34½	34½	34½
Dunlop J. Stephenson (M.)	42	—	41	—	40½	—	39¼	—	—	37½	37	36½	36	35½	35	34½	34½	34½
GolfWorks® Progressive Lady	42	—	41	—	40	—	39	—	—	37½	37	36½	36	35½	35	34½	34½	34½
H & B/Power Bilt Countess (L.)	41½	—	40½	40	40	—	39½											
H & B/Power Bilt Countess (M.)	41½	—	40½	—	40	—	39½											
Hogan Lady Hogan	42	—	41½	—	40½	—	39¾	—	—	37½	37	36½	36	35½	35	34½	34¼	34¼
Hogan Princess								—	—	37¼	36¾	36¼	35¾	35½	35¼	34	—	—
Louisville LMWH Metalwood	42	—	41	40½	40	—	39											
Louisville AGW Graphite	43	—	42	41½	41	—	40											
Louisville CMC								39½	39	38½	38	37½	37	36½	36	35½	35½	35½
Louisville CMR								39½	39	38½	38	37½	37	36½	36	35½	35½	35½
Louisville CMH								39½	39	38½	38	37½	37	36½	36	35½	35½	35½
Lynx Tigress G (M.)	42	—	41	40½	40	—	39½	—	—	37½	37	36½	36	35½	35	34½	34¼	34
Lynx Tigress Elegance (M.)	42	—	41	40	40	—	39	—	—	37½	37	36½	36	35½	35	34½	34¼	34½
Lynx Tigress SP (M.)	42	—	41	—	40	—	39½	—	—	37½	37	36½	36	35½	35	34½	34½	34½
Lynx Elegance (L.)	42	—	41	40½	40	—	39	—	—	37½	37	36½	36	35½	35	34½	34¼	34
Lynx Elegance Nouvelle (M.)	42	—	41	40½	40	—	39	38½										
Maruman Elicon Carbon (L.)	42	—	41	—	40	—	39	—	—	37½	37	36½	36	35½	35	34½	34	33½
Maruman Dangan 303	42	—	41	40	40	39½	39											
Mizuno Quad (L.)	42½	—	42	—	41¼	—	40¼	—	—	37½	37	36½	36	35½	35¼	35	34¾	34½
Mizuno Miz (L.)	42¼	—	41¼	—	40¼	—	40¼	—	—	38¼	37¾	37¼	36¾	36¼	35¾	35¼	35	35
Mizuno Altron SE	43¼	—	42¼	—	41¼	—	—	39¾	39¼	38¾	38¼	37¾	37¼	36¾	36¼	36	35¾	35¾
Northwestern Sandra Palmer Tour II (M.)	42	—	41	—	40	—	—	—	37½	37	36½	36	35½	35	34½	34	34	34
Northwestern Judy Rankin Pro Classic	42	—	41	—	40	—	—	—	—	37	36½	36	35½	35	34½	34	34	34
Northwestern Marlene Hagge Ult. (M.)	42	—	41	—	40	—	—	—	—	37	36½	36	35½	35	34½	34	34	34
Northwestern Team Lopez (M.)	42	—	41	—	40	—	—	—	—	37	36½	36	35½	35	34½	34	34	34
Northwestern Nancy Lopez NL35 (M.)	42	—	41	—	40	—	—	—	—	37	36½	36	35½	35	34½	34	34	34
Northwestern Judy Rankin Promaster Plus (M.)	42	—	41	—	40	—	—	—	—	37	36½	36	35½	35	34½	34	34	34
Toney Penna Lady Omega Steelwoods	42	—	41½	—	40½	—	—											
Toney Penna Lady Omega	42	—	41½	41	40½	—	—	—	37½	37	36½	36	35½	35	34½	34	34	34
Ram Golden Girl (G.)	42	—	41	—	40	—	40	—	—	37	36½	36	35½	35	34½	34	33¾	33½

LENGTH — LADIES'

GOLF CLUB MANUFACTURERS STANDARD SPECIFICATIONS — DURING PERIOD OF 1985 TO 1990

Mfg. & Model	#1 Wood	#2 Wood	#3 Wood	#4 Wood	#5 Wood	#6 Wood	#7 Wood	#1 Iron	#2 Iron	#3 Iron	#4 Iron	#5 Iron	#6 Iron	#7 Iron	#8 Iron	#9 Iron	Pitch Wedge	Sand Wedge
Ram Lady Laser (L.)	42	—	41	—	40	—	40	—	—	37½	37	36½	36	35½	34½	34	33¾	33½
Ram Laser LX (L.)	42½	—	41½	—	40½	—	40½	—	—	38	37½	37	36½	36	35½	35	34¾	34½
Slazenger Baroness	42½	—	41½	—	40½	—	40	n/a	38	37½	37	36½	36	35½	35	34½	34½	34½
Square Two PCX-Ladies	42	—	41	40½	40	—	40	38½	38	37½	37	36½	36	35½	35	34½	34½	34½
Wilson Patty Berg Staff	42	—	41½	41	40¾	—	40½	—	—	37½	37	36½	36	35½	35	34½	34	34
Wilson Tiara	41½	—	40½	40	39½	—	38½	—	—	37	36½	36	35½	35¼	34¾	34¼	34¼	32¼
Yamaha C-100	42	—	41	40½	40	—	—											
Yamaha XAM10								—	—	37½	37	36½	36	35½	35	34½	34	34
Yamaha The Secret III								—	—	37½	37	36½	36	35½	35	34½	34	34
Yamaha X-101	42½	—	41½	—	40½	—	40											
Yamaha Accurace (1989)								—	—	37½	37	36½	36	35½	35	34½	34	34
Yamaha X100	42½	—	41½	41	40½	—	40											
Yamaha Secret Pro	43	—	42	—	41	—	—	—	—	38	37½	37	36½	36	35½	35	34½	34½
Yamaha Accurace (1987)	42½	—	41½	—	40½	—	—											
Yonex Carbonex FL (G.)	42	—	41	40½	40	—	—	—	—	37½	37	36½	36	35½	35	34½	34	34
Yonex ADXFL	43½	—	41½	41	40½	—	—	—	—	38	37½	37	36½	36	35½	35	34½	—

GOLF CLUB MANUFACTURERS STANDARD SPECIFICATIONS — DURING PERIOD OF 1985 TO 1990

Mfg. & Model	#1 Wood	#2 Wood	#3 Wood	#4 Wood	#5 Wood	#6 Wood	#7 Wood	#1 Iron	#2 Iron	#3 Iron	#4 Iron	#5 Iron	#6 Iron	#7 Iron	#8 Iron	#9 Iron	Pitch Wedge	Sand Wedge
Browning 440 Gold	10	—	15	—	21	—	26	17	20	23	26	29	32	36	40	44	49	54
Browning Premier	10½	—	15	—	21	—	—	18	21	24	27	30	34	38	42	46	50	56
Browning Panache	12	—	15	—	21	—	—	16	18	21	24	28	32	36	40	44	50	55
Browning Maxim	13	—	16	19	21	—	25	—	21	24	27	30	34	38	42	46	50	56
Browning System 350	14	—	18	21	24	—	—	17	20	23	26	29	32	36	40	44	49	56
Browning Lady 440	13	—	16	19	22	—	25	—	21	24	27	30	34	38	42	46	50	56
Browning TLC	13	—	19	—	22	—	25	—	—	24	27	30	34	38	42	46	50	56
Cobra Steel Classics (M.)	12	—	16	—	19	—	23											
Cobra Baffler Blade Irons								15	18	22	26	30	34	37	40	44	48	54
Daiwa Lady Lite Touch (G.)	12	—	16	19	21	—	25	—	18	21	24	28	32	35	41	46	51	57
Daiwa Lady Exceler	13	—	17	20	22	—	25	—	—	23	26	30	34	38	42	46	51	57
Daiwa Escala	13	—	17	20	22	—	25	—	—	23	26	30	34	38	42	46	51	57
Dunlop J. Stephenson (M.)	12	—	15	—	20	—	21	—	—	22	26	30	34	38	42	46	51	56
GolfWorks® Progressive Lady	12	—	17	—	22	—	28	—	—	24	28	32	36	40	44	48	52	56
H & B/Power Bilt Countess (L.)	14	—	20	22	24	—	27											
H & B/Power Bilt Countess (M.)	13	—	16	—	22	—	24											
Hogan Lady Hogan	13	—	15½	—	21½	—	24½	—	—	23	26½	30	33½	37	40	44	49	55
Hogan Princess								—	—	23½	27	29	34	37	41	46	51	—
Louisville LMWH Metalwood	12	—	18	20½	24	—	28											
Louisville AGW Graphite	11	—	16	18½	21½	—	26½											
Louisville CMC Graphite								16	20	24	28	32	36	40	44	48	52	56
Louisville CMR Graphite								17	20	23	27	30	34	38	42	46	50	55
Louisville CMH Graphite								17	19	22	25	28	32	36	40	45	50	56
Lynx Tigress G (M.)	12	—	15	—	21	—	25	—	—	20	23	26	29	33	37	41	46	55
Lynx Tigress Elegance (M.)	13	—	19	22	25	—	28	—	19	22	25	29	33	37	41	45	49	57
Lynx Tigress SP (M.)	12	—	16	—	22	—	26	—	—	22	25	29	33	37	41	45	49	56
Lynx Elegance (L.)	13	—	19	22	25	—	28	—	—	22	25	29	33	37	41	45	49	56
Lynx Elegance Nouvelle (M.)	10/12	—	15	18	21	—	25											
Maruman Elicon Carbon (L.)	14	—	16	—	22	—	30	—	—	21	24	27	30	33	37	42	47	56
Maruman Dangan 303	15	—	17	20	23	25	27											
Mizuno Quad (L.)	12	—	15	—	20	—	23	—	—	22	25	28	32	36	40	44	49	56
Mizuno Miz (L.)	12	—	17	—	22½	—	26	—	—	21	24	27	30	34	38	42	47	54
Mizuno Altron SE	11	—	15	—	21	—	—	15	18	21	24	27	30	34	38	42	47	54
Northwestern Sandra Palmer Tour II (M.)	11	—	16	—	21	—	—	—	20	23	27	31	35	39	43	47	51	56
Northwestern Judy Rankin Pro Classic	11	—	16	—	21	—	—											
Northwestern Marlene Hagge Ult. (M.)	11	—	16	—	21	—	—	—	—	23	27	31	35	39	43	47	51	56
Northwestern Team Lopez (M.)	11	—	16	—	21	—	—	—	—	23	27	31	35	39	43	47	51	56
Northwestern Nancy Lopez NL35 (M.)	11	—	16	—	21	—	—	—	—	23	27	31	35	39	43	47	51	56
Northwestern Judy Rankin Promaster Plus (M.)	11	—	16	—	21	—	—	—	—	23	27	31	35	39	43	47	51	56
Toney Penna Lady Omega Steelwoods	—	—	15	18	21	—	—											
Toney Penna Lady Omega	—	—	15	—	21	—	—											
Ram Golden Girl (G.)	13½	—	17½	—	22	—	27	—	—	24	27	30	34	37½	42	46	50	55

LOFT — LADIES'

GOLF CLUB MANUFACTURERS STANDARD SPECIFICATIONS — DURING PERIOD OF 1985 TO 1990

Mfg. & Model	#1 Wood	#2 Wood	#3 Wood	#4 Wood	#5 Wood	#6 Wood	#7 Wood	#1 Iron	#2 Iron	#3 Iron	#4 Iron	#5 Iron	#6 Iron	#7 Iron	#8 Iron	#9 Iron	Pitch Wedge	Sand Wedge
Ram Lady Laser (L.)	13	–	17	–	22	–	27	–	–	21	24	27	30	34	38	42	47	53
Ram Laser LX (L.)	13	–	17	–	22	–	27	–	–	21	24	28	31	34	38	42½	47	53
Slazenger Baroness	12	–	19	–	23	–	27	n/a	21	24	27	30	33	37	41	45	49	55
Square Two PCX-Ladies	12	–	17	20	23	–	28	–	20	23	26	29	32	36	40	44	49	55
Titleist Titlette (1988)	12	–	16	–	21	–	–	–	–	–	26	30	34	38	42	46	53	–
Titleist Titlette (1986-1987)	12	–	16	–	21	–	–	–	–	–	26	30	34	38	42	46	53	–
Tommy Armour Butterfly	–	–	15½	18½	21½	–	25½	–	–	23	26	29	33	37	41	45	52	57
Wilson Patty Berg Staff	13	–	17	20	22	–	26	–	–	23	26	30	34	38	42	46	50	55
Wilson Tiara	11	–	16	19	21	–	25	–	–	23	26	30	34	38	42	46	–	–
Yamaha C-100	14	–	19	22	25	–	–											
Yamaha XAM10								–	–	22	25	28	32	36	40	44	45	54
Yamaha The Secret III								–	–	21	23	26	29	33	37	42	48	56
Yamaha X-101	14	–	20	–	26	–	29											
Yamaha Accurace (1989)	14	–	19	22	25	–	27	–	20	23	26	30	34	38	42	46	51	56
Yamaha X100	14	–	19	22	25	–	27											
Yamaha Secret Pro	12	–	17	–	23	–	–	–	–	21	23	26	29	33	37	42	48	56
Yamaha Accurace (1987)	13	–	18	–	24	–	–											
Yonex Carbonex FL (G.)	13	–	18	21	24	–	–	–	–	21	24	27	31	35	39	43	47	52
Yonex ADXFL	13	–	18	21	24	–	–	–	–	20	23	27	31	35	39	43	52	–

LIE — LADIES'

GOLF CLUB MANUFACTURERS STANDARD SPECIFICATIONS — DURING PERIOD OF 1985 TO 1990

Mfg. & Model	#1 Wood	#2 Wood	#3 Wood	#4 Wood	#5 Wood	#6 Wood	#7 Wood	#1 Iron	#2 Iron	#3 Iron	#4 Iron	#5 Iron	#6 Iron	#7 Iron	#8 Iron	#9 Iron	Pitch Wedge	Sand Wedge
Browning 440 Gold	55	—	56	—	57	—	57	56½	57	58	59	60	61	62	63	64	64	64
Browning Premier	55	—	56	—	57	—	—	56	57	58	59	60	61	62	63	64	64	64
Browning Panache	55	—	56	—	57	—	56	56	57	58	59	60	61	62	63	64	64	64
Browning Maxim	56	—	56	56	56	—	—	—	57	58	59	60	61	62	63	64	64	64
Browning System 350	55	—	56	57	57	—	—	56½	57	58	59	60	61	62	63	64	64	64
Browning Lady 440	55	—	56	57	57	—	57	—	57	58	59	60	61	62	63	64	64	64
Browning TLC	55	—	56	—	57	—	57	—	—	58	59	60	61	62	63	64	64	64
Daiwa Lady Lite Touch (G.)	55	—	56	56	57	—	57	—	—	58	59	60	61	62	63	64	63	64
Daiwa Lady Exceler	54½	—	55	56	58	—	57	—	57	58	59	60	61	62	63	64	64	64
Daiwa Escala	54½	—	55	56	57	—	57	—	57	58	59	60	61	62	63	64	64	64
Dunlop J. Stephenson (M.)	55	—	55½	—	57	—	56½	—	—	57	58	59	60	61	61½	62	62	63
Cobra Steel Classics (M.)	55	—	55	—	56	—	56	—	—	—	—	—	—	—	—	—	—	—
Cobra Baffler Blade Irons								56	57	58	59	59½	60	61	62	63	63	63
GolfWorks® Progressive Lady	55	—	56	—	57	—	58	—	—	58	59	60	61	62	63	64	64	64
H & B/Power Bilt Countess (L.)	55	—	57	57	57	—	57	—	—	—	—	—	—	—	—	—	—	—
H & B/Power Bilt Countess (M.)	55½	—	56	—	57	—	57	—	—	—	—	—	—	—	—	—	—	—
Hogan Lady Hogan	55	—	55½	—	56	—	58	—	—	58½	59½	60½	61½	62½	63½	64	64½	64½
Hogan Princess								—	—	57½	58	59	60½	61½	62	62½	64	—
Louisville LMWH Metalwood	54	—	55	55½	56	—	57											
Louisville AGW Graphite	55	—	56	56½	57	—	58											
Louisville CMC Graphite								55	56	57	58	59	60	61	62	63	63	63
Louisville CMR Graphite								56	57	58	59	60	61	62	63	64	64	64
Louisville CMH Graphite								58	58½	59	59½	60	60½	61	61½	62	63	63
Lynx Tigress G (M.)	54½	—	55	—	56	—	57	—	—	58	59	60	61	62	63	64	64	64
Lynx Tigress Elegance (M.)	54	—	55	55½	56	—	56	—	57	58	59	60	61	62	63	64	64	64
Lynx Tigress SP (M.)	55	—	56	—	56½	—	57	—	—	58	59	60	61	62	63	64	64	64
Lynx Elegance (L.)	55	—	55½	56	56	—	57	—	—	58	59	60	61	62	63	64	63	63
Lynx Elegance Nouvelle (M.)	54	—	55	56	56	—	56											
Maruman Elicon Carbon (L.)	57	—	57	—	58	—	60	—	—	59	60	60½	61	61½	62	62½	63	63
Maruman Dangan 303	55	—	57	57½	57½	58	58											
Mizuno Quad (L.)	55	—	55½	—	56½	—	57	—	—	58	59	60	60½	61	62	63	63½	63½
Mizuno Miz (L.)	55½	—	57	—	58½	—	60	—	—	58	59	60	61	61½	62	63	64	64
Mizuno Altron SE	54½	—	55½	—	56½	—	—	56	57	58	59	60	61	61½	62	63	64	64
Northwestern Sandra Palmer Tour II (M.)	55	—	55½	—	56	—	—	—	56	57	58	59	60	61	62	63	63	63
Northwestern Judy Rankin Pro Classic	55	—	55½	—	56	—	—											
Northwestern Marlene Hagge Ult. (M.)	55	—	55½	—	56	—	—											
Northwestern Team Lopez (M.)	55	—	55½	—	56	—	—	—	—	57	58	59	60	61	62	63	63	63
Northwestern Nancy Lopez NL35 (M.)	55	—	55½	—	56	—	—	—	—	57	58	59	60	61	62	63	63	63
Northwestern Judy Rankin Promaster Plus (M.)	55	—	55½	—	56	—	—	—	—	57	58	59	60	61	62	63	63	63
Toney Penna Lady Omega Steelwoods	55	—	56	56	57	—	—											
Toney Penna Lady Omega	55	—	56	—	57	—	—											
Ram Golden Girl (G.)	55	—	56½	—	57½	—	58½	—	—	57	58	59	60	61	62	63	64	65

LIE — LADIES'

GOLF CLUB MANUFACTURERS STANDARD SPECIFICATIONS — DURING PERIOD OF 1985 TO 1990

Mfg. & Model	#1 Wood	#2 Wood	#3 Wood	#4 Wood	#5 Wood	#6 Wood	#7 Wood	#1 Iron	#2 Iron	#3 Iron	#4 Iron	#5 Iron	#6 Iron	#7 Iron	#8 Iron	#9 Iron	Pitch Wedge	Sand Wedge
Ram Lady Laser (L.)	55	—	57	—	58	—	58	—	—	58	59	60	61	62	62½	63	63½	64
Ram Laser LX (L.)	55	—	57	—	58	—	58	—	—	60	61	62	62½	63	64	64½	65	65½
Slazenger Baroness	55	—	56	—	57	—	58	n/a	57	58	59	60	61	62	63	64	64	64
Square Two PCX Ladies	54	—	54	55	55	—	56	—	54	55	56	57	58	59	60	61	61	61
Titleist Titlette (1988)	54	—	55	—	57	—	—	—	—	—	59	60	60	61	62	62	63	—
Titleist Titlette (1986-87)	54	—	55	—	57	—	—	—	—	—	59	60	60	61	62	62	63	—
Tommy Armour Butterfly	54	—	55	55½	56	—	56½	—	—	58	59	60	60½	61	61½	62	62½	63
Wilson Patty Berg Staff	54	—	55	56	56	—	56	—	—	58	59	60	60	61	62	62	63	64
Wilson Tiara	55	—	56	57	57	—	57	—	—	57	58	59	60	61	62	62	—	—
Yamaha C-100	52	—	53	53½	54	—	—											
Yamaha The Secret III								—	—	59	59½	60	60½	61	61½	62	63	63
Yamaha XAM10								—	—	58	59	60	61	62	63	63	64	64
Yamaha X-101	54½	—	55½	—	56½	—	57											
Yamaha Accurace (1989)	52	—	53	53½	54	—	54½	—	57	59	59	60	60½	61	61½	62	63	63
Yamaha X100	54	—	55	—	56	—	—											
Yamaha Secret Pro	55½	—	56½	—	57½	—	—	—	—	59	59½	60	60½	61	61½	62	63	63
Yamaha Accurace (1987)	56	—	57	57½	58	—	—											
Yonex Carbonex FL (G.)	56	—	57	57½	58	—	—	—	—	57	58	59	60	61	62	63	64	64
Yonex ADXFL	56	—	57	57½	58	—	—	—	—	57	58	59	60	61	62	63	64	—

LADIES' — LENGTH, LOFT & LIE —
— FILL IN YOUR OWN TO KEEP UPDATED

GOLF CLUB MANUFACTURERS STANDARD OR CUSTOM SPECIFICATIONS

Manufacturer & Model	Year Specs. Published	#1 Wood	#2 Wood	#3 Wood	#4 Wood	#5 Wood	#6 Wood	#7 Wood	#1 Iron	#2 Iron	#3 Iron	#4 Iron	#5 Iron	#6 Iron	#7 Iron	#8 Iron	#9 Iron	Pitch Wedge	Sand Wedge	Third Wedge
Length:																				
Loft:																				
Lie:																				

APPENDIX 9

HOW A RUBBER GRIP IS MANUFACTURED

The following photos have been provided by the Eaton Corporation. They provide a sequence of the basic operations involved in manufacturing their rubber grips. The Eaton Golf Grip Plant shown in these photos is located in Laurinburg, North Carolina.

A9-1
The press operator removes the cured rubber grips from the injection mold using air to blow them off.

A9-2
The grips are installed on the mandrels of an automatic paint machine. When the grips pass under the spray guns to be painted, they are rotated to ensure complete paint coverage.

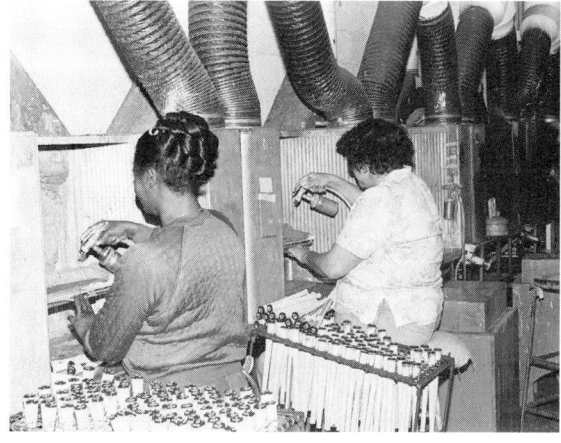

A9-3
Some grips are painted in more than 1 color. The additional colors are applied by manually spraying each grip after it has been placed under a mask.

A9-4
After painting, the grips are placed on racks and the paint is allowed to cure in a drying room.

A9-5
After the paint is fully cured, the grips are buffed. Buffing removes the paint from the surface of the grip and only leaves paint in the molded recesses or engravings.

APPENDIX 10

INTERNATIONAL GOLF

In 1963, there were approximately 6 million golfers in the U.S., or about 4% of the population was playing. By 1993, there were close to 25 million golfers, about a 12% participation rate. Golf in the U.S. is now in a mature phase and can no longer be considered "a rich man's game." However, golf in foreign countries is quite different from what we experience in terms of access, cost, marketing, fitting techniques and equipment.

In many countries, golf is still a game played mostly by high ranking government officials and businessmen. For instance, it has not been that many years ago that in South Korea, a sign of prestige was to have your driver (the club, not the chauffeur) hanging in the back window of your car. In Japan, club memberships are bought and sold in a commodities type market environment at some of the most prestigious retail stores.

One thing that all countries have in common is strong growth in the game. Some of this growth is due to an emphasis on making golf more affordable for the average resident. This is where the greatest number of new golfers must come for golf to continue on an upward path. In Europe for instance, there are about 6 million golfers but that is only a 2% participation rate. The participation rate in England is much higher because golf is so much more affordable. It costs about $30.00 per person with a cart during the weekend to play at a public golf course in the U.S. In the U.K., it is slightly higher. However, in Germany and France it costs close to $60.00 and in Spain almost $100.00. The drive towards low-cost golf in overseas markets is important to U.S. companies because a significant portion of their new sales will come from there. In the following pages, we'll take a look at specific subjects and how they differ in foreign countries from the U.S.

Golf Club Fitting

In the U.S., dynamic fitting techniques, in which the player actually hits balls using a variety of test clubs, is recognized as the most credible means of determining the right set of clubs for a golfer. The individual conducting the test observes the flight of the ball and how solidly it was hit with each different test club. The results of this ball striking test determine the right specification mix for the golfer.

In most foreign countries, fitting takes place almost entirely within the confines of the pro shop or retail store. Seldom does the player actually hit a shot. For example, at some pro shops in the United Kingdom, a player steps up to the screen of a computer terminal and responds to prompts with typed, single word answers on how the player perceives his or her game. Depending upon the combination of answers, the computer prints out a fitting recommendation upon which the player can act by ordering a set of clubs.

In New Zealand, the golf professional asks a similar series of questions but the session takes a peculiar turn when the golfer is requested to demonstrate their arm and back strength by pulling up on a bar that responds with a strength rating. This is the basis upon which the shaft flex recommendation is made.

Our staff was sent over to a large Japanese retail store to help set up an elaborate fitting room, complete with swing analyzer, video camera, fitting test clubs, etc. Those store employees who were assigned to the golf floor were then given extensive training for conducting a fitting. It was with frustration that our staff noticed that typically, after very thorough fitting sessions, the store customers were walked over to the part of the store in which racks of equipment were displayed and given the same standard specification clubs that he or she would have purchased without the fitting sessions. Elaborate steps had been taken to create a state-of-the-art fitting center that, at the time of our departure, was merely a facade.

Typically, however, most fitting sessions are confined to static methods that rely on rulers, charts or questionnaires that yield a suspect fitting recommendation. Of course, this was typical of the state of fitting in the U.S. during the early and mid 1980's because it was the manufacturer that was providing the testing methodology. Most manufacturers wanted to provide fitting techniques that were quick for the professional and at the same time, yield a recommendation for a set of clubs that were close to having standard specifications.

Today, manufacturers are upgrading their fitting systems to include more dynamic steps, drawn from my book *The Golf Club Fitting Plan*; thus yielding a more credible fitting system. For instance, Tommy Armour, Wilson and Titleist all have much improved fitting systems. Their challenge is to get the system into the hands of the people selling their product in foreign countries. Most U.S. manufacturers sell their clubs in foreign markets through a distributor. The distributor inventories the clubs and sells them, usually through a network of sales agents, to the golf professional or retail store. The problem to solve is that any credible fitting system is going to produce results that require custom specifications. If the distributors only warehouse stock equipment, they are unable to respond to custom requests; hence they have no interest in providing a companion fitting system with the manufacturer's clubs.

As foreign consumers become more aware of the value of the custom fitting process, they will look for those retail outlets that provide a credible fitting alternative before they purchase their new equipment. It is those outlets who are coming on the scene providing just such an alternative that are grabbing market share from the traditional equipment sources.

Marketing

There is a great demand for American golf equipment in foreign countries. Therefore, the challenge for all domestic companies is to satisfy that demand as easily and inexpensively as possible. It is for that reason that companies work through a distributor or agent in each of the countries in which there is demand for their product.

The difference between a distributor and an agent is significant. A distributor will take title to the product as soon as it leaves the shipping dock of a company. This usually means that payment has already been received through a wire transfer, letter of credit or some other form of prepayment. Although it is possible to recover money that is due from a foreign customer when they are in arrears, it can be very expensive and a time consuming process. An agent is more rare because they do not actually take title to the product. They simply receive the product, warehouse it and receive a commission for sales. Therefore, there has to be considerable trust between the company and the agent.

In both cases, an agent and distributor provide much needed benefits for the company; usually expert knowledge about the market and depending upon the market size, a sales force that will demonstrate and sell the product. A marketing strategy that works in the U.S. must be tailored to fit, for example, Singapore, Australia, Japan, etc. where consumers have their own unique tastes.

However, the old adage about the dog wagging the tail, the tail not wagging the dog accurately describes the view many companies take towards their foreign endeavors. Virtually all American golf companies' priorities are geared towards marketing their clubs to the domestic customer. Therefore, the materials and methods that are available for their marketing efforts in foreign countries are not always ideal and they are sometimes unable to respond in a way in which the distributor or agent would like. For example, consumers in Japan and Southeast Asia have historically been very brand conscious (this is slowly changing). To raise the level of consciousness about a golf club requires tremendous advertising expenditures in a countries' national or regional golf magazines or other periodicals, as well as on television. Since the number of golfers in any one country are relatively small compared to the U.S., it becomes difficult to justify spending the appropriate amount of money. Upper management in most companies wants to see results before spending more money on advertising while the sales people argue that best results can not be achieved without spending more money. As for the distributor or agent's view, the company who they represent is never spending enough money on advertising.

Equipment

The cost of golf equipment is significantly higher in foreign countries. In New Zealand, the wholesale price of a set of nine, steel shafted Callaway Big Bertha irons is $1,300.00 (U.S.). Assuming a modest margin, the price to the consumer will be around $2,200.00 (U.S.) or about twice the U.S. retail price. Much of the higher cost is due to transport, taxes, duty, agent commission and so on. The bottom line is that equipment is very expensive and has perpetuated the "rich man's game" label.

It is principally because of the relatively high cost of equipment from the major OEM's (original equipment manufacturers) that component usage is becoming much more widespread. Initially attractive to consumers of average means who wished to purchase an affordable set of clubs with which to start the game, components have now staked out a significant share of the market in countries like Canada, U.K., Australia and New Zealand because a credible argument is made that they are equal to OEM equipment. The challenge to component users and distributors is to dispel the myth that OEM equipment is superior. Component suppliers simply interrupt the traditional assembly process to deliver the separate components to their customer so that they can continue the assembly with a wider range of shafts, grips and heads.

For a long time, golfers in foreign countries were not as knowledgeable as their American counterparts. They did not, and to some extent still do not, have ready access to books and magazines that provide information that would make them more knowledgeable. This worked against them because it provided an opportunity for a few American companies to dump very inferior products into foreign markets. When I travel overseas and give seminars I am constantly amazed at the general poor quality of equipment that was purchased in the 1960's, 70's and early 80's. Even today, certain manufacturer's foreign clubs are inferior domestic clubs. This is principally due to the fact that these certain manufacturers send their components to their foreign agents who do the assembly themselves (in some countries the duty is lower on components than on assembled clubs). Their quality control is not as tight and shortcuts are taken which negatively impact the clubs. Overseas it is still common to find clubs with large quantities of lead in the shaft or lofts and lies that are way off. This of course undermines the image of the U.S. company and provides fertile ground for components.

Besides the occasional quality difference, clubs sold overseas are usually the same as those sold domestically. The only exception is in Japan and Southeast Asia where iron lofts are a couple of degrees stronger and the lengths are ¼" to ½" longer. This is intentional so that the average Japanese or Asian golfer can gain a few more yards with their shots. Of course, the longer length only makes the irons more difficult to control and would increase the percentage of off-center shots, but the overriding perception among the average golfer is that they absolutely need longer clubs for greater distance. Little headway would be made by the retailer who attempts to discourage that trend.

A10-1
One of the world's largest companies, $115 billion Mitsui & Co., distributes GolfWorks® products in Japan. They also run a highly successful GolfWorks® Repair School. Shown above is a picture of the front cover of a catalog they publish.

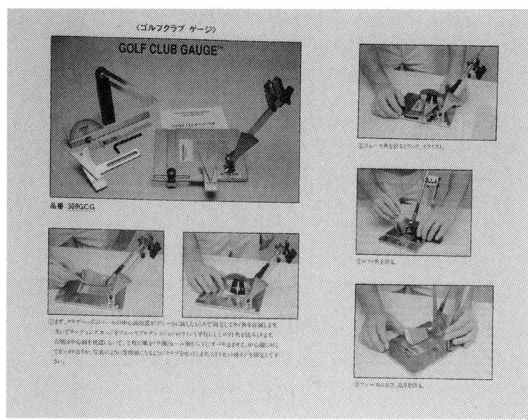

A10-2
This is one of the pages inside the catalog. The product shown is the "Golf Club Gauge."

A10-3
One of the most knowledgeable individuals associated with The GolfWorks® is Danny Seng of Singapore, who contributes articles to Asian golf publications. Articles like the one shown enhance the image of Danny and his company and help to drive his business.

INDEX